Henry Boyer Brumbaugh

The Weekly Pilgrim

Vol. 4

Henry Boyer Brumbaugh

The Weekly Pilgrim
Vol. 4

ISBN/EAN: 9783337293970

Printed in Europe, USA, Canada, Australia, Japan

Cover: Foto ©Lupo / pixelio.de

More available books at **www.hansebooks.com**

The Weekly Pilgrim.

"REMOVE NOT THE ANCIENT LANDMARKS WHICH OUR FATHERS HAVE SET."

VOL. 4. JAMES CREEK, PENNSYLVANIA, JANUARY 3, 1873. NO. 1

THE AUTUMN LEAVES ARE FADED

BY F. W. SURDAM.

Yes the trees are faded Jennie,
  Where once the yellow apples grew,
That we sat and ate together
  Beneath their shade, long months ago.

The shade is gone where then we sat,
  All bare the leafless branches spread,
Far scattered on the Autumn blast,
  The leaves lie withered now and dead

The happy song-birds, too, are gone,
  Far to the southern lands away;
No more their warbled echoes wake,
  The early dawning of the day.

Robed in a winding sheet of snow,
  Now lie the fields once green and fair;
Wild winds o'er faded nature shrieks,
  The sad requiem of the year.

Farewell to summer and its joys,
  Farewell green leaves and flowers gay;
Thou songbirds too, a kind farewell,
  For all things here must pass away.

And we, ere many years are gone,
  Down in the silent grave must lie;
While the storms and the winds above,
  Will sing our long last lullaby.

Yet 'tis alone our mortal part,
  With mortal things of earth must lie;
Unending life our spirit's find,
  Where leaves and flowers never die.

Free'd is that land of love and light,
  From winter's dreariness and gloom;
No frosts or chilling winds can blight,
  Its fair and everlasting bloom.

Sweet rest, may there the weary find,
  And progress upward, evermore;
With sin, and woe, and death behind,
  Eternal life and joy before.

Antwerp, Mich.

ORIGINAL ESSAYS.

For the Pilgrim.

A NEW YEARS DISSERTION.

For the first time in the history of the PILGRIM, do I, as a stranger among a great portion of the readers of this excellent and well conducted paper, attempt to write a friendly greeting. A stranger I say, but not to all, for quite a number of you I have met with before, and others no doubt, have seen me in person which to me are unknown. Let this be as it may, it is my porpose to write occasionally for the columns of the PILGRIM the present year, God sparing my life, and then, if the editors will accept and publish the same, you and I may form a closer intimacy ere the present year closes.

One thousand eight hundred and seventy-two is now to be numbered with the things of the past, adding one more year to the long column of years, from which time we date the christian era. Think, more than eighteen hundred years have passed by since the little babe of Bethlehem was circumcised after the custom of the Jewish law. Again thirty years after this event, was He publicly declared to be the Son of God, and then in the short time of three years following this event, was He publicly crucified on Calvery's summit. Thus we see that as year after year would roll back into eternity with the things then transpiring, other years with new occurrences would take their places. But in no instance could the succeeding year bring forward what the preceding one had carried along with itself in any other way than by memory. What a blessed gift *memory is!* With this we can retrace the ocean of time, and bring to our remembrance things that long since have happened and have passed away with the passing years. Some of these reminiscences of the past are of a pleasant, while others of a sorrowful nature. Some of them we would fondly cherish and often feel sad that we are so slow in bringing them up before our minds with all the little incidents connected therewith, while others we are as ready to have buried in the dark past.

Standing, as we are, upon a new era of time, we naturally look prospectively into the future of the present year, arranging things for the present and perhaps another year still farther away. Had we not as poor weak and perishable mortals, better first take a retrospective view? Let us look into the year just passed, and let us try and bring up some of the things that are now recorded in eternity. Husbands and wives, how many of you can recall to mind the happy hours you and your dear companions spent together on New Year's day just one year ago, or even later in the year. And where is one or the other of you now? Cruel death found his way to your domicils and carried one or the other a victim away, we hope, to a better world than this. Oh, the sighs and groans that then escaped from a heart that was bleeding for a loved one! I just now recall such scenes that happened in the past year. In what consist your present joy? Can you in truth say, "my joy and consolation is based upon the hope of meeting my partner in a country where years are not numbered and where the hand of God will wipe away all tears from our eyes?

Fathers and mothers, how many of you were called to the painful duty of standing by the bed side of a dying son or daughter, one that was near and dear to your hearts? Perhaps that son or that daughter was allowed by you, as Christian parents, to indulge freely in the vanities of the world, so much so that all their precious time of former years was entirely taken up in these sinful indulgences, and your ears were saluted with the words, "Papa, Mamma, O, I don't like to die, I am afraid to die, I am a sinner, pray for me." Many, yea very many have passed away with the past year uttering language of a similar nature.

Fathers and mothers, let me entreat you as a lover of your souls, ask yourselves the solemn question this New Years week, "have I done my duty to my children and family as God's word and my own good judgment would indicate that I should have done, first for myself, and secondly for my family at large, or may not some of my own children, they of my own household, stand up against me in the day of judgement?" O, do have an eye upon yourself and your children; and let this New Year cause you to form, within you, new resolutions for the better, and pray God that you may successfully carry them out?

Sons and daughters, how many of you were called during the year just passed to witness the last faint breathing of a kind Christian parent, one that often prayed with, and for you? Do you now recollect how the silent tear unbidden stole down your cheek, and perhaps fell upon the cold brow of your best loved friend on earth, how as orphans you sought the orphan's prayer, your heart broken and bleeding, almost, if not altogether willing to have the Savior to pour in oil and wines? Did you carry these feelings through all the past year and still out of the ark of safety, and do you mean to carry them through another year? Beware, there is danger ahead. Death may lay his icy hand on you before the present year closes, and lay your body low, and launch your spirit into eternity.

Ministers of the Gospel, have we been as faithful in our calling as we should, or could have been in the past year? Upon us hang weighty matters. Oh can we be so happy as to hear the Master of the house say, "you have been faithful in all my house, you have not shunned to declare the whole will and council of God. Now sit down with Abraham, Isaac and Jacob in the Fathers Kingdom." Such no doubt have passed away from our side, in the past year. Their voices are heard no more by us. Will we not double our diligence for the future? The present year may close the labors of quite a number of us. Who is ready when the Master calleth?

Editors of the PILGRIM, you too have entered upon a new year. Your labors of the past year is before us. Your work when viewed from the present new era, is, like all of ours, in many things it might have been better, but upon the whole so far as my knowledge goes, it has rendered satisfaction pretty generally. This should give you some encouragement to you as the publisher of the paper, but I trust you too with the rest of us, will try to improve, correct, &c., as you pass along in the present year, which I trust may be a pleasant and prosperous one, one that may amply reward you for your labors that you may bestow upon the PILGRIM, and for the good that may grow out of the same spirituality, a crown of everlasting life. Carefully examine the matter intended for its pages by the light of the Gospel of Christ. Let every sentence be formed under the influence of the Holy Spirit so that nothing may appear upon the face thereof that will cause a blemish to be brought upon the purity of Jesus, or his holy word or in the least stigmatize our holy religion that we have based upon the chief corner stone. Pray much and watch not a little.

To all brethren and sisters, old and young, may this year be a pleasant and happy one. May the church of Christ rejoice in seeing many souls return from sin and unrighteousness to holiness and righteousness, so that if the Lord of heaven and earth sees fit to make his appearing that many, many might be permitted to go in with Him and feast with Him in His Fathers kingdom. Even so Lord, Amen. C. G. LINT.

Dale City, Pa.

ORIGINAL HISTORY OF THE BAPTIST BRETHREN'S BEGINNING IN AMERICA.

This manuscript was intended for the *Pilgrim Almanac*, but crowded out, we therefore insert it in the PILGRIM, hoping that it will be satisfactory, both to the writer and our readers. The copy was written in the German and translated by L. Furry.

There came from Swartzenau, Germany, several families in the year 1719 to Germantown, Pennsylvania, and in the following year, 1720, 30 families more, all Baptist Brethren, also from Germany, with Peter Becker their preacher. They came from different places in Germany to Germantown and Philadelphia, Pennsylvania. These brethren organized a congregation at Germantown with their teacher, Peter Becker in the year 1821. After that, some of the Brethren moved to Conestoga, Lancaster county, some to Skippack, others to Oly and Falkens *Schwam fangus. Then had they, at different places, their meetings with Peter Becker, their preacher and overseer. (Then the brethren agreed to choose another preacher, and the choice, by a majority of voices, fell on brother Conrad Beissel for speaker, and John Hildebrand for deacon, assistants in the service at Conestoga, by the counsel of Peter Becker as †Bishop with the brethren at Germantown, because Peter Becker dwelled there. But Conrad Beissel at Conestoga soon caused some difficulty by commencing other ways (order) with the brethren of Conestoga and conceived an idea to keep the Saturday instead of the Lord's day as a seven dayer. After many and long admonitions, the church could not avail anything with Conrad Beissel to leave his own ways and to yield obedience to the Germantown brethren.) In the meantime, in December 1729, Alexander Mack, also arrived from Germany to Germantown. Then the congregation agreed with Mack to decide by voice of the majority of the congregation whether to keep the Sabbath or Sunday for the Lord's day, when 11 voices agreed with Conrad Beissel to keep with him, and 27 for Sunday, with Peter Becker and Alexander Mack. So Becker and Mack with the brethren in Germantown and Conestoga, proceeded as the majority decided. (But Conrad Beissel, upon his own hand, commenced the Cloister (or nunnery) at Ephrata to establish the seven dayer, (Seventh day Baptist) and he has for a considerable time priestridden several brethren and sisters.) After Alexander Mack had died at Germantown in the year 1735 was Michael Frantz chosen for speaker and John Landis for deacon. In the year 1735, at Conestoga, Lancaster Co., Pa., Michael Frantz was speaker and Bishop about 12 years, from 1735 to 1747 and then moved West: after that came Michael Pfoutz in his stead as speaker and bishop, from the 1747 to 1769, 22 years in the Conestoga Congregation, where he then died at the age of 50 years, the 4th of May 1759. Then came Christian Lengenecker in his stead as speaker and Bishop in the same Congregation from 1769 to 1772, a time of three years. After that, because the congregation had considerably spread, the Brethren concluded to divide the Conestoga into three districts in the year 1872, one district called Conestoga, the other White Oak and the other Swatara. Then were Peter Eichenberger and Jacob Stull appointed as overseer for Conestoga Congregation; Christ. Longenecker and John Zug for the White Oak, and Han Jacob Bashor and George Kline for Swatara, Berks Co. district.

In the year 1798 or 1800 was the Swatara district again divided into, two districts as Little and Big Swatara.

Now, or from this time, my manuscript covers the Conestoga Congregation only; written from time to time by Eichenberger and Jacob Stull. After Eigenberger went away, in the year 1801, was David Kemfer chosen to the ministry, and Jacob Stoll, Bishop. After that, while the Congregation increased, was in 1815 Jacob Pfoutz and Abraham Zug both chosen for speakers. In 1822 Jacob Stoll died in his 92 year. He was a Bishop 67 years.

In 1823 are Jacob Pfoutz and Abraham Zug, both, by the laying on of hands ordained to the office of Bishoprick.

1831 was Christian Bomberger chosen for speaker in Conestoga Congregation.

1832 David Kemfer died at the age of 81 years.

1841 Abraham Zug died; his age was 69 years, 4 months and 22 days.

October 5th, 1841, was organized the Tulpehocken Congregation from a part of Conestoga, a part of White Oak, and from a part of the Little Swatara, and John Zug was chosen for their minister. Named Tulpenhocken.

1810 Christian Rupp was chosen for a minister.

1844 Joseph Myers was chosen for a minister.

1845 Jacob Reinhold became a minister.

1849 Israel Myers was chosen for a minister.

1861 Bishop Jacob Pfoutz died, aged 87 years, 5 months and 25 days. Was a minister and Bishop 49 years in Conestoga.

Jan. 1864, again is the Conestoga Congregation divided into three districts, the one named Conestoga, the other Ephrata and the other West-Conestoga, and Samuel Harley chosen for minister.

1866 William Tries was chosen to the ministry.

1866 Samuel Myers and Jacob Hockman were chosen ministers.

1870 Isaac Sherk was chosen to the ministry.

1870 Israel Myers died, aged, 56 years, 4 months and 20 days.

C. BOMBERGER.

MAIN MISSION.

Dear Brethren:—Being aware that your readers feel a desire to hear or read something about the Main mission, and as we ascribe our success, (so far as we may call it such,) to the blessings of God, drawn down by the united, and unceasing prayers of our dear brethren and sisters in our behalf; of which praiseworthy exercise your readers doubtless, love an honorable share; I will gratify them with an article on that subject.

We landed on our field of labor on the first of Nov. On Sunday the third we preached for the first time, and likely, the first sermon ever preached by a Bro. in that State. It seemed the Lord had a hand in making and opening so that we could preach several times that day, for owing to wet weather, the minister in charge, did not attend, and so we were invited to fill the appointment, which we did as God gave ability, and we learned, with a degree of satisfaction. But not knowing their customs and habits, we, at first, rather felt ourselves slighted, as no one seemed to take in hand to make arrangements for further appointments, and when going to prayer, sometimes one or two, at other times none at all would kneel with us. At first we looked upon these things as indignaties offered unto us, but we soon learned otherwise, for some offered us their dwelling houses, at any time we seen fit to make an appointment, without first asking their consent, and as to kneeling in prayer, we also learned that mostly only those who audibly pray wil kneel; and the rest generally keep their seats. On the following Sabbath a similar vacancy gave us an opening at another Meeting-house. Thus we continued preaching, and visiting from house to house, until the evening of the first of Dec., when we had our last meeting with them, which made thirty-three meetings altogether. We had quite an affecting time when we bade them farewell, many tears were shed, many desires expressed to be remembered in our prayers: as well as desires made to return again.

The people among whom we labored are strictly moral, not only moral, but a majority of them are religiously inclined; in short, they answer very near to the testimony given to a Cornelius, "One that feared God, and gave much alms, and one that prayed always." Those Christian graces they measurably possess. Of this, we are witnesses; for that which they have been instructed in, they are quite zealous to carry out, whether Scriptural or traditional. As to almsdeeds, if we may judge by the hospitality bestowed upon us as entire strangers, we must decide they stand second to none with whom we ever formed acquaintance. Where-ever we came we shared the very best they had, and that with such a degree of cheerfulness that betokened the act to be done as "unto the Lord," "in the name of a disciple," "praying always," may be equivalent to regular attendants on prayer which we found these people to be who make a profession. Generally speaking they, are an intelligent, orderly, well informed people: especially well versed in the Holy Scriptures; at the same time like the Ethiopean Eunuch, have need that some one guide them, so that they may understand what they read. Some may wonder why we returned so soon when we had such a prospect before us. I will give our reasons which have been satisfactory, so far, to all we met. A severe New England winter was at the door, in fact, already set in. About 8 inches of snow was lying when we left, with a fair prospect of it accumulating every day, and which sometimes falls to the depth of from 5 to 6 feet, and then the horses nearly all sick so that those who could not wade the snow, were deprived of attending meeting, and we had no other way of getting from place to place. On account of the

*I had no other word for Schwam It would prefer overseer.

horse disease our labors are confined to quite a small circuit; which, for a time we much regretted, but afterwards considered it to have been providential, thus demonstrating that by perseverance an interest can be awakened among those people, which we could not have learned by going from place to place.

Love to all.

D. M. HOLSINGER.

NEW YEAR.

A cheering thought pervades many minds at the approach and opening of of New Year's day; it being the beginning of the year, and also the first in the year, January, which seems two faced, looking back over the past and forward upon the new.

While in meditation over the past, many meanderings come clustering around the mind, in drawing a picture of the workings amidst the human family, knowing that there is a supreme Being that rules in heaven and earth, who is unchangeable; yet many seek to find him in various places that he has not said he could be found.

When Christ was born he was searched for by many, even the wise of the world but he could not be found, only where he had told them through prophetic language. So with the first month, its only place among all the twelve is at the beginning. From this we learn that God cannot be approached, only by his appointed ways.

When we were brought into existence, his law controlled the same,and we learn that many live but a few minutes, hours, days, weeks, months, or years and pass away like the passing years. Some in sickness and sorrow all their days, some in luxury 'till near the last, not lifting their voices in thankfulness to the great I Am. How many can say with the beginning of the New Year, that I am a christian, my ways are of God's appointment, when God calls I obey, hear him, and answer, 'come unto me.'

Dear reader, are you as obedient as the New Year, or why can you not date your return to God with the year? When sickness prostrates you, you must obey, when death comes you will obey, and when God calls to judgement, obedience comes again,and when the words that all who are accountable can read or hear read, "come ye blessed, inherit the kingdom prepared for you from the foundation of the world," or "depart ye workers of iniquity into everlasting punishment prepared for the devil and his angels." What joy if the first salutes our ears, but what sorrow if the word depart? Remember you and I will obey one or the other. O, may we take heed to our ways while in the present life, knowing that we can look back over the past year and speak of its changes, drouth and moistening rains, of sickness and health, of joy and grief, families whole and broken, but of the present and coming year we know but little; but we hope for God's blessings and a fruitful year, with health and strength. Think what your feelings would be if you were to give me many rich gifts, but in return I would treat you unkind and unthankful, think! think!! Stop, and think how you have spent the past year, and what thy future career should be to be obedient.

Now dear PILGRIM your twelve months have closed and the new has begun, may your progress be with the progressing year as fruitful as the year is desired to be, ever abounding with truth, strengthening and encouraging brethren and sisters on their way home, with strong invitations to sinners to turn—bring food to the hungry and water to the thirsty that they may rejoice while the angels of heaven unite to praise God, that the lost is found the dead alive and the number of worshipers increased. Your pages have been welcomed by many, and may they be more so in the coming year, that no contentions find way to thy pages but peace, harmony and good feelings rule.

A happy New Year, a pleasant close, with the bright prospect of entering into the haven of eternal rest.

W. SADLER.

Nankin, O.

FROM OREGON.

Dear Brethren and Friends:—In compliance with the request of many of the brethren and friends that I met with in the state of Iowa, I will say that I left my present home on the 2nd. day of September enroute for Iowa. Stopped with the brethren in Jackson Co, Rogue River Valley, Oregon, four days, had one meeting. Preached the funeral of our respected young friend John Henry Wimer, who died the 28th. of Aug. in his 22nd. year, had a very attentive congregation. From thence we traveled to California, stopped with the brethren there near Lathrop only a few days, had one meeting, visited a few families, viz: Eld. George Wolf, Bro. Peter S. Garman, Bro. Jacob Shelly and Jacob F. Flory, and a few others, who all treated us very kindly. On Friday morning the 13th. of Sept. we took the emigrant train for Omaha, thence to Iowa. Arrived at Bro. Nathan Millers near Lacona, Warren Co. Iowa on Saturday the 21st., had four meetings here, one person was received into the church by baptism. We had a very pleasant time with the few brethren and friends who reside here, and others who met us.

On Tuesday morning the 24th, Bro. Jacob and sister Cynthia Shoup, who started for their residence in Marion Co. Iowa, took me in their conveyance. Had one meeting in their neighborhood and from thence they conveyed me to my old residence near South English, Keokuk Co., Iowa, at which place we arrived on Friday evening the 27th of Sept. Here I remained a little over one month attending to some temporal affairs, visited a great many of the brethren and friends, was present at three Communion Meetings, one near Dresden in Poweshiek Co., one near my old residence and one in the south-eastern part of Keokuk county, also was present at a good many other meetings. Was met with a very kind reception ,was very well treated, and enjoyed a feast of fat things. There were six persons baptized in Keokuk Co. while we were there. Saw many brethren with whom I had enjoyed happy seasons in days and years that are in the past; and while there it was renewed again. On the fourth Sunday in Oct. was the last meeting I was at in Keokuk Co. There was a very large collection of brethren and friends, the attention and order were very good and their seemed to be a very good feeling among the brethren. In all probability our next meeting will be in eternity.

On the first of Nov. we were again on board the cars enroute for the far West. Arrived at Altoona, Polk Co. Iowa next morning, stopped with Eld Georg R. Baker remained with them and other brethren over Sunday was present at three meetings. Here we also had a very pleasant season with the brethren, was very kindly received and entertained. Stopped a few days in Rogue River Valley, Oregan. Arrived at our present residence near Sublimity, Marion Co. Oregon the 20th of Nov. found all well. Thank God. Had a very pleasant trip and good health, traveled nearly six thousand miles over mountains, deserts, valleys and plains, exposed to dangers in various ways, but the good Lord watched over us and kept us from all danger. Thanks be unto his Great name. The brethren here are in usual health and there seems to be a growing interest among them. On last Sunday there was one person baptized making fourteen in all since we moved to Oregan, which was last Oct. a year ago. We have never yet regretted our moving to this place, the Lord is here and we can serve Him as well here as elsewhere.

Now I will close by tendering my heartfelt greeting of love to all, also my thanks to the brethren and friends for their kind treatment exercised toward me. Your unworthy servant would say to all our dear brethren everywhere, remember us in your prayers.

DAVID BROWER.

Sublimity, Oregon.

The apostle says we are "epistles, known and read of all men." They read us every day, while perhaps they have no desire to read God's word; and the information they get from reading our daily lives, is the evidence to them of the real value of the religion we profess.

FAMILY READING.

One of the most important duties of the head of a family is to supply its members with an abundance of good reading, carefully selected, to meet the wants, tastes and mental capacities of each. No parent can be negligent of this duty without incurring the greatest responsibility and violating a sacred trust. As good reading matter finds its way into a home, the very atmosphere of that home, gradually, it may be, but surely changes. The children begin to feel a new and brighter life opening before them in knowledge, duty and love; they talk about men and places, books and authors, the past and the future, and discuss the issues of the present. New fields of usefulness and pleasure open for them, and out of this number will come forth intelligent, and if the right kind of moral influence is thrown around them, good men and women to fill honorble places, and become useful members of the church and of society.

The periodical literature of the day is so abundant and so good in quality that by careful selection, the best thoughts of the greatest men may be reached, on all the branches of science, the industries and religion. The already long list of good books is constantly increasing, and at prices within the reach of even the poorest by a denial of useless, harmful and expensive luxuries, and appropriating the savings to such purposes. Then those who have imbibed a love of reading, study and improvement, and the investigation of new and useful topics are less likely to be led astray by the light and erroneous views that will certainly be presented to them all along their pathway through life.

A. B. BRUMBAUGH, M. D.

Huntingdon, Pa.

EARNESTNESS.

The late Rev. Rowland Hill, in once addressing the people of Wotton, raising himself, exclaimed, "Because I am in earnest, men call me an enthusiast. When I first came into this part of the country, I was walking on yonder hill, and saw a gravel pit fall in and bury three human beings alive. I lifted up my voice for help so loud, that I was heard in a town below at a distance of near a mile; help came, and rescued two of the sufferers. No one called me an enthusiast *then*: and when I see eternal destruction ready to fall on poor sinners, and about to entomb them irrecoverably in an eternal mass of woe, and call aloud on them to escape, shall I be called an enthusiast *now*. No, sinners, I am no enthusiast in so doing, and I call on thee aloud to fly for refuge to the hope set before thee in the gospel."

OUR ANTIETAM LETTER.

CHRISTIAN WORK.

"To do good and to communicate forget not." So says the Apostle Paul. I shall perhaps never forget these kind words, nor the manner in which they became deeply impressed upon my mind. On the occasion of one of our lovefeast meetings, a short distance from this place, about five years ago, I met the first time, a dear brother, Elder S. who lives beyond the mountains in Adams county. He bore the marks of age, his beard and hair being silvered with the frosts of advancing years. He was experienced in life. I, youthful and had but a few weeks before entered the ranks of the army of Jesus—"a new creature" in the gospel world. It was in the evening, at the close of my first communion with the church, I met him, and among other of his words, were the words introducing this letter. They were impressed at once, and remain indelible. It proved a *keepsake*, and if that brother's eye should trace these lines, I will take occasion to say, "thank you." The words gave me an earnest not to be a selfish Christian, but to say a word for Jesus, now and then, and thus communicate the grace and experience of our holy religion. "To do good" is to do as Jesus did, for "He went about doing good." Therefore, my christian readers, "let your light shine," and may we prove by exemplary and earnest lives that "none of us liveth unto himself," but for the purpose unto which we are called and fitted by the Gospel.

We are Christians, and by this we profess to be followers of Christ. We profess to have repented of our old, sinful life; to have faith in Jesus; to have been baptized as Jesus, our unique exemplar was in the flowing stream, and to have received this Spirit, to be "a new creature," and to "walk in newness of life;" to live by prayer and faith and love and hope; to represent our absent Master. How do we fulfill our high and holy calling? If by self-examination we find ourselves wanting, may God help to take heed, lest we fall short. "To do good and to communicate forget not." Yea, "*forget* not."

But says a correspondent, "How can I do any good?" You cannot of yourself. All our help must come from Jesus, therefore, He said, "Lo, I am with you always." As surely as we love Him, and "walk worthy of the vocation wherewith we are called," so surely will He go with us each day to help us say a word for His glory, say a word to create hope in some desponding breast, or shed a ray of light in some heart which is dark with sin, or a word of advice to "an erring brother," or a word of comfort to a bereaved heart. You feel an interest in those around you, then speak a word about their welfare, and thus help them as Jesus gives you help. So there are ten thousand ways to "do good" in the world. Please read 1 Tim. 4: 12 and Titus 2: 7.

You can all talk for your own personal interests, say something for the cause of Christ, also. Many of you can write letters, and I think too, you might write news and christian thoughts for the PILGRIM. The long evenings have come, and I trust we shall soon have plenty of good, cheering words coming through the public press. Let us have reports of news, statistics, &c., from every congregation. The grace of Christ be with you all. MONITOR.

Waynesboro, Pa.

A DIALOGUE BETWEEN GAMALIEL AND NICODEMUS.

For the sake of properly illustrating the early history of John the Baptist and Christ, we attribute the following conversation to Gamelial and Nicademus, and may be presumed to have taken place a short time after John commenced preaching in the wilderness.

Gamaliel. Well, Nicademus, which way this morning?

Nicademus. I think of going beyond Jericho, and perhaps near the Jordon.

Gam. Near the Jordon! What is going on there?

Nic. A somewhat strange and very peculiar person has been preaching there for the two last weeks; and I learn that the wilderness during the past few days has been almost alive with people, who never grow tired of hearing him preach.

Gam. What, a man preaching in the wilderness, who can he be?

Nic. By many who have heard him he is believed to be a young prophet.

Gam. Perhaps it would be much better for us to be very careful about such pretending prophets; as he may be another Judas of Galilee to rebel against the Romans.

Nic. He is not of Galilee; from what I have been able to gather, so far, it appears that he is from the hilly country south of Bethlehem.

Gam. What is his name, or has he any?

Nic. His name is John; the most of the people call him John the Baptizer.

Gam. The *Baptizer!* why is he called that, he don't *baptize* I hope?

Nic. Yes I have been told that all who are persuaded to follow him are baptized in the river Jordon.

Gam. He certainly cannot be a person of really great intellectual ability, or else he would certainly have visited that department of my school devoted to the "law and prophets."

Nic. He is said to be quite eloquent, and most remarkably well versed in every department of the Holy Scriptures.

Gam. You say he is from the hilly country, south of Bethlehem?

Nic. Yes, that is the general rumor.

Gam. Are you certain to what tribe he belongs, and who his father was?

Nic. I have not yet been able to ascertain the correctness of that matter: about ten years ago I saw a very handsome and intelligent young man in Hebron, who, I learned, lived not far from there, and the people called him John, and I concluded at that time that he might be the son of one of our priests, as I knew that one of them had a son by that name, and whether this is the same person, I am not quite able to tell; if he is then I know all about his parents.

Gam. [*Studies a few moments, and slowly says.*] Well now it slightly strikes my mind that I saw that very young man about ten years ago, and I am not certain but that I know him when he was a boy.

Nic. And indeed! is it possible! and where did you happen to see him?

Gam. One beautiful day in seedtime, when Luke, the eminent physician of Antioch, Matthew, the tax gatherer of Caperninm, and I were passing near the wilderness, we saw a noble looking young man seated upon a large rock that lay near a beautiful spring just at the foot of the Jordan bluff, with a measure of honey, and some locust by his side. He was reading from a small roll, which Matthew said was the book of Malachi, in the Hebrew language.

Nic. Did you enjoy the pleasure of conversing any with him?

Gam. When he saw us approaching, he gently folded the roll from which he was reading and placed it in his bosom. When we drew near where he was seated, he arose to his feet, and with a modest and humble bow saluted us with these beautiful words, "Grace and peace be unto you;" we much admired his manly courtesy, and greeted him with the salutation of our fathers "May thy days be long on earth" He bowed, but made no reply, though his countenance gave expressions of secret sadness, mingled with a ray of unknown hope. Never shall I forget the strange feelings that thrilled my bosom, when I heard the voice of the man of the desert. Silence prevailed for the space of one minute—all nature was still, then I simply remarked "I hope you are our kinsman by blood" He gently said "I am of the tribe of Levi: my father was of the course of Abia, and my mother whose name was Elizabeth, was of the daughters of Aaron"

Nic. Did you learn his fathers name?

Gam. Not for certain. Luke, who during this time was carefully contemplating our interesting stranger, remarked: "Gentle sir; are you not the son of Zacharias?" Just at this interesting moment we spied a band of Arab robbers making their way toward us, when the young man quickly said: "brothers make your escape, make haste." We rapidly made our way up a narrow vale, through the thick olive vines, and saw nothing more of our interesting Levite.

Nic. Did Dr. Luke know the young Levite's father?

Gam. While on our journey home he remarked that, he was of the opinion that he saw the same young man, some three years before that time. His father then lived among the hills, south of the city of David, and during his protracted illness, had called for medical aid, and it fell to his lot to visit him (being in Jerusalem at that time) and while there saw this young man, who was then about seventeen years old. Luke further remarked that when he saw him in his father's house he was reading the same roll that he had at the spring, and he thought he could recognize his features.

Nic. Do you remember anything of his appearance?

Gam. It was at least ten years ago that I saw him, and he was then a finely built young man, large black eyes, and hair of the same color. His complexion was somewhat affected by the desert sun, nevertheless his countenance strongly indicated a powerful mental capacity.

Nic. About what was his age?

Gam. Agreeable with what Luke intimated we judged him to be about twenty.

Nic. How was he dressed?

Gam. His manner of dress gave him the appearance of a prophet. Matthew conjectured that he might be a hermit.

Nic. Can you distinctly form an idea of what material his clothes were made?

Gam. He wore a large mantle, which presented a strange appearance and in all probability was made of camels' hair. This was drawn close to his body by means of a leathern girdle.

Nic. Did you learn whether he was living with his parents at that time?

Gam. Luke stated that if he was the son of the priest Zacharias, his parents were dead, having died some two years before that time; and Matthew remarked that he was living in a secluded cave not far from where we met him, and spent the greater part of his time reading the sacred rolls.

To be Continued.

Youth's Department.

WE ALL MIGHT DO GOOD.

We all might do good
 Where we often do ill;
There is always the way
 If there be but the will,
Though it be but a word,
 Kindly breathed or expressed,
It may guard off some pain,
 Or give peace to some breast.

We all might do good
 In a thousand small ways—
In forbearing to flatter,
 Yet yielding due praise;
In spurning all rumor,
 Reproving wrong done,
And treating but kindly
 The hearts we have won.

We all might do good,
 Whether little or great;
For the deed is not gauged
 By the purse or estate;
If it be but a cup
 Of cold water that's given,
Like the widow's two mites,
 It is something for heaven.

A TALK WITH THE LITTLE ONES.

It may be of some interest to you, my little readers, to tell you that after enjoying a pleasant trip from my home in Ohio, I arrived safely and well at the PILGRIM office. I never told you that I was going to make my home with the PILGRIM family, but the Editor knew it very well, and don't you think he requests me to write to you. Are you not glad that he remembers you? I am. I'm so glad he has introduced us. You see the Editor wants us to become acquainted. We thank him for it, but would feel more thankful could he think of some way to have us acquainted in the right way, but I suppose he knows his business, and thinks it best to remind us of a whole group of little wisdom seekers whom I have almost forgotten.

How I wish I could find some excuse for my long delay; but I can't, and if I could there would be no use of framing a whole column of excuses.

But what a slow way of talking this is. Excuse my little patience. I had almost forgotten how well you like to read, but what shall I write? How I wish some of our little readers were here in the office to-night to tell me what to write! I can half guess the many subjects you would have me write about. Some would want this, that and the other until I would get so tired listening that I would be tempted to tell some little mischievous urchin to pour all the ink out of the stand and fill it up with honey, so I might write a real sweet letter—one that would begin with love and end with love.

I wonder how you have spent your Christmas. May I not feel happy in believing you had a good time? I will tell you how I once saw a man spend Christmas. He spent it in a drunken fit; one of the worst kind of fits men, and sometimes boys, ever get. You see he thought it would look big to get drunk on Christmas, but, Oh, what a thought. I'll never forget that time as long as I live. A man drunk on Christmas. It looks bad enough to see a man drunk on any day, but will our little readers tell us why it looks so awful bad to to see a man drunk on Christmas?

F. M. SNYDER.

James Creek, Pa.

CARRIE'S STORY.

"Please, Carrie, put your sewing away and tell us a story? See its getting too dark to work."

"Well, what shall I tell you about?

"Little Willie and his dog, Captain."

"Wait one minute till I get Percy on my knee, and then I will commence."

As soon as they were all seated, Carrie began:

"In a country very far from here, there lived on the borders of the forest a poor wood-cutter. He had seven sons, the youngest of whom, Willie, was only eight years old. He was a good, obedient child, and was his father's favorite. One day the old wood-cutter felt so ill that he was obliged to stay in his hut, and not go out to his work at all. About noon he became so much worse, that he told Willie to go at one and fetch his brothers; and to tell them that their poor old father was dying. Willie ran as hard as he could to his brothers, and gave them their fathers message. The six brothers immediately set off for home, on the way disputing who would have the hut, who the ass, and who the large dog, Captain. When they came to the hut, the old man could scarcely speak. All he could say was,—"I give you all the hut, you six oldest, will have the ass, and my boy Willie, shall have the dog."

He then died.

Poor Willie cried as if his heart would break, but his brothers railed at him and told him to "hold his tongue."

The next day they buried the old man, and the day after they told Willie that they were going a day's journey into the forest and he would come with them. Willie asked if he might have Captain with him, and his brothers said "yes." In a few minutes all was ready, and they started off.

Just about dark they came to an open nook, and there they there stopped for the night. Soon they were asleep, and there was not a sound, except now and then the distant howl of a wolf. When Willie woke in the morning, he was *alone*. He called his brothers loudly, but there was no answer. His dog was still there with him and Willie said cheerily,—

"Come, Captain! we will go home." They set off through the dark woods. At dark Willie was not home, but had to stay in the forest. Just as they were asleep, a huge wolf sprang at them from a neighboring thicket. Captain sprang at the wolf, caught him by the throat and choked him. That night they slept little, and Willie was very glad when morning came. They pushed on all that day, and just as Willie was ready to sink from fatigue and hunger, he spied a light, not very far off. He struggled toward it, and at last came to a gate, which he opened and walked straight up to a large stone house. Willie knocked, and an old woman opened the door. She asked his name; he told her "Willie Bernard." She told him to come and bring his dog. She gave Willie some supper, and the dog a plate of scraps. After supper she asked his history, and told him he might live with her. Willie and she lived happily for the rest of their days.—*Young Folks' Rural.*

CORRESPONDENCE

A Reporter is wanted from every Church in the brotherhood to send us Church news, Obituaries, Announcements or anything that will be of general interest. To insure insertion, the writers name must accompany each communication. Our invitation is not personal but general—please respond to any call.

Dear Brethren and Sisters:—As the readers of the PILGRIM have been called upon to notice the account of a circumstance that transpired in London, perhaps it will not be amiss to promulge our view after surveying that given by Bro. Slifer as he earnestly inquires if there is anything wrong in the case. The service being called Dedication and Benediction of children in lieu of baptism is certainly sufficient for us to gather all we want regarding whether he expects the child to be baptized when it arrives to the age of discretion. The children of Israel killed the passover on the fourteenth day of the first month and roasted it with fire. Should they have killed it on the tenth day when they drew out and took it, struck the sideposts and lintel with the blood and then sod it in water in lieu of roasting and performed their ceremonies, we would hardly wonder if they intended to roast that which had been boiled: neither should we consider or make an ado whether they pleased God with their service, when God had said, "Eat not of it raw, nor sodden at all with water, but roast with fire." Ex. 12: 9. We are not under the jurisdiction of Levitical priesthood for which we should be thankful as the comers thereunto could not be made perfect. But the priesthood has been changed and there must of necessity be a change also of the law which required the violent to take it by force, and this force rent the veil of the temple from the top to the bottom and gives the scarlet dyed sinner, and the unclean access by accepting the conditions which "Wayfaring men, though fools may not err therein." Isa. 35: 8. It is said that there are over one thousand different forms of religion at the present day. If there were a thousand, exactly nine hundred and ninety-nine would be going wrong if Jesus' prayer availed anything when he implored the Father thus: "Holy Father keep through thine own name those whom thou hast given me, that they may be one, as we are." John 17: 11.

I do not rightly understand Bro. Slifer when he asks, if christian parents should ask us to bless their children. The prayers of the church should coincide with Jesus' prayer that we may be one; and I hope that our members may never become so sickly as to ask such a thing. Should the world make such request let us not publish them christian parents nor Christ-like people or we shall prefix and diminish God's word and be in danger of their blood being required at our hands.

Bro. Slifer inquires "who will say that he did wrong in thus gratifying them when he had such an illustrious precedent?" Jeroboam ordained a feast like unto the feast that was in Judah and offered upon the altar. But his priests were of his own make which had not been consecrated to communicate virtue. They had a precedent, their altar was fashioned like those in Judah, and yet they must hear from the man of God the lamentable cry, "O, altar, altar, upon thee shall priests be offered which offer incense upon thee, and men's bones shall be burnt upon thee.

It is claimed by various sects at the present day that men can bless each other and communicate the Holy Ghost by the virtue which is in them, but as our Savior gave us no such promise we may but expect to reap the reward of the ungodly by adding to "the prophecy of the book.

Peter told those on the day of Pentecost what to do for the remission of their sins. Ananias told Paul that it would wash his away, and this same Paul declares to the church at Corinth "that other foundation can no man lay than that is laid." And I have no fears that our elders in Annual Meeting will ever suffer a foundation to be laid to displease God, and rob his son Jesus Christ of the honor, "who has redeemed us with his own blood that he might purify unto himself a peculiar people zealous of good works." Pure religion and undefiled before God is to visit the sick; and when we visit our sick members; we should give all the comfort in our power to soul and body, what is more consoling to the afflicted christian than the promise connected with anointing. If we inform them of this, which is our duty, few would die without sending for the elders to anoint them in the name of the Lord. I have often been asked of infant consecration, &c., yet I have the first time to give the plea that our church don't do it. But my answer to them that are such is this: Jesus declared them fit subjects for his Father's Kingdom before he took them up in his arms. Although it was once said that the fathers had eaten sour grapes and put the childrens' teeth on edge, but God now says that we shall not have occasion to use this proverb again, as the son shall not bear the iniquity of the father, and attempting to purify or better that which God has made pure would be to hew out cisterns that can hold no water. And simultaneous to this, I fail not to tell them that while their babes are safe in the arms of Jesus that they are in a strange land and can only cross "by the washing of regeneration," Tit 3 : 5. which is the will of the father, and Jesus says that if any man will do his will he shall know of the doctrine, but no promise previous to this, after they have gone out of the way.

Yours in truth,

D. GIBSON.

New Market, Md.

MILLERSVILLE, Pa. }
Dec. 25th 1872. }

Dear Readers of the Pilgrim:—It has been some time since you have heard from me through the columns of the PILGRIM and now as I have a little recreation from the general routine of study I purpose leaving you hear from me, although I may not have much of interest to communicate to you. Since my arrival at school I have given myself wholly to study, consequently have not had time to write on subjects that would be of interest to the readers of the PILGRIM. I can assure you however that although I do not at present, take an active part in the work of publication, or in contributing to its columns, I am none the less interested. At some future time, perhaps not far distant, I expect to resume my labors with renewed energy. I am much interested and often feel like putting my hands to the work again—a work that we have the evidence of having been productive of good, and hope that it may be instrumental in performing a much greater work for the upbuilding and advancement of the Redeemers Kingdom in the future

On Friday evening Dec. 20th, school closed for one week. A large number of the students went to their homes to spend the vacation, but as it is some distance to my home, and the vacation being short, I remain in the vicinity of the school. It would have afforded me much pleasure to have returned to the old mansion house, and the PILGRIM home. If there is a place dear to me on earth it is home, and I claim there are many reasons why it should be. Cold and hard must be that heart that can be indifferent of it, especially when kind parents reside there. The feeling that clings to parents has more of heaven in it than earth. But our feelings are not always a rule of action, and I therefore deny myself of the pleasure that I might have realized from a visit to my home. On Saturday morning Dec. 22nd, I went to Lancaster City about four miles from Millersville. Here had the pleasure of meeting Bros. G. B. and H. B. Brumbaugh, who were on their way to Philadelphia, but stopped off here to remain several days. There was preaching at different places until Tuesday evening. The weather was very cold, yet the meetings were generally well attended, and some interest manifested. I accompanied Bros. during their stay here, and enjoyed myself much. I formed a number of acquaintances and found the brethren and sisters kind and sociable, alive and active in the performance of the Master's work. Bro. H. B. B. informs me that the prospects for the PILGRIM the coming year are good, and this information gives me encouragement. I hope that our brethren and sisters are going to take a greater interest in behalf of the PILGRIM than they have heretofore, and if so we can expect to accomplish more in the future.

On Tuesday morning Bros. went on to Philadelphia, and I returned to Millersville again. Things are very dull about here now. Of the five or six hundred students, there are perhaps not more than a hundred here now. I spend the time in my study, and feel much refreshed from having a little recreation.

It is now Christmas morning, the time that is hailed with joy and gladness by all. The stealthy steps of time have carried us on to the verge of another new period of time, and just before the old, shaggy, tattered year takes its flight, there is a general animation; the cold selfish feelings that are sometimes so prominent, are covered by those of kindness and love, every action indicates a heart in which burns a brilliant flame of love, and thus earth approaches nearer the likeness of a Paradise than at any other period of time, and why should it not? Surely the remembrance of that great event, the presentation of the greatest gift of which we can conceive should dispel all those narrow, contracted, selfish feelings and fill the soul with ecstasy. It is true we are receiving manifestations of God's goodness daily, and hourly, and these are reminders of this goodness, and should awaken feelings that should cause a perpetual flow of gratitude.

"But O, thou bounteous giver of all good,
Thou art of all thy gifts the crown."

His gifts, His kindliness and love are apparent wherever we look, but on this glorious morn, we have God manifest in the flesh, presented to us, and He is truly the crown of them all. This consideration is what should give the day its history, and to the Christian, it is a thought that awakens emotions of a higher type than those occasioned from any other source.

But I will perhaps become too lengthy. There is one subject I wish to direct attention to before we close. Since I have been here, I am more than ever impressed with the necessity of having a school conducted by the brethren, and situated among the brethren. If we had a school of this kind our brethren and sisters who wish to attend school could feel at home, and our children who are not connected with the church would be less exposed to influences that are productive of evil. The school here is not sectarian, and all sectarian feelings are, in a measure, avoided, but the influence is not such as is calculated to bring our children to the church. There are three here that belong to the church, and perhaps four or five of the brethren's children that are not members, and at the different schools in Pennsylvania alone, there are perhaps hundreds attending school. Now it would certainly be better if these were brought under the influence of the church. I have been making observations in reference to these things, and think I have been in positions to make them correctly, and my conclusions are that the schools generally are very dangerous places for our brethren's children. Even if the schools are unsectarian the general influence is to drift them into the popular current, and besides this, there are various amusements that are looked upon by popular christendom as being harmless that the Brethren look upon—and I think rightfully too—as being productive of evil. I do not suppose there are any of our brethren that would be pleased to have their children engage in dancing as an amusement, yet it is much practiced at some schools at least, and is looked upon as not being harmful. It is not necessary that I condemn it as an evil, I have my opinions in reference to these things, but do know that it has the appearance of evil, and should not be engaged in by Christians, and our youth should be taught to look upon it as improper amusement and of a low order. I might refer to many things of a similar nature that are carried on at schools that tend to evil. In all these things our brethrens children are as likely to engage as any other, and I was told of one that engaged in it very freely during this vacation. I suppose if those parents knew it, they would not appreciate that knowledge very highly. How much better for such if we had a school located near a church, and at such times have them attend preaching instead of engaging in such amusements They would enjoy themselves just as well, and be free from the many temptations that are presented at such times. Besides this, our brethren and sisters want a school where they can feel at home, where they can attend regularly, services conducted by the brethren, and enjoy their society. We cannot feel at home at many of the schools, and it is especially so with our sisters. There are many that neglect their education on this account, and I think it is high time that better educational advantages are placed within their reach, I believe that it is just as important that our sisters be educated as our brethren. It is not merely the attainment of facts that will fit us for some calling in life that we want, but we want culture, a strong, healthy, vigorous mind,—a mind that is capable of thinking clearly and accurately. This culture our sisters need as much as we. They have just as important positions to fill in life, and I see no reasons why their education should be neglected. I may have more to say in reference to this subject in the future. I hope that a move will be made soon towards the erection of school buildings designed especially for the church. I would enjoy myself much better if I could be surrounded by the church, and I believe this is the experience of all our brethren who are attending school.

J. B. B.

Dear Brethren:—I have been thinking of writing a little for the PILGRIM for some time, and as there is no meeting to-day that we can attend, I will improve my time in reading and writing. I have been wondering and thinking much of late as to how I could do some good to somebody, and seeing the liberality and kindness of the dear Editors of the PILGRIM in sending it for $1.25 in case any body wished to make any one a present of it. I adopted a plan, that is, to send the PILGRIM to a few dear friends that I think will like it and probably pay for it after they read it. If I don't see their name in the money list some time before the year is out I will pay for them myself. I expect there will be some that will think it, if they do not tell me, that I had better keep my money and let some wealthy members do that instead of me, as we are really poor folks, but I am afraid the rich ones would say they could not afford it.

Now dear brethren and sisters don't think hard of me for writing the way I do, I mean just what I say. Who is it that has not got some dear friends yet out of the ark of safety or on an erroneous path, probably, that might be saved yet before it is too late by simply reading the PILGRIM, as I think you will all admit that it contains much pure Gospel truth, and as the Gospel tells us that one soul is worth more than the whole world, and as there are so many erroneous teachers in this world, I think the brethren have more than they can do to preach the truth to everybody. I think the sisters ought to help in the great work by writing for our periodicals and sending them to all the outsiders they can, and by letting your neighbors read them after you have read them. I am convinced that most people like to read the PILGRIM whether members or not, and probably, like myself, they never had the Scripture so plainly explained before as it is in the PILGRIM as I must confess that it was through this paper that I had my eyes opened to the awful condition that I was in, and I think and hope that many more will see as I did before it is too late, and as it was through the kindness of a brother that sent the PILGRIM to us that I got acquainted with it. I feel as though I could not be thankful enough to him for the precious gift

LOVINA MARSH.

Dear Pilgrim:—Please give notice in your paper, that we intend, if no interfering Providence, to have a series of meetings at Spring Run meetinghouse, Mifflin Co. Pa. two miles from McVeytown Station P. R. R. commencing on the evening of the 8th of February 1873, to continue at least until the evening of the 14th. An invitation is given to members who wish to be with us, and we wish to be remembered by our ministering brethren of whom we do not wish to make special choice, but greatly desire to be remembered and have their ministerial aid. Think of us and help us.

JOSEPH R. HANAWALT.

Dear Brethren:—Please announce that we intend to hold a series of meetings in the Free Spring Church. Juniata Co., Pa., commencing on the 9th of January and to continue some 8 or 10 days. An invitation is given to the members to be with us, especially the ministering brethren.

MICHAEL BESHOAR.

The Weekly Pilgrim.

JAMES CREEK, PA., Jan. 3rd, 1873.

☞ HOW TO SEND MONEY.—All sums over $1.50, should be sent either in a check, draft or postal order. If neither of these can be obtained, have the letter registered.

☞ WHEN MONEY is sent, *always* send with it the name and address of those who paid it. Write the names and post office as plainly as possible.

☞ EVERY subscriber for 1873, gets a *Pilgrim Almanac* FREE.

OUR HOLIDAYS.

For a long time we looked forward to the holidays with the expectation of having a pleasant recreation, but as the time approached our labors seemed to increase and found that the only way to get free of office duties would be to leave. Bro. Geo. and ourself had, for some time, under contemplation, a trip East and concluded this would be our only chance. On Friday p. m. we started for Lancaster, Pa., and reached the home of Bro. Rinchold about 9 o'clock where we were kindly received and spent our time with this family until the next evening when there was an appointment for us at the Neffsville Church. Next A. M. (Sunday) at Enas, some 3 miles north of Lancaster and in the evening at Neffsville Church, also in Lancaster, we filling the appointment at the former place and Bro Geo. at the other. At these appointments we had the pleasure of the assistance and society of Eld. Rider from near Elizabethtown. Bro. Rider labors in the German and is a man of much Christian zeal, courteous, kind and sociable. He was accompanied by Bro. Gibble, a deacon, who gave testimony to our labors, as is the custom of some of the eastern churches.

According to arrangement, our time was now up for Lancaster, but as the meeting seemed to grow in interest, Bro. Rinchold prevailed on us to extend our time until Tuesday morning. On Monday we attended the funeral of brother Herr's child and in the p. m. visited the household of Bro. Peter Grosh who came into the camp at a late hour but abounds in love for the cause. We spent a pleasant season with the family and they seemed to be much encouraged. In the evening we held our last appointment in the Neffsville church. Notwithstanding the weather was extremely cold, the meetings were well attended and considerable interest manifested. Some three decided in favor of Jesus, and we believe a number of others were almost persuaded. This church is under the charge of Eld. Rinchold who seems to rule well and has the confidence and co-operation of his members. The membership is sociable and disposed to entertain those who place themselves within their households. We enjoyed our stay with them much. We made a pleasant acquaintance in the home of Bro. B. Evans. Here we met a young brother who accepted the call at the age of 12 years and seems to be quite consistent and faithful. His sister Sallie has also chosen the "good part" and there are several other brothers that we hope will follow their good example and flee the wrath to come before it may be too late. Bro. Evans intends to locate in Lancaster by Spring, having for one of his objects, the means of affording better facilities for the education of his children. This is right as we learned, by observation, that education to children is of far more importance than wealth. Wealth has been a great curse to the children of some of our eastern brethren.

During our stay at Lancaster we met our younger brother and PILGRIM associate, who is attending school at Millersville. He is deeply impressed with the necessity of having a Brethren's school in Pa., and has under contemplation to establish one in the vicinity of James Creek, as a better, more accessable and healthful location cannot be found in the State.

On Thursday morning we continued our journey to the city of Philadelphia and made our first call at the house of Eld, C. Custer where they were ready and waiting for us. In this family we call ourselves at home nor could we feel otherwise as there was nothing spared to make us feel comfortable. With his daughter, sister Mary, we have a special acquaintance as she had her first experience in teaching in our district and boarded with us. She is now teaching in Camden, N. J. and is succeeding finely.

The brethren in the city sold their old church in the Fall with the expectation of having a new one built again the Holidays, but were disappointed, so that we had not the pleasure of worshipping with the members in a church capacity, and the weather was so extremely unfavorable that we did not make many calls. On Thursday evening before leaving the city we stopped with Eld. Jacob Spanogle and spent quite a pleasant evening in his family. At 11:40 we took the train for home, but when we entered the coach it was jammed with people and what little space was left was filled with smoke. We then entered a sleeping coach where we were supplied with splendid beds—commended ourselves into the care of God and slept soundly until late next morning. On account of the heavy fall of snow and the storms we did not reach home until Friday morning, when we found all well and several hundred letters that had accumulated during our absence. Since then our lot has been one of incessant labor, often until the midnight hour, yet we do not complain, but feel greatly encouraged at the increased favor which the PILGRIM is receiving everywhere. From present indications its circulation will be largely increased for 1873 and hope there may be a proportionate increase in its usefulness.

PERSONAL.

I. J. ROSENBERGER, M. A. E. will owe us $1.00 on 1873.

LOVINA MARSH: Please tell us which names are to be credited with the $3.00 sent us.

GEO. W. JONES: S. L. M's name is booked for the *Phrenological Journal*. Due us $2.00.

JOHN ZUCK: S. E. G's PILGRIM is paid to No. 12, 1873.

F. W. DOVE: S. G. and G. G., are back on 1872, 40 cts. each.

C. C. ROOT: How much money did you send us under date of December 10th. Who for and what year?

WM. DOMER: If L. D. did not receive his paper for 1872, we will send it to him for 1873, by paying the extra 25 cts.

D. R. FRICKMAN: If J. B. did not get his paper we expect no pay. Tell him to try it again.

ELD. A. J. C.: The subject needs a hearing. Let us have it.

JOHN J. HESS: Your name has no credit for 1872. You will know, send us what you think is due. Your name is booked for 1873.

S. M. WELLS: Did not receive the $1.25. Last amount all right.

LAURA H. M.: The old contract will be continued, but a little oftener, please.

C. H. W.: $1.25 for Sarah B., not received.

J. W. B.: All satisfactory. The Almanac is sent to E. S. If she does not receive it, let us know.

GEO. KINNEY: Thos. Price's year will run to No. 19, 1873.

JOHN ARNOLD: The draft was received.

JESSE CONNER: Your subscription runs out with No. 50, 1872. Your name is booked for 1873.

C. C. ROOT: We have no specimen copies of the *Phrenological Journal* to spare. It is very cheap at the price we offer. All those who have paid $1.50 for the PILGRIM can have the Journal by sending the extra $1.00.

CATH A. FORNEY: You owe us $1.12½ cts.

M. BLSHOAR: Due us 50 cts.

J. C. R.: We cannot send the *Phrenological Journal* for a less time than 1 year at club rates. The Journal is ordered.

THE MAIN MISSION.—We received two reports of this Mission just a little too late for the last No. of 1872, and as they both contain about the same in substance, and Bro. Holsinger's was partly in type before Bro. Longenecker's was received, we hope he will excuse us in not publishing both.

PILGRIM ALMANACS.—On account of the large number of subscribers coming in we may possibly have made some mistakes in sending the Almanacs. If any have not received them before or with this number, let us know and we will supply.

BEHIND TIME.—On account of press of business we are a little behind time, but will be all right in a short time.

MARRIED.

WADSWORTH—ADAMS.—On the 25th of December, 1872, Mr. Elias Wadsworth and Miss Lucinda Adams, all of Cambria Co., Pa. S. HILDEBRAND.

GARVER—LEHMER.—By the undersigned, at his residence, Bro. J. B. Garver of Huntingdon co. and sister Sarah Lehman of Churchtown, Cumberland co., all of Pa. DAVID NEISLEY.

DIED.

GOCHNOUR.—In the Conemaugh Church, Cambria co., Pa., on the 14th of November, 1872, sister Margaret Gochnour, wife of brother Stephen Gochnour, aged 32 years, 9 months and 16 days.

SMITH.—Also on the 17th, brother Henry W. Smith, better known by some as the Indian Doctor, aged almost 73 years.

MARQUEDANT.—Also on the 15th of December, sister Lovina, wife of friend George Marquedant, formerly Lovina Gochnour, aged 31 years and a few mos. STEPHEN HILDEBRAND.

LEHR.—On the 7th of September last with Typhoid fever, near Elkton, Md., Philip Liehr, (cousin of F. P. Loehr, and schoolmate of his in Germany), in his 60th year. He was a very active and zealous professor of the Christian religion, with which his bereaved family and friends comfort themselves. F. P. L.

FREDERICK.—In Owl Creek Church, Knox co., Ohio, Dec. 21, 1872, Bro. Jacob Frederick, aged 79 years, 1 month and 19 days. Funeral conducted by Bro. David Workman, to a large concourse of relations and friends, from Isaiah 38: 1. "Set thine house in order for thou shalt die and not live.

He leaves a kind widow, sister in the church, and 8 children to mourn his loss, six of whom are members of the Church. They need not mourn as those who have no hope, for he expressed a willingness to go home to rest. He was a faithful member upward of forty years.

Dearest grandfather thou hast left us,
Here thy loss we deeply feel;
But it was God that hath bereft us,
He can all our sorrows heal.

AMANDA GOCHNOWER.

SNIDER.—In the Upper Deer Creek Church Cass co., Ind., Dec. 11th, Laura E., daughter of friend Samuel and Hester Snider and grand daughter of brother Wm. and sister Catharine Snider, aged 1 year, 8 months and 5 days. Funeral conducted by the writer to a large number of friends and relatives, from the 90th Psalm 12 verse.

Our sweet little Laura E is singing above,
Surrounded with angels, and feasting on love:
The Savior has called her away from our sight,
Away in yon heaven, all dressed in pure white.

HIEL HAMILTON.

JOHNSON.—A beautiful and tender branch cut down by death in the form of diptheria, Dec 1st, 1872, in Fayette co., W. Va., belonging to the family of bro. Hiram and sister Lydia Johnson, aged 3 years and five months

Little Sallie called so early to be an angel in heaven we hope, with the dear parents to meet thee in glory!

Sleep, little prattler, gently sleep,
Beneath thy new made earthy mound;
Whilst sunbeams through the osiers peep,
And birds make music all around.

Rest, little prattler, gently rest,
Thy little pilgrimage is o'er;
Now nestle in the Savior's breast,
Safe on the bright and shining shore.

J. S. FLORY.

MONEY LIST.

G. W. Mull,	$ 1.50	F W Dove	4.50
Jos. Hoover	4.50	Jos M Detirr	3.75
Andrew Trostle	1.50	Wm Hertzler	1.50
Eld J Murray	1.70	Thos E Coffman	1.35
Sam'l Plough	1.70	Benj Z. Eley	1.50
J Hollinger	1.60	W H *Robey*	3.25
Dr J Bughley	3.00	John Ptontz	1.50
J P Detrick	1.50	J Longnecker	1.38
Wm. Biddle	7.50	J H Linebaugh	2.85
Jos Snowberger	4.50	S Burget	1.50
S M Smith	1.50	Wm Biddle	1.50
A. F. Cross,	1.25	Isaac B. Trostle	4.25
S Gresnickle	1.25	Ella Williams	1.50
Emma'l Slifer	5.00	J J Blough	4.00
Daniel Bock	3.00	Jacob P Neff	5.00
Sam'l Brallier	1.50	Catharine Kline	1.75
J L Frantz	5.00	Tobias Blough	1.25
Josiah Burger	1.25	P M Correll	3.50
Lovina Marsh	3.00	D C Moomaw	75
Dan'l A Wine	5.25	J B Brumbaugh	2.00
Sam'l Gochnour	3.75	Fred. Showalter	1.00
John F Miller	1.50	John Zuck	7.32
B Ellis	4.50	J M Wells	5.40
M V Burck	1.25	Jos F Emmert	1.50
Dan'l Keller	7.80	John Neff	1.50
D R Saylor	5.25	E H Mahle	1.00
John Overholser	1.25	Morgan Leonard	1.00
J B Wolf	.50	C C Root	8.50
Sam'l Murray	13.40	S P Brumbaugh	2.25
Jno S Plank	10.50	David Brower	10.00
Henry Gephart	3.75	W A Clark,	7.00

Money List continued next week.

LITERARY NOTICES.

DON'T FORGET THE CHILDREN.

When providing your supply of reading for next year do not forget the children. They need a weekly paper as well as the older folks. Nothing better can be found for them than the weekly, BRIGHT SIDE AND FAMILY CIRCLE, which is designed especially for them. It is edited by C. G. G. Paine, A. M., a teacher in the Chicago High School, and has among its contributors some of the best writers of the country, such as Rev. Dr. Alden, Pres. of the N. Y. State Normal School, Prof. Sanborn Tenney, of Williams College, Mrs. A. E. Sherwood, Ina Clayton, Amelia E. Daley and others. It is designed to interest as well as instruct, and is such a paper as any parent or teacher may give to his children or pupils, assured that they will be benefitted by it. It is furnished at the low price of $1.00 per year, and every subscriber receives a handsome Chromo, the Calla Lilies. Published by the Bright Side Co., Chicago, Ill.

THE PHRENOLOGICAL JOURNAL for December, is a capital number of this most excellent monthly, and a worthy completion of its fifty fifth volume. Let us note a few of the topics considered: William B. Astor, the noted millionaire, with a fine portrait; Ancient Human Crania; Man as an Inhabitant of Two Worlds, Expression—the conclusion of the most valuable series of essays; Some Familiar Views of Society; The Pretty Man, and the Doll-faced Woman; Mr. Froude in America; How the Organs of the Brain were Discovered; Wm. H. Seward, with a splendid portrait; On the Formation of Character; "The One-Eyed Conductor," again; "Fanny Fern"; Origin of Metalliferous Deposits; Freckles and Beauty; Christian and Infidel, etc. 30 cts. for the number; $3 a year. Now is the time to send your subscription to S. R. Wells, 389 Broadway, New York.

THE
Scientific American.
FOR 1873.
Beautifully Illustrated.

The SCIENTIFIC AMERICAN, now in its 28th year, enjoys the widest circulation of any analogous periodical in the world.

Its contents embrace the latest and most interesting information pertaining to the Industrial, Mechanical, and Scientific Progress of the World; Descriptions, with beautiful engravings of new Inventions, New Implements, New Processes, and improved Industries of all kinds; Useful Notes, Facts, Recipes, Suggestions and Advice, by Practical Writers, for Workmen and Employers in all the various Arts.

Descriptions of Improvements, Discoveries, and Important Works, pertaining to Civil and Mechanical Engineering, Milling, Mining and Metallurgy; Records of the latest progress in the Applications of Steam, Steam Engineering, Railways, Ship-building, Navigation, Telegraphy, Telegraph Engineering, Electricity, Magnetism, Light and Heat.

The Latest Discoveries in Photography, Chemistry, New and Useful Applications of Chemistry in the Arts and in Domestic or Household Economy.

The Latest Information pertaining to Technology, Microscopy, Mathematics, Astronomy, Geography, Meteorology, Mineralogy, Geology, Zoology, Botany, Horticulture, Agriculture, Architecture, Rural Economy, Food, Lighting, Heating, Ventilation and Health.

In short the whole range of the Sciences and Practical Arts are embraced within the scope of the Scientific American. No person who desires to be intelligently informed can afford to be without this paper.

Farmers, Mechanics, Engineers, Inventors, Manufacturers, Chemists, Lovers of Science, Teachers, Clergymen, Lawyers, and People of all Professions, will find the SCIENTIFIC AMERICAN to be of great value. It should have a place in every Family, Library, Study, Office and Counting Room; in every Reading Room, College, Academy or School.

Published weekly, splendidly illustrated, only $3 a year.

The Yearly Numbers of the SCIENTIFIC AMERICAN make two splendid volumes of nearly one thousand pages, equivalent in contents to Four Thousand ordinary Book Pages. An Official List of all Patents issued is published weekly. ☞ Specimen copies sent free. Address the publishers, MUNN & Co., 37 Park Row, New York.

PATENTS. In connection with the SCIENTIFIC AMERICAN, Messrs. MUNN & Co. are Solicitors of American and Foreign Patents, have had over 35 years' experience, and have the largest establishment in the world. If you have made an invention, write them a letter and send a sketch; they will promptly inform you, free of charge, whether your device is new and patentable. They will also send you, free of charge, a copy of the Patent Laws in full, with instructions how to proceed to obtain a patent. Address MUNN & Co., 37 Park Row, New York.

Trine Immersion
TRACED
TO THE APOSTLES.

Being a collection of historical quotations from modern and ancient authors, proving that a THREE-FOLD Immersion was the only method of baptizing ever practiced by the Apostles and their immediate successors. The author, after proving Trine Immersion to have been the prevailing practice, in baptism, the first 1500 years of the Christian era, commences with the fifth century, and traces a Three-fold Immersion, to within 33 years of the apostle John's death, and then proves it to have been the Apostolic method of baptizing, while Single Immersion was invented not less than 326 years after the death of Christ.

Put up in a neat pamphlet form, with good paper cover, and will be sent, post-paid, on the following terms: One copy, 25 cts; Five copies, $1.10; Ten copies, $2.00.

Address, J. H. MOORE,
Urbana, Champaign co., Ill.
Oct. 22.

TUNE BOOK.

The Brethren's Tune and Hymn Book, is a compilation of Sacred Music adapted to all the hymns in the Brethren's New Hymn Book. It contains over 350 pages, printed on good paper and neatly bound. We will send it to any address, post paid at $1.25 per copy.

GOOD BOOKS.

A large number of our patrons are receiving our books as noticed below, as premiums, and express themselves highly pleased with them. Others who are not agents, have enquired whether we keep them for sale. We have now made arrangements with Mr. Wells to furnish any of their publicatio ns post paid at publishers prices. Orders for books must be accompanied with the cash, and plain directions for sending them.

Weaver's Works for the Young. Comprising "Hopes and Helps for the Young of both Sexes," $3.00.

Life at Home; or, The Family and its Members. A work which should be found in every family. $1.50. Extra gilt, $2.00.

Hand-book for Home Improvement: comprising "How to Write," "How to Talk," How to Behave," and "How to do Business," in one vol. 2.25.

Man and Woman: Considered in their Relations to each Other and to the World. 12mo, Fancy cloth, Price $1.00.

The Right Word in the Right Place. A New Pocket Dictionary and Reference Book. Cloth, 75cts.

Hopes and Helps for the Young of both sexes, Relating to the Formation of Character. Choice of Avocation, Health, Conversation, Social Affection Courtship and Marriage. Muslin, $1.50.

The Emphatic, Diaglott; or The New Testament in Greek and English. Containing the Original Greek Text of the New Testament, with an Interlineary Word for-word English Translation. Price, $4.00; extra fine binding, $5.00.

Oratory—Sacred and Secular; or, the Extemporaneous Speaker. Price $1.50.

Conversion of St. Paul. 12mo. fine edition, $1. Plain edition, 75 cents.

Man, in Genesis and in Geology; or, the Biblical Account of Man's Creation, tested by Scientific Theories of his Origin and Antiquity. One vol. 12mo, $1.00.

How to read Character, Illus. Price,	$1.25
Combe's Moral Philosophy,	1.75
Constitution of Man. Combe,	1.75
Education. By Spurzheim,	1.50
Memory—How to Improve it,	1.50

WANTED BOOK Agents FOR THE
GREAT INDUSTRIES
OF THE UNITED STATES;

AN HISTORICAL SUMMARY OF THE ORIGIN, GROWTH AND PERFECTION OF THE CHIEF INDUSTRIAL ARTS OF THIS COUNTRY.

1300 PAGES and 500 ENGRAVINGS.
Written by 20 Eminent Authors, including John B. Gough, Leon Case, Edward Rowland, Jos. B. Lyman, Rev. E. Edwin Hall, Horace Greely, Philip Ripley, Albert Brisbane, F. B. Perkins, etc.

This work is a complete history of all branches of industry, processes of manufacture, etc., in all ages. It is a complete encyclopedia of arts and manufactures, and is the most entertaining and valuable work of information on subjects of general interest ever offered to the public. It is adapted to the wants of the Merchant, Manufacturer, Mechanic, Farmer, Student and Inventor, and sells to both old and young of all classes. The book is sold by agents, who are making large sales in all parts of the country. It is offered at the low price of $3.50, and is the cheapest book ever sold by subscription. No family should be without a copy. We want agents in every town in the United States, and no agent can fail to do well with this book. Our terms are liberal. We give our agents the exclusive right of territory. One of our agents sold 133 copies in eight days, another sold 368 in two weeks. Our agent in Hartford sold 397 in one week. Specimens of the work sent to agents on receipt of stamp. For circulars and terms to agents address the publishers.

J. B. BURR & HYDE, *Hartford, Conn., Chicago, Ill., or Cincinnati, Ohio.*

Menno Simon's
COMPLETE WORKS.

In English, translated from the original Dutch or Holland, giving the whole of the great Reformers writings on the subject of Baptism. Price in full sheep $4.50; by mail $5.14.

Address, JOHN F. FUNK & BRO.
Elkhart, Ind.

MARIETTA NURSERIES.
AGENTS WANTED.

We want to employ active energetic Agents to canvass in Pennsylvania and Maryland, and local agents everywhere. Liberal workers will be liberally paid. Persons desiring immediate employment who can give good reference, will apply at once for terms, &c.

Address, ENGLE & BRO.,
Marietta, Lancaster Co., Pa.
Jan. 13t.

TRACTS.

"ANXIOUS BENCH RELIGION EXAMINED," BY ELDER J. S. FLORY. A SYNOPSIS OF CONTENTS. An address to the reader: The peculiarities that attend this type of religion. The feelings there experienced not imaginary but real. The key that unlocks the wonderful mystery. The causes by which feelings are excited. How the momentary feelings called "Experimental religion" are brought about, and then concludes by giving that form of doctrine as taught by Jesus Christ and recorded by his faithful witnesses.

COUNTERFEIT DETECTER
or
BAPTISM—MUCH IN LITTLE.

This work is now ready for distribution, and the importance of the subject will speak for it a large demand. It is a short treatise on baptism in tract form intended for general distribution, and is set forth in such a plain and logical manner that a wayfaring man though a fool, cannot err therein. Either of the above tracts sent postpaid on the following terms: Two copies, 10 cts, 10 copies 40 cents, 25 copies 70 cents, 50 copies $1.00, 100 copies $1.50.

1870 1872
DR. FAHRNEY'S
Blood Cleanser or Panacea.

A tonic and purge, for Blood Diseases. Great reputation. Many testimonials. Many ministering brethren use and recommend it. Ask or send for the "Health Messenger." Use only the "*Panacea*" prepared at Chicago, Ills., and by

Dr. P. Fahrney's Brothers & Co.,
Aug. 3-pd. *Waynesboro, Franklin Co., Pa.*

25 Ablest Tariff Journal in the U. S.
THE AMERICAN WORKING PEOPLE

Published monthly, is a welcome visitor at 100,000 Firesides. Finely printed, handsomely illustrated, ably edited—has no rival! $1.50 per year, sent on trial 3 months for 25 cents.

IRON WORLD PUB. Co., Pittsburgh, Pa.

25 THE **IRON WORLD** is the largest and most Valuable Metal Price Current in the world. $4.00 per year. Sent on trial one month for 25 cents. *All the State Geologists are Contributors.* IRON WORLD PUB'G Co., Pittsburgh, Pa.

$5 to $20 [illegible]

HUNTINGDON & BROAD TOP RAIL ROAD
Winter Arrangement.

On and after Tuesday, Oct. 4, 1872, Passenger trains will arrive and depart as follows:

Trains from Huntingdon South. *Trains from Mt. Dallas moving North.*

MAIL. A. M.	ACCOM P. M.	STATIONS.	MAIL. P. M.	ACCOM A. M.
le8 00	le5 30	Huntingdon,	ar3 20	ar9 00
8 08	5 57	Long Siding	3 12	8 53
8 24	6 10	McConnelstown	3 50	8 37
8 30	6 17	Pleasant Grove	2 50	8 30
8 45	6 30	Marklesburg	2 37	8 17
9 00	6 44	Coffee Run	2 23	8 01
9 07	6 52	Rough & Ready	2 15	7 53
9 20	7 05	Cove	2 01	7 40
9 24	7 10	Fishers Summit	1 57	7 35
9 44 / 9 54	ar7 30	Saxton	1 37	le7 15
10 10		Riddlesburg	1 10	
10 17		Hopewell	1 12	
10 34		Piper's Run	12 36	
10 52		Tatesville	12 38	
11 05		Bloody Run	12 24	
ar11 10		Mount Dallas	12 20	

JOHN M'KILLIPS, Supt.

SHOUP'S RUN BRANCH.

LE10 00	LE7 40	Saxton.	AR1 30	AR7 20
10 15	7 55	Coalmont.	1 15	6 55
10 20	8 00	Crawford.	1 10	6 50
AR10 30	AR8 10	Dudley	LE1 00	LE6 40

Bro'd Top City from Dudley 2 miles by stage.

Time of Penna. R. R. Trains at Huntingdon.

EASTWARD.		WESTWARD.	
H'b'g Ac.	9 24 A. M.	Cin. Ex.	2 10 A. M.
Mail	3 30 P. M.	Pe'f Ex.	7 45 "
Cin. Ex.	6 55 "	Mail	5 40 P. M.
Phil. Ex	11 15 "	W. Pass.	11 52 A. M.

The Weekly Pilgrim.

Published by J. B. Brumbaugh, & Co.
Edited by H. B. & Geo. Brumbaugh.

CORRESPONDING EDITORS.
D. P. Sayler, Double Pipe Creek, Md.
Leonard Furry, New Enterprise, Pa.

The *Pilgrim* is a Christian Periodical, devoted to religion and moral reform. It will advocate in the spirit of *love* and *liberty*, the principles of true Christianity, labor for the promotion of peace among the people of God, for the encouragement of the saints and for the conversion of sinners, avoiding those things which tend toward disunion or sectional feelings.

TERMS.

Single copy, Book paper,	$1.50
Eleven copies, [eleventh for Agt.]	$15.00

Any number above that at the same rate.

Address,
H. B. BRUMBAUGH.
James Creek,
Huntingdon county Pa.

The Weekly Pilgrim.

"REMOVE NOT THE ANCIENT LANDMARKS WHICH OUR FATHERS HAVE SET."

VOL. 4. JAMES CREEK, PENNSYLVANIA, JANUARY 14, 1873. NO. 2

POETRY.

MY BIRTHDAY.

BY LAURA.

"The years creep slowly by," we're older grown you say,
Ah, no! my friend, on lightning wings they speed away;
Another *year*! my heart throbs wildly with its loud Amen,
As cycling in its course the day has come to me again.

Upon the hills of life—how many have we gained?
What sights have seen, what lessons well attained,
While anxious care has left its trace upon our brow;
From childhood's happy *then* to woman's sadder *now*.

Ah, me! my friend we're older grown in worldly ways,
We love the trumpet tones, the magic voice of praise.
We've put aside our innocence with every childish toy,
And things of sense, too oft our precious time employ.

Did we but read aright the lesson of the hour,
Did we resist for aye the subtle tempter's power;
Could we temptation's luring snare evade,
Then not in vain would be the debt on Calvary paid.

Our feet have wandered far, Oh, God! to Thee we cry,
And to thy arm we haste, to thee for refuge fly,
For there, 'tis only there we'll find abiding rest,
And in thy loving smile, will be forever blest.

Then ever speed the years on lightning wings away,
Nor ask with tearful eyes for days and years to stay;
They've borne the echo back to "Him who dwells above,"
The record of our life—the golden gleam of love.

Easton, W. Va.

ORIGINAL ESSAYS.

A DIALOGUE BETWEEN GAMALIEL AND NICODEMUS.

Continued.

Nic. From what I have already learned, I believe that to be the very young prophet who is creating such intense excitement in the wilderness, and if so, I surely know much about his parents. His father and mother died about twelve years ago, leaving an only son, whose name was John. It has been nearly ten years since I last heard of him, and after summing up all that I have been able to gather so far, I conclude that the same John is preaching near the Jordan.

Gam. About what do you presume his age to be at the present time?

Nic. He is said to be about thirty years of age.

Gam. Well the young man that I saw near the large spring ten years ago, was about twenty, hence at this time he would be thirty. It is very likely that he is the same person who is preaching beyond Jericho. Were you acquainted with his parents?

Nic. Oh yes, I knew his father quite well, and have often seen his mother.

Gam. Who was his father?

Nic. Zachariah, he was a priest of the course of Abia, and his mother was Elizabeth, she was of the daughters of Aaron.

Gam. That agrees with what Luke remarked respecting his father, and while at the spring the young prophet told us that he was of the tribe of Levi, his father being of the course of Abia, and his mother, Elizabeth of the daughters of Aaron. But I am led to confess that I really don't believe that I was ever acquainted with his father.

Nic. Never knew old father Zacharias! You certainly have seen him quite often; he was at one time one of our priests of the course of Abia.

Gam. When?

Nic. Nearly thirty-one years ago; his term or days of ministration expired about twenty-one months before the death of Herod the Great.*

Gam. You certainly must be mistaken, I don't think he served in that course at that time.

Nic. You really ought to remember him, as, according to the custom of the priest's office, his lot was to burn incense at that time.

Gam. It may have been, but it fails to impress itself on my mind in that way.

Nic. There is one thing which I know you have not failed to remember.

Gam. What is that?

Nic. Nearly thirty-one years ago, and about twenty-one or two months before Herod's death, we were standing near the temple, when an aged priest of the course of Abia passed in to offer incense: he remained there so long that all the people marveled that he stayed so long in the temple, and when he came out he could not speak unto us, for he beckoned with his hand, and remained speechless, and we all concluded that he had seen an angel. Now you remember this, I know

Gam. Yes—certainly, I knew that pious old priest, and is this prophet in the wilderness his son?

Nic. From what I have been able to learn, so far, that is my impression for his name is John, and that is the only John that I know of among the Levites.

Gam. Well now I am glad to hear of that. Before my father, Simeon died, he used to talk a great deal about these good old people, who lived in the hilly country south of Bethlehem, and often wished to know how Elizabeth's cousin Mary, who resided in Galilee, was getting along.

Nic. Perhaps your father was well acquainted with these people, and also had some knowledge of their son John.

Gam. O yes! Since we have been conversing of these interesting events my memory is rapidly filling with the conversation of my father, respecting the Levite family. He knew the lad quite well, and admired him very much. But John, had a second cousin near his own age, living in the city of Nazareth, who appeared to awaken a remarkable interest in our family. I have not heard of him for quite a number of years. But more about the young prophet—is his appearance good?

Nic. His dress is similar to that you saw ten years ago in the wilderness, and his diet is said to be composed, principally, of Locusts and wild honey.

Gam. I think I must take young Saul with me, and go and hear that remarkable person, but for the present I must retire to my school-room.*

Nic. I would be pleased to learn something more of the prophet' second cousin who lives in Galilee, if you be pleased to tell me when we have more time.

Gam. Call some evening and after looking up the matter I think I can relate to you some very interesting accounts of his birth &c. [*They both seperate, and in the evening of the next day meet at the house of Gamaliel where their conversation was resumed.*]

Gam. Well Nicodemus, as you have just returned from the Jordan, I presume you can tell us all about the young prophet.

Nic. Soon after leaving you yesterday morning, I learned that the road near Jericho was infested with a band of Arab robbers, so I judged it safer to postpone my trip a few days.

Gam. I presume that you have been thinking very much over the remarkable events that are just now transpiring in our long forsaken land.

Nic. My mind has been employed during the last two days with these interesting events Everybody is making investigations.

Gam. I presume you have heard a great deal during the day.

Nic. Yes, I have been spending all my time talking and examining the sacred records. I presume you are ready to relate to me that story of Johns' second cousin, although I heard a great deal of him to-day, I was conversing with a man who resides near the sea of Galilee.

Gam. Did you learn his name?

Nic. He stated that his name was Zebedee. Two of his sons, James and John, were in company with him.

Gam. I know him well, he is one of the oldest fishermen on the coast of the sea of Galilee. I also enjoyed quite a pleasant interview with Matthew of Capernaum, who was on business here. But what did Zebedee reveal to you of John?

Nic. He said but little about John, only stating that he was well acquainted with his second cousin, and told me many things of this strange young man.

Gam. I am truly glad to learn more about him, though I formerly knew him in his younger days, and gained much information of him in my interview with Matthew. But then what had our fisherman to say of him?

Nic. He appears to know all about him, and a great deal of his parents

To be Continued.

*Herod surnamed the Great, died in the Spring of the fourth year, before the commencement of the Christian era.

*Gamaliel was a distinguished teacher of the Jewish law, and president of the Sanhedrin thirty-two years.

TO SISTER K. B. OF OHIO

My dear sister in the bonds of Christian love and union; I feel like penning a few words of encouragement for you, and all others, similarly circumstanced, who have our blessed Masters cause at heart. From personal acquaintance, and otherwise, I am fully persuaded you have an ardent desire for the well fare of souls, and the prosperity of Zion. Having, yourself in youth, consecrated your all to Jesus, it is natural you should have a concern for the young, and feel like devoting your life more and more to the purpose of causing them to enlist, as soldiers of the cross. In your love and zeal, you ask, "What can I do for Jesus?" It is to answer this question, that I now take up my pen.

I have no doubt, you feel the need of the assisting grace of God, in a work so important. We should all feel "that of ourselves we are nothing," then will we put our dependence in Him whose promises are so full of comfort. Believe it, though you are young, you can do much for Jesus. Remember that the *influence* of the young, falls with power upon the hearts of the same class, and, also have a peculiar, and beneficial bearing upon the minds of the more aged. All around you, you have young associates, some have named the name of Jesus with a hope of salvation, others have not, but are yet out, exposed to the lowering clouds of God's indignation and wrath! In your every day walk among them, and conversation with them, you may do *Much* for Jesus. Let them *see* and *feel*, that you really enjoy the peaceful and happy influence of "pure and undefiled religion," and that the simple pleasures of the world, and fascinating influences thereof, have no charms for you, but rather let them see, that with you, the cross of Jesus hath influences that are brighter, sweeter and dearer than aught else. With a meek and humble spirit, and chaste conversation, use every means in your power, to win their affections from the world, that they may turn them heavenward; and thus be the means of causing, through God's blessings, the wicked to turn from their evil ways, and cause your fellow soldiers to cling with a tighter grasp, to the cross of Jesus.

I would not advise the casting of "pearls before swine" but under fitting circumstances, let us not be ashamed to speak of Jesus, while in the society of the worldly minded, knowing, that often the right word in the right place, may be as precious seed, that may eventually bring forth good fruit. "A word fitly spoken, is like apples of gold in pictures of silver." In all things dear sister, "be as wise as serpents, and harmless as doves."

Next, we will speak of the Sabbath school, where you may do much for the glorious cause of Jesus. There you have labored in the capacity of a hand maid, in the nursery of the Lord, and I am glad to believe your labors, with those of all your co laborers, have not been in vain, and that you are encouraged with the knowledge, that in that relation, you are to be instrumental in the hands of God, of doing something for the building up of Zion. It is an important fact, that *first impressions* are of such a nature, that it is hard to remove them. Oh! then what a noble work it is, to labor week after week, to fasten upon the tender mind the truths of the Bible, and infuse within the precious young souls the love of a crucified Redeemer. In that sphere, dear sister, you can do much for your Savior, the church, and precious soul. Ask God to prepare you for the work, and enter upon your duties with convictions, that it is a matter of importance, no less than the eternal interests of dear and precious souls. Work with a will in all places, and at all times, and through the blessings of God, your labors will not be in vain in the Lord. Why should you spend your time and talents for Jesus? Ah! yes, why did Jesus lay aside His glory in Heaven, and come down here and labor in this world? Was it not to seek and save that which was lost? and that includes you and I. Shall we not then labor for that FRIEND who did so much for us, and shall we think it a hard task to labor a few days, for those precious ones around and about us, that they may be partakers with us in that great salvation? And again, we say, should we not work for Jesus, when we see just ahead, the glorious reward or gift of God which is eternal life—yea an eternal crown of glory, and a place of shining brightness, amid the stars of Heaven? O then dear sister K. we would say to you, and to all the dear ones of the household of faith, let us labor while we have time and opportunity, yes let us

"Work for the night is coming,
Work through the sunny noon;
Fill brightest hours with labor,
Rest comes sure and soon.
Give every flying minute
Something to keep in store;
Work for the night is coming,
When man works no more."

A few more days of labor, a few more seasons of meeting and parting here in this world, and then, if faithful, we die in the Lord, and *then* rest from our labors, and THIS mortal shall put on immortality and THEN meet to part no more. And there in the bright fields of living green, we will see the fruits of our labors brought to perfection through a Saviors love; see precious souls basking in the smiles of God's love, that were induced to take the first step upward through our influence and labors of love. Oh! the joy of meeting there, father, mother, brothers and sisters, associates' and an innumerable company of angels, all singing anthems of glory, honor and praise to Father, Son and Holy Spirit.

J. S. FLORY.

Orchard View, W. Va.

OUR CHRISTMAS GIFT.

This morning, Christmas day, we look back through the long train of time of 1872 years, to that when Christ, from the root of Jesse, made his appearance in the manger of Bethlehem, and we behold with joy the great and glorious promise of God fulfilled; "A child is born unto us." This scene caused the angels to rejoice when they brought the glorious news to the shepherds, who were shocked with fear, but the angel said, "Fear not, for we bring you good tidings of great joy which shall be unto all people, for unto you is born this day, a Savior in the city of David which is Christ the Lord." This caused the angels to shout through the air "Glory to God in the highest, peace upon earth good will to men." Now we see the Shepherds hasten to the place, when they had seen it they made known abroad the saying which was told them concerning this child. Next in turn, we see the wise men from the East coming to Jerusalem, who were moved by a star which they saw and they asked, "Where is the new born king? we have seen his star in the East and have come to worship him." This troubled king Herod with all Jerusalem, and Herod soon envied this child and sought to kill it, but God removed it from Bethlehem after the wise men had worshiped it and bestowed their gifts and treasures upon it. I heard it preached that the wise men committed an error when they went to Jerusalem to inquire from the king and his subjects, but it looks to me as if they had done what every wise man should do, go where they can get Scriptural evidence to find the way to Jesus who was born king, and it was not the case as we are told by some, that the wise men lost sight of the star because of stopping at Jerusalem, but there is the only place we learn the star first appeared unto them in all their journey and went before them, until it stood over and above where the child was, hence the wise men could not mistake themselves in their worshipping, because they had the Word of the Lord and the star to guide them in the right way and to the right place. They were not satisfied without having the testimony of God's Word in this matter. Let us all follow the wise men's example, always consult the word of God to tell us the way to Jesus, and then start the way the Word directs and God will not fail to send the star to accompany us all the journey through, 'till we come where He is that we may be there also, that we may see his glory and yield up all our treasures to Him. Let us always remember in all we do how great the love of God is to usward in this Christmas gift, who became the way for us, and he gave us many bright examples. Here is a good one for the youth of 12 years. When He began to be about His Father's business, and he was also subject to His parents, to give all the good children an example for them to follow Him, and finally come unto Him and obtain the Kingdom of Heaven. But young men and women, He also gave you an example and also told you that you shall keep the commandments. He also tells you that you cannot live by bread alone, and that you must give an account for every idle word you say. He told you you shall repent and believe the Gospel, and if you believe and are baptized, you shall be saved. He told you if you weep here you shall laugh, but if you laugh here then you shall weep. He gave you and I no example of sporting and laughing, but of weeping and praying, and of doing good to those around Him. He told us we shall take up our cross and follow Him daily or we cannot be H's disciples, that if we are ashamed of Him and of His words then will He be ashamed of us before His Heavenly Father and His holy angels. He also told us He would come again, and no one knoweth the day nor hour therefore He wants us to be ready, always to watch and pray, for in such an hour as we think not, He will come. And to those that will say the Lord delayeth His coming, such He will give their portion with the hypocrites in outer darkness where there will be weeping and gnashing of teeth.

Then my young friends, never spend the Christmas day in idle talk and foolish amusements, much less my brethren and Christian friends, do not be found at the idol of a Christmas tree or some pic-nic, but come to Christ the true Christmas tree. Upon him hangs all the fruit of eternal life, and He will give it to you without the aid of Santa Claus. Brethren, be not found in the preacher's gambling shops, but keep yourselves from idols is the prayer of your well wishing brother.

JOHN FORNEY.

Falls City, Neb.

For the Pilgrim.

TO A FREE PEOPLE.

The time has come in which it is necessary for all men and women who have within their breasts a single spark of love for their Creator, and the love of liberty to be on the alert. Secret societies have their organization in almost every known corner of our free and independent nation. What is the grand object of these institutions? What benefit can be expected from these organizations? Nothing. They are a curse not only to those who are outside these societies but also to those who belong to them. Every member of the order of Masons is bound by oath to disregard the law of Christ! Every member is bound to regard those who oppose them, as an enemy and oppose their progress in life in every possible manner! They are bound to support their own members in application for any office of trust or position of any kind, in preference to any one else, regardless of character! No one can fail to see the final result of such proceedings as these, and should use their utmost endeavors to root out from among the citizens of a free country, like ours, such corrupt organizations. But how shall it be accomplished? We think it may easily be brought about by the lovers of freedom providing they adopt the proper means. Let no lover of freedom countenance these associations either by supporting in office, or patronizing in business of any kind, any one who is known to hold a membership in these organizations. But says some devoted christian, if we do this we shall fail to obey the injunction to love our enemies, &c. Let me say to you, my christian brother, that this is not good reasoning; for there is no injunction upon record that requires any one to love the principles of the devil; but on the other hand, it is your duty as a christian, to do everything in your power to destroy these principles; then let no man have any dealings whatever with the members of these organizations, and save themselves and posterity from a form of slavery more direful upon the people than that to which the Africans were subjected, in times that are past and gone.

LIBERTY.

A memory well stored with Scripture and sanctified by grace is the best library.

There is some promise in your Bible exactly adapted to every trying hour.

TRIAL OF FAITH.

That "Without faith it is impossible to please God," is a truth so manifest throughout all the sacred pages, that it seems sometimes we had scarcely need again be told; and this is indeed acknowledged by all Christian professors. But when the faith of all is tried, oh what a precious and rare virtue is that faith which is unto the saving of the soul. Then when it has passed through all the fiery ordeals and escaped all without a visible mark of a test, except that by repeated trials, it has become stronger and brighter, as "gold tried in the fire." But the apostle Peter says of them who had received like precious faith with them, (the apostles), that the trial of their faith being much more precious, than that of gold that perisheth, though it be tried with fire, might be found unto praise and honor and glory at the appearing of Jesus Christ.

When the Bible is seldom read, and the divine sanctuary neglected, few trials of faith will be met, but if all that is commanded, and that is forbidden be carefully searched out, and held sacred and essential to our eternal well being, and a determination fixed to profit by them, notwithstanding any and every emergency, then sore and fiery trials will be met, and if the conscience then be kept void of offense, O, how precious that faith. Such a faith is not without works. Such is a living faith. To such a believer is the Gospel the power of God unto salvation. To such believers gave He power to become the sons of God. While faith as a mustard seed will remove mountains, what will such a faith not accomplish?

C. C. ROOT.

Mirabile, Mo.

SKETCH OF THE LIFE AND DEATH OF JAMES HIPES.

OF THE ROOT RIVER BRANCH.

The subject of this notice was born near Tengleaster, Va., March 4th 1804. In the year 1832 he emigrated to Ohio. Some time during the year 1836 both he and his wife came to the Church of the Brethren. In 1837 removed to Montgomery Co., Ind. From there, emigrated to the Territory of Minnesota, Fillmore County where he remained until his death, which took place on the morning of the 14th of July 1872. Between 3 and 4 o'clock in the morning, he winged his way to the Sunny Land from whence no traveler returns. His disease was not certainly known. He was afflicted for about seven years before his death, he very often had sick spells from which he would soon recover until the morning of the 13th he arose from his bed and dressed himself for the purpose of assisting a tenant who was living in one part of the house, (in case of sickness), and soon after he was dressed, he was taken sick. He walked to the barn, a distance of 6 rods, and returned to the house and sat down in the front door of the house, and in ten or fifteen minutes, he was treading the turf bound shores of an endless eternity. He gave mother and some others who were present the last parting hand, saying, "I must leave you now." Then to the celestial fields of glory, he quickly bent his way. He closed his eyes, and his spirit had taken its flight to a world unknown to us. Father lived a consistent member of the Church of the Brethren for about 35 years and we hope that he was prepared for that great and solemn change, from this mortal to immortality. Yes, father has gone over the river of death, but what a great consolation does the blessed hope afford us when we know that we shall meet beyond the Jordan of death, when this weary journey is done. Yes, we shall meet beyond the river where no farewell tear is shed, and how true the saying is, "When we are in the midst of life we are in death." Morning spread over earth her rosy wings, the Sun rose clear beyond the horizon, the gentle air whispered through the open door in which lay the still pale lifeless form of one who had been the joy of my aged mother and lonely niece, who was left standing at that lone post of death. All was still, the monster death had done his work—father was gone.

"When shall we meet again
Meet ne'er to sever,
When will peace wreathe her chain,
Round us forever."

WM. C. HIPES.

Preston, Minn.

MEMORIAL.

"Death loves a shining mark." This has been fully verified in the death of Sydney Hyder Johnson, who departed this life, December 7th 1872, at the residence of his cousin, Mr. W. H. Hitshew, Chambersburg Pa., in the 24th year of his age.

In writing this article, we feel that we are doing our duty, not only to a cherished cousin, but to our young friends who do not think of the uncertainty of life, and the vanity of this world. Sydney was not only a fine writer, as his contributions to many Journals testify, but he was a kind and dutiful son, a pleasant and agreeable associate. Of him it might truly be said, as of the young man in St. Mark's Gospel, "And Jesus beholding him loved him." Though he was not a member of any religious Society, he always entertained the greatest respect for religious sects, and to Rev. L. A. Gotwald of the Lutheran Church, who was assiduous in his attentions to him during his illness, he expressed the strongest hope of a blissful immortality beyond the grave. He had implicit faith in Jesus—and confided fully in Him.

What Baca valleys had to be passed, before we could say—Sydney is dead; he has gone from among us, his pleasant smile, and agreeable conversation will no more be enjoyed. How sadly will we look over his books, and his writing materials, which were such a delight to him. We hope God will give us all grace to bear this sad affliction, and to prepare to meet him at His coming.

OBITUARY OF JULIA MALOTT.

The subject of this obituary was one among the number of some forty, who were baptized into Christ, in that section of country, within the last few years. A few years ago there were no members at that place: the people being principly Old School Baptists. The Brethren's doctrine and the faith of Jesus being readily received, the little pilgrim band was moving along happily, until sister Julia sickened and died. On Christmas we received a message, (being with the brethren at Welch Run attending a series of meetings,) of her extreme illness. In company with brother Jerry Angle, deacon, we repaired next day, to her house, but she had fallen asleep in Jesus. A heavy gloom not only hung upon the heart of the husband and family, but upon the whole community. On the 27th we followed her remains to the grave. She was the first of the pilgrim band called to pass over to the other side. In her last moments she gave an unmistakable evidence of a living faith in Jesus, desiring to be absent from the body, and present with the Lord, regretting that her husband could not accompany her. She left in peace, receiving a faithful promise from Jacob, her husband, to accept Jesus and come after in the way. Our sister was beloved by all who knew her, she leaving an example for others to follow.

D. F. GOOD.

DILIGENCE.—We find in Scripture that most of the great appearances which were made to eminent saints were made when they were busy. Moses kept his father's flock when he saw the burning bush; Jacob is in prayer, and the angel of God appears to him; Gideon is thrashing and Elisha is ploughing when the Lord calls them; Matthew is at the receipt of custom when he is bidden to follow Jesus; and James and John are fishing.

INTENDED REFORMATION.—How dangerous to defer those momentous reformations which the conscience is solemnly preaching to the heart!

THE GREAT EVENT.

"Glory be to God in the highest and on earth peace, good will toward men." Luke 2: 14.

The above seraphic strain was heard in the night by those who watched their flocks by night, which caused the shepherds to say to one another; "Let us go to Bethlehem and see this thing which is come to pass, which the Lord made known unto us." When this was made known to them, they went in haste to Bethlehem, and when they came there they found Mary and Joseph, and the babe lying in a manger. When they had seen what was come to pass, they made known abroad what was told them concerning the child, and returned glorifying God for the things which they had heard and seen.

This glorious event occurred about eighteen hundred and seventy-two years ago, and it presents itself as fresh in our minds as if it had occurred in our age, for we derive the same benefits as those did who lived during the time the Saviour sojourned in this world.

This eventful circumstance caused the wise men from the far distant isles when they had "seen his star" to start from their distant land in search of the new born King to worship him. Psalms 72: 10. Isa. 60: 6. This was a time when the wise men opened their treasures and presented gold, frankincense and myrrh, which may have been of much advantage to Joseph and the mother of Jesus and the babe, as they had to take their flight to Egypt from the presence of a cruel king who sought to destroy the young child. When the child was but twelve years of age we may already learn a very important lesson from him, the time that his parents "found him in the temple, sitting in the midst of the doctors both hearing them and asking them questions, so that all that heard him were astonished at his understanding and answers." He went with his parents to their home and was subject unto them.

We find that the Savior was born into the world but the work of redemption was not yet complete, he had to lay down his life for his friends "and we are his friends if we do whatsoever he has commanded us." He had power to lay down his life and to take it again. "This commandment I have received of my Father." Here we can see the love of God in Christ Jesus concerning us, in sending his only begotten Son into the world to suffer and die, the just for the unjust to bring us to God. He suffered and died according to the scripture; yet the work was still not done, He had to be buried and rose again from the dead the third day, according to the scripture, which we find that he did, "Whereof He has given assurance unto all men in that He has raised Him from the dead." Now we find that "he has brought life and immortality to light through the gospel, and in order to have the full benefits of what the Savior has done for us, we must become His adopted sons and daughters. He has exemplified the way and the only way to become his children. We must submissively follow him in all the ordinances blameless as he delivered them to us. "If children, then heirs, heirs of God and joint heirs of Christ."

SAMUEL TEETER.

A FEW THOUGHTS.

Mr. Editor:—My mind is engaged at present, upon a subject which calls forth views which perhaps might be interesting to many of your readers, and which, with the blessing of God attending the weak effort, may produce good results. Time is moving onward carrying the human family on its rapid wings, not making any inquiry whether we are equipped for the journey or not. But while it is progressing, we are admonished almost momentarily as it rolls onward, that a preparation is necessary to journey down its rapid steps. We know not how soon we may be called from this stage of action. We have a plain directory, a sure and certain path to follow. All along that path we have written in unmistakable language: "Prepare to meet thy God", "My son give me thy heart", "Come unto me all ye who are weary and heavy laden and I will give you rest." Such and similar invitations are given throughout the entire law. We are traveling on a journey we expect never to return, we are only pilgrims journeying to a City whose builder and maker is God; that is, if we possess that pearl of great price, which was purchased on Calvary for sinful man.

The fountain is opened; the Savior has died and has risen, and is now interceding and pleading that we might live; offering a free salvation "without mony and without price", a free gift; only look and live, "forsake sin, cleave unto righteousness", "to-day if ye will hear His voice harden not your hearts". Here mercy is freely offered and forgiveness is obtained. We have the Holy Bible where it is all explained. Time's march is onward; the unceasing wheels move forward; we are on a great battle-field; our enemy is satan, our true friend is Christ. Satan desires to have us that he may sift us as wheat, but the Savior says that He has prayed for us, that our faith fail not. Then let us trust in Jesus, and abide under his wing; fix our treasure in Heaven, and secure that rich inheritance, that invaluable prize, that brilliant crown, that true diadem, that sparkling gem, that will deck the true Christian in the bright realms of glory.

W. B. SHANK.

Zanesville, Ohio.

SUGGESTIONS FOR NEW YEAR.

Inasmuch as it appears to me, as well as to some others, that there is but little practical religion in the world compared to the amount professed, I will try to give a brief view of what I think would meet the approbation of God for 1873.

First we must be engrafted into the true vine Jesus Christ. Paul says, we are the children of God by faith in Christ, and so many of you as have been baptized into Christ have put on Christ. Now the crown is not at the beginning, nor at the middle, but at the end of the race. If we are true branches, we will bear some fruit, and endure the purging so as to bear more fruit; we should therefore offer the sacrifice of praise to God continually, that is, the fruit of our lips, giving thanks to His name, &c. See Heb. 13: 14 15. How this "continually" should be understood. Remember the evening and the morning constitute the day, see also Exodus 29; 30 and to the end of the chapter. This should, at least, be a public sacrifice by those who are heads of families, twice a day, and if they see proper, seven times a day, and again at midnight, but those might be in the closet. And those of our brethren and sisters who are not heads of families, see that you honor your father and mother, or those with whom you dwell, in not putting any thing in the way of their family worship, and offer your private prayers continually, in behalf of all men. Love to God and love to man, should be the mainspring of all our actions. We should also strive to grow in grace, and a greater knowledge of the only true God and His holiness, and our sinfulness. Strive more and more to please God.

A BROTHER.

Youth's Department.

FOR THE YOUNG.

Dear Young Readers: Here I am for the first time with pen in hand, to tell you something, which we hope will not be inadmissable, about Jesus, as this name we know, sounds sweet to you. A long time ago, over 1800 years, in the days of Herod, who was a King, Jesus was born in Bethlehem of Judea, not a rich, fashionable town but poor people lived there. For this reason the rich Jews refused to receive Jesus as being the Savior. Jesus' parents went up to Bethlehem for a certain purpose and while there Jesus was born, and as there was no room for them in the inn, they were compelled to lay Him in a manger, a place in which horses are fed. Dear children, think how poor they must have been, no money to get a bed to lay him on, or friends to administer to their wants. Think of this dear young friends, you who have good warm clothes and beds, and friends to care of you. About this time, King Herod wanted to kill Jesus and to accomplish this, he sent forth his armies and slew all the children that were in Bethlehem and in all the surrounding country, thinking that by this, he would kill Jesus. But the angel of the Lord appeared to Joseph, the father of Jesus, and told him of Herod's work and that they must take Jesus and go to Egypt another country, which they did. So dear young reader, if you love Jesus, he will lead you out of all difficulties, yes, if the adversary tries to persuade you that it is no harm to put on fashionable things remember the story of Jesus, how poor, how despised he was by the fashionable, and that to be followers of him you must be plain, though the rich may laugh at you, Jesus was laughed at and was mocked. So Herod was defeated, and when Jesus arrived at the age of about 30 years, he was baptized of John, a man who "was sent from God," in the river of Jordan. Then he went up into a mountain and stayed there forty days eating nothing, when the adversary came and taunted him. Here is an important lesson to be learned from this. Jesus was hungry when the tempter came to him. Then he thought would be the best time to tempt him, he said, "if thou be the son of God, command this stone to be made bread." But Christ met him with truth and said, "it is written thou shalt not live by bread alone but by every word of God." So when satan tempts you to do anything wrong, tell him you cannot do so for Christ tells you not to do so. When Christ had ended his mission on earth, being taken by wicked men and put to death and laid in the grave, the third day an angel came down and rolled a stone away from the mouth of the tomb, which had been placed there by the Jews, and Jesus came forth, continued forty days, and then went up to heaven in a cloud, and now he is there, preparing a place for you, and if you love and obey Jesus, when you die you will go to him, and be happy forever.

J. M. WELLS.

You can never catch the word that has once gone out of your lips. Once spoken, it is out of your reach; try your best, you can never recall it. Therefore, take care what you say. Never speak an unkind word, an impure word, a profane word.

CORRESPONDENCE

A Reporter is wanted from every Church in the brotherhood to send us Church news, Obituaries, Announcements or anything that will be of general interest. To insure insertion the writers name must accompany each communication. Our invitation is not personal but general—please respond to our call.

INDIAN CREEK CHURCH, }
Newton Co., Mo. }

We give this as an item of history as it seems from what knowledge we have of the officiating Elders, that this is the first Lovefeast held by the "Congregational Brethren." We are pleased to learn that in their order there is no very great deviation and hope the proper efforts will be made to affect a union. We should by no means divide on such small differences.

Dear Pilgrim Brethren and Friends: As there has not been any report yet from this little Church, I have concluded to give you a short one myself, that the many readers of this valuable paper may know that we are yet alive, and still have the privilege of obeying high heaven by practicing these most sacred principles and ordinances handed down to us by God through his Son Jesus Christ which was, and is to be practiced while the world stands.

On the evening of the 10th of Nov., this little body assembled to wash feet and to partake of the bread and wine, the emblems of Christ's broken body, assisted by those dear Elders, some coming two hundred miles. Those who labored with us during the meeting were Elders Daniel and Franklin Hendricks of Jasper Co.; Elder Isem Gipson of Cater co., Mo., and Elders Hopping and C. Shank of Lawrence, Kansas. The day was passed in preaching the word, exhorting and prayer. In the evening, all things being ready, supper being served the brethren and sisters surrounded the table, making one link as we were baptized in one body, perfectly joined together. The minister, on reading the 13th chap. of John, coming to the 4th verse, Elder Gipson arose from supper, layed aside his garments and girded himself with a towel, after that poured water in a basin and washed his brother's feet and wiped them with the towel wherewith he was girded, so on around the table. Each two and two washed and wiped each others feet. After ending this ordinance, ate the supper, but while some did eat, the minister took the bread and blessed it and broke it with his brother, after that each two broke the bread between each other, so on around the table, consequently this ordinance was performed. In like manner he took the cup, gave it to his brother, after that two and two supped together, on around the table, serving alike to brother and sister, as we cannot read of but one cup being used. See Mark the 14:23. First Corinthians, 11: 25. What a glorious privilge this is, that we can obey the Savior in performing these commandments? How happy it makes us feel, when we obey the law and do our duty? Christ says, "if ye know these things happy are ye if you do them." If ye keep my commandments ye shall abide in my love, even as I have kept my Father's commandments and abide in his love. John 15: 10. Then if we strictly obey these commandments, we are a light to the world even as Christ says, "I am come a light into the world that whosoever believeth on me shall not be in darkness." Then dear young readers let us ever stick to the word and show our light by our works. Never shall I forget the order that was manifested at our little meeting in performing these ordinances. The world sympathized with us and said we were right. Bear with me dear readers for being tedious in stating to you our little meeting, for I would have you to know that we practice down here what we read.

As I promised that my letter would be short I trust you will bear with these few remarks. May God still add such blessings as we daily receive.

From a young pilgrim.

N. DICE.

Brother Brumbaugh:—I take the present opportunity to give you some church news for your worthy PILGRIM. Our church district was organized in June 1857, known as the Coldwater Church, and left in care of Elder Philip Moss who died in a few years after. Then we were left for some time without a shepherd, but the Lord protected the little flock, and some time after, others were elected to the ministry and placed in his stead, and the church slowly increased from time to time over a large territory until of late, it was thought necessary, for the sake of convenience and that there might be made a more extensive promulgation of the Gospel, to make a division and form two sub districts, which was fully established and ratified on last Saturday at our council meeting held for that purpose, by the assistance of Elders E. K., and Benjamin Beeghly of Waterloo Church. The newly organized district was then called Rock Grove district, with one minister, W. J. H. Bauman, who was in the second degree of the ministry. The church then thought it necessary to hold an election and the result was that Bros. H. N. Lane and Philip Workman were chosen to the ministry and brother W. J. H. Bauman promoted to the office of bishop to take the oversight of that district, while the writer has the charge of the original district as above named, with the assistance of his co-laborers in the Word, Bros. Benjamin Ellis, J. E. Eikenberry and T. C. Tallhelm.

Now as the Lord has prospered us, notwithstanding the many impediments that were thrown in the way by the enemy of souls, we trust that God will still bless us, and that we will all go forth as bold soldiers of the cross in letting our light shine, and adorning ourselves with meekness and Godly fear, for in so doing we may be able to advance the Kingdom of His dear son, our Lord Jesus Christ. By the way, I will further say that our meeting-house that we have in progress is now stopped, as the cold weather came on before the mason work was completed. It is all done up to the gable ends and I expect will have to stand so until Spring. Now as we are all helpless, needy creatures we desire the prayers of all God's children, especially may those of our young in the ministry be willing to take up the cross and labor for the Master's Kingdom is my prayer. J. F. EIKENBERRY.

Greene, Iowa.

Brother Henry:—I, in company with Bro. Joseph Snowberger, started on the morning of the 7th of Dec., on a mission of love to the brethren, sisters and friends in Bedford Co. Pa., met on the train at Cove Station. Stopped off at Bloody Run—was there met by brother Isaac Ritchy and conveyed to his house on Clear Ridge and in the evening went to the Clearville Meeting house, had a good meeting. After meeting went home with Bro. Ritchy. Next day, had meeting again at 10 o'clock, also in the evening. These meetings were well attended, good order and considerable interest manifested, After meeting in the evening, went home with friend Philip Grubb and was kindly entertained. Next morning, friend Grubb took us on his spring-wagon to friend Himes Grubb. In the evening, walked about three miles to the Werner school house, rather small congregation, weather disagreeable. After meeting, went home with friend James Grove and was kindly entertained by the family, much love and kindness manifested to us— have some reason to believe that they are not far from the Kingdom. In the evening, friend Grove accompanied us some three miles to the Clearville meeting-house, were requested, by different persons, to speak on the subject of baptism that evening, which we did as the Lord gave us ability. This was our last meeting at Clearville. After meeting went home with brother John Smith, was well entertained. Next evening, he and his wife and sons took us to the Clear Creek school-house full house and good meeting. After meeting, went home with brother Jacob Liegenfelter, well cared for. Next morning, went to Snake Spring Valley, had two meetings, 10 o'clock and evening. Next morning walked across the mountain, about seven miles, to Elder Steel's congregation, had four meetings, well attended and much interest manifested. On Monday morning we were taken to the funeral of old brother Frederick Oaks. Preached his funeral and returned home about four o'clock, found all well. We have great cause to be thankful to the good Lord for his protecting care exercised over us, while on this mission of love.

JOHN W. BRUMBAUGH.

Clover Creek, Pa.

CORINTH, W. VA., }
Dec. 8th, 1872 }

Dear Pilgrim:—I had thought not to give an account of our meeting at so late a date, but as church news is interesting, I have concluded to give a short sketch of our meeting.

On the evening of the 12th of October, the brethren assembled at our meeting house, Shiloh church, to attend to the ordinances of the Lord's house. The ministering brethren present were Martin Cosner and Wm. George from Grant Co., W. Va., and Solomon Buckalew and Z. Amon from Preston Co., W. Va., and others. Meeting opened by Bro. M. Cosner. Preaching by Bro. Wm. George to a large concourse of people. Good attention to the word preached. Followed by Bro. M. Cosner and Solomon Buckalew, with very appropriate remarks, after which the people were dismissed for a short time. Assembled again by singing, the brethren and sisters setting themselves around the table to engage in the most solemn thing belonging to the house of God. It is a solemn thing indeed to engage in these things, knowing that we must give account to him, the judge of quick and dead. We are truly glad to say that we had the best order manifested at this meeting for several years. Next day, met again for preaching at 11 o'clock. Sermon by Bro. Solomon Buckalew, to which good attention was given. Discourse from the following text: "Watch and pray always that ye may be counted worthy to escape all these things which shall come to pass and to stand before the Son of man." One baptised on Sunday. May the Lord help us to live in the future more conformed to his will, so if we meet no more upon earth, we may meet in the Celestial City where parting will be no more.

J. M. WELLS.

ALBION, MICHIGAN, }
Nov 30th, 1872. }

Dear Pilgrim:—I can not give you any church news, as most of the brethren can, but I love to read it, and that is the only comfort we have. We have not seen any of our ministering brethren in this state yet, but we hope to live, to see the day, that the Brethren may fulfill the command in this place, which our Savior gave to His Apostles, on the mountain, "Go ye therefore, and teach all nations, baptizing them in the name of the Father, and of the Son, and of the Holy Ghost, teaching them to observe all things whatsoever I have commanded you", as we believe the people here in this country, are not taught to observe all the commands. I hope and trust, that some of the brethren will come and teach the gospel in its purity. We would be very thankful, to have some of the ministering brethren come and hold meetings here. Yours in Christ.

MOSES MOIST.

Dear Brethren and Sisters:—On Sabbath morning, Nov. 10th, amid the inclemency of the weather, we felt very desirous of meeting with God's people in the Sanctuary, and after reaching there found, much to our surprise, that Bro. Daniel Snowberger of New Enterprise, Pa., would address us. After reading part of the 4th chapter of 2d Timothy, he selected for his text these words, "Preach the Word." We never had much of an opportunity of hearing Bro. S. preach, but we were deeply impressed with his sermon. By this text we understand that the whole Word of God is to be preached. This the Bro. tried to hold forth in its true light. We are not to take a part of the Word, and preach and practice it, and consider a part not to be observed and obeyed by us. Only a short time ago we were conversing upon the subject of Feet-washing when it was told us that Christ only washed His disciples feet to show his humility, and if we only *acknowledge* this humility of our Savior, it is not necessary that we perform the action. We *do acknowledge* that Christ showed his humility by washing his brethren's feet, but if I say I can be humble enough to wash my sister's feet, can any one believe it until I really show my humility by performing the action? Really not. The sermon was concluded by James A. Sell. Brother S. preached in a school house at first of Ten in the eve. Following Sabbath, November 10th, Bro. G. Myers addressed us at the school-house at Eldorado from John 1; 13. "Which were born," &c. Let us diligently strive for the religion of Christ that we may not be "born of the will of the flesh, nor of the will of man, but of God." Let us not give heed to perverse doctrine but follow the words and examples of Christ, that we may not be found guilty of failing in one point, and that we may win the crown of glory and sit at God's right hand for

"'Twill not be long our journey here,
Each broken sigh and falling tear;
Will soon be gone, and all will be
A cloudless sky, a graveless sea."

E. K. STIFLER.

Dear Brethren:—I will write a few lines for The PILGRIM. Brother S. S. Sherfy and I visited the brethren and friends in Washington Co., Va. We endeavored to preach to them the Word of the Lord a few days, had some good meetings with those kind friends. Thence we went to Ash Co., North Carolina. We found there a number of brethren, sisters and relations, and also kind friends. We preached the best we could by the help of the Lord, five or six days. We had good congregations and good attention to the word preached. The Lord opened the hearts of some, so that they brought forth fruits meet for repentance, and gladly received the Word and were baptized in the likeness of the death of the Son of God, and others made application. We bade farewell to those kind friends with tears, hoping that we will meet them again by and by. We set out for home, came by the way of Taylorsville in Johnson Co., Tenn.,—had a good meeting here, then we came again by the way of Washington Va., held a Communion meeting with the brethren and sisters;—a very large audience on Saturday night and also on the Sabbath. We then came home and found all well—had a happy meeting with the family. Thank the Lord for the blessing. May the grace of God and the Communion of the Holy Spirit rest upon all the Israel of God is our desire and prayer.

HENRY GARST.

Blountsville, Tenn.

Kind Editors:—With this we send the names of our patrons, to your worthy paper for the coming year. We however expect yet to add a few more names to the list. The PILGRIM meets with a warm reception with us, and we fondly hope that it may still continue in a manner that it may merit such patronage.

Our periodicals will aid us in performing our duties, if they give evidence to the wisdom that James speaks of as being "first pure, then peaceable, gentle, easy to be entreated, full of mercy and good fruits, without partiality and without hypocrisy." We do think that the character of the editorial labors in the church has much to do with the union and love that prevails in the church. An Editor sustains very much the same relation to his readers, that the minister does to his congregation. Every thought or sentiment that he edits he is to some extent, sowing that in the hearts of his readers; hence it very conclusively follows, that published matter should be "first pure."

The names we enclose are from the west branch of the old Rome congregation, under the eldership of Bro. J. P. Ebersole. We have a colony of about thirty-five members, a convenient house in which we meet every alternate Sabbath in humble worship—have had nine accessions during the summer. Yours in love.

I. T. ROSENBERGER.

Gilboa, Ohio.

Dear Editors:—Being at leisure this afternoon, I came to think over the past and found that we could have improved it better, and which is lost, therefore we should improve our time and spend every moment for some good cause since "God so loved the world that He gave His only begotten Son that whosoever believeth on Him should have everlasting life." My dear brethren and sisters in the faith, what great love God has manifested unto us. As the apostle says, "Behold what manner of love the Father hath bestowed upon us that we shall be called the children of God." Now since the grace of God has appeared unto all men, and blessed us with everything to make our bodies comfortable, also with a knowledge to serve Him in His own appointed ways Let us try to live faithful, improve our time by serving the Lord in love and sincerity that we may be prepared to follow the saints who have gone to their glorious reward.

The brethren of the Codorus Church, York Co., Pa., have built a meeting house this past Summer and Fall which is now finished. It is 70 feet long by 40 wide. We had the first meeting in it on the 14th of Dec. Saturday evening, Sunday forenoon and in the evening. Bros. Charles Royer and John L. Beaver of Union Co., Pa., were present during our meeting, preaching to us that glorious gospel of Jesus Christ, which Paul was not ashamed of, which is the power of God unto salvation. Our meetings were well attended, on Sunday evening the house was quite full of dear blood bought souls, listening to the Word preached by the brethren. May it have its effect through the grace of the Lord is my prayer.

On Monday the 16th the brethren left the vicinity of Loganville and went with Bro. Jacob Shamberger to Md., filling a few appointments there, they then left for the Upper Codorus Church where they ended their journey which they did on the 23d and then left for their respective homes. May God reward their labors with the crown of life.

CHRISTIAN NESS.

Loganville, Pa.

Dear Pilgrim:—This arm of the church is moving along slowly. There has been three added to the church by baptism, in the last year, and five by letter. There is a large field in this country, for the disseminating of the bread of life. When I hear of so many ministering brethren East, that travel mostly among large congregations, it makes me wonder why it is so. Brethren come out West among the scattered brethren, and labor for the cause; you can do much good. When traveling through this country, give us a call, as this is a good country, and room for all that wish a home.

BENJAMIN BASHOR.

Whitesville, Mo.

MARRIED.

LYNCH.—MASH.—October 10th, A. D. 1872 at 7 A. M. by the undersigned at His residence Mr. Robert Lynch to sister Mary Ellen Mash.

HOLLINGER—SHANK.—December 12th A. D. 1872 at 12 at noon, by the same, at the residence of the brides parents, Bro. John Edward, son of Bro. Jacob Hollinger to sister Mary Catharine, daughter of Bro. Martin Shank.

CHOICK.—STOUT.—On the same day at 3 P. M at the residence of the brides parents, Willson Klink, son of Bro. Christian Choick, to Miss Elizabeth, daughter of Bro. Michael Stout, all of Upper Cumberland District.

DANIEL HOLLINGER.

SNELL—PALMER.—On the 1st day of January 1873, by the undersigned at the house of brother Joseph Glick, brother Solomon G. N. Snell; of Rockingham Co., Va., to sister Aeliah Caroline Palmer, of Holt Co., Mo.

A. J. CORRELL.

BURKET.—NEARHOOF.—By the undersigned at the residence of the bride's parents, January 2d, 1873, Mr. William Burket to Miss Elly Nearhoof, both of Warriorsmark Valley, Huntingdon Co., Pa.

WILLIAM H. QUINN.

SHATHOWER—SPRINGER.—By David Goodyear, at the house of the bride's parents, Dec. 29th, 1872, brother George Shathower to sister Sarah Springer, all of Cumberland Co., Pa.

DIED.

ZIMMERMAN.—In the Mosco district, Augusta Co., Va., Nov. 4th, 1872, aged 78 years 5 months and 28 days. Funeral from Psalms, 36 : 9, by Eld Jacob Thomas and friend John Weaver.

Bro. Zimmerman leaves a widow and 6 children to mourn their loss, but we hope their loss will be his eternal gain. He was a faithful member. No matter how cold the weather, his seat was never found vacant in the church though he was a cripple. He has now gone to his reward.

JACOB ZIEGLER.

SHIVELY.—In the middle fork of Wild Cat Church, Clinton county, Ind. November 2 1872, brother Jacob Shively, aged 67 years, 3 months and 21 days. Disease, lung fever, only four days sick. He has been a deacon in this church for many years. Funeral services improved by the brethren from 1 Thes. 4 : 13-18.

STEPHEN SHIVELY.

DAILY.—At the residence of his son-in-law, George Row, in Summit county, Ohio, after an illness of 6 days, father Henry Daily, on the 14th day of October, 1872, aged 89 years, 9 months and 1 day.

He was formerly a citizen of Blair county Pa. His dwelling was on Clover Creek in said county. He leaves 5 children to mourn his loss, 4 sons and 1 daughter. He was a member of the Presbyterian church. Funeral services by the brethren Henry Brevantz and Wm A. Murray.

SELLERS.—December 7th, A. D 1872, in the Lower White Oak church Lancaster Co., Pa., sister Amanda, wife of brother Peter Sellers, aged 48 years, 1 month and 6 days.

She suffered much which she bore with christian patience, and when she felt that the time of her departure was at hand she made choice of Elder Bro. David Gerlach, Benjamin Eby and the writer to preach at her funeral. She then fully resigned herself to the will of the Lord and in her dying moments she left the strongest evidence of a glorious immortality. She leaves a husband and four daughters to mourn their loss which is to her, great gain. This family could scarcely be reconciled were it not for the words of the Apostle 2d Cor. 7 : 10, "since the ties of nature are broken," &c. On the 9th her remains were followed to their last resting place at Brethren's Meeting-house near Manheim (said Co.) by a large concourse who mourned the loss. An affectionate wife, a kind mother, a consistent and praiseworthy member has gone to her rest. Funeral services from 2 Cor. 4 : 17-18 and 5 : 1 by the aforesaid brethren.

DANIEL HOLLINGER.

MILLER—In the Sugarcreek church, Allen Co., Ohio, Dec. 23 1872, our much esteemed sister, Polly Miller, consort of Elder Daniel Miller, aged 54 years, 8 months and 8 days.

Thus has passed away a mother in Israel, leaving a vacancy in the church and family circle that cannot be filled. Her lungs were diseased for some years. Since early last Spring she was mostly confined to the room, and the last two months to her bed. She bore her affliction with christian fortitude, and in obedience to the demand of the apostle, called for the elders of the church and was anointed in the name of the Lord. In the morning of her departure, she addressed her youngest sons and said they were here and she was going to a better world—told them to obey their father and likewise called for other of the family and gave them the instruction of a christian mother and closed her eyes in death.

Funeral discourse to a large attentive congregation, from Phil. 1 : 21.

DANIEL BROWER.

[*Companion* and *Visitor* please copy.]

SNAP.—On the 1st day of December 1872, Mary Eliza, daughter of friend Samuel and Elizabeth Snap. Aged just 3 years. Funeral preached by M Swongur and the writer from Job 19 : 21. and Matthew 18 : 3.

J. L. Frantz.

HUDDLESTONE.—In the town of Ellsworth, Pierce Co., Wisconsin, William Whitdom, infant son of brother A. and sister Mary Huddlestone September 18th 1872, aged 1 year 3 months and 3 days. Of the same parents Ida Luella Huddleston, October 21st, 1872, aged 2 years, 11 22 days. Funeral by the writer from James 4th chap., latter clause of 11th verse.

Parents, weep not for your little loss it their eternal gain.

Yes they are gone, do not distrust.
But meekly to his wisdom bow,
He's laid the loved ones in the dust.
With angel spirits resting now.

WM. H. ROOSY

MILLER.—In the Valley District, Augusta Co., Va., our beloved sister Fanny, consort of Samuel Miller, November 17th 1872.

Her remains were taken to the Valley Meeting-house where the funeral occasion was served by Bro Levi Garber and others to a large congregation. She leaves a husband and three children and grandchildren and many friends to mourn their loss. But we hope our loss is her eternal gain. Age 61 years, 6 months and 10 days.

S. N. WINE.

SELL.—In the Yellow Creek branch Bedford Co., Pa., May 25, 1872, sister Susan Kagarice, daughter of brother John and sister Susan Sell, after an illness of only seven days. She was sensible to the last, and was resigned to the will of the Lord, and without a murmur or complaint peacefully passed from earth away.

She leaves a sorrowing husband and three little children, and a large circle of friends to mourn her untimely departure. The little children now loose the kind care of a loving mother, which they so much need in this cold and sinful world, but we hope the Lord will provide for them, and direct them into the paths of piety.

Funeral services by the brethren from Heb. 13: 14.

JAS. A SELL.

ZIGLER.—Dec. 28th, 1872, near Waterside, Bedford Co., Pa., Aaron Zigler, son of brother Jacob and sister Mary Zigler, aged 29 years, 8 months and 7 days.

Thus another young man had to leave without obtaining what he, undoubtingly, desired, as he had to go quite unexpectedly. Should serve as a warning to others in like circumstances. He was a quiet young man who never associating with bad company, addicted to reading, leaving one child and a disconsolate widow to mourn their loss. He was married by the writer just 5 days less than 4 years ago. Funeral occasion from Heb. 9 : 2 to a large audience by the writer.

LEONARD FURRY.

WARNER.—Near Salem, Montgomery county, Ohio, Nov. 28th, 1872, our much respected friend, Aaron, son of Bro. Jacob Warner, aged 29 years and some months.

He leaves a companion and one little daughter also a father and a step-mother and three sisters with many friends to mourn his departure. Funeral services by the brethren.

WARNER.—Fell asleep in Jesus, Sunday morning, Dec. 22nd 1872, in Salem congregation, Montgomery Co., Ohio, our much esteemed Bro. Geo. Warner, born in Bedford Co., Pa., aged 64 years, 9 months and 6 days.

He leaves a son and a daughter and six grand-children and many friends to mourn their loss. Funeral occasion improved by H. Davy and Jesse Stutsman from 2d Tim. 1st chap 10th ver.

JOHN H. BRUMBAUGH.

MILLER.—In Mt Union, Huntingdon co., Pa., Dec. 2nd, 1272, our much beloved brother Wm. Miller, (deacon), aged 53 yrs 11 mos. and 2 days. Funeral services by Jos. R Hanawalt and others. Text, 2. Kings; 22: 1.

He was afflicted for several months, but able to go about most of the time. The morning before his death, had visited some of his children in town, and came home about 1 o'clock, and said to his wife that he felt very queer, and then in a few moments fell with a stroke of apoplexy. He suffered seemingly in an unconscious state, and breathed his last about 5 o'clock, p. m. He left a kind widow, and seven intelligent and affectionate children to mourn their loss, but we believe their loss was his great gain. We believe he left the strongest evidence of a glorious immortality. Our beloved brother gave the strongest proof of a living faith in Jesus; his daily talk was religion, in his house and out of it; he read his Bible daily to his family and his life cast forth that bright and heavenly lustre that gave evidence that there was reality in the religion of Jesus. If space would admit, I could write pages in proof of his heavenly life. His desire was to be buried at the Spring Run Meetinghouse, Mifflin Co., Pa. The brethren at said place was at the station, awaiting the arrival of the deceased and friends with ample conveyances.

WM. H. QUINN.

The Weekly Pilgrim.

JAMES CREEK, PA., Jan. 14th, 1872.

☞ HOW TO send money.—All sums over $1.50, should be sent either in a check, draft or postal order. If neither of these can be obtained, have the letter registered.

☞ WHEN MONEY is sent, *always* send with it the name and address of those who paid it. Write the names and post office as plainly as possible.

☞ EVERY subscriber for 1873, gets a *Pilgrim Almanac* FREE.

NOW IS THE TIME.

There seems to be a time for everything and among the many things that should be done NOW is that of gathering subscribers for the PILGRIM. Our agents, generally, are doing finely and lists are coming in encouragingly, but we still have room for a large number more which we feel certain can be obtained if our agents and friends will make a little greater effort. Our No. 1 for 1873 seems to give satisfaction everywhere and all that is necessary to have a largely increased circulation, is to let it be seen. Brethren and sisters, try it. Take with you a copy of the PILGRIM and the *Pilgrim Almanac* and see what you can do. Do not wait on some person else, but try it *yourself*. It is true, times seem a little close and money scarce, but our terms are so easy that all can read the PILGRIM and pay for it. Those who do not have the money now, let them send in their names and pay for it as soon as they can. All we ask of you is, not to send us such names as you think will not pay at all. We cannot afford to send our paper free to any unless they are *really* poor. For such we do the very best we can, and if some of our wealthy brethren would send us a little that they could spare we would do much more. Some are doing nobly in sending the PILGRIM as presents to such friends as they think will appreciate the favor. Much good has been accomplished in this way and we hope that many more will take advantage of our liberal offer for that purpose. Remember, when the PILGRIM is sent as a present it costs only $1.25. Now brethren and sisters, let us hear from you and see what can be done. There are thousands in the Church, as well as outside of it, that would be benefitted by reading the PILGRIM. We are prepared to accommodate, at least, 1,000 with complete volumes and *Almanacs*, so that none need fear that they cannot be supplied. Let us hear from you soon and favorably.

OUR ADDRESSING MACHINE is on hands and part of the list set up, so that some will have their names printed on their papers this week, and in a short time we expect to have them all ready. We have the McFatrick Machine, the best that is made, and works like a charm, putting the names on as fast as the papers can be handled. Any of craft wishing a good and cheap Addressing Machine should enquire of us or call and see it operate before purchasing any other.

MARIETTA NURSERIES.—Our readers will please notice the advertisement of this responsible firm. From this Nursery we bought our trees which are now in bearing, and have, in every case, proved true to name which is quite an important feature in ordering trees. The proprietors are men of good standing and of known integrity, for whom our brethren can sell without risking their reputation. Any one wishing to enter a pleasant and profitable business during the winter and spring, should write at once for an agency.

THE *Pilgrim Almanac* is highly spoken of by all who see it, and are especially pleased with our improved "Ministerial Record." We still have a good supply and are waiting to give them FREE to every subscriber for 1873. To some we may have sent two copies; such would do us a favor by giving one to some person who would be willing to take the PILGRIM. Remember, we have none for sale.

THE *Herald of Truth* says: Bro. B. Warkentin of Russia, in company with Bro. Jacob Y. Shantz of Berlin, Ont., made a trip to Manitoba, in British America, north of Minesota, upon an invitation of the Canadian Government. They spent some two weeks there, after which Bro. Shantz returned home and Bro. Warkentin remained in Summerfield, Ill., where he intends to spend the winter. He seems to have been pretty well pleased with the countries in Manitoba.

CRITICISMS.—Bro. Slifer's article in No. 46, page 387, has called forth a large number of criticisms, but as it is sufficiently met by Bro. Gibbon in No. 1 for '73, we think it not profitable to insert any more while we have such an abundance of other matter that may be of greater interest. The writers will please excuse.

THE BAPTISM of John, whence was it, from heaven or of men? Under the above heading, Eld. B. F. Moomaw promises to write a series of papers. The first paper is before us and will appear next week. Eld. M. is a sound reasoner, and our readers can expect something worthy of notice.

PHRENOLOGICAL JOURNAL AND WEEKLY PILGRIM sent together for $3.50. Those who have paid us $1.50 for the PILGRIM, by sending $2.00 more can have the *Phrenological Journal*. Send us your names accompanied by the cash, and read the best Journal of the kind in the world.

A POP VISIT.—We, to-day, received a short call from our esteemed Bro. J. F. Oller, who manifests his usual life in the good cause. He thinks that Waynesboro, his place of residence, would be just the place for the PILGRIM Office. Had not James Creek such strong claims on us, we would certainly give the place a consideration.

HERALD OF TRUTH—is an interesting and ably edited monthly published by Jno. F. Funk & Bro., Elkhart, Ind., devoted to the interest of the Menonite Church. Published in English and German at $1.00 per year.

MONEY LIST.

Samuel Mohler, $1.50; Jno Hoover, 3.00; C F Wirt, 11.50; David Adams, 1.50; S M Goughnour, 4.35; Andrew Bechtal, 6.50; John A Clemant, 9.00; J W Blauch, 1.35; Jas L Fitzgerald, 1.25; Adam Appleman 16 35; Thos. B Mattocks, 3.00; A S Bechtal, 1.50; H E Bosserman, 6.00; John N Cripe, 1.50; Jacob Mohler, 15.00; Emanuel Hoover, 1.50; Ella Williams, 1 50; J A Cline, 15 25; Jas Brown, 7.45; Ja- Musser, 9 00, Fannie Hershberger, $10. Benj Landis, 1 50; Henry Garber, 15,00. Israel M Bennett, 1 50; Eliza Brandt, 1 50; Benj Kiser, 1 50; Isaac Garst, 2.85; David Long, 1.25; Jos Myers, 1.25; Martin Campbell, 1 50; Annie E Neal, 1.50; Rudolph Reigert, 1.50, J Blauch, 1 25; J C C., 1 50; J Lichtey, 1 50; J Bowers, 1.50, J Alcorau, 3.25; Uriel Hamilton, 7 50; M Beshoar, 9.50, Jacob Mohler, 1.60; F P Lehr, 1 00; Wm Forney, 1 50; Jno L Beaver, 5 75; Mary Kinoy, 50cts; A Barnhart, 1.50; Louisa Sappington, 1.50; F Dave, 2 00; J Garber, 1 50; Martin Eisenbour, 1 50; John Dale, 75cts; E B Shaver, 8.25; J Mohler, 2 50; J Bock, 3 50, J N Plank, 1.50; J C Richer, 5.50; Philip Workman, 1.25; Solomon Sprangle, 1.50; Keelin Leonard, 1.25; J Hertzler, 1.00; J B Tauzer, 4.50; New Bloomfield, 1 50; J R Lane, 12 00; H Reamer, 4.50; Nancy Schwartz, 1.00; Jos Saylor, 1.25; Jacob Troxel, 1 25; Mary Ross, 1 50; Martin Mohler 1 50; James Price, 7 58; Daniel Bower, 11.75; D Foglesanger, 7.50; Jacob Myers 1 25; Jacob Harnish, 1.50; Joseph Drury, 2 75; John Cripe, 2.25; D Bosserman, 2 75; A Lahr, sr., 1 50; H Beckman, 7.50; Henry Saiteman, 4.00; Jos Rittenhouse, 28 50; Jas Greenickle, 1.50.

GENERAL INTELLIGENCE.

A Church Floor Gives Way.

On Christmas night a congregation of three hundred adults and children were holding a celebration in a Baptist Church in the seventh ward of Williamsport Pa. The floor gave way and the whole assemblage was thrown into the cellar below. The oil lamps were broken, and the church took fire: the flames were soon extinguished, however. The scene was terrible. By 11 p. m., all the killed, fifteen in number, were removed. About fifty persons were injured, some fatally.

FLOODS.—Portions of the country in Leicester, Derby and Nottingham England, are submerged from the late floods. In some sections of these counties the tops of trees and hedges only are visible. A heavy landslide has occurred near Dover. Communications with that town are interrupted. The town of Petersborough, in Northampton county, is flooded, and many of the inhabitants are compelled to take refuge in the upper story of their buildings.

OFFICIAL TITLES.—By a government circular, all public officials in France, in their communications to the heads of departments, have been ordered to suppress the title of "his excellency," and merely to use the simple address of "to the Minister of, &c.," or "to the President."

Oregon, in October, 1871 exported to England $285,503 55 worth of wheat, and to South American ports over $35,000 worth of grain. She also sends into British North America not less than 200,000 bushels of grain to be used there.

It has been recommended that an intermediate census of the United States be taken in 1875, in order to ascertain the growth of the country during the first century of its existence.

EMIGRATION TO TEXAS.—The Mobile and Montgomery Railroad one day sold $1,256 worth of half fare tickets to texas, and the next $1,900 worth of emigtant's tickets.

HUNTINGDON & BROAD TOP RAIL ROAD

Winter Arrangement.

On and after Tuesday, Oct. 4, 1872, Passenger trains will arrive and depart as follows:

Trains from Huntingdon South. *Trains from Mt. Dallas moving North.*

MAIL A. M.	ACCOM P. M.	STATIONS.	MAIL P. M.	ACCOM A. M.
LE8 00	LE5 30	Huntingdon,	AR3 20	AR9 00
8 08	5 57	Long Siding	3 12	8 53
8 21	6 10	McConnelstown	2 56	8 37
8 30	6 17	Pleasant Grove	2 50	8 30
8 45	6 30	Marklesburg	2 37	8 17
9 00	6 44	Coffee Run	2 23	8 01
9 07	6 52	Rough & Ready	2 15	7 53
9 20	7 05	Cove	2 01	7 40
9 21	7 10	Fishers Summit	1 57	7 35
9 44 / 9 51	AR7 30	Saxton	1 37	LE7 15
10 10		Riddlesburg	1 19	
10 17		Hopewell	1 12	
10 34		Piper's Run	12 56	
10 52		Tatesville	12 38	
11 05		Bloody Run	12 21	
11 10		Mount Dallas	12 20	

JOHN M'KILLIPS, Supt

SHOUP'S RUN BRANCH.

LE10 00	LE7 40	Saxton.	AR1 20	AR7 10
10 15	7 55	Coalmont.	1 15	6 55
10 20	8 00	Crawford.	1 10	6 50
AR10 30	AR8 10	Dudley	LE1 00	LE6 40

Broad Top City from Dudley 2 miles by stage.

Time of Penna. R. R. Trains at Huntingdon.

EASTWARD.		WESTWARD.	
Hb'g Ac.	9 24 A. M	Cin. Ex.	2 13 A. M.
Mail	3 30 P. M	Pc'f Ex.	7 43 "
Cin. Ex.	6 55 "	Mail	5 40 P. M.
Phil. Ex	11 15 "	W. Pass.	11 32 A. M.

The Weekly Pilgrim.

Published by J. B. Brumbaugh, & Co.

Edited by H. B. & Geo. Brumbaugh.

CORRESPONDING EDITORS.

D. P. Sayler, Double Pipe Creek, Md.

Leonard Furry, New Enterprise, Pa.

The *Pilgrim* is a Christian Periodical, devoted to religion and moral reform. It will advocate in the spirit of *love* and *liberty*, the principles of true Christianity, labor for the promotion of peace among the people of God, for the encouragement of the saints and for the conversion of sinners, avoiding those things which tend toward disunion or sectional feelings.

TERMS.

Single copy, Book paper,	$1 50
Eleven copies, [eleventh for Agt.]	$15.00

Any number above that at the same rate,

Address,

H. B. BRUMBAUGH,
James Creek,
Huntingdon county Pa.

The Weekly Pilgrim.

"REMOVE NOT THE ANCIENT LANDMARKS WHICH OUR FATHERS HAVE SET."

VOL. 4. JAMES CREEK, PENNSYLVANIA, JANUARY 21, 1873. NO. 3

POETRY.

THE HOMELESS ONE.

"The foxes have holes, and the birds of the air have nests,
But the Son of Man hath not where to lay his head."

'Twas night-fall on Judea's hills;
The busy sounds of work were still,
The shepherd from the fold had gone
And sought his rest at home till dawn;
The busy sounds of childhood's play,
Had echoed from the hills all day.
And now from humble homes there floats
Soft lullabys—sweet mother notes;
The birds had sought their swinging nests,
The night winds rock them to their rest;
Not one of all the creatures here
But had some spot to it most dear.

The pale new moon had hardly set
Behind the brow of Olivet,
When slowly toiling up the steep
Came ONE who often came to weep
O'er man and all his woes.

The crowd had left Him—they had homes;
The beggar, even, who all day roams
In search of charity, had some shed
Where he could creep and lay his head.
But far upon that mountain height
Was ONE who knelt and prayed all night;
The dews fell cold upon his brow,
Bent low in supplication now!

He had no spot called home on earth,
He could not share in song and mirth;
He knew the bitter grief and pain
That must be his, ere he could gain
Redemption for lost, ruined man.
The courts and mansions of the skies
Were his, but he himself denies,
That he our woes and sins might feel,
And by his stripes mankind might heal.

Though wearied with his toil all day
Beneath the burning noontide's ray,
Night brought no rest to him, no home;
He knelt and prayed with heaven's blue dome
Stretched far above his weary head—
And this for thee! for thee were shed
His blood and tears, which cleanse from sin
And make us blest and pure within.

Oh! thou who longest for rest above!
Weary of all thy wandering here;
Take courage; rest upon his love;
In all thy grief he bore a share.

—*Christian Standard.*

ORIGINAL ESSAYS.

"THE BAPTISM OF JOHN, WHENCE WAS IT. FROM HEAVEN OR OF MEN?"

This is a question of superlative importance in these days of progress in ingenuity, and the devious ways in which the children of men endeavor to allure, deceive, and impose upon the credulity of the honest, and unsuspecting. It has become very common even in the exhibition of cabalistic performances, in order to quiet the scruples of the more conscientious, for the dramatist to pretend that it in some way possesses the sanctity of divine authority, or divine influences, and so also with what may be regarded the higher order of the inventions, and institutions of men. Thus Mahomet professed to have interviewed the angel Gabriel, from time to time, who revealed to him that he was chosen of the Lord a prophet; and communicated that religion, that he delivered to his people. So also the Pope of Rome claims that by virtue of Apostolical succession, and the power of inspiration, as God's Grand Vicar on earth, infallible, it is his prerogative to change "times and laws" Dan'l 7:25, to abolish institutions ordained by Christ and the Apostles, and establish such others in their stead, as may from time to time be suggested to his mind; and the same is true to a limited extent among protestant Christianity. This principle has at least obtained largely in the world, and is sanctioned and patronized by the church generally; and no marvel for men are men everywhere, and subject to the control of the same influences and if not sternly resisted the tendency is to flow in the same channel, that channel being popular, as we sometimes hear the idea expressed that we are living in a progressive age, the world is moving on, and we are compelled to move with it.

Of the unauthorized institutions alluded to we might mention, as unscriptural, *Free-masonery, Odd-fellowship, the various orders of temperance associations, &c. I would not be understood to object to these as moral institutions where nothing higher is pretended, but my idea is that they are entirely superceded by the pledge of Christianity and that Christians are unequally yoked when united in common Brotherhood with these associations. Therefore when we are brought within the range of any of these human institutions, and the temptation is presented to cooperate with them, we would do well to enquire in the language of the text at the head of this article, (with the necessary alterations). "Is Free-masonry, or this, that, or the other institution, from God, or is it from men?"

"If any man lack wisdom let him ask of God who giveth to all men liberally and upbraideth none." We need by no means be at a loss for the answer to any such question, for with a little care on our part to divest ourselves of human influence which may be brought to bear upon us by our surroundings, and "taking heed to the light of the sure word of prophecy," we shall most assuredly "be guided into the truth," for it is a peculiar trait in character of God's dealings with the children of men in communicating His will to signify it, in the most unmistakable language. In order then that we may know what we should do it is necessary that we have a command from God either directly expressed, or implied, "A command, says Wayland, involves three ideas. 1st That an act be designated. 2d. That it be somehow signified to be the will of God that the act be performed. 3d. That it be signified that we are included within the number to whom the command is addressed. Like an affectionate father, God has in all His intercourse with the human family from the giving of the law to Adam in the garden, down to the last command by our Savior and the Holy Ghost through the Apostles, signified His will in words and phrases suitably adapted to the human intellect, and farther He has given us the fullest assurance that he disapproves of everything that man presumes to do, apart from His authority, and that thereby His severest indignation is provoked.

MORE ANON.

A DIALOGUE BETWEEN GAMALIEL AND NICODEMUS.

Continued.

Gam. Did he inform you where the young man now resides?

Nic. Zebedee says he is living in the city of Nazareth, and John, who is about twenty-nine years of age, remarked that he sees him quite often, and that he and his brother James, have known him for a number of years.

James, who is well gifted in the use of words, proceeded to give the following description of him, as he appeared when he last saw him conversing with some of the learned in Capernaum: "He is of lofty stature and well proportioned; his countenance is truly noble. The hair of his head is the color of wine, and from the top of his head to his ears, very straight and without radiance, but it descends from the ears to the shoulders in shining curls, and even farther after the same magnificent manner. His hair is parted straight on the top of his head, after the manner of the Nazarenes, his forehead is smooth and clear, even without a wrinkle; his face free from blemish, and slightly tinged with red. His beard is the same color of the hair, and is forked, eyes very blue and brilliant. He has never once been seen to laugh, but many have seen him weep. In appearance, he is the most beautiful of the race of men."

Gam. Did they inform you what his name is, and how his parents are getting along?

Nic. James stated that all knew him by the name of Jesus, and he was living with his mother, whose name is Mary, but that when he was about thirteen years old, his father, whose name was Joseph died, leaving him to support his mother, which he did by working at the carpenter trade, which he in part learned of his father.

Gam. Did you learn how old Jesus is at this time?

Nic. Zebedee says that he is nearly thirty years old.

Gam. This is undoubtedly John's second cousin, whom we all loved so well.

Nic. You know that John is of the tribe of Levi, but Zebedee stated that Jesus is of the tribe of Judah, and how they can be cousins I have been trying to reconcile, as different tribes were not generally allowed to marry among each other.

Gam. That is perfectly clear in my mind since I examined the sacred records in the temple, and compared them with what I gathered from my interview with Matthew.

Nic. That is then one point which I wish you to clear up for me.

Gam. During my leisure, since I last saw you, I wrote down what I could gather of the genealogy of these two remarkable persons, and will simply read it to you: Mary, the mother of Jesus, was the only child of Eli, who was the son of Matthat. Unto Matthat was born two children the first was a son, whose name was Heli, and the second whose name I failed to ascertain, but will call her Rachel:—all these were of the tribe of Judah, having descended from David through his son Nathan. Rachel by the consent of the priesthood marries a man of the tribe of Levi, to them was born a daughter whom they named Elizabeth. Finally, Rachel's brother Heli become the father of a daughter, whom he named Mary, hence Mary and Elizabeth were first cousins. John and Jesus their children of course, are second cousins, though John by his father Zacharias was of the tribe of Levi, and Jesus of the tribe of Judah.

Nic. Well yes, that is clear now, but then there is another mystery in the matter which I have found no one who could properly solve it for me yet. I in company with Stephen the proselyte of Antioch, examined the sacred records and they do not appear to agree respecting the genealogy of Jesus.

Gam. In what respects do they differ? I think I can clear it up for you.

Nic. In the general record it is stated that "Jacob begat Joseph the husband of Mary," and in the private record it says that "Joseph the husband of Mary is the son of Heli: now then how Joseph could have two fathers, is not easily comprehended.

Gam. Well I can explain that. I was in the temple to-day, and Luke of Antioch was there, so we examined the records in relation to this matter, and found the same difficulty, but Luke who is well acquainted with both families gave the following solution of the problem: "If the general record is closely examined it will be seen that the genealogy of Joseph is traced through his ancestors to David, but in the private record it is traced from Heli to David; the difference is this: the general record traces the genealogy to David through his son Solomon, while the private record traces it to David through Nathan, the brother of Solomon. They are simply two distinct lines of descent. The first is the genealogy of Joseph, while the latter is that of Mary the wife of Joseph."

Nic. That is clear enough, but why is Joseph called the son of Heli, when Heli is the father of Mary?"

Gam. The reason is simply this: 'When Heli died he left Mary as the only heiress of what little property he owned in Bethlehem, and it was necessary that her genealogy be entered, in order to retain the estate of her father in the tribe to which he belonged. Then when Joseph married her, he became the son-in-law of Heli, but according to the law he was entered as the son of Heli, because he had married an heiress, and the estate

To be Continued.

FIFTY YEARS AGO AND NOW.

What must we do to bring about a uniformity in dress among the members of the church, and keep the brethren and sisters from dressing so much after the fashions of the world, and what plan are we to adopt to get back to our fore-fathers and mothers simplicity and uniformity of dress? This question has been asked me by some of our beloved members often, "Can you not write a plan and have it published in our periodicals that we all may see how to act in union to bring about the desired reformation?" Now my beloved brethren and sisters in Christ, I want you to hear me patiently and weigh the matter in the scales of reason and good common sense, and see whether you cannot say amen to the truth or at least, do not condemn me before I get through, as I do not intend to write anything but what I know to be truth, and has come under my own observation during the past fifty years, or a part of it. To write all the events, changes and admonitions that I have heard given by our elder brethren and sisters for us to take heed to, time would fail me to tell. I am well aware of the tenderness of some on these parts, therefore try to handle the subject as smoothly as truth and brotherly kindness will admit.

In the first place, I will have to take you all back with me fifty years to see how they worshipped God and how humble they all appeared to be. How they were all dressed, and how they had their children dressed. I will now try to show how we have gotten away from the good and right way, first, and then it will not be so hard a matter to see how to get back again to the old Landmarks that our fathers and mothers have set up. Now let us take a look at our brethren seated behind the table, all have on the rounded coats, their hair parted on top of their heads, meek and humble looking men, you cannot see any difference in their dress, they are all alike. Now let us take a look at the sisters. Here they all sit together, all have their heads covered with a plain swiss cap, no edgeing, no lace for a border, no ribbands to tie them on, the cap, border and strings all of swiss. All wear a short gown, their clothing worn at that time was made by their own hands. Here we again see all uniformed; sisters all meek and humble looking women,—no pride among them, how beautiful the sight! We discover at the same time, the great love they have for one another, honoring and preferring one another—no evil word spoken against each other thus fulfilling the command not to speak evil of any man. Do you not think, my dear sisters, with me that God's blessings rested upon those good, meek, lovable, loving sisters that lived fifty years ago?

We will now look at their children at church and see how they are dressed. Oh what a beautiful sight to see! All have on plain home made dresses with a waist-string to draw them to their bodies, plain three cornered handkerchiefs pinned around their necks, and swiss caps on their heads. "What!" says one, "have caps on their little girls at meeting? I cannot see what that was for." All their daughters had caps on at meeting from the little child up to age of 20 years, whether they were members or not. We could tell our brethren and sisters at that time at sight and not only them but their children in the same way. Their children were not ashamed of their plain caps, I have seen as high as twenty little girls from five to twelve years of age, sitting together with their beautiful plain caps on, looking and listening at the brethren who were speaking to us about the goodness of God, I could not help but inwardly exclaim, O, what beautiful little angels these are sitting before us! Now I will try to tell those who cannot see what dressing their children in that plain manner was for. It was because they were bringing up their children for Christ, so that they would not get puffed up with pride and thus become ashamed of Christ and His Church. I knew a little daughter who got her cap soiled that she could not wear it to meeting, she would not go being ashamed to go without it being only eight years old. What do you think of that little girl? Not being a member by profession, and yet was ashamed to be seen at meeting without a cap on and some of you, who have been members for years, are ashamed of being seen at meeting with a cap on. Here we can see, to train up a child in the way it should go, is the only right way for us to bring up our children in the nurture and admonition of the Lord.

Now let us go to church meeting and hear the admonition of the church as given in by the visiting brethren, what they had found when visiting the members. What do we hear? There is too much pride creeping into the church. Some good sister had discovered that some were making their little children's dresses too much like the worldly people, too much after the vain fashions. Some brethren did not come in the order they should, and others chewing tobacco in time of meeting, spitting on the floor so much that those who sat next to them could scarcely find a place to kneel down, in time of prayer, without getting their clothes soiled with tobacco, and a great many other things not necessary to name. Then listen to our beloved elder brethren admonishing us and telling what these things would lead to if we did not strive against them. These admonitions were given at every meeting but pride still increased. Here let me tell where we first began to get out of uniformity. Right at our little children in the cradle. As long as the little ones in our cradles were kept plainly dressed and nothing unnecessary put on them by their mothers nor tolerated by their fathers, in short, as long as pride and fashionable dressing was kept out of our cradles, it was an easy matter to keep pride and fashion out of the church, but as soon as it took root in our cradles, then its progress was more rapid in the church. In the cradle was the door opened for fashionable dressing in the church, and some may ask who opened that door, was it Eve again? No, not altogether, Adam is also complicated in it. The sisters may have led the way, but the brethren appeared to be satisfied well enough to say nothing against it. We soon saw the difference in the appearance of the brethren's children. No more plainly dressed little girls at meeting. The sisters laid aside their short gown except a few who still wear them, the others made plain dresses instead, and soon all were in uniformity in the uniform. It was not so far from the worldly style, therefore not so much of a cross. It was a step down and was easier to make.

Now dear sisters, do not think I am going to say all I have to say about you, just keep cool a while yet, then I will tell you about us brethren also. I just want to tell you how we got out of the good old way of our forefathers and mothers in Israel and then tell you how we must get back again if the Lord will. A. J. CORRELL.

To be Continued.

A FEW THOUGHTS ON THE LANDMARKS.

"Remove not the ancient landmark which thy fathers have set." Prov. 22: 28.

In noticing the foregoing injunction as a motto for the PILGRIM I was made to wonder whether the Editors ever gave those words a thorough consideration, to see what really, their spiritual signification or use may be to us; for, "All that is written before is written for our learning." The attentive Bible reader will readily perceive the practical application of those words under the former dispensation. When Israel were made possessors of Canaan, the land was divided to them by lot, but that division only related to the twelve tribes, and not to the sectioning out of each man's inheritance; or the patrimony of each head of a family. This became the duty of the leading men among them; such as Jethro advised Moses to appoint over the people, and whom he termed "captians," but are sometimes called elders, and at others fathers. And just as at this time, when a survey of lands is made, certain marks are left whereby said survey can be traced again at any time. Just so it was then, and these, in Bible language are "The *Landmarks* which the fathers did set," and by reference to Deut. 19 : 14 it is quite evident the Lord, through Moses, gave them His approval ; and 27 ; 17 a solemn curse is denounced against any one removing them. So now we have their literal definition, use and application pretty clearly before us. Let us try whether we can see what is therein contained for our learning. Jesus Christ procured an inheritance in which, not only every Israelite, but every son and daughter of Adam, has equal interest, in its broadest sense. But as there were tribes among Israel to be taken into the account of the general division of their possessions ; so there are classes to whom the teachings, the promises and threatnings of the Gospel are applicable ; so that the whole domain of that vast inheritance is all divided out, not by lot, or chance, but "By the determinate counsel, and unfathomable wisdom and love of God." Then as Palestine was promised to Israel in a general sense ; in that sense we all are equally interested in the Heavenly Canaan. These promises are gathered from the following texts: "Christ tasted death for every man" "So by the righteousness of one, the free gift came upon all men unto justification of life." "I bring you glad tidings of great joy, which shall be to all people." But when the tribes or classes have their apportionments allotted to them,—the lot or part that falls to the infantile and ignorant class is: "Of such is the kingdom of Heaven." "Where there is no transgression." "The first commandment with promise is, honor thy father and mother." "The times of ignorance God winked at," But to those of riper years and knowledge the apportionment is, "Repent and believe the gospel." "But now commandeth all men everywhere to repent" "Repent and be baptized every one of you * * for the remission of sins." &c. "Come unto me all ye that labor and are heavy laden, and I will give you rest." "And the Spirit and the Bride say come, * * and whosoever will let him take the water of life freely." "To you and to your children is the promise, and to all that are afar off."

Lastly, the other class, which are the, "Fearful and unbelieving, and the abominable, murderers, whoremongers, sorcerers, idolators, and all liars shall have their part (portion) in the lake that burneth with fire and brimstone; which is the second death." These quotations certainly include the destiny of all living, and may be said to stand parallel with the allotted inheritance of the ancient Hebrews, with this difference ; in the disposition of their inheritance by lot man had no choice, unless he utterly refused citizenship. In the "inheritance reserved in heaven," we see men can choose for himself or if he, forfeits that which had been intended for him, his doom is still unalterably fixed ; not by that which is the corresponding part with the "*Landmarks*," but by that which corresponds with the apportionment by the lot. Whenever we come to consider the parallel, or correspondence of these "Landmarks," we invariably find them of human origin or institution ; for such were they, but backed up with the divine sanction, as they also were. God delivered His people out of bondage ; He drove out the nations of Canaan before them ; He divided to them their land by lot, and now they must make such other regulations, as the nature of their circumstances require to promote and maintain love, union and peace among them ; for this very reason those "Landmarks" were set, so that each one knew precisely how far he may go.

So we, my brethren and sisters, were "delivered from the power of darkness, and translated into the kingdom of His dear Son." Our enemies are vanquished, and we are brought together into a church relation, or capacity, as they were; and now we must maintain love, union and peace in the church. Now as the God of Israel gave His sanction to those "Landmarks," or divisions, "Which the fathers did set" so has Jesus Christ given to His church, not only His sanction, but power to legislate, in the absence of positive law, saying : "Whatsoever ye shall bind on earth shall be bound in Heaven : and whatsoever ye shall loose on earth shall be loosed in Heaven." But knowing the evil propensities in man, and the number of temptations to which he is exposed, He has furnished us an outline with rules for this purpose. "If thy brother trespass against thee, tell him his fault between thee and him alone." * * * "Tell it unto the church." "But if he shall neglect to hear the church, let him be unto thee as an heathen man and a publican." Here I maintain the Savior gave His sanction to the desires of the church, just as the God of Israel had to those arrangements made by the fathers, for the regulation of their temporal affairs, and only the authorities that enacted, or set up, had power to repeal, or remove again. Thus, an Israelite being charged with removing his "neighbor's landmarks," is brought before the elders or judges of his city ; they are bound to investigate the case, but having no field-notes, plot, or draft in that law which Moses gave them, or in the division made by the lot, they must resort to, and investigate the "Landmarks" and subdivision made by the fathers ; and in doing so the guilt is fully established by the requisite number of witnesses. The curse or penalty attached to said offence, must now be inflicted with the same rigor or strictness, as if he had violated one of the ten commandments. Precisely so it is in the church of Christ. Difficulties do arise between brethren ; they are proceeded with in gospel order until the case is before the church. The leaven is at work, and if not purged out will leaven the whole lump. The whole body is endangered. But be it remembered it is the church that is to be heard now ; and nothing is said in this connection of hearing the Gospel. Then if the church can find no letter whereby to decide or dispose of said case, she must decide by the best light she has according to the spirit of the Gospel. But in case such a decision is passed by a majority of an individual arm or branch of the church, to the disowning of a party that neglects to hear the church, and the expelled party, with a minority, are dissatisfied with the proceedings hitherto, they now appeal to the highest authority in the church. Their case is laid before the District Council, but they fail to see alike ; or if they do agree they consider the query of a general character, and with their answer, send it up to Annual Meeting. That body now investigates the case, confirms the proceedings of the church, and it, being the highest acknowledged body in the church, its decisions are final and conclusive ; and can only be repealed, altered, or amended by that body which gave them its approval. Here I find a correspondence to "the ancient landmarks which the fathers did set ;" and of which we have quite a number in our borders : and yearly need more, as our borders are enlarged, and further subdivisions are made. And O! may none of us have the presumptions, or covetous disposition, to remove any of these "Landmarks" without legal authority, lest we draw upon ourselves the curse, or penalties annexed, which may be summed up in these words: "If any man shall take away from the words of the book of this prophecy, God shall take away his part out of the book of life and out

To be Continued.

IN MEMORY OF HANNAH FURRY.

Having been an intimate friend of the subject of this notice, whose obituary appears in another column, and also, a member of their little family during the past Summer, I therefore, pen a few thoughts on the death of her who was so much loved by all.

I had a great desire to visit her during her sickness, and often wished to be at her bedside, but as I could not, I daily waited for messages from her, which sometimes were favorable for her recovery, and which caused us still to have hopes for her, 'till at last the sad news, "Hannah is dead," reached our ears. Oh, how hard to realize that she is no more! She who was so young, so pure and innocent, is gone. In the school-room where she so much loved to go, there is a vacant seat ; schoolmates will meet her there no more. When Sabbath school opens again, her teacher will miss an interesting pupil from her class. A fond mother, a loved sister and little brothers, will no more be made glad to see her coming home, but Oh, the vacant place in the home circle! the void there that can never be filled! There where she daily moved with womanly grace and a sweet temper, shedding sunshine all around her, is where her absence will be felt the most. She who, with a willing heart, lightened their cares and welcomed them on their return will be thought of very often.

Many prayers, no doubt, were offered for her recovery, but God's ways are not our ways, and He saw fit to remove her from this world of trouble. All the prayers that were offered, the skill of physicians, the attention of kind friends and all the care an affectionate sister could bestow did not avail, He saw fit to remove her just in the bloom of youth, seemingly, a bud in the midst of full blown roses has been plucked. Grandfathers and grandmothers, whose locks are blooming for the grave, have been passed by, and death has taken one who was yet young, and promised a long life of usefulness.

Dear young friends, is not this a solemn call to you all? Remember, you too must die. Only a few months ago, I gave many of you the parting hand for awhile ; among that number was Hannah. How little did I think that would be the last time I would see her. You have often been called by the ministers of God, and in various ways to forsake sin, but this I think is a special call to you. The youngest of your circle has been taken from among you. Oh heed the call; for it may be the last one for some of you. Prepare while young for that *home* that Hannah spoke so much of going to during her last days on earth.

"Green grow the turf above thee
Friend of our early days ;
None knew thee but to love thee,
None named thee but to praise."

Pilgrim Office, EMMA MILLER.

A HOPE AND A PRAYER.

Since our last Annual Meeting, we have heard many express the hope that at our next meeting of the kind certain questions of difference will not so much as be mentioned. From experience it should be learned that the discussion of questions where there is such a difference of opinion as to forbid even the probability of a union is worse than useless. The design of our annual council is to foster love, union, and a oneness of mind, so much so as possible, touching the doctrine and regulations of the Church. That being the motive it would seem unwise to present to the meeting such a question as is calculated from its nature to produce discord rather than union and love, especially if it be a question that has been before the meeting time and again, and that too without bringing about the desired result, that of union of thought upon the subject. This subject is one of such importance that we have thought much upon it, and propose, out of love for the cause, a remedy. It is within the power of the district meetings to remedy the matter. Let the brethren in those councils, and in their deliberations keep one thing in view and let that be the welfare of the Church at large. Because they may have a trouble at home is no reason why the trouble should be carried into the whole "camp," to there cause a commotion and trouble that otherwise might have been avoided. If the question causing the trouble is entirely new and of a general nature it might be advisable to take it up to the Annual Council, but if it arises from a question that has been before the A. Meeting time and again, we do think it would be unwise to take it there, but rather try it in a way consistent to the principles of love to dispose of it at home, if that can not be done even by "*prayer and fasting*" let a committee be called and decide the matter according to the circumstances and the tenor of the Gospel and the decisions of the A. Meeting. It is then to be hoped, and fondly hoped that each district will act with such discretion and wisdom as to virtually say at the next A. M., as touching those vexed questions: "we can rule our house," or in other words, we can get along at home without the assistance of the A. M., we have wise men at home, we have a membership that are endowed with the Holy Spirit who manifest a spirit of love, union and forbearance. To see questions of a local nature or such as have been before the A. M., or of such a trivial nature that it looks like they might have been settled at home, certainly does not cast great credit upon the district that sent them. We are glad, when a district is called, to hear they have *nothing*: that answer means they have much of love and union at home. We not only hope but we pray that at our next A. Conference that *one* question on which so much has been said will not come up, if not we shall with thousands others be glad. Then those that would from the cause distract or dismember the body will be driven to the wall, and it is believed the mantle of peace will robe the church and prosperity follow her, even in those days of "perilous times." So may it be. J. S. FLORY.

KEEP IN THE RIGHT CHANNEL.

"Strait is the gate, and narrow is the way which leadeth unto life." &c.

Notwithstanding I am weak; Notwithstanding I am fallible; notwithstanding I may become excited; notwithstanding I am liable to go to extremes, yet, I say to us all, keep in the right channel.

Some years past, but I will never forget, I heard our old brother, John Brumbaugh, say, when preaching: "The middle course is the right course." He preached a number of years in Miami county, Ohio. I say, with the departed brother, the middle of the channel is the safest place for our ship. When we keep in the right channel, we are in the narrow way which leads right to the strait gate, and right along in the middle of the broad way. But the narrow way is marked out so plain, and "way marks" put up all along, so we can keep in the right channel if we only look up to the "way marks," hence we have to watch and be on our guard at home and abroad, but this is no mystery for we are so forgetful. We should learn to be temperate in all things, all learn to do all things, decently and in order, in our eating, in our drinking, in our talking, in all our walk and conduct, and particularly in using intoxicating drinks and tobacco. If we all would keep in the right channel, the tobacco question would go down, where it ought to be, and the Brethren will have no cause at our council meetings to take sides and go on: on extremes to the right and to the left, in their deliberations or discussions. I love all the brethren, but I was made sorry at our last A. Meeting, when we could discover that love was not, all the time, the controlling principle.

"Faith, hope and charity, these three, but the greatest of these is charity." 1 Cor. 13 chap. Read from 4th ver. to the end of the chap. Where charity rules we always keep in the right channel. We should not be offensive, as some members like to see clean faces, and they do not like to see so much tobacco juice spit on the floor, or on the stove or wall, but let us bear with one another in love. We hope till our next A. Meeting, things will be better, who may live to see it.

There has been much good counsel and admonition given to the members in regard to foolish, fashionable dressing, but will not affect much so long as the root is cherished, and some of our church officers are not in the right channel. But again, let love be the ruling principle.

In conclusion, I will, in this silent messenger, send greetings to all the brethren and sisters who know me in this life, east and west, north and south, especially to my two brothers and one sister in the flesh, who live in the west, Samuel and John Murray and Catharine Billhimer, and their families.

ELD. DAVID MURRAY.

Dayton, O.

LEARNING OBEDIENCE.

The lesson of obedience is one which all must learn. Hard and unwelcome as it seems, it will write itself in some way upon our hearts. We must learn to bow, to yield and to obey.

Man's fallen condition is a condition of willful rebellion against rightful power, of impotent resistance to wise and just authority; of unholy opposition to divine law and wholesome rule. This perverse opposition is Sin. "Sin is the transgression of the law," or more literally and forcibly, "Sin is lawlessness." It was the exercise of this lawlessness which first drove man from Paradise, and filled the world with trouble and distress. Rebellion against God involves all other rebellion. All authority is derived from, and delegated by the Almighty. Man rebelled against God, and creation has rebelled against man. Governors reject God's rule, and nations reject theirs. Husbands refuse to be subject to God, and wonder why their wives are not subject to them. Parents disregard the precepts of their Heavenly Father, and wonder that their children are also disobedient, unthankful, and unholy.

Thus we see lawlessness lies at the root of all human disorder, sin, and misery. Every violation of divine law, moral, mental, physical or social, whether written on the stones of Sinai, the fleshly tables of the heart, or in the very constitution of created things, draws after it a penalty and pain. Every obedience is a step in the way of life and peace.

Our first lesson then is obedience to authority. "Children obey your parents," is the first mandate of God to infant minds. Those who refuse to obey, heap up for themselves trouble, calamity and death. There are persons who deliberately refuse to regard anything but their own wills. They are too old to obey. They know enough to take care of themselves.

One such turbulent and ungovernable spirit in a community, or church, a workshop, or a family, is enough to break down all discipline, and tread under foot all authority. The faithful are discouraged in obedience, the young are encouraged in disobedience. Government is defied, rulers are condemned, and waywardness and confusion are the results.

Such persons must learn obedience. They are not exempted from the general necessity. They must learn that they are not almighty, and hence not independent. The lesson is severe—often it is tedious. They defy society, and become outlaws and vagabonds. They defy the church, and are excluded from its fellowship. They spurn the family-rule, and find themselves left outside to meditate upon their folly. They trample on the laws of health, and condemn themselves to years of pain and sorrow, sickness and distress. They defy the laws of God, and the afflictions of time and the judgments of eternity roll in upon them, to convince them of their dire mistake.

Rebellion is war. No man can resist God's law with impunity. No man can harden himself against God and prosper. Rebellion must end in defeat. Man must bow or fall, must bend or break. There is no escape. "As I live, saith God, every knee shall bow, and every tongue shall confess." Sooner or later all must yield,—if not now at mercy's altar, then at the judgment seat of Christ. If not here when pardon is offered, then hereafter, when mercy is fled.

The voice of wisdom calls us to obedience. Submit yourselves to God;—resist the devil and he will flee from you. Man must have a master. If he refuse to be God's servant he will become the devil's slave. Christ's yoke is easy; let us learn to wear it and find rest to our souls.—*The Christian.*

TEACH THE CHILDREN.—Teach your children early to love the religion of Jesus Christ. Bring them into vital communion with the people of God, teach them to enlist their interest in the church of Christ, love to work in it, support it by their money, and stand by it in after life.

If you neglect this your house will be full of young pagans, as many a prosperous man's house is to-day filled with children who are farther from any religious character than the Chinese or the North American Indians. It is a dismal day for any people when the little ones are turned over to wild and heartless materialism and atheism, for guidance and for help. The poorest church is better than a godless and inhuman creed. Organized religion is the corner stone of human society, and every fabric of it reposes on childhood as its living foundation, renewed and redeemed by the love and grace of Almighty God.

Make it a rule never to utter any unnecessary complaint or murmur, but in patience to possess your souls.

Youth's Department.

The following, is from a young pilgrim of 17 years of age who while quite young in life lost, both father and mother. We give it as a good example for our young readers, as we think he displayed great wisdom in accepting God as his father as he is truly a friend of sinners, and a father to the fatherless.

CLARION Co. PA.
Dec 2nd, 1872.

Dear Pilgrim:—I have read your page with interest, and am pleased very much with the good news it brings to the Christian readers. But there are many persons in the world who would rather read novels or some accounts of this world's folly. I dare say such is the case with many, at least, it used to be so with myself when I was traveling on the downward road to ruin, thinking of nothing but this worlds pleasure: not thinking of that ever near presence of God, who at his will could call us at any time, from our wild and wayward career, to meet the great Judge at the bar to pronounce our doom.

Oh! sinner stop for one moment and consider; you are standing on a slippery foundation, and sooner or later you may be cast off, and what is the result? You are cast into everlasting punishment, there to suffer in torment all through Eternity.

There are few who have not heard of the dangers of sin, therefore take warning before it is everlastingly too late. Turn at once and be saved from the wrath of God which awaits you at his coming. Oh, how unexpected many must meet God! In the full vigor of health they are cast into eternity prepared or unprepared. Yes, thousands of instances could be related but we have all heard and seen enough to know that God is infinite. Then turn, Oh! turn from the ungodly paths, and seek an interest in the wounds of a once crucified but now living Redeemer.

I earnestly thank God for what He has done for me, though it was His will to call from me at the age of three years, my father and mother; but it was His will and so I am content, knowing that He does everything for the best. I have not the pleasure that many have, to comfort their parents by kind words or sympathy, yet I hope to greet them, if it is God's will, when we meet in that land beyond the skies, where parting shall be known no more.

THOMAS. B. ZELLERS.

OPEN HEARTS AND READY HANDS.

One day a teacher said to his class, "Boys, you can all be useful if you will. If you cannot do good by great deeds, you can by little ones."

The boys said nothing, but the teacher saw by their looks that they thought he was mistaken. They did not believe that they could be of any use So he said:

"You think it is not so, but suppose you just try it for one week?

"How shall we try it?" asked one of them.

"Just keep your eyes open and your hands ready to do anything good that comes in your way all this week, and tell me next Sunday if you have not managed to be useful in some way or other," said the teacher.

"Agreed," said the boys, and so they parted.

The next Sunday those boys gathered round their teacher with smiling lips, and eyes so full of light that they fairly twinkled like the stars. He smiled, as they looked at them, and said:

"Ah, boys I see by your looks that you have something to tell me."

"We have, sir, we have," they said all together. Then each one told his story.

"I" said one, "thought of going to the well for a pail of water every morning to save my mother trouble and time. She thanked me so much and was so greatly pleased that I mean to keep on doing it for her."

"And I" said another boy, thought of a poor old woman whose eyes were too dim to read. I went to her house every day and read a chapter to her from the Bible. It seemed to give her a great deal of comfort, I cannot tell how she thanked me"

A third boy said, "I was walking along the street, wondering what I could do. A gentleman called me, and asked me to hold his horse. I did so He gave me five cents. I have brought it to put it in the missionary box."

"I was walking with my eyes open and my hands ready, as you told us," said the fourth boy, "when I saw a little fellow crying because he had lost some pennies in the gutter. I told him not to cry, and I would try to find his pennies. I found them, and he dried up his tears, ran off and felt very happy."

A fifth boy said, "I saw my mother was very tired one day. The baby was cross, and mother looked sick and sad. I asked mother to put the baby in my little wagon. She did so, and I gave him a grand ride round the garden. If you had only heard him crow, and seen him clap his hands, teacher, it would have done you good; and oh, how much brighter mother looked when I took the baby indoors again."—ex.

When the Christian is overtaken by the storm of adversity, or has been deserted by friends, or is called to bury a loved one, his heart is cheered and comforted by the voice, "It is I."

CORRESPONDENCE

A Reporter is wanted from every Church in the brotherhood to send us Church news, Obituaries, Announcements or anything that will be of general interest. To insure insertion, the writers name must accompany each communication. Our invitation is not personal but general—please respond to our call.

WELCH RUN, PA.,
Jan. 2, '73.

Dear Pilgrim: It has been sometime since I have written for your columns, and will try and give a few interesting facts of our series of meetings which was held at Clay Lick Meetinghouse, beginning on the 21st and ending on the 28th of December. The Brethren who labored for us were J. F. Oller and D. F. Good from Waynesboro, Pa., G. Mourer N. Martin, D. Miller and G. Bricker. We had a good meeting, one I trust that will not soon be forgotten by the brethren and sisters who attended. We feel to thank God that it was our happy privilige to meet day after day and night after night in the house of the Lord, and hear the glad tidings of salvation proclaimed aloud, by our beloved brethren who came to us on a mission of love. May God bless them for their labors of love and have souls for their hire, with grace sufficient for their day and trial, and finally grant them a home in Heaven, where sickness, sorrow pain and death are feared and felt no more.

When we sat under their pleadings with sinners to turn from their evil ways to God, we wondered how they could resist the spirit of God and cling to satan, the enemy of their souls who is hurrying them on to destruction and will soon, ah too soon, launch them into eternity unprepared. Think dear sinner before it is too late! Brethren and sisters, we should feel greatly encouraged in our race, for they urged us to press onward and upward to the mark and the prize of the high calling as it is in Christ Jesus. I can say, for one, that my soul burned with a strong desire to live a more holy life than I have done heretofore, and by the grace of God hope to do so. How sweet the time passed away when we were together in the sanctuary of the Lord, in singing, praying and praising God, and how loathe we were to leave the place were Jesus showed his smiling face, but time passed away and our meeting closed and we have returned to our homes. Let us not soon forget what we have heard, and be earnestly engaged in prayer for one another. Pray for us dear brethren, remembering that we often ask God to bless you and your families, and if we never meet in this vale of tears, may we all meet around God's throne in heaven where we will part no more.

"Where Jesus dwells my soul would be,
And faints my much loved Lord to see;
Earth twine no more about my heart,
For it is better to depart."

KATE ELLIOTT.

DELL DELIGHT, Benton Co., Mo.
Dec. 22, 1872.

Dear Editors of the PILGRIM and brethren in Christ I wish to drop you a few lines for the first time to give you an idea of our situation at this place. We have been living here nearly two years and we never had a meeting any nearer than forty-five miles to my knowledge. I am sorry to think that we cannot have meetings closer and oftener. We feel ourselves as lost sheep without a shepherd. If we only could have some of the brethren come and preach for us, it would do us so much good, and they would reap their reward. Our little flock is but small. There are but five members living here, but may the grace of God rest on each and every one of us, that we may, with the prayers of our brethren, and sisters, go on in the faith of the promise which we have in Holy Writ, that "Where two or three are gathered together in my name there am I in the midst of them." Dear brethren and sisters, you that have the privilege of going to meeting, think of us as we need your prayers in our behalf.

From your unworthy brother,

D. H. SAXTON.

HAMILTON, Mo.,
Dec. 11, 1872.

To the Brethren and Friends who intend to aid and assist us in building the Meeting House in the Hamilton Congregation, Daviess co, Mo.

Inasmuch as the building committee has been appointed and some of the building material already prepared, and remittances coming in very slow, we would say to those brethren and friends who wish to manifest their love, kindness, and liberality by true tokens, (*Means*,) to send in at once or as soon as convenient. Any amount will be thankfully received. Remittances can be made by express or registered letter to either of the subscribers. Brethren and friends please consider this matter and act without delay, we think it is a good cause, and the Lord will reward you for your labor of love.

Committee of Arrangement.

Hamilton Ex. Office, Geo. Witwer. W. B Sell, D. B. Sell and Jacob Naugle, Hamilton, Mo.

No Express Office. Dan'l Peffly, Altovista, Mo.

Dear Brethren—Please say to the churches of the Southern District of Ill., that the committee of arrangements for A. M., wishes to say to them that all the churches that wish to offer a location for the A. M. should send their request to the committee soon, as they expect to examine the places offered and determine the location this winter, and if no more places are offered before the committee will make their examination, they will make their selection out of the places now offered.

I would also say that I have yet a few copies of the Minutes of the District Meeting on reserve. If any of the churches in the district failed to get them, they can yet be supplied by notifying me.

DANIEL VANIMAN.

Virden, box 33 Macoupin Co., Ill.

An Abridged Report of a Trip to Pa., by Eld. John Knisley.

PLYMOUTH, IND., }
Dec. 23d, 1872. }

Dear Readers of the PILGRIM: In my notes of travel through the East, I promised to give a general report on my return home which promise I will now fulfill. On the 8th of Oct., I went west to Wanatah and thence south some fifty miles to a Communion Meeting at friend John Dobbins'. Eld. Jno S. Snowberger has the charge of this new district. From here I went to Monticello and attended a Lovefeast on the 11th. Here I met our esteemed Elder J. Quinter—had a very good meeting—Bro. Joseph Amich was ordained to the eldership. After the close of the meeting I went to the house of Bro. J. S. Snowberger's, and on the 13th we, J. S. Snowberger and wife, myself and Sister Dillinger were taken to Delphi to take the train for Pa. Arrived at Altoona on the 15th, at 7 p. m. From there we went to Martinsburg, Blair co., Pa., and was taken to the Yellow Creek Church to attend their Lovefeast. Jacob Miller has the oversight of this charge, assisted by L. Furry, D. Snowberger, Jno. Eshleman, S. A. Moore, John B. and J. Z. Replogle. This district is in Bedford co., and is thought to have a membership of 500. The Church seems to be in good order and in a flourishing condition.

From here we went to the Clover Creek Congregation, where they held a Lovefeast on the 17th. Elders Geo. and J. W. Brumbaugh preside here, assisted by G. W. Brumbaugh, Thos. B, Maddock, J. L. Wineland, and J. Snowberger. The meeting was interesting and much love manifested. From here we crossed the mountain and remained with Bro. Daniel Brumbaugh until next morning, when we took the cars at Coffee Run for James Creek. Here we met our dear Bro. H. B. Brumbaugh editor of the PILGRIM, and his kind wife, also two dear sisters, W. A. Clarke and Emma Miller, who are working in the PILGRIM Office. At this place I first heard from home and was very glad to hear from my children. Geo. Brumbaugh is the elder of the James Creek Church, assisted by H. B. and G. B. Brumbaugh. The members here all appear very kind and everything seems to be in good order. Their Lovefeast, commencing on the 18th, was one of much interest, and was a feast to the soul indeed.

On the 21st I, with Bro. D. Snowberger, took the train at New Pleasant Grove for Dale City, where we were met by the Brethren and conducted to their homes. I was here made to think how pleasant it is to meet the brethren. So will it be when Jesus comes, we shall all then meet to part no more. We put up for the night with Bro. P. M. Beachley, M. D. Next morning visited the *Companion Office* and then visited the kind family of H. R. Holsinger, was well entertained. On the 23d there was a Lovefeast held at the Elk Lick Church. Here is a large membership and is the place that the A. Meeting will be held for 1873. On the 25th, in company with J. S. and Dan'l Snowberger, went to Bedford where we held a meeting.

On the 26th went to our aged brother Andrew Snowberger, Elder of the Snakespring Congregation, where we had several meetings.

On the 27th had a meeting in Morrison's Cove. Here I and J. S. Snowberger separated, and I went to the Hopewell District. Bro. Jacob Steel is the elder, assisted by Henry and D. S. Clapper. From here was taken to the Yellow Creek Church again and held several meetings and then gave the parting hand to my travelling companions and returned to James Creek where I remained until the 12th of Nov. I then started in company with J. P. Brumbaugh, for Philadelphia, but missing the train at Huntingdon, we remained over night with Bro. A. B. Brumbaugh, M. D. The Doctor entertained us kindly, is a man of talent and commands a large practice. Next morning took the cars for the City, and made our first call in the city of brotherly love with Bro. C. Custer and kind family. In the p. m. went to Germantown and called on Bro. Davis Younce where I remained until the 16th, preached once and made a number of calls. Then returned again to Philadelphia and had two meetings.

On the 19th, started for Eld Moses Miller's Congregation, at Mechanicsburg, Cumberland co., Pa., had three meetings in Mechanicsburg Bro. Miller accompanied me on a visit to a number of the members which I enjoyed much. This congregation seems to be in good order and much love manifested. Then visited Elder J. R. Hanawalt's Congregation and attended eight meetings. At this place I got the sad news of the death of my son-in-law which ended the enjoyment of my trip and caused me to look homeward.

I started for James Creek where I had two more meetings and, one at Coffee Run. On the 3d of December I took my leave of the dear members and started for home where I arrived safely and found all well, but were sorry to find the vacant seats which were made by death during my absence. On the 5th our meeting commenced. Bro. Quinter failed to come, but Bro. J. Calvert and O. W. Miller were present, and labored for us to acceptance—one added by baptism and hope many more will come soon.

In conclusion, I will say that I never enjoyed myself so well as I did during this mission of love. I ask to be excused for not naming all the places that I visited, feel assured that you are all kindly remembered though not named. Brethren and sisters remember us in your prayers, and may we all hold out faithful until we meet on the other side of Jordan, never to part any more.

ALLENTOWN, PA., }
Jan. 15th, 1873. }

Dear Brethren Editors;—As no church news appears in the PILGRIM from this part of the Lord's vineyard, I will pen a few thoughts, if you think them worthy a place. On Saturday evening and Sunday last, Bros. Samuel Gettel and David Etter stopped with the little band of pilgrims and soldiers of the cross sojourning at Bethlehem, and preached for us. They gave many words of admonition, and urged us to remain faithful to the end so that we may obtain that pearl of great price, the crown that fadeth not away reserved in Heaven for those that fear God.

On Sunday afternoon we had a social meeting of singing and prayer. We felt that it was good to be together, and had a foretaste of Heaven indeed. I as a "babe in Christ" felt happy and overjoyed, and with renewed energy shall stand by the captain of our salvation in the thickest of the fight, plead boldly for the cause of the Redeemer, that I may once have a "clear title to a mansion in the skies," to a "city that has foundation whose maker and builder is God.

On parting, the farewell tears flowed freely, indeed many farewell tears were shed. I as a young brother never before knew that the dear brethren and sisters were so closely bound together. They are indeed blessed ties May God inspire us with His spirit to feel still a deeper love for each other, and for our fellow men who are yet out of the ark of safety, in the gall of bitterness, and unconcerned about their souls salvation, so that they can see by our walk, talk and conversation in life, that we are "a peculiar people, zealous unto every good work."

The PILGRIM is still a welcome visitor. May it continue its weekly visits to the brethren, sisters and friends, and be the means of calling many to righteousness. That the Lord may bless us, and all connected with the publication of the PILGRIM, and at last when the warfare is ended in this vale of tears, take us unto Himself, where He shall wipe all tears from our eyes and we shall reign with Him forever and ever, is the prayer of your unworthy brother in Christ.

H. F. ROSENBERGER

LEWISTOWN, PA,
Jan. 13th 1873.——

Dear Brethren:—By these few lines I will inform you that yesterday evening our series of meetings closed. Had one application for baptism, two reclaimed and many good impressions made by the brethren, namely: D. F. Good Jacob D. Trostle, and Jacob F. Oller. The Lord bless them for their labors, as they labored faithfully for both saint and sinner. The conviction of my heart is, that it will do us all good, and my prayer is, that the seed (or word of God) which has been sown broadcast amongst us by our beloved brethren, will bring much fruit to the glory of God, and to the conversion of sinners.

ELDER JACOB MOHLER.

MARRIED.

GEARHART—BUSH.—On the 31st of Dec. 1872, by the undersigned, Mr. Geo. W. Gearhart and Miss Francis Bush, both of Franklin co., Pa. JNO. ZUCK.

WILLIAMS—SHOUP.—On Thursday, January 9th, 1873, by the undersigned at the residence of the bride's father, Mr. Abraham L. Williams of Carroll co., Md. and Miss Mary E Shoup, of Beaver Creek twp., Greene co., Ohio.

B. F. DARST.

DIED.

BULGER.—In the Snakespring Church, Bedford co., Pa., Dec 28, 1872, our sister Hannah Bulger, aged 40 years, 9 mos. and 29 days. Funeral improved by the brethren from 1 Cor. 15: 51, 52.

DEGARMIN.—In the same Congregation, on the 29th of December, Mary Degarmin, aged 96 years, 9 mos. and 3 days

This aged mother was a member of the Lutheran church, and was much afflicted for the last 6 years. Funeral improved by the writer.

RITCHEY.—In the same community, on Dec 31st, 1872, Michael Ritchey, aged 39 years, 9 mos. and 21 days. Funeral discourse by A. Snowberger and the writer from Hebrew 9 chap. 27 ver.

The subject of this notice became alarmed in his last days about his future salvation, and made application to become a member of the church. We tried to encourage him in the good cause of Jesus, he being very weak in the flesh, and still weak in the faith, wished to wait till to-morrow, but that time never came to him. He leaves a sorrowing widow and 4 children to mourn the loss.

FOREMAN.—Also in the same Congregation, our much beloved sister Lydia Foreman, on the 11th of Jan., 1873 aged 76 years, 10 mos. and 29 days Funeral improved by the same as above from John 14th chap. 1 and 2 ver.

The departed was a sister to Eld. Jacob Steel, and has been a very pious, humble sister and, much beloved by all who knew her. We believe she has gained the heavenly mansion prepared for the children of God. HENRY HERSHBERGER.

FURRY. Jan. 10, 1873, near New Enterprise, Bedford co., Pa. Hannah Amanda Furry, daughter of bro. John B. Furry, dec'd, and sister Elizabeth, now Miller, grand daughter of bro. Dan'l Snowberger and the writer, aged 16 yrs., 10 mos. Disease, complicated Typhoid fever. Occasion improved by the brethren, from Matt. 24: 44. "Therefore be ye also ready" &c., to the largest audience I ever saw on such occasions.

The subject of this notice was remarkable for intelligence and strong memory, and by few excelled in education for her age. Since the death of her father, 9 years ago, she was adopted into the family of the writer, being an obedient child, tender hearted, beloved by many, and much attached to her grand parents; the loss of her, casts a gloom over the whole neighborhood, and especially over our fireside, as her vacancy in our hearts can never be filled 6 weeks of unremitting care on our part, and the skill of two eminent physicians were overruled by the fell-destroyer, through the intervening power from on high. It is the Lord, let him do as seemeth good in his sight. Thus ended the life of one, who was near and dear to many, and as was feared by the writer in the beginning of her disease, as he had a certain presentiment of her departure.

Dear Hannah! a few months was blooming in youth,
Now entombed with the dead attesting the truth;
That man has to die, whether old or in prime,
Strong warning from heaven, Oh, prepare all in time.

Her sweet voice in music no more we shall hear,
The loss in our family caused sorrow and tears;
May she in sweet anthems swell th' angelic choir.
Our loss gain associates with saints upon high.

Ye school-mates, remember, six weeks to the day,
She met you the last time, not thinking her stay;
On earth will be closed, in just such a short time,
Beware and prepare, for you may have less time.

LEONARD FURRY.

(*Visitor* please copy.)

PFALTZGRAFF.—In the Codorus Church York county, Pa., Jan. 7, 1873, brother Geo. Pfaltzgraff, aged 64 years, 8 mos. and 2 days. Funeral services from Matt 24: 44, by Andrew Miller and Thomas Gray.

Bro. Pfaltzgraff came to his death by a fall. He came out of his house, descended two steps from his porch, slipped and fell with his side on the edge of a step, broke in a rib, and bruised him inside, which caused a gathering of blood and ended his life in a few days. hope the people will take warning from the text, "Therefore be ye also ready, &c. CHRIST. NESS.

FREDERICK.—In the Owlcreek Church, Knox co., Ohio, Dec. 21, 1872, our beloved brother Jacob Frederick, aged 70 yrs. 1 mo and 19 days

This brother leaves quite a number of friends to mourn their loss. 9 children and 41 grand children, 14 great-grand children, and an aged widow who is beloved by all. This old brother and sister fared many a storm, being members of the church about 40 years and lived together 38 years. It seemed hard for the dear old sister to give him up. She went along to the funeral which took place on the 22d. He had quite a desire to depart this life. Just before he died, he said he would like to go to sleep and never wake up again in this world. Funeral discourse by the writer from Isaiah 38th chap. "Set thine house in order for thou shalt die and not live." D. N. W.

GREENAWALT.—Jan 12, 1873, in the James Creek Church, Huntingdon co., Pa., Elmer, son of bro. Samuel and sister Nannie Greenawalt, of croup and bronchitis combined; aged 2 yrs. 1 mo and 28 days. Funeral services by the editors.

The subject of this notice was rather a remarkable child, exhibiting more than an ordinary degree of mental powers. Although he was deprived of the power of speech by the affects of the terrible disease with which he died, yet his gestures and movements were that of a man rather than a child. But the time for his transplanting had come and he passed over the dark and dreaded scene of death with less suffering than was expected, but his removal has left an aching and painful void in the family and in the loving hearts of the parents and grand parents, which nothing on earth can fill.

Another plant removed from the family nursery to the fair climes of Heaven, another angel added to the happy throng, another glorified spirit joined to the celestial choir. Cease to mourn ye disconsolate ones. Let the sweet melody vibrate into your drooping souls; look up and hopefully follow on, and e'er long you shall meet on that beautiful shore in that sweet by and by. G. B.

MONEY LIST.

A Lichtenwalter, 5.80; Maria Herring, 1.25; Moses Miller, 16 25; John Custer, 5 00; M Brindle, 1 50; L Reed, 1.50; Barbara Price, 1.25; D Brumbaugh, 5 25; J R Royer, 1 00; Isaac Bright, 1 50; Jno Mohler, 3 50; Fred. W Kohler, 3 00; S P Maust, 1 20; North Manchester, 3 00; G Eby, 1.50; N D Hadsell, 1 50; D Troxel, 10 00; David Zook, 3.00; Enoch Eby, 1 50; D Goodyear, 1 50; Wm H Miller, 7.00; Jonas Price, 7.50; Jos F Heckler, 1.50; John Brown, 4 50; S M Kutner, 6 50; Eld Jno Murray, 1.70; Josiah Kimmell, 2 50; Isaac P Gaby, 6.00; H W Shenk, 1.50; Peter Kollar, 19.50; Jno D Norris, 5.30; C A Hartman, 1.50; J H Raffensparger, 7.62; Jos Detter, 1.50; Benj Rhodes, 1.25; Abram Bame, 1.50; S Mommert, 4.50; J F Oller, 1.50; Joshua Olinger, 4 50; John Gault, 6 25; E Brumbaugh, 1.50; Henry Brumbaugh, 1.50; Daniel Bechtel, 1.50; P. D. Fahrney, 2.50. F. P. Loehr, 9.00; H. Touthman 1. 50; D. F. Stouffer, 1.50; A. Louisa Roop, 1.50; D. G. Varner, 2 00; W J. Parsley, 1.70; M. H. Berger, 1.50 A. E. Shoemaker, 13 20; L. Hertzler, 2. 75; J. P. Brumbaugh, 1.00; S. S. Cresswell, 1.50; J. N. Dietrich 1.50; Samuel Moore, 6.00. Jacob Mohler, 1.50; Martin Bowers 1.50 Aaron Diehl, 4 50; H. W. Shenk, 15 00; D. F. Buck, 1.25; C. Ness, 1 50; John Zuck, 7.02; S. E. Miller, 1.25; D. O. Brumbaugh, 1.00; E. E. Parker, 1.50; M. J. C. Ecker, 1.50; Daniel Kinsel, 1.50; G. M. Snelker, 6.00; J. R. Lane, 6 00;

The Weekly Pilgrim.

JAMES CREEK, PA., Jan. 21st. 1873.

☞ How to send money.—All sums over $1.50, should be sent either in a check, draft or postal order. If neither of these can be obtained, have the letter registered.

☞ WHEN MONEY is sent, *always* send with it the name and address of those who paid it. Write the names and post office as plainly as possible.

☞ EVERY subscriber for 1873, gets a *Pilgrim Almanac* FREE.

HARD TIMES.

There is much said about hard times and there may be some truth in it as money seems a little scarce and hard to get in places, but this should not affect the circulation of the PILGRIM, and we believe that it would not by any means was its worth duly appreciated. Hard times may curtail the buying of farms and making investments for speculation, but when it comes down to the small consideration of $1.50 for the PILGRIM which brings its weekly portion of the bread of life to the hungry soul, it should not be taken into consideration, and is not by those who are not willing to live by bread alone, as we could abundantly show from a large number of letters like the following:

"*Dear Brethren*:—By this I inform you that I felt sorry on the receipt of the last PILGRIM, especially so, when I read that it would be the last number for the year. Oh, it seems to me as if I could do with a little less bread, rather than do without the weekly visits of the PILGRIM. Enclosed find $1.50, for which please send it on," &c. Such, brethren and sisters are the feelings, expression, and work of the poor, and how unlike it is from the grumbling that we sometimes see from the pens of brethren who count their wealth by thousands. Of course we do not mean that all of our wealthy members are uncharitable, not by any means, as some have done nobly in sending the PILGRIM to the poor, but as a rule there cannot be as much pure and vital religion found among the rich as there can among the poor, not the same thirsting after righteousness and religious reading. When we get as hungry for religious reading as the above writer, hard times will not stand in the way. Since we have commenced publishing the PILGRIM we have learned to place a much higher estimate on the zeal and integrity of the poor, and for their benefit especially have accepted in part, the credit system. Talk about losing by trusting our members! We would be ashamed to think that we have a brother or sister in the church that would deliberately cheat us out of our hard earned dues. No, brethren and sisters we will not believe that we have such among us until we are forced to the conclusion by actual experience. Therefore we continue to invite all of our members, no matter how poor, to take and read the PILGRIM. If you have not got the money now send us your names, and you can easily earn $1.50 within the next six months. *Try it*

ARE WE GROWING?

In all enterprises it is encouraging to the patrons to know that there is a growth or increase in usefulness. At first our circulation was confined to some 8 or 10 States. At present we have an actual circulation in the following States and Territories:

Pennsylvania	California
Ohio	Oregon
Indiana	Virginia
Illinois	Maryland
Iowa	Tennessee
Missouri	W. Virginia
Kansas	N. Carolina
Nebraska	New Jersey
Michigan	Kentuckey
Wisconsin	Massachusetts
Minesota	Maine
Decotah	New York

We also send one copy to Derbyshire, England, and almost daily they are coming in from places where our church was never before known. This fact alone should put our contributors on their guard as to what they send us for publication, as whatever is published in the PILGRIM is set upon a hill and cannot be hid. Let us cease grinding our petty little differences and set our Zion forth in its most beautiful robes. It is true, her outside garments may appear a little uncomely, but to know her aright is eternal life.

Now, brethren and sisters, if you are desirous of having our borders enlarged help us. We have done our part by letting the world know that there is a PILGRIM waiting for a call. Will not some of you give that call? If any of you have friends in Europe, Asia, Africa or anywhere else, send them a copy of the PILGRIM a year and you may accomplish a good work and be blessed in the deed. Any sending outside of the United States should send 20 cents extra to prepay postage.

TO OUR CONTRIBUTORS.

We feel truly grateful to the many who are supplying us with copy, but we hope that none will feel slighted on account of the non-appearance of their productions. We are trying to use such as will get out of season by being delayed, but still some of our correspondence is getting behind time, notwithstanding we are giving more than the usual space to this kind of matter. There is a variety of tastes in regard to this class of reading, some say not enough, and others, too much. We shall try to please both parties by keeping between the two extremes. We do not wish any to stop writing because we are a little flush just now. When we once get a little leisure, we shall boil some of it down and give only the substance.

PERSONAL.

NANCY SCHRANTZ, Your paper is paid to No. 39.

J. L. F. The eleventh copy is free. All over that, 10 per cent off.

JOSEPH DILLEY: R. B.'s PILGRIM for 1872 is 75 cents, also John J's.

ELD. G. W. That will do, send name and address with all those who pay.

J. M. ALCORAN. Your money was received and *Almanac* and PILGRIM sent. If you have not received them by this time, let us know.

A. R. SWITZER, O. S. & H. S., your year expires with No. 12 '73. Do you wish the PILGRIM continued for '73, and are they paid for 1872? They are not so marked in our book.

WRITE NAMES PLAINLY.—Our agents will confer us favor by writing all names as plainly as possible, also post offices. We get some written so badly that it is impossible to decipher them.

BRO. DANIEL SHOOK, wishes to know whether there are any brethren living in Davis Co., Kansas. If any of our readers know of any they will confer him a favor by giving him their name and address. His address is Junction City, Davis Co., Kansas.

NAME WANTED. Some person sent us $2.75 wishing the Tune Book and the PILGRIM, to be sent to Columbia City Indiana, and gives us no name. As soon as the name is sent us we will send both. Any one knowing the person will confer him a favor by informing him of his mistake.

SAMPLE COPIES. A number of our subscribers have been asking for specimen copies of the *Phrenological Journal*. To such and all others who may wish to accept our terms, (The WEEKLY PILGRIM and *Phrenological Journal* together for $3.50) we would say that we have now procured a number of sample copies of the *Phrenological Journal* and will send sample copy to such as think of subscribing by enclosing a three cent stamp to pay the postage.

GENERAL INTELLIGENCE.

It is reported that Merle d'Aubigne has left two nearly completed volumes on the Reformation, carrying his record to the death of Luther.

The library of the Escurial, which so narrowly escaped destruction a month or two since, contains over fourteen thousand MSS. in Hebrew, Arabic and and other languages.

The recent wonderful success of the French loan proves the French peasantry the wealthiest in Europe; the secret is economy, universal industry of women as well as men, and contentment with little.

Two Japanese priests have come to Berlin to obtain information about the Christian religion, and the Rev. Dr. Lisco is engaged in explaining to them the distinguishing features of the various Christian creeds.

A remarkable fog prevailed over New York last Friday. On the rivers navigation was suspended, and the ferry boats crossed slowly and irregularly. On the North River two boats collided, but happily without fatal results.

A gentleman in Iowa claims to have made the discovery that tea can be grown in Crawford county, in that State. The experiment has been tried, and it is said that 700 pounds of tea have actually been raised on one acre of land.

Arrangements have been completed for the organization of the Canadian Pacific Railway Company. The capital is to be subscribed among the Canadians, who seem anxious lest their undertaking pass into the hands of foreign and rival corporations.

FLORIDA.—The lumber business of Florida is increasing with rapid strides, and is an important source of revenue to the people of the State. The Lake country, at the head of the Ocklawaha river, is rapidly filling up with an intelligent and thrifty population. This section presents a fine opening for the cultivation of the orange, cotton and sugar.

HUNTINGDON & BROAD TOP RAIL ROAD

Winter Arrangement.

On and after Tuesday, Oct. 4, 1872, Passenger trains will arrive and depart as follows:

Trains from Huntingdon South. *Trains from Mt Dallas moving North.*

MAIL. A. M.	ACCOM P. M.	STATIONS.	MAIL. P. M.	ACCOM A. M.
le8 00	le5 50	Huntingdon,	ar3 20	ar9 05
8 08	5 57	Long Siding	3 12	8 53
8 21	6 10	McConnelstown	2 56	8 37
8 30	6 17	Pleasant Grove	2 50	8 30
8 45	6 30	Marklesburg	2 37	8 17
9 00	6 44	Coffee Run	2 23	8 01
9 07	6 52	Rough & Ready	2 15	7 52
9 20	7 05	Cove	2 01	7 40
9 24	7 10	Fishers Summit	1 57	7 35
9 44 / 9 54	ar7 30	Saxton	1 37	le7 15
10 10		Riddlesburg	1 19	
10 17		Hopewell	1 12	
10 34		Piper's Run	12 56	
10 52		Tatesville	12 38	
11 05		Bloody Run	12 24	
ar11 10		Mount Dallas	12 20	

JOHN M'KILLIPS, Supt

SHOUP'S RUN BRANCH.

le10 00	le7 40	Saxton,	ar1 20	ar7 15
10 15	7 55	Coalmont,	1 15	6 55
10 20	8 00	Crawford,	1 10	6 50
ar10 30	ar8 10	Dudley	le1 00	le6 40

Bro'd Top City from Dudley 2 miles by stage.

Time of Penna. R. R. Trains at Huntingdon

EASTWARD.		WESTWARD.	
Hb'g Ac.	9 21 A. M.	Cin. Ex.	2 19 A. M.
Mail	3 30 P. M.	Pc'f Ex.	7 45 "
Cin. Ex.	9 55 "	Mail	5 40 P. M.
Phil. Ex	11 15 "	W. Pass.	11 52 A. M.

The Weekly Pilgrim.

Published by J. B. Brumbaugh, & Co.

Edited by H. B. & Geo. Brumbaugh.

CORRESPONDING EDITORS.

D. P. Sayler, Double Pipe Creek, Md.

Leonard Furry, New Enterprise, Pa.

The *Pilgrim* is a Christian Periodical, devoted to religion and moral reform. It will advocate in the spirit of *love* and *liberty*, the principles of true Christianity, labor for the promotion of peace among the people of God, for the encouragement of the saints and for the conversion of sinners, avoiding those things which tend toward disunion or sectional feelings.

TERMS.

Single copy, Book paper,	$1 50
Eleven copies, [eleventh for Agt.]	$15.00

Any number above that at the same rate.

Address,

H. B. BRUMBAUGH.
James Creek,
Huntingdon county Pa.

The Weekly Pilgrim.

"REMOVE NOT THE ANCIENT LANDMARKS WHICH OUR FATHERS HAVE SET."

VOL. 4. JAMES CREEK, PENNSYLVANIA, JANUARY 28, 1873. NO. 4

POETRY.

THE CARELESS WORD.

'Twas but a word, a careless word,
 As thistle-down it seemed as light!
It paused a moment on the air,
 Then onward winged its flight.

Another lip caught up the word,
 And breathed it with a haughty sneer;
It gathered weight as on it sped—
 That careless word in its career.

Then rumor caught the flying word,
 And busy gossip gave it weight,
Until that little word became
 A vehicle of angry hate.

And then that word was winged with fire
 Its mission was a thing of pain;
For soon it fell like lava-drops
 Upon a wildly tortured brain.

And then another page of life
 With burning, scalding tears were blurred;
A load of care was heavier made—
 Its added weight, that careless word.

That careless word, oh! how it scorched
 A fainting, bleeding, quivering heart!
'Twas like a hungry fire that scorched
 Through every tender, vital part.

How wildly throbbed that aching heart!
 Deep agony its fountain stirred;
It calmed, but bitter ashes mark
 The pathway of that careless word.

ORIGINAL ESSAYS.

A DIALOGUE BETWEEN GAMALIEL AND NICODEMUS.

Concluded.

thus obtained must be kept in the family from which it is inherited." This is the explanation which Luke gave.

Nic. Well that is perfectly satisfactory respecting the genealogy of Joseph. You further stated that you knew Jesus when He was a boy.

Gam. He used to come with His parents to the passover every year, and the last I heard of Him till of late, was when he was about twelve years old. On that occasion he remained with the learned teachers of our law about three days, conversing with them on the divine law: asking and answering questions. He was the best informed, and the most comprehensive lad that I ever met with: there was not a single question connected with the teachings of the sacred rolls, which He could not accurately answer.

Nic. Have you ever seen him since that time?

Gam. All I learned of him is that about six months after that time his father died, and then he remained with his mother in Nazareth.

Nic. Do you remember when and where Jesus was born?

Gam. He was born in the city of Bethlehem, near the beginning of the seventh month (Sept.) or about seven months before the death of Herod the great.

Nic. What became of the estate which Heli left to his daughter Mary?

Gam. The estate left by Heli merely consisted of a dwelling house and necessary outbuildings, on a small tract of ground near Bethlehem. In this town Jesus was born, about the time Cyrenius * was governor of Syria. Mary and Joseph went there to be enrolled according to the decree of Cæsar Augustus and when the child was born angels made their appearance to some Shepherds who were watching their flocks by night in an adjoining field, praising the glory of the new born child. This circumstance prompted Joseph and Mary to conclude that they ought to make Bethlehem their home; as soon as they gained possession of their little residence they prepared to remain in this place.

Nic. Was this not the child that your good old father Simeon took in his arms and blessed, when he was brought to the temple to be presented to the Lord?

Gam. Yes, the same one, and also the same that the prophetess Anna thanked the Lord for the pleasure of seeing:—But then I have not finished my story of their property. About the time of the birth of the child a supernatural star appeared to some of the wise men beyond Babylon, and they immediately followed it to Jerusalem after a journey of about four months. On their arrival here, they enquired of Herod for the new born king of the Jews. Herod, finally, after consulting the chief priests and scribes, sent them to Bethlehem, requesting them when they found the child, to return and apprise him of his whereabouts. The wise men after paying homage to Jesus in the house at Bethlehem, returned to their own country by another way. When Herod saw that he was mocked of the wise men, he sent and slew all the children in and near Bethlehem. But the night previous to the slaughter of these infants, Joseph took the young child and his mother and went into the land of Egypt.

Nic. And left all their property in Bethlehem?

Gam. Yes, and during the tumult it was partly destroyed, and the remainder soon fell to ruin. They never realized anything for it.

Nic. If they went to Egypt, how came they in Nazareth?

Gam. They remained in Egypt 'till they heard of the death of Herod, when they returned to Israel, but on hearing that Archelaus did reign in his fathers' stead in the government of Judea, they feared their residing in Bethlehem would prove unsafe, and returned to their former home in Nazareth, where they remained.

Nic. And surely do you think this person to be more remarkable than John in the wilderness?

Gam. On that subject it is difficult to properly fix my mind. My father was in full faith of him one day being the strong arm who would redeem Israel.

Nic. And is he really older than John?

Gam. No, he is six months younger, he will not be thirty till about the first of the seventh month, and John, I learn, is at this time about thirty.

Nic. Surely I would be pleased to become acquainted with him, and perhaps when we visit John near the Jordan we will learn something more of Jesus.

Gam. Yes I will be happy to once more see the one my father so much loved and respected. When do you think the road to Jericho will be safe?

Nic. I think of trying it in a few days, and when I learn that the road is cleared of these Arabs I will inform you and we will be pleased to go.

Gam. Thank you, I will be pleased to do so.

J. H. Moore.

Urbana, Ill.

* The *learned* reader will notice that we retain King James' translation of Luke II. 2. The Greek is rendered thus by Wilson: "This was the first Registry of Quirinus (Cyrenius Governor of Syria." Facts teach us that King James' translation is incorrect, as Cyrenius was not governor of Syria till ten years after the Registry, but he executed the work, and was afterwards governor of Syria.

TO MY RELATIVES IN KENTUCKY.

Dear brother George:—You wrote me in your last letter that you did not enjoy yourself as well attending meeting in Kentucky as you did when you used to go to my meetings in Virginia, and you give as your reason, that there is too much pride. Thank the Lord, you are thus getting your eyes open to this fashionable religion which is becoming so prevalent in this our day, and it is in the hope that I may induce you and my uncles, aunts and cousins in that and the surrounding vicinity, to unyoke yourselves from the popular tide and seek consolation with the blessed hope of a future immortality in the wounds of an humble and loving Savior, I address you through the medium of the Pilgrim, the sweet white winged messenger, whose motto is "Remove not the ancient landmarks which our fathers have set."

I will now call your attention to the language of the beloved apostle, when he says "That which we have seen and heard declare we unto you, that ye also may have fellowship with us and truly our fellowship is with his Son Jesus Christ." The first Epistle general of John 1st chapter 3d verse. What we want is apostolic or primitive religion, and the way to gain this is to take heed to the apostolic doctrine as from them flows forth the living stream as it gushed from its fountain, the Son of God. They, that is the apostles, stand as living witnesses to direct our feet in the channel of truth, being ordained by the Savior Himself, for this very purpose that we could read their testimony and not be deceived. John, the author of the language under consideration, was one of the number that was thus ordained, and when he wrote this language he endeavored to fix our minds upon the entire cloud of Heaven, for He called to the stand the entire cloud of witnesses, when He makes use of the plural we, for, says John, "that which we have seen and heard." In contemplating upon this language, we will notice 1st, The things that the Apostle saw. 2nd, The things that he heard; 3d, The solemn importance of taking heed thereto, as it is the only way that we can unite ourselves in fellowship with the Son of God and with those that will sit upon twelve thrones judging the twelve tribes of Israel.

Man was created pure and holy, but fell from his holy state through the subtility of a wicked enemy, Gen. 3d chapter, and God in pronouncing judgment upon unhappy man, made a provision for his future happiness in the "promised seed" of the woman. See same chapter. But notwithstanding this, man sank deeper and deeper into the horrible pit of wickedness, until all of God's uncreated spiritual light seemed to be extinguished. But God in His love, would cause the light to spring up, as was plainly portrayed in the person of Able. When this light sprang up, subtility still existed. He blew upon the vital spark and made the earth to drink deep of its life giving principle, thus thinking that he would forever obliterate the name of the living God, but as time passed away and wickedness expanded, the tempter found that his plans had not altogether been successful, for in the days of Enos, men, in the place of a man, began to call upon the name of the Lord. The tempter seeing that all his former plans failed, began to invent new ones, so he induces the sons of God to take them wives from among the daughters of men, and as they thus married and were given in marriage, wickedness multiplied until the patience of God was tried, and his wrath revealed in the overthrow of the antidiluvian world, which was alive with human forms, and God's light only penetrating and shining through the avenues of one single family, namely, that of Noah's. Noah was righteous and stood as a living monument to warn the people. But it availed nothing, and God gave him the dimensions of an ark of safety which, if strictly followed, would bear him across the torrents of the mighty deep in which he could rest upon the face of the waters until his feet could stand in safety upon the pavilion of the new earth. This was strictly followed and it was so. What was so? Wickedness was annihilated, and a new era of things now exist upon the broad face of the earth. There is only eight souls that people it, and they are those that had found favor in the sight of God. One might think that in them and their posterity, that light and wisdom would spring up all around, but not so. The arch enemy, the prince of the power of sin appears. The seed of discord is sown, and soon its fruit begins to ripen into rebellion against God and His law. Time goes on, Peleg is born, the earth is divided and nations are made. Now begins war, commotion and bloodshed until God makes known the power of his vengeance by the overthrow of the cities of Sodom and Gomorrah. Even this, as terrible as it was, seemed not to stay the bilious tide that was then raging among the new born nations of the earth. This was the state of things when Abram the son of Heber, who was the progenitor of the Hebrew nation, appeared. Abraham was a man full of righteousness, had a perfect knowledge of the Great Deity, that made the Heaven and the earth, and so zealous was he in the cause, that he espoused that God was called the God of Abram, who was by the special appointment of God called Abraham, and God made a covenant with Abraham, giving him the seal of circumcision and the promise that in his seed all the nations of the earth should be blessed.

Again, a new era was ushered in, but it was not yet fully developed, the nations were still in darkness, the promised seed of Abraham were led into bondage. After the expiration of 200 years, God visits them through the medium of his servant Moses. Moses was a prophet, and God wrought great wonders by his hands which you can read at your pleasure. They are recorded in the book of Exodus. The new era that had been ushered in 200 years previous to this time, began now to develop itself. The commandments of God were given from Mount Sinai, and they were for the express purpose of instructing this peculiar organized body that they should not fall after the example of there progenitors. God's dealings with His people were very wonderful, His love and his patience were both exhibited. He committed unto them His oracles. He raised up unto them prophets, who would warn them of their wicked ways and foretell them of the glorious events that should and would happen, that a deliverer would come and turn away ungodliness from Jacob. Notwithstanding all of this host of heavenly witnesses and the still greater extension of Heavenly light, the human mind was so depraved, and its tendency so much downward, that high places were built up, God's teachers suffered martyrdom, and gods made of gold and silver, wood and stone were erected, but some, such as priests, scribes, Levites, Sadducees and Pharisees, still held to the law but they interpreted them wrong, giving out that this mighty Deliverer would come in the person of a mighty conqueror who would set upon the throne of David and rule as a mighty prince, bringing under his dominion all of the surrounding nations and thus according to the future covenant, they would be blessed. And while the people stood in high expectation, through tradition and the influence of these false teachers, there was a wonderful event took place. For behold it was written in the prophets, "I will send my messenger before thy face to prepare thy way before thee." The angels warn the shepherds by bringing good news unto men. The star appears, the wise men start and follow its course, king Herod is troubled, and the empire of Cæsar begins to tremble. Upon the lonely banks of the Jordan, stands one dressed in came's hair whose meat was locusts and wild honey, and he spoke, saying, "Think not within yourselves that ye have Abraham to your father, for I say unto you that God is able of these stones to raise up seed unto Abraham, and now behold the axe is laid unto the root of the trees, every tree therefore which bringeth not forth good fruit is hewn down and cast into the fire." Matt. 3d chapter. This my beloved, is some of the things that the apostle John saw, of them he saw as they stood upon the statute rocks, and some he saw with his own eyes, and they all stand connected with the things that he saw and heard. But he saw things that were still greater than they, for he was present when the last named prophet, John the Baptist, uttered the language, "Behold the Son of God that taketh away the sin of the world." He was present when the Son of God was made manifest by the descension of the Holy Ghost. He was present and witnessed the scene when the Son of God committed himself into the hands of his forerunner John, and was buried beneath the waves of the river Jordan. He was present and heard the voice from Heaven proclaiming; "This is my beloved Son in whom I am well pleased." He was ordained by that acknowledged Son of God and witnessed his three years mission upon the earth. He witnessed the mighty powers that was in him, when he turned the water into wine, delivered his sermon on the Mount, and when he made the blind to see, the lame to walk, the lepers cleansed, and he heard His voice when it penetrated the dark recesses of the cavern, saying 'Lazarus, come forth.' He was present at the memorable scene when the pall bearers of the last son of the widow of Nain, was conveying him to his grave. He witnessed the joyous acclamations of the multitude when the Son of God stopped the bier, reanimated the dead and delivered him to his weeping mother alive. He heard him utter the language; "I am the resurrection and the life, if any man believe in me, though he were dead, yet shall he live again." He saw and heard Him say; "I am the way, the truth and the life, and no man cometh unto the Father but by me." He heard him make his urgent appeals to the people, to come to a reformation of life in order that they might stand as living monuments of God's mercy, and enjoy the blessedness that is in reserve for them in the city of the living God, and also when he said unto the people, "Except ye repent ye shall all in like manner perish," that is, perish just as those Jews did whose blood Pilate mingled with the Jews sacrifices to be burned up with fire, and many other things the apostles saw which is too tedious to mention. They were with him when he was betrayed by Judas, when he healed the servants ear, and also when he was taken by the soldiers, taken from tribunal to tribunal, when he was insulted, scoffed at and spit upon, when his temples were pierced with thorns, when judgment was given against him and he going forth bearing the burden of his own cross. O, the dreadful scene that follows! He is marched to the top of Calvary's mountain, the Cross is erected, his flesh is pierced by the iron nails, Heaven and earth vails themselves from the sight, for the sun darkened, the rocks rend and the vail of the temple is rent in twain from the bottom to the top, and the prosecutor is made to exclaim, "Truly this is the Son of God." His life is taken from him, He is taken from the cross, his body deposited in the sepulcher, the stone is rolled at the door and sealed with the signature of Pilate, a cohort of soldiers is given, to stand as sentinels around the tomb, with the instructions that if the body was taken, death would be their doom. But blessed be the name of God, for Jesus was not to be confined to the narrow limits of the grave, for says He, "Destroy this temple and in three days I will raise it again." The third day came, the angel was dispatched, the sentinels trembled and became as dead men; the stone rolled away and the Savior was resurrected. He broke the bands of death, led captivity captive and gave gifts unto men.

This all happened to prove His power, to make reconciliation for the sin of Adam and to make a way possible that we, the posterity of Adam, might be restored to friendship and favor with God, and have the blessed hope within us that by following in the footsteps of our glorious Exampler that we too might attain to the resurrection of the dead.

After Jesus had been condemned to death and the sentence put into execution, those whom he had chosen and ordained for witnesses had their confidence shaken to that degree that they forsook their high calling and went back to their old occupations, but the Savior recalled them and when the twelve reassembled, the Savior appears unto them, and assured them that he had obtained all power in Heaven and in earth, and for this cause they are to go forth and "Teach all nations, baptizing them in the name of the Father, and of the Son, and of the Holy Ghost, teaching them to observe all things whatsoever I have commanded you, and lo! I with you alway even unto the end of the world." Matt. 28; 18-19-20. We notice that this language, beginning at the word teach, ending with the pronoun you in the 20th verse, bears out the idea of a repetition of action all through. We notice in the first place that the Savior says teach, after this, baptize in the name of the Father, then baptize in the name of the Son, then baptize in the name of the Holy Ghost, then comes the teaching them to observe all thing whatsoever He had commanded them, then the promise is annexed, of a continuation of His presence to the full consummation of time.

Now we will rehearse, "Go ye therefore," or for this reason, for what reason? Why for the reason that he had obtained all power. Where were they to go? Why to the nations of the earth. What were they to do? They were to teach them. What? Teach them that the promise annexed to the penalty in the Garden of Eden was realized, that the covenant made with Abraham had been made sure, that the promised seed that was to bless the nations had come, for he saith not, "and to seeds as of many, but as one, and to thy seed which is Christ." Gal. 3d chap. Christ had proven his power by raising the dead, Luke 8th chapter, by stilling the tempest and casting out a legion of devils. He had also suffered according to the Scriptures, John 19th chapter. His blood rested upon us. After these things have been fully made known unto us and we imbibe faith to believe it and thus see our deplorable condition, we must repent, "every one of us," Acts 2 36. What next? We must be baptized for the remission of sins, Acts 2; 33. This qualifies us for the gift of the Holy Ghost. Why was this baptism of water and the gift of the Holy Ghost necessary? "Except a man is born of water and of the spirit he cannot enter into the Kingdom of Heaven." John 3; 3. "In the like figure whereunto even baptism doth also now save us." Ist Peter, 3; 21.

I will now notice the mode of baptism. The sacrament is performed by going into the water, Mark 1st chapter, and Acts 8th chapter and 38th verse, and after we are in the water we must then be buried under under the water, Romans 6th chapter, and this must be performed by a face forward movement, for we must be baptized and planted together "in the likeness of his death." When Christ died, he bowed his head and gave up the Ghost John 19 ; 30.

The Savior, in the Commission, makes use of the singular name and not of the plural names, hence when we are baptized in the name of the Father it does not necessarily baptize us in the name of the Son, and when we are baptized in the name of the Son, we are not, by that action, baptized in the name of the Holy Ghost. We must first be baptized in the name of the Father, then be baptized in the name of the Son, and then in the name of the Holy Ghost. The commission is a compound sentence, which is made up of suppressed sentences, the sentences being suppressed by the use of an ellipsis, when we are baptized in the name of the Father the copulative conjunction, and, is introduced which means add to or fill up. Now when we complete the sentence we must make a pattern of the first, which is a complete sentence, hence we must insert the word, baptize, as that is the word which is understood, and so with the third sentence. Then we will read, baptizing them in the name of the Father, and baptizing them in the name of the Son and baptizing them in the name of the Holy Ghost. This is all essentially necessary to introduce us into the Church Militant. We must now do the commandments in order that we can enter the Church triumphant, for "not every one that sayeth unto me Lord, Lord, can enter into the Kingdom of Heaven, but he that doeth the will of my Father in heaven."

This brings us to the 3d division of the Commission, "Teaching them to observe all things whatsoever I commanded you." He commanded them to wash one anothers feet, with the penalty, "If I wash you not thou hast no part with me." John 13 chap. We are commanded five times, in the writings of the apostles, to salute one another with a holy kiss. The Scriptures also testify that if we are lovers of the world we are the enemies of God. We must be modest in our conversation. All of our talk must be coupled with fear. Our adorning must not be that outward adorning of plaiting the hair and wearing of gold or putting on of apparel, but it must be the hidden man of the heart, in that which is not corruptable, even the ornament of a meek and quiet spirit which is in the sight of God, of great price."

In conclusion, I would say unto you my relatives, who may read this, if I have made any impression upon your mind, O, do not let them slip. If you need more instruction, which in all probability you will, send for the PILGRIM. Remit $1.50 to the editors, for one copy one year, and you will never regret it, or take it in clubs and it will come cheaper. Let us all prepare for Heaven and immortal glory. We may never see one another in this life, but if we only prepare for death, we will meet on the other side of Jordan. Your brother, JOHN W. FITZGERALD.

Benlington, W. Va.

SALVATION.

Salvation is a word frequently used in the Gospel and is full of meaning; was and spoken for the benefit of the human race. The reason it was placed on record, was because there was need of something to elevate the condition of the human race, they had need of being elevated because they had fallen from their high and lofty position, which they once held, and which God designed them to occupy when they were created and placed in the garden of Eden, but sorry to say, that memorable command of God to them, "in the day thou eatest thereof thou shalt surely die," has entailed the curse upon the human family, and gave cause to say there is need of some plan for the salvation of the human race to bring them out of the dire calamity into which they have fallen, because of their disobedience of God's command to them given in the garden of Eden. Whether God was disappointed or not in the way things turned out, we will not now discuss, but surely man had now fallen from his high and holy estate, and in the great wisdom displayed by the Creator, in placing the cherubims and flaming sword to keep the way of the tree of life so man would not reach forth and also partake of it, and live forever in this fallen condition, but after living out his period of existence he would moulder to dust again from whence he was taken, but this was not enough to satisfy that benevolent Creator, this only pertained to the sufferings of the body.

Now from what we learn from the Holy Scriptures, man was composed of more than one part, for it is said that God breathed into his nostrils the breath of life, and man became a living soul. Again, it is said the body moulders back to dust, but the spirit goes to God who gave it, and it is very clearly set forth in the word of God, that the injury sustained reached higher than the body alone, for the spirit was also affected by the transgression, and the plan of salvation was more particularly for the benefit of that inner principle which lives forever.

O think of the wisdom displayed by the triune God; had to devise some plan to bring man out of this calamity which he brought himself into; think of the disinterested love displayed; the pain and suffering of the Son of God, so that the plan might be carried into effect which cost nothing less than the blood of a crucified Redeemer, which was shed on Calvary's bloody summit; think of the dying groans when he said, "if it be possible, let this cup pass from me nevertheless not my will, but thine be done."

Paul in writing to the Hebrews, 2d chapter, says, "If the word spoken by angels is steadfast, and every transgression received a just recompense of reward, how shall we escape if we neglect so great salvation, which at first began to be spoken by the Lord and was confirmed unto us by them that heard them." Here it is called by Paul a great salvation, and truly it is great, for when we contemplate what it cost and without its being carried into effect we never could have been brought to that standard of virtue to which we are brought through its merits.

Salvation means preservation from destruction or eternal death, then according to the defination of the term, the destiny of man was fixed, destruction from the presence of the Lord and from the glory of his power which he brought upon himself by transgression, and had not God interfered man would have remained in that condition, but God preserved him from this awful calamity by bringing salvation to bear upon them, to save them from the impending danger they were standing in. At that time, the Apostle says "by grace are ye saved, through faith and that not of yourselves it is the gift of God." Grace means favor, and it was given, but not merited, not earned, but bestowed. Thanks be to God for the favor, let us one and all make use of the means which has so richly been bestowed upon us that we may be again, reinstated into the favor of God.

Now what are the means? Answer, Repentance toward God, and faith in the Lord Jesus Christ, are among the first principles by which we may attain the benefits intended, and it requires an effort on our part rest assured, and sometimes no small one to extricate ourselves from the

To be Continued.

ANOTHER WAIL FROM THE CAMP.

In the *Baptist Record* published at Charleston, W. Va., of the date of Dec. 5th, 1872, we notice a "strike" at "*Mourners Bench Religion Examined*," over the initials 'M. E.' and under the caption "The 'Death Blow' Averted." If we were to look behind the veil "M. E." wears to hide his person we should not be surprised to see no less a character than Eld. M. Ellison the author of that stale and dead work called "Dunkerism Examined." The Eld. seems to have an aversion to "Dunkers" in general and myself in particular. From knowledge of the past I was prepared for almost anything from our opponent but was a little surprised to learn he had made a personal assault upon me under cover of a mask. Of all cowardice is there anything like stabbing at an opponent in the dark? If a "death blow" is worth resisting let it be done face to face or over the full signature. Such a medley of misquotations, misrepresentations and errors as are to be found in the article above mentioned we seldom see. We shall notice a few.

Among the first quotations he makes, or purports to have made, he has the following as our language: "wishes his right hand may be palsied, and his pen move no further, if any other motive prompts him than the welfare of souls." "M. E." is jubilant over this which he claims is a quotation from my tract; when the truth of the matter is there is no such quotation in the tract. What he says therefore relative to it amounts to nothing so far as it has reference to the tract. Again he says: "he (I) repudiates a person unless he has 'been born of the water three times.'" The words "born of the water three times," "M. E." has set forth as a quotation when it is evident no such a sentence is found in the tract he was examining, neither has such an idea ever went forth from our lips as an idea we claim, or from any other person so far as I know. In the name of common sense when will that long since exploded and thread bare argument of "three births,' 'three baptisms' &c., be laid aside. Does not every sensible person (free from bigotry and prejudice), know that in performing the ordinance of water baptism as commanded by Jesus Christ, there is but one going in and one coming out—but once commencing to perform the ordinances of that "one baptism" and but once completing the work of that "one baptism," and that in performing the work that belongs to the said ordinance, there are three special acts expressive of our faith in the triune God and *obedience* to the command of our Lord; yet some persist in calling it "three baptisms," or "three births," and such like inappropriate terms, all of which comes with a bad grace from those who believe in the Divine trinity.

"M. E." says: "To tell an inquirer to believe in Christ and he shall be saved, Mr. F. assumes not to be God's promise, but man's." Now I "assumed" no such thing! I know, as is plainly "assumed" in that tract, that "whosoever beleiveth in him (Christ) shall receive remission of sins." I also know and assume that we are not saved or justified by *faith alone*. But if we believe in Christ unto obedience to his word, we shall receive the remission of sins. God's promise is "he that believeth and is baptized shall be saved." Man's promise is "believe," and your sins are pardoned and you are saved *without baptism*. My assumption is in harmony with God's word and no other way will I "assume."

Again we quote "As the bitten Israelites looked upon the brazen serpent and was healed, so the anxious sinner believes in Christ and is saved. This is substantially what Elder Flory condemns." Instead of condemning I "substantially," in the tract as elsewhere, endorse the sum and substance of that text. The Israelites *obeyed* and lived. They were commanded to look and when they done so they lived. The sinner is commanded to "repent" after he believes in Christ and then "be baptized" in the name of the Lord Jesus "for the remission of sins" and then he shall live. But to tell the sinner to look with only an *assenting* faith, to Jesus and he shall be saved, "Is substantially what Eld. Flory condemns."

"M. E." refers (as usual) to the organization of the Brethren in a church capacity in Germany in 1708. For a man who lives "in a glass house to throw stones" so regardless of consequences is suicidal to say the least of it. The missiles he aims at the "Dunkers' have the effect to demolish his own "coveted retreat" so badly that it is "shivered to atoms" more than one hundred years this side of the "Dunkers" organization in Germany. And even if "M. E." would claim he is yet in the 'old hive' he has but little to boast of! All the evidence necessary to know whether we are in the line of 'Apostolic succession,' is this: Do we practice what they did as touching the doctrines of the Gospel. To know whether we are members of the Church of Christ we must 'examine ourselves to see whether we be in the faith' or not—in that faith that was delivered to the saints.

"M. E." further says "A large majority of these persons whose change dates from these meetings, would doubtless be accepted by Mr. F. as good Dunkers upon three immersions, without additional pious qualities." We would accept of them upon their confession of faith in the Lord Jesus Christ, evidence of their repentance toward God, and an expressed willingness to obey the gospel, trusting in a Saviour's love. A very exemplary member of the church was first "convicted" at a dance party, but we would by no means encourage dance parties as a suitable place to bring about the conviction of sinners. Neither can we recommend the mourner's bench as a necessary means to a genuine conversion.

In his concluding remarks 'M. E.' says "I am not blind to the fact that the 'anxious bench' as Mr. F. styles it may be imprudently used, but this abuse is no just argument against its prudent use, but the 'death blow is aimed at revival meetings in general." Why my dear sir! I never said one word against its "prudent" use, it was the "imprudent" use I was aiming the 'death blow' at. I endeavored to show how 'imprudent' it was used. I did not even attempt to lay a finger in the way of all that God may be doing in way of blessing such means to the good of souls, neither shall I. Now the question is how far may we go with the "mourner's bench" before it is "imprudently used." Well we will take the "law and testimony" to decide the matter. That decides it is not in the gospel, therefore not in the church. Then it follows the 'prudent use' of that auxillery to conversion stops just OUTSIDE *the Church*. There I am willing to leave it for nominal professors to lounge on!

"M. E." concludes by saying my "blow is lost in the air." And I prove "nothing" I promise to do. Passing strange that the blow is lost in the air and yet it hit somebody! Such nervousness as is perceptible in "The 'Death Blow' Averted" did not originate without a cause. And if it takes over two and a-half columns in a medium sized journal for "M. E." to disprove 'nothing,' how much space would he occupy to disprove *something*? That the 'blow' is lost in the air is simply a bare assertion, consequently worth nothing. I, as well as others, have evidence it has not been a blow struck in vain but to God be all the honor and glory ascribed for sending the 'shaft' from the "bow that was drawn at a venture" home to the heart of many who have awoke to the fact there is danger all around while reclining at ease in the chambers of Babylon. They have heard the voice, "*Come out of her my people that ye be not partakers of her sins, and that ye receive not of her plagues.*"

J. S. Flory.

Unwonted care is the creature of useless indulgence, or wanton extravagance; the really needful in life can be obtained without it.

A FEW THOUGHTS ON THE LANDMARKS.

Concluded.

of the Holy City, and from the things which are written in this book." I do not wish to set myself up as a judge, but I do sometimes fear there is a little of that removing disposition manifested, when brethren will speak so lightly, and disrespectfully of those decisions, when after much perplexing labor they are the very best that could be done for the time; or when brethren will not assent to the order of, or in fact to hear the church unless they are allowed to make the proviso, "If the order or demand is in accordance with the Gospel," this certainly is claiming what the Savior never granted, and is giving a key to every member whereby to open a *door*, the keeping of which He entrusted exclusively to the church.

And also, something of that spirit is manifested when brethren will say, such are only the decision of District or Annual Meeting, and hence only traditional. I appeal to our better judgment to decide who is in the right; those insubordinate members, or Christ the head of the body, or church. He virtually says hear the church, but they say you need not submit to all the decisions of District and A. M. If the Savior had said, if he neglect to hear the Gospel, it would materially change the matter; but as it is the church that is to be heard the inference is plainly drawn, that the church has full authority to dispose of difficulties between members, even to the disowning of those that neglect to hear decisions, although there may be neither precept nor example found in the Gospel on which to base her decisions. The power vested in her hands is amply sufficient. It is not claimed that the church or any part, independent of its HEAD is infallible, but the pledges given her by her supreme Head are claimed for by promise, not only till now, but, "Even unto the end of the world." These truths are taught by the faithful preacher of the cross. The true convert not only believes in Jesus as the only Savior, and in the Gospel as the only means or power of God unto salvation, or in His church as the only organization where the means of salvation are administered and carried out, but he also believes the promises alluded to above.

"Where two or three are gathered together in my name there am I in the midst of them." "Lo! I am with you always, even unto the end of the world." "Upon this rock will I build my church, and the gates of hell shall not prevail against it."

These, and many more, are the pledges given by her great Head, and believed by all her faithful children. Earth may shake to its center; kingdoms rise and fall, divide and subdivide, but the church, built on the "*Chief corner stone*" has stood, and will stand, unshaken, undaunted and undivided, through all the floods that the dragon may cast after her. Then stand to the "Ancient Landmarks" and you will stand right in the church, and be surrounded by an impregnable fortress, the promises of God to the Church, viz: "Though a mother may forget the child she bare, yet will not I forget thee O Zion!" The church cannot be divided, *never*! NO NEVER!

D. M. HOLSINGER

Youth's Department.

MAKE YOUR MOTHER HAPPY.

Children, make your mother happy;
Make her sing instead of sigh;
For the mournful hour of parting
May be very, very nigh.

Children, make your mother happy;
Many griefs she has to bear;
And she wearies 'neath her burdens—
Can you not those burdens share?

Children, make your mother happy;
Prompt obedience cheers the heart;
While a wilful disobedience
Pierces like a poisoned dart.

Children, make your mother happy;
On her brow the lines of care
Deepen daily—don't you see them?
While your own are smooth and fair.

Children, make your mother happy;
For beneath the coffin lid
All too soon her face so saint-like,
Shall forever more be hid.

Bitter tears and self upbraidings
Cannot bring her back again;
And remorseful memories
Are a legacy of pain

Oh, begin to-day, dear children,
Listen when your mother speaks;
Render quick and sweet obedience,
For your highest good she seeks

Loves you better than all others—
For your sake hers if denies;
She is patient, prayerful, tender,
Gentle, thoughtful, true and wise.

Never, while you live dear children,
Though you search the rounded earth
Will you find a friend more faithful
Than the one who gave you birth.

NOBLE CHILDREN.

We hear so often of noble men and women, that I thought it no more than just, I should tell a few of the noble actions of little children.

A few years ago, an aged couple were wandering along the streets of Nebraska City; they were in search of a certain doctor's office, but how were they to find him? The old man was blind, and the old lady did not know where he lived.

After wandering for some time, they met a number of little boys on their way to school. "Can you tell us where Dr. H. lives?" inquired the aged lady.

"Yes ma'am," answered one of the little boys. "Come, I'll show you where he lives." "You'd better come on to school; you'll be tardy and miss your perfect mark," called out one of the others.

"Go on, boys: I'll come directly," he called to his companions. Then taking hold of the blind man's hand he led them down the street, across it, then down the opposite side for some distance, when a man coming up the street, called; "Where are you going, Charlie?

"Why pa, this old man is blind, and they wanted to go to Dr. H.'s and didn't know the way. I'm taking them there" said the little fellow timidly.

"Well, I'll take them there; you may run back to school now," said the gentleman, kindly. Then he took them to the doctor's, and the little boy ran back to school. Children, don't you think he acted nobly? I do not know whether he missed his "perfect mark," or not; but I am pretty sure God put down a mark for him, worth more than all the "perfect marks" in the world.

One day a friend stopped at a little girl's house, on her way to a neighbor's, and wanted this little girl, whom I will call Edie, and her sister to go with her; but Edie's ma said one of them must stay to rock baby. Now, Edie wished her to say which should stay, but she said they better decide between themselves.

Here was a struggle; both wished so much to go. For a time neither spoke, but finally Edie said smilingly and cheerily,—

"You may go, sister. I'll stay and rock baby," and took her place at baby's cradle. She could hardly keep back the tears, but she smiled all over her face, and gave up sweetly to her sister. Now wasn't she a noble little girl? Could we give up our fondest delights and pleasures without a murmur, and as cheerfully as did this dear little girl?

In a school in a village in the East, was a poor girl subject to severe fits, and consequently, she would talk and act very strangely sometimes. One day I was standing at the schoolroom window, watching the girls, who were playing "ring," in the yard below. Poor Josephine went up and asked to play with them. "No! no" answered some of the girls. "Don't let her in, she's crazy!" "She shan't have hold of my hand!" "Nor mine, she's crazy!" Josephine burst into tears and turned away.

"Come back, come back, Josie, you can have hold of my hand!" cried Jennie W., running after her.

Jennie coaxed her to come back; and on seeing this some of the other girls relented,—for they all loved Jennie. Thus, the poor girl was allowed to play with the rest.

Poor Josephine is dead now; but she remembered kind Jennie to her dying day; and I think God will remember her, too.—*Young Folk's Rural.*

CORRESPONDENCE

A Reporter is wanted from every Church in the brotherhood to send us Church news, Obituaries, Announcements or anything that will be of general interest. To insure insertion, the writers name must accompany each communication. Our invitation is not personal but general—please respond to our call.

TRUTH.

Dear Pilgrim:—It is said that "truth is mighty and will prevail." How important then that we, at all times, speak the truth in all our actions and dealings. It is also said that "actions speak louder than words." How careful and watchful then should we be, that by our actions we do not speak an untruth. A falsehood or untruth may be acted out in many different ways, such as giving short weight, short measurement &c. Or suppose a man sells his produce to his neighbor for more than market value, the neighbor not being posted in regard to market prices, is he not taking advantage of his neighbor and acting out an untruth by taking more than lawfully belongs to him? Or for instance, a publisher says his paper is published weekly at $ — per year, when in fact he only publishes 50 numbers which do not make a year, neither does he publish his paper every week when he only publishes 50 numbers. Is he not then acting out an untruth? With the same propriety might the publisher of a monthly journal publish 11 numbers and call it a year. Let us all be consistent and make our words good and be honest, truthful and upright in all our dealings, not only in a temporal but also in a spiritual point of view, that we all speak the same thing.

A LOVER OF TRUTH.

Although this was not intended to be personal, yet as it may seem to touch our case, it makes it proper that we should make an explanation. In our business transactions it is generally accepted that custom makes law. According to our present labor system, laborers are hired at so much per day, when in reality they only labor ten hours, some eight and some less as the contract may be, yet they all labor for so much per day and by so doing, act out *no untruth*. Again teachers are hired for a certain compensation per month, but in that month they labor only twenty days, and six hours constitute their days labor. Their contracts are considered honorably fulfilled without acting any *untruth*. Just so, it has become a custom among a large number of publishers to issue fifty papers for a year. They agree with their patrons to publish a weekly paper at $—per year with the understanding that the year is to consist of fifty weeks or fifty issues. It occurs to us that such transactions are perfectly honest and that we act out no untruths in carrying them out.

UPTON PA., January 15th, '73

Beloved Editors of the Pilgrim:—This is to inform you that Bro. O. W. Bricker and I started on a mission of love to the brethren of the Aughwick Church, Pa., on Friday the 3d of January, stopped over night near Fannettsburg with brother Nashman, had preaching in Flickinger's school house in the evening. On Saturday morning started on our way to Hill Valley, stopped over night with Bro. John Spanogle. On Sunday forenoon preaching in the school house near brother Lanes'. On Sunday evening preaching in the Gilboa school house, over night with brother A. L. Funk. On Monday visited brother Enoch Lutz. In the evening, preaching again near brother Lanes,—over night with brother George Garver. Next morning on our way to Germany Valley stopped for dinner with Bro. Lane, in the afternoon stopped a few minutes with Bro. John Gleck, then went to brother George Eby's, preaching in the evening in the Union school house. On Wednesday morning went to the Germany Valley meeting house, for dinner with Bro. Benjamin Garver. In the evening, preaching again in the meeting house. On Thursday forenoon attended a council meeting at the meeting house, and for dinner with Bro. Samuel Lutz, preaching again in the evening, and over night with brother Andrew Spanogle. On Friday morning started on our way to Three Springs, stopped on our way at Bro. Lane's, for dinner. In the afternoon, on to the Three Springs, preaching in the evening in a school house. Over night with brother Samuel Bowser. On Saturday morning we started on our way to the Big Cove, stopped with friend Buckly at Fort Littleton for dinner. In the afternoon, went to McConnellsburg, called in town a few minutes with old sister Morton, then on to brother Melius, stayed over night with him, and preached in the evening about two miles distant. On Sunday morning, on to the school house near brother Hodges, in the afternoon, we crossed the Scrub Ridge into Licking Creek Valley, had preaching there in a school house, over night with brother Lake. Next morning started for home, stopped with a brother for dinner, then on home found our families well, thank the

Lord for His goodness over us while we were absent from each other, for from Him cometh every good as well as every perfect gift.

Now in conclusion, I will say, our love to all the brethren, sisters, and friends with whom we visited and preached on this trip. I had the pleasure of meeting quite a number of my blood connection whom I had not seen for a long time, and some of them I had never met before and it is quite likely it may be the last time for some of us until we meet on the other side of the Jordan of death. May God help us all so to live that we may meet in that glorious rest prepared for the people of God.

GEORGE MOURER.

HOLLIDAYSBURG, PA., Nov. 5th, 1872.

Bros. Brumbaugh:

We have again received another letter from our much-loved sister Hollowbush and by her request send it for publication. Perhaps some of the brethren and sisters may appreciate its contents as well as we.

E. R. STIFLER.

Dearly Beloved Sister:—The PILGRIM and your letter came in due season, for which I feel to thank you with a greatful heart. They came like gentle refreshing showers on the new mown grass. I love the Brethren's periodicals, they are so very encouraging. I have abundance of time to read and meditate, and death, the stern monarch of the grave, and eternity, seems to be the topic of my meditation. You will not wonder why it is when I tell you that he has visited our household four times in four years (one month more) and claimed four of its inmates for his victims. The first was a grand daughter three years old; the second was a grand son eight months old; the third was our son, the father of the little boy. He died, with the full assurance that he was going to obtain an inheritance incorruptible, undefiled, that fadeth not away. The fourth was my dear husband. One year ago last night he was at your place, (I saw it in his diary.) Then he was full of life and love, and had an ardent desire to do his Heavenly Master's Will O, how sad two thirds of the year has been to me! and what a loss! But I know it is his eternal gain. I am now sitting in the chamber where three of my dear departed ones breathed their last precious breath. I have much to think of that transpired during their sickness; to think of their prayers, and their last words of admonition. How oft my husband prayed that we might be one unbroken family in heaven. O, may his prayers prevail! Methinks they will, for "The fervent effectual prayer of the righteous man availeth much." It appears I have a heavy cross to bear, but I want to strive to bow with humble submission to the Divine Will of Him who tempers the blast to the shorn lamb. O, dear sister, I ought not complain of crosses or trials, for I am surrounded with many brethren, sisters and kind neighbors that are members of other denominations that seem to have great sympathy for me, and attend to my wants. I sometimes feel lonely, but Christians need not be lonely. They have the promise of the best of company if they will only accept of it. They have the company of Him who spake as never man spake; and who is chief among ten thousand and altogether lovely. We have the promise of the Comforter, who will come and abide with us forever. The Christian's privileges are great. He does not appreciate them as he ought, neither can he comprehend them.

On the 12th of October, we held our Lovefeast. We had a very happy time, and a large congregation The members were nearly all present to partake of the emblems of the broken body and shed blood of our blessed Lord and Master. whom we are trying to serve. The same day there was one added to the church by being buried with Christ by baptism, beneath the sparkling waves. Please tell Bro. G. Myers that it was Bro. Stern's daughter; tell him that the old grandmother who had her limb dislocated, when he was here, is perfectly well again. This afternoon our Sabbath school closed for this season. We had quite a serious time. Bro. Conner addressed the children very touchingly. He advised them to abstain from every appearance of evil; that they should never use the filthy weed nor utter profane language, but keep their mouths clean that they may praise God with their lips, for God is a God of purity, and as such we should worship Him. I cannot relate all he said, but it was true. Sister you wrote that your nephew was the first link broken from the chain of your family circle. I can greatly sympathize with you, for my near relations are nearly all gone. My parents are dead although they lived to a good age. They were both in their eighty-first year. I had but one brother, and he was killed while blasting rocks. I had six little grand-children, that were taken away by the hand of death. Two of them were accidentally killed, but I have full faith to believe that they are now chanting the songs of redeeming love in the very innermost courts of Heaven, for they never came under the power of the original sin, and of such is the kingdom of Heaven.

Then let us forbear to complain,
Since they have gone from our sight.
For we all may behold them again,
With new and redoubled delight.

My health is not as good as it was some time ago, yet I can still attend church for which I feel very thankful, but am fearful that when Winter comes, I may be confined to the house again. I am still striving to fulfill the last promise I made to my dear husband, that I would love the Lord for his sake. And I say to you press onward, yes *press onward*, dear sister, the prize is in view. There's a crown of bright glory awaiting for you. I will yet say that I have but one sister in the flesh and she is a worthy sister in the Lord. Her name is Susan Sidle. Perhaps you have seen her name in the C. F. C. I will now close and retire to rest hoping that goodness and mercy may follow us all our days, and that we may dwell in the house of the Lord forever.

HANNAH HOLLOWBUSH.

Pottstown, Pa.

A BRIEF SKETCH OF THE BRETHREN IN MIDDLETOWN VALLEY, MD.

Dear brethren:—A short time ago, I read in the PILGRIM a brief history of the brethren of Shenandoah Valley, Va., which was interesting to me, and no doubt to others. I will therefore give a similar account of our church, as it has existed in Middletown Valley, Frederick Co. Md., at least as far as I can recollect, and from what I have learned from others older than myself.

Among the first of the brethren who came to this state, at least in the vicinity where the writer resides, was John Slifer, the writers grandfather, who from the best date, emigrated here from Bucks Co., Pa., about the year 1780. I saw, in the year 1833 the very house in which he was born, and, also lodged there one night. Its location is near a village called Fryburg, Lehigh Co. Pa. With him, my grandfather, came his wife, her brother, whose name was Gaver, and a sister who had married a man by the name of Peter Miller. All those named except John Slifer were natives of New Jersey. All were members of the church. I never learned what part of New Jersey they came from, but presume it was across the Delaware river from Doylstown, as I understand there is a congregation of the brethren there yet. About the same time, there were several families also, in this Valley, yet north of this place some distance, by the name of Leatherman, Grossnickle, and Harshman.

When they organized a church I cannot tell. About the year 1810, their preachers were, Leatherman and Furguson; the latter was the first English preacher in this section, of the Brethren, or indeed any other denomination. I have been told that he always had large congregations to hear him.

About the year 1820 their preachers were Jacob Leatherman, Christian Hershman and John Holler, all of whom are dead. Then followed Daniel Brown and Christian Hershman who are also dead.

In 1840 Henry Koontz and Geo. Bear were elected. The latter died about a year ago. Bro. Koontz having moved out of the district, the writer was elected in his place in 1847. Since the latter period, the circuit in which the brethren named officiate, embracing the entire Valley of Middletown, has been divided, the National Turnpike being the dividing line. North of the turnpike the ministering brethren are Jonathan Baker and Geo. Leatherman, and the congregation is best known as the Grosnickle Church. South of said pike the congregation is known as the Brownsville Church. Brownsville is in Washington Co., Md. Those who minister in Holy things, in that congregation, are Cornelius Castle, Eli Yourtee and the writer.

With regard to the prosperity (spiritual) of those congregations, I presume it will compare favorably with others of our churches, as none of us are without our difficulties. But I think I may now say, for both divisions, that it is our purpose to endeavor to grow in the grace and knowledge of our Lord and Savior Jesus Christ, He being our Foundation and chief corner stone. It therefore behooves us to be careful as to the material we use in building thereon. Let it be that which is described by the apostle *Paul* as being superior to all the rest,—*gold*. There are other materials that are inferior, *silver, precious stone, wood, hay, stubble*. The best material possesses dross, showing that there is a necessity for the interceding prayers of our Saviour in our behalf,—having gone to prepare a mansion for us. Let us glorify His name.

EMANUEL SLIFER.

Burkettsville, Md.

FREMONT, NEB. Dec. 20th, 1872.

Dear Pilgrim:—Find enclosed a few lines to show how we are getting along out here. As for the brethren they are yet few in number, but we hope that in the future it will be better. We wish to inform your readers that we have a healthy and fruitful country, plenty of chances for home-seekers from the East; homesteads and wild land at low prices. If any of the brethren, let them be where they may, wish to emigrate to Nebraska to seek homes, call off at Fremont, Neb. before looking elsewhere, (especially laboring brethren.) I have traveled around over considerable of Neb. and finally located in Cedar Creek Valley, Boon Co., where I took a homestead of 160 acres of land, close to good water and mill power. There is yet plenty of good land to be had as homesteads, but is being taken up rapidly.

The land in Cedar Valley is level, very fertile and produces good crops of every kind. Those wishing to come out here had better not delay, as there is yet homes for many. For further information, write to Daniel Fouts, or Isaac P. Shively, Fremont, Nebraska.

MARRIED.

ALEXANDER—ROSE.—On Dec. 19th, 1872, by Martin Neher, at the house of bride's parents, in Piatt Co., Ill., Mr. B. F. Alexander, of Moultrie Co., Ill., to Miss Mary A. Rose of Piatt Co., Ill.

METZGAR—OAKS.—December 29th, 1872 by the same at the house of the bride's parents in Moultrie Co., Ill., bro. Andrew S Metzgar, of Clinton Co., Ind., to sister Mary Oaks, of Moultrie Co., Ill.

D. D. SHIVELY.

DIED.

BULGER.—Nov. 9th, 1872, in Morrison's Cove, Snakespring Valley Congregation, Bedford Co., Pa., sister Susannah Bulger aged 73 years, 7 mos. and 4 days.

At her request, she was the evening previous to her death annointed with oil in the name of the Lord, according to James 5th chap. Occasion improved by the Brethren from 1st Thess. 4th chap. latter part.

Also at the same place, Dec. 27, 1872, sister Hannah Bulger daughter of the above, aged 10 yrs., 10 mo. Occasion improved by the brethren, from 1 Cor. 15 latter part.

ZOOK.—Jan. 15, 1873, near Bakersville, in the Yellow Creek Congregation, Bedford co., Pa., sister Barbara Zook, wife of Jacob Zook, also daughter of the above, aged 47 years, 7 months and 3 days. Occasion improved by the brethren, from first four verses of 5th chap. 2 Cor.

Thus, in a little over two months, the mother and two daughters were called from time to eternity, truly a severe shock to the bereft. We truly sympathize with the bereaved relatives; but hope their bereavement is their eternal gain. The latter leaves a sorrowful husband and six children, three have preceded her into eternity while in innocency.

LEONARD FURRY.

(*Visitor* please copy.)

BRINDLE.—In Churchtown, in the Lower Cumberland Church, Pa., on the 15th of January, 1873, sister Sarah, wife of Bro. Geo. Brindle, aged 64 years, 1 mo. and 12 days. Funeral services by the Brethren from John 11: 25, 26.

Sister Brindle was for many years past a consistent member, and we hope died a christian. Leaving a dear husband and six children, two sons and four daughters all members save one, to mourn her loss.

M. MILLER.

ENK.—In the Ashland Church, Ashland co., Ohio., January 9th, 1873, our beloved sister Susannah Enk, aged 69 years and 11 months, less one day.

This sister was called upon to part with her husband, some thirteen years ago, and now she follows after, leaving quite a number of friends to mourn their loss. Some of them are members and some are not, but we hope the day may speedily come when we can call them all brethren and sisters, by adoption into the family of God. We hope our loss is her great gain. Funeral services by Eld. M. Weaver and the writer from first Thess.

D. N. WORKMAN.

(*Companion* please copy.

ZECH.—Near Young America, Howard co., Ind., September the 3d, 1872, Susannah Zeck, in the 56th year of her age, of dropsy, with which she suffered much and long.

She leaves 7 children, 3 sons and 4 daughters to mourn her loss. Funeral attended by brother Heil Hamilton. The text I have not heard.

ANNA M. TROXEL.

BRUMBAUGH.—In the Salem Church, Montgomery Co., Ohio, Jan. 6th, 1874, sister Elizabeth Brumbaugh, aged 89 yrs., 9 mos, and 7 days. Funeral sermon delivered by brethren Abraham Flory, Peter Nead and others from the words, "To live is Christ, to die is gain."

She lived a life consistent with her profession and died in the hope of a glorious resurrection. She was the widow of Henry Brumbaugh who, with his family, emigrated to Ohio from the farm now occupied by his nephew Isaac Brumbaugh near the James Creek Meeting House' Pa. She has 3 surviving sons and 5 daughters all members of the church.

D. H. BRUMBAUGH.

HESTAND.—On Jan. 6th, 1873, in Columbiana Co., Ohio., Ann J. Hestand, daughter of Bro. Isaac and sister Maria Hestand, aged 21 yrs, 10 mos. and 28 days. Funeral services by brethren D. Byers, L. Glass, and the undersigned, from Rev. 22: 7.

JOHN A. CLEMENS.

TROLL.—In the Maplegrove Church, Ashland co., Ohio, Jan. 2nd 1873, our beloved brother John Troll, aged 73 years, 11 mos. and 12 days. Funeral occasion improved by brother Wm. Sadler and the writer from Rev. 14: 13 to a very attentive congregation.

D. N. WORKMAN.

[*Companion* please copy.]

JORDAN.—In the Little Beaver Creek Congregation, near Dayton, Ohio, Dec. 31st, 1872, sister Anna Jordan, aged 85 yrs, 8 mos. and 22 days. Funeral services by brethren N. Brubaker, and Geo. Garver from 1st Cor. 15: 51.

The subject of this notice was a consistent member of the church for many years, and an example to the flock, and died in the triumphs of a living faith, with a full assurance of that rest that remains for those who love Jesus.

H. F. DARST.

The Weekly Pilgrim.

JAMES CREEK, PA., Jan. 28th, 1873.

☞ HOW TO SEND MONEY.—All sums over $1.50, should be sent either in a check, draft or postal order. If neither of these can be obtained, have the letter registered.

☞ WHEN MONEY is sent, *always* send with it the name and address of those who paid it. Write the names and post office as plainly as possible.

☞ EVERY subscriber for 1873, gets a *Pilgrim Almanac* FREE.

CAN'T DO WITHOUT THE PILGRIM.

On account of money being a little scarce, some of our former readers thought they would do without the PILGRIM, but when the time came for its usual visit there was an important visitor missing. The expression of such is' "Send on the PILGRIM again, we can't do without it." We are glad of this for several reasons. First, it shows us that the PILGRIM fills an important place in the home circle and it does us good' to know that it is missed. Secondly, we are made glad because we believe that we are doing a good work and that it will be a real benefit to such as are striving to gain the great reward, and lastly, because we need the aid and encouragement of all to make our work a success.

We sometimes feel like giving extracts from our numerous letters, showing to what degree the PILGRIM is appreciated by some of its readers. One says, "I have been a reader of your worthy paper for the last year, and have become so attached to its weekly visits that I cannot think of having it stopped, I am not a member of the Church, but think the time will not be long until I shall be numbered with the pilgrim band." Another is a poor widow who lives far from the places of meeting, and has no conveyance and therefore seldom gets to meeting. She says; "The dear PILGRIM comes almost like an angel visit, and when, in my lonely hours, I read from its pages the productions of my dear brethren and sisters and hear of the welfare of Zion, my heart overflows with gratitude. May God bless your labors that the welcome messenger may continue to go forth filling many precious souls with the bread of Life," &c.

Others have sons and daughters residing in the far West, who are out of Christ. To them the PILGRIM must be sent with the fond hope that it may be the means of their return to God. Another wants it sent to a friend who is no member, but thinks he will be after reading the PILGRIM a year. It truly makes our souls to rejoice when we have the assurance that our work goes forth on its weekly mission accompanied with the prayers of fond parents that it may be the means of converting their children and others that are yet out of Christ.

Brethren and sisters, have you the welfare of precious souls at stake? If so, improve the golden opportunity that is presented. Do not feel that you have done your duty until you have supplied every son and daughter, whether in or out of Christ, with the PILGRIM. It may be the means, in the hands of God, to save their souls, which is of more importance than if you were to give them great riches. The greatest good you can do in this life, is to labor for the salvation of your children and the world. Think of this and make use of the means that God has blessed to accomplish this end.

ARE WE LABORING FOR THE WELFARE OF ZION?

Had we not this blessed assurance, the oil of our lamp would not be consumed in the midnight hour. Even now while the busy millions are wrapped in the deep slumber of night, we are still at our post. Daily, we feel the weight of our position growing upon us, and we are made to think if our dear readers could experience the care that is bearing us down, least we should do or say something that might mar the peace or good of Zion, they would make every allowance for our failures.

We may have failed in carrying out our designs fully, and especially at this time as our labors are so great that we have not been able to give our contributors the attention they should have and in consequence, we may admit some papers that should have been modified, and left others out that should be admitted, but we have such faith in our brethren that we believe that all are laboring for the welfare of Zion and in this hope we excuse our neglect. That our work is greatly blessed seems evident from the general expression of our readers, and that still greater blessings may rest upon it is the burden of our prayer. We are deeply concerned for the welfare of sinners and the upbuilding of the Church and have determined to spend and be spent in laboring for the Lord and the cause of righteousness. Brethren and sisters, aid us by laboring for us in increasing our list of subscribers and enlarging our borders.

Subscribe for the PILGRIM.

PERSONAL.

WM. SADDLER. All right.

H. H. WINGER. Your PILGRIM is paid to No. 20, 1873.

NOAH FLORA. Please give us the name and address of the four first subscribers you sent us, so that we can mark the names paid.

JNO. W. FITZGERALD. The money was received and the Tune Books sent a short time ago. You will doubtless receive them all right.

CLARA M. BURKET. The $17.00 you sent us is received. Please send the names and address of those who paid it. Unless this is done, we can not know to whom to give the credit.

J. S, F. Your requests will be attended to. We cannot well send the PILGRIM every other week, but will send it every week for the amount named. What we give to the poor we hope will not be lost.

A CORRECTION. In No. 2 there was a blunder committed in a marriage notice, which we cannot account for. We have it Geo. Shathower and Sarah Springer, by David Goodyear, where it should be Geo. W. Shathower and Sarah E. Springer, by Eld. Moses Miller. The parties will please pardon, as it was done through a mistake.

ALMANACS. The complaint is, "we do not receive our ALMANACS." We do this business in such a way that we are sure they are sent. The trouble is most certainly with the mail and post masters. We have good evidence, to suspect some for detaining them in the office. We design that every subscriber shall have an ALMANAC, and therefore, are sending them the second time to such as did not get them.

ODD NO. WANTED.—Will some good brother, sister or friend who is not preserving the file, please send to my address, the PILGRIM bearing date May 21st 1872? Bro. B. does not have any, and I failed to get the No. It will confer quite a favor upon me, as I wish to have them bound.

E. B. STIFLER, box 72.

Hollidaysburg, Pa.

GREAT INDUSTRIES OF THE UNITED STATES, is one of the best and most interesting works of the kind ever published. It contains an historical summary of the origin, growth and perfection of the chief industrial arts of this country. in fact, it is a library of information that no man can well afford to do without. It is a work of 1301 pages and contains over 500 illustrations. This useful and interesting work will be sent free to any person who will send us 25 subscribers and $37.50.

MONEY LIST crowded out.

GENERAL INTELLIGENCE.

Sidney Rigdon, author of the Mormon Bible, is dead.

The earthquake shocks of Dec. 14, on the northwestern coast, are said to have been the first ever felt so far north. They do not appear to have been very severe, and caused but little damage. In Portland, Oregon, chandeliers vibrated and clocks were stopped.

Many of the Episcopal clergy in the Pittsburgh diocese, at a recent convention, advocated an abandonment of the Sunday School as an agency of spiritual instruction, and a return to the ancient method of making parents responsible for the work now committed to Sunday School teachers.

A well known clergyman was recently asked his opinion of a young lady much afflicted with the "Grecian bend." He replied that she reminded him of the woman mentioned in the Scripture, "who had a spirit of infirmity, and could in no wise lift up herself."

Sunflowers are raised in Watonwan Co., Minn for fuel. The oily seed in the flowers is found to make a hot fire, and the woody stock, when dried, furnishes a good substitute for timber, which is very scarce in that region. It is estimated that two acres will produce enough to last an ordinary family through a long winter.

The *Phœnix* tells us that phosphate digging in South Carolina is rapidly increasing. One company mined 15,000 tons during the last year, and the production from river deposits alone amounted to 40,000 tons in the last twelve months. It is thought that the entire products of the State will be increased not less than 40 per cent. during the present year.

A LONG BRIDGE.—The river Tay, in Scotland, is to be spanned by a bridge that will be the longest in the world. The Victoria bridge at Montreal, which has heretofore been the longest is 9,194 feet; that now being constructed over the Tay will be 10,321 feet. It lacks but eighty yards of being two miles in length. The work is to be finished in three years from May 1871. The greatest height of the structure will be eighty-eight feet above highwater mark.

HUNTINGDON & BROAD TOP RAIL ROAD

Winter Arrangement.

On and after Tuesday, Oct. 4, 1872, Passenger trains will arrive and depart as follows:

Trains from Huntingdon South. *Trains from Mt. Dal's moving North.*

MAIL. A. M.	ACCOM P. M.	STATIONS.	MAIL. P. M.	ACCOM A. M.
LE8 00	LE5 50	Huntingdon,	AR3 20	AR9 00
8 08	5 57	Long Siding	3 12	8 53
8 24	6 10	McConnelstown	2 56	8 37
8 30	6 17	Pleasant Grove	2 50	8 30
8 45	6 30	Marklesburg	2 37	8 17
9 00	6 44	Coffee Run	2 23	7 01
9 07	6 52	Rough & Ready	2 15	7 53
9 20	7 05	Cove	2 0.	7 40
9 24	7 10	Fishers Summit	1 57	7 35
9 44 / 9 54	ar7 30	Saxton	1 37	le 7 15
10 10		Riddlesburg	1 19	
10 17		Hopewell	1 12	
10 31		Piper's Run	12 56	
10 52		Tatesville	12 38	
11 05		Bloody Run	12 24	
ar11 10		Mount Dallas	12 20	

JOHN M'KILLIPS, Supt

SHOUP'S RUN BRANCH.

LE10 00	LE7 40	Saxton.	AR1 30	AR7 10
10 15	7 55	Coalmont.	1 15	6 55
10 20	8 00	Crawford.	1 10	6 50
AR10 30	AR8 10	Dudley	LE1 00	LE6 40

Bro'd Top City from Dudley 2 miles by stage.

Time of Penna. R. R. Trains at Huntingdon.

EASTWARD.		WESTWARD.	
Hb'g Ac.	9 21 A. M	Cin. Ex.	2 10 A. M.
Mail	3 30 P. M	Pc'f Ex.	7 45 "
Cin. Ex.	6 55 "	Mail	5 40 P. M.
Phil. Ex	11 15 "	W. Pass.	11 52 A. M.

The Weekly Pilgrim.

Published by J. B. Brumbaugh, & Co.
Edited by H. B. & Geo. Brumbaugh.
CORRESPONDING EDITORS.
D. P. Sayler, Double Pipe Creek, Md.
Leonard Furry, New Enterprise, Pa.

The *Pilgrim* is a Christian Periodical, devoted to religion and moral reform. It will advocate in the spirit of *love* and *liberty*, the principles of true Christianity, labor for the promotion of peace among the people of God, for the encouragement of the saints and for the conversion of sinners, avoiding those things which tend toward disunion or sectional feelings.

TERMS.

Single copy, Book paper,	$1.50
Eleven copies, [eleventh for Agt.]	$15.00

Any number above that at the same rate.

Address,
H. B. BRUMBAUGH,
James Creek,
Huntingdon county Pa.

The Weekly Pilgrim.

"REMOVE NOT THE ANCIENT LANDMARKS WHICH OUR FATHERS HAVE SET."

VOL. 4. JAMES CREEK, PENNSYLVANIA, FEBRUARY, 4. 1873. NO. 5

POETRY.

Selected by CATHARINE A. FORNEY.

THE ALTAR AT HOME.

Oh well I remember a long time ago,
While a stranger now lonely I roam;
The scenes of my childhood, the friends of my youth,
And the hallowed altar at home.

Where a mothers' devotion at evening with ours
Went up through the star-lighted dome;
And we knelt with a father to worship in prayer,
Round the hallowed altar at home.

At morn. our hymns with the songs of the birds,
Thrilled out on the soft balmy air;
And we knelt ere we went to the toils of the day,
Round that hallowed altar of prayer.

But the home of my childhood is desolate now—
We were gathered away one by one;
The light faded out from those beautiful scenes,
And the altar is broken and gone.

Yet faith to my rapturous vision unfolds,
A home in a city afar;
When I kneel on my journey to worship alone,
At my altar now everywhere.

And I know they are there at that happier home,
And that free from all sorrow and pain,
I soon shall be called from my altar below,
To join them in worship again.

Then let the glad years of eternity roll,
No anguish nor penitent prayer;
Or a desolate one with the cross all alone,
Will be heard at the altar up there.

Hudson, Ill.

ORIGINAL ESSAYS.

"THE BAPTISM OF JOHN, WHENCE WAS IT, FROM HEAVEN OR OF MEN?"

BY ELD. B. F. MOOMAW.

We noticed the fact in our former communication, that many of the impostors of our times were attempted to be palmed upon an honest and unsuspecting populace, by pretending for it divine authority, or at least divine sanction, and it is remarkable indeed that an intelligent public is so easily imposed upon, but strange as it is, it is not more strange than true. The critical student of the human character however, very soon discovers that the children of men are generally, if not universally either too credulous or too incredulous, too ready to beleive and adopt a theory of human invention, and too slow to accept and embrace a divine institution, ready, as it appears to endorse, and associate themselves with the institutions of men, upon the mere pretext of divine sanction with the slightest shade of testimony from the Book of God. Such testimony indeed, as to the careful and prudent observer would be no testimony at all, as is clearly exhibited in the arguments used in support of the different human institutions. The ingenuous partisan in these efforts with the pious inquirer invariably makes quotations from the Bible, which by the unwary is accepted as conclusive authority, when in fact there is no relevancy whatever, and which cannot, by any fair interpretation, have any application to the matter in question, and which, doubtless, never entered the mind as a basis for the foundation of these institutions, but a necessary after thought conceived and produced for them, while on the other hand, we demand the most demonstrative evidence in order to the exercise of faith in, and acceptation of a divine instiution. This is clearly seen in the history of the advent of Jesus Christ into the world, and the introduction of His holy religion, as well as in all his subordinate institutions, not to speak of the many similar circumstances under former dispensations, yea, notwithstanding the undoubted evidence that he has given to the world of his divine origin and attributes the clearness in which he has communicated his Father's will, and his positive declarations as to the advantage or disadvantage of believing, respecting and obeying or not obeying it, a large proportion of the intelligent world gives this all important subject little or no attention, while another large and respectable class, profess to believe, but treat it with utter indifference and disrespect, at least many of his commands and ordinances.

God in all his intercourse with men, well knowing the skeptical turn of the human mind, in things pertaining to godliness and designing the salvation and happiness of the human family, and that we should on our part be left without excuse, delivered His will in the most clear and unmistakable language, neither obscure nor ambiguous. Therefore, we conclude that what God designed that we should do, is clearly indicated in His word, and that for which we have no precept nor example in His word, He did not intend that we should engage in, however plausible it might appear. This idea, as it appears to me, furnishes us a safe rule by which we may determine upon the introduction or recommendation of any theory, from whence it is, whether it be of God or of men.

Concluded.

REFORMATION.

Dear Editors:—Reformation is very desirable, and indeed from the appearance of things at present it is much needed. But as long as people entertain a good opinion of themselves, and have an idea that there is a great deal of religion and righteousness in the earth, it cannot be expected they will become any better. Christ has said, "The whole need not a physician, but they that are sick," and it is certain that people will act according to this maxim, however sick they may be, if they imagine they are well. Many might have become good had they not judged themselves to be so while they were otherwise, hence, it follows that people must first see they are not right before they will seek after amendment, and while they are in a dark and bewildered state, the most glaring evils and inconsistencies are not easily perceived by them, and it is often a very difficult task to convince them of their impropriety. Indeed it is impossible to do this if they have so refused to receive the truth in the love of it, that God has sent them strong delusions to believe a lie. It requires no great degree of learning to prove that the Christian world is now in a very fallen and degenerated state, and that the number of those who possess true piety, is very few. And yet we find that the generality of professing Christians have an idea that religion is in a very prosperous condition, while some are almost ready to conclude that the Millenoial state of the Church is about to take place. But I would candidly ask, do we see anything characteristic of the true kingdom of God, which consists in righteousness and peace? Is not every man's hand, comparatively, against his neighbor, and was there ever a time when cheating, dishonesty and injustice was so general as at the present day? It is true, we now and then hear it said by one and another, that there is a great revival at such or such a place. If, by this, it is meant that people are becoming proselytes to some sect, I am willing to admit of its being correct, but at the same time I must remark, for people to come forward and unite themselves to some society is no proof that the world is getting any better, or that the persons themselves have become any better, for we seldom see them more humble or more inclined to do what is right than they were before, and in some instances they appear only to be worse. Now had the tree been made good the fruit would be good also.

It is clearly to be seen that even those few societies that were once zealous for the truth and bore a faithful testimony against the corruptions and evils in the Christian world, are fallen into decay, and many things which they have highly approved in their founders, they now condemn in others. Where is that regard for righteousness and that firmness in rebuking iniquity which we discover in the first preachers among them? These pious men have, no doubt, gone to receive the reward of their faithfulness, but little did many of them imagine that their labors in clearing away the rubbish and planting the good seed of the Kingdom, would be so soon lost, and briars and thorns spring up in the vineyard to choke the plants of righteousness.

These honest men, for so many of them were, began in the spirit, but their numerous followers are likely to end in the flesh. The friendship of the world which they have been led to embrace, is enmity with God, and it will be well for them to remember from whence they are fallen and repent and do their first works lest the candlestick be wholly removed out of its place.

No reformation can be expected as long as people suffer themselves to be led by blind guides and teachers, and they are looked upon as patterns to imitate, for I appeal to the impartial and candid observer, if there is not a greater degree of pride and outward grandure exhibited in the lives of the generality of those called ministers, in this day, than there is in their hearers to whom they pretend to teach humility, and do they not, like the false prophet in old time, prophesy smooth things, and with feigned words make merchandise of them, assuming to themselves, at the same time, the sole right to the key of knowledge to lock and unlock as they think proper, and if a congregation of people are rich, and will pay them the all, they will undertake to impart to them the knowledge of salvation, but if they are poor and cannot come up to their demands in pecuniary matters, they must remain ignorant. These things are but too true and until people come to exercise their own judgments, and examine for themselves in matters of religion, we shall see no change for the better.

A PILGRIM.

SOBER THOUGHTS FOR HONEST PROFESSORS.—NO 1.

Heaven-aspiring souls, and all ye that truly have a desire to walk in the light of divine truth, permit me to present to you, for serious consideration, a few thoughts touching that subject which we believe is dear to your hearts, viz; Salvation through the merits of a crucified Redeemer.

First, conceive the idea that it is possible, in this age of fanaticism and error, to be honestly in the wrong, and that many a snare is being set to entrap the unwary, and that we are all exposed to the cunning craftiness of Satans' agencies. Many unsuspecting persons unwittingly step into line with those that are rushing on in the tide of popular religion, and join hands with those who by learned criticisms mystify "the way, the truth and life" as it is in the gospel. The dark and muddy waters of allegorical exegeses are rapidly overflowing the prominent points of literal interpretation. The unreal is held forth for the real, imaginary things instead of the faithful promises of God. And thus the popular theology of the nineteenth century would sink into insignificance the "faith once delivered to the saints."

The world has really "gone mad" on the subject of religion, and amid the Babel confusion we hear one say, "here is Christ," another "lo here he is," and another "here, here" and so it is all through the streets of "Babylon." From amid this confusion of tongues, there is but one way of escape for those who feel they are not in the peaceful Kingdom of Jesus. Dear friends, let me implore you for the sake of your eternal interest to take the glass of the gospel and "examine yourselves whether you be in the faith or not." That will give naught but a true reflection. In that you will see in glowing colors of God's own painting, the characteristics of that religion exemplified by Jesus, to consist of love without dissimulation, humility without pride, gentleness without fierceness, faithfulness without deceit, hope without fear and steadfastness without wavering. Compare the *simplicity* of the gospel along side of popular religion, and Oh! what a contrast. The cross lies trailing in the dust, and pomp and pride hides from view the rugged brow of Calvary. Exaltation, and the desire to have the "chief seats in the synagogues" have put in the back ground a *kneeling praying* Jesus in Gethsemane, and paved with "roses" the paths in which the apostles trod. The love of gold has made such a merchandise of the gospel that devils might well stand amazed. *Pious gambling* (!) has turned the gaudy temples of worship into "dens of thieves." Pastors lounge at ease with folded hands, unless gold paves the way to congregated sinners. Fashions' votaries sing of "Jesus crucified" and with jewel-adorned fingers take the symbolic emblems of the broken body and shed blood of a meek and humble Savior. The commands of Jesus are ignorance, the spirit of the gospel hooted at, the power of the gospel denied, liberality of the conscience defended, the lust of the eye and pride of life the rule of government, that which is highly esteemed among men the idol of acceptance, and the world the theatre of pleasure. In the name of the holy religion of the Son of life and glory "come out of her my people that ye be not partakers of her sins." It is no *crime*, but commendable, to conscientiously change from error to truth. When new light and candid investigation of God's truths have opened our eyes it is our duty to come to "the light." No one can stand justified before God who clings to an erroneous doctrine, after it is known to be such, and it is our province to know it. Though to renounce it is like cutting off a hand, or plucking out an eye it must be done, or Heaven will be lost to us. Seek the approbation of God only, and now and now only is the time to investigate this important matter. The Word of God—the gospel—will a "tale unfold" to every candid inquirer that will sound to the believing heart like heavenly manna, and feed the hungry soul with manna from on High. Hear it, oh, ye sons and daughters, hear the Bible truths, and to them alone take heed and then you will never stand rejected at the bar of God, never hear the denunciation, "Depart from me ye workers of iniquity I never knew you." Oh! what a vast multitude will, it is feared, claim admittance that will be rejected because strangers to the Lord. Strangers from the fact they did not get in the "narrow way" with Jesus here, did not "learn" of Him who is "meek and lowly in heart," did not attain to friendship with the Lord, by doing whatsoever He commanded. Strangers to His *cross*, strangers to His spirit of humility and self-denial, and strangers to the "straight gate" and "narrow way." It is no marvel why Jesus will not know such. Dear reader, of all things that concern you there is nothing half so important as this of knowing whether "you are in the faith or not." Be assured *somebody is in error*, in matters of religion at the present day, it is utterly impossible for a thousand theories so widely differing one from another to all be right, touching a subject that admits of no *variation whatever*. While salvation through Jesus spreads her wings of glory to enfold the whole human family in her loving embrace, there is but one way,—absolutely but *one way*—of coming to God and securing the salvation of the soul through the merits of Christ. That way is God's own appointed way, opened up by His Son, and now it is indispensibly necessary that all must enter by Christ who is the "door" "the way, the truth and the life." Christ "has become the author of salvation to all them that OBEY Him."

In our next we shall endeavor to say something with a more direct reference to the means of salvation.

J. S. FLORY.

SHOULD IT BE HID?

"Now I praise you, Brethren, that you remember me in all things," &c.—Paul

It is very pleasant and agreeable, when we hear or read anything of our brethren that is praiseworthy; yet on the other hand it fills every true heart with sadness, and sometimes with grief, when the opposite is heard or read. Well might our beloved brother M. M. say, "Tell it not in Gath, &c." I have no doubt he expressed the sentiment of many brethren and sisters. And I would not disprove or speak disparagingly of this sentiment, for the spirit of criticism and fault-finding, is but too prevalent in every breast. And to throw the mantle of charity and forbearance, over the weakness of our fellow-men, is but carrying out the injunction, "Speak evil of no man."

I have no doubt every one that read the article of the old brother, that was ridiculed in the cars, by the two *would be gentlemen*, and he giving them lodging, and treating them as he did, was highly pleased and gratified; yet the actions of some nameless persons were exposed, and as that case represents hundreds of a like nature, let every one that reads the same, look into it as a mirror and make the application.

Whether it be right or wrong to present matters, that are true in the main, as the writer with the "Lantern" did, let the history of the Bible decide.

There are instances in our beloved brotherhood of unedifying proceedings, will not say of wrongs for Charity's sake, that cannot be remedied by the course proposed by M. M., and as there are many cases that need reformation, would it not be well to purge out the old leaven, like the Jews do, to the present day, taking a light and light it in every nook and corner of the house, holding a wing of a fowl in one hand with which they gather every impurity and burn it with fire outside of their premises? I would think it not wrong for the brother with the "lantern," though as for himself he would have to say, "I am not worthy to be called a brother, if he would bring every thing to light that is in a measure hid; and if he would have to say, "In this I praise you not that ye came together, not for the better but for the worse."

As for not exposing our weaknesses, the time was when the whole number, about 70, could be together in an upper room to hold big meeting as it then was termed, well might the Church have kept everything among themselves, but the times have changed and many things with it. Everything we now do, as a body, is done as if from the housetop instead of the secret chamber. The church is no longer hid. The war has compelled her to be known. Everywhere, people make it their business to find out and publish what they knew, and as they found things. Therefore it becomes the more necessary to take hold and purge out, or in other words to reform, and unless we know what is wanting, we cannot amend the wrongs. And as for the propriety of putting our faults in print, the whole Bible doth the same from Genesis to the final Amen of Revelation. Every good man that is spoken of in the Old Testament has his bad deeds also recorded and have been read by all generations and when we come to the record of the New, not only individual faults and transgressions are set forth to their shame and our warning; but whole churches are reproved, warned and corrected. Even the epistles to the seven churches, dictated by the Holy Spirit and recorded by John, are an exposition of the condition of the same. It is true, as I said in the beginning, it is very grevious to have our faults exposed, but some of us cannot be cured without it. Hence I argue that anything that is for our humiliation, to make us more meek and at the same time more forbearing towards our fellow-men and especially toward our brother, is as the Psalmist said, like oil upon our head.

Thus I have written not for controversy, but for eliciting or calling forth the reasonings and reflections of my brethren, since everything hath at least two sides. If my reasonings are faulty, it would do me no harm to correct the same. One thing, however, I have learned in living three score years and ten, that it goes very hard to change our mind, especially if we have given publicity to the same.

With the hope that our beloved fraternity may see the necessity of doubling their diligence. And if there is any praise, if there is any virtue, think of these things.

Your servant in love,

F. P. LEHR.

Bloomingdale, Mich.

AFFLICTIONS.

Loving brethren and sisters, for encouragement and comfort to those, who, like us, have tribulation, sorrows and afflictions, I pen these lines. God in His moral government sees proper to send afflictions, in order to correct us when we go astray. This is an evidence of His love to us as His children, and God-fearing people in all ages bore them with patience and resignation, "For whom the Lord loveth He chasteneth, and scourgeth every son whom He receiveth," O how necessary these corrections, for we are so forgetful of our duty we owe to our God, and toward one another. Let us then profit thereby like a David, "Before I was afflicted I went astray, but now I have kept thy word. It is good for me that I have been afflicted, that I might learn thy statutes." But amidst all these troubles and trials, the Lord promises to deliver us. "God hath seen my afflictions, and the labor of my hands, nevertheless my loving-kindness will I not utterly take from Him, nor suffer my faithfulness to fail." "Many are the afflictions of the righteous, but the Lord delivereth him out of them all." Hear the Savior, "In the world ye shall have tribulation; but be of good cheer; I have overcome the world." Our light afflictions are but a moment, then it worketh for us an exceeding and eternal weight of glory.

LEONARD FURRY.

Miscellaneous.

A NUT TO CRACK.

I will here present to those who think the "wise men" ought to understand the Scriptures, a "nut" for them to crack, and if they get any good out of it they are welcome to it.

Mr. Robert Dale Owen, who by the way is a Professor, says in a recent article that in order to get the correct age of the Patriarchs we must divide by *twelve* or that one of our months is as long as one of their years, therefore Adam was 77 years, 6 months instead of 930 years. Methusaleth 80 years and 9 months instead of 963 years, and so with all the rest. Now if the Professor is right, in the case of Shem, (Gen. 11 10) we have a father at 8 years and 4 months! A young father indeed! I would like to know the age of his wife. And in same chapter 24th verse, we have Nahor a father at 2 years and 5 mos. and at the age of a little over 15 years he begat sons and daughters! If the learned professor is correct, that was truly a fast age, ours is no comparison to it.

It is quite likely said professor belongs to the same class of "worldly wise men" that tell us baptize means to *sprinkle*! and that Christ when baptized did not go *into* Jordan, but only went *near* by, and a great many other things wherein they "wrest the Scriptures to their own destruction." May the Lord deliver us from the theology of all such!

J. S. FLORY.

QUERY.

Dear Editors:—We want you or some other brethren to give us an explanation, through the PILGRIM, on Math. 11: 7-8. ISAAC ULERY.

Bro. Editor:—Please give an explanation on 1st. Cor. 14: 34 in regard to women keeping silent.

JOHN GAULT.

Bro. Flory's "Criticism" below will give you the desired information. Ed.

A CRITICISM AND QUERY.

"Let the women keep silent, with all subjection. But I suffer not a woman to teach, nor to usurp authority over the man, but to be in silence." 1st. Tim. 2: 11-12.

The learned tell us that in the original it is *gune*—woman, a woman or the woman instead of "the women" as in our version. And also "in silence" in the original is *en esukia* meaning quietness, and not silence in an absolute term. This same word *esukia* in 2nd. Thess. 3: 12 is translated "quietness."

Where strict silence was required or intended the word *sige* is used as acts 21: 40, "there was made a great silence," also Rev. 8: 1, "there was silence in Heaven." If the translation above cited is correct, and we have no reason to doubt it, we would have the text to read "Let the *woman* (in the singular) learn in *quietness* with all subjection. But I suffer not a woman to teach nor to usurp authority over the man but to be in *quietness*" Such quietness as is opposed to turbulence, dictation, usurpation of rule, or the power of authoritative teaching. Such quietness as is meant in the Scripture "quiet and peaceable life," that is a life free from strife; and again, "a meek and quiet spirit," that is a spirit free from strife. Is it an error then, to understand Paul to mean that he suffered not a woman to *teach authority* over man or to *usurp authority* over him, but when she *prays, prophesies, teaches or learns*, let it be done in "obedience to man" that is in "quietness" or as being in subjection to her head? J. S. FLORY.

The *Christian Observer* in trying to show that when our Savior prayed "that they may be made perfect in one," had reference to a spiritual union and not external or the meeting of sects, gets off the following:

"It also ignores all the great evils that would certainly follow organic unity. It clamors for unity at all hazards. It has never considered that organic unity among Baptists, for example, would be a great blow to religion. If all Baptists were organically one, every Baptist pulpit would be open to the advocacy of trine immersion, and pledged not to oppose salvation through water, and other errors found among Dunkers, Mennonites and Campbellites. If this was not the case what would the organic unity be worth?

Why not say, If all Pedobaptists were organically one, every Pedobaptist pulpit would be open to the advocacy of salvation without water and other errors found among Presbyterians, &c. If advocating salvation through water is an error then is the scheme of redemption a vessel without bottom, and a cistern without water. It is declared that except a man be born of water * * * he cannot enter the Kingdom of Heaven. If a child can be born independent of a mother, then can a man be born again independent of water. The greater errorists are those who deny the "power of God unto salvation" by denying in part, the "Message" as delivered unto us. While we have no faith in this "lip union," we still detest the idea of forever condemning those who live humbly before God, and endeavor to walk in all His commandments and ordinances blameless. If our good brother of the *Observer* can get to Heaven without going *through water*, we have no objections to offer, for our part we prefer to be *born of water*, not at, or near it, but "buried with Christ in baptism."

SECRET SOCIETIES. The Alleghany Presbytery (United Presbyterian,) through a committee, to whom the subject was referred, has taken ground against secret societies which impose an oath of secrecy, including especially Odd Fellows and Masons, on the grounds that these orders are of pagan origin; that they selfishly confine their benevolences to themselves, instead of extending them to all men everywhere; that their oaths are administered by persons who have no right to do so, and are tendered and taken before the person swearing knows what he is about to swear; and that their religion is a false semblance, dishonoring the Savior. Pastors are *requested* to preach on the subject, sessions are *required* to enlighten the minds of the people as to their sin and inconsistency in belonging to these orders, and failing to do this, they are *directed* to proceed against" such members as they would against any other violation of the church, and the laws of God."

LAY REPRESENTATION.—The *Religious Telescope*, organ of the United Brethren, believes that the next change in the direction of progress in the Church must be the admission of laymen into the Church councils. There is no opposition to such a change but that it will come, sooner or later, cannot be doubted.

The progress of Christianity in Madagascar is attracting attention. During the last year the increase to the Christian community was 65,000 persons, including 18,000 church members. In three years the total addition has been about two-hundred and fifty-eight thousand converts.

SALVATION.

Concluded from last week.

pollutions of sin which we have fallen into, and which was brought upon us by disobedience to God's word. We have many examples given of the horrors that has befallen men ever after the conditions of salvation were made manifest, and brought so near that we could reach them, and why? We ask in all candor why? Because we neglect so great salvation, and do not make use of the means to obtain. Repentance means a turning from sin.

"O turn ye poor sinner, why will you die,
For God in great mercy is coming so nigh."

Above, we have said repentance toward God and faith in the Lord Jesus Christ, last but not least, is baptism, by which we are initiated into the family of God, for Paul says to the Galatians 3d chap. "As many of you as have been baptized into Jesus Christ have put on Christ, there is neither Jew nor Greek, there is neither bond nor free, there is neither male nor female, for ye are all one in Christ and have become Abraham's seed and heirs according to the promise." Again Paul says, "though an angel from heaven preach to you any other Gospel than that which we have preached, let him be accursed," this is pretty strong language, nevertheless true, as written by the inspired apostle, and given to us for our edification. One reason perhaps why we do not strive more earnestly to enjoy the benefits of salvation is, the way is a little too narrow, the gate is a little too straight, and we are filled a little too full of the corruptions of the world, and the sinful pleasures therein, and if we are not very careful, our day of grace will pass away, and we will not be any the better for being in it. Now, dear reader think of this, there is so much said, and so much done in the name of our Lord Jesus Christ, that, should your lot fall where the rich man is represented to be, that you would have to call to Lazarus for a drop of water to cool your tongue for the torment upon you, there is no possible hope of escape. Let that cause you to seriously reflect upon the great plan of salvation given for you.

Geo. Worst.

CHRIST THE MERCY.

FLAVEL.

"1-t. If Christ be the mercy of mercies, the medium of conveying all other mercies from God to men: then in vain do men hope for mercy out of Jesus Christ. I know many poor sinners comfort themselves with this when they come upon a bed of sickness, "I am sinful, but God is merciful. Plenteous in mercy; his mercy is great above the heavens, mercy pleaseth him, and all this; they, that are in Christ shall find experimentally to their comfort and salvation. But what is all this to thee if thou art Christless? There is not one drop of saving mercy that comes in any other channel than Christ to the soul of any man. You may enjoy the riches, honors and pleasures of this world for a season, but there are two bars betwixt you and all spiritual mercies, namely: The guilt of sin and the pollution of sin; and nothing but your own union with Christ can remove these, and so open the passage for spiritual mercies to your soul. But I will repent of sin, strive to obey the commands of God, make restitution for the wrongs I have done, cry to God for mercy, bind my soul with vows and strong resolutions against sin for time to come; will not all this lay a ground-work for hope of mercy to my soul?" No, this will not, this cannot do it. All your sorrows and tears for sin cannot obtain mercy, could you shed as many tears for any sin you have committed, as all the children of Adam have shed since the creation of the world, they would not purchase the pardon of that one sin; for law requires full satisfaction, and will not discharge any soul without it. The repentance of the soul finds, through Christ, acceptance with God, but out of him it is nothing. All your strivings to obey the commands of God and live more strictly for time to come, your vows and engagements to God for time to come cannot obtain mercy, being made in your own strength, it is impossible you should keep them: and if you could, it is impossible they should obtain remission and mercy, should you never sin more for time to come, yet how shall God be satisfied for past sins? Justice must have satisfaction, or you can never have remission. Rom. 3: 25, 26; and no work wrought by man can satisfy divine justice.

2nd. Is Christ greater and more necessary than all other mercies? Let no inferior mercy satisfy you for your portion. God has mercies of all kinds to give, but Christ is the chief, the mercy of all mercies. O be not satisfied without that mercy. When Luther had a rich present sent him he protested that God should not put him off so, and David was of the same mind, Psa. 17: 14, 15. If the Lord should give you the desires of your heart in the good things of this life, let not that satisfy you while you are Christless; for what is there in these earthly enjoyments whereof the vilest men have not a greater fulness than you? Job. 21: 7-12; Psa. 17: 10; and 73: 3-12; What comfort can all these things give to a soul already condemned as thou art? John 2: 18; what sweetness can be in them whilst they are all unsanctified things to you? Enjoyment and sanctification are two distinct things. "A little that a righteous man hath is better than the riches of many wicked." Psa. 37: 16; Prov. 10: 22; Thousands of unsanctified enjoyments will not yield your soul one drop of solid spiritual comfort, and what pleasure can you take in these things of which death must shortly strip you naked? You must die, and whose then shall all those things be for which you have labored? Be not so foolish as to think of having a great name behind you; it is but a poor felicity, as Chrysostom well observes, to be tormented where thou art, and praised where thou art not.

To be Continued.

WHAT IS LIFE?

Life may be compared to a river, beautiful in appearance and a smiling tender face, with sparkling eyes and rosy tints. Our course in youth, and maturity is along a wider and deeper flood, amid objects more lively and buoyant. Life bears us on like the stream of a mighty river. Our boat at first glides on down the narrow channel, through the playful murmuring of the little brook, and the winding of its grassy borders.

The trees shed their blossoms over our young heads. The flowers on the brink seem to offer themselves to our hands; we are happy in hope and we grasp eagerly at the enticements around us—the stream passes on and still our hands are empty. We are animated by the moving pictures of enjoyments, and all manner of sport so enticing. We are excited by some short-lived disappointment, and the stream bears us on, and our joys and our griefs are alike left behind.

Onward with a hurried step,
How smooth its dimpling waters wave:
The rocks beneath hath ever slept,
When the swan is want to lave.

Winding through the forest trees,
With tangling thorns and waving grass
Watering fowls and honey bees,
Without the aid of pitcher or glass.

Life is alone in a wilderness,
Like the river through wood and grove,
Innocent, murmuring and gentleness,
Like the cooing of the lonely dove.

What is life, Oh can you tell me?
What it is, and whence it came,
Why it is thus passing by me
The world is passing just the same.

Life is truth, we must confess it
Reality in its perfect state;
As it is none can undo it,
The ending may be soon or late.

The river 'mid its bubbling waves,
And confusion of its traveling;
Is firm and true, though lively joys,
Are mingling with its gabbling.

The moon looks down in calmness,
Into the mirror crystaline;
And the stars in all their sternness,
Are in splendor to be seen.

Tributaries of this wandering stream,
Are friendly and true-hearted;
And good and kind, but shun extreme,
Where all vanity first started.

The dense woods are filled with mirth,
So high above the shining brook,
'Tis nature for this mother earth,
To seek and wonder and to look

The quivering blasts have chilled thy blood,
The storms of winter threaten thee;
The sleet hath covered field and wood,
The icicles hang o'er shrub and tree.

This life is chilling just the same,
And threatened by the winter blast;
We're hastening toward the icy frame,
With steady step and eager grasp.

M. V. Michael.

Greenland, W. Va.

WINTER.

Stern winter has again approached with cold, snows and storms, and as we look around us and behold the barren appearance of the earth, at this season, it sometimes reminds us of the state we are liable to be in, spiritually, if we are not constantly on our guard as we should be.

There are many ways in which we may become careless or negligent of our duties toward our Maker, and thus become cold and indifferent.

We may begin to neglect our duties, and at first it will not be noticed by our brethren and neighbors, perhaps, but the longer we persist in such a course the further we will get from the true way, and the less desire we will have to hear or do anything concerning our eternal state. And if we persist in such a course, it will soon be seen and talked about by the world; they will see that we do not attend meeting as we formerly did, and the Church will observe that we absent ourselves from them when they assemble to worship our Father in Heaven; and if we were formerly instrumental members in the Church, we will now be a hindrance to the cause, and will not show by our fruits any good, but will appear as barren as the earth does at this time of the year.

Our desire for reading the Scriptures will become less, and we will perhaps begin to love to read novels or continued stories, and thereby lose the desire we once had for reading the Bible, the will of God.

Brethren and sisters, we cannot be too careful in this matter, for we can read, 2nd Peter 2: 20-21-22, the condition of those who have once turned their faces Zionward, and afterward become entangled in the pollutions of the world. I think if we are only willing to learn, and to know God's will all we can, and perform our duty as well as we know how, there would need be no fears of us becoming cold or negligent in this matter.

A. B. Lichtenwalter.

Thou preparest a table before me, in the presence of my enemies: Thou annointest my head with oil, my cup runneth over.

Youth's Department.

THE BATTLE OF LIFE.

Go forth to the battle of Life my boy,
Go while it is called to-day:
For the years go out, and the years come in,
Regardless of those who may lose or win
Of those who may work or play.

And the troops march steadily on my boy,
To the army gone before;
You may hear the sound of their falling feet,
Going down to the river where the two worlds meet;
They go to return no more.

There is room for you in the ranks my boy,
And duty, too assigned;
Step into the front with a cheerful grace,
Be quick, or another may take your place,
And you may be left behind.

There is work to do by the way, my boy,
That you never can tread again,
Work for the loftiest, lowliest men—
Work for the plow, adze, spindle and pen
Work for the hands and the brain.

The serpent will follow your steps my boy,
To lay for your feet a snare;
And pleasure sits in her fairy bowers,
With garlands of poppies and lotus flowers
Enwreathing her golden hair.

Temptations will wait by the way, my boy,
Temptations without and within;
And spirits of evil, in robes as fair
As the holiest angels in Heaven wear,
Will lure you to deadly sin

Then put on the armor of God, my boy,
In the beautiful days of youth;
Put on the helmet, breastplate and shield,
And the sword that the feeblest arm may wield
In the cause of Right and Truth.

And go to the battle of life, my boy,
With the peace of the gospel shod,
And before high heaven, do the best you can
For the great reward, for the good of man
For the kingdom and crown of God.
—*Little Sower.*

TO THE YOUNG.

Our blessed Savior said, "Suffer little children to come unto me and forbid them not, for of such is the kingdom of Heaven." I suppose we all know, that all those who die in their infancy will be received up into Heaven. I need not therefore talk to those the Savior had reference to, but to you who have left your infantile state, and have gone out into this sinful world.

Dear young reader let me warn you of some of the many dangers you are subject to. I would first try to impress upon your mind the great evil of intemperance. As you are starting out into this wide world of sin, intemperance will be about the first thing that may present itself before you. Let me warn you of the great sin of intemperance. It is one of the devil's best agents to lead the youth away from God; as he can draw you step by step by telling you there is no harm in taking a glass of strong drink, but let me tell you, kind reader, you may be led step by step, (which thousands are), down to degradation; down to a drunkard's grave; down to the confines of hell. Oh what an awful thought; be banished from the presence of God and all his holy angels forever, just for the sake of a few drops of poison to satisfy the craving appetite. Let me say to you dear young reader, whenever the temptation presents itself before you, always say, "Never a drop," and my word for it, you will never regret it when you grow up to man and womanhood.

Intemperance leads to the gambling saloon, to the many murders that are perpetrated now in our day. There are many other evils which the young, if not very careful, may be led into before they are aware of it. I would just here take occasion to say that the ball room, the festivals which are so common in our day and also the fairs and horse races which professors of religion take an active part in, and say there is no harm in it, but I would warn all young persons to stay away from such places, as they are an abomination in the sight of God. Then you may become useful men and women in this world, useful in the church, and finally reach the haven of rest.

Young readers, perhaps some of you have a little brother or sister in Heaven, whom you fondly loved. Would you not like to meet them there? Yes, I think you would. What a happy time that will be to meet our little brothers and sisters, fathers and mothers that have long gone before? They are inviting all to come and join them in that happy land where parting shall be no more forever.

We have but once to travel through this world, we should therefore make sure work, for if we miss Heaven we cannot retrace our steps. Then it will be too late, the door will be shut, then we will hear that awful sound, "depart from me ye cursed into everlasting fire prepared for the devil and his angels. Then let me say to you, "remember thy Creator in the days of thy youth before the evil days draw nigh."

There is another evil which I would wish to impress upon your minds, namely: pride (or fashion.) Dear young reader, I believe that pride is dragging thousands upon thousands down to a premature grave, yes, I will say down, down to the regions of dark despair, which were not prepared for boys and girls, neither for men and women, but for the devil and his angels. Be careful then that you are not debarred from the presence of God on account of decorating your body with all manner of foolishness, as it is an abomination in the sight of Almighty God.

In the last place, let me tell you how you can avoid all those things. Draw nigh to God and he has promised that he will draw nigh to you. Repent of your sins, believe you have so many to repent of, believe on the Lord Jesus Christ, and be baptized for the remission of your sins. Then you have the promise to receive the gift of the Holy Ghost. Let your light so shine before men, that others may see your good works, and glorify your Father which is in Heaven. The grace of God be with you all.

Greencastle, Pa.

LITTLE GEORGE'S TROUBLES.

Aunt Libby patted me on the head the other day and said, "George, my boy, this is the happiest part of your life."

I guess aunt Libby don't know much. I guess she never worked a week to make a kite, and the first time she went to fly it, got the tail hitched in a tall tree, whose owner would'nt let her climb up to disentangle it.

I guess she never broke one of the runners of her sled some Saturday afternoon when it was prime coasting. I guess she never had to give her biggest marbles to a great luberly boy, because he would thrash her if she did'nt.

I guess she never had him twitch off her best cap, and toss it into a mud-puddle. I guess she never had to give her humming top to quiet the baby, and have the paint all sucked off.

I guess she never saved all her pennies a whole Winter to buy a trumpet, and then was told she must not blow it, because it would make a noise! No; Aunt Libby don't know much. How should she? She never was a boy!—*Fanny Fern*

TOBACCO—A SPEECH FOR BOYS.

I go against tobacco, because it goes against me. I eschew it. I will not chew it. I will tell you why. 1st. I do not like the taste of it; it tastes worse than any medicine you can put to your lips, it is such sickening stuff. 2nd. I don't like the looks of it; when I see the tobacco I pity the mouth that chews it; and when I see the mouth that chews it, I pity the tobacco; it is of a dirty dirt-color. 3d. I don't like the effects of its use; it makes the teeth yellow and brown when they should be white; it makes the breath offensive when it should be sweet; it injures the voice so that those who chew cannot sing and speak to advantage. The voice breaks, and the chorister croaks like a raven when he should sing like a bobolink; the orator merely barks, and a tobacco bark is very disagreeable. 4th. I fear tobacco creates an appetite for liquor; it lights a fire in the throat which water may not put out.—*Bright Side.*

Surely goodness and mercy shall follow me, all the days of my life; and I will dwell in the house of the Lord forever.

Correspondence.

Report of the Treasurer of Middle District of Penna.

DICKENSON, PA.,
Jan. 21st, '73.

The former report published by me through the *Companion*, was made out and sent, on the 11th day of December, 1871. which report doth show the amounts of money which came into my hands, and the amounts paid out by me, for defraying the expenses of D. M. Holsinger while on his mission to Michigan.

The amounts received from the different churches up to Dec. 11th,	$122.23
Paid D. M. Holsinger,	95.35
Dec. 11, balance in my hands,	26 88
May 1, 1872, rec'd from Duncansville, Dunnings Creek, Upper Codorus and Marsh Creek churches the amount of	19 30
In my hands,	$46.18
May 1, 1872, paid to D. M. Holsinger $9.30 in receipts, $21.05 in money,	$30.35
Aug. 26, 1872, paid to same for expenses to meet the committee,	30.00
Paid out,	60.35
In hand,	46.18
Treasury short,	$14.17

I will also give a statement concerning the moneys received and paid out by me, for the travelling expenses of our representatives sent from the District Meeting to the A. M. as follows:

Received from the different churches up to May 31, 1871,	$87.25
Paid out at different times,	73.50
Balance left in my hands,	13.75
Rec'd from May 1, to June 15, 1872,	29.50
	43.25
May 24, sent to D. P. Saylor for expenses to Montgomery county,	$ 1 00
Solomon Garber expenses to Tenn.,	6.00
June 26, a check to J. R. Hanawalt exp's to A. M.	17.75
	24.75
In my hands,	$43 25
Paid out,	24.75
In my hands Jan. 21, '73.	$18.50

John W. Brumbaugh has not as yet, sent in his claim, so the churches of the Middle Penna. District, by this statement will see that this day, is a balance in my hands of only $[illegible]

I hope this statement will give satisfaction to those churches who asked me what their share to pay in was, but as to how much each district is to make up, I could not tell, so far, all used their own judgment, and those that did not pay in, for last years expenses, do know it. I hope so at least. DANIEL KELLER, SR.

Treas. of Middle Penn. Dist.

MIFFLINTOWN, PA., Jan. 27th, 1873.

Dear Pilgrim:—I would inform your readers that our series of meetings ended on the 20th. Brethren Daniel F. Good and Jacob Trostle were our ministers from a distance, and Brethren Wm. How and Archy Vandyke of Lewistown were also with us. They all labored faithfully as embassadors in Christ's stead, inviting sinners to turn to God and earnestly warning those who had covenanted with God to fear lest a promise being left them they might fall short.

The result of their labor was four precious souls were added to the Church by baptism, on last Sabbath, and many good impressions were made, so that some two or three more have made known their desire to be initiated into the Church militant. May the good Lord bless their labors with many souls for their hire. I would also add that Brother Trostle and Wm. How addressed the children in the Orphan's School at McCalisterville, giving them many wholesome instructions, such as were applicable to their age.

MICHAEL BESHOAR, SR.

CALVERSVILLE, Cumb. Co., Va., Dec. 30th, 1872.

Dear Pilgrim:—On the 14th of next February, it will be two years since we landed in this part of the country, and were the only brethren that ever had been in or through this part of Virginia. Now there are seven of us here. Next month two more expect to come, and some thirty or forty have visited this country during this time. All seemed to be well pleased, and they all acknowledged that there is as good or the best chance for brethren to colonize that they have ever saw. We had eleven meetings in nine months time. The people seemed to be well pleased with the preaching and general character of the Brethren. Yours in love,

WM. MALLORY.

Dear Pilgrim:—As there has nothing appeared in your columns from our district, I wish to say a few words that may be of some interest to your many readers.

Our Church, I think, is in a good and prosperous condition. A dozen or more were added to the Church during the last year.

On Saturday before Christmas we held a choice for a speaker at the house of Bro. and sister Hoff who have our thanks for kindness shown to all present. Eld. Jacob Berkey and two speakers from other districts were with us. Bros. Joseph Weaver and Joseph Eby were advanced to the second degree, and Bro. Benj. Fryfogle called to the ministry. Yours in truth. F. B.

Springfield District, Ind.

The follow we extract from a letter received from Eld. Geo. Wolf of Lathrop, Cal:

"Up to this date, January 20th, 1873, we have had the finest winter that I have seen in 16 years, since I have been in Cal. The mercury ranges at about 55 degrees above Zero, there was a few days in December at the coldest point, that the mercury fell to 16 degrees above Zero. The grass and grain-fields are green, stock does well, rain has fallen to wet the ground in the San Joaquin Valley two feet deep, a sufficient guarantee that we will have, (with our usual Spring rains) a bountiful harvest. Our seasons are more correctly named dry and wet, than summer and winter. We, like the Jews of Palestine, designate our rainy season by the early and latter rains. When the San Joaquin river overflows its banks by the 15th of February, it is a cause of rejoicing to us as well as it was to the Jews when their Jordan overflowed, as we will have a plentiful harvest.

Dear Pilgrim:—We are glad you are making your weekly visit to us again at the commencement of this year, and we also think you are very much improved, but how are you getting along in the way of getting your pay. Your Editors have been very generous and promise to wait those that have not the money at present, but is it right for those of us who could pay now just as well as at the end of the year, to take advantage of their generosity? They are at a heavy expense; their material has to be paid for, and their hands must be paid, and if they can't get money to meet expenses I fear you will have to stop, which we would regret very much, it is true, we sometimes see things in your columns that some of us think might as well be left out, but who of us could edit a paper and not make some mistakes, so we attribute the errors only to the head and not to the heart of the editors, and then it is also putting the agents to some trouble and inconvenience. The agent may receive two, three or five dollars which he will have to hold for a time, or ride probably 8 or 10 miles to get a check or postal order, and to send two dollars by postal order costs just as much as to send $20. Now friendly readers, what I have written I have written to stir up your pure minds by way of remembrance.

AGENT.

—Write for the PILGRIM, work for the increase of its circulation, and pray for its editors and contributors that it may be a power in favor of primitive Christianity.

MARRIED.

This notice was written on the same sheet of a private letter, and it being laid aside for future reference, the notice was overlooked. The parties will please excuse.

REDDIG—FUNK.—On the 12th of Dec., at the residence of the bride's parents, near Jacksonville, by the undersigned, Christopher Reddig, to Miss Catharine Funk, both of Cumberland Co., Pa.

SHADE—BASHOAR.—January 23d, at the residence of Bro. R. T. Myers, by Eld. P. S. Myers, Mr. B F. Shade, of Newton Hamilton, Pa., and sister Barbara Bashoar of Meyerstown, Pa.

SERENA MYERS.

DIED.

BAKER.—In the Union District, Marshall Co; Ind., Nov. 23d 1872, Emma Viola, daughter of brother Henry and sister Lucetta Baker, aged 3 years, 5 months and 15 days. Funeral sermon improved from Matt. 19; 13-14 by the writer.

WOLF.—Also, in the same district, January 13th '73, Catharine Fidily, daughter of brother Daniel and sister Catharine Wolf, aged 5 years, 8 months and 4 days. Funeral service improved from John 19; 20 by Eld. John Knisly and the writer.

ADAM APPLEMAN.

WHITER.—In the Jonathan's Creek Church, Ohio, some time in Febuary 1872 friend Thomas, husband of sister Catharine Whiter, of cancer in the stomach.

He suffered much, but like many others, put off his return to God and passed away, leaving a kind and affectionate wife and eight daughters, with other friends to mourn their loss. Funeral service by the writer.

HELSER.—Also in the same place, of spinal affection, on the 21st of April 1872, Hattie, youngest daughter of brother Levi and sister Catharine Helser, aged 7 years, 5 months and 5 days. She leaves father, mother, three sisters and three brothers behind, with many other friends to mourn their loss. Funeral service by the writer.

SNIDER.—Also in the same place, of old age, July 14th 1872, sister Elizabeth, wife of our old brother, elder Daniel Snider, aged 81 years, 4 months and 3 days.

She was afflicted a long time, but bore it with patience. Just one week before she died my wife and self went to visit her and other old persons were dying around her, and she made this remark, "Well that is the way it is, others can go, and I must still stay here. Oh well, perhaps my time will come too after while." Just one week from that day she died, and she died as she had lived, a consistent sister and very zealous. She was the mother of 8 children, 3 dead and 5 yet living, 38 grandchildren and upwards of 20 great grand-children. Though she is dead her example still lives among us. Funeral service by the writer.

HORN.—Also in the same Church, 13th of September 1872, Emma Jane, daughter of brother Daniel and sister Martha Horn, aged two years, 8 months and 21 days.

She leaves behind father, mother, brothers and sisters to battle with this world, but not long for some of them. Funeral service by the writer.

HORN.—Also in the same Church and of the same family, October 20th 1872, C. A. Horn, aged 8 months, and 29 days. Funeral service by the writer.

PLANK.—Also in the same Church, Oct. 12th, '72, sister Mary, wife of our old friend Adam Plank who fell dead some years ago, aged 73 years 9 mos. and 26 days.

She died at her son-in-laws, Bro. Peter Helser, where she had lived ever since her husband died. She had entirely lost her mind before she died. She leaves 3 brothers, 3 sisters, 4 sons and 3 daughters behind, besides many other friends. Funeral service by the writer.

LECKRONE.—Also in the same Church, Dec. 4th, 1872, brother Abraham Leckrone, aged 40 years, 10 months and 21 days, leaving an affectionate wife and one daughter, mother, brothers and sisters, and many friends and relatives to mourn his untimely departure.

The subject of this notice was confined to his bed for some months and suffered immensely, but bore it with Christian fortitude. He was a kind husband and father, a regular attendant at Church and a good neighbor. Funeral service by the writer.

COVER.—Also in the same Church and on the same day, our old and well known brother Samuel Cover, aged 71 years, 5 months and 26 days.

Brother Cover was always in a good humor and in good spirits. He was a very healthy man, but when disease took hold upon him, like many more, was compelled to go. I was sent for on the 5th of Dec., I went and stayed all night with him and in the morning, wrote his will and talked with him about his future prospects. He said he was ready and willing to go, that the Lord's will was his will in that as well as in all other matters. He leaves behind him a feeble but affectionate wife, a sister, one daughter, one grand-son and one great grand-son, all the family that is left.

VICKERS.—In the same Church on the 3d day of January '72, Joseph F., son of Bro. E. L. and sister Sarah Vickers, aged 11 months and 11 days. Funeral service by the writer.

Little Joseph thou art gone to rest,
While thy face we'll see no more;
Thy melodious voice is mingling with the blest,
On the farther shore.

WM. ARNOLD.

(*Visitor*, please copy the above obituaries.)

CARTER.—November 10th, 1872, in Union township, Sanjosquin Co., Cal. Benjamin Carter, aged 64 years. Funeral discourse by the writer from Matt. 24-44.

Friend Carter's remains lies in the Oak Grove Church Cemetery. Should his friends in the State of Wisconsin, see this notice, they can have the consolation of knowing that their friend and neighbor was highly respected here in Cal., and kindly cared for in a Christian-like manner, buried by his sons and neighbors. But kindness from relatives and friends cannot save us from the grave, for death hath all seasons and ages for his own.

REYNOLDS.—Also on the 28th day of December, 1872, Adaline, wife of Eldridge Reynolds, bid farewell, here below, to her husband, children and friends.

Her body sleeps in, and is the first bu in the new Cemetery, Union District, San-joaquin Co., California. Funeral discourse by the writer from 1st Cor., 15; 21-22-23

ELD. GEORGE WOLF.

MONEY LIST.

Samuel Miller	5.00
Eld John Knisley	2.75
David Bechtal	12.50
J S Snowberger	1.00
John A Clement	6.00
Jacob Arnsbarger	4.60
E S Miller	8.75
Daniel Bucher	1.50
Daniel Brower	1.50
Jno M Mohler	1.50
M Emma Rohrer	1.50
Samuel Musselman	.50
Engle & Bro	8.50
L H Dickey	16.20
Noah Flora	9.00
Wm H Boges	1.50
Eld David Bosserman	6.00
Thos Maddocks	1.70
Clara M Burket	1.50
John S Hull	1.25

John Ebie	1.50
Dan'l R Freeman	3.75
J D Blickenstaff	.75
Leonard Furry	20.00
Martin Garber	.50
T M Kauffman	.75
Danl W Stouffer	1.50
John Clingingsmith	1.50
Ed Raffe	4.05
Wm H Renner	9.45
Eld Jno Wise	12.50
Alma M Crouse	1.50
Jacob Link	1.50
Lewis Workman	7.00
Benj Hoover	4.25
A B Barnhart	1.50
V Reichard	15.00
Jonathan W Bleach	1.25
B F Moomaw	4.50
Wm Mallory	1.25
Lizzie F Miller	1.25
Marry Reddick	1.40
Jacob Mohler	1.50
Abraham Showalter	1.50
David W Shank	1.25
John Shank	4.25
Michael Youtzy	1.45
Mary Miller	1.50
L H. Dickey	1.25
D F Good	15.60
Michael Basboar	9.50
George Kinney	3.00
Libbie M Good	1.50
Israel Roop	4.50
John Rogers	1.50

The Weekly Pilgrim.

JAMES CREEK, PA., Jan. 28th. 1873.

☞ How to send money.--All sums over $1.50, should be sent either in a check, draft or postal order. If neither of these can be obtained, have the letter registered.

☞ When Money is sent, *always* send with it the name and address of those who paid it. Write the names and post office at plainly as possible.

☞ Every subscriber for 1873, gets a *Pilgrim Almanac* Free.

LET US BE REPRESENTED.

We have been making an effort to have the field of the Pilgrim enlarged and we are glad to learn that we are meeting with considerable success.

In addition to the list of States represented in No. 3, we now add New Hampshire and Washington Territory. The Pilgrim is now acknowledged by the religious press to be a first-class paper and is receiving favor from the same by way of "notices" for which we feel humbly grateful. The local press is also favoring us and we are especially indebted to the *West Carolina Record* for the favor conferred. This is a new paper published by Glendennin & Carpenter at Rutherfordton, N. C., at $2.00 per annum. Any of our readers interested in that part of the South, should read it.

The following States are not represented: Alabama, Arkansas, Connecticut, Delaware, Georgia, Louisiana, Mississippi, Rhode Island, South Carolina, Texas and Vermont. These we want represented by actual subscribers and we call upon our readers to help us. We have no doubt but what some of our readers have friends residing in all these States that would be benefitted by reading the Pilgrim a year. For this purpose it is sent for $1.25. Who shall we hear from first? We hope that in a short time, we can report a full representation. $1.25 is a small mite, yet for it, the Pilgrim can be sent and may be the means of opening new fields wherein much good may be accomplished. Our Church is getting alive to this way of introducing the truth and it is being blessed with good results. Let not your efforts be confined to the unrepresented States alone, but wherever there may be a door opened, let the Pilgrim go in.

OUR POOR LIST.

This list is so small that we almost forgot to publish it. Paper, ink and labor costs us money, and we cannot afford to give it away a particle better than the farmer can his corn and wheat, or the merchant his goods, yet we almost daily receive the names of such as are too poor to pay anything. Now brethren and sisters, what would you do? We have booked every name that has been sent in and are sending the Pilgrim just the same as if paid for. We do this first, because we cannot think of depriving the poor of the pleasure it affords them in reading it, and secondly, with the hope that some of our open-hearted brethren and sisters will assist us by donating a small amount for that purpose. The following was sent in for that purpose. This does not include those who sent in $1.25 to have it sent to their friends or such poor as they named themselves.

POOR LIST.

J. D. Rosenberger,	.50
A. P. Miller,	25
Daniel Back,	$1.50
Catharine Cline,	25

PERSONAL.

Jacob Mohler. You are right.

M. B. Hymnbooks sent by mail $4. 50.

Jno. Plank. You did not send Sarah Latimer's name. It is now booked and will come all right.

Israel Roop. We have been sending the Pilgrim to Geo. Dickey, Omer P. O. Seneca Co. Ohio. If that is not right, let us know.

Jno. S. Newcomer. Your name was overlooked in entering the new books. It is now entered and marked paid to No. 12. Is that right The tracts are sent again--had been sent before.

Wm. A. Murray.--Your last list is received and the Pilgrims are sent—The Tune Book is sent.

Correction.—At the end of Eld. B. F. Moomaw's article of this week the word "concluded" was placed instead of "continued," and part of the issue run off before it was noticed. We have now another paper on hands for next week and will still be continued.

D. W. Shank. We received $1. 25. Please notice the Pilgrim is $1. 50 The Almanac is sent.

Eld. Jno. Nicholson informs us that while cutting wood his ax glanced and cut his foot so badly that he will not be able to attend to his appointments for some time.

Your list and contribution did not reach us.

Bro. John W. Gish of Troutville Va. says; "We are having some very rough weather and considerable sickness, especially among the aged, among whom there has been a number of deaths. We are still well-pleased with the Pilgrim and hope it may continue to improve as it certainly has been since its commencement."

Lewis Workman. You say you sent us $7. 00 and gave us only three names that you say have paid, who is the $2. 50 for? Please inform us as it is important that we should know. In sending money always inform to whom it is to be credited.

Bro. D. D. Shively informs us that the brethren of Oak Haw church Ill., on the 25th of Dec. held a choice for deacon which resulted in the election of Bro. John Arnold to that office.

Also on the 27th. of the same month the brethren of Millmine Church held a choice for the same purpose, and brethren Daniel Mohler and Solomon S. Miller were chosen.

All Subscriptions must commence with the beginning of the year as long as we have back Nos. and *Almanacs* to supply the demand. We cannot afford to send the *Almanac* unless the Pilgrim is taken for a full year. We can still supply a goodly number with full Nos. Send along the new subscribers by the scores and by the help of God we will make the Pilgrim a power in the church and the world for good.

TO ALL WHO ARE CONCERNED.

We do, through this medium, inform the brethren and churches comprising the first district of Virginia, that Friday and Saturday before the fourth Sunday in April, is the time appointed for the holding of the Annual District Meeting, and will be held at that time no preventive providence, at the Valley Meeting-house in Botetourt Co., one mile south of Amsterdam. A full attendance is desirable. B. F. Moomaw.

LITERARY NOTICES.

Potter's Complete Bible Encyclopedia.—We are in receipt of a specimen Leaf of this recent and valuable work. If the "specimen" represents the work which it no doubt does, it will be a magnificent volume and will be a great addition to our religious literature. It is published by John G. Potter &Co. 917 Sansom St. Philada.

Trine Immersion Traced to the Apostles.—The first edition of this instructive and interesting work is exhausted and a copy of the 2nd. edition is on our table. The author, J. H. Moore informs us that he now has on hand a large supply and is prepared to fill all orders. This is a good work and should be circulated by the thousands. For price &c., see advertisement on last page.

The *Science of Health* though only a short time before the public, has gained a world-wide reputation, which it richly deserves. For the mass, it is the leading health journal of the United States, having for its motto, *Nature's remedial agencies are light, air, temperature' electricity, diet, bathing, sleep, exercise and rest.* All those wishing to enjoy long life and good health should read it. Published by S. R. Wells 389, Broadway, New York, at $2. 00 per annum.

Phrenological Journal for February is on our table, which, as usual, is fully up to its standard, and contains so many good things that we have not the space to enumerate all of them. There is no other publication comes to our office that we prize so highly. Each number contains from 70 to 80 pages of information for everybody. We notice that the publisher offers a premium of a new Chromo to new subscribers who send 30 cts. extra for postage and mounting. Published by S. R. Wells, 389 Broadway, N. Y., at $3.00 per annum.

We have made arrangements to send the Pilgrim and the *Phrenological Journal* together for $3.50. Those who have sent us $1.50 for the Pilgrim can have the *Journal* by sending $2.00 more. Sample copies sent on the receipt of stamp to pay postage.

Vick's Floral Guide for 1873. —The Guide is now published quarterly. 25 cents pays for the year, four numbers, which is not half the cost. Those who afterwards send money to the amount of one dollar or more for seeds may also order 25 cts. worth extra—the price paid for the Guide.

The January number is beautiful, giving plans for making Rural Homes designs for Dining Table Decorations, Window Gardens, &c., and containing a mass of information invaluable to the lover of flowers.—One Hundred and fifty pages, on fine tinted paper, some five hundred engravings and a superb colored plate and Chromo cover.—The first edition of 200,-000 just printed in English and German, and ready to send out.

James Vick, Rochester, N. Y.

GENERAL INTELLIGENCE.

HOW MUCH.

There is sufficient quantity of fermented and distilled liquors used in the United States, in one year, to fill a canal four feet deep, fourteen feet wide, and one hundred and twenty miles in length. The places where intoxicating drinks are made and sold in this country, if placed in rows, in direct lines, would make a street one hundred miles in length. If the victims of the rum traffic were there also we should see a suicide at every mile, and a thousand funerals a day. If the drunkards of America could be placed in a procession, five abreast, they would make an army one hundred miles in length. What an army of victims! Every hour in the night, the heavens are lighted with the incendiary torch of the drunken. Every hour in the day, the earth is stained with the blood shed by drunken assassins. See the great army of inebriates, more than a million strong, marching on to sure and swift destruction—filing off rapidly into the poor-houses and prisons, and on to the scaffold; and yet the ranks are constantly filled by the moderate drinker. Who can compute the fortunes squandered, the hopes crushed, the hearts broken, and the homes made desolate by drunkenness?—*Christian at work.*

THE LICENSE QUESTION.

The act passed by the last Legislature, and signed by Gov. Geary, prescribed that once every three years the citizens of the various counties shall vote upon the question of "license" or "no license." If, upon counting the votes, the majority in any county are in favor of no license then it shall not be lawful for the court of said county to grant any license for the sale of spirituous and intoxicating liquor during those three years. The first vote upon this question is to be taken at the Spring election coming. It will be noticed that the law does not call for a vote by election districts, as some suppose, but that the whole county is to be consulted whether or not liquor shall be sold within its limits. Which will we do, vote in favor of these hell houses, where our children are made drunkards, by staying at home, or go and vote it down? The issue is at stake and the decision will be made. Taverns or no taverns, that is the question.

The Weekly Pilgrim.

Published by J. B. Brumbaugh, & Co.
Edited by H. B. & Geo. Brumbaugh.
CORRESPONDING EDITORS.
D. P. Sayler, Double Pipe Creek, Md.
Leonard Furry, New Enterprise, Pa.

The *Pilgrim* is a Christian Periodical, devoted to religion and moral reform. It will advocate in the spirit of *love* and *liberty*, the principles of true Christianity, labor for the promotion of peace among the people of God, for the encouragement of the saints and for the conversion of sinners, avoiding those things which tend toward disunion or sectional feelings.

TERMS.

Single copy, Book paper,	$1.50
Eleven copies, [eleventh for Agt.]	$15.00

Any number above that at the same rate.

Address,
H. B. BRUMBAUGH.
James Creek,
Huntingdon county Pa.

The Weekly Pilgrim.

"REMOVE NOT THE ANCIENT LANDMARKS WHICH OUR FATHERS HAVE SET."

VOL. 4. JAMES CREEK, PENNSYLVANIA, FEBRUARY, 11, 1873. NO. 6

POETRY.

THE CHRISTIAN'S FATHERLAND.

BY DEAN STANLEY.

Where is the Christian's Fatherland?
Is it the Holy Hebrew Land?
In Nazareth's vale, on Zion's steep,
Or by the Galilean deep?
Where pilgrim hosts have rushed to lave
Their stains of sin in Jordan's wave,
Or sought to win by brand or blade,
The tomb wherein their Lord was laid?

Where is the Christian's Fatherland?
Is it the haunted Grecian strand,
Where Apostolic wanderer's first
The yoke of Jewish bondage burst?
Or where, on many a mystic page,
Byzantine prelate, Coptic sage,
Fondly essayed to intertwine
Earth's shadows with the light Divine?

Or is the Christian's Fatherland
Where, with crowned head and croziered hand,
The Ghost of Empire proudly flits
And on the grave of Cæsar sits?
Oh! by those world-embracing walls,
Oh! in those vast and pictured halls,
Oh! underneath that soaring dome,
Shall this not be the Christian's home?

Where is the Christian's Fatherland?
He still looks on from land to land—
Is it where German conscience woke
When Luther's lips of thunder spoke?
Or where, by Zurich's shore, was heard
The calm Helvetian's earnest word?
Or where, beside the rushing Rhone,
Stern Calvin reared his unseen throne?
Or where, from Sweden's snows came forth
The stainless hero of the north?

Or is there yet a closer band—
Our own, our native Fatherland?
Where Law and Freedom, side by side,
In Heaven's behalf have gladly vied?
Where prayer and praise for years have rung
In Shakspeare's accents, Milton's tongue,
Blessing with cadence sweet and grave,
The fireside nook, the ocean wave,
And o'er the broad Atlantic hurled,
Wakening to life another world?

No, Christian! no—not even there,
By Christmas hearth or churchyard dear;
Nor yet on distant shore brought nigh,
Nor Western Pontiff's lordly name,
Nor eastern Patriarch's hoary fame—
Nor e'en where shone sweet Bethlehem's star;
Thy Fatherland is wider far.

Thy native home is wheresoe'er
Christ's Spirit breathes a holier air;
Where Christ-like faith is keen to seek
What Truth or Conscience freely speak;
Where Christ like Love delights to span
The rents that sever man from man;
Where, round God's throne, His just ones stand—
There, Christian, is thy Fatherland.

ORIGINAL ESSAYS.

"THE BAPTISM OF JOHN, WHENCE WAS IT, FROM HEAVEN OR OF MEN?"

BY B. F. MOOMAW.

In support of the position that we have taken, and for the establishment of the principle contained therein, we next propose to present from the Bible, facts and circumstances there delineated.

First, we will briefly notice the command to Adam in Eden, setting forth his privileges and restrictions, thus commanding and saying to the man, "of every tree of the garden thou mayest *freely* eat, except the tree of knowledge of good and evil thou shalt not eat of it, for in the day thou eatest thereof thou shalt surely die." Gen. 2: 16-17. There was no possibility of being mistaken as to Divine authority of this command, as to the tendency and terrible consequences that would result from the want of a proper regard of this divine injunction, terrible consequences indeed! His expulsion from the lovely garden with all its comforts and luxuries; the withdrawal of God's presence; the cessation of those interviews in the dawn of the morning and in the twilight of the evening; the earth cursed for his sake; exiled to combat the thistles and thorns, to struggle for a subsistance until the seeds of death should be developed in the production of its legitimate fruits and he return to the earth, only to be succeeded by following generations, who in their turn, witness in sorrow and pain, the incalculable miseries that have been, now are, and shall be endured by poor fallen and suffering humanity in this world and by the impenitent in the world to come. All this because of yielding to the insidious temptation of the enemy and becoming dissatisfied with the ways and means of God—presumed to depart from them, and devise measures of his own. Oh fearful responsibility! awful presumption, and yet we have not profited by his sad experience, but as in very many instances, upon the presentation of theories of men, human origin, adopt them, without, as it appears, stopping to enquire "whence they are, of God or of men."

Secondly, We propose to examine the institution of the Sabbath, to see if we can arrive to any safe conclusion as to "from whence it is," then "to the law and to the testimony." In the history of the world's creation we learn, that on the seventh day, God ended His work which He had made, and rested on the seventh day from all His work which He had made. And God blessed the seventh day and sanctified it, because that in it He had rested from all His work which He had created and made. Gen. 2: 3 4. From this expression "sanctified it" which, in one sense means to set apart, we understand that God designed, as He had rested from His work, it should be consecrated to some special purpose and observed differently from the other six days; this conclusion is fully warranted by the many references and commands subsequently given relative to it, which we proceed to notice. See Ex. 16: 4-5. The Lord promised that for the children of Israel "He would rain bread from Heaven," and the people should go out and gather a certain rate every day, that He might prove them, whether they would walk in His law or not, and that on the sixth day they should gather twice as much as upon other days, doubtless for the reason that there should be no gatherings on the Sabbath 22 verse. And he said unto them, this is that which the Lord hath said, Tomorrow is the rest of the Holy Sabbath unto the Lord. And Moses said, eat that to-day, for to day is a Sabbath unto the Lord, to day ye shall not find it in the field. Six days ye shall gather it, but on the seventh which is the Sabbath, in it there shall be none. Six days shalt thou labor and do all thy work, but the seventh day is the Sabbath of the Lord thy God, in it thou shalt not do any work, thou nor thy son, nor thy daughter, thy man-servant nor thy maid-servant, nor thy cattle, nor thy stranger within thy gates, for in six days the Lord made Heaven and earth, the sea and all things that in them is, and rested the seventh day, wherefore the Lord blessed the Sabbath day and hallowed it." Exodus 20; 9-11. The same law reiterates 23: 12, see also 31: 12-17 the same law enjoined, accompanied with terrible denunciations, (refer to the passage as it too lengthy for insertion here.) See also Levit. 19: 30 "Ye shall keep my Sabbaths and reverence my sanctuary, I am the Lord." "And the Lord spake unto Moses saying speak unto the children of Israel and say unto them concerning the feasts of the Lord, which ye shall proclaim to be holy convocations, even these are my feasts. Six days shall work be done, but the seventh day is the Sabbath of rest an holy convocation, ye shall do no work therein, it is the Sabbath of the Lord in all your dwellings." Levit. 23: 1-3. The Lord having so positively commanded the observance of this institution and so frequently called the attention of his people to it, that it was impossible that they could misunderstand it, or be mistaken as to "from whence it came;" that it was the height of presumption to neglect or violate it. Hence when one was found in the camp of Israel, picking up sticks on the Sabbath, the Lord visited upon him summary punishment, and in order that their memories should be constantly refreshed commanded that a fringe should be put upon their garment, with a ribbon of blue, that they might look upon it and remember all the commandments of the Lord and do them, that they should not seek after their own heart and their own eyes. "That ye may remember and do all my commandments, and be holy unto your God. I am the Lord your God which brought you out of the land of Egypt, to be your God, I am the Lord your God." Num. 15: 37-41. For further testimony as to the obligation of keeping, and the awful consequences of neglecting it, we refer to Neh. 13: 16-18; Jer. 17: 25, and Ezek. 20: 16, 17.

We are thus particular in adducing testimonies so copiously, to impress the mind with the leading idea designed by this effort, that God's requirements of His intelligent creatures are clearly, definitely and fully expressed, that every thing that we are authorized to do is so plain that we may easily know "from whence it is, whether it be of God or of men."

To be Continued.

THE DESIGN OF BAPTISM.

Baptism is a command of the New Testament, and one of the many given as a means for our reconciliation with God. It is acknowledged by all professors of religion as far as I know that we are in an unreconciled state, those at least who are grown to a mature age, and know good from evil, and have transgressed the Law of God. We admit that, through the death of Christ we were reconciled from under the curse of a broken Law, so that the redemption holds good on the infantile part of the human family. They shall be saved through the merits of a crucified Redeemer, but for those who have grown to adult age and stepped out from under its protection, they will not be benefited by the redemption. There is, however, a code of Laws given for such that, by a proper use of the faculty, and a strict adherence to the letter of the law, may again enjoy the benefits and the glory God intended them to enjoy. And in order that we should be without excuse in the matter, he was very emphatic, thus clearly setting forth our obligations to him and no one need be deceived that desires the true knowledge of God, for it was given in plain simple language, so that high and low, rich and poor could all have the benefit of it. In proof of this, we need only show that it was given to poor humble fisherman at first for them to sow broadcast in the world. That there is a great principle involved in this, you may easily see, for had he given it to the high and opulent, the lowly not having such advantages or means of learning, they would not had any equal chance, and more than this, they would have been despised and looked down upon and perhaps thrust out of the synagogue as unworthy of being members of the family of God.

By reading the scriptures, you see among the great and noble, a disposition of pride manifested almost always. The all-wise God well knew that the evil nature in man would cause him to drift in that direction and hence the course which he pursued is undoubtedly the best, and even under this state of things, how often do we read, "Humble yourselves," and how both we are to do it.

That item in the great code of laws which we have under consideration at present, called baptism, we want to know what it was designed for. Above we have said, that the law was given in emphatic language. Then, can we not understand it? Surely we can, if we feel so disposed. Why then is there such a controversy about it? While one says it is only a cloak thrown around the economy of grace, another says it signifies something it does not. I hope none need fear the light of the gospel which God has been pleased to give us. "The gift of God is eternal life through Jesus Christ our Lord." God saw that man had not the means to purchase eternal life, therefore he sent his Son to present it to us as a gift. Now will we accept it as he gave it or will we try to make amendments to better suit our peculiar fancy? The form was drawn up in the Court of Heaven. The legislators of Heaven are the law-making power and, reader, let me assure you, you cannot alter or amend it, and the Savior has said, "not one jot or tittle of the law shall fail until all be fulfilled. Now that law was entrusted to trust-worthy men. Although humble fishermen, they were inspired, which empowered them to fulfill the design, and they were sent out to preach, that is, to tell the people what this law consisted of, and in what relation they stood thereunto, and those that believed, to them gave he the power to become the sons of God. Then faith in the word preached, is the first great principle, for if we will come to God we must first believe that he is, and that he is a rewarder of them that diligently seek him. This will bring us to the second step, which is repentance, and the third step is baptism. In obeying that command we promise God before men, that we will be faithful until death, and receive the promise of the gift of the Holy Spirit. By these three great and first principles in the economy of grace, we are initiated into the visible Church of the living God, the pillar and ground of truth. Now we ask, is this the order of the organic law of the Lord? Let us examine the inspired penman and see. Upon their testimony, we can build our hope with safety, and upon no other, for Paul says: "Though an angel from Heaven preach any other gospel than that which we have preached let him be accursed." The force of this language should be apparent to all.

After the resurrection of Jesus Christ he gave his commission to his disciples and said, "Go into all the world, teach all nations baptizing them in the name of the Father and of the Son and of the Holy Ghost teaching them to observe all things whatsoever I have commanded you, and lo, I am with you alway even unto the end of the world." This commission was the most important ever given to man, and for the faithful discharge of their duty he says again: "tarry at Jerusalem until you be indued with power from on high." They did not have to wait very long for that extra gift, and what did that bring to our view? There was a great, wonderful and magnificent scene—about an hundred and twenty disciples gathered together in one place, demonstrations from Heaven appeared, a rushing mighty wind which filled the house where they were sitting, and cloven tongues as of fire sat upon each of them and they were all filled with the Holy Ghost and began to speak with other tongues as the spirit gave them utterance."

When this curious phenomenon became noised abroad the multitude came together, and so the wonderful works of God began. But some mocked and said, "these men are full of new wine, but Peter stood up with the eleven and said, these are not drunken as ye suppose for it is only the third hour of the day; but is that which is spoken of by the prophet Joel." It is an outpouring of the spirit. He preached to them with power, clearly showing them that that Jesus whom they crucified had become both Lord and Christ, and on that account, these things were demonstrated before them and for their good. Their eyes were opened and they said to Peter and to the rest of the Apostles, "men and brethren what shall we do," an important question which required an answer, a direct answer, and in such language that they could understand. "Then Peter said unto them, repent and be baptized every one of you in the name of Jesus Christ for the remission of sins and ye shall receive the gift of the Holy Ghost," for the promise is to such. The promise of what? If you repent and be baptized you shall obtain the forgiveness of your sins, and according to Paul to the Gallatians 3d chapter, "put on Christ." For he says: "as many of you as have been baptized into Christ have put on Christ."

This is one of the many texts given for our instruction, showing us what the design of baptism is and what it will accomplish when done in the name of the Lord, with a full purpose of heart which can be testified to by many living witnesses and gives us the answer of a good conscience toward God.

To be Continued.

FIFTY YEARS AGO AND NOW.

Our sons and daughters are dressed as the sons and daughters of the world, and it does not stop here but we see it among the members. Why has all this come upon us? The only thing I see is we done it ourselves. We dressed our children after the world's vain fashion as long as we had the dressing of them, and they know no better than to keep on dressing fashionable when they have to dress themselves, and when they become members of the Church, the cross is too heavy for them to bear, that was not the case fifty years ago. They were brought up bearing the cross, and the burden was light. Is there any one especially to blame for all this? No, some commenced it and the rest of us let them go on in it until church members are unknown by their plain apparel. Sisters have on their heads the fashionable bonnet or hat instead of the plain cap, brethren also have on, fashionable coats, overcoats, hats, &c. Now dear brethren and sisters, have we not got too far from the meek and lowly Savior? If we have not got the spirit of fashionable dressing and pride, and really have the spirit of the meek and humble Jesus in our hearts, let us take down our signs that indicate pride and fashion. We all know when we pass through a city we judge the houses by the signs that we see posted above the doors, and so we may be judged by our signs of not living up to what we profess, and for fear of being judged wrong in this matter, let us take down the old man's sign, and put up the one that belongs to the Kingdom of Jesus. We need a reformation in this very thing, and how to do it without all are willing to reform I know not, unless we are willing to forsake the rudiments of the world and return to our first love by becoming more humble, and walking after the pattern as given by Jesus and exemplified by our forefathers. To accomplish this we must strive to keep in the spirit, and glory in the cross of Christ, and the God of our salvation, and not care about the outward adorning of our bodies, but more for the hidden man of the heart. How can we take the yoke of Christ upon us and instead of learning of Him, learn of the world, and instead of following our blessed Master, follow all the vain and sinful fashions of the world? I once felt sorry for a sister in the church, who raised five or six daughters, dressing them in height of fashion from little girls up to womanhood. The burden of her grief was that they went and joined a fashionable church that would require no change in dress. She said to me, "Bro. Andrew, I am so distressed I do not know what to do, three of my daughters have joined the ——, and father said, "I know there is no good there as there is nothing but pride and fashion in that church," O, brother Andrew, pray for my children." There I learned a lesson. If that good sister and brother had prayed for their daughters, and taught them to pray for themselves, and had not brought them up in the sinful fashion of the world and in pride, it might have been quite different. They trained them up to be the very subjects to become members of just such a church. They done all themselves. It is as easy to raise and train our children to become good members of the true church of Christ, as a fashionable one and much easier. "Train up a child in the way he should go, and when he is old he will not depart from it." That is the way with us, the most of our troubles are brought on us by ourselves, by wanting our children to look like other people's children, and they very often keep on looking and doing like other people. But to see if ever we can get back to our primitive purity again, is what those brethren wished to know. In the first place, we must get right ourselves and then keep the little ones right, in the cradle, and after they get out of it, train them in the nurture and admonition of the Lord, which is the only way that is right. Pray with our children and teach them that good and acceptable way of the Lord. In that way we may get back again into the old land-marks which our fathers have set up by the help of the Lord. But I never expect to see it, for I believe that the time of the coming of Christ is approaching, for as it was in the days of Noah so shall it be when the Son of man shall come. He also asked the question "When the Son of man comes, shall he find faith on the earth," a living faith of the righteous, the salt that preserves the earth? May our God enable us all to strive to enter in at the strait gate.

A. J. Correll.

Forest City, Mo.

GERMAN PAMPHLET.

The following is the Title and Preface of a little Pamphlet, written in the German language fifty years ago by a worthy brother in Virginia, supposed to be Ben. B.—who for the sake of delicacy, withheld his name. It is in my possesion, and as I believe few to be found; and as we see the truth verified, fifty years hence, of that part, at least, as regards the establishment of Christ's Kingdom by men, the undersigned would like to see it reprinted.

How much was accomplished in that period, towards a union of Christian denominations, and what success had men in bringing about universal peace upon earth? Experience will answer. Have we not seen, in these fifty years, denominations divided and sub-divided again and again, nations in commotion, kingdoms rent and others formed, subjects rebell against their leaders and government, causing the earth to be deluged with human blood? Now as the German is so little used among the Fraternity, the undersigned proposes through the Pilgrim to translate this work into the English language and have it printed, provided the brethren desire it, and are willing to help to bear the burden. It contains fifty small pages. Let us hear through the Pilgrim what you have to say, brethren. The work is worthy to be reprinted. Let us hear *soon* from every part of the brotherhood. A few words will do, for instance; approved or disapproved.

Yours in the bonds of Christian Union.

Leonard Furry.

TITLE.

A short and simple representation from the word of God, of the apostacy in the last time—and of the great tribulation under the beast of Antichrist—and ingatherings of the Elect to the Great Supper—of the conversion of the Jews—and of the general Judgment. Written by a lover of the Truth divine. Presented for consideration to all who seek their salvation. "Prove all things; hold fast that which is good." "Abstain from all appearance of evil." 1st Thess. 5:21-22.

PREFACE.

The reason of this little work is only as a warning to those who seek their salvation; since we have come into perilous times; sin, which is a lofty spirit of pre-eminence, has arisen, whose object is to unite and subdue all men under one head, as the beginning of the Millennial Reign of Christ, which is in opposition to the humble mind of Christ, and against the Holy Scriptures as this little tract shows. And yet there are many drawn from the Truth and thereby deceived, for Christ, through His own power without any human help shall establish *This Kingdom.* Therefore it is a deception and every effort of men shall fail. For this reason ought every one, *prove the spirits,* for Christ saith, "By the fruit ye shall know the tree."

Written in the year of the Lord 1823.

For the Pilgrim.

ASHAMED OF JESUS.

Shall we poor mortals, ever be ashamed of one who is far our superior, who holds the brittle cord of our existence, and on whom all our hopes of Heaven depend? But oh! how slow are we to yield submission to His holy word. What love He has shown toward us. He is ever willing to stand by us, to pardon our shortcomings, and how many of them we have. Have any of us such a forgiving spirit? I am afraid not, but let us try to have: let not the sun go down on our wrath toward any one. When the woes of life overtake us, and all hopes begin to fail, when all seems one dark cloud before us, there is one whose love never fails, always ready to comfort us. Let us never from His precepts depart, but strive every day with renewed energy to walk nearer to God—be this our highest aim.

I often wonder how many of us will be able to stand that judgment which awaits us at the last day. Could it then our glory be that Christ be not ashamed of us. Every day brings us closer to our eternal home than ever we have been before; yet how seldom do we think of it. We are swiftly sailing o'er lifes ocean and soon may we reach that eternal shore. Many changes have taken place during the last year; many loved ones have gone who at the beginning of the year, had as good prospects for a long life as you or I, but they are gone. Their gentle voice is stilled. May they be so fortunate as to obtain the heirship, that awaits the faithful. Let us wherever we go, show to the world by our conversation and dress, that we are not of the world, but that our calling is of a nobler one, and that we have set out to win the prize. God's promises are sure, His word shall stand when Heaven and earth shall pass away. How careful ought we to live. Are we letting our light shine that others may see our good works? Much is required of us. We have enlisted in a great warfare. Jesus is our captain and we are all soldiers under Him. Let us have our lamps well trimmed and full of oil, that we be not as the foolish virgins, who took no oil with them, and came and said, Lord open unto us, but the door was shut. He answered and said, "Verily I say unto you I know you not," but that it may be said, "Come ye blessed of my Father inherit the kingdom prepared for you from the foundation of the world." Happy thought!

M. E. Good.

Waynesboro, Pa.

THE LICENSE QUESTION

Dear Pilgrim:—I noticed in the *Companion*, a communication written by Eld. M. Miller in regard to the License Law which meets my approbation. This law has, for a long time been agitated in the state of Pa. on account of the evils of intemperance or the excession of spirituous liquors and the great evils resulting therefrom and firstly has been passed by the Legislature of 1872 in favor of Local Option or that each county, or its citizens, shall have the privilege of voting for license or no license. This privilege will be granted on the 21st day of March, 1873. The issue is a plain one for good or evil, but I do not intend to write much on the subject wishing merely to call the attention of the brethren in Pa. to this important matter. Perhaps many others, like myself, have not done as much for the cause as we should and as this seems to be an opportunity for us all to do good, it becomes us to give our influence in favor of that which may result in the moral and spiritual good of of the citizens of our state.

Viewing it in this light, dear brethren; would it not be well to give all timely notice of this chance to do good, if good there be in it, which I have no doubt there will if we cast our vote *for good.* Would it not be wisdom in the church of Pa. at their council meetings or otherwise to inform their members of this election, the design of it, and the beneficial results that are expected to be realized therefrom, so that all may be properly informed and thus enabled to vote intelligently and in favor of temperance?

May the Lord guide us to do his will in this as well as everything else we do.

Yours in love,

Samuel Myers, Sr.

WAYSIDE THOUGHTS.

An ounce of cheerfulness is worth a pound of sadness to serve God with.—*Fuller.*

What gift has Providence bestowed on man that is so dear to him as his children?—*Cicero.*

The Scriptures teach us the best way of living, the noblest way of suffering and the most comfortable way of dying.—*Flavel.*

A man that exhausts his energies endeavoring to pull down the enterprise, and destroy the character of his brother, will have nothing left to build up his own.—*Bastus.*

A man is the architect of His own future, so he is the author of all his "miseries," and men should not complain because they have dyspepsia and suffer, so long as they persist in using tobacco and gormandizing.—*Bastus.*

Our best hours are those we spend to our best interest, and the more of them we spend thus, the greater will be our future inheritance. If we sow to the flesh, we shall of the flesh, reap corruption, but if to the spirit, eternal life. Let us spend our hours in sowing to the spirit and enjoy our inheritance in reaping life eternal.—*B*[illegible].

Moments.—Moments well spent are the golden sands of life, each bright and valuable, and when cemented together, in the crucible of God's love, by the blood of a crucified Redeemer, make a treasure, safely laid up in heaven, of value a thousand times more precious than all the diamonds or gold of earth.

Moments unimproved are so many atoms of rust, that on a dying bed produce that terrible canker—remorse of conscience, which sets on fire the soul with the burnings of hell!—*J. S. Flory.*

CHRIST THE MERCY.

FLAVEL.

Continued from last week.

3. Is Christ the mercy of mercies infinitely better than all other mercies? Then let all that are in Christ be contented and well satisfied, whatsoever other mercies the wisdom of God sees fit to deny them, you have Benjamin's portion, a plentiful inheritance in Christ; will you yet complain? Others have splendid houses upon earth, but you have "an house not made with hands, eternal in the heavens." 2 Cor. 5: 1. Others are clothed with rich and costly apparel; your souls are clothed with the white pure robes of Christ's righteousness. "I will greatly rejoice in the Lord, my soul shall be joyful in my God; for He hath clothed me with the garment of salvation, He hath covered me with the robe of righteousness, as a bridegroom decketh himself with ornaments, and as a bride adorneth herself with her jewels." Isa. 61: 10. Let those that have full tables, heavy purses, rich lands, but no Christ, be rather objects of your pity than envy. God has not a better mercy to give than Christ, thy portion; in Him all necessary mercies are secured to thee, and thy wants and straits sanctified to thy good. O, therefore never open thy mouth to complain against the bountiful God.

4. Is Christ the mercy, in whom are all the tender mercies of God towards poor sinners? Then let none be discouraged in going to Christ by reason of their sin and unworthiness, His very name is mercy, poor, drooping sinner, encourage thyself in the way of faith; the Savior to whom thou art going is mercy itself to broken-hearted sinners moving towards Him. Jesus Christ is so merciful to poor souls that come to Him, that He has received and pardoned the chiefest of sinners—men that stood as remote from mercy as any in the world Tim. 1: 15; 1 Cor. 6: 11. Those that shed the blood of Christ have yet been washed in that blood from their sin. Acts 2: 36, 37. Mercy receives sinners without exception of great and heinous ones. "If any man thirst, let him come unto me and drink." Gospel invitations run in general terms to all sinners that are heavy laden. Math. 11: 28. When Mr. Bilney the martyr heard a minister preaching in this manner: "O, thou old sinner, who hast been serving the devil these fifty or sixty years, dost thou think that Christ will receive thee now?" O, said he, what a preaching of Christ is here; had Christ been thus preached to me in the day of my trouble for sin what glad tidings had it been: blessed be God. There is a sufficiency both of merit and mercy in Jesus Christ for all sinners, for the vilest among them whose hearts shall be made willing to come unto Him. So merciful is the Lord Jesus Christ that he moves first, Isa. 61: 1, 2; So merciful that he upbraids none. Ezek. 18: 22. So merciful that he will not despise the weakest desires of souls if sincere. Isa. 42: 3; So merciful that nothing more grieves him than our unwillingness to come unto Him for mercy. John 5: 40; So merciful that he waiteth to the last upon sinners to show them mercy, Rom. 10: 21; Math. 23: 37; in a word, so merciful that it is his greatest joy when sinners come unto Him that He may show them mercy. Luke 15 5: 22.

Objection. But it cannot enter into my thoughts that I should obtain mercy.

Answer. You measure God by yourself; "If a man find his enemy, will he let him go well away?" 1 Sam 24: 19. Man will not, but the merciful God will upon the submission of His enemies to Him, besides you are discouraged because you have not tried. Go to Jesus Christ, poor, distressed sinner; try Him, and then report what a Savior thou hast found Him to be.

Object. But I have neglected the time of mercy, and now it is too late.

Ans. How know you that? Have you seen the book of life, or turned over the records of eternity? Or are you unwarrantably intruding into the secrets of God which belong not to you? Besides if the treaty were at an end, how is it that thy heart is now distressed for sin and solicitous after deliverance from it?

Object. But I have waited long, and yet see no mercy for me.

Ans. May not mercy be coming and you not see it? Or have you not waited at the wrong door? If you wait for the mercy of God through Christ in the way of humiliation, repentance and faith, assuredly mercy shall come to you.

5. Has God performed the mercy promised to the fathers, Jesus Christ? Then let no man distrust God for the performance of lesser mercies contained in any promise of scripture. The performance of this mercy secures the performance of all other mercies to us; for Christ is a greater mercy than any which yet remains to be given. Rom. 8: 32. This mercy virtually comprehends all other mercies. 1 Cor. 3: 21–23; and the promises that contain all other mercies are ratified and confirmed to believers in Christ. 2 Cor. 1: 20; has God given thee Christ? He will give thee bread to eat, raiment to put on, support in troubles, and whatsoever else thy soul or body shall need. The great mercy Christ, makes way for all other mercies to the souls of believers.

6. How mad are they that part with Christ, the best of mercies, to secure and preserve any temporal mercies to themselves? Thus Demas and Judas gave up Christ to gain a little of the world. O, soul undoing bargain, how dear do they pay for the world that purchase it with the loss of Christ and their own peace.

Blessed be God for Jesus Christ the mercy of mercies.

METHOD OF GRACE.

THE MENNONITES IN PRUSSIA.

In Prussia there are also a number of Mennonites who are discussing the subject of emigrating to America, since there also, as many of our readers are aware, they are no longer exempted from military duty. There are however in Prussia only a few of the churches that are not willing to submit to the new military law. So far as is known to us, of the nineteen churches there, there are only two, the church in Heubuden and upper Nassau, which have steadily refused to accept the order requiring them to perform military service. Even in the last named churches there are a considerable number of members who are ready to forsake their old principles of non-resistance, and submit themselves to the service of the government. There are those also, however, in all the churches, whose adherence to the principles of non-resistance, is as it has ever been, a matter of conscience, and these are they, who now think of emigrating.

It appears that this matter has occasioned considerable trouble in the churches in Prussia, inasmuch as some of the leading bishops have consented to an unconditional submission to the law requiring military service of them; while on the other hand, there are others who will not allow any participation whatever in the practice of war.

There are at least three of the bishops who have, as the Mennonitischen Blätter informs us, resigned their office because their churches have declared themselves in favor of accepting the requirements of the new law; their consciences not permitting them to serve a church rejecting the principles of non-resistance. In other churches, it is said that even schisms have taken place on this account.

With feelings of the deepest sympathy and sincere pity, we look upon this whole matter which has caused our brethren in the faith in Prussia so much trouble to the detriment of the church.

It is, however, our most unquestionable privilege to inquire, Why is it, that in this civilized and highly enlightened nineteenth century, in which war is generally looked upon from other standpoints as a matter entirely inconsistent with the progress of the civilization of the times, and of christianity, that the privilege of exemption from military duty, which our brethren have so long enjoyed, should be taken from them? Is it not, perhaps, that the Mennonites generally did not understand properly to value this time-honored privilege, and that they did not feel sufficiently grateful to God for it? And may it not perhaps be the case, that the German government discovered, that among the Mennonites themselves, there are many to whom military duty is no longer a matter of conscience? Why then should the government hesitate any longer to require military duty of the Mennonites, when some of their own leading men express themselves in favor of it, in which preacher Manhardt has done in two articles in No. 6, 1872, of the *Mennonitische Blätter.* Such declarations do certainly not show an adherence to the old principles, as our fathers compiled and established them from the word of God; and they do not tend to cause the government to deal mildly with those who notwithstanding the unfaithfulness of others, still continue conscientiously, to hold fast to the old, and long accepted doctrines of the church.—*Friedensbote.*

FOR THE LAST TIME.

There is a touch of pathos about doing even the simplest thing "for the last time." It is not alone kissing the lips of the dead that gives you such a strange pain. You feel when you look your last upon some scene which you have loved when you stand in some quiet city street, where you know that you will never stand again, unless indeed, you come back, some day to the "old haunts," and wander among them an unwelcome guest. The actor playing his part for the last time, that singer whose voice is cracked hopelessly, and who after this once will never stand again before the eyes of upturned faces disputing the plaudits with fresher voices and fairer forms, the minister who has preached his last sermon—these all know the hidden bitterness of the two words "never again." How they come to us on birth-days, as we grow older. Never again young always nearer and nearer to the very last—the end which is universal, the "last thing" which follow all the other last things, are turn them, let us hope from pains to joys. We put away our boyish toys, with an old heartache. We are too old to walk any longer on our stilts—too tall to play marbles on the side-walks. Yet there was a pang when we thought we had played with our merry mates for the last time, and life's serious grown-up was waiting for us. Now we do not want the lost toys back. Life has other and larger playthings for us. May it not be these, too, shall seem in the light of some far off day as the boyish games seem to our manhood, and we shall learn that death is but the opening of a gate into the new land of promise?

Youth's Department.

GOOD NIGHT.

Good night, dear child, good night,
Sleep in thy little bed,
So soft, so lily white,
Beneath thy golden head.
Good night.

Like sunshine on a flower,
Thy tresses stray adown
The pillow in a shower,
And gild thy snowy gown.
Good night.

Feet, restless as the rain,
Your patter dies away
Till morning wakes again,
And calls you out to play.
Good night.

Good night, dear child, good night,
Breathed is thy evening prayer;
Thy watch of angels bright,
Comes through the silent air.
Good night.

We yield thee to their care
Until the shadows flee,
Content that they should share
In our felicity.
Good night.

MY LITTLE FRIEND.

I have a little friend living a few hundred miles from here, whose name I will call Annie, though that is not her real name. I call her by this name because it is a very pretty one, and one that I always loved.

Annie used to be one of my little scholars, when I lived in Ohio. She was not so very much better than most Annies, that I speak to the little readers of the PILGRIM of her, but she was so happy that I often think of her. But what was it that made her so happy? She didn't dress any finer than most of her school-mates, nor ride in a finer carriage, but she was happy, because she was good. And are all good children happy? Indeed they are. Annie's bright eyes and cheeks that beamed with rosy brightness, told that she was lovely, good and kind, and they must tell that she was happy. There was only a few times during the school that Annie seemed unhappy. A few times she happened to have poor lessons, not because she had not studied, but because the lessons were too hard for her. Then she did not look happy. Her bright eyes were made dim with tears, partly because she hadn't a good lesson, and partly because she feared she had offended her teacher by not studying harder.

Annie was careful not to offend any one; she spoke kindly to all. I never heard her speak one cross word, and she was so very gentle too. I have often thought, if the angels away up in that happy world, don't want her so much as not to let her live away from them and the good children there, she will one day become a good and useful woman. How many of our little readers will imitate Annie's good example? Would you always be happy, don't forget to be good and kind. Never let an angry word escape your lips. Be gentle; do all you can to make others happy, and then you will be happy too. We may call round sometime to see those little Annie's, Mary's and Minnie's, and we want to see them as happy as the little singing birds. Until then we will bid you a kind farewell, unless the PILGRIM will open the door of the Youths Department soon again for your friend,

F. M. SNIDER.

ACTING A LIE.

Ralph Royster ventured one day to toss his ball into the parlor. He knew it was wrong, but he wanted to do it, and did. Presently the ball fell on the table, and smashed a delicate glass that covered a beautiful collection of leaves.

"Oh," cried Ralph, "what shall I do now?"

After looking at the fragments with a rueful face for a few moments, he left the room feeling as if his heart was sinking down to his heels with a heavy load of guilt and fear, with which his disobedient act had loaded it. As he passed into the hall the cat rubbed against his leg. A bad thought arose in his breast, and putting the cat into the parlor, he shut her in and said:

"Stay there, Tabby! Mamma will think you broke that glass, and I shall escape a scolding. Hurrah for you, old Tabby! You are good for getting a fellow out of a scrape, if for nothing else."

At the tea table that afternoon, Mrs. Royster said to her husband:

"Pa, you must send Tabby away. I found her in the parlor to-day, and she had been on the table and broken the glass which covered those skeleton leaves."

Ralph blushed from his chin to the roots of his hair. His heart beat very quickly. The voice within whispered, "Be manly, be true. Confess that you broke it."

But Ralph was stubbornly silent. The poor cat was drowned for his misdeed, and he escaped a scolding by acting a lie.

I CAN PLOD—I CAN PERSEVERE.

When Rev. Dr. Carey, the great pioneer of mission-work in India, first proposed his plans to his father, he said: "William, you are mad!" And ministers and Christians replied to his proposition, "If the Lord should make windows in Heaven, then this thing might be."

His discouragements in first entering upon his work in India were appalling. When he found himself without a roof to cover his head, without bread for his sickly wife and four children, he made up his mind to build a hut in the wilderness, and live as the natives did around him. "There are many serpents and tigers, but Christ has said that His followers shall take up serpents," said this undaunted man.

God did not call him to this sacrifice, but to others, which required wonderful courage and persistence, before he achieved his final success which has made him famous the world over.

What was the secret that enabled the shoemaker's apprentice to become one of the most distinguished men of the age? What brilliant gift raised him from an obscure position to one of honor and fame, as the author of grammars and dictionaries, translations of the Bible and other books? He either translated or assisted in the completion of twenty-seven versions of Scripture, requiring a knowledge of as many languages or dialects.

He betrays the secret. In giving an estimate of his own character, he speaks of himself with Christian humility, but with full consciousness of the honor put upon him in the wonderful results he had been permitted to achieve. While not laying claim to brilliant gifts or genius, he says: "*I can plod—I can persevere.*"

He does not say, as we hear too often now a days, "I could always manage to get along, and keep up with my class in some way, without much study. I could jump at the meaning of my lessons; or I can catch up a trade without years of hard labor, "but I can persevere."

Plodding boys hold up your heads! You may seem to be left behind in the race by your so-called "smart" companions. Plod on. "The race is not always to the swift."

POLL AND THE CROWS.

One morning Mr. Herbert went out into the field near his house and shot at some crows that were pulling up his corn. He killed two of them, and when he went to pick them up, lo! on the ground he beheld Poll with a broken wing and leg. He had got out and had got into the company of the crows, and was walking about among them very grandly at the moment Mr. Herbert, while trying to kill the crows, shot and wounded him. When he carried the crows to the house, the children all said:

"But how is this, father! Here is poor Poll, (the parrot) all covered with blood and nearly dead!"

"Ah, yes," said Mr. Herbert; *bad company* has got poor Poll into trouble. If he had not been between the thievish crows, he would not have got hurt."

Mr. and Mrs. Herbert bandaged up the limbs of poor Poll, and it was weeks before he got well.

"What hurt you, Poll?"

"*Bad company,*" he would reply in solemn tones. And if he ever heard the children quarreling, or too noisy and ill-tempered in their sports, he would scream out, "*Bad company!*" and instantly good temper would prevail. Let children remember that almost always, evil occurs from going into bad company.—*Kind Words*

Correspondence.

A Reporter is wanted from every Church in the brotherhood to send us Church news, Obituaries, Announcements or anything that will be of general interest. To insure insertion, the writers name must accompany each communication. Our invitation is not personal but general—please respond to our call.

NOTES.

BY J. S. FLORY.

December 28th, in company with brother A. Evans (deacon) went by Railroad to Charleston, the capital of our State. At the home of brother J. Starkey met with a number of the brethren and sisters with whom we had a season of prayer, praise and church council and administration, after which we went afoot about 2 miles to friend W. Williards, where we had an appointment for preaching at night, found a waiting congregation who were attentive to the word preached. Next day, Sunday, meeting at Lynn S. H., after which we proceeded to the water side, and after having the ice cut which was about five inches thick, one willing soul entered and was baptized. Meeting at night again at the S. H, two more applicants for baptism, and others we were satisfied were almost persuaded to be Christians. Home to brother Starkey's in Charleston. Next day spent in visiting the members, and at night meeting at friend Frames; had a meeting and season of interest. Next day at 12 o'clock took the train "homeward bound;" all night at Bro. D. Harshberger's. Next day, New Years day, united together in the holy state of matrimony, sister Elizabeth Harshberger and a Mr. Wilson. Home in the evening, found all well, thank the Lord. During the past season in the bounds of our district, there has been 20 additions to the Church, about one fourth from the Missionary Baptists. To God the Father, and Jesus Christ the Son be all the glory now and forever.

Dear Pilgrim:—The Brethren of Maple Grove Ashland Co. Ohio, held a series of meetings that commenced on the evening of the 4th of January and was well attended by laboring brethren from a distance. The first sermon was preached by Wm. A. Murray from 1 Cor. 2; 1-7; 2d by John Nicholson, Eph. 2: 11; 3d by E. L. Yoder, Gen. 6: 3, followed by P. J. Brown; 4th by Murray, Titus 2: 11, 12; 5th by Nicholson and Brown, Isa 3: 11, 12; 6th by Christian Wise and Nicholson, Col. 1: 7th by P. J. Brown and Nicholson, 1 Tim. 3: 16; 8th by James McMullen, Rom. 6: 23; 9th by Yoder, Brown and Murray, Math. 22: 1,15; 10th by George Worst, Math. 7: 21, followed by Murray; 11th by Murray, Rom. 1: 11, 17, by P. J. Brown and McMullen; 12th by Yoder and Murray, Heb. 6: 1, 3; 13th by Worst, Mark 1: 14, 15, followed by Yoder;

14th by Murray and Worst, Heb. 10 34, 39: 15th by Worst and Murray, Acts 28: 30, 31; 16th by Murray, Acts 3: 22, followed by avid Witmer, and the 17th by Murray from Luke 17: 26. 20.

All these meetings were well attended, considering part of the time it was quite cold. Quite an interest was manifested by the brethren and sisters in attending and bringing their children and others; some sleds would convey as many as 17 persons at a time, and nearly all paid good attention to the word spoken. The zeal of the laborers, the interest taken by members and the power of God's word made good impressions on the congregation, and on Friday the 13th, two young women confessed that they were not ashamed to follow Jesus and were added to the church by baptism. While the congregation stood on the shore shivering and cold, they came out of the water rejoicing that their sins were washed away, and the great query among the people is, "How can they endure the coldness of the water?" the ice being about 18 inches thick. While they are in trouble or perplexed about the wonders of baptism in the winter, may they be led to think of the Hebrew children in the fiery furnace How did they endure it? Daniel in the lions' den &c. But to the unbelieving, this will always be a mystery, and the virtue unrealized until they are willing to say "Lord thy will be done," and his love is shed abroad in their hearts. In comparison, it is like a cup of pure water. It contains the properties that will slake thirst, but as long as not partaken of, the thirsty remain thirsty still, so those in the spirit feast of the spirit.

As many good impressions were made, may they be watered by the dew-drops from on High, that satan may be defeated so as not to be able to take all that has been sown by the faithful laborers in the Vineyard of the Lord, for I know that many cannot say they did not hear the words of eternal Truth, and if they do not practice the same in this life, in the judgment these things will condemn them. I feel very thankful to all my co-laborers and brethren and sisters that met with us. Other laborers were present from adjoining churches that did not labor, as they wished to hear others more distant, but all were willing to join in if needed. At one meeting there were twelve ministers present. May the blessing of God attend all, and if we meet no more on earth, may we strive to meet above.

W. SADLER.

Nankin, Ohio.

DRY VALLEY AND LOST CREEK MEETINGS.

Dear Editors:—On the 2nd of January, according to previous arrangements, I met with the brethren of Dry Valley, Mifflin Co., Pa., to help to preach the word of God to the anxious inquiring people of that place. By Saturday we were joined in the work by Elder J. D. Trostle of Md., and Elder P. S. Myers of Spring Run, also on Monday by our dear old brother Joseph Hanawalt of the same place. Under the supervision of elder and bishop Jacob Mohler, with his co-laburers, Wm. Howe, Archy Vandyke, Andrew Spanogle, G. S. Myers, J. Price and S. J. Swigart, the meetings were surely made pleasant, interesting, and we trust profitable. On the 9th, it seemed good to the brethren and the Lord, to take Bro. J. D. Trostle, accompanied by Bro. A. Vandyke, to Lost Creek, to help the brethren there to open their meeting, which was in connection with the Dry Valley. The meeting continued at Dry Valley until the evening of the 12th. The morning of the 13th, in company with Bro. William Howe and daughter, we repaired to Lost Creek, Free Spring Meeting-house, where we found brethren Trostle and Vandyke prosecuting their Master's business faithfully. The ministering brethren who stand by the side of their aged Elder to vindicate the cause of Christ, are Elder Solomon Sieber, Ezra Smith, Isaac Barto, A. Bashore. ——Landis and J. Cauffman, who seem fully efficient to the task and charge.

Brother Trostle left for home on the 16th. Brethren Howe and Vandyke also left the latter part of the same week, I remained with the brethren until the morning of the 20th. The meetings were all well attended; much interest manifested upon the part of the brethren, sisters and friends. A number were added to the Church, and many expressed a desire to be with, and for Christ very soon. While making this trip, I had the pleasure of visiting many of the brethren's families, besides enjoying their kind hospitalities, we shared with them in their private devotion around their altars. The pleasant social enjoyment of the rich feast, will be the source of many pleasant remembrances.

Our brethren's neighbors and their children are praiseworthy for their attention, their kindness and the interest they seemed to take in the preached word, and we fondly hope they may accept it and glorify the Lord with us.

To our dear brethren and sisters, we feel like saying yet, keep close to the 'ancient landmarks,' the gospel, that you may prove to the world that it is the right way of God to life eternal. Live the faith of Jesus practically, take it with you through all the routine of life, and it will "keep you through faith unto salvation ready to be revealed in the last times."

D. F. GOOD.

Bros. Brumbaugh:—As church news seem to be desirable I will give a short report of the Richland Church, Richland County, Ohio.

We have a snug little church house 30 by 40 about seven miles North-west of Mansfield. This church is composed of about eighty-five members, and as far as I know, at present, is in a prosperous condition, under the care of our beloved Elder Christian Wise, who has labored here in the ministry for twenty six years. During the year 1872 there were fifteen added to the church and one restored. We just closed our series of meetings, which continued one week, and we can truly say we had a good meeting. At the close we had two applicants for baptism, and we think good impressions were made on others, which we hope will not be lost. We have five speakers named as follows: Elder Christian Wise, Isaac Wisler, Israel Wisler, Peter Helphen and the writer. Brethren pray for us that we may all obtain that rest that is prepared for the people of God.

J. C. MCMULLEN.

Mansfield, Ohio.

Dear Editors:—The PILGRIM No. 3, this volume was received last evening, and before the evening hours were spent its contents was well perused. I was so well pleased that I remarked to my companion, I thought the PILGRIM had greatly improved since the commencement of the present volume, and I cannot see why some brethren are still opposed to the Brethren's periodicals.

I felt this morning to write a few thoughts, and if considered worthy you can insert, if not, I am just as well satisfied, as I think it very important that nothing should be published by the Brethren but what is consistent with our faith.

I have not been well for several weeks past and unable to go out, but as I sat in my chair this Sabbath morning and the fingers of the clock marked 10, I thought of the many places the brethren have now gathered together to worship here in Ill. My mind also wandered back to Pa., where we left nearly two years ago, where the brethren commenced to worship about one hour earlier, and before service closes here in Illinois, the brethren in California and the Pacific coasts will be ready to commence their service, and raise their songs of praises to the great Creator, and until their forenoon meetings close, the brethren in the East commence their afternoon service, so that nearly the whole of the Sabbath, songs of praise are offered to God by the Church. Would not that be enough to overflow our hearts with enraptures and joys if we could be so favored as to hear it all? It appears to me we would hardly be able to contain it in our limited minds, yet we believe it is all heard and taken into account by Him that sitteth on the right hand of the majesty on High. After trying to measure the capacity of the Church in its praises to God, we are led to think of what the Revelator heard. We think in the vision, were not only the present generation, but he heard as it were the voice of a great multitude, and as the voice of many waters, and as the voice of mighty thunderings, saying, Alleluia for the Lord God Omnipotent reigneth. There is where we believe all the faithful subjects of Christ's Kingdom will be present and lend their voices to swell the songs of everlasting praises, even unto the voice of thunderings, unto that great Creator. Who would not desire to be present there, and to help to raise that song and enjoy that full happiness? We think every human being. And to those that fully desire to be there, we would say we are all invited, and upon very easy terms. "Blessed are they that do His commandments, that they may have right to the tree of life and may enter in through the gates into the city."

JESSE Y. HECKLER.

MARRIED.

SMALL.—KAUFMAN.—On the 30th of Jan., 1873 at my residence, Mr. Hiram Small to Miss Anna M Kaufman, both of Franklin Co., Pa.

JOHN ZUCK.

DIED.

RHINEHART.—In the Upper Deer Creek Church, Ind., Dec 29th, 1872, David Rhinehart, aged 84 years, 8 months and 15 days.

He was born in Franklin Co., Va., April 15th, 1788, and moved to Preble Co., Ohio in the Fourmile arm of the church, where he was chosen a deacon in 18.., which office he filled to the satisfaction of the church and honor to himself for many years. For the last few years he resided in Cass Co., Ind. where the most of his children live, and where his son Abraham is bishop. Though not living near to the M. H. he was very sure to be there at the proper time and took a lively interest in the welfare of the church until a short time before his death. He departed this life with a bright hope of a blessed immortality. He had told his son some months before his death that he wished me to preach his funeral, but my health was so poor that it was postponed until last Sunday.

He was a member for nearly 50 years, and a deacon for nearly 40. He has now living 7 children, 42 grand children, 23 great grand children, and one great great grand child.

Funeral occasion from *Rev.* 14: 12, 13, to a very large and attentive audience.

HIEL HAMILTON.

(*Visitor* please copy.)

GROVE.—On the 18th of Jan. 1873. Mary Ann Grove departed this life, aged 25 years, 11 months, and 12

She leaves her husband, (John Grove and many friends to mourn her loss. Funeral occasion improved by Jos. Hess of the River Brethren, Bro. Jos. Gipe, and the writer, from Amos 4: 12

JOHN ZUCK.

SMITH.—Williamsburg, Clover Creek church, Blair Co., Pa., Jan 31st, 1873, sister Mary, wife of Bro. Adam R Smith, aged 35 years, 6 months and 9 days.

The funeral occasion improved by the Rev. Ounue, and Bro. Joseph Snowberger, from Rev. 14: 13. "Blessed are the dead which die in the Lord from henceforth, yea saith the spirit that they may rest from their labors and their works do follow them." These words it appears had been selected by the sister while on her sick bed

A. S. BRECHTEL.

SHOOK.—On the 5th of Jan., 1873, in the Coldwater district, Iowa, Magdalena, daughter of friend Abram and sister Ruth Shook, aged 15 years, 1 month and 18 days. Funeral services improved by the writer in the town of Greene to a large congregation from Amos 4: 12, last clause.

E. J. EIKENBERRY.

SHOOK.—In the Root River congregation, Fillmore Co., Minn., on the 31st of Dec., 1872, Marella, daughter of Bro. John and sister Shook, aged 14 years, 11 months and 27 days. Funeral occasion improved by brethren Joseph Ogg and Wm. Ryles on the 1st day of the New Year, at the Prairie Queen School House, to a large and attentive audience from 1st Pe. 1:21, 25.

JOSEPH DRURY.

AARON.—Very sudden on the 25th of Jan. 1873, in Pattonsville, Bedford Co., Pa., Peter Aaron, father of W. H. Aaron of Pattonsville, aged 60 years, 5 months and 22 days. Occasion improved by ——— Shoemaker, German Reformed, from 1st Thes. 4, 13, 14, to a large audience. He was a member of the G. Reformed church and of a good christian deportment.

LEONARD FURRY.

LITERARY NOTICES.

AN EXCELLENT PEN.—We have been favored with a sample card of the celebrated Spencerian Steel Pens, and after trying them quite thoroughly are convinced of their superiority. These pens are comprised in fifteen numbers, each differing in flexibility and fineness of point, so that the most fastidious penman cannot fail to find among the fifteen just such a pen as suits him. The Spencerian Pens are famous for their elasticity of movement, smoothness of point and great durability, and are a nearer approximation to the real Swan Quill Pen than any thing hitherto made. They are manufactured in England under the supervision of the original inventor of Steel Pens, the venerable Josiah Mason, and Joseph Gillott—the latter making a few of the numbers after the models of the late P. R. Spencer, the famous penman. They are used very largely in the common schools of the United States, in all the principal commercial colleges, in the government offices at Washington, and in the banks and commercial offices throughout the country, the sale reaching an enormous quantity annually. For the convenience of those who wish to try them, a sample card of the Spencerian Pens may be had by mail by enclosing 25 cents to Messrs Ivison, Blakeman, Taylor & Co., 138 and 140 Grand Street, N. Y., or the pens may be bought at almost any store where pens are sold.

HEARTH & HOME is a large, beautiful and highly illustrated weekly journal, full of instructive and interesting reading matter, adapted to the wants of every family. It is acknowledged to be the best periodical of its kind published and has a tremendous circulation. With it every subscriber gets a beautiful Chromo, "The Strawberry Girl," size 14x21, in 18 colors. For the Chromo there must be 25 cents extra sent to pay postage or still better, send 50 cts. extra and have it mounted and varnished ready for framing. Published by Orange, Judd & Co., 245 Broadway, New York, at $3,00 per annum.

FLOWERS! FLOWERS! No home in the land can afford to do without these natural decorations, especially when we can have them sent to our doors at prices within reach of all. We are just in receipt of Briggs & Bro's mammoth *Quarterly* flower and vegetable catalogue of 136 pages, containing cuts, with a number of beautifully colored plates, of a large number of the most beautiful flowers and best vegetables grown. This hand some, useful and beautiful publication is sent to subscribers quarterly at the small cost of 25 cts. per year. Send for it and you will never regret the investment. Address,

BRIGGS & BRO.,
Rochester, N. Y.

The Weekly Pilgrim.

JAMES CREEK, PA., Feb. 11th. 1873.

☞ HOW TO SEND MONEY.—All sums over $1.50, should be sent either in a check, draft or postal order. If neither of these can be obtained, have the letter registered.

☞ WHEN MONEY is sent, *always* send with it the name and address of those who paid it. Write the names and post office as plainly as possible.

☞ EVERY subscriber for 1873, gets a *Pilgrim Almanac* FREE.

OUR MOTTO.

Our "Motto" has been so variously understood, defined and interpolated that it may puzzle the minds of some to know how to understand it, notwithstanding we have at different times, explained how we understand it. If others wish to give it different interpretations it matters not to us as long as they give it as *their* opinion, but we are not anxious to have others tell us how we are to understand it, neither do we suppose that any wish to do this, at the same time, the opinions of others, admitted, may seem to infer our assent.

Eld. D. M. Holsinger in No's 3 and 4, give a very good exposition of the original design of the text, and while we assent to the application in the main, there is a part from which we feel to dissent when accepted as our motto.

That we should publish the PILGRIM in defence of such decisions as were made by the Brethren in the absence of direct scripture would be a small work and not worthy of the sacrifice. To do this would be equivalent to admitting that there was a single period of time in which the Brethren had reached perfection and that since then the great tendency is to diverge from that perfect period and its decisions. While we honor and respect the zeal and wisdom of our forefathers, we beg leave to honor and respect *still more* the "landmarks" as set by Jesus Christ and his Apostles. Advocating and upholding the decision and councils of men has been the great curse of the Christian Church, in all ages and with great reluctance would we advocate anything not based upon the "Word." When brethren say they are willing to accept the decisions of the church as far as they are founded upon the truth, we say, amen, as no brethren, or set of brethren, are invested with any authority to make any others. Our Law, as given by Christ is a *perfect* law and meets every case. If there be cases for which we have no direct example or precept, the spirit of those examples and precepts will reach them indirectly, for instance, we have no direct scripture for sisters to wear the cap, but in the injunction of Paul we have it indirectly. So in all other cases. Independent of the scriptures we advocate nothing. It has been well said; "Search the scriptures for in them ye think ye have eternal life and they are they which testify of me." We have ever been strong advocates of the Brethren and are yet, but we wish to have it understood that we do not stand in defence of such decisions as have neither example nor precept in the scriptures as a basis, neither do we believe that the Brethren make such decisions, but such things may happen through fallibility and for us to accept them as the laws of the Medes and Persians would be a great error and heap upon us a code of laws which might well be called "the traditions of men." Our forefathers were fallible men just as we. All the light they had they received from the scriptures. We have the same scriptures to-day with greater facilities of understanding them, and we believe we have now, just as wise, as holy and pious men in the Church as there ever were, therefore, why look back? The divine injunction is "forward" and "upward." With the chart of salvation, which contains all of our landmarks, in our hands and the spirit as a lamp for our feet, let us go onward with the blessed assurance that we shall reap if we faint not. The PILGRIM will labor in defense of the "landmarks" as set by Jesus Christ and revealed unto us by his chosen witnesses which "landmarks" we believe are carefully observed and held forth by the Brethren.

OUR MEETINGS

During last Fall the brethren of James Creek built a Church, some five miles south of the James Creek Church, and notwithstanding the early and severe Winter, got it completed, and on the first day of February commenced a series of meetings in it which were both interesting and we hope profitable. On account of a negligence on our part we had not as much ministerial aid as we perhaps would have had, had we published it according to orders. Though our help was small in number, yet it was quite efficient. Brethren Stephen Hilderbrand and J. S. Burkhart, of Conemaugh were with us, also J. S. Snowberger of Clover Creek.

On account of sickness in the family, we had not the pleasure of attending a number of the appointments, but those who were present say the meetings were well attended, interesting, and that the brethren labored with much zeal for our Master's cause, for which they have our grateful thanks.

Bros. Hildebrand and Burkhart, were with us in the PILGRIM Office where we made their acquaintance which was quite agreeable, and we hope, will not soon be forgotten. They expressed themselves much pleased with the membership of James Creek, and we are sure that the members were quite well pleased with the ministerial aid, so that we hope both parties may soon have the pleasure of again enjoying each others society. Our meetings closed on Tuesday evening for want of help, and on account of the break in the weather.

Brethren, in making their ministerial visits, will please not forget James Creek.

PERSONAL.

J. L. BEAVER. The Hymn books were sent. Call at the Express Office and if they have not arrived, let us hear from you.

DANIEL SAYLER. We have no account of receiving a letter from you containing money. The PILGRIM is now sent.

JACOB J. KINDIG. Letter and money was not received. The PILGRIM is sent.

D. BOCK. You will oblige us by giving the names and address of subscribers you sent, not going to Miamisburg and Dayton.

J. H. GOODMAN. Our father's name is John, a brother to Jacob, of whom you speak.

DAVID GOODYEAR. The first volume of the PILGRIM was issued in the year 1870, therefore for 67, 68 and 69 there are none. Volume 1st 1870, we can send you post paid for $1.25.

R. B. R. Your money was rec'd but your name was overlooked in booking. Of Nos. 22, 48 we have none. Any persons having these Nos. who do not wish to preserve them, will confer us a favor by sending them to the PILGRIM Office, if not too much soiled.

MONEY LIST.

Jonas Price	$1.50
Lizzie F Miller	4 00
Jno N Barnhart	1.50
Stephen Hildebrand	3 00
Louisa Lawyer	1.50
Samuel Hoke	1.50
Moses Kling	.50
John D Norris	1.45
Daniel Bock	27 00
John Newcomer	1.50
B F Flaine	3 25
Jno H Goodman	1.50
Samuel Warcham	2 00
Isaih Jarner	11.75
S J Garber	8.75
Jesse Conner	1.50

GENERAL INTELLIGENCE.

Seventy-five members of the Ecumenical Council have died since it was opened in Rome, in December, 1869.

Deaths in 1872: Chicago, 10,000; St. Louis, 7,027; Cincinnati, 5,472; New York, 32941; Philadelphia, 20,-554; Baltimore, 8,703.

INTENSE COLD.—This winter has been marked by an unusual amount of intensely cold weather. On the 18th inst., the temperature at Sparta, Wis., was 45 degrees below zero; Lacrosse, Wis., 31; St. Paul 31; Minneapolis, 34 below; Milwaukee, 8 above.

BEST TIME FOR PAINTING HOUSES. The best time for painting the exterior of buildings is late in autumn or during the winter. Paint then employed will endure twice as long as when applied in early summer or hot weather. In the former it dries slowly and becomes hard, like a glazed surface, not easily affected afterward by the weather, or worn off by the beating of storms. But in hot weather the oil in the paint soaks into the wood at once, as into a sponge, leaving the lead nearly dry and nearly ready to crumble off. This last difficulty, however, might be guarded against, though at an increased expense, by first going over the surface with raw oil. By painting in cold weather, one annoyance might certainly be escaped, namely, the collection of small flies in the fresh paint.

HUNTINGDON & BROAD TOP RAIL ROAD

Winter Arrangement.

On and after Tuesday, Oct. 4, 1872, Passenger trains will arrive and depart as follows:

Trains from Huntingdon South. *Trains from Mt. Dallas moving North.*

MAIL. A. M.	ACCOM. P. M.	STATIONS.	MAIL. P. M.	ACCOM. A. M.
le7 40	LE	Huntingdon.	AR1 00	AR
7 45		Long Siding	3 55	
8 00		McConnelstown	3 45	
8 05		Pleasant Grove	3 35	
8 22		Marklesburg	3 22	
8 40		Coffee Run	3 07	
8 45		Rough & Ready	3 00	
9 00		Cove	2 40	
9 05		Fishers Summit	2 45	
9 15		Saxton	2 35 le	
9 40		Riddlesburg	2 15	
9 47		Hopewell	2 05	
10 05		Piper's Run	1 50	
10 32		Tatesville	1 30	
11 05		Bloody Run	1 20	
10 40		Mount Dallas	1 15	
11 08		Bedford	2 11	

G. F. GAGE, Supt.

SHOUP'S RUN BRANCH.

LE 9 25 LE	Saxton.	AR2 15 AR	
9 40	Coalmont.	2 00	
9 4[illegible]	Crawford.	1 55	
AR10 00 AR	Dudley	LE1 45 LE	

Broad Top City from Dudley 2 miles by stage.

Time of Penna. R. R. Trains at Huntingdon

EASTWARD.		WESTWARD.	
Hb'g Ac.	9 24 A. M	Cin. Ex.	2 19 A. M.
Mail	3 30 P. M	Pac'f Ex.	7 45 "
Cin. Ex.	6 55 "	Mail	5 40 P. M.
Phil. Ex	11 15 "	W. Pass.	11 52 A. M.

The Weekly Pilgrim.

Published by J. B. Brumbaugh, & Co.

Edited by H. B. & Geo. Brumbaugh.

CORRESPONDING EDITORS.

D. P. Sayler, Double Pipe Creek, Md.

Leonard Furry, New Enterprise, Pa.

The *Pilgrim* is a Christian Periodical, devoted to religion and moral reform. It will advocate in the spirit of *love* and *liberty*, the principles of true Christianity, labor for the promotion of peace among the people of God, for the encouragement of the saints and for the conversion of sinners, avoiding those things which tend toward disunion or sectional feelings.

TERMS.

Single copy, Book paper,	$1.50
Eleven copies, [eleventh for Agt.]	$15.00

Any number above that at the same rate.

Address,

H. B. BRUMBAUGH.
James Creek,
Huntingdon county Pa.

The Weekly Pilgrim.

"REMOVE NOT THE ANCIENT LANDMARKS WHICH OUR FATHERS HAVE SET."

VOL. 4. JAMES CREEK, PENNSYLVANIA, FEBRUARY 18, 1873. NO. 7

POETRY.

SEND ME.

BY REV. DANIEL MARCH, D. D.

Hark, the voice of Jesus crying,
 Who will go and work to-day?
Fields are white and harvests waiting,
 Who will bear the sheaves away?
Loud and long the Master calleth,
 Rich reward He offers free;
Who will answer, gladly saying,
 "Here am I, send me, send me!"

If you cannot cross the ocean,
 And the heathen lands explore,
You can find the heathen nearer,
 You can help them at your door.
If you cannot give your thousands,
 You can give the widow's mite,
And the least you give for Jesus
 Will be precious in his sight.

If you cannot speak like angels,
 If you cannot preach like Paul,
You can tell the love of Jesus,
 You can say He died for all.
If you cannot rouse the wicked,
 With the judgment's dread alarms,
You can lead the little children
 To the Savior's waiting arms

Let none hear you idly saying,
 "There is nothing I can do,"
While the souls of men are dying,
 And the Master calls for you.
Take the task he gives you gladly,
 Let His work your pleasure be:
Answer quickly when He calleth:
 "Here I am; send me, send me."

ORIGINAL ESSAYS.

SOBER THOUGHTS FOR HONEST PROFESSORS.—NO 2.

J. S. FLORY.

Paul says the Gospel "is the power of God unto salvation to every one that believeth." From this we evidently learn that the Gospel is all sufficient to govern us in matters of salvation—we need not look elsewhere for light to illumine our pathway, other than that which is vouchsafed unto us from God as a blessing, the result consequent upon our faith in and obedience to the Gospel. Salvation is the one thing of all others needful for our present and eternal happiness. Believing the query to be in the minds of our readers, "what shall I do to be saved," we purpose to present a few practical illustrations, drawn from the New Testament Scriptures, applicable to the premises under consideration.

First, we introduce the case of the Philippian jailor, Acts 16, as one who, probably never had heard of salvation, through Jesus,—fearful that he must die, he inquired of Paul and Silas what he should do to be saved. As an answer, relative to eternal salvation he was told to "believe on the Lord Jesus Christ and thou shalt be saved." Faith was necessary to salvation because "without faith it is impossible to please God." The apostles spoke unto him and his household the word of the Lord and we learn baptism followed. In this instance, we see baptism belongs to the "word of the Lord"—evidently it was water baptism for he went where there was water. Never for a moment be deluded with the idea that this man was baptized in his house, for it is evident he was not, because after his baptism he "brought them into his house," which he could not have done, had he not gone out of his house, for he was in when the apostle "spake to him and all that were in his house." In the case of the Ethiopian Eunuch, Acts 8, we have also one who when He learned of Jesus it was required of him that he should believe. When Philip preached unto him "Jesus" he preached *water baptism*, and believing, he, the Eunuch was baptized *in* water.

Next, we will call attention to those on the day of Pentecost Acts 2, who when they *believed*,—believed that Jesus was the Christ and they had crucified him &c., asked what they should do. Peter did not tell them to believe, for it was evident they were already believers, but he told them to "*Repent* and be baptized every one of you for the remission of sins and ye shall receive the gift of the Holy Ghost." Having believed, it was now necessary to take another step, and that was repent and then *be* baptized—that is suffer yourselves to be baptized *in water* as the Lord had commanded, "and ye shall receive the gift of the Holy Ghost,"—shall receive it from God, who it is that baptizes with the Holy Spirit as He had *promised* He would.

Now we wish to call attention to the case of Paul Acts 9: 22. Owing to his miraculous conversion he was made to believe, and believing he became a penitent man for "behold he prayeth." After he received his sight he "arose and was baptized" and Ananias said unto him, why tarriest thou, arise and be baptized and wash away thy sins, calling on the name of the Lord." Now here we have a character that had believed and no doubt repented and yet had not his sins washed away. Why? the answer is plain, because he had *not yet* been baptized. "Be baptized" here, as well as elsewhere, undoubtedly means *submit to the ordinance of water baptism*. Mark you it does not say arise and ye *shall* receive the baptism of the Holy Ghost as some would have us to believe it *ought* to read. No, no, it is just as it should be, and as in other cases water baptism was necessary that he might receive remission of sins. From these cases we have presented, we are forced to conclude that faith, in a certain measure, is the first step, *repentance* the second, and *water baptism* the third. By a faithful compliance with those prerequisites we have the promise of the washing away of sins through the merits of Christ and cleansing efficacy of His blood, and THEN ye shall receive the gift of the Holy Spirit. The adopting principles of the Gospel in all its primary bearings beautifully harmonizes with the above conclusions. "He that believeth and is baptized shall be saved." "Except a man be born of water and the spirit he can not enter into the kingdom of God." "Saved us by the washing of regeneration and renewing of the Holy Ghost." Titus 3:5. "Therefore we are buried with him by baptism into death; that like as Christ was raised up from the dead by the glory of the Father even so we also should walk in newness of life; for if we have been planted together in the likeness of his death, we shall be also in the likeness of His resurrection." Rom. 6:45. "Buried with him in baptism wherein also ye are risen with Him through the faith of the operation of God. In these positive scriptural truths we have salvation *following* baptism—born of the spirit *after* born of the water,—the renewing of the Holy Ghost *after* the washing of regeneration,—are in the likeness of His resurrection after having been planted in the likeness of his death,—walk in newness of life *after* having been buried with Him by baptism into death,—are risen with Him through the faith of the operation of God *after* we have been buried with Him in baptism,—and ye shall receive the gift of the Holy Ghost *after* having been baptized in the name of Jesus Christ,—be baptized *for* the remission of sins. In the face of all these incontrovertible facts, hundreds and thousands teach differently, and we are pained to the heart to see so many honest unsuspecting ones led astray thereby. That my candid and unprejudiced readers may see the inconsistency of erroneous views along side the truth, we will make an exposition of a few points. The tenet of faith of some of our popular religionists claim the reception of the Holy Spirit *before* baptism,—the remission of sins *before* baptism—born of the spirit *before* being born of water—the renewing of the Holy Spirit *before* the washing of regeneration—are in the likeness of His resurrection *before* being planted in the likeness of His death—walk in newness of life *before* having been buried with Him by baptism into death—are risen with Him through the faith of the operation of God *before* having been buried with Him in baptism. And that baptism is *because* of the remission of sins. That we are saved by *faith alone*, when James says "ye see then how that by works a man is justified, and not by faith alone." And we are told that Jesus saves all who come to Him by faith, while Paul says "He became the author of eternal salvation unto all them that *obey* Him." However we will admit that all who come to Christ with that faith that is of a living, saving nature and prompts the professer to obey the commands of God, will be saved. To expect salvation short of the promises of God is hazardous in the extreme. Does not the Gospel plainly teach that the doctrine of salvation is to believe on the Lord Jesus Christ "as the Scriptures hath said;" thoroughly repent of sin, and be baptized in the name of Jesus Christ for the remission of sins and then the Holy Spirit shall be received? Now the Lord has plainly specified the conditions upon which He will become reconciled to man and "Remember their iniquities no more." He "was in Christ reconciling the world unto Himself," and now we have the promise of the pardon of our sins through the same Jesus upon conditions we meet God at the point He has designated. He would have the material man *buried* in a material element—water—an outward washing significant of that inward cleansing He is willing and promised *shall* take place through the atoning blood of Jesus, that was shed "once for all," and as the seal of His covenant and promise, the soul—the immaterial principle of man is baptized with an immaterial gift, nothing less than the Holy Spirit or Holy *life* and are thus truly regenerated,—recreated after the image of God—and is recognized as a son of God—a new creature in Christ Jesus, and, therefore, must walk in newness of life. Thus in this great work of regeneration, the sinner "comes to God"—meets God at the point His mercy called him, and then Jesus meets the sinner, and oh! what a meeting! Contrition on the part of the sinner, love, grace, mercy and pardon through His Son's atoning blood on the part of God. Now the adopted child of God becomes a "fellow citizen with the saints of the household of God" and running the race set before, forgets not to learn of Jesus that he may know how to run and keep the commandments of his Lord and Master, having the spirit of his Heavenly teacher, he will be "meek and lowly in heart," will not aspire to high things but condescend to men of low estate,—will never cavil about the commands of Jesus, but bow submissively to the *all* things knowing that after having done all he is but an unprofitable servant, yet has the promise of glory, honor and and immortality through the free grace of God. Oh that we might all look well to our ways and fear lest a promise being left us we should come short of it, knowing "there is a way that seemeth right unto man but the end thereof is death." Let us get in the way that *is right*, which is the *Gospel way*. Come all ye that love the Lord and let us walk *that* way together, and we will soon all be at home in Heaven.

FOR THE READERS OF THE PILGRIM.

I herein present a query for every sincere soul to solve for their own benefit, and if any lack wisdom, let them ask of God who giveth liberally to all men and upbraideth not, and it shall be given them. The Savior said, "Seek first the Kingdom of God," and again "Whosoever loveth anything more than me is not worthy of me." Paul says, "I beseech you therefore, Brethren, by the mercies of God, that ye present your bodies a living sacrifice holy acceptable unto God which is your reasonable service, and be not conformed to this world, but be ye transformed by the renewing of your minds, that ye may prove what is that good, acceptable and perfect will of God." From the foregoing texts, we ask whether it is not our duty to cut off every unnecessary thought, desire and action? We do admit that sincerity and perfection are two things, yet we think we cannot be Christians without the first, and we do not comprehend how we can possess the first without desiring the latter. "Blessed are they that hunger and thirst after righteousness for they shall be filled," hence a continual uneasiness and warfare, but blessed be God, it is not without a promise. And now by way of solving the query, I would ask, how much unnecessary expense and time is lost by chewing tobacco, smoking, snuffing, extra tending at tables in serving up the luxuries and unnecessaries of life, and I ask how much of it is in conformity to this world? Yea, I would understand it to be an obstacle in our way of knowing the perfect will of God. My idea is that all that is done to gratify the lust of the eye and the pride of life, is sinful unless it is as Paul said, "Whether ye eat or drink, or whatsoever ye do let it be done to promote God's glory and our eternal welfare."

Now, as our highest obligations is to love God supremely and our neighbor as ourselves, if by cutting off the luxuries of life we can do good to suffering humanity, are we not under obligations to do it? Christ undoubtedly was rich, and might have been happy without us, but for our sakes He became poor, took upon Himself suffering and shame. If we are His we have His spirit, and will we not deny ourselves of the superfluities of life for those whom we are to love as ourselves? If we but cut off and dispense with these things that are calculated to destroy our constitutions rather than make them healthful and vigorous, those things which do us no real good but the gratifying of the carnal mind which is enmity to God and is as the poet says:

"How vain are all things here below,
How transient and how fair;
Each pleasure hath its poison too
And every sweet a snare."

Yea, if we would do away all vanity, and live soberly, righteously and godly in this present world, and appropriate our surplus to the cause of Christ and His Brethren, what a vast amount of good might be done in our own fraternity, besides the world at large? And how much more would we be as lights to the world and salt to the earth, and our Heavenly Father be glorified thereby and we at the end would hear the happy applaud of "Well done good and faithful servant," &c., whereas I fear many of us will be charged not with using and not abusing the world, but with abusing and wasting the Master's goods, and many will be speechless not having the wedding garment on. Therefore love, (charity) should be the main spring of all our actions, and in all we do we should have an eye single to the glory of God, to the promotion of His Kingdom here on earth and to the edification of immortal souls. Thus when we come together in our assemblies for worship we ought to meet quietly, as near the appointed time as possible, and as much as convenient, meet and greet each other quietly with an unfeigned salutation, remembering that it required Aaron and Hurr to stay up the hands of Moses so that Joshua could prevail, and ascend our supplications Heavenward in behalf of our ministering brethren that they may divide the word of Truth aright, and draw from the sacred records things old and new, to the glory of God and to the benefit of the church. And when we meet upon Communion occasions, we ought to be very solemnly impressed and pay strict attention to the examination admonitions, and at the supper, or feast of charity, look forward with a happy anticipation of a glorious feast with Abraham, Isaac and Jacob and the saints of old, when Jesus Himself will serve, which by way of illustration, perhaps might be termed the Millenium feast, and when we partake of the bread and wine in remembrance of Jesus' dying love, we should look back with profound and august solemnity to the crucifixion of the Son of God. And as I believe the design and intention was and still is to impress the mind anew of the sufferings of that immaculate Lamb of God, profound silence would be better calculated to promote the cause and bring about the end than singing, and when the commandments of the Redeemer have been observed in silence, truth and sincerity, we might to the glory of God and our encouragement sing with the spirit and understanding:

Rejoice, the Lord is King,
Your God and King adore;
Mortals give thanks and sing,
And triumph evermore.
Lift up your hearts, lift up your voice,
Rejoice again, I say rejoice," &c.

or something else that would be as appropriate.

May God grant that the Church in 1873 be more like that described in the Song of Solomon, looking forth as the morning, fair as the moon, clear as the sun and terrible as an army with banners.

D. Bosserman.

Gettysburg, Pa.

THINGS TO BE PRAYED FOR.

OUR FATHER

Merciful and gracious, thou gavest us being, raising us from nothing to be an excellent creation, forming us after thy own image, tenderly feeding us and conducting and strengthening us all our days. Thou art our Father by a more excellent mercy, adopting us in a new birth to become partakers of the inheritance of Jesus

WHICH ART IN HEAVEN.

Heaven is thy throne and earth thy footstool. From thy throne thou beholdest all the dwellers on earth and triest the hearts of men, and nothing is hid from thy sight. And as thy knowledge is infinite, so is thy power uncircumscribed as the utmost orb of heaven, and thou sittest in thy own essential happiness and tranquility immovable and eternal. That is our country and thither thy servants are traveling. There is our Father and that is our inheritance. There our hearts are, for there our treasures are laid up till the day of recompense.

HALLOWED BE THY NAME.

Thy name, O God, is glorious, and in thy name is our hope and confidence. According to thy name so is thy praise unto the world's end. They that love thy name shall be joyful in thee for thy name which thou madest to be proclaimed unto thy people, is the Lord God, merciful and gracious, long suffering and abundant in goodness and truth, keeping mercy for thousands, forgiving iniquity, transgression and sin, and that will by no means, clear the guilty. In this glorious name we worship thee O, Lord.

THY KINGDOM COME.

Thou reignest in heaven and on earth. O do thou rule also in our hearts, advance the interest of religion, let thy gospel be placed in all the regions of the earth and let all nations come and worship thee, laying their proud wills at thy feet, submitting their understanding to the obedience of Jesus, conforming their affections to their holy laws. Let thy kingdom be set up gloriously over us and do thou reign in our spirit by thy spirit of grace.

THY WILL BE DONE ON EARTH AS IT IS IN HEAVEN.

Thy will, O God, is the measure of holiness and peace, thy providence, he great disposer of all things, tying all events together in order to thy glory and thy good for thy servants, by a wonderful mysterious chain of wisdom. Let thy will also be the measure of our desires, for we know that whatsoever thou doest is good. Grant that we may submit our will to thine, being patient of evils which thou inflictest; lovers of the good which thou commandest; haters of all evil.

GIVE US THIS DAY OUR DAILY BREAD.

Thou, O God, which takest care of our souls, do not despise our bodies, which thou hast made and sanctified and designed to be glorious. But now we are exposed to hunger and thirst, nakedness and weariness, want and inconvenience. Give unto us neither poverty nor riches, but feed us with food convenient for us and clothe us with fitting provisions according to that state and condition wherein thou hast placed thy servant, that we may not be tempted with want nor made contemptible by beggary, nor wanton or proud by riches, nor in love with anything in this world, but that we may use it as strangers and pilgrims, as the relief of our needs, the support of our infirmities and the oil of our lamps, feeding us till we are quite spent in thy service.

FORGIVE US OUR DEBTS AS WE FORGIVE OUR DEBTORS.

O dear God, unless thou art pleased to pardon us, in vain it is that we should live here, and what good will our life do us? O, look upon us with much mercy, for we have sinned greviously against thee, O God. Pardon the adherent imperfections of our life, the weakness of our duty, the carelessness of our spirit,—our affected ignorance, our intelligence, our rashness and want of observations, our malice and presumptions.

LEAD US NOT INTO TEMPTATION.

Gracious Father, we are weak and ignorant, our afflictions betray us and make us willing to die. Our adversary, the devil, goeth up and down seeking whom he may devour. He is busy and crafty, malicious and powerful, watchful and envious, and we tempt ourselves running out to mischief.

BUT DELIVER US FROM EVIL.

From sin and shame from the malice and fraud of the devil, and from the falseness and greediness of men, from all thy wrath and from all our impurities. Good Lord, deliver thy servant.

FOR THINE IS THE KINGDOM, THE POWER AND THE GLORY FOREVER. AMEN.

So shall we, thy servants advance the mightiness of thy kingdom, the power of thy majesty and the glory of thy mercy from generation to generation forever. Amen.

TOBIAS M. KAUFFMAN.
Neffsville, Pa.

TEMPTATION.

This subject is one of great importance to all men, especially to professors of religion. Wherefore seeing we also are compassed about with such an innumerable cloud of witnesses we should lay aside every weight and the sin which doth so easily beset us, that we may run the race which is set before us with patience.

The tempter is daily watching our movements, our progress and our life, but his greatest concern is our negligence. Let us consider Him that endured such contradiction of sinners against Himself, lest we be weary and faint in our minds. Perhaps we have not yet resisted unto blood striving against sin. If we consider how, through all the meandering scenes of life that Satan, in various ways, makes an effort to temporize our path to eternal glory by smoothing it a little, making it easier to get along with our worldly affairs and all that men in general are engaged in. It almost makes us shudder to think of it. But it raises joy in our hearts to peruse the greatest annal that ever was dispersed through America viz: the Gospel, and there learn that Christ died for the propitiation of our sins, and not for ours only but for the sins of the whole world, also leaving us an example in all things, He being baptized in Jordan and that being sanctioned by a voice from Heaven acknowledging Him as His Son; then He was led up of the Spirit to be tempted of the devil, and when He had fasted forty days and forty nights was an hungered. Then the tempter tempted Him and said: if thou be the Son of God, command that these stones be made bread. This is the joy that we have, that Christ gave us an example in this even when we are tempted how to overcome evil with good. Now seeing that the destroyer is a crafty being taking the advantage of our blessed Master by holding out such inducements as would be almost impossible for us to overcome, it becomes us to take instruction.

In our age of the world, there are people who might believe that the Spirit tempted them, but we understand it to mean, if we go on unforbidden ground (such there are many in the world) and give place to enticements; certainly we are not in the bounds of our duty, and God hath not promised the comforter. There, then, he might suffer us to be tempted. The Spirit will lead us into all truth, but when ever we are out of our bounds we have no promise of not being tempted. Therefore, being negligent in our daily duty, God may suffer us to be tempted. Thus mortal man has many temptations to overcome or to be thrown into. Just as cunning as the enticer was in ancient times, he is to this hour, for he has already the current flowing by every wind of doctrine, making professors of religion believe there are nonessentials written in the word of God. Others are induced to believe that the Spirit of God will follow them to gatherings of the world, and may be connected with the world in almost all respects. Therefore, in due time let us one and all meditate upon the Gospel of truth and not annihilate even the church of Christ by disobedience or selfrighteousness, but be obedient in all things. Although we frequently stray upon paths that are devious in our pilgrimage, let us not be negligent in our daily devotion to God, for we know that He is faithful and will not suffer us to be tempted above that we are able, but will with the temptation also make a way of escape that we may be able to bear it; therefore we should be careful not to receive the grace of God in vain, and let him that thinketh he stand take heed lest he fall.

ANOMALOUS.

THE HOUSE OF THE LORD.

Of all places on earth, methinks the sweetest one is in the house of the Lord,—where Christians meet to worship the Most High, and where Jesus has promised to be in the midst, if assembled in His name. Cold and indifferent must be the heart that does not esteem this as a pleasant duty, and a privilege that is calculated to qualify us better for the various responsibilities incident to life. Weary with the toils, trials and excitement which we meet with while engaged in our earthly vocations, yet we can look forward with bright anticipations to the hour when we will for a time, lay these aside as belonging to the cares of this life, and go up to the house of the Lord, and there have our souls fed with the Bread of Life. To those who go up to this sacred place with full determinations to worship "in spirit and in truth," it is none other than "the house of God and the gate of Heaven," but those who go to the house of prayer careless and unconcerned, it is not likely that they will receive much benefit from the beautiful and instructive truths that are there presented by those whose duty it is to proclaim the Gospel to a dying world.

Many may prefer to frequent the ball-room or some other vain and sinful amusement which the world participates in, but our highest joy should consist in attending the house of the Lord. These scenes should be dear to every heart, as they are bright spots strewn along our pathway through life, and if entered into with solemnity and a desire to be instructed in the right paths, will produce great and lasting benefits.

This world would indeed be a dreary waste were it not for the solemn assemblies where God's people congregate to worship Him, and where they are encouraged to go on in the good cause which they have espoused,—to labor with renewed zeal in the Master's cause, thus securing unto themselves a rich inheritance, and showing to those around them that they have been with Jesus and learned of Him, that they too may be constrained to frequent the house of prayer and praise and thereby glorify their Father in Heaven. May we ever esteem it a high and sacred privilege to meet in the sanctuary of the Lord while here on earth, that when we are done meeting and parting in these earthly temples, we may be so unspeakably happy as to meet in our Father's house in that beautiful land on High.

"You may sing of the beauty of mountain or dale,
Of the silvery streamlet and flowers of the vale;
But the place most delightful this earth can afford,
Is the place of devotion, the house of the Lord."

W. A. CLARKE.
Pilgrim Office.

PATIENCE.

"But let patience have her perfect work, that ye may be perfect, and entire, wanting nothing. James 1:4.

Nowhere else in the Bible is this ennobling principle so often spoken of, in so few of the sacred pages as in the epistle of James. The Apostle knew its worth by inspiration as well as by experience and natural philosophy. He studied its results and found it most provident of good, that it tended unto perfection, and as having a tendency to prepare its possessor for any and every emergency, being "entire," and as providing for him all things so that he be "wanting nothing." Thus do all Christians study this virtue and thus do they find it. Patience is the foundation from which flows an incense, that sweetly flavors all passions. It causes happiness, joy and peace in the family circle. It causes glad hearts when father returns home. It causes affectionate accents and expressions of love; terms of reverence, acts of kindness, longsuffering and forbearance toward all. As it gladdens hearts when fathers return home, so does it secure and preserve cheerfulness when mothers retire for a few hours from the cares and toils of home. Patience is an indispensible link in the chain which suspends those eight grand characteristics which, if they "be in you and abound they shall make you that ye shall be neither barren nor unfruitful in the knowledge of our Lord and Savior Jesus Christ." But if this link be broken, then shall three of these fall, of which one is Charity, which Paul says is greater than faith or hope.

C. C. ROOT.

THE DESIGN OF BAPTISM.

Continued.

God is a God of order, and his organized law is a law of order, and we are required to obey it in the order in which it is laid down, which is both consistent and clear to every unprejudiced man or woman. But through philosophy and vain deceit we become contaminated with the rudiments of the world, influenced by the power of satan, and we soon begin to set up our judgment against God and His holy apostles, hence, the great confusion in christendom at the present day.

A series of Essays came under my notice a short time since on the subject above treated, and the writer when referring to the sermon of Peter, in regard to baptism for the remission of sins, would try to make us believe that the word for, meant *because of*, and therefore sins must first be remitted before a candidate is fit for baptism, and that baptism, is only a right signifying that sins are remitted. I would here say, that brings him into a dreadful dilemma, for Peter says repent and be baptized for the remission of your sins, then if the word *for*, means because of, it would read thus: repent and be baptized because you have your sins remitted, about as glaring a fraud as could possibly be practiced against the messengers of Christ.

Again, he says, when referring to I Peter, 3: 21. "The like figure whereunto even baptism doth also now save us, (not the putting away of the filth of the flesh," &c. It seems to me that the outward washing in baptism is here, by Peter, called the putting away of the filth of the flesh. Why does he say so? Not because Peter says so, for Peter says right to the contrary. Now whose testimony will we take, Peters or J. H.'s? Oh, consistency, thou art a jewel. Again, "We must be baptized into Christ not in water," and many more like expressions which are not worthy of comment. Any who have a desire to see the essays I will refer you to the *Church Advocate*, published in Lancaster, Pa., dated Oct. 2d, 9th and 16th, but the writer is a resident of our county.

Now I will show you dear reader that Peter meant what he said, on the day of Pentecost, and that it corresponds and corroberates with the general tenor of the gospel. All other inspired writers give testimony that in the general order of God's dealing with men it required a duty to be performed. That duty is repentance and baptism for the remission of our sins, and that is the design of it and what it will accomplish when complied with according to gospel order. We will now take you back to the ushering in of the gospel dispensation and see what was then preached, Matt. 3: 1. In those days came John the Baptist preaching in the wilderness of Judea and saying, Repent, &c. in the 6th verse, and were baptized of him in Jordan confessing their sins not upon their remission. Oh, but says one, John's baptism was not Christian baptism. Well, let us pass on to 13th verse of same chapter we read, "Then cometh Jesus from Gallilee to Jordon unto John to be baptized of him." Now if that which is said above be true then we find here Jesus guilty of an unchristian act, for Matthew the Evangelist says, John baptized him, and when he was baptized he went up out of the water, (which is another thought worthy of our attention, especially those of you who are in the habit of going through the formula in the house), Jesus said it was becoming so that all righteousness might be fulfilled. Another might say, Jesus was not baptized for the remission of sins, we admit and say more, he was not required to repent, either; then that is an exceptional case. The reason of this is, he had nothing to repent of, and whenever we find one among you having nothing to repent of we will say the same. But such is not the case, then we will treat you as John treated the people of Jerusalem and the Land of Judea, that is, have you baptized in the water confessing your sins. That is so plain that any man not blind with prejudice or otherwise can see, and as for John's baptism not being Christian is so thin it seems as though some one would frighten at their own shadow. I would ask who sent John? That is enough. The Savior once asked the Jews this question, "The baptism of John, was it from Heaven or of men? Again it is said, the lawyers and Pharisees rejected the counsel of God against themselves and were not baptized of John. Were John's disciples rebaptized? I would like to see an account of a case? If not, then it was valid baptism and approved of by God and Christ, giving us an example. And out of the number of those whom John baptized, Christ chose twelve to be his witnesses whom he sent forth to preach his word. Now does their word and works correspond with the word and work of John. Of Peters' history I have already given. We will now come to Paul, one born out of due time, not receiving his instruction in the same way that the others did, but getting it direct from heaven after the resurrection of Christ from the dead, for at the time the other apostles were busily engaged in spreading the gospel. Saul, as he was then called, was persecuting the followers of Christ, being brought up at the feet of Gamaliel as many of the divines of the present day, but when God saw proper to call him from his wicked career and put him to a more noble purpose, and that, at a time when he was very busily engaged, having received authority from the rulers, was on his way to Damascus to bring to Jerusalem those disciples of Christ and punish them because they did not obey Gamaliel, but God met him in the way and said, "Saul, why do you persecute me?" Saul was astonished at this bit of information but said what shall I do Lord? Now if as we hear so much from our friends who so bitterly oppose us in the setting forth of the gospel as it is delivered unto us, why not have Saul's sins forgiven where the Lord met him, why did he have to go through the hands of one of his faithful disciples? Answer, because it is the order of God's dealing with men. Was it contrary to the course delivered by Peter on the day of Pentecost? If it was, then there is two orders. I tell you nay. There is one plan for our salvation, and as already said, it is clearly set forth, not shrouded in mystery as some would have us to believe. We will now take Paul's own language of the formula which he underwent when he was initiated into the family of God. Turn to the 22d chap. of the Acts of the Apostles 16th verse, which reads, "And now, why tarriest thou, arise and be baptized and wash away thy sins, calling on the name of the Lord." This was his own language long after he was converted, at the time he was making his defence in Jerusalem. I have given three positive cases under three different orders, that is, one before Christ's death and resurrection, one immediately after by one of his chosen witnesses, and one especially called to bear his name before the Gentiles; a perfect agreement in their order of procedure having received their authority from the court of Heaven, in which we do not find such a divided state of things as in this fast age.

SEEDS.

Who can tell what a world of life is wrapped up in the tiny acorn, as it lies unnoticed half buried in the soil? The brown earth, out of pity, hides it away in her bosom and nourishes the little germ. Soon two shining green leaves peep above the earth, and in a short time they are grown to a shrub. The hand of a child might pluck it up and yet all the form of life manifested by the giant oak is contained in it. The smallest of seeds, the mustard, produces a plant from seven to nine feet high, approximating a tree, where the fowls of the air may find shelter among its branches. The winds and ocean currents bring the seeds and plants from every shore and deposit them upon the coral reefs, in time, render them a fit habitation for man. Here the cocoanut grows and the palm tree spreads its broad leaves to protect him from a tropical sun. Who can tell from a seed what the plant may be? The germ of the towering pine is contained in a much smaller seed-coat than the acorn. The smooth, light seed of the thistle which the wind carries to and fro over the fields, does not indicate the trouble that the farmer has to root up the noxious plant that injures the grain. A husbandman passing by a neighbor's field saw a thistle growing alone. Instead of pulling it up as his first impulse was, he went on, and the next year he found dozens of the same plants in his own fields. We may learn from this to regard the faults of others with charity, for sin may have scattered the same seed in our hearts. The time for different species of seeds to germinate is varied. Some germinate in a few days, some in a few weeks, while others remain buried for a whole season.

The good seed of truth often lies buried long after the sower has gone to his reward. The growth of plants also depends upon the nature of the soil and the manner in which it has been prepared. The pastor's field is wide. Thorns and thistles are springing up among the plants and he needs to work diligently to destroy these. Many an earnest minister has wept over the seed he has sown, for he saw no prospect of a harvest, "only the leaves, no gathered sheaves." Another comes in his place and the field having been cultivated by his predecessor, reaps his labors in a precious ingathering of souls. The field of the Sabbath school teacher is smaller and he can more carefully watch the tender plants and by the help of the Master may be able to gather the fruit of eternal life, but a mother gone to her rest may have scattered the seed.

The spirit of christianity that is mingling with the atmosphere of many nations to-day, is not the product of our generation, but the spirit and teachings and struggles in which Luther, Whitfield, Calvin, the Pilgrims, Roger Williams, Judson and many others have sowed precious seed. We are reminded of the scripture, "Except a corn of wheat fall into the ground and die it abideth alone." The seeds that are sown in tears, we are told, shall be reaped in joy. Into every christian heart God has poured the good seed and commands us to scatter it abroad. He alone can give the increase. Then let us commit all that we do to his care, praying that while we try to sow the precious seed that we may be kept from scattering also the tares.

MAGGIE SPIFLER.

Hollidaysburg, Pa.

A merry heart doeth good like a medicine.—*Bible.*

Youth's Department.

THE CHILD AND THE RILL.

CHILD.

Beautiful rill,
Sparkling and bright,
Gliding so still
From morn to night,
Who taught thee to flow?
Who ordered thy course?
And thy fount below,
Who gave it its source?

RILL.

'Twas God, my dear child,
Who gave me my source;
He taught me to flow,
And ordered my course,
'Neath the shade of the trees,
By the side of the hill,
'Midst the grass and the flowers,
So gentle and still

And this is the place
For me to do good;
At the foot of the hill,
In the shade of the wood,
I water the herds;
I refresh the tall trees;
I nurture the flowers,
And cool every breeze.

And if, my dear child,
God e'er fixes your lot
At the foot of the hill,
Come, oh, come to this spot.
Hear the beautiful birds
Sing among the thick bowers,
And see the blithe bees
Sipping sweets from the flowers.

See what beauty and love,
And what happiness to,
Spring up by my side,
And your pathway pursue:
Nor sigh to be great,
Like the ocean or flood;
But, like the small rill,
Be content to do good.

"NO ONE TO LOVE ME NOW."

How sad it is to think of orphan children! Here they are in our picture. Their mother has just died. Before retiring to rest that night, sister Martha went into her mother's room. There she found her little crippled brother, Eddy, crying bitterly, as he raised the cold hand that lay beside him.

"Mother! O mother, speak to me! Tell me you'll not go away! Oh, I will be good! If you leave me, I shall have nobody to love me!"

He paused for an answer, and then receiving none, he said again, in a voice of sorrow which pierced Martha's heart;

"Mother, dear mother, do speak to me!"

Martha went up quietly to him, and laying her hand gently on his shoulder, she whispered "Eddy!"

The little boy raised his face. Oh, how pale and wan it was!

"Eddy, mother is in Heaven now: she cannot hear you speak to her."

"Oh, she must hear me! She always listened to me before."

"But she can't now, Eddy, because God has taken her away."

"And will she never come back?"

"No; but if you ask the Lord Jesus Christ, He will take you to be with her some day."

"But there is no one to love me now."

"I will, Eddy;" and she drew him tenderly into her arms, and kissed him almost as fondly as his mother had done. Eddy looked up into her face, and there seemed to be something there which he could trust, for by degrees his sobs became less violent; and bidding his sister good-night, quietly, he went up to bed.

Both the brother and sister cried themselves to sleep that night.

God pity and bless the poor orphans. How good He is to permit us to say:

"When my father and my mother forsake me, then the Lord will take me up."

EASIER NOW.

"It is my birthday, grandpappa," said the boy; "I have so many presents—a top and a ball, and some books."

His grandpappa looked rather sadly at the child and said—"I hope you will grow up a wise and good man, Arthur, and a happier man than I have been."

"Why, grandpapa?" asked the boy.

"I did not remember my Creator when I was young, my boy. I was always putting it off till another day, and when my friend here used to say that youth was the best time to think of God, and to give my heart to Him, I would say there was time enough yet, and I forgot God, in whose hands my life was. Then came the cares of life, and I seemed to have no time. I had to work for my living; to toil all the long days, and sometimes nights, in my counting room, at my books, and I found it difficult then to think of God. At last I was very ill; God took away the health for which I had never thanked Him, and the strength which I had thought was all my own; but in illness, and during nights of pain and bitter suffering, I found I could not think of God nor study the Bible which I had neglected, nor learn of Jesus, whom I had rejected. God raised me up again, however; but then I had other sorrows and cares, and it still seemed as if there was no time for religion. I have at last, I hope, found Jesus my Savior; but how sad is the thought to me that I have nothing but a world-weary heart to offer Him! I can do nothing for God, for I have so little strength either of mind or body."

The boy looked grave. His grandparent went on, "It is an easy yoke that Christ bids us take. Is it not, friend Gray?"

"It is indeed," said the other old man with a quiet smile.

"Bear this in mind, dear boy, that serving God in youth saves us from many sorrows, and it does not take away from us one real pleasure. Don't let your birthday pass away without praying that God would help you to remember Him now in the days of your youth."

The child lifted up his heart and God heard his prayer.

THE VOICE OF THE BELL

A boy whose only religious education was obtained in a Sabbath school, discovered the worth of his soul at a very early age, and became convicted of sin. Christian friends looked forward to the time when he would be useful in the service of Christ for he appeared to be truly converted. But he formed the acquaintance of careless and wicked boys, and, by degrees, he absented himself from Sabbath school, and from church. At last he forsook both entirely, and said he was "ashamed to be a Sabbath scholar now, as he was a big boy." He went on from bad to worse, till he became a young man.

One Sabbath morning, he with some of his wicked companions, had set forth to spend the day in sport. They happened to pass the church where, when a boy, he had attended the Sabbath school. Just as they reached the steps, the bell pealed out its solemn tone.

He started; to his ears it spoke as plain as human voice: "Come, come, come!" Then and there the Spirit arrested him. He went on, but every peal rang in his ear, "Come, come now!" As the last stroke died away he turned to his companions, saying: "I'll not go with you to-day; I am going back to church." They laughed and tried to stop him; but he turned from them, and went back to the church, the days of his boyhood in that Sabbath school walking with him in the visions of memory every step of the way. The sermon was from the words, "Come unto me," etc. Then and there the Savior said to his soul, "Come;" and he went. To this day he is one of the most zealous workers in the vineyard of Christ. List to "the sound of the church-going bell," and see if it says not to you: "Come, come, come now."—*Sunday School Messenger.*

DO IT IN TIME.

Only two or three inches—that was all. If the switchman had moved the track only that little distance, all would have been right. But he forgot; and the train that was passing the station ran furiously into the heavy freight cars, and dashed itself to pieces!

"What was the cause?" everybody asked, when the news of the great accident spread about town.

"Oh! a switch was out of place," was the answer. "The switchman was careless. Perhaps he was drunk."

How true it is, as Solomon said "There is a time for everything." If we do not attend to it at the right time, it is just as bad as if we did not do it at all.

Correspondence.

A Reporter is wanted from every Church in the brotherhood to send us Church news, Obituaries, Announcements or anything that will be of general interest. To insure insertion, the writers name must accompany each communication. Our invitation is not personal but general—please respond to our call.

BLACKSBURG, VA.,
Feb. 4th '73.

Dear brethren:—I received yours dated January 29th this morning, and was pleased with the Christian spirit that dictated it. In response to its contents, I will say that the ever welcome PILGRIM has not reached me this year yet, and that I was growing impatient for its weekly visits. I believe I wrote substantially in my last to be recognized as a permanent subscriber, if not, regard me so from henceforward until it is directed otherwise. I regret very much my inability to communicate for its pages at present.

My health is very much impaired at this time, and I am contemplating a visit to "Our Home" New York, to try the virtue of its healing agencies. Should I go there, I will try and send you a remembrance, occasionally if my health will permit. I am now barely able to get about the house, and have been compelled, though reluctantly, to suspend the labors of the ministry indefinitely. As soon as I revive sufficiently, I will devote a full share of my time and energies to the good cause which you are carrying forward. May the Great Physician bless His feeble servant with His presence to enable him to suffer for the cause of salvation, and may you likewise receive a due share of Heaven's gifts.

Your brother,
D. C. MOOMAW.

REMARKS. The above is the expression of a large number of our readers. Some have said, "Send it on until I order it stopped," others, "as long as it is is published," &c. but of course, we cannot remember these things, and as they are generally such as are in the habit of writing to us, we made no note of it, expecting that they, like all others, would notice our present arrangement, and inform us of their wish of having it continued, but it seems that they may have been waiting and depending on their "life-lease" for reading the PILGRIM. We highly appreciate such abiding faith in our Christian integrity, but are sorry that they were disappointed in not receiving the PILGRIM. We especially sympathize with our much esteemed brother Moomaw in his affliction, and hope that through the aid of our Great Physician and from the benefits to be derived from a treatment at "Our Home" he may soon be restored to health and be again enabled to preach the unsearchable riches of Christ.

THE NAME OF JESUS SOUNDS SO SWEET.

These are words that have left a lasting impression on my mind, from the fact, that they came from the dying lips of a departed friend.

Three years ago I had a dear brother. His manly strength was not surpassed in all the country. His health was very good. To look at him you would think death would never overtake him, but alas, disease took hold on his manly frame and brought him down to a bed of sickness. He was unable to attend to business for eight long months. He did not profess to be a follower of the meek and lowly Jesus but often remarked to me that he intended to be a christian, and wanted to be a true follower of Christ, but he was deprived of ever attaching himself to the church, but thank God, he had a lingering disease, and I feel satisfied he made peace with Him who is able to forgive the worst of sinners. While our dear old mother was attending to his wants and spending many sleepless nights over him, he saw her weeping and said, "mother do not weep for me, but be up and doing for yourself." Just before his death, while some friends were singing the hymn, "Jesus lover of my soul," he said, "how sweet the name of Jesus sounds," and soon left this vale of tears. I feel satisfied he reached that happy home where parting will be no more, and now I will say to father, mother and sisters, do not get weary serving the Lord, but prepare to meet thy son and our dear brother. We have one more dear brother who is out of the ark of safety and still sporting on the brink of ruin. May God be merciful to him, and may he flee the wrath to come before it is too late and prepare to meet death and hear the welcome plaudit, "well done thou good and faithful servant, that he may inherit the kingdom prepared for the people of God."

"Vain brother thy mad pursuit forbear,
Repent, thy end is nigh;
Death at the farthest can't be far,
O, think, before you die."

Now in conclusion, I will say dear brethren and sisters in the Lord, be up and doing and if you have friends still walking the downward road, try and pursuade them to turn from their evil way. They may be snatched from time to eternity without one moments warning. There is a work for us all to do. If we cannot preach we can talk. Let us all do our part, and do it without delay, and try to bear each others burdens while traveling through this world of trouble is the desire of your unworthy follower of Christ. C. P. F.

WITH.

"I indeed baptize you with [en] water unto repentance: but he that cometh after me is mightier than I, whose shoes I am not worthy to bear he shall baptize you with [en] the Holy Ghost, and *with* [not in the Greek] fire." Matt. iii. 11.

The Greek preposition *en*, which is here translated *with*, is found not less than 290 times in Matthew's gospel; and out of the 290 times which it occurs in the *Greek* Testament, it is rendered *in* 215 times in King James' translation. It is rendered *among*, 12 times; *within*, 3 times; *for*, once; *under*, once; *through*, once; *at*, once; *unto*, once; *upon*, once; *because*, 2 times; *at*, 7 times; *on*, 4 times; by miscellaneous terms, 4 times; *by*, 26 times, and is rendered *with* but 11 times; so that our authority for saying that John baptized with water is without foundation. It should be rendered *in*; "I indeed baptize you *in* water." "He shall baptize you *in* the Holy Ghost, and (*in*) fire."

For the benefit of the readers that are not acquainted with the Greek I, will refer to a few places where the Greek *en* (in) is found.

Matt. iii, 6. Baptized of him *in* (*en*) Jordan.
" iv. 21. *In* (*en*) a ship with Zebadee.
" " 23. Teaching *in* (*en*) their synagogues.
" v, 12. Your reward *in* (*en*) Heaven.
" " 15. All that are *in* (*en*) the house.
" vi, 9. Our Father which art *in* (*en*) Heaven.
" ix, 10. Sat at meat *in* (*en*) the house.

J. H. MOORE.

Bros. Brumbaugh:—We had a meeting in the Rock Run District, Indiana, last week. Brother Jesse Calvert was with us. The weather was cold and very stormy and the lanes were drifted full, but they were shoveled open and a good attendance was had and a great interest taken in the meeting by everybody.

On Saturday, ten were baptized, notwithstanding the ice, snow and cold winds.

Also the week previous, a meeting was held in the Shipswaney district by Bro. Jesse Calvert and Isaac L. Berkey. There was no Meeting-house, but the neighbors and friends all agreed to stop the school during the meeting as the weather was so very cold. Four more were made willing to enter the Kingdom of Jesus and were taken to the Lake, the ice, 30 inches thick, cut open, and there buried with Christ in Baptism. Many more seem to have made up their minds to come into the Church, for which purpose there is another meeting of several days appointed, commencing on the 12th day of April. The good work of the Lord is still going on. JACOB BERKEY.

FOREST CITY, MO.
FEB. 3d., 1873.

Dear Pilgrim:—We have had a very cold winter so far. At present it is moderating and the snow is thawing rapidly. It had been 24 degrees below zero about Christmas with an average of about 8 degrees below zero for six weeks. I hope that the coldest weather is over, at least we are willing that it should be. (So are we. Ed.) I recalled all our appointments for meetings at a distance from us until the first Sunday in March, it being too cold and icy to travel any distance. The horse disease is also among us, but few have died and it is about over.

We are still slowly increasing in number here in the Bethel Church under the blessing of God, and we hope and pray that a continuation of those blessings may attend our weak efforts which we hope still to make in favor of the good cause.

Love to the saints.

A. J. CORRELL.

Brother's Brumbaugh: As church news are solicited, I would say that we, the brethren of the Ridge District are moving along slowly, not many accessions. Sinners, like Pharoah, are willing to put it off a day longer. Brother Daniel Hollinger was with us at a school house near where I live and preached three successive evenings, and also on Sabbath at the Etter Meeting House. He labored faithfully, hope he will be rewarded for his labors of love and that the seed sown may produce a bountiful harvest. We are glad when brethren come to preach for us. Yours in the bonds of Christian love.

DAVID M. FOULKSANGER.

POTTSTOWN, PA.,
Feb. 4th, 1873.

Editors of the Pilgrim: We the members of the North Coventry Church, have had quite a refreshing time. We have been made to sit in heavenly places with Christ Jesus. We had a continued meeting of two weeks. Bro. J. Myers, D. Hollinger, D. Yountz, S. Zug and others were with us. There were sixteen added to the Church and several more are expected to join in with us. May the Lord bless the brethren for their labors of love.

HANNAH HOLLOWBUSH.

MARRIED.

KEIM—HERSHBERGER.—At the residence of the bride's parents, (Elder Henry Hershberger,) by Eld. S. C. Keim, on Feb. 6th, 1873, Bro. Sam'l C Keim of Salisbury, Somerset Co., Pa., to sister Fannie Hershberger, of Everett, Bedford Co., Pa. M. W. KEIM.

GLASS—KENSINGER.—At the residence of the undersigned, New Enterprise, Bedford Co., Pa., Feb. 6th, 1873, Martin F. Glass and Lydia D. Kensinger, of Blair Co., Pa. S. A. MOORE.

MILLER—ANDES.—By the undersigned, at the house of the bride's parents, Holt Co., Mo., Feb. 2d, 1873, bro. John Miller and Miss Susannah Andes, both formerly of Rockingham Co., Va.

A. J. CORRELL.

SHANK—MYERS.—By the undersigned, Feb. 4th, 1873, Jacob H. Shank and Miss Susan Myers, all of Franklin Co., Pa.

G. W. BRICKER.

BAUM—McCOLLY.—On January 23, 1873, by the undersigned, at his residence, Mr. L. Baum and Miss H. McColly, both of Columbiana co., Ohio.

HESTAND - KELLY.—On the evening of Feb. 6, at the bride's parents, in West township, by the undersigned, Mr. Frank L. Hestand and Miss Nancy E. Kelly both of Columbiana Co., Ohio.

JOHN A. CLEMENT.

DIED.

SNAPP.—Near DeGraff, Logan Co., Ohio, Jan. 19, 1873, friend Wm. Snapp, aged 44 years, 11 mos. and 15 days.

Disease, Lung fever, leaves a kind companion, sister in the Church and six children to mourn their loss. Funeral preached by the writer and M. Swonger from 1 Cor. 15: 22, 23. J. F.

ANDRIST.—Died on Feb. 1st, in Columbiana Co., Ohio, Emma, daughter of John and Magdalena Andrist, of Minnesota, while here on a visit with her mother, aged 3 years, 2 mos. and 1 day. Funeral services by the undersigned.

JOHN A. CLEMENT.

SNAPP.—Also at same place, and out of same family, Jan. 26, 1873, Jabez L., son of Wm and Mary Snapp, aged 16 years, 6 mos. and 8 days.

Disease, Lung fever. Funeral preached by the writer and M. Swonger, from 90th Psalm, 9 and 10th verses. So we see, just in one week's time, father and son were taken out of one family. Let us take warning. J. L. FRANTZ.

MILLER.—In the Cherry Grove Congregation, Carroll co., Ill., Jan. 23, 1873, Emma Miller, aged 10 years, 8 mos. and 5 days.

Thus is another one joined to the happy throng. She was a pleasant little girl, loving and loved by all, and especially the family. She was the youngest and the pet of the family. Funeral services by the brethren, from John 4: 40.

KATE ESHELMAN.

MONEY LIST.

Leonard Furry	$20.00
G. W. Bricker	1.50
Mahlon P Lichty	.50
Jeremiah Rothermel	1.12½
H A Switzer	3.00
Hannah Hollowbush	.50
Benj. Brumbaugh	1.50
H H Fleck	5.00
P D Fahrney	.50
John Brumbaugh	1.50
Daniel Brower	7.50
Kate Eshelman	12.00
Mrs. Rosa Speck	1.50
S A Moore	1.00
Rebecca J Reynolds	.50
D Bolsbaugh	4.30
S E Miller	.50
Henry Sperline,	1.00
Elias Latshaw	1.50
J L Frantz	10.00
Levi Swigart	1.25
Jacob Kinsel	1.50
M F H Kinsel	1.50
Joseph Dunmire	1.50
Wm A Murray	18.20
J R Miller	6.00
E P L Dow	10.50
Mathias Frantz	1.50
C C Root	8.50
Wm Sadler	21.50
J H Moore	9.00

Money List crowded out.

The Weekly Pilgrim.

JAMES CREEK, PA., Feb. 18th, 1873.

☞ How to send money.—All sums over $1.50, should be sent either in a check, draft or postal order. If neither of these can be obtained, have the letter registered.

☞ When Money is sent, *always* send with it the name and address of those who paid it. Write the names and post office as plainly as possible.

☞ Every subscriber for 1873, gets a *Pilgrim Almanac* Free.

SPRING RUN MEETING.

On last Saturday, February 8th, after passing through a very busy week, we concluded to unyoke ourself from office duty and give the McVeytown brethren a short visit, it being the commencement of a series of meetings to be held at that place.

At 3.20 p. m. we took our leave of the office, and making the connection at Huntingdon, arrived at McVeytown a little before sundown. On leaving the car, we soon learned that brethren J. R. Lane and G. Hanawalt were also on the train. It so happened that each got into a different car without the notice of the other, of course we would not have made the point any sooner, but we lost the opportunity of a friendly chat which we always enjoy. Sometimes luck meets us at every corner, so it was in this case, brother Geo's son had brought a sleigh to convey him home and in it, we found just enough room for our accommodation, and in a short time we were landed at his home where our bodily wants were attended to, and then off for the meeting, which, by the way, was a little late. When we entered the church we found a large audience which was being profitably addressed by brother J. R. Lane, who was the only strange minister present except those of the adjoining congregation, Lewistown. Bro. Lane delivered quite an interesting discourse, followed by Bro. Archy Vandyke, who speaks with considerable earnestness and power.

After service, Elder Hanawalt concluded to divide the labors making three appointments for Sabbath a.m. The other brethren were to fill the outside appointments, and we were left to fill the one at the church. The arrangements all made, we were taken to the home of P. S. Myers, (resident minister), where we were kindly cared for, brother Lane was also present. Next morning we repaired to the church with the weight of our duty heavily upon us, but to our great satisfaction we there met our brother D. M. Holsinger, who on account of bad connection arrived too late for the evening meeting. Of course, we waived the position and brother Daniel gave the audience quite a solid sermon, faith being the subject. He is not apt in stirring up the animal feelings, neither is it his desire, but deals in evident facts which cannot well be gainsayed. We followed with such ideas as were at command. After meeting, we were taken to the house of our old brother Samuel Myers where we dined. His family has become quite small, his children all being married, and have left the old homestead except Reuben, who lives in the same house and has charge of the farm. Two sons and two sons-in-law are in the ministry, one a deacon and the others all members except two. Again next March, if they are spared, will be the fiftieth year that they have lived together in wedlock and have in contemplation, a golden wedding,—except the gold, which he thinks is a little too scarce to have it displayed very much,—that they may be enabled once more before being gathered to the fathers, see all their children together, which is possible as they are all yet living, and what is remarkable, he informed us that in keeping house fifty years, they never had a death in their house. We hope the old father and mother may be spared to realize their desires.

In the evening, there were services again at the Church, and we led off with the ability given, followed by D. M. Holsinger. After services we were taken to Elder Hanawalt's, in company with D. M. Holsinger, where we enjoyed ourself much and had quite an interesting evening and morning entertainment. Bro. Joseph is zealous of his charge and rules well, leaving nothing undone that he thinks might be for the advancement of the good cause. The move now on foot for the abolishing of the hell nurseries with which our country is cursed, is by him, receiving due attention, and he is not ashamed to let the brethren and the world know that the Church of the "Brethren" *is a* temperance Church, and that he regards it a sacred privilege to slay the demon in the bud. Brethren, a word. Remember, we oppose Temperance Societies on the basis that the Church has it *all*. That is right, —our position exactly. The principle is good, very good, but the practice, *the practice*. There is where we may commit ourselves. The issue is before us and we *must* cast an influence for or against. Make it a subject of prayer, weigh it well and then with the light which God will give, act. The time passed so pleasantly, that before we were aware of it, the hour, to go up to the house of the Lord had arrived, where we resorted and enjoyed another very pleasant waiting in the Sanctuary. We now took leave of the brethren, and was taken out to Bro. Abram Myers, also a resident minister, near the depot, that we might take the p. m. train for home. Here we met Eld. Wm. Howe and brother and sister Shellenberger who had come this far on their way to meeting. At this place we spent our time pleasantly, and we trust profitably. In the evening we took the train for home but remained over night in Huntingdon for want of connection—were hospitably entertained in the house of our brother A. B. Brumbaugh M. D., and next morning reached home and found all things well.

The brethren at Spring Run, (McVeytown) intend continuing the meeting during the week, and we hope the result may be a realization of their fondest expectations—souls converted to God.

THE GREAT WONDER.

The great wonder to strangers is, how James Creek can produce such a ponderous mail. They can scarcely be made to believe that so small a place can contain a printing office with so large a circulation, and in so short a time, but it is a fact and teaches us not to despise the day of small things. Like the tiny snowball, we commenced from a small center and rolled on and on, until our dimensions became of such a magnitude that we cannot escape observation. The humble Pilgrim now travels the United States from center to circumference and weekly makes glad the hearts of thousands, and still the voice from the North and South, East and West is come. The last week has been a propitious one for us, adding largely to our list. And so it will continue, brethren and sisters, if the proper effort is kept up. The Pilgrim for 1873 is acknowledged by all to be a great improvement upon those of the past and all that is needed to leave its circulation doubled, is to be seen. For this purpose we will send, free of postage, a number of specimen copies to any and all who wish to labor for us. Our terms are so liberal to such as are honest and *will* pay as soon as they can, that it makes it an easy matter to gather subscribers for us. There is very little risk to run if you can get a brother or sister to subscribe as it is an important part of our religion to pay our honest dues, and any that refuse to do it have denied the faith and are not worthy of the name. It is true, we have a large amount of money standing out, but we think it safe, because it is in the hands of brethren. On account of our money lists not being very large a few of our friends entertained fears that our ends might not meet, but we say, calm your fears, our money list is no index to our circulation. It is the result of our liberality and the *bulk* of our money is back yet. Because we are liberal should make none ungrateful. The more liberality we show towards our patrons, the more gratefulness should be extended to us, or else will our charity be abused. Please think of these things and favor those, especially, who favor you.

AGENTS WANTED.

We want a good active agent in every congregation in the brotherhood and anywhere else that a periodical defending Primitive Christianity is desired. Any persons wishing to labor for us will be supplied with an Almanac, prospectus and sample copies free of charge. Now is the time to work, and there are hundreds that would gladly read the Pilgrim if the opportunity was offered. We have still a goodly number of back No's and Almanacs on hand, so that all can be supplied.

PERSONAL.

Geo. W—. Als. 20 cts, ad $3. 00

John Arnold. That will do. The name is booked.

Jonathan Davis. The Pilgrim is sent as directed.

John Custer. The money was received and credited.

Abraham Sell. You can get what you want by addressing Fouse Bros., Crum & Co, York, Pa. None of the books on hand.

Jesse Cover. The letter containing $1. 50 for Joseph Halderman was not received. We have now booked his name and send the Pilgrim to Schwenksville, Pa. is that right?

J. W. Beaver. All right now. Tune Books will be sent as soon as another lot arrives.

D. R. Freeman. Your name, with the others, was overlooked in transferring from the old book. They will come right now. We have on our book Elias Rarick. Is this the one you mean or is there another?

John Brown. We took John and John B Brown to be the same name and sent only one paper. The list letter sent us containing postal order for $3, 00 and the names Jacob Cover and Wm. Badenburg was not received. They are now booked and if the postal order is lost another one can be had on application.

GENERAL INTELLIGENCE.

A citizen of Bedford county, Va., has just perfected an apparatus to melt snow and ice on railroad tracks, by means of a flame "sufficiently intense to produce the effect instantaneously." According to the plan of the inventor, the flame has to be shut from the fore part of the engine, and is relied upon to do its work without causing the slightest impediment to the progress of the train.

"I am glad," said a missionary to an Indian chief, "that you do not drink whiskey; but it grieves me to find that your people use so much of it." "Ah, yes," said the red man, and he fixed an impressive eye on the preacher, which communicated the reproof before he uttered it, "we Indians use a great deal of whiskey, but we do not make it."

The Kochive of Egypt is reported to be the richest person in the world, his annual income being $50,000,000. He is also the most extensive farmer, and does large business as a merchant, banker, manufacturer and ship builder.

The Weekly Pilgrim.

Published by J. B. Brumbaugh, & Co.

Edited by H. B. & Geo. Brumbaugh.

CORRESPONDING EDITORS.

D. P. *Sayler*, Double Pipe Creek, Md.

Leonard Furry, New Enterprise, Pa.

The *Pilgrim* is a Christian Periodical, devoted to religion and moral reform. It will advocate in the spirit of *love* and *liberty*, the principles of true Christianity, labor for the promotion of peace among the people of God, for the encouragement of the saints and for the conversion of sinners, avoiding those things which tend toward disunion or sectional feelings.

TERMS.

Single copy, Book paper,	$1.50
Eleven copies, [eleventh for Agt.]	$15.00

Any number above that at the same rate.

Address.

H. B. BRUMBAUGH.
James Creek,
Huntingdon county Pa.

The Weekly Pilgrim.

"REMOVE NOT THE ANCIENT LANDMARKS WHICH OUR FATHERS HAVE SET."

VOL. 4. JAMES CREEK, PENNSYLVANIA, FEBRUARY, 25, 1873. NO. 8

POETRY.

NOTHING GOOD SHALL EVER PERISH.

SELECTED BY REBECCA J. REYNOLDS.

Nothing good shall ever perish,
Only the corrupt shall die;
Truth, which men and angels cherish,
Flourishes eternally.

None are wholly God-forsaken,
All his sacred image wear;
None so lost but should awaken
In our heart's a brother's care.

Not a mind but has its mission—
Power of working woe or weal
So degraded none's condition,
But the world his weight may feel.

Words of kindness, words of warning,
Deem not thou may'st speak in vain;
Even those thy counsels scorning,
Oft shall they return again.

Though the mind, absorbed in pleasure,
Hold the voice of counsel light,
Yet doth faithful memory treasure
What at first it seemed to slight.

Words of kindness we have spoken,
May when we have passed away,
Heal, perhaps, some spirit broken,
Guide a brother led astray.

Thus our very thoughts are living,
Even when we are not here;
Joy and consolation giving
To the friends who hold us dear.

Not an act but is recorded,
Not a word but has its weight;
Every virtue is rewarded,
Outrage punished, soon or late.

Let no being, then, be rated
As a thing of little worth;
Every soul that is created
Has its part to play on earth.

ORIGINAL ESSAYS.

For the Pilgrim.

ANOINTING THE SICK.

"Is any sick among you? let him call for the elders of the church; and let them pray over him, anointing him with oil in the name of the Lord:

And the prayer of faith shall save the sick and the Lord shall raise him up; and if he have committed sins they shall be forgiven him. James 5:14-15.

Dear readers and fellow-pilgrim, travelers to an endless eternity, and more especially to you brethren and sisters, and all that name the name of Christ, is it not astonishing that such a plain commandment, attached with such great promises, and enjoined by Christ, whom all Christian professors acknowledge to be the Head of the Church, and so emphatically taught by James, one of His inspired apostles, is so little observed and even by many extinct? Why those Christian associations have lost sight of this plain command, whose teachers, on whom they entirely rely, can mystify and spiritualize any plain commandment and change it so to suit their own fancy or preconceived notions, we do not so much wonder; but why it is that those who with us believe in the literal observance of all the commandments of the Son of God, do not teach and observe it, we can not understand; and, especially, that it is so much neglected by our own fraternity.

Brethren and sisters, let us examine ourselves in this matter whether the fault does not lie with us. Do we teach our young members the necessity of this wholesome ordinance, when we visit our afflicted and distressed members? Every individual can be a teacher in this respect, but ministers should preach it publicly and frequently in their solemn assemblies when they meet together in the holy Sanctuary. I think this part of doctrine is too much dispensed with in some localities among the Brethren. *This ought not so to be.* Can we say with the Apostle Paul that we "have not shunned to declare unto you all the counsel of God," if we omit to teach that part? May we so solemnly declare that "we are free from the blood of all men" and neglect this point? Let every one answer for himself in the fear of God. I am well aware that some conceive the idea that as long as the disease is not considered dangerous, or likely to prove fatal it is unnecessary to attend to this injunction. We were called once to perform this ordinance on a dangerously sick sister and when we got there she was much better and considered convalescent, some proposed to omit it for fear if she recovered and would sin or commit faults through weakness it would not be forgiven her. We said it was only complying with the command of the Lord and in so doing we are always on the safe side and under the promise, for perhaps as many recover as die; but this I say when this ordinance is performed, the patient as well as the minister that performs it must be fully resigned to the will of the Lord. But as regards dangerous illness to be required, we have no "thus saith the Lord" The apostle does not qualify sickness; he says simply "Is any sick among you." We do not know the mind of the Lord; slight diseases, *by His will* can in a moment of time turn fatal, and if no effort is made to comply with this command an important promise may be lost, *lost*, yea LOST, and that forever. Brethren and sisters let us think on these things.

It was ever considered by the Brotherhood that the anointing should not be performed more than once in one sickness, but if the brother or sister gets well, as is often the case, and gets sick again it should be done again and as often as they get sick it should be repeated, for the apostle does not say how often, but merely "if any get sick among you." But a particular request on the part of the sick must be made to the elders; hence the necessity of teaching our members. Unless doing so from time to time, young members especially, would be ignorant of this fact and we may be chargable for their ignorance. The order of anointing is laid down in the Brethren's Encyclopedia under the head, Anointing, but as some have not access thereto, I will give the order we observe: When we are called on such occasions, if circumstances permit, we first sing a suitable hymn, if not, we dispense with singing; then exhort briefly and follow with prayer: then we read James 5th chap. so much as accords with the subject. And it requires two, since *He saith* "Let him call the elders of the church, and let them pray over him." If expedient, brief comments are made on the subject, and efficacy of anointing, then if possible, the sick is raised in the bed to a sitting posture, and the elder brother reaches forth his hand, the other brother pours the oil upon it which he first puts upon the head of the sick, and thus three times saying the words of the apostle: First, Thou art anointed with oil in the name of the Lord," unto the strengthening of thy faith. Secondly, unto the comforting of thy conscience. Thirdly, and unto a full assurance of the remission of thy sins; and then both put their hands on the sick, even as is done when a brother is ordained and pray briefly for the sick member. Such an example we have of the Savior as we see in Mark 6:13 and 19:18. Brethren also who are not ordained may administer it in cases of necessity. I am well aware that some professors speak lightly and even vilify this ordinance because the Roman Church practice what they call, Extreme Unction, and sometimes even after they are dead. But let it be known that we have it not from Papal authority; We have learned it from the word of God, and and that shall stand though Heaven and earth passeth away. Under the Jewish ceremony the Priests were anointed with oil and under their theocracy kings were also anointed with oil; both orders, first, to show to themselves their noble station and high authority, and, secondly, signifying to their subjects the same, and the indispensible necessity of honoring and obeying them as Priests and Kings. Now the believers in Christ are represented in the Gospel as a *Royal Priesthood*—both dignities verged in one, Hence, let no follower of Christ think it beneath his or her dignity to have the Holy Anointing administered in case of sickness for the promise is, *salvation, restoration and pardon.* For the prayer of faith shall *save* the sick, because he obeys the Savior through faith, and *He* is the only *one* that can *save*. And the Lord shall raise him up—if stricken down with pain, overwhelmed in affliction, cast down with sorrow, the strength of the Lord will uphold him, and through his unwavering faith, obtain the victory over sin, death and the grave, through the merits of Jesus Christ the Lord. LEONARD FURRY.

THE DESIGN OF BAPTISM. (Concluded.)

BY ELD. GEO. WORST.

Many more circumstances might be referred to but let that suffice, in the mouth of two or three witnesses shall every word be established. We will refer you to one case which was not a natural one but a miracle wrought for the benefit of Peter and those with him, which you will find in the 10th chapter of the Acts of the Apostles, the conversion of Cornelius and those of his house, who we learn received the Holy Spirit before baptism. It says nothing of the remissions of his sins, but we intend to be consistent for we believe it to be contrary to the nature of God to grant the Holy Spirit to any that were yet in their sins. Therefore from the nature of God he would not give the Holy Spirit, and from the nature of the Holy Spirit it would be impossible to dwell where sin is, so from this stand point we assert, that he had received the remission of sin before baptism, and to prove that his was not God's natural way of dealing with the children of men, needs only an examination of the circumstances pertaining to it. Peter receiving the charge he did from his Master, which was, go not into the way of the Gentiles or any city of the Samaritans enter ye not, but go only to the lost sheep of the house of Israel, and the vision of the sheet let down to him from heaven, filled with all manner of beasts and fowls of the air, and the voice, "arise, slay and eat," caused him to go with the messengers sent from Cornelius, and after he did go he would not likely have baptized him if it had not been for the demonstrations of the Holy Spirit which caused him to say, "who can forbid water that these should not be baptized seein; they have received the Holy Ghost as well as we." He did not say to him repent and be baptized for the remission of your sins. Furthermore we find that Peter had to answer to his brethren when he returned, and had to explain to them the nature of the circumstances attending his mission which satisfied them that the Gentiles had also a right to be numbered with the children of God. Paul, in writing to the Romans 6th chapter, says, "Ye were the servants of sin, but God be thanked ye have now obeyed from the heart that form of doctrine which was delivered you being then made free from sin ye have become the servants of righteousness." You see, after obedience, deliverance comes. God's storehouse is ever full, he is ready to pay, but his manner of doing is to pay when the work is accomplished. He has never promised to pay beforehand. If he should see proper to give any one the Holy Spirit before baptism, it will not benefit our case in the least, and we have no assurance of it in the word of God. He gave it to Cornelius for a special purpose, and the gospel does not point to any other case or the need of any other that any specialty should be used, therefore I would advise to follow strictly the prescribed plan laid down.

For the better understanding of the subject, we will ask, what is repentance? Let the apostle answer. He says repentance toward God and faith in the Lord Jesus Christ. Again, repentance from dead works to serve the living God. This shows a turning from, and a turning to. Repentance is simple and easily understood if we let the apostle explain it. We will now give you a case. Saul started from Jerusalem to Damascus to perform a work, in the gospel sense it would be a dead work. Jesus met him in the way, and said, "Saul, why persecutest thou me?" He repented from his rash act, that is, turned from his intended work and turned to the service of the living God. But there was a time intervened between the time he turned from and turned to, and in that time, he was relieved of his sins and the way he was relieved he will tell you if you turn to the 22d chapter of the Acts of the Apostles. Now to illustrate, when we repent of our sins we turn, we stop committing sin, we see that it is not well pleasing in the sight of God. Then the evil spirit will have nothing to do, He will leave, he will not stay where he cannot be engaged in doing something. We are now not committing any sin but look at the fearful catalogue of sins charged against us from the time we became accountable until now. Will it do merely to ask God to forgive us? If that will do, why need baptism? Why, says one, it is an outward sign of an inward purification. Cannot God see the heart? Who cares what man says, if God and I are reconciled. Whose business is it? "Be not deceived, evil communications corrupt good manners, awake to righteousness and sin not." Your sins will not be remitted until you have an application of the blood of Christ and He says whosoever doeth the will of my Father in Heaven the same is my brother and sister and mother. Paul says, "How shall we that are dead to sin live any longer therein? Know ye not that as many of us as were baptized into Jesus Christ were baptized into his death, therefore we are buried with him by baptism into death." Into what kind of death? Getting rid of the last dregs of pollution and that long list of crimes charged against us we go down into the water in the name of Jesus Christ and are buried beneath the wave leaving our load of sin there. The rest will come to walk in newness of life. What a beautiful figure of the resurrection? As Christ was raised from the dead, so we also should walk in newness of life. Peter, perhaps for fear that man would take a wrong view, was very explicit in telling us that it was not to take away the filth of the flesh but the answer of a good conscience toward God by the resurrection of Jesus Christ." If a few drops or a handful of water would have been used only, on such occasions, Peter would not have reminded us of the danger of misunderstanding the design of it.

Another beautiful figure we find in the children of Israel passing thro' the Red Sea. Before they came to the Red Sea they refused to work for the Egyptians, but were not out of danger of being taken back into slavery again until the sea closed over and drowned the Egyptians. Then the Israelites on this side of the Sea could sing the song of deliverance. Paul says, "they were all baptized unto Moses in the cloud and in the sea. Another illustration may be made to show that in the act of baptism our sins are remitted. Col. 2: 11, 12 we read, "In whom also ye are circumcised with the circumcision made without hands in putting off the body of the sins of the flesh by the circumcision of Christ. Buried with him in baptism wherein also ye are risen with him through the faith of the operation of God who hath raised him from the dead. Circumcision means cutting around. Then, by repentance we cut around our sins or deaden them, or crucify them. Then after they are crucified they must be buried before we get them out of our way. Buried with Christ in water baptism, and leave the dead body in the water, but the new man which is created in righteousness unto good works, will be resurrected to walk in newness of life. "For God so loved the world that he gave his only begotten Son, that whosoever would believe in him should not perish but have everlasting life." John 3: 16.

That Son suffered death upon the cross for the redemption of the human family. While upon the cross, he said, "it is finished," the work of redemption is accomplished. Paul to the Hebrews, says, "a testament is of force after men are dead, otherwise it is of no strength at all while the testator liveth" While in life, he was engaged in writing out, or making known the Will, and when it was finished, he sealed it with his blood, and made it effective even to the remitting of our sins by a compliance therewith, having faith in its merits. If it were not for the emmissaries of satan, it would not be a hard matter to enlighten the minds of men and turn their feet into the ways of piety and truth, but the law of the Lord is so contrary to the evil nature in man that satan's force, which is "Legion," gains the ascendency of and the power over us, so that we are ever ready to give heed to his devices rather than to the simple truth of the gospel. He has so wisely arranged his plans thro' his emmisaries, that you can be accommodated in any manner of worship and retain the disposition you was possessed with before conversion. This makes worship such an easy task in appearance that many bite at the bait to their utter condemnation. The motives of these emmisaries are many and various, some for the love of gold and some for honor, some for power, and some that they may gain a great name in the world, all under the name of religion. To accomplish their ends they set up their judgment against the plain testimony of Jesus and his holy apostles, setting at naught some of the ordinances laid down and substituting traditions of their own devices, which are foreign to the gospel, and enforcing them upon their followers, promising them salvation. Well did the Savior say, ye have made the word of God of no effect through your tradition, ye hypocrites how can you escape the damnation hell?

In conclusion, we would say, examine our remarks closely, and compare them with the general tenor of the gospel and act the part of wisdom, for your eternal destiny depends upon your strict observance of all the commandments and ordinances laid down in the gospel. The Savior says, "I am the way, the truth and the life and no man cometh to the Father but by me, and he that entereth not by the door the same is a thief and a robber." If we enter by the door, we will receive the remission of our sins and the Revelator John, says, "the door is open and no man can shut it." Although they may stand at the door with their weapons of eloquence trying to mystify the way, no man need be deceived in this enlightened land of ours, neither will there be excuse for us if we get deceived, for we all have access to, and the free use of the Gospel—can read it for ourselves and choose the way our father's trod. Peter, Paul, and many more who sealed the testimony of Jesus with their blood, are examples of faith for us to well consider what they endured having the hope of a blessed immortality beyond the grave.

CHARITY.—A crust of bread given to the poor through motives of pure philanthropy, would, in the sight of God, outweigh and sink into insignificance even the charity of Peabody, if given from no other motive than to secure the praise and approval of men. —*J. S. Flory.*

A LEVELING SYSTEM.

"Every vally shall be filled up and the hills shall be made low, the crooked shall be made straight and the rough be made smoothe,and all flesh shall see the salvation of God."

Dear brethren and sisters, these lines which your unworthy brother is now penning is, intended for the good of all, therefore do not condemn them before you give them a serious consideration.

The Savior brought a light into the world to enlighten every man that cometh into the world, and his forerunner John (the Baptist), was sent to prepare or show the children of men how to prepare themselves, in order that they might see that light, and the "leveling system" above mentioned is the way to get to that light or see the salvation of God. If so, where is the scribe, where is the wise? Hath God not made foolishness the wisdom of this world? Why is this? Because they must come down to men of low estate, and like the Eunuch, must acknowledge, "How can I except some man instruct me." They cannot see the Kingdom and salvation of God except they be born again. Now if the "leveling system" has brought us to that light and we continue to walk in the light, then are we his disciples indeed, and we shall know the truth and the truth shall make us free.

If we abide within the limits of this "leveling system," we will be a distinct and separate people from the world, so that everybody that sees us will know that we are the light of the world and the salt of the earth. Our light is not put under a bushel or under the bed, but on a candlestick so that all that are in the house can see it.

This is the confession that the Lord requires of us, that we should not be ashamed of our appearance or conduct when it agrees with the pattern laid down by the Scriptures, so that we can know each other and be known by the appearance, that the world may see the light and glorify our Father in Heaven. If we do this, we need no private signs as do the secret societies, but our appearance and conduct will show to all that we are the people of God. If the world wish to know our signs, let them go and search the Scriptures, and there they will find all that is necessary for the children of God to have.

Now dear brethren and sisters, please bear with your humble servant while he drops a few words concerning the different appearances that are so prevalent among us. O, let us get still closer together so that we can see eye to eye. Let us now keep in view, the "leveling system" while here on our pilgrimage. The things which Moses commanded the children of Israel was a shadow of that which was to come, and it was said to them that they, with their houses, men-servants, maid-servants, &c., were to keep the Sabbath holy. Let us try to make use of this knowledge, for if Jesus had brought them rest, he would not have spoken of another day. There is therefore a rest remaining for the people of God, and that rest will be obtained when we take the yoke of Jesus upon us and learn that meekness and lowliness of heart that was manifest in Him. If this be manifested in us, it is a good confession and must shine as a light to the world.

Now concerning the Sabbath that was foreshadowed in the Mosaiac dispensation, it did not only require from the heads of families to see that the Sabbath was kept holy, but they were made accountable for all that were about them

We have considered the hull and now get at the kernal a little. Our commander tells us to walk in newness of life, and, will it do for us, as fathers and mothers, to keep that Sabbath or maintain that humility on our persons and forget to examine our houses or the adorning that is in them, or our children, that they are brought up in the way that the Lord would have them, or that our men and maid-servants be instructed in the ways of the Lord, and our animals that we use for our convenience, do we put anything about them for a show to the world, or to gratify our carnal desires? As I did not wish to be lengthy, I only touched the points of the subject, hoping that what I have said may be for our general good. JACOB STEEL.

Yellow Creek, Pa.

WINTER REFLECTIONS

Oh how drear! Stern Winter art thou here? Hast thou appeared and with thy chilling blasts put to flight the pretty plumed birds; driven into his hive the working bee and chilled to death my most favorite flowers? Thou hast come: thou didst not forget thy speedy return. Nevertheless, we must welcome thee. Thou hast found the weak inhabitants of a terrestrial globe with hearts colder than thou canst make them. Thy winds are cold and fierce. Without wood thou hast found the drunkard's widow, without bread his children. Oh! God pity the drunkard's widow, pity his children who cry every day for bread.

O man, art not thou ashamed? Hast thou departed so far from the Sun of Righteousness that shineth in the meridian of glory, that those genial rays will never reach you? O ponder. Think seriously. Look about you. Look upon a frozen world. Compare your own heart with the mundane sphere on which you reside. Is all well? If not, will you continue to live a life that is little better than death? Are you so near frozen that the warm heart of Jesus pressed to thine own, will not melt thee? Great God! Infinite Mercy! ye concerned hosts of Heaven, ye, *all ye* sympathizing inhabitants of the earth, may we not command thy sympathy, all thy love? Has Jesus lived for naught? Has He died in vain? Cannot we, by viewing the past, make amends for the present? Are we not to hope better things for the future? May we not pray God to proffer mercy and stay vengeance yet awhile, since there are many that can aid in the great work of reformation? *Can aid?* Yes, but will you? Will you work for Jesus? Will you live for Him who died you? Will you reflect upon the past? Or are your sins so great that you would blush to look, aye, to think of them? Can it be that you have held the world's *pride* and *licentiousness*, as your idol and God? O foul sin, what hast thou done for the past? Wilt thou do even more for the future? Friendly alien, we love thee too well to have you hug any longer, the vain delusion that drove you from redeeming love. Fall into the ranks of Jesus while proffered mercy bleeds for you. The Heavenly host is concerned for you. You have resisted long, too long. Your service is needed, though previously spent for satan—spent for the enemy of all good, the enemy of all true joy. Be no longer alarmed at your sins *i. e.* that they are too numerous to get rid of. Christ's greatest pleasure is in saving the worst of sinners, though they have greived Him.

F. M. SNYDER.

HOME.

There is not another term in our language so sweet to all as *home*. Heaven, to the saint is as dear a word, as sweet a thought, but when the sinner thinks of home or hears the term, though Heaven, or the thought of Heaven may be to him a dread, yet even home, O, how sweet to him. To the truly moral but unregenerate, home is even yet a name sweeter, lovelier and freer of remorse than any other. To the sainted pilgrim, the thought of home, the enjoyment of what is here called home, or to hear of home, becomes dear because only that they savor a little of that which they call their home in Heaven. Because they bring to the soul a faint foretaste of their "house not made with hands eternal in the Heavens." Because the word home is heard, and no sooner is heard the echo in the sky, home, HOME. I have said that even the sinner, and the moral unregenerate, love the thought of home, one why is it that you love that home so dear, which so soon will deny you entertainment, which will toss you away as if an odious adhesion, or a venomous infection; and who can claim exemption from this doom? Then after this merciless and sure banishment which is rapidly and daily nearing us then where will we take up our abode and call it home? Then oh, for a home in Heaven. It is true, here we enjoy home, but then we shall need a more enduring substance. It is equally true, now our joy and happiness is at home, and our sweetest memories are at home; but then shall we want "a far more exceeding and eternal weight of glory," then death shall have no sting—the grave shall have no victory, "but thanks be to God who gave us the victory through our Lord Jesus Christ."

C. C. ROOT.

Mirabile, Mo.

FAITH.—Living faith hath life through the Holy Spirit which is the gift of God. Such faith hath footmarks—it is the incentive to "the prayer of faith" so he that asketh of God doeth so without doubt. He that obeyeth, "obeyeth from the heart." He that warreth with sin and Satan, fighteth the "fight of faith." Would we live the life of a Christian, we must "live by faith." Would we please God it must be "by faith." Faith maketh a man "alive to God," he liveth a life consecrated to the service of God. His mouth speaketh of the goodness of God—his tongue praiseth the Lord of life and glory.—his eyes look upon "His handiwork" with radiance and adoration. His hands open when the cause of the Lord calls for help—his feet are ready to walk the "narrow way," yea, that one that is "justified by faith" is a stranger and pilgrim seeking a better country like father Abraham who "walked by faith,"—that promised land is on ahead, the faithful shall inherit it. Those who "live by faith" shall conquer through faith, and when they "die by faith" shall seize the substance, and the things "not seen as yet" shall then appear in all their beauty, grandeur and immensity.—*J. S. Flory.*

BEAUTIFUL DEATH.—A girl of thirteen years, was dying. Lifting her eyes toward the ceiling, she said softly, "Lift me higher." Her parents raised her with the pillow, but she faintly said, "No, not that but there," again looking earnestly toward Heaven, whither her happy soul flew a few moments later. On her grave stone these words are carved:—Jane B.—aged 13, "Lift me higher." How beautiful is death when connected with such scenes.—*Eliza Warner.*

How seldom can we see all things working together for good. But it is better discipline to [illegible] —*McDuff.*

THE DESIRE OF ALL NATIONS.

And the desire of all nations shall come. Haggai, 2: 7.

The chapter preceding our text, is mainly spent in reproving the negligence of the Jews, who, being discouraged from time to time, had delayed rebuilding the temple, and in the meantime, employed their care and cost in building and adorning their own houses; but at last being persuaded to set about the work, they met with this discouragement, that such was the poverty of the time that the second structure would no way correspond with the magnificence and splendor of the first. In Solomon's days the nation was wealthy, now it was poor; so that there would be no proportion between the second and the first. To this discouragement, the prophet applies the relief, that whatever was wanting in external pomp and glory should be more than recompensed by the presence of Jesus Christ in this second temple, for "the desire of all nations," said he, shall come into it; which, by the way, may give us this useful lesson, that the presence of Jesus Christ gives a more real and excellent glory to places of worship than any external beauty whatsoever we can bestow upon them. Our eyes like the disciples, are apt to be dazzled with the goodly stones of the temple, and in the meantime to neglect and overlook that which gives it the greatest honor and beauty.

In these words we have both a description of Christ and an index pointing at the time of his incarnation. He is called "the desire of all nations," and the time of his coming in the flesh is plainly intimated to be whilst the second temple should be standing, here then we find just cause to bemoan the blindness that is happened to the Jews, who, owning the truth of this prophecy, and not able to deny the destruction of the second temple many hundred years since, yet will not be persuaded to acknowledge the incarnation of the true Messiah.

Christ was to come into the world in the time of the second temple, and after grevious concussions and revolutions which were to make way for his coming; for so the prophet here speaks, "I will shake all nations, and the desire of all nations shall come," to which the apostle alludes. Heb. 12: 26, applying this prophecy to Jesus Christ, here called "the desire of all nations."

The desires of God's people in all kingdoms, and among all nations of the earth, are, and shall be drawn out and fixed upon the Lord Jesus Christ. Christ is not given to any one nation in the world, but intended to be God's salvation to the ends of the earth. "There is neither Greek nor Jew, barbarian or Scythian, bond nor free, but Christ is all and in all." Col. 3: 11. In the explication of this point two things must inquired into; why Christ is called the desire of all nations, and upon what account the people of God, in all nations, desire him.

1st. That God the Father has appointed him as a remedy for the sins and miseries of his people in all parts of the world. If God had not appointed him for, he could not be desired by all nations, and herein the grace of God admirably shines forth in the freeness of it, that even the most barbarous nations are not excluded from the benefits of redemption by Christ. This is what the apostle admires, that Christ should be 'preached unto the Gentiles.' 1 Tim. 3: 16. To a people who seemed to be lost in the darkness of idolatry. "Ask of me and I shall give thee the heathen for thine inheritance and the uttermost parts of the earth for thy possession," Psa. 2: 8.

2nd. Christ, the desire of all nations, plainly indicates the sufficiency there is in him to supply the wants of the whole world. As the sun in the heavens suffices all nations for light and influence, so does the Sun of righteousness suffice for the redemption, justification, sanctification and salvation of the people of God all over the world. "Look unto me and be ye saved, all the ends of the earth." Isa. 45: 22.

3rd. It implies the reality of Godliness, it shows that religion is no fancy, as the atheistical world would persuade us; for this appears in the uniform effects of it upon the hearts of all men, in all nations of the world that are truly religious, all their desires, like so many needles touched by one and the same loadstone, move towards Jesus Christ. Were it possible for the people of God of all nations, kindred and languages in the world to meet in one place, and there compare the desires and workings of their hearts, as face answers to face in a glass, so would their desires after Christ answer to each other. All hearts work after him in the same manner; what one says, all say. These are my troubles and burdens, these my wants and miseries, these my desires and fears, one and the same spirit works in all believers throughout the world, which could never be if religion were but a fancy as some call it.

Christ, the desire of all nations, implies the vast extent of his kingdom in the world out of every nation under heaven some shall be brought to Christ, and to heaven by him; and though the number of God's people, compared with the multitudes of the ungodly in all nations, be but a remnant, a little flock, and in that comparative sense there are few that shall be saved; yet considered absolutely and in themselves, they are a vast multitude which no man can number. "Many shall come from the east and from the west, and shall sit down with Abraham, Isaac and Jacob, in the kingdom of heaven." In order to this, the gospel like the sun in the heavens encircles the world. It arose in the east and takes its course towards the western world; rising by degrees upon the remote idolatrous nations of the earth; out of all which a number is to be saved. Even "Ethiopia shall stretch out her hands unto God." Psa. 68: 31. And this consideration should move us to pray earnestly for the poor heathen who yet sit in darkness and the shadow of death. There is yet hope for them, we are to inquire upon what account Christ becomes the desire of all nations; yet he is the desire of all the people of God dispersed and scattered among those nations. When God touches their hearts with the sense of sin and misery, Christ, and none other, is desirable and necessary in the eyes of such persons. They are all by nature under condemnation, Rom. 5: 16, 18, under the curse of the law; against which nothing is found in heaven or earth able to relieve their consciences but the atoning blood, the pure and perfect righteousness of the Lord Jesus, and hence it is that Christ becomes so desirable in the eyes of poor sinners all the world over, when the light of the gospel shall shine upon the nations, they shall see that by reason of sin they are all barred out of heaven, and none but Christ can open an entrance for them into the kingdom of God; that no man cometh to the Father but by him, John 14: 6. Neither is there any name under heaven given among men whereby they must be saved, but the name of Christ, Acts 4: 12, and this will make the Lord Jesus incomparably desirable in their eyes.

To be Continued.

Universalism in a Nutshell.

"I am a Universalist," said G. K. boastingly, "and you orthodox are not fair in saying that our system is inconsistent with reason." "I will prove the irrationality of your system," said his friend. "You believe that Christ died to save all men?" "Yes, I do." "And you don't believe there is a hell?" "No, I do not." "You don't believe there is any punishment hereafter?" "No, I do not; men are punished for their sins in this life." "Well, now let us put your 'rational system' together. It amounts to just this, that Christ the Savior died to save all men from nothing at all. Not from hell, because according to you, there is none. Not from punishment in the future state of being, for he receives his whole punishment in this life. Yours is the absurd spectacle of ropes and life preservers thrown, at an immense expense to a man who is on dry land, and in no danger of being drowned."

Religious News.

ILLINOIS.—The Journal of the Illinois Convention for 1872, reports: Baptisms—infants, 1,073; adults, 183; total, 1,256. Communicants, 5,440. Confirmations, 671. Marriages, 432. Burials, 538. Sunday school teachers, 787; scholars, 6,647.

THE OLD CATHOLICS lately held a conference at Otten, Switzerland, which was attended by 150 delegates, and a congregation of 3,000. Prof. Reinkens, from Germany, preached constantly both in Catholic and Protestant churches.

SEXTON AND PREACHER.—The expenses of Plymouth Church for the last year amounted to nearly $14,000, and were distributed as follows: Salary of pastor, H. W. Beecher, $20,000; assistant, Rev. S. B. Halliday, $3,000; first sexton, $3,500; second $1,200, music, $8,000; current expenses, $7,000; insurance, $500: Plymouth Library, $700.

CONGREGATIONALISM IN CHICAGO.—Though but twenty years since Congregationalism had existence in Chicago seperate from Presbyterianism, there are now in Chicago nineteen Congregational churches.

ONE FIFTH of all the Lutheran ministers in the United States are found in Pennsylvania, of whom 35 reside in Philadelphia, 22 in York county, and Adams, Allegheny and Berks have each 20. Nine counties have no Lutheran ministers.

The *Christian Standard* reports the following accessions to the Christian Church for last week: Pennsylvania, 4; West Virginia, 3; Ohio, 70; Indiana, 9; Illinois, 3; Iowa, 18; Missouri, 4; Texas, 7; England, 15—total, 133.

THE MORMONS.—The movements of the United States troops toward Utah is the absorbing topic of interest in Salt Lake City. The *News* (Mormon), says that devoted Mormons "will welcome this opportunity to prove faithful even unto death."

The expulsion of a Methodist minister for getting up a lottery for his church is a good thing. Let the leaders of all Christian churches understand that a raffle or lottery in a church fair is an offence against good morals and punishable under the laws of the State.

Youth's Department.

GOOD COUNSEL.

Guard, my child, thy tongue,
That it speak no wrong;
Let no evil word pass o'er it;
Set the watch of truth before it,
That it speak no wrong!
Guard, my child, thy tongue.

Guard, my child, thine eyes;
Prying is not wise:
Let them look on what is right;
From all evil turn their sight:
Prying is not wise.
Guard, my child, thine eyes.

Guard, my child, thine ear,
Wicked words will sear.
Let no evil word come in
That may cause the soul to sin:
Wicked words will sear.
Guard, my child, thine ear.

Ear, and eye, and tongue,
Guard while thou art young:
For, alas! these busy three
Can unruly members be.
Guard while thou art young,
Ear, and eye, and tongue!

ROSA'S THEFT.

BY WILLIAM TELL.

Rosa's work was all done; her lessons all learned, and she had gone out on the steps of her father's large house to play, when a rather coarse looking boy came along carrying something under his arm which proved to be a cage containing a bird of very beautiful plumage. When he saw Rosa he stopped, and Rosa looking up at him said:

"What kind of a bird is that?"

"A golden pheasant," replied the boy, setting the cage down where Rosa could see it. She exclaimed, clapping her hands:

"O, my, how beautiful! I wish it was mine!"

The boy stepped nearer, and said in almost a whisper:

"You may have it for two dollars. The cage cost more than that."

"O, dear I haven't got any money," replied Rosa.

"Perhaps you can borrow it," said the boy, looking disappointed.

"I don't think I can, papa and mamma have both gone out, but they never give me more than my weekly allowance anyway. O, perhaps Jane will lend it to me," said Rosa, suddenly brightening up. "She has got some, I know. Will you wait till I run and see her?"

"Yes," said the boy, sitting down, "if you will be quick."

Rosa ran into the kitchen but Jane was not there, so running up stairs, she hunted through all the rooms, and then down stairs again till she came to the sitting room, where she saw her uncle George's pocket-book lying on the stand half open, with a lot of bills in plain sight. For a moment Rosa stood still looking at it, and trembling all over.

"O," she thought, "If uncle George were only here. He'd lend it to me, I know."

A secret voice seemed to whisper in her ear, "Take it Rosa, Take it! uncle George will never miss it."

Then stepping up to the stand Rosa pulled out a two dollar bill. After this she stole down stairs looking in every direction to see if any one was watching her.

"Did you get it," asked the boy, as Rosa came out on the steps.

"Yes," said Rosa, looking guilty and handing him the bill. She then took the bird and went into the house. When all of a sudden a great difficulty arose in her mind, and she thought:

"O! what shall I tell mamma if she asks where I got the bird." Then a thought suddenly struck her, "I'll say Laura Jay gave it to me."

Laura Jay was a little girl who often came to see Rosa, and who lived ten or twelve blocks away.

When the family came home they were very much pleased with the bird, and of course believed Rosa's story, but when uncle George came Rosa's heart seemed to stand still.

But uncle George quickly walked to the stand; picked up his pocket book, put it in his pocket and remarked: "How careless of me, I thought some one had picked my pocket."

That night Rosa could not say her prayers. For she knew she had stolen, and then told a wilful lie to conceal it, so she went to bed and left them half finished.

But she could not master courage enough to tell how foolish she had been, and so kept the guilty secret, which weighed so heavily on her mind and heart.

In the afternoon she again took the bird out on the steps to let it get fresh air, where a small crowd of little children soon gathered around to gaze at its beautiful plumage, when a policeman sauntering by stopped.

"Ho," said he, "This is the very bird, let's look at this cage little girl."

Whereupon he lifted the cage and found the name of Ida Wilder written upon the bottom.

"Yes, this is it, here is her name. I say, little girl, where did you get this?"

"I bought it of a boy for two dollars," said Rosa, trembling, and very much scared.

"You bought it for two dollars, yes a very likely story, such a bird and cage as that for two dollars, you stole it," and the policeman took hold of her.

Just then uncle George came out.

"What's this fuss here, policeman, let that little girl alone."

"This bird has been stolen," said the officer of the law, "and it's my business to see about it."

And Rosa was obliged to explain all, which she did with many tears and much tribulation. She was not taken to jail, but her punishment was great, and thus uncle George thought, and so did her mamma for that night she helped Rosa to say her prayers, and gave her words of counsel which were never forgotten.

And let all my young readers take warning from Rosa's experience, and never steal to gratify a passing desire, and never tell a lie for it is sure to become a burden to your conscience, even if it is not found out, you are left in shame.—*Bright Side.*

EFFIE'S CONFESSION.

"Oh, Laura, just see what I,ve done!"

Laura stopped running, and came back to the place where Effie was standing and looking at a flower border.

"What's the matter? What have you been doing?" said she.

"Why I've broken one of these lovely lilies that father wanted to keep till Aunt Marion comes. As I was running past here, I went too near this side of the path, and my dress caught and broke the stem. Just look at it."

"Oh, what a pity! What will your father say? Do you think he'll scold you?"

"I don't know. What shall I do about it?"

Laura thought a moment, and then said—

"I'll tell you! I've got a capital plan. Lets go and let Towser out of the house, and then come back here, and he will be sure to follow us, and then we can say he broke it."

"Why, Laura Graham, that would be telling a dreadful falsehood, and I won't do it."

"But what will you say if your father asks who did it?"

Effie looked at Laura and then at the broken lily. A bright thought seemed to strike her, and she said, "I'm going right to father to tell him just how it was," and she walked off very fast, as if she were afraid her courage would give out, while Laura followed slowly.

They found Mr. Neville in the library, reading the newspaper, and Effie walked up to him and stood by his chair, waiting for him to look up.

Presently he said, "Well Effie?"

Then she told him all about it, without trying to excuse herself. Her father waited for her to finish; then drawing her to him and kissing her, told her he had seen the whole from a window, and watched to see what she would do, and as she had been truthful, and came and confessed her fault, he would gladly forgive her.—*Bright Side*

Correspondence.

A Reporter is wanted from every Church in the brotherhood to send us Church news, Obituaries, Announcements or anything that will be of general interest. To insure insertion, the writers name must accompany each communication. Our invitation is not personal but general—please respond to our call.

MY EXPERIENCE.

Brother Pilgrim:—Many days have come and gone since my mind and pen, as co workers together, have been engaged in speaking to you, through this medium, fearing most of all that when I come to you, as my custom is, I may not bring food for the soul, and again, that I may be found burdensome to our editors, and an intruder in the columns of the PILGRIM, by filling space that might be devoted to a better purpose. But "as there is a time for all things under the sun," I will try my hand to the work, and if I have not the wherewith to polish my ideas as I go, just take them as you find them.

I will now proceed, and say with one of old, "Few and evil have been my days." There is nothing that I can gather from my experience since I have enlisted in the army, that would be of interest, but my mind runs back to my early childhood days. The recollection of those days come to me as days not long passed. I very well remember the first prayer I offered to our Heavenly Father. As a general thing, those who pray to God very young have been taught so by Christian parents. Whether this be right or not I have my ideas. We cannot read in the Bible of children being commanded to pray. I think they should be taught the principles of Christianity as soon as they become able to know good from evil. To learn the little one to pray before they have the knowledge they should have, seems to me like plucking fruit from its mother stem before it becomes ripe. There can be no positive benefit derived from it. Before I attained to this knowledge, I was under the protecting care of Christian parents. They knew my wants, and my desires were to them. As regards a spiritual life I knew nothing. As to temporal things, my parents supplied my wants. And as soon as I became spiritual minded, then I must look to a higher or spiritual power. As in temporal things I had a resource, my earthly parents, so in spiritual things, I must look to my Heavenly Father. His spirit striving with me, made me feel the need of prayer, and the first striving, I am made to believe, had the effect of leading me to commune with God in secret. This was my first prayer. I continued my secret devotions for a number of years. This brought me to the studying of the Scriptures.

The Bible was my favorite book. No other book was half so interesting. I have oftimes thought, how pure my thoughts were then. There was no unbelief, no doubts, no thoughts to disturb my mind, but by and by a change came, time was wafting me down,—a little wrong here and a little there. I began to get uneasy. I needed something and prayed earnestly. I now began to learn that my parents could not supply all my wants. I was growing more and spiritual minded, but my wants still unsupplied led me to seek God in prayer. The effect of prayer bid me read the Word, and it led me to become a child of God by adoption, by complying with the requirements of the atonement. As my parents became dead to me, so far as my spiritual wants were concerned, I began to stray from my Father's house, I was now led to return and be adopted into the family of God. Now began the warfare, such as mortals have to fight. I, having set my feet "homeward bound," the devil no doubt saw that I was making for the "straight and narrow way," and commanded a halt, and began to reason and promise me many things upon which I could feast. As I was not so easily taken into his service in this, he strikes at my weaker points. As my nature was to be very backward, (and is not very much changed yet) he tries his hand here, and to my knowledge I never having heard the Brethren explain how applicants were received, this caused a stand still, I not having energy sufficient to make my wants known, thinking probably it would be my duty to explain what I believed and how I felt, &c., and my courage failed me. O, if I just had known that the church was of such a lovely nature, and how welcome I would have been, my heart would have been given wholly to the Lord much sooner than it was. Here ministers may gather an item that may be improved. These things caused me much trouble, but still I trusted in my Heavenly Father, I prayed and I wept, but ah, how soon was I changed, for at a certain time, as I was returning from prayer, where I was holding sweet communion with God, my mind changed, but not as I hear sometimes at prayer-meetings, where the forgiveness of sins and peace to the hardened soul is found, but I was changed from a praying boy to an infidel. O, sad to tell, I who never doubted to the existence of a God, a Savior and a future life, was now a disbeliever. Doubts began to arise in my mind whether there was any such thing as a hereafter, O, how gloomy was my soul! The twelve months under which I labored in this condition, all seemed darkness and gloom beyond the tomb. There was no light to my benighted mind, if I then should have taken a leap into the dark. I prayed, but all such prayers were not such as cometh from the heart. What to do I knew not. I attended preaching, but there was not the place for me, There I heard of death, O, must I die and go where no living never come, in the cold and silent tomb? But I believe in all this there was a hand unseen to me. The spirit of God left the house, but it was not swept and garnished. The devil seeing the house vacated, enters in for the spoil. For a little while, God is dethroned, angels weep, devils laugh, and I am made to tremble. I wept, I mourned. As a mother weeps for her little babe that is lost to her, so I mourned my condition. Thank God my Redeemer was living. He knew the eruptions of my heart. He pitied my condition. As the angry waves of the ocean arise with foaming madness, when the hissing wind, with fury disturbs its peace, so was I comparatively speaking. I was hurled into the ocean of despair, where the angry waves lashed my frail bark, but there was a power which once calmed the turbid water away back in the land of Judah, that spoke peace to my troubled soul; "peace be still," was heard in an hour of great need. I reasoned with myself of the creation of all things, and came to the conclusion that there must be a creative power. Who created God? and thus I began to speculate, when there was "a still small voice" seemed to whisper in my ear, "And who created that principle of unbelief in thy heart?" Get thee hence satan, thou savorest not the things that be of God, but of men. Old satan, I never as much as thought of him while in the arms of his power. He could infuse into my heart the thot's of a disbelief in God, but not once did he let me reason whether there was a devil. Just as soon as I thought of my mind being changed to unbelief without any reason on my part, that soon was my eyes opened so that I might behold the devil in his masked form.

This ends my experience prior to my conversion, and here it shall end with you. But I could speak of the time when my sins were pardoned, or rather, when I began to feel the burden of sin removed, and effects of religion. I might fill many more sheets, but will not now, at some other time you will hear from

ONE WHO KNOWS.

Dear Pilgrim:—I was at church to day and heard an interesting sermon delivered by Eld. John Wise. No doubt, his words touched many hearts with a sense of the duty they owe to God. As we sang the last stanza of the 923d hymn in the Brethren's Hymnbook, a sweet dream came to mind which I dreamed last night of my sister, who died a year ago. I dreamed I saw her, shook hands with her, kissed her and conversed with her. It was a happy meeting after being separated one year. But I soon awoke and found that it was only a dream. Oh reader if the dream of meeting death-divided friends is sweet, what must the reality of it be. Let us take fresh courage and lay aside every weight and the sin which doth so easily beset us and run with patience the race set before us, looking unto Jesus the author and finisher of our faith. Let us put on the whole armor of God that we may overcome all evil. Then soon we will reach that happy shore where death-divided friends at last shall meet to part no more. There will be no more death, neither sorrow nor crying nor pain, but God will wipe away all tears from their eyes. There the wicked cease from troubling and the weary are at rest. Then will we realize the following precious promises as they are only unto him that overcometh.

"To him that overcometh will I give to eat of the tree of life which is in the midst of the paradise of God." Rev. 2:7. "He that overcometh shall not be hurt of the second death." Rev. 2:11. "To him that overcometh will I give to eat of the hidden manna and will give him a white stone and in the stone a new name written which no man knoweth saving he that receiveth it." Rev. 2:17. "And he that overcometh and keepeth my words unto the end, to him will I give power over the nations. And he shall rule them with a rod of iron; as the vessels of a potter shall they be broken to shivers even as I received of my Father. And I will give him the morning star." Rev. 2:26. "He that overcometh the same shall be clothed in white raiment and I will not blot out his name from the Book of Life, but I will confess his name before my Father and before His angels." Rev. 3:5. "Him that overcometh will I make a pillar in the temple of my God and he shall go no more out and and I will write upon him the name of my God and the name of the city of my God which is new Jerusalem which cometh down out of Heaven from my God and will write upon him my new name." Rev. 3:12 "To him that overcometh will I grant to sit with me on my throne even as I also overcame and am set down with my Father on His throne." Rev. 3:21. These, brethren and sisters, are glorious promises, and should be a happy consolation to every regenerated soul.

HANNAH E. SMITH.

Tenmile Village. Pa.

ALMENA, MICH.,
FEB. 1873

Dear Editors, brethren and sisters in the Lord:—Inasmuch as we love to read the church news, and hear from the different arms of the church how the Lord is prospering them, we have thought it would not be out of place to drop you a few lines informing you of our progression in our Masters cause We have had a series of meetings here in our school house, conducted by our elder and worthy brother F. P. Loehr and brother M. T. Baer, and assisted for a few evenings, by brother Peter Wrightsman, M. D. of South Bend Indiania.

Our meeting was largely attended and with good order, and all seemed to be edified. After the close of the ten o' clock services on Sunday we went to the water, and five were inducted through the holy rite of baptism into the Church, and one week from that time, after the close of our meetings, six more souls manifested to the world their humble intentions, by being baptized in to Christ. May the good Lord send more abundantly the convincing Spirit, until all may see the error of their way and accept of God's mercy before it is everlastingly too late, is my prayer. Yours as ever in the Lord.

J. J. SOLOMON.

Dear Editors:—Through the kind mercies of God I am permitted for the first time, to write to you. I am requested by two of our German brethren who cannot write in the English, that I should write for you to send them the PILGRIM. This is the first year that we have had the pleasure of reading your paper, and we are well pleased with it and hope it will keep close to the gospel, and hold forth nothing that is not in harmony with it, so that the world can have no opportunity of disputing its name as not being a pilgrim.

I will now inform the brethren and sisters that there are but few members here in the East end of the Oks Church. Old Abraham Ritch is our speaker in this end. He is beloved by all who know him. Brethren and sisters wishing to come West, will here find a very good country, and also railroad conveniences, one crossing at Lovington and one at Sullivan, the county seat, 9 miles south of this place. If any come to Lovington and wish to stop with brethren, enquire for Samuel Early or Daniel Oaks who live near the station, and will gladly accommodate.

PERTHENIA EARLY.

Lovington, Ill.

SAD INTELLIGENCE.

Just rec'd by letter, sad intelligence from Franklin county Va., announcing the death of our much esteemed brother, Elder Abraham Naff, after a short and painful attack of pneumonia.

In the death of brother Naff, the community has lost one of its most valuable citizens; as a husband, he was all that can be expressed; as a father, kind and affectionate, as well as a faithful guardian of the best interest of his children; as a neighbor, he was obliging; as a member of the church, an ornament; as a minister, zealous and efficient; as a counsellor, wise and prudent; in a word, he will be very much missed in every department of the society in which he moved, especially, as a faithful watchman over the principles of Apostolical Christianity, and the preservation of peace and harmony in the churches within his reach. So highly were his services valued that whenever a committee was wanting to settle any matter, he was almost invariably one of the number. What I say, I speak knowingly as it very frequently happened that he and myself labored together, having traveled together many thousand miles. The last time we were together we served as a committee, and at that time were appointed to attend in another important case, and agreed to meet on the 31st of Jan., but the day previous I rec'd a communication from him, informing me of his illness, and consequent inability to serve, and requested me to inform him of the result of the labor assigned us. Accordingly, I wrote on the evening of Feb. 2nd., which, as I am informed, reached his residence on the 4th., but alas! too late, as he had fallen asleep in death, a few hours before it arrived. So it only remains for us to be resigned, to "be still and know that the Lord is God." Our prayer is, that his mantle may fall on another, that the vacancy occasioned by his death may be filled, and that blessings such as they may need, may be bountifully dealt out to the dear sister, and the entire household, is the sincere prayer of their brother and friend.

B. F. MOOMAW.

ANNOUNCEMENTS.

Please announce through the PILGRIM that our District Meeting will be held on the 13th of May in the Cook's Creek Congregation, Rockingham Co., Va.

SOLOMON GARBER.

The District Meeting for North Missouri will be held on the 7th and 8th of March in the Smith Fork Branch, Clinton Co., (near Plattsburg), in the Brethren's Meeting-house. A general representation desired. Those coming by R. R. will stop off at Plattsburg.

GEORGE WITWER.

Please make the following announcement in the WEEKLY PILGRIM. The District Meeting of West Virginia, will be held in Seneca District, eight miles west of Mouth of Seneca, at Union School House, in Dry Fork township, Randolph Co., on Friday and Saturday, 9th and 10th of May. For any further information address the undersigned at Mouth of Seneca,

Pendleton Co., W. Va.

By order of the Church.

ASA HARMAN.

MARRIED.

DICE—DINE.—On Feb. 5th, 1873, at the residence of the bride's parents, by the undersigned, Bro. N. Dice of Newtonia, Mo., to Miss Sarah E. Dine of Xenia, Ind.

REV. SAMUEL SWADLEY.

CURP—SMITH.—On the 5th inst., at the residence of the bride's parents, by Eld. Geo. Witwer, Mr. Wm. Curp and Miss Margaret Smith, both of Caldwell Co., Missouri.

DIED.

HASSLER.—In the Falling Spring Church, Pa., on the 6th of February, 1873, Saml. F. Hassler, aged 37 years, 1 mo. and 27 days, after a brief illness of Pneumonia.

He leaves a dear widow, sister in the church, and two children to mourn his loss. Funeral services by Eld. Henry Koontz and J. Gipe, from Heb. 9: 27, 28.

D. H. BONEBRAKE.

(*Companion* please copy.)

STUCKMAN.—On Feb. 10th, 1873, Clara Emma, daughter of our dear friend M. S. Stuckman, of spotted fever, aged 5 years, 3 mos. and 6 days. The occasion was improved by Bro. John Miller and the writer from Matt. 24: 44, to a large and attentive congregation.

JESSE CALVERT.

PATE.—In the Fall Creek Church, Henry Co., Ind., January 23rd, 1873, Charles Pate, aged 1 year and 7 months. Also, on Feb. 3rd, Dora Belle Pate, aged 1 yr., 8 mos. and 12 days, children of Wm. and Martha Pate, and grand children of Bro. Isaac Livesey. Funeral exercises by Geo. Hoover.

NEFF.—Also in the same Church, Feb. 1st, 1873, at the house of her son, Bro. Levi Neff, Sarah Neff, aged 88 years, 4 months. Funeral exercises by Geo. Hoover from Amos 4th chapter and latter clause of the 12th verse. She was a member of the Lutheran church.

ETTER.—Also in the same Church, Feb. 10th, 1873, sister Elizabeth Etter, aged 98 years and 4 months.

She was a member of the church of the Brethren for 35 years. Funeral services conducted by Martin Rodicap and George Hoover, from Rev. 3: 11, 12.

D. F. H.

BENNITT.—On Feb. 11th, 1873, in the Winamac District, at North Bend, Parthena Alice, daughter of Bro. James Y. and sister Hannah Bennitt, aged 13 yrs., 6 months and 25 days.

Bro. James is in the ministry. It was a hard stroke to give up their child as she was an obedient daughter and much loved, and was taken away unexpectedly, as she was sick only three days; disease, inflammation of the brain. The child expressed a willingness to go home and we need not mourn for her as those who have no hope. Funeral service by Bro's. A. Appelman and D. R. Freeman, from John 16: 20.

The Weekly Pilgrim.

JAMES CREEK, PA., Feb. 25th, 1873.

☞ How to send money.—All sums over $1.50, should be sent either in a check, draft or postal order. If neither of these can be obtained, have the letter registered.

☞ WHEN MONEY is sent, *always* send with it the name and address of those who paid it. Write the names and post office as plainly as possible.

☞ EVERY subscriber for 1873, gets a *Pilgrim Almanac* FREE.

WHAT HATH GOD WROUGHT?

When we look around us and view the fields of nature, only half explored, we behold wonders upon wonders, and the query flashes upon our mind, 'What hath God wrought.' Notwithstanding, nature in its primeval state, presented mysteries as a book unpaged, yet, like the glory of Solomon, half was untold, until made manifest through the agencies of man.

Were the fathers, who have been sleeping for centuries, to return and drop in among the modern achievements of man, they would scarcely know in what world they had appeared. They seem truly wonderful to us who have been brought up among them, but how much more wonderful would it be, if all were to flash upon our minds at once. Though the achievements and inventions of men are legion, yet there are a few that have taken the lead through the civilized world. Among these first in importance we name that of Printing. What this has done for the world, cannot be estimated. Truly, "what hath God wrought." By it, under the blessing of God, the Gospel has been preached in every tongue, and every clime has been made to sing the songs of redeeming love. It is the great civilizing power of the world and to have it removed would leave a blank which nothing else could fill.

Another great advance in the sciences, is the invention of the power and utility of steam. Fulton was looked upon as a visionary enthusiast, but his invention has become the bone and sinew of the manufacturing world, and to-day, the rushing iron-horse owes his speed to his inventive genius, and thousands upon thousands of engines throughout the length and breadth of the land, speak forth his praise. But the great modern wonder is that of domesticating the fiery element electricity, and making it subservient to our daily wants. The honor of this great achievement partly belongs to the late Sam'l F. B. Morse, to whom Emperors, Kings and Queens afterwards, delighted to pay homage. But what makes our subject the more interesting is the fact that it was the first message or dispatch that was ever transmitted by Telegraph, which occurred at 8. 45 A. M. on the 24th of May, 1844. Mr. Morse was a man of undaunted courage and, had learned to rough his way through, but when he presented his Telegraph to Congress, requesting an appropriation of $30.000 to enable him to give it a fair test it was rec'd with such bad grace that he became discouraged, and was making arrangements to leave, when a daughter of Hon. Henry Ellsworth brought him the happy intelligence that his bill had passed. The tidings so overjoyed him that he took the lady by the hand and declared that she should send over the wires, the first message, as her reward, and that message was, "What hath God wrought?" The message strikes us as being altogether appropriate and reflects great credit to the one who suggested it. It throws the honor just where it belongs, while Prof. Morse was the instrument, God was the author. "And without him was there not anything made." These are the three great inventions of the world and their spheres of usefulness are so blended together that neither one seems to be independent of the other. By Electricity, the messages are sent to the Press. By the Press they are multiplied by the hundreds, thousands and millions, and through the agency of steam, they are distributed over the world, so that we seem equally indebted to Laurentius, Fulton and Moore for the great privileges and conveniences which we now enjoy, for which we should thank God, because he wrought them all.

ODD NUMBERS of the PILGRIM will be supplied to such as will distribute them and solicit subscribers. We have a good supply of some numbers and will gladly send them to such as may apply. If our brethren and sisters generally would accept this offer, our list might be largely increased, as there are many in the church who would subscribe for it if they could once see a copy of it, and not only in the church, but there are many others who would gladly read it, had they an opportunity. A few weeks ago, a copy of the PILGRIM was accidentally left lay in the seat of a Railway car, the conductor took it home with him and his wife was so pleased with it that it was sent for immediately. Brethren and sisters, the PILGRIM is getting to be a great missionary, and by the blessing of God and your aid, we hope to be able to introduce the humble doctrines of Jesus into the homes of many that have not learned them aright.

PHRENOLOGICAL JOURNAL & PILGRIM sent together for only $3.50. The Journal alone costs $3.00. It is decidedly the most important Journal published, free from all fiction and love stories, and can with safety, be introduced into our families and will in all cases, make favorable improvements on the minds of those who read it. Those who have paid us $1.50 for the PILGRIM, by sending us $2.00 more can have the Journal. Specimen copies for examination, will be sent by enclosing a 3 cent stamp to pay postage.

CORRECTION.

In PILGRIM No. 4, under the caption "Another wail from the camp;" second paragraph, you have the type to say the quotation "M. E." made from "Mourner's Bench Religion Examined," reads "*wishes his right hand* may be palsied" &c., when it should be "*wishes his sight* may be palsied" as that is the way "M. E." uses it, therefore I was justifiable in saying "there is no such quotation in the tract.

J. S. FLORY.

THE HERALD OF TRUTH is a valuable religious monthly published by J. F. Funk & Bro., Elkhart, Indiana, in both English and German, at $1.00 per year. It is the organ of the Mennonite Church of America, and contains much interesting reading for everybody. Specimen copies sent free on application.

OUR CHURCH PAPER is a new weekly published by the Pittsburg synod of the Reformed Church. It is ably edited by Rev. Geo. B. Russel, and from [illegible] is receiving a liberal share of patronage.

THE CHURCH and the duties of her members. A series of papers under the above caption is under way of preparation for the PILGRIM, by one who is fully able to do the subject justice, and will appear in due time.

QUERY.

Will some kind Bible student inform me through the columns of the PILGRIM who David's mother was. It is not recorded in the Book, but history or tradition I presume has [illegible]

[illegible] I. H. M[illegible]

"Unquestionably the best sustained work of the kind in the World."

HARPER'S MAGAZINE.

NOTICES OF THE PRESS:

The ever-increasing circulation of this excellent monthly proves its continued adaptation to popular desires and needs. Indeed when we think into how many homes it penetrates every month, we must consider it as one of the educators as well as entertainers of the public mind, for its vast popularity has been won by no appeal to stupid prejudices or depraved tastes.—*Boston Globe.*

The character which this *Magazine* possesses for variety, enterprise, artistic wealth and literary culture that has kept pace with, if it has not led the time, should cause its conductors to regard it with justifiable complacency. It also entitles them to a great claim upon the public gratitude. The *Magazine* has done good and not evil all the days of his life.—*Brooklyn Eagle.*

SUBSCRIPTIONS.—1873.

TERMS:

HARPER'S MAGAZINE, one year $4 00

An extra copy of either the MAGAZINE, WEEKLY, or BAZAR will be supplied gratis for every club of Five Subscribers at $4.00 each, in one remittance; or, Six Copies for $20.00, without extra copy.

Subscription to HARPER'S MAGAZINE, WEEKLY, and BAZAR, to one address for one year, $10 00; or two of Harper's Periodicals to one address for one year, $7.00.

Back Numbers can be supplied at any time.

A Complete Set of Harper's Magazine, now comprising 45 volumes, in neat cloth binding, will be sent by express, freight at expense of purchaser, for $2.25 per volume. Single volumes, by mail, post-paid, 3.00, Cloth cases, for binding, 58 cents by mail, postpaid.

The postage on Harper's Magazine is 24 cents a year, which must be paid at the subscribers post-office.

Address HARPER BROTHERS,
New York.

THE

HOUSEHOLD TREASURE.

Containing several hundred Valuable Receipts for cooking well at a moderate expense, making Dyes, Coloring, Cleaning and Cementing. This book also points out in plain language, free from Doctors' terms the diseases of men, women and children, and the latest and most approved means used for their cure, to which is added a description of the Medicinal Roots and Herbs, and how they are to be used in the cure of diseases.

This is a work of considerable importance and we offer it to our readers as being a valuable accession to every household. Sent from this office to any address, postpaid, for 25 cents.

Bee Books, Bee Books!

On receipt of 50 cts. I will send by mail a valuable *Bee Book* treating on over one hundred subjects. No Bee keeper should be without it. It tells just how to make bees profitable. *Italian Queen* Bees bred from imported mothers, each $3.00. Orders solicited. Address

E. J. WORST,
New Pittsburgh, Wayne co., O.
Feb 18-4t.

Menno Simon's COMPLETE WORKS.

In English, translated from the original Dutch or Holland, giving the whole of the great Reformers writings on the subject of Baptism. Price in full sheep $4.50; by mail $5.14.

Address, JOHN F. FUNK & BRO.
Elkhart, Ind.

LAND, LAND, LAND!!

The completion of the Chesapeake and Ohio Trunk Line Railway, has opened up to the world much of the fine TIMBER LANDS, rich COAL FIELDS and cheap FARMING LANDS of W. Va. Now is the time to get cheap homes and invest money with the prospect of a handsome profit. For further particulars inquire of the undersigned, agent for lands here. J. S. FLORY,

Orchard View, Fayette Co., W. Va.
Jan. 10.

Trine Immersion.

A discussion on Trine Immersion, by letter between Elder B. F. Moomaw and Dr. J. J. Jackson, to which is annexed a Treatise on the Lord's Supper, and on the necessity, character and evidences of the new birth, also a dialogue on the doctrine of non-resistance, by Elder B. F. Moomaw. Single copy 50 cents.

GOOD BOOKS.

A large number of our patrons are receiving our books as noticed below, as premiums, and express themselves highly pleased with them. Others who are not agents, have enquired whether we keep them for sale. We have now made arrangements with Mr. Wells to furnish any of their publications post paid at publishers prices. Orders for books must be accompanied with the cash, and plain directions for sending them.

Weaver's Works for the Young. Comprising "Hopes and Helps for the Young of both Sexes," $3.00.

Life at Home; or, The Family and its Members. A work which should be found in every family. $1.50. Extra gilt, $2.00.

Hand-book for Home Improvement: comprising "How to Write," "How to Talk," How to Behave," and "How to do Business," in one vol. 2.25.

Man and Woman: Considered in their Relations to each Other and to the World. 12mo, Fancy cloth, Price $1.00.

The Right Word in the Right Place. A New Pocket Dictionary and Reference Book. Cloth, 75cts.

Hopes and Helps for the Young of both sexes, Relating to the Formation of Character. Choice of Avocation, Health, Conversation, Social Affection Courtship and Marriage. Muslin, $1.50.

The Emphatic, Diaglott; or The New Testament in Greek and English. Containing the Original Greek Text of the New Testament, with an Interlineary Word for-word English Translation. Price, $4.00; extra fine binding, $5.00.

Oratory—Sacred and Secular; or, the Extemporaneous Speaker. Price $1.50.

Conversion of St. Paul. 12mo. fine edition, $1. Plain edition, 75 cents.

Man, in Genesis and in Geology; or, the Biblical Account of Man's Creation, tested by Scientific Theories of his Origin and Antiquity. One vol. 12mo, $1.00.

How to read Character, illus.	Price, $1.25
Combe's Moral Philosophy,	1.75
Constitution of Man. Combe,	1.75
Education. By Spurzheim,	1.50
Memory—How to Improve it,	1.50
Mental Science, Lectures on,	1.50
Self-Culture and Perfection,	1.50
Combe's Physiology, Illus.	1.75
Food and Diet. By Pereira,	1.75
Natural Laws of Man,	.75
Hereditary Descent,	1.50
Combe on Infancy,	1.50
Sober and Temperate Life,	.50
Children in Health—Disease,	1.75
The Science of Human Life,	3.50
Fruit Culture for the Million,	1.00
Saving and Wasting,	1.50
Ways of Life—Right Way,	1.00
Footprints of Life,	1.25
Conversion of St. Paul,	1.00

BOOK AGENTS

WANTED FOR THE

GREAT INDUSTRIES OF THE UNITED STATES;

AN HISTORICAL SUMMARY OF THE ORIGIN, GROWTH AND PERFECTION OF THE CHIEF INDUSTRIAL ARTS OF THIS COUNTRY.

1300 PAGES and 500 ENGRAVINGS.

Written by 20 Eminent Authors, including John B. Gough, Leon Case, Edward Howland, Jos. B. Lyman, Rev. E. Edwin Hall, Horace Greely, Philip Ripley, Albert Brisbane, F. B. Perkins, etc.

This work is a complete history of all branches of industry, processes of manufacture, etc., in all ages. It is a complete encyclopedia of arts and manufactures, and is the most entertaining and valuable work of information on subjects of general interest ever offered to the public. It is adapted to the wants of the Merchant, Manufacturer, Mechanic, Farmer, Student and Inventor, and sells to both old and young of all classes. The book is sold by agents, who are making large sales in all parts of the country. It is offered at the low price of $3.50, and is the cheapest book ever sold by subscription. No family should be without a copy. We want agents in every town in the United States, and no agent can fail to do well with this book. Our terms are liberal. We give our agents the exclusive right of territory. One of our agents sold 133 copies in eight days, another sold 368 in two weeks. Our agent in Hartford sold 397 in one week. Specimens of the work sent to agents on receipt of stamp. For circulars and terms to agents address the publishers.

J. B. BURR & HYDE, *Hartford, Conn., Chicago, Ill., or Cincinnati, Ohio.*

TUNE BOOK.

The Brethren's Tune and Hymn Book, is a compilation of Sacred Music adapted to all the hymns in the Brethren's New Hymn Book. It contains over 350 pages, printed on good paper and neatly bound. We will send it to any address, post paid at $1.25 per copy.

TRACTS.

"ANXIOUS BENCH RELIGION EXAMINED," BY ELDER J. S. FLORY. A SYNOPSIS OF CONTENTS. An address to the reader: The peculiarities that attend this type of religion. The feelings there experienced not imaginary but real. The key that unlocks the wonderful mystery. The causes by which feelings are excited. How the momentary feelings called "Experimental religion" are brought about, and then concludes by giving that form of doctrine as taught by Jesus Christ and recorded by his faithful witnesses.

COUNTERFEIT DETECTER
or
BAPTISM—MUCH IN LITTLE.

This work is now ready for distribution, and the importance of the subject will speak for it a large demand. It is a short treatise on baptism in tract form intended for general distribution, and is set forth in such a plain and logical manner that a wayfaring man though a fool, cannot err therein. Either of the above tracts sent postpaid on the following terms: Two copies, 10 cts, 10 copies 40 cents, 25 copies 70 cents, 50 copies $1.00, 100 copies $1.50.

Trine Immersion TRACED TO THE APOSTLES.

The SECOND EDITION is now ready for delivery. The work has been carefully revised, corrected and enlarged.

Put up in a neat pamphlet form, with good paper cover, and will be sent, post-paid, on the following terms: One copy, 25 cts; Five copies, $1.10; Ten copies, $2.00. 25 copies, $4.50; 50 copies, $8.50; 100 copies, $16 00.

Address, J. H. MOORE,
Urbana, Champaign co., Ill.
Oct. 22.

DYMOND ON WAR.

An inquiry into the Accordancy of War, with the Principles of Christianity, and an examination of the Philosophical reasoning by which it is defended. With observations on some of the causes of war and on some of its effects. By Jonathan Dymond. Sent from this office, post-paid, for 50 cts.

1870 1873

DR. FAHRNEY'S Blood Cleanser or Panacea.

A tonic and purge, for Blood Disease. Great reputation. Many testimonials. Many ministering brethren use and recommend it. Ask or send for the "Health Messenger." Use only the "*Panacea*" prepared at Chicago, Ills., and by

Dr. P. Fahrney's Brothers & Co.,
Aug. 3-pd. *Waynesboro, Franklin Co., Pa*

New Hymn Books, English.

TURKEY MOROCCO.

One copy, postpaid,	$1.00
Per Dozen,	11.25

PLAIN ARABESQUE.

One Copy, post-paid,	75
Per Dozen, "	8.50

Ger'n & English, Plain Sheep.

One Copy, post-paid,	$1.00
Per Dozen	11.25
Arabesque Plain,	1.00
Turkey Morocco,	1.25
Single German, post paid	50
Per Dozen,	5.50

$5 to $20 per day! Agents wanted! All classes of working people, of either sex, young or old, make more money at work for us in their spare moments or all the time than at anything else. Particulars free. Address G. Stinson & Co., Portland, Maine.

HUNTINGDON & BROAD TOP RAIL ROAD

Winter Arrangement.

On and after Tuesday, Oct. 4, 1872, Passenger trains will arrive and depart as follows:

Trains from Huntingdon South. *Trains from Mt. Dallas moving North.*

MAIL. A. M.	ACCOM P. M.	STATIONS.	MAIL. P. M.	ACCOM A. M
le7 40	LE	Huntingdon,	AR4 00	AR
7 45		Long Siding	3 53	
8 00		McConnelstown	3 45	
8 05		Pleasant Grove	3 35	
8 22		Marklesburg	3 22	
8 40		Coffee Run	3 07	
8 45		Rough & Ready	3 00	
9 00		Cove	2 40	
9 05		Fishers Summit	2 45	
9 15		Saxton	2 35 le	
9 40		Riddlesburg	2 15	
9 47		Hopewell	2 05	
10 05		Piper's Run	1 50	
10 52		Tatesville	1 30	
11 05		Bloody Run	1 20	
10 40		Mount Dallas	1 15	
11 06		Bedford	12 44	

G. F. GAGE, Supt

SHOUP'S RUN BRANCH.

LE 9 25	LE	Saxton.	AR2 15	AR
9 40		Coalmont.	2 00	
9 45		Crawford.	1 55	
AR10 00	AR	Dudley	LE1 45	LE

Bro'd Top City from Dudley 2 miles by stage.

Time of Penna. R. R. Trains at Huntingdon.

EASTWARD.			WESTWARD.		
Hb'g Ac.	9 34	A. M	Cin. Ex.	2 19	A. M.
Mail	3 30	P. M	Pc'f Ex.	7 45	"
Cin. Ex.	6 55	"	Mail	5 40	P. M.
Phil. Ex	11 15	"	W. Pass.	11 52	A. M.

The Weekly Pilgrim.

Published by J. B. Brumbaugh, & Co.

Edited by H. B. & Geo. Brumbaugh.

CORRESPONDING EDITORS.

D. P. Sayler, Double Pipe Creek, Md.

Leonard Furry, New Enterprise, Pa.

The *Pilgrim* is a Christian Periodical, devoted to religion and moral reform. It will advocate in the spirit of *love* and *liberty*, the principles of true Christianity, labor for the promotion of peace among the people of God, for the encouragement of the saints and for the conversion of sinners, avoiding those things which tend toward disunion or sectional feelings.

TERMS.

Single copy, Book paper,	$1.50
Eleven copies, [eleventh for Agt.]	$15.00

Any number above that at the same rate,

Address.

H. B. BRUMBAUGH.
James Creek,
Huntingdon county Pa.

The Weekly Pilgrim.

"REMOVE NOT THE ANCIENT LANDMARKS WHICH OUR FATHERS HAVE SET."

VOL. 4. JAMES CREEK, PENNSYLVANIA, MARCH, 4, 1873. NO. 9

POETRY.

FOR THE NIGHT COMETH.

Haste! beloved, the night cometh swiftly!
The night wherein never man can work—
With its chilling blasts, and its gloomy shadows
Where the ghosts of neglected duties lurk.

Now, while the daylight is gleaming o'er us,
Earnestly labor while yet we may,
Then when the night-shades gather around us
Gladly we'll put our toils away.

Day is given for labor unceasing,
Night is the season for peaceful rest,
Haste! for the hours are surely passing,
The sun is reaching toward the West.

Shrink not away, but cheerfully labor
Each at the task which the Master gave,
Though the hours be never so long and weary,
Still let the heart be strong and brave.

What though the task may seem too mighty
For hands so feeble and frail and small—
The Lord who gave it hath still a purpose,
Which worketh ever with us, through all

Even though failure seem all our portion,
Lift up the eyes with weeping dim!—
Haply the lesson He meant to teach us
Was just—our weakness apart from Him

Ours is the duty of cheerfully striving;
His to judge if the work shall be blest.
Labor, then while the daylight lingers,
Leaving, in meekness, to Him the rest
—*Christian Standard.*

ORIGINAL ESSAYS.

CHRIST THE RISEN SAVIOR.

"Now is Christ risen from the dead."

We learn from this text that some of the Corinthians had denied the doctrine of a resurrection, probably explaining away the apostolical language, as figurative, and, as only meaning conversion or that change which took place in the world by the introduction of Christianity.

In confuting this error the apostle called their attention to the resurrection of Christ, as an undeniable fact and showed that the denial of a resurrection was equivalent to saying that Christ was not risen, and thus tended to subvert the foundation of Christianity and to destroy the hope and comfort of believers. "If there be no resurrection of the dead, then is not Christ risen, and if Christ be not risen, then is our preaching vain and your faith is also vain, yea and if we are found false witnesses of God, and if Christ be not raised ye are yet in your sins. Then they also which are fallen asleep in Christ are perished." "If in this life only we have hope in Christ, we are of all men most miserable." All the joy and supports of Christians are inseparably connected with future and eternal felicity, without the hope of which they would have nothing to counterbalance their peculiar trials and conflicts. If Christ were not risen, believers were yet in their sins and even the martyrs had perished. But were not the primitive Christians converted from idols to serve the living God? Did they not repent and do works meet for repentance? Were they not exemplary in the practice of all good works, and did they not meet death for the sake of a good conscience toward God? How, then could they yet be in their sins, as none of these things could atone for their transgressions, and if Christ were not risen, no effectual atonement had been made. They must therefore, have still continued under condemnation and been exposed to the curse of the law which they had broken—a most conclusive proof that the death of Christ was a satisfaction for sin, and, that none can be saved who are not interested in, that atonement he then adds the words, "Now is Christ risen from the dead."

Though true Christians have a witness in themselves which in general satisfies their minds as to the certainty of the things they have believed, yet in seasons of temptation, an acquaintance with the evidence of Christianity would tend greatly to their establishment. And in these times of infidelity all who would continue earnestly for the faith once delivered to the saints should be able to give a reason for their hope to every inquirer or objector both to defend themselves from the charge of enthusiasm, and to preserve young persons, perhaps their own children, from the fatal contagion. It is therefore greatly to be lamented, that pious persons are in general, so little furnished with this sort of knowledge of which they might make such important use. It is commonly said that the New Testament is built upon the foundation of the Old, and must stand or fall along with it, and there is a truth in this sentiment, though it be somewhat diverse in its nature from that which is supposed. Our Lord and His apostles have so frequently quoted the Old Testament and almost every part of it as the Scripture, the word of God, the oracles of God and the language of the Holy Ghost, that their credit must be connected with the divine inspiration of the books thus attested by them. We are able to prove that the Canon of the Old Testament in those days, differed very little, if at all, from that which we have at present, yet our Lord referring to different parts of it, says, thus it is written and thus it must be the Scriptures must cannot be broken, the Scriptures must needs be fulfilled. And the apostles say: "All Scripture is given by inspiration from God." "Holy men of God spake as they were moved by the Holy Ghost." This consideration completely establishes the whole of the Old Testament as a divine revelation with all those who duly reverence the words of Christ and His apostles. In all other respects, the New Testament stands on its own basis and is proved to be the Word of God by distinct evidence. It affords unspeakably more support to the Old Testament than it receives from it, and the resurrection of Christ alone is sufficient to authenticate the whole sacred volume.

The restoration of the dead body to life, is no more difficult with God than the production of life at first. The Divine operation is in both respects alike, incomprehensible.

As we continually observe life to be communicated in a certain way, we call that the law of nature, though we understand not our own meaning and cannot explain how causes produce their effects. But dead bodies do not return to life in the ordinary course of human affairs, we therefore suppose some laws of nature to the contrary, the violation of which in any particular instance, we should call a miracle, that is a divine interposition and operation, to produce an effect above or contrary to the general energy of second causes. Some persons, indeed pretend that this is impossible, but why should it be thought incredible with you that God should raise the dead? The power is no greater than that by which thousands of infants receive new life every day. And who will now say that God cannot or shall not exert his power in any way which they have never before? If a sufficient reason can be assigned for His interposition and the fact be indisputably proven, it becomes as credible as other well attested events, many of which do not coincide with our expectations or ideas of probability.

A PILGRIM.

To be Continued.

WHOSE CHILDREN ARE YOU ?

Whosoever doth not righteousness is not of God. 1st John, 3:10.

When we look abroad upon the earth and behold the many wonders connected with it, we are led to confess that there is a Supreme Being worthy of our best praises, and when we come to our own bodies and contemplate their structure and the dependence of each member, their sympathy one for another, we are led to say, how wonderful! what wisdom! While viewing these we should ask ourselves, who formed all these parts and gave them their office, and are they filling the sphere for which they were created? The answer must come, God formed all.

But a question of importance presents itself, whose children are we, or whose child am I? Here we call a number of children together and ask them, one will answer, "I am J. C's child," another, "I am J. J.'s son," another, "I do not know," and a fourth, "I am Mr. B's by adoption." So we might go on questioning children, and what a variety of answers. Some will tell us promptly what family they belong to and some do not know. Why is it? Because it frequently happens that children's parents die when they are young and they never hear their names, but mark the sadness of that child when it says, "I do not know." How lonesome it feels when it sees other children enjoying the comforts of a pleasant home. Now the inference is drawn from the three classes of answers from the children, that but one of them will stand the test before God, and that is of adoption. There are many who claim to be the children of God but are not; like the Ethiopian that went to Jerusalem to worship, Acts 8:27, when properly instructed, he changed and then knowing his duty, he did it. And Saul, who claimed to be a child of God, believing he was doing God's service but had yet to be adopted. While some say, "I do not know," they appear to be in doubt, saying: "I have done this, and that, but there is a part I do not fully understand. I would willingly do all if I could only believe it necessary, and my teachers ought to know for they make it their study. They are good men and if they can get to Heaven without it I can too," yet they hardly know whose children they are. But the child of adoption says, "I must obey, for when I was adopted the law was made known to me. I have a copy and can read it and hear from it from day to day; and the law says: "If ye love me keep my commandments." A claim to the inheritance is gained by obedience and the child of adoption will ever affirm its right to do a thing because its father did it. Why does it pray? Because it was taught it. How does it know its prayers are answered? Because it asks according to the law. If it disobeys God, it asks forgiveness, and then if it has been offended it forgives, and knows it is forgiven because the word says so. Then the natural conclusion is, that we are all the children of some one be service, and in whose service are we? Now this can be answered by the word of God. It will stand when Heaven and earth pass away, and the children of God are the children of light, and light will shine in darkness. Again, children do not like to hear their parents evil spoken of, they all want honorable parents. Now which is the greater honor, to be God's child or a child of the devil? We are one or the other—can not be both. Let the solemn question come to us all, that in the judgment there will be but two classes of children, and I am to be of one class, and where will my lot fall, on the left or right? If on the left, I will be a child of the devil. Sad thought! What kind of a home has he for me? A lake of fire is his home, and I with him must dwell. What is the order of his house? Weeping and gnashing of teeth, dying and never dead, gloomy prison. Dreadful thought! But on the right hand, "Come ye blessed inherit the kingdom prepared for you from the foundation of the world." What is the order of that house? We are made heirs and joint heirs with Christ, we will sit around our Father's table and Christ will serve, go in and out and find pasture, drink of the pure waters and unite with the Heavenly hosts to praise God. Dear reader, let you be old or young, whose child are you? Remember one thing, this question will be answered some day and we are writing the answer while we live, and as death finds us so will the judgment. Then if you have not done so, set thy house in order, for this night thy soul may be required of thee. And if we never meet on earth may we be the children of God, and meet in that happy Home prepared for us above, where sickness and sorrow, pain and death are strangers.

WILLIAM SADDLER.

Nankin, Ohio.

MY NEW HOUSE.

I married a wife at the age of twenty-three, settled down on a tolerable good farm and was what might be called a well to do farmer. For a number of years we, (wife and I) fought manfully with the ups and downs that attend this very honorable vocation until finally, we could see the day of success dawning, and our labors crowned with a reward.

All this time there seemed to be but one object worthy of our labor, and that was, to get a clear title for our home and the necessary conveniences. The house, though tolerable good when we commenced farming, was beginning to be insufficient for home comforts and it seemed to me, if we just had a good comfortable house, the end would be gained and we would be contented.—The last payment had been made two years before, and by good luck and management we had gathered enough to make a commencement in building, and I presented the matter to my wife.

"Sarah, we have now been laboring for a long time, and have at last succeeded in getting our farm paid for and have some left; had we not better build a house, as this one is very uncomfortable and is not worth repairing anymore?

"You are right, husband, our house is not as comfortable as it might be and I have wished that we could have a better one, but of late my mind has been fixed upon another subject. It is now twenty-three years since we commenced keeping house. All this time God has dealt graciously with us in granting us health and in giving us this comfortable home, but how ungrateful we have been. We are now growing old and our bodies, like our house, are failing and soon may fall. Do you not think it is high time that we commence building houses for us that will not fail, but be eternal in the Heavens? To have a new house would be very desirable, but it will not secure us from death, and oh how dreadful the thought of dying unprepared—without that spiritual home as a refuge for the soul. I have made up my mind, since God has spared me thus long, to put off the important work no longer, but now, seek the Kingdom, and I hope you will do the same and then we can have the promise that "all things will be added," and if among those, we get a new house, so much the more can we prove thankful."

I often sat and heard the powerful preaching of the word, unmoved, but this one stroke came as a thunderbolt and I was slain. The awful truth was presented to me in all its fullness, and I determined that no opportunities should be lost until the Kingdom was secured. Together we sought the mercy-seat—covenanted with God to live faithful until death, by being buried with Christ in baptism.

We lived to realize the promised "added blessings," and to have a new house, but the partner of my trials and joys is gone—her earthly house failed and is now lying beneath the green turf of the valley, but the *new* house was ready, and her spirit has entered its eternal abode. Your unworthy servant is still abiding his time, but this earthly house is rapidly failing, and soon I expect to be unclothed that I may be clothed upon with that spiritual house which is eternal in the Heavens. I feel that I am nearing the stream, but death has lost all its terrors. Dear PILGRIM, sweet messenger of salvation, may God spread your wings and help you go forth to warn sinners of their lost condition and persuade them to build for themselves houses that that will abide beyond the grave.

A BROTHER.

LOVING OUR ENEMIES.

But I say unto you, love your enemies; bless them that curse you; do good to them that hate you, and pray for them who despitefully use and persecute you.—Matt. 5; 44.

This is the language of our Savior, and there is probably no command given us that is more in opposition to the human nature than the one contained in the above text. We are so apt to return evil for evil, forgetting as it were the command of our blessed Redeemer, "Love your enemies." Oh, that this were carried out to its full extent! Would to God we had more of that forgiving spirit within us that was exercised by our Savior, who when He was reviled, reviled not again; when He suffered, He threatened not, and looked down even from the cross and prayed to His Heavenly Father to forgive them for they knew not what they did. Such was the spirit of Christ.

> Oh! how benevolent and kind
> How mild, how ready to forgive;
> Be this the temper of our mind,
> And these the rules by which we live

Paul says if a man have not the spirit of Christ, he is none of His. Brethren and sisters, let us examine ourselves, and see whether we are in possession of that spirit that is mild and ready to forgive. If we are, we will readily forgive those who misuse us, we will not hold a feeling of revenge against any one, but will have a feeling of love toward all, not only our brethren and sisters, but also those that are without. We will let our light shine that others may see our good works and glorify our Father in Heaven. For if we love them which love us what reward have we, and if we salute our brethren only, what do we more than others, do not even the publicans the same? Let us try and be the children of our Father which is in Heaven, who maketh His sun to rise on the evil and on the good, and sendeth rain on the just and on the unjust. If we have not a loving disposition toward our enemies, we have not the spirit of Christ within us, consequently we are not His children, for the Word says so. That Word that will stand either for or against us at a coming day; that Word that is quick and powerful and sharper than any two edged sword, piercing even to the dividing asunder of soul and spirit, and of the joints and marrow, and is a discerner of the thoughts and intents of the heart.

Brethren and sisters, let us take the admonition of the Apostle Paul, who says, "Be kindly affectionate one to another, with brotherly love," again, "Recompense to no man evil for evil, and as much as lieth in you live peaceably with all men, not avenging yourselves but rather give place unto wrath, for it is written, vengeance is mine, I will repay, saith the Lord." Let us endeavor to keep the unity of the spirit in the bond of peace, that we may with propriety say, "Forgive us our trespasses as we forgive those who trespass against us." May the Lord be our helper and we His faithful servants.

M. T.

Nankin, Ohio.

A SPIRITUAL mind has something of the nature of the sensitive plant. I shall smart if I touch this or that. There is a holy shrinking away from evil.—*Cecil.*

AN EXTRACT.

Brethren, I wish to give an extract from the report of an editor upon a sermon preached in our county town by a Methodist minister from the following text:

"And they all with one consent began to make excuse."—St. Luke, 14: 18.

The editor says: "In the evening he discussed—in the second branch of his subject—the effect and excuses offered for rejecting religion. Among others he mentioned the following: The mysteries of the Bible; the number of denominations; inconsistency of professors of religion; fear of failure of success; fear of failure to be able to hold out faithfully to the end; don't feel as to it. In reference to the number of orthodox denominations, he said that he recognized them all as integral, component parts of the Kingdom of God, each performing its proper office and function, that a single Church would result in ecclesiastical despotism and spiritual tyranny, that this experiment was tried for a thousand years, but that God would never again entrust the reins of spiritual power to the hands of any spiritual Church: that he spoke the sentiments of his heart when he said, that rather than have the Methodist or any other church reign supreme in this country, he would have the summit of every mountain in this beloved State, the crater of a blazing volcano, with its sides covered with molten running lava, and every stream from its source to the sea filled with blood instead of pure, limpid sparkling water."

It seems that the speaker recognizes all orthodox denominations as integral, component parts in the Kingdom of God, each performing its proper office and function. Now friendly reader, out of the hundreds of different Churches that we are told are in existence, what part can each one perform and perform its proper office and function? The speaker thinks if God would trust the reigns of spiritual power to a single Church it would result in ecclesiastical despotism and spiritual tyranny. What! the church founded on the Apostles and prophets, Jesus Christ himself being the chief corner stone, run into despotism and spiritual tyranny, when Christ has promised to be with his people always even to the end of the world! Where is men's faith, when they say they are honest and say they would rather see every mountain in this State break forth with volcano eruptions and every stream filled with blood rather than see the Church that Christ has established here on earth reign supreme?

"And they all with one consent began to make excuse." Are there not excuses that will not be worth any more at the great and coming day than the excuses those persons made that were bidden? The one had bought a piece of ground, the other had bought oxen and the third had married a wife and therefore neither of them could come, but in this age of the world it has become popular for people to believe if they only have religion it don't make any difference whether they follow Christ or not, all will be well, when Christ says, "I am the way." This just reminds me of a conversation that took place between a professor and non-professor not long ago. They met on the road to Stanton, our County seat, and commenced talking about religion. The non-professor asked the other some questions and he would say, "what of that, if a man only has religion." There was a county fair near town that day where the professor was going, the other was also going to the town, but not to the fair, and before they parted he asked the professor if he thought it was right to go to the fair where they were horse racing, &c. He answered, he did not know that it was exactly right but what of that if a person had religion.

S. J. GARBER.

THE DRUNKARD'S TREE.

"Wine is a mocker, strong drink raging; and whosoever is deceived thereby is not wise." Prov. 20: 1.

"Drunkards shall not inherit the kingdom of God." 1 Cor. 6: 10.

The
sin of
drunken-
ness ban-
ishes human
reason; drowns
the memory; cau-
ses disease of the
system; changes the
joy which it promises
into madness; destroys
the beauty of person; im-
pairs the strength; vitiates
the healthy appetite; paraly-
zes the feelings; makes the
blood impure; allures to vice;
makes a man an offensive hospital, full of wretchedness, causing internal and external, incura-
ble diseases; in whose train is shame,
poverty, cares and sorrow; bewitches
the mind; is a plotter of mischief against
the soul; a thief of the purse; reduces to
beggary; brings woe to the wife; sorrow to
the children; of a man it makes a brute;
a suicide who drinks in anothers health,
and robs his own, whose days
are few and inglorious. And
this is not all; they bring
upon him the wrath of God
in this world, and after
death eternal destruction.
These are some
of the innumerable evils which
spring from the evil root of drunkenness.
—*Herald of Truth.*

Intemperance has slain its thousands and unless checked, will curse millions yet unborn.

SIMPLICITY.

Simplicity of manner and plainness of speech has ever been peculiar characteristics of the "Brethren." Some one writing for the PILGRIM, No. 8, '73, seems to have forgotten whom he is, or entirely lost this peculiar feature. On "*Winter Reflections*," he first addresses the *winter*, then *God*, then *man*, then *Great God! Infinite Mercy! Concerned hosts of Heaven, all ye sympathizing inhabitants of the earth*, &c., in the same sentance. Then he talks to *pride* and *licentiousness* as familiar friends. The article is full of words and phrases the meaning of which is not very plain to his readers, and doubtless not to himself. "Terrestrial Globe," —why not *say the earth*,—"Mundane sphere"—why not say *the world*? Who are the "concerned hosts of Heaven?" Why "pray God to *proffer* mercy and stay vengeance" when he says "*proffered mercy*" bleeds for you? There are many things in this article that we do not understand, and we greatly wish that we too were learned and had the ability to see all these bright visions set forth therein.

A. B. B.

DRIFTING AWAY.

With proud, exultant step we may tread to the very verge of the future in the journey of life; but we can go no farther; there it becomes lost to us in the realities of the present; we are left to look forward to a new future, while behind us lies the past, from which we are rapidly drifting. Often our hearts grow weary, our eye-lids wet with tears, as we pause to look back at the receding shore, and through the dim distance, seem to catch glimpses of the forms we loved in other days—our idly friends, whose hands we were wont to clasp in fond, familiar greeting, but whom now we meet no more as in the old en time, for on the restless sea of change our barks have drifted far apart. Far more vividly than all, come to us visions of the old homestead, from whose portals we went forth with brave hearts, to try the realities of the world which lay beyond the precincts of our own quiet home. Half impatiently we had looked forward to the time when, no longer bound by the restraints of home, we should take our place upon the stage of active life; but often the path has proved a thorny one, our feet have grown weary, and with yearning hearts we have longed for the quiet joys from which we have forever drifted.

No more do we gather an unbroken circle beneath the shelter of the old home tree; loved ones grown weary with life's burdens, and borne on the river of death, have drifted away to the unknown shore. It is sometimes sad to feel that we are receding from all that our hearts hold dear. From our childhood years with their innocent joys—from the sacred ties of home and early association—but more sad, more bitter than all, comes to us the knowledge that on the current of worldly pleasure we are floating from the love of our Heavenly Father; that with thoughtless feet we are treading each day nearer the grave, unmindful of what may lie beyond its dark borders.

There are moments when our better natures are awakened within us—when we turn heart-sick and weary from the vanities of the world, and pause to contemplate whither the stream of life is carrying us. Then it is that we feel the need of a stronger arm than earth can give to lean upon; and could we but throw off the shakles of sin, and with renewed energy and earnest purpose press forward in the path of duty—aiming to fulfill the mission of which Our Savior has left an example in His Holy word—our lives would be purer, our influence more ennobling, and we far more happy: that when our eyes grow dim with age, and we await our summons home, there may come to us no regret for the joys from which we have drifted away, but rather golden gleams of the home to which we are hastening.—*Rural New Yorker.*

RELIGION.—The religion that goes in golden slippers, never takes its way through the "straight gate" along the thorny road which Heaven-bound pilgrims travel. That religion that glows only when the sun shines dies out when the storm rages and the clouds thicken. But that religion that has Jesus crucified in it, goes even barefooted over the burning sands of the "desert" and is a light and lamp to the feet of the "meek and humble" pilgrim while pressing onward through storms and tempests to the promised land—the land of eternal rest.—*J. S. Flory.*

EDUCATION, like money, is a power for good or evil. A man of good education is a man of large talents, and places him under large responsibilities, but it should be remembered that ignorance will not lessen our responsibilities, as the improvement of our talents implies a duty, and that duty can only be fully discharged by surrounding ourselves with such circumstances as will enable us to successfully meet the great responsibilities of life and improve our talent to its full extent. There was a man of three score told us, the other day, that he would now give $1,000 if he had a good English education. He was a minister, and lacked education. Young reader, think of this. Perseverance and application now to a few tie money now, will give you what thousands cannot when you are old. —*Bloss.*

THE DESIRE OF ALL NATIONS.

Concluded.

Inference 1st. Is Christ the desire of all nations? How vile a sin is it then in any nation, upon whom the light of the gospel has shone, to reject Jesus Christ? These say, "depart from us, for we desire not the knowledge of thy ways," Job. 21: 14. They thrust away his worship, government and servants from amongst them, and in effect say, "we will not have this man to reign over us." Luke 19: 14. Thus did the Jews, they put away Christ from among them, and thereby judged themselves unworthy of eternal life. Acts 13: 46. This is at once a fearful sin and a dreadful sign, how soon did vengeance overtake them like the overthrow of Sodom; O let it be for a warning to all nations to the end of the world. He would have gathered the children of Israel under his wings as a hen doth her brood, even when the Roman eagle was hovering over them, but they would not; therefore their houses were made unto them desolate, their city and temple made an heap.

2nd. If Jesus Christ be the desire of all nations, how incomparably happy must that nation be that enjoys Christ in the power and purity of his Gospel ordinances; if Christ under a veil made Canaan a glorious land. Dan. 11: 41. What a glorious place must that nation be which beholds him with open face in the bright sunshine of the Gospel. O, my country, know thy happiness and the day of thy visitation, what others desired, thou enjoyest; provoke not the Lord Jesus to depart from thee by corrupting his worship, longing after idolatry, abusing his messengers and oppressing his people, lest his soul depart from thee.

3rd. If Christ be the desire of all nations, examine whether he be the desire of your soul in particular, else you shall have no benefit by him. Are your desires after Christ true spiritual desires? Reflect, I beseech you, upon the frame and temper of your heart. Can you say of your desires as Peter did of his love to Christ? Lord, thou knowest all things, thou knowest that I desire thee. Try your desires by the following tests: Has Christ the supreme place in your desires? Do you deem all things but dross in comparison of the excellency of Jesus Christ your Lord? Do your desires after Christ lead you to effort, to use all the means of accomplishing what you desire? You say you desire Christ, but what will you do to obtain your desire? If you seek him carefully and incessantly in all the ways of duty; if you will strive in prayer, labor to believe, cut off right hands and pluck out right eyes, that is, be willing to part with the most profitable and pleasant ways of sin that you may enjoy Christ, the desire of your souls, then are your desires right, are your desires after him permanent, or only a sudden fit which goes off again without effect? If your desires after Christ abide in your heart, if your longings are at all times for him, then are your desires right. Christ always dwells in the desires of his people; they can feel him in their desires when they cannot discern him in their love or delight. Do your desires after Christ spring from a deep sense of your need of him? Has conviction opened your eyes to see your misery, to feel your burdens, and to make you sensible that your remedy lies only in the Lord Jesus? Then are your desires right, bread and water are made necessary and desirable by hunger and thirst, by these things try the truth of your desires after Christ.

4th. Do you, upon serious trial, find in you such desires after Christ as above described? O, bless the Lord for that day wherein Christ the desire of all nations, became the desire of your souls, and for your comfort know that you are blessed in this, that your eyes have been opened to see both the want and worth of Christ. Had not Christ applied his precious eye salve to the eyes of your mind, you would never have desired him; you would have said, "he hath no form nor comeliness, and when we shall see him there is no beauty that we should desire him," Isa. 53: 2, or as they to the spouse, "what is thy beloved more than another beloved?" Sol. Song, 5: 9. O blessed souls enlightened of the Lord to see those things that are hid from them that perish; you are blessed in that your desires after Christ are a sure evidence that the desire of Christ is toward you, we may say of desires as it is said of love, we desire him because he first desired us; you are blessed in that your desires shall surely be satisfied. "Blessed are they that hunger and thirst after righteousness for they shall be filled." Matt. 5: 6. "The desire of the righteous shall be granted." Prov. 10: 24. You are blessed, in that God hath guided your desires to make the best choice that ever was made, whilst the desires of others are eagerly set upon gaining riches, pleasure and honor in the world, any good will satisfy some men's happy soul, if none but Christ can satisfy thee, Psa. 4: 6. You are blessed, in that there is a work of grace certainly wrought upon thy soul; and these very desires after Christ are a part thereof, blessed in that these desires after him keep thy soul active and working after him continually in the way of duty. One thing have I desired, that will I seek after. Psa. 27: 4, Desire will be a continual spring to diligence and industry in the way of duty; the desire of the end quickeneth to the use of means. Others may fall asleep and cast off duty, but it will be hard for those to do so whose souls burn with desire after Christ, you are also blessed, in that your desires after Christ will make death much the sweeter and easier to you. "I desire to be dissolved and to be with Christ, which is far better." Phil. 1: 23. When a christian was once asked whether he was willing to die, he returned this answer; Let him be unwilling to die, who is unwilling to go to Christ.

5th. Let me exhort and persuade all to make Jesus Christ the desire and choice of their souls. This is the main scope of the Gospel. Every creature naturally desires its own preservation, do not you desire the preservation of your precious and immortal souls? If you do, then make Christ your desire and choice. Do not your souls earnestly desire the bodies they live in? How tender are they of them, how careful to provide for them, though they pay a dear rent for those tenements they live in. And is not union with Christ infinitely more desirable than the union of soul and body? O, covet union with him; then shall your souls be happy when your bodies drop from them at death, 2 Cor. 5: 1-8. How do the men of this world desire the enjoyments of it? They rise early, sit up late, &c., and all this for very vanity. Shall a worldling do more for earth than you for heaven? Shall the creature be so earnestly desired and Christ neglected? What do all your desires in this world benefit you if you go Christless? Suppose you had the desire of your hearts in these things, how long should you have comfort in them if you have not Christ. Blessed be God for Jesus Christ, the desire of all nations.

Method of Grace,

FLAVEL.

Religious News.

The highest average salary to clergymen in New York are paid in the Protestant Episcopal Church, two ministers receiving $12,000 each.

Miss Sarah E. Smiley, the Quakeress preacher, has recently received the ordinance of baptism, and formally declared herself no longer a Quaker, but a member of the church universal.

From the *Advent Christian Times* we learn that a Jonas Wendell of Edenboro, Pa., has written a work, entitled "Present Truth," on prophecy and chronology, setting forth the end of this age, this present year, 1873.

Spurgeon the London Baptist Divine has so far recovered from his late illness that he has commenced preaching again, and is expected to visit Brooklyn soon, as the guest of Dr. Talmage, and will probably preach for him in the Tabernacle.

FROM RUSSIA.—Recent dispatches from Berlin, in Germany, state that there is an extensive emigration movement to America, among the German colonists in Russia. One hundred and twenty families are said to have left Beresina alone. We must however not place too much confidence in these dispatches.—*Herald of Truth.*

Beecher says that religion that isn't "mixed" with politics and the business of life, is worth about as much as yeast that is never mixed with flour.

Yes, as far as dollars and cents are concerned, Beecher knows how to make things pay. With religion on one shoulder and politics on the other we have a nice mixture and no doubt it will *raise*.

Benjamin Franklin, a self-made man, Editor-in-chief of the *American Christian Review*, Cincinnati, now sixty-two years of age, has served as an evangelist thirty-seven years, and as an editor thirty-five years. He is the most noted evangelist among the Disciples, having visited more States, travelled more extensively, and held more protracted meetings, than any other man among this people. He has baptized with his own hands over 8,000 people.

The following is a clip from the *Christian Standard*: With the word of the Lord before me, no person is born again until he is baptized; no person is converted until he is baptized; no person is regenerated until he is baptized. A person may be baptized and not be born again, but born again he cannot be without being baptized. A person may be baptized and not be converted, but converted he cannot be without being baptized. A person may be baptized and not be regenerated, but regenerated he can not be without being baptized.

The Missionary Herald states that the field of Christian missions in what is distinctively known as the heathen world embraces a population of 700,000,000. Of these seven-eighths are attached to one or other of the three great systems—Mohammedanism, Hindooism and Buddhism. The first as yet relatively untouched, still pushes its proselytism in Africa and everywhere stands as a barrier to the Christian faith. In India even university graduates celebrate the degraded rites of Hindooism. And Buddhism, with its 300,000,000 votaries, has hardly been touched by Christian influences. The *Herald* draws the conclusion that there is a great deal of hard work to be done yet.

Youth's Department.

LITTLE GEORGIE.

BY J. H. HAFF.

Death comes alike to all. The young, the little boys and girls, tripping lightly and gayly along the flowered pathway of life, are as suddenly called away as the old, those who have ripened through long years for the grave. The little ones with their blooming cheeks and their bright eyes are the flowers of earth. They gladden all around them with their presence. The glad sunshine of their young faces, and the merry gushing of their young hearts enliven the less cheerful journey of the old fathers and mothers.

But some flowers die in the early Spring-time, before they have had time to fully open their petals to the bright sunshine and mature into the ripe fruit.

So little boys and girls are often called by our good Heavenly Father from the happy home circle on earth, and the fond embrace of their parents, to bloom forever in the beautiful land that Jesus makes glad by His presence. I am going to tell you a short story of little George W———, who died thus early but who went away happy because he loved Jesus, and knew that Jesus loved him.

Georgie was just seven years old, a bright, happy little boy who loved everybody and whom everybody loved. He had a good papa and mamma who taught him to pray and to be good. He had a pretty home in a pretty town, in a pretty part of the country. His father and mother loved everything beautiful and good. Their beautiful little cottage was surrounded with beautiful flowers and vines and evergreen trees, that made it look like a paradise. The rooms of the cottage were hung with beautiful pictures, and good and beautiful books were on the tables and in the book-cases.

We used to pass this beautiful home every day, where Georgie and his brothers and sisters lived so happily with their parents. We knew the little boys and girls of this home were happy and good, because they had such good parents, and had so much beauty and goodness around them; and boys and girls that always have things good and beautiful about them, grow good and beautiful themselves.

But grief and sorrow came suddenly and unexpectedly to the happy hearts of this pretty home, and although several years have passed, when the recollection of the hour comes back, there also comes back the quick pang of pain and sorrow.

One evening just at the hour when the fading beams of the sun were kissing the flowers around the cottage, good-night, little Georgie, taking his whip in his hand, and bidding his mamma an hour's good-by started to meet his papa at the store. On his way he had to cross the railroad, and just as he passed it the puffing engine rolled by dragging heavily a long train of cars. Little Georgie turned around to look at the rattling train. He struck at the wheels with his whip. The lash became entangled, and little Georgie in his endeavor to tear it loose, stumbled and fell under the car, and several wheels, carrying their heavy load, passed over him. His tender limbs were almost severed from his body. A strong man seeing him fall, leaped from the train and picked up the poor crushed form and carrying it home laid it tenderly on the sofa, where the smiles of the pictures and the breath of the sweet flowers might be above him and around him as his young life ebbed away.

Then strong men and tender women gathered in and all mingled their tears with the sorrow-stricken hearts that bowed around the dying boy. But the bravest heart there was little Georgie. Not a tear dimmed his eye, not a groan escaped him, and as drop by drop his young blood flowed from his mutilated form, he sang snatches of his Sunday school songs. Conscious that he was dying he told his dear papa and mamma that he was going home. He called for his young playmates and with smiling face he bid them good-by, telling them of his love for them and his dear parents and brothers and sisters, but that he loved Jesus too, and would soon be with him. Just before he died he asked his papa to lay him once more in his little bed, but he could not be moved; and just six hours after the heavy wheels had passed over his tender form his young spirit took its flight.

We bowed our head with the rest in the sorrowing crowd. We assisted to dress the poor crushed boy and to fold his little hands across his breast. It was a painful death for one so young and promising, and yet it was happy. It was young and innocent childhood passing away before the taint of earth had fastened upon it, yet it was childhood passing away almost as if with the wisdom of age.

Such was the life and death of little Georgie. We laid him away where the flowers bloom and the green trees wave their branches over his grave; in a spot where the beauty of the home where he lived and died might flourish where his crushed body sleeps. I hope all the little boys and girls who read this story may aim to be as good as little Georgie was and to love the dear Savior as he did. And we hope the parents of the same little boys and girls may aim to make the homes of their dear children as happy as Georgie's parents made his.—*Christian Standard.*

Correspondence.

A Reporter is wanted from every Church in the brotherhood to send us Church news, Obituaries, Announcements or anything that will be of general interest. To insure insertion, the writers name must accompany each communication. Our Invitation is not personal but general—please respond to our call.

EASTON, W. VA.,
February 14, 1873.

Dear Pilgrim:—You still make your weekly visits to my home, away up here among the hills and valleys of West Va. I know I would miss you greatly were you to "pass me by" in going to and fro over the world. The work our periodicals have to do is immense, they are silent teachers, and penetrate where the living voice of God's ministers cannot, or do not go. And too, that which is read in the circle at home is often more effective than many sermons. The mind is more at rest, and seems to be withdrawn from the excitements and amusements of the outside world. The "mind itself a kingdom is," wherein is fought the battle of life and the victory gained over the adversary.

Since last I took up my pen to write to you, death has been walking up and down through our land, knocking at almost every door. Our little circle was ruthlessly invaded and one of the fairest and best was called to "spirit life." Calmly and fearlessly she went down to the Jordan of death for her hope was in Jesus, an anchor to bear her above the chilling waves. Life was bright before her, and the radiance from the golden future shed its light around her pathway. But God's ways are not our ways. He saw not as we see—with a glance of his omniscient eye He scanned the plain, and seeing the evil to come, said come up higher, thy life work is done. Sad sorrowing hearts find their only comfort now in looking beyond the brightness of the stars, beyond the dimness of the earth, to the Celestial City where the white-robed angels dwell. On earth we have the melancholy satisfaction of going where raised mounds and hallowed inscriptions tell of the loved dead. Ah! How blessed the righteous when he dies." It is the "never-forever" that wrings the heart with agony, never here—forever there. Life at the longest, can't be long, and ere many years roll away, the angel Azrael will come for us, and bear us away from care and toil. May we too be able to say as did our dear one, —"Don't you see the Father and Jesus are with me"—then why need we fear to cross over.

"Snow-white hands are folded," for their work is done—the record is closed—the golden bowl is broken, the silver cord is loosed, the pitcher is broken at the fountain and the wheel at the cistern, and the light that never was on sea or land, the light of divine love, glorified the face of the dead.

Let us then live that when our summons comes we can draw our robes around us, like one who lies down to pleasant dreams. We know that our loss is her gain, but it is hard, Oh! so hard to say "Thy will be done," and bow in meek submission to His will. We know that He who is the resurrection and the life will help in every trouble. Therefore let us leave all to Him, knowing He doeth all things well.

In the one hope, L. H. M.

TIPTON, CEDAR CO IOWA,
February 18th, '73.

Dear Pilgrim:—I will pen a few lines for the brethren in the ministry upon the charge given by the Savior to His servants, "Occupy till I come." As every one has received at least one talent to put the same to usury, or make use of the same in such a way as to accumulate an increase by his talent, and consequently every one that is a faithful servant will be diligently engaged in meditating often in what way and manner he may make the best use of his talents, so that he can know his labor is profitable and not hid in a napkin, no matter what the napkin be, "convenience," "afterwhile," "some other time," or anything else. Now I do not want my brethren to understand me to charge any one of not making any use of his talents, but I wish to be understood in the language of the Savior, "Go into all the world, and preach the Gospel," and also in the language of St. Paul, "Preach the word in season and out of season," &c.

I have noticed, very often, in some districts, four, five and more laboring brethren, sitting at the stand the same time, where one or two are sufficient for to conduct a meeting and to preach the Word there, and some of these brethren may not make use of their calling but a few times in a year. Others again we notice who are laboring faithfully in the Master's cause, are also embarrassed with "convenience," &c., for often we hear that such meet with the brethren in large congregations, where they have large meeting-houses, churches organized for many years, and plenty of able brethren in the ministry, although there may be there at the same time, six, eight or more able speakers together to attend the preaching for the day. Now there are newly organized churches in their infancy, and quite young and weak, even suffering for the want of help where such could find the very place to find labor desired, and where the talents of such would be crowned with the very desired fruit of their labor, when like here in Cedar Co., Iowa, the calls come from so many places repeatedly, "Come preach for us, come and give us a meeting," where many are inquiring for the good old way to walk therein.

A very large territory is open here for laborers, as they are few in number here, and we can only hold meetings at some places every eight weeks and at some four weeks, and at some places from where the calls are repeated, not at all, consequently some will at last wander astray and will follow such teaching which will finally lead them to destruction and be lost. Therefore brethren now could make the best use of their talents here, and in such a way where their labors would be profitable, and perhaps more so than if they would even go to the far East or West, North or South, among Pagans, heathens or Gentiles.

I see there are calls for laborers from many places, and I think not any without a good cause, but perhaps not many places where such a fair prospect is open, and where laborers are more needed than here. Our Church is in a good and prosperous condition, the Lord has done great things for us during the last two years. We number about 50 members, considerably scattered, and the way is open for brethren to come and settle down with us, where they will find a large field to labor in. Land is very fertile, and all improved, generally good buildings, timber and water plenty, and can be bought as cheap or cheaper than any one can go into new land and make the necessary improvements.

Your brother in love,
SAMUEL MUSSELMAN.

Dear Pilgrim: The health and prosperity of this arm of the Church at present is pretty good, with a little exception. We had seven accessions this fall, one of the seven, Samantha Collins living in Lockport, tells us the way she came to know the Brethren. One day she was at the house of a proprietor of a Paper Mill in the village, and saw a part of a book lying on a stand. She asked to read it. The lady, gave it to her and said it came there among the rags brought on the Canal boat which they had bought. When she read it she found it was a part of a book written by Elder Peter Nead of Dayton, Ohio, known as "Nead's Theology." In that work she found a people who obeyed the Gospel in its primitive purity, and that was the church she had been seeking for, for the space of seven years. She said she believed there was a church that did obey the commandments of Christ all this seven years seeking, but knew not where to find it until she found part of Nead's Theology. From that time on she sought the Church, and as the writer was passing through that vicinity and preached in the town in which she lived, he became acquainted with her and she requested the whole book. He gave it to her, and she read it and gave it to her neighbor, a Lutheran lady, and at our Communion in September, both of them came the distance of fifteen miles and were baptized. Sister Collins above named, was a member of the Baptist Church. She said at one time she called upon her minister to give an explanation of the 13th chapter of John. His response was, "if my feet are dirty, I wash my own feet." She said to him, "you are a pretty minister, you profess to preach the whole Gospel to us, and inasmuch as you make light of this chapter you make light of your Savior, &c."

How remarkably strange sometimes things occur. In the case above the book was thought to be entirely useless, sold by somebody in rags, was separated and laid aside and pronounced worth nothing. But in it there was a message (though secreted in rags), a message that directed the soul to the Church of God. I believe that God had a hand in this matter, and that He has a great work for her to do, and our prayer is, that sister Collins, with all others, may be bright and shining lights in the Church.

JOHN NICHOLSON.

Dear Pilgrim: — As you request Church news, I thought to write a few lines for your columns that may be of some interest to those that read it. We appointed a meeting on the 10th of December, for brethren Jacob Berkey and Jesse Calvert, but the latter failed to come, yet we had five very interesting meetings, and a good feeling was manifested among the people.

On Sunday following, being the 19th, brethren Jesse Calvert, David Hostettler and Isaac Berkey came to us unexpectedly. We appointed an evening meeting at our school-house, on Monday at sister Hannah Baumgardner's house, and in the evening at the school-house, had a large congregation. The teacher and neighbors were much interested, and all were willing to stop the school for the week. On Thursday the 23d was very cold, and snowed all day, we baptized three persons, the ice being nearly two feet thick, which took much labor to cut through, but the brethren were willing to labor to get poor souls in the fold of Christ. On Sunday the 26th, one more, a motherless daughter, was added to the church by baptism, while many more were almost persuaded to be Christians, and others contemplate uniting with the Church soon. May the prayers of the Church go up to God in their behalf that they may not put it off until it is too late. The Lord reward those brethren for their labor, and that the word spoken by them may be as bread cast upon the waters that may be gathered not many days hence.

SAMUEL LUPOLD.
Lagrange Center, Ind.

Editors of the Pilgrim: — I had not seen a number of your paper for a long time, until lately I was at Bro. J. H. Flora's where a meeting was held. He was endeavoring to make up a club for the PILGRIM, and seeing that the paper had improved much, it induced me to try it for the present year. A few days since I received the PILGRIM and Almanac, and am much pleased with them. I have read the PILGRIM and it contains many good lessons. It, like many other things, is condemned by many, (brethren not excepted), upon these grounds, they say, all that is written is nothing more than men's opinions. Admitted; so is preaching mens opinions, out always when we hear or read religious conversation we should not condemn it until we have examined the Word of God, and if it does not harmonize with that, then we can truly say that it is only doctrines of men.

Dear brethren, when you write, let your pen be governed by the spirit of the Gospel, but we contend for no doctrine save that which was once delivered to the saints, but strive to keep in view the landmarks that our ancient fathers have set. So we hope the PILGRIM will visit us weekly and bring us interesting items that cannot be condemned by the words of eternal Truth. Let us prove all things, and hold fast to that which is good, is the prayer of your unworthy servant.

JEREMIAH BARNHART.
Retreat, Va

Editors Pilgrim: — We desire to contribute our mite of church news to the brethren through the PILGRIM, by stating that through an invitation, Elder H. D. Davy came to us on the 25th of January, and on the evening of that day and the next morning, (Sunday), preached two sermons at the Rowland Meeting-house, near Canton, brethren Conrad Caylor, W. Murray, Noah Longenecker and Aaron Shively also being present and taking part in the exercises. On Sunday evening we repaired to the Canter Meeting house, and continued to meet day and evening until Tuesday evening, brother John Clement also coming to us. We had very good meetings, a full house and good attention. We earnestly pray that the good seed sown may not all have been sown in vain, but that some may have fallen upon good ground, spring up and bring fruit unto eternal life, some thirty, some sixty and some a hundred fold. Yours in love,

B. B. BOLLINGER.

CORDELIA, CAL., }
FEB. 12th., 1873. }

Dear Editors: — Perhaps a few words from this part of the world would interest you. The first topic is "the weather." Our winter has been an unusually fine one. We had some hard frosts, but light freezes. I saw ice about a quarter of an inch once or twice this winter and that was cold for our ever fine climate. We have green vegetables the year round, such as turnips, radishes, lettuce and onions. Almond trees blossomed some time ago and the peach trees are almost out.

Our growing grain looks promising and every available spot of land is being sown with the expectation of reaping a bountiful harvest. Farmers say, we have had sufficient rains to insure a crop even if we should get no more, but our rainy season continues up to May, though generally no very heavy showers in the Spring months, they are only occasional.

More Anon.
CARRIE P. FOSTER.

Dear Pilgrim: — On the first Sunday of the present month, (Feb.) the brethren of the Brownsville Church, Washington Co., Md., commenced a meeting, and continued for some six days. The ministering brethren present were Brown and Gibbons of the Bush Creek Congregation, Frederick Co. Md., and Daniel Wolf of Washington Co. Md.

Part of the time the roads were in bad condition for travel, yet there was pretty good attendance by the people of the community, and good attention paid to the preaching, and although there were none added to the church, I am sure good impressions were made on many who attended, and the prospects are that some will yet declare on the Lord's side, and will say, that they started to think about their souls best interest at this meeting. The Church was built up by the efforts then made to extend the Redeemer's Kingdom.

EMANUEL SLIFER.
Burkettsville, Md.

MARRIED.

HORNBECK—ROTHROCK.—On Jan. 30, 1873, at the house of the bride's father, by the undersigned, Samuel Hornbeck and Miss Mary E. Rothrock, both of White Co., Ind. JOS. AMICK.

DIED.

FLORY.—Near South English, in the English River District, Keokuk Co., Iowa, February 17th 1873, Salomon O., youngest child of brother Joel and sister Susan Flory, of Lung fever and Erysipelas combined, aged 2 years, 1 month and 25 days. Funeral discourse by the brethren from 2d Samuel, 12th chapter 23rd verse.

Thus has one more glorified spirit been added to the happy throng in Heaven. Oh, that we may all be permitted to meet it with all the Redeemed around the throne of God. B. F. FLORY.

(*Visitor* please copy.)

ENGLAR.—In the Pipe Creek Church, Carroll Co., Md., February 14th '73, E. M., daughter of Josiah and Caroline Engler, aged 14 years, 5 months and 25 days.

The subject of this notice was an amiable, intelligent girl, and though full of life and mirth, her amusements and enjoyments were of such a nature that her parents, and those with whom she was surrounded, were led to conclude that she had not yet crossed the line of accountability. She died of Consumption. May the Lord comfort the stricken parents, brothers and little sisters, and help them and us all to remember the solemn words of the wise man that were used on the occasion, "Rejoice, O, young man, but know thou that for all these God will bring thee to judgment."

E. W. STONER.

(*Companion* please copy the above.)

NEHR.—In the Sugar Creek branch, Allen Co., Ohio, son of brother Samuel and sister Rebecca Nehr, aged 4 years, 9 months and 7 days.

MILLER.—Also January 25th, 1873, Lavella V., daughter of brother John E. and sister Miller, aged 8 weeks.

BANSHOTTOM.—Also in the same branch Feb 4th 1873, brother Wesley B. Banshottom, aged 51 years. Funeral occasion of all the above by the Brethren.

The subject of this notice had been for some years an expelled member, but when he found the disease (Erysipelas), was likely to prove fatal, he became alarmed, and not willing to die out of the Church, he sent some ten miles for the elders of the church to visit him immediately and receive him into the church, which was attended to on the 4th, at which time he much regretted his living so long outside of the Church, but thanked God that he had been earnestly engaged in prayer and believed his prayers were heard, and on the morning of the 5th he breathed his last. Funeral occasion of all the above by the brethren.

DANIEL BROWER.

ETTER.—On Feb. 17th, 1873, in the Lower Cumberland Church, Pa., brother Samuel Etter, aged 69 years and 11 days. Funeral services by brethren D. Keller and Jacob Hollinger, from Isa. 38: 1.

M. MILLER.

FISHEL.—In the Hopewell Church, Feb. 14th, 1873, sister Christina Fishel aged 31 years, 9 mos. and 6 days. Funeral services by Eld. Jacob Steel and S. A. Moore, from 1st Thess. 4. 13.

OAKS.—In the Hopewell Church, Bedford Co., Pa., Dec. 14th, 1872, brother Frederick Oaks, aged 81 years, 9 mos. and 10 days. Funeral services by John W. Brumbaugh and J. Snowberger, from Rev. 14: 12, 13.

OAKS.—In the same Church, sister Elizabeth Oaks, wife of the above aged 72 yrs. 9 mos. and 22 days. Funeral services by Elders Jacob Steel and John W. Brumbaugh from Hebrews 13: 14.

HENRY CLAPPER.

ANNOUNCEMENTS.

Please announce through the PILGRIM that our District Meeting will be held on the 13th of May in the Cook's Creek Congregation, Rockingham Co., Va.

SALOMON GARBER.

The District Meeting for North Missouri will be held on the 7th and 8th of March in the Smith Fork Branch, Clinton Co., (near Plattsburg), in the Brethren's Meeting-house. A general representation desired. Those coming by R. R. will stop off at Plattsburg.

GEORGE WITWER.

Please make the following announcement in the WEEKLY PILGRIM. The District Meeting of West Virginia, will be held in Seneca District, eight miles west of Mouth of Seneca, at Union School House, in Dry Fork township, Randolph Co., on Friday and Saturday, 9th and 10th of May. For any further information address the undersigned at

Mouth of Seneca,
Pendleton Co., W. Va.

By order of the Church.

ASA HARMAN.

TO ALL WHO ARE CONCERNED.

We do, through this medium, inform the brethren and churches comprising the first district of Virginia, that Friday and Saturday before the fourth Sunday in April, is the time appointed for the holding of the Annual District Meeting, and will be held at that time no preventive providence, at the Valley Meeting-house in Botetourt Co., one mile south of Amsterdam. A full attendance is desirable.

The undersigned also informs his brethren that he has a number of New Hymn Books on hand for sale. B. F. MOOMAW.

SEND for old numbers of the PILGRIM for free distribution. We desire to put a copy in the home of every brother and sister in the land, and all others that might be benefited by reading them. How many will aid us by ordering copies for distribution? Send in your orders and thus assist us in the good work.

The Weekly Pilgrim.

JAMES CREEK, PA., Mar. 4th. 1873.

☞ How to send money.—All sums over $1.50, should be sent either in a check, draft or postal order. If neither of these can be obtained, have the letter registered.

☞ WHEN MONEY is sent, *always* send with it the name and address of those who paid it. Write the names and post office a plainly as possible.

☞ EVERY subscriber for 1873, gets a *Pilgrim Almanac* FREE.

TRINE AND TRIUNE.

The above words seem to be the subject of some inquiry, and we have been requested to give the definition of each, and show the difference of meaning, if there is any, which seems to be a matter of doubt with some who regard them as synonomous terms. These conclusions, no doubt, have been arrived at from the manner in which they are generally used.

That there is a difference, is very evident when we trace up their origin and definition.

Trine, is from the Latin word *trinus* and signifies, threefold or thrice repeated.

Triune is from the Latin words, *tri—three*, and *unus*, one, together *tri—one*—three in one.

With the word immersion attached to it, as our querist has it, we have Trine Immersion, which is equivalent to three immersions, or being immersed thrice.

In Triune Immersion, we have three immersions in one immersion or three actions to complete one immersion which so beautifully harmonizes with our mode of baptism that it occurs to us that it would be much more appropriate for us to accept the term Triune Immersion, instead of Trine Immersion. Trine Immersion really signifies three immersions, and to fully carry out the sense, in baptism, it would necessitate the administrator, each time, to lift the subject entirely out of the water and give three distinct immersions which would entirely destroy the trinity and unity of the God-head. But in Triune Immersion we have three in one, by the subject being taken in the water and the lower part of the body immersed in the water, *unus*, and remain there while the upper part is immersed in each of the names of the Trinity, *tri*, thus making three immersions in one immersion which makes a beautiful figure of the God-head and fully coincides with the commission, baptizing them in the name of the Father, and of the Son and of the Holy Ghost.

CRITICISMS.

Of late, a number of criticisms have been sent us, one of which we admit this week, under the caption, "Simplicity." This we do, not to discourage but for improvement.

Criticisms, wisely administered, are just the things we need, and would greatly improve and elevate our standard of literature, and we would open a special department for this purpose were we assured that our contributors would *bear* it. There should be no possible offence taken from friendly criticisms, especially among children, (as such we claim to be) when it is done for our benefit and improvement.

When we attended school, in our Literary Societies, there was a critic appointed to criticise, not only our compositions, but the manner in which we stood, gestures &c., and that in the most *rigid* manner. We not only bore it, but we *desired* it, because we knew it was for our own improvement. In this spirit exactly we wish our contributors to receive any criticisms that may be offered on their compositions.

As a timely hint we would say; study brevity. Write only when you have something to write about, and let that be to the point. Remember, apologies are a waste in paper, ink, and time of writing them; a waste of postage, a waste in compositor's time, and a waste in reading, in fact, it is waste all around because there is nothing at all in them. Do not apologize but write with such ability as God may give, be brief and to the point and we will exact no more.

We are in want of a large number of plain practical articles and we hope our readers will get to work and supply us promptly. The world is God's great book of instruction and a living witness of the Bible. Whenever and where-ever there is an idea suggested that might be of general interest, make it the subject of an article for the PILGRIM.

CAN'T DO WITHOUT IT. The following is the sacrifice some are willing to make that they may read and have others read the PILGRIM.

Brother Brumbaugh:—I am taking that good paper, THE WEEKLY PILGRIM. It comes every week a welcome visitor and I could not do without it and borrowed the money to send for it. I am a widow and have to work for my living, but I must have another copy sent for my daughter. She has not yet found that sweet rest promised to the righteous. Enclosed find, &c. S. E. M.

Jefferson, Ind.

If our whole Church was made up of such material, our circulation would be increased by the thousands. How much better to spend money thus, than to waste it in decorating our daughters with the frivolities of fashion which impart no knowledge, but tend to the destruction of the soul. Fathers and mothers, if you have sons and daughters, see that they are supplied with the PILGRIM. Some have done it, and there are hundreds more that should do it. Think of this.

PERSONAL.

ABRAHAM L. NEFF: The money was not received.

JAS. AMICK. All postal orders must be made payable at Huntingdon.

L. WORKMAN: You say Susa Long paid $2.50 but this information will do us no good unless we have her address.

D. MILLER: M. J. McClure's papers are sent and we suppose he gets them now. His address is changed to Prospect, as ordered.

JOSEPH RITTENHOUSE: J. P. and D. W. are marked paid on our list. Sarah Hull's name is not on our list. Shall we send the PILGRIM to her?

DANIEL BOCK: All right now. Your list was right but we always want the names of those who pay, sent with the money, so that we can give them credit for the money he pays.

MONEY LIST.

E. W. Stoner,	$15.00
G. H. Shafer,	1.25
J. R. Reese,	1.50
C. Custer	1.50
G W Bricker	1.50
D M Foglesanger	1.50
C F Wirt	2.75
F W Kohler	1.50
S P Maust	75
Catharine E Tesler	1.50
J J Howard	3.00
Solomon Garber	1.50
Daniel Hoover	15 00
John W Blauch	2.15
Edward Ball	1.50
J J Kessler	1.50
Isaac Cripe	11.00
John Brubaker	2 00
Asa Hammer	2.50
George Kinney	3.75
A C Neff	4 25
Frederick B. Weimer	1.50
J P Hetric	1.50
L H Dickey	1.30
Jesse Calvert	3.00
Noah Horne	1.50
John R Riffe	70
Peter Knavel	4.50
Dr. J J Solomon	4.50
Peter Knavel	1.50
Abraham Good	1.50
David Bossler	1 00
S M Kintner	6.50
D B Sell	5.50
M Emma Rohrer	1 25
Isaac Brumbaugh	2.60

VALUABLE RECEIPTS.

The following are a few of the hundreds of valuable receipts contained in the "Household Treasure." No Family can afford to be without it for the trifle it costs. See advertisement on last page.

BRONCHITIS.—Avoid exposure to cold or damp air; and refrain from reading aloud, public speaking, singing, or blowing instruments; keep clear of stimulants, and use a diet of milk and vegetables, take some soothing syrop to allay the irritation; wear no cravat or other bandage about the neck, a light ribbon is sufficient; let the neck have plenty of fresh air, and apply cold water to it every morning when you wash.

COUGHS AND COLDS.—Keep the bowels open by pills or senna—soak the feet in warm water, and drink freely of herb tea, such as catmint or spearmint. Use for the cough, a syrup of life-everlasting, and thoroughwort, boiled in molasses.

WHOOPING COUGH.—Take salts of tartar twenty grains, cochineal ten grains, loaf sugar one ounce, dissolve in three gills of water. Dose for a child, four to five years old, a teaspoonful three times a day, and also a little when the cough is troublesome.

RED ANTS.—To keep them away from cupboards, keep one pint of tar, in two quarts of water, in an earthen vessel in your closets, and you will not be troubled with little red ants. When first mixed, pour the water on hot.

CHEAP SPONGE CAKE.—Four eggs, three cups of sugar, one cup of milk one tea-spoonful of saleratus, flour enough to make a good stiff batter, a little salt and spice, quick oven. Bake it twenty minutes.

LAND, LAND, LAND!!

The completion of the Chesapeake and Ohio Trunk Line Railway, has opened up to the world much of the fine TIMBER LANDS, rich COAL FIELDS and cheap FARMING LANDS of W. Va. Now is the time to get cheap homes and invest money with the prospect of a handsome profit. For further particulars inquire of the undersigned, agent for lands here. J. S. FLORY,

Orchard View, Fayette Co., W. Va.

Jan. 10.

Trine Immersion.

A discussion on Trine Immersion, by letter between Elder B. F. Moomaw and Dr. J. J. Jackson, to which is annexed a Treatise on the Lord's Supper, and on the necessity, character and evidences of the new birth, also a dialogue on the doctrine of non-resistance, by Elder B. F. Moomaw. Single copy 50 cents.

Bee Books, Bee Books!

On receipt of 50 cts. I will send by mail a valuable *Bee Book* treating on over one hundred subjects. No Bee keeper should be without it. It tells just how to make bees profitable. *Italian Queen* Bees bred from imported mothers, each $5.00. Orders solicited. Address

E. J. WORST,

New Pittsburgh, Wayne co., O.

Feb 18-tf.

THE MUSICAL MILLION.
AND
FIRESIDE FRIEND.

ALDINE S. KIEFFER, EDITOR.

A large sixteen page Monthly Magazine, devoted to the interests of the Character-Note System of Musical Notation, Music, Poetry, and the dissemination of a Pure, Chaste, Home Literature.

Each number contains from six to eight pieces of New Music for the Choir, Home Circle and Sabbath School. It contains charming stories of Faith, Hope, Love, and Temperance. Its aim is to make the heart better, and Home happier.

☞ Terms:—Fifty Cents a Year! ☜

PREMIUMS!!

One hundred subscribers one year $50.00

Premiums to agents who send us clubs of 100, First a Silver watch worth $20, or 2nd. 100 copies Glad Hosannas by express, 3rd, 100 copies of Our School-Day Singer by express, or a package of 25 Christian Harp, 25 Glad Hosannas, and 50 copies each of the Morning and Evening Star Songster.

Fifty Subscribers one year, $25.00

Premiums to agents, just one-half of the above rates in books, or $7.50 in Greenbacks.

Twenty-five subscribers, one year, $12.50

Premium to agents, a copy of WEBSTER'S NATIONAL PICTORIAL DICTIONARY, worth $5.00. Now is the time. Or we will send books to the amount of $3.50 selected from our Catalogue, at trade prices.

Ten Subscribers, one year $5.00

Premium to the club agent of Ten copies of the Morning Star Songster, and Twenty copies of the Evening Star Songster. This enables the agent to offer an inducement to persons who subscribe to him, by giving each one a copy of the Songster.

Four subscribers, one year, $2.00

Premium to the club agent, Woods' Household Magazine, or a Tuning Fork, Key of A or C, or a copy of the Song Crowned King.

A sample copy of the Musical Million, containing a List of premiums sent free.

In forming clubs, Subscribers need not all reside at the same office, but may be from a dozen different places.

☞ Address all orders, for either Book or papers to

RUEBUSH, KIEFFER & CO.,

SINGER'S GLEN,

Rockingham Co., Va.

THE

HOUSEHOLD TREASURE.

Containing several hundred Valuable Receipts for cooking well at a moderate expense, making Dyes, Coloring, Cleaning and Cementing. This book also points out in plain language, free from Doctors' terms the diseases of men, women and children, and the latest and most approved means used for their cure, to which is added a description of the Medicinal Roots and Herbs, and how they are to be used in the cure of diseases.

This is a work of considerable importance and we offer it to our readers as being a valuable accession to every household. Sent from this office to any address, post-paid, for 25 cents.

GOOD BOOKS.

How to read Character, Illus.	Price, $1.25
Combe's Moral Philosophy,	1.75
Constitution of Man. Combe,	1.75
Education. By Spurzheim,	1.50
Memory—How to Improve it,	1.50
Mental Science, Lectures on,	1.50
Self-Culture and Perfection,	1.50
Combe's Physiology, Illus.	1.75
Food and Diet. By Pereira,	1.75
Natural Laws of Man,	.75
Hereditary Descent,	1.50
Combe on Infancy,	1.50
Sober and Temperate Life,	.50
Children in Health—Disease,	1.75
The Science of Human Life,	3.50
Fruit Culture for the Million,	1.00
Saving and Wasting,	1.50
Ways of Life—Right Way,	1.00
Footprints of Life,	1.25
Conversion of St. Paul,	1.00

BOOK AGENTS

WANTED FOR THE

GREAT INDUSTRIES
OF THE UNITED STATES;

AN HISTORICAL SUMMARY OF THE ORIGIN, GROWTH AND PERFECTION OF THE CHIEF INDUSTRIAL ARTS OF THIS COUNTRY

1300 PAGES and 500 ENGRAVINGS.

Written by 20 Eminent Authors, including John B. Gough, Leon Case, Edward Howland, Jos. B Lyman, Rev. E. Edwin Hall, Horace Greely, Philip Ripley, Albert Brisbane, F. B. Perkins, etc.

This work is a complete history of all branches of industry, processes of manufacture, etc., in all ages. It is a complete encyclopedia of arts and manufactures, and is the most entertaining and valuable work of information on subjects of general interest ever offered to the public. It is adapted to the wants of the Merchant, Manufacturer, Mechanic, Farmer, Student and Inventor, and sells to both old and young of all classes. The book is sold by agents, who are making large sales in all parts of the country. It is offered at the low price of $3.50, and is the cheapest book ever sold by subscription. No family should be without a copy. We want agents in every town in the United States, and no agent can fail to do well with this book. Our terms are liberal. We give our agents the exclusive right of territory. One of our agents sold 133 copies in eight days, another sold 368 in two weeks. Our agent in Hartford sold 397 in one week. Specimens of the work sent to agents on receipt of stamp. For circulars and terms to agents address the publishers.

J. B. BURR & HYDE, *Hartford, Conn., Chicago, Ill., or Cincinnati, Ohio.*

TUNE BOOK.

The Brethren's Tune and Hymn Book, is a compilation of Sacred Music adapted to all the hymns in the Brethren's New Hymn Book. It contains over 350 pages, printed on good paper and neatly bound. We will send it to any address, post paid at $1.25 per copy.

TRACTS.

"ANXIOUS BENCH RELIGION EXAMINED," BY ELDER J. S. FLORY. A SYNOPSIS OF CONTENTS. An address to the reader: The peculiarities that attend this type of religion. The feelings there experienced not imaginary but real. The key that unlocks the wonderful mystery. The causes by which feelings are excited. How the momentary feelings called "Experimental religion" are brought about, and then concludes by giving that form of doctrine as taught by Jesus Christ and recorded by his faithful witnesses.

COUNTERFEIT DETECTER
or
BAPTISM—MUCH IN LITTLE.

This work is now ready for distribution, and the importance of the subject will speak for it a large demand. It is a short treatise on baptism in tract form intended for general distribution, and is set forth in such a plain and logical manner that a wayfaring man though a fool, cannot err therein. Either of the above tracts sent postpaid on the following terms: Two copies, 10 cts, 10 copies 40 cents, 25 copies 70 cents, 50 copies $1.00, 100 copies $1.50.

Trine Immersion
TRACED
TO THE APOSTLES.

The SECOND EDITION is now ready for delivery. The work has been carefully revised, corrected and enlarged.

Put up in a neat pamphlet form, with good paper cover, and will be sent, post-paid, on the following terms: One copy, 25 cts; Five copies, $1.10; Ten copies, $2.00. 25 copies, $4.50; 50 copies, $8.50; 100 copies, $16.00.

Address, J. H MOORE,

Urbana, Champaign co., Ill.

Oct. 22.

DYMOND ON WAR.

An inquiry into the Accordancy of War, with the Principles of Christianity, and an examination of the Philosophical reasoning by which it is defended. With observations on some of the causes of war and on some of its effects. By Jonathan Dymond. Sent from this office, post paid, for 50 cts.

1870 1873

DR. FAHRNEY'S
Blood Cleanser or Panacea.

A tonic and purge, for Blood Diseases. Great reputation. Many testimonials. Many ministering brethren use and recommend it. Ask or send for the "Health Messenger." Use only the "*Panacea*" prepared at Chicago, Ills., and by

Dr. P. Fahrney's Brothers & Co.,

Aug. 9-pd. *Waynesboro, Franklin Co., Pa*

New Hymn Books, English.

TURKEY MOROCCO.

One copy, postpaid,	$1.00
Per Dozen,	11.25

PLAIN ARABESQUE

One Copy, post-paid,	75
Per Dozen, "	8.40

Ger'n & English, Plain Sheep.

One Copy, post-paid,	$1.00
Per Dozen	11.25
Arabesque Plain,	1.00
Turkey Morocco,	1.25
Single German, post paid	50
Per Dozen,	5.50

$5 to $20 [illegible]

HUNTINGDON & BROAD TOP RAIL ROAD

Winter Arrangement.

On and after Tuesday, Oct. 4, 1872, Passenger trains will arrive and depart as follows:

Trains from Huntingdon South. *Trains from Mt. Dallas moving North.*

MAIL. A. M.	ACCOM P. M.	STATIONS.	MAIL. P. M.	ACCOM A. M
LE7 10	LE	Huntingdon,	AR4 00	AR
7 45		Long Siding	3 55	
8 00		McConnelstown	3 45	
8 05		Pleasant Grove	3 35	
8 22		Marklesburg	3 22	
8 40		Coffee Run	3 07	
8 45		Rough & Ready	3 00	
9 00		Cove	2 40	
9 05		Fishers Summit	2 45	
9 15		Saxton	2 35	
9 40		Riddlesburg	2 15	
9 47		Hopewell	2 05	
10 05		Piper's Run	1 50	
10 52		Tatesville	1 30	
11 05		Bloody Run	1 20	
10 40		Mount Dallas	1 15	
11 08		Bedford	2 14	

G. F. GAGE, Supt.

SHOUP'S RUN BRANCH.

LE 9 25 LE	Saxton.	AR2 15 AR
9 40	Coalmont.	2 00
9 45	Crawford.	1 55
AR10 00 AR	Dudley	LE1 45 LE

Bro'd Top City from Dudley 2 miles by stage.

Time of Penna. R. R. Trains at Huntingdon

EASTWARD.		WESTWARD.	
Hb'g Ac.	9 29 A. M	Cin. Ex.	3 25 A. M.
Mail	4 15 P. M	Pc'f Ex.	7 27 "
Cin. Ex.	7 24 "	Mail	5 45 P. M.
Phil. Ex	11 29 "	W. Pass.	11 50 A. M.

The Weekly Pilgrim.

Published by J. B. Brumbaugh, & Co.

Edited by H. B. & Geo. Brumbaugh.

CORRESPONDING EDITORS.

D. P. Sayler, Double Pipe Creek, Md.

Leonard Furry, New Enterprise, Pa.

The *Pilgrim* is a Christian Periodical, devoted to religion and moral reform. It will advocate in the spirit of *love* and *liberty*, the principles of true Christianity, labor for the promotion of peace among the people of God, for the encouragement of the saints and for the conversion of sinners, avoiding those things which tend toward disunion or sectional feelings.

TERMS.

Single copy, Book paper,	$1.50
Eleven copies, (eleventh for Agt.)	$15.00

Any number above that at the same rate.

Address,

H. B. BRUMBAUGH.

James Creek,

Huntingdon county Pa.

The Weekly Pilgrim.

"REMOVE NOT THE ANCIENT LANDMARKS WHICH OUR FATHERS HAVE SET."

VOL. 4. JAMES CREEK, PENNSYLVANIA, MARCH, 11, 1873. NO. 10

POETRY.

CHEER UP

BY [illegible]

Lonely pilgrim on the journey of Life,
Oppressed with fear's, with cares and sighs,
Cheer up, cheer up, fear not the world's sad strife,
For thou art heir of Paradise.

Awake, ye drooping despondents arise,
And bid an adieu to thy grief,
For peaceful rest, and joy that never dies,
Comes to the weary soul's relief.

Cheer up, cheer up, from the darkness of night,
Ye careworn mourner old and gray,
Fix thy weary eye on the distant light,
Let not thy hopes all pass away.

Cheer up, cheer up, ye young hearts drooping low,
Dry thy tears and sigh no more,
Though "the dark seas roll and the wild winds blow,"
Cast thy hopes on the distant shore.

For there in purest rays of heavenly light,
Undying joys forever bloom,
And fair, celestial beings, pure and bright,
Earth's lonely wanderer, welcome home.

Antwerp, Mich.

ORIGINAL ESSAYS.

THE BAPTISM OF JOHN. WHENCE WAS IT, FROM HEAVEN OR OF MEN?

In resuming the train of thought on the subject of divine and human institutions, after an absence of several weeks, I very much regret that I could not have pursued the subject regularly, and presented it to the readers of the PILGRIM in an unbroken chain through each successive number, but circumstances, beyond my control, directed otherwise and the only remedy left, is for me to ask those in whose mind an interest has been or shall be awakened upon this, as I regard it, important subject, to preserve the papers containing it, and read in connection, that they may be able to judge of the merits of the question, and the force of reasoning adduced.

The causes combined which has prevented me, was the burning of my son Jas. C. Moomaws' barn with all his corn, forage, a large quantity of cloverseed, all his farming implements and machinery (a full assortment,) all his harness, together with four valuable horses, cows, and other stock. In the meantime, I was called upon to visit an afflicted son some thirty miles distant, with whom I spent several days. The subsequent burning of another barn and stock &c., in the immediate vicinity of my son's that was burned, the arrest of the supposed incendiaries, and their trial in which I felt somewhat interested. It resulted in the conviction, in the mind of the minister of justice, and all present, with a strong probability of the guilt of the accused, and he was remanded to prison to await a future trial. Why those who have suffered should have been selected as victims of such an atrocious outrage, is a mystery that perhaps only eternity will reveal, it being notorious that two more quiet, kind, and inoffensive men could not be found in that or any other community.

Asking the forbearance and pardon of the reader for the above digression, by way of apology and explanation, we will resume the subject by again calling attention to the carefulness of our rightful sovereign in the injunction of all duties imposed upon his subjects that we may assuredly know from "whence they come from God or from men."

Let us then notice forsooth, the authority in the divine law for the observance of the passover and its concomitants, the feast of unleavened bread, &c., Ex. 12th chap., "And the Lord spake unto Moses and Aaron in the land of Egypt saying. This month *shall* be unto you the beginning of months; it *shall* be the first month of the year to you, speak ye unto all the congregation of Israel, saying. In the tenth day of this month, they *shall* take to them every man, a lamb according to the house of their fathers, a lamb for an house." 5th ver. "Your lamb *shall* be without blemish a male of the first year, ye *shall* take it out from the sheep, or from the goats; "And ye *shall* keep it up until the fourteenth day of the same month, and the whole assembly of the congregation of Israel *shall* kill it in the evening." And they *shall* take of the blood." "And they *shall* eat the flesh in that night, and with bitter herbs they *shall* eat it." 10th ver. "And ye *shall* let nothing remain of it until the morning, and that which remaineth until morning ye *shall* burn with fire." "And thus *shall* ye eat it," "and ye *shall* eat it in haste, it is the Lord's passover," &c. Thus we see in the divine command for this feast we have the verb *shall* used in the imperative moode seventeen times. And in the reiteration of the command by Moses we have the following. See same chap. 21st verse, Then Moses called for all the elders of the children of Israel, and said unto them *draw out and take you a lamb according to your families* and kill the passover." "And ye *shall* take a bunch of hysop and dip it in the blood that is in the bason, and strike the lintel and the two side-posts with the blood," &c. In this Moses fixes the obligation to observe, keep and perpetuate this institution by repeating the command, to draw out and take "ye *shall* take, ye *shall observe*" and "ye shall say it is the sacrifice of the Lord's passover." "And the people bowed the head and worshipped." Six times satisfied that it was from God, the children of Israel went away and did as the Lord had commanded Moses and Aaron, so did they."

In the same connection we have the command for observing the feast of unleavened bread and holy convocations not less than nine times so that there cannot possibly be any mistake as to "from whence it was," and therefore the people bowed the head and worshipped.

In pursuance of the investigation of these feasts we ascertain that command is repeated very frequently in the scriptures, after leaving the point of its first institution. See references, Lev. 23: 5-8; Num. 9: 1-14; 28: 16, 17. Deuteronomy 16: 1-8; 2nd Kings, 23: 21 23; Ezekial 45: 21. In addition to the frequency and urgency of this command, and the penalties denounced against the unfaithful, we have in the Old and New Testament, twenty three references at least, thus indelibly fixing it in the mind of every believer, in the divine authenticity of the Bible, that these are divine institutions, and that they might not be neglected by those for whom the command was intended without incurring the most fearful responsibility.

Passing from the ritual of the Old Testament to the new dispensation, reviewing the duties, obligations, privileges and prerogatives, enjoined and awarded under the teachings we will content ourselves with examining a few of these institutions, supposing that will be sufficient to fix the principle in our minds, the point aimed at throughout these communications, that is when we adopt and connect ourselves with any enterprise, religiously, that we are sure that we know "from whence it is from heaven or of men."

Commencing with the institution of baptism what a stream of thought rushes into the mind. First we behold the rough man of the woods, without the benefit of refined society, or the advantage of human literature, emerging from his obscure retreat, preaching in the wilderness of Jordan the unsearchable riches of Christ, whose harbinger he was, preaching "the *baptism* of repentance for the remission of sins," attracting by his profound wisdom and superhuman eloquence, all Jerusalem and Judea, and the regions around and about Jordan. The farmer leaving his plow in the furrow, the smith his anvil, the carpenter his bench, the woodman his ax, the milliner her half finished garment, the merchant his counter, the clerk his desk, the banker his books and his safe, the lawyer his library and the bar, the judge his dignified seat, the priest and the people all rush to the unparalleled scene, and yielding to the divine influence, overwhelmed by the proof that it was "from heaven and not of men" thousands submitted and received the divine institution at the hands of him whom God had sent, and yet this is not all, but in the midst of this grand and sublime array of divine influence. Oh what do we see? The Son of God himself emerging from the midst of the surrounding press, with a halo of glory surrounding his head, which eclipsed the grandeur of the scene, though already superlatively grand. He submitted to and thus approved by his act, his own institution, in confirmation of which the heavens were opened, the Holy Ghost descended, rested upon him, the voice of the Father was heard proclaiming, "this is my beloved Son in whom I am well pleased." Subsequently, John bare record, saying, I saw the Spirit descending from heaven like a dove and it abode upon him. And I knew him not, but he that sent me to baptize with water, the same said unto me, upon whom thou shalt see the Spirit descending and remaining on him, the same is he which baptizeth with the Holy Ghost. And I saw, and bear record that this is the Son of God. John 1: 32-34. With such an array of testimony before us, who can doubt for a moment, "from whence it is?" No marvel then that these recreant Scribes and Pharisees writhed when the question in the language of Christ, under which we write was proposed to them. How appropriate the question asked by the Prophet Jeremiah 13:25, "What will ye say when He shall punish thee?" John obtained his commission from Heaven as we have seen, but "he must decrease and his superior must increase". Hence at the time appointed Christ assumes His high prerogatives, unfurls His banner, which then, and still is floating in the breeze, with the great law of baptism inscribed. "All power is given to me in Heaven and on earth, go ye therefore and teach all nations, baptizing them in the name of the Father, and of the Son, and of the Holy Ghost, &c." It being clearly demonstrated that the baptism of John was from Heaven, and he testifying that Jesus Christ was the Son of God, having accomplished the object of His mission he resigned, in favor of his superior, resting from the field of his successful labors. The messenger of the covenant, whom we delight in, came to His own temple, invested with full power, assumes His rightful prerogatives as leader and commander of the people, and says: "Go therefore." The command to baptize was only once actually given by Christ, yet it was so well understood that it was faithfully attended to by the apostles, and frequently commanded by them, as in the case of Ananias to Saul, and Peter to the Pentecostians, and well understood by all who desired to know the will of the Lord, as the Ethiopian Eunuch, and the jailor who received baptism at the hands of Paul and Silas, &c. So well was it understood that we have it literally commanded and referred to about seventy-two times, and figuratively, not less than five times, sufficient to enable us to determine of a truth that it is from Heaven and not of men.

To be Continued.

A LETTER OF LOVE UNTO THE CHURCH AT FALLS CREEK, IND.

Editors of the Pilgrim:—Please publish this letter enclosed, written by John J. Hoover, Marmaton, Kansas, to the brethren and sisters of Fall Creek, Henry Co., Ind. And the brethren and sisters wish me to request of you to add thereto, that we entertain a feeling of gratitude and respect for brother John for the sympathy, and love that is manifested for this Church in the following letter and feel thankful for the friendly admonitions and instructions that he gave us, hoping they will have a good effect and eventually prove an inestimable blessing to us all. Brother John was elected to the ministry in this Church, and during his stay with us was ever prompt and at his place; ever ready to instruct the brethren and sisters and encourage them to press forward and be true to their profession. May he ever hold out to do so and obtain "souls for his hire now, and in the world to come eternal life."

Yours most respectfully,
DAVID K. TEETER
Sulphur Springs, Ind.

Grace be unto you, and peace from God the Father, and the Lord Jesus Christ, to whom be all praise, honor, glory, power and dominion forever.

Dearly beloved brethren and sisters in the Lord, whom I love dearly, and whom God has also chosen to be the followers of His Son Jesus Christ and called from the dead works of a sinful world, and hast set thee apart from the world to be His children, according to the glorious promises revealed in His word. Although thou art yet surrounded by the world, and temptations may arise on every side, yet if thy face be set Zionward and thine eye be single to the glory of God, those temptations will fly from before thee, as the chaff is carried before the wind.

Being absent from you in the body, dearly beloved, I write unto you, to stir up your pure minds, by way of remembrance, for thou art well aware that God was in Christ Jesus reconciling the world unto Himself, and when thy sins were upon thee, thou went about seeking rest but finding none, and when thy sins arose before thee like unto mountains, thou sawest thy condition then, retracedst to thy Fathers house, and thou hast well done, that thou hast returned while the door is yet open, for the door of Gospel grace is open night and day. But many of your heads are growing gray, the frosts of many winters are telling upon you and soon you will be wafted o'er the cold stream. There is no repentance in yonder world to which you are fast hastening, the door of grace will soon be closed with you, and if you have made a proper use of the means of grace granted, all will be well with you when the change comes. And knowing the terror of the Lord, we persuade you as dear brethren to be watchful and hold fast that thou hast, that no man take thy crown, always showing that true light that becometh the true followers of Christ. I plead with you to receive the good counsels and wholesome instructions given you by those that have the charge over you, knowing that they are working for the interest and salvation of your never dying souls, and this is all the pay they ask of you, obedience and submission to the Divine requirements. If obedient members, you are living in peace one with another, and not looking back again into the beggarly elements of the world, then the chastening rod is withheld, and not stretched out among you. Then doth charity reign among you, and the blessings of Almighty God are flowing freely upon you. O I remember the many seasons of worship, yes many times did we kneel together in prayer, and our hearts were thrilled and made to overflow with gratitude to our Heavenly Father for the unsearchable riches of His grace, but soon, ah soon, dark clouds arose, a brother here or a sister there, has broken the charm, they have stepped over the mark, they have reached out their hand, they have partaken of the forbidden fruit, and worse than all, they contend that it is not wrong to take a few things of the world along, only a few, the switch or chignon, and ruby with a few ribbons interwoven, are as good a covering for the head as I desire, and I don't need your plain caps," says the sister, and "I am sure if this flounce or grecian bend don't hurt me it ought not to hurt any one else." And says the brother, "I don't see any harm in trimming and coloring my hair and beard to suit myself, and then this paper collar is a very little thing, and my fashionable coat, pants and vest suit me very well." But suppose the Savior would come to you in person, clothed with flesh as He once was, what do you think He would say? Would He say, "O ye of little faith," or would He say "ye fools and blind," or "you belong to the world" and are of your father the devil, or that you are lukewarm and "I will spew thee out of my mouth. If there be any such among you dear brethren, in the language of the apostle "we pray you in Christs stead be ye reconciled unto God," and "be not conformed to this world but be ye rather transformed by the renewing of your minds, that ye may prove what is that good, acceptable and perfect will of the Lord," for we are instructed in the law, "that to be carnally minded is death, but to be spiritually minded is life and peace, for the carnal mind is in enmity against God, and is not subject to the law of God, neither indeed can be." If there be any among you, that would turn away, let them remember the words of the apostle Peter when the Savior said to the apostles, wilt thou also turn away? Peter said "Lord where will we go, thou hast the words of eternal life?" and John in his epistolary writing says, "my little children, these things write I unto you that ye sin not, and if any man sin, we have an advocate with the Father, Jesus Christ the righteous; and He is the propitiation for our sins and not for ours only, but for the sins of the whole world, and hereby do we know that we know Him if we keep His commandments." And again we learn that His commandments are not grievious, but by obeying the same we are made partakers of His grace and we become fit subjects for our Masters' use, for "God is not unrighteous to forget your work and labor, which you have showed toward His name, in that ye have ministered to the saints and do minister, and we desire that every one of you do show the same diligence to the full assurance of hope unto the end."

And you, dear brethren and sisters who have the rule and oversight, how is it with you, are you always ready and willing to discharge every duty encumbent upon you, in holding the little flock to-gether, and also in calling others into the pasture of the Lord that there may be an increase in the fold of Christ, and that He may have His own with usury at His coming? And have you not a few lambs of your own yet, that have not been gathered into the fold? If so, have you used every means in your power to get them in? Have you implored the divine aid at all times to assist you in gathering them in, or do ye rather, like the children of Israel, when they went to take Ai? they went without imploring the divine aid, and they were smitten and driven back in disorder, and caused Joshua to rent his clothes, &c. See Joshua 7th chapter. When you go to them go in the fear of the Lord, and use every means of grace given you, as Joshua did when he took Jericho. He used all the means given him by the Father, and they in using the very last and very simple means, that of blowing a blast with the rams horn and raising a great shout, made the walls of Jericho fall. So you should never stop until you have exausted every means of grace given you, and then the walls of satan will be sure to tumble down, so that when you appear at the judgment bar of God, you can say: "here am I Lord with those that thou hast given me." Be very careful brethren, lest perhaps you may loose those things which you have wrought and finally not be permitted to receive a full reward. And dearly beloved, in conclusion I would ask you all to remember your son in the faith, whom you have chosen, and set as a watchman upon the walls of Zion. Let your prayers ascend the hill of Zion as the prayers of one man in my behalf. And now unto Him that is able to keep you from the hour of temptation, and to present you blameless before God, unto Him be all honor, glory, power and dominion forever and ever, amen.

JOHN J. HOOVER.
Marmaton, Kan.

SIMON MAGUS AND SIMON PETER.

We have in the 8th chapter of Acts an account of those two ancient characters, and an interview between them. Simon Magus seems to have been a very extraordinary man, and exceedingly popular in a very eminent city, Samaria. The inhabitants of all ranks regarded him with high veneration, and had done so for a long time. At the time Simon Peter appeared in that city, Simon Magus seems to have been highly respected in a religious point of view. He was to them as an oracle of God, and seemed invested with power almost divine. He asserted his own dignity and gained the ear of the people so that all from the least unto the greatest gave heed to him saying, this man is the great power of God. And a chief engine of his fame was his power of working wonders which others could neither explain nor imitate. Simon Peter was not a person of high renown among such people as the inhabitants of Samaria. He was a low bred man, and his speech marked with a provincial vulgarity. He had been, originally, neither a prophet nor a prophet's son, nor a doctor of the law, but men had taught him to take fishes from his youth, howsoever, the Founder of Christianity having all power in Heaven and earth had, by this time, made him a successful fisher of men. He was qualified for the work with wondrous powers in particular, when by divine guidance, he laid his hands on believers, they received the Holy Spirit, and were also endowed with wonder working gifts. Previous to his arrival at Samaria, Philip, one of his friends had preached the Gospel there, and it had been confirmed with signs following, hence many believed the Gospel and acted under its influence. Simon Magus too, by the different nature and tendency of the wonders wrought was overpowered into a profession of that Gospel which was so confirmed. He was still more astonished when he observed the gifts of the Holy Spirit communicated by laying on of the hands of Simon Peter and others. Whatever knowledge of the truth he had thus attained he still labored under a great mistake. He thought the teachers of Christianity made a trade of it, and also that they acted by their own skill or power, hence as he could teach others to imitate his own miracles, he thought perhaps the apostles could do so too, and as he had no higher aim than the gaining of money, he thought they were like himself, hence he proposed to purchase the power. This proposal was so repugnant to the whole spirit of that system which levels every mountain and exalts every valley,—so hostile to the nature of a kingdom not of this world, the king of which voluntarily appeared in this world as an indigent dependant, and promised his subjects the same kind of treatment which himself had experienced, and so derogatory to the gift itself, which was not of temporal but of eternal importance, that Simon Peter at once saw the character of the man and the nullity of all his pretentions to Christianity, and filled with holy indignation, he thus reprehended him: "Thy money perish with thee because thou thoughtest the gift of God could be purchased with money thou hast neither part nor lot in this matter, thou art yet in the gall of bitterness and bond of iniquity, repent of this thy wickedness, and pray God if perhaps the thought of thine heart may be forgiven thee." At this reprehension Simon Magus stood confounded and convicted, and requested an interest in the other prayers. Indeed his sin seems to have been exceedingly heinous, and it did not so much consist in the single act of offering the money to the apostles as in that erroneous state of mind from which it flowed.

This reprehension then must apply to every act which betrays the same erroneous state of mind. Simon's sin consisted in the thought of his heart, that money could purchase what was the gift of God. This error appears in two views. He is guilty of it who thinks that any sum, however great, is of any avail to purchase such an engagement. He is equally guilty of this error who thinks any sum, however small, absolutely necessary to the attainment, since without money and without price is the motto to them all.

These principles may be brought to a practical application to officers in the Church. I shall consider Simon's error as it bears on these offices. Every office in the Church which has the warrant of God is God,s gift to the person invested with the office, accordingly the Elders of the Church of Ephesus are enjoined to take heed to the flock over which the Holy Spirtt had made them overseers. Acts 20. Now whatever plan of Church puts this office within the reach of the person who has money, or out of the reach of the person who has it not, must involve the error of Simon Magus. And every church which renders such offices attainable by wealthy societies, and unattainable by those who are poor, renders this gift an article purchasable with money, and is deeply tinctured with the error of Simon. God gave to the Church, pastors, but for want of money, the poor little society cannot obtain the gift. Perhaps they fix on an object and present a call, if so, the question is, "What salary ?" If this be too little, the affair is ended, they cannot support the gospel, and they shall not get it in that way. A similar plan is in the quantity and quality of the gift. These are distributed as nearly as can be guessed in the exact ratio of the wealth of the societies. One very poor gets a sermon but once a month, and a little more wealthy may observe public worship three times a month, but it is so contrived that the most despised preacher is sent to the most despised society. While this is the case of poor societies, those which are wealthy, have public worship every Lord's day and may have a plurality of pastors, and those of the most esteemed and accomplished sort. Thus the poor society is frequently deprived of its pastor. These hints claim the regard of many small societies.

A PILGRIM.

FAITH ALONE DOCTRINE.

After listening to some of the popular preachers of the present day, on the "Faith alone doctrine," I became so aroused on the subject that I feel that our sanctified press as well as they that occupy the sacred desk, should give this subject a more and more earnest study and investigation. When I contemplate the many thousand souls of the present day who are deluded by their leaders and preachers crying peace, peace, where there is no peace, I feel that it is time that we become awake to the subject. "Only believe," say they, and you shall be saved ? Verily nay. And in this way, poor people are deluded and do not realize what they' are promised and what they expect and become sceptic and infidel. Oh ! who can comprehend the fearfulness of the destruction of the great numbers of lost precious souls by the "faith alone doctrine." Is it not brethren a similar method to that of satan with our first parents in Eden's garden in telling them part truth only ? But what does St. James say 2 : 20, "But wilt thou know, O! vain man, that faith without works is dead." &c. Those blind guides appear to make great demonstrations to awaken them to a sense of duty and when the query is put "what they must do to be saved," they tell them, "only look to Jesus by faith, that is all that is necessary to salvation and arise and give God thanks, he saved a thief upon the cross by faith and he can save you by faith—believe, you are blessed and it is done." They do not for one moment, think that believing a thing does not make it so if it was not so before they believed it.

Now Brethren, I have not so learned of Christ. The way to salvation, but faith and obedience is the more excellent way. The way Saul was commanded after he believed. He was commanded to be baptized in order to wash away his sins, by repentance, faith and baptism. Acts 8 : 39. "What doth hinder me from being baptized ?" When he had believed on the Lord Jesus Christ. And further, Peter on the day of Pentecost, Acts 2 : 41, "They that gladly received his word were baptized and the same day there were added to the church about three thousand souls." They not only believed but continued steadfast in the Apostles doctrine. The Phillippian Acts 16 : 33. and he took them the same hour of the night and washed their stripes and he was baptized he and all his household." Taking all these, as well as many other examples and positive commands into consideration, how can the "faith alone doctrine" stand the test in the great day of accounts. I have been made to wonder hearing the advocates of this doctrine to appeal to such examples, as for instance, Naaman the leper, or Moses raising the brazen serpent on a pole to enforce faith, and thus resting the scriptures to their own destruction, when those examples are purely practical to enforce obedience to ordinances of God's house. One of these advocates of "faith alone" in my hearing, declared to a large audience that all the water baptism Christ had reference to in telling Nicodemus he must be born of the water and the spirit, was the water that flowed out of his side pierced by the soldiers' spear, so you see dear friends the necessity, in these latter days of scepticism, of us proving the spirits whether they be of God and contend earnestly for the faith once delivered to the saints, not only believe, but *do* the commandments and we shall have a right to the tree of life and enter through the gates into the city.

And again, Abraham the Father of the faithful, was likewise justified by obedience in offering up his only son. Obedience is better than sacrifice and to hearken than the fat of rams, while stubborness is idolatry, and disobedience as witchcraft. Was not Moses obedient as well as believed in every word and work of the Lord, except one transgression, for which he was deprived of entering the promised land, and the Son of God our Lord Jesus Christ, was obedient in all things even to the death on the cross that we through his obedience might be saved. And now if we know these things happy are we if we do them. If any man have not the spirit of Christ he is none of his. He obeyed his Father's commands and we must obey his, for he says, "if ye love me keep my commandments."

G. R BAKER.

Altoona, Iowa.

—While Christ represents us in heaven, it is our duty to endeavor to represent him on earth ; and thus to be living "epistles of Christ,—known and read of all men."

—Fortune does not change men ; it only unmasks them.—*Madame Riccoboni.*

For the Pilgrim.

A CONVERSATION ON DRESS.

Mrs. A. Well elder, I declare it is almost discouraging for persons to be picked at, and have so many stories told about them as they tell about me.

Elder. Indeed, what is the trouble now: I am not posted in regard to the stories, and think we all have about all we can do to build over against our own house, without spending too much time in watching our neighbors. You are aware that I oppose backbiting, and claim if we see a wrong in a brother, our duty is to go to him in a proper spirit and tell him his fault to his face.

Mrs. A. Well, somebody has started the story that I went to Mr. —— s to a dinner party on the Sabbath, dressed in the gayest manner possible. Now the facts are, I never went to a party to Mr. ——s house, and I never went to his house on the Sabbath. I went there one Sunday to dinner with my son and his wife by invitation, and I don't think people need find fault with that.

Eld. Probably this can all be explained in this wise, sister; you know some people call Sunday the Sabbath. It might have been casually mentioned at first, that you were at Mr. —— to dinner on the Sabbath, meaning Sunday; others may have heard of it, and supposed it was on the Seventh-day, the day you profess to keep. We want to look upon all with all the allowance possible, and not to think they are designing to injure us unless we have direct evidence to that effect.

Mrs. A. Well, I have not so much charity perhaps as I ought to have, and I think it is a small matter any way to be noticing people's dress, I am sure I have not purchased any new dresses lately. My clothing is all old, and as for my gold chain, broach and cuff-buttons, I wear them when I go out into company, and it is necessary to do so when you move in respectable circles.

Eld. Well, sister, Christ is represented as our pattern, and we are admonished to learn of him; there would be an amazing contrast between the silks, satins and gold jewels of some and the plain vesture of Christ.

Mrs. A. I think it is a small business to descend to notice such things, and I confess I do not want to associate with people who pick flaws about such little things. People that move in the circle in which I do, must dress according to those they associate with, or they will have no influence.

Eld. I have always supposed that to be a Christian was to be like Christ, and we are admonished not only to have the mind that was in Christ, but He is given as a pattern, that we should walk in His steps, I should think it would be our duty to follow Him and go with the humble ones who are trying to imitate Him instead of disowning our profession for the sake of securing influence in what is called by men, high circles. We should remember that, "what is highly esteemed among men is an abomination in the sight of God."

Mrs. A. Well, my broach and sleeve-buttons are useful articles, and I could not get along without wearing them.

Eld. Let us see, you wear your broach to fasten your collar. A jet or vulcanized rubber pin, costing twenty-five cts., would keep your collar to its place, and look much more neat, plain and tidy than a cameo two by three inches, set on a plate, costing twenty-five or thirty dollars; your gold cuff-buttons one inch in diameter are worth from ten to fifteen dollars; your cuffs could be secured with nice jet buttons not costing over twenty-five cts.

Mrs. A. I don't care anything about them, I'd just as willingly wear an old rag or a piece of pewter as my broach so far as my own feelings are concerned, but we are responsible for the influence we exert upon others.

Eld. That is true; and you would not wear pewter or an old rag, for that would not be neat or tasty. I am glad you feel responsible for the influence you exert upon others, but sister, have we any right to take a course to influence others contrary to the teachings of the Bible?

Mrs. A. If you people should all dress in that plain manner, you could never gain influence over such as Mr. —— and ——, you ought to think it an honor to have people come in among you that move in such high circles.

Eld. Well I don't know that it helps the cause any to have persons espouse it that feel above the simplicity of the truth; and as for these men you mention, with all their avaricious over-reaching disposition and pride, what could we do with them? What help would they be to us? God is not so straitened for means as to have the standard of truth lowered to gain them. I say here that unless such men can come down to the simplicity of the Gospel, I would rather they would not come among us, for it is no benefit to them or to the cause of God.

Mrs. A. I have thought your preaching would have a better influence if you did not say any thing about dress. Preach the great and glorious truths and let these little things alone.

To be Continued.

Religious News.

THE ANNUAL CONFERENCE of the "Brethren" for 1873 will be held at Dale City, Pa., and for 1874, in the Otter Creek Church, Macoupin Co., Ill.

The Friends have six hundred and sixty two houses of worship in this country, including Orthodox and Hicksite. They have lost in the last decade nine per cent of their membership.

THE Moravians report 1,156 converts on the Labrador coast. The Bible complete, in the Esquimaux language, has recently been distributed among the heads of families. In South Africa, the Moravians reckon 8,814 converts; in Surinam, 23,703.

FROM an exchange, we learn that there are 97,105 orthodox Friends or Quakers in the United States. From religious statistics it appears that they are decreasing in number on account of their children not embracing their faith.

Millerism is reviving in Vermont. The world, it is there affirmed by some, is coming to an end toward the close of the present year. Others think that the catastrophe will occur during the present Winter. There are a good many meetings, and there is a good deal of preaching and excitement.

REPORTS from the interior of Russia, state that the Baptists are making a large number of converts, and that they are rebaptizing by the scores, in the rivers and in the sea, despite the biting cold.

Such news is not very cheering when we learn that thousands of humble Christians are compelled to leave the same country to be freed from learning the arts of war and human butchery.

The Baltimore *Sun* says that the Eutaw Place Baptist church unanimously agreed to increase the salary of their pastor Rev. Dr. Fuller, but he politely declined their generosity. At their next meeting they reunited after services and again unanimously resolved to insist upon their pastor to comply with their resolution. The *Sun* remarks: "We never heard of such a difficulty before." Rather rare we suppose.

THE UNITED BRETHREN originated among the German population of this state in the year 1760. They now claim a membership of 140,000 distributed among forty three conferences, has four bishops, supports eight colleges, publishes five regular periodicals and sustains three hundred missionaries in the home work.

This shows what energy and zeal combined will do. While others are spending their thousands to propagate their respective creeds we seem to be holding our purse strings with an iron grasp. Brethren right here we are diseased, and if not cured it will form a putrifying sore which will finally infirm and weaken the effective working force of the whole body. One of the hardest lessons we have to learn, is that our wealth and means belong to the Lord, and that it is our duty to use it for the furtherance of His cause and the glorifying of His name.

ELD. ADDISON PRATT.—This prominent Mormon preacher died Oct. 14th, 1872, at the house of his daughter in Anaheim, Los Angeles Co., Cal. He was the son of Henry Pratt, Esq., the celebrated organ builder. He was ordained Elder at Nauvoo, Ill., in 1842. In 1843, he was sent on a mission to the South Pacific Islands where he was successful in converting many to the faith of the "Latter Day Saints." In 1852, he returned to San Francisco. After remaining with his family a number of years, he went to his daughter where he might enjoy a milder climate, hoping to be relieved of a disease which was aggravated by the cold winters of his home. At this place he passed away in the full enjoyment of his faith, thus demonstrating that conscience is no guide whatever in religion, as a man can die happy in any religion, no matter how absurd, if he can only die *in the faith*.

AGAINST CHURCH FAIRS.—The General Council of the Diocese of Florida has expressed by resolutions, "its decided condemnation of balls, fairs, festivals, concerts, theatrical representations, and all such public entertainments in aid of religious objects, believing all these modes of obtaining money for the services of God to be contrary to the spirit of the Gospel, opposed to the teachings of the church on the subject of offertory, and calculated to lower that spiritual standard which ought to be aimed at by every Christian in the devotion of his substance to the service of God."—*N. Y. Observer.*

This is certainly a move in the right direction. The desire for having costly edifices for worship is becoming so great that some churches have resorted to any and every means to obtain the funds, above that of direct stealing. The gambling and chance games played off at these church fairs are practically stealing, or to be a little more mild, robbing the devil to serve God.

Youth's Department.

FAITH.

In the gloaming, when my darlings,
In their dainty robes of white,
By their mother's knees have murmured,
"Jesus keep us through the night,"

To their little crib white-curtained,
Where the upper shadows fall,
Nestled in my arms, I take them
Through the long, unlighted hall.

Swift, in rayless silence round us,
Close the deepening shades of night;
"Dark!" my blue-eyed Bertie whispers,
Half in awe and half in fright.

"Dark!" the baby brother echoes,
With a hush upon his glee;
When my Bertie, nestling nearer,
Whispers softly, "*Papa, see!*"

Blessed, blessed faith of childhood,
Father, grant this faith to me;
Dark the shadows round me gather,
But I know that Thou dost see.

THE PATH OF THE WISE

Let me ask my little PILGRIM friends what is the most excellent of all knowledge? You will all answer immediately, "To know the path of the wise man and how to walk therein." "The path of the wise" is the highway to eternal excellence and glory. Let us look at the truly wise man. His gait is firm, his language purity, his voice a melody, a smile of grace lights his countenance, mercy, truth and faith flash from his eye. Though his forehead is deeply furrowed with care yet the expression there, is untouched by the blight of life's autumn. He rises from his couch at early morn., and tunes his harp to mingle his notes of praise with the sweet song of birds, he pours out a prayer of praise as he mounts upon the golden chain of faith. As the day advances, the wise man still pursues his holy course, he is girt about with the habiliments of active life, he feasts at the table of plenty and simplicity, and drinks at the fountain of innocence. At evening he throws aside the implements of labor, considers the privileges and blessings of the day, consigns himself into the hands of an efficient and powerful Creator, and wraps himself in sweet repose, while angels guard his peaceful slumbers. Thus has passed away the truly wise man. Who of us are ready to follow in his footsteps? It is foolishness, error and wrong to seek wealth, honor power, save that *wealth, honor and power* that guides us in the path of wisdom and prepares us for filling our mission in life and fits us for glory beyond.

CARRIE FOSTER.

Cordelia, Cal.

JOHNNY'S MISTAKE

Little Jonny H—— came running home from school one day, and asked his mother's permission to go out in the morning with a party of boys to shoot wild ducks.

Mrs. H——readily gave her consent, and Johnny hastened to bring out the old rifle, which had grown somewhat rusty by disuse, and commenced cleaning and polishing it.

While Johnny was thus engaged, his mother sat nearby, quietly watching his movements until he was ready to put in the charge, when she said to him, "Johnny, you had better not load your rifle to-night; I'm afraid some accident will happen."

"O mother," replied Johnny, "there will be no danger, and then I shall be all ready for an early start in the morning."

"But," continued his mother, "something might happen, and at all events it will be safer to put it away just as it is."

Johnny made no further reply, and his mother soon left the room.

Johnny was usually a very good boy, and prompt in obeying his mother's wishes; but this time he kept looking at his rifle, and wishing he might load it, and the more he looked and wished, the harder it became for him to put it away.

At last, saying to himself, "mother wouldn't care if she knew there was really no danger, and I'll be very careful." Johnny took the last step which parleying with temptation almost always leads to, loaded the rifle and set it behind the door.

Early the next morning, before any one else in the family was astir, Johnny crept down stairs and hastened to join the boys in their sports. So eager was he to be on his way, he actually forgot his rifle, until he was fairly out of the house. Then he turned and went back for it, but somehow, in opening the door, the rifle was knocked down, its contents discharged, and the ball entered one of Johnny's knees.

And now what do you think were the first words that passed his lips? Did he call for help? Did he utter an exclamation of pain? No, this is what he said, "I thought I knew better than my mother."

How many other boys, and girls too, have made the same mistake that Johnny did. They may not find it out so quickly and surely, but sooner or later they will think, if not say, "After all mother knew best."—*Child's Paper.*

A CHILD'S MORNING PRAYER.

Many a Christian mother, who, at evening receives at her knee her little one, with folded hands and closed eyes to say, "Now I lay me," before going to rest, has been puzzled to find an equally brief and suitable form of words in which to conduct the morning devotions of said little child. Possibly it would be a kindness to some such mothers if you should publish the accompanying stanza, which has done acceptable service in the circle where it had its origin in a mother's heart:

Jesus hear me while I pray;
Please to take my sins away;
Make me gentle, make me mild,
Make me thine own little child.
Amen

—*Congregationalist.*

Correspondence.

A Reporter is wanted from every Church in the brotherhood to send us Church news, Obituaries, Announcements or anything that will be of general interest. To insure insertion, the writers name must accompany each communication. Our invitation is not personal but general—please respond to our call.

Dear Pilgrim:—As you and the brethren at large, have not heard from this arm of the Church this Winter, I will state that we, the brethren of the Mohican Church, Wayne Co., Ohio, commenced a series of meetings on the 8th of Feb., and continued until there was 18 appointments filled. We gave some special invitations and a general one. When the time came for the meeting we had to commence under rather unfavorable circumstances, no strange brethren made their appearance, but we began. Bro. Jacob Garver, our Elder, preached the first sermon on Saturday evening, and on Sunday the writer tried to preach the second. By Sunday evening help began to come in, a force of three brethren, which made us rejoice. Third sermon by J. B Shoemaker, of the Shipswaney Church, followed by Moses Weaver from the Ashland Church, to a very attentive audience. Fourth by Wm. Saller, of the Maple Grove Church, brother Shoemaker, P. J. Brown and Garver being called away a short distance to visit a sick man. Fifth by brother Saller, followed by brother Shoemaker. In about the midst of the meeting, brother Christian Wise of Mansfield Church arrived, which caused a thrill of joy to us all, seeing our ministerial aid increasing and the interest of the meeting also increasing from time to time. Sixth by brother Wise. Seventh by Shoemaker, followed by Wise. Eighth by Wise and Witmer from the Ashland Church, and ninth by Wise, Witmer and Brown. While brother Wise occupied the floor it seemed as though the entire audience were held spell-bound, every countenance riveted upon the speaker while he was engaged in delivering to them the word of God with power and effect.

On Thursday morning, the 15th, brother Joseph N. Kauffman of Logan Co., came to our assistance, and some of those that were with us returned to their homes, but still left enough for all necessary demands. Tenth sermon by brother Kauffman, followed by Wise. Eleventh sermon by Kauffman and Wise,—interest still increasing, congregation enlarging, and attention and good order praiseworthy. At this point Bro. Wise returned home. We now gave the matter more fully into the hands of Bro. Kauffman, who preached day and evening until Sunday evening, a series of discourses taking a broad field, throwing his net out a great ways and drawing it together by degrees until he brought it to an end by a baptism sermon, which was truly a master piece discourse. He made popular religion quake, and the sinner tremble. We expected to close on this evening, but as we were informed that two precious souls had become tired of sin, we thought good to have a meeting on Monday, and when we came together two more made application, therefore after the sermon, we went down to the water and received four into the Church by baptism, which made us all truly rejoice in the God of our salvation, seeing He is still willing to call sinners through the labors of his servants. From visible indications, we think many more will, from time to time knock at the door for admittance. Taking it all in all, it was truly a time of refreshing to us all. May we long remember what we have heard, and all put it to practice, for it was dealt out to saint and sinner, each one received his due portion in due time. May it be watered by the dew-drops of Heaven, so that His Satanic Majesty may be made to tremble and the borders of Zion be enlarged, is our prayer.

GEORGE WORST.

New Pittsburg, Ohio.

ALLEN, PA.,
February 29th 1873.

Dear Brother:—I am receiving the PILGRIM, and I love it because it holds to the old order of the Brethren. I do love that order. I am not in favor of those modern styles in dress which are now getting so common. Some say, dress to please yourselves, but we should not thus do, we should follow Christ and His people, and if we do not, it is a strong evidence that we do not love them, and if we do not love the brethren whom we have seen, how can we love Christ whom we have not seen? I do think if we are not willing to follow our old brethren as they followed Christ, we have not yet fully cast off the old man. The beloved Apostle says, "Be ye followers of me even as I also am of Christ." If we are not willing to come to the humble order of the Church, I think we yet love the world too much. John in his epistle, says, "Love not the world neither the things that are in the world, if any man love the world the love of the Father is not in him." Again, "We know that we have passed from death unto life because we love the brethren, he that loveth not his brother abideth in death." O, then, brethren, let us love one another with a pure heart, and that which our brethren love to see, let us not shun or decline to wear. I believe that we are in times in which we should be up and doing, for in such an hour as we think not the Son of Man cometh, and O, if He should find us asleep, how awful it would be. I am afraid we would open our eyes where the rich man did, but the Savior says, "Blessed is the man who, at my coming, shall be found watching." Yes, he will indeed be blessed and will be conducted to that Heavenly home. DAVID GOODYEAR.

Dear Pilgrim:—This morning I feel to inform your readers that I am well and have been ever since my trip in Pa., and all our members are also well as far as I know. There is not much sickness at present in our neighborhood and, we feel thankful to God our Heavenly Father for His kindness conferred on us.

I have not forgotten and hope never shall, the dear brethren, sisters, their kind children and all the friends that I met in Ind. and Pa. last fall. My mind often travels the rounds and when I think of their kindness, I ask God to bless them all.

I will now say that I traveled through the Brotherhood in part of Northern Ind., found all well with a few exceptions, attended many meetings, had large congregations and very good attention to the word preached. I had three meetings in Milford, Ind. in the Campbellite or Christian Church. They were very kind. I think the brethren ought to preach there often. While I was in Milford I visited our much respected friend Allen Gilkerson, and Mary his wife, she being a kind sister, and I hope that he also will soon become a member, as I think he loves the brethren and the order they practice. He is a reader of the PILGRIM and told me that he could not well do without it. I think there should be good admonitions in our papers for our dear friends and children, and all our brethren should take the periodicals at least one of them, and the older ones could take more, or get some for the poor. Our children should read these good admonitions and when they have read them, we should give them to our neighbors that they may read them, if there is not too much criticism, of which I disapprove; at any rate dear members, we cannot do too much good, but we can very easily do too little, and I fear if we are not careful, we may labor too much for the world and not enough for the Lord. If we have so much concern for the things of this world we are so apt to neglect our duty towards God and one another, and we will find fault with long meetings and short ones too, and after a while we may forget where the Lord has promised to meet with us. I mean if we do not watch and pray. Well may the Savior say "what I say I say unto all watch." If we do not watch we may get proud and buy everything that the world buys, and become defiled, or we may become stingy which is covetousness, and such will not make themselves comfortable for others. But if our affections are above where Christ sitteth on the right hand of God, we are not so apt to be in our duty, and not be too slothful or too worldly-minded; and I do think we will have the right kind of courage in every direction. We will pay a debt while we have money, and do without what we do not need, however much our eyes may covet it; have the courage to speak our mind when necessary, and to hold our tongue when prudent; have the courage to speak to a friend in a plain and modest apparel, even though you are in company with a rich one and richly attired; have the courage to make a will and a just one before your dying hour, have the courage to tell a man and the most agreeable acquaintance we have when we are convinced that he lacks principle. A friend should bear with a friend's infirmities, but not with his vices. Have the courage to show your respect for honesty in whatever guise it appears, and your contempt for dishonest duplicity by whomsoever exhibited. Have the courage to wear our old clothes until we can pay for our new ones, have the courage to obey our Maker at the risk of being ridiculed by man, have the courage to acknowledge our ignorance rather than to seek credit for knowledge under false pretense, have courage to stand for God, even if we must stand alone, have the courage of two evils to choose the last, but of two wrongs, to choose neither, and have courage to believe in God with all your heart, and own His name everywhere. JOHN KNISLEY.

Plymouth, Ind.

ANNUAL MEETING OF 1874.

Editors of the PILGRIM, please say that the committee of arrangements, after carefully examining the many places offered for holding the A. M., of 1874, have finally decided, all things considered, that Joseph Filburns have the best facilities for the accommodation of the A. M., therefore the Lord willing, it will be held in the Otter Creek Congregation, MaCoupin Co., Ill., 25 miles south of Springfield at the residence of brother Joseph Filburns, only about 200 yards from the St. Louis, Alton and Chicago Railroad. You can also say to the brethren of Southern Ill., that the money subscribed for procuring a tent for the benefit of the churches in the Southern district of Ill., is not sufficient, and that the project is therefore a failure for the present. DANIEL VANIMAN.

Virdin, Ill.

ANNOUNCEMENTS.

Please announce through the PILGRIM that our District Meeting will be held on the 13th of May in the Cook's Creek Congregation, Rockingham Co., Va.

SOLOMON GARBER.

The District Meeting for North Missouri will be held on the 7th and 8th of March in the Smith Fork Branch, Clinton Co., (near Plattsburg), in the Brethren's Meeting-house. A general representation desired. Those coming by R. R. will stop off at Plattsburg. GEORGE WITWER.

Please make the following announcement in the WEEKLY PILGRIM. The District Meeting of West Virginia, will be held in Seneca District, eight miles west of Mouth of Seneca, at Union School House, in Dry Fork township, Randolph Co., on Friday and Saturday, 9th and 10th of May. For any further information address the undersigned at Mouth of Seneca,

Pendleton Co., W. Va

By order of the Church.

ASA HARMAN.

TO ALL WHO ARE CONCERNED.

We do, through this medium, inform the brethren and churches comprising the first district of Virginia, that Friday and Saturday before the fourth Sunday in April, is the time appointed for the holding of the Annual District Meeting, and will be held at that time no preventive providence, at the Valley Meeting-house in Botetourt Co., one mile south of Amsterdam. A full attendance is desirable.

The undersigned also informs his brethren that he has a number of New Hymn Books on hand for sale. B. F. MOOMAW.

Please announce that the District Meeting of Western Maryland, will be held the Lord willing in the Welsh Run Congregation in the Broad Fording Meetinghouse, five miles north-west of Hagerstown on the second Thursday in April, 1872.

NICHOLAS MARTIN.

Please announce that the District Meeting of Northern Indiana and Michigan, will be held in the Brethren's Meetinghouse, ½ mile west of Goshen, Elkhart Co., Ind., commencing on Thursday the 1st day of May, 1873, at 10 o'clock, a. m.

JESSE CALVERT, Clerk.

Champaign Lovefeast.

The brethren in Champaign Co., Ill., have appointed their Communion Meeting on Saturday and Sunday, June 7th and 8th, 1873, at Bro. Geo. Dilling's, five miles east of Urbana. We extend an invitation to all, especially the ministering brethren.

J. H. MOORE.

Urbana, Ill.

MARRIED.

STAHL—LACKINGS.—On Dec. 5, 1872, by the undersigned, John M. Stahl and Mary C. Lackings, both of Franklin Co., Pa.

SHANK—BURKHERT.—Dec. 19, 1872, by the same John S. Shank and Anna Burkhert both of Franklin Co., Pa.

PITTINGER—HERSHY.—Dec. 24, 1872, by the same, Robert H. Pittinger and Mary Hershey, both of Washington Co., Md.

JONES—HANES.—Feb 4th, 1873, by the same, John W. Jones and Susan M. Hanes both of Washington Co., Md.

GROVE—MILLER.—Feb. 18, 1873, John S. Grove and sister Anna E. Miller, both of Franklin Co., Pa.

JOHN SHANK.

DETRICK—LAHMAN.—On January 16, 1873, near Greencastle, by the undersigned, at the residence of the bride's parents, Mr. Calvin Detrick to Miss Francis Lahman. GEO. H. HARRISON.

DIED.

SHELLER.—In the Welsh Run arm of the Church, Nov. 20th, 1872, near Broad Fording, Washington Co., Md., brother Christian Sheller, aged 74 yrs., 6 mo., and 18 days.

He left an aged widow, two children and grand children to mourn their loss, but not to mourn as those who have no hope.

Asleep in Jesus, O, for me,
May such a blissful refuge be;
Sacredly shall my ashes lie,
Awaiting the summons from on high.

MARY E. MARTIN.

(*Gospel Visitor* please copy.)

CRUME.—In Noble Co., Ind., Feb. 19th, 1873, Willie, infant son of brother Levi and sister Mary Crume, aged 8 months. Funeral service by brother Christian Weaver from Matt. 19: 2, 3.

MILLER.—In the Welsh Run arm of the Church, near Broad Fording, Washington Co., Md., Feb. 17th, 1873, sister Katie Miller wife of bro. Abraham Miller, aged 52 yrs, 9 mos and 7 days. Disease, palsy, died very suddenly. Funeral discourse by Elder Christian Keefer and the brethren.

Sister Miller was a consistent member of of the Church for a number of years and was beloved by all around her. She leaves a kind husband and family of children to mourn their loss, but not without hope.

NICHOLAS MARTIN.

(*Gospel Visitor* please copy.)

SNAPP.—In Logan Co., Ohio, on Feb. 19, 1873, of Lung fever, our old friend Jno. B. Snapp, aged 73 years, 1 month and 27 days.

He was a member of the Baptist Church. He leaves an old companion, three children, 18 grand-children and many relatives to mourn their loss. Funeral preached by the writer in the English and by John P. King minister of the Omish Church in the German, by request, from Rev. 14: 13.

J. L. FRANTZ.

DUBBS.—On Feb. 25, 1873, Daniel Dubbs of dropsy, aged 81 years, 4 months and 18 days.

FOX.—On Feb. 25, 1873, of Typhoid Fever, Catharine Fox, aged 23 years and 13 days. I preached both funerals in one day. JESSE CALVERT.

COFFMAN.—Near South English, in the English River Church District, March the 1st, 1873, our beloved brother, Benjamin F. Coffman, formerly of Rockingham Co., Va., aged 39 years, 8 months and 6 days. Disease Typhoid fever.

He leaves a widow, two children and a large number of relations and friends to mourn their loss, but they mourn not as those who have no hope for all feel assured that he rests in the Paradise of God. His last audible words were, "all is well, let me go in peace." A kind husband, an affectionate father, a good citizen and an humble exemplary follower of Christ were some of the characteristics of his life. A few days before he passed from earth he called for the Elders of the church and had the Holy Unction of annointing with oil administered to him. Though his sickness was of short duration, only two weeks, he suffered but little or no pain, but slowly and silently passed through the gates of death and peacefully landed in the haven of eternal rest. O that we might all so live, that when we die we can also die in peace and meet all our dear brethren, sisters, friends and all the holy Fathers around the throne of God. The funeral services were attended to by the brethren, to one of the largest collections of mourning and sympathizing friends ever assembled in this part of the Lord's heritage. The words of Jesus addressed to Martha, as recorded in John 11: 23. "Thy brother shall rise again," were improved upon on the solemn occasion. B. F. F.

(*Visitor* please copy.)

BENNITT.—On Feb. 11th, 1873, in the Wammee District, at North Bend, Parthena Alice, daughter of Bro. James Y. and sister Hannah Bennitt, aged 13 yrs., 6 months and 25 days.

Bro. James is in the ministry. It was a hard stroke to give up their child as she was an obedient daughter and much loved, and was taken away unexpectedly, as she was sick only three days. Disease, inflammation of the brain. The child expressed a willingness to go home and we need not mourn for her as those who have no hope. Funeral service by Bro's. A. Appelman and D. R. Freeman, from John 16: 20

The Weekly Pilgrim.

JAMES CREEK, PA., Mar. 11th, 1873.

☞ How to send money.--All sums over $1.00, should be sent either in a check, draft or postal order. If neither of these can be obtained, have the letter registered.

☞ When Money is sent, *always* send with it the name and address of those who paid it. Write the names and post office as plainly as possible.

☞ Every subscriber for 1873, gets a *Pilgrim Almanac* Free.

QUERY AND ANSWER.

Will the Editors of the Pilgrim please give us an explanation on the following Scripture: "If there come any unto you and bring not this doctrine, receive him not into your house neither bid him God speed." 2d John 1st; 10.

What house is here referred to, our dwellings or the house of public worship?

Wm. B. Sell.

The souls of all men are equally precious in the sight of God and should so be considered. To refuse any man the common charities of life seems not to be in harmony with the spirit of Christ, therefore we conclude that it is not the man that we are so specially to guard against as the doctrine which may not be in accordance with the truth, hence if any bring among us a doctrine that does not comport with the Word of God and is not calculated for the salvation of the soul, we are to afford him no opportunity to preach that doctrine, no matter whether it be a private house, a tent or a Church-house. It is the doctrine that we are to exert our influence against. To do this will not necessitate us to deny them the common charities, such as entertaining them as strangers or feeding them when hungry.

TAKE THE BACK NO'S.

All subscriptions should commence with the beginning of the volume, as the first Nos. contained some very interesting articles some of which are still continued. It will also make a complete file and make the volume valuable for binding. We can still supply all subscribers with numbers from the beginning of the year. New subscribers are still coming in quite encouragingly and we can assure you, they are welcomely received. We have room for many more, send them along and we will accommodate all.

Bro. Stephen Hildebrand, of Mineral Point, Cambria Co., Pa., says: "One month has elapsed since I took my leave of the brethren and sisters of James Creek and of the Pilgrim Office. I arrived home same evening—found all well. I often think of the privilege I had of meeting with you, brethren, and I am so well pleased with the zeal and appearance of the brethren and sisters that I hope the time will not be long until we can meet again. Further, I think it would do our brethren and sisters good to visit James Creek, especially, sisters."

We feel glad that those who visit James Creek are generally favorably impressed as we always contended that good men ought to have a good reputation at home. Perhaps some brethren flatter the James Creek Church a little, but one thing we are glad to acknowledge, we have peace among us and try to contend for the faith.

PERSONAL.

D. Brower. That will do

Jacob Link. We don't publish the Pilgrim in the German.

Jacob Weaver. H. E's paper is now paid to No. 40 73.

Jeremiah Rothermel. The money you speak of is received—Almanac and No. 7 sent.

D. F. Hady and others. The Tune Books have now arrived and all orders are filled.

B. A. Leiter. Your name with several others was on the book but overlooked in putting them in the addressing galley. They will come all right now.

—Brother D. Youre intends to leave the charge at Germantown, but where he intends to locate we have not yet learned.

—Elder Isaac Cripe of Pyrmont, Ind., has been unwell during the winter but is now recovering.

Eld. Geo. Wolf. We received $8.00 from you about the 24th of November, but have no account of receiving any since. You say you sent $8.00 January 20th, how did you send it? Was it by postal order, check or how?

--S. M. Shuck of Preston, Minn., informs us that their Church is in a good condition and that they have been prospering. During the winter, they added eight to their number by baptism.

—Elder J. W. Brumbaugh of Clover Creek, and J. T. Myers of Somerset, Pa., gave us a call. Had preaching on last evening at the James Creek Church,—this evening service will be in our new Bethel.

—Sister M. M. Custer informs us that the brethren at Pottstown Pa., were holding some meetings, and that twenty-five were to be baptized on Saturday March the 1st.

—From Elder J. W. Brumbaugh, we learn that the church at Snake Spring, Pa., on the 22d of February, held a choice for a speaker and two deacons. The charges fell upon Bro. Wm. Ritchy for speaker, and Thomas Dibert and John Baker deacons.

—A brother says, "The winter here in Marion Co., Oregon has been very mild up to this date, February 20th, health good, the wheat looks well and the grass growing.

—From brother J. B. Diehl we learn that Elder C. Long, of Adel, Dallas Co., Iowa, has had bad health during the winter and seems to be declining some, but in his religious deliberations and zeal, remains unchanged.

—The following very good advice is received from a brother in the West: "Try your best to keep out controversaries as our people are not inclined to patronize a paper of that character. Exhibit a mild and gentle spirit through the columns of your paper, and then I have no doubt that the circulation of the Pilgrim will be an entire success.

—The building of a church near Hamilton, Caldwell Co., Mo., will fall through unless the Brotherhood comes to their aid more liberally. In brother W. B. Sell's last letter, he says: "On next Sabbath I have an appointment to fill at a distance of 13 miles and no way to get there but walk. Brethren, think of these things, and then help them to build a house for worship.

—Sister Kate Gambel of Cordelia, Cal., has been on a trip to Yosemite Valley and among the "Big Trees," and has given an account of it for the the entertainment of our readers,—will appear next week. Sister Kate, notwithstanding she is isolated from the general Brotherhood, remembers the poor by sending $1.00 along to make glad the fireside of some poor lonely widow. Brethren and sisters, what have you done towards supplying the poor with good religious reading? You would be surprised to learn that we have or are giving $400,00 for this purpose and cannot afford it a particle better than many hundreds of our subscribers.

Continue to work for the Pilgrim. A number of our agents who had done quite well before, made a second effort and almost doubled their lists. There are many more could do equally as well if they would try a little. One of our agents last week took a Pilgrim to their council meeting and obtained nine new subscribers.

LITERARY NOTICES.

The Phrenological Journal for March contains a good portrait and sketch of William F. Havemeyer, Mayor of New York City; The Problem of Life; Driven to Death; Indian Relics, and our Indian Policy, a well illustrated and sensible article; A Penal Colony for Criminals; Mrs. Mary Somerville, the Scientist, with portrait; What Shall our Boys do? Dreams and their causes; Longevity in the Professions; "I Cannot Quit It," or the Inebriate's Plea; A Good Memory, how to acquire and retain it; The Celt; The Red Deer of America; Hugh Stowel Brown on Americans, etc. Price 30 cts. A year's Subscription, with a "taking" Chromo, $3.00. Address S. R. Wells, 389 Broadway, N. Y.

Science of Health for March is on our table. As usual, it is filled with just such information as every family needs. If the money wasted for patent nostrums was spent for this invaluable periodical, people might have wiser heads and less aches and pains. Only $2.00 per year. Address S. R. Wells, 389, Broadway New York.

The Rock is a new weekly published by T. J. Shelton, Arcola, Ill. It is to be devoted to whatever is honest, pure, just, true, lovely and of good report.

MONEY LIST.

Daniel Bright	1.60
J C Coover	1.50
Thos. B Maddocks	6.00
Eld M Miller	.50
W G Cook	2.50
B B Bollinger	10.00
D Gibbon	8.75
Samuel Mohler	1.50
Daniel Brower	1.50
Lovina Marsh	2.00
J R Miller	1.50
G W Shively	5.62½
D H Barrick	1.35
E Slifer	1.60
Jacob Weaver	3.30
D Vaniman	1.50
Jos Amick	8.55
J L Frantz	1.50
J B Lair	2.75
Jacob M Mohler	1.50
S B Furry	.30
Annie Brower	2.75
Elizabeth Longenecker	.25
Jno G Snider	1.50
S C Miller	1.50
D Brower	1.90
Daniel Petry	.25

NEWS ITEMS.

The thermometer registered 79 degrees in the shade at St. Augustine, Florida, on the 3d of January.

There is a Japenese proverb which says, "The chief glory of the sword consists in its resting quietly in its sheath."

The coldest day, except one, for a hundred years, was the 30th ult., according to the averment of Professor Loomis of Yale College.

The Catholic Church in Great Britian has about 2,500 priests, 1,020 churches, 82 religious communities for men, 280 for women, and 4,500,000 lay members.

It is reported that President Grant will shortly make a tour through a number of the Southern States, among them Virginia, North Carolina Georgia, and South Carolina.

Six thousand men are now grading the Texas Pacific Railroad, and track-laying will begin as soon as the rise in the Red River enables the necessary supplies to be brought up.

New York is to have an underground railway. A large number of men are at work upon it. The underground lines in London are a success; their is no reason why they should not be in New York.

HUNTINGDON & BROAD TOP RAIL ROAD

Winter Arrangement.

On and after Tuesday, Oct. 4, 1872, Passenger trains will arrive and depart as follows:

Trains from Huntingdon South. *Trains from Mt. Dal's moving North.*

MAIL. A. M.	ACCOM P. M.	STATIONS	MAIL. P. M.	ACCOM A. M.
LE7 40	LE	Huntingdon,	AR4 00	AR
7 45		Long Siding	3 55	
8 00		McConnelstown	3 45	
8 05		Pleasant Grove	3 35	
8 22		Markleshurg	3 22	
8 40		Coffee Run	3 07	
8 45		Rough & Ready	3 00	
9 00		Cove	2 40	
9 05		Fishers Summit	2 45	
9 15		Saxton	2 35	le
9 40		Riddlesburg	2 15	
9 47		Hopewell	2 05	
10 05		Piper's *Run*	1 50	
10 32		Tatesville	1 30	
11 05		Bloody Run	1 20	
10 40		Mount Dallas	1 15	
11 08		Bedford	12 14	

G. F. GAGE, Supt

SHOUP'S RUN BRANCH.

LE 9 25 LE	Saxton.	AR2 15 AR
9 40	Coalmont.	2 00
9 45	Crawford	1 55
AR10 00 AR	Dudley	LE1 45 LE

Bro'd Top City from Dudley 2 miles by stage.

Time of Penna. R. R. Trains at Huntingdon

EASTWARD.			WESTWARD.		
Hb'g Ac.	9 29	A. M	Cin. Ex.	3 25	A. M.
Mail	1 15	P. M	Pc'f Ex.	7 27	"
Cin. Ex	7 24	"	Mail	5 45	P. M.
Phil. Ex	11 29	"	W. Pass.	11 50	A. M.

The Weekly Pilgrim.

Published by J. B. Brumbaugh, & Co.

Edited by H. B. & Geo. Brumbaugh.

CORRESPONDING EDITORS

D. P. Sayler, Double Pipe Creek, Md.

Leonard Furry, New Enterprise, Pa

The *Pilgrim* is a Christian Periodical, devoted to religion and moral reform. It will advocate in the spirit of *love* and *liberty*, the principles of true Christianity, labor for the promotion of peace among the people of God, for the encouragement of the saints and for the conversion of sinners, avoiding those things which tend toward disunion or sectional feelings.

TERMS.

Single copy, Book paper,	$1.50
Eleven copies, [eleventh for Agt.]	$15.00

Any number above that at the same rate.

Address,

H. B. BRUMBAUGH.
James Creek,
Huntingdon county Pa.

The Weekly Pilgrim.

"REMOVE NOT THE ANCIENT LANDMARKS WHICH OUR FATHERS HAVE SET."

VOL. 4. JAMES CREEK, PENNSYLVANIA, MARCH, 18. 1873. NO. 11

POETRY.

"IS YOUR LAMP BURNING?"

Say, is your lamp burning, my brother?
I pray you look quickly and see.
For if it were burning, then surely
Some beams would fall bright upon me.

Straight, straight is the road, but I falter,
And oft I fall out by the way:
Then lift your lamp higher, my brother,
Lest I should make fatal delay.

There are many and many around you
Who follow wherever you go;
If you thought that they walked in the shadow,
Your lamp would burn brighter, I know.

Upon the dark mountain they stumble;
They are bruised on the rocks, and they lie
With their white pleading faces turned upward
To the clouds and the pitiful sky.

There is many a lamp that is lighted;
We behold them anear and afar:
But not many among them my brother,
Shine steadily on like a star.

I think, were they trimmed night and morning,
They would never burn down or go out,
Though from the four quarters of heaven
The winds were all blowing about.

If once all the lamps that were lighted
Should steadily blaze in a line,
Wide over the land and the ocean,
What a girdle of glory would shine!

How all the dark places would brighten!
How the mist would roll up and away!
How the earth would laugh out in her gladness
To hail the mellennial day!

Say, is your lamp burning, my brother?
I pray you look quickly and see;
For if it were burning, then surely
Some beam would fall bright upon me!

—*Friends Review.*

ORIGINAL ESSAYS.

SIR, WE WOULD SEE JESUS.

JOHN 11: 21.

This phrase, addressed to Philip by certain Greeks who were among them that came up to Jerusalem to worship at the feast, seems very natural from the attending circumstances. It may have contained a sincere desire to see Jesus and hear Him converse, or it may have been mere idle curiosity. All Jerusalem was astir over the Personage who spoke as one having authority, and whose miracles none could gainsay. The Pharisees said among themselves, "Perceive ye how ye prevail nothing? behold, the world is gone after them." His entry into Jerusalem had been triumphant—the people had cut down branches of palm trees and strewed them in the way proclaiming before Him, "Hosanna, Blessed is He that cometh in the name of the Lord." That a notable miracle had been performed, no one could deny, and indeed the chief priests consulted concerning putting Lazarus to death, because on account of Him many believed on Jesus. The multitudes that followed Him were great, and from different motives; some because others did, some from the benefits derived for themselves or friends, some from curiosity. He granted all requests to see Him, and to each meted a portion in due season. Zaccheus, we remember desired greatly to see Him, but thought His house would not be honored by the Great Teacher, but we remember the words of Jesus, "Zaccheus, make haste and come down for to-day is salvation come to thy house, and he made haste and received Him joyfully." The people beheld Him as Isaiah says, "A man of sorrows and acquainted with grief." They beheld Him as one whom the Scribes and Pharisees could not entangle. To the woman at the well of Samaria He spoke in simple terms. To Nicodemus, He spoke immediately of the new birth; and when he marveled, answered "Art thou a teacher in Israel and knowest not these things?"

Let us contemplate Him in a few of the scenes through which He passed while tabernacling in the flesh. We see Him walking up the streets of Jerusalem alone toilworn and weary, we see him by the sea of Gallilee, teaching the waiting people, when they hung upon His word until the "day was far spent," when He had compassion on the multitude and said to His disciples, "Give ye them to eat." And when they hesitated whence to get bread to satisfy them in the wilderness, He commanded them to sit down in companies and with a few loaves and a couple of fish, fed the multitude. We see Him rebuking the boisterous waves, and shrieking wind, and *immediately* there was a great calm. We see Him at the grave of Lazarus, manifesting both His human and divine nature, in the temple exhibiting zeal for His Father's house, when He made a scourge of small cords and drove out them that bought and sold therein. We see Him toiling up the rugged ascent of Tabor with His three disciples. We know not of the conversation that passed between them there, but we have an account that His face did shine as the sun, and His raiment was white as the light, while He held communion with Moses and Elias just from the courts of Heaven, who doubtless spake of His decease and resurrection, while over all spreads a bright cloud. No wonder awe steals over the disciples at this holding high converse with the skies. No wonder all things earthly are forgotten, and Peter in the fullness of his soul exclaims, Lord it is good for us to here, let us remain. We see Him in the large upper room, when the preparation for supper being ended He riseth therefrom and poureth water into a basin and began to wash His disciple's feet. We see His agony in the garden, when the weight of the world's salvation rested upon Him—when sympathy from God and man seemed denied. We see Him on the resurrection morn, when He addressed words of cheer to the weeping Mary; when He led captivity captive and gave gifts unto men; when He journeyed with two of His disciples to Emmaus, how their hearts burned within them while He unfolded to them the Scriptures! Again, we see Him on the day of His ascension when He led His disciples out as far as Olivet, and when a cloud received Him out of their sight. We see Him as the Mediator, made a priest forever after the order of Melchisedec. Again we shall see Him when this mortal shall have put on immortality, and this corruptible, incorruption, for we shall be like Him.

HATTIE F. MILLER.

CHASTENING LOVE.

The love that chastens is the love that saves. Yearning over the sinner, it hates and abhors the sin. Twining itself about the wayward child, it restrains and recalls the wandering feet from every sinful path. "As many as I love I rebuke and chasten." And that God whose love will not allow us to sin unrebuked, nor tolerate wrong doing in us, will yet defend His children and deliver and bless and save them forever.

"Two Rabbis," says a Jewish legend, "as they drew nigh to Jerusalem saw a fox running upon the hill of Zion. At the sight Rabbi Joshua wept, but Rabbi Elizer smiled. 'Wherefore dost thou smile?' asked the one who wept. 'Nay, wherefore dost thou weep?' said the other. 'I weep,' replied the Rabbi Joshua, 'because I see fulfilled what is written in the Lamentations: "Because of the mountain of Zion, which is desolate, the foxes walk upon it."'

"'And therefore do I smile,' said Rabbi Elizer, 'for in the sign that God hath fulfilled His threatenings, I see a pledge that not one of His promises shall fail!'"

So in every affliction and trial which comes upon us, we may recognize the Father's hand correcting us, or the Father's love permitting every grief, and may take comfort in the assurance that all things are working together for good to them that love God, and that He who chastens and afflicts us for our profit in this world, shall fulfill each promise of blessing made to us for days to come, and crown us with the joy and glory of His Heavenly home.—

The Christian.

Make the best possible use of wealth while living. You cannot take it to the grave, and it will only be a curse to your children if they are made to believe they have no aim in life, but to wait until you choose to leave them all your accumulations.

THE BAPTISM OF JOHN, WHENCE WAS IT, FROM HEAVEN OR OF MEN?

B. F. MOOMAW.

In resuming our reflections upon the principle involved in this question, we next in order, consider briefly the ordinance of Feet-Washing.

As a matter of faith, the Christian world stands united upon this subject, nor could it possibly be otherwise, because in matters of faith we have no power over our volition, but are compelled by the laws of our organization to decide according to the weight of evidence adduced. This being in the case before us, so overwhelming, no intelligent person would risk their reputation by denying that it was a divine command, it fully embracing the three ideas according to Wayland, "an act designated, signified to be the will of God, that it be performed, and that we are included within the number addressed.

The discrepancy only arises when *opinion* is substituted for faith. One is of the *opinion* that it is intended as a social institution, to be performed literally in the family circle. A second is of the *opinion* that it is to be understood figuratively, and implies an act, or actions of hospitality and benevolence, and is fully met in all its demands by feeding the hungry, clothing the naked, supplying the wants in any way of the destitute. Comforting the oppressed, visiting the sick, literally washing the feet of the weary traveller, or others when filthy, or forsooth, blacking the boots and foraging the horse of the minister. A third party believes that all these, minus the blacking of boots, &c., are obligations devolving upon Christians, fully enjoined by divine authority, and that they need not be coupled to the command of Feet-washing. Hence that it may legitimately be practiced as an act of kindness when necessary, and should be performed by the Church according to the example and command of our blessed Lord and Master, and that when this is performed it secures to the believer great and precious promises, "If ye know these things happy are ye if you do them." We are of the latter party, and why? "because it is from Heaven and not from men."

It is not our purpose to discuss the comparative merits of these different propositions here, but only to show that it has the sanction of a divine command, and "that it is not of men." This is the point that I desire should be constantly kept in view. "Then to the law and to the testimony."

It is a fact well understood, that God's people, under the old covenant dispensations, performed many and various ablutions and among them was the washing of feet, both socially and sacramentally. Socially as in the case of Abraham in the plains of Mamre, Genesis 18: 4. Lot in the city of Sodom, the Levite in Bethlehem in the land of Gibeah, Judges 19: 21. Abigail at Carmel, 1 Samuel 25: 41, the exhortation of David to Uriah, 2 Samuel 11: 8, and the church represented in Songs of Solomon. 5: 3.

Sacramentally, Ex. 30:17-21, "And the Lord spake unto Moses saying, thou shalt also make me a laver of brass, and his foot also of brass to wash with all, and thou *shalt* put it between the tabernacle of the congregation and the altar, and thou shalt put water therein, *for* Aaron and his sons *shall* wash their hands and their feet thereon. When they go into the tabernacle of the congregation, they shall wash with water that they die not, or when they come near to the altar to minister, to burn offering made by fire unto the Lord. So they shall wash their hands and their feet—that they die not, and it shall be a statute forever unto them, even to him and to his seed throughout their generations.." Moses, Aaron and his sons are the parties to whom this command was given. They well understood what was required of them, and the fatal consequence of neglecting, changing or modifying it, hence we see them as faithful stewards and true believers, obeying it to the letter. See Ex. 40:30-32, "When they went into the tent of the congregation and when they came near to the altar they washed as the Lord commanded Moses."

In the above we have a striking analogy, a counterpart in the examples and commands of Jesus Christ, the Moses like prophet, the author of our blessed Christianity. Here we see Shilo assembling his chosen, from the world apart, "among them as one that serves," laying aside his garment, fulfilling the object of his mission, delivering his Father's will, honoring it by His own example, threatning excommunication upon those refusing submission, declaring that they should have no part with Him. Oh, fatal denunciation! Like in the case of Aaron and his sons, must "wash that they die not, but otherwise if ye know these things, happy are ye if ye do them," that ye may have life, and have it more abundantly," John 13th chapter. What care and what labor has our Savior taken to convince and satisfy our skeptical minds that this, as well as other institutions, is from Heaven, and not of men. May it not with propriety be said of this generation as to the disciples on the way to Emmaus, "Oh fools and slow of heart, to believe the things that are written in the Prophets, and in the Psalms concerning me."

The Lord's Supper and the eucharist standing in the same connection with, and so closely allied to the ordinance of Feet-washing, it is not necessary so far as our present purpose is concerned, to go into a detailed review of the evidences upon which their divine authority is predicated. The facts and circumstances establishing these also, hence no difficulty in determining "from whence they are."

The salutation of the kiss, we think deserves from us a passing notice in this connection. Standing, as it does, somewhat isolated, we conclude that it has rather a special significance, having many examples in the Old Testament of it being observed by many persons eminent for their piety and devotion to the glory of God, and the best interests of humanity, in connection with the example of the Master and the apostles, as well as the frequency of Apostolic command in the New Testament, we conclude "that it is from Heaven;" and fixes the obligations upon the servants of God to practice it, but as the when and the where is not expressed, this must be supplied according to the nature and design of the institution, which we now proceed to consider.

First, It is significant of reverence, 1 Sam. 10: 1. Samuel annointing Saul. "Then, Samuel took a vial of oil and poured it upon his head, and kissed him, and said, is it not because the Lord hath annointed thee to be a captain over his inheritance." 1 Kings 19: 18. And the Lord said unto Elijah, "Yet have I left me seven thousand in Israel, all the knees which have not bowed unto Baal, and every mouth which hath not kissed him."

2nd. Of submission to Christ, Psa. 2: 12. David addressing the sovereigns of earth, "Be wise now therefore O ye kings, be instructed ye judges of the earth, serve the Lord with fear, and rejoice with trembling, kiss the Son lest he be angry and ye perish from the way when his wrath is kindled but a little. Blessed are they that put their trust in him.

3rd. Of love, Gen. 27: 26, 27. Isaac blessing Jacob, "said unto him, come near now and kiss me my son, and he came near and kissed him." 1 Sam. 20: 41. Jonathan and David whose hearts were knit together in affection kissed one another, and wept one with another, until David succeeded." In the observance of this duty we should constantly have these three points before the mind, reverence unto Christ, who has assured us that "what we do unto a disciple in his name, we do unto him." Thus we salute our brethren in the name of the Lord, because they are his disciple, and in submission to his authority because he has signified by his example and the express command through inspired instruments that the faithful should salute one another with an Holy kiss, and of love, signifying that fraternal affection, christian fellowship and common brotherhood that characterizes every well regulated family, especially the family of Christ. Taking this view of the subject as we do, it is clearly implied when and where it ought to be observed. Not only as an act of devotion to be performed at places of worship, but when and wherever brethren, who have been separated for a time, meet together, and when we separate not knowing whether we shall ever meet again, as well as on other occasions when circumstances demand an expression of love and fidelity. So I understand it and so the spirit moves within, and I doubt not but it will be blessed by the smiles of an approving Providence.

(*To be Continued.*)

STRIKE AT THE ROOT.

It cannot but be considered the duty of the ministers of the Gospel and every professed follower of Christ to oppose evil of every shade and color, whenever and wherever they possibly can, not however, to select out some particular one and make it a hobby upon which to continually ride, and pass all others by without a notice. I know some who make a hobby of intemperance. It is their Alpha and Omega. The whole power of their intellect and talent is engaged in a warfare against this evil while they pay no attention to others. There are other vices besides intemperance, which must be met and conquered by the love of truth and temperance, and there are more virtues to contend for than temperance. Still intemperance is an evil of such immense proportions and wide extent that it behooves all lovers of order and good government to rise up as a man and sweep it away, root and branch.

Our penitentiaries, jails, alms-houses, and lunatic asylums are constantly crowded with the victims of this terrible vice. The only way to effectually combat the evil is to strike at its root, License.

In voting upon this question at the coming election, is there any one professing to be a christian that will stultify their sense of justice and right by voting license? What! Shall we vote liberty to those who have no more conscience than to poison our children, ruin our homes, crush our hearts, and blast our hopes. Go to some of our large cities and visit the dens of squalid poverty and then you can get a just conception of the ring of misery and wretchedness there. You will find the poor mother hanging over the smouldering embers with her little ones hovering around her piteously asking for bread. What causes this misery and woe? Nine cases out of ten, RUM. Shall we grant license to that which robs the wife of her husband and home, the children of their friend and father? The thought is preposterous. The license law has proved a failure and its results do not justify its retention and the only remedy at present is, NO LICENSE. I am not afraid that whisky will hurt me but I am afraid, and have good reason to be afraid that it will hurt ten thousand others, therefore I am opposed to it and whatever else will work detrimental to the good of my fellowman. Young men are not, as a general thing, as thoughtful and considerate as men of age and experience, and being naturally of a more active, lively temperament, they are more apt to be led astray, in the years of early boyhood. I heard a gentleman quote a verse which has never faded from my memory. "The drunkards will never be dead." I will tell you the reason. The young grow up before the old one's die." Alas how true! Nine-tenths of the drunkards of to-day were led astray when they were young. We seldom see a person who has arrived at the years of manhood, start in the downward course of the common drunkard. They learn to love liquor when young and it grows with them as they grow older. Let us take a look at some of the statistical reports and see the terrible amount of vice and crime that is the result of this nefarious traffic in ardent spirits.

Rum pauperism costs the United States annually $35,000,000. Rum sickness, $1,000,000 annually. The number that die drunkards 80,000; the number sent to prison, 200,000; the number of young men who annually become drunkards, 600,000; the number of children reduced to a state worse than orphanage, 200,000. Only think of it, two hundred thousand little ones upon the cold charities of the world every year. Thousands grow up in ignorance and vice, the girls not having the necessary care, admonition and instruction to shield and guide them, fall victims to the lusts of man. The boys, exposed to all the temptations of vice, grow up thieves and pickpockets and end their career in State prison or on the gallows. I am told that religion costs the United States annually $12,000,000 and crime $40,000,000. Lawyers $70,000,000; Rum, $200,000,000. Think of that, child of God, enough spent for Rum to send a missionary to every dark and benighted corner of the earth.

The local option law may not be adequate to accomplish the desired end, but then it is a step in the right direction and the best we can do for the present is to make use of it. If we cannot have a perfect plan to oppose evil, better have an imperfect one than none at all. It is, or should be an object of every professed Christian to save some from the ultimate ruin of the world. What can you do with a drunken man, can you reason with him? You might as well preach to the stars as to him. What can we do with a man that is enslaved to liquor? I think I am safe in asserting that not one out of a thousand break the chains of their thralldom and gain or regain a respectable position in society. Then why not make use of the helping hand the government holds out to us and with it endeavor to remove the source of so much crime and misery, and one of the greatest obstacles that impedes the progress of the cause of Christ. He is a wise man that knows his opportunity and makes use of it.

BENJAMIN BOWMAN.

CHRIST THE RISEN SAVIOR. NO. 2

"Now is Christ risen from the dead."

Universal History, observation and experience prove that the world lieth in wickedness, idolatry, superstition and impiety, and every kind of vice and misery has, in all ages, covered and desolated the earth. But it hath pleased God, of His infinite mercy, to reveal Himself to sinful men to make known a way in which they might be reconciled to Him and recovered to holiness, and thus to introduce a religion suited to rectify the disorders of the world, and unite the honor of His name with the eternal happiness of innumerable millions. Miracles, and the resurrection of the Redeemer, especially formed a suitable demonstration that this religion came from God and served to arrest the attention of mankind, for alas! sinners in general, are too much concerned about the affairs of this life to notice those things which relate to God and their eternal state. There are reasons assigned for a divine interposition on this occasion. The Jews, the most inveterate enemies of Christianity, preserve with profound veneration and scrupulous care, the books of the Old Testament which have been handed down in the same manner, from generation to generation during a long succession of ages. These books contained a system of prophecy centering in the person and redemption of the Messiah, and among other particulars, His sufferings and death are foretold with clear intimations of His resurrection and subsequent glorious Kingdom. We know also that the gospels were made public in the earliest ages of Christianity, for they are continually quoted and referred to by those writers whose works have been preserved, and from them we learn that our Lord predicted His own death, and resurrection on the third day in so explicit a manner that the Jewish rulers were aware of it and took their measures accordingly. Yet when the body of Christ was delivered to Joseph they were so fully satisfied by what they saw and heard of His being dead, that they made no objection on that ground, but they requested Pilate that the sepulcher might be securely closed and guarded by Roman Soldiers until the third day was past, lest the disciples should steal His body and say that He was risen again.

After all their precaution, the body was gone and they were never able to show by whom it was taken or what became of it. Here let us pause that we may consider the credibility of testimony. One consistent witness of sound understanding and fair character, who has no apparent interest in deceiving, is often deemed sufficient to determine the sentence of life or death, the most important of all temporal concerns. But if three or four such witnesses should agree that they saw such a murder committed by the prisoner at the bar, no sober man could doubt the fact or scruple to pronounce him guilty. Now there were twelve appointed witnesses to the resurrection of Christ, of plain, good understanding, and unexceptionable character; for Peter's denial of his Lord through the force of sudden temptation forms no impeachment of his integrity, seeing he so honestly confessed his guilt and so fully proved the sincerity of his repentance by his subsequent conduct. And when Judas by transgression fell, another was chosen in his place. These witnesses had constantly attended Jesus during some years and must have been competent to know Him from all other men. They were remarkably incredulous respecting His resurrection, and His crucifixion seems almost to have extinguished their hopes. How then can it be supposed that they would have attempted to overpower or deceive the vigilant and valient soldiers, and to steal the body of Jesus. In so desperate an undertaking they would have been sure to excite the combined rage of both the Jewish and Roman rulers and success could only expose them to hatred, persecution and all kind of hardships and sufferings. It is manifest that from the time they began to bear witness to the resurrection of Christ, they renounced all prospects of worldly interest, ease or greatness, and willingly embraced poverty, labor, contempt, bonds, stripes and perils as their portion so that no possible account can be given of their conduct unless it be ascribed to a principle of conscience. The strict and exact morality of their writings demonstrate that they could not be actuated by false principles, for they do not allow, in any case, to do evil that good may come, and they condemn all kinds of impositions with the most decided severity. Is it then possible for human beings deliberately to choose temporal and eternal misery, and to persevere in decided adherence to a plan which on their own principles, insures their damnation in another world as well as a complication of miseries in this present life?

The witnesses of our Lord's resurrection survived that event for a long time, some of them nearly forty years, and John still more. They were after a while, separated into different parts of the world and seemed to have no common interest except in the success of Christianity. They passed through a series of the severest trials and almost all of them died martyrs in the cause. But no change of circumstances or situation no promises or threatenings of men, no repeated tortures or impending dangers induced one of them, in the smallest degree, to waver in His testimony. They declared unanimously that on the third morning after the crucifixion a vision of angels told some of their company at the sepulcher that their Lord was risen; that afterwards they all saw Him repeatedly; that they examined His hands, feet and side; and were sure it was the same body which had been nailed to the cross; that He ate and drank with them several times; that at length, after giving particular instructions relative to their future conduct, He ascended from among them until a cloud intercepted their sight of Him; and that two angels appearing unto them, declared He was gone to Heaven. Such an unwavering, persevering testimony of twelve persons whose holy lives, diligent labors, disinterestedness and patient sufferings, evince their sincerity and form complete proof

A PILGRIM.

To be continued.

WHAT TO TAKE HOME.—A loving heart and a pleasant countenance are commodities which a man should never fail to take home with him. They will best season his food and soften his pillow. It were a great thing for a man that his wife and children could say of him: "He never brought a frown or unhappiness across his threshold."

"The gospel of the Kingdom ... is the burden of every true ministry, the life of every sincere church, the inspiration of every devout soul, and the hope of deliverance and salvation to every lost sinner.

CONVERSATION ON DRESS

Continued from last week.

Eld. Well, sister, what shall I do? "Preach the word" as Paul admonished Timothy, or cripple the truth, and come down to pander to the follies of the ages? How can I do otherwise than to proclaim against this thing, when Paul says for women to adorn themselves in modest apparel, with shame-facedness and sobriety; not with braided hair, or gold, or pearls, or costly array?

Mrs. A. That is only Paul's opinion, you know that some things which he said were only his opinion.

Eld. Paul says, "If any man think himself to be a prophet, or spiritual, let him acknowledge that the things that I write unto you are the commandments of the Lord." Wherever he said anything that was not the commandment of the Lord, he has taken express pains to tell us so. Peter also speaks of this matter in a similar manner.

Mrs. A. I was not aware that Peter said anything about it.

Eld. Oh yes; Peter says: "Whose adorning let it not be that outward adorning of plaiting the hair, and of wearing of gold, or of putting on of apparel." 1 Pet. 3:3.

Mrs. A. Well they did not mean we should not wear any gold, but that we should not go to excess and pride in these things. I don't think actually, that the Lord cares what we wear, if we don't have our affections on it. I do not believe in going to excess in this thing, I never did care anything about finger-rings, and could see no use in them.

Eld. Why was it not just as easy for Peter and Paul to say, Don't have your affections on your dress, as to say in plain terms, not to "put on" or wear gold. You are aware that when people pattern after another, the tendency is for each person to go a little farther than his pattern. For instance, if you wear those articles you are pleading for, the next one might for four or five finger-rings; and the next one for a bracelet; and so on without limit. Now you say these texts condemn extremes in jewels and dress; and as you question the manner in which I apply them, won't you be so kind as to tell me where to lay down a line of distinction, so that, in instructing the people, they may know what is excess in jewels.

Mrs. A. Well don't say anything about it at all, let every one's conscience be the guide in these matters.

Eld. But sister, you are aware that conscience is the result of instruction. To have a good conscience the mind must be properly instructed. The poor Hindoo mother who throws her child into the jaws of the crocodile, is prompted to it by her conscience. She is instructed that he is the river God, and that his open jaws are an invitation to give her child to her God. Our minds should be instructed by the Bible, and our conscience be such that we should tremble at the Lord's word. We should not seek to please ourselves, and bring God's word to our terms.

Mrs. A. I think it is descending to small particulars to pay any attention to such things, and in dress I think every one should be left to do as they please.

Eld. Well sister, it would be a strange way to train up children, to let them always do as they please. Christians are admonished as "new born babes to receive the sincere milk of the word" that they may grow thereby. How else shall we make progress than by being admonished of our errors, submitting to the Lord's word, and putting away our sins.

Mrs. A. Well, it will only bring the frown of other denominations upon us, to be so particular.

Eld. But are you not aware that the Methodists in their discipline protest against wearing gold, and refer to these testimonies in Timothy and Peter to enforce their positions. If they fail to live up to their discipline that is no reason why we should fail live up to the Bible. On this account, where there is such a tendency with the masses to go into excess in dress and pleasure-seeking, I think it is important for those who would have the Lord's favor, and "shine as lights in the world" to carefully seek in all things to comply with his word.

Mrs. A. Well, I had thought of being baptized and uniting with the Church, but I do not wish to connect myself with a people who are going to watch me all the time. I presume I can find somebody who will baptize me, as for organization I am suspicious of it.

Eld. I presume, sister, there are many who will take in members, and let them do as they please, if they keep up a form of religion; but the question is whether such things are going to stand the test of the judgment. It seems to me it is the proper way to learn all our wrongs here, and put them away, that we may be prepared for the judgment. I should not wish to belong to a Church that watched me to pick flaws with my endeavors to do right, but if they watched over me for good, and meekly tried to instruct me in the right way, above all people, I should consider them my best friends.

Mrs. A. Well, I must be going. Good day.

Eld. Sister do not decide these matters hastily. Pray over them carefully; consider us as your friends.

J. S. L.

Religious News.

For 1872, the different Baptist Churches claim 100,000 additions.

BRIGHAM YOUNG wants a kingdom. One of the Sandwich islands, he thinks, would answer his purpose. He is convinced that nothing short of this will save his pet relic from destruction.

The General Baptists seems to be in earnest in making a move towards establishing churches in towns and cities. We know of another church that should imbibe more of this spirit.

EXPULSION FOR COVETOUSNESS.—The *American Christian Review*, in referring to the statement that men are never excluded from the churches for the grave sin of covetousnes, asserts its knowledge of five men, all in good circumstancess and good standing in the community, who were expelled at one time from the Disciples church in Little Flat Rock, Indiana, for that sin. No other charge was made against them. They had refused to pay their proportion of the cost of a new meeting-house.

The Herald of Truth says: "Thro' a letter from M. C Hazard of Chicago, we are informed that the Northern Pacific Railroad Company has succeeded in making an arrangement with the trans-Atlantic transportation companies by which the fare for the Mennonites who wish to emigrate from Russia and settle upon the lands on the line of their road, is reduced to £10,4, or about $50,00 American money. This makes the expense of the journey very much less than usual.

FOREIGN.—Victor Emanuel of Italy is reported in a precarious condition of health. The Spanish Republic has not yet reached unruffled seas. A second ministry has been elected since the revolution, and the aspirants to the throne are becoming more clamorous. The Carlists claim 35,000 men in the field. Families are flying in great numbers to France. An immense fraud on the Bank of England has been discovered. The supposed perpetrators are Americans.

Among other amendments to the Constitution of the United States the following is proposed:

TO THE HONORABLE THE SENATE AND HOUSE OF REPRESENTATIVES.

The undersigned citizens of the United States petition your honorable bodies for such an amendment to the Constitution of the United States as shall suitably express our national acknowledgment of Almighty God as the source of all authority in civil government, of the Lord Jesus Christ as the Ruler of nations, and his revealed will as of supreme authority; and thus indicate that this is a Christian nation, and place all the Christian laws, institutions and usages of the government on an undeniable legal basis in the fundamental law of the land.

A STUPID ROW.—There has been a stupid row in Alpena, Mich. The small-pox prevailing, the authorities, to prevent contagion, ordered the schools and churches to be closed. The Rev. Mr. Saktew, of the Catholic Church, refused to close his place of worship, upon the ground that he was "under superior orders."

The Mayor sent a body of policeman to prevent the church from being opened on Sunday, but some of the congregation getting in by the back door, the priest recommended them to set the law at defiance, and come again at 3 o'clock p.m. Trouble and perhaps bloodshed would have occurred had not the matter been laid before the Bishop, who at once ordered the priest to obey the law.

MORAVIANS.—At Bethlehem, Pa., is the principal Moravian settlement in this country, and a unique and interesting community it is. Well to do in this world's goods, the members devote their large receipt almost exclusively to church and educational purposes. Their house of worship is large, and the regular congregation of the village averages a thousand members, who are divided into choirs or societies. One is composed of children, another of boys and girls, another of unmarried women and still another of married people; and each of these societies has its meetings and love feasts from time to time, which are generally delightful social occasions. The Moravians give heed to their music, for a huge choir leads the congregation, and singing occupies a large portion of the service.

THE NEW YORK OBSERVER is discussing the propriety of amending their system of educating men for the ministry. Under the present system the Church is obligated to educate all students furnished by the different Presbyteries whether they seem adapted to the calling or not. The reform contended for is to educate only such as have special abilities for that calling. Notwithstanding the Presbyterian ministry is largely of such as have called themselves, yet they profess a divine calling as the following will show: Every young man called of God to preach, would in good time be brought into the ministry without the aid of a church institution to help him. But as we have the Institution, it must be so administered as to sift out the dull, and educate as nearly as possible only those whom God has called.

Youth's Department

WHAT CHILDREN CAN DO.

It is not much that we can give
  In doing good to others;
But we in joy and peace can live
  With sisters and with brothers.

To playmates all we can be kind,
  And fill their hearts with gladness;
Our parent's wishes we can mind,
  And crown their lives with gladness.

And more than all we can obey
  The precepts of our Savior;
And prove our love to Him each day
  By goodness of behavior.

So, whether short, or whether long
  The life that is assigned us;
A memory like a pleasant song
  We all may leave behind us.

FOUR SERVANTS OF SATAN.

Dear young friends, Satan has a great many servants, and they are very busy, running about doing all the harm they can. I know four of them, and some of the mischief they have done. I found out their names, and I want to put you on your gaurd against them, for they are very sly. They will make you believe they are your friends. They appear sociable, easy, good-natured, and not too much in a hurry. They seem to wait your own time, and entice you when you least expect it.

"O, we want you to enjoy yourselves," they say, "and not be so particular:" and the arguments they use are very taking, at least I must think so, since so many of the young listen to them and are led away by them.

And all I believe, because they did not know, in the first place, who was speaking to them. They were deceived. They did not see it was satan's uniform they had on. Do you ask for their names? Here they are;

"There's no danger." That is one.

"Only this-once." That is another.

"Everybody-does-so" is the third, and "By-and-by" is the fourth.

If you are tempted to leave God's house, and break the Sabbath day to go for a sail or a ride, and "Only this once" or "Everybody-does-so" whispers at your elbow, know it is false. The great evil of one sin is, that you bring your heart and conscience into such a state that you will be likely to go on sinning: for there is not half so much to stop you as there was to prevent you setting out at first. Hold no parley with "Only-this-once," or "Everybody-does-so." Listen to their dangerous counsels, no, not for a moment.

Are you thinking seriously about the welfare of your soul? Has the Holy Spirit fastened upon your conscience the solemn warnings of a faithful teacher, and brought to mind a tender mother's prayer for your conversion? Does the tear start in your eye, and are you almost persuaded to choose Christ and that better part which cannot be taken from you? That is a moment when "By-and-by" hovers near to snatch your confidence and persuade you to put away serious things. It succeeded with poor Felix when Paul preached to him, and the Roman ruler was "almost persuaded to become a Christian." "By-and-by" whispered in his ear. He put off his soul's salvation to a more convenient season, and it never came.

"By-and-by is a cheat as well as a liar. By putting you off, he means to cheat your soul of Heaven. God says now; "Now is the accepted time and the day of salvation." He never asks you to postpone it. He makes no promises and no provisions for "By-and-by."

Dear children, be on your gaurd against these four servants of satan, in little things as well as in great ones for their only aim is to harm and ruin you.—*British Messenger.*

HENRY AND HIS HABIT.

Henry Town is a good enough boy in some respects. He is amiable and truthful, and pleasant in his manners, but in matters where he is required to take upon himself any burden of responsilibity or trust, he is a broken reed.

"Henry," says his sister, "will you be sure to put this letter in the post-office for me?"

"Oh! certainly."

"Now you won't forget it?"

"No, really I won't."

"It is to uncle Thomas about meeting me in New York, and if he doesn't get it and come to the station for me, I shall hardly know what to do."

"Oh! I'll be sure to put it in," and Henry takes the letter and goes off. He really intends to go to the post-office the first thing, but on the way down he meets a companion, who has something to say about a sailing party, and Henry forgets the letter entirely, until about three hours after the mail. Then he drops it in and thinks no more about it, only to answer, "Oh! yes," when asked if he had done his errand.

The consequence is, that when his sister gets to New York, where she has never been before, there is no one to meet her. She has to find her way to the other side of Brooklyn alone; takes the wrong car, and only finds her friends at the end of a very troubled, distressed anxious day. She is not well or strong; the fatigue and the worry made her ill for a week, and the whole pleasure is spoiled because Henry could not take the trouble to keep his mind on one subject long enough to post a letter.

I might multiply instances of the worry, disappointment, and wear and tear of the tempers and feelings of others occasioned by Henry's habits, but one is enough.

Henry is always very sorry, and never means to do so again; but the trouble is he does not mean not to do so, and I fear he will never reform, unless he takes to heart the lesson, "What thy hands find to do, do with thy might."—*Child's World.*

MANNERS.

Manners are more important than money. A boy who is polite and pleasant in his manners will always have friends, and will not often have enemies. Good behavior is essential to prosperity. A boy feels well when he does well. If you wish to make everybody pleasant about you, and gain friends wherever you go, cultivate good manners. Many boys have pleasant manners for company, and ugly manners for home.

We visited a small railroad town, not long since, and were met at the depot by a little boy of about eleven or twelve years, who conducted us to the house of his mother, and entertained and cared for us in the absence of his father, with as much polite attention and thoughtful care, as the most cultivated gentleman could have done. We said this to his mother before we left her home, "You are greatly blessed in your son; he is so attentive and obliging.',

"Yes," she said; "I can always depend on Charlie when his father is absent. He is a great help and comfort to me." She said this as if it did her heart good to acknowledge the cleverness of her son.

The best manners cost so little, and are worth so much, that every boy can have them.—*Youth's Guide.*

UPWARD AND ONWARD.

BY LORAIN S. HULBERT.

This should be the watchword of every American boy. Striving against the wrong, overcoming all evil habits, let us persevere in all we do. Let us be fair and honest in all our dealings with every one.

We should be truthful in small things as well as in great, ever working our way upward and onward. Let us remember that, "If at first you don't succeed, try, try again." If we would win fame we must work for it. It will never do to be idle. If we would make our mark in the world, we must begin while we are boys. It is not necessary that, to be great, we should be rich. Many men, such as Lincoln, Franklin and others, were once poor boys; they worked up and on to high positions in life, esteemed by all who knew them. If others have done it, why should not we? We can if we only try. Let us all, therefore, struggle to this end.

Upward and onward ever,
  Battling 'gainst wrong in our youth,
Let us put forth every endeavor,
  And struggle for virtue and truth.

—*Young Folks Rural.*

Correspondence.

VISIT TO THE YOSEMITE VALLEY.

The following was intended for the Youth's Department, but as it will be of general interest to all our readers, we give it a place under this head. We speak for our young readers in behalf of an account of the Geysers and hope sister Kate will send it without further invitation. Ed.

CORDELIA, CAL.
February 22d,'73.

Dear PILGRIM *readers*:—I have long thought of writing for your edification if Bros. Brumbaugh will give it a place in their worthy paper. I am taking the PILGRIM and think it a good paper. I often see good articles from dear sisters which encourages me to try to write a little. I only wish I was able to do justice to the subject I wish to write about. I know there are very many dear children and others who will never get to visit this country and see the wonderful curiosities that are here. I have traveled around a good deal, and saw many things which I would love to speak about, but I will only give you a short history of our trip to Yosemite Falls and the Big Trees.

I left home August 6th in company with my husband and three little ones my sister Lou Reader and her husband, and a Mr. George Reader, lately from Illinois. They were out here on a visit and did not like to return without seeing as much of California as they could. We took our conveyance and camped out, as we have no fear of rain here in the dry season. I think this one of the best countries in the world to travel in, we can camp for months and not get rained upon. The first night from home we camped near the foot of Mount Diabalo, a noted Mount. They have numerous earthquakes there and the best coal in the State is found on Mount Diabalo. The next night we stayed at brother Overholsers on the SanJoaquin, where we were kindly cared for. There we met sister Goan, who lives on the Sacramento river, next day we called on brother H. Eby, but did not stay long as they were in the midst of threshing. We crossed the SanJoaquin river and stopped with brother Haines' folks for dinner and spent the afternoon there, had a very pleasant visit and a good time, enjoyed it very much—they have a nice home and are well provided with the necessaries of life. From there we went to brother George Wolf's where we were kindly received by all the family,—that evening brother and sister Pennington came and we had some good singing, Bros. John and Joseph and his wife all being good singers, and being well supplied with singing books. After a season of prayer, we retired for the night, next morning, with sister Wolf's assistance, we did some more cooking preparatory to starting, as we knew we would be out several days before reaching Yosemite Falls. They also provided us with some of their nice cans of honey which were quite a luxury. After leaving brother Wolf's we had several days travel among strangers, but we met with great kindness everywhere. I forget how many days we were out, but we traveled 'till we could no farther with our wagons, and then camped for the night. Early next morning our men folks went to the hotel and hired saddles for the day at $1.00 a piece, so we mounted our horses and mules and began to descend. The first half mile was pretty good, but it kept getting worse and worse 'till our trail looked almost like a thread winding around the steep rugged mountains, it was just all we could do to stick to our horses. It was so rough and steep in many places, that several times I began to think we could never make the trip. If our horses had made a misstep we would have been hurled down thousands of feet some places almost perpendicular into the Merced river as it went foaming and gushing below us. There are a great many ladies who have to be lashed fast to the animal they ride, and then just give the animal the rein and not pretend to guide them and they go down all right. They have good steady mules and ponies on purpose for the trip.

My sister and I thought we would rather take the chances than to be tied fast to our horses. It is 2½ miles down into the valley, and the valley is 5 miles long and the scenery on the whole route is so beautiful and grand that it is beyond description. There are thousands of persons visit the valley every year for the purpose of seeing the Yosemite Falls. They are said to be the highest in the known world. There are other Falls in the valley but none so high as the Yosemite. They have a good hotel in the valley and are doing a little farming there, but everything has to be packed down.

I will give a list of altitudes at Yosemite Valley of the principal waterfalls. First cataract 900 feet, Bridal veil Falls 980 feet. It is rightly named, it looks like a long white gauze veil, 'tis beautiful. Next is Yosemite, this is in three falls, first fall 1,600 feet, second 600 feet, third 134 feet, total, 2,634 feet. Varial 350 feet, Nevada 700, South Fork 600, Royal Arch Falls 1,000 feet.

The valley is surrounded with very high mounts, and some of them perpendicular and so smooth nothing could climb them. They all have names, will only give a few. One is called Elespitor, Indian name, Tatockamula, signifies great chief of the valley, so named by the Indians. About two-thirds of the way up the mountain is a good picture of a man with hat on and side whiskers. It is the work of nature as no human being could ever get there. It is 3300 feet high. Sentiral Dome 4,500, Cap of Liberty 4,000, Mt. Star King 500, Clouds Rest 6,034 feet. As we came from Yosemite Falls we came by the grave of Big Trees, situated in Carveras Co. They are said to be the largest in the world. There are perhaps one hundred or more, and they are all named. Some of the bark off of the mother of the forest was sent to the woald's fair. They have been badly used, some of them dead and others badly burned. One, called uncle Tom's Cabin, was burned so much that my little boy rode in horse back and turned around. The father of the forest has been dead a long time. It is rather the largest of any in the grove, having a length of 480 ft. It is partly burned out for quite a distance. We rode through that for curiosity's sake. There is another large tree cut down and a saloon or dancing'hall on the stump of it. We were in it, I believe it is about 31 ft across. We also got to see the Mariposa trees, but they are not quite so large as the Colveras Grove. I believe there are trees in South America that is said to be taller than these, but not near so large around. We collected quite a numuer of things while out on our trip, were out about three weeks and traveled about 500 miles, we also got to see one of the natural bridges, which is quite a curiosity. We went over it and under it, it is on the Stanislaus river and a very perfect bridge.

Now dear children I have told you of this to show you how many beautiful things God has made for us and to show His goodness, power and wisdom. We know that He is all-wise and has created everything for some good purpose. Although there are many things that we cannot see what they are for, yet they are for some purpose, as nothing was made in vain. Now I ask of you to be good children, read the PILGRIM, for in it you will get much instruction, it is a good paper and I love to look over its pages. If you request, I will give a sketch of the Great Guysers at some time as I have been there also.

KATE GAMBEL.

Bros. Brumbaugh:—Permit me to drop a few lines in the PILGRIM for the purpose of informing the brethren and sisters that we, according to previous arrangements, had brother H. D. Davy to come on the 8th of February and preach for us. He came according to promise, and delivered thirteen sermons with power and demonstration of the spirit, to the satisfaction of those within and without as was made manifest in a few days, by the surrendering of the carnal mind. Six precious souls came forward and demanded baptism. Many more had their affections taken from earth and placed on things above, and are "counting the cost." O may they speedily get through, and come for refuge into the Kingdom that Christ set up while in the woald.

Brethren and sisters, how long are we going to remember the good counsels and admonitions given by our beloved brother. Let us ever remember them and profit thereby. Let us not be "hearers only" and thereby be deceived, "but be ye doers of the word," then the blessing.

The impressions made were deep and lasting I think, both in saint and sinner. The meetings were well attended, good order and good attention given to the word spoken. Bro. Davy spoke as the spirit gave him utterance, so let God be praised for all the good done by mortal man, and we his subjects, benefitted. Our meeting was held in the brick meeting-house, near Hagerstown, Indiana.

JOSEPH HOLDER.

Dear Editor:—I thought to write a few lines for the PILGRIM, I am well pleased with it and want you to continue it. About Church news, I cannot say much as there is no church organized here. There are 9 members here within ten miles. We had two meetings here this winter held by brother Isaac Hershy. The people were all well pleased with his sermons and want him to come back. The people here seem to be very anxious for the Brethren to come here and locate. The news was before the Rutland Center Farmer's Club that there was a colony of Dunkards coming West, and they made arrangements to meet them in Kansas City to bring them here to Montgomery Co., also made preparations to accommodate them while looking around for homes. Now brethren you can see that the people here are desirous of you coming. Whether this colony is coming I do not know, but was discussed as given, in my presence.

I will now say a little about our country here. We have one of the best countries in the State, well watered and a great deal of good timber, and land is cheap yet. Land sells from $5.00 to $20.00 per acre with good improvements. If any wish more particulars about the country, address,

WM. MERKY,
Independence, Montgomery Co. Kan.

ANNOUNCEMENTS.

Please announce through the PILGRIM that our District Meeting will be held on the 13th of May in the Cook's Creek Congregation, Rockingham Co., Va.

SOLOMON GARBER.

The District Meeting for North Missouri will be held on the 7th and 8th of March in the Smith Fork Branch, Clinton Co., (near Plattsburg), in the Brethren's Meeting-house. A general representation desired. Those coming by R. R. will stop off at Plattsburg.

GEORGE WITWER.

Please make the following announcement in the WEEKLY PILGRIM. The District Meeting of West Virginia, will be held in Seneca District, eight miles west of Mouth of Seneca, at Union School House, in Dry Fork township, Randolph Co., on Friday and Saturday, 9th and 10th of May. For any further information address the undersigned at Mouth of Seneca,

Pendleton Co., W. Va.
By order of the Church.

ASA HARMAN.

Please announce that the District Meeting of Northern Indiana and Michigan, will be held in the Brethren's Meetinghouse, mile west of Goshen, Elkhart Co., Ind., commencing on Thursday the 1st day of May, 1873, at 10 o'clock, a. m.

JESSE CALVERT, Clerk

Champaign Lovefeast.

The brethren in Champaign Co., Ill., have appointed their Communion Meeting on Saturday and Sunday, June 7th and 8th, 1873, at *Bro.* Geo. Dilling's, five miles east of Urbana. We extend an invitation to all, especially the ministering brethren.

J. H. MOORE,
Urbana, Ill.

TO ALL WHO ARE CONCERNED

We do, through this medium, inform the brethren and churches comprising the first district of Virginia, that Friday and Saturday before the fourth Sunday in April, is the time appointed for the holding of the Annual District Meeting, and will be held at that time no preventive providence, at the Valley Meeting-house in Botetourt Co., one mile south of Amsterdam. A full attendance is desirable.

The undersigned also informs his brethren that he has a number of New Hymn Books on hand for sale. B. F. MOOMAW.

Please announce that the District Meeting of Western Maryland, will be held the Lord willing in the Welsh Run Congregation in the Broad Fording Meetinghouse, five miles north-west of Hagerstown on the second Thursday in April, 1872.

NICHOLAS MARTIN.

You will please announce through the PILGRIM that the Brethren in the Middle District of Iowa, purpose holding their District Council Meeting with the Brethren in Dallas Co., in their Meetinghouse, on Monday the 19th day of May, 1873. We expect a good representation of delegates, also a general invitation to the brethren to be with us.

J. S. SNYDER,
Cor. Sec'y.

MARRIED.

SIPP—DOMER.—On Jan 12, 1873, at the residence of the bride's parents, Mr. Fredrick Sipp, of Buena Vista, Tuscarawas Co., Ohio, to sister Margaret Domer, of Holmes Co., O.

M. H. SHETT.

DIED.

POULUS.—In Elkhart Valley Congregation, Elkhart Co., Ind., Feb. 19, 1873, Frank Wesley Poulus, son of Henry and sister Poulus, aged 1 year, 4 mos., and 25 days. Funeral services by S. Leer, H. Rule and others.

P. H. K.

MILLER.—In Yellow Creek Congregation, Elkhart Co., Ind., Feb. 23, 1873, Henry Gilbert son of Delila Miller, of spotted fever, age 17 years. Funeral services by D. B. Stadsman and others.

P. H. KURTZ.

SNOEBERGER.—On Feb. 21st, 1873, near Lattasburgh, Wayne Co., Ohio, friend Frederick Snoeberger, aged 60 yrs., 9 mos. and 27 days.

He leaves an aged wife, a sister and five children to mourn their loss. Funeral preached by P. J. Brown and the writer from Isa. 38: 1, to a large concourse of people who assembled to pay their last respects to the dead.

GEO. WORST.

KABRICK.—On March 1st, 1873, in Union District, Marshall Co., Ind., Adam Marion, only son of bro. John and sister Elizabeth Kabrick, and grandson of Eld. John Knisley, aged 3 yrs. and 5 months. Funeral services from Acts 17: 28.

D. W. M.

SEIDER.—In Union District, Marshall Co., Ind., March 8th, 1873, Margaret Emily, daughter of Bro. Jacob, and sister Margaret Seider, and grand-daughter of Eld. John Knisley, aged 0 yrs., 10 mo. and 28 days. Funeral services from 2nd Peter, 1: 4. O. W. MILLER.

(Visitor please copy.)

GARBER.—Of the Flat Rock District, Va., March 8th, brother Jacob Garber, aged 77 years, 10 months and 25 days. Funeral services by Eld. Jacob Wine, Samuel H Myers and the writer from 2d Tim. 4: 7. JOHN NEFF.

(Visitor and Companion please copy.)

The Weekly Pilgrim.

JAMES CREEK, PA., Mar. 18th, 1873.

☞ How to send money.—All sums over $1.50, should be sent either in a check, draft or postal order. If neither of these can be obtained, have the letter registered.

☞ WHEN MONEY is sent, *always* send with it the name and address of those who paid it. Write the names and post office as plainly as possible.

☞ EVERY subscriber for 1873, gets a *Pilgrim Almanac* FREE.

A TALK WITH OUR READERS.

Five months ago we announced our departure from the PILGRIM office for the purpose of attending school. Now we are happy to inform you that we are again at home, and as we have been absent for some time, of course we feel like talking a little to our readers. During our absence we were in a measure cut off from the relation which we sustain to our patrons, at least we had not access to the private correspondence, and it is through this medium that we receive our greatest encouragement. If we were to publish the many words of encouragement and approval it would require more space than should be given for this purpose. Our readers can feel assured however that these good words are not lost. They have done much towards strengthening and animating us in our labors in the past. Since our arrival at home, we are informed that our private correspondence this year is full of these words of cheer and encouragement, and indeed the general approval with which the PILGRIM is meeting is all that can be expected and desired. It is true the circulation is not as large as it should be, but there are reasons for this. Money is very scarce and there are many places in the Brotherhood where the PILGRIM is unknown. In view of this we are patient, feeling assured that if we are faithful, and try at all times to be governed by correct Christian principles, our labors must finally be crowned with success. "God helps those who help themselves," and we shall try to do all in our power to make our undertaking a success, and effectual to the furtherance of the good cause, and then if it be in consonance with God's will we may expect His help. In view of the many words of encouragement, and a consciousness of right we look forward with bright hopes, hoping that our brethren and sisters may be moved and stirred up from their lethargy in regard to our periodicals, that they will be more and more impressed with them as means for disseminating truth and exposing error. It is true our periodicals may often be impregnated with impurities, and on this account some object to them. But this is no reason why they should be discarded. The clear sparkling rivulet that meanders through the valleys, and the bubbling spring present the idea of purity, but as they course their way from their source they become impregnated with impurities; yet impure as they are, the trees, the shrubbery and flowers along their course receive moisture that gives vigor, and besides all this, the thirst of thousands of beings is quenched. So it is with reference to our periodicals. They claim to point the reader to Jesus the great fountain Head from whence issues the clear bubbling stream of the waters of life. The source—the intentions are all right, but as men attempt to convey this truth who are all polluted with sin and uncleanness, it becomes tarnished with the most prominent corruptions of our nature. But impure as it may be, if we have been learning of Jesus, we may, like the tainted waters of the rivulet, give nourishment. Our brethren and sisters may be strengthened, and even the poor famishing sinner may come and drink. Brethren, if we are only honest, and go directly to the great fountain Head for our knowledge, it it does become slightly impregnated with the corruptions of our nature, it may still do its work.

The PILGRIM at times, may have been found to contain a large per cent of dross. Help us readers to make improvement. When you write be sure that you have an object in view, and let that object be the honor and glory of God. Endeavor to feel what you write and also the responsibility. Remember words have power, and a small drop of ink falling like dew upon a thought, produces that which may mold the mind of thousands. If all our contributors will be influenced by the good Spirit when they write, our periodicals must certainly become a power for good.

In conclusion, we make an urgent request that our readers continue their efforts to increase our circulation. This year we will be obliged to spend considerable in order to carry on the publication of the PILGRIM successfully. In this we know that many are anxious that we shall be successful, and will no doubt rally to our aid. A long pull, a steady pull and a pull altogether, is all that is needed to largely increase our circulation.

J. B. B.

TAKE THE BACK NO'S.

All subscriptions should commence with the beginning of the volume, as the first Nos. contained some very interesting articles some of which are still continued. It will also make a complete file and make the volume valuable for binding. We can still supply all subscribers with numbers from the beginning of the year. New subscribers are still coming in quite encouragingly and we can assure you, they are welcomely received. We have room for many more, send them along and we will accommodate all.

The following articles demand a careful reading: "Sir, we would see Jesus," by Hattie F. Miller, "From whence is it?" by Elder B. F. Moomaw, "Strike at the Root," by Benj. Bowman, and the "Risen Savior" by A Pilgrim.

PERSONAL.

ANNA TROXEL. Your letter was not received.

CORRECTION. In PILGRIM No. 8, Perthenia Early's correspondence, Oks Church should read, Okkan Church.

GEO. M. SIZER. Your remittance was overlooked and your name not credited. The numbers are now all sent and marked paid to No. 20, 73, Nos. 42 volume 3 are sent.

J. DEURY. If you give us Martha Rollin's post office we can give you the desired information. We had your list all right except one name and that is now attended to.

J. B. LAIR. The money was received and your name changed. They must come right now. If there are any missing Nos. inform us what they are and we will supply them.

BRO. JOHN NEFF says; "To-day I attended the funeral of old Jacob Garber (son of Martin Garber) a member of the Flat Rock Dist., Upper Shenandoah, Va. I have no doubt that many of the brethren remember of him, as in his time he was called a great peacemaker.

BRO. E. SLIFER says that much to his regret and that of his church, the name of Bro. Ephraim Stoner was omitted in his report of their meetings. Bro. Stoner was with them during their meeting and labored to general acceptance. The mistake may have occurred in the office but cannot now determine.

BRO. TOBIAS M. CAUFFMAN of Neffsville, Pa., says, "We had a series of meetings in Lancaster City with very good results, eight souls having decided in favor of Christ.—We had a very good meeting and believe the spirit of the Lord was with us. Brethren Daniel Longenecker, Peter Myers and David Garlach were with us."

THE "Household Treasure" seems to be just the thing wanted and the demand for it quite lively. Our first lot is all gone, but in a few days we will have another supply, when we can fill all orders. It is a little work that every family should have and will prove worth many times its cost.

Money List crowded out.

A new ERA in JOURNALISM.

The Great Achievement of the Nineteenth Century.

THE

DAILY GRAPHIC

All the News and Full of Pictures.

The Daily Graphic is the title of a newspaper, published in New York, which is achieving the most remarkable journalistic success ever chronicled. It is an eight-page evening paper (three editions daily), elegantly printed, and conducted by the ablest editorial talent attainable.

As a newspaper The Daily Graphic stands in the first rank, and contains regularly

The very Latest and Fullest News from all parts of the World.

Its great feature consists in the fact that it is not only a newspaper, but an Illustrated Newspaper as well. Four of its pages are filled with choice reading matter—telegrams, editorials, general and local news, items, gossip, and correspondence on the freshest and most interesting topics. The remaining four pages consist of

SPLENDID ILLUSTRATIONS.

executed in the most faultless and artistic style, and portraying accurately and fully all leading events within twenty-four hours after their occurrence. Those who have made journalism a study, and fully appreciate the great enterprise manifested in the collection and publication of news by the aid of the telegraph, steam presses, and the development of journalistic talent, have been fond of advancing the theory that the next advance in that field would result in a newspaper furnishing in its regular issues pictures of all current prominent events. That theory is a theory no longer; the newspaper of the future is the newspaper of to-day, and that paper is The Daily Graphic. The processes which render this marvellous achievement an existing fact are the result of the most careful study and endless variety of experiments, gradually perfected during the past twelve years. They depend upon improvements in lithography and the application of the photographic camera. By their aid a picture is made ready to print in from twenty minutes to two hours. Costly and elaborate plates, works of art, scenes of interest, are reproduced and pictured forth with equal facility and the most scrupulous fidelity. Illustrations of leading events are engraved and prepared for the press even before the accompanying written narrative or description leaves the hands of the compositor.

For the proper practical working of so great an enterprise, The Graphic Company was formed, with a Capital of

$500.000 in Gold.

months and months before the first issue of The Daily Graphic, the most extensive preparations were made, and to-day The Graphic Company has

The Largest and Most Complete Newspaper Establishment in the United States.

In the great work of illustrating the events of the day an extensive corps of the best known and most accomplished artists are constantly engaged.

The Daily Graphic aims to be in its strictest sense a newspaper. Striving always to be just and truthful, it discusses all questions independently and impartially. It is not the organ of any party, sect, or creed. It is always high toned, and contains nothing to offend any taste. Its contents give it an immense advantage over the "old fashioned" papers. The annual subscriber gets a

PICTORIAL HISTORY OF THE YEAR,

a volume of twenty-four hundred pages, constituting a valuable record of events and a graphic panorama of our time and progress. It possesses not merely a local interest, but is a paper for every reader of the language. It is, emphatically, The Paper for the Household.

Terms, $12 per year, or $3 for three months.

Address,

THE DAILY GRAPHIC.

39 and 41 Park place, New York City.

LAND, LAND, LAND!!

The completion of the Chesapeake and Ohio Trunk Line Railway, has opened up to the world much of the fine TIMBER LANDS, rich COAL FIELDS and cheap FARMING LANDS of W. Va. Now is the time to get cheap homes and invest money with the prospect of a handsome profit. For further particulars inquire of the undersigned, agent for lands here. J. S. FLORY,

Orchard View, Fayette Co., W. Va.

Jan. 10.

Trine Immersion.

A discussion on Trine Immersion, by letter between Elder B. F. Moomaw and Dr. J. J. Jackson, to which is annexed a Treatise on the Lord's Supper, and on the necessity, character and evidences of the new birth, also a dialogue on the doctrine of non-resistance, by Elder B. F. Moomaw. Single copy 50 cents.

THE GROUNDS FOR A

FORWARD and BACKWARD

MODE OF

BAPTISM.

Briefly, yet *carefully* examined; and the TRUE and CORRECT mode so clearly set forth that none can help but understand

This little book contains 36 pages, neatly put up in paper cover. Price per doz. $1.25, add 10 cts. for postage. Two copies, 25 cts 1 copy, 15 cts., free of postage.

Address, SAMUEL KINSEY,

Mar 11-tf. Dayton, O.

Bee Books, Bee Books!

On receipt of 50 cts. I will send by mail a valuable *Bee Book* treating on over one hundred subjects. No Bee keeper should be without it. It tells just how to make bees profitable. *Italian Queen* Bees bred from imported mothers, each $3.00. Orders solicited. Address

E. J. WORST,

New Pittsburgh, Wayne co., O.

Feb 18-4t.

$5 to $20 [illegible]

THE

HOUSEHOLD TREASURE.

Containing several hundred Valuable Receipts for cooking well at a moderate expense, making Dyes, Coloring, Cleaning and Cementing. This book also points out in plain language, free from Doctors' terms the diseases of men, women and children, and the latest and most approved means used for their cure, to which is added a description of the Medicinal Roots and Herbs, and how they are to be used in the cure of diseases.

This is a work of considerable importance and we offer it to our readers as being a valuable accession to every household. Sent from this office to any address, postpaid, for 25 cents.

GOOD BOOKS.

How to read Character, illus. Price,	$1.25
Combe's Moral Philosophy,	1.75
Constitution of Man. Combe,	1.75
Education. By Spurzheim,	1.50
Memory—How to Improve it,	1.50
Mental Science, Lectures on,	1.50
Self-Culture and Perfection,	1.50
Combe's Physiology, Illus.	1.75
Food and Diet. By Pereira,	1.75
Natural Laws of Man,	.75
Hereditary Descent,	1.50
Combe on Infancy,	1.50
Sober and Temperate Life,	.50
Children in Health—Disease,	1.75
The Science of Human Life,	3.50
Fruit Culture for the Million,	1.00
Saving and Wasting,	1.50
Ways of Life—Right Way,	1.00
Footprints of Life,	1.25
Conversion of St. Paul,	1.00

BOOK AGENTS

WANTED FOR THE

GREAT INDUSTRIES

OF THE UNITED STATES;

AN HISTORICAL SUMMARY OF THE ORIGIN, GROWTH AND PERFECTION OF THE CHIEF INDUSTRIAL ARTS OF THIS COUNTRY.

1300 PAGES and 500 ENGRAVINGS.

Written by 20 Eminent Authors, including John B. Gough, Leon Case, Edward Howland, Jos. B. Lyman, Rev. E. Edwin Hall, Horace Greely, Philip Ripley, Albert Brisbane, F. B. Perkins, etc.

This work is a complete history of all branches of industry, processes of manufacture, etc., in all ages. It is a complete encyclopedia of arts and manufactures, and is the most entertaining and valuable work of information on subjects of general interest ever offered to the public. It is adapted to the wants of the Merchant, Manufacturer, Mechanic, Farmer, Student and Inventor, and sells to both old and young of all classes. The book is sold by agents, who are making large sales in all parts of the country. It is offered at the low price of $3.50, and is the cheapest book ever sold by subscription. No family should be without a copy. We want agents in every town in the United States, and no agent can fail to do well with this book. Our terms are liberal. We give our agents the exclusive right of territory. One of our agents sold 133 copies in eight days, another sold 368 in two weeks. Our agent in Hartford sold 397 in one week. Specimens of the work sent to agents on receipt of stamp. For circulars and terms to agents address the publishers.

J. B. BURR & HYDE. *Hartford, Conn., Chicago, Ill., or Cincinnati, Ohio.*

TUNE BOOK.

The Brethren's Tune and Hymn Book, is a compilation of Sacred Music adapted to all the hymns in the Brethren's New Hymn Book. It contains over 350 pages, printed on good paper and neatly bound. We will send it to any address, post paid at $1.25 per copy.

TRACTS.

"ANXIOUS BENCH RELIGION EXAMINED," BY ELDER J. S. FLORY. A SYNOPSIS OF CONTENTS. An address to the reader: The peculiarities that attend this type of religion. The feelings there experienced not imaginary but real. The key that unlocks the wonderful mystery. The causes by which feelings are excited. How the momentary feelings called "Experimental religion" are brought about, and then concludes by giving that form of doctrine as taught by Jesus Christ and recorded by his faithful witnesses.

COUNTERFEIT DETECTED

or

BAPTISM—MUCH IN LITTLE.

This work is now ready for distribution, and the importance of the subject will speak for it a large demand. It is a short treatise on baptism in tract form intended for general distribution, and is set forth in such a plain and logical manner that a wayfaring man though a fool, cannot err therein. Either of the above tracts sent postpaid on the following terms: Two copies, 10 cts, 10 copies 40 cents, 25 copies 70 cents, 50 copies $1.00, 100 copies $1.50.

Trine Immersion

TRACED

TO THE APOSTLES.

The Second Edition is now ready for delivery. The work has been carefully revised, corrected and enlarged.

Put up in a neat pamphlet form, with good paper cover, and will be sent, postpaid, on the following terms: One copy, 25 cts; Five copies, $1.10; Ten copies, $2.00. 25 copies, $4.50; 50 copies, $8.50; 100 copies, $16.00.

Address, J. H. MOORE.

Urbana, Champaign co., Ill.

Oct. 22.

DYMOND ON WAR.

An inquiry into the Accordancy of War, with the Principles of Christianity, and an examination of the Philosophical reasoning by which it is defended. With observations on some of the causes of war and on some of its effects. By Jonathan Dymond. Sent from this office, post-paid, for 50 cts.

1870 1873

DR. FAHRNEY'S

Blood Cleanser or Panacea,

A tonic and purge, for Blood Disease. Great reputation. Many testimonials. Many ministering brethren use and recommend it. Ask or send for the "Health Messenger." Use only the "*Panacea*" prepared at Chicago, Ills., and by

Dr. P. Fahrney's Brothers & Co.,

Aug. 3-pd. *Waynesboro, Franklin Co., Pa*

New Hymn Books, English.

TURKEY MOROCCO.

One copy, postpaid,	$1.00
Per Dozen,	11.25

PLAIN ARABESQUE.

One Copy, post-paid,	.75
Per Dozen, "	8.50

Ger'n & English, Plain Sheep.

One Copy, post-paid,	$1.00
Per Dozen	11.25
Arabesque Plain,	1.00
Turkey Morocco,	[illegible]
Single German, post paid	[illegible]
Per Dozen,	[illegible]

HUNTINGDON & BROAD TOP RAIL ROAD

On and after February 9th, 1873, Trains will run on this road daily (Sundays excepted) as follows:

Trains from Huntingdon South. *Trains from Mt. Dallas moving North.*

MAIL. NO. 1. A. M. P. M.	STATIONS.	MAIL. NO. 2. P. M. A. M.
LE7 40 LE	Huntingdon,	AR4 00 AR
7 45	Long Siding	3 55
8 00	McConnelstown	3 45
8 05	Pleasant Grove	3 35
8 22	Marklesburg	3 22
8 40	Coffee Run	3 07
8 45	Rough & Ready	3 00
9 00	Cove	2 58
9 05	Fishers Summit	2 15
9 15	Saxton	2 35 le
9 40	Riddlesburg	2 15
9 47	Hopewell	2 05
10 05	Piper's Run	1 50
10 25	Tatesville	1 30
10 37	Bloody Run	1 20
10 40	Mount Dallas	1 15
11 08	Bedford	12 44

G. F. GAGE, Supt

SHOUP'S RUN BRANCH

LE 9 25 LE	Saxton,	AR2 15 AR
9 40	Coalmont,	2 00
9 45	Crawford,	1 55
AR10 00 AR	Dudley	LE1 45 LE

Bro'd Top City from Dudley 3 miles by stage.

Time of Penna. R. R. Trains at Huntingdon.

***Mail No. 2 makes connection at Huntingdon with Mail going East on Pennsylvania Railroad at 4.15 p. m., and West at 5.45 p. m. Mail No. 1 leaves Huntingdon at 7.40 a. m. on arrival of Pacific Express West.

Trains on this road connect with trains on Bedford & Bridgeport, and Cumberland & Pennsylvania Railroads.

The Weekly Pilgrim.

Published by J. B. Brumbaugh, & Co.

Edited by H. B. & Geo. Brumbaugh.

CORRESPONDING EDITORS.

D. P. Sayler, Double Pipe Creek, Md.

Leonard Furry, New Enterprise, Pa.

The *Pilgrim* is a Christian Periodical, devoted to religion and moral reform. It will advocate in the spirit of *love* and *liberty*, the principles of true Christianity, labor for the promotion of peace among the people of God, for the encouragement of the saints and for the conversion of sinners, avoiding those things which tend toward disunion or sectional feelings.

TERMS.

Single copy, Book paper,	$1.60
Eleven copies, (eleventh for Agt.)	$15 00

Any number above that at the same rate.

Address,

H. B. BRUMBAUGH.

James Creek,

Huntingdon county Pa.

The Weekly Pilgrim.

"REMOVE NOT THE ANCIENT LANDMARKS WHICH OUR FATHERS HAVE SET."

VOL. 4. JAMES CREEK, PENNSYLVANIA, MARCH, 25, 1873. NO. 12

POETRY.

HOPE.

Never despair! The darkest cloud
That ever loomed will pass away,
The longest night will yield to dawn—
The dawn will kindle into day.
What if around thy lonely bark
Break fierce and high the waves of sorrow,
Stretch every oar! there's land ahead!
And thou wilt gain the port to-morrow.

When fortune frowns, and summer friends
Like birds that fear a storm, depart,
Some, if the heart hath tropic warmth,
Will stay and nestle round thy heart.
If thou art poor, no joy is won,
No good is gained by sad repining,
Gems, buried in the darkened earth,
May yet be gathered for the mining.

There is no lot however sad,
There is no roof however low,
But has some joy to make it glad,
Some latent bliss to soothe its woe.
The light of hope will linger near,
When wildest beats the heart's emotion;
A talisman when breakers roar,
A star upon the troubled ocean.

The farmer knows not if his field
With flood, or drought, or blight must cope;
He questions not the fickle skies,
But ploughs, and sows, and toils in hope.
Then up, and strive, and dare, and do,
Nor doubt a harvest you will gather;
'Tis time to labor and to wait,
And trust in God for genial weather.

ORIGINAL ESSAYS.

THE CHURCH AND DUTIES OF HER MEMBERS.—NO. 1.

I purpose, in these papers, to present to the consideration of my dear brethren and sisters a few thoughts upon the duties and obligations that necessarily devolve upon each member of the Body of Christ in their relative calling and station. First I propose to speak of the laity or private members, so called. Secondly, of the deacons. Thirdly, of the ministers in the first and second degree. Fourthly, of Elders or Bishops, and lastly, of the whole Church in a comprehensive sense as one united body. In the first place then to begin with the,

LAITY.

We would remark that those who are, by way of distinction, so classed constitute the body in the main, and the officers of the church are an outgrowth, in one sense of the word, from the same. Inasmuch as the body of each individual member, born of God, is the temple of the Holy Ghost, so the Church—body of Christ,—should be truly a holy habitation for the indwelling of the Divine light and life. As the ocean is made up of drops of water, so the Church is composed of individual members. If all the drops of water that fall into a reservoir be pure, the whole body of water will be pure. On the other hand, just in proportion to the impure drops that fall in, in the same proportion will the body be impure. So with the Church, the purity of the same depends upon the individual members that compose the body. Just in proportion to the number of working members there are in the Church, in that proportion the body will be an active working body. There are degrees in life and activity. One man may be alive and capable of action to some extent, but because of diseased and crippled members of his body he can barely breathe, and his action is sluggish, and in that condition he can accomplish little or nothing. Another has more of the vitalizing principles of life, his members but little injured by disease, such a one may go forth and brave the dangers of life,—bring any energy into play—and in the end accomplish much. Just so with the Church. If every member of the body is alive and healthy, much may be accomplished, otherwise, if the members are sluggish and sin-diseased, but little will be accomplished in the conversion of the world. What is true in this relation of the whole Church, is true of local churches or congregations. When the vital principles of "pure and undefiled religion" predominate over everything else in the members, the body will be a "light to the world and salt to the earth," but if the light be darkness, great is the darkness indeed. If the salt lose its savor, how shall the earth be salted—how the world be saved from the corrupting influence of sin? Enough has been said, we hope, to show to every reflecting mind that each and every member of the Church has weighty duties to perform, and the obligations resting upon them are of no little moment. Sometimes we come across members who live and act as though nothing more was required of them than to retain their membership in the Church. Being a member of the Church seems to be the height of their ambition. The essence of their religion seems to be wrapped up in "I am a professor," independent of the duties and obligations that devolve upon a *possessor* of pure religious principles. They live as though nothing was required of them other than what tends to their own individual interest.

Peter in his first epistle says; "Laying aside all malice and all guile, and hypocrisies and envies, and all evil speaking, as new born babes, desire the sincere milk of the word, that ye may grow thereby, if so be ye have tasted that the Lord is gracious. To whom coming as unto a living stone, * * ye also, as lively stones, are built up a spiritual house, a holy priesthood, to offer up spiritual sacrifice, acceptable to God by Jesus Christ."

Believers coming to Christ, come as to a "living stone" and receiving His spirit, they become as "lively stones" working together in love, that the Church may be a "spiritual house," full of life, zeal and activity. A "holy priesthood"— a "peculiar people" such as are acceptable to God —are truly His people. Believe it then individual member, although you belong to the laity, as a member of the organization to which you belong, you are duty bound to labor, with the rest in the common salvation. Think not that because you are a member in a private capacity, you are exempt from duty such as tends to the building up of Zion. Who in the armies of the living God in ancient days were instrumental, in the hands of God, of bringing about victory? We answer, in a great measure, it was the [illegible]. The captains gave [illegible] hopes of success lay in the courage and demeanor of their private soldiers. With drawn weapons of warfare they pursued the enemy close and strong and victory perched upon their banners. So it is with the armies of God's people. The Captain of our salvation may command, the officers of the Church herald the orders but success depends, in a great measure, upon the *valor* and *conduct* of the "private" soldiers of the cross. "What can or what must the private soldier do may be asked? The answer is, "do what you can," obey the orders of your Captain,—the Lord Jesus Christ. You may live isolated from the body of the congregation to which you belong, yet you have no right to be "off duty." You have a desire for your neighbors to be enlisted in company with you. Occasionally the truth is preached, but the desired effect is not produced. Is there not a cause? Look to it brother or sister, and see if the cause is not in the fact you have not on the "whole armor of God" therefore the enemy shifts you along in the popular current. When your neighbor jests in an unbelieving manner, you may encourage the same by a manner of levity, or perhaps put in a word to help along, when a silent, grave look of reproof might have gone home to his heart. Or when your neighbor "drinks" you *drink*, just in a sociable way you know! Or when he talks politics and of worldly things, generally you seem to be a fit companion for him. Can you wonder when the truth you profess is preached it falls [illegible] on your neighbor's heart. The truth may be preached with power, but if there is not a favorable expression from those who profess to be [illegible] to the truth, the preacher's word [illegible] often a dead upon the hearers. Neighbors go on groping in darkness because there is little or no light in the life of the professor, souls are [illegible] ing and [illegible] his very eye [illegible] a lack of savor in the salt.

We take another case by [illegible] illustration. One may feel living apart from church facilities, but in that loneliness the child of God feels God is nigh, that His eye is upon them, and His ear ready to hear the cries of His children. Only a private member, yet they feel the obligations resting upon them as professors of the holy religion of Jesus. Having on the whole armor of God they live out what they profess, not only the name "professor" is written on their "breast-plate" but also "holiness to the Lord." With meek and lowly heart, chaste conversation and godly conduct, their life is a light for their neighbor, and their walk "a savor of life unto life." When the word is preached, the hearers see a beautiful expression of the Truth in the professor's daily walk, so that others fall in love with true religion and the "lone star" soon has others of a kindred nature within the circle and bonds of the Kingdom of Heaven." The isolated member that has the cause truly at heart is not slow to subscribe to one or more of the Church periodicals, and after reading them lends them to his neighbors, an interest is gotten up, religious subjects are often talked of. The isolated grain of "salt" is at work, both openly and in secret prayer, so that the cause is made to prosper and souls to rejoice in the truth as it is in Jesus.

We now turn to the laity that live in close proximity one to another, and under the influence of the congregation in general. Here sometimes members may be found that live seemingly careless of their duties and obligations, as much as to say, "Let others attend to the matters that belong to the church, I am only a private member,—don't matter what I do, just so I am careful enough to escape censure from the church, or come up to the standard of this or that brother or sister's general religious character." Awake from that dream dear soul and remember there are no blessed promises to the "drones" or nominal professors. You must be one of the "lively stones" or you may never fit into the Heavenly house of habitation. Duty demands you help bear one anothers burdens. You may claim you can stay at home from public worship and do just as much good reading your Bible. That expression has no wider range than your own individual interest or ease. How will it be with the brother who has to bear the heavy cross of preaching the Word when he finds your seat empty? Will he be encouraged? How can he speak fervently of the blessedness of the religion of Jesus, when he remembers those of his flock are seemingly so indifferent? And how about those neighbors of yours, think they will fall in love with that religion you seem to care so little about? Will they go out to hear that one preach or to that house of worship that you do not seem to care enough about to go to any trouble to get there? And again remember many diseases are contagious. The evil of neglecting to attend religious worship or council meetings is of a contagious nature. One member stays at home, then another follows suit, and so the influence spreads the evil, until a coldness—something like a *death chill*—comes over the Church. The discouraged ministers go through with the form of worship,—do the best they can probably, but under the circumstances their best accomplishes but little. But now we turn to the subject under more favorable circumstances. Suppose every member feels the obligations of their calling—have an earnest zeal for their Master's cause, and goes to work with a will. First, set a watch over their own hearts and have kindled within their soul a love for the welfare of others, especially those of the household of faith. Keep love burning through the medium of private prayer. When the day for going to public worship comes they *hunt* not for excuses to stay at home—will brave the storm for the sake of Jesus and the duty they owe to God. The ministers heart is gladdened to see them in their seat—their earnestness has influenced others out. Duty demands the members should pray for their preacher as well as others—it is the house of prayer. God is there—the Holy Spirit is there—Jesus in the love and pleadings of His sublime words is there—sinners tremble and turn to God,—saints are "built up." In the outpourings of God's love, grace and mercy "Holy Manna is showered all around." A consummation so glorious that we may even "walk in Heavenly places in Christ Jesus" here can not be brought about without a hearty coöperation of the private members of the Church. Seeing then that it is within your power, through the mercy of God, to enliven the Church and keep burning upon her altar the fire of a Savior's love, watch and pray lest your individual indifference bring the Church into a cold or luke-warm state. In council meetings let any one that can, be out on duty and help cast out Satan if he has found foothold anywhere. "Know no man after the flesh,"—let all things be done with an eye single to the glory of God and welfare of Zion. If the body is healthy and full of love and life, a diseased member, though it be *the head*, may be brought to a healthy state of action. In pecuniary matters you have no right to say "I have begotten my money and it is mine to do as I will." You are the *Lord's* steward, be careful then that you waste not His money upon your lust, when the cause demands it, give as the Lord has prospered you, not grudgingly but cheerfully. It is a true adage, "If the able horse will not pull, the willing one must, able or not able." If the rich hold a closed hand on the *dollars*, the poor must open and give the *dimes*, or the cause will suffer. In short remember the duties and obligations of the lay members are such that a failure on their part will clog the wheels of the car of salvation, and make the gospel a stumbling block to the world. But a strict compliance with their duties will give such an impetus to the ark of the Lord as to cause her to outride the breakers of persecution,—induce thousands to enter and sail for the harbor of rest. Up, up, then, and to work dear brethren and sisters,—on with the whole armor of God. Keep the sword unsheathed—be not content with the uniform alone, but pray for courage and strength that you may acquit yourselves as becometh valiant soldiers of the cross,—fighting under that Banner that always leads to victory.

J. S. FLORY.

THE BAPTISM OF JOHN. WHENCE WAS IT, FROM HEAVEN OR OF MEN?

B. F. MOOMAW.

Having now considered the authority upon which the foregoing institutions are based, and as we think fully sustained the position in which we embarked in this investigation, that for everything that God designed that his intelligent creatures should observe and do, he has signified it to them in language clear and unmistakable, and impressed it by his own illustrious example.

In the next place, we propose to show, that our prerogatives are limited and circumscribed by this charter. He being wise enough to devise his own means for the accomplishment of his purposes, and just in requiring that his authority should be respected, and mighty to avenge himself upon those who shall take from, add to, substitute for, modify or amend them, they having been pre-arranged in the councils of Heaven. "Where is the wise, where is the scribe, where is the disputer of this world? Hath not God made foolish the wisdom of this world?" For after that in the wisdom of God, the world by wisdom knew not God, it pleased God by the foolishness of preaching to save them that believed." 1 Cor. 1: 20, 21. "Oh, the depth of the riches both of the wisdom and knowledge of God, how unreasonable are his judgments and his ways past finding out. For who hath known the mind of the Lord, or who hath been his counsellor? Rom.—11: 33, 34.

As a suitable commentary upon this subject I quote from Goulburn's Personal Religion, chap. 10, page 158. "It would be well in considering the various ordinances of Religion we began by narrowly examining their charter, as it exists in God's Holy Word. How shall we ascertain their true character? How shall we know what we may expect from them, and what we may not expect? How, in short, shall we secure ourselves against a false estimate of them, otherwise than by looking into their original constitution? The exact limits of a patent or prerogative granted by the government of a country to any individual, can only be ascertained by consulting the terms of the patent. Let the holder abstract from the public records, and hide away the parchment on which those terms are written, and there are then no powers which he may not assume, on the general vague representation that the patent is his."

In the absence of a proper regard to the principle involved in this general idea, what has the religious world not assumed in all ages from Adam in Eden, to the present day. The adversary is not wanting in ingenuity nor argument to install insiduously into the human mind an infusion of unbelief, if not successful in the first effort, to induce the final and fatal step, as in the case of our progenitors in the garden, yet step by step he proceeds to final success, as in the case of ancient Israel; the commands of God, as revealed in his charter, are superceded by traditions which are of men. This truth is so fully delineated in the Bible that to undertake elucidation of it would appear to be a work of supererogation. Nothing more is necessary than a reference to the history as given in the Bible of that age of the world, as to the conduct of those then living, their final, terrible overthrow and destruction, because of their disregard of the terms of their charter, and the assumption of prerogatives not awarded them. And yet while these facts are fully sustained it must be admitted that those unfortunates are entitled to some respect for honesty of purpose, and purity of motives, or at least for the plausibility of their pretentions; but erred in supposing that the Lord would be pleased and his name glorified by the introduction of *helps* of their own invention outside of the limits of their charter "upon the vague representation that the paint was theirs," which however was offensive to God and visited by his deep displeasure and awful retribution, as exemplified in the circumstance of King Saul. See 1 Sam. 15th chapter. The Lord commanded Saul to go and destroy the Amelekites, to fight against them until they were utterly consumed, but he kept the king of Amalek, Agag, alive, and permitted the people to take the best of the flocks and of the herds to offer an unauthorized offering at Gilgal; and yet he, as it appears, was honestly under the impression, that he had obeyed the voice of the Lord, see his declaration in the chapter above referred to 20th verse, and was not sensible of his mistake, until too late to make amends, until he had lost his crown, then he was awakened to the fact that it was not "from Heaven but of men." He then confessed that he had sinned, having transgressed the commandment of God, and obeyed the voice of the *people*, ver. 24. Please indulge our departure at this point, that we may criticise Saul's apology. "he feared the people and obeyed their voice." He, the king of Israel by divine appointment, in the exercise of Royal powers, and feared the people. How is this? Did he fear that they would assassinate him or inflict any personal injury upon him? Certainly not for we have no intimation whatever that his people were mutinous or rebellious. We opine that he simply feared the opposition of sentiment, and that thereby he would risk the loss of popular applause, and his shares of the honors of the gratuitous offering at Gilgal. Here is the weakness of our nature, desiring to be like other associations by which we are surrounded, like the Elders and people of ancient Israel, though faithfully forewarned by the Lord, through his servant Samuel of the consequence of rejecting him, determined to have a king over them, that they might also be like all the nations and that their king might judge them and go before them and fight their battles." 1 Sam.—10: 19, 20.

Again, "when ye come to appear before me" saith the Lord "who hath required this at your hands, to tread courts, bring no more vain oblations, incense is an abomination unto me, your new moons and appointed feasts my soul hateth, they are a trouble unto me, I am weary to bear them." Isa.—1: 12, 14; Jer.—7: 22, 23; Hos.—6: 6, 7; Mic.—6: 6-8.

Thus it has ever been with the children of men, social in our nature, we yield to popular influence, and step by step move along assimilating ourselves more and more with our surroundings, almost unconsciously until becoming *like them*, and first to one thing, and then another, accept their ideas, adopt their ways and means, without properly considering "from whence it is, from Heaven or of men," justifying ourselves in the conclusion that the end justifies the means, and so introduce the measures resorted to by our neighboring associations in the use of which they have succeeded in the accession of numbers, In proportion as we have departed from the usages divinely authorized, we notice a departure from the narrow path of humility and self-denial. We may use these human instrumentalities cautiously at first, and whilst under the control of those who first adopt them, they may be and are likely to be so guarded, as not to produce very mischievious results, but passing into second hands, and so on, the departure becomes wider and wider, until we get in the broad way with those popular associations, that have one after another respectively been lost in the broad sea of popular Christianity. We have a very striking example of this truth in the history of what is known as the reformation of the nineteenth century. When that reformation was first introduced, its advocates sternly and steadily objected to all extraordinary means, such as the mourner's bench, promiscuous singing and praying, rubbing the hands, &c., by which undue excitement and illegitimate conversions were produced, contending that the word preached, was the only instrument by which genuine conversions were produced; but now, even at this early day, while so far as is known to me, the successors have not introduced the bench, I venture the assertion, that they have adopted so many of those practices, and devised others in the use of which, they excel in producing excitement and premature conversions. The principle that we in this communication have aimed to establish is, that institutions having the sanction of divine authority, will be, and these alone, in the final day, approved by the commander in chief, the command having been issued by him, and delivered to the sons and daughters of men; the reverencing him, and respecting his authority "obey from the heart" is reported back. The Lord, the head of department recognizes, and approves *his own* work, pronounces the welcome plaudit, "well done thou good and faithful servant enter into the joy of thy Lord." Whereas on the other hand, if we shall add to, or take from the prophecies of *the Book*, the plagues shall be added that are threatened, and our part taken out of the Book of Life and out of the Holy City, and from the things which are written in the book.

To be continued.

God's Love.—It is the bright sun behind the cloud that gives it the silver lining and golden edging, so it is the genial rays of God's love that causeth us to see, by an eye of faith joy in tribulation, hope in adversity and in the darkest hour of trial a smiling Jesus bidding us "Be not afraid." [illegible]

CORRECTION.

In the Pilgrim of March 11, No. 10, page 73, Bro. Moomaw says: "Thus we see in the divine command for this feast we have the verb *shall* used in the imperative mood seventeen times." Shall, in all the instances mentioned, is an auxillary of the indicative mood, first future tense. For the benefit of writers we will here say that the indicative mood indicates or declares a thing, or asks a question; while the imperative mood commands, exhorts, entreats or permits, and must always be from a speaker to a second person addressed. In the article referred to, the speaker is the Lord, and the persons addressed are Moses and Aaron. After some preliminaries, the Lord says to them "Speak ye unto all the congregation of Israel." The verb speak in this sentence is in the imperative mood, while the verbs "shall take, shall be, &c.," in the following sentences are declarations of what the people of Israel are to observe. In the Commission we have "Go and teach" in the imperative mood. The Savior speaking and the disciples spoken to.

We considered it our duty to make this correction, lest some designing reader might censure the author unjustly. It does not destroy the sense and force of his article in the least, for all know that "shall" represents a duty to be performed.

S. B. Furry.

Martinsburg, Pa.

Remarks.—Of many of the sciences it is said, they are stubborn facts, but of grammar not so, as there are more exceptions embodied in it than there are rules. We do not wish to undervalue Bro. Furry's knowledge of grammar as in the main he is certainly right, but at the same time, we are not willing to admit that Bro. Moomaw is altogether wrong. In all such cases we make grammar succumb to the force of language and circumstances, and justify our course in the exceptions. In the *indicative mood* we have facts. The *subjunctive* implies a doubt or supposition, and in the *potential mood* we have possibility expressed, but in the *imperative* there is *command*. Imperative is from the Latin *imperativus* and expresses positive command, hence any word or sentence that expresses a command, we call it in the *imperative mood*. The word under consideration in Bro. Moomaw's article, though somewhat mixed in person, in every instance express a positive command, therefore call it an auxillary, if you please, and [illegible] it in the *imperative mood* [illegible] shall in the instances [illegible] expresses a command. Imperative means to command and mood means manner, he then spoke in a commanding manner.

Again. Our author or grammar says; "When *shall* is used in the sense of *must* it belongs rather to the *potential mood* and when emphasized, to the imperative." In Webster we have; "If the auxillary (shall) be emphasized the command is made *more imperative*, more positive. If emphasizing makes it *more* imperative it certainly must be imperative in its most ordinary sense.

Again. In the case of the laws being delivered to the people, Moses was simply God's mouth-piece by which he delivered His messages to the people and in reality, spoke directly to the people, hence in the present tense and second person. In analyzing the sentence, "Your lamb *shall* be without blemish * * ye *shall* take it out from the sheep," &c., the pronouns, you and ye certainly do not refer to Moses and Aaron alone, but to the whole congregation of Israel. This certainly strengthens the position that shall may be in the *imperative mood* and until Bro. Furry shows us that the word *shall* in the case referred to does *not* express a positive command we shall hold to our position although we admit that he has the weight of authors on his side.

HOW TO OPPOSE FEET-WASHING.

I am not much in favor of committing sermons to memory, but I presume that if all those who have a desire to oppose Feet-washing upon *gospel grounds*, would commit the 13th chapter of John to memory, and then preach that, and nothing else on the subject, that no one on earth would ever become convinced that Feet-washing is a non-essential.

I have heard and read many sermons on Feet-washing, but would not give the sermon that Jesus preached on the subject for a million of such.

When you preach your next sermon on this subject, please say what Jesus said. When you oppose Feet-washing, say what your Master said nothing more. When people ask your opinion on this commandment, say what Jesus did. At the close of every argument introduced against Feet-washing, stop just one moment and give Jesus time to say "Y[illegible] ought to wash one another's feet," and I'll run the risk of you convincing the people that Feet-washing is unnecessary.

J. H. A.

[illegible]

WHEREVER you are, dear friend, though you must be in the world, take care that you be not of it. "Come ye out from among them; be ye separate, saith the Lord, touch not the unclean thing, and I will receive you, and will be a Father unto you, and ye shall be my sons and daughters, saith the Lord Almighty." It is only in the lonely path of the true disciple of Christ, who follows the Lamb whithersoever he goeth, that you can realize your adoption, and cry, Abba, Father. Come out from the world; confess yourself to be on the Lord's side, and then your fellowship with God shall be sweet beyond degree! Range yourself under the divine banner and by God's grace remain a separatist from the world until life's latest hour. So shall you, like Abraham, be a sojourner with God. "Dwell deep, O inhabitants of Dedan," right away from the world's customs and sins, and above all, from its selfish spirit and grovelling aims! Dwell deep in the solitudes where Jesus dwelt—in the lonely holiness which was fostered on the cold mountain's side, and then shone resplendant amid temptation and persecution! Commit yourself unto no man; call no man master; lean on no arm of flesh; walk before the Lord in the land of the living, and so dwell deep, as did your Lord.—*Spurgeon.*

THE dark cloud may hover over us, but the cross of Christ will be the lightning-rod that will take the bolt out of it. You have seen people invalids, and after a while, under some tremendous stroke of disease, their entire temperament seemed to be changed, and they come out of that sudden sickness strong men. So it is with many of those who are going along invalids in the Christian life, very weak in the service of God. After they have passed through some great disaster—that disaster having been sanctified to their souls—they become strong men in Christ Jesus. These Christians who are swarthy now—do you know how they got their swarthiness? It was by sweltering at the forge of affliction. Their battle-axe was dull enough until it was sharpened on a gravestone.—*Talmage.*

PRAYER is a haven to the shipwrecked mariner, an anchor to them that are sinking in the waves, a staff to the limbs that totter, a mine of jewels to the poor, a security to the rich, a healer of diseases, and a guardian of health. Prayer at once secures the continuance of our blessings, and dissipates the cloud of our calamities. O blessed prayer! thou art the unwearied conqueror of human woes, the firm foundation of human happiness, the source of ever-enduring joy, the mother of philosophy. The man who can pray truly, though languishing in the extremest indigence, is richer than all beside; whilst the wretch who never bowed the knee, though proudly seated as monarch of nations, is of all men most destitute. —*Chrysostom.*

HEAVEN and earth, with all castles of kings and emperors, could not make a dwelling-place for God, but in the man that keeps his word there he will dwell.

Isaiah calls the heavens his throne and the earth his footstool, but not his abode. We may search long to find where God is, but we shall find him in those who hear the words of Christ.

For the Lord Christ saith, "If any man love me, he will keep my words, and we will make our abode with him."—*Luther.*

WHEN the heart of man is bound up by the grace of God, and tied in golden bands, and watched by angels, tended by those nurse-keepers of the soul, it is not easy for a man to wander; and the evil of his heart is but like the ferity and wildness of lions' whelps. But when once we have broken the hedge, and got into the strengths of youth, and the licentiousness of an ungoverned age, it is wonderful to observe what a great inundation of mischief in a very short time will overflow all the banks of reason and religion.—*Jeremy Taylor.*

THERE is no receiving of Christ to dwell and live with us, unless we turn all other guests out of doors. The devil, you know, would not take possession of a house till it was swept and garnished; and dares any man imagine that a heart defiled, full of all uncleanness, a decayed ruinous soul, an earthly sensual mind, is a tabernacle fit to entertain the Son of God? Were it reasonable to invite Christ to sup in such a mansion, much more to rest and inhabit there? *Chillingworth.*

WHEN the church is cold and dead, those hymns which were written by God's saints, in moments of rapture, seem extravagant, and we walk over them on dainty footsteps of taste, but let God's Spirit come down upon our hearts, and they are as sweetness on our tongues; nay, all too poor and meagre for our emotions, for feeling is always tropical, and seeks the most intense and fervid expression.—*Beecher.*

THE whole world is full of miracles, but our eyes must be pure, lest, because they are so common to us, they become dim.—*Luther.*

HEIRS OF GOD.

The Christian cannot realize in this world what a glorious privilege it is to be an heir with God and a joint heir with Christ. Those who expect to inherit an earthly fortune, do not mind so much the privations of their present lot. But the poorest child of God is heir to an inheritance, beside which the wealth of this world is as nothing. Although we generally look at this inheritance as lying beyond the vale, yet we may claim the priviliges of an heir. If adverse winds blow, and the waves of sorrow rise high about us, we may rest assured it is because we are beloved children of God that we are thus afflicted. Even if poverty and want become our portion, we need not despair, for our Father hath taught us to ask him for our daily bread, and he has enough and to spare; all the resources of the earth are at his disposal; so if we, like dutiful children, do the work laid to our hands, trusting in him, we may claim the promises of future good.

We may gather something of the exceeding glory of our inheritance, when we reflect that Christ with whom we are joint-heirs, "shall have dominion from sea to sea;" that one day the kingdoms of this world shall become the kingdom of our Lord, and he shall reign forever and ever. A mansion in the heavenly city, far more beautiful than any palace of earth, an unfading crown of life, and a kingdom that shall never end; what a glorious prospect is this, and how it should daily cheer and animate the believer's heart.—*The Christian.*

Religious News.

REV. F. B. HUDSON, pastor of the Methodist Church, at Lyons, N. Y., was stricken by paralysis while preaching in his pulpit on Sunday morning, March 2nd. A local paper in giving the particulars, states that he had read about half his discourse—his voice as firm and distinct as on previous occasions. Suddenly he stopped, and requested that a window be let down to admit fresh air. For a moment he stood pressing his hands to his forehead, and leaning forward to the desk; then, as if rallying all his strength for the effort, he began again, and uttered the words of his sermon—"These days are passing away," and as the last syllable left his lips he sank back on the sofa insensible. He was taken to his residence, and died in the evening.

AN OLD CHURCH.—"Old Donegal Church" in Pa., was founded in 1722. It still exists, but is very feeble, being in the midst of a community composed almost entirely of Mennonites, and being also only about three miles from the towns of Marietta and Mt. Joy. The Church received a large grant of land from the Penn family, and has now a fund of $8,000, and has regular preaching most of the year in connection with the Mt. Joy Church. The graveyard connected with this Church is an object of considerable interest, some of the inscriptions on the tombstones dating back one hundred and forty years, and some graves without any mark, being even older.

THE PRESBYTERIANS.—The Free Church of Scotland has a congregation in Rome, and for many years the Established Church of Scotland has also had a congregation there during the winter months. The two congregations are now to meet as one. The Rev. Dr. Macgregor, of the Established Church, in Edinburgh has agreed to visit Rome in order to take a term of the Sabbath services.

TEMPERANCE LEGISLATION.—The Indianapolis *Sentinel* says: "The temperance movement which has just ended—or just begun in this State, by the passage of the bill in the Legislature—seems to be a part of a tidal wave, so to speak, that at present is surging through the Mississippi Valley. In the house of the Minnesota Legislature a bill has passed, and is now hanging tremblingly around the doors of the Senate, to become a law, which in effect is similar to that of Indiana. It puts the power of license in the hands of the community; puts the cost of the license from $50 to $300; provides that every seller of liquors shall give a bond in the sum of $1,000 to $3,000, with two or more sureties not to sell liquor on Sunday, nor sell to any minor or habitual drunkard, and to pay all damages that may result."

CRUSHED BY A FALSE ALARM.—While Rev. Mr. Talmage's congregation was at worship on Sunday night the 2nd inst., in Brooklyn, in the Academy of Music, the cry of fire was raised, and in the consternation following several persons were badly crushed.

The Episcopalians have a theological school in Colorado established by Bishop Randall. The building was erected by a munificent layman of Boston, Nathan Mathews, Esq.

The African Methodist Church of South Carolina held its annual Conference at Georgetown recently. It claims to have 170 preachers 48,000 members.

A Roman Catholic Cathedral is to be erected in Hartford at a cost of $400,000.

Youth's Department

BIRTH OF OUR SAVIOR.

SELECTED BY HETTIE L. MOHLER

How much better I'm attended,
Than the Son of God could be;
When from Heaven He descended,
And became a child like me.
Soft and easy was my cradle,
Coarse and hard my Savior lay;
When His birth place was a stable
And his softest bed was hay.

Lo! He slumbers in a manger,
Where the horned oxen fed;
Cold the air and full of danger,
Whistling by His blessed head.
See the kinder shepherds round him,
Telling wonders from the sky;
Where they sought Him, there they found Him,
With His virgin mother by.

From the East the wise men pressing,
In their arms rich jewels bring;
To receive the precious blessing,
Of their long expected King
Yet to read the shameful story,
How the Jews abused their King;
How they served the Lord of glory,
Makes me angry while I sing.

'Twas to save us all from dying,
Save us all from burning flames;
Bitter groans and endless cryings,
That our blest Redeemer came.
May we learn to know and fear Him,
Love and serve Him all our days;
Then go dwell forever near Him,
Seek His face and sing His praise

A FEW WORDS TO THE CHILDREN.

Children, have you all homes and kind parents? I presume not. I well remember when my two brothers and three sisters and I formed a family of children with our kind parents, but death has taken the mother, two brothers and one sister, and whose turn will come next God only knows. Do you love your parents? God tells you to love them. Do you obey them and honor them? It is God's will that you should. When you attend school do you try to learn, so you can read God's word and learn of His wisdom? What beauties are contained therein! Be active, enquiring and you can learn who created all things. If you have homes, try to be kind one to another, to father, mother, sister, brother and all, for in Heaven there is no quarreling, no disputing, no bad names called, no lying, no stealing, swearing nor tattling.

So if you wish to get there you must be good children, and not abuse one another. When meeting strangers, speak kindly and make no sport or fun of any lameness, or cripples, but feel sorry for their condition and help them all you can, for if you can not be kind to such here, what would you think of meeting them in Heaven? Those of you who have no settled earthly home, which was my lot when young, perhaps you feel the want of it, but then there is a home prepared in Heaven for all good children. There is no sickness, pain, death, nor sorrow, neither want, all will be happy. What a pleasant sight to see a company of children all enjoying each others society in peace. It makes glad fathers, mothers, sisters and brothers, and is the admiration of visitors.

Do not hurt your playmates. "Do as you wish to be done by;" live in peace: thank God for all His blessings, such as food, clothes, health and strength, kind parents, and all good things. Speak the truth, and if we never meet on earth, if we are good and kind we may above. Good-bye for the present.

W. SADLER.

Nankin, Ohio.

THINKING.

There is hardly a fault which the young are more generally blamed for than thoughtlessness. It is natural for boys and girls, being unused to thinking for themselves, and acting on impulse, as they always do, to forget or leave undone things which ought to be attended to. This ought not to be, however. We should have our wits about us at all times.

How often we hear the reply, "I didn't think," or "I forgot." How easily, by a moment's deliberation, might that "I didn't think" have been changed to an "I did think."

Thoughtfulness is an indispensible element of character, and no one can secure the confidence of those about him until he learns to practice thinking. Learning to think is a part of the education of the young, and it is as essential to their full development as any other branch of study. A man without his thoughts about him is like a ship without a rudder—drifting about where the winds send it, just as he is drifted about and driven by impulse to do that which after a moment's care he would have refrained from doing.

Thinking has accomplished much, for everything in the way of improvement requires its exercise. It is only by deep, concentrated thought that so many great ends are accomplished by man. When Sir Isaac Newton was asked how he made so many discoveries, he replied; "By thinking." Now, boys and girls, though it is a natural characteristic of you to be thoughtless and impulsive, still, we should endeavor to throw off this careless way of doing, and cultivate a thoughtful character; for our success in life depends upon this one thing.—*Young Folks Rural.*

SERMON TO THE BOYS.—Boys, did you ever think that this world, with all its [illegible] and mountains, oceans, seas and rivers; with all its steamboats, railroads and telegraphs; with all its millions of grouping men, and all the science and progress of ages, will soon be given over to the boys of the present age—boys like you. Believe it, and look abroad on your inheritance, and get ready to enter upon its possession. The presidents, emperors, kings, governors, statesmen philosophers, ministers, teachers, men of the future, all are boys now.—*Young Folks Rural.*

Correspondence.

Dear Pilgrim:—As I am in receipt of many letters from the brethren and friends in the Atlantic States North and South, East and West, making inquiries about our country here in the far West, or Pacific slope, I thought it good to answer some of them through the PILGRIM, provided its Editors will publish the same.

We reside in the North-west portion of Oregon, in the Willamatte Valley, said to be about 130 miles in length, north and south, and about 40 miles in width east and west, with the Willamatte River—navigable for Steam Boats a portion of the year—running through its entire length. Also the Oregon and California Rail road passing through near the center of the Valley. This Valley in many things, reminds me very much of the Shenandoah Valley in the State of Virginia. We have some very good soil, some very poor, some level land, some a very nice rolling elevation, and some very hilly. Our good soil is well adapted to the raising of Fall and Spring wheat, rye, oats, barley, tame grass and vegetables, provided the land is well cultivated, but we cannot raise corn, cane, sweet potatoes, successfully, our nights in Summer are too cool and Summers too dry, yet they raise some of each. We have a very good fruit country, excellent water, clear, cool and soft, and very good water-power for machinery. In portions of the Valley springs are tolerably plenty. Our mountains are covered with timber, such as fir, pine, white cedar, hemlock, &c. Our Valley has some of the above kinds, with white oak, maple, balm, alder. Notwithstanding we are in a Northern latitude we have a very mild climate; true, our winters are very rainy, but not cold. This has been a very mild winter. The winds in Winter are generally from the South, and in Summer generally from the North, very pure air, can see an object a great distance when the day is fair. Our Summers are very pleasant indeed. Land rates here from 8 to 40 dollars an acre, owing to improvements, locality, soil, &c. Near Salem, our county seat, which is also the capital of the State, land is as high as $100,00 per acre, no Government lands or very little. We think we have a healthy country, yet along the large streams it is somewhat unhealthy. We have advantages and disadvantages, some things we like very well, and there are other things we do not like. It is no paradise, far from it, yet upon the whole we think we have the making of a very good country.

Now as regards spiritual affairs, the good Lord is here and is as near and as dear to His children as anywhere, and we can serve Him as well here as in the East, and we think if we live faithful, and the Lord will help, the good work will prosper here. True, we are very few in number, and very much scattered, yet there seems to be a good feeling among the brethren generally. Truly the harvest is great but the laborers are very few. Think of us dear brethren in the East, and when it goes well with you, pray for us. To those of my correspondents who have made inquiries about Oregon, I have given you some of my views about this Valley, and we would be very glad if you would move to this country, settle down among us and help to build up the Church and our country, provided you would like this country. My expenses on the emigrant train from Omaha Neb., to San Francisco Cal., was $50,00 a passenger; from San Francisco to Portland, Oregon on the steamer Steerage, passage $15 in gold, and from Portland to Turner Station, our nearest Railroad station, about eleven miles west of us cost $3,00, making $98 a passenger from Omaha Nebraska to Turner Oregon, boarding and other expenses not counted. This is the cheapest way that I know of to come from the Atlantic States to this part of Oregon. Those who prefer can come on the express train, first class cars, from Omaha to San Francisco for $100,00 a passenger, thence to Portland on the Steamer Calvin, passage $30,00 in gold. Thence to Turner $3 00, or from San Francisco or Sacramento, Cal., to Turner, Salem, or Portland, by overland Railroad and stage, fares from 50 to $90,00 a passenger. The distance to stage about 300 miles.

Now in conclusion, let me say I have given some of my views of this country. Others may come and look at it in a different light, have different views, therefore I can not tell how others might view it. I might say much more about the advantages of Oregon, but let this suffice. For further particulars let the brethren and friends write to me.

DAVID BROWER.

[illegible], Marion Co., Oregon.

I started with brother David Clapper from Hopewell Congregation, February 27th, lodged that night with brother Isaac Ritchy next day we went to Shiling Hill Valley, dined with brother [illegible] Dishong, and then went to brother Alpheus Melott's, as as they expected we would come from. [illegible] that day the roads being badly drifted, though our arrival would likely [illegible] for an appointment. The next day March the 1, had two meetings in the Morgan Schoolhouse, one at 11 A. M., and in the evening. Next day, being Sunday, we we [illegible] Daniel Lake's, had two meetings with crowded houses and good attention. Two persons desired to be received into the Church. An occurrence took place just at the commencement of the evening services, which caused some excitement and stopped our proceedings a few moments. A widow woman being sick and by the powerful conviction she was brought under, was thrown into spasms, but quiet being restored we proceeded. After meeting she wished to be received, but her son and daughter opposed, and we thought it advisable in the condition she then was in, not to be too hasty; we advised her to wait till her mind was more composed, but to be careful then not to put it off for a more convenient season, which we hope she will do, as we understand her children are not opposed provided she is in a proper condition, they being friends of the Brethren.

March 2nd. had preaching in Cross Road School House at 11 A. M., and also in the evening; lodged with Br. Jonas Melott, where we stayed three nights. This family made us very comfortable, and we felt at home. Next day we had two meetings at Castner's S. H., but a sale being near by, the day meeting was small. We felt discouraged and wanted to recall the evening meeting, but those present would not suffer it; hence we went to friend — Simpson's, three miles distant for dinner, as we could do no better; no other invitations were given. We were kindly received and had a pleasant friendly interview on Scriptural topics, chiefly on church discipline and ordinances. They seem not far from the Kingdom of God; they invited us to have meeting there the next time we came and bid us God speed in the noble work in which we were engaged. That evening we had a crowded house, good attention and we hope good impressions were made; had an invitation to stay all night near, but as Bro. Jac. Myers from Millstone Point met us here he preferred to go home after meeting five miles distant. So we went along it being moonlight but cold. Stayed all night and the next night also. Bro. Myers is a deacon in that branch of the Church which is under the oversight of Bro. Christian Keefer of the Welsh Run district. The brethren built a comfortable Meeting house here some years ago, called Bark Cabin. Here we had meeting at 10 A. M. and in the evening; had very interesting meetings. This is what they call Little Cove, about five or six miles below Hancock, Washington Co. Md. The members seem to be alive to their interest in Christ. In the afternoon we were called to see an afflicted and aged brother, John Miller, who desired to be anointed with oil in the name of the Lord, (James 5th chapt.) which was performed through faith in the fear of the Lord. In the evening after meeting had an applicant for baptism.

March 7th went back to Cross Road S. H. and as it was sixteen miles distant we had meeting only in the evening. Another applicant for baptism but not for immediate admission. House crowded and good attention. Next day went to friend Caleb Winks at Licking Creek. Had meeting at 10 A. M. and in the evening in his house. As many could not get in, there was some disorder outside among the children of Belial in the evening. This is the only place that we observed any notable disorder in all our meetings.

March 6th being Sunday, went to Absalom Melotts, had two meetings in the Turkeyfoot S. H. Met brethren Daniel Young and Geo. Harman from Franklin Co. Bro. Harman led the exercises in the evening. O how we felt encouraged to meet with our fellow watchmen on the walls of Zion, but our stay together was short, only one night at Bro. James Lakes. They had meeting there at 10 A. M. on the 10th, and we had to go eight miles to Bro Daniel Melotts to preach the same hour that day in his house, where we also had meeting in the evening which ended our mission for this time.

Next day went home, found them reasonably well, God's name be praised. Much love was manifested by all and we were treated with much more kindness and hospitality than we deserved. We heartily thank them for the same and pray God to reward them in the resurrection of the just. Calls were repeated: "Come and preach for us" by saint and sinner. Preached 19 times and traveled 191 miles. May our weak labors be crowned with success.

LEONARD FURRY.

New Enterprise, Pa.

Dear Pilgrim:—As it gives me much satisfaction to read Church news, I feel to give some which may be satisfactory to some at least. Having had a desire for some time to visit the brethren in Illinois I, in company with brother Zachariah Troyer, took the train at Walkerton on the morning of the 14th. of Feb. at 2. o'clock. Arrived at Chicago at 7. A. M., visited D. P. Fahrney's office and returned to the Depot just in time for the train at 10 A. M. Made good time and landed at Girard about 6 P. M. Stayed over night with Bro. Jonathan Brubaker and his kind family. On Sunday we met with the brethren for the first time at the Pleasant Hill M. Macoupin Co. Ill. Our dear Bro. and Eld. John Metzker also met with us; met again for preaching in the evening. Eld. David Frantz from Macon Co. was added to our company; met again on Monday evening; two more Elders met with us, Joseph Hendrick from *Macon* and David Wolf from Adams Co. We continued to labor together morning and evening until Wednesday. Then I went to Montgomery Co. Bro. Metzgar to Sangamon and the other brethren remained 'till Friday morning. I can truly say this was a season of refreshment to me, meeting with many brethren and sisters whom I had once known, from Va., Ohio and Ind. and forming happy acquaintances with many whom I never saw before. On Wednesday evening and on Thursday I had meeting in the neighborhood of brother J. E. Studebakers. On Friday went to Morrisonville in Christian Co., in company with Bro. Daniel Vaniman and others. Had meeting in town that evening. Next day, met with the brethren in Church council. Here we were met again with bro. J. *Metzker*. Bro. Abraham Lear was advanced to the second degree. He is the only minister in that district, which is newly organized. Here I would say to the brethren who wish to move west, this is a good country, land can be bought very reasonable and the little flock seems to be in a healthy condition. Had preaching in the evening and on Sunday. On Sunday night, in company with Bro. J. Metzker, took the train at 12 o'clock, arrived at Cerro Gorda at 3 a. m., met with Bro. Isaac Barnhart when we got off the train, I went with him to his house, and after breakfast I went to Bro. J. Metzker's and stayed till after dinner. Then we made Bro. J. Hendrix a short visit, went to Bro. David Fratzer's, took supper with them, went to their meeting house and had meeting that evening. This ended our meeting with the brethren in Illinois, and I must say that I feel very thankful to all the brethren and sisters for their kindness shown to us while among them, and further, I was much pleased to see how earnestly they contend for the faith once delivered to the saints, and how very zealous they are in keeping up the landmarks which our father's have set.

JOHN N. BARNHART.

Walkerton, Ind.

RAVENSWOOD, W. VA., }
March 2, 1873. }

Dear Brethren:—I will tell you of my situation here in this country. I have been living here for four years and during this time my health has been very bad, and I have had considerable trouble. I have lost my horse and cow and have three helpless children, and have not heard the pure Gospel preached since I have been living in Jackson Co. At this time I am in destitute circumstances. I desire to read your paper if you please to send it to me. I read one of your PILGRIMS this winter, and I would love to have them to read regularly. One of the brethren wrote to me to know if I was still in the faith of the Gospel as I was when I made my baptismal vow. I answer I am and expect to be in the same faith while I live in this world of sorrow.

A. E. B.

Dear Brethren and Sisters, such are the frequent requests made of us, what do you think of it? Here is a sister, like hundreds of others, isolated from the Brotherhood, deprived of the benefits of meeting in the sanctuary with the children of God. Is there any wonder if such would grow cold in the faith. She desires to read the PILGRIM because, in it she obtains food for the soul and learns of the welfare of Zion. She shall have it and we hope to her it may prove to be the bread of Heaven, but while we thus administer to the spiritual wants of our Father's hungry children, can we not prevail on some of our well circumstanced and liberal brethren and sisters to open their hearts and aid us in the good work? Many could spare from $1,00 to $5,00 without making any sacrifice whatever. "Feed my lambs."

GRANT, MO., }
March 10, '73. }

Some of my brethren or sisters have been so kind as to send me the PILGRIM to comfort me in my lonely hours. I have been confined to the house and to the bed for months, and how welcome does the PILGRIM come to me. I am now trying to write a few lines for its columns. Afflictions are God's most effectual means to keep us from losing our way to Heaven. Without this hedge of thorns on the right and on the left, we should hardly keep the way. If there be but one gap open, how ready are we to find it and turn out at it when we grow wanton, worldly or proud. Every Christian, as well as all good men, may call affliction one of the best schoolmasters, and with David may say, "Before I was afflicted I went astray, but now I have kept thy word." Many thousand recovered sinners may cry, "O helpful sickness, O comfortable sorrows, O greatful losses, what would our proud hearts be if all was health and prosperity?" Your sister,

FANNIE BENSON.

Dear Pilgrim:—Another Sabbath is here bringing with it more snow. Every flake is an expression of the Father's goodness to us as they come one after another filling the air with purity. While watching those beautiful messengers I was impressed to write a few lines to my brethren and sisters hoping to say something to cheer them as they journey onward.

I have been a professor of religion forty years of my life, but not knowing what Church suited my views best, did not unite with any until about a year and a half ago. I attended a series of meetings held by our much esteemed and trustworthy brother Moses Baer of Bloomingdale, this State, Mich. By comparing his teachings with those laid down by our Savior, I decided what Church to join and I became a member of the Brethren, feeling persuaded that to live a true Christian life I must obey the commandments in full. May the service of the Lord be our delight, remembering that passage of Scripture from Matthew 28th chapter 20th verse which says, "Teaching them to observe all things whatsoever I have commanded you, and lo I am with you alway even unto the end of the world."

MARY BURNS.

Bro. Keelin Leonard of Lanark, Carroll Co., Ill., says that he was raised in North Carolina, but left there in 1825, leaving a large number of friends from whom he has not heard since. He wishes the address of some who live there that he may correspond with them. If you give the county and post-office to which you came, you may get the desired information.

ANNOUNCEMENTS.

Please announce through the PILGRIM that our District Meeting will be held on the 13th of May in the Cook's Creek Congregation, Rockingham Co., Va.

SOLOMON GARBER.

The District Meeting for North Missouri will be held on the 7th and 8th of March in the Smith Fork Branch, Clinton Co., near Plattsburg, in the Brethren's Meeting-house. A general representation desired. Those coming by R. R. will stop off at Plattsburg.

GEORGE WITWER.

Please make the following announcement in the WEEKLY PILGRIM. The District Meeting of West Virginia, will be held in Seneca District, eight miles west of Mouth of Seneca, at Union School House, in Dry Fork township, Randolph Co., on Friday and Saturday, 9th and 10th of May. For any further information address the undersigned at Mouth of Seneca, Pendleton Co., W. Va.

By order of the Church.

ASA HARMAN.

Please announce that the District Meeting of Northern Indiana and Michigan, will be held at the Brethren's Meetinghouse, 4 mile west of Goshen, Elkhart Co., Ind., commencing on Thursday the 1st day of May, 1873, at 10 o'clock, a. m.

JESSE CALVERT, Clerk.

Champaign Lovefeast.

The brethren in Champaign Co., Ill., have appointed their Communion Meeting on Saturday and Sunday, June 7th and 8th, 1873, at Bro. Geo. Dilling's, five miles east of Urbana. We extend an invitation to all, especially the ministering brethren.

J. H. MOORE,
Urbana, Ill.

TO ALL WHO ARE CONCERNED.

We do, through this medium, inform the brethren and churches comprising the first district of Virginia, that Friday and Saturday before the fourth Sunday in April, is the time appointed for the holding of the Annual District Meeting, and will be held at that time no preventive providence, at the Valley Meeting house in Botetourt Co., one mile south of Amsterdam. A full attendance is desirable.

The undersigned also informs his brethren that he has a number of New Hymn Books on hand for sale. B. F. MOOMAW.

Please announce that the District Meeting of Western Maryland, will be held the Lord willing in the Welsh Run Congregation in the Broad Fording Meetinghouse, five miles northwest of Hagerstown on the second Tuesday in April, 1873.

NICHOLAS MARTIN.

You will please announce through the PILGRIM that the Brethren in the Middle District of Iowa, purpose holding their District Council Meeting with the Brethren in Dallas Co., in their Meetinghouse, on Monday the 19th day of May, 1873. We expect a good representation of delegates, also a general invitation to the brethren to be with us.

J. S. SNYDER,
Cor. Sec'y.

Please announce through your paper, the Lord willing, the District Meeting for the North-eastern District of Ohio, will be held in the Jonathan's Creek Congregation, Perry Co., Ohio, on Tuesday the 20th day of May, 1873, being the second Tuesday before the A. M. All persons coming to the meeting [illegible] brethren and sisters, must come to Newark, Ohio, thence down the Newark, Somerset & Straitsville Railroad to Glenford Station, there the brethren will meet those who come and convey them to the place of meeting, 3 miles off. Those who intend to come will please write us and we will have the necessary arrangements made.

W. ARNOLD.
Somerset, Perry Co., O.

Companion and *Visitor* please copy the same.

ANSWER TO QUERY.

L. H. Miller asks who David's mother was.

Answer; Nahash.

The book tells us Abigail, (David's sister) was the daughter of Nahash, sister to Jeremiah, Joab's mother. 2 Samuel 17: 25.

And Jesse begat his first-born Eliab, and Aminadab the second, and Shimma the third, Nathaniel the fourth, Raddai the fifth, Ozem the sixth, David the seventh, whose sisters were Zeruiah and Abigail.—1 Chronicles 2: 13-19.

WM. NOFFSINGER.
Defiance, Ohio.

DIED.

ZARGER.—In the Falling Spring Congregation, Jan. 30, 1873, sister Zarger, aged 86 years, 9 mos, and 24 days. Funeral services by Bro. Jacob A. Stover and the writer.

SHANK.—In the same Congregation, near Chambersburg, Feb. 2, 1873, bro. Jacob Shank, aged 67 years, 10 mos, and 6 days. Funeral services by Jacob A. Stover, from Phil.—1: 23.

BAKER.—In the same Congregation, in Shady Grove, Feb. 12, 1873, Ann Maria Baker, daughter of bro. Adam and sister Elizabeth Baker, aged 11 years, 1 mo, and 12 days. Funeral service by Eld. Jacob Price and the writer.

STOVER.—In the same Congregation, Mar. 1, 1873, sister Mary Stover, aged 71 yrs., 5 mos, and 2 days. Funeral services by Bro. Abram Golley and the writer from 1 Thess.—1: 14.

JOHN ZUCK.

UMBAUGH.—In the Maple Grove Congregation, Feb. 27, 1873, sister Susan Umbaugh, aged 69 years, 6 months and 23 days. Funeral services by the brethren from Rev.—2: 17, in the presence of a large and attentive congregation.

WM. SADLER.

LEONARD.—In the Elkhart Valley Congregation, March 8, 1873, Angeline, consort of David Leonard, aged 47 years, 1 month, and 12 days. She was followed to her grave by a large concourse of relatives and friends to mourn her loss.

P. H. KURTZ.

MONEY LIST.

Abram Baum	$ 1.25
D M Rittenhouse	3.00
Wm. Angle	11.75
J W Brumbaugh	1.50
Jacob Brumbaugh	1.50
Kate Gandel	4.00
David Shong	.25
Samuel Rebert	.10
P H Kurtz	3.00
John Burkholder	.35
Odin Clark	1.50
Harman Heilman	1.50
Geo S Wine	13.60
George Worst	11.70
Geo W Jones	2.00
Daniel Kinsel	2.75
Daniel Brower	1.50
E. B. Shaver,	.90
A Anderson,	.70
C. H. Roop,	1.50
John F Reiman,	1.00
Mary Burns,	.62
Dr. Solomon,	6.50
S. N. Wine,	9.15
John Zuck,	10.00
Jonas Berkey,	19.25
Martha Hutton,	1.75

The Weekly Pilgrim.

JAMES CREEK, PA., Mar. 25th, 1873.

☞ How to send money.—All sums over $1.50, should be sent either in a check, draft or postal order. If neither of these can be obtained, have the letter registered.

☞ WHEN MONEY is sent, *always* send with it the name and address of those who paid it. Write the names and post office as plainly as possible.

☞ EVERY subscriber for 1873, gets a *Pilgrim Almanac* FREE.

A WORD TO ALL.

From present indications we can congratulate our readers in the expectation of more than an ordinary amount of interesting and instructive reading during the present year. With such aids as Furry, Moomaw, Flory, Moore, Worst and a large number of others, we expect to make the PILGRIM all that the Brotherhood can reasonably expect. It is true, we have disappointed a few in not publishing their productions, which we feared might be the cause of engendering strife without being any advantage to the Church, but on the whole the PILGRIM is acknowledged to be as carefully conducted as well could be, under existing circumstances, and we hope the disappointed few, after mature deliberations will justify the course we are pursuing, especially when we assure them that we do nothing out of personal preferences, but for the sake of the glorious cause which we are trying to advocate. We remember the time that we wrote things, under the impulse of the moment, that we sorely regretted afterwards and felt very grateful to the editor for withholding it from the public. Just so we may all do and feel. We claim no superiority over our brethren generally, but our position and relation to the Brotherhood gives us advantages that many others do not have, hence, in a general way, we should be better able to judge what is for the welfare and prosperity of the Church than those who do not have these advantages. Out of the thousands of letters received and those largely from the working part of the membership, we have very excellent facilities for learning the sentiments and wants of the Church. From knowledge thus attained we set our feet upon the "Ancient Landmarks" and imploring divine aid, we endeavor to steer the ship as independent of all personal preferences, not forgetting the advice of those who are our superiors in age and in the divine life.

This week will be noticed the first number of a series of articles by Eld. Flory on "The Church and the duty of her members" for which we ask a careful reading. In a few weeks, we will commence a series of papers containing some fifteen chapters, entitled "A Light to the World," by J. H. Moore. The following we have before us: Chapter I. "The Bible." Chapter II "Obedience." Chapter III "Baptism." Chapter IV "Immersion" Chapter V "Infant Baptism." Chapter VI "Backward and forward Baptism." With these productions, and those of our many other contributors, our patrons can certainly feel hopeful, especially when it is taken into consideration the large amount of Church news and other miscellaneous reading we give each week. In conclusion, we tender our thanks to contributors, agents and patrons for their generous co-operation, and hope by the end of the year we may all feel that the PILGRIM has been for our mutual good.

TAKE THE BACK NO'S.

All subscriptions should commence with the beginning of the volume, as the first Nos. contained some very interesting articles some of which are still continued. It will also make a complete file and make the volume valuable for binding. We can still supply all subscribers with numbers from the beginning of the year. New subscribers are still coming in quite encouragingly and we can assure you, they are welcomely received. We have room for many more, send them along and we will accommodate all.

HUNTINGDON & BROAD TOP R. R. Summer arrangement. After March 23, there will be two trains daily. The Mail leaves Huntingdon southward at 7.45 a. m. and returns at 1.00 p. m. The Passenger at 6.00 p. m. and arrives at 8.25 a. m. The new arrangement will be properly indicated in the "Time Table" next week.

AN INQUIRER.—To those who have paid $1.50 for the PILGRIM we will send the *Phrenological Journal* by sending $2.00 more. The price of the *P. Journal* is $3.00, the PILGRIM $1.50, making $4.50, we send them both together for [illegible]. Now is the time to subscribe.

ANONYMOUS NAMES.—We prefer that writers give their full names to their productions, but if any through modesty wish them withheld we will gratify them, but in all cases, we must have the writer's name.

SPECIAL NOTICES.

Seeds, Plants, Trees,—Prepaid by Mail.

My new priced descriptive Catalogue of Choice Flower and Garden Seeds, 25 sorts of either for $1; new and choice varieties of Fruit and Ornamental Trees, Shrubs, Evergreens, Roses, Grapes, Lilies, Small Fruits, House and Border Plants and Bulbs; one year grafted Fruit Trees for mailing; Fruit Stocks of all kinds, Hedge Plants, &c.; the most complete assortment in the country, will be sent gratis to any plain address, with P. O. box. True Cape Cod Cranberry for upland or lowland, $6 per 1000; $1 per 100; prepaid by mail. Trade List to dealers. Seeds on Commission. Agents wanted. B. M. WATSON,

Old Colony Nurseries and Seed Warehouse, Plymouth, Mass. Established 1842.

$50,000

Will be distributed this year, to the subscribers for the AMERICAN WORKING PEOPLE, a large quarto, 16 page Monthly, costing but $1.50 per year. It gives a premium to every subscriber, varying from 25 cents in value up to $2, $5, $10, $20, $100, $200, and $500 in Greenbacks, besides Watches, Sewing Machines, Parlor Organs and numerous other premiums of value. Send for specimen and circulars to

CAPRON & Co.,
Mar. 18-2m. Pittsburgh, Pa.

WANTED. We will give men and women

Business that will Pay

from $1 to $8 per day, can be pursued in your own neighborhood; it is a rare chance for those out of employment or having leisure time; girls and boys frequently do as well as men. Particulars free.

Address J. LATHAM & CO.,
292 Washington St., Boston, Mass.

Trine Immersion
TRACED
TO THE APOSTLES.

The SECOND EDITION is now ready for delivery. The work has been carefully revised, corrected and enlarged.

Put up in a neat pamphlet form, with good paper cover, and will be sent, post-paid, on the following terms: One copy, 25 cts; Five copies, $1.10; Ten copies, $2.00, 25 copies, $4.50; 50 copies, $8.50; 100 copies, $16.00.

Address, J. H. MOORE,
Urbana, Champaign co., Ill.
Oct. 22.

DYMOND ON WAR.

An inquiry into the Accordancy of War, with the Principles of Christianity, and an examination of the Philosophical reasoning by which it is defended. With observations on some of the causes of war and on some of its effects. By Jonathan Dymond. Sent from this office, post paid, for 30 cts.,

LAND, LAND, LAND!!

The completion of the Chesapeake and Ohio Trunk Line Railway, has opened up to the world much of the fine TIMBER LANDS, rich COAL FIELDS and cheap FARMING LANDS of W. Va. Now is the time to get cheap homes and invest money with the prospect of a handsome profit. For further particulars inquire of the undersigned, agent for lands here. J. S. FLORY,

Orchard View, Fayette Co., W. Va.
Jan. 10.

TUNE BOOK.

The Brethren's Tune and Hymn Book, is a compilation of Sacred Music adapted to all the hymns in the Brethren's New Hymn Book. It contains over 250 pages, printed on good paper and neatly bound. We will send it to any address, post paid at $1.25 per copy.

GOOD BOOKS.

How to read Character, illus. Price,	$1.25
Combe's Moral Philosophy,	1.75
Constitution of Man. Combe,	1.75
Education. By Spurzheim,	1.50
Memory—How to improve it,	1.50
Mental Science, Lectures on,	1.50
Self-Culture and Perfection,	1.50
Combe's Physiology, Illus.	1.75
Food and Diet. By Pereira,	1.75
Natural Laws of Man,	.75
Hereditary Descent,	1.50
Combe on Infancy,	1.50
Sober and Temperate Life,	.50
Children in Health—Disease,	1.75
The Science of Human Life,	3.50
Fruit Culture for the Million,	1.00
Saving and Wasting,	1.50
Ways of Life—Right Way,	1.00
Footprints of Life,	1.25
Conversion of St. Paul,	1.00

A large number of our patrons are receiving our books as noticed below, as premiums, and express themselves highly pleased with them. Others who are not agents, have enquired whether we keep them for sale. We have now made arrangements with Mr. Wells to furnish any of their publications post paid at publishers prices. Orders for books must be accompanied with the cash, and plain directions for sending them.

Weaver's Works for the Young. Comprising "Hopes and Helps for the Young of both Sexes," $3.00.

Life at Home; or, The Family and its Members. A work which should be found in every family. $1.50. Extra gilt, $2.00.

Hand-book for Home Improvement; comprising "How to Write," "How to Talk," How to Behave," and "How to do Business," in one vol. 2.25.

Man and Woman: Considered in their Relations to each Other and to the World. 12mo, Fancy cloth, Price $1.00.

The Right Word in the Right Place. A New Pocket Dictionary and Reference Book. Cloth, 75cts.

Hopes and Helps for the Young of both sexes, Relating to the Formation of Character. Choice of Avocation, Health, Conversation, Social Affection Courtship and Marriage. Muslin, $1.50.

The Emphatic, Diaglott; or The New Testament in Greek and English. Containing the Original Greek Text of the New Testament, with an Interlineary Word for-word English Translation. Price, $4.00; extra fine binding, $5.00.

Oratory—Sacred and Secular; or, the Extemporaneous Speaker. Price $1.50.

Conversion of St. Paul. 12mo. fine edition, $1. Plain edition, 75 cents.

Man, in Genesis and in Geology; or, the Biblical Account of Man's Creation, tested by Scientific Theories of his Origin and Antiquity. One vol. 12mo, $1.00.

$5 to $20 per day! Agents wanted! All classes of working people, of either sex, young or old, make more money at work for us in their spare moments or all the time than at anything else. Particulars free. Address G. Stinson & Co., Portland, Maine.

THE
HOUSEHOLD TREASURE.

Containing several hundred Valuable Receipts for cooking well at a moderate expense, making Dyes, Coloring, Cleaning and Cementing. This book also points out in plain language, free from Doctors' terms the diseases of men, women and children, and the latest and most approved means used for their cure, to which is added a description of the Medicinal Roots and Herbs, and how they are to be used in the cure of diseases.

This is a work of considerable importance and we offer it to our readers as being a valuable accession to every household. Sent from this office to any address, post-paid, for 25 cents.

WANTED BOOK AGENTS

FOR THE

FUNNY SIDE OF PHYSIC.

800 *Pages,* 250 *Engravings.*

A startling expose of Medical Humbugs of the past and present. It ventilates Quacks, Imposters, Travelling Doctors, Patent Medicine Venders, Noted Female Cheats, Fortune Tellers and Mediums, and gives interesting accounts of Noted Physicians and Narratives of their lives. It reveals startling secrets and instructs all how to avoid the ills which flesh is heir to. We give exclusive territory and liberal commissions. For circulars and terms address the publishers. J. B. BURR & HYDE,

Hartford, Conn., or Chicago, Ill.

AGENTS WANTED FOR THE

UNCIVILIZED RACES OF MEN

In all countries of the world.

Being a comprehensive account of their Manners and Customs, and of their Physical, Social, Mental, Moral, and Religious Characteristics.

By REV. J. G. WOOD, M. A., F. L. S.

500 *Engravings,* 1500 *Super Royal Oc. Pages*

In two Volumes, or two Volumes in one. Agents are making over $100 per week in selling this work. An early application will secure a choice of territory. For terms address the publishers,

J. B. BURR & HYDE,
Hartford, Conn., or Chicago, Ill.

TRACTS.

"ANXIOUS BENCH RELIGION EXAMINED," BY ELDER J. S. FLORY. A SYNOPSIS OF CONTENTS. An address to the reader: The peculiarities that attend this type of religion. The feelings there experienced not imaginary but real. The key that unlocks the wonderful mystery. The causes by which feelings are excited. How the momentary feelings called "Experimental religion" are brought about, and then concludes by giving that form of doctrine as taught by Jesus Christ and recorded by his faithful witnesses.

COUNTERFEIT DETECTER
or
BAPTISM—MUCH IN LITTLE.

This work is now ready for distribution, and the importance of the subject will speak for it a large demand. It is a short treatise on baptism in tract form intended for general distribution, and is set forth in such a plain and logical manner that a wayfaring man though a fool, cannot err therein. Either of the above tracts sent postpaid on the following terms: Two copies, 10 cts, 10 copies 40 cents, 25 copies 70 cents, 50 copies $1.00, 100 copies $1.50.

Trine Immersion.

A discussion on Trine Immersion, by letter between Elder B. F. Moomaw and Dr. J. J. Jackson, to which is annexed a Treatise on the Lord's Supper, and on the necessity, character and evidences of the new birth, also a dialogue on the doctrine of non-resistance, by Elder B. F. Moomaw. Single copy 50 cents.

THE GROUNDS FOR A

FORWARD and BACKWARD

MODE OF

BAPTISM.

Briefly, yet *carefully* examined; and the TRUE and CORRECT mode so clearly set forth that none can help but understand.

This little book contains 30 pages, neatly put up in paper cover. Price per doz. $1.25, add 10 cts. for postage. Two copies, 25 cts 1 copy, 15 cts., free of postage.

Address, SAMUEL KINSEY,
Mar 11-3t. Dayton, O.

Bee Books, Bee Books!

On receipt of 50 cts. I will send by mail a valuable *Bee Book* treating on over one hundred subjects. No Bee keeper should be without it. It tells just how to make bees profitable. *Italian Queen* Bees bred from imported mothers, each $3.00. Orders solicited. Address

E. J. WORST,
New Pittsburgh, Wayne co., O.
Feb 18-4t.

1870 1873

DR. FAHRNEY'S
Blood Cleanser or Panacea.

A tonic and purge, for Blood Diseases. Great reputation. Many testimonials. Many ministering brethren use and recommend it. Ask or send for the "Health Messenger." Use only the "*Panacea*" prepared at Chicago, Ills., and by

Dr. P. Fahrney's Brothers & Co.,
Aug. 3-pd. *Waynesboro, Franklin Co., Pa*

New Hymn Books, English.

TURKEY MOROCCO.

One copy, postpaid,	$1.00
Per Dozen,	11.25

PLAIN ARABESQUE.

One Copy, post-paid,	75
Per Dozen, "	8.50

Ger'n & English, Plain Sheep.

One Copy, post-paid,	$1.00
Per Dozen	11.25
Arabesque Plain,	1.00
Turkey Morocco,	1.25
Single German, post paid	50
Per Dozen,	5.50

HUNTINGDON & BROAD TOP RAIL ROAD

On and after February 9th, 1873, Trains will run on this road daily (Sundays excepted) as follows:

Trains from Huntingdon South. *Trains from Mt. Dallas moving North.*

MAIL. A. M.	NO. 1. P. M.	STATIONS.	MAIL. P. M.	NO 2. A. M.
le7 40	LE	Huntingdon,	AR1 00	AR
7 45		Long Siding	3 53	
8 00		McConnelstown	3 43	
8 05		Pleasant Grove	3 35	
8 23		Marklesburg	3 22	
8 40		Coffee Run	3 07	
8 45		Rough & Ready	3 00	
9 00		Cove	2 50	
9 05		Fishers Summit	2 45	
9 17		Saxton	2 35 le	
9 40		Riddlesburg	2 15	
9 47		Hopewell	2 05	
10 05		Piper's Run	1 50	
10 25		Tatesville	1 30	
10 37		Bloody Run	1 20	
10 40		Mount Dallas	1 15	
11 08		Bedford	2 44	

G. F. GAGE, Supt.

SHOUP'S RUN BRANCH.

LE 9 25	LE	Saxton,	AR2 15	AR
9 40		Coalmont,	2 00	
9 45		Crawford,	1 55	
AR10 00	AR	Dudley	LE1 45	LE

Bro'd Top City from Dudley 2 miles by stage.

Time of Penna. R. R. Trains at Huntingdon.

**Mail No. 2 makes connection at Huntingdon with Mail going East on Pennsylvania Railroad at 4.15 p. m., and West at 5.45 p. m. Mail No. 1 leaves Huntingdon at 7.40 a. m. on arrival of Pacific Express West.

Trains on this road connect with trains on Bedford & Bridgeport, and Cumberland & Pennsylvania Railroads.

The Weekly Pilgrim.

Published by J. B. Brumbaugh, & Co.

Edited by H. B. & Geo. Brumbaugh.

CORRESPONDING EDITORS.

D. P. Sayler, Double Pipe Creek, Md.

Leonard Furry, New Enterprise, Pa.

The *Pilgrim* is a Christian Periodical, devoted to religion and moral reform. It will advocate in the spirit of *love* and *liberty*, the principles of true Christianity, labor for the promotion of peace among the people of God, for the encouragement of the saints and for the conversion of sinners, avoiding those things which tend toward disunion or sectional feelings.

TERMS.

Single copy, Book paper,	$1 50
Eleven copies, [eleventh for Agt.]	$15.00

Any number above that at the same rate.

Address,

H. B. BRUMBAUGH.
James Creek,
Huntingdon county Pa.

The Weekly Pilgrim.

"REMOVE NOT THE ANCIENT LANDMARKS WHICH OUR FATHERS HAVE SET."

VOL. 4. JAMES CREEK, PENNSYLVANIA, APRIL 1, 1873. NO. 13

POETRY.

SING ME MOTHER'S SONGS.

Sing me the songs that my own mother sung
As she rocked me on her knee;
For the songs my infant ears first heard
Are the sweetest, aye, to me.
Warble them softly, as she used to do
When my head lay on her breast,
Oh! I know of no other place so sweet
Where the weary head may rest.

Sing me the songs that my own mother sang,
And my fevered brow will feel
The soft, soothing touch of her cool, white hand—
Ah! such balm my wounds might heal;
And this bounding heart will be calm for awhile,
And my pulse will throb no more,
And I'll think I sit 'neath the hawthorn shade,
As I did in the days of yore.

Sing me the songs that my own mother sang
In the years of long ago.
Sing them softly; they will ease my pain
As their soothing numbers flow
And I think I stand by her side once more,
As in childhood's happy days,
Ere these weary feet had yet learned to tread
In the world's lone, gloomy maze.

Sing me the songs that my own mother sang;
They have hushed my feeble wail,
And my childish sorrows they have lightly tossed,
Deep in oblivion's vale.
Even the angels that watched while I slept,
And to dreamland led the way,
Enraptured stood when they heard her melting voice,
As she trilled her roundelay.

Sing me the songs that my own mother sang
In our home so far away,
And I'll think I am lisping my evening prayer
By her knee at the close of day;
And the little cottage will rise to view,
The streams, the meadows, and flowers;
And I saw them then, to my infant gaze,
They seemed like elfin bowers.

ORIGINAL ESSAYS.

THE CHURCH AND DUTIES OF HER MEMBERS—NO. 2.

BY J. S. FLORY.

DEACONS.

The word "Deacon" in its primitive sense meant a servant, one who attended his master, waiting on him at table and elsewhere. Deacons are spoken of in the early Christian Church. In Acts 6th we find some murmured, "because their widows were neglected in the daily ministration." We find it was the custom in those days to have "all things common," so that those who had lands and horses sold them and laid the proceeds at the apostles feet. The needy men, doubtless, came forward and got what they needed, but the widows were neglected; the apostles had much to attend to as ministers of the Word so they could not—or it was not expedient they should leave the Word of God, and serve tables, hence the necessity to choose men to attend to this matter. They chose seven men from among themselves—that is the multitude of disciples chose the men. The nature of the calling demanded they should be men of "honest report and full of the Holy Ghost." The qualifications of Deacons are set forth by the apostle Paul in first Timothy, 3: "Likewise must the deacons be grave, not double tongued, not given to much wine, not greedy of filthy lucre, holding the mystery of the faith in a pure conscience, * * * ruling their children and their own house well." While it is stated by Paul, "Let the deacons be the husband of one wife," we do not understand him they must necessarily be married, but if married let them have *only one wife at a time*. From what we have quoted above relative to the qualifications of deacons, it will be readily inferred the office imposes weighty duties and solemn obligations upon those that are called thereto. Their duties may be defined to consist, in part, to that of being treasurer, and to distribute to the needy or to any object the Church may order,—to attend to the "Church visit" as often as the Church directs, in consequence of this duty they are often called "visiting brethren,"—to superintend the preparations at our Communion meetings that everything may be in readiness at the proper time and in order. To those then is often and in general laid the unpleasant task of visiting members who may be in an unreconciled state with each other, or members who may have committed offense against the Church in their careless walk and conduct, and report the matter to the Church. Liberty is generally given to the deacons to read the Scriptures in public at our seasons of public worship, to pray also at said meetings, and in some places to bear testimony to the word preached. In some places, especially where ministers are scarce, liberty is given to the deacon to "open meetings" by giving out a hymn, exhortation to prayer, &c., in like manner close meetings in accordance with the wish and liberty given by the minister. And in cases where the minister fails to attend appointments the deacon is priviliged to read a chapter, give an exhortation, and close by singing and prayer. Of course these liberties vary in proportion to the number of ministers present and the ordinary customs of the congregations. Deacons wives are sometimes called deaconesses, and in many things the same duties devolve upon them that do upon their husbands, especially when their own sex are the persons to be attended to. Paul says also of them "Even so must their wives be grave, not slanderers, sober, faithful in all things."

The calling of the deacons is a calling of an official nature, therefore they must feel their duties in many respects are different from the private members. They wield an influence of no small effect. In fact a corpse of live energetic deacons may engineer life and prosperity in the Church. Deacons, if in your official duties, walk and conduct you manifest a spirit in harmony with your required qualifications, and use your office well, you purchase to yourselves "a good degree, and great boldness in the faith which is in Christ Jesus." The more you are exalted by the Lord the more you should become humbled through the grace of God. Duty requires you should cultivate a spirit of prayer in your families as well as abroad. In matters of trying to bring about reconciliation between parties, let *patience, love* and *prayer* persuade your hearts. Labor and admonish in such a way that the parties may feel you are in earnest about their eternal interests. Feel if possible, that the salvation of precious souls may hang upon the efforts you are making and your labors of love. Know that personal influence goes along way, therefore try to so live that your influence may be a strong argument in matters requiring admonitions. It makes the heart sad to have to hear, as we sometimes do, that deacons give good reason for transgressors to say to them in answer to their advice, "*Physician, heal thyself*, then talk to me." No wonder Paul would have them grave, honest, not given to much wine &c. He would have them models of Christian character in whom the noble characteristics of the Son of life and glory, were exemplified in their daily lives. It is the duty of all to love not the world nor the sinful things of the world, but to those in office this should be considered in the fullest sense of its importance. If those who are in official stations set good examples by their daily walk and conversation, with propriety and a greater show of success they may expect their admonitions to be successful in keeping the branches trimmed of superfluous outgrowth,—such things as tend to the overthrow of the Christian graces. The privileges and opportunities that necessarily accompany the office of deacon are such that they may, as instruments in the hands of God, do much toward keeping the Church in the "unity of the spirit" and the prosperity of Zion depends in part upon how they use the office of the deaconship. Also the converting influence of God may be made to penetrate the heart of the unregenerate through their labors of love. Time spent in the performance of their duties is not time lost, it is as treasures laid up in Heaven. May the deacons with their wives, remember the blessing of "a good degree" is to those who "use the office of a deacon well." Not such an empty degree as is conferred by men upon one another in the secret societies, but a degree to be conferred by God. "A good degree" in the favor of a Savior's love,—"a good degree" with Him "of whom the whole family in Heaven and earth is named." "A good degree" amid the "stars" of Heaven,—yea, "a good degree" with those that shall wear the crown of glory and walk the streets of the new Jerusalem. In the language of Paul to the saints, bishops and deacons at Philippi, we would say; "Grace be unto you, and peace from God our Father and from the Lord Jesus Christ!"

TO THE UNCONVERTED.

"And it is appointed unto men once to die, but after this the judgment; so Christ was once offered to bear the sins of many; and unto them that look for him shall he appear the second time without sin unto salvation."—9: 27, 28.

It is evident that the apostle in the above named chapter, is treating, in the first place, on the first covenant which stood in meats and drinks and in diverse washings and ordinances imposed on them till the time of reformation. Now we learn that on account of the weakness and imperfection of the law: the comers thereunto could not be made perfect, although they were obedient in offering divers sacrifices and offerings and burnt-offerings and offerings for sin; yet there was a remembrance made of sins every year. This was because the law was a mere figure or shadow of good things to come, but we thank God we live under the new covenant; for it is able to make us wise unto salvation, for it was not possible that the blood of goats and calves could take away sin, hence it pleased the Father of the universe, to send his Son, in whom dwells all the fullness of the Godhead bodily, to offer himself once for sin; and by so doing he hath brought life and immortality to light through the Gospel. Hence it is in the gospel of Christ that we learn that here we have no continuing city, and that it is appointed unto men once to die. Therefore we wish to warn the unconverted man and women, to flee from the wrath to come and take hold of eternal life, while it is yet called today with them; because death will soon come, and when once the icy arms of death encircles around us like the sable curtain of the night, then all creature help will fail. Therefore I earnestly entreat you my dear reader, to seek the Lord while he may found, and call upon his name while he is in the way, that he may have mercy upon you, in the present time and in eternity. Oh think of eternity, of incomprehensive eternity; without beginning or end! While you are in health is the time to serve the Lord. Jesus calls for you today by saying: "Come unto me all ye that labor and are heavy laden, and I will give you rest, take my yoke upon you, and learn of me, for I am meek and lowly in heart, and ye shall find rest unto your souls; for my yoke is easy, and my burden is light." My dear reader, this is the rest I desire you and me to enjoy after death, that we may reign with Christ and the saints, where we shall feast upon joys that are unspeakable and full of glory; and in order to enjoy that rest, we must believe in the Lord Jesus as our only Savior, earnestly contending for the faith once delivered to the saints.

Now dear reader, in the exercise of faith that works by love, the heart or mind is entirely changed from evil thoughts to good thoughts, and instead of thinking about evil things, we will endeavor to do good to all men as far as lays in our power. It is repentance that changes our conduct, from evil works to good works, such as God hath before ordained, that we should walk in them, and by being baptized in the name of the Father and of the Son and of the Holy Ghost, we are brought into the kingdom of God's dear Son, in whom we have redemption through his blood, according to the riches of his grace; even the forgiveness of our sins, &c. And as it is appointed unto men once to die, and after this the judgment, so we learn in the last clause of this verse that death is not the end of man, for Christ will sit upon the throne of His glory, and separate the righteous from the wicked; the righteous he will place on his right hand and the wicked on his left hand, &c., Matt.—25th chap. There we shall be able to discern between the righteous and the wicked, and him that serves God and him that serves him not. Christ once offered to bear the sins of many. Now the reason why Christ was once offered to bear the sins of this world is this, that Adam, our representative in sin, by disobedience fell from that state of holiness wherein he was created; hence it was not possible, that fallen man could be restored again into the favor and friendship of God without a mediator, and Inspiration teaches us that there was none found in heaven or on earth, that could redeem man from the dilemma in which he placed himself by disobeying God's holy law, save the Son of God, therefore Christ came into this world of sorrow, and became obedient unto death even to the death of the cross; and in doing so, he hath brought life and immortality to light, that whosoever believes in him should not perish, but have eternal life. Now dear reader, by the above we learn, that by the disobedience of one man many were made sinners, and by the obedience of Christ many may be made righteous. Oh, dear sinners, remember how God loved you, and gave himself in the person age of his Son to reconcile you again into God's favor and friendship. Then look to the tree of the cross, and remember that our redemption cost the blood of Christ. Oh how the Lord of glory suffered for you and me; we soon will have to leave this place of abode, and go to the spirit land, from whence no traveler hath returned; and dear reader, remember, that not every one that saith unto me, Lord, Lord, shall enter into the Kingdom of Heaven, but he that doeth the will of my Father which is in Heaven.

Now to them that look for him (that is for Jesus,) shall he appear the second time without sin, unto salvation. According to the signs given by our Savior, we may look for him to make his second advent soon; and if so, brethren and sisters, let us labor to enter into the rest that is prepared for the children of God. Oh, let us all take warning, by the admonition of the Lord, when he saith, "be ye also ready, for in an hour when ye think not the Son of man cometh," and when he comes he will gather his elect from the four quarters of the earth, and they that have been faithful laborers in the vineyard of the Lord, shall be changed in a moment, in the twinkling of an eye, and ascend up with those who are resurrected and meet the Lord in the air and ever be with him in glory.

Now, dear reader, if this will find its way to you through the PILGRIM, I hope you will find some encouragement in it to press on toward the prize of our high calling in Christ Jesus. May the grace of God, and the Communion of the Holy Spirit, rest upon the Israel of God, is my hearts desire and prayer.

I find by reading the PILGRIM that the brethren have good meetings in some places. I hope that the time is not far distant when those good meetings, may be more general all over the world, that much good may be accomplished in these last times, for Christ's sake and so Amen.

HENRY GARST.

CHRIST THE RISEN SAVIOR.

Continued from No. 11.

"Now is Christ risen from the dead," that in any other case he who should not be satisfied with it would be deemed skeptical almost to insanity.

This is, however, but a very small part of the evidence afforded us in this important affair. Saul, the persecutor, was a man endowed with superior talents, cultivated by education, and possessed of peculiar advantage for rising in the world of which he was evidently availing himself while gratifying his implacable enmity to the gospel, yet was he all at once converted into a most zealous preacher of that faith which he had attempted to destroy, and renouncing all his former principles and worldly prospects, yea, expatiating above measure his powerful patrons and employers, he spent all the remnant of his days in the most self-denying labors, hardships and sufferings, endured with the greatest alacrity for the sake of Christ and the gospel, and at length sealed his testimony with his blood. How can this fact be accounted for unless we allow the truth of his narrative concerning the manner of his conversion, and if that be allowed, the resurrection of Christ is demonstrated in this chapter. This man declares that Christ appeared after his resurrection to above five hundred brethren at once, of whom the greater part remained to that time. This was our appeal to nearly three hundred living witnesses of that truth. But no one ever attempted to disprove the truth of his assertion, though false teachers would have concurred with open enemies in such an attempt, had it been practicable. The testimony of the apostles to the resurrection of Jesus, implied a charge of the most complicated wickedness against the rulers of the Jewish Nation. These had power in their hands and were ready to vindicate their characters and punish those who thus accused them. This might readily have been done had they produced the Roman soldiers in court to testify that the body of Jesus had been stolen, or to state in what way it had been removed from the sepulchre. But in fact, they had *bribed the soldiers to circulate* a self-contradictory report on this subject which would not bear investigation, and when St. Matthew soon afterward charged this publicly upon them, and declared that story was generally current among the Jews, to that time no one attempted to deny or disprove the charge. In every case of this nature silence must be construed into a confession of guilt, and if the rulers could have accounted for the removal of the body without either admitting the charge of Matthew or our Lord's Resurrection, no doubt can reasonably be made, but that they would have done it in the most public manner. Every reflecting person must perceive that the evidence is completely satisfactory, provided it can be made clear that their books were published at the time to which they refer. To obviate therefore, every doubt and without engaging in an argument I would inquire at what subsequent time it could have been possible to obtain credit to writings of this description. If manuscripts said to have been long concealed in some library, be produced, or published as the work of an eminent author, who flourished two or three centuries ago it immediately is subjected to a severe scrutiny, and imposture in such cases seldom escapes detection. But writings which contain a circumstantial narrative of things not done in a corner, but in the open view of mankind, during several years connected with an epistolary correspondence resulting from them, could never have obtained the least credit in the world.

If published after the times referred to, with an express appeal to mankind that they all have been familiarly acquainted with, then such an insolent attempt to persuade whole nations out of their senses and understanding must have excited universal astonishment and indignation, or had it been possible to convince a few individuals that they had received these books from their ancestors, and been taught from infancy to revere them as the writings of the apostles, when in fact neither they nor any other persons had ever before seen or heard of them. The effrontery of the deceiver and the credulity of the deceived, must have constituted an unprecedented event and marked the age in which it occurred. As therefore no one can be mentioned when any attempt of this kind is so much as hinted at by either Christian, Jewish, or Pagan historians, we might be confident that the writings in question extant, and well known in the church from the very period in which they are said to have been published, even had we no other evidence. But no impartial man of learning can be imposed upon by any pretense of this kind, having access to abundant proof of another nature, that the books of the New Testament were extant in the early ages of Christianity, and this argument is principally advanced for the benefit of those who have neither leisure nor advantages for these investigations. We should also remember that on the day of pentecost, immediately following the resurrection of Christ, the Holy Spirit was poured out on the assembled apostles with such extraordinary circumstances as drew together vast multitudes who then resided at Jerusalem. In the presence of all these witnesses they spake fluently and correctly in the language of several countries from which their hearers were collected, though it was certainly known that they had not the opportunity of learning them, and this miracle together with Peter's sermon on the occasion was made effectual to the conversion of three thousand persons. The gifts of tongues and of working miracles in the name of Jesus were ever after continued to them and were frequently exercised in the most public and undeniable manner before numerous witnesses; enemies as well as friends. The same powers were likewise communicated to many others by the laying on of the Apostles hands. The time, places, occasion and circumstances of these extraordinary transactions are frequently specified in their writing. Thus the inhabitants of many cities and countries were appealed to, and the enemies of Christianity were challenged to disprove their pretensions, but none ever attempted to do it for the Jews themselves do not.

To be continued.

PRAYING WITHOUT CEASING.

During a series of meetings, held by brethren D. F. Good, J. F. Oller, M. Miller and G. Mourer, there was much said on the subject of prayer. I read an article lately on praying without ceasing which I think worthy of being published.

"A number of ministers were assembled for the discussion of difficult questions, and among others it was asked how the command to pray without ceasing could be complied with. Various suppositions were started, and at length one of the number was appointed to write an essay upon it to read at the monthly meeting, which being overheard by a female servant, she exclaimed, 'What, a whole month wanted to tell the meaning of the text! It's one of the easiest and best texts in the Bible.'

"Well, well, Mary, said an old minister, what can you say about it? Let us know how you understand it. Can you pray at all times?

O yes sir.

What, when you have got so many things to do?

Why sir the more I have to do the more I can pray.

Well Mary, do let us know how it is for most people think otherwise.

Well sir, said the girl, when I first open my eyes in the morning, I pray the Lord to open the eyes of my understanding, and while I am dressing I pray that I may have strength equal to my day; when I begin to kindle the fire, I pray that God's work may revive in my soul and as I sweep the house I pray that my heart may be cleansed from all its impurities, and while preparing breakfast I desire to be fed with the hidden manna, and the sincere milk of the word, and as I am busy with the little children I look up to God as my Father, and pray for the spirit of adoption, that I may be his child, and so on all day, everything I do furnishes me with a thought for prayer.

Enough, enough, cried the old divine, these things are revealed to babes and often hid from the wise and prudent. Go on Mary, to pray without ceasing. As for us, my brothers, let us bless the Lord for this exposition, and remember that He has said the meek will guide in judgment."

Dear brethren and sisters, if we all could pray without ceasing what a blessing it would be to us. We would not have room for so many unnecessary things, we would be so much happier.

LOUISA C. BUTERBAUGH.
Clay Lick, Pa.

THE GRAVE.

Dear Pilgrim, have you ever thought of the solemn word, "The Grave?" Oh how solemn. Who is it that has not followed some near friends to the grave. Dear pilgrims let us all try and be ready to meet the pale white horse and not be alarmed at his coming for we will all have to go to the grave whether prepared or unprepared as we are going down every day, and methinks when I see the coffin lid closed for the last time over these smiling faces, can it be that this is the last look forever in this world. Oh how solemn to think over these solemn thoughts while we are traveling to the grave, for God is no respector of persons. Thus it is that death often [illegible] from the sickly to the healthy and from aged to the strong man in his prime, from the miserable wretch who longs for the grave to the smiling babe in its mother's arms. He pours his putrefying breath and leaves nothing in that mother's house but lonesomeness. All that is now left you is the little grave. How sad and lonely is the mother who is called to weep the loss of her departed infant, who is called to give up that loved one whose smiles were so bright and fair as she lays it in the cold damp earth and returns home to her house of mourning. There she sees her empty cradle, no friend can fill the place of her lost one.

Young mother, what can friendship say
To soothe the anguish of the day?
I've felt it all, alas, too well, I know
How vain all earthly power to hush thy
woe.

I've sat and watched by the dying bed,
And burning tears of anguish shed.
I've gazed upon the sweet but pallid face,
And there I've tried some comfort to trace.

I've listened to the short and struggling
breath,
I've saw the cherub eye grow dim in death
Like thee I've veiled my heart in gloom.
And laid my first born in the tomb.

A LEAF FROM MY KNOWLEDGE DRAWER.

Jesus never did anything that was not necessary; it was not necessary for him to go into the water to be sprinkled; but Jesus did go into the water; therefore he was not sprinkled.

Those who obey Jesus the best love him the most, and those who love him with all their heart, obey him with all their might.

Those who refuse to be baptized, do not follow in the foot-steps of Jesus, since the way that Jesus trod lay through the gate of baptism.

The Bible never once calls either sprinkling or pouring baptism; hence if either sprinkling or pouring is baptism, those who wrote the Bible either did not know it, or refused to tell what they did know.

Our English word *baptism* is from the Greek word *baptisma*, the meaning of which is dipping; hence "One Lord, one faith, one dipping."

Our English word *baptize* is from the Greek word *baptizo*; the meaning of which is dip or immerse.

If Paul referred to single immersion when he said "one baptism" then that method of baptizing must have been in use at that time. But single immersion was not invented until nearly 300 years after Paul's death. Therefore he did not refer to single immersion when he said "one baptism."

J. H. MOORE.

DARKNESS AND LIGHT.—Exclude light from a plant and it becomes sickly and unprofitable, so with the soul devoid of spiritual light and influence, it soon becomes sickly and unprofitable, and is cast out into "outer darkness" where there is "weeping and gnashing of teeth."

The plant that grows in the light and warmth of the sun is clothed in verdure,—flowers expand and fruit matures. So with the soul that is lit up with "the light of the world" it flourishes in the verdure of a life "hid in Christ." The christian graces bloom in great beauty, and fruits immortal are gathered when the eternal harvest comes.—*I. S. Flory.*

HAVE A FIXED PURPOSE.—Small is the number of human beings who follow any definite or particular plan during life. Millions spend a long and healthful life without having accomplished comparatively anything. A large majority of mankind set out at the beginning of maturity, without a fixed purpose, and while numbers come out almost anywhere thousands end life the next thing to nowhere. Have a fixed purpose in life, and stick to it. Though you may not be great, there is a noble chance to be wise and useful, and these are the secret corner stones of true greatness.—*J. H. Moore.*

SCRIPTURES.—A noble book! All men's book! It is our first, oldest statement of the never ending problem,—man's destiny, and God's ways with him here on earth; and all in such free-flowing outlines,—grand in its sincerity, in its simplicity, in its epic melody, and repose of reconcilement.—*Carlyle.*

I HAVE read it through many times; I now make a practice of going through it once a year. It is a book of all others for lawyers, as well as divines; and I pity the man who cannot find it a rich supply of thought and rule for conduct.—*Daniel Webster.*

Selections.

THE Lord, our Shepherd coming out to hunt the lost sheep, puts on no regal apparel, but the plain garment of our humanity. There was nothing pretentious about it. I know the old painters represent a halo around the babe, Jesus, but I don't suppose that there was any more halo about that child than about the head of any other babe that was born that Christmas eve in Judea. Becoming a man, he wore a seamless garment. The scissors and needle had done nothing to make it graceful. I take it to have been a sack with three holes in it, one for the neck and two for the arms. Although the gamblers quarrelled over it, that is no evidence of its value. I have seen two rag-pickers quarrel over the refuse of an ash-barrel. No! in the wardrobe of heaven, he left the sandals of light, the girdles of beauty, the robes of power. The work of saving this world was rough work, rugged work, hard work; and Jesus put on the raiment, the plain raiment, of our flesh. The storms were to beat him, the crowds were to jostle him, the dust was to sprinkle him, the mobs were to pursue him. O Shepherd of Israel! leave at home thy bright array; for thee, what streams to ford, what nights all unsheltered! He puts upon him the raiment of our humanity, wears our woes, and while earth and heaven and hell stand amazed at the abnegation, wraps around him the shepherd's plaid.—*Talmage.*

THE Christian wants to know no new thing, but to have his heart more elevated above the world, by secluding himself from it as much as his duties will allow, that religion may affect this its great end, by bringing its sublime hopes and prospects into more steady action upon the mind. Recollection is the life of religion.—*Cecil.*

BUT what is a trust in God good for that departs when you need it, and comes again only when you can't get along without? What is a ship good for that is safe in the harbor but unsafe on the ocean? What is a sail good for that is sound in a calm, but splits in the first wind? What patience is that which only lasts when there is nothing to bear? Courage, when there is no danger; firmness where is no pressure; hope, when everything is before the eyes—what are all these worth? But such is not the trust which most Christians have in God. It has no virtue in it. It is like a lighthouse that burns only in daylight, and is extinguished at sundown.

SOME malady which you do not understand troubles and alarms you. The physician is called. Thinking that the illness proceeds from a certain inflammatory process on a portion of your skin, you anxiously direct his attention to the spot. Silently but sympathizingly, he looks at the place where you have bidden him look, and because you have bidden him look there, but soon he turns away. He is busy with an instrument on another part of your body. He presses his trumpet-tube gently to your breast, and listens for the pulsations which faintly but distinctly pass through. He looks and listens there, and saddens as he looks. You again direct his attention to the cutaneous eruption which annoys you. He sighs and sits silent. When you reiterate your request that something should be done for the external eruption, he gently shakes his head, and answers not a word. From this silence you would learn the truth at last, you would not miss its meaning long.

O! miss not the meaning of the Lord when he points to the seat of soul's disease: "Ye will not come." These, his enemies, dwell in your heart.—*William Arnot.*

A JUDICIOUS silence is always better than truth spoken without charity. The most powerful remedy against sudden starts of impatience is a sweet and amiable silence. However little one speaks, self-love will have a share in it, and some word will escape that may sour the heart and disturb its peace for a considerable time. When nothing is said, and cheerfulness preserved, the storm subsides; anger and indiscretion are put to flight, and nothing remains but a joy pure and lasting.—*Francis de Sales.*

To be despised, reprehended, or accused by wicked men, is pleasant to a man of good heart; but to suffer blame or ill-treatment from the virtuous, or from our friends and relations, is *the test* of true patience. Be patient not only with respect to the subject of the affliction which may befall you, but also with regard to its accessories or accidental circumstances. We must preserve the whole interior of our breast always sweet.—*Francis de Sales.*

ONE WORD.—Madge had a spoiled day. It was just one little word that did it all. Madge had sprung out of bed that morning determined to try to do good; but when Ned happened to spill his coffee on her new dress, she forgot her good resolutions, and declared that he was the most provoking fellow in the world. Then Ned grew angry and "answered back," and after that everything went wrong all day, for never a day goes pleasantly that begins with angry words.

Religious News.

DEBATE.—There will be a debate four miles north of Marysville, commencing on Tuesday, April 8th, at half past nine o'clock a. m. to continue four days, between A. C. Hanger of the Christians, and J. J. Moss of the Disciples, on the following questions:

1. "Do the Scriptures teach that repentance toward God, and faith in our Lord Jesus Christ, without baptism, are for remission of sins?" A. C. Hanger affirms.

2. "Do the Scriptures teach that baptism is as essential for remission of sins, as repentance toward God and faith in our Lord Jesus Christ?" J. J. Moss, affirms.

UNION MEETING HOUSE, Union Co., O.

RELIGIOUS FREEDOM.—Rev. J. L. M. Curry, LL. D., of Richmond, Va., recently delivered a lecture in Hanson-Street Baptist church, Brooklyn, N. Y., on the subject of "Baptists and Soul Liberty," in which he says: "For their championship of religious liberty the Baptists have suffered ignominy, insult and persecution from the State and from other denominations. They have been imprisoned in Berlin, butchered in France, oppressed in England whipped in Massachusetts, sent to jail in Virginia. They have been banished, burned, starved, drowned, and slain by the sword, for maintaining that God alone is Lord of the conscience. In Virginia the House of Burgesses taxed its ingenuity to the utmost to devise punishments for those who preached the gospel without Episcopal ordination. These facts are recorded by historians of other denominations, and the records of jails in Virginia to-day contain the proofs of Baptist faithfulness and martyrdom."

Foreign.

EVANGELIZATION IN LIBERIA.—Three are waiting to be baptized in Monrovia, Africa, and twelve in Caldwell. At the Baptist Mission in New Georgia eighteen were baptized a few Sabbaths ago. Seven at Freeman station were also candidates. *Most* of these converts are native and half civilized Congoes.

JEWISH CONVERTS.—Sixty years ago, there was hardly a Jewish convert to Christianity in Great Britain. Now there twenty thousand converts on the Continent and three thousand in England, of whom one hundred are clergymen of the Church of England. In the University of Berlin twenty-eight of the professors are converted Jews.

THE JAPAN MISSION.—When the missionaries of the Reformed Church reached Japan, before they had time to learn the language, a door of usefulness was opened to them the Japanese youths, who were eager to learn the English language. Soon Bible classes were formed in all their schools. The presence of so many Japanese studying in our American schools is a direct result of their labors.

CHURCH DESTROYED.—During the prevalence of a severe storm on the 2nd inst., the church of Little Beaver, Presbytery of Shenango, Penn., was blown down. Services had been held in the morning, and was announced for in the evening; if a congregation had been present at the time of the calamity, there certainly would have been a great loss of life. The building was repaired and renovated some two years ago at considerable outlay. Rev. David Harrison, of the Presbytery of Blairsville, had just been called to the pastorate. The loss will fall heavier on the people, who will receive the sympathy of others.

Constance the scene of martyrdom of John Huss and Jerome of Prague, had just been the scene of a demonstration in favor of the Old Catholic cause. On Sunday, Feb. 9th, Professor Michelis and Friedrich addressed an enthusiastic meeting of between two and three thousand people from all parts of the land bordering on the lake, and with such effect, that the next day a *plebiscite* was taken of the Constance Catholics, when 653 declared their non-adherence to the Infallibility party. The scene, so report the papers, was most exciting, all work was stopped, and the greatest interest stirred up; the priests had sent out fly sheets, urging the people to vote against the Reformers, but in vain. The Swiss reform movement had infected the neighboring Badeners, and they flocked to the poll. Two Churches are forthwith to be demanded from the Government.

Bells and Church Divisions.

A writer in the *Baptist Weekly* says: A very hard-hearted clapper in an old church tower professed the intensest distress because its bell was hopelessly cracked. Many people thought it a pitiable position, and wished the sad-hearted clapper a better bell. But just then the Ghost of ancient Diogenes, the sage, floated in through the window, and whistled most angrily: "Master Clapper, cease your noise, and remember, in the first place, *you* cracked the bell; and, secondly, nobody would have known it had you not told them." I have observed often that those who bemoan divisions in a church are those who make them; and I also observed sometimes that they who make them are most ready to publish the fact; I have observed another fact, *viz.* that all clappers are not as good metal as the bells they crack.

Youth's Department

SPEECH OF "KING ALCOHOL."

DEAR FRIENDS AND COADJUTORS:—Let me first briefly consider what I have done in the past. As I turn the pages of history, and glance back down the ages, I almost feel constrained to ask: What have I *not* done in the past? From my very birth, I have trod the earth, conquering and to conquer. I have brought ruin to kings and to kingdoms. I have crushed poets and scholars, sculptors and scientists, orators and artists, as worms beneath my heel.

I have crushed the best feelings of the human heart. I have brought the gray hairs of the aged to the grave in sorrow. I have made widows weep and orphans mourn. I have separated families, broken the hearts of wives and mothers, and blighted the lives of little children. I have caused vice, crime and ignorance. I have caused starvation, disease and death. I have changed men into demons. Wherever I have gone, there have also gone slavery, war and bloodshed. I have stalked in the halls of legislation, and blasted the fair hopes of friends of learning. I have built poorhouses and filled them with paupers. I have built jails and prisons, and filled them with criminals and convicts. I have built asylums, and peopled them with orphans. I have erected scaffolds and caused man to murder his fellow man; to take a human life, to blot out all that strength and courage which make him famous among men; "all the probabilities in life of a gifted man; the renown, the position, the pleasures, the profits, the keen, ecstatic joy, that never could be made up,—all ended quite," nothing left but the unsightly corpse, which must soon be buried from sight. All this have I done, and then smiled as I fastened the rope around his neck that was to launch him forth into eternity.

At present, I am spreading disease, desolation, death, misery, vice, crime, jails, prisons and scaffolds, and filled orphan asylums throughout the civilized world. I know it is said that free schools, colleges, universities, seminaries, and, in fact, all places of learning, science and art, the press and the pulpit, are retarding my progress. No doubt but they will retard my progress in every way possible; they are my enemies and ever have been. But they cannot stop me. *Stop me!*

They might as well attempt to dam up the Niagara, or let the ocean into the heart of Vesuvius. I never was more prosperous than at the present moment. Hear what *they* themselves say of me. "He is yearly destroying 600,000 lives in the United States alone. He is yearly sending to prison 100,000 men and women. He is annually sending to the poorhouse 200,000 children." (A large per cent. of these children will grow up in ignorance and want, and eventually consent to become my servants). "He is yearly causing 300 murders to be committed; he annually causes 100 suicides. He annually bequeaths to private and public charity 200,000 orphans." All this, in *United States alone!*

When my enemies are forced to make this acknowledgment, who says my power is waning? Nor is this all. My traffic against the laws of God and man is rapidly increasing. I am yearly gathering strength and marshalling my forces for the conflict that is surely approaching—the conflict that is either to leave me victor in possession of the field, to scatter my seeds of hell at pleasure, and to my harvests of drunkenness and vice at will, or to witness my utter annihilation, to see me lie down to sleep my last sleep, to hear the rattle in my throat, to see my eye swim in agony (blessed sound and blessed sight to the friends of temperance, peace and love), and see me buried so far from the memories of men that to future generations my name will be unknown. But until that day *does* come, until the last hour of my existence, this shall be the motto, written in letters of blood upon the black banner under which I march: "To make countless thousands mourn."—*The Young Folks Rural.*

CULTIVATE THAT PLANT.

You have a plant on your window—a rare plant. You expect that in due time it will bring forth a flower. You are careful of it. You attend to it regularly. You think of it often, and supply its wants. You watch its growth and developments. You show it to your friends. In short, it is your favorite—your nursling, and the hope of your heart.

Now, my young friend, we find no fault with what you do. It is rather a taste which we would encourage: for the heart is always improved when it loves, and is interested in something that is lovely. What we wish to say is this: you have *within you* such a plant, which, if properly cultivated, will bring forth a far lovlier flower than any earth has ever yielded. Your own spirit may be made to blossom in heaven, covered with all the graces of the Spirit. Cultivate it carefully. Have it always in your thoughts. Watch its growth; labor for its improvement; make it the favorite, and hope of your heart. It is of more value than many flowers.

The same bread feeds angels and and men, souls in glory, and travellers in grace.

Correspondence.

A Reporter is wanted from every Church in the brotherhood to send us Church news, Obituaries, Announcements, or anything that will be of general interest. To insure insertion, the writers name must accompany each communication. Our Invitation is not personal but general—please respond to our call.

In Memory of Sister Sarah Furgason, Dec'd.

The subject of this notice was born on the 16th of November, A. D., 1850, being the third child of our esteemed Bro. Robert and sister Susan Furgason. Surrounded by the hallowed influences of a christian home, she grew to the age of womanhood, and entered the gay society that is in the world, and is so attractive to the young mind, carnally inclined to imbibe the errors that are cast abroad for truth at the present day. Still her heart was of a religious and God-fearing turn, and she manifested a disposition to do the bidding of Him who saith, "If any man will come after me, let him deny himself and take up his cross and follow me."

Her first religious impressions to which she gave heed so as to inquire for the ways of salvation, were received at a protracted meeting conducted by the "Brethren in Christ," or as they are more familiarly known, "Shumakarians." She entered into Church relation with them, and continued that union until after her health began to fail, and then her mind still remained for a while apparently unchanged, as to her future welfare for time and eternity. Neither knew we any change in her mind religiously, until during the winter of 1872, when Bro. Jesse Calvert, from Milford, Ind., was with us, and preached to all that assembled the sure testimonies of the Lord. It was then that the messenger of the Covenant came to her once more through his preached gospel and in silent meditation, that caused her mind to undergo a change, when she concluded to change the Church relations and made application to be received into the Church, and afflicted as she was, in her affliction, with dropsy in its loathsomeness, and quite weak, in the midst of the cold, on the 23rd of January, A. D., 1872, she was conveyed to the water in a sleigh, and then we led her down into the liquid water and there, according to the appointment of her divine Lord, she was baptized, and though the water was at the freezing point; with a warm heart and strong faith in the promises of the Savior, she endured as a faithful soldier of the cross of Christ, and was enabled to rejoice with joy unspeakable and full of glory.

Before Bro. Calvert bade us farewell she was annointed with oil in the name of the Lord according to the direction of the Lord, James—5: 14, 15. Meanwhile all that skill and kindness could do was done to relieve her sufferings. Tapping was resorted to by the physicians and was performed successfully eleven times, and thirty-two gallons of water taken from her. This all along, gave her more or less relief until the last time, which was not so effective, as it appeared that death had marked her for his own, and on the morning of March 4th, the sorrow stricken family and some waiting friends gathered in her room, round her bed, to see the king of terrors do his work. Her last hours were peaceful, as upon the bosom of Jesus she leaned her head and realized that "Jesus can make a dying bed feel soft as downy pillows are."

There lay the body of clay, lifeless, to be laid on the cooling board by kind though reluctant hands. On the following day the remains were escorted to the narrow house by a large escort of mourning relations and sympathizing friends. There she lies among the remembered dead. Yes there all that is mortal of sister Sarah sleeps the long, dreamless sleep of death till the "Lord himself shall descend from the heavens with a shout, with the voice of the archangel and with the trump of God, and the dead in Christ shall rise first." And dear father, mother, brother and sisters, friends and relatives, old and young, she being dead yet speaketh to you in well-known accents, which exhort you, to choose the Savior she has chosen, to cultivate the virtues which she has recommended, to live disinterestedly, live for immortality.

"It is not all of life to live.
Nor all of death to die."

On Sunday the 10th of March the friends and community generally assembled at our meeting house, to listen to the funeral services of our sister which we conducted as God gave us utterance from 2 Cor.—5: 1. And we had as interesting an audience as is necessary to have on such an occasion as this.

It seems, *it is sad* to give sister Sarah up at the youthful age of 22 yrs., 3 mos. and 18 days, yet we have the bright anticipation of meeting her once more, not on any earthly shore, not beneath any changing sky, but on the sunny shore of the river of life, beneath the smiling presence of God, and with her roam the Father's house of many mansions where parted friends will meet again to exchange kindliest greeting with each other.

"When, O, thou city of my God.
Shall I thy courts ascend,
Where congregations ne'er break up.
And sabbath's never end?

"Apostles, martyrs prophet's there,
Around my Savior stand,
And soon my friends in Christ below
Will join the glorious band."

J. P. Hetric.

Oakland, Pa.

STILL ONWARD.

Dear Pilgrim:—I feel encouraged now, and desire to inform you and your many readers of our pilgrimage here in Missouri. It is now just nine years since I penetrated my way through the centre of northern Missouri, westward into Kansas; at that time not knowing of any brethren anywhere in Mo. I learned since however, that there were a few members in Knox and Schuyler counties, and a few in Clinton Co., and one sister in Cedar at that time. When the war closed emigration began to pour into this state from the East, North, and West, and congregations were soon organized here and there throughout the state. But up to four years ago our district was composed of Mo., Kansas, and I believe Nebraska. Last May this State was divided into two districts after having composed one district for three years. The districts are called North and South Mo. districts. On the 7th of this month—March—the North Mo. district met for the first time, and organized for council, choosing for moderator, brother George Witwer, and for clerk brother Eli Metz, for assistant clerk and corresponding secretary C. C. Root. Of the ten congregations of which the district is composed, six were represented, all by delegates. Out of the six churches, ten ministers were present, and four absent. What an interesting council would North Mo. afford were it fully represented! Twenty three ministers according to the proportion of the churches represented, besides other delegates and members. Now according to the above statistics is not the word *onward* an appropriate motto for pilgrims here. But to this date of our pilgrimage here let us rear up a pillar in our hearts and call it Ebenezer.

COR. SECRETARY.

ROSEVILLE, O.,
March 11, 1873.

Bro. Brumbaugh:—I have read some eight or nine Nos. of the PILGRIM and I can truly say that I am much pleased with the paper. We think that there might be much good accomplished if we could induce our neighbors and friends to take the PILGRIM or some other one of the Brethren's periodicals. Brethren and sisters we can all do something toward enlarging Zion's borders. There are not many of us but what have some friends or neighbors out of Christ, and Oh! let us think for one moment; are we using every means in our power to bring them into the fold of Christ? If we are not it is high time we make an effort. Let us be up and adoing while it is called day for when the night cometh no man can work. Brethren and sisters let us be alive in the cause of our Master. Oh may we let our light shine so that our friends and neighbors may take knowledge of us that we have been with Jesus and learned of Him. Let us remember there is more joy in heaven over one sinner that repenteth than over ninety and nine just persons that need no repentance. Let us use every available means in our power to bring sinners to Christ, and not hide our talent as did the slothful servant, but let us improve it. Yes, improve it to the honor and glory of God and the salvation of souls. Let us be willing to spend and be spent in the cause of our Master and ever remember that our work will soon be done. God grant that all may live and work as we will wish we had done when we come to die that it may be said to us, "come up higher."

NOAH HORN.

Dear Pilgrim:—This evening through the mercies of God, I am spared and am enjoying one of the best of blessings, good health, and am thankful this evening that the great privilege is given me to correspond with so valuable paper as the PILGRIM. What a great blessing it is to weak humanity that through the silent pen we may converse with distant friends.

Dear PILGRIM, since it is your motive as well as mine to work in the Master's cause in trying to build up Zion, we will put our trust in God and work together for good hoping that if this is worthy of your columns that it may find its way to some lone heart, and that to do good. I believe there is work for you and me to do as well as for all others who love to see sinners come to Christ. I am young in the Master's cause and it is a sore regret to me that I did not give my heart to God at an earlier time than I did. Dear PILGRIM, the friend of sinners, press onward and upward, strive that you may send glad tidings of joy to every heart and home, and God grant that you may hurl the Gospel news to every family where fictitious reading covers mantle and shelf. Time may not be long any more, therefore dear brethren and sisters, let us work for Jesus. The best we can do will not repay those drops of blood that stood on our dear Redeemer in Gethsemane Garden. We cannot repay the great agony the Savior underwent for us poor sinful creatures. We do not deserve Heaven as home if we think of ourselves alone, when there are thousands that know not Christ. A Christian's life is marked with trials and troubles on the way, and many temptations are in our path daily, but our trials here will only make it brighter there if we prove faithful to the end. What if the waters may be deep, dark and rapid. What if they do threaten to engulf us in their angry waves, is not God on the other side? Yes he is there on that evergreen shore, and beckons us come on. If we only trust in him his grace is sufficient for us all. He has promised to be with us and will lead us safely through the valley and shadow of death and when life with all its sorrows and cares are over we may meet those dear old Fathers, those dear old Mothers and all those loved ones gone before, where crowns of life are laid up for all those who love God. May we all pray that there may be at least one star in that crown for us, and may we all meet in that better world where parting will be known no more, there to sing God's praise through endless ages of eternity on Canaan's peaceful shore.

From your unworthy correspondent,

LOVINA H. BURKHART.

ANNOUNCEMENTS.

Please announce that the District Meeting of Northern Indiana and Michigan, will be held in the Brethren's Meetinghouse, ½ mile west of Goshen, Elkhart Co., Ind., commencing on Thursday the 1st day of May, 1873, at 10 o'clock, a. m.

JESSE CALVERT, Clerk.

Champaign Lovefeast.

The brethren in Champaign Co., Ill., have appointed their Communion Meeting on Saturday and Sunday, June 7th and 8th, 1873, at *Bro.* Geo. Dilling's, five miles east of Urbana. We extend an invitation to all, especially the ministering brethren.

J. H. MOORE,
Urbana, Ill.

TO ALL WHO ARE CONCERNED.

We do, through this medium, inform the brethren and churches comprising the first district of Virginia, that Friday and Saturday before the fourth Sunday in April, is the time appointed for the holding of the Annual District Meeting, and will be held at that time no preventive providence, at the Valley Meeting-house in Botetourt Co., one mile south of Amsterdam. A full attendance is desirable.

The undersigned also informs his brethren that he has a number of New Hymn Books on hand for sale. B. F. MOOMAW.

Please announce that the District Meeting of Western Maryland, will be held the Lord willing in the Welsh Run Congregation in the Broad Fording Meetinghouse, five miles north-west of Hagerstown on the second Thursday in April, 1872.

NICHOLAS MARTIN.

You will please announce through the PILGRIM that the Brethren in the Middle District of Iowa, purpose holding their District Council Meeting with the Brethren in Dallas Co., in their Meetinghouse, on Monday the 19th day of May, 1873. We expect a good representation of delegates, also a general invitation to the brethren to be with us.

J. S. SNYDER,
Cor. Sec'y.

Please announce through your paper, the Lord willing, the District Meeting for the North-eastern District of Ohio, will be held in the Jonathan's Creek Congregation, Perry Co., Ohio, on Tuesday the 20th day of May, 1873, being the second Tuesday before the A. M. All persons coming to the meeting (*i. e.*) brethren and sisters, must come to Newark, Ohio, thence down the Newark, Somerset & Straitsville Railroad to Glenford Station, there the brethren will meet those who come and convey them to the place of meeting, 3 miles off. Those who intend to come will please write us and we will have the necessary arrangements made.

W. ARNOLD.
Somerset, Perry Co., O.

Please announce through the PILGRIM that our District Meeting will be held on the 13th of May in the Cook's Creek Congregation, Rockingham Co., Va.

SOLOMON GARBER.

Please make the following announcement in the WEEKLY PILGRIM. The District Meeting of West Virginia, will be held in Seneca District, eight miles west of Mouth of Seneca, at Union School House, in Dry Fork township, Randolph Co., on Friday and Saturday, 9th and 10th of May. For any further information address the undersigned at Mouth of Seneca, Pendleton Co., W. Va.

By order of the Church.

ASA HARMAN.

The District Meeting of Middle Penna., will be held, the Lord willing, at the Clover Creek Meeting-house, Blair Co., on Tuesday the 13th day of May, '73. Brethren coming by Railroad will come to Altoona, thence by Hollidaysburg and Morrison's Cove branch to Martinsburg, which is two miles from place of meeting. Those coming Via. Harrisburg, should be sure to be there by 1 P. M. to meet the mail train, so they get to Martinsburg at 9 P. M., if later, they must lay over.

It is the desire of the church here, that some of our dear ministering brethren be with us over Sunday, and have meetings at four or five different places. Now those who feel willing to do so, will please notify Bro J. W. Brumbaugh, Clover Creek, Blair Co., Pa., informing him when they expect to arrive, and conveyance will be ready to take them to the different points.

D. M. HOLSINGER.

DIED.

WAGONER.—In the North Fork of Wildcat Church, Pyrmont, Carroll Co., Ind., February 28, 1873, sister Catharine, wife of brother David D. Wagoner, aged 21 years, 8 months, and 8 days. Funeral services by Elder Isaac Cripe and Samuel Ullery.

She leaves a sorrowing husband and two little step-sons to mourn their loss. The evening previous to her death she was anointed with oil in the name of the Lord.

CATHARINE D. MICHAEL.

MILLER.—Near Dayton, Ohio, Jan. 21, '73, brother Joseph B. Miller, aged 27 years, 6 months and 21 days. Disease strangulated brain. Funeral service by brethren Nead, Brubaker and others, from Rev. 14:13.

The noiseless foot-steps of death crossed the threshold and removed the center of family attraction and delight. Brother Miller was afflicted several months, and suffered much. He bowed in humble submission to the afflicting hand of Providence, and was resigned to the Master's will, to live or die. Seeing the will of the Lord concerning him indicated a departure to the spirit land, he arranged his temporal affairs, providing liberally for his dear, but now bereft companion, whom he committed to the "widow's husband" above. In the early part of his illness, he called on the Elders of the church, and was anointed with oil in the name of the Lord. He calmly met the approaching message, and resigned his departing spirit to the care and keeping of the Savior.

Whilst in the tomb our father lies,
His spirit rests above;
In realms of bliss it never dies,
But knows a Savior's love.

W.

FISHER.—In the Monticello District, White Co., Ind., Feb. 4, '73, Bro. Samuel Fisher, formerly of Franklin Co. Va., aged 48 years and one day. Also Feb. 2, '73, Elizabeth F., daughter of the above, and sister Rebecca Fisher, aged 8 years, 1 month and 9 days, both died of brain fever, being sick only a few days.

On the 6th their remains were conveyed to their last resting place by a large concourse of sympathizing friends and neighbors, and both laid in one grave. Truly a solemn scene to see father and daughter lie side by side in the cold embrace of death, warning old and young to prepare to meet their God. The occasion was improved from the words, "For me to live is Christ, and to die is gain," by brother Jos. Amick and the writer, and we hope the warning will not altogether be in vain. May God graciously smile upon the bereaved widow and the rest of her family, who have had to undergo some severe trials since they made their home among us. In the Spring of 1868 one of their sons was killed by lightning, and in the Spring of 1872 one died with brain fever, and now father and daughter at one time are taken from our dear sister. O that the remaining children may strive to meet them in a better world, where no such solemn trials are to be endured, but where friends can meet with immortal bodies, and sing, O death, where is thy sting! O grave where is thy victory?

MISNER.—On the same farm, old mother Misner January 22, and on the 25th, a little grand-daughter of hers. Funeral improved by the writer.

J. S. SNOWBERGER.

The Weekly Pilgrim.

JAMES CREEK, PA., April 1, 1873.

☞ How to send money.—All sums over $1.50, should be sent either in a check, draft or postal order. If neither of these can be obtained, have the letter registered.

☞ When Money is sent, *always* send with it the name and address of those who paid it. Write the names and post office as plainly as possible.

☞ Every subscriber for 1873, gets a *Pilgrim Almanac* Free.

EDUCATIONAL.

In a communication to the Pilgrim several months ago, we noticed briefly the propriety of the Brethren in the East making a move towards the erection of school buildings, and the establishment of a school that would meet the apparent want of the Church. Of late this question seems to be more agitated, and the project in some localities meets with a degree of approval, that promises fair for a move in this direction. In view of this we are stimulated to again take up our pen, and drop a few thoughts relative to this important project.

We are aware there are those who differ from us, as to the propriety of having a school under the supervision of the Brethren, but we always regard the opinions of others with deference, and are not disposed to look upon our own as always being right, and those of others as always wrong. We hope then that those who think differently, will allow us the privilege of giving our sentiments without any unpleasant reflections.

Some of our aged brethren look upon schools as an innovation, and one too, that is likely to bring about direful results. We do not by any means censure them for having these fears, and indeed they are not without grounds. There is a tendency to glide into the popular current in reference to this matter, and if we will allow ourselves to move with this current, it will certainly result in the downfall of our glorious Zion.

We will notice briefly some of the objections that are brought against schools. Says a brother, "Colleges lead pride into the Church." We agree that Colleges *might* lead pride into the Church as well as *might* many other things. But Colleges has never led pride into the Church of the Brethren, nor is it likely they will very soon; therefore the result of colleges cannot exist, and our brother, we think, would better not make a positive declaration in reference to a thing that does not exist, nor was never known to exist. We have a school that, as far as known to us, is in successful operation, but the term *college* is really, we think, not appropriate. There are hundreds of institutions in our land to-day denominated colleges that are far from being such, and would we not, brethren, better adopt the name "Brethren's School," and avoid high sounding titles, especially when such titles are not strictly appropriate? We do not mean by this to cast any reflections on those who are immediately concerned in the school already in progress, as it no doubt meets their ideal of a college. We have *one* school in the Church, and we do not know what effect it is producing, but we feel confident that if it is nursing pride, the fault rests with those who have charge of it, and not in the school. Pride may be coming into the Church, but it is most likely entering through a wider door than that of schools. There are many ways through which pride may enter the Church, and might it not be that the watchman have conceived the idea that this is *the* way, while other places are left unguarded.

But will school lead pride into the Church? If our schools are properly conducted, and under the supervision of those who are influenced by Christian principles, there certainly cannot be as much danger as is anticipated. It is a well known fact to all, that we are greatly influenced by those who surround us, and a school under the auspices of the Church will certainly throw its influence in favor of the Church. It must have an influence, and if that influence is not for the Church, it is because it is devoid of the principles of the Church. Pride is governed greatly by surrounding circumstances. We see more of it in some localities than in others, and in some churches than others, all of which depend on the nature of the prevailing influence. Then let the influence of our schools be against pride, as well as other evil, and its influence must certainly have a salutary effect. There are hundreds of our fraternity and their children attending school, and is it not evident to every thinking mind that if these were sent to a school under the influence of the Church, that they would more likely inculcate its principles? If then, the principles of the Church are to fight against pride, which they certainly should be and our schools be governed by these, may they not be a means to keep pride out of the Church?

Again, it is said to be something new, and therefore some object to schools. Schools among the Brethren may be something *new*, but whether they should have been so is question upon which we might differ from some, but we will not discuss it at this time. The subject and the discussion of it, however, is nothing new, and indeed it is becoming old enough, if there be any virtue in age, to demand some attention. The subject was agitated years ago, and nearly as much accomplished then as now. Schools are nothing new. They have existed for centuries, and we as a Church have, to a limited extent, availed ourselves of the advantages to be derived from them. This we may still continue to do, but unless we will ourselves take hold of the work of education the surrounding influence will certainly lead many, that might be bright and shining ornaments in the Church, away from it. This fact has been so frequently demonstrated that it ought to cause every one to reflect seriously on this subject. Many parents have learned to their sorrow the power of the influence exerted over their sons and daughters while attending school. We can call to mind a number of instances in which brethren's children have united with other churches, all of which their parents attribute to the influence brought to bear upon them while at school. Now if this influence can be avoided, should not the Church make an effort to do so? The Divine injunction is, "Be harmless as doves and wise as serpents," and would there not be wisdom in trying to protect our youth from the influences of the world?

There is an idea extant among part of the Brotherhood at least, that were we to establish schools the design would be to prepare our brethren for the ministry, and that our ministers would finally drift into the same channel with other churches. It is to be feared that there are a few who might favor an idea of this kind, and it is perhaps the sentiments of this few, though very indirectly expressed, that forms a basis for this idea. But if there be such at all, they are certainly very few, at any rate this is not the idea, and we can assure you, brethren, that were this so, we would be among the number that would oppose schools. We do think that mental culture might be an advantage to some of our ministers, and we have heard a number of them regret their deficiency in this respect, but if mental culture can be made available in meeting and contesting with the great enemy of souls, our laity need it as much as the ministry. Our ministers are watchmen on the walls of Zion, but when it comes to the contest the laity must help fight the battles. When the great Captain of our salvation wants more watchmen, He will call them through the instrumentality of the Church, and if we keep the apostolic method of calling our ministers, we need not fear these innovators.

Now brethren, we have given our opinion in reference to schools in a very brief form, and hope we are understood. Our desire is that the propriety of the Brethren having schools, which may screen our youth from the contaminating influence of the world, receive some thought, and that whatever may be done, will result in good, and tend to the prosperity of the Church, and the furtherance of the Redeemer's Kingdom.

J. B. B.

Almanac for 1874.—We have now opened a book in which we wish to correct all the errors in our "Ministerial List," also, to add all such as are not in and those called and may be called up to time commencing our next years Almanac. We intend to commence the work in time so we may be enabled to have things in better shape than that of the present year. We kindly solicit all such as are not in the list to inform us of it, giving the address in full. Any information of standing value to the church is also solicited. We give this timely notice that all may be prepared to give us the desired information.

Briggs & Bro., will please accept our thanks for their magnificent Chromos received at our office.

No. 1. embodies sixteen colors and multiform tints, and is composed of forty-three different varieties of flowers, with a key, naming each variety.

No. 2. is a very fine Chromo of eighteen colors and multiform tints representing thirty-two different varieties of flowers. The colors are rich and very beautiful.

No. 3. is a magnificent Lily Chromo of eighteen colors and sixteen varieties. It is lovely and cannot help but be admired by all.

No. 4. is the Grand Chromo of the season. It embodies twenty different colors and is agreeably interspersed with figures that are intended to enhance its beauty.

These Chromos are 19x24 inches and sent post paid, for 75 cents each, by Briggs and Bro., who also publish a mammoth Illustrated Floral Quarterly and seed catalogue which will be sent to all for 25 cents. Address Briggs & Bro., Rochester, New York.

Latham & Co., have sent us a pair of their beautiful crayons of "Raphael's Cherubs." Size 20x24. The original, in the possession of the King of Saxony, is regarded not only as the gem of the Dresden Gallery, but of the whole world of art. They are so pretty that we have not words at command to describe them.

[illegible]

Father Hyacinth is expected to resume the pulpit at Geneva at the invitation of the liberal Catholics. By the way, 'Old' Catholics, 'Liberal' Catholics, etc., sounds as if Rome's boast, that she has no sects, can no longer be uttered.

SPECIAL NOTICES.

Seeds, Plants, Trees.—Prepaid by Mail.

My new priced descriptive Catalogue of Choice Flower and Garden Seeds, 25 sorts of either for $1; new and choice varieties of Fruit and Ornamental Trees, Shrubs, Evergreens, Roses, Grapes, Lilies, Small Fruits, House and Border Plants and Bulbs; one year grafted Fruit Trees for mailing: Fruit Stocks of all kinds; Hedge Plants, &c.; the most complete assortment in the country, will be sent gratis to any plain address, with P. O. box. True Cape Cod Cranberry for upland or lowland, $6 per 1000; $1 per 100; prepaid by mail. Trade List to dealers. Seeds on Commission Agents wanted. B. M. WATSON,

Old Colony Nurseries and Seed Warehouse, Plymouth, Mass. Established 1842.

$50.000

Will be distributed this year, to the subscribers for the AMERICAN WORKING PEOPLE, a large quarto, 16 page Monthly, costing but $1.50 per year. It gives a premium to every subscriber, varying from 25 cents in value up to $2, $5, $10, $20, $100, $200, and $500 in Greenbacks besides Watches, Sewing Machines, Parlor Organs and numerous other premiums of value. Send for specimen and circulars to

CAPRON & Co.,
Mar. 18 3m. Pittsburgh, Pa.

WANTED. We will give men and women

Business that will Pay

from $4 to $8 per day, can be pursued in your own neighborhood; it is a rare chance for those out of employment or having leisure time; girls and boys frequently do as well as men. Particulars free.

Address J. LATHAM & CO.,
292 Washington St., Boston, Mass

Trine Immersion

TRACED

TO THE APOSTLES.

The SECOND EDITION is now ready for delivery. The work has been carefully revised, corrected and enlarged.

Put up in a neat pamphlet form, with good paper cover, and will be sent, post-paid, on the following terms: One copy, 25 cts; Five copies, $1.10; Ten copies, $2.00. 25 copies, $4.50; 50 copies, $8.50; 100 copies, $16 00.

Address, J. H MOORE,
Urbana, Champaign co., Ill.
Oct. 22.

DYMOND ON WAR.

An Inquiry into the Accordancy of War, with the Principles of Christianity, and an examination of the Philosophical reasoning by which it is defended. With observations on some of the causes of war and on some of its effects. By Jonathan Dymond Sent from this office, post-paid, for 30 cts..

TUNE BOOK.

The Brethren's Tune and Hymn Book, is a compilation of Sacred Music adapted to all the hymns in the Brethren's New Hymn Book. It contains over 350 pages, printed on good paper and neatly bound. We will send it to any address, post paid at $1.25 per copy.

GOOD BOOKS.

How to read Character, illus. Price,	$1.25
Combe's Moral Philosophy,	1.75
Constitution of Man. Combe,	1.75
Education. By Spurzheim,	1.50
Memory—How to improve it,	1.50
Mental Science, Lectures on,	1.50
Self-Culture and Perfection,	1.50
Combe's Physiology, Illus.	1.75
Food and Diet. By Pereira,	1.75
Natural Laws of Man,	.75
Hereditary Descent,	1.50
Combe on Infancy,	1.50
Sober and Temperate Life,	.50
Children in Health—Disease,	1.75
The Science of Human Life.	3.50
Fruit Culture for the Million.	1.00
Saving and Wasting,	1.50
Ways of Life—Right Way,	1.00
Footprints of Life,	1.25
Conversion of St. Paul,	1.00

A large number of our patrons are receiving our books as noticed below, as premiums, and express themselves highly pleased with them. Others who are not agents, have enquired whether we keep them for sale. We have now made arrangements with Mr. Wells to furnish any of their publications post paid at publishers prices. Orders for books must be accompanied with the cash, and plain directions for sending them.

Weaver's Works for the Young. Comprising "Hopes and Helps for the Young of both Sexes," $3.00.

Life at Home; or, The Family and its Members. A work which should be found in every family. $1.50. Extra gilt, $2.00.

Hand-book for Home Improvement; comprising "How to Write," "How to Talk," How to Behave," and "How to do Business," in one vol. 2.25.

Man and Woman: Considered in their Relations to each Other and to the World. 12mo, Fancy cloth, Price $1.00.

The Right Word in the Right Place. A New Pocket Dictionary and Reference Book. Cloth, 75cts.

Hopes and Helps for the Young of both sexes, Relating to the Formation of Character. Choice of Avocation, Health, Conversation, Social Affection Courtship and Marriage. Muslin, $1.50.

The Emphatic Diaglott; or The New Testament in Greek and English. Containing the Original Greek Text of the New Testament, with an Interlineary Word for-word English Translation. Price, $4.00; extra fine binding, $5.00.

Oratory—Sacred and Secular; or, the Extemporaneous Speaker. Price $1.50.

Conversion of St. Paul. 12mo. fine edition, $1. Plain edition, 75 cents.

Man, in Genesis and in Geology; or, the Biblical Account of Man's Creation, tested by Scientific Theories of his Origin and Antiquity. One vol. 12mo, $1.00.

$5 to $20 per day! Agents wanted! All classes of working people, of either sex, young or old, make more money at work for us in their spare moments or all the time than at anything else. Particulars free. Address G. Stinson & Co., Portland, Maine.

THE

HOUSEHOLD TREASURE.

Containing several hundred Valuable Receipts for cooking well at a moderate expense, making Dyes, Coloring, Cleaning and Cementing. This book also points out in plain language, free from Doctors' terms the diseases of men, women and children, and the latest and most approved means used for their cure, to which is added a description of the Medicinal Roots and Herbs, and how they are to be used in the cure of diseases.

This is a work of considerable importance and we offer it to our readers as being a valuable accession to every household. Sent from this office to any address, post-paid, for 25 cents.

WANTED BOOK AGENTS

FOR THE

FUNNY SIDE OF PHYSIC.

800 *Pages*, 250 *Engravings*.

A startling expose of Medical Humbugs of the past and present. It ventilates Quacks, Impostors, Travelling Doctors, Patent Medicine Venders, Noted Female Cheats, Fortune Tellers and Mediums, and gives interesting accounts of Noted Physicians and Narratives of their lives. It reveals startling secrets and instructs all how to avoid the ills which flesh is heir to. We give exclusive territory and liberal commissions. For circulars and terms address the publishers. J. B. BURR & HYDE,
Hartford, Conn., or Chicago, Ill.

AGENTS WANTED FOR THE

UNCIVILIZED RACES OF MEN

In all countries of the world.

Being a comprehensive account of their Manners and Customs, and of their Physical, Social, Mental, Moral, and Religious Characteristics.

By REV. J. G. WOOD, M. A., F. L. S.

500 *Engravings*, 1500 *Super Royal Oc. Pages*

In two Volumes, or two Volumes in one. Agents are making over $100 per week in selling this work. An early application will secure a choice of territory. For terms address the publishers.

J. B. BURR & HYDE,
Hartford, Conn., or Chicago, Ill

TRACTS.

"ANXIOUS BENCH RELIGION EXAMINED," BY ELDER J. S. FLORY. A SYNOPSIS OF CONTENTS. An address to the reader: The peculiarities that attend this type of religion. The feelings there experienced not imaginary but real. The key that unlocks the wonderful mystery. The causes by which feelings are excited. How the momentary feelings called "Experimental religion" are brought about, and then concludes by giving that form of doctrine as taught by Jesus Christ and recorded by his faithful witnesses.

COUNTERFEIT DETECTER
OF
BAPTISM—MUCH IN LITTLE.

This work is now ready for distribution, and the importance of the subject will speak for it a large demand. It is a short treatise on baptism in tract form intended for general distribution, and is set forth in such a plain and logical manner that a wayfaring man though a fool, cannot err therein. Either of the above tracts sent postpaid on the following terms: Two copies, 10 cts, 10 copies 40 cents, 25 copies 70 cents, 50 copies $1.00, 100 copies $1.50.

Trine Immersion.

A discussion on Trine Immersion, by letter between Elder B. F. Moomaw and Dr. J. J. Jackson, to which is annexed a Treatise on the Lord's Supper, and on the necessity, character and evidences of the new birth, also a dialogue on the doctrine of non-resistance, by Elder B. F. Moomaw. Single copy 50 cents.

THE GROUNDS FOR A

FORWARD and BACKWARD

MODE OF

BAPTISM.

Briefly, yet *carefully* examined; and the TRUE and CORRECT mode so clearly set forth that none can help but understand.

This little book contains 30 pages, neatly put up in paper cover. Price per doz. $1 25, add 10 cts. for postage. Two copies, 25 cts 1 copy, 15 cts., free of postage.

Address, SAMUEL KINSEY,
Mar 11-3t. Dayton, O.

LAND, LAND, LAND!!

The completion of the Chesapeake and Ohio Trunk Line Railway, has opened up to the world much of the fine TIMBER LANDS, rich COAL FIELDS and cheap FARMING LANDS of W. Va. Now is the time to get cheap homes and invest money with the prospect of a handsome profit. For further particulars inquire of the undersigned, agent for lands here. J. S. FLORY.
Orchard View, Fayette Co., W. Va.
Jan. 10.

1870 1873

DR. FAHRNEY'S

Blood Cleanser or Panacea.

A tonic and purge, for Blood Diseases. Great reputation. Many testimonials. Many ministering brethren use and recommend it. Ask or send for the "Health Messenger." Use only the "*Panacea*" prepared at Chicago, Ills., and by

Dr. P. Fahrney's Brothers & Co.,
Feb. 3-pd. *Waynesboro, Franklin Co., Pa*

New Hymn Books, English.

TURKEY MOROCCO.

One copy, postpaid,	$1 00
Per Dozen,	11 25

PLAIN ARABESQUE.

One Copy, post-paid,	75
Per Dozen, "	8.50

Ger'n & English, Plain Sheep.

One Copy, post-paid,	$1.00
Per Dozen	11.25
Arabesque Plain,	1.00
Turkey Morocco,	1.25
Single German, post paid	.50
Per Dozen,	5.50

HUNTINGDON & BROAD TOP RAIL ROAD

On and after March 22d, 1873, Trains will run on this road daily (Sundays excepted) as follows:

Trains from Huntingdon South. *Trains from Mt. Dallas moving North.*

MAIL. A. M.	PASS P. M.	STATIONS.	MAIL. P. M.	PASS. A. M.
LE7 45	6 00	Huntingdon,	AR4 00	AR8 25
7 50	6 05	Long Siding	3 55	8 20
8 10	6 17	McConnelstown	3 45	8 18
8 17	6 25	Pleasant Grove	3 35	8 02
8 30	6 40	Marklesburg	3 20	7 45
8 45	6 55	Coffee Run	3 07	7 32
8 55	7 03	Rough & Ready	2 57	7 23
9 05	7 12	Cove	2 47	7 13
9 08	7 18	Fishers Summit	2 45	7 10
9 20	7 30	Saxton	2 27	6 55
9 40	7 50	Riddlesburg	2 10	6 33
9 47	7 58	Hopewell	2 02	6 25
10 02	8 12	Piper's Run	1 47	6 11
10 17	8 30	Tatesville	1 32	5 55
10 30	8 40	Everett	1 20	5 45
10 35	8 45	Mount Dallas	1 15	5 40
11 08	9 20	Bedford	12 44	5 00

G. F. GAGE, Supt.

SHOUP'S RUN BRANCH.

LE 9 25 LE		Saxton.	AR2 15 AR
9 40		Coalmont.	2 05
9 45		Crawford.	1 55
AR10 00 AR		Dudley	LE1 45 LE

Bro'd Top City from Dudley 2 miles by stage.

Time of Penna. R. R. Trains at Huntingdon.

***Mail No. 2 makes connection at Huntingdon with Mail going East on Pennsylvania Railroad at 4.15 p. m., and West at 5.45 p. m. Mail No. 1 leaves Huntingdon at 7.40 a. m. on arrival of Pacific Express West.

Trains on this road connect with trains on Bedford & Bridgeport, and Cumberland & Pennsylvania Railroads.

The Weekly Pilgrim.

Published by J. B. Brumbaugh, & Co.
Edited by H. B. & Geo. Brumbaugh.

CORRESPONDING EDITORS

D. P. Sayler, Double Pipe Creek, Md.
Leonard Furry, New Enterprise, Pa.

The *Pilgrim* is a Christian Periodical, devoted to religion and moral reform. It will advocate in the spirit of *love* and *liberty*, the principles of true Christianity, labor for the promotion of peace among the people of God, for the encouragement of the saints and for the conversion of sinners, avoiding those things which tend toward disunion or sectional feelings.

TERMS.

Single copy, Book paper,	$1.50
Eleven copies, (eleventh for Agt.)	$15.00

Any number above that at the same rate.

Address,
H. B. BRUMBAUGH,
James Creek,
Huntingdon county Pa.

The Weekly Pilgrim.

"REMOVE NOT THE ANCIENT LANDMARKS WHICH OUR FATHERS HAVE SET."

VOL. 4. JAMES CREEK, PENNSYLVANIA, APRIL, 8, 1873. NO. 14

POETRY.

Selected by HATTIE F. MILLER.

PRAY WITHOUT CEASING.

1 THESS. 5:17.

Pray—for the year is ending,
The last thou ere may'st see;
And the life thou would'st be mending
May be never more to be.

Pray—the New Year will open
With hopes that must deceive;
And many a heart be broken,
That's now too proud to grieve.

Pray—for the tempter trieth
The wiles that failed before,
In every path there lieth
The last year's snare and more.

Pray—for death's poisoned arrows
Are flying thick and fast;
And this year's coming sorrows
May be greater than the last.

Pray—for the dark wave's sighing,
That overwhelms the whole;
And winter winds are sighing
A requiem for thy soul.

Pray—now the Savior's waiting
To show thy sins forgiven;
And the Holy Ghost entreating
To seal thee *heir* of *Heaven*.

ORIGINAL ESSAYS.

A LIGHT TO THE WORLD.

What is Safe and what is not Safe; What is Right and what is not Right.

BY J. H. MOORE.

Chapter I.

THE BIBLE.

The Bible should be our guide in all religious matters, pertaining to the salvation of sinners. This book we know is right, whether other books are right or not. When we get and obey the Bible we get and obey a book that all religious denominations admit to be safe; a book the correctness of which none will question. When we obey this book, we obey a book that all admit to be right, and therefore must acknowledge that our conduct is right, so far as it agrees with the rules of the book. Though other rules found in other books, may be too short to reach heaven, those prescribed in the Bible are not. Though other books may be wrong, the Bible is not, and never can be.

We accept the Bible as our *rule of faith* and *practice*. All admit this to be right. Many try to prove that the books that contain the rule of *their* faith and practice are right, because they are so near like our book. There is no dispute about the Bible, but about their books. We all know that the Bible is both safe and right, and it makes no difference what becomes of their books of discipline. The Bible as a rule of faith and practice does not contradict itself, but their books of faith and practice do from the fact they don't agree. If we adopt the Bible as the only *rule* of our faith and practice, it makes no odds what they say about other rules, they cannot condemn ours unless they condemn the wisdom of heaven itself. It makes no difference how much they oppose other books they cannot oppose ours.

We are not to be judged by the rules in other books, but by those contained in the Bible. If other books contain the same rules that are found in the Bible, then all right; the more of such rules the better the book, but it can never be *better* than the Bible. It is not questioned whether the rules in the Bible are right, but are those right that are not in the Bible? It is by the rules in the Bible that we are to be judged in the last day, and not by those that are not in the Bible. Though other books may not be opened on the day of judgment we know the Bible will. People do not say that our rule is *nearly* right, but they will admit it to be *exactly* right. They do not say that it is as safe as any, but it is *safer* than any other. They do not say that the Bible is as *good* as any book, but it is *better* than any other. There is not a commandment in the world that has anything to do with the salvation of sinners, that is not in some shape or form found in the Bible, though, there are commandments of men found in other books, that are not in any shape or form connected with the salvation of any person. The Bible contains all the laws that pertain to our salvation though other books may not. When we are in possession of this book we are in possession of all the laws and rules that are demanded in order to secure the salvation of sinners. Furthermore, when we get the Bible, we get the *whole truth* respecting religion, and nothing but the truth—our entire duty toward God and man. In this noble volume we have all that God requires at the hands of his children, and nothing that he does not require. There are no non-essentials in the work; God is not the author of such productions. We have all that he has commanded, and nothing that he did not command. God never required men, or set of men, to do that which he did not want them to do, nor to obey a law that he did not want them to obey. He does not demand at our hands that which he did not intend that we should do. He never put laws in the Bible to be violated, they were put there to be obeyed. There is no use talking about non-essentials in the Bible, there are none there; the rules were put there to be obeyed.

Chap. II.—OBEDIENCE.

God never punished men simply because they obeyed his commandments. It never was unsafe or wrong to obey all the commands of the Creator, but it has always been unsafe *not* to obey them. It is not a question whether it is safe to obey the holy book? But is it safe *not* to obey it? All will agree that God will not punish a man for obeying *all* his commands, but the important item is will he not punish him if he does *not* obey them? All will agree that the man who obeys the Bible is not only right but safe too, but then is a man either right or safe does *not* obey it? God has in times past punished men for not obeying his commands, and as he is unchangeable in his manner of dealing with the children of men, it certainly follows that he will do the same in the future.

It is not questioned whether or not there is a place of happiness? All agree that there is a place reserved in the future for those who love and serve God. This ground is undisputed, none has the least reason to doubt this;—but then is there a place of punishment in the future for the wicked? is the question that we wish to settle. There are those who state that there is no place of future punishment, though it is mentioned in the Bible. The same revelation that proves that there is a heaven in the future, also states that there is a hell. Strange to conclude that the good book means just what it says when speaking of heaven, and reverses the order when speaking of hell, and means something else. You show me a man who don't believe in a future punishment of the wicked, and I will show you a man who does not obey the Bible entire. Whenever I find a man who obeys from the heart that form of doctrine once delivered to the Saints, I always, without failure, find one who, not only believes that the righteous have the promise of eternal life, but that there is a place of future punishment reserved for those who obey not God's holy commandments. That the righteous occupy safe ground has never been questioned by any, but do the wicked occupy grounds that are either right or safe, is the point to be settled, this is the doubtful ground; this is the unsafe ground if there is any to be found. If there is none here, then there is no such a thing as unsafeness in the universe. If there is no danger then, no one can be hurt and we may all as well be still. Even those who believe that all mankind will be saved anyhow, whether they obey the gospel or not, are all the time preaching their doctrine as tho' a man *had to believe it* in order to be saved.

I see no use in crying fire! fire!! when there is no fire. What is the use of telling people to flee the wrath to come, when there is no wrath to come? What sense would there have been in Noah's building an ark to save himself and family from flood, if there had been no flood? What would be the use of Jesus telling us to fear him who is able to cast both soul and body into hell, w...

there is no hell? How in the name of all reason could the rich man die, be buried, and then lift up his eyes in hell, when there was no hell? How could he be in torment when there was no torment to be in? How could there be a wide gulf between him and Lazarus when they were both in the same place? Neither Christ nor his apostles ever taught that there is no hell, and that all mankind will be saved whether they obey the gospel or not. Being that all agree that there is a place of happiness in the future—a fact which all admit—now then the question is, who shall enjoy that happiness in the future world? That those who obey the gospel will, is admitted by both saint and sinner. This much is settled. Then we know that they are safe whether any body else is or not. There is not one particle of doubt about this. The righteous then are safe whether there is any hell or not. If there is no hell then of course they can never go to any place but heaven, and if there is no hell then their home is in heaven anyhow. But now comes the fearful question; can those who do not obey the gospel be safe? This is where the doubts come in. There are no doubts respecting the destiny of the righteous, but that of the sinner is all uncertain. There is but one way for him to escape future punishment, and that is if there will be no punishment in the future. The righteous we know are safe, but sinner what say ye of your condition?

To be Continued.

THE CHURCH AND DUTIES OF HER MEMBERS.—NO. 3.

BY J. S. FLORY.

THE MINISTRY.

Probably the most prominent meaning of the word *minister* is servant. Joshua was called the minister of Moses. Elisha the minister of Elijah, also they are termed their servants. Servants not menial, but honorable, and in due time succeeded to the station or office of their masters. John Mark was *minister* to Paul and Barnabas who themselves were ministers or servants. Hence we call these servants, ministers who explain and promulgate the word of God in a public manner, and conduct the services of God in a manner agreeable with the liberties and licence granted them by the Church. That there are degrees in the office or calling of ministers in the Church militant, the Scriptures fully testify. The Church has adopted regulations in this matter that seem to work well, and we have no doubt they meet the approbation of God, being, so far as we can see, in harmony with the tenor of the Gospel. For sake of distinction we may call the degrees first, second and third. In certain points their duties are the same, but in others of a special and relative sense they differ. Without stopping to inquire as to the why and wherefore of making those distinctions, we will pass on, and in the first place speak of the duties and obligations of those in the

FIRST DEGREE OF THE MINISTRY.

Under this head we may be a little lengthy in way of giving advice, inasmuch as it has been requested that I do so, and that too by such as feel the cross a heavy one, and knowing we had to pass through the trying ordeal, ask for counsel, which we will cheerfully give so far as our judgment and experience in the matter will admit of. We are conscious of the fact, and would say to our brethren, it is no "childs play," to stand up between God and man to attempt to preach the Gospel. The duties and obligations of the ministry are such that we never could see how any man, feeling the weight of responsibility attending the calling, could stand forth voluntarily a candidate for that station. But when the Lord, through His Church by the prompting of His Holy Spirit, calls you, dear brother, to that high and holy calling, it is your duty to bow in humble submission to His will. Jonah tried fleeing from duty, but the Lord overtook him in a summary manner. Our advice is, yield to the voice of the Lord Paul like, and say "Lord what will ye have me to do?" And in obedience to the command of Jesus, "Go preach my Gospel," go fully impressed with the great responsibilities and importance that cluster around the sacred office. Notwithstanding your privileges as a public speaker may be to some extent circumscribed, the limits of your field of action is all sufficient for present purposes. Do all you can in the station you are placed and you will find not a little to do. You may herald the tidings of salvation to a ruined world, at such places and times, as your brother minister higher in office, or the Church may give liberty. Learn to submit to the will and judgment of your elders in office or the wish of the Church. While undue forwardness is to be avoided, we also would advise you to guard against unnecessary backwardness. The most commendable state of deportment is between the two extremes. We here might speak of certain things worthy of note by those who are just putting their hand to the work of the ministry. You should have enough self-confidence to overcome timidity and that want of self-trust which so often stands in the way of duty. On the other hand beware of that spirit of exaltation and self dependence that seems to *chill* the hearers. Dedicate yourself to the Lord; put your dependence in Him. Having no special qualifications of your own that you may pride in, so much the better. Borrow no man's words, no man's jestures nor no man's deportment; simply be yourself in the stand and out of it. Just as certain as any one tries to appear in somebody's garments other than their own, just so certain will the audience discover that they *don't fit the speaker*. Let me whisper in the ear of the youthful servant in the calling of the ministry, the secret of all secrets to efficiency in their calling. It is *often and earnest prayer to God in closet.* It is the golden key that unlocks God's storehouse of love, grace and mercy, and fills the soul so full of "Jesus crucified" that he may go forth as a vessel fitted and prepared for the Master's use, and then having a confiding trust in God, the gold and silver truths of God's word may be handed out to the "poor and needy" souls,—the Holy Spirit, unrestrained, will give the "true ring" to the sound of the blessed Gospel. Solemn earnestness will sweeten the "Bread of Life" to hungry starving souls. We would earnestly recommend a careful study of the Scriptures. In studying certain subjects, gather up the "fragments;" become familiar with their relative and analogous bearings. Fill the mind with matter, store the house full of material, such as solid Scriptural truths, and imagery in harmony with God's revealed scheme of redemption; but when it comes to sermonizing leave that arrangement to the Lord, through the medium of the Holy Spirit, who from a well stored mind may readily send forth the precious seed into the hearts of the hearers.

Avoid a tedious manner of discoursing; also beware of falling into the habit of using repeatedly, stereotyped sayings. A straight line is the nearest way to a given point, so the plain simple truth is more readily sent home to the heart in a plain simple manner. Roundabout flourishes, lofty flights and glowing pictures will do to fill up the *vacuum* of expansive minds that are destitute of Jesus and Him crucified!

Long sermons are sometimes allowable with the experienced, but with the beginner they are seldom looked upon in a judicious manner. Of all other things, especially avoid personal allusion to other denominations by way of censuring them for their doctrine. Such a course is bad enough if indulged in by the "chiefest Apostles.". Also avoid the tendency to be harping continually upon such doctrinal points that are subject to great controversy. I have learned by experience, the better way is to labor to get the world to see they are woefully diseased by sin, and when they see their sickness and look to Jesus with a longing desire to be healed, then tell them how to take the antidote.

Speaking in a monotone—the voice at the same pitch—either high or low is to be avoided. A variation in the voice is more effective and easier on the speaker. A contracted habit of some nature is often injurious to the efficiency of the minister; and sometimes it is let run on until it becomes almost as a second nature. To avoid such objectionable habits, let it be mutually agreed with brethren that they tell each other of their faults or objections others may find in them that they may guard against them, or let brethren that see these things in others tell them. Surely they should love brethren for this kindness. We will remember of a brother, almost a stranger, who told us of a habit we had contracted of using a word many times out of its place. We were ignorant of the habit. Our attention called to it, we labored against it until we overcame it. I shall ever love that brother for that kind act.

Again, we would say to young ministers, make but few apologies, it often is worse than time lost. If you don't feel like speaking or that you can not say anything to profit, the congregation will know it soon enough without you telling them. If you feel like speaking they will doubtless know it. When you speak, if possible, throw the promptings of your very soul into your words. Cultivate a passion for souls, and preach as though your words were your *dying counsel* to *dying persons* before you. Learn to know when you are done and then quit!

Being a minister of the Lord to preach the everlasting Gospel, look well to your ways. Now, if not before done, is the time to lay aside every weight and the sin that so easily beset us. Now is the time to labor diligently that you may be "a workman that needeth not to be ashamed."

Personal influence is of the utmost importance. If of a godly nature, it will tend to preparing the heart of your hearers for the reception of the good seed. Otherwise, and it will tend to forging the shackels of satan tighter upon the sinner. Here is a duty and obligation you should ever keep before you; to so walk that others may be influenced to come to Jesus. Oh! think of it; a careless and crooked life may cause precious souls to fall into eternal burnings. How then shall you meet your God! having preached the Gospel and then be yourself cast away! Join not arms with the world, be not a "party man" in the broils of political contention; stand aloof as one crying aloud to sinners to flee the wrath to come. A watchman chosen to stand upon the walls of Zion should be careful how he goeth down into the valley of Achor to hunt the "Babylonish garments," "gold" or "silver" that belongeth to the enemy! In other words beware of the entanglements of the world and the danger of riches.

In conclusion, we would say to those who feel they are too weak and unworthy to fill a station of so exalted a nature, put your trust in God who is "strength." Wherein ye lack ask of God who giveth bountifully. Ever say,

"Father I stretch my hand to thee,
No other help I know."

Be faithful over the few things God hath entrusted to you and he will make thee ruler over many things; and say "enter than into the joy of the Lord."

A CHRISTIAN'S LIFE A HAPPY ONE.

That the life of a true Christian, in the main, is a very happy one, we need not to tell an humble follower of the Lord Jesus Christ, for he certainly has experienced and tasted that the Lord is gracious; his great burden of sins, as a ponderous load, has been removed; his stricken conscience set at ease, and his poor, troubled, sorrowful soul made to rejoice in the God of his salvation. He hath tasted the good word of God, and the powers of the world to come; hath tasted of the heavenly gift, and has partaken of the Holy Ghost: hence furnished with the necessary equipment to carry on the holy warfare of his Christian pilgrimage with celestial joy and angelic delight. Behold his weapon! They are not carnal, but mighty through God to the pulling down of strongholds; casting down imagination, and every high thing that exalteth itself against the knowledge of God, and bringing into captivity every thought to the obedience of Christ."

His stand is a noble one; first against his own flesh and blood, then against principalities and against powers; next against the rulers of the darkness of this world and spiritual wickedness in high places, and above all, against the cunningly artful devices of the arch-traitor, the devil, the enemy of God and men. His loins are girt about with a snow-white linen girdle of truth, with a bright, glistening golden breastplate of righteousness; his feet shod with shoes of clemency, pity, mercy, and benevolence, well furnished with the Gospel of Peace; with the glittering, brazen helmet of salvation; the ever-ready and unmistakable shield of faith; the anchor of souls, to withstand the breakers, quicksands, rocks, and quench the fiery darts of the wicked; and with the two-edged weapon, the sword of the Spirit which is the word of God. Thus furnished the Christian goes forward with joy, courage, delight and consolation; hath nothing to fear, though the heavens tremble, the earth reels to and fro, the fountains of the great deep may open, fiery streams may issue forth, boiling water shooting up, the airy elements charged with electricity, may dart the flashes of lightning from pole to pole; the mighty crashes of thunder may shake the earth from center to center; the dreaded pestilence may rage and sweep away its thousands, yet amidst all these terrible judgments of God, the staple christian is protected, for he has entered the ark of safety. The God who overrules the universe, rides upon the clouds, and is reigning in the gloomy deep, surrounded with light and darkness, is his God; and he, in whom dwelleth all the Godhead bodily, is his salvation. Though the iron hand of death would enclose his frail body, and bring his mortal remains to dissolution, yet the pains of death cannot hold him, for his lively hope is in Christ, who loosed the pains of death and triumphed over the grave, led captivity captive, and gave gifts to men. If the Christians life is a life of pleasure, cheerfulness and enjoyments, as I have shown in my former article, why are men so negligent, careless and unconcerned? Even Christian professors, that named the name of Christ, live like the world, so destitute of christian vitality, that even their actions, deportment and rule of life is condemned by the moral worldlings in truthfulness and punctuality. O, brethren and sisters where are you found? Let us examine ourselves closely whether we are on the side of vitality, or on the side of formality. May God forbid that the devil should use any of us as an instrument to be a stumbling block to pure and undefiled Christianity. There are certainly enough without us, and yet it is to be feared, numbers will be weighed in the balance and found wanting.

Permit me to ask some questions and let every one answer the same by his own acts: Have you solemnly and sincerely repented of all your sins and cherished a decided hatred to every thing that is evil? Did you join the church of God for the sole purpose of honoring and loving God and to promote his glory? Can you love your enemies, pray for them that persecute you, bless them that curse you, feed your enemies, give them to drink and clothe them when necessary? Do you pray that part of the Lord's prayer, "Deliver me from evil" consistently, by using every effort by moral suasion on your part, to remove every evil with which you are surrounded, and your neighbor, and your children your neighbors children, who may not be strong enough to withstand those evils, or will you stand neutral and see them one by one ensnared thereby and drawn down the road to hell? Will you assist by liberally throwing in your mite for the purpose of spreading the pure Gospel, to enlightening benighted souls, who by a spurious Gospel are led to perdition? Have you a family altar erected and gather your children around your own fireside regularly to admonish them to refrain from evil, pray with them and thus bring them up in the nurture and admonition of the Lord? Is the worship of God your chief delight, and has the service of the Lord the preponderance over earthly things? Are you one of those who leaves the seat in church vacant, when weather is unpleasant, or perhaps you feel a little tired; you and your horses overworked in order to accumulate wealth which many times proves a curse to the children?

Pardon my digression. Happy as the Christian is while tabernacling in the flesh, while doing the commands of the Lord, and even under affliction, crosses, trials, temptations, sorrows and disappointments, which seem strange to the carnal minded, yet tenfold more happy is he in eternity. The christian lives for eternity, his aim is to enjoy God in felicity; he lives in anticipation of realizing that blessed hope of a glorious immortality, where Christ, the hope of glory, will lead him to fountains of living water, and God shall wipe away all tears from his eyes. O, that blissful hope! The soul reviving hope! May I be permitted to see the day, so long desired, and anxiously waited for, and endured so many trials, hardships, crosses, mockings, and derisions in anticipation of being found worthy, through the atoning blood of my Savior, to realize his presence at his coming. May I rejoice, seeing him brilliantly arraigned robed in glory, decked with majesty, clothed with power and splendor, accompanied with Saints clothed in white linen, seated upon white horses. O, heavenly beauty! Victorious army! Seraphic brilliancy! Almighty conqueror! King of glory, mighty in battle; the Alpha and Omega; thou wast dead and art alive. Behold thou livest for evermore; thou hast the key of hell and death. Amen. Unlock death and open the portals of heaven and give admittance to thy humble unworthy servants in order to assist in swelling the music of the Angelic choir in heaven in company with the redeemed, the full fruition of happiness, glory, joy, peace, and love. May God prepare us for that happy meeting. LEONARD FURRY.

New Enterprise, Pa.

HOME.

By the term home is generally understood the place of abode, the dwelling house; but its import may be properly confined to the family circle, the place where kindred spirits are assembled, those who are near and dear to us, by the ties of nature, as well as those who are allied to us socially or by the ties of christian unity. Where these are and remain is home, no difference how unattractive the surroundings may be. It is the society of the good, those who have correct moral principles, those in whom love, as emanates from God, is the ruling power, that give a place its lustre. The most beautiful mansions in which love is not the predominating element, is indeed a dark and gloomy spot. Home in reality is the family circle in which love warms every heart.

Home! home! how much feeling is embodied in this little word. Speak the word and the sound vibrates on chords that make music for the soul, —music that has no sadness, music that falls, like evening dew, on the withered flower. It animates, it revives, it stretches out every wrinkle in our drooping desponding natures and the downcast forlorn countenance becomes all radiant with hope.

There are perhaps few words that have a more pleasing thought than the word home, and especially is this so, when we speak of our eternal home. The thought of our earthly home is a pleasing one, but when we lift the curtain and take a look beyond this time, although our vision is clouded by fogs and mists, we see a home that is more glorious. It is the thought of this home that fills the soul to the brim with ecstasy. The feelings of joy awakened from a contemplation of this home is limited to a certain class of individuals. There are many, very many, who cannot look beyond this time with the assurance of having a home there, and to such, the word home, as viewed from this standpoint, can have no charms. It is a dull, meaningless word, and although, like the grain of wheat, full of life and vitality, the pod in which is embodied that which will nourish and enliven the soul, yet there is no soil in which to germinate and develop itself. The word home, in order to produce an animating effect, must have a soil in which to stretch out its tiny fibres,—a heart rich in goodness and warmed up by the Sun of Righteousness.

To the Christian,—those who have enlisted under the Banner of Jesus and are battling for truth and right is the word home an endearing appellation. When the fight is the hardest, and Satan's darts are being hurled at us with a sure aim,—our souls wracked with pain and the inner man becomes languid, then the thought of this home gives us courage and nerves us afresh for the contest. O what a glorious thought! This world is truthfully a dark and thorny desert, and while encountering with the ups and downs, we can look beyond to the time when we shall arrive at home,—a home where, if we were to travel from pole to pole, take all the pleasures this life can afford, and multiply each through endless years, they would not be worth one minute of time in our heavenly home.

There are positions in life in which the word home becomes doubly endearing. We appreciate our earthly home more when away from it, and especially is this so when in adverse circumstances. So it is with those who, like the prodigal, have wandered far away from their heavenly Father's house. They come to want; the vain and perishable things of this life will not satisfy the soul, and a longing desire is felt for the Father's house wherein there is bread enough and to spare,—bread upon which angels feast,—bread that strengthens and supports the soul. This is the feeling of many a poor famishing soul, and it is in this condition the thought of home is a pleasing one indeed.

Reader, are you making preparations for your arrival at this home? Are you complying with the conditions that will warrant you an inheritance there? Do you look forward to the time when you will arrive there with pleasure? Surely when we think of the blessedness of that home and the joy to be realized there, we should truthfully feel that this world is not our home. J. B. F.

Selections.

"PAPA TEACHES ME."

"If I were old enough, I would smoke cigars, mamma," said a boy of six summers, as he stood looking out at the window.

"O no, my son, smoking is not a nice, cleanly habit, it is injurious to health, leads people into other bad habits, and into bad company. Besides, it wastes a great deal of money that might feed and clothe poor little wretched children, or give the Bible to those who have never heard anything about Jesus, our Savior. Don't you see that such a useless, wasteful habit would be very wrong, my dear boy?"

"Yes, mamma, I did not think of those things, but papa teaches me to smoke, and he is good."

"Papa teaches you? He would not teach you a bad habit for the world. What makes you say so?"

"He smokes himself, mamma!"

Christian father, is the fine promising boy, growing up by your side, upon whom you look with joy and pride, to be impressively taught by your silent example, to begin a career of self indulgence, which will lead him by slow, but sure steps, to idle lounging, sinful expenditures, evil company, and perhaps to profanity, intemperance, and the worst of vices? O stop, stop, when you are nearest to God in your closet, and consider well your ways, consider them especially in reference to your child. Think how potent is the influence of your example, even in little things, in this forming period of his character, and how lasting is its power. A wrong step now—a little step into the path of doubtful self-indulgence, and out of the path of unquestionable moral rectitude, your child will be quick to see, and the sight may be a death blow to pure, unyielding moral principle, in his heart forever! O, Christian parent, you would not, as you fear God, for any present pleasure, peril the temporal and eternal future of your confiding child.—*The Christian.*

TO YOUNG MEN

Prove worthy of your charge. Into your keeping will soon be given all the vast and grand machinery of this great era of progress. The fairest heritage of earth is yours; its mineral resources to hammer and forge; its agricultural wealth to garner; its seas to whiten with commerce; its growing mind to guide and control, and, more sacred trust, the upholding and sweeping onward of banners of Christianity, shaping the destinies of nations for coming time.

Your work is to be done only by vigorous and persistent endeavor. Think that every hour you spend in a frivolous manner is time belonging to imperative duty. Every act by which you mar and blacken the physical being is theft from the life given you by God. Every word no matter how light or trivial, may exert an influence for good or evil. Open ears are ever around you catching and treasuring the merest words. See that such treasures are good.

Men are like planets, ploughing along their separate orbits, free and yet guided and held in their pathway by the influence of others. Look to it that your guiding influence shapes to the true course.

Fill your position whether high or humble—fill it to the uttermost. Crowd to the brimming measure every requirement of your duty. Know that the highest meed of praise is one's own approbation of the still small voice of God, saying, "Well done, good and faithful servant."

Young man, go forth and God speed! Be true to yourself and God, and the people shall rise up and call thee blessed.

A RIGHT KIND OF RELIGION.—We hear much about experimental religion—a religion of feeling, a religion of work, of action, of theory or idea, but the religion we want is a religion of faith. That is the kind of religion well pleasing in the sight of God, the religion the heart wants, the religion that comforts the soul—the religion the church needs—the religion necessary to the conversion of the world. That religion which is the result of an implicit and abiding trust in God through faith—not simply assenting faith, but such a trust and belief that takes God at his word and "works by love" and produces not only rest, peace, hope, joy, and happiness, but a holy life full of works in perfect harmony with God's word. Such a religion of faith that shows to the world entire consecration to Jesus and him crucified. Having such a religion "profession of religion" sinks into insignificance along side of possession and confession is but the shadow—possession the substance.—*J. S. Flory.*

Commentary upon commentary. If the Word of God is not understood, it will not be for want of what are called helps. We see it stated in a London paper that Rev. Professor Plumpre, with the assistance of several scholars and divines, is engaged in the preparation of a work on an extensive scale, illustrative and explanatory of the various books of the Bible.

GOD'S LOVE, NOT MINE

Some years ago two gentlemen were riding together, and as they were about to separate, one addressed the other thus: "Do you ever read the Bible?" "Yes, but I get no benefit from reading it, because, to tell the truth, I feel I do not love God." "Neither did I," replied the other; "but God loved me." This answer produced such an effect upon his friend that, to use his own words, it was as if one had lifted him out of the saddle into the skies. It opened up to his soul at once the great truth that it is not how much I love God, but how much God loves me."

Religious News.

Bro. F. P. Loehr says: "Prospects are flattering all around us; our preaching is admitted to be the Word of the Lord, and although there are but two of us that go to preach from home, we are seldom together, but fight the battles single hand, even without an "armor bearer." My wife formerly went with me, but this winter I am alone. You will know that I answered the call of brother Moses Moist near Albion, Michigan, I was there twice, and on the 17th of next month I promised to be there to baptize. I know not yet how many, but this much I can say that many people that were disgusted at all professors and their preaching, expressed their unaffected approbation at my preaching and desire me to come back often. One man that would not let any preacher come in his house, although his wife is a Methodist, after hearing me the first time, expressed his approbation and desired to be visited, which was done to mutual satisfaction, and when I was there the second time, he sent me one dollar to pay expenses of coming there again. At the series of meetings we held near Almena, in this Co., a certain woman was baptized whose husband had threatened to shoot the preacher who would do it and also his wife in case she would be baptized, but now attended our meeting and brought his wife to the water in all kindness where she was immersed. I relate these things to show you how much good could or might be done if proper exertions were used. But in preaching to the world it requires almost more self-denial than a man of three-score years and ten is capable of enduring. I might with great pleasure travel among the churches in old settlements like a nearly worn out plow in cultivated soil, and be kept from rusting, but cannot stand hard knocks and pushing," &c.

Those who would visit the Holy Land, and go up to Mount Zion before the holy quiet of these sacred regions is disturbed and desecrated by the sound of the locomotive, must start upon the pilgrimage soon. The surveys for the projected railway from Jaffa to Jerusalem have been completed, and the plans were sent off on the 7th inst. to the Minister of Public Works at Constantinople. The Pope and the chiefs of the Greek Armenian, and Jewish faiths, not only in the East, but even Paris and London, have been informed that 1,500 tickets for the journey from Jaffa to Jerusalem and back will be annually and gratuitously placed at their disposal for the use of poor pilgrims. How many tickets are to be distributed among poor Protestants we do not learn.

Egypt is no longer "the basest of kingdoms." Recent information shows that some of its cities have increased with more than American rapidity. When Napoleon the first was in Alexandria the city contained 7000 inhabitants, in 1842 this number was nearly nine times as great, twenty years later the population had risen to 164,000, and the consular reports for 1872 place its population at 200,000. The increase throughout Northern Egypt has been in a like proportion, and the country now contains more than five millions of people. This is due in a good degree to the British overland route to India, and the enterprises of French engineers and agriculturists.

Abraham Jaeger, a converted Jewish Rabbi, has prepared a volume on Judaism and Christianity giving his own experience in coming into the light of truth. He and his book are highly spoken of by the good men of Chicago who knew him personally, and the warm feeling, strong purpose, and thorough learning evinced in his volume commend it to the Christian public.

The Committee now revising the Constitution of Pennsylvania has adopted a provision that "no appropriation, except for pensions or gratuities for military services, shall be made to any person or community, nor to any denominational or sectarian institution, corporation or association for charitable, educational, or benevolent purposes."

The Lutheran Sunday school of Mifflintown, Pa., has thrown out of its library all such books as are commonly termed "Sunday school novels," and the managers express their determination to buy no more books of that character for their library.

The religious excitement in Geneva, Switzerland caused by the preaching of Father Hyacinthe, is increasing. The reverend gentleman is meeting with great success, and the Ultramontanes are much exasperated.

Youth's Department

GOD BLESS THE LITTLE CHILDREN

God bless the little children,
We meet them everywhere;
We hear their voices round our hearth,
Their footsteps on the stair;
Their kindly hearts are swelling o'er
With mirthfulness and glee;
God bless the little children,
Wherever they may be.

We meet them 'neath the Gipsy tents,
With visage swarth and lean,
And eyes that sparkle as they glance
With roguery and fun;
We find them fishing in the brook,
For minnows with a pin,
Or creeping through the hazel bush
The linnet's nest to find.

We meet them in the lordly hall,
Their stately father's pride!
We meet them in the poor man's cot—
He has no wealth beside.
Along the city's crowded street
They hurl the hoop or ball;
We find them 'neath the pauper's roof
The saddest sight of all.

For there they win no father's love,
Nor mother's tender care,
Their only friend is God above,
Who hears the orphans prayer.
But dressed in silks or draped in rags,
In childish grief or glee,
God bless the little children,
Wherever they may be.

BEND OR BREAK

I was on a visit to a friend in the country. His house stood beside a little stream, on both sides of which were trees growing. At the back was a range of hills, down which the wind swept at times with great power. One of the days of my visit, the night set in with signs of a storm. And a stormy night it was. The wind roared, and whistled, and the sound was louder as it rushed through the trees and swept them two and fro.

When morning came, we found that though the storm had ceased it had left evidences of its violence. Flowers and shrubs, where much exposed, were torn, and in some cases battered to the earth. Leaves were hurled together into corners, branches were torn from the trees, and in one case a large elm was broken down.

One of the ladies of the family had gone into the garden to see how it had fared with her flowers; As she did so, two little girls passed. The younger of the two had seen the tree, and had told her neighbor about it, and they were discussing its fate. How had that tree been broken and blown down, was the question, while the other trees around had stood? "O," answered the elder, "when the wind came and blew harder and harder and harder, the tree said 'I won't bend;' and so, as it wouldn't bend, the wind broke it and tore it up; but the others said, 'I'll bend;' and as they bent they were not broken or blown down." When informed of this on the lady's return, I thought, There's a good lesson for some of my little friends, and I must tell the story to them.

It had better been for some boys I know if they had said in their heart, "I'll bend," when their parents sought to train them right; but they would not yield, and now they are broken. O, how sadly! And some at school wouldn't bend but rebelled, and were punished and expelled, and they are broken now. And some, when affliction came upon them, would not yield their hearts to God, as He wished, but hardened their necks; and they have been broken. And some, who were servants to others, would not bend to the will of their masters, though it was right; and they are now as useless as the broken tree.

A proud rebellious spirit is not a good one. It is sure to bring him who cherishes it to wreck and ruin. "Pride goeth before destruction, and a haughty spirit before a fall. Better yield obedience than be stubborn. Better "obey your parents in the Lord; for this is right." Better do your duty to those you have engaged to serve, as the Bible bids. And it is better far not to "despise chastening of the Lord. Yield your will to Him. This will keep you from bending when you ought not, and save you from being broken and ruined when you should have bent and persevered.—*Early Days.*

EYES AND NO EYES.

You have all read the story in the school books of the two boys who went over the same road, one with his eyes open and the other with his eyes shut. It is old, but worth remembering every day. So many things worth knowing go on right under our eyes without being noticed.

I knew a man, I think I may have told you of him before, a busy man, who had very little time for reading or study, but whose mind was a perfect store-house information on almost every subject.

"How does it happen that you know so much more than the rest of us?" asked him one day.

"Oh," said he, "I never have time to lay in a regular store of knowledge, so I *save up all the bits* that come in my way, and they count up a good deal in the course of the year."

That is just the thing: save all the bits.

"That boy," said a gentleman, "always seems to be on the look-out for something to see."

So he was; and, while waiting in a newspaper office once for a package, he learned, by the use of his eyes what he never could have guessed, that slips rooted best in nearly pure sand.

"This is lapis lazuli," said the jeweller to his customer, "and this is 'chrysoprase.'" And the wide-awake errand boy turned around from the door to take a sharp look, so that in future, he knew just how those two precious stones looked. In one day he learned of the barber what became of the hair clippings; of the carpenter how to drive a nail so as not to split the wood; of the shoemaker, how the different surfaces of fancy leathers are made; of a locust, that his mouth was no use to him in singing; from a scrap of newspaper, where sponges are obtained; and from an old Irish woman, how to keep stove-pipes from rusting. Only bits and fragments of knowledge, but all of them worth saving, and all helpful to increase the stock-in-trade of the boy who meant to be a man.—*Picture Magazine.*

SPEAK CORRECTLY.

Boys and girls should learn to speak correctly while they are children, for it will be hard to correct wrong habits when they become older.

"The other day a little girl asked: 'Shall you go to-morrer?' The answer was, 'I dunno.' How much better to pronounce the words, and to say to-morrow and don't know. Never say, sech fine apples; but such fine apples. Jest as live is another improper expression. You should say, just as lief. And don't say, I ain't. There is no such a word as ain't in the English language. You should say I'm not, or it isn't.

"I heard a boy say, 'I never saw sech figgers' That was very bad pronunciation. Another said, 'I can holler louder than you;' but a bright little fellow replied, 'I don't think I can holler at all, though I can hallou so as to be heard a quarter of a mile.'

"Now, children, try hard to speak properly, and never use such words as these:

To-morrer	Ain't
Dunno,	Holler,
Sech,	Figgers.

"There is one mistake which almost everybody makes in saying 'He don't.' It is well enough to say 'I dont,' or 'they don't,' but it should be, "He doesn't.

BOYS, DO YOU HEAR THAT?

A New Orleans paper tells of a printer who, when his fellow-workmen went out to drink beer during working hours, put in the bank the exact amount he would have spent if he had gone out to drink. He thus kept his resolution for five years. He then examined his bank account, and found that he had on deposit $521.86. In the five years he had not lost a day from ill health. Three out of five of his fellow-workmen had, in the meantime, become drunkards, and were discharged. The water-drinker then bought out the printing office, went on enlarging the business, and in twenty years from the time he began to put by his money, was worth $100,000. The story, whether new or old, teaches a lesson which every boy and young man should lay to heart.

Correspondence.

A Reporter is wanted from every Church in the brotherhood to send us Church news, Obituaries, Announcements, or anything that will be of general interest. To insure insertion, the writers name must accompany each communication. Our Invitation is not personal but general—please respond to our call.

Dear Pilgrim:—I feel like giving a little Church news for the satisfaction of those who may feel interested. Nine years ago I visited, for the first time, this State, Michigan, in June, and found a few members in this Co, Vanburen; preaching several times to general satisfaction. Winter following, that is in 1865, wife and I came back here again and spent the month of February, being good sleighing all the time, yet not very cold, so we concluded to move here, which was done the latter days of April, when we found less than 20 members, and until this time there was no church organized in the State, although there was a small number of members in Cass Co., the southwest corner of the State, who were under the care of Jacob Miller de'd, and David Miller from St. Joseph Co., Ind. The whole number known at this time was considerable less than one hundred.

We had meeting every Sunday here and there through the Summer seasons, and in Winter went forth in the sleigh with some brother or my wife, looking up the scattered lambs in the counties of Alegan, Kent, Ionia, Barry, Clinton, Eaton, Calhoun, Kalamazoo, St. Joseph and Cass. There are members scattered all thro' the State, besides such as cannot join in with the popular churches, especially such as came from Pa., Ohio and Indiana. Many of the Eastern people are disgusted at all so called Christian religion, but when they hear our doctrine they desire us to preach for them. There are a goodly number of places, where in one years time small churches could be established by holding series of meetings, as the people desire to have, for say they, we would like to know the whole truth, how you believe and practice, and you cannot give full satisfaction in one or two meetings at a time. But you see, dear brethren, the field is too extensive for one or two laborers, so a large portion of the harvest is not gathered, the seed is sown by the reading of the Word of God, it only wants the minister to gather them in bundles or organizations, and with the influx of emigration, Michigan might count its thousands of the meek followers of Jesus.

There are now at this time six or seven organized churches with about five hundred members, and less than twenty ministers, of whom four or five are ordained. There is a move made to apply to next District Meeting to be struck off into a separate district, as the distance to D. M. is too great for those North of us to attend.

Now if there are any of the ministering brethren that may not have elbow room, where ten or twelve are sitting behind the table, come over to Michigan. The harvest is whitening and the laborers are but few, and although this is a Northern clime yet the hearts of the people are warm if touched with the Gospel fire.

We are no respector of persons, the black, the white, the rich and the poor are all seated around the table of the Lord, as well as at our home board. The above will answer those inquiries who say, "What is Bro. Loehr doing?" He is wearing out gradually, but his zeal for the cause is unabated, and his love to the Church is not measured.

F. P. LOEHR.

MAINE MISSION.

The attention of the churches of the Eastern and Middle Districts of Pa., is hereby called to the Maine Mission." Below I give extracts of a letter in my possession, from which it will be seen that there still is a desire among the people there to have "the way of God expounded more perfectly." There are still other facts set forth in those letters, more encouraging than those given below, but of such a nature that I deem it not expedient to publish them, but will submit them to the meetings of both districts when in session, and whatever more may be obtained during the intermediate time will also be laid before them. My opinion is, there is still a work for us, as a church, to do in those remote regions that ought not to be neglected. But it requires a sacrifice of the enjoyment of home and friends, which are just as near and dear to the minister who goes, as to any one else. And it requires means at the hands of the Church, so that those willing to make said sacrifice, and approved of by the Church, may be brought on their way; hence this appeal is made to the churches to give the subject their prayerful attention.

The first letter under date of Dec. 22, says: "There is still a hungering for the word of life. I often hear people say, I wish those ministers from Penna., were here to preach to us the things pertaining to our everlasting well being." Same letter: "All the people to whom I showed your letter say to me; send him my best respects—tell him he must come back," &c. Under date of March 16, the same correspondent writes as follows: "After giving the result of another visit they have had since we left, he says: "But there are a number here that would be glad to see you and hear you preach the word, and if you will write what inducements and encouragements you wish held out, I will make enquiry and see if they can be given." I replied to the above enquiry and will give the result at the proper time.

D. M. HOLSINGER.

Clover Creek, Pa.

EXPLANATORY.

We are sorry to intrude on your valuable paper with a subject destitute of spiritual food, and ask your indulgence and the pardon of your readers this once yet. Your concluding remarks tingled somewhat challengingly, induced us to explain. The phrase, "*the imperative mood*," we understood technically; and as such thought the writer to have used it. Substitute *an* for *the*, and that technicallity is in a manner *erased*,—and *then* we would prefer manner instead of mood, as the latter term is invariably connected with grammatical modifications of verbs in manner. Hence technically so used.

But if intended according to your expression to "make grammar succumb to the force of language and circumstances," we have to yield. The grammars are very prolific in exceptions, and indeed must be; yet when they come to the formula of parsing, all yield to the same technical terms. For instance, *shall* in the indicative mood, 2nd person, 1st future tense signifies command; while in the 1st and 3rd persons, determination. *Must* in the potential mood, 2nd person, present tense, signifies command more emphatic yet; while 1st and 3rd persons, stern necessity. We confess to be ignorant of the author who places any of those auxiliaries in the imperative mood technically. So we looked at the subject. Are we wrong?

S. B. FURRY.

Martinsburg, Pa.

REMARKS.—We are strongly in favor of words having but *one* meaning. We become cognizant of each others ideas, wishes and wants by the use of combination of sounds, either vocalized or represented by characters. These sounds, when combined, are called words, representing distinct ideas. Imperative is expressive of the idea of a command, and shall, when used in the sense of must, as in the cases referred, to, implies a positive command, therefore becomes imperative, hence we simply contended that Bro. Moomaw's expression, according to the force of language and the circumstances, was admissable. We were aware that, according to the technicalities of grammar, our position was not tenable, although Kerl says that shall, when used in the sense of must, does not properly belong to the indicative mood but to avoid *troublesome distinctions* is so considered. Therefore we still affirm that shall in the cases referred to is used in an imperative sense and may be so considered. In making our criticism we had an object in view which we hope both parties understand and now drop it, hoping that we have done justice to both without doing any injustice to ourselves.

Dear Pilgrim:—I feel like writing a little which I hope you will give place in your columns. I am a reader of the PILGRIM and would not like to do without it, as in it I read so many letters from sisters and others which gives me much pleasure in reading. Sisters, I feel like encouraging you to write more. Perhaps if we were all more interested in the PILGRIM's welfare and labor more for it we might give considerable aid to the editors.

I will now tell you how I came to join the pilgrim band. I was baptized when an infant and brought up in the Lutheran faith and became a member of that Church. While on a visit among my relatives, I was told that there was to be a Dunkard meeting in the neighborhood, and that there were to be some baptized and that we would all go and see the sight. We all went and indeed we did see a sight, one that I never saw before. After the baptizing was over we had some conversation about these strange people, and as I was a good reader at that time, I argued that their baptism was right according to the Scriptures, which gave occasion for them calling me a Dunkard but I cared not. After a short time I again returned home and months and years passed away with the convictions received at that meeting resting upon my mind, finally my father was called to the spirit-land leaving a poor mother and eight children to be cared for in a cold and pitiless world. My former convictions still bore heavily upon me and I went to the Brethren to live and provide for myself. They took me often to their meetings and once to a Lovefeast, the first one I ever attended. I noticed closely to see how their practice would correspond with the Word, and when I beheld how beautifully the primitive order of the Gospel was carried out, I was astonished that I stood where I did. Eld. John Metzgar and others spoke so much of Jesus and so perfectly illustrated the divine precepts and principles of religion, also the love and compassion of Jesus, His forbearance, forgiveness, meekness, holiness and simplicity that I was perfectly charmed, and was pursuaded that it was impossible for any to read His history with an unprejudiced mind without acknowledging that He was none other than the one spoken of by the prophet who said: "His name shall be called Wonderful Counsellor, the Mighty God, the Everlasting Father and the Prince of Peace." One more text, "How oft would I have gathered you under my wings * * * and you would not." "And ye will not," sounded loudly in my ears until I was constrained to cast my all on Jesus, and my lot with the people of God.

Then I was young, but now I have passed my two score and my sight is beginning to grow dim. My life has been a mixture of sorrow and joy but day by day I am nearing deliverance and can truly say "the Lord will never forsake the righteous, no never.

Dear sisters, do not grow weary in well doing, as we have the promise that we shall reap if we faint not.

"If you meet with troubles and trials on the way,
Cast your burden on Jesus and don't forget to pray."

ANNA TROXEL.

Milmine, Ill.

MARRIED.

SPITLER—SHOUP.—On Tuesday, March 11, '73, by the undersigned at the residence of the bride's father, Mr. Moses Spitler of Montgomery Co., and Miss Amanda A. Shoup, of Beaver Creek, Green Co., Ohio.

B. F. DARST.

DIED.

KINSEL.—In Spring Run Congregation, Mifflin Co., Pa., March 10, '73, Salome Heeman, youngest daughter of brother Michael F. H., and sister Eva E. Kinsel, aged 5 years, 8 months and 13 days. Funeral sermon by Eld. P. S. Myers, from these words: "For the thing which I greatly feared is come upon me, and that which I was afraid of is come unto me. I was not in safety, neither had I rest, neither was I quiet, yet trouble came."—Job 3: 25; 26.

Sallie, as she was commonly called, was an amiable little girl, and much beloved by all who knew her, and more especially by the family; but her stay on earth was short, and now she is an angel and gone to dwell with her Savior, where you, parents, brothers and sister, with all of us can meet her if we obey, from the heart, all of Christ's commandments.

S. W. BOLLINGER.

SMITH.—In the Woodland Church, Barry Co., Michigan, March 15, '73, sister Mary, wife of brother Isaac Smith, aged 35 years, nine months and 24 days.

She leaves a husband and four children to mourn their loss, but we hope and believe that their loss is her gain. Funeral service by the writer from 1 Thess., 4: 13, 14.

ISAAC MILLER.

(*Companion* and *Visitor*, please copy.

MORGAN.—Near South English, Iowa, March 24, '73, Eva, only child of Charlie and Priscilla Morgan, and grand daughter of Rev. David Brower of Marion Co., Oregon, aged nine months and 11 days. The funeral exercises were attended to by the brethren to a large concourse of sympathizing friends. Text last verse of the 6th chapter of *Romans*.

Thus has another plant been removed to the fair climes of Heaven; another angel added to the happy throng, another glorified spirit joined to the celestial choir. Let us all follow on and ere long we shall meet on that beautiful shore, in that sweet by and by.

B. F. F.

WAGONER.—In the Auglaize Church, Auglaize Co., Ohio, February 23, '73, Sarah E., daughter of C. Wagoner, jr., aged 4 years, 9 months and 23 days. Funeral service by the brethren from Mark 10: 13-16.

BALIFF.—Also in the same branch, March 25, sister Tena Baliff, aged 35 years, 2 months and 27 days. Funeral on the 27th, in the Christian Church, by the brethren to a large and attentive concourse of people, from 1 Thess., 4: 13-18.

The subject of this notice was ailing for some time, and when she thought the time of her departure was near at hand, she sent for the elders of the Church and was anointed in the name of the Lord. She leaves a sorrowing husband and five children to mourn their loss, which is not without hope.

DANIEL BROWER.

MILLER.—In the Snake Spring Congregation, Bedford Co., Pa., in the South end of Morrisons Cove, March 19, '73, Bro. John P. Miller, aged 73 years, 2 months and 13 days. The above is a brother to Eld. Jacob Miller of Yellow Creek Congregation. The funeral was improved by the brethren from 1 Thess., 4: 14.

H. HERSHBERGER.

STEAMBERGER.—In the Springfield District, Noble Co., Ind., March 24, '73, sister Ellen, wife of friend George Steamberger, aged 43 years, 9 months and 16 days. Funeral services by Bro. Christian Weaver, from Rev. 14: 13

JOHN B[illegible]

ANNOUNCEMENTS.

Please announce that the District Meeting of Northern Indiana and Michigan, will be held in the Brethren's Meetinghouse, ½ mile west of Goshen, Elkhart Co., Ind., commencing on Thursday the 1st day of May, 1873, at 10 o'clock, a. m.

JESSE CALVERT, Clerk.

Champaign Lovefeast.

The brethren in Champaign Co., Ill., have appointed their Communion Meeting on Saturday and Sunday, June 7th and 8th, 1873, at Bro. Geo. Dilling's, five miles east of Urbana. We extend an invitation to all, especially the ministering brethren.

J. D. MOORE,
Urbana, Ill.

TO ALL WHO ARE CONCERNED.

We do, through this medium, inform the brethren and churches composing the first district of Virginia, that Friday and Saturday before the fourth Sunday in April, is the time appointed for the holding of the Annual District Meeting, and will be held at that time no preventive providence, at the Valley Meeting-house in Botetourt Co., one mile south of Amsterdam. A full attendance is desirable.

The undersigned also informs his brethren that he has a number of New Hymn Books on hand for sale. B. F. MOOMAW.

Please announce that the District Meeting of Western Maryland, will be held the Lord willing in the Welsh Run Congregation in the Broad Fording Meetinghouse, five miles north-west of Hagerstown on the second Thursday in April, 1872.

NICHOLAS MARTIN.

You will please announce through the PILGRIM that the Brethren in the Middle District of Iowa, purpose holding their District Council Meeting with the Brethren in Dallas Co., in their Meetinghouse, on Monday the 19th day of May, 1873. We expect a good representation of delegates, also a general invitation to the brethren to be with us. J. S. SNYDER,
Cor. Sec'y.

Please announce through your paper, the Lord willing, the District Meeting for the South eastern District of Ohio, will be held in the Jonathan's Creek Congregation, Perry Co., Ohio, on Tuesday the 20th day of May, 1873, being the second Tuesday before the A. M. All persons coming to the meeting (i. e.) brethren and sisters, must come to Newark, Ohio, thence down the Newark, Somerset & Straitsville Railroad to Glenford Station, there the brethren will meet those who come and convey them to the place of meeting, 8 miles off. Those who intend to come will please write us and we will have the necessary arrangements made. W. ARNOLD.
Somerset, Perry Co., O.

Please announce through the PILGRIM that our District Meeting will be held on the 13th of May in the Cook's Creek Congregation, Rockingham Co., Va.

SOLOMON GARBER.

Please make the following announcement in the WEEKLY PILGRIM. The District Meeting of West Virginia, will be held in Seneca District, eight miles west of Mouth of Seneca, at Union School House, in Dry Fork township, Randolph Co., on Friday and Saturday, 9th and 10th of May. For any further information address the undersigned at Mouth of Seneca,
Pendleton Co., W. Va.
By order of the Church.
ASA HARMAN.

The District Meeting of Middle Penna., will be held, the Lord willing, at the Clover Creek Meeting-house, Blair Co., on Tuesday the 13th day of May, '73. Brethren coming by Railroad will come to Altoona, thence by Hollidaysburg and Morrison's Cove branch to Martinsburg, which is two miles from place of meeting. Those coming via. Harrisburg, should be sure to be there by 1 P. M. to meet the mail train, so they get to Martinsburg at 9 P. M., if later, they must lay over.

It is the desire of the church here, that some of our dear ministering brethren be with us over Sunday, and have meetings at four or five different places. Now those who feel willing to do so, will please notify Bro. J. W. Brumbaugh, Clover Creek, Blair Co., Pa., informing him when they expect to arrive, and conveyance will be ready to take them to the different points.

D. M. HOLSINGER.

The brethren in the Little Swatara Church have appointed their Communion meeting on Thursday and Friday, the 12th and 13th of June '73, at brother Henry K. Bixler's, two miles North-East of Jonestown, Lebanon Co., Pa. Ministering brethren going or coming from the East to the Annual Meeting, by their return are invited to stop off with us and give us their assistance. Those coming by Railroad will stop off at Jonestown, within two miles of the place of meeting. By the order of our Elder, David Merkey.

(*Companion*, please copy.)

J. HERTZLER.

Please announce that the District Meeting for 1873 of the Middle District of Ind., will be held in the Bachellor Run Church at their lower Meeting-house, commencing on the second Friday after Good Friday. Brethren coming by Railroad from East or West will stop off at Ino station, on the Camden and Frankfort road. A full representation is desired. Ino is 1½ mile from place of meeting. J. S. SNOWBERGER.

The Weekly Pilgrim.

JAMES CREEK, PA., April 8. 1873.

☞ How to send money.—All sums over $1.50, should be sent either in a check, draft or postal order. If neither of these can be obtained, have the letter registered.

☞ WHEN MONEY is sent, *always* send with it the name and address of those who paid it. Write the names and post office a" plainly as possible.

☞ EVERY subscriber for 1873, gets a *Pilgrim Almanac* FREE.

HELP US.—Through judicious advertising we have daily calls for sample copies of the PILGRIM from places where the truth, as we preach it, was never heard, and we fondly hope it may be the means of planting the standard of Christ in many new sections where Primitive Christianity was never preached. Brethren and sisters you can greatly aid us in the good work by sending for sample copies and distributing them to such as may receive them gladly. For this purpose we always keep a supply on hands. We will send them by the hundreds if you will be kind enough to just send us money enough to pay the postage.

The postage on PILGRIMS is one cent for every two copies, or eight cents per pound. Brethren and sisters continue to labor to increase our circulation. There are hundreds and thousands that would be benefitted by reading the PILGRIM. Subscriptions may commence at any time and run one year, or back No's can still be furnished.

WE are informed that on the 23d of March a son and daughter of Eld. David Long and a daughter of Bro. V. Reichard of Manor Congregation, Md., were inducted into Christ's kingdom by holy baptism. We should have scores of such reports every week as there is no reason why any sane person should remain in the employ of satan who has no reward to offer but misery and everlasting destruction.

IN CORRECTING our galleys we found a number of mistakes. They are corrected as far as possible but if there should be any more, please let us know as soon as possible so that all corrections can be made and all receive their papers. In writing for lost copies please state what Nos. are wanted and we will supply them.

PERSONAL.

F. W. DOVE.—Right.

SAMUEL WAREHAM. — Due us $1.00.

JACOB WEAVER.—You are right; it was $6.50.

D. BROWER.—The $1.50 was received and the PILGRIM sent.

ELIZABETH HUFFERD.—In the Tune Book is used the character or square notes.

LOST COPIES.—All lost copies will be supplied if we are informed what Nos. are missing.

J. J. KINDIG.—All sums under $1.50 are at our risk if carefully put up and addressed.

CHANGE OF ADDRESS.—J. B. Miller of Alumbank Pa. has changed his address to New Paris, Bedford Co., Pa.

WM. B. SELL is our agent for Hamilton, Mo. We will be responsible for all money paid to him for books, subscription, &c.

DANIEL BOCK.—We have no account of the $3.00. If you would give us the names and address we could then tell whether or not it was received.

MATHIAS FRANTZ. — The order was received and names credited but by oversight the amount was not published. Bro. Pelley's name is right in our book.—Missing Nos. sent.

N. D. HADSELL of Garrett, Kansas, under date of March 23, says: "We have had nice weather during the whole of this month thus far. The farmers have been ploughing for several weeks for Oats. Wheat looks well for the chance it had and grass has started nicely on the prairies.

LITERARY NOTICES.

THE SANITARIAN is a new monthly journal devoted to the protection of public health and the preservation of human life. It is ably edited by A. N. Bell, contains over fifty pages of useful information and is published by A. S. Barns & Co., 111 and 113 William St., New York, at $3.00 per annum.

IOWA'S RESOURCES.—We have just received a pamphlet of over 150 pages, giving the manufacturing, agricultural and industrial resources of Iowa, with reliable information to capitalists seeking the best fields for investment, also, valuable information for emigrants seeking new and desirable homes. Any person desiring a copy may obtain it gratuitously by addressing A. R. Fulton, at De Moines, Iowa. Secretary Iowa State Board of Immigration.

AMERICAN SUNDAY SCHOOL WORKER.—The last number of this Journal contains an able article by one of its editorial committee. Rev. T. M. Post, D. D., on Early Conversions, and a variety of choice, selected and origional articles. Intelligence, Book Notices, &c., besides twelve pages given to the elucidation of the International Lessons.

It is published by J. W. McIntyre, No. 4 South Fifth Street, St. Louis, at $1.50 a year. Single copies 15 cents.

SCRIBNER'S MONTHLY for April is on our table. One of the leading articles is "An Hour among the Greenbacks" which is well worth a reading as it gives, in detail the whole process through which the much sought for pieces of paper are made to pass. There is one signature which no doubt almost everybody noticed, but few have had the pleasure of deciphering. That mysterious chirography when translated is F. E. Spinner, the treasurer. He is a rare specimen of humanity but you can learn much of his character by reading the April No. of Scribner. It also contains many other papers that are high interesting and instructive. Terms $4.00 per year.

Address, Scribner & Co., 654 Broadway, N. Y.

MONEY LIST.

Lydia Showalter	$1.25
D M Negley	50
David Coble	1.50
Levi Ridenour	1.25
Wm H Carrier	50
Michael Beshoar	1.25
Joseph Markly	1.50
Samuel Moyer	6.00
Susanna Keiser	50
John Beckley	50
E E Miller	1.50
F W Dove	40
Jacob Weaver	6.50
Daniel Brower	23.25
D M Fogglesanger	3.00
Mathias Frantz	1.50
J N Shellabarger	1.25
Catharine A Forney	1.12
Jacob Mohler	4.12
Lewis Workman	8.50
Kate Eshelman	3.00
Susan Brumbaugh	1.50
J S Snowberger	2.00
Andrew Forsyth	1.50

It is said that the emperor of Germany is of the opinion that he and other monarchs of Europe are reaping a larger harvest from his overwhelming victory over Napoleon III. than is enjoyable. From that followed a republic in France, and from that republic, he thinks comes the new one in Spain. This is more than be fought for. However, unless there are fewer changes in their ministries, and a manifestation of more stability in their government, it is probable that the conquering William's peace of mind, so far as the establishment of republican governments in Europe is concerned, will be fully restored.

Seeds, Plants, Trees,—Prepaid by Mail.

My new priced descriptive Catalogue of Choice Flower and Garden Seeds, 25 sorts of either for $1; new and choice varieties of Fruit and Ornamental Trees, Shrubs, Evergreens, Roses, Grapes, Lilies, Small Fruits, House and Border Plants and Bulbs; one year grafted Fruit Trees for mailing; Fruit Stocks of all kinds; Hedge Plants, &c.; the most complete assortment in the country, will be sent gratis to any plain address, with P. O. box. True Cape Cod Cranberry for upland or lowland, $6 per 1000; $1 per 100; prepaid by mail. Trade List to dealers. Seeds on Commission. Agents wanted. B. M WATSON,
Old Colony Nurseries and Seed Warehouse, Plymouth, Mass. Established 1842.

$50.000

Will be distributed this year, to the subscribers for the AMERICAN WORKING PEOPLE, a large quarto, 16 page Monthly, costing but $1.50 per year. It gives a premium to every subscriber, varying from 25 cents in value up to $2, $5, $10, $20, $100, $200, and $500 in Greenbacks besides Watches, Sewing Machines, Parlor Organs and numerous other premiums of value. Send for specimen and circulars to
CAPRON & CO.,
Mar. 18-3m. Pittsburgh, Pa.

WANTED. We will give men and women

Business that will Pay

from $4 to $8 per day, can be pursued in your own neighborhood; it is a rare chance for those out of employment or having leisure time; girls and boys frequently do as well as men. Particulars free.
Address J. LATHAM & CO.,
292 Washington St., Boston, Mass.

Trine Immersion

TRACED

TO THE APOSTLES.

The SECOND EDITION is now ready for delivery. The work has been carefully revised, corrected and enlarged.

Put up in a neat pamphlet form, with good paper cover, and will be sent, post-paid, on the following terms: One copy, 25 cts; Five copies, $1.10; Ten copies, $2.00; 25 copies, $4.50; 50 copies, $8.50; 100 copies, $16 00.
Address, J. H. MOORE,
Urbana, Champaign co., Ill.
Oct. 22.

DYMOND ON WAR.

An Inquiry into the Accordancy of War, with the Principles of Christianity, and an examination of the Philosophical reasoning by which it is defended. With observations on some of the causes of war and on some of its effects. By Jonathan Dymond. Sent from this office, post-paid, for 50 cts.

TUNE BOOK.

The Brethren's Tune and Hymn Book, is a compilation of Sacred Music adapted to all the hymns in the Brethren's New Hymn Book. It contains over 350 pages, printed on good paper and neatly bound. We will send it to any address, post paid at $1.25 per copy.

GOOD BOOKS.

How to read Character, illus. Price,	$1.25
Combe's Moral Philosophy,	1.75
Constitution of Man. Combe,	1.75
Education. By Spurzheim,	1.50
Memory—How to Improve it,	1.60
Mental Science, Lectures on,	1.50
Self-Culture and Perfection,	1.50
Combe's Physiology, Illus.	1.75
Food and Diet. By Pereira,	1.75
Natural Laws of Man,	.75
Hereditary Descent,	1.50
Combe on Infancy,	1.30
Sober and Temperate Life,	.50
Children in Health—Disease,	1.75
The Science of Human Life,	3.50
Fruit Culture for the Million,	1.00
Saving and Wasting,	1.50
Ways of Life—Right Way,	1.00
Footprints of Life,	1.25
Conversion of St. Paul,	1.00

A large number of our patrons are receiving our books as noticed below, as premiums, and express themselves highly pleased with them. Others who are not agents, have enquired whether we keep them for sale. We have now made arrangements with Mr. Wells to furnish any of their publications post paid at publishers prices. Orders for books must be accompanied with the cash, and plain directions for sending them.

Weaver's Works for the Young. Comprising "Hopes and Helps for the Young of both Sexes," $3.00.

Life at Home; or, The Family and its Members. A work which should be found in every family. $1.50. Extra gilt, $2.00.

Hand-book for Home Improvement: comprising "How to Write," "How to Talk," How to Behave," and "How to do Business," in one vol. 2.25.

Man and Woman: Considered in their Relations to each Other and to the World. 12mo, Fancy cloth, Price $1.00.

The Right Word in the Right Place. A New Pocket Dictionary and Reference Book. Cloth, 75cts.

Hopes and Helps for the Young of both sexes, Relating to the Formation of Character. Choice of Avocation, Health, Conversation, Social Affection Courtship and Marriage. Muslin, $1.50.

The Emphatic, Diaglott; or The New Testament in Greek and English. Containing the Original Greek Text of the New Testament, with an Interlineary Word-for-word English Translation. Price, $4.00; extra fine binding, $5.00.

Oratory—Sacred and Secular; or, the Extemporaneous Speaker. Price $1.50.

Conversion of St. Paul. 12mo. fine edition, $1. Plain edition, 75 cents.

Man, in Genesis and in Geology; or, the Biblical Account of Man's Creation, tested by Scientific Theories of his Origin and Antiquity. One vol. 12mo, $1.00.

$5 to $20 [illegible]

THE

HOUSEHOLD TREASURE.

Containing several hundred Valuable Receipts for cooking well at a moderate expense, making Dyes, Coloring, Cleaning and Cementing. This book also points out in plain language, free from Doctors' terms the diseases of men, women and children, and the latest and most approved means used for their cure, to which is added a description of the Medicinal Roots and Herbs, and how they are to be used in the cure of diseases.

This is a work of considerable importance and we offer it to our readers as being a valuable accession to every household. Sent from this office to any address, post paid, for 25 cents.

WANTED BOOK AGENTS

FOR THE

FUNNY SIDE OF PHYSIC.

800 *Pages*, 250 *Engravings.*

A startling expose of Medical Humbugs of the past and present. It ventilates Quacks, Imposters, Travelling Doctors, Patent Medicine Venders, Noted Female Cheats, Fortune Tellers and Mediums, and gives interesting accounts of Noted Physicians and Narratives of their lives. It reveals startling secrets and instructs all how to avoid the ills which flesh is heir to. We give exclusive territory and liberal commissions. For circulars and terms address the publishers. J. B. BURR & HYDE,
Hartford, Conn., or Chicago, Ill.

AGENTS WANTED FOR THE

UNCIVILIZED RACES OF MEN

In all countries of the world.

Being a comprehensive account of their Manners and Customs, and of their Physical, Social, Mental, Moral, and Religious Characteristics.

By REV. J. G. WOOD, M. A., F. L. S.

500 *Engravings*, 1500 *Super Royal Oc. Pages*

In two Volumes, or two Volumes in one. Agents are making over $100 per week in selling this work. An early application will secure a choice of territory. For terms address the publishers.
J. B. BURR & HYDE,
Hartford, Conn., or Chicago, Ill.

TRACTS.

"ANXIOUS BENCH RELIGION EXAMINED," BY ELDER J. S. FLORY. A SYNOPSIS OF CONTENTS. An address to the reader: The peculiarities that attend this type of religion. The feelings there experienced not imaginary but real. The key that unlocks the wonderful mystery. The causes by which feelings are excited. How the momentary feelings called "Experimental religion" are brought about, and then concludes by giving that form of doctrine as taught by Jesus Christ and recorded by his faithful witnesses.

COUNTERFEIT DETECTER
or
BAPTISM—MUCH IN LITTLE.

This work is now ready for distribution, and the importance of the subject will speak for it a large demand. It is a short treatise on baptism in tract form intended for general distribution, and is set forth in such a plain and logical manner that a wayfaring man though a fool, cannot err therein. Either of the above tracts sent postpaid on the following terms: Two copies, 10 cts, 10 copies 40 cents, 25 copies 70 cents, 50 copies $1.00, 100 copies $1.50.

Trine Immersion.

A discussion on Trine Immersion, by letter between Elder B. F. Moomaw and Dr. J. J. Jackson, to which is annexed a Treatise on the Lord's Supper, and on the necessity, character and evidences of the new birth, also a dialogue on the doctrine of non-resistance, by Elder B. F. Moomaw. Single copy 50 cents.

THE GROUNDS FOR A

FORWARD and BACKWARD

MODE OF

BAPTISM.

Briefly, yet *carefully* examined; and the TRUE and CORRECT mode so clearly set forth that none can help but understand.

This little book contains 30 pages, neatly put up in paper cover. Price per doz. $1.25, add 10 cts. for postage. Two copies, 25 cts 1 copy, 15 cts., free of postage.
Address, SAMUEL KINSEY,
Mar 11-3t. Dayton, O.

LAND, LAND, LAND!!

The completion of the Chesapeake and Ohio Trunk Line Railway, has opened up to the world much of the fine TIMBER LANDS, rich COAL FIELDS and cheap FARMING LANDS of W. Va. Now is the time to get cheap homes and invest money with the prospect of a handsome profit. For further particulars inquire of the undersigned, agent for lands here. J. S. FLORY,
Orchard View, Fayette Co., W. Va.
Jan. 10.

1870 1873

DR. FAHRNEY'S

Blood Cleanser or Panacea.

A tonic and purge, for Blood Diseases. Great reputation. Many testimonials. Many ministering brethren use and recommend it. Ask or send for the "Health Messenger." Use only the "*Panacea*" prepared at Chicago, Ills., and by

Dr. P. Fahrney's Brothers & Co.,
Feb. 8-pd. *Waynesboro, Franklin Co., Pa*

New Hymn Books, English.

TURKEY MOROCCO.

One copy, postpaid,	$1 00
Per Dozen,	11.25

PLAIN ARABESQUE.

One Copy, post-paid,	75
Per Dozen, "	8.50

Ger'n & English, Plain Sheep.

One Copy, post-paid,	$1.00
Per Dozen	11.25
Arabesque Plain,	1.00
Turkey Morocco,	1.25
Single German, post paid	50
Per Dozen,	5.50

HUNTINGDON & BROAD TOP RAIL ROAD

On and after March 22d, 1873, Trains will run on this road daily (Sundays excepted) as follows:

Trains from Huntingdon South. *Trains from Mt. Dal's moving North.*

MAIL. A. M.	PASS. P. M.	STATIONS.	MAIL. P. M.	PASS. A. M.
le7 45	6 00	Huntingdon,	AR4 00	AR8 25
7 50	6 05	Long Siding	3 53	8 20
8 10	6 17	McConnelstown	3 45	8 10
8 17	6 25	Pleasant Grove	3 35	8 02
8 30	6 40	Marklesburg	3 20	7 45
8 45	6 55	Coffee Run	3 07	7 32
8 55	7 03	Hough & Ready	2 57	7 23
9 05	7 12	Cove	2 47	7 13
9 08	7 18	Fishers Summit	2 45	7 10
9 20	7 30	Saxton	2 27	6 55
9 40	7 50	Riddlesburg	2 10	6 35
9 47	7 58	Hopewell	2 02	6 25
10 02	8 12	Piper's Run	1 47	6 11
10 17	8 30	Tatesville	1 33	5 55
10 30	8 40	Everett	1 20	5 45
10 35	8 45	Mount Dallas	1 15	5 40
11 08	9 20	Bedford	12 44	5 00

G. F. GAGE, Supt.

SHOUP'S RUN BRANCH.

LE 9 25 LE	Saxton.	AR2 15 AR
9 40	Coalmont.	2 00
9 45	Crawford.	1 55
AR10 00 AR	Dudley	LE1 45 LE

Bro'd Top City from Dudley 2 miles by stage.

Time of Penna. R. R. Trains at Huntingdon.
*, *Mail No. 2 makes connection at Huntingdon with Mail going East on Pennsylvania Railroad at 4.15 p. m., and West at 5.45 p. m. Mail No. 1 leaves Huntingdon at 7.40 a. m. on arrival of Pacific Express West.

Trains on this road connect with trains on Bedford & Bridgeport, and Cumberland & Pennsylvania Railroads.

The Weekly Pilgrim.

Published by J. B. Brumbaugh, & Co.

Edited by H. B. & Geo. Brumbaugh.

CORRESPONDING EDITORS.

D. P. Sayler, Double Pipe Creek, Md.

Leonard Furry, New Enterprise, Pa.

The *Pilgrim* is a Christian Periodical, devoted to religion and moral reform. It will advocate in the spirit of *love* and *liberty*, the principles of true Christianity, labor for the promotion of peace among the people of God, for the encouragement of the saints and for the conversion of sinners, avoiding those things which tend toward disunion or sectional feelings.

TERMS.

Single copy, Book paper,	$1.50
Eleven copies, [eleventh for Agt.]	$15.00

Any number above that at the same rate,
Address,
H. B. BRUMBAUGH,
James Creek,
Huntingdon county Pa.

The Weekly Pilgrim.

"REMOVE NOT THE ANCIENT LANDMARKS WHICH OUR FATHERS HAVE SET."

VOL. 4. JAMES CREEK, PENNSYLVANIA, APRIL 15, 1873. NO. 15

POETRY.

LIFE.

At the portals of the morning
 Stood a child with dainty feet,
All about him golden sunshine,
 Pearly dews and blossoms sweet;
And with tender, dimpled fingers
 Plucked he flowers fresh and fair,
And the overhanging branches
 Showered the dewdrops in his hair.

Looking forward o'er life's pathway,
 Saw he broader fields of green;
Skies with snowy clouds so fleecy,
 Here and there blue shreds between;
And with swiftly flying foot-steps,
 Started he for fields more bright;
But in vain he hurried onward—
 They were always just in sight.

Warmer, brighter grew the sunshine,
 Broader, rougher grew the way;
But with green fields just before him,
 Nothing could his footsteps stay,
So he wandered on 'till manhood
 Took the place of childhood fair,
Then he threw aside his flowers,
 Wiped the dew-drops from his hair.

Onward, onward, toiling, striving,
 Helping others with his might;
Learned he that the blooming green fields
 That are always just in sight
Lay beyond the cold, dark river;
 Here we only longing wait,
Till the Master calls us over,
 And unbars the pearly gate.

The noontide sunbeams o'er him fell,
 Then came the evening calm
With its golden, golden sunset,
 The dying day's sweet psalm.
The boy from the morning portals,
 At even with snowy hair,
Crossed when the Master called him,
 To the green fields "Over there."

ORIGINAL ESSAYS.

THE BAPTISM OF JOHN. WHENCE WAS IT, FROM HEAVEN OR OF MEN?

B. F. MOOMAW.

In our examination of what we regard as the institutions of men we propose to begin with Freemasonry, as probably the most ancient, and no less honorable, humanly speaking, than any other in the catalogue of these associations. In pursuing this subject it is my desire to treat it in all fairness and to exercise the largest degree of charity possible. As a moral institution I have no doubt but that it has accomplished a great deal of good, and if persons are not inclined to adopt the Bible as the *all sufficient* and infallible rule of faith and conduct perhaps they would do well to associate themselves with this order, for doubtless if the precepts of Masonry, so far as what is revealed is concerned is consistently followed it will have a very beneficial effect upon the moral character, by restraining the natural passions, and inculcating the practice of virtue by limiting the desires and inordinate affections and cultivating the higher order of our nature in the exercise of the principles of justice, benevolence and charity, and the establishment of the golden rule, "doing unto others as we would," our circumstances being reversed, "that they should do unto us." As to the secrets and mysteries of the order what they teach is altogether a different matter. Of what is done by them in secret, as Paul would say, "it would probably be a shame even to speak," all that we can know about it is that the most strict precaution is used to prevent them from being known, and our Savior says that "light has come into the world, and men loved darkness rather than light because their deeds were evil."

We introduce here a scrap on instructions to Masons, when in presence of strangers who are not Masons.

"Before those who are not Masons you must be cautious in your words, carriage and motions; so that the most penetrating stranger shall not discover what is not proper to be intimated. The impertinent and ensnaring question or ignorant and idle discourse of those who seek to pry into the mysteries and secrets committed to you, must be prudently answered, and managed, or the discourse wisely diverted to another subject as your discretion and duty shall direct." For the purpose too the lodge room is always in an upper room to prevent being seen through the windows. Why this guarded secresy I never could define, if their works were lawful or good. "If there is light why put it under a bushel? Why not put it on a candlestick that its reflection might illuminate the world around, but a thought has occurred to my mind while contemplating this subject, that this secresy is the secret of success else why the astonishing progress of the craft? There being no public declamation nor lectures, but very few tracts or published documents of Masonic literature, little or no effort made by the members to induce persons to initiate, but men ever curious to pursue and possess that from which they are barred like our progenitors in the garden become more and more anxious and finally make the fatal step, from which when once taken it is impossible to recede, and so when once initiated into the craft, there is no remedy that will effectually relieve them, but are joined to their idol of man's invention as we assert. Whether our assertion can be maintained against the arguments advanced by its votaries who claim for it the sanction of divine authority the sequel will show. We propose then to review these arguments that we may see how far the premises are supported, "whether it is from Heaven or of men."

One week ago to-day we wrote the foregoing, was taken quite unwell, unable to set up, consequently had to suspend, but now through the mercy and grace of God, I am able to resume. One hour in the past my mail messenger arrived bringing in the PILGRIM dated March 25th, glancing over its pages my eye soon fell upon brother S. B. Furry's criticism of my language used in a former communication, and his criticism criticized by Bro. editor. so I looked upon the subject when I said that the verb shall was used in the imperative mood, that God was really the person speaking. Moses, Aaron and the children of Israel the second person, or persons spoken to, Moses simply the instrument through which the Lord spake, and had it been necessary to have used an indefinate number of instruments, in my opinion it would have made it no less imperative, just as the command of baptism and every other Christian duty has been communicated to the children of men through an unlimited number of instruments and yet the command is no less imperative. But I will leave brethren Furry and PILGRIM to discuss questions of grammer, and I will try to pursue a little further the train of thought on the subject of institutions human and divine.

Freemasonry being the subject now under consideration with a view to the discussion and settlement of this question it becomes primarily necessary to enquire what Masonry is. At the present day it has two meanings under the style of operative and speculative Masonry, by the former it is according to the explanation of Masons. Made to conduce to man's temporal wants by furnishing shelter from the weather, and by the appliances of architectural symmetry, varied by the tastes and talents of succeeding generations, has imprinted its existence in every country and clime where civilization prevails, by these magnificent structures which are the pride and admiration of every nation.

By speculative Masonry, we mean virtue in its most extended sense, as taught by the daily exercise of brotherly love. Relief and truth, and which compells the initiated to subdue the passions, act upon the square, keep a tongue of good report, maintain secresy and practice charity. It is so intimately connected with religion as to lay its professors under the strongest obligation to pay to the Deity that rational and heart emanating homage which at once constitutes their duty and happiness. Reasoning, then from this acknowledged data it will not be necessary to detain the reader with a long account of the origin of Masonry. Certain it is, and must be, that when the first man was found in the image of God, the principles of Masonry as a divine gift from Heaven were stamped upon his heart by the great architect of the universe. It is worthy of remark that it is claimed for Masonry, that it is a divine gift from Heaven stamped upon the heart of man by the architect by which he [illegible] provide shelter from the inclemency of the weather, &c. As in the case of Adam when expelled from the garden of Eden, built an habitation for himself and family, and no doubt, say Masons, instructed his descendents in the science and its application, to whatever craft was convenient for those early times. Cain also being pre-instructed in the principles of architecture built a strong city and named it after the name of his oldest son Enoch, whose race following his example improved themselves not only in Masonry but made discovery of several other useful arts. Seth, Mathuselah, Noah, Nimrod or Belus, are all claimed as patrons of Masonry.

From Shinar the science, say they, were carried to distant parts of the world, notwithstanding the confusion of the dialects, and which is presumed to have given rise to the universal practice of conversing without speaking and communicating between Masons by tokens and signs. Abraham, Isaac, Jacob, Joseph and Melchisedec are all claimed as belonging to the craft. That the Israelites practiced Masonry in Egypt is a well authenticated fact from the Bible (Masonic language.) We read they were trained to the building up of two cities with stone and brick, for the Egyptians, and it was undoubtedly the design of the most High, to make them expert Masons, before they should possess the promised land.

The city of Tyre was built by a great body of Sidonian Masons from Gabala, under a grand master and a number of princes.

In after times Ahibal king of Tyre, repaired and beautified that city, and so did his son Hiram being also a Mason. He became one of the principal architects of that stupendous edifice which has been and always will remain the admiration of the world, viz: Solomon's temple. So much for the pretended divine authority for such an institution or organization, if indeed there is any proof of an organization in all the testimonies introduced. So far, I cannot perceive any, simply that men were endowed by their creator and maker of all things, with a mechanical talent capable of being cultivated as circumstances from time to time seemed to demand. If this constitutes Freemasonry I would ask are not all mankind Freemasons? Have those calling themselves Masons more or have others less of this endowment? Have not the females of our race their share of mechanical genius? Why then are they excluded from its secrets and mysteries? No, nor does it stop here, upon the same hypothesis do we not plainly see that the inferior animals come in for their share of the honors of Masonry. Passing by the red man of the forest with his Booth or his wigwam, his moccasin and well arranged strings of beads, &c. We invite attention to the beaver, the otter, the muskrat, and many other of the inhabitants of the water and the woods. The eagle too, wisely selecting his site beyond the reach of danger, displaying the most consummate skill in the arrangement of its building for the comfort and protection of its tender brood, and among many of the more inferior of the feathered tribes do we discover an equal share of Masonic or if you please architectural skill. Coming next to the insect family, we introduce the honey bee as a great past master Mason who surpasses all others in architecture, in the methodical arrangement of his habitation for the comfort and convenience of his colony.

So much then for the divine authority for the craft as exhibited in the organization of operative Masonry but it must pretend as a basis in some way or other to have the sanction of divine authority, or else the pious portion of society would not for a moment entertain a favorable thought toward it and could not be induced to participate, but as we have said in a former chapter of this essay all these pretended evidences of authority from Holy Writ is merely a necessary afterthought and never was thought of as a foundation originating the craft, even of operative Masons, much less speculative, according to the present form. We next propose to show the true origin of the craft from Masonic history.

To be Continued.

A LIGHT TO THE WORLD.

What is Safe and what is not Safe; What is Right and what is not Right.

BY J. H. MOORE.

Chap. III.—BAPTISM.

It is never questioned whether it is safe to be baptized, but is it safe not to be baptized? Other things considered, we know that a man does right when he is baptized, but the doubtful point is, does the man do right who is *not* baptized? We know that it is not against the Bible to be baptized, but then is it against the Bible *not* to be baptized?

In the time of the apostles we know that there were persons in the Church who had been baptized, but the point to be settled is, were there any in the church who were *not* baptized? It is a simple fact that a man can be *baptized* into Christ, but can he get into Christ and *not* be baptized? The former is not only admitted to be right but it is safe, while the latter is neither right nor safe.

We all agree that God will never condemn a man simply because he has been baptized, but then will he not chastise him if he refuses to submit to this institution? Christ says: "He that believeth and is baptized shall be saved, but he that believeth not shall be damned." This much is then settled—that the man who both believes and is baptized shall be saved from his sins. Then the point is, has a man the forgiveness of his sins who simply believes and is not baptized? If he has, then all the devils are safe for they also believe and tremble, Jam.—2: 19. Peter said on the day of Pentecost, "Repent and be baptized every one of you * * * for the remission of sins." Acts—2: 38. Why must they be baptized? Ans. "For the remission of sins." Was it either safe or right to submit to Peter's instruction on this occasion? If it was not then the Pentecostians did wrong for "they that gladly received his word were baptized," Acts—2: 41. Were not they on safe ground when they believed, repented and were baptized? All must answer they were. Well then were those safe who simply believed and were not baptized? Here is where the doubts come in. There is not one particle of uncertainty about the baptized believers, but about the unbaptized. God has promised pardon to all those who believe, repent and are baptized, and no one doubts this—that the penitent baptized believer has been pardoned of his past sins; but the question is has the man received pardon who is not baptized? This is the only point of doubt in the entire matter. We are certain that we are saved from past sins when we have faith, repentance and baptism, but have we the promise without baptism? is the turning point. The man who takes the former we know is safe, but is the man who adopts the latter safe? This is the question for every man to answer who has never been baptized. There are simply two positions and two only in this whole matter—one is to be baptized and the other is not. The first we know is safe, no one doubts this, but then is the latter safe? Here are all the doubts. Then friendly reader which position will you occupy? You know that both Christ and the apostles were baptized, and further, you know that they occupied grounds that were both safe and right, now then are you willing to stand side by side with them, or will you refuse to be baptized and occupy grounds that are exceedingly doubtful? Jesus says: "If ye love me keep my commandments." John—14: 15.

To be Continued.

For the Pilgrim.

THE ENJOYMENTS OF A CHRISTIAN RELIGION.

Man in his natural state or carnal mind has no proper conception of the beauty of a true christian religion; the glorious enjoyments it affords, the happy feelings, encouragements, and the consolation in the proper exercise therein to be realized. O, when the love, the sacred flame that issues from the fountain head warms up the soul of its possessor with kindness, and love towards his brethren and sisters who like him have embraced the religion of Jesus Christ, love divine, as a powerful magnet will draw them together closer and closer till a like feeling pervades them all; whether joy or grief, gladness or sorrow that they will "rejoice with them that do rejoice; and weep with them that weep; bear with one another in adversity, and guard one another in prosperity." Actuated by this God-like principle the church will prosper, God's blessing will be dispensed over it, the Holy Spirit will dwell in it, and joy and peace will be the habitation thereof. O who would not desire to have a dwelling place upon Mount Zion, a seat in his holy temple, a title in the sanctuary of Jehovah; in order to swell the music of heaven; peace be within its walls, and prosperity be within its palaces. Sooner be a door-keeper in the house of the Lord than dwell within the tents of the wicked. Beautiful is the church upon Mount Zion which can not be moved, yea, the gates of hell can never prevail against. Such is the glowing description of the church of God and the permanancy thereof. Delightful is worship in the beauty of its holiness. "Behold how good and how pleasant it is for brethren and sisters to dwell together in peace and unity and worship the great God and praise his holy name in the city of our God in the mountain of his holiness." Beautiful for situation, the joy of the whole earth is Mount Zion, on the sides of the north, the city of the great King. We, as thy children in our adoption have thought, yea, experienced, of thy loving kindness. O God in the midst of thy temple, according to thy name O God, so is thy praise unto the ends of the earth. Come sinner, yea come all the ends of the earth and be saved, for the Lord's right hand is full of righteousness. He is no respecter of persons. All who are willing to abandon sin, fear him, worketh righteousness and accept of the condition of pardon shall be accepted of him. Then let Mount Zion rejoice, let the daughter of Judea be glad when the number of God's children be multiplied because of his righteous judgement. O brethren and sisters, God's children, redeemed of the Lord, cleansed through obedience to his word, your sins washed away by the atoning blood of Jesus Christ, properly applied to your soul by walking in the light of the Lord, by keeping all his commandments. Come yea now, see the glory of the church, view the beautiful serving of God, walk about Zion, and go round about her; tell the towers thereof. "Mark ye well her bulwarks, consider her palaces that ye may tell to the generations following." For this God, whom we serve is our God forever and ever; he will be our guide even unto death. "He maketh us to lie down in green pastures; he leadeth us beside the still waters; he restoreth our souls; he leadeth us in the paths of righteousness; for his name's sake, yea, though we walk through the valley of the shadow of death, we will fear no evil; for thou art with us, thy rod and thy staff they comfort us." If this be the glorious comfort and the blessed enjoyments of the children of God, why so few enlist under the gladsome banner of King Emanuel? Is it not evident then, that the unconverted have poor conceptions of the kingdom of God? The reasons may be various but one grand reason which centers in all others is, because the "god of this world has blinded the minds of them that believe not, lest the light of the Gospel of Jesus Christ, who is the image of God, should shine unto them." They do not desire the service of Jesus. Unbelief, the devil's hook and battering ram to tear down and break into fragments the worship of the true God by teaching them that a historical belief in God alone is sufficient to save them, without any practical faith accompanied by a strict obedience to all the commandments of our Lord Jesus Christ. Mystery Babylon, the great, the mother of Harlot, with her daughter through the deceitful doctrine of unessentiality and optionality leading millions to ruin and ever lasting burnings. Only look and believe in Jesus and all is right, no matter how you drop and how you live; the lust of the flesh, the lust of the eye and the pride of life you need not abandon. Drinking saloons, tippling houses, lotteries, gambling, celebrations, festivities, circus shows and theatre houses ill fame, playing the harlot, cursing, swearing, together with the practical denying of the sufficiency of the Gospel for salvation, by associating, and uniting together in secret order, swearing to their secrecy the most dreadful and abominable oaths the prince of darkness could invent, and this all under the cloak of christianity. Such is the doctrine or at least allowable by these emmissaries. These adherents of these abominable vices are all practical infidelity, and no comfort and permanent enjoyment, when uniting with them can possibly be realized. But dear children, who by one spirit are all baptized into one body and thereby made the children of one God thereby becomes one family, consequently one common interest in that high calling. O let us be knit together in love the center attraction, the bond of perfection, the fulfillment of the law and the glueing liquid which cements us together as one heart, one body and one soul here on earth, will bring us home to rest and gather us together in heaven where full fruition of our love will only be realized. True we have our troubles here, sorrows to endure, conflicts to meet, all is not sunshine. Clouds and darkness roll over us; adversity treads on the heels of prosperity; tempest follows serenity; troubles succeeds joy; temptation often comes after feeling the presence of Jesus and enjoying his smiling countenance for a little season; but amid all these trials when we look through the dark vista with an eye of faith to our future abode in heaven we can still rejoice, knowing that all things work together for our good if we love God. Hence to my dear brethren and sisters in Fulton Co. We sang together the glorious songs of Zion; we felt love flowing together centering in Christ our head, we labored together in the cause of Christ, and we have felt the sweetness of heaven. Now let us hold out faithful to the end is my prayer.

LEONARD EMMRY.

New Enterprise.

FEASTING.

This is a prevailing custom among a certain class of people in our larger cities, and wealthy country towns, and also among the rich in farming communities, and in fact we are scarcely at liberty to say anything in reproof to it, for fear of hurting the feelings of some of the frequenters and indulgers in this evil if I may be allowed to call it so. However the words feasting and festivals has become a little obnoxious to the ears of some of the religious populace, and in order to obviate this difficulty they in some localities, call them social meals, dinners or suppers, by adopting this or a similar modest name, the most of Christians have adopted the custom. This thing of modifying terms is a great fort of the enemy of men. Look at the word gambling. There is scarcely a religious sect in the country that does not consider gambling and gambling shops the very filth of a civilized community, even the laws of our beloved country speaks against the great evil. And of late the word has been modified to such a degree that church members and preachers not only take an active part in it but encourage the practice. That monster is now named Fair instead of Gamble, and to take all the evil stench away thay have recently christened it Church Fair, allowing the monstrous practice of gambling to be carried on in the house solemnly dedicated to the service of God. To the honest christian man or woman the change of name has no bearing from the fact that the practical part is near about the same.

No dear brethren and sisters the name has not much to do with these things, it is simply a hiding place and that only for the time being. I do not want you to draw the conclusion from the above that I class feasting with gambling as being of equal magnitude for evil. I brought up this subject to show how eager men and women are to rush into evil, that, under one name they discard, speak, pray and preach against, they will under cover of a more mild name, in works and practice show forth the very thing that the first name indicated.

But to feasting, I still hold however, that there is an evil in this practice, name it what you will. That a considerable change has taken place in the manner of preparing and conducting these meals, I will admit, and I shall give the honor to those that it belongs to, the Good Templars, with their uniting zeal for temperance, have in many cases been the cause of having the wine cup dispensed with on occasions of this kind. Oh how many young men and young ladies too, have laid the corner stone of a drunkards life at the bacqueting table of their father and mother, uncle, or rich neighbor. I admit that the more considerate have improved a great deal in this respect, and because the wine glass is omitted they say the evil is entirely away. Let us see. It has a strong tendency of leading our children into pride and arrogance, making them of an aristocratical turn of mind, overlooking the absolute wants of their poorer neighbors children, and in after life they will do just as their progenitors did, and by doing so make their poorer friends and neighbors feel very uncomfortable in their community, and not only so, but it follows them into our churches and Sunday Schools, in many cases keeps such from singing and praying with us, and laboring with us in the Sunday School. This may seem strange to some of you but be assured there is too much of this among the so called religious world.

But again, I consider them wrong from a Biblical standpoint. Under this head I include all these dinners and suppers or feasts that are now becoming among neighbors including members of our own beloved church. You no doubt are ready to say, "we can do as we please with that which we call ours." This is true, you can make just as many feasts, or dinners and suppers as you please and there is none can say aught against it. This is not the wrong or where the evil lieth. Would to God there were more of our rich brethren willing and ready to get up these feasts, for in this the evil does not seem to be if our motives are good, pure and Biblical. But I am persuaded to believe that, taking the Bible and the general practice now prevalent among the people, the motives are not prompted of true Christianity. For I am of the opinion that just as soon as the feast is projected, every one or nearly so of the party, are also pointed out, and who are they? Invariably such that are able to repay again! Who dare deny? Dear brethren and sisters, if you of your abundance feel like making a feast that your souls may be blessed thereby, go by the Savior's directions on this subject and you will receive a blessing, and if you think you cannot do so, rather have none at all, than to have them in direct opposition to God's word, and thereby commit a sin. Hear the Savior on this subject. "Then said he (the Savior) also unto him that bade him, when thou makest a *dinner* or a *supper*, call not thy friends, nor thy brethren, neither thy kinsmen, nor thy *rich neighbors*; lest they also bid thee again, and a recompense be made thee. But when thou makest a feast, call the poor, the maimed, the lame, the blind: and thou shalt be blessed; for they cannot recompense thee: for thou shalt be recompensed at the resurrection of the just. Luke—14: 12-14.

Living up to the above order of things we are sure of obtaining a blessing. It may be possible that some of those that freely indulge in these things will answer me by saying we are not doing these things with the expectation of receiving a blessing from God, but do it simply as an act of friendship or charity, expecting to have the compliment returned, at some future time. Brethren, such arguments or excuses may do for the world to make use of, it will never be becoming a true child of God. And if this is the object for getting up these feasts, they are doubly sinful. In the first place you call not the proper subjects, and in the second place you violate the apostles injunction, hear him, "Whether therefore ye eat or drink, or whatsoever ye do, do all to the glory of God." 1 Cor.—10: 35. Whenever we do a thing simply to gratify the wishes of men we come short of glorifying the name of God. The better plan brethren for us to do in this matter, is to weigh it in the scales of Biblical knowledge and if we can't do it to the glory of God, do it not at all. First for your own sake and second, for the sake of your dear children and thirdly for the sake of your poorer neighbors, for remember while you and your select party may be sumptuously feasting, your poor neighbors and their children may not even have [illegible] bread with which to stay hunger. Ye rich forget not the poor, for [illegible] is the Maker of us all.

Ash [illegible], P[illegible]

Selections.

THE BITTER SPRING.

A little river in Scythia, Herodotus tells us, has a marvelous sweetness in its waters until a certain bitter spring mingles with it. Henceforth its waters are all tainted and unfit for use.

What a type of the young heart is this stream at first; and how like that heart when one corrupt teacher has beguiled it, is its course after meeting the spring. One wicked lad in school has well nigh destroyed all the rest. Some gray-haired men seem to spend their lives in destroying our youth. "Their sleep is taken away except they cause some to fall."

I have seen a youth urged and pressed into a bar-room, with great mirth and jesting, by a party of young men. He hung his head and went most unwillingly at first, but he soon became a regular visitant there.

An infidel merchant took great pains to instil his view into the minds of all in his employ. Any young man of especial intelligence was sure to receive his most marked attention. His books were loaned freely and pressed upon him, and he did not rest until he felt he was fairly won to infidelity. He has gone to give up his account; but he could not bury his influence. It was like a poisoned well whereof hundreds may drink to their eternal death.

Christ says of such a corrupter of youth, "It were better for him that a mill-stone were hanged about his neck and that he were drowned in the depth of the sea." That was a terrible punishment sometime inflicted on malefactors, but it was light compared with what God has in store for those who cause to offend these little ones.—*Am. Mess.*

THE SWEETNESS OF HOME.

He who has no home has not the sweetest pleasure of life; he feels not the thousand endearments that cluster around that hallowed spot to fill the void of this aching heart, and while away his leisure moments in the sweetest of life's joys. Is misfortune your lot, you will find a friendly welcome from hearts beating true to your own. The chosen partner to your toil has a smile of approbation when others have deserted, a hand of hope when all others refuse, and a heart to feel your sorrows as her own. Perhaps a smiling cherub with prattling glee and joyous laugh, will drive all sorrow from your careworn brow, and enclose it in the wreathes of domestic bliss.

No matter how humble that home may be, how destitute its stores, or how poorly its inmates are clad; if true hearts dwell there, it is yet a home—a cheerful, prudent wife, obedient and affectionate children, will give possessors more real joy than bags of gold and windy honors.

The home of a temperate, industrious and honest man will be his greatest joy. He comes to it weary and worn but the music of the merry laugh and the happy voices of childhood cheer him. A plain but healthful meal awaits him. Envy, ambition and strife have no place there, and with a clear conscience he lays his weary limbs down to rest in the bosom of his family, under the protecting care of the poor man's friend.

THE LOVE OF CHRIST.

Oh, how shallow a soul I have to take in Christ's love; for let worlds be multiplied, according to angels' understanding, in millions, till they weary themselves, these words could not contain the thousandth part of his love! O that I could join in among the throng of angels, and seraphim, and now glorified saints, and could raise a new love song to Christ before all the world! I am pained with wondering at new-opened treasures in Christ! If every finger, member, bone and joint were a torch burning in the hottest fires in hell, I would that they could all send out love praises, high songs of praise for evermore to that plant of renown, to that royal and high prince, Jesus my Lord.

Oh that my hairs, all my members and all my bones were well tuned tongues, to sing the high praises of my great and glorious King! Help me to lift up Christ upon his throne, and to lift him up above all the thrones of the clay kings, the dying scepterbearers of this world!

FOR US.

It is a blessed thought that the Bible was written for us. That the Spirit of God looked along the ages and saw that in such an event or circumstance of life, we should need just such counsel and help. And then he inspired men to write it down. Not for our good only, but for thousands who have gone before and who will come after. No promise is there but has been proved thousands of times, no warning, but many have taken it home.

It is like a good chart, which has everything on it, that a mariner in every sea may need. Its truths never wear out. Says one who has been a deep student of it, "The Bible will bear a thousand readings, and the man who has gone over it the most frequently and carefully, is the surest of finding new wonders there."

Religious News.

RELIGIOUS STATISTICS.

The following is an extract from the Cincinnati *Gazette* and goes to show in what an awkward position our multiplicity of names place us. It is perfectly absurd for us to be known as Dunkards, Tunkers, Old Brethren, German Baptists and "The Brethren." By common consent we have universally acknowledged the name "Brethren" which is applicable and significant of our fraternal feeling as a church. Why then cling to that meaningless name (when applied to us) German Baptists. If we would have any respect for the meaning of the terms it would be far more consistent to call ourselves English Baptists, but neither would be appropriate and we hope our brethren will, at their Council, District and Annual Meetings, agitate the question until we adopt the name "Brethren" and acknowledge none other.

In regard to statistics returned in the census, it may be stated generally, as a proposition, that the census statistics fall in almost all instances below the facts. The reason is obvious; those who take the census and its statistics cannot put down anything but what they find and know. It is very evident they can not find and know all that is true. For example: There are several quite numerous religious sects who do not know their own statistics. This is to be regretted, because a religious society with any organization whatever ought to know its own churches and its own members. If it does not, how can it maintain its own discipline? For example, the society of the "United Brethren" in Ohio claim (as stated by their officers) two hundred more churches than are given in the census; but those could not be found. Hence they are not in the census. So the "Methodists," as contradistinguished from the "Methodist Episcopal," claim more churches than census gives them. The most curious case of error in the census is putting the "Christians" and the "Disciples of Christ" under the *same head* as "Christians." In the introduction to the census, it is said that it was impossible to separate; that some of the churches did not know themselves what the difference was! That may be, and yet the difference is both definable and palpable. The churches properly called "Christian" were founded about a century ago, the first church in this country being founded in, I think, 1763. Of this church there is only one in Cincinnati—the Bible Church of Dr. Summerbell, on Center street. The "Disciples of Christ," which is their official name, are what are called "Campbellite Baptists," that is, they are mainly those who separated from the regular Baptist Church under the preaching of Campbell and his disciples. There were some others, mostly known as "New Lights," who came out in the extraordinary revivals in Kentucky and some other states sixty years ago. There are in all seven varieties of Baptists, most of whom are contained under the head of "Regular Baptists," "Disciples of Christ," "Christians," "Free-Will baptists," "Tunkers" and "Mennonites. I give these examples just to show under what difficulties the Deputy Marshalls labored to give not only the numerical view of the churches, but a just view showing their real and distinctive differences.

OHIO.—The state statistician of Ohio has been delving in the census reports, and other official unofficial documents, in search of the truth about the churches in that state. He finds the number of church organizations to be 6,489; church edifices 6,282; church organizations without edifices, 206. The Presbyterians have about 800 congregations; the Congregationalists, 200; the Methodist Episcopalians, 1,900; other Methodists, etc., 250; Baptists, 500. The Presbyterian is the wealthiest denomination in proportion to its members; and the Methodists wealthiest in the aggregate. Mr. Mansfield says, further, that the Roman Catholics have in Ohio, in round numbers, three hundred churches; their number, according to the Roman Catholic Almanac is about two hundred and fifty thousand. As that is less than a *tenth* part of the population of the state, nobody need feel alarmed about them.

STATISTICS.—The total number of churches belonging to the Congregational church in North America is 3,366, of which 3,263 are in the United States, and 776 of these last are vacant. The number of ministers is 3,224 in all, and 3,201 are in the United States. The net increase of the denomination for the year is 61 churches, 6,862 members, 2,145 Sunday School scholars, and 77 members The greatest number of churches are in Massachusetts, being 503, followed by Connecticut, 291; New York, 253; Illinois, 241; Maine 239; Iowa 213; Ohio, 204; Vermont, 201; New Hampshire, 187; Wisconsin, 182; Michigan, 180.

PHILADELPHIA. — The assessors' estimate of the value of Moravian churches, as lately published gives the following figures; First church, including cemetery, $50,000; Second church, $28,000; Third church, $2,500; Fourth church, $5,900. Together, $86,400, which is about 25 percent less than their market value, so we are assured.

BIBLE REVISION.—The Old Testament Revision Company having gone a first time through the pentateuch, have now arrived in their final revision at the Book of Numbers. Many members of the company are favorable to an immediate publication of the Pentateuch.

THE Rock Creek Church in east Tennessee, composed of emigrants from Wales, although without a pastor, keep up regular Lord's day convocations, weekly prayer meetings and singings. They are not ashamed to sing, pray nor talk of Jesus.

The Nevada Legislature has passed the compulsory educational act.

Youth's Department

WATCHING FOR PAPA.

She always stood upon the steps,
Just by the cottage door,
Waiting to kiss me when I came,
Each night, home from the store.
Her eyes were like two glorious stars,
Dancing in Heaven's own blue,
"Papa," she'd call, like a wee bird,
"I's lootin' out for you."

Alas! how sadly do our lives
Change as we onward roam;
For now no birdie voice calls out
To bid me welcome home.
No little arms stretch out to me,
No blue eyes dancing bright,
Are peeping from the cottage door,
When I come home at night.

And yet it comforts me to think
That when I'm called away
From scenes below, to those of bright
And everlasting day,
A little angel at the gate,
With eyes divinely blue,
Will call with birdie voice, "Papa,
I's lootin out for you."

—Selected.

KIND WORDS.

When I was quite young I learned the value of kindness. Previous to this I considered it but a duty to be performed by men and women only, to each other. As an example of this, I supposed if a person were sick, her neighbor should sit by her and talk in such a manner as not to be rude: or if a person were sad or had trouble, his neighbor should sympathize with him.

I was nine years old when we moved to a village where we knew no one. The first woman with whom we got acquainted was one of those persons who deem their neighbors inferior to themselves. Accordingly we (our family) had formed an opinion of each person in the place, from what she had told us. This person was rough in her manners; another kept an unclean house; Mrs. C. wasn't accommodating at all.

At school I did not like the appearance of my schoolmates. I chose one of these as my friend in all things. At no time was I so happy as when in Ella's company. This was in June, and there were many flowers in a slough near the school-house, that we used to gather after school.

One day when Ella took her dinner to school she wanted me to ask her mother if she might go with me after flowers that day. What! ask that woman who walks past with her head so high, and looks so hateful? At last I said I would. After dinner I went to her. "Mrs. Ferris, please may Ella go with me for flowers after school?"

"Yes, most certainly she may," she answered pleasantly.

Dear friends, have you any idea how I felt as I went to school? I told mother of her gentle reply. From that time until now I never have paid any attention to slander, and ever after Mrs. Ferris and my mother were firm friends.—*Young Folks Rural.*

THE DEVIL'S WORKSHOP.

Where is the devil's workshop? Is it in the "bad place?" Let us tell you where it is. It is in the *idle mind.* Think of that. The wicked one finds out every idle mind, and goes into it with all his tools, and begins to work. What kind of work does he turn out? Oh, he makes a good job of it. Let us see. There are evil thoughts, bad feelings and bad passions. He makes the boy or girl think about wicked things, feel vexed at everything and everybody; nothing goes right with them. They cannot do things and have things like others. They are disappointed, cross, sour, whine and whimper about everything. Nothing suits them, nothing pleases them, and they want nobody to love them. They don't care. They don't want to get their lessons, don't want to practice, don't want to go to school, don't want to do anything. Hate brothers and sisters, won't obey papa and mamma, quarrel, fight, pout and scold, and do many other bad things.

Did you ever see a little boy or girl in this condition? If you did, you saw the kind of work the devil does in every idle mind, for an "idle mind is the devil's workshop." Whenever you find yourself thinking, and feeling and acting this way, put your mind to work on some hard study, pleasant book, or useful employment.—*Young Pilgrim.*

DON'T BOYS.

Don't be impatient, no matter if things do sometimes go wrong.

Don't give the ball a kick, and send it into the nearest mud-puddle, because it won't go straight when you throw it. Don't send the marbles against the fence, and break your best glass alley, because your clumsy finger could not hit the centre. Don't break your kite-string all to pieces, because it will not bring your kite down from the tree with the first jerk; it will take you full three times as long to get it down afterward. Don't give your little brother an angry push and a sharp word, if he cannot see into the mysteries of marble-playing or hoop-rolling with the first lesson. You were once just as stupid as he, though you have soon forgotten it.

What in the world would become of you if your mother had no more patience than you? If, every time you came to her when busy she would thrust you off with a cross word? Dear, kind, loving mother, who never ceases to think of you, to care for you; who keeps you so nicely clothed, and makes such nice things for you to eat! What if she were to be so impatient that you would be half the time afraid to speak to her, to tell her about your troubles in school and at play! Ah, how you grieve that mother by your impatience and crossness!

Correspondence.

A Reporter is wanted from every Church in the brotherhood to send us Church news, Obituaries, Announcements, or anything that will be of general interest. To insure insertion, the writers name must accompany each communication. Our Invitation is not personal but general—please respond to our call.

CONSISTENCY.

Dear Pilgrim:—Consistency is a jewel I think all should possess, for without it we would often be left to doubt and in darkness. We often find portions of Scripture that do not seem to exactly harmonize, but with this little jewel we can connect one passage with another so as to form a perfect chain, and they then become easy of comprehension.

I want to notice in particular, one verse of Scripture found in the first epistle of John, 2 chapter and 15th verse. It reads as follows: "Love not the world, neither the things that are in the world, if any man love the world the love of the Father is not in him." Now I ask, is there not anything in this world that we should love? What does other Scriptures tell us concerning love? Does it not tell us to love our children, our husbands, our wives, and even our enemies? And are they not often times of the world, and entirely wrapt up in it? It seems necessary to at once call forth the little jewel and it will tell us we must love God better than all things else. And it says that love from us is due, in a certain degree, to all God's creatures, but we should not love the vain amusements, and pleasures of the world, nor anything that is sinful. We should hate sin and shun it, knowing that when it is finished, it bringeth forth death.

Many other portions of Scripture might be brought forth and compared in this same manner, but I think there is enough already to show us how much the jewel of consistency is needed to reconcile one passage of Scripture with another. And not only is it necessary to reconcile Scriptures, but also church custom, order, &c., by comparing the same with Gospel authority, and then find out which seems to be consistent with Gospel. Then as a matter of course, the inconsistencies will in a manner be brought to light. We will now take into consideration the Churches that think the subject of dress of so small importance that it is beneath their notice, consequently their members indulge in all the vain and frivilous fashions of the age and of wearing of gold and of costly apparel. Is this consistent with Paul's first epistle to Timothy, 2:9-10. They read thus: "In like manner also, that women adorn themselves in modest apparel, not with braided hair, or gold, or pearls, or costly array, but which becometh women professing godliness with good works." I think many will say at once, that their custom of dressing is indeed very inconsistent with the Gospel.

I will next notice the Seventh day Adventist. They claim to be, strictly speaking, a Bible people, having no Discipline but the Word of God. Nevertheless they are obliged to except of Ellen G. White's visions, as being a later revelation from God. No matter what the vision may command, the Church must obey or they will be called to an account by a special vision for them, pointing out their faults, &c. As a Church, their Christian character cannot be gainsayed. Mrs. White claims that, in a vision, the Church was to wear a certain style of dress, and an angel gave her the pattern. The womens dress is to be short with pants of the same material, they also wear a short saque, a plain white collar, but no ornaments allowed. They have no particular style for male members clothing. I would ask, is it necessary for us to have a special revelation to make our place, calling, and election sure with God? Let us hear what Paul says in 2 Tim. 3: 15 16 17 and see if this vision government is required or consistent. "And that from a child thou hast known the Holy Scriptures which are able to make thee wise unto salvation thro' faith which is in Christ Jesus. All Scripture is given by inspiration of God, and is profitable for doctrine, for reproof, for correction, for instruction in righteousness, that the man of God may be perfect, thoroughly furnished unto all good works." Now if we can be made perfect, and be thoroughly furnished unto all good works through the Gospel, would it not be very inconsistent for us to look for anything farther? There cannot be anything better than that which will make us perfect. Again we see that consistency is indeed a jewel. As I have been noticing other Churches, it seems right for me to look home, or to the Church of which I am a member, called the Church of the Brethren. Although I have been a member only about one year, yet I think I understand at least, a portion of the rules and order of the Church, this much I do know, the established order is to have our garments made after a particular style and the sisters are required to wear a cap as a covering as found in 1 Cor. 11. Here our sister presents an argument relative to the covering which she will please excuse us for omitting, as we believe after she has been in the fold awhile longer her views will be changed. To try to make it appear that the hair is the covering referred to by Paul is evidently out of the question. The subject is prayer, and the requirements of the woman is *that she be covered*. If the hair is the covering meant, it certainly is a grave question to know how our sisters would put that covering on and take it off again on those special occasions. We are in favor of any reasonable amount of forbearance in such cases, and would advise that our brethren lead in such cases instead of driving.—ED.]

And now in conclusion, I would say to the Brethren, those that hold office and claim power to enforce order. If any cannot see that it is required of them by the Gospel, do not I beseech you, add insult to injury by saying that because they do not fully come up to the order, they have not God in their hearts, or He would work to the outside. Who is it that judges the heart? Is it not God? I feel thankful that we are not left to the mercies of man, neither are we to be judged by men, but the God whom we adore is full of love and tender mercies. It is Him that justifieth, who is he that condemneth? It is Christ that died, yea, rather that is risen again, who is even at the right hand of God, who also maketh intercession for us. Do ye look on things after the outward appearance: If any man trust to himself that he is Christ's, let him of himself think this again, that as he is Christ's so are we Christ's. Brethren and sisters, one and all, let us as the followers of Christ, have our words and acts correspond with His example of love, mercy, and forbearance. Then with consistency we may claim to be His children. As a lover of God, His people, truth, charity and justice, I claim to be, though very unworthily, a sister.

M. J. GOBLE,

Pine Grove Mills, Michigan.

Dear Brethren: After a long silence as usual, I again direct my thoughts in a practical form to the sanctum of the PILGRIM. It looks rather selfish I confess to receive its precious weekly visits without so much or so little as a word of cheer or welcome, coming as it does with its pleasant smiling face teeming with good things such as a hungry soul loves. I wish to say privately brethren that you are a head and shoulders above your former selves in the superior quality and mechanism of your paper, and although it does not contain as much as it could be made to carry, yet that defect is abundantly redeemed by the wisdom and forbearance of its management, the excellence of its contributions, &c. The old fable of the retort of the lion on the fox is apropo at this point. You remember that.

Well as the Lord has blessed me with restored health it does not become a greatful heart to refuse a public acknowledgement. I am now in a better condition as regards the body, I think, than I have been for some time, but I had to pass through a severe furnace of affliction. Nervous dyspepsia is not the most acceptable ill that flesh is heir to, but as we have not the liberty to choose the rod that our Father chastises us with, we will not quarrel about the means, but pray that the end or purpose might be hallowed to the glory of the loving Father and the winnowing and purifying of the soul.

My restoration is the work of the Lord through the agency of means which are abundantly at his command, of which I will write in the future, and now it behooves me to use the blessing thus conferred to the advancement of the cause of truth. May the Lord of the Vineyard give me grace to serve him faithfully and effectually.

Your Fellow Servant,

D. C. MOOMAW.

WEVERTON, MD., April 3rd, 1873.

Dear Friends:—I came across a few pages of one of the WEEKLY PILGRIMS, and in it I saw a piece, "How to oppose Feet-washing" by J. H. Moore, referring to what Jesus said in the 13th chapter of John. Man to be honest, must admit Feet-washing to be right because Jesus said so. Now what does Jesus say about the Lord's Prayers, also about moral laws or the government of Cesar? Now we propose that where there is no simplicity there is no law as simplicity makes purity. If Christ is truthful can man get to heaven and not obey his commandments? God is honorable and just. He is the author. Now one more question. Can man obey the law of God and not confess his sins? also what does St. John mean in Revelations by the City of Babylon on the old whore? If you give this an insertion in your paper and send me one for three months I will be pleased to come and see you at times.

"Remove not the ancient land-marks which our fathers have set."

GEO. G. BINGHAM.

A CORRECTION.

The following we received from the associate editor of the *Baptist Record* and as we wish to do justice unto all men, we insert it hoping that whatever misunderstanding may exist between Elder Flory and friend Ellison may be amicably adjusted on Christian principles.—ED.

Mr. Editor:—In your issue of 28th January, 1873, Elder J. S. Flory has introduced me to your readers under colors not the most desirable and, although a stranger to you and your readers, I ask a little space in your paper, not to discuss the issues between Mr. Flory and myself, but to set myself right before your readers. 1st. Elder F. implies that I "have an aversion to 'Dunkers' in general and himself in particular." I disclaim such aversion, and strive as a christian, to be a real friend to all my race.

2nd. Elder F. censures me sharply for signing my review of his Tract "*Moomaw's Dunck Religion Examined*," with M. E. instead of my full name. As an associate editor of the *Baptist Record* that is my usual and well known signature, and, instead of concealing the writer as Mr. F. assumes, identifies him, and is no "mask." 3rd. The "*misquotations*" complained of were mainly typographic errors. The M.S. to the *Record*, reads: "Wishes his right arm may be palsied and his pen move no further, if any other motive prompts him than the welfare of precious souls." It is erroneously printed, "*sight* may be palsied" &c, "wishes" is used instead of the term "*May* my right arm be" &c. I cannot see that any injustice is done to the original idea.

4th. In the terms, "born of water *three times*" the quotation marks were improperly placed after the words "*three times*." It is my language and not Elder Flory's. Other mistakes occur of less moment which I will not occupy your space to correct.

In friendship and love,

I am yours, &c.

M. ELLISON.

Dear Editors:—We are living here in Lacrosse, Wis., and seem to be all alone as there are none of the Brethren that we know of living within 150 miles. If any of the brethren when passing through here would stop off at North Lacrosse, Wis. and enquire for D. R. Hurlburt and come and see us we would be thankful indeed. We connected ourselves with the Brethren last Fall while on a visit to Indiana, believing it to be the only church that lives up to the commands of God. Notwithstanding we are here alone we thank God and the Lord Jesus Christ that we are still trying to live Christians and striving for the crown that the Lord will give us at that day and not to us only, but to all those who love his appearing.

D. R. HURLBURT.

Lacrosse, Wis.

DIED.

FARMER.—Near Golden Corner, Wayne Co., Ohio, February 23, '73, Mrs Elizabeth Farmer, aged 25 years, 6 months and 27 days. Her remains was taken to the Beech Grove burying ground where the funeral services were preached by Bro. Yoder and J. H. Shoemaker to a large concourse of people who had assembled to pay their last respects to the dead. She leaves a husband and two small children, and many other friends to mourn her loss.

M. A. F.

SWARTZ.—In the Hopewell district, Bedford Co., Pa., April 3, '73, sister Catharine E., wife of brother George Swartz, being his third wife, aged 33 years, 10 months and 4 days. She leaves a sorrowing husband and a small family of little children to mourn their loss which we hope is her gain. Funeral occasion improved by Bro. John Rush and the writer, from Rev. 14:12-13.

D. S. CLAPPER.

FURGASON.—In the Indian Creek Church Westmoreland Co., Pa., Feb. 25, 1872, Benjamin F., son of brother Robert and sister Elizabeth Furgason, aged 21 years, 5 months and 27 days. Funeral occasion improved by D. D. Horner and others, from 1 Thess. 4:14.

COVER.—In the same branch, Feb 26 '73, Susan, daughter of brother Michael and sister Elizabeth Cover, aged 26 years, 2 months and 27 days. Funeral service improved by D. D. Horner and others.

The subject of this notice died with Consumption. She lingered a long time and shortly before she died she awakened from her slumber and said there was something that she neglected 'till too late. She wished to be baptized but she thought she was too weak, and she wanted to be annointed which request was granted and her wishes were, if the Lord would spare her she would be baptized, and so she was received.

FURGASON.—In the same branch, March 15, '73, sister Eliza, wife of brother Robert Furgason, aged 48 years, 10 mos. and 11 days. Funeral occasion improved by James Bennett and others from Heb. 11:13. She has left a sorrowing husband and dear children to mourn their loss, but we hope their loss may be her great gain.

J. FOYST.

GILBAUGH.—In Filmore Co., Minn., of scarlet fever, Annie M., aged 3 years, 2 months and 17 days, and Samuel, aged 9 months and 7 days, daughter and son of brother Peter and sister Mary Gilbaugh. Funeral discourse by the writer from Luke 18;16.

WM. C. HARRIS.

BUCK.—In the Yellow Creek Church, Bedford Co., Pa., April 4, '73, brother David F. Buck, aged 55 years, 12 days. His disease was a lingering complication, asthma and bronchitis. He devoted his last years to the service of God, and in his last days was much concerned about his children. The solemn rite of annointing was performed by request some three weeks before his departure. He leaves a disconsolate widow, four children, an aged father and mother, brother and sister, to mourn their loss. Occasion improved from 1 Thess., second chapter last two verses to a very large concourse of people. He was the only son, or only child of Samuel and Mary Buck, who is now in his 84th year, and takes it hard to see his son going before him, but God does all things well, and we must yield to His will.

Nine years ago little Sadie went home,
To rest in the mansions of glory above;
Now papa is gone, for to meet her at home,
To embrace her with joy in the fullness of love.

Soon, soon some more of the family may go,
Who will be the next? let each be concerned;
And prepare to meet God, to escape the sad woe,
Of missing the two in the Paradise of God.

LEONARD FURRY.

(*Visitor*, please copy.)

BROWER.—In the Lower Twin Creek Church, Preble Co., Ohio, April 3, '73, our much beloved brother Henry Brower, aged 40 years, 3 months and 7 days. Funeral improved by the Brethren from Rev. 3:21.

The subject of this notice was confined to his bed about three months. He bowed in humble submission to the afflicting hand of Providence and was entirely resigned to the will of God. During his affliction he called for the elders of the Church and was annointed. He leaves a sorrowing wife, (a sister), 4 children and many friends behind but O, the consoling thought, they need not sorrow as those that have no hope.

DANIEL BOCK.

CORRY.—In Champaign Co., Ohio, March 17, '73, Manda, daughter of brother John and sister Mariah Corry, disease Typhoid Pneumonia. Funeral preached by the writer to many sympathizing friends, from Matt. 18:3.

J. L. FRANTZ.

BLOUGH.—Near St Clairsville, Bedford Co., Pa., March 6, Rosanna, wife of Bro. Noah B. Blough, aged 38 years, and 27 days, see C. F. C. No. 13, page 209, disease cancer. Also March 12, Emma S. Blough aged 8 years, 10 months and 28 days. Disease of last two Diphtheria.

Thus we see in less than two weeks brother N. B. B. deprived of the happy enjoyment that once existed in the family band. Now they are gone. Companion and children are gone to that land from whence no traveler returns. Bro. B. is left with 5 children to mourn [illegible]

We hope the loss so deeply felt here is the departed ones great gain. Funeral occasion improved by the writer, assisted by J. H. Zuo, Lutheran pastor, from Heb 4:2

FRIEND.—Near New Enterprise, Bedford Co., Pa., March 20, '74, Phebe Friend, aged 57 years, 6 months and 9 days. Funeral occasion improved by the writer and D. C. Long, Seventh Day Baptist minister, from John 12:46.

S. A. MOORE.

ANNOUNCEMENTS.

Middle District of Pa., at Clover Creek, May 15.

West Va., Seneca District, Randolph Co., 9th and 10th of May.

Middle District of Iowa, in Dallas Co., on the 19th day of May.

Northern Indiana and Michigan, ½ mile west of Goshen, Ind., May 1st.

Northeastern District of Ohio, Jonathan's Creek Congregation, Perry Co., on May 20th.

Middle District of Ind., Bachelor Run Congregation, Lower Church, second Friday after Good Friday.

First District of Virginia, on Friday and Saturday before the fourth Sunday in April, at the Valley M. H., Botetourt Co., 1 mile south of Amsterdam.

Please announce through the PILGRIM that our District Meeting will be held on the 13th of May in the Cook's Creek Congregation, Rockingham Co., Va.

SOLOMON GARBER.

Please notice through the PILGRIM that the District Meeting of Western Pa., will be held at the Fairview Meeting house in the George's Creek branch, Fayette Co. Pa., on Wednesday 21st of May, '73.

J. FOUST.

Please announce that the District Meeting of North-Western Ohio will be held, the Lord willing, with the brethren of Crawford Co., at the house of brother John Brillhart, on the Base Line on the 23 day of May, and on the 24, the day following, there will be a Communion meeting at the same place. A general representation is desired.

ISRAEL ROOP.

LOVEFEASTS.

Champaign Co., Ill., at Geo. Dillings, 5 miles east of Urbana, 7th and 8th of June.

Little Swatara Church, at Bro. Henry K. Basler's 2 miles northeast of Jonestown, Lebanon Co., Pa., 12th and 13th of June. Brethren returning from A. M., are invited to stop.

Please announce that the Hudson Church, McLean Co., Ill., have appointed a Lovefeast on the 14 and 15 of June, to commence at 10 o'clock A. M., at the house of J. Y. Snavely. The usual invitation is given.

THOMAS D. LYON.

MONEY LIST.

Samuel C Miller	1.50
J F Allen	4.50
Jacob Wise	2.00
David Hilderbrand	3 00
Jonathan Davis	4.50
J B Miller	10.80
Eli Beagle	9 50
Geo Heistrman	1.50
Daniel Bock	1.50
Joseph Kongh	.50
Eld J Wagoner	1.50
Daniel Brumbaugh	1.50
Kate Brenizer	1.25
Benj. Beshoar	1.50
Adam Appleman	18 00
Henry Hackleberger	1.50
James P Harris	1.60
Jacob H Isoopple	13.25
Israel Roop	1.60
Daniel Mohler	2 00
I J Rosenberger	13 00
David Miller	25.00

The Weekly Pilgrim.

JAMES CREEK, PA., April 15, 1873.

☞ How to send money.—All sums over $1.50, should be sent either in a check, draft or postal order. If neither of these can be obtained, have the letter registered.

☞ WHEN MONEY is sent, *always* send with it the name and address of those who paid it. Write the names and post office as plainly as possible.

☞ EVERY subscriber for 1873, gets a *Pilgrim Almanac* FREE.

ADMONITIONS.

"The best friends are those who tell us of our faults and teach us how to correct them."

We occasionally get a gentle reprimand for mistakes we make in presenting matter before the public which it is thought would be better withheld. While we entertain the best of feelings towards those who have the goodness thus to give us their opinions, we hope they will make due allowance for us under the circumstances which we are often placed. We, just like other people, are often deceived in the motives of our writers. Not being informed on both sides of the question we sometimes admit articles that we afterwards regret it as deeply as do our readers. The position of an editor of a religious paper is a peculiar one and none can fully understand it but those who have learned it by experience. Our first and leading object is to please God and labor for the promotion of his cause or the salvation of his people, and secondly, so far as is possible, meet the wishes and expectations of our patrons. To fully meet the desires of all is impossible as in attempting to please one by granting a special request we may displease hundreds of others, so that when our judgment anticipates such results we always think it prudent to disappoint the few rather than offend the many and we hope all of our readers will justify us in this position even if it should cause some of their productions to meet their destiny in the waste basket. There is one thing we wish distinctly understood; the basis upon which we accept and reject is merit and demerit, with as little favoritcism as possible. We are fully aware of the responsibilities under which we are placed and therefore wish to discharge our duty in such a way as to meet the approbation of God rather than of man, therefore we always accept, kindly, the ideas and suggestions of our brethren and sisters relative to our labor and duties and endeavor to be profited by them.

FEASTING.

We call special attention to the above subject as treated by Eld. Lint on another page. This very thing is greatly stirring up the minds of many of our conscientious and good thinking brethren and sisters and we know it will be considered a timely stroke in the right direction. But you see we are growing rich (in this world's goods) Our old houses have been torn down and larger one's built with their spacious and well-furnished parlors. The tables are decorated with the most modern style of dishes and is made almost to groan under its load of luxuries. Now it would seem just grand to have our rich neighbors and kinsman come and see these things. Then the compliments we get! Why really it makes us feel ever so good. "You have a splendid parlor, and your carpets are really grand." Chairs, sofas, lounges, pies, tarts, jams, jellies and a hundred and one other things make subjects of complimentary notice, and has been the pride of many a good housewife—but here comes Bro. Lint with his Bible quotations and spoils the whole thing.

Well, to be carnally minded is death but to be spiritually minded is *life* and *peace*, and as life and peace is more to be desired than a gorged stomach and empty applause, we suppose that it would be better after all, to follow out the divine injunction of our blessed Master, and bestow our good things upon the poor and needy like God our most indulgent Father is doing unto us, as the best of us must, in his sight appear as miserable beggars, and shall a beggar despise a beggar? Nay, verily, God is the Father of us all and *we are brethren*.

PLEASE NOTICE.

As we wish to have some of our brethren stop with us on their way to District Meeting, we have appointed services for Saturday evening, (May 10), Sunday and Sunday evening, in the James Creek Church, with the expectation that some of the brethren will make arrangements to stop with us.

By taking the Broad Top Road at Huntingdon will save about $1.00 in fare, and will have only 1½ miles further to walk from the Railroad. Those coming to James Creek on Saturday can either take the morning train which leaves Huntingdon at 7.45 A. M., or the evening at 6.00. Brethren intending to stop with us will please inform us as soon as convenient.

Dear Editors: Are we excusable in the sight of God in submitting ourselves to the fellowship of town idlers and getting into conversation and dispute about religion, politics and the news of the day, such as finding fault with our neighbors, &c., with the children of profanity and bad habits of every description. Paul to the Corrinthians says: "Be ye not unequally yoked together with unbelievers, for what fellowship hath righteousness with unrighteousness, what communion hath light with darkness, and what concord hath Christ with Belial?"

J. B.

REMARKS. In these things we should exercise good judgment and be governed by the influence we may exert over those with whom we associate. To dispute about religion with those who lack piety and have no disposition to come to the truth, is casting pearl before swine. To talk politics is a loss of time and belongs to the other kingdom. We are to redeem time and our conversation is to be holy. To talk about and find fault with neighbors to say the least, is low and mean and does not become a child of God.

PILGRIM ALMANACS.—As we have on hands several hundred more *Almanacs* than we need for distribution, we will send them to any address, free of postage on the following terms. Single copy, 10 cents, 6 copies 40 cents, and 12 copies 70 cents.

A BROTHER from Iowa writes; "Enclosed find $1.25 for which I desire the WEEKLY PILGRIM sent to my son-in-law and daughter in Ohio, in whose spiritual welfare I feel much interested * * * * * send all back Nos. to them for this year for I believe the PILGRIM to be a power in the land in circulating the truth and should be read by all who desire to obtain a saving knowledge of Jesus. * * * * *

The Brethren here are building a large stone church which when completed, will reflect credibly for the zeal the brethren here have for the cause in erecting a suitable place for the worship of God.

OUR CONTRIBUTION BOX

Our box is unusually full of original essays just now, and some of our contributions are, are, getting the attention that they should have on account of the series of articles that we have now under way of publication and for want of time to prepare them. We hope that none will feel discouraged at the non appearance of their efforts. Every paper will be examined in due time and nothing of merit will be lost. We are glad to have a good supply on hand as the busy season is now setting in, and the probability is that our contributors will not have as much leisure as they had during the winter.

It will take $1,500,000 to pay the back pay the Congressmen voted themselves.

The Wisconsin Legislature has refused to pass any compulsory educational law.

The Legislature of Rhode Island has legalized marriage between blacks and whites.

The Portugese dictionary, which was begun nearly one hundred years ago by the Academy of Sciences, has now brought down its information to the end of letter C. Senhor Domingos Vieira is now the editor of the work.

TRACTS.

"ANXIOUS BENCH RELIGION EXAMINED," BY ELDER J. S. FLORY. A SYNOPSIS OF CONTENTS. An address to the reader: The peculiarities that attend this type of religion. The feelings there experienced not imaginary but real. The key that unlocks the wonderful mystery. The causes by which feelings are excited. How the momentary feelings called "Experimental religion" are brought about, and then concludes by giving that form of doctrine as taught by Jesus Christ and recorded by his faithful witnesses.

COUNTERFEIT DETECTER
OR
BAPTISM—MUCH IN LITTLE.

This work is now ready for distribution, and the importance of the subject will speak for it a large demand. It is a short treatise on Baptism in tract form intended for general distribution, and is set forth in such a plain and logical manner that a wayfaring man though a fool, cannot err therein. Either of the above tracts sent postpaid on the following terms: Two copies, 10 cts, 10 copies 40 cents, 25 copies 70 cents, 50 copies $1.00, 100 copies $1.50.

Trine Immersion.

A discussion on Trine Immersion, by letter between Elder B. F. Moomaw and Dr. J. J. Jackson, to which is annexed a Treatise on the Lord's Supper, and on the necessity, character and evidences of the new birth, also a dialogue on the doctrine of non-resistance, by Elder B. F. Moomaw. Single copy 50 cents.

THE GROUNDS FOR A

FORWARD and BACKWARD

MODE OF

BAPTISM.

Briefly, yet *carefully* examined; and the TRUE and CORRECT mode so clearly set forth that none can help but understand.

This little book contains 38 pages, neatly put up in paper cover. Price per doz. $1.25, add 10 cts. for postage. Two copies, 25 cts 1 copy, 15 cts., free of postage.

Address, SAMUEL KINSEY,
Mar 11-3t. Dayton, O.

LAND, LAND, LAND!!

The completion of the Chesapeake and Ohio Trunk Line Railway, has opened up to the world much of the fine TIMBER LANDS, rich COAL FIELDS and cheap FARMING LANDS of W. Va. Now is the time to get cheap homes and invest money with the prospect of a handsome profit. For further particulars inquire of the undersigned, agent for lands here. J. S. FLORY.

Orchard View, Fayette Co., W. Va.
Jan. 10.

New Hymn Books, English.

TURKEY MOROCCO.

One copy, postpaid,	$1.00
Per Dozen,	11.25

PLAIN ARABESQE.

One Copy, post-paid,	.75
Per Dozen, "	8.50

Ger'n & English, Plain Sheep.

One Copy, post-paid,	$1.00
Per Dozen	11.25
Arabesque Plain,	1.00
Turkey Morocco,	1.25
Single German, post paid	50
Per Dozen,	5.50

HUNTINGDON & BROAD TOP RAIL ROAD

On and after March 22d, 1873, Trains will run on this road daily (Sundays excepted) as follows:

Trains from Huntingdon South. *Trains from Mt. Dal's moving North.*

MAIL. A. M.	PASS. P. M.	STATIONS.	MAIL. P. M.	PASS. A. M.
LE7 45	6 00	Huntingdon,	AR4 00	AR8 55
7 50	6 05	Long Siding	3 53	8 20
8 10	6 17	McConnelstown	3 45	8 10
8 17	6 25	Pleasant Grove	3 35	8 02
8 30	6 40	MARKLESBURG	3 20	7 45
8 45	6 55	Coffee Run	3 07	7 32
8 55	7 03	Rough & Ready	2 57	7 23
9 05	7 12	Cove	2 47	7 13
9 08	7 18	Fishers Summit	2 45	7 10
9 20	7 30	Saxton	2 27	6 55
9 40	7 50	Riddlesburg	2 10	6 35
9 47	7 56	Hopewell	2 03	6 25
10 02	8 12	Piper's Run	1 47	6 11
10 17	8 30	Tatesville	1 32	5 55
10 30	8 40	Everett	1 20	5 45
10 35	8 45	Mount Dallas	1 15	5 40
11 08	9 20	Bedford	12 44	5 08

G. F. GAGE, Supt.

SHOUP'S RUN BRANCH.

LE 9 25 LE	Saxton.	AR2 15 AR
9 40	Coalmont.	2 00
9 45	Crawford.	1 55
AR10 00 AR	Dudley	LE1 45 LE

Broad Top City from Dudley 2 miles by stage.

Time of Penna. R. R. Trains at Huntingdon.

**Mail No. 2 makes connection at Huntingdon with Mail going East on Pennsylvania Railroad at 4.15 p. m., and West at 5.45 p. m. Mail No. 1 leaves Huntingdon at 7.40 a. m. on arrival of Pacific Express West.

Trains on this road connect with trains on Bedford & Bridgeport, and Cumberland & Pennsylvania Railroads.

The Weekly Pilgrim.

Published by J. B. Brumbaugh, & Co.
Edited by H. B. & Geo. Brumbaugh.
CORRESPONDING EDITORS.
D. P. Sayler, Double Pipe Creek, Md.
Leonard Furry, New Enterprise, Pa.

The *Pilgrim* is a Christian Periodical, devoted to religion and moral reform. It will advocate in the spirit of *love* and *liberty*, the principles of true Christianity, labor for the promotion of peace among the people of God, for the encouragement of the saints and for the conversion of sinners, avoiding those things which tend toward disunion or sectional feelings.

TERMS.

Single copy, Book paper,	$1.50
Eleven copies, [eleventh for Agt.]	$15.00

Any number above that at the same rate,

Address,
H. B. BRUMBAUGH.
James Creek,
Huntingdon county Pa.

The Weekly Pilgrim.

"REMOVE NOT THE ANCIENT LANDMARKS WHICH OUR FATHERS HAVE SET."

VOL. 4. JAMES CREEK, PENNSYLVANIA, APRIL, 22, 1873. NO. 16

POETRY.

OVER THE RIVER.

BY REV. J. H. WELTY.

Over the river's a mansion of rest,
A home for the weary, a cheer for the blest.
Jesus is there as the centre of light,
The essence of love, and the sense of delight.

Over the river the dead are at home,
But we on this side yet in weariness roam.
O that we safely were housed on that shore,
We'd sing the sweet praise of the Lord evermore.

Over the river that's flowing between,
They tell us the fields are so lovely and green.
Mansions are there that shall never decay,
Whose loveliness never shall vanish away.

Over the river by faith I descry
The mountains of glory that tower on high;
There I behold the fair city of love,
Jerusalem shining in glory above.

Over the river I'm longing to go
Where joy is unbroken by seasons of woe.
Some have departed; we bade them farewell,
In mansions across they peacefully dwell.

Over the river! I wish I were o'er.
Will some one not guide me to yonder bright shore?
Yes, says the Savior, I'll pilot thee o'er
And safely I'll land thee on Canaan's bright shore.

Come then, dear Savior, I'll sail in Thy boat,
For over the river of death it will float.
Tempests may rage and the thunders may roll,
I know Thou wilt still them, and comfort my soul.

When we are safe in Immanuel's land
We'll join the glad chorus of Heaven's fair band;
Shoutings of welcome in triumph we'll raise
And roll to His throne the sweet anthems of praise.

—*Reformed Messenger.*

ORIGINAL ESSAYS.

THE CHURCH AND DUTIES OF HER MEMBERS.—NO. 4.

BY J. S. FLORY.

Second Degree of the Ministry.

When the second degree (so called) is conferred upon the minister his privileges are extended so that he now has a right to go forth and make appointments, fill them by preaching to all who come to hear and baptize as many as truly believe. Of course it is expected they will be submissive to the rightful wishes of the Elders and the Church and act in harmony with the same. Also, they now have the right to solemnize the marriage of parties when called on and in some other respects their privileges and duties are extended which are regulated in a great measure by the surrounding circumstances. As their duties thus are extended their obligations are of a more responsible nature. Therefore it is expected that as they make advances in their calling they will make progress in their Christian life so as to become more zealous and self-sacrificing in the cause of their blessed Master. Become more and more patterns of humility and Christian piety. What has been said in reference to those in the first degree in a great measure, is applicable to the ministry in any position and what we may say further here may apply likewise to all. It is generally looked upon by the non-professor as well as others that the Minister of the Gospel should be a great deal better than other Christians. Therefore such things that hardly engage attention when belonging to the Laiety are in the case of the Minister magnified into wonderful monstrosities. In consideration of this fact we ought to use *double* dilligence in looking well to our way. Jesting is often freely indulged in by men and women considered very pious without causing a passing reproof, but in the case of ministers we often hear such remarks, that we have felt ashamed because too often guilty. We have seen, as we thought, solemn impressions entirely erased from the mind of hearers, by the jesting and levity of the preacher just after having finished his discourse. Ministers are men of like passions with others but these things ought to be avoided as much as possible, especially before a mixed multitude where there may be dear souls laboring under a burden of conscious sin. If we have to give an account to God for any idle word that seems to drop harmless how shall it be with us when we have to give an account for those idle jesting words that destroy in a measure our influence for good? Here brethren is something not only to think about but something to pray about, that it be less prevalent. While we abhor the sanctimonious countenance and demeanor of the hypocrite, we would love to *feel* and *see* cheerfulness seasoned with such love, courteousness and the christian graces in general, that was free from sin and lightmindedness. Cheerful gravity and happy joyful conversation can not be condemned where chastity and moderation give tone to the social circle. While remembering that the tongue is an unruly member it would be well for us all to adopt the language of the Psalmist when he says: "I said I will take heed to my ways that I sin not with my tongue; I will keep my mouth with a bridle, while the wicked is before me." Psa.—39: 1. The wicked are always watching to catch something from the professor especially from the minister, that they may justify themselves by saying, "I am about as good as those that make a profession." How necessary then that the Heralds of Truth talk and walk so that the ungodly cannot have room to ease their wicked consciences in that way.

An old Brother minister once said he believed, that in proportion to the number that profess religion there would be more preachers lost than of any other class! If true, and why should we doubt it, is it not a fearful thought? The responsibility so great and flesh so weak! But God has promised to be with the weak and that too unto the end. Shirking the responsibility, Jonas like, will never mend the matter at all, hence the only alternative, to insure the blessing, is, dear fellow watchmen, to fulfill the calling whereunto we have been called, to the best of our ability. Do all we can and leave the rest to God and the co-laborers of his that may follow in our footsteps. Let us not fall out on the way. Right here we feel to make a remark or so. Nothing insures such unity in the Church and force to the preached word as love and union among the ministers who all seem to be laboring to the one grand end of building up Zion and saving precious souls. But too often jealousy is seen eking out from under the ministerial robes; Self is a stubborn imp that has his throne in the flesh and often wants to be a gem in the eyes of world worshippers. Jesus and Him crucified should always keep self on the background hid behind the wreaking cross of the suffering Son of God. Suppose "I myself" did want to preach and somebody else done all the preaching, if sinners were made to feel and God's name glorified you Bro. "I myself" will not be held accountable for your silence, but if envy was playing in your heart when earnest prayer ought to have filled it, you might be accountable for something! "Preferring one above another" is no where more commendible than with the ministers. But then it should not be adopted with such effects as to become ludicrous in the eyes of the congregation or to forcing up a brother who well knew that it was not his time to preach. Circumstances generally are such that brethren may know if it is prudent for them to get up, and when they are conscious of this, let them do so without being urged. I remarked above one would not be accountable for their silence when the time was well taken up by another. But I fear there are times the ministers do not do their duty that is when lounging at home often half the Sundays out of the year when there are cries not far off to "come and preach for us," or at least an effectual door would be opened if a little effort was made to introduce the true Gospel. Go into all the world and preach the Gospel and then there need be none complain because they don't get to preach as often as they desire. The world is large and sinners plenty and God's mercy great, go then brother, go and preach the Word, be instant in season and out of season.

To be Continued.

This life of ours—what is it? A very few soon-ended years, and then—the ceaseless psalm and the [illegible] Sabbath of the soul.

THE BAPTISM OF JOHN, WHENCE WAS IT, FROM HEAVEN OR OF MEN?

H. P. MOOMAW.

In a treatise on Masonry published in 1792, by William Preston, Master of the Lodge of Antiquity the origin of Masonry is traced from Creation. Ever since symmetry began, and harmony displayed her charms (says he) our order has had a being." We have seen above how it has existed from creation. Its introduction into England he likewise supposes to have been prior to the Roman invasion. There are, according to him, the remains of some stupendous works executed by the Britons, much earlier than the time of the Romans, even this displays no small share of ingenuity of invention; so that we can have no doubt of the existence of Masonry in Britain even during those early periods." Truly if the mechanical arts proves the existence of Masonry, then Masonry has always existed. But as seen by the following, these arts were not confined to any particular class, but indeed common to all people. Mr. Preston further says: "The Druids are likewise said to have had among them many customs similar to those of the Masons, and to have derived their government from Pythagoras; but the resemblance betwixt their usages and those of the Freemason Societies now existing cannot be accurately traced even by the Masons themselves.

Masonry is said to have been encouraged by Cæsar and many of the Roman generals who were appointed governors of Britain'; but though we know, that at this period the Fraternity were employed in erecting many magnificent fabrics, nothing is recorded concerning their Lodges and Conventions and we have a very imperfect account of the customs which prevailed in their assemblies."

It is vaguely supposed that Lodges and conventions were introduced during the fifth century under the auspices of General Carausius who ambitiously hoped to be the founder of a British empire, to accomplish which he encouraged learning, collecting also the best artificers from many different countries, and appointing Albanus his steward, the principal superintendant of their assemblies. Lodges or conventions of the fraternity, began now to be introduced, and they be regularly carried on." "This Albanus, or St. Alban is said to have been a great friend of Masons, and gave them two shillings per week, besides three pence for their cheer: while before that time they had no more than one penny per day and their meat." He likewise obtained a charter from the king and his council, for them to hold a general council, which was named an Assembly.' The same circumstances are mentioned in a M. S, written in the time of James II, only this increases the weekly salary of the Masons to 3s. 6d. and 3d. per day for the bearers of burthens. It is exceedingly doubtful, and it is doubted by intelligent Masons themselves whether Freemasonry is entitled to the credit of so great antiquity as a mechanical association or organized society. But say they if this story of St. Albans is not believed, doubtless the order has great antiquity. Now then let us see what is the facts in the case as confidently relied on by intelligent Masons themselves for which I quote the language of John Dove the Grand Secretary of the Grand Lodge of Virginia. "Freemasonry denotes the system of mysteries and secrets peculiar to the society of free and accepted Masons. The origin of the society is very ancient but we have no authentic account of the time when it was first instituted, or even what was the reason of such an association of people under the title of *Masons* more than of any other mechanical profession. In Dr. Henry's History, we find the origin of Freemason's Society, in Britain attributed to the difficulty found in former times, of procuring a sufficient number of workmen to build the multitude of Churches, monasteries, and other religious edifices, which the superstition of those ages prompted the people to raise. The Italians, says he, with some Greek refugees and with them French, Germans and Flemings joined into a fraternity of architects, preparing Papal bulls for their encouragement, and their peculiar priviliges; they styled themselves Freemasons and ranged from one country to another as they found Churches to build." By other accounts, however, (says our author) the antiquity of Masonry is carried up much higher even as early as the building of Solomon's temple. In Britain the introduction of Masonry has been fixed at the year 674, when glass making was first introduced, and it appears, indeed, that from this time many buildings in the Gothic style were erected by men in companies, who are said to have called themselves free because they were at liberty to work in any part of the kingdom. Others have derived the institution of Freemasons from a combination among the people of that profession not to work without an advance of wages. At this time it appears that a combination of these mechanics were employed under the direction of Edward the III, to assist in rebuilding and enlarging the castle together with the church and castle of St. George at Windsor. At this time it was said that Masons agreed on certain tokens by which they might know and assist each other against being impressed, and not to work unless free and on their own terms. Further accounts of their history shows that the society was not permanently organized until the year 926, which occurred at York under the patronage of Elwin, the kings brother who obtained for them a charter from Athelstane and became grand master himself. Our author further says, "there is indeed great reason to believe that York was the original seat of Masonic government, no other place having claimed it and the whole fraternity, having at various times owned allegience to the authority then established. Hence at the present day all regular Masons are called and known among themselves as York Masons. What, we would ask, does these historical facts prove to the enquiring mind? It proves first that operative Freemasonry as a mechanical society is absolutely and exclusively of men and not from heaven, that it has not the semblance of divine authority and that all such pretentions is a myth and an imposture, of which the too credulous world ought to be faithfully warned, and second that it was simply conceived in the mind of shrewd and ingenious mechanics, of different orders and an organization formed, that in their combined resolutions they might control the compensation for their services determined "not to work only upon their own terms." This organization, let it be remembered was not founded earlier than A. D. 500, and probably not earlier than 674, and most probably, not until 926, after Christ, and the 4926th year of the world and without one word of authority from the Bible, hence it is not from Heaven.

To be Continued.

WALK IN THE LIGHT.

This then is the message which we have heard of him, and declare unto you that God is light, and in him is no darkness at all. If we say that we have fellowship with him and walk in darkness, we lie, and do not tell the truth, but if we walk in the light as he is in the light, we have fellowship one with another, and the blood of Jesus Christ, his Son, cleanseth us from all sin. 1 John, 1: 5, 6, 7.

Then to ascertain how we may correctly walk in the light, we go to the law and testimony. We ask then, what is the language of the New Testament in speaking of the ordinance as included in the commission of Christ's ministers? As to the ordinance of baptism we find it instituted, enjoined and practiced, but to all appearance, it is thus presented as an ordinance which was to follow the preaching of the Gospel, and the conversion thereby of the souls of men to the faith of Christ. Hence we see that through the instrumentality of the Gospel we come to the light by hearing it preached, or by reading and contemplating it sincerely. To walk in the light we must conduct ourselves in every respect consistent with the Gospel. Then the blood of Jesus Christ his Son will cleanse us from all sin. Now mark, I will in this treatise give the Gospel plan by which every sinner can place himself in a condition where the efficacy of the blood of Jesus Christ will reach his case and cleanse him from all sin. Then I hope the caviling in regard to receiving remission of sins and the gift of the Holy Ghost will stop wherever this may come. Hence we introduce divine law with testimony. In the commision, Christ says, "preach the Gospel to every creature, he that believeth and is baptized shall be saved, but he that believeth not shall be damned. Mark 16: 15, 16. Here, evidently, is the divinely indicated order in the work of the ministry. 1st, preaching the Gospel. 2nd, its effect—conversion unto faith. 3rd, the outward expression of this effect, baptism. This order the first ministers of Christ appear to have uniformly followed. We will give the uniform order as it is given to us in the Gospel. The Apostles adhered to the counsel of Jesus, and tarried in Jerusalem, until they were endued with power from on high. Then they preached to the multitude in Jerusalem, and the people heard them preach, and consequently the guilty were convicted and said, "what shall we do." Peter said, "repent and be baptized every one of you in the name of Jesus Christ for the remission of sins and ye shall receive the gift of the Holy Ghost." Acts 2: 37, 38. Hence when Philip preached Christ unto the samaritans, and they believed the things concerning the kingdom of God and the name of Jesus Christ, and were baptized both men and women. Acts 8: 5, 12. Also same chapter, 35th verse. "Then Philip opened his mouth and began at the same Scripture and preached unto him Jesus. They came to a certain water and the Eunuch said, See here is water; what doth hinder me to be baptized? Philip demanded and obtained of him a profession of his faith in Christ, and then baptized him in the water. 37, 38. Again, when Saul of Tarsus was so wonderfully converted by the Lord himself he must needs go and listen to the counsel of Ananias, then arose and was baptized. Acts 9: 18. Also Acts 22: 16. Also when Peter carried the Gospel to the Gentiles he began with preaching "peace by Jesus Christ," assuring them that "through his name, whosoever believeth on him shall receive remission of sins." (This is a context and must be connected with other texts when the sense is given.) And when his preaching had been blest to their conversion, then "he commanded them to be baptized in the name of the Lord. Acts 10 : 36, 48. And again, when Paul and Timothy spoke to the women at the river side, the Lord opened the heart of Lydia to attend to the things that were spoken, and she was baptized. Acts 16 : 13, 14, 15. And when Paul and Silas prayed and sang praises unto God at the midnight hour, in their prison, when the anxious jailer of Philippi came in with the inquiry, "sirs, what must I do to be saved?" the reply was, "believe on the Lord Jesus Christ and thou shalt be saved and thine house." Then spake they unto him the word of the Lord and to all that were in his prison, and believing in God with all his house, he was baptized, he and all his, straightway. Acts 16: 30, 31, 32, 33.

The foregoing is the legal plan given by divine authority whereby we can place ourselves in a condition that our sins will be remitted by the blood of Christ, and then and then only is the poor creature a fit subject for the indwelling of that Holy Spirit or power, consequently we do not claim that the element water remits sin or washes away sin, and to say that by faith and repentance, without baptism, our sins are remitted is inconsistent with the tenor of the Gospel, and to claim that a person is a fit subject for the reception of the Holy Spirit or power while living in disobedience to the holy commands of God is an error as we will here prove. "Jesus answered and said unto him, if a man love me he will keep my words, and my Father will love him, and we will come unto him, and and make our abode with him. John 14 : 23. (Mark the phrase, keep my words.) And we are his witnesses to these things and so is also the Holy Ghost whom God has given to all them that obey him." Acts 5: 32. "And being made perfect, he became the author of eternal salvation unto all them that obey him." Heb. 5: 9. "He that saith I know him and keepeth not his commandments is a liar and the truth is not in him." 1 John 2 : 4. Then if baptism is a commandment, (which we all admit) and we keep it not, we are styled a liar, and common sense would say, a liar is not a fit subject for the indwelling of the Holy Spirit. Hence it becometh us to adhere to the whole counsel of God that we may walk in the light as he is in the light, and the blood of Jesus Christ, his Son, will cleanse us from all sin. More might be said but let this suffice for the time. We hope our friend J. H. of Ohio will also take a lesson from this as he has some good ideas and methinks would not take much to convert him if he is an honest man.

ELD. DAVID MURRAY.

Dayton O.

A LIGHT TO THE WORLD.

What is Safe and what is not Safe; What is Right and what is not Right.

BY J. H. MOORE.

CHAPTER IV.—*Immersion.*

It is not questioned whether immersion is right; but are sprinkling and pouring right? this is the question. All admit immersion to be safe, but then are sprinkling and pouring safe? Here is where all the doubts come in. Nobody denies immersion being either right or safe, but all the doubts in the whole matter are in relation to sprinkling and pouring. Immersion we know is right

All are agreed that *baptizo* * means immersion, but the question to settle is, does it ever mean sprinkling or pouring? Nobody denies it meaning immersion; this much is a fact; this much is settled, we know this is right; but then does it mean sprinkling and pouring? this is not settled this is not admitted to be either right or safe, but it is an exceedingly doubtless position.

It is a settled fact that John did baptize in water, this much is a fact, nobody denies this, but then did he ever baptize *out* of water? Here is the trouble; here is where all the doubts come in; here is where the disputing is. We know, and it is a settled fact that John baptized where there was *much* water, but did he ever baptize where there was *not much* water is the point of doubt. We are certain that it is right to baptize in water, because John did the same, but we have no definite account where either he or any of the apostles ever baptized *out* of the water. It is then not a question whether those do right who baptize in water, but are those right who do *not* baptize *in* water. We know that baptism can be performed *in* water, but then can it be performed *out* of water is where all the difficulty comes in.

There are simply two sides to this matter. One is to baptize *in* the water and the other is to baptize *out* of the water. It is a very easy matter to find instances in the Testament where persons were baptized *in* the water, about this there is no difficulty, but all the difficulty has been in trying to find some one who was baptized *out* of water. It is quite an easy task during the first centuries of the christian era to find persons by the hundreds that were immersed, but all the trouble has been in trying to find some person who had been sprinkled or poured.

Nobody seems to deny immersion being baptism; all seem to know and be certain that immersion is baptism, but all the doubt seems to be about sprinkling and pouring. Everybody knows that immersion is right, and not only right but safe. None are dissatisfied with immersion, but all the trouble is about sprinkling and pouring, in trying to prove that they are right. The position is very doubtful, there is not one particle of safety about it. The world, or only a part of it, has been trying for the last 300 years to prove that sprinkling and pouring are right, but they seem to be losing ground rapidly; let them lose it, we will not occupy it, for the simple reason it is not safe; we will cling to immersion; that we know is safe.

To be Continued.

* BAPTIZO is the Greek word used by the sacred writers when speaking of baptism. In the Greek language they have *baptizo* dipping, *rantizo* sprinkling, and *cheo* for pouring. When the apostles spoke of baptism they employed *baptizo*, and when speaking of sprinkling they used *rantizo* The two words are never used interchangingly.

AND THEN.

Man of the world, live on in the way you call pleasant. Laugh when fortune smiles on you, bow to the caprices of fashionable surroundings, drink with merry associates, the demon sparkling cup. On with the dance—this world to you is only a theatre of present enjoyments. But ah! remember life is but a passing shadow, all your pleasures are but momentary, your hopes,—your gains—your honors and titles are all fleeting shadows—think of it, death is in your path just ahead! And then, yes, and then, the grave, the cold grave is awaiting you,—and then—and then!—

Woman, one of fashions votaries, how like the butterfly that flits from flower to flower. Thou art jumping from folly to folly, seeking to catch the dazzling beams of vanity that, like meteors, dart hither and thither in the world. Faster, than those fleeting bubbles pass before your eyes, your life is passing. Your smiles of to-day give place to expressions of sorrow and disappointments to morrow. To day your fashioned disfigured body may be an object of notice to mortal eyes, to-morrow, food for worms that crawl into the prison cell! To-day, in life and health, to-morrow, in death, and then,—and then! The future echoes, *and then*! Eternity—awful eternity answers in mockings of woe,—*and then*! The thunderings of God's indignation and wrath replies, *and then*! AND THEN!—the pangs of hell get hold the soul!!

But ye faithful followers of the "meek and lowly" One, ye chosen of God, soldiers of the cross, pilgrims seeking a better country, "walk by faith," run the race set before you, "fight the fight of faith,"—travel on in the narrow way, though in treading the thorny desert we leave bloody tracks along the way, and a burning sun beat the sweat upon our temples like unto scalding tears, we hope to keep in view the tracks of Jesus, left upon the shores of time, and ever listen to the echoing voice of Him who said "follow me." We can almost feel the lavings of Jordans' waves at our feet, and see beyond the stream, "the land of rest" for weary pilgrims. We will abide our time,—wait 'till we are called to lay our armor by, and then! Yes dear pilgrims, and then,—and then we will cross over by and by, to meet to part no more. To the faithful "*and then*," is not a term full of sorrow and despair, but a note of sounding joy. We must sleep in Jesus—*and then*, comes the glorious resurrection, and then eternal life with God, *and then* the crown of glory, *and then* to be like Jesus, *and then*—Eternity only can tell the rest.

J. S. FLORY.

GOOD BY.

It is a hard word to speak. Some may laugh that it should be, but let them laugh. Icy hearts are never kind. It is a word that has choked many an utterance, and started many a tear. The hand is clasped, the word spoken, we part, and are upon the ocean of time—we go to meet again, God only knows where. It may be soon; it may be never. Take care that your "good-by" be not a cold one—it may be the last one that you can give. Ere you meet your friend again, death's cold hand may have closed his eyes and hushed his lips forever. Ah! he may have died thinking you loved him not.

Again it may be a very long separation. Friends crowd around and give their hand. How do you detect in each good-by the love that lingers there; and how do you bear away with you the memory of those parting words many, many days? We must often separate. Tear not yourself away with a careless boldness that defies all love, but make your last words linger—give the heart its full utterance—and if tears fall, what of it? Tears are not unmanly.—*Musical Million.*

Try what you can make of the broken fragments of time. Glean up its golden dust; those raspings and parings of precious duration; those leavings of days and remnants of hours which so many sweep out of existence. And thus, if you be a miser of moments, if you be frugal and hoard up odd minutes and half-hours and unexpected holidays, your careful gleanings may eke out a long and useful life, and you may die at last richer in existence than multitudes whose time is all their own.—*James Hamilton.*

A TRUMPET CALL TO THE WEAK.

BY REV. THEO. L. CUYLER.

The Christian church is not all that it might be in spiritual power and usefulness; and for the simple reason that each individual in it is not all that he might and ought to be. Multitudes in the eternal church are mere weaklings. If alive, they are barely alive. Their pulse is low. Their faith is feeble. Their joy's are few. Their assurance is so scanty and scrimped that they can only say, "Well, I *hope* that I am a Christian. I really think that I was once converted. I hope that I shall be admitted among the rest when my journey is over. It is up-hill work; I often stumble along in the dark. To tell the truth I have very little religion, and the little I have is of very little use to myself or to others."

There are thousands of Christian professors who, if they were to utter their honest convictions, would make substantially such a confession. There is no vigor in their faith, no ring in their prayers, no power in their lives. They manage to float with the current, but have no strength to make head against one. They have never known what it is to be "*Strong in the Lord* and in the power of his might." A regiment of such Christians would never convert one sinner from the error of his ways. A church entirely composed of such members would not contain "salt" enough to preserve society from putrefaction.

Perhaps this copy of the Messenger may fall into the hands of many who are thus dragging out a weak and unhappy existence. Let me say a frank word or two to such in the spirit of love.

1. You are to be pitied; but none the less to be blamed. Your spiritual condition is entirely your own fault. Whatever your "constitutional infirmities," or however unfavorable may be your situation in life, it is possible for you to be strong, cheerful, useful, effective servant of the Lord Jesus. That you are not one is wholly owing to your own sin. God never made a more complete free agent than you are. He never made more bountiful offers or precious promises to any human being than he has to you. "My grace is *sufficient* for you" is in your Bible, and was meant for your benefit. If Astor should draw a note in your name for a million of dollars, it would not be a more personal possession than is God's promise to "strengthen you mightily in the inner man." The Creator never made you to be a failure. The Savior never refused to be your intercessor. The Holy Spirit never refused to "work in you mightily." No one in the universe is accountable for your dwarfish condition and almost useless life, but your own sinning self. Admit this, or there is no hope of anything better and brighter in the future.

2. How shall you be strengthened? I answer in two or three words. "IN THE LORD." Paul condenses the answer in that short, simple line he wrote to the people at Ephesus: "Be strengthened *in the Lord.*" A man may be strong in self-will, or strong in intellect, or in business capacity, or in social standing, or in natural enthusiasm, or in many other ways, and yet be a very weak Christian. The sap of his nature all runs off into the limbs of his selfish undertakings. He is not strong in the Lord. His name may even loom large on the roll of the church, but he is worth less to his Lord than the poor seamstress who communes with Christ every day over her needle, and opens her little room for a "cottage prayer-meeting" at night. Her life is *hid with Christ* in God.

You have been trying to live *out* of the Lord Jesus. Your reliance has been on some old experience of "conversion many years ago, and on a decently respectable church-membership. There has been but little actual "indwelling of Christ in your heart by faith." Faith is the door; you have barred it up! Faith is the artery of connection with Jesus; you have practically severed it! Having amputated a living, grasping, upholding faith, you had really nothing to hold by and no arm to work with. He who could "do all things" for you has not been *asked* to do really anything; for having so little faith, you have lived well nigh prayerless!

Before you can ever be a stronger Christian, you must believe it *possible* to become one. Take Paul's wonderful declaration in the last chapter of his letter to the Philippians—"I have strength for all things in HIM which giveth me power." [This is the literal reading of the verse.] Believe that! Start with that, as James Watt started with the principle of the expansive power of steam. Fairly and fully try the experiment of living in Christ and on Christ. All the sap of your daily being has been drawn off into other things. Now give yourself to Jesus. Cut off the sinful intimacies of your soul, and seek a new intimacy. Seek the inflow of that power which is from on high!

When our college professor of electricity wished to test the power of his lectric machine, he used to place a student on an insulated stool with glass legs. The stool was thus cut off from all contact with the rest of the room. As soon as the machine was set in motion the student became *charged* with the electric current, and if touched, his body gave of the keen bright spark. Now you must *insulate* yourself from sinful alliances and practices, if you would become filled with the current of heavenly influences. Cut off the world! Cut off favorite sins! They have drained away your life. Open your soul to baptism from on high!

I close with reëchoing the watchword, "Be strong in the Lord!" Be filled with the Spirit! Resolve on your knees that this shall be the strongest and best year of your life. Make it a *bearing year!* You ought to outgrow last year's narrow and scanty garments. Along the shores of the sea there are creatures that every year cast off their shell that they may wear a newer and a larger coat of mail. The eagle sheds his feathers, that with a brighter plumage and a broader pinion he may soar up to meet the sun in his coming. I beseech you then, begin a new life! 'Mount up with wings as eagles!" Try the full power of prayer! Try the full power of HIM in whom dwelleth the fulness of the God-head!

Oh, how many a glorious record
Had the angels of you kept!
Had you *done* instead of doubted,
Had you *run* insterd of crept!

—*American Messenger.*

Religious News.

The *Christian Cynosure* pitches into H. W. Beecher and the managing Editor of the *Union* in the following comparative style:

"Oliver Johnston, we are told, is the real managing editor of the *Christian Union*, while Beecher is editor-in-chief. Mr. Johnston and I were abolition lecturers together in our youth and I loved him as a faithful and fearless friend of the oppressed. He too, like Beecher, has stumbled at the "stumbling stone"—Christ. Mr. Johnston told me at our last interview in the *Independent* office, that he did not and could not believe that Jesus Christ was conceived by the power of God, or that any miracles recorded of him in the New Testament are facts! And the difference between him and Beecher is, that he tells frankly what he does and what he does not believe, while Beecher has no fixed religious belief whatever; nor, indeed, any moral principle, but could always preach Minie rifles and cannon shot as "means of grace" to slave-holders in Kansas; and, the instant the popular breeze was turning, give a thousand dollars to a Kuklux College of which the unrepentant arch-traitor Lee was president. Under the teachings of such men

No pledge is sacred and no home is sweet."

MORMON CONFERENCE.—The semi-annual Conference of the Mormons was held last Sunday in Salt Lake City. There were present about 6,000 persons from all parts of the Territory, including 400 or 500 Gentiles as spectators. At the morning services Apostles Taylor and Cannon spoke. The latter thought the prospects of the Mormon Church never were more bright and encouraging. All the powers of the world could not put down the Church and thwart divine design. God's people would reign here. In the afternoon Brigham Young, looking in the best of health, denounced the fashions of the ladies, caricaturing the "Grecian bend" across the platform, much to the amusement of the audience. He expected his people to cling to the old ways. The discourse was disjointed and discursive, but enforcing the assertion that the Mormons were God's people and ought to pay tithing. The attendance was not so large as usual. A number of missionaries are to be sent to foreign parts.

One of our exchanges of the Presbyterian faith give the following as a reason why their people do not object to them going back to the Abrahamic covenant for a proof of infant baptism:

One reason why no opposition is is made in our church to thus going back to Abraham for authority to administer infant baptism is because there is no money to be paid by parents in connection with it. If there were, one half of the Presbyterian Church would join the Baptist.

The Second Adventists of Groton, Vermont, have designated April 12, 1873, as the last great day.

How many more prophets and "ends" are we to have? The credulity of the people in this age of intelligence is a problem unsolvable. The day has passed like all other modern prophetic days and the world yet stands and will stand until God's own time will come "the day and the hour of which no man knoweth."

Six hundred Christian people are said to be still in prison in Japan, persecuted for Christ's sake. But they will soon be set at liberty, we doubt not, as the Japanese Government is seriously set upon reform. Many of these so-called Christians are Jesuits, who, for political, not religious reasons, have been imprisoned.

CHURCH LOTTERIES IN OHIO.—A bill has passed the House of Representatives of Ohio, prohibiting lotteries and gift enterprises of every description. An amendment to exempt churches, newspapers and public libraries from its operations, was voted down decisively.

The *Christian Standard* reports the accessions to the Disciple Church for last week as follows:

Pennsylvania, 28; Ohio, 43; Indiana 145; Illinois, 135; Iowa, 121; Missouri, 173; Nebraska, 1; Oregon, 30; Kentucky, 57; Texas, 27; North Carolina, 9—Total 791.

Youth's Department

SATURDAY NIGHT.

The supper is over, the hearth is swept,
And in the wood-fire's glow,
The children cluster to hear a tale
Of that time so long ago—

When grandmamma's hair was golden brown
And the warm blood came and went,
O'er the face that could scarce have been sweeter then,
Than now in its rich content.

The face is wrinkled and care-worn now,
And the golden hair is gray;
But the light that shone in the young girl's eyes
Has never gone astray.

And her needles catch the fire's light,
As in and out they go,
With the clicking music that grandma loves,
Shaping the stocking toe.

And the waking children love it, too,
For they know the stocking song
Brings many a tale to grandma's mind,
Which they shall hear ere long.

But it brings no story of olden time,
To grandmamma's heart to-night—
Only a ditty, quaint and shore,
Is sung by the needles bright.

"Life is a stocking," grandma says,
"and yours is just begun;
But I am knitting the toe of mine,
And my work is almost done.

"With merry hearts we begin to knit,
And the ribbing is almost play,
Some are gay colored, and some are white,
And some are ashen gray.

But most are made of many a hue,
With many a stitch set wrong,
And many a row to be sadly ripped
Ere the whole is fair and strong.

"There are long plain spaces without a break
That in youth are hard to bear;
And many a weary tear is dropped
As we fashion the heel with care.

But the saddest, happiest time is that
We court and yet we shun;
When our Heavenly Father breaks the thread,
And says that our work is done."

The children come to say good night,
With tears in their bright young eyes;
While in grandma's lap, with a broken thread,
The finished stocking lies.

LITTLE CHILDREN.

Our Savior loves the little ones. When the disciples would have pushed them aside as not worthy of the Master's notice, Jesus rebuked them, and said, "Suffer the little children to come unto me, and forbid them not for of such is the kingdom of Heaven. And He took them up in His arms and blessed them." At another time they came unto him saying, 'Who is greatest in the Kingdom of Heaven? And Jesus called a little child unto Him, and set him in the midst of them, and said, Verily I say unto you, except ye be converted and become as little children, ye shall not enter into the Kingdom of Heaven; and whoso shall receive one such little child in my name, receiveth me;" thus setting them as examples for us, and commending them to our love and care.

Precious treasures are these "little ones." Childish and dependent, they wield a mighty influence in the home circle, and in the world. Stern faces are made to smile and sad hearts forget their sorrows in the loving prattle and innocent glee of little children, who, while they weary the arms, cheer the hearts of those whose God-given task it is to tend and rear them. Wicked and hardened men have been melted and won by some loving word spoken in the lisping accents of an infant tongue.

Journeying at a certain time, my attention was attracted to a beautiful babe, on the lap of its mother who was seated just in front of me. The car was crowded, and as the passengers hurried along in quest of seats, the little fellow shrank back with a look of fear and wonder; but as his eye met that of his mother, the troubled look gave place to a smile of peace. The whistle sounded; the cars rolled along; and the hills, the trees and the houses, as he watched them from the window, all seemed to be running away. Every now and then he would turn his wandering gaze to his mother, as if he would ask the meaning of all this strange commotion. But no sooner did he behold her smile than his fears were gone and he laughed and crowed again in innocent glee.

At last, wearied with looking, he nestled his little head on mother's arm and laid himself down to rest. He knew not where he was going; everything was new and strange, but no matter; mother was there; her arm was around him; her loving eye was over him, and he felt as safe as if at home in his own little cradle. His infant heart knew just enough to trust implicitly in mother, and thus he sweetly slept.

Just so our Heavenly Father wo'd have us lean upon His arm and trust in Him. We cannot fathom the mysteries of life's journey; we know not where it may lead us nor when it will end, nor can we foretell what a day or an hour may bring forth. We can neither control the elements which God has created; not overrule the circumstances in which we are placed; nor give a reason for the way that we take; but God knows it all. He sees the end from the beginning. His eye is upon us, and His Almighty Arm is around and underneath the children of God. As "little children," then, let us trustingly, confidingly, rest in His love, "casting all our care upon Him for He careth for us;" and leave Him to mark out our way, and guide and protect us through life's journey, and at last receive us home as "little children" to our Father's house.
—*The Christian.*

GIVE me the treasures of redemption; my food is manna, and my wine is love; my sweet pillow the bosom of the Son, and my strong defence the arm of the Almighty God; my home that palace eternal in the heaven, where angels' harps supply the music, and, woven of Jesus' righteousness, the robes are fairer than angels wear.

Correspondence.

A Reporter is wanted from every Church in the brotherhood to send us Church news, Obituaries, Announcements, or anything that will be of general interest. To insure insertion, the writers name must accompany each communication. Our Invitation is not personal but general—please respond to our call.

MIRABILE, MO.,
March 30, '73.

To those to whom Church news from Missouri is interesting, I will here give a few thoughts in addition to the history of the Brethren here, the formation of Districts, and the report of the first District Council of the North District of Mo.

The attendance at our regular appointments in this North-western portion of Mo., has hitherto been remarkably good as a general rule, but I foresee in the future already at hand that things will in this respect change for the worse, and the reasons for this will undoubtedly be plausible to all, which are these: Our country, like all others of like promising success in agricultural, commercial, as well as mechanical and other worldly pursuits, is improving rapidly, and wealth, pride and popularity are the more and more taking the sway. Popular Christendom is being extended and multiplied. Church-houses are being erected by the various denominations on every hand, whereas three or four years ago school-houses and private dwellings were the common places of meeting for worship. In this respect the Brethren, owing to their scattered condition and limited circumstances, are being left far behind, and that natural disposition of man to be comfortable and popular is manifest in society here and elsewhere, and of course school-houses will be passed by and those new meeting-houses thronged, not so much for choice of doctrine as to be up with the times. Now in view of the above facts, and having a large acquaintance of brethren of "well to do" circumstances in a temporal point of view, and being well acquainted with the brethren of the Hamilton Branch, Daviess Co., Mo., who are soliciting aid in their struggle to overcome the results of the above fate, I would fearlessly say, brethren if you have any means to lend to the Lord, this is a safe depository for your donations. The calls from that Church are promptings and motives of the most ardent zeal and devotedness in the good Master's cause. In this congregation are vested of our greatest and most eminent ministerial powers and energies, and many fruits are conspicuously seen to ripen as the results of the same. These facts I offer not as being myself interested more than others of foreign congregations, nor as being asked to solicit, but rather to encourage such as might be willing to contribute it they were more familiar with the Church at Hamilton. I would here state that they do not mean to build a showy, fashionable house in town, but a plain Brethren's Meeting-house in a newly opened farming community four miles North of town.

Fraternally yours,
C. C. ROOT.

Dear readers of the Pilgrim:—I this evening pen you a few lines stating that we in the Black Water Church, Franklin Co., Va., and adjoining churches were called together to-day to pay the last tribute of respect to one of our beloved old sisters, namely, Hannah Flora, aged 84 years, 3 months and 17 days. She has been a consistent member of the Church for many years, leaves five daughters and three sons, one a minister and elder of the above named Districts. The other two sons are deacons in the Church. Her children left to mourn her loss, no doubt look forward to the day that they shall meet their mother and father in that upper and better world. She also left many grand-children and great-grand-children, and I would say to them and myself, will we and all that knew her, endeavor to follow her bright examples as we are drifting speedily to the grave? Remember how kind she was, how faithful, how humble, how plain, how much we loved her. Yes, dear reader I often think how important it is that we should try to imitate our old fathers and mothers as respects our plainness in dress, but we are sorry to say and see that as our fathers and mothers go that that plainness and humbleness goes out with them. This ought not so to be, but we should be a separate and distinct people from the world. But as soon as we become contentious about these things and every one have their own order and cut of dress, we can no more recognize each other but will be with the current of the world. Then our confession is gone. Bear in mind, we all promised to renounce satan and all his pernicious ways, we have put away the old man with his deeds and have put on the new man, so then let us not love the world nor the things that are in the world, for in the world is the lust of the flesh and the pride of life which is not of the Father but of the world and the world will pass away with the lust thereof. Yea, I firmly believe that pride will be the downfall of the Church if not checked. It is rapidly growing and who is to stop it? You who are set as watchman, should warn the brethren and sisters of the danger as respecting this matter. We fear it is not done in all congregations. Not to flatter ourselves nor our brethren, but here in old Franklin Co., we have but little trouble in this respect. The brethren and sisters seem to be contending for nothing but the faith that was once delivered to the saints. Oh that we could all see eye to eye and mind the same thing and be governed by the same rule, that is the Gospel. Let us live for Him who died for us so that when our imperfect labors shall end on earth we may cross the Jordan of death to meet those who have washed their robes and made them white in the blood of the Lamb. J. BARNHART.

Retreat, Va.

NOTICE TO ALL.

As the Communion season is near at hand, it would be, doubtless, a good plan to have a package of my pamphlets, TRINE IMMERSION, on hand at each Lovefeast throughout the Brotherhood for general circulation. From 25 to 50 copies might be sold at each meeting, thus convincing the world and confirming the Brethren. I insist that some one from each arm of the Church order a package and have them ready till the meeting. From some several hundred letters I select the following: Eld. Jacob Miller, of Va., says, "I think they should be sent far and wide among the Brethren and others." A brother in Ill. who has sold some 40 copies in his neighborhood, says, "They have kicked up quite a dust around here, and perhaps it will yet end in a debate." J. S. Flory of Va., says; "I am anxious that your pamphlet should be widely circulated. It is, in my opinion, *just the right thing in the right place at the right time.*" For terms see my advertisement on the last page of the PILGRIM. J. H. MOORE.

Urbana, Ill.

TO THE BEREAVED.

My dear brethren and sisters; —I feel, this beautiful Sabbath morning, like saying something to you through the columns of this good paper. Among the many thoughts my mind was drawn upwards to that blissful abode where all those that love and serve God those that have washed their robes white in the blood of the Lamb have gone, and are waiting for their friends to come and join in the throng to sing the loud hallelujahs for ever and ever.

I have near and dear friends gone before whom I hope to meet there when done toiling here below, yes, among the happy throng I have one dear little grand-son whom I saw laid in the silent tomb a few days ago. Dear little Charlie, he was too sweet for earth and Jesus said come up higher. The dear parents are almost heart broken to see their only darling boy suffer and be taken from them so soon after the Lord gave it to them, but dear parents, I would say to you in your great bereavement. I know it was hard for you and for me and hard for any parents to bid farewell to their dear sweet little ones, but the Savior says, "Suffer little children to come unto me and forbid them not for of such is the Kingdom of Heaven." I know it has touched a very tender chord and has severed a tie of nature that cannot soon be forgotten. Oh yes, I would have loved to have seen sweet little Charlie one time more but when I arrived the dear heart broken mother met me in the yard weeping very bitterly, saying, "Oh, mother, my darling is gone." Yes, dear mother, you can go to him but he can never come to you. I hope you will set about the work without delay and never give it up 'till you have found peace at the feet of a crucified Redeemer. I hope you are both saying in your hearts, "This is done of the Lord for our good and we are determined to try, by the help of God, to meet our dear little Charlie up yonder in that better world, where there is no more sickness, no more sorrow pain nor death, and where parting is no more." Yes, strive to meet your little one there in that Heaven above. Dear children, I would say to you, try to live in that way and manner that you may raise the little ones that you have left in the nurture and admonition of the Lord. Grieve no longer for little Charlie, but weep for yourselves, and say with good old Job, "The Lord gave and the Lord hath taken away, blessed be the name of the Lord."

"Only a little baby,
Gone to its heavenly rest;
Only a little lamb,
Safe on the Savior's breast.

Only a little angel,
Amid the hosts above;
Only another little voice,
Singing, God is love."

NANCY CROUSE.

Fayetteville, W. Va.

THE MAINE MISSION.

As there is a call for the publication of Elder Daniel Longenecker's report of the Maine Mission also, we will now give it, believing it may now be in place, as the District Conference is near at hand and the Mission question will likely receive some attention. Ed.

Dear Pilgrim:—As there has been an article sent to the press I will only give a sketch of a few points that may be of interest to some of your many readers.

When we came to the place where we intended to commence our labors we were kindly received. After handing in our letter of recommendation we were conveyed to a friend near a Church where we remained during the night. Next morning (Sunday Oct., 3.) we were taken to an appointment made for a Freewill Baptist, but as he did not come we were introduced to a friend who introduced us to the congregation as ministers of the Gospel from Penna., and desired us to take the stand, which we did and preached for the first time in the State of Maine. From there, we were taken to Elder Dennis and held meeting in his house. Here we got privilege to hold meetings in dwelling houses at night, and during the day we attended to calls for visits believing that visiting would accomplish as much good as preaching, giving us the privilege of speaking face to face, answer and ask questions, and expound the Scriptures as believed and taught by the Brethren, laboring to be as wise as serpents and as harmless as doves. We reasoned together in Christian faith and love without giving offence and thus became as familiar as if we were one of the family. Being invited, we went from house to house. On our arrival we were always kindly received by the mistress, invited in and recognized as messengers of glad tidings—treated with respect, politeness and hospitality. In the morning the Bible was placed on the stand and liberty was gived to read and pray, the family all being present at seasons of worship.

After preaching we gave liberty to all who felt to give testimony to what had been said, and one of the ministers and his wife and a deacon and his wife stood up in the congregation and gave testimony to the word as presented. Almost every night some gave testimony to what had been said, bidding us God speed and praying that we might have souls for our hire.

There are three kind of Baptists or immersionists here. The Freewill, Calvanistic and Adventists, and in order to introduce the truth as we believe it, it was necessary to show the difference between them and ourselves or the Brethren. * * * [Here is given an exposition of order and practice which we omit for want of space, Ed.] We had many pleasant seasons with this people both in preaching and private conversation, but to give all that was preached and said would be impossible.

DANIEL LONGENECKER.

MARRIED.

BEERY—WAGNER—March 23, '73, by brother Menno Stouffer, brother Ephraim Beery to sister Lydia Wagner, both of Macon Co., Ill. ISAAC WAGNER.

DIED.

BILLINGS.—In Botany District, Pattawattamie Co., Iowa, April 3, '73, G. C. *Billings*, of Consumption.

He was confined to his bed from the 29th of May 1872. Towards his last, he became reconciled and desired to be immersed, but was so weak that it was not administered. What a warning this should be to all, not to put off our duty until it may be too late. God can just as suddenly call us all, as He can cast us on the bed of affliction, and may not have the opportunity to prepare as our friend *Billings* had. His hopes seemed to be bright before him. He had a desire to go but O, how dangerous it is to neglect our best interests until our last. He requested his funeral discourse to be preached by the writer, which was done to a very attentive congregation from these words, "It is appointed unto men once to die, but after this the judgment." Heb. 9 : 27.

H. H. FOLCK.

AINSWORTH.—In the Manor Church, Md., March 30, Mary Lizzie, daughter of brother Wm., and sister Louisa Ainsworth, aged 14 years, 5 months and 15 days. Funeral services by the Brethren

We wish to inform our young readers of a death that occurred in our neighborhood lately which makes us feel very sad. A little girl has been taken from our midst that was much admired by all who knew her for her amiability and lovely disposition. We see in the departure of little Mary Lizzie, that death is no respecter of persons. If beauty and loveliness could have bribed him then she would not have died. But this could not be done, all the sympathies of friends and admirers could not avail.

"So fades the lovely blooming flower,
Frail, smiling solace of an hour;
So soon our transient comforts fly,
And pleasure only blooms to die."

S. A. COFFMAN.

ANNOUNCEMENTS.

Middle District of Pa., at Clover Creek, May 13.

West Va., Seneca District, Randolph Co., 9th and 10th of May.

Middle District of Iowa, in Dallas Co., on the 10th day of May.

Northern Indiana and Michigan, ½ mile west of Goshen, Ind., May 1st.

North-eastern District of Ohio, Jonathan's Creek Congregation, Perry Co., on May 20th.

Middle District of Ind., Bachelor Run Congregation, Lower Church, second Friday after Good Friday.

First District of Virginia, on Friday and Saturday before the fourth Sunday in April, at the Valley M. H., Botetourt Co., 1 mile south of Amsterdam.

Please announce through the PILGRIM that our District Meeting will be held on the 13th of May in the Cook's Creek Congregation, Rockingham Co., Va.

SOLOMON GARBER.

Please notice through the PILGRIM that the District Meeting of Western Pa., will be held at the Fairview Meeting house in the George's Creek branch, Fayette Co. Pa., on Wednesday 21st of May, '73.

J. FORNEY.

Please announce that the District Meeting of North-Western Ohio will be held, the Lord willing, with the brethren of Crawford Co., at the house of brother John Brilharts, on the Base Line on the 23 day of May, and on the 24, the day following, there will be a Communion meeting at the same place. A general representation is desired. ISRAEL ROOP.

Western Maryland District Meeting.

The Western Maryland, District Council, met in the Broad Fording Meetinghouse, Washington Co., Md., on the 10th day of April, 1873, and after considering a number of Queries, concluded to send up but *two* to the Annual Meeting. The Council was conducted with great harmony.

At the close of business of a general character, the delegates of the following Congregations, made the subjoined arrangements for their Lovefeast meetings this Spring, and authorized me to announce them with the usual invitations:

Beaver Creek, Wednesday May 4, at 1 P. M.

Manor Church, Tuesday May 13, commencing at 9 o'clock A. M.

Welch Run, Thursday May 15, commencing at 1 o'clock P. M., continuing next day till noon. E. SLIFER.

LOVEFEASTS.

Champaign Co., Ill., at Geo. Dillings, 3 miles east of Urbana, 7th and 8th of June.

Little Swatara Church, at Bro. Henry K Bixler's 2 miles northeast of Jonestown, Lebanon Co., Pa., 12th and 13th of June. Brethren returning from A. M., are invited to stop.

Please announce that the Hudson Church, McLean Co., Ill., have appointed a Lovefeast on the 14 and 15 of June, to commence at 10 o'clock A. M., at the house of J. Y. Snavely. The usual invitation is given. THOMAS D. LYON

Bros. Brumbaugh:—We wish you to announce through the PILGRIM, that we intend the Lord willing, to hold our Lovefeast at the Spring Run Church, Mifflin Co., Pa., on the 27th. and 28th. of May and extend an invitation to our brethren and sisters especially ministers to come and give us a helping hand. P. S. MYERS.

Please announce in the PILGRIM, that we intend, the Lord willing, to hold our Lovefeast, four miles north of Falls City, Nebraska, on the 3rd and 4th, of May, preceding the State Council of Kansas and Nebraska, which will be held on the 5th of said month. By order of the Church.

C. FORNEY.

Please announce that the Brethren in York Co., Pa., in Codorus Church, have appointed their Communion Meeting, on Tuesday and Wednesday, 10th and 11th of June, 1873, at the East Codorus Meetinghouse, 8 miles south of York and about 1 mile east of Logansville. An invitation is extended to all desiring to come especially the ministering brethren.

CHRISTIAN NESS.

Please announce in the PILGRIM, that the Brethren in the Shade Creek Congregation, Somerset Co., Pa., have appointed their Lovefeast on the 29th day of May next, commencing at 10 o'clock.

A hearty invitation to all the Brethren and sisters, especially the ministering brethren. Those coming by rail road, east or west, will stop off at Johnstown and will be conveyed to place of meeting, if notified in time. Ministering brethren coming from a distance will be conveyed to Annual Meeting.

By order of the Church.

HIRAM MUSSELMAN.

John O. Stauffer, after you left my house we found your memorandum book and pencil lying in the yard, which I suppose dropped from your pocket when you carried your coat out to your wagon. S. J. GARDNER.

New Hope, Va.

The Weekly Pilgrim.

JAMES CREEK, PA., April 22, 1873.

☞ HOW TO SEND MONEY.—All sums over $1.50, should be sent either in a check, draft or postal order. If neither of these can be obtained, have the letter registered.

☞ WHEN MONEY is sent, *always* send with it the name and address of those who paid it. Write the names and post office as plainly as possible.

☞ EVERY subscriber for 1873, gets a *Pilgrim Almanac* FREE.

CURRENT EVENTS.

One among the outrages of the times was that of members of congress voting into their own pockets thousands of dollars, thus robbing from honest laboring men to get means to play the harlot with. We are glad to see that those who favored the acts with those who are willing to touch the pilfered gains, have brought upon themselves a stigma of reproach which ought to forever debar them from receiving another position of trust from the people. We are commanded to pray for our rulers, but our prayer is that we may have as few of such as possible.

The hanging of Foster, the car-hook murderer, is another event that has been and is yet commanding considerable comment, not on account of the greatness of the culprit, but the circumstances connected with his imprisonment and execution. Notwithstanding the crime was one of the darkest hue and unprovoked, yet every conceivable effort was made to save him from the affixed penalty of the law. One of the pleas was, because he was *drunk*, just as if drunkenness was a virtue and that a man was more than justified in it. In addition to the privileges of a common citizen, he is allowed to make a fiend of himself and slay his fellow man at pleasure. When the American people once pays a premium on drunkenness then will every man's life be in his neighbor's hands. Notwithstanding he never showed any fruits of repentance during his imprisonment, yet several prominent ministers made a saint of him and followed him up with their empty prayers even on the scaffold, and there prayed so long that it became necessary for the executioners to stop them. He was as dead and unconscious of their empty petitions as the noose that was placed around his neck. We are to pray for sinners that they may be saved from their sins, but to pray for an unborn, unregenerated sinner to have him saved in his sins, is an outrage on our holy religion.

We do not say that there is no mercy for such if truly penitent, but these popular, clerical preliminaries might all be ended in the culprits cell and thus avoid the hypocritical sham which is now played off on the scaffold, to be seen of men.

Another event, and a sad one too, just now presents itself to our mind, we mean the loss of the Atlantic and the fate of a large portion of her crew. We can almost see the hopeful crew get aboard the vessel which is considered altogether safe. The embarking a ship is an important event and often cuts asunder the dearest ties that unite loving hearts together. The morning in Liverpool was fair and promising, and as hopeful ones gathered to the port, many a greeting was given and farewell tear shed. Fathers and mothers took leave of their children, brothers and sisters gave the parting hand, tenderly and hopefully were they entrusted into the bosom of the mighty ship with the expectation that it would carry them over the turbulent waves and land them safely on the shores of American freedom, but how vain are human expectations, instead of this, it carried them to a watery grave. This truly is a world of destruction and there is no refuge that will secure us from the grim monster death. We are all aboard the ship of life and every moment is rapidly wafting us down, down towards the rock of destruction and unless we have our "Life Boat" prepared we will be hopelessly lost. Jesus has prepared an ark for us that will outride every storm and land us safely on the other shore. Brother, sister, how is it with us? Dear sinner, how is it with you? Have you entered that ark? If not, you are in danger of being shipwrecked every moment and your fate may be far worse than those of the ill-fated Atlantic, you will be engulfed into the whirlpool of destruction and sunk into the eternal burnings.

LOVEFEAST.

The time for holding our spring Lovefeast is approaching, notices of which are coming in from every direction. There are seasons that exert a happy influence throughout the brotherhood and should be regarded as means of grace for which we should feel truly grateful indeed as it is declared that unless we eat His body and drink His blood we have *no life in us*. It is by participating in these feasts our inward man becomes renewed in strength day by day. Here it is where kindred spirits meet and partake of the living emblems of our blessed Lord and thus have our hungering and fainting souls filled with the "Bread of life" and our thirsting spirits quenched with the "Living Waters." Here it is that many of us have met for the first time as adopted children of God and formed attachments which will only end in death to be renewed in heaven. Truly such are blessed occasions and we hope, at the coming feasts, many will have the pleasure of partaking of the emblems of Jesus that a year ago were strangers and aliens to the commonwealth of Israel.

As these are times when brethren and sisters meet from far and near they afford very excellent opportunities of introducing and distributing the PILGRIM. For this purpose we will send to any of our readers who desire to labor for us as many sample copies as they can use to advantage. Will not our agents send for some and continue their efforts in enlarging our circulation? With specimen copies and a little effort 10 or 15 names might be raised at each meeting. We can still supply back numbers or subscriptions may commence at any time and run a year or from April 1st to end of year $1.10. Brethren and sisters, let us hear from you as we are assured there are many who would read the PILGRIM had they an opportuny.

PILGRIM ALMANACS.—As we have on hand several hundred more *Almanacs* than we need for distribution, we will send them to any address, free of postage on the following terms. Single copy 10 cents, 6 copies 40 cents, and 12 copies 70 cents.

PERSONAL.

D. BOCK. Received all right.

HENRY GROFF. The PILGRIM is sent to Samuel Showalter, Nebraska City, Neb.

J. RITTENHOUSE. Your letter was received and we have been sending the PILGRIM to Sarah Hull and M. A. Hanna with all back Nos.

ELD. GEO. WOLF. The mistake must have occurred through an oversight. We have now given you credit for the amount, and the PILGRIMS changed as requested.

A PRESENT. Some person sent us $1.25 to send the PILGRIM to Louisa Stiernogle, Forsythe, Mo., but the post master informs us that there is no such person there. Where is the mistake?

LITERARY NOTICES.

BEHIND THE SCENES IN WASHINGTON, is the title of a new work of which we have received advance sheets. It promises to be a work that will interest the mass, as it shows up things generally about the capital, tells how the public money is spent and gives a complete and graphic account of the credit mobilier investigation, the congressional rings, political intrigues, workings of the lobbies, ect Giving the secret history of our national government, in all its varied branches, and showing how the public money is squandered, how votes are obtained, etc., with sketches of the leading senators, congressmen, government officials, etc., and an accurate description of the splendid public buildings of the federal capital, by Edward Winslow Martin, author of "Secrets of the great city," etc., etc. Illustrated with numerous fine engravings of the public buildings and noted scenes in Washington. National publishing company, Philadelphia, Pa.; Chicago, Ill.; Cincinatti, Ohio, St. Louis, Mo.

THE MEMORIAL PULPIT.—Under this title A. S. Barns & Co., of New York are publishing in pamphlet form, a sermon each week, by Rev. Charles S. Robison of the Presbyterian Memorial Church. The following sermons are now published: The Gospel no Shame," "A picture and its Lessons," "A Man asleep," "Spiritual Dreaming," "Ladder of Life," "Nearing Salvation," "Our Christian Names," "Onliver his Welcome," "Ladder of Doctrine, and Faith and Failure." Terms, 10 cts single or $3 00 per year.

NEWS ITEMS.

California anticipates a wheat crop this year of over 50,000,000 bushels.

Alexandria in Egypt has grown more rapidly than any other city on the eastern continent. In 1812 its population was about 60,000, and now it is nearly 300,000.

INCREASE OF SALARIES.—Both Houses have adopted a bill, known as Ben Butler's Compensation Bill, making a sweeping increase of salaries. The President,s salary is increased to $50,000, and those of members of Congress and other officers, largely increased.

WOMEN AS SCHOOL DIRECTORS.—"Women of the age of twenty-one years and upward shall be eligible to any office of control or management under the school laws of this state." These words have been adopted in committee of Constitutional Convention as a new section for the organic law of Pennsylvania.

JAPANESE PAPER MONEY.—A Japanese 10 cent note is thus described: The note is made of heavy yellow silk paper, about 2½ by 1½ inches and is printed in black with "tenchest letters" in a very tasteful manner. Upon one end is stamped a peculiarly shaped adhesive stamp, printed in purple with a curious arabesque design in which the words "Imperial Treasury of Japan" (in English) are frequently repeated. Three seals are imprinted on the note in red ink.

The Weekly Pilgrim.

Published by J. B. Brumbaugh, & Co.

Edited by H. B. & Geo. Brumbaugh.

CORRESPONDING EDITORS.

D. P. Sayler, Double Pipe Creek, Md.

Leonard Furry, New Enterprise, Pa.

The *Pilgrim* is a Christian Periodical, devoted to religion and moral reform. It will advocate in the spirit of *love* and *liberty,* the principles of true Christianity, labor for the promotion of peace among the people of God, for the encouragement of the saints and for the conversion of sinners, avoiding those things which tend toward disunion or sectional feelings.

TERMS.

Single copy, Book paper, $1.5[illegible]
Eleven copies, (eleventh for Agt.) $15.00
Any number above that at the same rate.

Address,
H. B. BRUMBAUGH.
James Creek,
Huntingdon county Pa.

The Weekly Pilgrim.

"REMOVE NOT THE ANCIENT LANDMARKS WHICH OUR FATHERS HAVE SET."

VOL. 4. JAMES CREEK, PENNSYLVANIA, APRIL, 29, 1873. NO. 17

POETRY.

The Old Man In The Stylish Church.

SELECTED BY N. THAPP.

Well wife, I've been to church to-day—
been to a stylish one—
And seein' you can't go from home, I'll
tell you what was done:
You would have been surprised to see
what I saw to-day;
The sisters were fixed up so fine they hardly bowed to pray.

I had on these coarse clothes of mine, not
much the worse for wear,
But then they knew I wasn't one that
they called a millionaire;
So they led the old man to a seat away
back by the door;
'Twas bookless and uncushioned—a "reserved seat" for the poor.

Pretty soon in came a stranger with gold
ring and clothing fine;
They led him to a cushioned seat far in advance of mine.
I thought that wasn't exactly right to seat
him up so near
When he was young, and I was old, and
very hard to hear.

But, then, there's no accountin' for what
some people do;
The finest clothing nowadays oft gets the
finest pew.
But when we reach the blessed home, all
undefiled by sin,
We'll see wealth beggin' at the gate while
poverty goes in.

I couldn't hear the sermon, I sat so far
away,
So, through the hours of service, I could
only "watch and pray;"
Then the doins' of the Christians sitting
near me round about—
Pray that God would make them pure
within as they were pure without.

While I sat there, lookin' all around upon
the rich and great,
I kept thinking of the rich man and the
beggar at his gate;
How, by all but dogs forsaken, the poor
beggar's form grew cold,
And the angel bore his spirit to the mansions built of gold;

How, at last the rich man perished, and
his spirit took its flight
From the purple and fine linen to the home
of endless night;
There he learned, as he stood gazin' at the
beggar in the sky,
"It isn't all of life to live; nor all of death
to die."

I doubt not there were wealthy sires in that
religious fold
Who went up from their dwellin's like the
Pharisees of old;
Then returned home from their worship
with a head uplifted high,
To spurn the hungry from their door with
naught to satisfy.

Out! out with such professions, they are
doin' more today
To stop the weary sinner from the Gospel's
shinin' way
Than all the books of infidels, than all that
has been tried
Since Christ was born at Bethlehem—since
Christ was crucified.

How simple are the works of God, and yet
how very grand!
The shells in ocean caverns, the flowers on
the land,
He gilds the clouds of evenin' with the gold
light from his throne,
Not for the rich man only—not for the poor
alone.

Then why should man look down on man
because of lack of gold?
Why seat him in the poorest pew because
his clothes are old?
A heart with noble motives—a heart that
God has blest—
May be beatin' heaven's music 'neath that
faded coat and vest.

I'm old—I may be childish—but I love
simplicity,
I love to see it shinin' in a Christian piety.
Jesus told us in his sermons in Judea's
mountain's wild,
He that wants to go to heaven must be like
a little child.

Our heads are growin' gray, dear wife; our
hearts are beatin' slow;
In a little while the Master will call for us
to go.
When we reach the pearly gateways, and
look in with joyful eyes,
We'll see no stylish worship in the temple
of the skies.—*Sunday Republic.*

ORIGINAL ESSAYS.

THE SAINT'S LEGACY.

"Peace I leave with you, my peace I give unto you.—John 14: 27.

Who was better qualified and authorized to leave such a legacy than the Savior? An angel was despatched from Heaven to Shepherds, and subsequently joined by a multitude of the Heavenly host praising God, saying, "Glory to God in the highest," and announcing on earth "peace, good will toward men." Hence He is called the Prince of peace, His word the glad tidings of peace, His ministers the messengers of peace, and His Kingdom the kingdom of peace. Let us for a moment consider under what circumstances our Master uttered His parting legacy. To His disciples he said, "Little children, yet a little while I am with you. Ye seek me, and as I said unto the Jews, whither I go ye cannot come so now I say unto you." This evidently occasioned gloomy thoughts, and they began to be troubled. But now He says encouragingly, "Let not your hearts be troubled, ye believe in God, believe also in me. In my Father's house are many mansions; if it were not so, I would have told you, I go to prepare a place for you." While He was thus preparing them with the sad intelligence of His death, He leaves them this legacy, "peace I leave with you." This verily was a part of His last will and testament. Lands, houses, goods and silver and gold He had none; as a stranger He sojourned here, and had not where to lay His head, but such as He had He gave them. Why does He bestow it in the manner He did? First, to make it dearer to them, and second, to make it surer. It was the remembrance of their dying Lord and Savior. Anything left by a dying friend is dear and cherished, and considered of almost inestimable value. Second, to render it sure. If it be but a man's will and is confirmed, no man can disannul it, but here it is the Lord's testament, and every thing concurs to establish confidence. The will is written, witnessed and sealed. The testator dies, for the testament is of no force while the testator lives. The executor is true and honest, and will see all punctually fulfilled. This is His executor, "The Comforter, which is the Holy Ghost, whom the Father will send in my name He shall teach you all things, and bring all to your remembrance whatsoever I have said unto you." Though He Himself bequeathed peace at His death to His disciples personally, it is still not confined to them. In receiving this assurance, they stood as the representatives of all His people, to the end of time. If we love and follow Him, we are as much included in the bequeathment as if we were mentioned by name. "Neither pray I for these alone, but for them also which shall believe on me through their word." We consider a legacy of earthly possessions very valuable, because it secures us a home while abiding here. But what is it in comparison with the legacy left by our Savior? If we have no peace of mind what are we? All the earthly possessions will not make us happy. Remorse of conscience and despair will seize hold on us, and will render us miserable and wretched beyond description. Earth is full of sorrows and Heaven cannot heal them. Why is this? Because we do not avail ourselves of the Savior's legacy. We do not love Him sufficiently "to observe all things whatsoever He has commanded us;" and to such only who obey Him in all things is His peace promised. If in possession of that legacy, we look from earth to Heaven,—have our meditations there, though prone to wander, yet that spirit of adoption with all our infirmities enables us to cry, "Abba Father." We have that consolation within ourselves, though the world hate us, God is our friend our hope and our refuge, and when the earthly curtains are drawn across our eyes, and all the noise and tumult are shut from our ears, it is then only to behold the effulgent glory beyond this vale of tears, and to hear the welcome plaudit and invitation, "Well done, thou faithful servant, enter thou into the joys of thy Lord." Then it is that we shall realize the final and glorious inheritance which the Savior has prepared for us. Hear Him once again. "Ye have heard how I said unto you, I go away and come again unto you. And if I go and prepare a place for you, I will come again and receive you unto myself, that where *I am*, there ye may be also." O, the blessed assurance of the Savior's company in the trying hour of death! "*I will come again.*" To conduct us to the mansions in the skies. "Yea" saith the Lord. Welcome, thrice welcome, Lord, speak, thy servant heareth.

S. B. FURRY.

Martinsburg, Pa.

THROUGH PASSENGERS.—People in the Church are like passengers in the cars. It is easy to see that some are through passengers; they have fixed for the journey, and are quite composed and resolved. They never leave the train because others leave. They intend "to finish their course." They know before they start of the trussels, tunnels, dangers and expenses, and count the cost of all. Others only set out for *Gain Station* or *Popularity depot*, and never go quite to *Castello.*

For the Pilgrim.

"THE LAYING ON OF HANDS."

The above is one of the prominent features of the doctrine of revealed religion; unhappily however, it has like many other of its tenets grown almost extinct in modern christendom. We purpose in the fear of the Lord, to hold forth in this essay, the doctrine of the above subject as portrayed in the Word of Divine Truth. We shall notice it under the following heads; viz., first, when initiated. Second its design. Third its perpetuation. Fourth, its objections.

1. *When instituted.* We find no occasion of its practice until after Pentecost. It is true, the Savior laid His hands on diseased persons at different times, thus restoring them to health, but as a religious rite, it was never in vogue until the apostles were fully qualified for the work. The first instance recorded under our notice, is Acts 6th chapter, where the Apostles called seven persons to their assistance in the labors of the church, "whom they set before the apostles and when they had prayed, they laid their hands on them."

2. *Its design which is two-fold.* First, with a view to receive the Holy Ghost. We have in 8th chapter of Acts narrated the event of Samaria's receiving the word through Philip's preaching, who it seems baptized converts, but omitted the laying on of hands (either for want of qualification or omission of duty.) "But when they at Jerusalem heard these glad tidings, they sent unto them Peter and John, who when they were come down prayed for them that they might receive the Holy Ghost, for as yet he had fallen on none of them only they were baptized in the name of the Lord Jesus. Then they laid their hands on them and they received the Holy Ghost." A second instance setting forth the design of this ordinance, is seen in the 19th chapter of Acts, where Paul found certain disciples who it seems had been baptized as they supposed unto John's baptism, but had not so much as learned that there was any Holy Ghost. Paul preached Christ to them and when they heard this they were baptized in the name of the Lord Jesus. And when Paul had laid his hands on them the Holy Ghost came on them." We have now given two instances which clearly proves the fact that the laying on of hands was observed with a view to impart the Holy Ghost. Kind reader, have you been baptized? If so, have you had the hands of the administrator laid upon you in connection with prayer? If not the work is deficient, and we urge upon you in harmony with the example above, to send for those who are qualified to complete the work.

A second design of the laying on of hands, was to set persons apart for an especial work. This was the case in the 6th chapter of Acts alluded to above. Those seven persons were chosen and set apart to aid the apostles in their labor. Again Acts 13 chapter affords us with one more evidence of the above truth, where we observe that there "Were certain prophets and teachers at Antioch, who administered unto the Lord; and while they fasted, the Holy Ghost said; separate me Barnabas and Saul to the work whereunto I have called them. And when they had fasted and prayed, they laid their hands on them and then sent them away." Paul had preached before, but he had never been set apart, never been fully qualified for his mission, until prayer, fasting and the laying on of hands was observed; then they (Barnabas and Paul), went forth fully qualified for their mission. We now have given two evidences showing the second design of the laying on of hands, and the Savior tells that "In the mouth of two or three witnesses every word may be established."

We have in the above, in part, sustained our third point, *i. e.*, its perpetuation. But under this head we wish especial attention given to the thought that the apostles, as we see above, practiced it in the first stages of their labors. Paul was subject to its observance and, in turn, like the faithful became teacher of the same doctrine. In 2d Timothy 1. 6, he remarks. "I put thee in remembrance that thou stir up the Gift of God which is in thee by the putting on of my hands." Here we learn the fact that Timothy was subject to the imposition of hands by Paul. And in 1 Timothy, 4: 14, he tells Timothy "Not to neglect the gift that is in thee by the putting on of the hands of the presbytery." Also 1 Timothy 5: 22. "Lay hands suddenly on no man." but as he elsewhere remarks, "Let them first be proven." Many churches have suffered much by not heeding the connected thought of the last two quotations. Laying hands suddenly on those in the church who are not proven is not commendable. We remember some years since of seeing a letter in some of our periodicals from the West, warning brethren against the evil of "laying hands suddenly on brethren for the Eldership, who were not proven, but were mere novices." It is certain that many congregations have suffered much, from a want on the part of those who have the care of the church. All evils are contagious let them prevail in any rank in religious society they will: but when it exists in the official department of the Church, the evil is greatly augmented; hence we see the propriety of the apostle so minutely setting forth the character of Elders or Bishops and Deacons. In Hebrews 6th chapter, the apostle takes occasion to enumerate several christian duties, and among them is that of the "Laying on of hands." From the above testimonies we think it evident, that the "Laying on of hands" was perpetual. *Imposition or the laying on of hands was an ancient and venerable rite used in the primitive church on several occasions, particularly in ordination, in absolution of penitents, in healing the sick, in conferring the gifts of the Holy Ghost." Burkit.* Buck also sanctions the above historical statement.

Lastly, we come to notice the objection, a prominent one of which is, that the laying on of hands was practiced by the apostles in the day of miracles, and as the day of miracles has ceased the laying on of hands should cease also. To this objection we would simply remark that if all was to cease that originated in the day of miracles our *holy religion* would be included. The imparting of the Holy Ghost by the laying on of hands is *no* miracle, although not unlike many other religious duties, originated and was performed in the day of miracles. We would call the attention of the reader to the fact that we baptize "for the remission of sins," by which the evil inhabitant is driven out, "the house is empty swept and garnished. Now in turn as a next step we observe "the laying on of hands," by which the holy occupant is invited in. In the above we fail to see, which of the two steps are the most miraculous, they are both important attainments, to which we arrive by a simple train of obedience. In the second place our opponents remark that "The laying on of hands" was observed with a view to impart the gifts of tongues. "*Wherefore tongues are for a sign not to them that believe but to them that believe not.*"—1 Cor. 14: 22. Here we have the object of the gift of tongues clearly stated. It is true we have one instance, in which the gift of tongues followed the gift of the Holy Ghost, which was consequent to the laying on of hands, Acts 19: 9. And two instances in which it followed the miraculous gift or descent of the Holy Ghost, Acts 2: 4, and 10: 4 6, but that the gift of tongues was not the uniform result of the laying on of hands is evident; neither had they a promise to that effect. It is further to be observed that the gift of tongues always followed and never preceded the reception of the Holy Ghost, for it is quite conclusive that no one was fully empowered to the work of miracles until their conversion was matured.

A third objection we are called upon to notice is, that "the laying on of hands" originated and ceased with the apostles. This is a mere assertion; and assertions in the absence of proof either *pro* or *con* avail nothing. We have seen in the above that the apostles (direct of the Savior) practiced it. Paul, "who was not taught of man, neither did he receive it of man, but by revelation," not only was subject to it but pressed it upon the Hebrews; and in his dying words urged Timothy not to neglect it.

It is true as we remarked above, it originated in the Apostles time and not in the Savior's, simply because we only had the promise of the Holy Ghost or comforter, after the Savior's departure.

We have noticed its origin, design, perpetration and its urgent command to be perpetuated; and are wholly unable to find even a hint of its having ceased. In conclusion "to the law and to the testimony if they speak not according to this word it is because they have no light in them."

I. T. ROSENBERGER.

Gilboa, O.

For the Pilgrim.

GOVERNMENT AND POLITICAL STRIFE.

Man has a King and a government already provided him; with a code of laws comprehending every emergency. This King is God himself, whether represented by Christ or the Father. He said to man, "I will be thy King" Hosea—13: 11. We are bound to accept him, and consequently to reject everything which stands opposed to him. "Fear God, and keep his commandments, for this is the whole duty of man," Eccles.—12: 13. This is the standard or rule of man's duty. Everything else must be in subordination, nothing to conflict. No opposing laws are required to complete our duty. All should be simplified in harmony with this. "And the government shall be upon his shoulder: and he shall be called—The Prince of Peace." Isa.—9: 6. All this was conferred on Christ. He was and is the Supreme Lawgiver of the whole human family, notwithstanding all the prevailing opposing influences. These can never change the duty of man. When government requires us to kill our fellowmen, God commands "Thou shalt not kill." The vengeance of the Almighty to the amount of seven-fold was incurred on any who might kill the murderer Cain. Man was never allowed to have an earthly king until he refused and rejected God. Then God gave him one in his anger. "I gave thee a king in mine anger, and took him away in my wrath." Hosea—13: 11. They had their choice, but not without the woeful consequences. They would lose their "goodliest young men" and much of their valuable possessions by rejecting God as their King, as seen in 1 Sam.—8. God frequently gives men up to destruction when they wilfully persist in an evil course. In like manner the young man was told to rejoice in his course. "Rejoice, O, young man in thy youth, and let thy heart cheer thee in the days of thy youth, and walk in the ways of thine heart, and in the sight of thine eyes; but know thou that for all these things God will bring thee into judgment." Eccl.—11: 9. But those who truly appreciate Christ "The Prince of Peace" and wish for the happy consequences will seek to obey his Word rather than the commandments of men. It will afford them the safest protection. But to trust in man as a lawgiver is always attended with danger when his laws are not in subordination to the higher law. When government is prepossessed of or assumes the power to take human life, we term it a war government. This is not in subordination to God, and for this reason dangerous to vote under such a goveronment for any purpose however proper or good, in itself considered when liable to involve political strife. To attempt to force men from the use or sale of strong drink or from any other evil by making laws to be enforced under a war system, might tend to lay the foundation of rebellion as truly as the efforts to abolish slavery did. This is no visionary idea, it has been proved by sad experience. Many men of good intentions in former years, by taking an active part in seeking by their right of suffrage to eradicate slavery from the land while under a military government, laid the temptation to yield to the war system to accomplish their purpose, and it resulted in one of the most horrid and bloody butcheries the country ever witnessed. When we know what has passed, how can we venture again in such a broad way leading to destruction? We earnestly caution and entreat all those who do not want another bloody rebellion to shun the first steps toward such a calamity. "It is an honor to cease from strife." Prov.—20: 3. "Leave off contention before it be meddled with" 17: 14. Cease to vote or to take any active part in war government. Were the principles of warfare or human butchery totally eradicated from government, it might be safe to co-operate in political affairs in projecting any reform. But while it is not, it is quite unsafe and inconsistent for the followers of the "Prince of Peace." We think it proper for all true friends of peace to hold on to the peace principle and avoid taking any part in what may lead to carnal war. We should shun the place of political suffrage as truly as we should the house of "the young wanton," fearing the end might be deplorable. "Her house is the way to hell, going down to the chambers of death." Prov.—7: 27. So is every place where the elementary principles of war originate. It is political strife in making laws, then of putting them in force. The next step is frequently attended with human butchery. But the only proper way is to seek to God for help and obey his Word according to Eccl.—12: 13.

T. F. Tukesbury.

Brentwood, N. H.

CHRIST THE RISEN SAVIOR.

Continued from Page 98.

"Now is Christ risen from the dead."

Thus the inhabitants of many cities and countres were appealed to, and the enemies of Christianity were challenged to disprove their pretensions, but none ever attempted to do it for the Jews themselves do not deny that many extraordinary works were performed by Jesus and his disciples, and the way in which they try to account for them is, that from the first their ancestors had nothing to object. In this manner the witnesses and proofs of our Lord's resurrection were multiplied in almost every part of the vast Roman empire, yea, God also bore them witness both in signs and wonders and with divers miracles and gifts of the Holy Ghost. And can any man suppose that a general belief could ever have prevailed through whole nations of such public and extraordinary events without any person attempting to deny them, if they had not actually happened, and been so notorious as to be incontrovertible. The chosen witnesses of our Lord's resurrection were likewise the principal writers of the New Testament, and the whole was doubtless written under their inspections. Now in these books prophecies are inserted which have been fulfilling ever since to the present day. "The people shall be led away captive into all nations and Jerusalem shall be trodden down of the Gentiles until the times of the Gentiles be fulfilled." Has not this been actually the case with the Jews and with Jerusalem during eighteen hundred years? Could human sagacity have foreseen such an unparalleled series of events, or would God have thus confirmed the testimony of impostors, and does not this prophecy thus wonderfully accomplished, demonstrate the resurrection of Christ and the truth of Christianity?

The coming of the man of sin with lying, miracles, doctrines of demons worshipping of angels, prohibitions of marriage and commands to abstain from meat, the inquisitions, usurpations and persecutions of the Roman antichrist with various other particulars were most exactly and circumstantially predicted by the several witnesses of our Lord's resurrection, and the accomplishment of these prophecies are many divine attestation of their testimony for the satisfaction of all succeeding generations.

The Jewish ritual or the Pagan theology was intimately connected with the foundation of the several governments then existing in the world and all the learning, ingenuity and authority on earth were engaged in their support, yet a few unarmed, obscure, unlettered men, by preaching a crucified and risen Savior in the midst of persecution and sufferings, established Christianity on an immovable basis and their successors following their example, so wonderfully prevailed that at length Judaism and Paganism fell before them, and the religion of Jesus was professed by many nations, and however corrupted or despised, it subsists to this day. Whatever men may insinuate concerning the ministers of religion, it is an undenied fact that plain preaching, fervent prayer, holy lives and patient sufferings were the only weapons that the primitive preachers of the Gospel, used to oppose all the authority and learning of the world which were resolutely implanted against them and yet they decidedly triumphed in a contest apparently so unequal. As wise men will always allow that every effect is produced by some adequate cause, but what adequate cause can be assigned unless we allow that Christianity was of God, and men could not overthrow it.

We may now, I trust, confidently say that no other past event was ever proved by such a body of evidence. Who doubts whether Alexander conquered Darius, yet who can produce the tenth part of the proof in respect of this event which hath even at this time been stated of our Lord's resurrection? But men can believe that Alaxander conquered Darius without either parting with their sins or feeling uneasiness of conscience while the truth of the gospel is very alarming to all who walk according to the course of the world and neglect the salvation of Christ. It would be the grossest inconsistency and the most absurd trifling to contend earnestly that Christ is risen, and then overlook or deny the peculiar doctrines which His resurrection was intended to authenticate. We infer therefore from our subject that Jesus is indeed the Son of God. On account of various expressions which He used in speaking of Himself, He was charged with blasphemy and with making Himself equal with God. For this crime He was condemned by Caiaphas and the Jewish council who said before the Roman governor, "We have a law and by our law he ought to die, because He made Himself the Son of God." The Centurion who attended His crucifixion could not but know for what crime He suffered, when therefore he witnessed the miracles which accompanied His death, he cried, "Truly He was a righteous person, truly this was the Son of God." When incredulous Thomas was at length, convinced that Christ was risen, from all that he had before heard, seen, believed or hoped, seems at once to have rushed into his mind and he exclaimed in adoration, "My Lord and my God." Thus was Jesus declared to be the Son of God with power by the resurrection from the dead. He was demonstrated to be the promised Messiah, the seed of the woman, the seed of Abraham, the son of David, Emanuel, the mighty God, the everlasting Father, the Prince of Peace, Jehovah our righteousness, and whatever the prophets, from the beginning had spoken concerning the expected glorious Redeemer. All that had been spoken of Himself was likewise thus fully proven to be true. It now was manifest that He was warranted to say, "I and the Father are one." "He that hath seen me hath seen the Father. Before Abraham was, I am. I am the way, the truth and the life, no man cometh to the Father but by me. No man knoweth the Father but the Son, and he to whom the Son shall reveal Him. I am the light of the world, I am the resurrection and the life, if any man thirst let him come unto me and drink. The Father judgeth no man but hath committed all judgment to the Son, that all men should honor the Son even as they honor the Father. He that honoreth not the Son honoreth not the Father that sent Him. In short, the resurrection of Christ not only demonstrates the truth of Christianity, but the infallible certainty of all its doctrines, and authenticates the whole Scripture as divinely inspired. His testimony proves it in respect of the Old Testament and the new was written by His chosen witnesses and attested by all the miracles which they wrought in His name.

A Pilgrim.

To be Continued.

Editorial From Page 135

Our space is unusually crowded this week and a number of items left out that we intended for insertion. Money List, Obituaries, Correspondence and Editorial. We call special attention to "Laying on of Hands." In it are suggested of ideas of vital importance to the Church and demands a prayerful consideration. Next week will appear "The origin of the Antioch Bench, by Eld. D. P. Sayler."

A LIGHT TO THE WORLD.

What is Safe and what is not Safe; What is Right and what is not Right.

BY J. H. MOORE.

CHAP. V.—*Infant Baptism.*

Many people ransack the New Testament from beginning to end to find where some infant was baptized, and when they find none, instead of returning to the ark like Noah's dove, they imagine some in somebody's family. They had an idea before they looked that such things were to be found, and when they find themselves disappointed they will not remain so, but imagine that neither Lydia nor the Jailor could have families without children. They can imagine a host of things, but it seems an utter impossibility for them to imagine that all their children could have been grown up at that time. Such people can imagine a multitude of things; they can even see or seem to see all the waters of Jordan all dried up from the beginning to the end; they can even imagine that over one million of people could live, from year to year, in the city of Jerusalem where there was not even water enough to immerse a few thousand persons; they can imagine that the Eunuch was so forgetful, that he came all the way from Ethiopia to Jerusalem, and even forgot to put a cup of some kind in his chariot to drink out of, and consequently had to climb down out of the chariot into the water and get his feet all wet, just to have Philip sprinkle a little water on his head, all because he forgot to put a cup in the wagon. You may tell such people that baptism is for the remission of sins, and they will tell you that there is not one particle of virtue in baptism, and that it has nothing to do with the salvation of anybody; then they will turn right round and have their children baptized, as though the harmless little things could not be saved without it. They can imagine the thief on the cross as being perfectly safe without being baptized, but cannot bear the idea of sending their children to the grave without baptism, as though the sinless creatures were worse than the thief.

There is not one single instance in the Testament showing that infants were baptized, but adults were baptized by the thousands. It is then not a question whether adult baptism is right, but is infant baptism right? Here is the turning point. We are commanded to baptize believers and not unbelievers; children cannot believe, hence to baptize them would be to baptize unbelievers. Children cannot believe, and furthermore God does not require it of them; they are not sinners, from the fact there is no law for them to transgress. They do not need baptism, they are perfectly safe without it,

We propose to hold to the baptism of penitent believers, those who know the Lord, who love and are willing to obey him. This much we know is right, nobody disputes it; all the dispute is about infant baptism. This is not right, but we know that adult baptism is. All the doubting and disputing to be found in the whole matter is about infant baptism, not one word is heard against adult baptism. Everybody admits this to be both safe and right. Nobody denies adult baptism being either right or safe—all the fuss is about infant baptism, about the baptism of penitent believers there is no uncertainty, this we know is safe grounds, hence we will occupy this, and this only.

To be Continued.

OPPORTUNITIES are everywhere running to waste, like the rich golden fruit of the overburdened orchard. They are not confined to any particular locality. In running after them, we are the more certainly running away from them. They who do not, without delay, seek an interest in the salvation offered in the Scriptures, and secure an heirship to heaven, are madly running away from the most valuable *opportunities*, and losing the highest priviliges to which any can attain. Reader embrace this golden opportunity of becoming a christian. —*A. B. Brumbaugh.*

HEAVEN and earth, with all castles of kings and emperors, could not make a dwelling place for God, but in the man that keeps his word there he will dwell.

Isaiah calls the heavens his throne and the earth his footstool, but not his abode. We may search long to find where God is, but we shall find him in those who hear the words of Christ.

For the Lord Christ saith, "If any man love me, he will keep my words and we will make our abode with him."—*Luther.*

As the tempest tossed mariner hails with joy the rent in the cloud through which he sees the light blue sky, so the sin tossed soul that feels the rocky reefs of destruction nigh beholds the "cleft" in the "Rock of Ages" and with faith and hope flees hither for safety.—*J. S. Flory.*

A THIEF, coming to rob a house, said, "I dare not, there is a light in it." God grant that we may have the light of grace burning in our hearts as the best preservative against our spiritual enemies.—*Hill.*

Religious News.

C. H. SPURGEON of the London Tabernacle, it is said, is offered $50,000 to deliver fifty lectures in the United States, but the report is, he has declined the offer.

Henry Ward Beecher has nearly completed the second volume of the "Life of Christ." He is said to have become heartily tired of his work, having found it much more of a task than he had anticipated. Cynics intimate that he lacks sympathy with his subject.

THE Roman Catholics of the Canton of St. Gall, have adopted a new style of arguments against the Old Catholics. A number of young women have resolved that they will not dance with any young men who incline to the new heresy of denying the infallibility of the Pope. This must be to the young men worse than excommunication by the Pope.

THE sale of the pews in Mr. Hepworth's new church in New York City, on Monday, resulted very satisfactorily, the bidding being higher than generally anticipated. The first choice of the $1,200 pews was taken at $1,000, and the premiums varied from this sum to a few dollars for the cheaper pews. Among the principal bidders were Judge Hilton, Mr. Sniffin, the builder, and Mr. Anthony, who purchased from four to twelve pews each. The gross sum realized at the sale from the 347 pews was not far from $250,000.

LOSS OF THE ATLANTIC.—It is now currently reported that the loss of the Atlantic is laid to the charge of drunkenness. When we tell you that for the first months of the year there were totally lost, five hundred and eighty-six vessels you will conclude that to sail on the ocean is extremely dangerous but when the fact is established that three-fourths of all these disasters are the result of drunkenness it will be admitted that intemperance has more to do with it than the ocean. This demon is not only the curse of the seas but thousands and millions have been shipwrecked by it on dry land.

THE POPE'S ILLNESS.—The Catholic Church seems to be under a cloud of sorrow on account of the dangerous illness of Pope Pius IX. From latest accounts there seems to be no hopes for his recovery. Last May he passed his four score years. He stands high in the estimation of the Church and has passed through a number of trying ordeals the severest of which was when Victor Emanuel relieved him of his temporal power. The Cardinals now living are nearly all at Rome with the expectation of a speedy election of another Pope after the death of Pius IX.

MORMANISM.—Brigham Young the living wonder of the age has resigned some of his positions of secular affairs, with the intention of retiring somewhat from active duties He is now seventy-two years of age and is represented as being a shrewd business man and immensely rich. The railroad and telegraph, he looks upon as his greatest enemies and are filling Salt Lake the capital of his kingdom and the Mormon Paradise, with a Gentile element, that is very uncongenial to his way of thinking and it is now currently reported that he with a large body of his followers will strike for Arizona and there build up another city out of the reach of railroads, telegraphs and civilization.

SPIRITUALISM EXPOSED.—R Cev. P. McCarthy, a Universalist clergyman stated at the meeting of a Radical club in Philadelphia, the other day, that he had fully and carefully investigated the subject of spiritualism, had attended in London more than five hundred spiritual seances, and was therefore, justified in saying that there are no grounds for the belief that disembodied spirits ever visit this mundane sphere to move furniture or do other such work. He had, himself, often sat at the table at which the immortal Shakespeare had kept up a conversation, the effect of which was to surprise the speaker that there was so much falling off in the beauty of diction of Shakespeare's conversation when compared with the writings of the poet while in the flesh.

THE INDIAN POLICY.—It is a well known fact that the Quakers, time and again, requested the government to give them charge of the Indians of our frontiers with the hope of naturalizing them according to their "peace principles," but there were so many money leeches around Washington that it did not seem expedient. The result is, the Indian policy has been a miserable failure as far as Indians and peace is concerned but a grand success to those sent, in the way of realizing fortunes. At a late interview, General Canby and Dr. Thomas were deliberately murdered as the outgrowth of the miserable policy that always characterized the dealings with the Indians. That peace policy which alone can subdue the wild and savage passions of the red man, if wisely administered, is now condemned and to be abandoned, the cotton and extermination to be substituted. This is one of the modern blunders as the "peace policy" can never be condemned until fairly tested by peace men, as peace never thrives well behind bristling bayonets and the sword.

Youth's Department

COTTAGE BY THE SEA.

BY J. D. THOMAS.

Childhood days now pass before me,
Forms and scenes of long ago.
Like a dream they hover o'er me,
Calm and bright as evening glow.
Days that know no shade of sorrow,
There my young heart pure and free,
Joyful hailed each coming morrow,
In the cottage by the sea.

CHORUS.—In the cottage by the sea,
In the cottage by the sea,
Joyful hailed each coming morrow
In the cottage by the sea.

Fancy sees the rose-tree twining
Round the old and rustic door,
And below the white beach shining,
Where I gathered shells of yore,
Hears my mother's gentle warning,
As she took me on her knee;
And I feel again life's morning,
In the cottage by the sea.

What though years have rolled above me,
Though mid fairer scenes I roam,
Yet I ne'er shall cease to love thee,
Childhood's dear and happy home!
And when life's long day is closing,
Oh! how pleasant it would be,
On some faithful heart reposing
In the cottage by the sea.

KIND WORDS.

When I was quite young I learned the value of kindness. Previous to this I considered it as but a duty to be performed by men and women only, to each other. As an example of this, I supposed if a person were sick, her neighbor should sit by her and talk in such a manner as not to be rude; or if a person were sad or had trouble, his neighbor should sympathize with him.

I was nine years old when we moved to a village where we knew no one. The first woman with whom we got acquainted with was one of those persons who deem their neighbors inferior to themselves. Accordingly we (our family) had formed an opinion of each person in the place, from what she had told us. This person was rough in her manners; another kept an unclean house; Mrs. C. wasn't accommodating at all.

At school I did not like the appearance of my schoolmates. I chose one of these as my friend in all things. At no time was I so happy as when in Ella's company. This was in June, and there were many flowers in a slough near a schoolhouse, that we used to gather after school.

One day when Ella took her dinner to school she wanted me to ask her mother if she might go with me after flowers that day. What! ask that woman who walks past with her head so high, and looks so hateful! At last I said I would. After dinner I went to her.

"Mrs. Ferris, please may Ella go with me for flowers after school?"

"Yes, most certainly she may," she answered, pleasantly.

Dear friends, have you any idea how I felt as I went to school? I told mother of her gentle reply. From that time until now I never have paid any attention to slander; and ever after Mrs. Ferris and my mother were firm friends.—*Young Folk's Rural.*

BE HONEST CHILDREN.

I suppose some of the little boys who read this will say, when they look at the title of the piece, "That's easy enough; I am honest; I never took anything that did not belong to me in my life." Well, that is right; but there is more in being truly honest, perhaps than you think. I will tell you a story, and then you will understand me.

In a country school—the school of which I am teacher—a large class was standing to spell. In the lesson there was a very "hard word" as boys say. But I put the word to the scholar at the head and he missed it. I passed it to the next, and the next, and so on through the class, till it came to the last scholar, the smallest of the class, and he spelled it right at least I understood him so, and he went to the head, above seventeen boys and girls all older than himself. I then turned and wrote the word on the blackboard, so that they might all see how it was spelled. But no sooner had I written it than the little boy at the head cried out, "O, I didn't say so Miss W———. I said e instead of i!" and he went back to the foot of his class, of his own accord, quicker than he had gone to the head. Was he not an honest boy? I should have always thought he spelled it right, if he had not told me; but he was too honest to take any credit that did not belong to him.

SIX SHORT HINTS FOR THE YOUNG.

1. Never neglect daily private prayer; and when you pray, remember that God is present, and that He hears your prayers. (1 John 5: 15.)

2. Never neglect daily private Bible-reading; and when you read, remember that God is speaking to you, and that you are to believe and act upon what He says. All backsliding begins with the neglect of these two rules. (John 5: 39.)

3. Never let a day pass without doing something for Jesus. Every morning reflect on what Jesus has done for you, and then ask yourself, "What am I doing for Him?" Matt. 5: 13-16.)

4. If you ever are in doubt as to a thing being right or wrong, go to your room, and consider whether you can do it in the name of Jesus, and ask God's blessing upon it. (Col. 3: 17.) If you cannot do this it is wrong. (Rom. 14: 23.)

5. Never take your Christianity from Christians, or argue, because such and such people do so and so, that, therefore, you may. (2 Cor. 10: 12.) You are to ask yourself, "How would the Lord have me act?" Follow Him. (John 10: 27.)

6. Never trust your feelings, or the opinions of men, if they contradict God's Word. If authorities are pleaded, still "Let God be true, but every man a liar." (Rom. 3: 4.)

"Renew my will from day to day;
Blend it with Thine, and take away
All that now makes it hard to say,
Thy will be done."

Correspondence.

A Reporter is wanted from every Church in the brotherhood to send us Church news, Obituaries, Announcements, or anything that will be of general interest. To insure insertion, the writers name must accompany each communication. Our Invitation is not personal but general—please respond to our call.

HARD TIMES.

Dear Pilgrim:—Hard times is the general cry with everybody and I have been made to wonder whether any one has considered why times are hard. Every thing is a good price wages are good but all cry, hard times, and why? Now let each one think for themselves. Perhaps we have spent money for that which was neither good for the soul nor body, then it must have been ill spent, and done us harm, and made times harder with us, but the hardest is not yet come. We perhaps, have spent money for things that are abominable for we are likely to spend for that which is pleasing to the eye and we are told that which is pleasing to the eye is an abomination in the sight of God, and what seems to be the most pleasing to the eye at the present time? I suppose all will admit it is that of dress. Now when we are decorating our bodies with those abominable fashions which are uncalled for we are doing something that is neither good for cold or heat and even uncomfortable and causes us to cry out hard times. Ah how much better could we have spent those hours that we spent in making ourselves abominable in the sight of God, had we been in our closets or some lonely place asking God to feed and clothe our bodies with the necessaries of life and to feed our souls with the heavenly food. How lamentable it is to think of the time when we will have to appear before the judgement seat with all those abominations staring us in the face, and will be made to cry out for the rocks and mountains to fall upon us and hide us from the face of him that sitteth upon the throne. Is it not enough to make the heart of stone burst into tears when we reflect that those abominations which we now have upon us will banish us from the presence of God and heaven's eternal happiness, and cast us down into a dismal hell, and in its indescribable torments. Then we can only look back and say, I done it myself, I had no need of doing it, I seen others that did not have those abominations on and they stood as high in society as I did. What folly. Things have caused us hard times in this world, and may cause us much harder in the next. Let all conclude to follow the meek and lowly Jesus so that we may have a hope of striking glad hands on the sunny banks of eternal deliverance.

WM. MALLORY.

Carterville, Va.

Dear Reader:—Out of a feeling of love I pen a few lines for the PILGRIM on the subject of pride which I think is one of the growing evils of the Church. Do we ever think back and remember what we promised at the water-side in our baptismal covenant before God and a large congregation of brethren, sisters and friends? We there promised to renounce satan, all sinful practices and ungodly lusts, and how many of us are doing so today? I fear the number is alarming ly small. Why is it that our garments must be cut after the fashion of the world, our hair worn after the latest style and many other little things, and some big ones that is not in accordance with the order of the Church and the spirit of the Gospel.

We say we are not proud yet we wear, desire and have about us those unnecessary and forbidden things. No matter what we may say, it is pride or we would not have them about us. It is either on account of a lusting after such things or a fear that the world will laugh at our plainness.

A few words to our sisters. Do you leave off these small things which generally lead to large ones if not guarded against. How often do we see our sisters with an unnecessary amount of ribbons and edging on their apparel, which is to be modest, some without caps and their fingers loaded with rings. Be careful, these things are not of God but of the world. Let us all be on our guard and see that we live out a profession and remain true to the covenant we have made.

G. W. FESLER.

Anderson, Ind.

WEVERTON,
April 11th, 1873.

Dear Mr. Editor:—I take the earliest opportunity to acknowledge your very welcome paper. My object is to improve the occasion some, and to exchange ideas. I see you have some professional Christians among your contributors, but one thing I can say, they have not gone so far as I have. I notice one on "Cosmetics?" Men cannot love God unless he first obeys his law. The gift of the Holy Ghost come by prayer. Prayer itself is satfaction or the evidence of faith, after this the law of God, the commandments, and the law of Jesus Christ. God requires a practical acknowledgment. Without this you are not subject to his consideration. You are supposed to be an enemy of God without this absolute submission. The tree of Knowledge in the Garden of Eden was the foundation of law. Without law man would not be perfect. We see where man is by this disregard of God's command. Every man is a free moral agent. He must submit to God's will or perish. His punishment is hell fire. The law of God means what it says. Figures of speech is not wise unless it explains itself. It will do in conversation but it will not do as a law to hand down to man. The world could not do without science but keep it away from God's word. If God's law is not made to meet the intelligence of man it is no law. Christ says, "man must not be ashamed to confess me. He that does not live up to the commands of God makes a compromise and perverts the walks of God. It is hard to give up this world when we do not see anything in return, consequently the necessity of faith. I see people having more than their brethren. Some with great riches. Who are they? They are not God's people, they are generally people that control. God help them. Their reward is on earth. They are loud in faith to God but every act proves them to be servants of satan. All the world must go to destruction for want of some one brave and honorable enough to serve his Master. So long as it will not touch our pockets or interrupt the pleasures of this life it is all right, but where are those three hundred thousand souls that have passed away and what causes all the persecution and misery on the earth? The church must kneel to Baal's god and no one dare shoulder the cross and say that Christ is king. I do not wish to complain. We are brothers. Christ must be acknowledged king. Man is the temple of God. If so, can he be destroyed at the pleasure of man? No, God controls all to the glory and honor of his name. The day shall come when they will murder you and think they do God's service. This world is an enemy to God. Heaven is the home of the Christian. When man can see in this manner then and not till then, will he not love the things of this life.

GEO. S. BINGHAM.

SHIPPENSBURG, PA.
April 19, '73.

Dear Pilgrim:—On the morning of the 8th inst., I in company with brother P. P. B., started for Shippensburg, Cumberland Co., Pa. The morning was a beautiful one; winter like a sliding car seemed to be taking its departure, and in its place approaching the ever welcome Spring. The general animation observable by all nature, and the apparent appreciation of God's goodness, gave enchantment to every view, and as we went dashing through valleys, forests, tunnels, towns, and along rivers, we saw much to please and entertain. On, on, we went and in a short time we were at McVeytown Station. Here we had but time to take the hand of our much esteemed Eld. Joseph R. Hanawalt who informed us that he had buried two of his children, and that several more were not expected to live. This intelligence, and the sadness depicted in the countenance of our brother made us feel that this world is truthfully a mixture of grief and sorrow. While some hearts throb with joy, others are sad; the opening bud of the inverted year brings to some a bitter cup, and many are the prayers, "If it be thy will, let it pass by." Bro. Joseph is naturally fond of children, and this affliction will wound him severely. There are but few who will form the acquaintance of a family of children, and gain their confidence and respect like brother Hanawalt. When a boy it was a happy time when he came to visit us, and well do I remember those few words that touched my heart, and aided me in enlisting in the service of Jesus.

About noon we arrived at Harrisburg and in a short time we were off for Shippensburg, but as brother P. P. B. had some business in Mechanicsburg, we stopped there. While here we called upon Bro. Burkholder, and another brother whose name we cannot now remember. Both are in business, and from appearance there is not the least probability that there business is driving *them*. We arrived at Shippensburg in the evening and then wended our way to the place where I expect to make my home for a few months. I will stop with David Newcomer who resides about one hundred yards from the State Normal School at Shippensburg. As the school was not to open until next Monday and having a desire to visit some in the vicinity of Waynesboro, we passed on to that place. Here we were met by our friend Anson Good, whose acquaintance I formed at the Millersville Normal last winter. We were glad to meet him, and his kindness, shown toward us will be long remembered. Our visit to his home was a pleasant one indeed. We also met and formed the acquaintance of Bro. J. Zook, Jr. He is teaching in the Waynesboro School and appears to be pursuing his calling with energy and zeal. Bro. Zook is a graduate of the State Normal School at Millersville and has not only what is comprehended in the science of education but elocation as an art, and consequently prepared for teaching. We hope that the church at no far distant period will feel that it needs such brethren to labor in its own limits and that it will give them an opportunity to work. We also met Bro. D. B. Mentzer and a number of others with whom we had been acquainted for some time, and feel indebted to all for the kindness shown toward us.

On Sabbath we had the pleasure of attending the Brethren's Sabbath School which was being organized. The brethren at the helm seem to be in earnest, and they will, no doubt have an interesting Sabbath School. On Monday morning we returned to Shippensburg and on Tuesday attended the opening exercises of the school. The examinations for classification commenced early in the morning and continued until noon. In the afternoon a number of addresses were given to a very large audience. This School building is said to be one of the finest Normal buildings in the State and has every appearance for a grand success. It opened out with 300 students, and there are now perhaps nearly four hundred. This week was spent principally in classifying and it will be a few days yet before things will be in good working order.

In conclusion, I will say to the brethren, my object in going to school is not to make a display of education but to enable me more fully to discharge the duties that are devolving upon me in the position in which I am now placed, and the advantages to be derived from it when lawfully used.

J. B. B.

BLACKSBURG, VA.
April, 16, 1873

Dear Bros. Brumbaugh:—In chronicling the death of friend Etzler (see obituary) and the circumstances which preceded it seem to justify more than ordinary publicity.

About six years since he had the first stroke of paralysis. Three years later he had the second stroke, both on the right side, from which he never fully recovered. This is the third year since, and he and his friends had presentiments that this would be his last. He lived near Christiansburg, the county seat of this county, about 15 miles from this place, and as his wife's relations lived in this vicinity, they had a great desire to visit them before the expected summons came. Accordingly they set out on Saturday the 12th. He was enjoying usual health and was in a pleasant and cheerful mood. About 3 o'clock, p. m., when within a few hundred yards of our house he was smitten with the third stroke in the left side. His wife held him in the buggy till she drove to the gate when he was carried into the house and laid on the bed. His friends and relations were notified of the sad affair and came promptly to our aid and everything that affection could suggest was applied to effect his restoration but all was vain. Fifty hours after he was brought into the house his spirit departed from the earthly tenement. The funeral services were performed here at 11 o'clock of the 15th by Rev. W. Gardiner of the Methodist church, assisted by the brethren. The text of his discourse was the interrogators of Job, "If a man die shall he live again?" He spoke very impressively, assuming the affirmative as regards believers, and the negative as regards unbelievers. He was followed by Bro. A. Crumpacker, who, in his usual forcible style, testified that those things were true and abundantly proved from the Scriptures the verities of eternal life for the righteous and eternal death for the wicked. A large concourse of sympathizing friends were present and a deep solemnity pervaded the assembly. He was then buried in the graveyard one mile distant. He was a consistent member of the Methodist church for about fifty years. This sad event adds another to the numerous admonitions to be *always ready* for death. Without a moments warning he was an unconscious paralytic. We are equally liable to the same swift agency. His lonely widow is left childless to descend the western slope of life, and it was sorrowful indeed to see her return from the grave to the house of a stranger and gather up his hat and clothing and finish her journey alone without the pleasant company of her devoted husband. May she realize the comforting truth that the Christian's God is the especial protector of the widow, and, reposing her confidence in his promises, receive that strength and consolation that is the unfailing heritage of all the faithful.

D. C. MOOMAW.

Dear Pilgrim:—Please announce that the Spring Creek Church, composed of part of Dauphin and Lebanon counties have appointed a Lovefeast on the 16th and 17th of May next at the house of Bro. Jacob Long about 2½ miles south of Annville. We cordial invite ministerial aid.

Also some of our members wish the District Meeting published, still, therefore please say our District (eastern Pa.) Meeting will be held on the 15th of May next, but the delegates have to meet on the 14th. A previous conference fixed the meeting of delegates at 4 o'clock p. m., that is, to arrange matters and get business ready to commence on the morning of the 15th, at 8 oclock. Place of meeting is at Bro. Pfantz's about one mile from Lititz, Lancaster county Pa.

WM. HERTZLER.

[*Companion* please copy.]

Brother Brumbaugh:—Please announce in the PILGRIM that we will (if the Lord will) have our Lovefeast in the Dry Valley Meetinghouse, Mifflin Co., Pa., four miles east of Lewistown, ¼ miles from Maitland station, on the Sunbury and Lewistown R. R., on the 25th day of May next, commencing at 10 o'clock a. m., and dismissing at 12 o'clock, assembling again at 4 o'clock p. m. for evening services. Preaching next day in the forenoon. We give an invitation to all who have a desire to be with us, especially to ministering brethren.

JACOB MOHLER.

Notice to Brethren and Sisters Going to A. M.

I, to-day made arrangements with the Baltimore and Ohio R. R. company, and with its branches, from Baltimore to Washington, Weaverton to Hagerstown, Harpersferry to Harrisonburg, and Grafton to Parkersburg for half fare. No farther West however than Wheeling, friend Cole having no authority to control the division west of the Ohio river in such matters.

The conditions are the same as they were on former occasions on this road. Those going will start where they choose and pay their full fare to Cumberland, asking no questions, as agents along the line know nothing at all about it, and of course can give no information. At the place of meeting I will furnish all who apply and have complied with the conditions, with a certificate which will pass them to the place of starting free of charge.

If some one would, or could arrange with some line west of the Ohio river to connect these arrangements at Wheeling or Bellair, this would be the route for all west, and south of west to take. And whereas the B. & O. R. R. Co. has never refused to grant the brethren half fare privileges, while the Pittsburg, Fort Wayne & Chicago Co. has rarely, if ever granted it, I think the brethren are in duty bound to consider it. Last year they refused to abate one cent of my full fare going and coming, while the Pittsburg & Conellsville road, through the brethren, sent me, by telegraph, a pass to return free over the road.

D. P. SAYLER.

P. S. I am already furnished with the return certificates.

DIED.

GARVER.—In Germany Valley, Aughwick Congregation, Huntingdon county, Pa., March 25, '73, Bruce J., only son of B. F. and Sallie E. Garver, aged 1 year, 4 months and 5 days. Funeral services by Eld. John Spanogle.

Farewell dear Bruce, a long farewell,
For we shall meet no more
'Till we are raised with thee to dwell,
On Zion's happy shore.

The blooming cheek, the sparkling eye,
The form once brisk and gay,
Must now within the church-yard lie
Though you be far away.

His childish voice you'll hear no more,
No, no, 'tis silent here;
But it has joined the Heavenly choir,
In strains more sweet and clear.

The grass will each returning Spring.
Wave o'er his lowly bed;
And sweet song-birds his requiem sing,
For little Bruce is dead.

ANNIE M. BRIGHTEL.

MILLER.—In the Beaver Creek Congregation, near Bridgewater, Rockingham Co., Va., March 31st, '73, brother Joseph Miller, aged 49 years.

His sickness was of short duration, he leaves a sorrowing companion, (a sister), and 7 children, and a large connection of friends and relations to mourn their loss, but we hope their loss is his eternal gain. He was a good husband, a good neighbor and a good citizen and prominent brother, —was beloved by all who knew him. His remains were taken to Beaver Creek on the 2d of April, where the occasion was improved by brother Solomon Garber and others from Rev. 14:13-14

MILLER.—In the same congregation; near Sangersville, Augusta Co., April 11, '73, sister Christena Miller, aged 80 years, consort of Abraham Miller dece'd.

She leaves a large connection of children and grand, and great grand children, and sympathizing friends and relations which are scattered through different States. She was confined to her bed for several weeks. A few weeks prior to her death she called for the Elders and was anointed in the name of the Lord. She desired to be absent from the body and be present with the Lord. Her life was one that is worthy of imitation. On her death bed she selected the 528th hymn to be sung at her funeral. Occasion improved by brother Geo. Wine and others, from Rev. 14:13. S. N. WINE.

BOCK.—In the Dry Creek Congregation, Linn Co., Iowa, April 12, '73, sister Mary, oldest daughter of brother Samuel, and sister Catharine Bock, aged 19 years, 3 months and 23 days.

The subject of the above notice contracted a severe cold some time during last Summer, which produced that dreadful scourge of the human family, consumption. In November she had to quit work, and from that time she gradually wasted away and became weaker to the last. One week previous to her death, she was taken down into the watery grave and there buried with Christ in baptism. On Sunday her remains were followed to the grave by an immense concourse of people. Funeral services by the brethren from 1 Peter, 1: 24: 25.

JACOB BOCK.

NOFFSINGER.—In the Lower Miami Church, Montgomery Co., Ohio, April 12, '73, sister Mary Noffsinger, aged 80 years, and 3 months. Funeral occasion improved by the brethren from 2 Tim. 4: 6 7-8.

She was a member of the Church for many years, and truly a mother in Israel. During her affliction she called for the Elders of the Church and was anointed with oil in the name of the Lord. She bore her affliction with christian fortitude,—was submissive to the will of the Lord, and waited patiently for the change, having this hope that being absent from the body she would be present with the Lord.

(*Vindicator*, please copy.)

DANIEL BOCK.

SHOWALTER.—In the James Creek Congregation, Huntingon Co., Pa., April 15. '73, sister Jane, wife of brother Frederick Showalter, aged 33 years.——Funeral services by the editors, Eld. Geo., and H. B. Brumbaugh, to a large and sympathizing congregation.

The death of our sister was unexpected and her sickness of short duration. In the morning she was as well as usual, at about 9 o'clock A. M., she took convulsions and coutinued to have one after another until death released her sufferings which occurred in the evening of the same day. Truly, in the midst of life death is at the door.

GOUGHNOUR.—In the Desmoins Valley church, Iowa, our much beloved sister Mary Goughnour, April 11, '71, aged 73 years, 2 months and 19 days. Funeral discourse improved by the brethren.

She was a much beloved sister, had been a very exemplary member of the church for many years. She leaves a large circle of friends and acquaintances to mourn their loss, but her eternal gain. O. R. BAKER.

(*Companion*, please copy.)

TETWILER.—In the Clover Creek congregation, near Williamsburg, Pa., April 10, '73, sister Maggie, wife of brother Andrew Tetwiler, age between 31 and 32 years. She leaves a sorrowing husband and three small children to mourn their loss. Funeral by the brethren from Rev. 14: 13. JOS. S. SNOWBERGER.

ETZLER.—At the residence of the writer Montgomery county Va., on the 14, ult. Mr. John Etzler, of Paralysis, in the 67, year of life. Funeral services by Rev. W. Gardiner, assisted by the brethren.

O. C. MOOMAW

ANNOUNCEMENTS.

Middle District of Pa., at Clover Creek, May 15.

West Va., Seneca District, Randolph Co., 9th and 10th of May.

Middle District of Iowa, in Dallas Co., on the 19th day of May.

Northern Indiana and Michigan, ½ mile west of Goshen, Ind., May 1st.

North-eastern District of Ohio, Jonathan's Creek Congregation, Perry Co., on May 20th.

Middle District of Ind., Bachelor Run Congregation, Lower Church, second Friday after Good Friday

Please announce through the PILGRIM that our District Meeting will be held on the 13th of May in the Cook's Creek Congregation, Rockingham Co., Va.

SOLOMON GARBER.

Please notice through the PILGRIM that the District Meeting of Western Pa., will be held at the Fairview Meeting house in the George's Creek branch, Fayette Co. Pa., on Wednesday 21st of May, '73.

J. FOUST.

Please announce that the District Meeting of North-Western Ohio will be held, the Lord willing, with the brethren of Crawford Co., at the house of brother John Brilharts, on the Base Line on the 23 day of May, and on the 24, the day following, there will be a Communion meeting at the same place. A general representation is desired. ISRAEL ROOP.

LOVEFEASTS.

Falls City, Nebraska, May 3, and 4.

Spring Run, Mifflin county, Pa., May 27, 28.

Beaver Creek, Wednesday May 4, at 1 P. M.

Manor Church, Tuesday May 13, commencing at 9 o'clock A. M.

Shade Creek Congregation, Somerset co. Pa., May 20, commencing at 10 a. m.

Champaign Co., Ill., at Geo. Dillings, 5 miles east of Urbana, 7th and 8th of June.

Colorus, York county, Pa., on the 10th and 11th of June at the East Colorus M H.

Welch Run, Thursday May 15, commencing at 1 o'clock P. M., continuing next day till noon. E. SLIFER.

First District of Virginia, on Friday and Saturday before the fourth Sunday in April, at the Valley M. H., Botetourt Co., 1 mile south of Amsterdam.

Little Swatara Church, at Bro. Henry K. Bixler's 2 miles northeast of Jonestown, Lebanon Co., Pa., 12th and 13th of June, Brethren returning from A. M., are invited to stop.

The Weekly Pilgrim.

JAMES CREEK, PA., April 29, 1873.

MEMORIAL.

Seldom were we called upon to receive so sad an intelligence as that of the departure of our departed sister, wife of Bro. F. Showalter. It seems only a few years since we saw them setting out on life's uneven journey together having pledged to each other to live together for their mutual good. Sister Jane was a woman of fair intelligence and her first thought seemed to be to set her house in order and devote herself and time to the service of the Lord. This she done as a wise master builder, by digging deep and making the foundation sure, building alone on Christ the Rock of Ages.

After a few years of struggling with the stern realities of life, and they had secured for themselves a place which while on earth we call home. Beside them were growing up two little branches, Ida and Effie, which seemed to complete their ideal of home on earth. They, no doubt, often looked forward into the then promising future with lively expectation—but what are human expectations! They are as the morning vapor or the dew that clings to the tender blade for a moment and then passes away. God had given them, and in His wisdom He saw good to take them away. About two years ago and the happy jubilant little spirits were taken home and their bodies tenderly conveyed to the grave over which God has now spread his mantle of green. This was a sad bereavement to the fond parents and made a wound which nothing but the hope of a reunion in heaven could heal. Again God has called and mother is taken home to meet her loved ones on the "Shining shore" beyond the stream of death. The expectant family, on this side, is now small, only a bereft father and a motherless little daughter. According to the ties of nature this seems hard but we would have our brother know that it was the hand of the Lord and that he doeth all things well. First the cloud, then the storm, then the rain, then the calm and *then*, thank God, the sun comes forth in all its loveliness. So it will be with you, brother, and so it will be with us all if we love Jesus and abide our time. Our days are numbered and one after another of us will be called to lay our armor by and go to our reward, therefore it behooves us all not so much to mourn for the sainted dead as for ourselves and our children.

Sister Showalter lived as we have reason to believe she died, a faithful servant of Jesus and for her we have a lively hope. She ever lived true to the profession she made and was loved and respected by those with whom she associated, and in the family circle and church her presence will be greatly missed, but our consolation is that our loss will be her great gain.

JAMES CREEK.

As before announced we have appointed meeting for over Sunday prior to our District Meeting and invite some of the brethren to stop with us. Those stopping will take the "Broad Top" road at Huntingdon and get a ticket for Marklesburg. By coming this way it will cost something over a dollar less and not more than 1½ miles further to walk. It will be across a mountain but there is a good pike and also a hack from the morning train. Had arrangements been made for all delegates to pass over the "Broad Top" road, which would have been cheaper and better, we could have received excursion tickets. Those stopping at James Creek can take, at Huntingdon, either the morning or evening train. The morning train connects with the Pa. Central and the evening with the Pacific Express. We will be glad to hear from those who intend to stop with us.

GENERAL INTELLIGENCE.

ATTEMPT TO KILL FATHER GAVAZZI.—The *Swiss Times*, of a recent date, says that when Father Gavazzi was preaching on the suppression of religious corporations, two men, one of them a taylor from Faenz, thirty years of age, and the other a Roman student, eighteen years of age, were discovered in the act of firing a large bombshell, full of iron and powder, on the door of the Evangelical chapel, in Via del Corallo. The two miscreants, taken in the act by the guards of the Questura, were arrested before they could accomplish their infernal design. It was, indeed, most fortunate that the bomb did not explode, or it must have caused great damage, the room being full of people. The arrested men were immediately given up to the Procuratore del Re, to whom also was delivered the sequestered bomb. The above-mentioned student had been arrested once before for injury to the arms of Savoy, for having taken part in a demonstration on the death of a Pontificial gendarme.

An Indiana Sunday-school man writes to a Bible firm in New York: "Send me on some Sunday-school papers and books. Let the books be about pirates and Indians as far as possible."

This is a joke; but the query comes in whether much of the reading which is already furnished to the children does not foster a taste for something stronger in the shape of pirates and Indians?

$50.000

Will be distributed this year, to the subscribers for the AMERICAN WORKING PEOPLE, a large quarto, 16 page Monthly, costing but $1.50 per year. It gives a premium to every subscriber, varying from 25 cents in value up to $2, $5, $10, $20, $100, $200, and $500 in Greenbacks besides Watches, Sewing Machines, Parlor Organs and numerous other premiums of value. Send for specimen and circulars to

CARSON & Co.,
Mar. 18-2m. Pittsburgh, Pa.

WANTED. We will give men and women

Business that will Pay

from $4 to $8 per day, can be pursued in your own neighborhood; it is a rare chance for those out of employment or having leisure time; girls and boys frequently do as well as men. Particulars free.

Address J. LATHAM & CO.,
292 Washington St., Boston, Mass.

DYMOND ON WAR.

An inquiry into the Accordancy of War, with the Principles of Christianity, and an examination of the Philosophical reasoning by which it is defended. With observations on some of the causes of war and on some of its effects. By Jonathan Dymond. Sent from this office, post paid, for 50 cts.

TUNE BOOK.

The Brethren's Tune and Hymn Book, is a compilation of Sacred Music adapted to all the hymns in the Brethren's New Hymn Book. It contains over 350 pages, printed on good paper and neatly bound. We will send it to any address, post paid at $1.25 per copy.

GOOD BOOKS.

How to read Character, Illus. Price,	$1.25
Combe's Moral Philosophy,	1.75
Constitution of Man. Combe,	1.75
Education. By Spurzheim,	1.50
Memory—How to Improve it,	1.50
Mental Science, Lectures on,	1.50
Self-Culture and Perfection,	1.50
Combe's Physiology, Illus.	1.75
Food and Diet. By Pereira,	1.75
Natural Laws of Man,	.75
Hereditary Descent,	1.50
Combe on Infancy,	1.50
Sober and Temperate Life,	.50
Children in Health—Disease,	1.75
The Science of Human Life,	3.50
Fruit Culture for the Million,	1.00
Saving and Wasting,	1.50
Ways of Life—Right Way,	1.00
Footprints of Life,	1.25
Conversion of St Paul,	1.00

A large number of our patrons are receiving our books as noticed below, as premiums, and express themselves highly pleased with them. Others who are not agents, have enquired whether we keep them for sale. We have now made arrangements with Mr. Wells to furnish any of their publications post paid at publishers prices. Orders for books must be accompanied with the cash, and plain directions for sending them.

Weaver's Works for the Young. Comprising "Hopes and Helps for the Young of both Sexes," $3.00.

Life at Home; or, The Family and its Members. A work which should be found in every family. $1.50. Extra gilt, $2.00.

Hand-book for Home Improvement: comprising "How to Write," "How to Talk," How to Behave," and "How to do Business," in one vol. 2.25.

Man and Woman: Considered in their Relations to each Other and to the World. 12mo, Fancy cloth; Price $1.00.

The Right Word in the Right Place. A New Pocket Dictionary and Reference Book. Cloth, 75cts.

Hopes and Helps for the Young of both sexes. Relating to the Formation of Character. Choice of Avocation, Health, Conversation, Social Affection Courtship and Marriage. Muslin, $1:50.

The Emphatic, Diaglott; or The New Testament in Greek and English. Containing the Original Greek Text of the New Testament, with an Interlineary Word for-word English Translation. Price, $4.00; extra fine binding, $5.00.

Oratory—Sacred and Secular; or, the Extemporaneous Speaker. Price $1.50.

Conversion of St. Paul. 12mo. fine edition, $1. Plain edition, 75 cents.

Man, in Genesis and in Geology; or, the Biblical Account of Man's Creation, tested by Scientific Theories of his Origin and Antiquity. One vol, 12mo, $1.00.

$5 to $20 per day! Agents wanted! All classes of working people, of either sex, young or old, make more money at work for us in their spare moments or all the time than at anything else. Particulars free. Address G. Stinson & Co., Portland, Maine.

THE

HOUSEHOLD TREASURE.

Containing several hundred Valuable Receipts for cooking well at a moderate expense, making Dyes, Coloring, Cleaning and Cementing. This book also points out in plain language, free from Doctors' terms the diseases of men, women and children, and the latest and most approved means used for their cure, to which is added a description of the Medicinal Roots and Herbs, and how they are to be used in the cure of diseases.

This is a work of considerable importance and we offer it to our readers as being a valuable accession to every household. Sent from this office to any address, post-paid, for 25 cents.

WANTED BOOK AGENTS

FOR THE

FUNNY SIDE OF PHYSIC.

800 *Pages*, 250 *Engravings*.

A startling expose of Medical Humbugs of the past and present. It ventilates Quacks, Imposters, Travelling Doctors, Patent Medicine Venders, Noted Female Cheats, Fortune Tellers and Mediums, and gives interesting accounts of Noted Physicians and Narratives of their lives. It reveals startling secrets and instructs all how to avoid the ills which flesh is heir to. We give exclusive territory and liberal commissions. For circulars and terms address the publishers. J. B. BURR & HYDE,
Hartford, Conn., or Chicago, Ill.

AGENTS WANTED FOR THE

UNCIVILIZED RACES OF MEN

In all countries of the world.

Being a comprehensive account of their Manners and Customs, and of their Physical, Social, Mental, Moral, and Religious Characteristics.

By REV. J. G. WOOD, M. A., F. L. S.
500 *Engravings*, 1500 *Super Royal Oc. Pages*

In two Volumes, or two Volumes in one. Agents are making over $100 per week in selling this work. An early application will secure a choice of territory. For terms address the publishers.

J. B. BURR & HYDE,
Hartford, Conn., or Chicago, Ill.

TRACTS.

"ANXIOUS BENCH RELIGION EXAMINIED," BY ELDER J. S. FLORY. A SYNOPSIS OF CONTENTS. An address to the reader; The peculiarities that attend this type of religion. The feelings there experienced not imaginary but real. The key that unlocks the wonderful mystery. The causes by which feelings are excited. How the momentary feelings called "Experimental religion" are brought about, and then concludes by giving that form of doctrine as taught by Jesus Christ and recorded by his faithful witnesses.

COUNTERFEIT DETECTER
or
BAPTISM—MUCH IN LITTLE.

This work is now ready for distribution, and the importance of the subject will speak for it a large demand. It is a short treatise on baptism in tract form intended for general distribution, and is set forth in such a plain and logical manner that a wayfaring man though a fool, cannot err therein. Either of the above tracts sent postpaid on the following terms: Two copies, 10 cts, 10 copies 40 cents, 25 copies 70 cents, 50 copies $1.00, 100 copies $1.50.

Trine Immersion.

A discussion on Trine Immersion, by letter between Elder D. F. Moomaw and Dr. J. J. Jackson, to which is annexed a Treatise on the Lord's Supper, and on the necessity, character and evidences of the new birth, also a dialogue on the doctrine of non-resistance, by Elder B. F. Moomaw. Single copy 50 cents.

Trine Immersion

TRACED

TO THE APOSTLES.

The SECOND EDITION is now ready for delivery. The work has been carefully revised, corrected and enlarged.

Put up in a neat pamphlet form, with good paper cover, and will be sent, postpaid, on the following terms: One copy, 25 cts; Five copies, $1.10; Ten copies, $2.00, 25 copies, $4.50; 50 copies, $8.50; 100 copies, $16.00.

Address, J. H MOORE,
Urbana, Champaign Ill. tno
Oct 22.

LAND, LAND, LAND!!

The completion of the Chesapeake and Ohio Trunk Line Railway, has opened up to the world much of the fine TIMBER LANDS, rich COAL FIELDS and cheap FARMING LANDS of W. Va. Now is the time to get cheap homes and invest money with the prospect of a handsome profit. For further particulars inquire of the undersigned, agent for lands here. J. S. FLORY,
Orchard View, Fayette Co., W. Va.
Jan. 10.

1870 1873

DR. FAHRNEY'S
Blood Cleanser or Panacea.

A tonic and purge, for Blood Diseases. Great reputation. Many testimonials. Many ministering brethren use and recommend it. Ask or send for the "Health Messenger." Use only the "*Panacea*" prepared at Chicago, Ills., and by

Dr. P. Fahrney's Brothers & Co.,
Feb. 3-pd. *Waynesboro, Franklin Co., Pa*

New Hymn Books, English.

TURKEY MOROCCO.

One copy, postpaid,	$1.00
Per Dozen,	11.25

PLAIN ARABESQE.

One Copy, post-paid,	.75
Per Dozen, "	8.50

Ger'n & English, Plain Sheep.

One Copy, post-paid,	$1.00
Per Dozen	11.25
Arabesque Plain,	1.00
Turkey Morocco,	1.25
Single German, post paid	.50
Per Dozen,	5.50

HUNTINGDON & BROAD TOP RAIL ROAD

On and after March 22d, 1873, Trains will run on this road daily (Sundays excepted) as follows:

Trains from Huntingdon South. *Trains from Mt. Dal's moving North.*

MAIL. A. M.	EXPS. P. M.	STATIONS.	MAIL P. M.	EXP'S. A. M.
LE7 45	5 30	Huntingdon,	AR4 00	AR8 25
7 50	5 35	Long Siding	3 55	8 20
8 10	6 10	McConnelstown	3 45	8 10
8 17	6 20	Pleasant Grove	3 35	8 02
8 30	6 35	MARKLESBURG	3 20	7 45
8 45	6 50	Coffee Run	3 07	7 32
8 55	7 00	Rough & Ready	2 57	7 23
9 05	7 10	Cove	2 47	7 13
9 08	7 13	Fishers Summit	2 45	7 10
9 20	7 28	Saxton	2 27	6 50
9 40	7 50	Riddlesburg	2 10	6 35
9 47	8 00	Hopewell	2 02	6 22
10 02	8 15	Piper's Run	1 47	6 05
10 17	8 32	Tatesville	1 32	5 42
10 30	8 45	Everett	1 20	5 35
10 35	8 50	Mount Dallas	1 15	5 30
11 08	9 20	Bedford	12 44	5 00

SHOUP'S RUN BRANCH.

LE 9 25 LE	Saxton.	AR2 15 AR
9 40	Coalmont.	2 00
9 45	Crawford.	1 55
AR 9 55 AR	Dudley	LE1 45 LE

Bro'd Top City from Dudley 2 miles by stage.

Time of Penna. R. R. Trains at Huntingdon.

***Mail No. 2 makes connection at Huntingdon with Mail going East on Pennsylvania Railroad at 4.15 p. m., and West at 5.45 p. m. Mail No. 1 leaves Huntingdon at 7.40 a. m. on arrival of Pacific Express West.

Trains on this road connect with trains on Bedford & Bridgeport, and Cumberland & Pennsylvania Railroads.

G. F. GAGE, Supt.

The Weekly Pilgrim.

Published by J. B. Brumbaugh, & Co.
Edited by H. B. & Geo. Brumbaugh.
CORRESPONDING EDITORS.
D. P. Sayler, Double Pipe Creek, Md
Leonard Furry, New Enterprise, Pa.

The *Pilgrim* is a Christian Periodical, devoted to religion and moral reform. It will advocate in the spirit of *love* and *liberty*, the principles of true Christianity, labor for the promotion of peace among the people of God, for the encouragement of the saints and for the conversion of sinners, avoiding those things which tend toward disunion or sectional feelings.

TERMS.

Single copy, Book paper,	$1.50
Eleven copies, [eleventh for Agt.]	$15.00

Any number above that at the same rate.

Address,
H. B. BRUMBAUGH,
James Creek,
Huntingdon county Pa.

The Weekly Pilgrim.

"REMOVE NOT THE ANCIENT LANDMARKS WHICH OUR FATHERS HAVE SET."

VOL. 4. JAMES CREEK, PENNSYLVANIA, MAY 6, 1873. NO. 18

POETRY.

ONE STEP MORE

"A man's heart deviseth his way; but the Lord directeth his steps." Prov 19:9.

What, though before me it is dark,
Too dark for one to see?
I ask but light for one step more,
'Tis quite enough for me.

Each little humble step I take,
The gloom clears from the next;
So, though 'tis very dark beyond,
I never am perplexed.

And if sometimes the mist hangs close,
So close I fear to stray,
Patient, I wait a little while,
And soon it clears away.

I would not see my further path,
For mercy veils it so;
My present steps might harder be,
Did I the future know.

It may be that my path is rough,
Thorny and hard and steep;
And knowing this, my strength might fail
Through fear and terror deep.

It may be that it winds along
A smooth and flowery way;
But, seeing this, I might despise
The journey of to-day.

Perhaps my fate is very short,
My journey nearly done;
And I might tremble at the thought
Of ending it so soon.

Or, if I saw a weary length
Of road that I must wend,
Fainting, I'd think, "my feeble powers
Will fail me ere the end."

And so I do not wish to see
My journey or its length;
Assured that, through my Father's love,
Each step will bring its strength.

Thus, step by step, I onward go,
Not looking far before;
Trusting that I shall always have
Light for just "one step more."

ORIGINAL ESSAYS.

ORIGIN OF THE ANXIOUS, OR MOURNER'S BENCH.

Dear Editors and Brethren:—It becoming known that I was making efforts to ascertain the origin of the "Mourners, or Anxious Bench," I have been strongly solicited and urged by many brethren to have it published as soon as I found it; some nameing one, and some another one of our papers, &c. I have at last found it in the LIFE AND LABORS OF JAMES QUINN, BY JOHN F. WRIGHT. Although the work was published in 1851, it is nevertheless out of print, and I had a long and tedious time before I procured a copy in a second-hand book store in Baltimore. And whereas our brethren, and many thousand of our readers are not overmuch concerned in procuring biographies of Methodist preachers, I will, for their information, give the historical extract, and that all may know it, I will write a copy for the *Visitor*, one for the *Companion*, and one for the PILGRIM.

"This year (1838), he (Rev. James Quinn,) frequently invited penitent souls to the seats vacated for their accommodation, that they might have the advantage of the instruction of himself and others, and receive the concentrated sympathy, solicitude, and prayers of such as had access to the throne of grace, and influence at the court of heaven. About this time the question was agitated as to the distinguished individual who first introduced the practice of inviting penitent persons to the mourner's bench. Hear Mr. Quinn on this subject:

"Something has been said, in a late number of the *Christian Advocate* and *Journal*, on the subject of inviting mourners to the vacated seats or railing around the communion table—for I dislike the term altar, or altar for prayer on such occasions. A Jew or Catholic may use the term consistently with his faith on the subject of altar and sacrafice, but an enlightened Protestant believers, where he thinks, speaks, sings or worships, extends his views beyond temples made with hands. But to return. The writer (in the paper referred to) seems to think that L. Dow first introduced the practice in 1802-3; but the first I (Quinn) ever saw or heard of it was in 1795 or 6 at a watch night held at the house of that mother in our Israel, the widow Mary Henthorn, near Uniontown, Pa. The person who conducted the meeting was that holy, heavenly minded man, the Rev. Valentine Cook—blessed man; In imagination I view him now, near or quite six feet in stature, quite stoop shouldered, dark complexion, coarse, black, bushy hair, not much taken care of, small, deep set black eyes and full of the fire of intelligence, strong, well arched brows, high cheek-bones, and an unusually large mouth. He was not handsome; but when he conversed on the subject of religion—and it was almost his constant theme—and more especially when he preached, there was a sweet and almost heavenly benignity beaming in his countenance, presenting rather an unearthly attraction. It was next to impossible for the heedless to remain uninterested under the sound of his voice. Mr. Cook's subject was the qualification, duties, and awful responsibilities of the watchman. His sermon was close and argumentative, giving to the greedy and sleepy dogs, as the prophet styles the avaricious and slothful watchmen or ministers, their portion observing, as he passed along that those who were the least laborious were often the most clamorous for their worldly gain. The sermon was closed with an almost overwhelming exhortation, which appeared as it must carry all before it. Then came the invitation to the mourners to come to the vacated seats to be prayed with and for. I think this was new, perfectly new for the people appeared panic stricken; and I confess I was greatly moved, for it appeared to me as if the two world's were coming together. Verily, methought the very hairs of my flesh stood up. He, however was very particular in giving the scriptural character of a true penitent, and, in the most affectionate and convincing manner, invited such, and none but such, to come; alleging at the same time, that if any should dare to act as did Ananias and his wife, they might be met as these were. O, it was an awful yet glorious time of the precious power and presence of God! Several souls found peace with God through our Lord Jesus Christ, and some obtained the blessing of perfect love. But brother Cook, and most of those who united with him in that meeting have passed away; yet have they a more distinct recollection of what then and there took place than the old man, who by the forbearance of God, lives to write about it. Since that time I have heard many inviting mourners to the place prepared for the purpose—have not always been suited, have often attempted it myself, and frequently failed; and it does appear to me that a combination of time, place, persons, talents, etc., must concur; otherwise, not only no good, but some harm may be the result of a misguided and premature effort. We may have seen, as well as read of sparks of our own kindling."

My dear brethren the above is all I can find written on this subject; and I feel assured that a general knowledge of the origin of this *man made idol* will do more to overthrow this BAAL than all the essays, treaties, or tracts we can write on the subject. Mr. Quinn was admitted into the itinerant ministry of the M. E. Church, May 1st, 1799, and served in it till 1847 when he died after 48 years service, and hence he knows whereof he affirms. It appears that Cook the originator was very cautious what class of mourners he at first invited, and it does not appear that the plan was generally adopted. Mr. Quinn writing of camp meetings in 1804-6 says: "There were no altars, no mourner's benches, or anxious seats, in those days, nor were any invitations given to seekers of salvation to present themselves for the prayers of the Church."

By the minute description Quinn gives of V. Cook a physiognomist will declare him one of the most violent fanatics, full of electricity, and competent of the wildest freaks of a fanatic. This is the man who is the creator of the *Mourner's Bench*, which Mr. Quinn said was *new*, "*perfectly new*," and at its birth "panic struck the people," and made the very hair on his flesh stand up, is now the idol of the day, and has assumed such popularity in certain quarters that to say aught against it stirs up the fires of hell, and woe to the man who dare stand in its range. Well brethren, I am the man that will stand before the hottest fire, and will not be afraid to open my mouth against it, (if the editors are not afraid to print it.) Valentine Cook being the creator of it, and is its god, and his spirit is the spirit of it, and they who are born by it, or under its influence are born of Cook, and not of God. This being so, is there any wonder its converts are what we see and know them to be. From this idolatry good Lord deliver the people. Amen.

D. P. SAYLER.

THE CHURCH AND DUTIES OF HER MEMBERS.—No. 4.

BY J. S. FLORY.

ELDERS.

The word Elder, Bishop, Overseer and Presbyter seem to have a synonymous meaning. The same persons that are called Elders are called Overseers. For proof we refer to Acts 20th chapter and 17th to 29th verse, where we learn Paul sent to Ephesus and called the Elders of the church, and when they had come he spoke to them, and among other things said, "Take heed therefore unto yourselves and unto all the flock, over which the Holy Ghost hath made you overseers to feed the Church of God which he hath purchased with his own blood." Also that the same persons that are called Elders are spoken of as Bishops. See Titus 1 : 5, 7: "For this cause left I thee in Crete that thou shouldest set in order the things that are wanting, and ordain Elders in every city, as I had appointed thee; if any be blameless * * * * * for a Bishop must be blameless, &c., &c. And those who were empowered to attend to the rite of laying on of hands are denominated by Paul as constituting the Presbytery. 1 Tim. 4 : 14. It were the Apostles and probably teachers and prophets, (Acts 13 : 1, 2, 3,) who were enforced, therefore they were Presbyters.

Without stopping further to speak about the name we will pass on to the duties of those who hold the chief office in the Church under our great head Jesus Christ. The station in the Church being the highest, the duties are the most weighty and the considerations and responsibilities are indeed of a solemn nature. The minister who is only required to preach the Word, be instant in season and out of season, does not feel that weight of responsibility that hangs over him who has to keep a vigilant oversight over the flock entrusted to his charge. As they are to be examples to the flock, it is no wonder the Apostle requires such a high standard of qualifications. Hear him, "a Bishop must be blameless." "The husband of one wife, having faithful children not accused of riot or unruly. Yes, "blameless as the steward of God; not self-willed, not soon angry, not given to wine, no striker, not given to filthy lucre, but a lover of hospitality, a lover of good men, sober, just, holy, temperate; holding fast the faithful word as he hath been taught, that he may be able by sound doctrine, both to exhort and to convince the gainsayers." Can dust attain to such a standard? Only through the power of the Holy Ghost. The nearer the character of the Elder or Bishop comes up to those qualifications the more successful he will be in his calling. He, as one that constitutes in a great measure, the head of the congregation or flock over which he presides, yields a wonderful influence for good or for evil. In this age of worldlymindedness and disposition to depart from the simplicity of the Gospel, the *overseers* have indeed a mountain of opposition to face. They cannot be idle and do their duty. Think of it—the word of truth to preach to a perishing world, infidelity in every conceivable phase to meet, wolves in sheep's clothing prowling for admittance into the fold to keep at bay; within the fold, troubles and contentions often to quell, the flock to feed, to cherish and encourage. And this too it is expected, must be done in the spirit of love, humility and forbearance; however not such forbearance that will permit members to indulge in things of a nature calculated to foster pride and a departure from the narrow way and simplicity of the Gospel. In such cases it is the duty of the Elders in particular to admonish the parties to a sense of their duty in such a way as will more likely insure the desired end. Right here at this point much might be said, as it is one of the most important in the whole course of Church government. To nip the "appearance of evil" in the bud so as to accomplish a good work requires that we "be wise as serpents and harmless as doves." To lord it over God's heritage will, by no means do. An iron rule which has "*must*" and "*shall*" for bands to bind and force members to duty we have but little faith in. *Forced religion* is unknown in God's covenant of grace. There is a way to proceed in such cases where members have deviated from the path of duty and broken their vows to some extent, that we seldom see fail. First let *them feel* we are deeply concerned about their soul's interest, by our words of love and tender sympathy, and next stir up within them, if possible, a spirit of penitence and desire to please God, impress upon their minds that those matters are such that tend to their eternal interest and that if they expect God to forgive them they should freely ask forgiveness of the Church, or if individual cases, ask forgiveness of the parties interested; Or if only cases requiring admonition to a sense of duty in Church matters that will tend to a more consistent life and better example to the world and Church, let them feel we have a desire to see them and the Church prosper in matters of piety. A seemingly indifference on the part of the "head" as to how the members conduct themselves is inclined to cause the members to become careless or indifferent, inasmuch as Jesus Christ condescended to be like unto his brethren, the overseers of his Church should condescend to put themselves along side with their brethren and sisters, in matters of trials and difficulties, that is, not act as though we are more holy than they, that we are always saints and they *sometimes* sinners. Touching this idea we have forcibly brought to our minds a case that came under our observation. A sister was before the Church council, on a charge of trespass; *hours* were spent in order to get her make an acknowledgment, but nay, she could not be brought to that point. As nothing desirable could be accomplished the case was dropped until after adjournment when a committee of three were selected to talk to her about the matter, apart from the Church. I shall never forget the impressive manner in which a brother brought the matter to bear upon her mind. He talked to her as though he and she were both little children who loved each other, both he said had faults, he often done things he ought not to and asked her if she did not; "yes," she said, and I seen the the tears begin to flow. Then said the brother when I knew I had done wrong and did not feel well until I had confessed my fault and asked forgiveness. Now the reason I do so is because I want to go to heaven and be with God with all my dear brethren and sisters and with *you!* Now sister ——— I know you want to be happy which you never can be unless you confess your faults if you have any. So now just do all that God requires of you, make acknowledgment and there will be joy in heaven, joy in your heart and joy in the Church. God will forgive, and the Church can not but forgive you. It is needless to say she readily acknowledged her fault and soon the whole matter was settled.

A worldly minded professor when found classed with the laity is a matter to be regretted but such a character in the office of Elder or Bishop would be lamentable indeed. In such a case the flock would also be inclined to feed in the same pasture and drink at the same fountain. In a great measure the prosperity of the Church depends upon the character of the Elders. This being so, how important that they be as Paul would have them be. "Blameless, not self-willed, sober, just, temperate, &c., &c." "Holding fast the faithful word as he has been taught." In this latter particular it is feared, owing to *outside pressure*, too many are inclined to *let go* instead of *hold fast* the faithful word and cling to the "old paths" learned of our fathers. We need not try to hide the fact that the Church is moving "*worldward*." Nothing but a bold and determined effort on the part of the *Overseers*, and a refreshing shower of Divine Grace in the Church in general, can arrest and keep back the restless spirit that is striving for a broader platform and an easier cross than was known to our fathers even back in the days of the Apostles. We would call special attention to the sentiments of one of our most prominent Bishops, as expressed to me in a private correspondence lately. In speaking of the prospects of the Church he says: "I do not expect that we in the wealthy and fashionable parts of the world will ever again be able to record a large increase in the Church unless we do more or less, depart from the self-denial doctrines of the Gospel, and assimilate with, or pander to the usages of our fashionable surroundings, and this I am pledged, both to my God and the Church never to do, and which by the help of God I mean to keep." Did we all stand upon that resolution and carry out such a noble determination the Church would be safe. A giving away at one point encourages the enemies of the cross to press harder upon another point. Just as it was with the nonresistent in the great rebellion. Because a few denied their principles the others had to be put to a severer test. Let every elder of the Church stand up for true Christianity, such as the Apostles heralded to the world, which I consider we are pledged to do, and by the help of God may do. As stewards over God's heritage we are duty bound to keep inviolate the principles of the Church in at least as pure a state as we found them when the government of the Church passed into our hands. Time, customs and surroundings cannot grant us license to deviate from the narrow way mapped out by our blessed Savior and hallowed by the walk and teachings of the Apostles. In that narrow self denying way we must use every effort on our part to keep the ark of the Lord, or as it was with Moses we shall be denied an entrance into the Promise Land.

In closing the eyes for nightly rest, it is good to say, "He giveth his beloved sleep;" and in opening them: when night is past, to say, "When I awake I am still with thee."

For the Pilgrim.

DEATH.

We may look where we will, we see evidences of death. Whether among the high or low, rich or poor, weak or strong, all is tending toward dissolution. We ask, what is death? It is a seperation of parts, a dividing asunder of that which composes the whole man. Without a separation of it, it would be impossible to produce death according to the decrees of God.

We learn from Holy Writ, when God made man he formed him from the dust, and blew into his nostrils the breath of life, and he became a living soul. This is proof sufficient to show that he was composed of at least two positive principles the dust, and that which emanated from God or which was added to what God formed out of the dust. Now we believe, had it not been for certain causes this separation would not have taken place and therefore death would not be known. There would not be such a thing as death visible in this wide range of knowledge. The cause is that which we wish to investigate.

We read in the epistle of James—1: 14, 15, "But every man is tempted when he is drawn away of his own lust and enticed. Then when lust hath conceived it bringeth forth sin; and sin when it is finished bringeth forth death." This gives us the key to the whole subject solemn as it is. Had not our mother Eve lusted after the forbidden fruit, after God told them "in the day thou eatest thereof thou shalt surely die," there would have been no death, but she was enticed by the artful entreaty of the serpent, and did partake, and gave to her husband and he did eat. The yielding to the entreaty was the conception of sin, and the eating was the sin finished and behold it brought forth death as God declared it should, and death passed upon all, and we see its work of destruction wherever we turn our eyes. In Ecclesiastes we learn that the body returns to the dust from whence it was taken but the spirit goes to God who gave it. This is the disposition made of man at his dissolution or seperation. There is, however, another death spoken of more terrible than this, that is, the second death. If the first death is a separation of parts, which it is, the second is also a separation of parts. The first death is brought about by separating the spirit from the body, but from divine revelation we learn the doctrine of the resurrection when these bodies will be raised and reunite with their spirit again. Perhaps after the earth shall have undergone a renovation or cleansing from the effects of the curse pronounced upon it by the transgression, but of the second, we have no knowledge of any reuniting whatever. That principle given to the natural body is a part of God, and at its dissolution returns to God again, but if man engages in sin and lives and dies in the same, when that spirit returns it cannot remain in the society of God, for God cannot look upon sin with the least degree of allowance, therefore another separation must take place which is the second death. That part of man that God gave to the body which returns again, will be now separated from sin forever and "punished with an everlasting destruction from the presence of God and from the glory of his power," so says Paul to the Thessalonians 2nd letter, 1: 9. There are also two resurrections as well as two deaths. The Revelator says, "blessed and holy is he that has part in the first resurrection, on such the second death has no power." Then, since inspired and holy men have told us that it is appointed unto man once to die, and from observation we see it is true, for many circumstances have forced themselves within our view to demonstrate this fact without the possibility of doubt, then upon the same ground we may, with safety, argue that all that has been said by those holy and inspired men is true. They have also said there is a second death but we are glad to know they have given us instructions how we may avert that second death.

The commission of sin brought about natural death and brought man so low in the scale of morals that he could not raise himself to anything like respectability without some assistance from a power superior to his own. God shows a willingness by reaching forth a helping hand in time of need, for John says, "God so loved the world that He gave His only begotten Son that whosoever believeth on Him should not perish but have everlasting life." Natural death is the wages of sin, and the spiritual death would follow as a natural consequence if the gift of God could not be attained. The apostle kindly informs us that eternal life is the gift of God, and the gift of God is His Son which He gave as a ransom for all, and whosoever will believe in Him shall not perish or the second death shall have no power over him and shall also have part in the first resurrection.

These are thoughts that are worthy of our serious and candid attention for we look upon death with a degree of terror and solemnity, but it is nothing compared with the second death. The Evangelist says; "Fear not them that kill the body and after that can do no more, but I tell you whom you shall fear, He that can destroy both soul and body in hell." When we contemplate all these in the light of the Gospel, and with an eye of faith behold the terror of the Lord, we persuade men and women to forsake their evil ways and try to shun the calamity hanging over us and brought upon us by sin which is the transgression of the law which God had given and which at first was disobeyed, but withal has given a way that we may avert the dreadful calamity of the second death, but the first cannot be avoided so long as the signs appear, which is, "thorns and thistles shall it bring forth to thee and thou shalt eat the herb of the field." While this sign is seen the body must return to earth from whence it is taken and the spirit return to God who gave it, and if it were not for the wisdom and mercy displayed by a kind and benevolent God we would be irretrievably lost. "But after that the kindness and love of God our Savior towards man appeared, not by works of righteousness which we have done but according to His mercy He saved us by the washing of regeneration and renewing of the Holy Ghost which He shed on us abundantly through Jesus Christ our Savior, that being justified by His grace we should be made heirs according to the hope of eternal life." Titus 3: 4-5-6-7.

Now friendly reader, let us think upon our way. There is much to be gained and also much to be lost, one soul is of more value than all the world, for if we were to gain the whole world and lose our own soul what would we have? I will tell you, we will have for our company false prophets, wicked men and devils in a prepared hell. If we do not desire such company and such a place we may avoid it by obedience to God and His word. GEORGE WORST.

For the Pilgrim.

TEMPTATION.

Continued from page 51.

I shall still try to present a few thoughts to the readers of the PILGRIM for the edification of our souls. In fact, we believe, there is no other word to be found anywhere that should draw our attention more closely than temptation. For when we consider these special forms of temptation, in general they give rise to many evils that are connected with mankind. We should be accurate in examining our former temptations and prepare ourselves to withstand the enticer, for we all know, giving way to the destroyer is sinning and sin has derived from the devil.

The origin of sin is generally traced back to the garden of Eden and in our way of thinking, we must conclude that the real origin is derived therefrom, for there was the first transgression made by the human being. Lucifer transgressed the laws of heaven and thereby fell from his majesty and has become the enemy of souls. He it was that introduced sin into the world, and he it was that conversed with mother Eve in the Garden of Eden. There he made an effort to temporize and he also conquered and we believe has won many more since the creation. Man came from his maker pure and holy, in the likeness of God's own image, and would have remained so if they had not given way to temptation. Death was the consequence of their sin and eternal death will be the result of our transgression. The weak point is the basis of his work, his cunning eye seeing we also are connected with some favorite object, he holds out inducements as will meet our approbation, and if possible win us. We cannot serve God and mammon. If we have made use of partiality on our pilgrimage to another world we should do so no more. If we have one part of our religion connected with the kingdom of this world and the other part with the kingdom of God we are standing on the brink of destruction, for there may be an open link for the destroyer to creep in. The present world in which we now reside is only a transitory home and we should consider it as the grass of the field unworthy of our attention in comparison to the worth of our souls. This world was created for the abode of man, and since the creation, has been the cradle, home and the grave of our race. But the glorious event is fast approaching when the Lord shall make his appearance in the clouds of heaven to take vengeance upon those that have given way to temptation and know not their God. If we profess to be believers we should have our affections set upon things that are above, there should be our treasure and our heart. If we are oftimes oppressed and darkened by clouds of temptation and doubt, and oftimes beset with bitter trials and sorrow, we should still look above. No tears are shed by the inhabitants of that celestial sphere, all is joy and contentment in that perfect bliss which awaits us in that heavenly home.

Now knowing that our life is of a short duration and die we must, let us keep upon the path of virtue for soon we will be out of temptation's reach and when life is extinct and time is no more, may we be forever happy with God in heaven is my prayer. ANOMALOUS.

WITTY sayings are as easily lost as the pearls slipping off a broken string; but a word of kindness is seldom spoken in vain. It is a seed which, even when dropped by chance, springs up a flower.

WORLDLY honor is a bubble which bursts at the slightest touch.

THE HISTORICAL ARGUMENT FOR IMMERSION.

BY PROF. C. F. LOOS.

It is also true that, if there were nothing certain in the word *baptizo* itself, the historical argument for immersion would still be complete. *It is certain* that, if we were to reject as inconclusive this historical argument we must, in like manner, also utterly abandon the historical argument for the authenticity and genuineness of the Holy Scriptures, especially of the New Testament, for that is of the same kind and extent, not a whit stronger in the first centuries, where its whole force rests. You say, we have the scriptures themselves; so we have immersion, in a wide, unbroken stream from the beginning, in all the lands were Christianity was born and first lived.

THE TRUE POSITION.

The true position for the advocates of apostolic baptism to take, is that there is no real ground for this controversy at all. This opposition to immersion is without a shadow of right. In the light of all kinds of evidence bearing upon it, no part of Christian doctrine is more clearly decided before the Christian world than that of the external act of baptism—that it is an immersion of the body in water, and nothing else. The whole scope of evidence positively forbids, we repeat it, all reasonable doubt and all justifiable controversy against it. *This* is the position to be taken, and, in clear and, bold definition, to be declared and maintained before the world. First, because it is true. Secondly, because we hold immersion, not as a matter of opinion, but as a part of the doctrine of Christ. As men would say, "it is an article of belief;" and no man should hold anything as a matter of Christian faith that admits legitimately of doubt, differences and controversies in any important respect. We do not allow that the Godhead of Jesus Christ, the atonement through his blood, salvation through faith in him, the inspiration of the scriptures, the everlasting destruction of the wicked, legitimately in the light of the word of God, admit of doubt and debate in anything affecting the essential nature of these great truths, and that, too, in spite of the fact that the Christian world is full of essential differences and fierce disputes about them. These truths are opposed and debated, but we deny the lawfulness of such oppositions and such hostile controversies. And so about baptism. The anti-immersion denominations have all introduced, in a high place, baptism into their creeds, and yet they hold that it is a subject of lawful and wide difference of opinion. This is wholly illegitimate and inconsistent. *Whatever is not above all reasonable doubt and debate, has no right in the creed of a man*, as it necessarily belongs only to the domain of the indifferent, and therefore of free opinion. Lastly, the clear and uncompromising, persistent affirmation of a great truth, and that in all the fullness of this truth, awakens men to its reality and importance, and has much to do in leading it to victory. To admit, in the full light of the evidence, the lawfulness of doubt and difference, is already half defeat—at least, a great unnecessary loss. Justice to the truth, justice to ourselves, justice to the world to be convinced, to be led from error to truth, demands imperiously the constant, fearless proclamation of the full truth.

To show that in what we have said here of the *certainty* of the claims of immersion, we have not exaggerated, or spoken as a partisan, we cite a series of eminent authoritative testimonies. Note, it is not simply as general witnesses to immersion that we refer to the following statements, but because of the strong emphatic manner in which they declare the certainty of the claims of immersion as the primitive baptism. This testimony is an argument of strong force and that must be felt, as it comes from eminent learned men, in practice on the opposite side:

Luther: Sermon on Baptism, 1519 (Luther's Werke, Erlangen, vol. 21); it opens as follows:

"Firstly, *Tauf* in Greek is called *baptismus*, in Latin *mersio*: that is, when we dip something entirely into the water, that it closes together over it. And although in many places it is no longer the custom to plunge and dip the children entirely into baptism, but only water is taken from the baptism and poured on them, nevertheless it should not be so; and it would be proper according to the meaning of the word baptism, to sink the child, or any one that is to be baptized, entirely into the water, and thus to baptize, and then draw it out again." Luther here knows nothing of an undetermined or various meaning of this word *baptismus*; to him it is perfectly clear and settled. His whole sermon rests throughout altogether on the idea of immersion; take this out and nothing is left.

Calvin—On Baptism: "Though the word baptize itself signifies immersion, and *it is certain* that the rite of immersion was observed by the ancient church."

Turretin, of Geneva (of the Reformation period, and a man of great eminence): "And, indeed, baptism was performed in that age, and in those countries, by immersion of the whole body in water."

Limborch: "Formerly those who were to be baptized were accustomed to be immersed with the whole body in water."

Augusti: Christ Archæology (In his work a whole volume is devoted to baptism): "That the rite of immersion was the common form of baptism in the ancient church *can not be denied*; and the most zealous defendants of aspersion must admit that in ancient times, aspersion occurs only as an exception, in cases of extreme necessity."

Brenner—a German Catholic historian—in a learned work on baptism, says: "For thirteen hundred years, baptism was universally, and in regular form, an immersion of the person under the water, and only in extraordinary cases an aspersion or an affusion. The latter were indeed as proper forms of baptism, and, in fact, forbidden.

Schaff: Church History, p. 489, note: "As regards the *form* of baptism, the unprejudiced historian *must concede the right to the Baptists*; as also most of the German scholars (*forscher*, those who have searched into the facts) do as Neander, Knapp, Hoefling, etc." Again, in the text, p. 488: "Finally, as regards the manner and form of the external act of baptism, without doubt immersion, and not aspersion, was the original, normal form. *This is clear* already, from the meaning of the Greek words, *baptizo, baptisma, baptismos*, by which this rite is designated; then the analogy of the baptism of John, who performed the act *in* the Jordan (*en*, and also *eis ton Jordanen*); further, from the New Testament comparisons of baptism with the passage through the Red Sea; with the flood, with a bath, with a burial and a resurrection; finally, *the universal custom of ecclesiastical antiquity that always baptized by immersion* (as the Oriental and Russo-Greek Church does yet in our day), and only allowed of affusion and aspersion in extreme cases of necessity, that is, with the sick and dying."

Bishop Taylor (Church of England), in his *Doctor Dubitantium*, after making a number of references in proof of immersion, says: "All which are a *perfect conviction*, that the custom of the ancient churches was not a sprinkling, but immersion, *in pursuance of the sense of the commandment and the example of our blessed Savior*."

Dean Stanley, in his History of the Eastern Church, p. 117, finally makes this most explicit statement:

"THERE CAN BE NO QUESTION that the original form of baptism—the very meaning of the word—was complete immersion in the deep baptismal waters; and that at least four centuries, any other form was either unknown, or regarded, unless in the case of dangerous illness, as an exceptional, almost a monstrous case. To this form the Eastern church still rigidly adheres; and the most illustrious and venerable portion of it, that of the Byzantine empire, absolutely repudiates and ignores any other mode of administration as essentially invalid." Dean Stanley is Regius Professor of Ecclesiastical History in the University of Oxford; and as a ripe scholar of the first rank, especially in ecclesiastical history of the East, speaks with the highest authority on this question. But the Dean is also a man of free thought and speech. How diminutive, by the side of these free, scholarly words of such eminent men appears this small, servile tortuous agony—these unscholarly, "cunning, exegetical artifices and acts of violence," as Dr. Schaff says, "of the narrow-minded opponents of the Baptists"!

In the passages cited we have italicized the words to be especially noted. The list of these citations may be greatly lengthened, but this must suffice. Now let any *one* carefully look at these declarations, and ask himself, how could such men have possibly come to such conclusions? Dean Stanley has stated the whole truth in the right way—"THERE CAN BE NO QUESTION;" this is precisely what we claim.

We have finished what we intended to say in these articles. The argument has been confined to a very limited range and is only partial. In any direction opened in it, it might possibly have been extended much further; but we believe enough has been offered to meet the case.

In concluding, we would earnestly commend to the men of the present anti immersion camp the judgement presented by eminent men on their own side, on the character of this argument against immersion. The judgment is severe but merited. It will be seen that what we have said of the "tortuous molepaths" of this argument is not originated by us. Gentlemen! may you ponder the words of your brethren, and may they indeed be to you "a kindness and an excellent oil!"

Dr. Geo. Campbell, on the attempts to evade the force of *baptizo*, says: "It is to be regretted that we have so much evidence that even good and learned men *allow their judgments to be warped* by the sentiments or customs of the sect which they prefer. The true partisan or whatever denomination, always inclines to *correct the diction of the Spirit by that of the party*.

Monthly Review (England): "Hitherto the anti-pedobaptists (or Baptists) seem to have had the best of the argument on the mode of administering the ordinance. The most explicit authorities are on their side. Their opponents have chiefly availed themselves of *inference, analogy and doubtful construction*.

Dr. Schaff: "*Baptizo* denotes in the classics always an entire or partial *immersion*, and not every manner of the application of water, as affusion or aspersion, without any reference to the quantative relation of the object to be bathed, as many *prejudiced opponents* of the Baptists—for example, Dr Dick—by *all manner of exegetical artifices* and *strokes of violence* have sought to prove."

Dr. Nevin (German Reformed), in the *Mercersburg Review*, May, 1850, on the mode of baptism, says: "*It needs but ordinary scholarship and a mind unpledged to a mere party interest* to see and acknowledge here a certain advantage on the side of the Baptists. The original sense of the word is, on the whole, in their favor." Then, in detail, he shows this advantage in church history, in the opinions of the Reformers, etc. The words we have italicized truly characterize the anti-immersion argument, as it was and yet is; and we need add no more.—*Christian Standard*.

AN escape from the second death and an eternal, immortal, and never-ending life can only be obtained by a living union with Christ "who has brought immortality to light through the Gospel.—*J. S. Flory*.

LIFE Insurance is a most valuable means of providing for a family in case of a failure in business, or an unexpected and premature death.—*Rufus*.

THE three things most difficult are to forget an injury, to keep a secret and make good use of leisure moments.

Youth's Department

MY LETTER FROM THE KING.

BY MARIE S. BUTLER.

One day, a long, long time ago,
As little children do,
I read a story o'er and o'er,
And longed to find it true.

T'was of a great and mighty king,
Who ruled a famous land;
And on a fairy hill-top built
A palace vast and grand.

Then, by an order from the king,
The gates wide open stood;
And messengers went far and wide
To call the brave and good.

But somewhere on the winding way,
A giant lived in state;
And fought the pilgrims day by day,
Who passed his castle gate.

He conquered some, and some were killed,
And some, with many a sting
Of cruel arrows, reached at length
The palace of the king.

And there at last, the story said,
They all are living still,
With fairies flitting in and out
The palace on the hill.

I used to find my story true,
To know the "famous land;"
And here's my letter from the king,
Whose gates wide open stand.

His palace is beyond the clouds,
And all the stars on high
Are only golden lamps hung round
His palace in the sky.

So I go on, and day by day
Grow gladder while I sing,
Nearing the "city on the hill"—
The "palace of the King."

I often meet the giant too—
My giant's name is sin—
I fight him at his castle gates,
And will not enter in.

And I shall meet him yet again,
But angels help me still—
These are the fairies of my king,
The servants of his will.

My King is called the "Wonderful,"
The "Mighty" and the "Fair"—
His names are in your Bible;
My letter too is there.

When I am sad I read again
My letter from the King,
And looking toward the open gates,
Grow gladder while I sing.

—*Standard.*

LITTLE GRAVES.

A short time ago I was called up on to visit a graveyard and while there was surprised to see so large a number of little graves, some quite short. Underneath those little mounds sleeps the bodies of dear little children and the blighted prospects of many fond parents. No doubt many of my young readers have witnessed those little bodies laid in their narrow houses and have shed many bitter tears at the loss of a brother, sister or dear little playmate, perhaps with the sad thought that you will never see them any more—that they are dead and never will come forth again. This is a mistake. They are not dead but only sleeping. The little spirit that was so lively and full of joy came from God and cannot die. The body that now lies in the grave will continue to lie there until our blessed Savior comes, when it will return again and enter the body to live forever with the Lord.

But the question is; will good boys and girls and bad ones all share alike in the world to come? In answering this question I will have to go around a little. We are all condemned or rewarded according to the knowledge we have and the manner in which we use it. You no doubt have read how Adam and Eve fell by being disobedient, how that by their eating of the forbidden fruit we all became sinners by nature. Ever since that time children are born into the world with a disposition to sin and they will become small sinners or great sinners in practice according to the influence by which they are surrounded.

Those who have godly fathers and mothers will likely be taught to be good children, but those who have ungodly and wicked parents will most likely raise bad children. Now these children have just as good a reason to be bad as you have to be good, therefore it would not seem fair that they should be punished for doing that which they could not well help. Now that God who preserves you every day is good, holy and just, so that we all became sinners and there was no way to escape, He sent His Son to suffer and die that we might be saved and gave us a law or plan of salvation. In this death we are released from the sin that Adam and Eve brought upon us and all we have to account for is the sins we commit *knowingly.* Those who are not taught the will of Jesus and to be and do good, if they commit sin and bad deeds, do it ignorantly and therefore are not accountable and if called away in that condition Jesus will spare them just the same as your kind parents spares or forgives you when you do some some very bad things thorough ignorance.

But I wish to impress upon your minds the fact that you will not always remain in this unaccountable condition. While I noticed many little graves I also noticed that there were larger ones. The longer the grave the greater will be the responsibilities of those who lie in them and as you do not all expect to fill little graves it becomes the more necessary that you strive to do and be good so that you may not only prepare yourselves to fill large graves but may aid those children who have not the advantage which you have, to become good, and thus grow up to become useful men and women.

It is because Jesus said; "Suffer little children to come unto me and forbid them not for of such is the kingdom of heaven," that I have such a preference for little graves. But when children grow out of being little, they also grow out of this promise and thus become accountable to God and to be saved, must be born again by believing in Jesus, repenting of sins and becoming obedient to all the commands of the Lord. Hoping that the little PILGRIM readers will all learn that, to them, most important of all commandments, "Obey your parents for that is right," I now close promising to let you hear from me again.

UNCLE HENRY.

Selected for the Pilgrim.

GOOD MANNERS

Young folks should be mannerly. How to be so is the question. Many a good boy and girl feel that they can't behave to suit themselves in the presence of company. They feel timid, bashful or self-distrustful the moment they are addressed by a stranger or appear in company. There is but one way to get over this feeling and acquire easy and graceful manners: that is to do the best they can at home, as well as abroad. Good manners are not learned by arbitrary teaching so much as acquired by habit. They grow upon us by use. We must be courteous, agreeable, civil, kind, gentlemanly and womanly at home, and then it will be a kind of second nature to be so everywhere. A coarse, rough manner at home begets a bit of roughness which we cannot lay off if we try when we go among strangers. The most agreeable people we have ever known in company are those who are perfectly agreeable at home. Home is the school for all good things, especially for good manners.

H. BEELMAN.

Correspondence.

A Reporter is wanted from every Church in the brotherhood to send us Church news, Obituaries, Announcements, or anything that will be of general interest. To insure insertion, the writers name must accompany each communication. Our invitation is not personal but general—please respond to our call.

In Memory of Fannie Emmert.

Died, April 17th, 1873, aged 12 years, 10 months and 21 days.

"A mother dear laments thy loss,
Two sisters wept around thee,
A brother too did show his love
By weeping o'er thee."

We can extol the virtues of the dead, we can forgive them their vices. We can point in pride to where they last kneeled in prayer; to the last words of endearment given a darling sister or brother, or the last embrace given an affectionate mother. We can do this but we cannot recall them back to us. Such were our reflections as we stood by the side of the dying. She lay an a bed utterly unconscious of her surroundings, or the friends that wept around her. Yet even here she appeared so beautiful, so lovely, so everything that solicited our sympathies, asked our protection and excited our admiration. It seemed like that of calm resignation to a seemingly cruel fate. Even while contending with the demon Death a smile seemed to play over her naturally intelligent features; but it was the smile of heaven rather than that of earth; it was the will of angels predominating over that of man. The night wore heavily away as we stood by her bed and with it passed the dead. At half past two we looked for the last time. A few minutes later the immortal part of herself had taken its flight to other worlds than this, and left the body with her weeping friends. The morning dawned, and the news went forth that she was dead. It was then that not only a mother, two sisters and a brother, together with many associates, but old age itself gave way to the tender sympathies and wept.

Hard in deed doth appear the lot to one so young to be thus called away from all her companions and from the trees and flowers that she loved so well. But death is a relentless hand, it touched the flower ere it had fully bloomed and scattered its fragrance on the morning air. Thus died Fannie, honored, praised, and loved by all who knew her. Her short though virtuous life can be beautifully illustrated by the following pathetic lines, from "Gray's elegy."

"Full many a gem of purest ray serene,
The dark unfathomed caves of ocean bear;
Full many a flower is born to blush unseen,
And waste its sweetness on the desert air."

EFFIE GROSSNICKLE.

Editors of the Pilgrim:—Dear brethren, I would like to drop a few thoughts in regard to the *Pilgrim Almanacs.* I don't want to dictate as we are personally strangers, but not so by reputation, as I have from the first been a reader of the PILGRIM and have been trying, in my weak way to labor for its support and will continue so to do as long as it keeps in Gospel bounds, trying to keep us in that narrow path which leadeth unto life, as there be few that find it. The *Almanac* is a beautiful supplement; it has become a household necessity. The calendar is in perfect order, all that could be desired. The Ministerial List is very convenient. Now I come to the point where I would like to give my advice as I feel interested. That space occupied with the Biographies of our forefathers might be better occupied. There is no advantage in us knowing where the founders of the church in America were born, lived and died. Our hope must be founded on the word, the Gospel of Christ. There are many of the brethren who can preach and write with power and with spirit. Commit some of their sermons to writing, and you have something for the *Almanac* that will benefit the world. There are many who read the *Almanac* that never read the PILGRIM.

H. BEELMAN.

REMARKS.—As the PILGRIM and its "supplement" is published for the benefit and convenience of its patrons we shall always be glad to hear from those concerned. Last year's *Almanac* was gotten up in too much haste to make it what we desired it to be, but for the coming year, we hope to do something better in that direction. To accomplish this, we have now opened a book in which we wish to add all the names of the ministers not heretofore published, correct all mistakes and changes in this year's list and note changes of address, also have it arranged in alphabetical order. Now brethren this list will be just as complete as you help us to make it. We hope some brother in every Church district will be interested in this matter and carefully examine the present list and make a note of all mistakes, add all names and addresses of those omitted and send it to us at your earliest convenience. As to what other matter it shall contain, we wish to be governed by the wishes of our patrons. While some prefer biographies of our prominent ministers, others, like Bro. Beelman, will prefer something of a more instructive and beneficial nature. All those who feel to contribute to its pages will do so as soon as convenient and we will place all on file and from what we may receive, its pages will be filled.

OUR MISSION.

On the 12th of January, 1873, I left home for Crawford Co., Pa., according to promise and arrangement, met Bro. John W. Brumbaugh on the 13th at Altoona, where he had meeting on Saturday evening, Sunday and Sunday evening. Bro. John being our leader, (and a very good one), we got aboard the first west bound train, which was at 2:20 p. m. We were informed this was the accommodation train and were not disappointed in the least, if frequent stops are considered accommodations. At 7 p. m., we reached a place called Derry. Here we took refreshments and at 7:20 we resumed our place on our accommodation train, arriving at Pittsburgh at 10:25, went to St. James Hotel, kept on European plan, registered our names, and retired for the night—had a comfortable night's rest. Morning of 14th. Porter called at door. "*Six o'clock, up!*" After asking God's blessing on us, which we all so much need, we repaired to the dining room and partook of refreshments. Then to depot, obtained tickets for Lionsville. At 7:40 aboard the train and up the Pittsburgh & Erie R. R. Here we had about as much accommodation as the day previous, the railroad being thickly strewed with villages, towns and iron manufactories of different kinds. The villages and towns are of modern character, seemingly much attention given to houses and surrounding shrubbery, while the streets and sidewalks receive little or no attention at all, at any rate, the condition of them would represent to the pedestrian, no attention given to streets or sidewalks, the streets being overlaid with mud 4 or 5 inches deep while the sidewalks were covered with a substance equally solid. We might name some of the towns of note, and talk of their advantages, &c., but towns and cities are not our object. Something of more importance now, directly concerns us who advocate the "Missionary cause," as we shall now try to show. At 12 m., arrived at Lionsville, where we met our friend, (brother in principle, hope soon will be by practice), A. J. Williams awaiting our arrival, took refreshments at hotel, then aboard A. J. W's. sled and then towards his home where we arrived safely at 3:30 p. m., found his companion and family all well. Here we felt at home. Everything was done on the part of Mr. and Mrs. Williams to make us comfortable. Well truly Bro. John and myself did highly enjoy ourselves while here. It was with some difficulty that A. J. W., obtained a place for public preaching, he succeeded however, in securing the Academy of Hammonsburg, which we thought was very good for public preaching, the people there feeling a delicacy in giving their homes for preaching not knowing whether we were orthodox (as they say.) According to the arrangement, on the evening of the 15th we tried to preach. We were agreeably disappointed as the house was quite full of eager listeners, seemingly ready to receive the word in its purity. After service two or three persons offered their Churches. We rested the matter in the hands of A. J. W., to decide as to the place, he accordingly chose the U. P. Church, 4½ miles north of Hammonsburg, where we met daily for preaching, up to Sunday evening, the 19th, when we closed our labors, on this mission.

We think good impressions were made and inasmuch as this was the first time the Brethren were known to preach in Crawford County, we left with the promise that some brethren should return to them again early in May, or as soon as arrangements could be made. We are very positive there is one there who desires to be a member, and in full communion with the Brethren.

We now appeal to the Middle District of Pa., to consider this matter, and say who shall or who shall not go. Where are the brethren that advocate so very strongly the "*go ye!*" Here is an opportunity to go, turn up the goers. We long to see the day, when every call will be filled.

This short and imperfect report was withheld to this late day, in order to stir up the pure minds, by way of remembrance at District Meeting.

S. A. MOORE.

New Enterprise, Pa.

NOTES.

ORCHARD VIEW, W. Va.,
April 18, 1873.

The cry still comes from every side to "come and preach for us." Since the long, cold winter has apparently come to an end we have set out to try to fill some of the many calls. The 6th of the month 3 willing souls in this neighborhood, were inducted into the Lord's kingdom by baptism, and there are several other applicants for that initiary rite. The prospects are encouraging for which we feel to thank God.

At noon the 11th. inst., I got aboard the cars here near me and after a pleasant ride of 5 hours on the Chesapeak & Ohio R. R. I was in Huntington on the Ohio river. Huntington is improving rapidly. Put up at a hotel kept by a Mr. Samples, formerly from McVeytown, Pa., who had just arrived with his wife and son-in-law, a Mr. Mathews; he also has a son-in-law living in the city by the name of Young from Frederick Co., Md., I found an agreeable acquaintance with them all, I was treated with that marked kindness so characteristic of Penna. hospitality. Next day at 10 a. m., returned as far as St. Albans, mouth of Coal River, was met by Bro. S. Meadows who kindly conveyed me to his home near the Upper Falls of Coal. Meeting at night at friend and sister Adkins, found brother P. A. Fisher and family sojourning with them for a few weeks until he builds on his new purchase. Had an interesting meeting. I was glad to meet once more with the dear brethren and sisters of that section, some of whom are young in the Church as well as young in life—they manifest a zeal for the cause they have espoused. Next day, Easter, at 11 a. m., good turn out, at 4 p. m., meeting at Falls School House, said by some to have been the largest turnout ever seen at that place, one baptized. All night with Bro. S. Meadows, next morning walked to St. Albans and at 12 m. arrived at Charleston, was taken by friend T. C. Fitzwater to his home, meeting at night in the city, at Bro. J. Starkey's, good turn out, next day was taken by Bro. Starkey to Lynn S. H., meeting at 11 a. m., one baptized, returned to the city and made several family calls, meeting at night at friend Fitzwater's house, attentive congregation. Hope the Lord will abundantly bless all the brethren, sisters and friends for their kindness and my prayer is they may continue faithful, keep themselves "unspotted from the world," and as chaste virgins finally be presented unto Christ, the coming "bridegroom."

Returned home the 16th and found all well. Praise the Lord.

In my series of articles "The Church" &c., I notice a number of typographical errors, of such a nature, however, that the reader may readily correct them in the mind.

To-day we are having some snow—the fruit trees are in bloom. Truly winter lingers in the "lap of spring."

We expect to have a Communion meeting the 17th of May. Come over brethren and help us.

Yours in love,
J. S. FLORY.

Dear Pilgrim:—Please announce that the Brethren of Winona county, Minn., near Lewiston, intend, the Lord willing, holding a communion meeting on the 7th and 8th of June next. Services to commence on Satday 10 o'clock A. M. A general invitation is extended to all and especially ministering brethren. All those coming by public conveyance will get off at Lewiston station on the Winona & St. Peter R. R. and call on J. S. Lewis.

C. F. WIRT.

CORRECTION.—In the Biography of Eld. John Flory in "*Pilgrim Almanac*" an oversight appears, he was the father of ten children, the name of one of his sons, that of *Michael*, is left out.

In "Meeting Calander" in Almanac in place of "Boyer's Ferry" read SEWELL. J. S. FLORY.

Railroad Arrangement to A. M.

I, to-day made arrangements with the Baltimore and Ohio R. R. company, and with its branches, from Baltimore to Washington, Weaverton to Hagerstown, Harpersferry to Harrissonburg, and Grafton to Parkersburg for half fare. No farther West however than Wheeling, friend Cole having no authority to control the division west of the Ohio river in such matters.

The conditions are the same as they were on former occasions on this road. Those going will start where they choose and pay their full fare to Cumberland, asking no questions, as agents along the line know nothing at all about it, and of course can give no information. At the place of meeting I will furnish all who apply and have complied with the conditions with a certificate which will pass them to the place of starting free of charge.

If some one would, or could arrange with some line west of the Ohio river to connect these arrangements at Wheeling or Bellair, this would be the route for all west, and south of west to take. And whereas the B. & O. R. R. Co. has never refused to grant the brethren half fare privileges, while the Pittsburg, Fort Wayne & Chicago Co. has rarely, if ever granted it, I think the brethren are in duty bound to consider it. Last year they refused to abate one cent of my full fare going and coming, while the Pittsburg & Conellsville road, through the brethren, sent me, by telegraph, a pass to return free over the road.

D. P. SAYLER.

P. S. I am already furnished with the return certificates.

PHILADELPHIA,
April 26th, 1871.

Editor of the Pilgrim:—Please notice that an arrangement has been concluded with the Penn. C. R. R. Co. for the benefit of our brethren going to the Annual Meeting to be held at Dale City, Somerset Co. Pa., commencing the third day of June.

The excursion will be open on the 20th

of May, the tickets to be on sale to the 3rd of June and be good to return to the 14th of June.

All who go to the Annual Meeting living east of the mountain will buy excursion tickets at the main stations on the main road or main stations on the branch roads, via Huntingdon, over the Huntingdon & Broad Top R. R. through to Bridgeport on the Connellsville road.

All living west of the mountain (except Pittsburg) will buy excursion tickets at main stations on the main road or main stations on the branch road via Greensburg through to Connellsville. Those from the east to Bridgeport, and those from the west to Connellsville, will at those places buy tickets for a short distance over the Connellsville road to Dale City, the place of meeting.

Those from the east ought to be at Huntingdon at or before 7:40 in the morning, and those from the west ought to be at Greensburg at or before 10 o'clock in the morning. They will then go through to place of meeting by daylight.

Those who intend to stop off must inform the conductor of their intention to do so. Their tickets will then be endorsed on the back and honored by the next conductor. Those who fail thus to inform the conductor will lose the advantage of the excursion rates and have no redress.

The branches are, Columbia branch, Bald Eagle branch, Ebensburg branch, Waynesburg branch, Hollidaysburg, Morrison's Cove and Newry branches, Tyrone and Clearfield branch, Western Pennsylvania division, Lewistown division, Mifflin and Centre county branch, Indiana branch, Butler extension and Bedford division.

The above excursion arrangement extends to those living in the state of Pennsylvania only.

C. CUSTER.

NOTICE.

HAMILTON, MO.,
April 22nd, 1873.

To the Brethren in Kansas, Nebraska and Mo. who wish to attend our A. M. I wish the names of all who wish to attend at once as I expect to be able to make arrangements for half fare permits for all our members on the Chicago, Burlington and Quincy R. R from Quincy to Chicago and probably also on the Hamilton and St. Joseph from St. Joseph to Quincy. From Chicago to Pittsburgh the arrangements have already been made by brother John Beghly. Brethren to meet there on the 28th or morning of the 29th of May and take the Pan Handle route. Brethren in Ill. who have no season or yearly permits on the C. B. & Q. road and may wish to take that road are also included.

GEORGE WITMER.

ANNOUNCEMENTS.

Middle District of Pa., at Clover Creek, May 13.

Middle District of Iowa, in Dallas Co., on the 10th day of May.

North-eastern District of Ohio, Jonathan's Creek Congregation, Perry Co., on May 20th.

About 1 mile from Lititz at Bro. Pfautz's, Lancaster Co., Pa, May 15th. Delegates to meet the afternoon before.

Please notice through the PILGRIM that the District Meeting of Western Pa., will be held at the Fairview Meeting house in the George's Creek branch, Fayette Co. Pa, on Wednesday 21st of May, '73.

J. FORST.

Please announce that the District Meeting of North-Western Ohio will be held, the Lord willing, with the brethren of Crawford Co., at the house of brother John Brubarts, on the Base Line on the 25 day of May, and on the 21, the day following, there will be a Communion meeting at the same place. A general representation is desired.

ISRAEL ROOP.

LOVEFEASTS.

Spring Run, Mifflin county, Pa., May 27, 28.

Beaver Creek, Wednesday May 14, at 1 P. M.

Shade Creek Congregation, Somerset co. Pa., May 29, commencing at 10 a. m.

Champaign Co., Ill., at Geo. Dillings, 5 miles east of Urbana, 7th and 8th of June.

Codorus, York county, Pa., on the 7th and 8th of June at the East Codorus M. H.

At the house of Bro. Jacob Long, 3½ miles south of Annville, 16th and 17th of May.

Welch Run, Thursday May 15, commencing at 1 o'clock P. M., continuing next day till noon.

E. SLIFER.

Dry Valley Church, Mifflin Co., Pa, May 22th, 10 o'clock A. M., ½ mile from Maitland on the Sunbury and Lewistown R. R.

The Weekly Pilgrim.

JAMES CREEK, PA., May 6, 1873.

☞ HOW TO SEND MONEY.—All sums over $1.50, should be sent either in a check, draft or postal order. If neither of these can be obtained, have the letter registered.

☞ WHEN MONEY is sent, *always* send with it the name and address of those who paid it. Write the names and post office as plainly as possible.

☞ EVERY subscriber for 1873, gets a *Pilgrim Almanac* FREE.

CHURCH NEWS.

We hope our brethren and sisters will continue to keep us posted on the condition and progress of the Church. When the disciples learned of each other and the success of the work of the Lord, they took courage and thanked God. If they needed good tidings to encourage them on the way, we need it none the less. During our late rebellion, when any part of the great army was repulsed by the enemy, the whole was affected and indeed, the nation was made to mourn, but when there was a decisive victory it infused every soldier with renewed courage. Just so it is with us. We are in the midst of a great rebellion, the whole camp of satan is arrayed against us and sometimes we meet with reverses, the foe out generals us and we are ready to despond, but when we learn that in other parts of the army, victories are being won we take courage and go forth with renewed zeal to fight against the kingdom of darkness. Every time that there is a soul converted there is a glorious victory achieved, even of greater value than the whole world. From the thousands of valient soldiers that are now faithfully engaged in the contest there must be a large number of victories, many souls converted to God. Why not report them that others may take courage. Brethren and sisters, let us hear from every congregation in the brotherhood and thus keep us posted on the good news of the kingdom. The Communion season will soon be here when the great brotherhood will assemble at their respective places of worship and there feast on the living emblems of Christ. A report of these meetings are generally interesting and will be duly appreciated if not too lengthy. In conclusion, let us have a report of everything transpiring that may be of a general interest to our readers.

THE ELDERS.

We wish to manifest no partiality to our writers, but we are, sometimes, partial to their subjects. Bro. Flory's "Duties of the Elders" of this week, is a subject of vital importance to the Brotherhood and is the basis from which our prosperity must be expected. With Christ for our head and good ruling elders for a basis, Zion will come forth in her most lovely garments and the world with all its deceitfulness and power cannot clog its progress. It is a high position of trust and the responsibilities are important and great and those placed in it should not fail to feel it. The subject is well treated and we hope it may go forth accomplishing the great desire of the Church, that our elders may be instructed, encouraged and fully qualified for that most high calling in which they have been called, that the flock may be cared for and receive the meat in season and that many yet without may be constrained to enter the fold and live.

PERSONAL.

S. C. SHOWALTER. The PILGRIM is sent to the poor sister.

ELD. JACOB MOHLER. All right,—sorry to give you so much trouble.

JAMES BARTON, The letter ordering PILGRIM sent to Joseph Forney was not received. It is now sent.

BENJ. J. EASH, PILGRIM to end of the year, $1.00. Put it in a common yellow envelope, direct and seal it carefully and it is at our risk.

MINUTES OF D. M's. Secretaries of our District Meetings will confer a favor by sending us a copy of their minutes. We will print Minutes at the following rates: 100, $6.00, 200, $8.00, and 300, $10.00

CHANGE AND CORRECTION. The Lovefeast at Codorus, York Co., Pa, has been changed from the 10, and 11 of June to the 7, and 8. The Beaver Creek, Md., should be on the 14, of May instead of the 4.

PILGRIM ALMANACS.—As we have on hand several hundred more *Almanacs* than we need for distribution, we will send them to any address, free of postage on the following terms. Single copy 10 cents, 6 copies 30 cents, and 12 copies 60 cents.

THE HELPING HAND. All orders for the "Household Treasure" will now be filled with the "Helping Hand." This is a recent work containing all that was in the "Treasure" with the addition of considerable other important information. We intend to keep it on hand instead of the Treasure at the same price. All orders promptly filled.

RAILROAD ARRANGEMENTS. Last week we gave the privileges tendered by the Southern roads, and this week we give those of the Eastern and Western. The favors granted are about as complete as could be expected. The Pa. Central, as well as all other roads who grant the privilege, go to considerable trouble to accommodate and should be held in grateful remembrance by the Brethren.

Those who go to A. M., on excursion tickets should take the copy of the PILGRIM containing the arrangements with them.

W. ARNOLD of Somerset, O., wishes us to say to those coming to their District Meeting, via Mansfield, Ohio, that they must arrive there on Monday the 19th of May, at 10:27 a. m., in order to reach the place in time. Also states if there are any who wish to come and spend Saturday and Sunday with them they will be heartily welcome.

D. F. R. "Dymond on War," is a book of 124 pages well bound in flexible cloth and is acknowledged to be one of the best works written on the subject, and is well worth the price asked for it, (see advertisement). All those wishing to become well posted on the important subject of non-resistance should not fail to secure a copy of this valuable work.

OUR POSITION is a tract written and published by Isaac Errett, editor of the *Christian Standard*. It gives the distinctive features of the plea for reformation urged by the Disciples of Christ. It has the following divisions: *First*. That in which they agree with the parties known as evangelical. *Second*. That in which they disagree with all. *Third*. That in which they differ from some but not from all. The tract is written by a master hand of the denomination who is fully able to define their position.

MONEY LIST.

Henry Groff	$1.25	T M Kaufman	3.25
Jacob Troxel	50	J W Fitzgerald	12.00
Nicholas Trap	2.75	Saml Kinsey	5.00
Eld Geo. Wolf	3.00	M A Hoofstitler	1.25
A. H Snyder	50	N Kauffman	1.50
Wm Forney	1.50	Jos Zobin	2.88
Isaac Price	1.00	Ad Baker	3.00
Geo A Branscon	70	Mathias Frantz	3.00
J W Eller	7.50	Elihu Moore	3.50
Eli Smith	3.00	D R Freeman	2.10
D Brumbaugh	2.20	Henry Sprankle	6.40
S M Haley	1.00	E Slifer	1.50
H C Monningstar	3.00	Jacob Mohler	1.20
E Slifer	3.00	Samuel Murray	7.25
E W Stoner	1.35	Wm H Clark	3.00
S M Smith	1.25	Barbara C Price	1.50
A Pilgrim	75	Joel Sherfy	1.25
Wm C Teeter	1.50	Jacob Beck	1.50
G S Bingham	1.50	Joseph Stover	1.50
D H Bonebrake	1.00	Andrew Bechtal	1.50
A B Brumbaugh	1.70	H A Switzer	4.25
D Bosserman	6.00	Leonard Furry	20.00
Jacob Mohler	3.64	John Showalter	2.50
Benj Sprecher	1.50	James Brandt	3.00

(Obituaries crowded out.)

GENERAL INTELLIGENCE.

THE necessity for the abolition of the franking privilege must be apparent to every one from the statement in the Washington *Star* of the 15th inst., that there now leaves the post-office in that city daily from 30,000 to 50,000 pounds of franked matter. It may be safely asserted that not a tithe of this matter is of any use to the Government or the people. The franking privilege should be denominated a scheme to make and keep voters. How the mails will rejoice on the 1st of July, and how the people, male and female, will rejoice that the Post-office Department is to be appropriated to legitimate uses!

MONSTER RAILWAY MAP.—There has been on exhibition in this city for a few days past a map of the route of the Pacific Railway, which is to be exhibited at the Vienna Exposition. The map is the largest ever made in the country, measuring 12 feet by 10, and representing an area of 655,200 square miles. The measurements are from old surveys and maps, corrected in many instances by the surveys of the road itself. Executed in water colors and showing at a glance the contour and general physical characteristics of the whole immense stretch of country, this map was yet only five weeks in preparation. Four landscapes in water color in vacant corners represent the City of Duluth, the valley of the Upper Yellowstone, Shadow Lake, Montana, and the St. Louis River Minnesota.

HUNTINGDON & BROAD TOP RAIL ROAD

On and after March 22d, 1873, Trains will run on this road daily (Sundays excepted) as follows:

Trains from Huntingdon South. *Trains from Mt. Dallas moving North.*

MAIL. A. M.	EXPS. P. M.	STATIONS.	MAIL. P. M.	EXP'S. A. M.
LE7 45	5 50	Huntingdon,	AR4 00	AR8 25
7 50	5 55	Long Siding	3 55	8 20
8 10	6 10	McConnelstown	3 45	8 1[illegible]
8 17	6 20	Pleasant Grove	3 35	8 02
8 30	6 35	MARKLESBURG	3 20	7 45
8 45	6 50	Coffee Run	3 07	7 32
8 55	7 00	Rough & Ready	2 57	7 23
9 05	7 10	Cove	3 47	7 14
9 08	7 13	Fishers Summit	2 45	7 10
9 20	7 28	Saxton	2 27	6 50
9 40	7 50	Riddlesburg	2 10	6 35
9 47	8 00	Hopewell	2 02	6 25
10 03	8 15	Piper's Run	1 47	6 05
10 17	8 32	Tatesville	1 32	5 45
10 30	8 45	Everett	1 20	5 35
10 35	8 50	Mount Dallas	1 15	5 30
11 08	9 20	Bedford	12 44	5 00

SHOUP'S RUN BRANCH.

LE 9 25 LE	Saxton.	AR2 15 AR
9 40	Coalmont.	2 00
9 45	Crawford.	1 55
AR 9 55 AR	Dudley	LE1 45 LE

Bro'd Top City from Dudley 2 miles by stage.

Time of Penna. R. R. Trains at Huntingdon.

**Mail No. 2 makes connection at Huntingdon with Mail going East on Pennsylvania Railroad at 4.15 p. m., and West at 5.45 p. m. Mail No. 1 leaves Huntingdon at 7.40 a. m. on arrival of Pacific Express West.

Trains on this road connect with trains on Bedford & Bridgeport, and Cumberland & Pennsylvania Railroads.

G. F. GAGE, Supt

The Weekly Pilgrim.

Published by J. B. Brumbaugh, & Co.

Edited by H. B. & Geo. Brumbaugh.

CORRESPONDING EDITORS.

D. P. Sayler, Double Pipe Creek, Md.

Leonard Furry, New Enterprise, Pa.

The *Pilgrim* is a Christian Periodical, devoted to religion and moral reform. It will advocate in the spirit of *love* and *liberty*, the principles of true Christianity, labor for the promotion of peace among the people of God, for the encouragement of the saints and for the conversion of sinners, avoiding those things which tend toward disunion or sectional feelings.

TERMS.

Single copy, Book paper,	$1.50
Eleven copies, [eleventh for Agt.]	$15.00

Any number above that at the same rate.

Address,

H. B. BRUMBAUGH.
James Creek,
Huntingdon county Pa.

The Weekly Pilgrim.

"REMOVE NOT THE ANCIENT LANDMARKS WHICH OUR FATHERS HAVE SET."

VOL. 4. JAMES CREEK, PENNSYLVANIA, MAY 13, 1873. NO. 19

POETRY.

FATHER IS GONE.

BY LAVINO H. BURKET.

On The Death of Brother Funk.

Schoolmates, weep not for your father,
He has only gone to rest;
Gone to sleep that sleep in Jesus,
Happy father, he is blest.

First your dear and sainted mother
Journeyed through the shades of death—
Through that valley Jesus led her,
To a land of life and health.

Yes, in Heaven your dear mother
Beckons you to meet her there—
Watching for her children's coming,
Those she loved and cared for here.

Then your sister crossed the river
Leaving husband, children, friends;
Home and all her earthly treasures,
For a world that never ends.

Now your father too has left you
But 'twas Jesus bid him come;
He had done with earthly sorrows—
God has took him to his home.

What to them were earthly treasures
On the waters dreadful roar,
On the other side the river
They have viewed fair Canaan's shore.

You will miss him, ah, I know it,
I have lost a father too;
Well I know that deep, deep sorrow
When some dear one's hid from view.

Death has robbed me of two brothers
Who was ours to love and own;
And a darling little sister
Now an angel at God's throne.

Schoolmates, mourn not for your father
He will dwell at God's right hand;
Fields of pasture, fresh and fragrant,
Blooming in that better land.

He has passed across the Jordan
And has landed without fear;
Oh, dear children do not tarry,
Try to meet them over there.

All your brothers now are walking
In the road your parents trod;
And a sister too is trying
To be owned a child of God.

Though a Christian's road is often
Marked with trials on the way,
Yet an Advocate is promised,
Oh, then come and don't delay.

Come to Jesus, long delaying
Won't insure that blest retreat—
Putting off all timely warning,
You may lose that mercy seat.

Dearest schoolmates, come to Jesus,
He is Father, Brother, Friend;
Pray that He may choose our pathway,
And guide us safely to the end.

ORIGINAL ESSAYS.

For the Pilgrim.

THE SOURCE OF CHRISTIAN ENJOYMENT.

Ye were sealed with that Holy Spirit of promise.—Eph. 1: 13

Having in my former articles spoken of the enjoyment and happiness a christian life affords, I will now say something of the source from whence these delights flows and gives the unmistakable assurance of terminating in unending happiness in the world to come.

True, Jesus Christ is our salvation, He redeemed us to God by His own blood. He paid the debt due for sin, "in becoming sin for us that we may be made the righteousness of God in Him." For we are "not redeemed with corruptable things, as silver and gold, from our vain conversation received by tradition from our fathers, but with the precious blood of Christ, as of a lamb without blemish and without spot." The regenerated souls that have embraced the faith in Jesus and being baptized into His death, have put on Christ the hope of glory, and are justified in Him from all sins whether actual or inherited, from which they could not be justified by the law of Moses, for an implicit obedience of faith in the gospel of Christ is the power of God unto salvation." It is said of the believer, "But of him are ye in Christ Jesus, who of God is made unto us wisdom, and righteousness, and sanctification and redemption. In whom we have redemption through His blood, the forgiveness of sins according to the riches of His grace." Hence the true Christian is delivered from sin, and consequently enjoys a present salvation, although the body is still the same corruptible mortal, clothed with flesh and blood, hence liable to err and subject to deception. Though the mind is changed, the actions different, his promptings heavenward, his aim to glorify God in his spirit and in his body, yet he stands in need of help from above as a pledge, and as an earnest of his future inheritance and purchased possessions in Heaven when the body is redeemed. This assistance is afforded us in the third person of the Godhead, by being sealed with that Holy Spirit of promise. "O, the depths of the riches, both of the wisdom and knowledge of God! How unsearchable are His judgments, and His ways past finding out." Behold the wise arrangement in the plan of salvation! The Triune God, displayeth his power through the trinity of His Godhead by giving each part their work to perform in the plan of salvation and eternal redemption. How wise how appropriate the [illegible] given in the three [illegible] in the ordinance of christian baptism, as each person in the Godhead has its important work to perform, so each one has to be honored in its own name by baptizing the subject into the *name* of the Father, and into the *name* of the Son, and into the *name* of the Holy Ghost. The Father draws and enlightens the sinner by the spirit of His grace. The Son saves through the redemption of His blood in delivering him from his sins, and by his triumphant resurrection redeems his body from corruption, and through His victorious ascension to Heaven, opened the portals of bliss, and gives admittance into the paradise of God. The Holy Spirit sanctifies, leads into all truth, guides him through the uneven path of life, seals his promise of redemption, and is an earnest or pledge of an eternal adoption as God's children, and consequently heirs of that "inheritance which is incorruptible, undefiled, and that fadeth not away." O how important, brethren and sisters, that we "grieve not the Holy Spirit of God whereby we are sealed unto the day of Redemption." "Therefore let all bitterness, and anger, and clamor, and evil speaking be put away from you, with all malice, and be ye kind one to another, tender-hearted, forgiving one another, even as God for Christ's sake hath forgiven you."

The sinner, by hearing the word of truth preached unto him, receiveth it, trusts in God for his salvation, and yields obedience to His faith in submitting to the conditions of pardon. Repentance, faith and baptism has the assurance of the remission of his sins and the gift of the Holy Ghost. See Acts 2 chapter. "In whom ye also trusted *after that ye heard the word of truth*, the gospel of your salvation, in whom also *after that ye believed*, ye were sealed with that Holy Spirit of promise, which is the earnest of our inheritance until the redemption of the purchased possession unto the praise of His glory." That there is a time limited to the Holy Spirit as the earnest [illegible], [illegible] [illegible] *[illegible]*. See German version, [illegible] inheritance shall [illegible] is intimated by "*until*," understanding till another [illegible] shall commence, [illegible] try to get at the proper meaning of the apostle in order to see when that time shall be, and what the redemption of that purchased possession signifies. The spirit of God is our pledge certainly as long as we are in this life, that the redemption which has been procured for us by Christ shall actually be ours, and whether it will end in death I shall leave to every ones own opinion, but allowing the consciousness of the soul between death and the resurrection, which we must do if we believe the spirit of the Scripture, I incline to the belief that it will reach to the morning of the first resurrection, when mortality is swallowed up of life, and the immortal soul reunited with the body redeemed from corruption. That there is a redemption of the child of God and a redemption of the body in the future is evident from Romans 8, and a deliverance from the bondage of corruption to the glorious liberty of the children of God, where second death has no power, is equally evident, and even that the whole creation groaneth and travaileth in pain, it is the earnest expectation of the creature of humanity, and waiteth for the manifestation of the Son of God. And not only they, but ourselves also which have the first fruits of the spirit, even we ourselves groan within ourselves, waiting for the adoption, to wit, the redemption of the body,—likewise the spirit helpeth our infirmities. Is it not conclusive then, that Christians, the first fruit of the spirit, God's elect, yea, the first born of His creatures, the begotten of God, have need of being sealed with the Holy Spirit of promise? But what is the purchased possession? The purchased possession includes, in a general sense, the whole human family, for Christ tasted death for every man. He purchased with His own blood, all kindred, nations, tongues and people. Humanity strayed away from God, lost as sheep having no shepherd, were dead in trespasses and sins. Christ came, rescued them, "died for all, then were all dead." "And that he died for all, that they which live should not henceforth live unto themselves, but unto him which died and rose for us." O the glorious resurrection, Christ died and rose again. Soul-cheering and soul-reviving hope, the perfection of our faith, the consummation of sin, the finishing stroke of Redemption, the end of our justification, the key to Heaven and the diploma to admit us into the presence of God. But here is offered a conditional salvation for all those who have lost their title in Christ by trampling under foot the blood of the New Covenant wherewith they were sanctified by turning again to God, comply with that condition and live faithful unto Christ. They, with the innocent children, are in a more particular sense called the purchased possession and will be alike redeemed from corruption at the first resurrection and taken home to Christ as His own blood bought people, to realize that inheritance for which the Holy Spirit was their pledge.

LEONARD FURRY.

To be Continued.

GOD'S DESIGN IN CREATING MANKIND.

In the beginning God created man in His own image, male and female, to enjoy themselves with Him and to be fruitful, multiply, replenish and subdue the earth, and have dominion over the fowls of the air, the fishes of the sea and every living thing that moveth upon the earth, and were allowed to eat of every herb bearing seed, and of every tree in the which is the fruit yielding seed, but of the tree of knowledge of good and evil they were not to eat of, for in the day that they ate thereof they should surely die. Die from what? From the enjoyment with Him and be doomed to be with the beasts of the field and be under the curse with the earth by it, not yielding its full increase, and producing thorns and thistles and enslaving man the more to replenish it, and also brought mankind subject to diseases and finally death, and then to be rewarded according to their doings. Eve being beguiled of the serpent to eat of the forbidden fruit, she also tempted Adam to sin and knowing then good from evil, knowing they were naked and perceiving that they can do as they please, by using the opportunity in many things to the extreme and out of place, being responsible for their acts and being inclined to do evil, God gave them again consolation that the seed of the woman shall bruise the serpents head, and the seed of the serpent shall bruise his heel to restore mankind to enjoy themselves with God, to praise and adore Him for He is worthy of all honor, dominion and praise. And the holy prophets prophecied of Christ's coming who should bruise the serpents head. Perceive the love of God by not sparing His only Son, born from the tribe of Judah, to give His life for the sins of the world in the which we are also interested. He had been suffering also for us, to redeem us that we may be heirs with Him and enjoy ourselves in God's presence. O, what condescending love and great mercy for the Son of God to lay down His life for His friends, and He loved us even when we were enemies and aliens from the commonwealth of Israel or the children of God. He left His abode with God, put on human flesh, turned water into wine, healed the sick, cleansed the lepers, healed the maimed, gave sight to the blind, raised the dead and to the poor He preached the gospel, and such as gave heed to hear him. Therefore every one of us should give heed to His teachings, that is the will of His Heavenly Father which He has left us for information how to become heirs with Him, to be exalted and honored almost like the Son of God after being such depraved, sinful and unprofitable servants, scarcely worthy of anything. Therefore we should stop at once and not grieve God any more by sinning or disobeying His will. Let us be up and doing, in watchfulness and prayer, so that we may see and hear and understand aright and forsake the evil ways of the world. Love God with all our heart, soul, strength and mind, so that whatever we do it may be done for the wellfare of our soul and body and the welfare of others and the honor and glory of God, that we may become worthy to praise Him with Christ and His throng, in due reverence.

Let us lay aside all filthiness and superfluity of knowledge, and with meekness receive the ingrafted word of God which is able to save our souls, which says that we must believe that He is the only true and living God, and Him only should we worship, and that He is the rewarder of them that diligently seek Him. How seek Him? By doing according to the requirements of His will. We shall not take the name of God in vain, but give honor and reverence to Him on the Sabbath, which is a type of the glorious rest of the righteous in the mansions prepared of God to exercise with Christ. We shall honor our father and mother, be subject in accordance to the word of God, even for the sake of prosperity in this life. We shall not kill, abuse or misuse our brother, sister, neighbor, nor even our enemies, nor offend if it can be reasonably avoided, not commit adultery, nor cause strife or disturbance in families, but rather introduce forbearance, correction unity and love, and we shall not steal, not only goods, but allow each others rights and privileges, and encourage one another to faith and good works, bearing no false witness against one another or our neighbors, but rather speak words of truth and verity, and such as may induce others to turn from their errors, neither shall we covet anything that is our neighbors or that is belonging to somebody else. We oftentimes see things good and useful, and pleasing to have, we should not be tempted to get it by fraud or deceit, but do unto others as we ourselves wish to be done by.

Again, God wants us to make ourselves useful in this world, we shall be diligent in business, fervent in the spirit, serving the Lord, striving to improve our talents in some way in the Church, and in some occupation in laboring with our own hands, that we may also have something to give to the needy. We may wield our influence in many ways by following the example of Christ in the spirit of meekness and quietness, encouraging one another to faith and good works, by avoiding the foolish talking and evil doings of the world and the false professions thereof. Some think if the heart is right all is right, but if the heart is right we are willing to do all the commandments and to put down all pride that is above commonness and the knowledge of God, casting away our own conceits and imaginations, and unlawful lusts of the eyes for things of vanity and show. Let us take heed to Him that spake from Heaven, and spake as never man spake, that we do not neglect so great a salvation, which was at first spoken of by Moses and the Prophets and confirmed to the apostles that heard Christ speak, so that we may enter in through the gates into the city and have a right to the tree of Life, which yieldeth twelve manner of fruits, and the leaves of it are for the healing of the nations, where we may rest from our labors and our works do follow us. On such the second death has no power. I greet you in the name of God through the grace of Christ, to meet Him and one another in peace.

T. H. WISLER.

Honor, Ohio.

A LIGHT TO THE WORLD.

What is Safe and what is not Safe; What is Right and what is not Right.

BY J. H. MOORE.

CHAP. VI.—*Backward and Forward Baptism.*

We do not propose at this time to settle the question whether it is possible to obey any of the commandments by going *forward*? But the question is can we obey any of them by going *backward*? We do not intend to settle the question whether God is pleased with the *forward* action in baptism, but will he sanction the *backward* action? Here is where we get into difficulties. Nobody disputes the forward action being either right or safe, but the entire trouble is about the backward motion. We all know that our great Law giver has given commands that required a forward motion to obey—about this there is no dispute, this is safe ground, but did he ever, since the world began, give a command that required a backward motion? Here is a work for somebody who has been for years ransacking the Bible to find a divine commandment that must be performed *backward*. They can find them by the hundreds that are forward but these don't suit them.

There are people who see, or seem to see a world of things, but for their lives they cannot see the children of Israel passing through the Red Sea *forward*, which is a type of our forward baptism; they even fail to see Noah going into the ark forward, "The like figure whereunto even baptism doth also now save us." They see clear through the fact that we are baptized in the likeness of Christ's burial, when Paul says: "that so many of us as were baptized into Jesus Christ were baptized into his death," not his burial; his death took place on the cross when he bowed his head *forward* and gave up the Ghost, and how in the name of all reason can we be baptized in the likeness of his death by laying the body *backward* when he bowed *forward*?

All leading religious denominations agree that the face forward action is both safe and right, but the great difficulty is about the backward motion, is it either safe or right? We know that the forward is, and furthermore, we are certain that in the time of the apostles the administrator placed his right hand on the head of the candidate and gently bowed his head *forward* till he was fully immersed. I don't know of a single instance in the practice of the early Christian's, where they ever practiced the backward posture. Nor did the backward motion come into use among those who immersed till sometime after the commencement of the Reformation. [A. D. 1517.] It was then introduced by a class of people, who imagined that our Savior was buried on his back, hence in the likeness of that *imaginary burial* they commenced laying the body backward in the water. And the various religious denominations that have sprung from them still use the backward motion, not because it was ever practiced by the apostles or any of their immediate successors, but almost unconsciously has it crept from generation to generation, even down to our time and even now in this enlighted age there are those who regard it as of divine appointment.

And what is more surprising than

even all of this, is, that there are multitudes who condemn sprinkling and pouring because they are human inventions, and then turn right around and practice the backward method, which is not yet four hundred years old, lacking not less than 1440 years of being as old as Christian baptism. Those who undertake to trace the practice of immersion to the apostolic age, have to perform nearly their entire journey upon the forward method.

To suppose that God will sanction the backward baptism, is to simply put the inventions of men on an equal footing with the *thus saith the Lord*. We are not aware that he ever did sanction the introduction of a human invention in the room of a divine appointment, and to suppose that he will do so in this one case is neither reasonable nor necessary. It is then not even so much as questioned whether the forward baptism is right, but is the backward right? Here are all the doubts in the whole matter. We will stand on safe grounds and go FORWARD in the likeness of our Savior when he bowed his head and gave up the Ghost. Those who have a desire to go backward in the likeness of Eli who fell from his seat backward and broke his neck [1 Sam. 4: 18,] can do so.

All the communities of believers established in the early ages of Christianity either by the apostles or any of their immediate successors, practiced the forward method of baptizing. In the early times no one ever dreamed of baptizing any other way; they had but one method and that was the forward, the same as is now practiced by the Brethren. The Waldenses also practiced the same mode, while none have used the backward method only those who have in some way sprung from the English Baptist. Even their own historians regard them as the inventors of this modern method of baptizing. All the evidence in existence, both scriptural and historical, is decidedly in favor of the position that the Lord Jesus was baptized by bowing forward under the hand of John the Baptist, and those who propose to follow Jesus rather than man, should submit to no other method. This we are certain is not only right but safe. "I am the way the truth and life, no man cometh unto the Father, but by me."—*Jesus*.

YE ARE THE LIGHT.

Ye are the light of the world, a city that is set on a hill cannot be hid.—Matthew 5: 4.

This, we think is a text that should often be preached in our day, since the world thinks there is no reality in religion, and we know that it does not consist in saying Lord, Lord, but in doing what Jesus has commanded. It took then, and does now what is often preached, that faith and true repentance with a godly sorrow over sin, and baptism for the remission of sins to make them the light of the world. Now if we, who make this good profession before the world, are seen going into the saloons and there drink with the world, and when asked for our tobacco box, pass it freely, and are heard jesting and joking and talking foolishly, I would like to know how that light shines. Now brethren and sisters, Jesus meant that we should not be seen or take part where such things are going on, or we can not be the light of the world. Even men who are honest seekers must find a better state of things to convince them that there is a genuine or pure religion.

Again, if we are not transformed from the world in all things, how can we be the light of the world? If we have money to loan, and take from men out or in the Church, more than lawful interest, the light needs considerable trimming in my estimation of the text, since through the chaste conversation and godly walk, the world may be constrained to love God and keep His commandments. There is not much danger that these things are done before the Church, but always before the world where our light should shine. It was the world that Jesus came to save and is now gone up to Heaven, and has commanded us to preach His gospel and to see that it is lived out before the world so that there can none be mistaken, and as the apostle says, "What ye do, do all in the name of the Lord Jesus giving thanks to God by Him." Seeing then that we should be different from the world to be the light of it, seems almost sufficient, but it must be told a little plainer, for not only the laity, but those who are set apart are hardly willing that these things should be touched with the pen and indeed not willing to lay them aside, but it takes us all to watch that the light does not get too dim for the world to see it for they are to see it.

Now if the Church is to be as a city on a high hill, and if we would see a large city on a high hill or mountain, it would surely draw our attention. So if the world can see our good works it must come to the conclusion that there is reality in religion.

Brethren and sisters, let us remember that we also are the salt of earth, and if we lose our saving qualities, we certainly will be cast out to be trodden under foot of men. Now brethren and sisters, I do not want to censure the Church, but merely to stir up our pure minds in way of remembrance while so many temptations are before us.

JACOB BERKEY.

Goshen, Ind.

WHAT DO WE LIVE FOR?

In noticing the manners and daily walk of the mass of the people in this our day and time, we arrive at the conclusion that there are those, and in fact not a few, that do not know what they live for. They seem to drag through life as though they come by chance, and as if there was no just God, no deceitful devil, neither Heaven nor a soul to save. They seem to have nothing to do but to make the number more while living and less when dead, as though God did not demand anything of them, and as if the devil did not tempt them, they are as the chaff before the wind. "But why stand ye all the day idle? Doth not wisdom cry and understanding put forth her voice? Well may the Psalmist ask, "What is man that thou art mindful of him?" "For the ways of all men are before his eyes." "These seven things doth the Lord hate, a proud look, a lying tongue," &c., of which the world seems to be made up of nowadays. Some strive for wealth only, others for pleasure, while some few dare to live godly. But in order to make our lives profitable, "let us incline our ears unto wisdom, and apply our hearts to understanding, for happy is the man that findeth wisdom, and the man that getteth understanding." And "Keep our hearts with diligence, for out of it are the issues of life," and "Ponder the path of our feet, let our ways be established and turn neither to the right nor to the left," but say:

It's not for worldly goods I live,
But for the sparkling crown;
It's not for vain corrupted things,
But *Heaven's* high renown.

I'll live for good while here I stay,
And not for wretched woe;
I'll live for Heaven's eternal day,
And then to glory go.

I'll live and learn how I must die,
To gain that *Heavenly* rest;
I'll live to meet my God on high,
And be forever blest.

May the God of truth and grace teach us all what to live for, and what our duty in life is toward Him is the prayer of your unworthy servant.

J. B. LAIR.

Mexico, Ind.

For the Pilgrim.

FRIENDSHIP.

How dear is friendship. It sweetens the bitter cup, and smoothes the thorny path of life. How pleasing the idea! How animating the thought that we have friends. How much to be prized is a true friend in whom we may always confide. But some may ask, who are my friends, and how may I know them? Let me ask, how did the man that fell among thieves know which was his friend? You would readily answer, the Samaritan, because he showed mercy.

A true friend whose heart is drawn out in sympathy for those around, who is ready to speak a word of consolation to the afflicted and whose hand is ready to administer relief without expecting recompense, is to be prized among the sparkling gems of earth, but a false friend is more to be dreaded than an avowed enemy, for we know the design of an enemy is to injure, but a false friend is like a serpent coiled in the grass lying in ambush for its prey, and its unhappy victim is ensnared before he is aware that danger is near. Some will be our friends while prosperity blooms along our pathway, then all goes on pleasantly, but when adversity, with its chilly blast, sweeps away the flowers of prosperity, and naught but the leafless stock, the recollection of the past remains, then we look around for our friends. Alas! they are gone, yes, gone when we most needed them.

But to obtain true friends, we have a part to act. We must show ourselves friendly to our brethren and sisters and friends, and those with whom we associate. Many of us have had our family circles broken by the impartial hand of death, we have seen a kind father, an indulgent mother, or both consigned to the silent grave. Many of us have received the unwelcome tidings of the death of parents and friends; unwelcome to us indeed it is, while perusing the pages of the fatal letter which bore the message, that made our hearts ready to burst with grief. Painful thought, that we had not the privilege of standing by their couch of pain and administering to their varied wants, or of hearing their farewell advice, nor of seeing the last flicker of the lamp of life as it was gently extinguished by the hand of death. Then how alleviating to the afflicted soul it is to have a friend that will sympathize with us in our deep affliction, and with kind and consoling words, pouring the oil and wine into the bruised heart. Again, if anything transpires to add happiness to the contented mind how brightly that spark will kindle when shared with a true and faithful friend. Under considerations like these, ought we not to show ourselves friendly to all. If we meet with a stranger, treat that stranger kindly, for we know not what secret sorrow is his. We little know what painful emotions are throbbing in his bosom. A mild word, or friendly look or some little act of kindness may be the means of alleviating much heartfelt sorrow. Happy thought.

HARRIET E. HUMMER.

Marsh Creek, Pa.

He that always complains is never pitied.

RESTORATION OF ISRAEL.

That this is, by many, considered an abstruse subject, one not connected with a Christian's duties or welfare and hence not profitable for discussion, I am well aware, and yet I am also aware that there are others who have given the subject more than a passing notice, in fact, considerable study; and as a result, even Brethren, have arrived at different conclusions, and I, being one that has arrived at one conclusion after reading and studying the prophecies relating thereto, would fain offer an opinion, with all due respect for the opinions of others, and if I am in error those in possession of better light and knowledge will please correct, as it is not my wish to disseminate incorrect opinions.

That Israel has a promise of restoration at some certain period of time is admitted, I believe, by all, but the points of difference, are, 1st. What is Israel to be restored from? 2nd. What is Israel to be restored to? 3d. Who are Israel?

In considering this subject we will first ascertain the definition of the words used. Restoration according to Webster, means, 1st. Act of being restored. 2nd. State of being restored. Restore means to bring back from a state of ruin or decay.

Now, first, we claim Israel is to be restored from ruin or decay or both, and in establishing this position, will quote certain prophecies of the olden time. Just here I wish to call the attention of the reader to the fact that many writers, in attempting to elucidate this subject, have used the prophecies relating to the punishment of the Jews for disobedience and the rewards or blessings they were to receive for repentance and obedience; and also those having reference to the return of the Jews from the Babylonish captivity, which prophecies I propose to eliminate and use only such as remain to be fulfilled.

In pursuance of that I shall first quote Isa. 11: 11. "And it shall come to pass in that day, that the Lord shall set His hand again the second time to recover the remnant of his people which shall be left from Assyria, and from Egypt, and from Pathros, and from Cush, and Elam, and from Shinar, and from Hamath, and from the islands of the sea."

Assyria is one name applied to the the empire under which the Jews suffered their seventy years bondage but Isaiah could not have had reference to that bondage from the fact that he mentions several other countries and the islands of the sea while only the one term of Assyria or Babylon, (which are synonymous) is used in connection with the seventy years captivity. It may be argued that these different countries were but integral parts of the Assyrian Empire: admitted—but such was not the case for many years after. I also deduce from the quotation above, that Israel was in an advanced state of decay and consequently of ruin, from the fact that there was only a remnant to be recovered, whereas if my understanding is correct, there was more brought back than went into captivity in Babylon. "And I will gather the remnant of my flock out of all countries whither I have driven them, and will bring them to their folds; and they shall be fruitful and increase. And I will set up shepherds over them, which shall feed them; and they shall fear no more, nor be dismayed, neither shall they be lacking, saith the Lord." Jer.—23: 3, 4.

It is evident from the foregoing prophecies that Israel was or would be in a deplorable condition, in a ruined state, for in what worse condition could any people be than to be without the favor and friendship of God, to be without the civilizing, the refining, the Christianizing influences of religion, to be without the soul-cheering presence of the spirit of God, bearing witness with their spirits that they were the children of God and to be subject to all the wiles and machinations of a powerful adversary as well as all the ills that flesh is heir to without one assuring hope of rest in this world or in the world to come? It will be admitted this is, or would be, a ruined condition and any people placed in such a condition would naturally deteriorate and decay. And it was from just this predicament that I understand Israel was to be restored. For further support of this, see the fifth, the eighth, and especially the fifteenth and sixteenth chapters of Jeremiah.

The second question is, what is Israel to be restored to? I have placed these in the line of rotation in which they are usualy treated, because it required the greatest amount of argument to make the answer, usually given to this second question acceptable, for it is almost invariably shown or attempted to be shown, that Israel must be restored to nationality first, and afterward would come to a restoration spiritually, but as according to my understanding of the question, this is reversing the two positions Israel was destined to occupy, I will, for my own convenience in treating the subject, transpose the questions and treat the third question first and the second can be easily and briefly answered, especially, as I shall only speak of Israel in a spiritual sense; not that I deny that Israel will be restored to nationality, but simply, that I do not understand Israel is to be settled in Palestine at all or that Israel is to be formed into a nation before its restoration spiritually. And now I will answer the third question, Who is the Israel to whom the promises are made?

The word Israel, when translated means, a prince of God; who prevails with God; hence I do not understand that Jews are Israelites at this day because when we consider the definition of the term it cannot be said they are Princes of God or that they prevail with God.

Again, when the promise was made to Abraham, that in him and his seed all the nations and kindreds and families of the earth should be blessed, said promise was made as a reward for implicit faith manifested by obedience, and as the Jews are notoriously an unbelieving race, rejecting entirely the Savior and the Testament, He gave, thereby manifesting a want of faith not only in Christ but also in the word of God spoken through the mouths of His prophets since the world began concerning Christ. Hence I argue that the promises of restoration have found or will find fulfillment, not in the Jews but in the true and faithful followers of Christ, for be it remembered that God, by the mouth of the prophet Jeremiah, says: "Behold the days come saith the Lord that I will make a new covenant with the house of Israel and with the house of Judah." Jer.—31: 31. And Paul, in writing to the Hebrews, treating this subject, says: "For if that first covenant had been faultless, then should no place have been sought for the second." "In that he saith, a new covenant, he hath made the first old. Now that decayeth and waxeth old, is ready to vanish away. Heb. 8: 7, 13. Then if the first covenant is old and has been superceded by a new and better covenant, established, as Paul says, "on better promises," and again in speaking in relation to this same subject, "Then said he, Lo, I come to do thy will, O God. He taketh away the first that he may establish the second." Now if by Christ fulfilling, He taketh the first covenant away, and the Jews claiming and accepting no other covenant, on the contrary they emphatically repudiate that second covenant which Paul says "was made on the better promises," wherein is their promises contained, seeing that "by the deeds of the law no flesh shall be justified?" I understand that the unbelieving Jew stand in the same alienated relation to God that the unbelieving unregenerate gentiles and unless he believes and repents of his sins that he will suffer the same consequences for a sinful life, the unrepentant Gentiles will, for Paul, in writing to the Romans, argues this fully, and the conclusion that he seems to arrive at, is, that through the faith that Abraham manifested, he was accounted righteous without circumcision, and that circumcision was given unto him as a seal of his righteous faith for, says Paul, the promise that he should be heir of the world was not made to Abraham through the law, but through the righteousness of faith." For, says he, "if they which of the law be heirs, faith is made void, and the promise is of none effect." In another place Paul says, "Who are Israelites: to whom pertaineth the adoption, and the glory, and the covenants, and the giving of the law, and the service of God, and the promises?"

For they are not all Israel who are of Israel; neither because they are the seed of Abraham are they all children: but, in Isaac shall thy seed be called." Again, "but Israel which followed after the law of righteousness hath not attained to the law of righteousness.

Wherefore, because they sought it not by faith, but, as it were, by the works of the law, for they stumbled at that stumbling stone." Paul also says that "he that is circumcised Christ shall profit him nothing;" and I also read that "there is no other name given under Heaven or among men whereby we must be saved only in the name of Jesus." Hence I can not believe that the promises of restoration are made to the unbelieving Jew, but to all those who believe on the Lord Jesus Christ, be they Jew or Gentile, bond or free, and I thank God that it is so, for if it were not so, those who Paul calls the Israel of God would lose much of the future joy that I have always thought would be theirs.

Now in regard to the question, what Israel is to be restored to, I will only say, restored to the favor and friendship of God, restored to the serving God and so living that we may, through the atonement of our Savior, meet God in peace and ultimately be received into his family above.

There might be much more written on this subject but this article is already larger than it was designed to be and if the ideas are erroneous it is too large now.

M. J. McClure.

Lower Fall Creek, Ind.

The things that tend to elevate a person into noble self-sacrifice, generosity, purity of life and communion with God are good; but the things that lead out to selfishness, penury, hatred and the development of the animal instincts are evil. Let every one ask the question—which way am I tending? Are the influences by which I am led elevating me into a higher life or are they tending to degrade me into lust and sin?—*J. B. B.*

Youth's Department

THE GOOD SHEPHERD.

A giddy lamb one afternoon,
Had from the fold departed;
The tender shepherd missed it soon,
And sought it heavy hearted.
Not all the flock that shared his love
Could from the search delay him;
Nor clouds of midnight darkness move,
Nor fear of suffering stay him.

By night and day he went his way
In sorrow till he found it:
And when he saw it fainting lay
He clasped his arms around it.
And closely sheltered in his breast,
From every ill to save it,
He brought it to his home of rest,
And pitied and forgave it.

And so the Savior will receive
The little ones who hear him:
Their pains remove, their sins forgive,
And draw them gently near him;
Bless while they live, and when they die,
And soul and body sever,
Conduct them to his home on high,
To dwell with him forever.

—*Childrens Friend.*

A TALK ABOUT FLOWERS.

Spring time is now here in all its loveliness and no doubt, many of my little readers have real nice times gathering the pretty flowers that our kind God has strewn so plentifully everywhere. Flowers are real pretty and the smell is so deliciously sweet that I do not blame you if you do spend a few hours daily amongst them.

But flowers, like boys and girls, are not made to be admired for their beauty alone. If your playmates had no loveliness about them but their beauty, you would soon grow weary of their company. Just so it would be with the pretty flowers that you now so much admire. If they would always remain the same beautiful flower you would soon grow weary of them, their bright colors would lose their loveliness and the sweet fragrance grow insipid and stale, the fact is, you would become so accustomed to it that after awhile you would hardly notice its presence at all. It is the changing from one thing to another that we so much admire. First we notice the little bud, it swells and the shell, that has so long protected it from the cold winds, snows and frosts, burst and the beautiful flower spreads itself in all its lovely colors, with its odor shedding a fragrance all around. A few days of sun and shade and the fragrance grows less and less, the pretty colors fade away and it drops to the ground just as if that was all it was made for, but if you examine the place from which it fell, you will find that it had a purpose and that its work was accomplished, there is the tiny fruit already forming into shape and in a few weeks and months it will be grown or matured in the shape of a delicious cherry, peach, plum or pear or something else equally good. First the bud, then the flower and then the fruit. So you see, everything has its place and order. If there were no buds there could be no flowers, and without flowers there could be no fruit.

I hope you will excuse me for going around so far to tell a short story but I want to set you to thinking. It would be shocking to think of people being born big men and women at once. We could not think of it. The fact is, it would spoil all our enjoyment and we would become weary for want of change. How glad then we ought to feel that everything is made just right. If you will take the trouble to read several of the first chapters of Genesis you will there learn that after God had labored six days he looked upon all he made and he said it was good. The little buds he made were good, the flowers were good, the fruit was good and, did I say the little boys and girls which he makes are also good? Yes, that is what I intended to say. That chubby little brother or sister of yours is the bud, and you, my young readers, are the flowers, but the great question is, will you ever mature any fruit? If not, you do not fill your purpose nearly so well as the flowers we were just talking about. Hundreds and thousands of little boys have lived and died without bearing any fruit just because they were naughty to their comrades and disobedient to their parents. If you wish to be pretty and lovely flowers, OBEY YOUR PARENTS, love your little brothers and sisters and be kind to your playmates and to all whom you meet. Such things are most beautiful flowers and will produce such fruit as will never fail you. Be good children and you will hear from me again.

UNCLE HENRY.

ISAAC'S MISTAKE.

"Please, brother Isaac, won't you go with me after the cows?" asked little Peter Case of his elder brother. "They go in all directions," he continued, "and I have to run everywhere." "Don't bother now, Peter, I want to finish this book to-night," replied Isaac, "perhaps I'll get through in season to stop their going down after the apples though." "Oh! do, for that will help so much," and Peter hurried away, for the sun was almost down and he feared to be late.

"You may bring in the chips, Susan," said Mrs. Case, "Isaac is very busy reading and I do not like to interrupt him. He'll be a wonderful man some day if he keeps at his books." So, while Isaac pored over the printed page the other children did the chores readily and without a shade of discontent, for Isaac was believed to be a rare genius, a wonderful prodigy, who took to learning as naturally as a duck to water.

"He doesn't seem interested in pigs or sheep or chickens, same as other children be," said Mrs. Case proudly, "but I do believe he'd read from morn till night week in and week out. I do hope his health won't give way, he's such a promising child. Some folks say 'tis hard, hard work to study, but bor' me, our Isaac just likes it, he does. He'll 'stonish the world some time with his learning."

In short, the whole family for years cherished the fond hope that one of their number was to achieve greatness. The parents, as you may suppose, had not enjoyed the advantages of good instruction in their younger days, and later the cares of providing for physical wants gave little time for improvement, and as too often happens, that little was neglected. But times had bettered of late; books and papers were easily obtained, and they resolved that no expense should be spared to give Isaac a liberal education. The other children must be content with lesser advantages. Now Isaac shared in all the fond anticipations of future fame, yet if the truth must be spoken, he was of so indolent a disposition that he chose reading merely because it was easier to turn the leaves of a book than the sods in a potato patch. As his teachers did not perceive his extra scholarship, they were voted dull and commonplace, quite unable to guide and assist his soaring genius. So he was permitted to select his own books and study by himself as he pleased. But when little Peter would question him as to what was in some big book, he would either say, "You don't expect me to remember everything, do you?" or, "I can't explain it to a boy."

"But I can tell what I read about to day and explain every point in my lesson," persisted Peter.

"Pshaw! that's nothing," said lazy Isaac, "you only read a page while I have read hundreds."

"One thing well learned is better than a dozen passed over without any attention, my teacher says," replied Peter.

Isaac shrugged his shoulders, saying, "She doesn't know much, I guess."

But as the years rolled away, Peter, who could only be spared an hour or two a day from manual labor, in mental discipline and strength far outstripped his elder brother, who read continually without reflection. The books and papers he devoured without order or method would fill a whole library, but their contents were only stumbling blocks to real progress, and too late he learned that merely glancing at other men's thoughts, however learned or conclusive their arguments may be, will never make one either learned or wise, respected or esteemed.—*School-day Magazine.*

Correspondence.

A Reporter is wanted from every Church in the brotherhood to send us Church news, Obituaries, Announcements, or anything that will be of general interest. To insure insertion, the writers name must accompany each communication. Our Invitation is not personal but general—please respond to our call.

Dear Editors:—As it is a great pleasure for me to read the PILGRIM, I will relate an occurrence, which, simple as it may appear, I hope will be worthy the attention of your readers. A young lady became convinced of the drawings of the Father which led her to consider the duties she owed to her Lord and Master. Being determined to accept the call, she made her wants known to her parents, which was a matter of great rejoicing to them. She then requests her mother to accompany her to her sisters, and as they were on their way, she noticed her brother in the field plowing and says:

"Mother, see yonder is my brother, may I go and talk to him?"

"Yes, daughter, you can go, but don't stay long."

She then goes to him and says:

"Brother, I have made up my mind to forsake my sinful ways and serve the Lord. I intend to be baptized, will you not go along with me?"

The brother at first seemed to give little heed to her appeals, but a sisters love cannot be put off as long as there is hope, so she followed him several times around his plot, telling him of her determination and the duties she owed to her Lord, exerting all the influence she could command to get him to go with her, until finally he stopped his plow and said:

"Sister, your arguments are too strong for me, I must yield, I will go with you and aid you in fighting the battle of the Lord."

She then returned to her mother and said:

"Oh mother! I have gained my brother."

The mother, on this intelligence, was made greatly to rejoice and, no doubt, the angels in heaven were made to rejoice with them.

Thus dear young brethren and sisters, you can see what can be done when we exert our influence in favor of the blessed cause of our Master and for the salvation of souls.

K. L.

Cherry Grove, Ill.

Dear Pilgrim:—While items of interesting Church news are carried to the homes of our beloved brethren and sisters upon the pages of our periodicals, we desire also to have a little space that we may encourage others on the way as we have been encouraged by our brethren. On the morning of the 26th of April a snow was on the ground about two inches deep but as the sun arose the snow disappeared, and at 9 o'clock our beloved brethren and sisters gathered in groups in and around the Centre Meeting-house to hold the Annual Council. Bishops Conrad Kahler, George Irwin and John B. Shoemaker being present, council was commenced and immediately after dinner a choice for two Deacons was held, and the solemn responsibility of filling the duties of this office fell upon our beloved brethren Simon Peter Eby and Michael Gehman, who, after expressing their willingness, were installed into office. On the evening of the same day brethren Kahler and Shoemaker delivered each a short sermon—"that came from the heart and went to the heart." The meetings were continued on Sunday and Sunday evening, brother George Irwin also taking part in preaching with zeal and energy. Now the seed is sown and we look with earnest expectation and desire for the fruit thereof. "Paul may plant, Apollos may water, but it is God that giveth the increase."

B. B. BOLLINGER.

Louisville, Stark Co., O.

Dear Pilgrim:—By your permission, I will present to your readers a few thoughts on the character and deportment of ministers, churches, &c. That there is a looseness of Christian principles manifested must be evident to all and there was never a time that the following advice given by Paul to Timothy is more needed.

I Charge thee therefore before God and the Lord Jesus Christ who shall judge the quick and the dead at his appearing and his kingdom, preach the word." Tim.—4 : 1.

Here is a charge before God and the Lord Jesus Christ for every minister of Christ to preach the Word of God. Now let us see how many of the so called Ministers of God preach the Word, or how many of the members of the different Churches live up to God's holy law. Can any of them be told from the rest of the world by their daily walk and conversation? Can any man or woman go into one of their churches and pick out their member from the rest of their congregation? Do not the members dress in the very height of fashion and do their preachers tell them it is contrary to the will of God? "In like manner also that women adorn themselves in modest apparel, with shamefacedness and sobriety, not with broidered hair, or gold, or pearls, or costly array, but which becometh women professing godliness, with good works." If a person wishes to join their Church and be baptized, the minister will sprinkle, pour or immerse at their pleasure or convenience. Was Paul sprinkled, Peter poured and John immersed? They admit of three different baptisms but Paul says: "There is one God, one faith, one baptism. Eph.—Eph. 4 : 5. Now, if there is only one, why do they preach three different baptisms? Paul says: Romans—6 : 4. "Therefore we are buried with him by baptism.

Again, they will have their festivals and buy and sell, have oysters and ice cream and sell things at auction and their ministers say it is right Christ says, in His Holy Word, Mat. 21 : 12, 13, And Jesus went into the temple of God and cast out all them that sold and bought in the temple, and overthrew the tables of the money changers and the seats of them that sold doves, and said unto them, it is written my house shall be called the house of prayer but ye have made it a den of thieves." They eat the Lord's Supper but do they wash the disciples feet? Why not? because it is stooping too low, it is not popular, it would be a disgrace to get down so low and wash a brother or sisters feet. "Who art thou, , O man that makes thyself better than God." Read John 13th chapter. Again, do they salute a brother with a holy kiss, or would it shame them? We are commanded to salute one another in several places in the Bible and why be ashamed of that which was commanded of God?

Dear brethren and sisters and all you that desire to live Godly lives, flee such doctrine and live righteously in the sight of God, for if we ever get to Heaven we must keep all of God's commands, 1 John—2 : 4, "He that saith I know Him and keepeth not His commandments is a liar and the truth is not in him." And again, Jas. 2 : 10, "For whosoever shall keep the whole law and yet offend in one point, he is guilty of all, therefore if we wish to live Christians in the sight of God and the Lord Jesus Christ, we must keep even the very least of his commands, love one another and lay aside all pride and vanity and foolish fashions of the world. 2 Cor.—6 : 17, "Wherefore come out from among them and be ye seperate saith the Lord." Let us therefore dress ourselves and our children in modest apparel and in the fear of God, and let us take upon ourselves the whole armor of God that we may stand against the wiles of the devil. Let us strive to enter in by the door into the fold of Christ, for "he that climbeth up some other way is a thief and a robber."

In conclusion I will say, in the name of God and of the Lord Jesus Christ, when you preach, preach the word, don't try to preach anything that is not in the Bible as the Gospel of Christ, but preach boldly against this so-called popular religion and the fashions of the world. Gal. 1 : 8, "But though we or an angel from heaven preach any other Gospel unto you than that which we have preached unto you let him be accursed."

D. R. HURLBUT.

Lacrosse, Wis.

ROANOAK, ILL., May 4, '73.

Dear Pilgrim: For the first time I take my pen in hand to give you a little news from this part of God's moral heritage. Four weeks ago the brethren met at our meeting-house and organized a Sabbath school for the first time in this part of the country among the Brethren, and it is very largely attended, and there appears to be great interest taken in it by the brethren and the friends in general, and I must say we use the best of all books and that is the Bible. We object to those books, that are generally used in Sabbath schools, with those long stories and fables that never transpired. Our prayer is that our school will be a pleasant one, and that great success will accompany it, as we have a great many young people in this part of God's moral Vineyard, and thank the good Lord we had the opportunity, after meeting to-day, of going down to the water-side to attend to one of the ordinances of the Lord's house, namely, baptism. I just thought that many more might follow the same example and make the angels in Heaven rejoice as well as the saints on earth.

Now I must say in conclusion, I am well pleased with the PILGRIM so far as this is the first year I have taken it. It gives us a large amount of good instruction which if we will adhere to, will be good for us in time and eternity. GEO. W. GISH.

ANNOUNCEMENTS.

Bro. Editor: — Please announce to the readers of the PILGRIM that we intend, God willing, to hold a Lovefeast in the Yellow creek Church near New Enterprise, Bedford, Co., Pa., on Wednesday the 28th of May, 1873, commencing at 4 o'clock p. m. Meeting next day forenoon. General invitation is extended.

By order of the church.

LEONARD FURRY

Dear Brother of the Pilgrim:—Please announce that the Lick Creek Church, Williams Co., Ohio, have appointed a Lovefeast on the 10th and 11th of June to commence at 10 o'clock a. m., at the house of David Rittenhouse. A general invitation is given. If any one come by railroad stop off at Bryan. The place of meeting is about 15 miles north of Bryan. Conveyance will be attended to.

JOHN BROWN.

Please announce a Communion Meeting in Canton Church, Stark Co., O. at Bro. John Seefing 3 miles north of Louisville, on the 8th of June. Ministers specially invited.

B. B. BOLLINGER.

Dear Pilgrim:—Please announce that the Lost Creek Church, Juniata Co., Pa., have appointed a Lovefeast on the 20th and 21st of May next, commencing at one o'clock at the Goodwill meeting-house, 10 miles east of Mifflin station, and about 7 miles north of Thomsonstown station. If those ministering brethren that proposed being with us would inform us by letter whether they could be at one of the above named stations on the 17th we would make several appointments for them. One of our regular places for meeting is 2 miles north of Mifflin station on the 18th.

M. BESHOAR, SR.

Bro. Henry—Please announce in the PILGRIM that we, the Brethren in Snake Spring congregation, Bedford Co., Pa., have appointed our Lovefeast on the 30th day of May, commencing at 10 o'clock. Also meeting next day. A hearty invitation extended especially to ministering brethren.

HENRY HERSHBERGER.

Please announce that the brethren of the Jacobs' Creek Church, Somerset Co., Pa., intend to hold a Lovefeast on the 24th and 25th of May. Brethren please make your arrangements to stop with us returning from District Meeting. The meeting is to be held at Bro. John Meyers, 3 miles south of Mt. Pleasant. By order of the Church. F. B. WEIMER.

Bro. Brumbaugh: — Please announce that the brethren of Falling Springs Church, Pa., intend holding a Lovefeast at Hades' Church on the 16th of May. The usual invitation given.

D. H. BONEBRAKE.

NOTICE.

This informs all that will attend the District Council in Perry Co., of north-eastern O. I have got the grant of half fare on the Baltimore and Ohio R. R. from Mansfield and all stations. So you must all pay full fare going and at the meeting you will get a return certificate free. I want a full representation of brethren at said meeting when the company shows such liberality.

WM. SADLER.

To the brethren of the north western district of Ohio. As there is a surplus fund in the hands of the undersigned from last A. M., we request a general representation to district meeting on the 23rd of May, where a distribution of the same may be expected.

DANIEL BROWER.

QUERIES.

Will some brother or sister please give, through the PILGRIM an explanation on Luke 16 : 9, and more particularly on the latter part of the verse; "That when ye fail, &c.," fail in what?

JACOB BOCK.

Will some brother give an explanation of John tenth chapter and latter part of the ninth verse.

MARTIN J. McCLURE.

DISTRICT MEETING.

Middle District of Pa., at Clover Creek, May 13.

Middle District of Iowa, in Dallas Co., on the 19th day of May.

North-eastern District of Ohio, Jonathan's Creek Congregation, Perry Co., on May 20th.

About 1 mile from Lititz at Bro. Pfautz's, Lancaster Co., Pa., May 15th. Delegates to meet the afternoon before.

Please notice through the PILGRIM that the District Meeting of Western Pa., will be held at the Fairview Meeting house in the George's Creek branch, Fayette Co. Pa., on Wednesday 21st of May, '73.

J. FOUST.

Please announce that the District Meeting of North-Western Ohio will be held, the Lord willing, with the brethren of Crawford Co., at the house of brother John Brilharts, on the Base Line on the 23 day of May, and on the 24, the day following, there will be a Communion meeting at the same place. A general representation is desired. ISRAEL ROOP.

LOVEFEASTS.

Spring Run, Mifflin county, Pa, May 27, 28.

Beaver Creek, Wednesday May 14, at 1 P. M.

Shade Creek Congregation, Somerset co. Pa., May 20, commencing at 10 a. m.

Champaign Co., Ill., at Geo. Dillings, 3 miles east of Urbana, 7th and 8th of June.

Codorus, York county, Pa., on the 7th and 8th of June at the East Codorus M. H.

At the house of Bro. Jacob Long, 2½ miles south of Annville, 16th and 17th of May.

Welch Run, Thursday May 15, commencing at 1 o'clock P. M., continuing next day till noon. E. Slifer.

Dry Valley Church, Mifflin Co., Pa. May 27th, 10 o'clock A. M., ¼ mile from Maitland on the Sunbury and Lewistown R. R.

MARRIED.

GEHRETT—NORRIS.—At the Pilgrim office, by the Editor, May 8th, 1873, Mr. Oliver Gehrett and Miss Susan Norris, all of Huntingdon Co., Pa.

DIED.

ROW.—In the Vally River Congregation, near Bealington, *Barbour* Co., W. Va., our beloved sister Delila F. Row, aged 32 years.

Sister Row had been a member of the Church for 18 months, and during that time she lived a consistent Christian, walking in the laws of the Lord blameless. Her chief delight was to always be about her Father's business. Pleading for His word in its original order was one of her chief characteristics, and when sickness at last deprived her of attending public worship, she was not an idler in the Vineyard of the Lord, but when her friends and relatives would come to see her she would always make occasion to speak in behalf of her Master. Her last moments seemed to be her happiest ones. She plead with her husband, who is not a brother, to serve God, and so warm was her pleading that he promised to follow her example and serve his Master. Brethren pray that the promise may be realized. After complying with the last injunction by being annointed she expressed her willingness to go and her gentle spirit took its flight. Funeral sermon by the brethren from the words, "She hath done what she could," to a large and attentive congregation. She leaves a husband, eight children and many friends to mourn their loss.

J. W. Fitzgerald.

(*Vindicator*, please copy.)

ZAHN.—In the Fairview District, Ind., on the 11th of April, '73, our dear and well beloved sister Jennie Zahn, aged 30 yrs. 5 months and 20 days.

She had come to the Church from the entire outside world, and was a very faithful sister, made her home a place of hospitality and died in the true faith of the christian religion, leaving a dear husband and five children with many friends to mourn their loss. Funeral services from 1 Peter 1: 24-25, by the writer and others to a large concourse of people.

CRIPE.—In the North Fork, of the Wild Cat District, Ind., April 20, '73 brother Daniel Cripe, aged 57 years, 6 months and 10 days. Funeral occasion improved by Isaac Billheimer and others from 2 Timothy 4:6-7-8, to a very large audience. He was a faithful watchman upon the walls of Zion in the second degree of the ministry. No doubt but that the Church will greatly feel his loss, but we sincerely believe their loss will be his eternal gain.

(*Companion*, please copy.)

Samuel Carey.

COFFMAN.—In the Manor Church, near Brethardsville, Md., April 28, '73, of Appoplexy, sister Lydia, wife of David Coffman, aged 61 years, and 13 days.

Thus an affectionate mother has been separated from a kind husband, and dear children, but we trust that those who are left behind will continue looking unto Jesus in their bereavement. She was a dear mother, and has always been regarded as one that was respected and beloved by all who knew her. She was a faithful sister in Christ, and finally fell asleep in Jesus.

Dear children, let faiths' consoling power,
Forever restrain your tears of love;
For who that witnessed my parting hour,
Could wish my enrapured soul from above.

ANDERSON.—In the James Creek Congregation, Pa., March, 18 '73, Nancy M., daughter of Anthony and Sarah Anderson aged 11 years, 3 months and 8 days. Funeral preached in the Bethel, April 27, by the Editor.

Nannie was a bright and hopeful little girl, much loved by her parents who greatly mourn their loss, though they have the blessed assurance that she has gone home to Jesus, who has said, "Suffer little children to come unto me and forbid them not, for of such is the Kingdom of Heaven."

HARMINSON.—Near Ogden, Champeign Co., Ill., Mary E., daughter of brother and sister Harminson, April 12, '73, aged 1 year, 3 months and 24 days. Funeral services by the brethren. J. H. Moore.

EMMERT.—In the Beaver Creek Church, Washington Co., Md., April 17, '73, Fannie Victoria, youngest daughter of sister Susan Emmert, widow of late Dr. Andrew Emmert, aged 12 years, 9 mos. and 21 days. Disease Dropsy. The funeral service improved by brethren D. F. Stouffer and A. Cost from Mark 5; 39, "The damsel is not dead, but sleepeth."

We loved her, yes, no tongue can tell,
How much we loved her, and how well;
God loved her too, and He thought best,
To take her home to be at rest.

E. G.

(*Companion*, please copy.)

SPRINKLE.—Near Lancaster Indiana, March 30, '73, of spotted fever, Ella, daughter of brother Levi and Christena Sprinkle, aged 12 years and 12 days. Funeral discourse by Geo. W Jewett and others. Matthew 10: 13.

BRUMBAUGH.—Loonereek, Huntington Co., Ind., April 9, '73, Charlotte Fridly, daughter of Henry and Rebecca Brumbaugh, aged 22 years, 2 months and 13 days. The occasion to be improved by J. S. Leedy and the writer on the fourth Sunday of May. G. W Jewett.

TRAYER.—In Huntersville, Madison Co., Ind., April 18, '73, of Inflamation of the bowels, Silas A Trayer, aged about 48 years.

The deceased was not a member of any Church, but that he was respected as a citizen was attested by the unusually large attendance at his burial. Funeral preached on the 27th of April from Job 14 chap. and first clause of 14 verse by the writer and Samuel Bock. M. J. McClure.

(*Visitor*, please copy.)

BOGGINS.—In Fayette Co., W. Va. October 19, '72, of whooping-cough Robert K., son of friend Samuel and sister Mary Boggins, aged 18 months.

KINCADE.—In the bounds of the Fayette Co. Church district, W. Va., January 28, '73, sister Sarah Kincade, aged 61 years. She died in hopes of a blessed immortality. J. S. Flory.

SMITH.—In the village of Stonerstown, Bedford Co. Pa., (*Hopewell Church*,) April 22, '73, sister Eliza Jane, wife of brother David Smith, aged 46 years, 11 months and 12 days. Funeral occasion improved by the writer and D. S. Clapper from Rev. 14: 12-13.

S. A. Moore.

BEAR.—In Shady Grove, Pa., Mary H *Bear*, died April 11th, A. D., 1873, aged 33 years, 11 months, and 1 day. Funeral services by Bro. J. A Stover and the writer, from Amos 3: 12.

MILLER.—Bro. Jacob H. Miller, in Greencastle Pa., on the 21st of April, A. D., 1873, aged 59 years, 4 mo. and 18 days. Funeral services by bro. Abram Golly and the writer.

DECKER.—Fanny Decker, on the 28th of April, 1873, aged 5 years 10 months and 22. Funeral services by the brethren from Jas. 4: 14.

John Zuck.

JORDAN.—In the Bachlor Run Church, Carroll Co., Ind., March 10th, 1873, Nancy Elizabeth, daughter of friend Josiah and sistre Elizabeth Jordan, and consort of David Eikenberry: aged 20 years, 2 months and 23 days. Funeral occasion improved by Elders Hiel Hamilton and Isaac Eikenberry from 17 Psalm, 15th verse.

The above notice was married on last New Year's day to David Eikenberry, son of Eld. John F. and Elizabeth Eikenberry of Butler Co., Iowa; went to Iowa last Fall with the expectation of returning home by next Fall with his wife, but instead of that she has gone to her long home. She was taken with a severe attack of lung fever and from that to hasty consumption, which soon done its fatal work. This is a solemn warning to those of her young associates who have not made their peace with God. May they too make preparation before the icy hand of death takes them to their eternal home. J. Eikenberry.

(*Companion* please copy.)

BEEGHLY.—In the Cove district, Md., Oct 15, 1873, Wm. R. M., twin son of Daniel and Sally *Beeghly*, aged 1 year and 3 months. Funeral services by the writer and Jacob M. Thomas, in the Lutheran Church, Bear Creek, Md.

TURNEY.—Sister Hannah Rebecca Turney, formerly the widow of William Fike and daughter of Michael M. Thomas. She was annointed with oil in the name of the Lord and the bread and wine or the communion administered shortly before her death. She died in the triumph of faith, aged 33 years, 9 months and 2 days. She leaves a sorrowing husband and 4 children and father and sister and brothers and friends to mourn the loss. Funeral service by Eld. Jacob M. Thomas and the writer from *Isaiah*, 38th chapter and latter part of the first verse, "Set thine house in order for thou shalt die and not live." Jacob Beeghly.

(*Companion* and *Visitor* please copy.)

The Weekly Pilgrim.

JAMES CREEK, PA., May 13, 1873.

☞ How to send money.—All sums over $1.50, should be sent either in a check, draft or postal order. If neither of these can be obtained, have the letter registered.

☞ When Money is sent, *always* send with it the name and address of those who paid it. Write the names and post office as plainly as possible.

☞ Every subscriber for 1873, gets a *Pilgrim Almanac* Free.

A SAD DISASTER

In glancing over our exchanges our attention was called to the Dixon, (Ill.) disaster which occurred Sunday, May 4th. We have not got the occurrence in detail, but from what we have we glean the following: Baptism was being administered in Rock river at Dixon where a large number had assembled to witness the ceremony. At this place there was an iron bridge across the river on which there were some three hundred persons witnessing the baptisms that was being administered just below, but in an unexpected moment part of the bridge gave way and the multitude were precipitated down into the river, many of them to fill a watery grave. At latest account it is supposed that there were between 90 and 100 lives lost.

To our mind, this sad occurrence has presented quite a chain of reflections. It is a notable fact that the ordinance of baptism administered by immersion is as a sign spoken against everywhere and when it is known that persons are to be thus baptized it generally insures a large crowd, a goodly percentage of which are scoffers. A bridge would be a very fair position for persons thus disposed, and the fact seems to be presented to our mind that many of those who met this sad fate might have been of this class. These impressions have forced themselves upon our minds from observations made at such baptisms. Our hearts have been pained at times when this sacred ordinance was performed, to notice groups of the vain, the gay and the scoffers taking the most prominent eligible position and there talk, laugh and scoff at those who were humble enough to be buried with Christ in holy baptism. Baptism to the prepared penitent is a passing from death to life but it makes us shudder to think what it may have been to some of those who were immersed by the precipitating of the bridge. Our imagination perhaps is too lively, but we can see so many faces changed from the scornful laugh to that of devilish despair, that we are inclined to think it may have been a judgment of God to warn a gainsaying world.

The pedo baptists were so desirous to get a case in which some person was drowned in being immersed that a number of imaginary ones were made. Here now are almost a hundred of real cases. Hundreds and thousands of both saints and sinners have lost their lives in this element, but of the millions that have been been baptized by immersion, not one real case of loss of life can be adduced. This thing of scoffing at the ordinances of God's appointment is a most heinous crime and it is a miracle of mercy that judgment is not meted out more frequently than what it is.

RESOLUTIONS.

The following resolutions we extract from the Minutes of the first district of Virginia, and think them worthy of being accepted by the Church generally. The time is here that we should make available, every practicable means of sowing, broadcast, the truth as it is in Jesus. A good religious literature freely distributed will have its effect and produce a copious harvest.

Whereas the District Meeting recognizes the importance of adopting more efficient measures to spread the doctrine of the Brethren, we do therefore advise:

1st. That the Elders of each congregation, by and with the consent of their congregation, appoint a committee of one Deacon whose duty it shall be to act as receiver and disburser of all funds voluntarily contributed for the purchase of the Brethren's publications and testaments.

2nd. That these publications be selected by the Elders, with the approval of their congregations, and distributed where the Gospel is imperfectly or altogether unknown as understood by the Brethren.

3d. That these distributions be made by the traveling ministry or any other safe or practicable means.

4th. That these books be sold at cost and when loaned or bestowed, the party so doing, will report to their congregation.

5th. That the several committees keep a record of their transactions and report annually to the District Meeting.

6th. That our Ministry be exhorted often to a more vigorous effort, to spread the Gospel, and that the congregations aid, encourage and assist them in so doing.

7th. That this District adopt these resolutions as instructed by Y. M. of 1871, Art. 7.

☞ The minutes of this D. M. can be had by sending 10 cts. to Eld. B. F. Moomaw, *Bonsacks*, Roanoke Co., Va.

BOOK NOTICES.

Under this head we will notice such books &c., sent us for examination that are in harmony with the general character of our work. No fiction or obscene literature of any character will receive any attention whatever. We wish our notices to be a benefit both to publishers and our patrons.

THE REPUBLIC is a neat 64 page monthly magazine devoted to the dissemination of political information; published by "The Republic Publishing Company, Washington, D. C. at $2.00 per annum.

HOW TO GO WEST, is a well gotten up pamphlet of some seven pages sent us by the Chicago, Burlington and Quincy R.R., containing several important maps of their territory, the Union Pacific R. R route with all the stations and distance between them from Omaha to Sanfrancisco, with a general description of all the important towns along their part of the road. Persons going West should send for it as it will be sent to all free of charge. Address D. W. Hitchcock, Chicago, Ill.

Prof. Fowlers Greatest Work.

The National Publishing Company of Philadelphia, have just issued a really valuable and important work, by Prof. O. S. Fowler, on Manhood, Womanhood, and their Mutual Interrelations: Love, its laws, power, etc.,—The science of Life. It is a masterly exposition of the laws which control the relations of the sexes, and their duties toward each, and we hesitate not to pronounce it the most valuable and timely publication of the age.

Every good book sold and read in a community adds to the intelligence and power of that community. We recommend this work to the careful consideration of every man and women in our land. It is pure and elevated in its style and ideas, and furnishes a practical solution of many of the most perplexing questions of life. It should be read by the young and old, the married and single, and especially by those contemplating marriage. It thoroughly discusses questions of the greatest moment and in which every married person is greatly interested.

All friends of morality and purity in social life will hail the advent of this book with delight. It contains a vast amount of those *heart* truths calculated to promote pure, virtuous love and connubial concord, and will be a real blessing to the public. Its low price brings it within the reach of all and the information it contains is beyond value. It is sold by subscription only and agents are wanted in every county.

A. B. B.

The Weekly Pilgrim.

Published by J. B. Brumbaugh, & Co.

Edited by H. B. & Geo. Brumbaugh.

CORRESPONDING EDITORS.

D. P. Sayler, Double Pipe Creek, Md.

Leonard Furry, New Enterprise, Pa

The *Pilgrim* is a Christian Periodical, devoted to religion and moral reform. It will advocate in the spirit of *love* and *liberty*, the principles of true Christianity, labor for the promotion of peace among the people of God, for the encouragement of the saints and for the conversion of sinners, avoiding those things which tend toward disunion or sectional feelings.

TERMS.

Single copy, Book paper, $1.[illegible]
Eleven copies, [eleventh for Agt.] $1[illegible]
Any number above that at the same rate.

Address,

H. B. BRUMBAUGH.
James Creek,
Huntingdon county Pa.

The Weekly Pilgrim.

"REMOVE NOT THE ANCIENT LANDMARKS WHICH OUR FATHERS HAVE SET."

VOL. 4. JAMES CREEK, PENNSYLVANIA, MAY 20, 1873. NO. 20

POETRY.

THE TWO HERMITS WHO COULD NOT QUARREL.

Dwelt together hermits twain,
Simple men were they--
Part in prayer and part in toil
Spent they every day.

And they loved each other well--
Peaceful was their life--
Never knowing discontent,
Never knowing strife.

Spake one evening brother Paul,
"Surely you and I
Are most ignorant of men!"
"*Tell me, brother, why?*"

"All men, save ourselves, I know
Quarrel now and then;
Only we not knowing how,
Still in peace remain."

"*Teach me*," mild spake brother John,
"*How to do my part:*
I will then if you so wish,
Try with all my heart."

"Lo this brick," said brother Paul,
"Here I place in view,
And you stoutly must maintain
It belongs to you.

"I shall say that it is mine,
And if both can well
Do our part, there shall arise
Quarreling in this cell.

"Now we will begin—I say,
This is mine own brick;"
"*Nay, I'm sure that it is mine*,"
Cried the other quick.

"If 'tis yours," said Brother Paul,
"Take it if you will;"
Smiling when they saw that strife
Lay beyond their skill.

Saw that they must be content,
Ever to remain'
'Mid the contests of the world
Ignorant old men.

ORIGINAL ESSAYS.

THE BAPTISM OF JOHN, WHENCE WAS IT, FROM HEAVEN OR OF MEN?

B. F. MOOMAW.

In resuming our sketch of the "royal craft" and presenting an analysis of its origin and operations, in following Masonry through its intricate, obscure and mystical workings, we discover that from the time at which we date its true origin as relied on by honest and intelligent Masons themselves, that is to say, in the year 926 or 4926th year of the world. It had its advances, and it had its reverses, sometimes more, and sometimes less flourishing. Following its path through the space intervening, and arriving at the time of the reign of James the second, we discover that Masonry was very much neglected, about this time. A. D., 1685 Sir Christopher Wren was elected to the office of Grand Master, who appointed Gabrael Cibleer, and Edward Strong his wardens, yet notwithstanding the great reputation and abilities of this celebrated architect, Masonry continued in a declining state for many years, and only a few lodges were held in different parts of the kingdom. Sir Christopher Wren continued at the head of the fraternity till king Williams death in 1702.

During the reign of Queen Anne, Masonry made no considerable progress, Sir Christopher's age and infirmities drew off his attention from the duties of his office, and the number of Masons considerably diminished. It was therefore determined that the privileges of Masonry should not be confined to operative Masons, but that people of all professions should be permitted to participate in them, provided they were regularly approved and initiated into the order.

The former privileges were still allowed to remain to the four old lodges then extant. In consequence of this the old masons in the Metropolis visited all their inherent privileges as individuals in the four old landmarks to be infringed. It is therefore, to this day a fixed principle in Freemasonry that there is to be no changes or inovations allowed in the order, and that in the initiation as a prentice, or, taking the degree of fellow Craft, as well as subsequent degrees, the initiated are pledged most solemnly to strictly observe these landmarks.

An assembly and feast was held in London on the 24th of June, 1719, when Dr. Dersaguliers was unanimously elected Grand Master, at this feast the old regular and peculiar toasts were introduced; and from this time we may date the rise of Freemasonry on its present plan, known as speculative Masonry. That we may better understand what is meant by speculative Masonry we will bear in mind, that under the term of operative Masonry, they claim extraordinary and superior architectural skill, in performance of which they use the compass, square, rule, plumb and level. The assumed object of speculative Masonry is building up, and beautifying the moral character of society, drawing conclusions from the symmetry of highly perfected architecture, to the cultivation of a high degree of moral refinement, for which purpose they introduce the working tools used in mechanical operations as emblems mystically to produce these results. The compass forsooth to limit our desires to those things that is useful, necessary and expedient, to restrain all excesses and all superfluous and hurtful indulgences. The plumb being used by operative workmen to try perpendiculars, and teaches speculatively that we should be truthful, correct and honest in our deportment. The square in their work teaches that we should square our lives by the rule of right, doing unto others as we would have them do unto us, and by the level we prove horizontals, by which we are reminded that although a crown may adorn the head, and a scepter in the hand, yet the blood in our veins is derived from the same Almighty Parent, and is no better than the humblest citizen, and teaches us that we are traveling on the broad level of time, to the undiscovered country from whose bourne no traveller returns.

The trowel, an emblem of the Master Mason, is an instrument operatively used to spread the cement by which the building is united into a common mass, but is symbolically used for the spreading the cement of brotherly love and affection, which is to unite us into one sacred band or society of friends and brothers, a temple of living stones, among whom no contention should ever exist, but that noble contention, or rather emulation of who can best work or who can best agree.

In connection with the mechanical tools Masons have introduced a number of emblems, such as the Lambskin apron, an emblem of innocence by which we are reminded that purity of life and conduct is essentially necessary to gaining admittance into the celestial lodge above, where the supreme architect of the universe presides.

The twenty four inch guage an instrument used by operatives to measure and lay out their work, is a symbol used speculatively to teach how properly and profitably to divide our time, a portion for secular employment, a second portion rest and refreshment and a third portion for devotion and the service of God. The common gravel or hammer used by mechanics to break off the corners of rough stones the better to fit them for the builders use, are used as a symbol by speculative Masons for the purpose of divesting our hearts of all the vices and superfluities of life, thereby fitting our minds for the spiritual building, "that house not made with hands, eternal in the heavens.

Three pillars are erected also, in Masonic lodges as emblems of wisdom, strength and beauty, which is necessary to adorn all great and important undertakings. The starry decked heavens, is with them an emblem indicating the aims and hopes of Masons that they may there arrive at last.

The Theological ladder which Jacob saw in his vision ascending from earth to heaven, the three principle rounds of which, are denominated Faith, Hope and Charity, which say they, "admonishes us to have faith in God, hope in immortality, and charity to all mankind. Among the emblems of Masonry are what are termed by them movable jewels called the rough Ashler, the perfect Ashler, and the Trestle Board, or what we would call the rough rock, the smooth rock, and the board for drafting, by which we shall be reminded of our rude and imperfect state of nature, that perfect state at which we may arrive by a virtuous education, our own endeavors, and the blessing of God. The rules and designs laid down by the master workman. So should we endeavor to erect our spiritual building agreeably to the rules and designs laid down by the Supreme Architect of the Universe, in the great book of nature and revelation, which is our spiritual and moral Trestle Board.

The Linets of Masonry, purports to be brotherly love, relief and truth. The cardinal virtues four in number temperance, fortitude, prudence and justice.

The principles proposed to be taught

by these emblems, Tenets and Mottoes, are in themselves excellent, and are entitled to the denomination of virtue itself, and why? because they are of Masons who are men." Certainly not but because they are of God from Heaven, laid down upon his own Trestle Board the book of Revelation.

Masonry to make its beauties known,
Must mingle colors not her own.

We propose, therefore, to show that these emblems are unnecessary, idolatrous delusive and deleterious in its tendencies to the interests of the soul. The necessity of them is wholly superseded by the fact that the principles that they propose to cultivate are all clearly taught in the Holy Scriptures, which is a sufficient rule but it is the only rule for our faith and practice.

The compass to teach us to limit our desires is unnecessary because we are taught in the Bible that we should "not covet our neighbor's house, our neighbor's wife, nor his manservant, nor his maidservant, nor his ox, nor his ass, nor anything that is our neighbors." Ex.—20: 17. Be ye therefore followers of God as dear children and walk in love as Christ also hath loved us and hath given himself for us." Eph.—5: 1.

But fornication and uncleanness or covetousness let it not once be named among you as becometh saints. Neither filthiness, nor foolish talking nor jesting which are not convenient but rather give thanks. "For this ye know that no whoremonger, nor unclean person, nor covetous man who is an idolater, hath any inheritance in the kingdom of Christ or of God." Eph.—5: 5. "Mortify therefore your members which are upon the earth fornication, uncleanness, inordinate affection, evil concupiscence, and covetousness which is idolatry." Col. 3: 5 Coupling the scriptures with the history of our great mother in Eden's garden, lusting and then perpetrating the terrible act, that destroyed her own happiness and deluging all posterity in ruin and woe, without calling the mind to the numerous passages besides in which we are commanded and forewarned on this point, we will certainly conclude that it is enough to limit our desires and suppress extravagance, without introducing the compass or any such appliances.

In pursuing this train of thought, I beg leave to be permitted to call to mind the fact that we have set forth in the commencement of this treatise that for all that God designs for us to do and teach, He has been so lavish in his teachings, giving line upon line, and precept upon precept, &c., that for every willing mind there is quite a sufficiency to enlighten the mind, however inactive the intellect may be, with this truth constantly upon the mind of the reader we may be saved the herculean task of giving the many references that might be adduced and will therefore content ourselves with a few in each point

The plumb then is unnecessary because we are taught in the Bible that we should not lie nor steal, that if we do the devil is our father, and that he is a liar and the father of liars, and that all shall have their part with him "who loveth and maketh a lie." We are taught in the scriptures to be careful correct and to "provide all things honest in the sight of all men."

We have no need of the mechanics square, because we are commanded in the scriptures to do unto others as we would have them do unto us, and as an offset to envy we are commanded to "in honor prefer one another." The level to teach that all the children of men are in many respects parallel is superfluous, because the Bible teaches that "God made of one blood all men to dwell upon the whole earth and hath determined the times before appointed, and the bounds of their habitation" "that we all came into the world one way and that we all will go out one way" and that "there is no respect of persons with God." Nor is there any necessity for the trowel, to impress the obligation to love the brethren or our neighbors for the command and exhortations and the denunciations upon, and connected with this subject is legion. Second only to the first and great commandment to love the Lord our God with all our soul, mind and strength, and indeed like unto it, to love our neighbor as we love ourself. To say more on this point would seem almost like an insult to the intelligence of the reader, we therefore forbear. The Lambskin as an emblem may be classed with the rest, because the life and character of Christ we have a perfect model of innocence, not only inoffensive in his behavior but sacrificed for a time the joys of heaven and the glory he had with the father, laid aside the robe of royalty took upon himself the form of a servant, suffered a life of sorrow and grief, privation and persecution, "bore our griefs, carried our sorrows, the chastisement of our peace was upon him and by his stripes we were healed." "Led as a sheep to the slaughter and as a lamb before his shearers is dumb, so he opened not his mouth," thus commending his love while we were his enemies, he died for us, and accordingly commanded us that "we should not return evil for evil but to return good for evil." If our enemy hunger feed him, if he thirst give him drink, and that we should not avenge ourselves of our enemies, but refer all to the arbitrament of him who holds in his hand the scale of justice accompanying our verdict with our earnest petition for clemency and pardon, with this array of light "from Heaven," where is the necessity of such appendages "from men."

To be Continued.

THE SOURCE OF CHRISTIAN ENJOYMENT.

The subjects of Christ's purchased possession, as we have seen in our former article are "they that follow the Lamb withersoever he goeth. These were redeemed from among men, being the first fruits unto God and to the Lamb. "And in their mouth was found no guile; for they are without fault before the throne of God." John the Divine, in a vision, saw the bride, the Lamb's wife at the consummation of the marriage as a glorious scene delightful to behold; when the "voice of the mighty thunderings, proclaimed, Alleluia, for the Lord God omnipotent reigneth. Let us be glad and rejoice, and give honor to him, for the marriage of the Lamb is come, and his wife has made herself ready. And to her was granted that she should be arrayed in fine linen, clean and white: (the emblem of purity, O, may not our departed innocent children be among the number; our heart rejoices, and our soul is enraptured with the pleasing tho't that they will be there), for the fine linen is the righteousness of the Saints. And he saith unto me, write "Blessed are they which are called unto the marriage supper of the Lamb. And he saith unto me, these are the true sayings of God. Brother, sister, would you like to be one of that number? O, yes, seems to be the language, then let us have our lamps brightly burning and our vessels well supplied with oil, ever ready to meet the bridegroom, lest we may be left behind. Trust in God, pray to him in the name of your Advocate, for he has commenced the work and will finish it according to the good pleasure of his own will. "Of his own will begat he us by the word of truth, that we should be the first fruits of his creatures." "Now he which establisheth us with you in Christ, and hath anointed us is God; who hath also sealed us, and given the earnest of the spirit in our hearts." What more would we want? If the seal of God's Holy Spirit is stamped upon our hearts, and the love of God shed abroad into our souls; we can glory in tribulation, be cheerful in suffering, rejoice in persecution and delight in reproaches; feeling glad to be worthy to suffer for the sake of the Lord Jesus Christ, esteeming the reproach of Christ's greater riches than the treasures and sinful pleasures of this ungodly world, having ever respect to the recompense of reward. Christians are pilgrims here, this is not their home, men have no continuing city here, hence they look for a city whose builder and maker is God. Such being the seekings of the children of God their hope of glory, their joy in the worship of God, their delights in the enjoyment and society of one another, their gladness in the knowledge of being the heirs of God, their happy prospect of being redeemed from corruption and in anxious anticipation of a glorious resurrection; and amidst all these enjoyments, they are patiently waiting; looking for the blessed hope of the glorious appearing of the great God and our Savior, the Lord Jesus Christ An appeal to you dear friends, outside of the fold of Christ; sinners, worldling, moral citizens, nominal professors, callous christians and backsliders, a warning voice declares loudly, you are on slippery grounds, your road is dangerous to travel, darkness and blackness surrounds you; your life is suspended on a tender little thread over a dreadful chasm, the gulf of despair ready any moment to swallow you up, and sink you down into the abyss of woe and everlasting misery. Where is your hope of serving the God of this world, the shrine of fashion? Is there any comfort in the attendency of the Bacchanalian feasts, or in the dancing-rooms, the tipling-houses, or any other places of sinful amusement? Would you wish to be found in hells of gambling, cursing, swearing, and blaspheming your lovely Savior's name when the iron clasp of death shall transport you from time to eternity? O, stop and think! Ponder well, reflect thou hast a soul to save, one that cannot die, that must ever live either in hell or in heaven. O, think of death and eternity! Remember every secret thing thought or action is known to him, who is to be your judge, and if unrepented will be made manifest in the day of judgment. God who made you, and who loved you, and gave his only begotten Son to redeem you by shedding his precious blood to save your undying soul, who has made known his will in the Gospel you have heard preached from time to time, who hath operated upon your soul by the spirit of His grace; that same God whom you have slighted, turned your back and trifled with his word, and whose ministry you have derided, slandered and evil-spoken of, and perhaps cursed, "that same God will be your judge at the dreadful day of the Lord." How shall or may you abide the day of his coming? And who shall stand when he appeareth? "For behold, the day cometh, that shall burn as an oven; and all the proud, yea, all that do wickedly, shall be stubble; and the day that cometh shall turn them up, saith the Lord of Hosts, that it shall have them neither root nor branch." This being the fearful fate of the ungodly: we as lovers of your souls urge you to speedily return, forsake your evil ways, turn to God. "Let the wicked forsake his ways and the unrighteous man his thoughts and let him turn unto the Lord for he is merciful, and to his God for he will abundantly pardon." A word to you my dear young friends, you are placed in this world for a noble purpose and you have the advantages of a Christian-like education, you have the privileges of learning to read, a talent is given to every one of you to make you a child of God, an heir of Heaven, by a proper improvement of that talent, you can, Apollo-like, become mighty in scripture; make yourselves well acquainted with the contents of the word of God, it is able to make you wise unto salvation, especially the practical part of the Holy Scripture. Discriminate well what you read, and be willing to obey the demands of the Gospel, be humble, prayerful, watchful, guard against the wiles of the enemy, mark well his artful devices, and shun the company and association of emissaries, do not accompany them to their places of amusements, though they may be represented to you as innocent, yet depend upon it, there is poison in the bowl or death in the pot. Be not ashamed to separate yourself from the proud, the haughty, the wicked and gay, silly and light-minded. Come out from among them, it does not detract anything from your character, or honor, or esteem among sensible persons of a well balanced mind; and besides will afford you pleasure, in your dying hour, enjoyment in health, consolation in sickness, delight in death, admits you into glory and c. use us to shine as the bright stars in the galaxy of Heaven. We are passing away and you are soon called to fill our station in life, therefore qualify yourself to fill that responsible station that the work of the Lord may be successfully carried on when we are dead and gone.

Finally, let us all do our duty that we all may meet in Heaven above, where all is love, where we never more need to part, where all the redeemed of the Lord shall meet with gladness, and forever bask in the beautiful smiles of their glorious Redeemer, and God shall wipe away all tears from our eyes. Amen.

LEONARD FURRY.

For the Pilgrim.

A NEW CREATURE.

Therefore if any man is in Christ he is a new creature, old things are passed away, behold all things are become new. 2 Cor. 5: 17.

This language spoken by the Apostle Paul to the Corinthians is worthy of our every notice that if we are not in Christ we are without hope and without God in this world and consequently we cannot participate with him in glory. It is clearly set forth in the Scriptures of divine truth that we are of a corrupt nature and are prone to evil. Our inclinations are such that will still draw us farther away from Christ, and in order to become new creatures we must undergo a great change, changed from nature to grace. As long as we are in an unreconciled state with God we are strangers to grace, our rational powers, we will very readily admit, are dreadfully impaired, and the soul weakened by sin. The animal passion is strong and corrupt and opposes the dictates of the spirit of God and in such a disordered state we cannot please God until we are created anew in Christ Jesus unto good works—born again as the Apostle says, not of corruptible seed, but of incorruptible by the word of God which liveth and abideth forever. As long as the children of men are under the power or control of the carnal mind they are dead in trespasses and sin, and unless they become awakened to a lively sense of duty they will not make the necessary change in order to become new creatures. Paul would say to such, "Awake thou that sleepest and arise from the dead and Christ will give thee light." Ephesians 5: 14. Paul says, "to be carnally minded is death, but to be spiritually minded is life and peace, because the carnal mind is enmity against God, not subject to the law of God neither in deed can be, so then they that are in the flesh cannot please God." Romans, 8: 6, 7, 8. Hence we understand that the carnal mind must be brought in subjection to the will of God, our carnal inclinations must be subdued and brought under the power and influence of the Holy Spirit. The Apostle says, "that ye put off the former conversation, the old man, which is corrupt according to the deceitful lust, and be renewed in the spirit of your mind, and that you put on the new man which after God is created in righteousness and true holiness." Ephesians 4: 22, 13, 24. Our former life and conduct must be changed, put off the old man with his deeds. So thorough and radical is the change that it is best described as putting off our former selves, having been made willing to hate and forsake sin, all the sinful pleasures of an evil world by repentance toward God and faith in the Lord Jesus Christ. Repentance always means a change of purpose, a godly sorrow that worketh a repentance unto salvation not to be repented of having within a living faith, a faith that works by love, throwing ourselves entirely upon the promises of God, believing that his grace is sufficient for us and that by making the right application of the blood of Christ our sins will be washed away and thus become new creatures in Christ. We here would ask the question, can this be done by repentance and faith alone? Some are ready to say, Yes, but we beg leave to differ with such for we do not understand it in that way. Remember the subject: "Therefore if any man is in Christ he is a new creature." We will bring up Paul about this matter, Romans 4: 3, 4, 5, 5. "Know ye not that so many of you as have been baptized into Jesus Christ were baptized into his death Therefore we are buried with him by baptism into death that like as Christ was raised up from the dead by the glory of the Father even so we also should walk in newness of life, for if we have been planted together in the likeness of his death we shall be also in the likeness of his resurrection, knowing this that the old man is crucified with him that the body of sin might be destroyed, that henceforth we should not serve sin." As the death and resurrection of our Savior were both necessary to complete our redemption and salvation, our matured love of sin and inclinations to commit, which is represented in the old man must be crucified and buried. 'Buried with him in baptism wherein also ye are risen with him through the faith of the operation of God who hath raised him from the dead, buried with him in baptism, by openly renouncing sin, publicly professing to hate and forsake it, risen with him from their death in sin, by believing on him, and thus experiencing in their own persons the same divine power which raised Christ from the dead and thus rise to newness of life. The apostle also says that as many of us as have been baptized into Jesus Christ have put on Christ, thus we see that by the believer being baptized we put on Christ and if any man is in Christ he is a new creature. It is sometimes said that we put too much stress on baptism, but it is the command of the Savior for he says, "He that believeth and is baptized shall be saved." We infer from this that the believer must be baptized in order to be saved from his past sins while it would not benefit an unbeliever though he were baptized he would yet remain in his sins. Much might be said about the utility of baptism yet notwithstanding it is an outward washing it has its inward cleansing. Peter says, "the like figure whereunto even baptism doeth now save us, not the putting away of the filth of the flesh but answer of a good conscience toward God by the resurrection of Jesus Christ." Let this suffice. We would say to all, search the Scriptures and whatsoever thy hand finds to do, do it. Therefore if any man is in Christ he is a new creature, united to him by faith created in Christ Jesus unto good works, old things are passed away, our former views and feelings are changed, we enter a new field of labor where as we once delighted in the way of sin, we now delight in the law of the Lord, are willing to take the word of God for the man of our counsel. Behold all things are become new, we have new hopes and new prospects, the child of grace has new rules of action and pursues a new course of conduct, having now obeyed from the heart that form of doctrine and being made free from sin become the servants of righteousness we have our fruit unto holiness and in the end, everlasting life.

DANIEL BOCK.

Miamisburg, Ohio.

CONTENTMENT.

Is there any one human being upon the face of the earth that is really contented and happy? The good book says, "A contented mind is a continual feast," and again it says; "Contentment with godliness is great gain." The rich are not contented because they have too much of this world's goods, and the poor are not contented because they think they have not enough of the things of this world. Money making seems to be the main object now a-days with rich and poor, old and young. St. Paul says, we ought to be contented with such things as we have. Those of us who are professors of religion are not contented with what we have. Those who have so much of this world's goods stored away in their houses, and who turn the poor away from their doors empty, are not contented because they have not done their duty. The Lord has placed us here as stewards over what he has given us, and if we do not our duty what will be our condition, what will be our doom when that great day of wrath shall come? And what will be the end of those who are yet out of the ark of safety? They are not contented, because they know their duty and do not do it.

M. C. K.

Parnassus, Va.

SEEK not to isolate yourselves; imprison not your soul in sterile contemplation, in solitary prayer, in pretending to a grace which no faith not realized in works can enable you to observe. You can only save yourself by saving others. God asks not: what have you done for your soul? but what have you done for the brother's souls I gave you? Think of these. Leave your own to God and his law. Labor unweariedly for others good. Such is the holiest prayer. —*Mazzini.*

THE CHURCH AND DUTIES OF HER MEMBERS.—No. 6.

BY J. S. FLORY.

ALL IN A BODY.

Having spoken of the members of the Church in their separate calling, we now, in this concluding paper, propose speaking to them in general terms as constituting the body of Christ, and God's family of children on earth. We learn that in the Church there are "diversities of gifts but the same spirit" "and there are differences of administrations, but the same Lord." "And there are diversities of operations, but it is the same God which worketh all in all." Hence it mattereth not what be our gifts or calling, how we administer or what be the operation, we are all controlled by the same spirit, governed by the same Lord, and the same God "worketh within us to will and to do." Paul gives a beautiful illustration of the Church and the individual members being dependent on one another, &c., in the 12th chapter of 1 Cor., says he: "For as the body is one and hath many members, and all the members of that one body being many, are one body; so also is Christ. For by one spirit are we all baptized into one body * * * have all been made to drink into one spirit. For the body is not one member, but many. If the foot shall say, because I am not the hand, I am not of the body; is it therefore not of the body? and if the ear shall say, because I am not the eye, I am not of the body; is it therefore not of the body? If the whole body were an eye, where were the hearing? If the whole were hearing, where were the smelling. But now hath God set the members every one of them in the body, as it hath pleased him. And if they were all one member where were the body. But now are they many members, yet but one body." Here we see the members constitute the body and those members God hath set in the body as it hath *pleased* him. Therefore we see all are necessary in their place to which God hath assigned them, whether they be in the laity or in some official position. The private member cannot say he or she is not of the body no more than the Bishop can say he is not of the body. Neither can one say we have no need of the other. The eye cannot say of the hand I have no need of thee; or the head to the feet I have no need of thee. All have need of the other that the body might be a body working together harmoniously through a concert of action on the part of the members. Paul further says, "much more those members of the body which seem to be more feeble are necessary." Yes, often we see it those members who seem to be weak or backward in lending assistance to some new order of things, are *necessary* to keep the Church from rushing into some trouble or departure from the faith.

"God hath tempered the body together * * * that there should be no schism in the body; but that the members should have the same care one of another, and whether one member suffer all the members suffer with it; or one member be honored, all the members *rejoice* with it. Now ye are the body of Christ and members in particular."

If by one spirit we have all been baptized into one body, one member should have the same care for another. We know if the foot meets with an accident the hand will care for it, and if the hand suffers the whole body will be pained and there will be a corresponding sympathy throughout every member of the body. So it should be in the Church. If one member meets with a trouble, the sympathy of all should flow that way and do all that can be done to restore that one to a state of health and "comeliness." And if one is honored all should rejoice with it. But often it is feared there is not much rejoicing with some when one in the same station is praised and religiously honored and the name of Jesus through him glorified. Now as we all are members in particular of the body of Christ, let us feel our responsibilities and as "lively stones" work together, one with another that we may truly be "built up a spiritual house, a holy priesthood to offer up spiritual sacrifices, acceptable to God by Jesus Christ."

Think of it, private members, much depends on you. Honor your standing by walking worthy of the vocation wherein you are called; honor those who have a rule over you, not with empty honors such as the world delights in, but honor them by being obedient to their rightful councils and admonitions that they give out of love for you and the Church. Did you know how often in secret prayer they call to God to bless you, and how often they spend sleepless hours and wet their pillows with tears because of some troubles in the flock, you would methinks, be more careful of your walk and ways. As a father loves his children so those that are over you love you. How it makes their soul glad to see you take up the cross and follow Jesus in that self-denying path—to see you in your seat at times of worship, and by your chaste conversation and godly walk manifest to all you have consecrated your life to the service of God. As a mother loves her darling babe or a father his obedient child so is the obedient member loved by those that have the charge over them. And the love of Jesus. Oh! how sweet to those that are his disciples indeed.

And ye Deacons of the Church of the living God! Think of the position you hold. Adorn your calling with the spirit of meekness and humility. And ye ministers who hold a commission from God to preach his everlasting word, "Preach the word, be instant in season and out of season, reprove, rebuke, exhort, with all long suffering and doctrine." "Study to show thyself approved unto God, a workman that needeth not to be ashamed, rightly dividing the word of truth." And ye "stewards of the Lord's choosing that have in charge his people." "Be not many masters," nor "Lord it over God's heritage," but "be examples to the flock" which are to be fed by you, "taking the oversight thereof, not by constraint but willingly; not for filthy lucre, but of a ready mind." And then "when the chief shepherd shall appear, ye shall receive a crown of glory that fadeth not away."

One and all of the household of faith, let us labor together in love that the glorious principles of the religion of Jesus may be perpetuated, that hundreds and thousands more of Adam's sons may taste of redeeming love flowing so free from Calvary's brow. That crimson flood has not lost its power, the gospel is yet the power of God unto salvation to them that believe, but the number of the enemies of the cross is "legion." The dying groans of the Son of God is scarcely heard amid the din of a worldly religion. The wreaking cross is almost hid by the shining mockery of a popular money-loving priesthood. But amid all the clamor made by "the devotees of Moloch" we can yet hear the pleading, loving voice of the Lamb of God whispering "*Come unto me.*" "I am meek and lowly in heart." "Learn of me." Yes beloved, we must learn of Jesus or we will learn amiss. Infidel hands would pluck the Christian ensign from the blood-stained standard and trail it in the dust of science. But nay, we must fling it to the breeze, for under no other banner can we hope to conquer. 'Tis the only banner of liberty for condemned souls. The Church of God has stood the storms of persecution for over 1800 years. We hope by the the grace of God her influence may never wane while time lasts. But let me say once more, much, very much depends upon our courage and valor as soldiers of the cross. Let us draw on the whole armor of God that we may successfully combat with error and innovations that we sometimes see looming up in battle array even at the very threshold of the Church. Would we maintain the honor of Jesus we must fight. Would we keep the Church as the Savior adorned it we must fight, would we come out conquerers in the end we must fight—fight the fight of faith. Satan is pressing hard, but the weapons of our warfare are "mighty to the pulling down of strongholds." By and by our warfare will be over, then when the smoke of battle clears away and we "lay our armor by" we will see the light of eternal day, and the shining splendors of a holier clime. —the soldiers home—the saints rest. Where the Church of God shall exist in the light of God's continuance and *love* as a rainbow encircles her forever and ever.

For the Pilgrim.

THE SAINT'S PROMISE.

Lo, I am with you always, even unto the end of the world. Matt. 28 : 20.

This was the parting address of the Savior. He was just about leaving his disciples corporeally, but not without first promising his spiritual presence to remain with them. Let us consider him as just upon the verge of entering upon his ultimate glory, taking his position upon the right hand of his Father and our Father—his God and our God. O, to have seen him! To have glanced at the features and emotions of his countenance just then. His great solicitude for his disciples on previous occasions must then have manifested itself with mingled sorrow and sympathy. He well knew what temptations, persecutions and torture awaited them. Thank God we can with the eye of faith, behold him at present as such; and hear him say, "Lo, I am with you alway, even unto the end of the world." The promise extends into the future, to the end of the world;—and not only to *us*, but to our children, to those afar off, even to as many as the Lord our God shall call. With this blessed assurance, let us also consider it as a demonstration of his divinity. Who less than God could have given such a promise? He does not say my blessing shall be with you, but *I am* with you. This necessarily supposes omnipresence. How else could he be with so many individuals at one time in the various parts of the earth? He not only left the promise of his presence with us individually, but also collectively. While he was at Capernaum, and but a short time after his transfiguration, he said, where two or three are gathered together in my name, there am I in the midst of them." As to place, he does not designate. In our private houses he is with us as well as in the sanctuary, in the grove as well as in the field. Neither does he designate as to time; for he is the same yesterday, to-day and forever." But as to manner he says, *in my name*. The number of the assembly, however small, is nothing to him; but to be gathered together in his name is very essential. If we have any objects in view aside of worshipping in the spirit and in truth, it is not in his name. Our affections must be set upon things in heaven, not upon things on the earth. All temporal thoughts should give place to spiritual meditation. His presence wherever we meet, will then be in the midst of us. There is always something impressive in the company of human beings, especially if some distinguished personage is present.

Think of Jesus, the Master, being present whenever his saints are assembled. "God is greatly to be feared in the assembly of the saints, and to be had in reverence of all them who are about him. "Nothing short, but God with us," not corporeally but spiritually. When we enter the sanctuary, we place ourselves immediately under his view. Let us then guard against wandering thoughts, drowsiness, formality, or hypocrisy. Let it impress us with the importance and sacredness of divine worship. Let it stimulate us to make use of the means of grace vouchsafed to us. Some think it needless to repair to the sanctuary, because the minister is unable to tell them more than they already know. This is very questionable. If granted, do you know more than your Master? Are you so holy that you need no further blessings? We should not only go because the minister is there, but because the Savior himself is there, whose sufficiency is divine. O, what a privilege, to hold sweet converse, and that he can be touched with the feelings of our infirmities. If we are indifferent to the David's gracious presence here on earth, what right have we to expect his glorious presence in heaven? But if we have his presence here; at death we shall only remove to his temple above, where tribulation and poverty, pain and anxiety, persecution and oppression will be no more; and where all tears shall be wiped away from our eyes. There we shall be before the throne of God, and bask in the sunshine of eternal glory; with Jesus as our companion, and God as our King, who is King of kings and Lord of lords, and whose palace is the universe.

S. B. FURRY.

Martinsburg, Pa.

For the Pilgrim.

THE CITY OF OUR GOD.

And the city was pure gold like unto clear glass. And the foundations of the wall of the city were garnished with all manner of precious stones &c. And the twelve gates were twelve pearls, every several gate was of one pearl, and the street of the city was pure gold as it were transparent glass. And he shewed me a pure river of water of life clear as crystal proceeding out of the throne of God and of the Lamb.

Such, dear reader, is a part of the description of the holy city which as given by John the Revelator in the 21st and 22nd chapters of Revelations, and it is this city that we may all become heirs to and inhabitants if we are only willing. Dear reader, think for one moment, are we not willing to comply with the will of our heavenly Father and become an inhabitant of such a beautiful place as this, and even more than this, for we are told "that eye hath not seen ear hath not heard, neither hath it entered into the heart of man the joys the Father hath prepared for them that love him. Can we not, will we not love such a kind Father who has prepared all this for such unworthy creatures as we. Think, dear reader were such a place to be obtained in this world would we not strive with all our power to obtain an inheritance in it which would only continue for a season, and is this not worth far more which will continue through an endless eternity, and the terms are easy through which we can obtain an inheritance in this happy place, for he says, "My faith is easy and my burden is light." Friendly sinner, think of your condition, should the messenger death call you now where is your hope for eternity? do you know why you stand where you are trying to satisfy yourselves with the fleeting pleasures of this world?

What are the pleasures earth affords,
How transient and how few,
Compared with heavens eternal joys,
And pleasures ever new.

Dear sinners, let me entreat you as one that loves your precious souls, fly, Oh, fly for refuge to the arms of a merciful Savior, who will receive all who come to him and give you an inheritance in the city of our God.

MARY HOOVER.

Chatham Ohio.

Youth's Department

A CHILD'S REVERIE.

A little girl I am indeed,
And little do I know:
Much help and care I yet shall need,
That I may wiser grow;
If I would ever hope to do
Things great and good and useful too

But even now I ought to try
To do what good I may;
God never meant that such as I
Should only live to play,
And talk and laugh, and eat and drink
And sleep and wake, and never think.

Then let me try each day and hour
To act upon this plan:
What little good is in my power,
To do it while I can.
If to be useful thus I try,
I may do better by-and-by
—*Child's Paper*

YOUTHFUL CHARITY.

There is nothing so lovely among children as the exercising of charity. It has such good effects that I am persuaded that a short chapter on it will be both interesting and useful to my young readers.

There are so many ways of practicing this grace that I shall not atempt to tell all of them as there is scarcely an hour of your lives pass but what you can have an opportunity of practicing it. I just now remember of a little occurrence which happened last Winter which I will relate. This will show you one way of being charitable.

A little brother and sister, on their way to school, were overtaken by a snow-storm and being thinly clothed, they soon became chilled and cold. The little sister being the oldest, had a cloak along which properly belonged to her, as mother made it expressly for her use. Now if this little sister would have had no charity she would have folded it all around herself and left the little brother shiver in the cold wind, but she had learned to be charitable and therefore offers to share it with her brother. She offers to wrap it around them both, but the little brother thought it was not large enough to cover them both, and rather than rob his sister of her comforts he would stand the storm, but the sister says, "Come brother, it will be large enough for us both, I will stretch it a little."

Was not that noble? Stretch it a little, how many things, dear children, you might stretch a little for the comfort of your little brothers and sisters! It proved sufficiently large for both and under that cloak two warm and loving hearts were protected and kept snugly warm until the storm was over, when they could go on their way greatly benefitted just because they were charitable.

I hope my little readers will often think of stretching a little, their comforts so the others also may enjoy them.

No matter what you may have, If your little brothers and sisters could be made happy by sharing it with them, stretch it a little and give them part and you will always find it large enough, and you will feel much better than if you had enjoyed it all yourself

UNCLE HENRY.

"DIDN'T THINK."

Susie "didn't think," and so she put a scuttle of coal on the stairs, and it was the cause of her little brother's falling and injuring himself very severely. Days of suffering and months of protracted weakness were the result of that one moment of thoughtlessness. O, if she could only recall the past!—Such was her distressing exclamation when too late. She became a thoughtful girl after this, which simply proved that she might have been so before and it was sad to her to think that it should have required so painful an accident to teach her, when she could have become so without all this suffering to her brother. Lawrance "didn't think to leave a letter at the post-office for his sick father on his way to school, although reminded by his mother; and the delay of a few hours was the means of a heavy loss of property.

But why blame a boy for forgetting, or a girl for not always being thoughtful? Because boys and girls of the ages just mentioned—from eleven to fourteen—are old enough to take a little thought, to consider what will be the consequence of a slight carelessness or a moments forgetfulness. It would not hurt them to try to acquire habits of thought and consideration; besides, this might save much suffering to themselves and others. It is better to take a little pains now, and avoid much misery hereafter.

"Didn't think" has burnt houses and steamboats, and even cities, thereby destroying many valuable lives. The thoughtless throwing of a cigar or matches among combustible materials, the firing of a cracker among such has caused great conflagrations. In this way the city of Portland was set on fire, and millions of dollars worth of property destroyed thereby.

"Didn,t think" may be called guilty of mans'aughter,; since this reckless character has sent hundreds of souls without warning, into eternity; although never intending to commit crime. That imperfect boiler ought to have been attended to long ago, but Mr. "So and so" "didn't think," and the result is the loss of hundreds of lives. That railroad switch ought to have been sooner replaced, or that signal hoisted; but the man 'didn't think,' and his fellow creatures are hurled out of life by the score, as well as life-long suffering entailed on many of the survivers.

Beware of entertaining for a moment that disreputable personage "didn't think." He is often found in companionship with that lawless character. "Don't care," and the two combined may work irreparable ruin and misery beyond the power of conception, causing an unutterable wretchedness to thousands who, but for them, might have had much happiness.—*Bright Side.*

GOD'S BLESSINGS. —God often reproves our want of faith by bringing us blessings sooner than we expected. A man has concluded that at such a time he will receive something he greatly craves, or that it will come upon the occurrence of some event. But God sends the blessing sooner. He does not wait for the event. It is His own time, and He has brought it about in his own way; but it is also in reproof of the limiting faith which hampered the prayers with conditions and circumstance. Earnest, eager Christians have looked forward to the conversion of their friends, making it depend on some contingency; but God supersedes their plannings by gracious arrangements of his own. How it should deepen our trust when he does better for us than we know how to ask or think!

There is but one breath of air and beat of the heart between this world and the next.

Correspondence.

A Reporter is wanted from every Church in the brotherhood to send us Church news, Obituaries, Announcements, or anything that will be of general interest. To insure insertion, the writers name must accompany each communication. Our Invitation is not personal but general—please respond to our call.

THE GREAT GEYSER SPRINGS OF CALIFORNIA.

I will now give you a sketch, or short history, of the Geysers according to promise, as I see you request it. These celebrated springs are situated in Sonoma county, and as a natural curiosity, there is no part in the United States that can compete with them. The scenery is mild, picturesque and grand in the extreme. The Plutoo or Sulphur Creek runs through i s whole extent, and on the north side is the wonderful Geyser Canon and all the celebrated Geysers or medicinal springs which render this place such a wonderful curiosity. Among the natural, is an eye water that has effected some extraordinary cures, also soda water, sulphur and acidolated springs in both a cold and boiling state. Descending from the hotel about 75 feet, we first meet the spring of iron, sulphur and soda, temperature 73 degrees from Fahr. The first spring going up the Geyser gulch is the tepid Alum or Iron, temperature 97 degrees. Twenty ft. from this we pass the Geyser Bath, temperature 88 degrees and containing amonia epson salts, magnesia, sulphur, iron &c. Higher up is the spring of boiling alum and sulphur. This has a temperature of 155 deg., so also the black sulphur, quite near it. The epson salts springs has a temperature of 146 deg., and within six feet is a spring of iron, sulphur and salts at boiling point, then comes the boiling black sulphur spring roaring and tearing continually. We wander over rocks, heated ground and thick deposits of sulphur, salts ammonia, tartaric acid, magnesia, &c., then we come to the witch cauldron, it is over 7 feet in diameter and of unknown depth, and is boiling just as hard as it can. The conten's are thrown two or three feet high in a state of great ebullition and very black looking, and the steam that rises from it looks like it might be from a large mill or machine shop. It is one of the most frightful looking places I think I ever beheld, approaching as near as we dare, and looking in, we could see the black waters boiling and tearing in mad and pitiless fury, foaming around the sides of their prison. We put some eggs in a can and made it fast to a pole and held them in the cauldron nearly five minutes and they were cooked quite hard, and we were very much overcheated ourselves in the operation for the steam would almost completely cover us sometimes, and from a hundred vent holes above our heads the steam would rush out in terrible jets. The ground where we were standing was so heated we could scarcely stand on it, I never beheld anything so awful in its appearance, its temperature is said to be about 500 degrees. Opposite the witches cauldron is a boiling alum spring, and near by, is a scalding spring, from which issue streams and jets of boiling water, sometimes throws the water 15 ft.

The next great curiosity is the steam boat Geyser, sounding just like a steam boat blowing off steam. Just above this the gulch divides, up the left or western one, are many hot springs, 150 ft above apparent action, is found a smooth plastic beautiful clay, temperature 167 deg. From this point we could overlook the ceaseless action, the roar, steam, groans and bubbling of a hundred boiling medicated springs, while the steam ascends many feet above them all, following the usually traveled path, we pass over the Mt. of Fire with its hundred orafires, thence through the Alkali Lake, then we pass cauldrons of black sulphurious boiling water, one white sulphur spring quite clear and up to boiling point. Over most all the ground we traveled, magnesia, alum, salts, tartaric acid, nitre, iron and sulphur abounded. At a thousand places there was hot scalding steam escaping and forming beautiful deposits of sulphur crystals.

Our next visit carried us up to the pluton, past the ovens, hot with escaping steam. We also come to a soda and iron spring 15 feet by 8 and 12 feet, above is cold soda and iron, strong tonic not very inviting, temperature 56. It is 12 feet by 5 and affords a large supply. The pluton in the shade was 61 degrees with fine pools for bathing, and a little way above was nice for trout fishing. There are a great many springs of which I cannot speak. There is one red paint spring. It is a nice paint, we brought some away, then there is another called the devil's ink stand. The black liquid is boiling up all the time and is sufficiently black for writing purposes, I have written letters with it. There is one spring that has splendid tasted water, by adding a little sugar it just tastes like lemonade. There is one place in the side of the canon, near the cauldron that sounds just like a machine shop in operation. It makes a great noise and is called devil's machine shop, I do not know why they give such names. The Indian springs are nearly a mile down the canon. This is the old medicated spring where many a poor Aborigine has been carried over the mountains to have the disease driven out of him by these powerful waters. On its outer wall, runs a cold stream of pure water, temperature 96 deg., and another impregnated with iron and alum, it is beautifully and romantically situated. We have mentioned nothing like all the springs, we pass some at almost every step. They have a whistle attached to one of the springs that is continually blowing off steam and can be heard three miles and is only a small whistle too.

You need not think that desolation, fire and brimstone reign supreme. One of the wonders of the place is, that grass, shrubs and huge trees grow on the very edge and even overhang the seething cauldrons below. The most varied wood abound there, oak, pine, sycamore, laurel, willow, alder and madrone. The scenery is very fine, I wish I could do justice to the subject of which I am writing about. I have been there twice and then did not see near all the curiosities, I believe a person could spend weeks there and still find something new. One great feature of the Geysers are the hills of crude sulphur for chemical manufactories, such as gun powder, sulphuric acid, &c., of which it is said half million tons are consumed annually. We visited the great sulphur banks also, quite a distance from the Geysers. That was quite a curiosity, sometimes it takes fire and the flames shoot up very high and is very grand to behold.

KATE GAMBEL.

Cordelia, Cal.

WHY IS IT.

Why is it that the brethren and sisters are allowed to use the affirmation, when Christ teaches us in his sermon on the mount: "But I say unto you, swear not at all, neither by heaven, for it is God's throne, neither by the earth, for it is his foot stool, neither by Jerusalem for it is the city of the great King, neither shall thou swear by thy head because thou canst not make one hair white or black, but let your communication be yea, yea, and nay, nay, for whatsoever is more than these cometh of evil." Matt. 5: 34, 35, 36, and James 5: 12, says; "But above all things my brethren, swear not, neither by heaven, neither by earth neither by any other oath; but let your yea be yea, and your nay, nay, lest ye fall into condemnation."

Now I would suppose the affirmation would be one of the "any other oaths that the apostle speaks of, which, I claim is merely a modified oath, and just as binding as the real oath. Then why not let your yea be yea, and your nay, nay?

Why is it that some of our brethren pray for kings and rulers that are in authority, that they might enact such laws that we may lead a quiet and peaceable life in all Godliness and honesty? I Tim. 2: 2. Why not pray for their conversion, that they might obey the divine law? In the 1st verse of the 9th chapter we are told to pray for all men, and in the 4th and 5th we see; "For this is good and acceptible in the sight of God our Savior, who will have all men to be saved and to come unto the knowledge of the truth." Let the kings and those that are in authority make their laws and we will be subject to the law for so we are commanded to be subject and not pray for them to enact &c., but pray for their conversion.

SARAH J. MILLER.

Milford, Ind.

ACKNOWLEDGMENT.

I am very thankful to some kind brother or sister for sending me the PILGRIM. I have not the privilege of meeting with the Church often, but it does my soul good to read the many instructions and kind admonitions of the brethren and sisters through the PILGRIM.

SAMANTHA COLLINS.

Railroad Privileges.

The Pittsburgh, Fort Wayne & Chicago R. R. will carry brethren and sisters to A. M. from Chicago and all intermediate points, where 20 or more will get on, at 4 cents per mile. You will pay the whole amount as you go and get a return ticket. Tickets will be sold from 27th of May and good until 15th of June. This is much shorter than by the Cincinnati road and quicker and cheaper.

JESSE CALVERT.

Brother John Mahn has made arrangements with the C. V. R. R. Company for excursion tickets to persons going to A. M. Brethren and sisters traveling over this road will inform the ticket agent that they are going to A. M., and from him they will receive their excursion tickets.

ANNOUNCEMENTS.

Dear Pilgrim:—Please make the following announcement for a Communion meeting in Union Church, Marshall county, Ind., 5½ miles west of Plymouth on the 10th of June, beginning at 10 o'clock. A general invitation is extended. All those coming on the mail train will stop off at the summit, 3 miles west of Plymouth where they will be met by members to convey them to their home. Those coming on the fast train will stop off at Plymouth where they will be cared for.

JOHN KNISLEY.

The brethren of South Bend district, St. Jasper Co., Ind., will hold their Communion meeting on the 12th day of June next, at the house of Zachariah Troyer, 14 miles from South Bend, near North Liberty. A general invitation is given and we hope at least some of our western ministering brethren, in returning from Annual Meeting, will stop and stay during the meeting. Those that come over the Pittsburgh Fort Wayne & Chicago R. R. will stop at Plymouth and take the I. T. & C. R. R. and stop at Walkerton. From there they will be conveyed to place of meeting.

ZACHARIAH TROYER.

CERRO GORDA, ILL.,
May 9th, 2873.

Dear Ed. of Pilgrim:—Please publish that the brethren in the Church of Oneaw in Piatt and Macon county, Ill., have appointed their communion meeting on Tuesday, the 10th day of June, 1873 at George Funks, 5 miles south-west of Cerro Gordo, Ill. An invitation to all especially to ministering brethren.

J. P. REPLOGLE.

LOVEFEASTS.

Spring Run, Mifflin county, Pa., May 27 28.

Beaver Creek, Wednesday May 14 at 1 P. M.

Shade Creek Congregation, Somerset co Pa., May 29, commencing at 10 a. m.

Champaign Co., Ill., at Geo. Dillings, 5 miles east of Urbana, 7th and 8th of June

DISTRICT MEETING.

Middle District of Iowa, in Dallas Co on the 19th day of May.

North-eastern District of Ohio, Jonathan's Creek Congregation, Perry Co., on May 20th.

Please notice through the PILGRIM that the District Meeting of Western Pa., will be held at the Fairview Meeting house in the George's Creek branch, Fayette Co. Pa., on Wednesday 21st of May, '73.

J. FOUST.

DIED.

KNEPPER.—In the Falling Spring Congregation, Franklin Co., Pa., April 26th 1873, sister Annie E., eldest daughter of brother Alexander and sister Sarah Knepper aged 19 years, 7 months and 22 days.

The subject of this notice was afflicted with consumption for several years, and, unwilling to die out of Christ she desired to be baptized, and on the 31st of March she was carried to a neighboring mill-dam and was baptized into Christ. A few days after, by her request, she was annointed in the name of the Lord. She endured her suffering with patience and resignation to the will of God, calmly awaiting her deliverance Funeral services by the brethren, from Rev 14 : 13, by her request,

"No sickness or sorrow or pain.
Shall ever disquiet her now,
For death to her spirit was gain,
Since Christ was her life when below.

Her soul has now taken its flight,
To mansions of glory above.
To mingle with angels of light,
And dwell in the kingdom of love.

DAVID BOCK.

EBERLY.—In the Yellow Creek district. Waterside, Bedford Co ; Pa., May 4th, John Wilson Ellsworth, son of John and Malkia Eberly, aged 10 years, 10 months and 14 days, of heart disease. Funeral services from Matt. 6 : 33, by Rev Shoemaker.

JOS. Z. REPLOGLE.

NISLEY —In the Lower Cumberland Church, Pa , May 5th, 1873, John Nisley, aged 78 years, 9 months and 11 days. Text 2 Cor. 5 : 9.

BEARNING, — Same congregation as above, May 4th, Catharine Dorathy Hearning, aged 77 years and 8 months.

Funeral by the brethren.

CUPP.—Departed this life, Feb. 27th, 1873, in the Sugar Creek branch of the church, Allen county Ohio, brother John Cupp ; age, 63 years, 9 months and 10 days. He leaves a sorrowing widow, children, and many sympathizing friends to mourn their loss.

Funeral occasion improved from Rev., 14: 13 by the brethren. DANIEL BROWER.

HERSHEY.—Died in the Neosho Valley church, Woodson county, Kansas, sister Susan Hershey, wife of elder Isaac Hershey, aged 58 years, 6 months and 8 days. The death of our dear sister was a sore affliction to her husband and children but they have hope that her end was that of the righteous. She was much beloved by all who knew her. Funeral service by Jesse Studebaker, from 1 Peter 1 :24, 25

NANCY E. STUDEBAKER.

EVERGAN.—In the Raccoon church, Montgomery county, Ind , February 17, 1873, Elizabeth Ann Evergan, aged 30 years, 1 month and 8 days. She was the daughter of Matthias and Sally Frantz, had been a member of our church about two years. She suffered nearly a year almost entire confinement to her bed, but in all her affliction, blessed with great patience and unwavering faith and hope in The blessed Savior, desiring to obey the whole will of her Heavenly Father, she was annointed a few days before her death the day she died she asked her husband and her father to sing for her while she would sleep, so we see the dying christian whose hope and trust was in God. longed to hear the songs of Zion, greeting them last on earth and first in Heaven She left a husband and four children, an aged father and mother, one brother and sister-in-law, but many friends and relatives, especially brethren and sisters in the church, to mourn her loss. Funeral services before she was buried, in presence of a large congregation by John ... of Woodford county, Ill., and R H Miller, from Rev. 14 : 13.

R H. MILLER

The Weekly Pilgrim.

JAMES CREEK, PA., May 20. 1873.

DISTRICT MEETING OF MIDDLE PA

On last Friday evening we had the pleasure of a call from Daniel Keller and Daniel Hollinger. Though the weather was unpropicious and the roads extremely muddy, we had a pleasant and interesting little meeting in the Church,—next morning according to their arrangement they left us to remain with the brethren at Clover Creek over Sunday. For Saturday evening we had the promise of brethren John Spanogle and J. R. Lane to be with us but in the evening we were pleasantly disappointed by Bros. D. F. Good and J. P. Larew stepping into our home. Notwithstanding the bad roads, the meetings were well attended and the congregation well entertained by the four above named brethren.

On Monday morning we all took the train for the District Conference to be held at Clover Creek. After a pleasant walk across Taurus mountain we landed at Bro. J. W. Brumbaugh's who resides only a few rods from the church. After dinner we were favored with a horse and went over to Martinsburg to make a short call at the *Echo* office, where we found Mr. Lehman, our former help in the PILGRIM office, but now proprietor of the *Echo*, in the best of spirits and quite hopeful of his enterprise. Mr. Lehman is a man of good moral worth and the citizens of Morrisons Cove should study their own interests and give him, a liberal support.

In the evening we returned to the church again where we met quite a number of delegates and others who had gathered to attend the meeting. As the brethren there had decided to have no public preaching that evening we had a meeting composed principally of ministers and those living in the immediate neighborhood. Preachers preaching to preachers proved to be quite interesting and many felt that it was good to be there.

On Tuesday morning after some appropriate remarks by Bres. Grabill and Isaac Myers, the meeting was opened by prayer and organized by the last years officers. An election was then held for the ensuing officers with the following result. Grabill Myers, Moderator, George Brumbaugh Clerk, and H. B. Brumbaugh Assistant Clerk. Out of the 24 churches of the District, 22 were represented in person, one by letter and one not represented.

There was not much business before the meeting, and what was there was principally all of such a character as had been acted upon by A. M. This not being of a general interest we shall not burden our readers with notes. There was one move made in the right direction in which we feel interested, and hope it may prove a success. Altoona is said to be a field of promise for gathering a congregation. The brethren have been preaching there for some time and report an increasing interest in the meetings but they have no house, and the house in which they now worship can be had only for a short time, therefore there must either be a house purchased or built, or the meetings must stop. The place lies between two congregations and they do not feel able to build a house unless they can get assistance, and as the members residing there and those interested in the meeting are not from these districts alone, but from surrounding districts both East and West a large number of these being brethren's children, it was tho't proper and advisable to call upon the whole Middle District of Pa., to assist in building a house, accordingly, it was presented to the delegates of the D. M., and arrangements made to make an effort in that direction. The move was favorably received by the meeting. The delegates were called upon to express their sentiments in regard to the matter and, with a few exceptions, all manifested a willingness to do what they could by presenting the case before their several churches and then report the result. For this purpose, George Brumbaugh, Grafton P. O. Huntingdon Co., Pa., was appointed as the person to whom all reports are to be sent. Each church or individual member, is to report, between this and the first of July, how much they are willing to give, but no money to be sent until it is known that the move will be a success. John Spanogle, J. W. Brumbaugh and P. S. Myers are appointed as an investigating committee, whose duty it is to determine on the proper location, plan and size of the house and appoint a building committee if the house is to be built.

Now brethren, this is an important matter and we hope that every church will take the matter to heart and act as if souls were at stake which undoubtedly, is the case. Because you have one to build at home is no reason that you should not aid in this. We are only a small congregation, only in moderate circumstances, built a church last Summer, are building one this Summer and yet expect to do our share in this. Brethren, we do not boast, but we believe that the money which we lend to the Lord, is the best investments that we make.

Another important move was made at the meeting in sending Leonard Furry and J. W. Brumbaugh on a mission to fill a call from Crawford Co., Pa. The meeting was one of considerable interest and everything passed off pleasantly and with the best of feelings.

MINUTES of the Middle District of Pa., can be had of us at 10 cents per single copy, or 60 cents per dozen, post paid.

OUR ARRANGEMENT.

Our brethren of James Creek had intended appointing a Communion Meeting with the expectation of having our Eastern brethren stop with us on their way to A. M , but as the time that we would have preferred holding our meeting was taken by the brethren East of us, we have concluded to have no Communion services, but have appointed meeting at the James Creek Church for Saturday evening to be continued over Sunday, hoping that our brethren will still make arrangements to stop with us. By coming this far on Saturday, (May 31), the place of A. M. can be reached by Monday evening. By noticing the "Time Table" on eighth page you can see the connection of trains at Huntingdon. Those who intend stopping off will inform the conductor of their intention so that they may have their tickets attended to. This can be done when he calls for the tickets. For convenience we will make arrangements to have the evening train of May 31 stop at the church. Our brethren will please remember this arrangement as we will be pleased to have all stop who feel like giving us a call.

PERSONAL.

J. ZUCK.—Due from E. B. W. 95 cts.

WM. C. TEETER—That is right. We expect our agents to reserve sufficient to cover expenses.

G. R. BAKER.—The letter containing D. H's. subscription was not received. PILGRIM is now sent.

HYMN BOOKS.- We are now out of books but have ordered. We have booked the orders sent in and will fill them as soon as the books arrive.

FOR WANT of names a number of communications are lying in our manuscript box. We have given frequent notices that no contributions will receive any attention unless we are informed of the name of the writer.

THOSE WHO do not get the *Phrenological Journal* will please write to the publisher of the Journal stating what Nos. are missing and they will be promptly supplied. Change of address &c., must be made with the publisher and not with us.

ADDRESS WANTED. Martin Lehman, formerly of Lower Cumberland Church Pa., will learn something of importance by letting his whereabouts be known to the undersigned. Any person knowing his address will confer a favor by sending it. Address Daniel Hollinger, Dickinson, Cumberland Co., Pa.

ANNOUNCEMENTS.

Please announce a Communion Meeting in Canton Church, Stark Co., O. at Bro. John Seetung 3 miles north of Louisville, on the 8th of June. Ministers specially invited.

B. B. BOLLINGER.

Please announce that the brethren of the Jacobs' Creek Church, Somerset Co., Pa., intend to hold a Lovefeast on the 24th and 25th of May. Brethren please make your arrangements to stop with us returning from District Meeting. The meeting is to be held at Bro. John Meyers, 3 miles south of Mt. Pleasant. By order of the Church. F. B. WEIMER.

Bro. Henry—Please announce in the PILGRIM that we, the Brethren in Snake Spring congregation, Bedford Co., Pa., have appointed our Lovefeast on the 30th day of May, commencing at 10 o'clock. Also meeting next day. A hearty invitation extended, especially to ministering brethren.

HENRY HERSHBERGER.

Dear Brother of the Pilgrim:—Please announce that the Lick Creek Church, Williams Co., Ohio, have appointed a Lovefeast on the 10th and 11th of June to commence at 10 o'clock a. m., at the house of David Rittenhouse. A general invitation is given. If any one come by railroad stop off at Bryan. The place of meeting is about 15 miles north of Bryan. Conveyance will be attended to.

JOHN BROWN.

Bro. Editor: — Please announce to the readers of the PILGRIM that we intend, God willing, to hold a Lovefeast in the Yellow creek Church near New Enterprise, Bedford, Co., Pa., on Wednesday the 28th of May, 1873, commencing at 4 o'clock p. m. Meeting next day forenoon. General invitation is extended.

By order of the church,
LEONARD FURRY

Please announce that the District Meeting of North-Western Ohio will be held, the Lord willing, with the brethren of Crawford Co., at the house of brother John Brillhart, on the Base Line on the 23 day of May, and on the 24, the day following, there will be a Communion meeting at the same place. A general representation is desired. ISRAEL ROOP.

The Weekly Pilgrim.

Published by J. B. Brumbaugh, & Co.

Edited by H. B. & Geo. Brumbaugh

CORRESPONDING EDITORS.

D. P. Sayler, Double Pipe Creek, Md.

Leonard Furry, New Enterprise, Pa.

The *Pilgrim* is a Christian Periodical, devoted to religion and moral reform. It will advocate in the spirit of *love* and *liberty*, the principles of true Christianity, labor for the promotion of peace among the people of God, for the encouragement of the saints and for the conversion of sinners, avoiding those things which tend toward disunion or sectional feelings.

TERMS.

Single copy, Book paper,	$1.50
Eleven copies, (eleventh for Agt.)	$15.00

Any number above that at the same rate.

Address,

H. B BRUMBAUGH.
James Creek,
Huntingdon county Pa.

The Weekly Pilgrim.

"REMOVE NOT THE ANCIENT LANDMARKS WHICH OUR FATHERS HAVE SET."

VOL. 4. JAMES CREEK, PENNSYLVANIA, MAY 27, 1873. NO. 21

POETRY.

CHRIST IN THE GARDEN.

SELECTED BY MOLLIE UMBAUGH.

While nature in stillness was sinking to rest,
The last beam of daylight shone in the West;
O'er fields by moonlight, my wandering feet,
Sought in meditation some lonely retreat.

While passing the garden, I paused to hear
A voice faint and plaintive from one that was there;
The voice of suffering affected my heart,
While in agony pleading the poor sinner's part.

In offering to Heaven his pitying prayer,
He spoke of the torments the sinner must bear;
His life as a ransom He offered to give;
That the sinners redeemed in glory might live.

I listened a moment, then turned me to see
What a man of compassion this stranger could be;
I saw him low kneeling upon the cold ground,
The loveliest creature that ever was found.

His mantle was wet with the dew of the night,
His locks in the sunbeams were glistening bright;
His eyes, bright as diamonds, to Heaven were raised,
While angels in wonder stood around him amazed.

So deep were his sorrows, so fervent his prayer,
That down o'er his bosom rolled sweat, blood and tears;
I wept to behold him, I ask him his name,
'Tis Jesus, he answered, from *Heaven* I came.

I am the Redeemer, for thee I must die;
The cup is most bitter, but I cannot pass by;
Thy sins like a mountain are laid upon me;
And all this deep anguish I suffer for thee.

I heard with deep sorrow the tale of his woe,
While tears like a fountain of water did flow;
The cause of his sorrows to hear him repeat
Affected my heart, and I fell at his feet.

I trembled with horror, I loudly did cry,
Lord, save a poor sinner! Oh, save or I die!
He smiled when he saw me and said to me "live!
Thy sins which are many I freely forgive."

How sweet was the moment he bade me rejoice,
His smiles, O how pleasant, how cheering his voice!
I fled from the garden and spread it abroad,
I shouted "salvation! Oh glory to God!"

I'm now on my journey to mansions above,
My soul's full of glory, of light, peace and love;
I think of the pardon, the prayer, and the tears
Of that loving stranger who banished my fears.

The day of bright glory is rolling around,
When Gabriel descending the trumpet shall sound;
My soul, in rapture to glory shall rise,
To gaze at the stranger with unclouded eyes.

ORIGINAL ESSAYS.

A LIGHT TO THE WORLD.

What is Safe and what is not Safe; What is Right and what is not Right.

BY J. H. MOORE.

CHAP. VII.—*Trine Immersion.*

It seems neither reasonable nor necessary that we should be called upon to settle the question, whether *trine* immersion is either right or safe (?) there are but few if any who, doubt this. The main difficulty is not about *trine* but *single* immersion.

Among the unlearned the question is, what was the apostolic method? But not so among the learned immersionists, all their able writers, with only a few exceptions among modern critics, agree that the apostles and their immediate successors practiced a three-fold immersion. Nor are they alone, all the ancient writers, without one single exception known to me, who speak of the primitive method of baptizing, state it to have been trine immersion; about this there is no dispute, all the controversy has been about the antiquity of single immersion.

The origin of trine immersion, no man either modern or ancient, has ever found this side of Christ. You may as well try to find the origin of Christianity itself this side of Jesus as to try to find the introduction of trine immersion this side of the same period. But not so with single immersion, no man on earth can more clearly trace Mahommedanism to its early fountain head, than we can trace single immersion to its very beginning near the middle of the fourth century. Even those that first used it knew that it was not of divine authority. And how has it came down to us? I answer through the Roman Catholic Church, who claims to herself the prerogative to change, create and abolish ordinances at her pleasure. Why did she adopt this human invention? Tell me why she adopted sprinkling and pouring, and then you have a key that unlocks the entire mystery.

This method of baptizing, like many other errors, has found its way into many, if not the majority of modern churches, and some now claim for its authority the teachings of the apostles. And even a majority of those who patronize the single immersion, do not doubt the validity of the three-fold immersion, knowing that in it is embodied all the elements that can possibly be connected with the form of Christian baptism. Let the commission given by Christ, and recorded by Matt.—28: 19, teach what it may, either single or trine immersion, there is no sane man on earth who will say that trine immersion does not contain all that is therein taught.

I have yet the first man to find who contends that trine immersion does not meet all the demands of the commission, all the trouble has been in trying to get single immersion to meet all the demand which the commission requires. About trine immersion doing the work there is no dispute, then this is safe, whether the other is or not. If I take a candidate into the water and say "I baptize thee into the name of the Father," [*then dip him*], "and of the Son," [*dip him*] "and of the Holy Ghost" [*dipping him the third time.*] there is no man who would say that I did not do just what I said I would? Will any one say that the candidate was not "baptized into the name of the Father, and of the Son, and of the Holy Ghost;" about this there is not nor can there be one particle of dispute. This we know is right, it can't help but be right. But if to the contrary I should say "I baptize thee into the name of the Father, and of the Son, and of the Holy Ghost" *then dip him*, it is questioned whether I have done just what I said I would do. If in the former case I did what I said I would, then in the latter I did not. If in the former I obeyed the commission, in the latter case I violated it. No one will say that I did not do precisely what I said I would in the former case, and in the latter case I used precisely the same words, but acted differently. The former we know is right, but all the doubts in the whole matter are about the latter. The former we know is on safe ground, but all the doubts in the entire matter are about the latter being on safe ground. "Prove all things, hold fast that which is good."

As early as nine years after the death of Christ we have an account of a church in Antioch, and this body of Christians continued the apostolic method of baptizing till long after the close of the fourth century, and during this entire period has never been known to practice anything but trine immersion. Chrysostom was one of the most learned bishops that Antioch ever boasted of, and he tells us that "Christ delivered to his disciples one baptism in three immersions," when he gave to them the last commission. He was a native Greek scholar, and fully competent to examine and determine the meaning of the Greek commission. It is then a settled fact that trine immersion was preached in Antioch; about this there is no uncertainty, all the difficulty in the whole matter has been in trying to find single immersion there. In all my reading and researches of antiquity, I must state that I have not found one single instance of single immersion in this Church of antiquity, nor do I believe that any one else has. While this is true respecting Antioch, the same may be affirmed of Cesarea, where trine immersion still prevailed in the fourth century. But we are not yet through with this matter of antiquity; there is more weight attached to this than is generally presumed by the careless thinker. The church at Jerusalem, the mother church of the whole world, was founded by Christ and the apostles, and I here remark as a matter of fact that in all antiquity they have never been known to practice single immersion, while the three-fold immersion has always been the prevailing practice at that place.

Cyril a learned bishop of Jerusalem, was born only 215 years after the death of the apostle John, and he declares that they at that time used trine immersion in Jerusalem. There is then no trouble about finding trine immersion in the first church organized by Christ and the apostles, the only trouble has been in some fruitless attempts to find single immersion there. About trine immersion being practiced in all the leading churches there is not one particle of doubt, all the doubts are about single immersion. Even the church at Rome continued the practice of trine immersion till after the sixth century, while the church at Milam continued it much longer, and it was the general practice all over the Christian world till the seventh century. The Catholic church in the west, did not adopt the single immersion till A. D. 633, while on the eastern part of christendom never would consent to a change. When the new method appeared the candidate was baptized into the name or death of the Lord Jesus only, and not "into the name of the Father, and of the Son, and of the Holy Ghost. All from the least to the greatest knew that the commission taught trine immersion; and in those times the commission was regarded as an unanswerable argument in support of this method. This can readily be discovered in the writings of Tertullian, Chrysostom, Monulus, Jerome and Theodoret, all of whom state that the commission teaches a three-fold immersion. However in course of time some of the Eunomians seemed to have changed their formula, and "baptized in the name of the Father, and of the Son, and of the Holy Ghost," by dipping once only, although it was a glaring perversion of language, still during the dark ages the people in part became accustomed to it, so that when the reformation commenced it did not appear so ridiculous as at first. Although as a method of baptizing it did not become general till after A. D. 1517, it soon found its way to the Baptist churches, and has by them been nourished even till our time. Right here is a fact worth knowing by all, and that is the Campbellite Church has received her method of baptizing directly from the Baptists. Campbell was formerly a member of the Baptists and when he ushered into existence his reformatory movement, instead of adopting the apostolic method, which consists in dipping the candidate three times face forward, he incorporated the Baptist method, which was never practiced by any of the churches established by Christ and the apostles. Perhaps there are many of them who are not aware of this painful fact, and when informed that their method of baptism is not yet 400 years old, are struck with perfect amazement. It is therefore high time that every member in the Church, be up and doing. Labor to restore Christianity to its primitive order; preach the entire gospel everywhere, and give the people not only a chance to believe but to obey it.

Single immersion by a backward action is being spread all over our entire land, under the name *Christian Baptism*, when the facts in the case teach us that it lacks more than 1200 years of being old enough to reach the apostolic age. Several attempts have been made to trace immersion to the apostles, but nearly the entire journey from the reformation, has been performed upon the royal highway of trine immersion, but this from the facts of antiquity and immersion ceases to have an existence beyond the middle of the 4th century, and sprinkling and pouring remain in everlasting possession of the contested field.

The formula of baptism, "baptizing them into the name of the Father, and of the Son, and of the Holy Ghost," as it stands recorded by Matthew is very elleptical, and, filling up the ellipsis will read as follows, "Baptizing them into the name of the Father, and baptizing them into the name of the Son, and baptizing them into name of the Holy Ghost." This is what Paul calls "one baptism" or as the Greek has it "one dipping" not one dip but dipping; this is the true meaning of the Greek *baptisma*, and was so intrepreted by the ancient Greeks, in whose mother tongue the New Testament was first written. In the commission there are three distinct names—Father, Son and Holy Ghost, and it is into these three distinct names that we are to be baptized, which possibly cannot be done short of three distinct actions. About being baptized into these three distinct names with three distinct actions there is not one particle of dispute; all confess it can be done, none say it cannot, this then is not only safe but right, and all the difficulty and trouble has been in trying to baptize a person into three distinct names with one action, on this hang all the doubts connected with the whole subject. In the former case there can be no uncertainty, neither can it be doubted, but the latter is where men's faith and understanding fail them.

No one who has ever been lawfully baptized by trine immersion is dissatisfied with his method of baptizing, none doubt it being either right or safe, all the doubts come from the man who has been baptized by single immersion, he is the one who doubts the validity of his method, if there are any doubts at all. All concede trine immersion to be a good baptism, hence it is safe, and not only safe but right. It is so good in the estimation of people in general, that they will patronize it in their own Churches. No one of any note doubts its validity, all the doubts are about single immersion.

For the Pilgrim.

SAUL VERSUS PAUL.

We first get acquainted with this man from the 7th chapter of Acts of the apostles, at a time when there was a great persecution of the followers of Jesus Christ, some time after the mission of Christ was ended on earth, and the will of Heaven made known to man. Introducing this kingdom was a mighty work, and was especially intended for the benefit and restoration of man to his primitive glory and enjoyment. The rules and regulations laid down, were so different and so at variance with the customs of the people that it caused quite an excitement among them, although having received their authority from Moses, their Lawgiver, who was authorized by the Most High God to deliver to them a law which was to govern them until the time prophecied for the coming of the Messiah. But they became so wise in their own conceit that they introduced traditions to that extent that the Savior was compelled to tell them that they had made the word of God of none effect through their tradition, and by heeding their tradition they so far lost sight of the prophesied Messiah which was to come and did come, that they did not know Him, and indeed rejected Him, although proving Himself by signs and miracles. But with all that, they condemned Him to death and crucified Him, which was considered the most shameful death, or punishment that could be inflicted upon criminals in their day. Think of the shameful death inflicted upon the Son of God. Yet this disposition was not universal, God be thanked, for there were some that did believe on Him and were willing to enlist under His banner, walk in His footsteps, and gladly suffer persecution for the name of Jesus if need be.

The Evangelist John, in his first chapter, says; "He came to His own and His own received Him not, but as many as received Him, to them gave He power to become the sons of God." Out of that number, He chose witnesses to witness of His life, of His death and of His resurrection. To them gave He power to carry on the great work which He begun, yet they were not fully equipped until after He was crucified and ascended to Heaven to His Father again. Then the Holy Spirit was poured out upon them profusely, and actuated them to that degree that they preached the Word with great effect, so much so that great numbers were converted on the day of Pentecost, were made to feel that they were guilty of shedding the blood of the Son of God, and without repentance of their sinful acts, they would be eternally damned. The work did not stop there for the Savior told them while He was yet with them, "Go ye into all the world and preach the gospel to every creature," and faithful to their trust, they went on with mighty power, demonstrating the Word of God with signs and miracles, so that fear came upon every soul because many wonders and signs were done by the apostles, by this means, proving beyond a doubt that their authority was from above. When this became more generally known, it began to arouse the fury of the adversaries of Jesus and His followers, and persecutions began to rage to a fearful extent, yet this did not intimidate the disciples in the least, they would suffer chastisement in various ways, scourgings, imprisonments and terrible threatenings, but with all this before them, by the help of God, they would stand before the unholy councils and declare whether they should hearken unto God more than men, they might be the judge but preach they would and did.

Now, seeing the field so large and the labor so extensive, they saw proper to call more laborers into the field to help them. Among them was a Stephen, a man with great eloquence and power, who disputed with the great men, yet they were not able to resist the wisdom and the spirit by which he spoke. Then they suborned men to say, "We have heard Him speak blasphemous words against Moses and against God." and set up false witnesses which said, "This man ceaseth not to speak blasphemous words against this holy place and the Law, for we have heard Him say that this Jesus of Nazareth shall destroy this place and change the customs which Moses delivered us."

Kind reader, think of what the followers of God had to suffer in the primitive age of Christianity and compare it with the privilege you enjoy, the zeal you had, and that will show you how much Christianity is on the decline, although much talked of at the present day. But it is nearly all popular religion, and of the same stamp possessed by the Libertines, Cyrenians and Alexandrians of that day, who are disputing with the humble followers of Christ, setting aside some of the commandments and ordinances of the house of God, and adding some traditions to make it suit their peculiar fancy and, by their fervent zeal, collect large numbers to them and lead them along in their blindness, getting well paid for it. Stephen suffered death by the hand of those adversaries who engaged in presenting the followers of the meek and lowly Jesus, by a shower of stones cast upon him, and to facilitate their work of destruction, they threw off their outer garments and laid them down at a young man's feet whose name was Saul, who was also consenting to the dreadful deed under contemplation, who was honestly giving his consent; being brought up at the feet of Gamaliel and taught according to the perfect manner of the Law, as he afterwards confessed. Some people are very tenacious about what their conscience dictates, believing it to be a true guide to action, but this case proves to a demonstration that it is a creature of education, assisted by reason and governed by understanding. When these great principles are well developed in us, we are always able to determine which is true and which is false, having access to the truth of God's Word. But when led about by Gamaliel and taught his doctrine, we are in danger of getting to where Saul was and be conscientious in it, and all be wrong in the sight of God. Oh, how many Gamaliel's there are at the present day! traveling from place to place, teaching for doctrines the commandments of men, and with success fearful to look upon. Can it be possible in this enlightened age of literary attainments and Biblical knowledge that we should thus be led astray by such sensational divines, for whom we will not say anything better than they aim at fleecing instead of feeding the flock. To prove this, is only to look around in your vicinity and you will at once see, as those increase in theological attainments, they want their salaries increased or they will say, "God has called me some where else," where a greater salary is offered.

We trace this man Saul a little farther, and find him zealously engaged in retarding the spread of the gospel, although young in years, yet we see what a powerful influence for evil a man can have. In the 8th chapter and 1st verse we read; "And Saul was consenting unto his death, and at that time there was a great persecution against the Church at Jerusalem. But there were devout men who carried Stephen to his burial and made great lamentation over him. As for Saul he made havoc of the Church, entering into houses and hailing men and women, committing them to prison." So terrible was his zeal for the promotion of that cause which he learned of Gamaliel, and led on in this matter until he was prompted to extend his persecutions into strange cities. Therefore he desired and obtained letters of authority from those standing at the head of Government, from whom we should think better things, but they granted him power to go and bring bound to Jerusalem such as he could find of that persuasion, for the purpose of compelling them to desist from their course of worship. We think the object was to annihilate the followers of Jesus and strengthen the cause of Gamaliel. In the 9th chap. of Acts we read a vivid picture of the doings of Saul. We see him starting for Damascus with a cohort of assistants, no doubt fully bent on wreaking out his vengeance on all he came in contact with who were engaged in the service of Jesus and His word, Jesus standing at the right hand of God looking on with pity and compassion. And when Saul drew near to Damascus, his heart beating with hope at the good report he could bring his employers on his return, and the number of prisoners he could bring them. The applause and esteem he expected to receive at their hands caused him, no doubt, to quicken his pace,—but when he drew near to Damascus, lo, suddenly, there shone round about him a light from Heaven which was so dazzling he could not bear up under it, but fell prostrate to the earth, and heard a voice saying unto him, "Saul, why persecutest thou me?" Dear reader, can you imagine the astonishment that must have been experienced by him when he heard that voice from on High, accompanied with the great light? He said, "Who art thou Lord?" The answer was, "I am Jesus whom thou art persecuting," and he trembling with astonishment, said, "Lord what shall I do?" The Lord said, "Go into the city and there it shall be told thee what thou must do." Astonishing, for him to go to the place for instruction where he intended to capture prisoners for Gamaliel! But such is the command of God. The Lord's ways are not our ways, nor his thoughts our thoughts, or else we would often do differently from what we do. Those with him stood speechless, hearing a voice but seeing no one, being also shocked by the power of God because they were also assisting in the wicked work. They then took hold of their peer, leading him down to Damascus and left him there with his guilty fear pressing him so terribly that he could neither eat nor drink for three days, in which time the Lord prepared one of His servants and sent him to comfort Saul, for he is now earnestly engaged in prayer to be relieved of his enormous iniquity resting upon his soul. Ananias, the Lord's servant, coming into the house where Saul was said, "Brother Saul, the Lord even Jesus that appeared unto thee in the way as thou camest, hath sent me that thou mightest receive thy sight and be filled with the Holy Ghost.

To be Continued.

PURE RELIGION.

There are various and erroneous opinions about religion. Religion we learn is derived from the Latin word *religio*, which signifies oath, because it binds or imposes duties on its followers. So we conclude that when a man receives the Christian religion that he becomes a sincere believer in the gospel of Jesus Christ, which is the plan and principle of salvation, and enters into a covenant with the Lord to obey the same and this faith in the Gospel brings about a repentance which will result in a reformation of life. We also learn that pure and undefiled religion is this: to visit the fatherless and the widows in their afflictions and to keep unspotted from the world.

We may infer, from the above quotation, that the religion of Jesus Christ requires its followers to visit the fatherless and widows in their afflictions and to administer to them as we see their circumstances require. By keeping unspotted from the world, we understand that we must forsake all evil habits and not follow them any more but press forward into all the ordinances and commandments of the Lord as they are recorded in the Gospel. And that we must lay aside all superfluity of naughtiness, gaudy apparel, &c. So we learn from the above definition of religion, that it is a principle to be wrought out and that the christian religion is the principle of eternal life and salvation, which is taught by Jesus Christ and his apostles, and in order to obtain eternal life and salvation which is taught by Jesus Christ and his apostles, we must embrace this religion and work it out with fear and trembling. We have said that when a man receives the christian religion that he becomes a sincere believer, so when a man has properly received this religion he becomes willing to deny all selfish inclinations, to renounce all the works of the devil and live a life of peace devoted unto the service of the Lord.

THOMAS OWENS.

Romeo, Tenn.

A WORD TO MOTHERS.

And ye fathers, provoke not your children to wrath but bring them up in the nurture and admonition of the Lord." This is a very good admonition, how we should train our children and not to provoke them. Oh, mothers, how many of us are provoking our children! We think there is more than one way of provoking them. There are a great many provoked about the holidays, when mother's are distributing their gifts among their children, when some receive a gift and others none. Mothers, think upon this weighty subject ere another year rolls around. Let us not be drawn by the allurements of satan, for he is going round like a roaring lion seeking whom he may devour. He is setting traps every day, some in the fashionable way of dress, and some in giving gifts to part of the family and others receive none. Oh, how many children are slighted at home, around the fireside. Perhaps some of our neighbor's children are now sitting at the saloons smoking cigars or drinking rum. Oh, mother, think! Have you not slighted some of these children when they gathered home at their father's house and some would return back with their basket filled while others would return home with them empty? Is this not provoking our children to wrath, for God is no respecter of person and is it right for us mother's to be a respector of our own flesh and bone? Methinks not, for we ought to try and encourage our children on the way to Zion. I fear, sometimes, mothers are most too negligent in training those little ones. They are left have their own way too much when young and when they get older they are harder to bend. And then they are slighted around the fireside and will begin to see that mother thinks more of one than she does of another, and the slighted one will begin to start out in the world for himself and satan will do all in his power to help him along, and thus have him to join his army. Oh mothers, be careful how you are using your children at home and do not provoke them to wrath. I have been made to weep when I see old tottering mothers make such a vast difference in their own children.

In conclusion let us mothers be careful and not provoke our children to wrath but bring them up in the nurture and admonition of the Lord.

SARAH RITTENHOUSE.

Chatham, O.

THE MEEK.

Blessed are the meek, for they shall inherit the earth. MATT.—5: 5.

The Savior, in preaching the sermon on the mount, pronounces a blessing on the meek. Meekness is one of the essential graces of the child of God. When we approach a throne of grace we must come with a meek spirit. It is meekness which characterizes the child of God. We have an example set before us by our Savior, in His sufferings, when he was clothed in a gorgeous robe and crown upon his head, when they smote him so that the blood trickled down over his face. He did not even turn an angry look upon them, that none but the most wicked hands could do it. He looked upon them with such a meek and forgiving look that even the hard-hearted Pilate could not meet his glance without being awed into pity. Brethren let us all pray for meekness, and holiness. Then there will be no disputings and quarrelings in our midst, but we shall all dwell as one happy family here in this world. Then, peace shall reign here, and when death shall come it will find us prepared. May we all meet in Heaven is the prayer of your unworthy brother.

JACOB LONGANECKER.

Goshen, Ind.

ALMS are the salt of riches.

THE BAPTISM OF JOHN, WHENCE WAS IT, FROM HEAVEN OR OF MEN?

S. F. MOOMAW.

The twenty-four inch guage is no less superfluous because the light "from heaven" is by no means insufficient, if we will only open our eyes that its rays may reach the organ of vision, the necessity of all such appliances will be wholly obviated. The great architect has wisely divided the time into periods, the year into seasons, spring, summer, autumn and winter, and so disposed his providences as to assign to each, duties peculiar to itself. Into weeks of seven days with the command that "Six days shalt thou work and do all thy labor and the seventh is the Sabbath of the Lord, in it shall no work be done." Into days and nights, the day for work. A day consists of twelve hours. See John 11 9. In these twelve hours we are to perform the work that we find for our hands to do, whether it be of a secular or spiritual character, the necessary hours for refreshment and recreation excepted, these labors necessarily vary according to circumstances. Some days entirely devoted to secular business, mental exercises excepted, and other days altogether employed in duties of a spiritual character. "The night cometh in which no man can work." So arranged to afford a season of rest for body and mind, hence there is no need of the twenty-four inch guage for these purposes. Nor when the Bible can be procured is there need of the mason hammer to remind us of the depravity and sinfulness of our character, because this is clearly seen in all the ways of unregenerate men, besides it is abundantly taught in the Holy Scriptures, in the history of Adam as well as in the deluvian and antideluvian world. "God made man upright but he has sought out many inventions." "From the crown of the head to the sole of the feet, full of wounds bruises and putrefying sores, which have not been bound up nor mollified with ointment" therefore in "order to fit our minds for the spiritual building" we must "break off our sins by righteousness." This requires an effort on our part. "The kingdom of heaven suffereth violence, and the violent take it by force" and the sure word of the prophecy exhorts that the wicked man forsake his ways and the unrighteous man his thoughts, return unto the Lord and he will have mercy upon him, and unto our God and he will abundantly pardon. With these Scriptures and the man's parallels before us we may dispense also with the hammer.

It appears that having so fully shown the uselessness of all these appliances we may dismiss this point without noticing particularly the other items under this head, that is the pillars, the starry skies, the ladder, the rough and smooth Ashler, believing that enough has been said to satisfy every intelligent reader that all these things are superfluous and offensive to God, having in our hand the grand trestle board on which we have fully portrayed our origin, our true condition, God's entire will concerning us, an infallible index by which we may shun the awful chamber of death and find our way through the blackened paths of this sin cursed world to mansions of the blessed, having erected our spiritual building agreeably to the rules and designs laid down by the supreme architect of the universe in the Gospel, it being the power of God unto salvation. We regard these symbols as being Idolatrous because they are the inventions of men, and in opposition to the command of God, where he says, "Whatsoever I command you observe to do it, thou shalt not add anything to it nor diminish anything from it." Deut. 12: 32, Rev. 21: 18, 19. "Thou shalt not make unto thee any graven image or any likeness of anything that is in heaven above, or that is in the earth beneath, or that is in the water under the earth. Thou shalt not bow down thyself to them nor serve them, for I the Lord am a jealous God visiting the iniquity of the father upon the children to the third and fourth generation of them that hate me, and showing mercy unto them that love me and keep my commandments." God has nowhere either directly or indirectly commanded these things and therefore they are Idolatrous and sinful.

We regard them as being delusive because it is assumed that the craft is of divine origin, and sustained by divine sanction, and these emblems coupled with the inspired, the less intelligent at least regard them as being equal to it, and attach as much if not more importance to them as to the world itself and risk their eternal interest upon them concluding that if they are pretty good Masons that they are good enough, hence we regard the institution so far as vital christianity is concerned dangerous in its tendencies, and deleterious in its consequences, by engaging the attention and satisfying the mind of the initiated, so that they inquire no farther about the way of salvation, unlike the laborers in the market in the days of Christ, idle, waiting to be employed, they being occupied with Masonry, it is not convenient to undertake any other arrangement.

I wish also to note the failure of Freemasonry in a moral point of view, of accomplishing its assumed object of improving society, for in its practical effects we can discover no advantage whatever in favor of Masons. Morally they are no better than other men exhibiting in their life, character, conversation and their transactions with their fellow-men, visibly all the marks of depravity and degradation.

Before dismissing this royal craft I propose to show its inconsistency with itself professing to be consolidated bound together by the cement of brotherly love when in fact they are politically and religiously in antagonism. Masons of one section meeting Masons of another section on the battle field, engaging in all the horrors of mortal strife, and while as you have seen, Masons are uncompromisingly tenacious for the landmarks of the order, they pander to the prejudices and superstitions of all orders of society, speaking of the qualifications and duties of candidates for Masonry, they inform us that in ancient times the Christian Masons were charged to comply with the Christian usages of the country when they sojourned or worked being found in all nations and of divers religious persuasions, yet is now thought most expedient that the brethren in general should only be charged to adhere to the essentials of religion, in which all men agree.

Lodges, say they, were anciently dedicated to king Solomon, who was our first most excellent grand Master. But *Masons professing Christianity* dedicate theirs to St. John the Baptist and St. John the Evangelist, but to whom Mahomedans dedicate theirs they don't inform us but they do inform us that Lodges were formed in the Ottoman Empire, at Constantinople, Smyrna and Aleppo in 1738. I suppose however they would dedicate them to their prophet or some of his principal votaries, either Allen Beer or Allen Taleb. So then we have according to them, Jews, Mahommedans and Christians, Catholic and Protestants of all grades, including Mormons I suppose.

As a qualification for initiation into the order it is required that the candidate believe firmly in the eternal God, and to pay that worship that is due him. But to accommodate the case to a Jew or a Mohammedan our Savior Jesus Christ must be ignored and left out of the question, thus, after all sapping and undermining our blessed Christianity, dishonoring and insulting the Father, who gave his Son, the only competent mediator, through whom and through whom alone the Father can be approached, for says our blessed Lord, "No man can come to the Father but by me," which proves conclusively that it is not from heaven but of men.

To be Continued.

THE VOICE OF GOD.

God calls to us in various ways. Who is it that has not heard his voice, in one way or the other? How often has he called to us through sickness and death, by removing from our side those who were near and dear to us? God calls very loudly to us in this way, in language like the following: "Be ye therefore ready also." He tells us by almost daily observation, and His word teaches us, that this world is not our abiding place; but that we are fast hastening to eternity, and the time and place that now knows us, will shortly know us no more and that forever. Therefore knowing as we do, that we are but pilgrims and sojourners here in this unfriendly world beset with sin on either side, would it not be wisdom in us to prepare for that solemn change which awaits us, and which we all have to undergo sooner or later. "As it is appointed unto man once to die and after this the judgment?" Another way in which God calls to us is when he sends that "still, small voice," whispering to us that all is not well. My dear young friends, have you not heard it? It you have, Oh, turn it not away. It you do, it may never return to you again. Remember, God says: "My spirit will not always strive with man." "To-day if you hear his voice harden not your hearts," and the Savior says, "Behold I stand at the door and knock, if any man hear my voice and open the door I will come in to him and sup with him and he with me." Therefore see that ye refuse not him that speaketh for if they escaped not that refused him that spake upon earth much more shall not we escape if we turn away from him that speaketh from heaven. And if the word spoken by angels was steadfast, and every transgression and disobedience received a just recompense of reward, how shall we escape if we neglect so great salvation, which at first began to be spoken by the Lord and was confirmed unto us by those that heard him?" He tells us "to-day." Do not wait until next year, or perhaps a few years hence, for a more convenient season. Before that convenient season comes around, death may throw its icy arms around you and claim you as its victim, and you may be hurled into eternity without a moments warning, there to appear before the all-scrutinizing eye of Jehovah, and when the messenger of death calls, you will have to obey whether you are willing or not, whether prepared or unprepared. That will be a call that you cannot resist. Why not obey him now, while you are young and in your prime. "while the evil days come not, nor the years [illegible] nigh [illegible] pleasure in them." Dear young friends, we would say to you in the language of one of old, "Stand still and see the salvation of the Lord." Consider for a moment, look back with me to Calvary's rugged summit, and behold there what our adorable Redeemer endured for you and for me. Well might the apostle say, "Behold what manner of love." It was love toward sinful man that permitted the Savior to leave the shining courts of Heaven, and to suffer the ignominious death upon the cross, and to become the propitiation for our sins, and not for ours only but for the sins of the whole world. He died for all, there is none excepted. You who are still holding out the puny arm of rebellion against him, he has made atonement for you. "Oh yield to his love's redeeming power, and strive against your God no more." "For the Lord Jesus shall be revealed from heaven in flaming fire, taking vengeance upon them that know not God, and that obey not the gospel of our Lord and Savior Jesus Christ." Those who have withstood him will then have to exclaim, "The harvest is past, the summer is ended and we are not saved." You will then have to be banished from the presence of the Lord and the glory of his power. But to those that hear his name will the sun of Righteousness arise with healing in his wings. They shall be mine, saith the Lord, in the day when I shall come to make up my jewels, and I shall spare them as a father spareth his own son that serveth him."

Brethren and sisters, let us press onward. There is a crown in reservation for us if we are faithful and endure unto the end, a crown of glory undefiled and that fadeth not away. May the Lord impart unto us grace to do his will here on earth, and when our earthly career is ended take us home without the loss of one to sing his praises, with all those who have washed their robes and made them white in the blood of the Lamb.

MARTHA TROXEL.

Nankin, O.

FORETHOUGHT—AFTERTHOUGHT.—The former is a fountain of good in itself—the latter, alone, is only a source of sorrow, as it is born too late to be of service. Life is so short that forethought is needed from its beginning to its close. Not a few undervalue it. Their hope is in circumstances, chance and day-dreaming they call thinking. Forethought calls for work, self-denial and economy, and promises a satisfactory reward. It is an insurance office, of which the young man is president and cashier, and the profits are all his own. Afterthought and its result is a blessing.

THE tongue is not steel, but it cuts

Youth's Department

THE BETTER LAND

SELECTED BY SENETH SNYDER.

I hear thee speak of the better land,
Thou call'st its children a happy band;
Mother, oh, where is that radiant shore?
Shall we not seek it and weep no more?
Is it where the flower of the orange blows,
And the fireflies dance toward the myrtle boughs?
Not there, not there, my child!

Is it where the feathery palm trees rise,
And the date grows ripe under sunny skies?
Or 'mid the green islands of glittering seas,
Where fragrant flowers perfume the breeze?
And strange bright birds on the starry wings,
Bear the rich hues of all glorious things?
Not there, not ther, my child!

Is it far away in some region old,
Where the rivers wander o'er sands of gold?
Where the burning rays of the ruby shine,
And the diamond lights up the secret mines,
And the pearl gleams forth from the coral strand,
Is it there, sweet mother, that better land?
Not there, not there, my child!

Eye hath not seen it, my gentle child!
Ear hath not heard its deep sounds of joy;
Dreams cannot picture a world so fair,
Sorrow and death may not enter there.
Time doth not breathe on its fadeless bloom
Beyond the clouds, and beyond the tomb.
It is there, it is there, my child!

AFTERWHILE.

The above word is so frequently used that I have concluded to have a talk about it for the benefit of my young readers.

I object to it, first because it is kind of a home made expression, or rather a throwing two words together in such a shape as to make nothing at all as it is not to be found in the dictionaries nowhere, and it is very important that young persons should always use good language or proper words. But there are a great many words used outside of dictionaries, and they generally have a meaning too. If they always meant some good trait or act I would not have any special objections to them, but some of them are decidedly improper and objectionable.

Mother told Annie that she should run home quick and see that no fire had fallen out of the stove. The answer was: "Yes, mother I will go after while," but after while was just a little too late, the fire had dropped on the floor and the alarm was not given until it was too late, and the house was burned.

The little boy had an offer of a good situation and was to meet his employer at just 9 o'clock, but he concluded to have a game of ball first and go afterwhile, 9 o'clock came but the boy was not there. The conclusion was, if he is tardy and breaks the first engagement, he will break many more, and word is left for the boy that he is not needed. The house was burned and the boy lost a good position all on account of using "afterwhile" instead of "now."

The present is always the best time for making a mark in whatever we intend to do. The time spent between "now" and "after while" is always lost when there is anything to do done. Poor old Felix, that you can read of in the Bible, was made to fear and tremble under Paul's preaching, but instead of getting right to work and doing his duty he adopted the word "after while" or the more convenient season, which means the same thing, and we are not told that it suited him any better "afterwhile" and it is probable that the convenient season never came. It should be remembered that "after while" never comes. No matter how long you wait it is still "afterwhile" How many of my young readers, like Felix, have been made to tremble on account of their sins, but you still put off your best friend with "afterwhile." You wait days and weeks and even years, and you are no better—no nearer Jesus than you was at the first call, and the fact is, you get farther away every day. Whenever there is anything to be done, the only way is to get at it at once and do it and then "afterwhile will not give you any more trouble. Before closing, I will tell you a word I like much better and you can find it in your dictionary. It is NOW. Adopt it and it will never leave you in want.

UNCLE HENRY,

SWEET JESUS

He is ever near, never fear. He is much loved by all His dear and dying friends of this earthly sanctuary. Don't be afraid to work for Jesus for He will reward you greatly for all you do in His favor. Do not fail to do your duty toward Him whilst on this plue of sin for this is not our home, our home is built on high, far, far above the starry sky.

Farewell, ye dreams of night,
Jesus is mine;
Lost in this dawning light.
Jesus is mine;
All that my soul has tried,
Left but a dismal void,
Jesus has satisfied—
Jesus is mine.

SUSIE COFFMAN.

DON'T TATTLE.—Children, don't tell tales about each other. Don't call one of your school-mates ugly, another stingy, another cross, behind their backs. It is the meanest kind of sin. Even if they are ugly, stingy or cross, it does no good to repeat it. It makes you love to tell of faults, it makes you uncharitable—your soul grows smaller—your heart loses its generous blood, when you tattle about your friends. Tell all the good you know about them and carry their sins in your own heart; or else tell them to God, and ask Him to pardon them. That will be Christ-like. If anybody says to you, "Oh, that Mary Willis did such a naughty thing!" all to mind some virtue that Mary possesses and hold it up to her praise. For your own sake, learn to make this a habit.

SPRING WATER FOR CHILDREN.—Spring water for a child to drink is not only the best beverage for his bodily health, but likewise for his mental and for his moral health—tending to keep his mind clear and his morals pure. It is a sin and a shame to give an innocent and healthy child either beer or wine. It makes him love that which, as he grows up to manhood, may, and proably will, become his bane and his curse. The world is full of drunkards, and many of that fraternity were taught to drink—were initiated into the mysteries of drunkenness from their childhood!

THISTLES IN THE HEART.—Bad habits are the thistles of the heart, and every indulgence of them is a seed from which will spring a new crop of weeds. A few years ago, a little boy told his first falsehood. It was a little solitary thistle seed, and no eye but God's saw him plant it in the mellow soil of his heart. But it sprung up, oh, how quickly! and in a little time another and another seed dropped from it to the ground, each in its turn bearing more seed and more thistles; and now his heart is overgrown with this bad habit. It is as difficult for him to speak the truth as it is for the gardener to clear his land of the hurtful thistle after it has once gained a footing in the soil. "Lying lips are an abomination to the Lord, but they that deal truly are His delight."—*Observer.*

CHILDREN MAY GIVE.—Children should be taught to give just as they should be taught to love or to pray. Giving is as clearly a duty as it is a privilege. But children in the Sunday School should be trained to earn or save what they give; not to ask it from father or mother, as if it was a tax on Sunday School attendance. Children usually enjoy giving of their own little treasures a great deal more than their parents enjoy giving it out of their abundance, for avarice is not a child's vice. Calls to giving judiciously may increase the attractiveness to children of any Sunday School, even among the very poorest in the community. It is a great mistake to refrain from asking poor children to give into the Lord's treasury through fear that they will be repelled from the Sunday School when they are thus called on. The proper way is to make giving a part of their training in life, as surely as cleanliness of person, decency of speech, or uprightness in conduct.

Correspondence.

A Reporter is wanted from every Church in the brotherhood to send us Church news, Obituaries, Announcements, or anything that will be of general interest. To insure insertion, the writers name must accompany each communication. Our Invitation is not personal but general—please respond to our call.

OUR DUTY, WHAT IS IT?

Mr. Editor :—You say you have no preference to your contributors but you do not like some of their subjects. The greatest enemy man has are the institutions of this world, and the greatest apparent enemy to man's condition in this world, is the law or word of God.

We are commanded to pray for those who persecute or badly use us, —to forgive under all circumstances. There is no limit this is the sense of the law as I understand it. Now Mr. Editor what is the duty of a Christian? Is it not his duty to combat all kingdoms that are against God and to love man as his brother? Can man serve two masters? What is the New Testament, is it not the Church or government of Christ and is that not perfect within itself? Is it not intended to meet all the wants of this world and do we not live under a government absolutely antagonistic to the principles of God's law? St. Paul tells us to be subject to the powers that be, that is powers that become of God. Who took the lives of St. Paul and the apostles, was it not the authorities that be? Was not Christ Crucified for instituting a kingdom against the will of the powers that be? Are we not brethren and are we not entitled to the privileges that God gives us? If we do not serve him we know the consequence. Has any man a right from God to take my freedom from me and does not the authorities that be do this? A Christian cannot serve his Master and allow any man's freedom to be taken from him under any circumstances. We are commanded to pray without ceasing, to forgive those that trespass against us, or our heavenly Father will not forgive us. Is there any limit? Have we time to take the life or liberty of any man, no matter what the crime is, or will we set all the day long and see our brethren do this and never a caution from the Christian? Mr. Editor, how does civilization come, does it come through the pulpit or the bayonet? If it come by the bayonet at any time, is there not a soul lost in establishing this civilization? Most assuredly man must not fight his brother under any consideration, there is no limit here, God's laws are absolute, the law judges man not I. Men in authority, know me, I preach nothing I do not practice. 'Tis hard to give up the world—pity those men and do your duty. God is able to protect and save the world. Man must deny himself, he cannot serve two masters.

GEO. G. BINGHAM.

Waterton, Md.

REMARKS.—While we object to some subjects we also object to the style that some men use in presenting their ideas without subjects, especially the interrogative style of our contributor, friend Bingham. We protest from the fact that it presents too many subjects without presenting clear ideas on any. That some of the institutions of man are opposed to grace is evident, but the law of God should be man's best friend and greatest consolation, and is, unless he is determined on rejecting, in which case, it will certainly be a powerful enemy that none can withstand.

The precept of divine love as taught in the command, "Love your enemies and pray for those who despitefully use us," is from above and needs no limit, as the spirit of it is in the letter and, if carried out, will produce the designed effects, "Love thy neighbor as thy self," and who would fight, abuse and persecute his own flesh?

It is the imperative duty of every Christian to combat against the kingdoms of darkness, using the lawfully prescribed weapons, "the sword of the spirit, &c," and we hope that every loyal soldier of the kingdom of Christ is on duty.

The New Testament *is* the Christian's law, and in it is contained the whole duty of man, but that it will ever become the law of nations is not in harmony with the spirit of its teachings.

That our present government is absolutely antagonistical to the principles of God's law, may be a question of serious doubt, as it is justly termed the asylum of the oppressed, financially and spiritually, and it becomes us as a Christian people, to tender our grateful acknowledgments that we can yet worship God according to his revealed will, under our own vines and in homes that we are allowed to call our own.

The "powers that be" are *allowed* of God and we are to be subject only so far as they do not conflict with the "higher powers." Our liberties are allowed of our King (Jesus) and can only be fully realized when we get into the kingdom proper, or triumphant. The position in which we are now placed is mightily contested and we can only claim the liberties of a good soldier, to fight for our King. This warfare is continual and only victorious in death.

Civilization may be effected by the sword and also, by the power of the Gospel. The sword may civilize but it will not Christianize, the power of the Gospel will do both.

To practice what we preach is considered honorable and just provided our preaching is honorable and orthodox, but to preach a false doctrine is wrong and to live it out is still worse.

We highly prize the productions of those who, when they write, have subjects and present logical reasoning thereon. In writing we should have only two objects in view, first, to obtain information and second, to give information. These are both laudable and we hope that all those who desire to assist us in presenting a good and interesting paper to the world will think of these things.

R. R. Privileges.

Members going to A. M. over the Va. & Tenn. R. R. will pay full fare going and return on my certificates of attendance, and for the Orange, Alexandria and Manasses R. R. they will present a certificate of membership to the agent where they take the cars on that road, and the agent will give them round tickets for the price of fare one way.

B. F. MOOMAW.

NOTICE.

To brethren and sisters going to Annual Meeting, I received a grant today from the Baltimore & Ohio R. R. Company for half fare from all of its stations west of Belair, on the Ohio division. Pay full fare from place of starting to Cumberland, and you will be returned free by a certificate from Bro. D. P. Saylor to Belair and this arrangement will bring you on home by obtaining a certificate from a brother sent from our District Council.

WM. SADLER.

Naukin, O.

ANNOUNOMENTS.

Please announce that we, the brethren and sisters of the Desmoines Valley Church, expect, the Lord willing, to hold our Lovefeast on the 28th and 29th days of June, 1873, at Elkhart, Polk Co., Iowa, about 16 miles northeast of Demoines City. The general invitation is given, and especially to the ministering brethren to be with us.

S. M. GOUGHNOUR.

Companion please copy.

Dear Editor :—Please publish that we, the brethren of the Woodland Church, Mich., intend holding our Communion meeting on the 15th of June, commencing at 10 o'clock. We wish all our dear brethren and sisters that can to be with us. Those from the East will come to Jackson, Mich., there take the valley road to Nashville. Those from the South and West, will come on the Penisulair road to Charlott where they will take the Valley road to Nashville, where they will be met with conveyance. The meeting will be held at the house of the undersigned.

ISAAC SMITH.

[*Companion* please copy.]

Please announce that the Brethren in Welch Run intend, the Lord willing, to hold a Lovefeast in the western end of the said district, on the 7th. and 8th. of June, commencing on Saturday at 1 o'clock and meeting the next day at Jacob Mallott's in Licking Creek Valley. General invitation extended. By order of the brethren.

G. W. BRICKER.

Please announce that our Communion will be held in our Meeting house in the Spring Creek Congregation, 14 miles S. E. of Warsaw, on the 20th. day of June next. All are invited.

DANIEL MILLER.

Pierceton, Ind.

DIED.

OGG.—In the Root River branch, Fillmore Co., Minn., on May the 7th, William Ogg, aged 5 years, 10 months and 4 days. He was a son of our beloved elder Joseph and Susan Ogg. Burial occasion was improved from the 90th Psalm, from the 1st to the 12th verses to a large and attentive audience by brother William Hipes.

J. D.

DRURY.—Also in the same branch, April 2nd, 1873, Henry Edward, infant son of George and Catharine Drury, aged 4 weeks and 1 day. Occasion improved from Matt. Gospel, 18th chapter 2nd 2[illegible]th, verses, and 19th chapter and 14th verse by brother Joseph Ogg.

Why is it that God calls such little harmless infants that knows no sin, and leaves a father and mother that is living away from the pales of the church? The answer may be found in the parable in St. Luke's Gospel, the 13th chapter. (Read the parable.) The dresser of the vineyard, has no doubt been digging about the parents of that little tender branch to see if they will not bring forth fruit—to give them another chance to turn in with the overtures of mercy. Dear brother and sister, Christ requires fruit at your hands Christ may come presently and call upon one or both of you for fruit at your hands because he desires fruit from you that may stand to your account as a sweet smelling odor, a sacrifice, acceptable and well-pleasing to God. It may be that God, for Christ's sake, required fruit at your hands, he came and found none, so he took that little tender branch from you because it was prepared to meet its Lord and Savior Jesus Christ in peace, and you, yourselves was not, so I would say to you with the psalmist, "Oh Lord so teach us to number our days that we may apply our hearts unto wisdom."

JOSEPH DRURY.

LIVENGOOD.—Fillmore county, Minn., John, youngest son of brother John and sister Livengood, of the Root River branch of Spinal Meningitis, age 7 years, 3 months and 14 days.

Only about 30 hours from the time he was taken sick until he plumed his snowy pinions, till he folded them to rest mid the welcome song of rapture on a loving Savior's breast. Funeral discourse by the writer from James 4 : 14, latter clause.

WM. C. HIPES.

RICHARD.—In the Woodstock congregation, Shenandoah county, Va., January 10th, sister Mary Richard, aged 73 years, 4 months and 5 days. Funeral occasion improved by brother Wakeman and the writer from Rev. 14 : 13.

TABLER.—In Frederick, county, Va., eld James D. Tabler, aged 65 years, 10 months and 14 days. Funeral occasion improved by elder G. Shaver, J. Wakeman and the writer, from Proverbs 14 : 13.

Sister Tabler, his wife preceded him to the tomb about two years. She was in her 68th year.

SAMUEL A. SHAVER.

[*Visitor* please copy.]

POTEET—In Fayette Co., W. Va., Mar. 25th, Andrew Poteet son of Bro. William and sister Mary Poteet, aged 13 months.

How suddenly the cold hand of death plucked from the family circle this dear pet. 'Tis gone but not lost; 'tis sleeping awaiting the glorious immortal waking when the same little one shall come forth in a glorified state to meet the angels in the sky. Parents, brothers and sisters, Oh may you so live that you may meet all the dear ones gone before in that blessed land where death is a stranger and troubles never come.

J. S. FLORY.

BARNHART.—In the Germantown district, Franklin Co., Va., May the 13th, 1873, elder Abraham Barnhart departed this life. His disease was bronchitis. He was sick some 8 days. He leaves an old sister widow and 5 sons all in the ministry and 2 daughters that are sisters. His age was 77 years, 6 months and 24 days. The funeral was attended by a number of relatives and friends. Preaching by the brethren, from Rev. 14 : 12, 13. We need not mourn as those that have no hope. He has been laboring in the ministry for nearly 40 years. It surely would be wisdom in us to try and imitate his example.

NAFF.—Magold district. Franklin Co., Va., May the 11th, 1873, uncle and brother Jacob Naff, aged 73 years, 3 months and 29 days. He had been afflicted about 4 years with paralysis. He got better again so he could walk about some with sticks until about a year ago he got so bad that he was confined to his bed for more than a year and suffered a great deal. He leaves a widow sister and 3 daughters that are sisters in Christ, and 5 sons. We hope our loss is his great gain. He was a deacon in the Church for a long time. His funeral was attended by the brethren. Text the 14th chapter of Rev., 12th and 13th verses.
J. P. NAFF.

SANGER.—March 21st, in Fayette county, W. Va., Charles Earnest, infant and only son of Joseph F. and Hannah Sanger. May this dispensation of God's providence bring to the remembrance of the beloved parents with solemn thoughts that they too must die and may they prepare to meet their God and dear son in that happy land where all is joy and peace forever.
J. S. FLORY.

The Weekly Pilgrim.

JAMES CREEK, PA., May 27. 1873.

☞ HOW TO SEND MONEY.—All sums over $1.50, should be sent either in a check, draft or postal order. If neither of these can be obtained, have the letter registered.

☞ WHEN MONEY is sent, *always* send with it the name and address of those who paid it. Write the names and post office as plainly as possible.

☞ EVERY subscriber for 1873, gets a *Pilgrim Almanac* FREE.

RADICALISM VERSUS LIBERALISM.

Some people seem to think that it is really necessary to have two extremes in order that there be a mean, forgetting that it is pleasanter and more safe to be on the middle of a balance than at either end. It is a notable fact that while some of us are too radical in our views, others are too liberal. Both of these are extremes and just so long as one is indulged the other will follow as a consequence.

One clamors for the letter while the other contends for the spirit. Radicalism is dangerous when connected with our own views, and it has been a stumbling block to its thousands. It is so affianced to the letter theory, that anything beyond it has no virtue or shade of comeliness, and some of our own brethren are deeply tinged with it, the result of which, is the extremes that we now have to contend with. It should be remembered that the letter without the spirit is dead. Yes, as dead as a body without a soul.

All the ritual services of the Church have a spiritual import and in the observing of them, more care should be manifested that the design should be realized than that the letter should be carried out. To undertake to strictly carry out the letter of the ordinances of the Lord's house is rank radicalism and leads to very great extremes. Some of these extreme views now threaten to rip the foundation of the Church, destroy propriety and bring in damnable heresies. Some will ransack the whole Bible through to prop up some letter, pet theory and thus entirely lose the benefits of the great design for which God intended them. Many instances might be adduced to establish our position, but we think that the "signs of the times" portray facts in such unmistakable terms that none can fail to see the issue. It is necessary that there be clouds that we may have rain, as without clouds it could not rain, but rain is the object and if we get it in due season we are little concerned about the clouds, their color, height in the atmosphere or the direction from which they came. Just so it is with the ordinances of the Lord's house, we must have them, as they are the avenues through which God showers His grace upon us, but grace and divine favor is the object and end to be obtained. Therefore we should not parley about the shell at the risk of losing the kernel. Baptism is the sign of regeneration, the burial of the old man and the resurrection of the new. Water is the element, but we are not so radical in carrying out the letter as to resort to Jordan or the waters about Enon to be buried with Christ in baptism. In the Communion, we sip of wine as being emblematical of the blood of Christ, but we are not so careful in ascertaining its qualities, believing that the efficacy is not in the wine but in that which it represents. Again, Feet-washing, we all agree is intended to inculcate the principle of humility, humility then is the object and not the washing and wiping, but in all these things, some have made shipwreck of their faith by prying after the letter and thus losing the spirit. These are the results of radicalism when carried to extremes.

Liberalism has a tendency of running in the other direction, ever contending for the spirit and thus depreciating and ignoring the letter altogether. We also have, among us, an element of this kind, but to be candid, we look upon this as being the more excusable from the fact of it being the attending result of the other extreme. While rituals may be justly termed the shell or hull yet the kernal cannot exist or mature without it. A hull may grow and mature without a kernal, but a kernel cannot grow without its shell. Just so it is in religion. A man may live a ritualistic or outward Christian without the spirit or inward grace, but no man can possess and live out vital Christianity without the outward adorning, or complying with those things which have been ordained by Christ the great head of the Church, for our salvation. This is a subject of weighty importance and it is to be hoped that all true followers of Jesus will endeavor to imbibe more of His humble and self-sacrificing principles. The old German proverb comes beautifully in place in this connection. *Mittleweg: die beste strass.* This truly is the best way and the *only* way that will keep our blessed Zion harmoniously together. A little more radicalism in points of doctrine and more liberalism in the observing of those things in which there is no point of doctrine at stake, such as contending for the letter in the Salutation, the Supper and Feet-washing. The letter in these things kill and if persisted in, will cause schisms in the Church which will be difficult to heal. In these things we plead for liberality, *liberality*, LIBERALITY.

REPORT OF A. M.

The question now is, "do you intend to give a report of A. M.?" We expect, no providential interference, to be there and do the very best we can. We hope that we may have a more favorable report to give than on former occasions. We hope that our dear brethren will consider the importance of the meeting and go up to the place with the determination of working for the Lord and the upbuilding of Zion. Those who are in the habit of taking an active part and especially those who allow themselves to become excited should take heed to their ways and bridle their tongues as some of the leading papers of the country will be represented by their reporters who will catch their words on the wing and sow them broadcast over the land. A hint to the wise should be sufficient.

ATTENTION, PLEASE.

As a number of our readers and agents promised to pay us at A. M. we would just say, please prepare a list of the names for which you intended to pay, with the address as we will not be able while there to know who has or who has not paid us. By attending to this you will confer a favor and much oblige.

BROAD TOP EXCURSION.

We are making arrangements to have excursion tickets to A. M. sold at the following stations: Marklesburg, Coffee Run, Cove, Hopewell and Everett. Those going will make it a point to get tickets at the above named stations.

NOTICE.

Those intending to stop at James Creek over Sunday on way to A. M. and wishing to visit the PILGRIM OFFICE which we would be glad to have them do, should try and come up on the Saturday morning train.

MINUTES.—We have a small number of the Minutes of the District Meeting of Middle Pa. Those who neglected to order at the meeting can still be supplied by forwarding soon. Single copy, 10 cents, 6 copies 40 cents post-paid.

MICHAEL FORNEY.—We do not publish any paper adapted to Sunday School purposes. *The Children's Paper* published by Bro. H. J. Kurtz, Dayton, Ohio, we think, would suit you. He will send you specimen copies and price by addressing him as above.

BREVITY is very desirable in obituaries, notices, and those writing will please not be too lengthy. On account of the unusually large number for last week we were compelled to abridge some for which we hope those concerned will excuse us.

COMPLETE VOLUMES.

We are still prepared to furnish complete volumes of the PILGRIM, commencing with No. 1, of Jan. 1st., 1873, at $1.50. Our back numbers are all perfect and filled with reading that is well worth preserving. Some of the articles are continued from early numbers of the year which makes it more important to commence with the volume which, when completed, will make a handsome volume for binding. Those who prefer it can have the remainder of the year or from Annual Meeting for 80 cts.

MARRIED.

SNUFFER—SPANGLER.—By the undersigned at the residence of the bride's father, May 1st, 1873, Isaac F. Snuffer and sister Rasmus Spangler, all of Raleigh Co., Va.
W. H BAILY.

MONEY LIST.

Isaac Rohrer	$1.50
S P Brumbaugh	1.50
John Bollinger	1.50
Mollie E Heneks	50
John Zuck	3.00
Luke G Williams	1.50
J A B Hershberger	1.60
J W. Blauch	50
Daniel Brown	1.50
Wm C Teeter	1.70
Mary A Hockman	25
Samuel Kinsey	1.50
W A Maust	25.
Margaret Deardorff	30
Michael Myers	1.50
D F Good	5.00
J P Lane	6.25
J R Lane	1.40
Andrew Miller	95
Joseph Shelly	1.25
Jesse Crumpacker	1.50
J H Raffensparger	1.80
Jacob Hoover	1.50
David Bechtal	1.70
Daniel Diehl	2.75
Michael Bechtal	1.50
Henry Hershberger	6.00
J H Staudenour	4.00
Kate Gambel	1.00
Samuel J Miller	1.50
Jno W Fitzgerald	1.25
Isaac Flory	4.50

BOOK NOTICES.

Under this head we will notice such books &c., sent us for examination that are in harmony with the general character of our work. No fiction or obscene literature of any character will receive any attention whatever. We wish our notices to be a benefit both to publishers and our patrons.

GOOD READING.—In reading, everybody has an object, or at least should have. If they have not the probability is that their reading will make an object for them, hence it is the more important what we read. We have, just now, before us the June No. of the *Phrenological Journal* and in looking over its contents it wonders us how Mr. Wells succeeds in filling so large a magazine with such fresh, live and interesting reading. Any person wishing to be posted on the living and stirring events of the day cannot well afford to do without it. With the July No. commences a new volume. Published by S. R. Wells, 389 *Broadway* New York at $3.00 per year.

Lives of the Governors of Pennsylvania.

We have received from James K. Simon, Publisher, No. 29, South Sixth Street Philadelphia, Pa., through J. C. Blair, Huntingdon, a work under the above title, by Major W. C. Armor whose connection with the Executive Department of the State offers him superior opportunities for the task he has so successfully accomplished.

It is a very handsome octavo volume of about 640 pages, including the portraits, 29 in number finely and correctly executed; is printed on fine white paper with large clear-faced type and handsomely bound. It contains the biographies of the Governors of the State from its earliest settlement to the present time; and in connection with these embraces a complete epitome of the history of the State, including the events of its early settlement, its proprietary government, the wars of the Revolution; and 1812, and the rise and fall of the Rebellion.

It is a book which should be secured by every citizen of the State as a knowledge of the lives and characters of our public men cannot fail to be useful and interesting, and the vast number of important facts and incidents which it contains must form a valuable adjunct to, and stimulate the intelligence of our great commonwealth. It is sold by subscription and agents are wanted in every county in the State. Address as above. A. B. B.

"BEHIND THE SCENES IN WASHINGTON."—The National Publishing Co., of Philadelphia, has just issued one of the most remarkable and interesting books of the day, bearing the above title.

Of late the whole land has been ringing with the most startling and appalling reports of corruption at Washington—the highest officials—men whose names have hitherto been without a stain, have been implicated in the charges, and the press has rung with accusations and denunciations which have caused all good citizens, without regard to party, to fear for the future of the country. All have an interest in discovering the truth of these reports, and all have an interest to know more of the practical workings of affairs at Washington.

A truthful picture of life "Behind the scenes in Washington" cannot be otherwise than deeply interesting. The low price at which the book is issued, brings it within the reach of all, and no one who wants to know the truth about men and things at Washington, should fail to read this work. It is sold by subscription only, and agents are wanted in every county.

WANTED. We will give men and women

Business that will Pay

from $4 to $8 per day, can be pursued in your own neighborhood; it is a rare chance for those out of employment or having leisure time; girls and boys frequently do as well as men. Particulars free.

Address J. LATHAM & CO.,
292 Washington St., Boston, Mass.

DYMOND ON WAR.

An inquiry into the Accordancy of War, with the Principles of Christianity, and an examination of the Philosophical reasoning by which it is defended. With observations on some of the causes of war and on some of its effects. By Jonathan Dymond. Sent from this office, post-paid, for 50 cts.

TUNE BOOK.

The Brethren's Tune and Hymn Book, is a compilation of Sacred Music adapted to all the hymns in the Brethren's New Hymn Book. It contains over 350 pages, printed on good paper and neatly bound. We will send it to any address, post paid at $1.25 per copy.

GOOD BOOKS.

A large number of our patrons are receiving our books as noticed below, as premiums, and express themselves highly pleased with them. Others who are not agents, have enquired whether we keep them for sale. We have now made arrangements with Mr. Wells to furnish any of their publications post paid at publishers prices. Orders for books must be accompanied with the cash, and plain directions for sending them.

How to read Character, illus. Price,	$1.25
Combe's Moral Philosophy,	1.75
Constitution of Man. Combe,	1.75
Education. By Spurzheim,	1.50
Memory—How to Improve it,	1.50
Mental Science, Lectures on,	1.50
Self-Culture and Perfection.	1.50
Combe's Physiology, Illus.	1.75
Food and Diet. By Pereira,	1.75
Natural Laws of Man,	.75
Hereditary Descent,	1.50
Combe on Infancy,	1.50
Sober and Temperate Life,	.50
Children in Health—Disease,	1.75
The Science of Human Life,	3.50
Fruit Culture for the Million,	1.00
Saving and Wasting,	1.50
Ways of Life—Right Way,	1.00
Footprints of Life,	1.25
Conversion of St. Paul,	1.00

Weaver's Works for the Young. Comprising "Hopes and Helps for the Young of both Sexes," $3.00.

Life at Home; or, The Family and its Members. A work which should be found in every family. $1.50. Extra gilt. $2.00.

Hand-book for Home Improvement: comprising "How to Write," "How to Talk," "How to Behave," and "How to do Business," in one vol. 2.25.

Oratory—Sacred and Secular; or, the Extemporaneous Speaker. Price $1.50.

Conversion of St. Paul. 12mo. fine edition, $1. Plain edition, 75 cents.

Man, in Genesis and in Geology; or, the Biblical Account of Man's Creation, tested by Scientific Theories of his Origin and Antiquity. One vol. 12mo, $1.00.

Man and Woman: Considered in their Relations to each Other and to the World. 12mo, Fancy cloth, Price $1.00.

Hopes and Helps for the Young of both sexes, Relating to the Formation of Character. Choice of Avocation, Health, Conversation, Social Affection Courtship and Marriage. Muslin, $1.50.

$133 33 ... from any or all Publishers. Send for Circulars. J. C. BLAIR, S. S. Book-Store, Huntingdon, Pa. $100

Trine Immersion
TRACED
TO THE APOSTLES.

The SECOND EDITION is now ready for delivery. The work has been carefully revised, corrected and enlarged.

Put up in a neat pamphlet form, with good paper cover, and will be sent, post-paid, on the following terms: One copy, 25 cts; Five copies, $1.10; Ten copies, $2.00, 25 copies, $4.50; 50 copies, $8.50; 100 copies, $15 00.

Address, J. H. MOORE,
Urbana, Champaign co., Ill.

Oct 22.

GIVEN AWAY.

A FINE GERMAN CHROMO.

We send an elegant chromo, mounted and ready for framing, free to every agent for

UNDERGROUND
or,
LIFE BELOW THE SURFACE.

BY THOS. W. KNOX.

942 Pages Octavo. 130 Fine Engravings.

Relates Incidents and Accidents beyond the Light of Day: Startling Adventures in all parts of the World Mines and Mode of Working them; Under-currents of Society; Gambling and its *Horrors*; Caverns and their Mysteries; The Dark Ways of Wickedness; Prisons and their Secrets; Down in the Depths of the Sea; Strange Stories of the Detection of Crime.

The book treats of experience with brigands; nights in opium dens and gambling hells; life in prison; Stories of exiles; adventures among Indians; journey through Sewers and Catacombs; accidents in mines; pirates and piracy; tortures of the inquisition; wonderful burglaries; underworld of the great cities, etc., etc.

AGENTS WANTED

for this work. Exclusive territory is given. Agents can make $100 a week in selling this book. Send for circulars and terms to agents.

J. B. BURR & HYDE,

HARTFORD, CONN., or CHICAGO, ILL.

TRACTS.

"ANXIOUS BENCH RELIGION EXAMINED," BY ELDER J. S. FLORY. A SYNOPSIS OF CONTENTS. An address to the reader: The peculiarities that attend this type of religion. The feelings there experienced not imaginary but real. The key that unlocks the wonderful mystery. The causes by which feelings are excited. How the momentary feelings called "Experimental religion" are brought about, and then concludes by giving that form of doctrine as taught by Jesus Christ and recorded by his faithful witnesses.

COUNTERFEIT DETECTER
or
BAPTISM—MUCH IN LITTLE.

This work is now ready for distribution, and the importance of the subject will speak for it a large demand. It is a short treatise on baptism in tract form intended for general distribution, and is set forth in such a plain and logical manner that a wayfaring man though a fool, cannot err therein. Either of the above tracts sent postpaid on the following terms: Two copies, 10 cts, 10 copies 40 cents, 25 copies 70 cents, 50 copies $1.00, 100 copies $1.50.

Trine Immersion.

A discussion on Trine Immersion, by letter between Elder B. F. Moomaw and Dr. J. J. Jackson, to which is annexed a Treatise on the Lord's Supper, and on the necessity, character and evidences of the new birth, also a dialogue on the doctrine of non-resistance, by Elder B. F. Moomaw. Single copy 50 cents.

$5 to $20 per day! Agents wanted! All classes of working people, of either sex, young or old, make more money at work for us in their spare moments or all the time than at anything else. Particulars free. Address G. Stinson & Co., Portland, Maine.

THE
HELPING HAND.

Containing several hundred Valuable Receipts for cooking well at a moderate expense, making Dyes, Coloring, Cleaning and Cementing. This book also points out in plain language, free from Doctors' terms the diseases of men, women and children, and the latest and most approved means used for their cure, to which is added a description of the Medicinal Roots and Herbs, and how they are to be used in the cure of diseases.

This is a work of considerable importance and we offer it to our readers as being a valuable accession to every household. Sent from this office to any address, post-paid, for 25 cents.

1870 1873

DR. FAHRNEY'S
Blood Cleanser or Panacea.

A tonic and purge, for Blood Diseases. Great reputation. Many testimonials. Many ministering brethren use and recommend it. Ask or send for the "Health Messenger." Use only the "*Panacea*" prepared at Chicago, Ills., and by

Dr. P. Fahrney's Brothers & Co.,
Feb. 3-pd. *Waynesboro, Franklin Co., Pa*

New Hymn Books, English.

TURKEY MOROCCO.

One copy, postpaid,	$1.00
Per Dozen,	11.25

PLAIN ARABESQUE.

One Copy, post-paid,	75
Per Dozen, "	8.00

Ger'n & English, Plain Sheep.

One Copy, post-paid,	$1.00
Per Dozen	11.25
Arabesque Plain,	1.00
Turkey Morocco,	1.25
Single German, post paid	50
Per Dozen,	5.50

HUNTINGDON & BROAD TOP RAIL ROAD

On and after March 22d, 1873, Trains will run on this road daily (Sundays excepted) as follows:

Trains from Huntingdon South. *Trains from Mt. Dal's moving North.*

MAIL. A. M.	EXP'S. P. M.	STATIONS.	MAIL. P. M.	EXP'S A. M.
el7 45	5 50	Huntingdon,	AR4 00	AR8 25
7 50	5 55	Long Siding	3 55	8 20
8 10	6 10	McConnelstown	3 43	8 10
8 17	6 20	Pleasant Grove	3 35	8 03
8 30	6 35	MARKLESBURG	3 20	7 45
8 45	6 50	Coffee Run	3 07	7 32
8 55	7 00	Rough & Ready	2 57	7 23
9 05	7 10	Cove	2 47	7 13
9 08	7 13	Fishers Summit	2 45	7 10
9 20	7 28	Saxton	2 27	6 55
9 40	7 50	Riddlesburg	2 10	6 31
9 47	8 00	Hopewell	2 02	6 23
10 02	8 15	Piper's Run	1 47	6 05
10 17	8 32	Tatesville	1 32	5 48
10 30	8 45	Everett	1 20	5 35
10 35	8 50	Mount Dallas	1 15	5 30
11 08	9 20	Bedford	12 44	5 00

SHOUP'S RUN BRANCH.

LE 9 25 LE	Saxton.	AR2 15 AR	
9 40	Coalmont.	2 00	
9 45	Crawford.	1 55	
AR 9 55 AR	Dudley	LE1 45 LE	

Bro'd Top City from Dudley 2 miles by stage.

Time of Penna. R. R. Trains at Huntingdon

*** Mail No. 2 makes connection at Huntingdon with Mail going East on Pennsylvania Railroad at 4.15 p. m., and West at 5.45 p. m. Mail No. 1 leaves Huntingdon at 7.40 a. m. on arrival of Pacific Express West.

Trains on this road connect with trains on Bedford & Bridgeport, and Cumberland & Pennsylvania Railroads.

G. F. GAGE, Supt.

The Weekly Pilgrim.

Published by J. B. Brumbaugh, & Co.

Edited by H. B. & Geo. Brumbaugh.

CORRESPONDING EDITORS.

D. P. Sayler, Double Pipe Creek, Md.

Leonard Furry, New Enterprise, Pa.

The *Pilgrim* is a Christian Periodical, devoted to religion and moral reform. It will advocate in the spirit of *love* and *liberty*, the principles of true Christianity, labor for the promotion of peace among the people of God, for the encouragement of the saints and for the conversion of sinners, avoiding those things which tend toward disunion or sectional feelings.

TERMS.

Single copy, Book paper,	$1 50
Eleven copies, [eleventh for Agt.]	$15.00

Any number above that at the same rate.

Address,
H. B. BRUMBAUGH.
James Creek,
Huntingdon county Pa.

The Weekly Pilgrim.

"REMOVE NOT THE ANCIENT LANDMARKS WHICH OUR FATHERS HAVE SET."

VOL. 4. JAMES CREEK, PENNSYLVANIA, JUNE 3, 1873. NO. 22

POETRY.

FRIENDSHIP.

There is an emotion of the soul
More kin to Heaven than earth;
'Tis friendship, beauteous attribute,
We never learn its worth.
Its influence so sweet, so pure,
If we ourselves are true,
Through this sweet agency we may
Work for our Master do.

In meditating on God's gifts,
Enjoyed by us while here,
All wisely suited to our tastes,
And each so very dear:
Were all beside it left to me,
And I bereft of this,
Something I'd feel that I had lost,
That I should ever miss.

To all the ills and woes of life
We can be more resigned,
If sympathy from some dear friend
Thrills us with accents kind:
And in misfortune's gloomy hour,
Our saddest thoughts is when
We need words of encouragement,
And are deserted then.

These sweetest feelings of the heart—
O, cruel thought—may change
For these we deemed so true, we may
Forever be estranged.
Slander's poisoned breath can taint
An atmosphere of love,
And friends oft tried, whom we thought true,
Will sometimes faithless prove.

But there is One who ever loves,
If unto Him we pray;
Give Christ your love, make him your friend,
He never will betray.
Man's friendship only is the bud,
Which withers in an hour;
Christ's lasts through all eternity,
And is the full-blown flower.

ORIGINAL ESSAYS.

CAMPBELL'S GREAT MISTAKE.

It seems a very easy matter for those who are somewhat versed in the history of great reformers, to readily discover that they have frequently incorporated numerous errors, which are imbibed during the early years of life. Though many of them have accomplished a vast amount of good, none seems to have been entirely free of fatal errors. Had these false principles of religion, extended no farther than the mere practice of the reformers themselves, the mistake would not be of such great moment. Those who look upon such characters as the true embassadors of Christ, have, and are still following closely in the footsteps, and are rapidly perpetuating the growing evil.

Though Alexander Campbell, as a practical religious reformer, has accomplished a great deal of good, neither his teachings nor practice has been entirely free from many great errors which time has stamped upon the minds of the religious part of the world. Few, if any, have done more than he to prove conclusively that baptism is essential to salvation, while immersion is the apostolic method of baptizing. In these he was correct, while his early training almost indelibly stamped single immersion, as well as the backward action upon his mind; and when he ushered into existence, his grand reformatory movement, it contained these fatal errors, that had found their way into the world, sometime after the close of the third century. Had Campbell, in an early period of his life, been able to have moved the Baptist spectacles from his eyes, rolled back the curtains of time, and quietly looked into the three first centuries of the Christian era, he would have found neither the backward action, nor single immersion among any of the early Christians, who followed in the footsteps of the Lord. He, however imbibed these errors, either directly or indirectly, from the Baptist Associations, who from time to time contracted them from those who made it their business to change times and laws.

Thousands who are zealously engaged propagating the same principles under the name Christianity, are not aware that the Gospel which they are circulating, contains practices that are no more evangelical than sprinkling and pouring. Though they are right, in their faithful efforts exerted in defence of immersion, they are teaching and practicing the backward action, that is not half as old as either sprinkling or pouring, while single immersion another element in their teaching and practice, was not invented till after the middle of the fourth century. And why all this? Simply because Campbell made a great mistake, when he incorporated into his plan of salvation the Baptist method of baptizing, instead of the Evangelical mode taught by Christ, when he said: "Baptizing them into the name of the Father, and of the Son, and of the Holy Ghost." Matt. 28: 19. The great trouble is, too many read the scriptures with both the backward action and single immersion in the eye, and look upon the phrase "One baptism" Eph. 4: 5, as refering to a single dip only, not remembering that this "one baptism" mentioned by Paul is the same method that is taught in the last commission given by Christ and recorded by Matthew, i. e. "baptizing them into the name of the Father, and of the Son, and of the Holy Ghost." This is the only method of baptizing ever taught by Christ, or practiced by the apostles, and no one ever dreamed that this commission taught single immersion till long after the rise of the controversy respecting the Trinity, nor did such an idea receive much encouragement till after the commencement of the reformation, A. D. 1517. Among the writings of the first Christians, there is about as much evidence in support of the commission teaching single immersion, as there is in support of it teaching sprinkling and pouring. And when those who did invent single immersion they refused to claim for its support the authority of the commission—"baptizing them into the name of the Father, and of the Son, and of the Holy Ghost"—knowing that this taught trine immersion, and therefore in order to justify their human invention, they simply baptized "in the name of Christ" or "in the death of Christ," and then dipped the candidate but once, and not three times according to the directions of Christ. Finally however, as errors and heresy multiplied, and ignorance increased there were those who ventured to baptize in the three names by dipping once only, which, when first introduced looked about as logical as immersion by sprinkling, or pouring by immersion.

I have given Campbell's writings a very careful examination, and I discover that he has failed to show me one single instance where single immersion was practiced by any of the primitive Churches, while the numerous extracts which he has made from the writings of ancient historians, prove conclusively that trine immersion was the apostolic method of baptizing, and universally prevailed in West as well as in the East during the first centuries of the Christian era. These, as well as a hundred other facts that sustain trine immersion, we would cease to defend, if any of his learned followers, or any one else could convince us that we are wrong in stating that trine immersion was the apostolic method, or show to the world that we are in error, when we assign the origin of single immersion to the fourth century, and the origin of the backward action to the English Baptists who were in error respecting the ancient method of baptizing. They of course, thought the eastern nations, like the English buried on the back, and when they read the phrase "buried with him by baptism," they at once tho't of an English burial and commenced laying the body backward in baptism. The consequence has been that all the Baptists in the world who have either directly or indirectly, sprung from the English Baptists have practiced the backward method of immersion. But from the beginning it was not so. In the time of the apostles the administrator placed his right hand on the head of the candidate and dipped him three times face forward, at the mentioning of the "name of the Father, and of the Son, and of the Holy Ghost."

Not one single writer, whose productions have come under my notice, has been able to find any trace of single immersion beyond the middle of the fourth century, while to find one single instance where it was ever practiced in or near Jerusalem, the mother Church of the world, seems to be an utter impossibility. Not one of the learned writers, who advocate a change in times and laws, has ever been able to find single immersion practiced in any of the churches established by the apostles, till some time after the close of the fourth century. While this is true respecting their efforts to sustain single immersion, their researches of antiquity after the backward action has been more than three-fold worse In addition to this array of painful facts it is sufficient to remark that they have failed to produce the testimony of one single ancient author, who states that the last commission given by Christ and recorded by Matt. 28: 19, teaches single immersion, or anything short of trine immersion. You may as well labor to prove that baptize means sprinkling as to attempt to prove that the commission teaches single immersion. This commission has come down to us in the Greek language, and all the ancient Greek and Latin authors, who have commented upon the subject, without one single exception, have given it in favor of trine immersion. And if it was not designed to teach the method of baptizing, it seems remarkably strange that none of the native Greeks, in whose mother tongue the commission was written, were ever able to understand the simplest command ever written in their language. The same evidence that is brought forward to prove that *baptizo* means immersion, proves conclusively that the commission teaches a three-fold immersion; and to reject the authorities in the latter, presupposes the right to reject them when introduced in support of the former.

Many have looked upon the Brethren as practicing a method of baptizing unauthorized by the Gospel, not having the least idea that their own mode was a human invention in a two fold sense. There has never been a period since the time of Christ and the apostles when trine immersion, as a method of baptizing, did not exist, while single immersion "In the name of Jesus" only, single immersion in the names of the Trinity, as well as the backward action have all found their origin this side of the close of the third century, not one of them being old enough to have been the apostolic method.

Single immersionists should cease to look upon our practice with disrespect, since they can neither find its origin this side of Christ, nor trace their single immersion and backward baptism to anything like near the close of the apostolic age.

Though Campbell did some useful work, there is yet room for reformation. He gave to the world a religion that does not contain Christian baptism, unless it be proven that Christian baptism was not introduced till after the middle of the fourth century, and that it took a thousand years longer to bring it to perfection by associating it with the backward action. Had he gone one, or perhaps two steps farther and reproduced not only trine immersion but the forward action more than six hundred thousand of his mistaken followers would now be facing the world with evangelical baptism. But as it is, he has made a great mistake and thousands are in his footsteps, and why all of this? Simply because Campbell made a mistake.

Nor is this all, his system contains no feet washing, while the Gospel introduced by Christ does. Neither does it contain the Holy kiss as found in the religion of the Christian Church, and all of this simply because the perfect Gospel was not reproduced, and now thousands fail to practice either feet-washing or the holy kiss not because they are not taught in the Gospel, but because Campbell failed to teach this part of the Gospel. What a blessing it would be if such able minds had not shunned to declare the whole counsel of God, neither adding thereto nor taking anything from the perfect law.

The Holy Spirit by the mouth of Paul has said, "If any man preach any other Gospel to you than that ye have received, let him be accursed." Gal.—1: 9.

J. H. Moore.

SAUL VERSUS PAUL.

(*Continued from page* 163.)

See how condescending and how kind that Jesus was, after being persecuted so long by this wicked Saul, that he immediately renders relief by showing him, through his servant, how he could be relieved of his sins. The plan here laid down, is not excepted by the Gamaliels of the nineteenth century, to arise forthwith, when their eyes are opened and receive baptism at the hands of the Lord's servants, but prefer a probationary state for six months or so and by that time the greater portion backslide, as they call it, which was not the case with Saul. After his baptism, as soon as he received meat, he was strengthened and in a few days began to preach Christ in the Synagogue, that He is the Son of God, and those that heard him were amazed and said, "Is not this the man that destroyed them that called on this name in Jerusalem and came here for that intent that he might bring them bound unto the chief priests?" But this did not terrify him for he was truly converted to God, and no more a servant of Gamaliel. Now the fury began against him. The enemies of Christ lost a prominent leader which proved a heavy blow against them, but true to his natural gift "zeal," he now brings it to bear against the enemies of the cross, battling for the Lord with the power of his might, and did great execution by his eloquence and fortitude, being willing to spend and be spent for the name of Jesus. We see him traveling to and fro, calling to the people, come to the Lord, do not spend your time in sin and folly. He sometimes demonstrated his power by performing a miracle as in the case of Elymas, where he is also called Paul. "O, full of all mischief, child of the devil, enemy of all righteousness, perverting the right ways of the Lord, thou shalt be blind not seeing the sun for a season." The Lord caused it to come to pass which caused no little astonishment to the deputy, seeing a demonstration of the power vested in the doctrine of the Lord.

Again we see him traveling by sea and land until he came to Philippi, the chief city of Macedonia, and on the Sabbath they went out of the city by a river side where prayer was wont to be made and speaking to the women that resorted thither, one Lydia, whose heart the Lord opened, attended to the things spoken of Paul, and was baptized and her household, and abiding with Lydia a short time, a certain damsel possessed with a spirit of divination met him, which brought her master much gain by soothsaying. After following Paul and acknowledging him to be the servant of the Most High God, and showing the way of salvation, he commanded the spirit in the name of Jesus Christ, to come out of her which obeyed. But it had a tendency to arouse the fury of those that were benefitted, and calling to their assistance the magistrates, they laid many stripes upon them (Paul and Silas), and cast them into prison, into the inner prison, and made their feet fast in the stocks, but that did not quiet their tongues for in the night they prayed and sang praises unto God which caused the earth to quake and shook the foundation of the prison. Alarming the jail keeper, seeing the state of things, he drew his sword for the purpose of killing himself, but Paul instantly cried with a loud voice, do thyself no harm for we are all here, as a failure to perform, to the letter the duties of a jail keeper would forfeit his life under that tyrannical government, as the case of Peter's apprehension and liberation clearly shows. But God works by use of means, for when the Jailer saw and heard, by the mouth of Paul, that the prisoners were all safe, his mind was no doubt attracted to the cause of the commotion and quickly perceiving that Paul must be a man of God, said, "Sirs, what must I do to be saved?" The answer was: "Believe on the Lord Jesus Christ and thou shalt be saved, and thy house, and after he preached to them the word of the Lord, the jailer took Paul and Silas, and washed their stripes, and was baptized, and all his household," perhaps in the same river that Lydia was baptized the next morning. He is liberated and becomes a guest at the house of Lydia again, but he travels on and we soon find him in the idolatrous city of Athens standing in the midst of Mars Hill declaring to them that they are too superstitious, for their devotions are to a God of their own make. Then he declares to them the true God, tells them there was a time that God winked at ignorance, but now commandeth men everywhere to repent. He preached Jesus and the resurrection, some believed and some mocked. He then departs from here and goes to Corinth and finds a man by name, Aquilla, lately from Italy, by occupation a tent maker. He abides with him and works at his trade, he also being of the same craft, not a hireling, not a salaried preacher, but works for his living and preaches the gospel of Christ free of charge. Jesus says, "He that is a hireling, when he seeth the wolf coming fleeth, and lets the wolf catch the sheep, and because he is a hireling, careth not for the sheep."

Some at the present day say Paul took no pay from the churches because they were too poor to pay him, but recommends to pay the preachers well for their labors. After Paul having remained there one year and six months, reasoning every Sabbath day out of the Scriptures and laboring through the week at his trade, he took his leave of the brethren and sailed into Syria, and from there to Ephesus. Passing through the upper coast he found certain disciples and asked them, "Have ye received the Holy Ghost since ye believed? We never heard there was any Holy Ghost but were baptized unto John's baptism," of course John did not baptize them, for he taught that there was a Holy Ghost, and he had no authority to confer that power on any others, therefore they were not baptized by the proper person, so Paul required them to be baptized in the name of the Lord Jesus, and when he laid his hands upon them they received the Holy Ghost, and in his sojourn at this place God wrought special miracles by his hands which magnified him so as to cause the people to bring their books of curious arts together and burned them to the amount of fifty thousand pieces of silver. So mightily grew the word of God and prevailed, and soon Demetrious, and those of like occupation, began to tremble, fearing the profits of their business would suffer, which was making silver shrines for the great goddess Diana, whom Asia worshipped. Although Paul finding more congenial spirits at this place, he was permitted to retire from the scene with little or no persecutions; for the town clerk recommended to have things decided in a lawful manner fearing they would be called to account for the days uproar caused by Demetrious and his fellow craftsmen. Paul after this called the elders of the Church from Ephesus to Miletus and said; "Ye know after what manner I have been with you at all seasons, serving the Lord with all humility of mind and with tears and temptations which befell me by the laying in wait of the Jews, and how I kept back nothing that was profitable unto you, testified to Jew and Greek, repentance toward God and faith towards our Lord Jesus Christ, and now I am bound to go to Jerusalem not knowing what shall befal me there save the Holy Ghost witnesseth that bonds and afflictions await me, but I count not my life dear to me so I might finish my course with joy, but I declare that you shall see my face no more, wherefore I take you to record this day that I am pure from the blood of all men, for I have not shunned to declare to you all the council of God, but I know after my departure, shall grievious wolves enter in among you not sparing the flock." My field of labor lies in another direction, after I have gone up to Jerusalem and there withstood the trials and persecutions then I must also see Rome.

He was but a few days at Jerusalem until he was apprehended and charged before the council where every effort was made to condemn him to death but God had more labor for him, therefore his fate was postponed, then brought before Felix, then before Festus where he is declared innocent, and might have been set at liberty had he not before this time appealed to Cesar not wishing to be tried before the Jews who were thirsting for his blood. Therefore unto Cesar he must go and was sent to Rome, over the boisterous sea where they were once shipwrecked and with great difficulty saved from a watery grave. But God was with him and preserved his life and brought him safe to Cesar. Three days after, he called the chief of the Jews together, stating that he delivered a prisoner from Jerusalem into the hands of the Romans, for this cause have I called to see you and speak unto you, because that for the hope of Israel I am bound with this chain. Then they appointed him a day when they came to his lodging to whom he expounded and testified the kingdom of God concerning Jesus, out of the law and out of the prophets, from morning until evening. Thus we see that age did not diminish his zeal, nor persecutions thwart his prophetic mission, for he dwelt two whole years there in his own hired house and received all those that came in unto him, preaching the kingdom of God and teaching those things, which concern the Lord Jesus Christ, no man forbidding him. He here begins to write letters to the different churches, which he before established which are so famous and full of instruction and edification for the government of God's people, and the warnings which he so clearly elucidates, putting his diciples on their guard against parties and factions which should arise to pervert the truth. And when his days were almost ended he said, "I have fought a good fight, I have finished my course and I have kept the faith, therefore there is laid up for me a crown of righteousness and not for me only but for all those that love his appearing." and when the time of his execution arrived, the sword was drawn by his executioner and with one stroke his head was severed from his body and Paul was no more a living acting being, but his name lives and is revered by all civilized nations on earth for the zeal he had for his God from the time became acquainted with him until his death and for the many good and wholesome lessons we have received through his arduous labors.

GEORGE WORST.

THOUGHTS FOR CONSIDERATION.

I devote some of my time to reading, and make extracts of what I read of such passages as appear adapted to enforce the subject treated. Lately, on looking over some of these, I found the following which I offer to the editors for insertion.

"It has been said that a revival of religion scarcely continues longer than one generation, and that there never was any institution, however wise and good, but, in the lapse of time it has been abused." The same writer remarks, if it be prudent or necessary therefore to inquire into the cause or causes of degeneracy in the affairs of State, it is much more so with regard to religion or the various denominations of those who profess it. If upon a calm and dispassionate observation, some cause or causes seem to be operating, or likely to operate, for the worse among any body of religious people, it cannot be deemed unreasonable or uncharitable to point them out in order to prevent, or in some degree to check their growth. When a revival of religion takes place says Baxter, it begins in the ministry. This remark will be warranted by referring to the History of the Reformation by the instrumentality of Luther and his faithful cotemporaries in the ministry, as also of a later period, by Wesley, Whitfield and others, all of whom appeared to have been inspired by reading the Holy Scriptures, meditation and prayer. When corruption gets into the Church, it generally gains admittance through the same channel, diffusing its baneful influence down through every order until death, unless prevented by amputation, has sealed their destiny and the candlestick is removed out of its place. This observation deserves some consideration, when we call to remembrance the history of the Church at Rome. That Church retained her primitive purity through a scene of suffering and persecution, unparalleled, almost, in the history of human transaction. But that which could not be effected by prisons, flames and tortures, was soon brought about by a new state of things taking place. When Constantine, Emperor of Rome, became a Christian and poured honors and wealth on the clergy, then ease and luxury soon engendered pride and arrogance and the offspring of these, a desire of power, which meeting with gratification, soon enabled them to lord it over the poor heritage of Christ, laying the foundation for a system of errors and corruption, at war with the civil and religious liberties of the Christian world. This ought to serve as an eternal warning to all succeeding generations, never to place in the power of the clergy to play the same game.

Let all denominations consider that the department which God has assigned his embassadors is to be examples to their flocks, of meekness, humility and love, totally renouncing the world with all its pomps and vanities, a spirit as opposite to the spirit of the greater part of the ministers in this our day as humility is to pride, or as righteousness is to vice, and yet all acknowledge the preceding to be the character of our Lord and his apostles. Humility indeed was the lesson Christ constantly taught his disciples by example and precept. The princes of the Gentiles, said the blessed Savior, exercise authority over them and they that are great, dominion upon them, but it shall not be so among you, but whosoever will be great among you, let him be your servant, even as the Son of man came not to be ministered unto, but to minister and to give his life a ransom for many.

We find our Lord, on a certain occasion, when supper was ended, took a towel and girding himself, after pouring water into a basin, he began to wash his disciples feet and to wipe them with the towel wherewith he was girded. Considering the dignity of this person, engaged in this lowest and most menial office, that of washing the feet of his disciples, can we wonder at Peter, exclaiming, "Thou shalt never wash my feet?" But hear our Lord explain this astonishing transaction, so contrary to worldly usages and to the views of men who could not conceive that true greatness consists in true humility. Said the divine Redeemer, "If I your Lord and master have washed your feet ye also ought to wash one anothers feet, for I have given you an example that ye should do as I have done to you." As though he should have said, do not suppose that the kingdom I am about to establish, has a tendency whatsoever to cherish pride or gratify the ambition or carnal nature, by creating higher or lower orders in the administration of its government. On the contrary, my design by the example I have set before you, both on this occasion and throughout my whole life, is to teach you the necessity of self-abandonment, meekness and love that you may be led to imitate me your Lord and Master in lowliness and meekness, each esteeming the other better than themselves and in proportion as these heavenly virtues evidence themselves in your whole deportment, the farther you will be removed from a desire of having the pre-eminence over one another and thereby promote the best interests of my spiritual kingdom on earth.

A PILGRIM.

A WORD TO THE BRETHREN AND SISTERS IN GENERAL.

I often wish I was better qualified and had more time to write. I could wish for no greater pleasure than to write for the PILGRIM and help to spread the truth, as I consider it a duty that is enjoined upon the faithful followers of Christ as we are told to "work while it is day for the night cometh wherein no man can work," and I think that night is fast approaching, as every day brings us some wonderful things never before heard of. We are told that great tribulation and wonders shall come to pass and false prophets shall arise. What else do we hear daily preached by many of the fashionable and highly educated preachers but falsehood? They twist the truth into such a shape that it just suits their own fancy, no matter whether it is just exactly as Christ gave it to us or not. It is perfectly shocking to see so many people say they don't believe this or that that is in the Bible and yet profess to be Christians. It is awful to hear such expressions from such that we always thought were true believers. Is it any wonder that we frequently hear people talk, as I did the other day. There was an old friend of mine told me that he was sent to catechism and was taken into the Church and never knew any better but what it was all right, especially, according to his catechism, but when he began to read the Scripture for himself, he began to see it in quite a different light. So I suppose a great many more could say, if they would read the Scripture carefully and prayerfully. But so many read the Scripture and say they cannot understand it and yet it tells us that a fool cannot err therein. Why should it be such a task for those that are well educated if they really want to understand it? We now frequently hear people say that the Bible is not the same as it was several hundred years ago. How that is I do not know but I cannot believe that it would be changed so much that we could not still know enough or learn enough from our present Bible to find the way to heaven by reading and obeying the same. But it is too much of a task to obey what is in our Bible, yet still some claim there are things in the olden Bibles that ours says nothing about. I never saw one of those old Bibles but should like to see one. If any brother or sister that reads these lines can tell me of any infant baptism in the old Bible or of any thing of the kind I will be glad to hear of it. I was told that it did speak about infant baptism in the old editions but unless I hear more of it I cannot believe it. Please inform me if there are such, as I suppose there is some of our readers who have the old Bibles yet.

LOVINA MARSH.

REMARKS.—If you have been so informed in regard to old Bibles being different from present editions, your informant was either ignorant or malicious in design. The only change that has been made is in orthography and phraseology, but the intent or meaning remains the same. Infant baptism is based upon very obscure inferences as not a single instance ever was or ever can be found in the New Testament when a child was baptized. Believers only are fit subjects for this holy ordinance.

THE SUFFERER'S REST.

BY ANNA STOUFFER.

On the death of her little neice, Laura Olive Trostel.

'Twas God gave the sufferer rest,
He called her early, he knew best.
Jesus took the beautiful, dutiful child,
She died mid blooming youth and joy.

Weep not for me dear father and mother,
Soften your grief, sister and brother;
In heaven she went to draw our thoughts after,
To think if we, like her, could face our Master.

She left example for friend and mate,
For them that sobbed if their hearts would break;
"Come to me, cousin, come to me brother,
O! meet me," she prays. "Sister, father, mother."

In the churchyard corner alone she sleeps
And we wish her not again;
For Jesus, we know, safely her keeps,
Till we meet her in Heaven.

Clearspring, Pa.

Selected by L. A. Anglemyer.

CHARITIES THAT SWEETEN LIFE.

Pleasant words! Do you know, reader how potent a spell lies in pleasant words! Have you not often thought of its power to soothe, to charm, to delight, when all things else fail? As you have passed on through the journey of life, have you not seen it smoothing many a ruffled brow, and calming many an aching bosom? Have you not noticed it in the house and by the way, at the fireside and in the place of business? And have not felt that pleasant words are among the "charities that sweeten life?" Ah! yes and their influence has come over your own soul. Not long since when you went bending to the earth, oppressed and weary with life's manifold sorrows, when dark clouds hovered over you, when you were ready to yield in despondency the pursuit of happiness, and give yourself up in unmitigated gloom, when no object of life seemed desirable, oh! who can tell how in such an hour the sound of a cheerful voice—one pleasant word has dispelled the gloom, and given you to the world again, a man, a hopeful trusting man. You can tell us how like an angel whisper was the kind inquiry of that companion, and how the tone of cheerful sympathy sent the dark clouds rolling from your sky, and revealing the light of day, showing you that earth is not all a wilderness, nor man a being utterly deserted to wretchedness.

Or when you come from the counting room or work-shop careworn and weary, when your brow has been furrowed and your thoughts perplexed, when troubles of the present and anxieties of the future have crowned every peaceful feeling from your heart, when you almost dreaded to return to your own fireside, lest the sight of dear ones there should increase your distress, tell us what has been the influence of a pleasant word at such a time. Tell us how that, ere you opened your door, the sound of glad voices reached your ear, and as you entered, how the troubles of your soul were laid at rest; and cares, for the present and for the future, fled before the pleasant words of your smiling children and the gentle greeting of your wife.

Or, when the ire of your spirit has been roused, and indignant feelings have reigned supreme in your heart, when the angry threat was just rising to your lips or the malignant wish about to burst from your heart, what mighty spell caused the storm to subside, and spoke the turbulent waves so quietly to rest? Did the soft answer turn away your wrath.

Among the multitudes of the earth, how small the number who habitually and from principle speak pleasantly. You have met them. Now and then they have crossed your path, and I doubt not that your whole soul has blessed them as it ought, for the words which were balm to your wounded spirit. And did you not wish you were like them? Did you not feel that earth would be a paradise indeed, if all the tones of that matchless instrument, the human voice, were in harmony with the kind thoughts of a thoroughly kind heart? But, while you thus wished did you resolve to add one to their number? Did you determine to imitate their example? You think it a small matter requiring little effort. But I assure you it might cost you many a struggle ere you could learn to speak in pleasantness to all whom you might chance to meet, even in one short day; and if you accomplished it perhaps it would be a better days work than you ever did, and you might lay your head on the pillow of rest at night with feelings akin to those of spirits around the throne.

Speak pleasant words to all around you, and you shall ever be lighted by the smiles of those who welcome your coming and mourn your departing footsteps.

Mother, speak gently to the little ones who cluster around you, speak ever pleasantly, and be assured that answering tones of joy and dispositions formed to constant kindness shall be your reward.

Sister, brother, friend, would you render life one sunny day, would you gather around you those who would cheer you in the darkest hour? Let the law of kindness rule your tongue and your words be pleasant as "the dew that descended on the mountains of Zion."

Leeds, Ind.

READ THE NEW TESTAMENT.

What is a testament? A declaration of one's will, to test, to be a witness, &c., hence the New Testament referred to above is God's divine will or law, recorded in a volume, a book called the New Testament, the New and last covenant God gave to his people, the new economy of grace and salvation. Why and wherefore read the New Testament? because therein you will learn your duty to God and man, therein you will learn what you must do, that when you die you can go to heaven, or inherit eternal life—therein we learn how to judge ourselves that we be not judged; therein we know what is necessary to know to make us competent judges, to judge when we hear preaching whether it is consistent with God's divine will or not; therein we learn, that many false prophets are gone out into the world. 1 John 4: 1; therein we learn there were false prophets among the people even as there shall be false teachers among you. 2 Pet. 2: 1; therein we learn that in the last days perilous times shall come. 2 Tim. 3: 1; therein we learn that this is the last time. 1 John 2: 18; therein we learn that Paul charged Timothy to preach the word; that the time would come when they will not endure sound doctrine, &c. 2 Tim. 4: 1, 2, 3; therein we learn to prove all things and hold fast to that which is good. 1 Thes. 5: 21. Truly we have much good reading matter in our religious papers but I say again, read the New Testament.

ELD. D. MURRAY.

Dayton, O.

SILENT INFLUENCE. It is the bubbling spring which flows gently, the little rivulet which runs along day and night, by the farm house, that is useful, rather than the swollen flood or warring cataract. Niagara excites our wonder, and we stand amazed at the power and greatness of God there as He "poured it from the hollow of His hand." But one Niagra is enough for the continent or the world, while the same world requires thousands and tens of thousands of silver fountains and gentle flowing rivulets, that water every farm and meadow, and every garden, and that shall flow on every day, and every night, with their gentle, quiet beauty. So with the acts of our lives. It is not by great deeds, like those of the martyrs, that good is to be done; it is by the daily and quiet virtues of life—the Christian temper, the meek forbearance, the spirit of forgiveness, in the husband, the wife, the father, the mother, the brother, the sister, the friend, and neighbor, that good is to be done.

A MOTHER'S LOVE.—A mother's love (says Washington Irving) is never exhausted; it never changes; it never tires. A father may hate his child, brothers and sisters may become inveterate enemies, husbands may desert their wives, wives their husbands. But a mother's love endures through all; in good repute, in bad repute, in the face of the world's condemnation, a mother still loves on, and still hopes that her child may turn from his evil ways and repent; still she remembers the infant smiles that once filled her bosom with rapture, the merry laugh, the joyful shout of childhood; the opening promise of his youth; and she can never be brought to think him unworthy.

A GOOD conscience is to the soul what health is to the body. It preserves a constant ease and serenity within us, and more than countervails all the calamities and afflictions that befal us.

As welcome as sunshine
In every place,
Is the beaming approach
Of a good-natured face.
—*What Next*

Religious News.

PENNSYLVANIA SABBATH SCHOOL CONVENTION meets in convention at Titusville, June 3, 4 and 5, '73. Each Sunday School is requested to send two delegates. Pastors of all denominations are invited to be present.

Brigham Young says that, when he went into Utah with his people, the Indians were all about him; but by dealing with them fairly at all times, keeping all his promises and never deceiving them, he had no trouble with them. He thinks the Modocs treated the Peace Commissioners just as they believed they would have been treated if they had fallen into the power of the white men.

Law is more sacredly regarded in New York than it was a few months ago. A decided impression for good is made on courts, juries, and the public generally. There is a prevailing opinion that life and property are safer now than they have been.

So says the *Observer*. The cause is attributed to the fact that in a few cases it has been honored by allowing justice to overbalance the power of bribery.

A REPORT. Bro. Addison Baker of Carthage Mo., informs us that the brethren at their District Meeting, without a dissenting voice, agreed that the report of the committee sent by last A. M. to settle difficulties in Iowa, Mo, and Kansas shall be sent for publication in the PILGRIM. With such authority, we will be pleased to publish it, but hope it may be written in the spirit of moderation with a due regard for the influence it may exert on the general Brotherhood and the outside world.

GERMAN BAPTISTS.—Two out of every three of the German Baptists in this country take the German Baptist paper, published at Cleveland, Ohio. There are 6,000 German Baptists in America, and their paper has a circulation of 1,000.

Those of our brethren who still

clamor for retaining the above, to us, insignificent title, will please make a note of these facts. The German Baptists above alluded to are German Baptists because they speak the German language and read a German paper, but to call the Brethren, German Baptists who have become so English that we cannot support a German paper is both unreasonable and absurd.

Modoc War. From present indications, this heathen butchery will soon terminate. At latest accounts, about one half had made an unconditional surrender and it is thought that the remaining party will soon be captured How strange it is that because a few untutored savages, who believed that they had been shamefully abused and deceived, committed murder, the whole tribe must be annihilated while the Modocs of New York and our other large cities can commit cold blooded murder and it takes months and even years of judicial proceeding, with an expense of thousands, before the law can be honored and the public safety insured.

Sabbath Schools, notwithstanding some good and zealous brethren protest against them, seem to be gaining favor in the Church, and there is a considerable inquiry in regard to suitable books and papers for their use. The Brethren at New Enterprise, Pa., has perhaps the largest school in the State, numbering, if we are not mistaken, as high as 240 scholars. That this school has been a power for good all readily admit that have any acquaintance with that community, and the same happy results might be enjoyed in every Church where there is a sufficient number of children to form a school. There are quite a number of others that are in successful operation that we hope may be attended with equally good results.

Whiskey Versus $100.000.—The late Thaddeus Stevens in his will bequeathed to his nephew about $100.000 providing he would abstain from the use of intoxicating drinks In case he would fail to comply with these conditions the amount was to be used to found an Orphan's Home in Lancaster, Pa. From late accounts it appears that he has broken the will and arrangements are now being made to erect the Orphan's Home.

To money has been accorded, the power that moves the world, but how passingly strange it is that the demon alcohol has a power that even exceeds that of money. Though the nephew loses the fortune, the old father, in his judicious will, may still befriend his blood by preparing a home for his orphans. How great must be that power that makes man its willing slave, strips him of his earthly possessions, lowers to a brute level and finally debars him from the joys of Heaven!

Youth's Department

For the Pilgrim.

SHE DWELLETH IN HEAVEN.

BY LOVINA B. BURKHART.

She dwelleth in Heaven no more upon earth,
Will her voice swell the cadence, of music or mirth;
She dwelleth in *Heaven*, your darling is there,
Yes May is an angel in Eden so fair.

She dwelleth in Heaven a blossom so bright,
It can never be injured by dews of the night.
She is singing God's praise on that evergreen shore,
Where angelic choristers weep never more.

She dwelleth in *Heaven*, her life here was brief.
Her God will protect her from sickness and grief.
Dear parents don't mourn for the one that is gone,
She's happier now than the wayfaring one.

She dwelleth in *Heaven*, she's waiting for you;
Awaiting and watching 'till you bid adieu,
To the world with its pleasures and trials combined,
To the will of our Father we should be resigned.

She dwelleth in Heaven in robes of pure white,
While her dear little sisters now roam with delight
Through the wood-land and grove in their innocent glee,
Dear Ollie and Ida how happy and free.

She dwelleth in Heaven, no chilling winds blow,
No tempest can ever her pleasure o'erthrow.
There night never comes, dear parents prepare
To meet May an angel in Heaven so fair.

Wilmore, Pa.

JESUS WHEN A LITTLE BOY.

One time when Jesus was a little boy, only twelve years old, he managed to get away from his parents to talk with some very learned men. I don't know that he ever had seen them previous to this time. I don't believe he did. And how he introduced himself, I am unable to say. Whether he said to those big men, "I'm little Jesus," or whether he at once, told them that he was the Son of the great God, I cannot say. But we know that he did want very much to talk to those learned men who thought they knew it all, when they did not even so much as know that there was a Savior born into the world. Whether they found Jesus out enough to know that he was the one to save the world; the one to set up his Kingdom in the world, I do not really know. But, after he had heard them and asked them some questions, I think we can learn from what then happened, that he had given them a hint of his mission from Heaven into such a sinful world.

It happened while little Jesus was talking so earnestly to those men, so that they wondered at his words, his parents came to him. They had been searching for him for some time, and were becoming very much alarmed, thinking they might never find Jesus. You see they loved him—loved him much more than many persons do now, who don't care whether they *ever* find Jesus. They told Jesus how they had been seeking him, "sorrowing." Jesus was very much surprised on hearing this, and said: "Wist ye not that I must be about my Father's business? Don't you know I left my home in Heaven to save the world?" *To save the world!* Yes my little readers. And what a useful lesson Jesus teaches you in that he engaged in his "Father's business," while so very young. There is no telling how much a little boy or girl can do for Jesus if an effort is only made. Annie is one of the most peevish and disagreeable scholars in school. She don't like her teacher, nor scarcely any of the scholars. Yet I'm sure, if you speak kindly to her, she can't help loving you. If you then try to get others to love her, you will do something for Jesus for which you will be happy. Every kind word you speak; every good act you do, will make you useful to Jesus.

F. M. SNYDER.

THE RUNAWAY KITTEN.

Three or four years ago in the village near us there lived a family that had a very pretty kitten but it would not stay at home, but ran away to the neighbors and to one of the stores, where it was stepped on and abused (as runaways are apt to be), until finally it followed two of my sisters home. We thought it was so pretty we would let it live here. We fed it, and it soon began to like us, but it was so very sore that we could hardly touch it without it scolded or spit at us. It was but a kitten when it came here, but it has been here four years and now it is quite a large cat. He has a very beautiful coat and is admired by all that see him. His coat is a velvety black and dark gray. He spends much time on it and is very choice of himself. When he comes in he looks all around for a cushioned chair and then waits and sometimes he goes to the parlor door and begs to go in. He is marked very singular; has an M in his face right above his nose, and then he has almost a perfect heart on one of his sides. There are some who think he stands like a tiger.

We think him a very intelligent cat too, for he seems to understand much we say to him. If we ask him if he wants a mouse he pricks up his ears and does not wait to be called long, but comes and begins to smell around and spring at everything that moves. He always seems very much pleased when he catches one and most always comes back for the second. If he does not find one he seems very much disappointed and does not stop hunting for some time after we leave him.

If he does not have his new milk morning and night it always seems to make him feel all out of sorts. Sometimes when he is teasing, we ask him if he is hungry? He will answer back as long as we talk to him. It is very amusing to see him when some strange dog comes here; if the dog comes near, he will growl and spit at it and then run to the house with his tail as big as he can make it. He does not seem to be afraid of our own dog, but a strange dog he cannot bear. He still retains his old habit of running away, and sometimes will be gone a day or two, but he always comes back hungry and I should think glad to be at home again.

We once had a black and white kitten which we all thought a great deal of, he was so playful and useful too. If he caught a mouse he would play with it a long time and when he got tired he would eat it. I have known him several times to lose a mouse playing with it, and then he would begin to cry, as if imploring help to find it again. If we went to help him and found it he was perfectly satisfied. One morning he was sick and went away and we saw no more of him until one day we found him dead.—*Young Folk's Rural.*

THE FOOLISH FOX.

In the depths of the forest there lived two foxes. One of them said, "Let's quarrel."

"Very well, but how shall we begin?"

"O, it cannot be difficult," said fox number one; "two-legged people fall out; why not we?"

So they tried all sorts of ways, but it could not be done, because each one would give way. At last number one fetched two stones.

"There!" said he, "you say they're yours, and I'll say they're mine, and we will quarrel, and fight and scratch. Now I'll begin. These stones are mine!"

"Very well, you are welcome to them."

"But we will never quarrel at this rate!" cried the other, jumping up and licking his face. "You old simpleton, don't you know that it takes two to make a quarrel?"

So they gave it up as a bad job and never tried to play at this silly game again.

What are thy crosses to thy comforts, thy miseries to thy mercies, thy days of sickness to thy days of health, thy days of weakness to thy days of weakness to thy days of strength, thy days of scarcity to thy days of plenty?—*Thomas Brooks.*

Correspondence.

A Reporter is wanted from every Church in the brotherhood to send us Church news, Obituaries, Announcements, or anything that will be of general interest. To insure insertion, the writers name must accompany each communication. Our Invitation is not personal but general—please respond to our call

AN EXPLANATION.

By special request of the brethren of California we admit the following, but of the facts of the case we have no acquaintance. It is written in the spirit of love and we trust is the prompting of honest and sincere hearts. There is an apparent discrepency somewhere but we hope there is enough charity among the brethren concerned to have it set aright.

Bro. Brumbaugh:—We brethren of California desire to make some explanation through the PILGRIM of the position we occupy toward Bro. Gipson, who the standing committee of last A. M. cut off. The reason we desire this is, that the facts may be known to the general brotherhood and thereby we will stand on the merits of the case. We know we have been strongly censured by many for fellowshipping Bro. Gipson after he was cut off by said committee.

In order to give a correct idea of the case we will review from the time the Church in Macoupin Co., Ill., called for a committee of Elders from the churches around them, to hear the case. The committee met with the church and heard the grievances from both parties and rendered a decision.

Eld. D. B. Sturgis, who afterwards visited Cal., was chairman of said committee. In their decision they laid an admonition on the church in MaCoupin Co., and an acknowledgment on Bro. Gipson. The matter was not reconciled at that time and Bro. Gipson removed to Cal. He told us how he stood and his statement was afterwards confirmed by letter from the brethren in Ill. There were several letters passed between Eld. Wolf and the brethren in Ill. They expressed a strong desire that brother Gipson might be reconciled to the Church, for said they, he is a valuable man. Thus the matter rested until Elds' Miller and Sturgis came to Cal., clothed with power from the brethren in Ill., and appointed by A. M. also a letter of recommendation to us from the brethren of Indiana, which we thought was credentials sufficient to act in any case of difference between two brethren or more.

It was in my presence that Bro. Sturgis had his first interview with brother Gipson. It seems Bro. Gipson labored under a mistake in regard to the extent of the acknowledgement required of him. He tho't they required of him to recant his former conviction or belief in the single mode of Feet-washing. When he heard from Bro. Sturgis what the committee that tried the case, required of him he was perfectly willing to make the acknowledgment and did so in my presence to Bro. Sturgis. Then we went in the house (for we had retired to talk the matter over privately), where the brethren of Cal. were assembled in church council.

Bro. Sturgis introduced the matter and spoke with much warmth and love, feeling glad that his labors were crowned with success and that reconciliation was made. Bro. Gipson arose and made the acknowledgment before the church. Then the brethren gave him over to the church in California, and they received him in full fellowship.

The following was drawn up by Bro. Sturgis and signed by the brethren the day after the Church Council, and the last act of the Brethren in Cal:

San Joaquin Dist., Dec. 10, '70.

In Church council assembled, A. P. Gibson accepts the decision of the Church with the committee in Macoupin Co., Ill, and confesses his faults and asks forgiveness. We accept the same in behalf of the Church of Macoupin Co., and he is now received by the Church here as a private member.

DAN'L B. STURGIS,
JACOB MILLER
A. P. GIPSON.

Witnessed in behalf of the Church of Cal., by ELD. G. WOLFE.
" J. MYERS.

When the Brethren saw fit, they advanced Bro. Gipson to the ministry and he labored with us in word and doctrine and was at peace and in perfect union with the Church when we were informed that the standing committee had cut him off, and that too, without preferring a charge against him, and to this time, have given us no reason for their action, only informed us we should not fellowship him any further.

It was promised that the whole matter would come out in our periodicals but we have seen nothing of it since. I do not wish to criticise the action of any of the Brethren for some of them are gone and will have to give an account of their stewardship to that judge that does not only see their actions but knows the motive that prompts them to act. With these facts before you brethren, where is there a Church that would have done different from the Church in Cal?

We don't claim to be perfect but if we err I trust we shall ever do it on the side of mercy.

Sent for publication by request.

ELD. J. MYERS.

WHY IS IT?

In PILGRIM No. 20, current volume, an article appears under the above heading, written by Sarah J. Miller asking the above question, why the brethren and sisters are allowed to use the affirmation, and then quotes the language of Christ which he spake in reference to swearing recorded in Matt. 5: 34, 35, 36, and also that of James 5: 12. on the same subject. And then says; "Now I would suppose the affirmation would be one of the 'any other oaths' that the apostle speaks of, which, I claim, is merely a modified oath, and just as binding as the real oath. Then why not let your yea be yea and your nay, nay?"

Now for the information of the sister I would say, when we make use of the affirmation, we do just what the Savior and James say that we should; we say no more than yea or nay. This is not an oath, not even in *modified* form. We are asked by the magistrate: "do you solemnly and sincerely declare and affirm that you will speak the truth, the whole truth and nothing but the truth?" Then we answer, yea. Now there is nothing in this interrogatory that has the appearance of an oath. The government must have some form, and when we are to be put upon the witness stand and are thus interrogated and we answer yea, we merely promise what we intend to do, and by all means should do, that is, speak the truth. The words *declare* and *affirm* are defined, the former, to make known publicly, and the latter, to establish or ratify, to declare positively. This is required of us to satisfy the "powers that be" that we are qualified for the witness stand. The officers of the law know very well that there are many who consider themselves more under obligation to speak the truth when they are on oath, or even have been affirmed, than they would without an oath or affirmation. And as there is nothing in the form of affirmation used by the Brethren and others that conflicts with the Gospel, it is our duty to obey the law.

But that this is just as binding as the real oath, I admit; for the Christian religion, without any oath or affirmation, binds us to speak the truth. I once heard a man say that he would just as soon speak an untruth when he was on oath, as tell a lie without an oath, for, said he, we read that "all liars shall have their part in the lake that burneth with fire and brimstone," and he could not see how there could be a greater punishment for such as would speak an untruth with an oath.

The sister also finds fault with those brethren who pray for kings and rulers that are in authority over us, that they might exact laws that we may lead a quiet and peaceable life &c., and says; "why not pray for their conversion," To this I would reply that the brethren do this because the apostle exhorts us to do so, and from his words, 1 Tim. 2: 1, 2, we plainly infer that he means that we should pray that they would rule well, for he says; "that we may lead a quiet and peaceable life, &c. Now if we would pray for their conversion and our prayers would be answered that is, if they would be converted (which it is not likely that all of them will) they would cease to be kings and rulers in the kingdom of the world, and then others would fill the vacancy and there would still be kings and rulers; and while the present state of things exist, God will need such as his ministers to protect the children of God and to punish the evildoers, and keep them in check and to them he has given the sword. But when the Millenium dispensation will commence he will not need those rulers any more. Christ will then reign and his saints shall reign with him. So there is no impropriety in praying that they might rule well and enact and wise good laws, &c.

DANIEL SNOWBERGER.

New Enterprise, Pa.

Answer to Query.

HUDSON, Ill.,
May 18, 1873

Dear Pilgrim:—In No. 19 I find a query propounded by Bro. M. J. McClure, found in the latter part of the 9th. verse of the 10th. chap. of John, thus, "I shall go in and out and find pasture."

Our Savior here uses a metaphor taken from a custom then prevailing in the East, namely: by going before the sheep, while the sheep as faithfully follow the shepherd, who led them from the fold to the pasturage; where they grazed upon the green grass, until evening, when they followed their shepherd to the fold again. Here is the point to be considered. The sheep realized a real pleasure in partaking of the green grass through the day, or while they were *out*, and again at night, when they are *in*, they will ruminate upon what they had so much enjoyed when they were out, here they realize a double pleasure, and no doubt the second, is by far, the greatest. So with Christ's followers, while complying with the outward ordinances it affords a real pleasure, because Heaven has commanded it and promised a blessing upon it. The willing hands, the penitent hearts, yea the whole soul is fixed upon the thing signified. Faith now is strong that the end will be accomplished, by the power of God, while the humble suppliant is complying with the means of Heaven's own appointment.

Now this child of God will, within himself, have a real pleasure of knowing that he has obeyed from the heart, that form of doctrine delivered to him; hence, when he goes within, there is a new creature, and when he goes out, here he uses or has used the means that secures the end.

T. D. LYON.

LATHROP, CAL.,
May 15th, 1873.

Dear Pilgrim:—Our crop will not be as bountiful in the San Joaquin this harvest as we anticipated in January and February from the fact that our Spring or latter rains, was nearly an entire failure. Therefore if we get a half crop this harvest it is as much as we can expect. Heading grain will commence in the San Joaquin valley in two weeks. Haying is about done. On the coast and other valleys north, the yield of grain will be equal to other good seasons.

ELD. GEO. WOLF.

QUERY.

Dear friend Brumbaugh will you or some of the members of your Church give an explanation through the PILGRIM of the 6th chapter 16th verse, Matt. which reads as follows: "Moreover when ye fast be not as the hypocrites, of a sad countenance for they disfigure their faces that they may appear unto men to fast, verily I say unto you, they have their reward. Romans 10th chapter 13th verse, "For whosoever shall call upon the name of the Lord shall be saved. 1 Cor. 5th chapter, 11th verse, "but now I have written unto you not to keep company. If any man that is called a fornicator, or covetous, or an idolater, or a railer, or a drunkard, or an extortion with such a one no not to eat.

A FRIEND TO THE PILGRIM.

The Weekly Pilgrim.

JAMES CREEK, PA., June 3, 1873.

☞ How to send money.—All sums over $1.50, should be sent either in a check, draft or postal order. If neither of these can be obtained, have the letter registered.

☞ When Money is sent, *always* send with it the name and address of those who paid it. Write the names and post office as plainly as possible.

☞ Every subscriber for 1873, gets a *Pilgrim Almanac* Free.

THE TRUE CHURCH.

We have been asked, "Is the Church of the Brethren the true Church?" This is an important question, and one that every man and woman has a right to have answered. But that answer must rest on a basis sufficiently sure to make it safe. Every right and wrong, true and untrue, is determined by law. Law is the basis of all judgment and without it, no decision can be made. Then, to answer our querist, we must first determine whether we have a law by which we can decide, and second, whether that law will admit of us being called the true Church. The first proposition, it is not necessary for us to prove, as all religiously disposed persons are ready to admit that the New Testament *is* the Christian's law, and that it, finally, will either condemn or acquit us.

Admitting this, we are ready to enter our second proposition and determine, according to that law, who or which is the true Church. As this law is universal in its application and all are to be judges, we would say to the querist and all who are interested in regard to the true Church, *come and see*, for thus saith the Lord. "Stand ye in the ways and see, and ask for the old paths, where is the *good* way, and walk therein, and ye shall find rest for your souls." In the matter of determining the true Church we want all to have equal privileges as we are all equally concerned and have the same law. Our great King and Law Giver would say; "Ye are the judges, hear what I say." The True Church consists of that people that acknowledges Jesus, as the Christ and His word as their law. Now it is altogether rational to conclude that the organization or Church that endeavors to walk in all the commandments and ordinances of the Lord blameless, must be the true Church. This is what the Brethren do, and just so far as they come short of this effort so far are they short of being the True Church. But says the querist; "If you are the True Church, will all others be lost?" Judgment is not given into our hands neither do we desire to pass judgment. This is not our mission, neither was it that of our blessed Redeemer. He says; "I judge no man—but the words which I speak, they shall judge you in the last day." It is our duty to preach the truth, the whole truth and the truth alone. Such preaching, if accepted, will produce a True Church and nothing short of this will do it, because it consists of God's people and God's people will comply with this law. "If ye love me, keep my commandments," is a point of law and forms a test whereby the True Church can be known. "He that saith he loveth me and keepeth *not* my commandments is a liar and the truth is not in him." Then, stand in the ways and see; take the chart of salvation in hand, view them well, ever remember ing that, in the day of judgment, we shall not be judged by the creeds of men, but by the gospel of truth. Keeping these facts in view, it is scarcely possible that any should fail in finding the True Church. Our convictions are that the Church of the Brethren is the True Church, because there is no other Church known that walks so nearly, in all the ordinances and commandments of the Lord blameless. What will be the end of those who are not willing to comply with all the requisitions of the Lord will only be determined in the day of final accounts, when every one shall be called upon to have their lives squared by the living oracles of God.

Broad Top R. R. is now supplied with new engines, two baggage cars and four splendid new traveling coaches of the latest style and modern finish. As they pass along they present a grand and glittering display and reflect great credit to the company. The road is also in a better condition than it has been for a number of years and nothing is left undone by the gentlemanly Superintendent and conductors to make travelers feel safe and comfortable. It richly deserves the large increase of patronage it has received under the new superintendency and may justly be considered a road of first class accommodations.

Next Week's Pilgrim will be some behind time on account of ourself and some of our help attending Annual Conference. We expect to make good use of the time and give our readers as much information in regard to the business there transacted as possible.

Only 80 cents.—The Pilgrim will be sent from A. M. to the end of the year for 80 cents. Our agents and those interested in the welfare of the Pilgrim will please make this known and solicit a few more names for us.

Excursion.—Last week in giving the offices at which excursion tickets will be sold on the Broad Top line we omitted Saxton. We expect this paper to reach its destination in time to make this correction.

Tune Books.—Orders for Tune Books will be filled as soon as we get another supply.

HUMAN BUTCHERY.

The following is the sentiments of C. H. Spurgeon on war as expressed in regard to the French and German war. It is plain pointed and powerful and should cause all men to examine well the grounds taken to defend honorable human butchery.

"Did either of you ever think of what war means? Did you ever see a man's head smashed, or his bowels ripped open? Why, if you are made of flesh and blood, the sight of one poor wounded man, with the blood oozing out of him, will make you feel sick. I do not like to drown a kitten; I can't bear to see a rat die, or any animal in pain. But a man? Where's your hearts, if you can think of broken legs, splintered bones, heads smashed in, brains blown out, bowels torn, hearts gushing with gore, ditches full of blood, and heaps of limbs and carcasses of mangled men? Do you say my language is disgusting? How much more disgusting must the things themselves be? And you make them! Do you fancy that your drums and fifes, and feathers and finerics, and pomp, make your wholesale murders one whit less abominable in the sight of God? Do not deceive yourselves; you are no better than the cut-throats whom your own laws condemn; better, why you are worse, for your murders are so many. Think, I pray you, for your poor people will have to think whether you do or not.

Is there so little want in the world that you must go trampling on the harvest with your horses and men? Is there so little sorrow that you must make widows by the thousand? Is death so old and feeble that you must hunt his game for him, as jackals do for the lion? O, kings, their souls are as precious in God's sight as yours; they suffer as much pain whenever bullets pierce them as ever you can do; they have homes, and mothers, and sisters, and their deaths will be as much wept after as yours, perhaps more. It will be hard to think of the blood you have shed when you lie dying, and harder still to bear the heavy hand of God when he shall cast all murderers into hell. Have pity upon your fellow-men. Do not cut them with swords, tear them with bayonets, blow them to pieces with canon, or riddle them with shots. What good will it do you? What have the poor men done to deserve it of you? You fight for glory, do you? I am a plain-talking Englishman, and I tell you the English for glory is DAMNATION, and it will be your lot, O, kings, if you go on cutting and hacking your fellow-men. Stop this war, if you can, at once, and turn to some better business than killing men. Before the deep curses of widows and orphans fall on you from the throne of God, put up your butcher knives and patent men-killers, and repent."

ANNOUNCEMENTS.

Please announce that we, the brethren and sisters of the Desmoines Valley Church, expect, the Lord willing, to hold our Lovefeast on the 28th and 29th days of June, 1873, at Elkhart, Polk Co., Iowa, about 16 miles northeast of Demoines City. The general invitation is given, and especially to the ministering brethren to be with us. S. M. Goughnour.

Companion please copy.

Please announce that our Communion will be held in our Meeting house in the Spring Creek Congregation, 14 miles S. E. of Warsaw, on the 20th. day of June next. All are invited. Daniel Miller.

Pierceton, Ind.

Eds. Pilgrim:—Please announce Communion Meetings which were arranged at the District Meeting of North-eastern O., and to all of which meetings we are requested to invite our beloved brethren and sisters and especially the ministering brethren. They are as follows:

June the 7th, Sandy Church at brother Abraham Hestands. Those coming by railroad will stop off at Homeworth station.

June 8th, Canton Church at brother John Seefong, three miles Northeast of Louisville Station.

June 10th, Tuscarawas, at brother Joseph Shively's, about six miles south of Canton, O.

June 13th, Springfield at Brethren's meeting house, about six miles South east of Akron, O.

June 15th, (was to be on 12th.—time changed at D. M.) Chippewa at brother Hestands, Wooster Summit in sight of the place where last A. M. was held.

June 17th, Ashland at brother Emanuel Hershey's.

Arrangements will be made to convey those that come by Railroad to the above named places by the Brethren and further directions will be given.

Josiah Kerm.
B. B. Bollinger.

Please announce that the Richland Church, Richland county, Ohio, will, the Lord willing, hold a Lovefeast at Bro. John Kendell's seven miles North-west of Mansfield on the 21st and 22nd of June. A general invitation is given.

J. C. McMullen.

Please announce that the Hudson Church, McLean Co., Ill., have appointed a Lovefeast on the 14 and 15 of June, to commence at 10 o'clock A. M., at the house of J. Y. Snavely. The usual invitation is given. Thomas D. Lyon.

BOOK NOTICES.

In this department we will notice such NEW BOOKS, *as may be sent us by publishers, that are in harmony with the character of our work. A. B. Brumbaugh, M. D., Huntingdon Pa., literary editor, to whom all books must be sent.*

BOOKS RECEIVED.

From Claxton, Remson and Haffelfinger, Publishers Philadelphia. Price $1.50 each. For sale at Blair's; Huntingdon, Pa.

TWICE CROWNED. A story of the days of Queen Mary. By Harriet B. McKeever.

BONNE et NOIR. A tale of Baden—Baden, from the French of Edmond About By E. R.

CLYDE WARDLEIGH'S PROMISE. By Macy D. Numan.

THE HEMLOCK SWAMP and a season at White Sulphur Springs. By Elsin Leigh Whittlesy.

HARD WORDS.—We have before us, a beautiful little volume—Lily's HARD WORDS: a story for little people, written by Margaret Hosmer. It is published by Claxton, Remson, and Haffelfinger of Philada., and for sale by Blair, Huntingdon, Pa.

We cannot refrain from putting in a plea for the children. They are not usually provided with a sufficient amount, and variety of reading matter. They need food for reflection, and we doubt not that by reading this book, many a little boy and girl would be enabled to solve the meaning of these *hard words*, and learn the lessons of *Helpfulness*, Patience, Prudence, Forgiveness, Unselfishness, etc. etc., and as they grow up, to weave these lessons into their lives to make them beautiful and good. A. B. B.

MAGAZINES.

HARPER for June leads off with "Cheap Yachting," occupying 15 pages with engravings, representing different scenes that are both interesting and pleasant to those who have the good fortune to see and enjoy them. Next follows "The Marquois of Hastings in America," delineating events connected with the Revolutionary times and full of interest. The Wine Islands of Lake Erie, Harz Mountains and a large number of other papers, which makes it of sufficient scope to suit the taste of all classes of intelligent readers. Published by Harper and Bros. Franklin Square, New York. at $1.00 per year.

"THE ASCENT of Mount Hayden," a modern chapter of Western discovery beyond the Rocky Mountains, graces the first pages of *Scribner* for June and will be read with pleasure, especially by those who are curious to learn of things that are rare and strange. "Our postal car service" is also a paper of very general interest and is worthy of a careful reading, with a large amount of other information for everybody. Published by Scribner & Co., 654 Broadway New York, at $4.00 per year.

THE AMERICAN PROTESTANT is a 48 page monthly published in defence of American principles and Institutions, and exposing the secret workings of Romanism in our nation. "Under the Ban" is a paper of rare interest; "The Abduction;" "Romish Premiums;" "The Porch and the Alter," and number of others are among the leading articles for June. Terms, $1.75 per annum. S. M. Kenedy, No. 8, North Seventeenth st., Philadelphia.

THE ADVOCATE OF PEACE for May is received. It is certainly devoted to a good cause, having for its motto, "On Earth Peace, * * Nation shall not lift up sword against nation, neither shall they learn war any more."

"Not too fast," is the leader, and shows up facts that should be generally known, *i. e.* the Modocs hostility is the offspring of white counsellors. The *Advocate* is a 16 page monthly published by the American Peace Society, Boston, Mass., at $1.00.

DYMOND ON WAR.

An inquiry into the Accordancy of War, with the Principles of Christianity, and an examination of the Philosophical reasoning by which it is defended. With observations on some of the causes of war and on some of its effects. By Jonathan Dymond. Sent from this office, post-paid, for 50 cts.

TUNE BOOK.

The Brethren's Tune and Hymn Book, is a compilation of Sacred Music adapted to all the hymns in the Brethren's New Hymn Book. It contains over 350 pages, printed on good paper and neatly bound. We will send it to any address, post paid at $1.25 per copy.

GOOD BOOKS.

A large number of our patrons are receiving our books as noticed below, as premiums, and express themselves highly pleased with them. Others who are not agents, have enquired whether we keep them for sale. We have now made arrangements with Mr. Wells to furnish any of their publications post paid at publishers prices. Orders for books must be accompanied with the cash, and plain directions for sending them.

How to read Character, Illus. Price,	$1.25
Combe's Moral Philosophy,	1.75
Constitution of Man. Combe,	1.75
Education. By Spurzheim,	1.50
Memory—How to Improve it,	1.50
Mental Science, Lectures on,	1.50
Self-Culture and Perfection,	1.50
Combe's Physiology, Illus.	1.75
Food and Diet. By Pereira,	1.75
Natural Laws of Man,	.75
Hereditary Descent,	1.50
Combe on Infancy,	1.50
Sober and Temperate Life,	.50
Children in Health—Disease,	1.75
The Science of Human Life,	3.50
Fruit Culture for the Million,	1.00
Saving and Wasting,	1.50
Ways of Life—Right Way,	1.00
Footprints of Life,	1.25
Conversion of St. Paul,	1.00

Life at Home; or, The Family and its Members. A work which should be found in every family. $1.50. Extra gilt, $2.00.

Hand-book for Home Improvement: comprising "How to Write," "How to Talk," How to Behave," and "How to do Business," in one vol. 2.25.

Man, in Genesis and in Geology; or, the Biblical Account of Man's Creation, tested by Scientific Theories of his Origin and Antiquity. One vol. 12mo, $1.00.

Man and Woman: Considered in their Relations to each Other and to the World. 12mo, Fancy cloth, Price $1.00.

Hopes and Helps for the Young of both sexes, Relating to the Formation of Character. Choice of Avocation, Health, Conversation, Social Affection Courtship and Marriage. Muslin, $1.50.

The Emphatic, Diaglott; or The New Testament in Greek and English. Containing the Original Greek Text of the New Testament, with an Interlineary Word for-word English Translation. Price, $4.00; extra fine binding, $5.00.

The Right Word in the Right Place. A New Pocket Dictionary and Reference Book. Cloth, 75cts.

Trine Immersion

TRACED

TO THE APOSTLES.

The SECOND EDITION is now ready for delivery. The work has been carefully revised, corrected and enlarged.

Put up in a neat pamphlet form, with good paper cover, and will be sent, post-paid, on the following terms: One copy, 25 cts; Five copies, $1.10; Ten copies, $2.00. 25 copies, $4.50; 50 copies, $8.50; 100 copies, $16.00.

Address, J. H. MOORE, Urbana, Champaign co., Ill.

Oct 22.

GIVEN AWAY.

A FINE GERMAN CHROMO.

We send an elegant chromo, mounted and ready for framing, free to every agent for

UNDERGROUND

OR,

LIFE BELOW THE SURFACE,

BY THOS. W. KNOX.

942 Pages Octavo. 130 Fine Engravings.

Relates Incidents and Accidents beyond the Light of Day; Startling Adventures in all parts of the World Mines and Mode of Working them; Under-currents of Society; Gambling and its *Horrors*; Caverns and their Mysteries; The Dark Ways of Wickedness; Prisons and their Secrets; Down in the Depths of the Sea; Strange Stories of the Detection of Crime.

The book treats of experience with brigands; nights in opium dens and gambling hells; life in prison; Stories of exiles; adventures among Indians; journey through Sewers and Catacombs; accidents in mines; pirates and piracy; tortures of the inquisition; wonderful burglaries; underworld of the great cities, etc., etc.

AGENTS WANTED

for this work. Exclusive territory is given. Agents can make $100 a week in selling this book. Send for circulars and terms to agents.

J. B BURR & HYDE,

HARTFORD, CONN., on CHICAGO, ILL

TRACTS.

"ANXIOUS BENCH RELIGION EXAMINED," BY ELDER J. S. FLORY. A SYNOPSIS OF CONTENTS. An address to the reader: The peculiarities that attend this type of religion. The feelings there experienced not imaginary but real. The key that unlocks the wonderful mystery. The causes by which feelings are excited. How the momentary feelings called "Experimental religion" are brought about, and then concludes by giving that form of doctrine as taught by Jesus Christ and recorded by his faithful witnesses.

COUNTERFEIT DETECTER
or
BAPTISM—MUCH IN LITTLE.

This work is now ready for distribution, and the importance of the subject will speak for it a large demand. It is a short treatise on baptism in tract form intended for general distribution, and is set forth in such a plain and logical manner that a wayfaring man though a fool, cannot err therein. Either of the above tracts sent postpaid on the following terms: Two copies, 10 cts, 10 copies 40 cents, 25 copies 70 cents, 50 copies $1.00, 100 copies $1.50.

Trine Immersion.

A discussion on Trine Immersion, by letter between Elder B. F. Moomaw and Dr. J. J. Jackson, to which is annexed a Treatise on the Lord's Supper, and on the necessity, character and evidences of the new birth, also a dialogue on the doctrine of non-resistance, by Elder B. F. Moomaw. Single copy 50 cents.

THE

HELPING HAND.

Containing several hundred Valuable Receipts for cooking well at a moderate expense, making Dyes, Coloring, Cleaning and Cementing. This book also points out in plain language, free from Doctors' terms the diseases of men, women and children, and the latest and most approved means used for their cure, to which is added a description of the Medicinal Roots and Herbs, and how they are to be used in the cure of diseases.

This is a work of considerable importance and we offer it to our readers as being a valuable accession in every household. Sent from this office to any address, post-paid, for 25 cents.

1870 1873

DR. FAHRNEY'S

Blood Cleanser or Panacea.

A tonic and purge, for Blood Diseases. Great reputation. Many testimonials. Many ministering brethren use and recommend it. Ask or send for the "Health Messenger." Use only the "*Panacea*" prepared at Chicago, Ills., and by

Dr. P. Fahrney's Brothers & Co.,

Feb. 3-pd. *Waynesboro, Franklin Co., Pa*

New Hymn Books, English.

TURKEY MOROCCO.

One copy, postpaid,	$1.00
Per Dozen,	11.25

PLAIN ARABESQUE.

One Copy, post-paid,	75
Per Dozen, "	8.50

Ger'n & English, Plain Sheep.

One Copy, post-paid,	$1.00
Per Dozen	11.25
Arabesque Plain,	1.00
Turkey Morocco,	1.25
Single German, post paid	50
Per Dozen,	5.50

HUNTINGDON & BROAD TOP RAIL ROAD

On and after March 22d, 1873, Trains will run on this road daily (Sundays excepted) as follows:

Trains from Huntingdon South. *Trains from Mt. Dal's moving North.*

MAIL. A. M.	EXPS. P. M.	STATIONS.	MAIL. P. M.	EXP'S A. M.
LE7 45	5 50	Huntingdon,	AR4 00	AR8 25
7 50	5 55	Long Siding	3 55	8 20
8 10	6 10	McConnelstown	3 45	8 10
8 17	6 20	Pleasant Grove	3 35	8 02
8 30	6 35	MARKLESBURG	3 20	7 45
8 45	6 50	Coffee Run	3 07	7 32
8 55	7 00	Rough & Ready	2 57	7 23
9 05	7 10	Cove	2 47	7 13
9 08	7 13	Fishers Summit	2 45	7 10
9 20	7 28	Saxton	2 27	6 55
9 40	7 50	Riddlesburg	2 10	6 35
9 47	8 00	Hopewell	2 03	6 22
10 02	8 15	Piper's Run	1 47	6 05
10 17	8 32	Tatesville	1 32	5 48
10 30	8 45	Everett	1 20	5 35
10 35	8 50	Mount Dallas	1 15	5 30
11 08	9 20	Bedford	12 44	5 00

SHOUP'S RUN BRANCH.

LE 9 25 LE	Saxton.	AR3 15 AR
9 40	Coalmont.	2 00
9 45	Crawford.	1 55
AR 9 55 AR	Dudley	LE1 45 LE

Bro'd Top City from Dudley 2 miles by stage.

Time of Penna. R. R. Trains at Huntingdon

*.*Mail No. 2 makes connection at Huntingdon with Mail going East on Pennsylvania Railroad at 4.15 p. m., and West at 5.45 p. m. Mail No. 1 leaves Huntingdon at 7.40 a. m. on arrival of Pacific Express West.

Trains on this road connect with trains on Bedford & Bridgeport, and Cumberland & Pennsylvania Railroads.

G. F. GAGE, Supt.

The Weekly Pilgrim.

Published by J. B. Brumbaugh, & Co.

Edited by H. B. & Geo. Brumbaugh.

CORRESPONDING EDITORS.

D. P. Sayler, Double Pipe Creek, Md.

Leonard Furry, New Enterprise, Pa.

The *Pilgrim* is a Christian Periodical, devoted to religion and moral reform. It will advocate in the spirit of *love* and *liberty*, the principles of true Christianity, labor for the promotion of peace among the people of God, for the encouragement of the saints and for the conversion of sinners, avoiding those things which tend toward disunion or sectional feelings.

TERMS.

Single copy, Book paper,	$1.50
Eleven copies, [eleventh for Agt.]	$15.00

Any number above that at the same rate.

Address,

H. B. BRUMBAUGH.
James Creek,
Huntingdon county Pa.

The Weekly Pilgrim.

"REMOVE NOT THE ANCIENT LANDMARKS WHICH OUR FATHERS HAVE SET."

VOL. 4. JAMES CREEK, PENNSYLVANIA, JUNE 10, 1873. NO. 23

POETRY.

STRENGTH IN ADVERSITY.

Pilgrim on life's rugged road,
Toiling, fainting 'neath thy load,
On the Lord ,thy burden roll;
He with strength renews thy soul:
Hath not Jesus said to thee,
"As thy day, thy strength shall be."

In the bitterness of grief,
Though thy prayer find no relief;
Bowed, forsaken, and forlorn,
Though thy sighs prevent the morn,
Tarrying long he comes at length,
To revive thy fainting strength!

Though thy Savior long forbear,
He will hear his people's prayer!
What though he, when sorrowing sought
Make as though he heard thee not?
Watch, and without ceasing pray,
That thy strength be as thy day.

When temptation cometh in,
With a surging flood of sin,
And the burning billows swell
From the lowest depths of hell;
O my Savior! say to me,
"As thy day, thy strength shall be."

Some distrustful of their Lord,
Fear to lean upon his word;
One day, by the hand of Saul,
They are fearful they shall fall!
Still that word is sweet to me,
"As thy day, thy strength shall be."

What though his approach be late?
It is good on God to wait:
He will prove his promise true,
By his gifts, not small, nor few:
His salvation thou shalt see,
"As thy day, thy strength shall be."

When wild winds thy vessel sweep
O'er the dreary boisterous deep,
And thy prostrate strength shall fail
As she drives before the gale,
Then cry mightily and say,
"Let my strength be as my day!"

Dark may be the midnight hour,
With Death's shadow covered o'er;
Yet how drear soe'er the night,
God hath said, "Let there be light!"
Jesus can, if thou wilt pray,
Turn thy darkness into day.

Art thou tempted oft to say,
God with thorns hath hedged my way?
Dost thou sit alone and weep,
Doth thy heart sad vigils keep?
Weeping may endure a night,
Joy shall come with morning light.

As Thy people once were fed
With the heaven-descended bread
Feed me thus in righteousness
In life's howling wilderness;
And, when fainting by the way,
Let my strength be as my day.

O thou comfortless and lost,
In thy Lord and Savior trust!
Lo! the dayspring from on high
Speaks thy great Deliverer nigh!
Leave thy fatherless to me;
"As thy day, thy strength shall be!"

Oh! when Death, with iron blow,
Strikes some dearly loved one low,
Vale of Shadows! though Despair
Walk in awful silence there;
Light in darkness thou may'st see,
"As thy day, thy strength shall be!"

ORIGINAL ESSAYS.

BAPTISM OF JOHN, WHENCE WAS IT, FROM HEAVEN OR OF MEN?

B. F. MOOMAW.

It might probably be expected that we would next notice as an institution conceived and introduced by men without divine authority the order of Odd Fellowship, but as I have not the means at hand of securing a knowledge of the order sufficient to warrant a critical examination of it, and as it is comparatively of little magnitude, simply an outgrowth of Freemasonry, with similar aims and objects, we will therefore class it with other unauthorized inventions of men and pass it by.

In passing along through this promiscuous world and interviewing the various institutions, human and divine, we necessarily meet in social intercourse with Sunday School's. And in prosecution of our undertaking we must inquire "whence is it from God or of men," and associating again in the mind the facts as presented in our investigations. In the first several chapters of this treatise of institutions of universally acknowledged divine authenticity, that the scriptures so fully abounds with commands and exhortations that it leaves no room for a doubt as to whence they come. And in that the subject of this article is so extremely barren, destitute of precept or example in the history of primitive Christianity that I am compelled to doubt whether it is "from Heaven" or that it is divinely approved, neither am I prepared to admit that it can be made to subserve the best interests of vital Christianity. It is true that quotations are made from scripture in support of the institution, but are they, or are they not, susceptible of question, whether they are merely an afterthought to sustain, and not the basis of the organization. Let us notice for a moment the relevancy of these quotations, Eph. 6: 4. contains the language which is invariably used when scriptural authority is demanded. "Fathers provoke not your children to wrath, but bring them up in the nurture and admonition of the Lord." But the reader will please notice that this scripture is a part of the apostles instructions upon family regulations. The duty of children to parents, parents to children, of servants to their masters and masters to and their servants, nothing here, as I opine that would ever have suggested the idea of Sunday Schools. And it is probable that it was the awakening in the mind of this fact, that induced the convention of Episcopal ministers at Pittsburg (the place where Sunday Schools were first established in the United States) to abandon them and throw the responsibility upon parents of bringing up their own children, as noticed in the PILGRIM of recent date. One more passage is sometimes referred to as sustaining Sunday Schools, "And God has set some in the Church first, Apostles; secondarily, Prophets; thirdly, teachers; after that miracles, then gifts of healing, helps, government, diversities of tongues." The application of this passage is that we may employ "helps" as our judgment may suggest and hence the expediency of Sunday Schools. If such latitude is allowable, then the promiscuous singing and praying, the relating thrilling anecdotes, the rubbing the hands, the mourner's bench with all the altar exercises of modern revivals is in place. Surely if the above was designed by God as authority for Sunday Schools, it is a great departure from his usages on other institutions, and the apostles and all Christians were very slow to perceive, in that sixteen centuries were suffered to pass away before the discovery was made.

The origin of Sunday schools is said by some to date back to the reformation to the beginning of the reformation of the sixteenth century. Dr. Sears says, "that as early as 1527, ten years after the commencement of his great work, Luther laid the foundation of these schools, &c." "Eustace in his 'classical tour' speaking of the celebrated Charles Borromeo who died in 1584 says, many of his excellent institutions yet remain and amongothers that of Sunday Schools."

From Frieselanders, State of the poor in Germany, we learn that in 1773, a respectable ecclesiastic named Kindermann formed a Sunday School and that his example was soon followed by others."

In 1767 John Frederick Oberlin, pastor of the Waldbach in the Ban de la Roche, commenced his Sabbath School. Joseph Allien, Miss Hannah Ball and others, came in for their share of the honors of the introduction of Sunday School's. But finally Robert Raikes of Gloucester, England, is by the world regarded as the honor instrument, who stamped perplecity on the system and made it known to the world by publishing it in the *Gloucester Journal* of Nov. 3d, 1783.

The first Sunday School in the United States upon the present plan as said above was established in Pittsburg in Pennsylvania in the year 1809, in 1811 in Delaware and in New York. In 1816 the first Sunday School was organized in Virginia at the Baptist Church, called Ground Squirrel in the following manner, Captain Charles P. G sold at the April muster of a militia company, he formed the men into a hollow square and invited all who were friendly to the cause, to meet him on the next morning, being the Sabbath with their children at the Ground Squirrel Meetinghouse, to organize a Sunday School, free of charge.

The above is the account of the origin of the system and as given by professed Christians, but Robert Owen the infidel, who declares that all religion is founded upon ignorance, and that it is the true source of all the crime and misery existing in the world, contests the claim, and charges the votaries of Christianity with borrowing the idea of infant schools from himself, he having first introduced them at New Lanark, five years before they were introduced elsewhere. But the priesthood, says he, has laid hold of these institutions, and are now moulding the children with them, to their own purposes. Whether Kindermann, Oberlin, Raikes or Owen, is entitled to the honor of the invention, the conclusion is inevitable, that it is of men and not from Heaven and belongs to the same class as Freemasonry, &c. One of the objects as claimed by its friends is to afford an opportunity, and encourage the indigent and neglected children, to learn to read, &c., that they may be able to read the Scriptures. It is certainly important that all should have this benefit, but looking at the subject from a literary standpoint, I regard it as secular in its nature and as such, to attend to it would be a desecration of the Sabbath day. This difficulty appears to have existed in the mind of some in the early days of its existence, to obviate which it is said that a right reverend bishop of that day gravely proposed to remove it, by suggesting that the Sunday Schools should be held on the Saturday afternoon.

Much has been claimed by the advocates of Sunday Schools for the cultivation of morality among the children and youth where they are in progress. On this point I can only say that I have been a close observer of its operations for nearly half a century and have failed to see the beneficial effects in that direction. In my youth I was an attendant at Sunday Schools for a considerable time, and have been surrounded by them all my life, some families patronized them others did not, and I have yet to see any advantage derived to those who attended over those who did not. If any difference the others have it. Our brethren as a class have never had anything to do with them, and I challange investigation to-day, and then if we do not show a better record than others in point of freedom from crime and evidence of high-toned morality, I yield the point.

The above is my experience and observation, and I am not alone on this subject, for I have before me a quotation from an author of the early history of the institution in England, as published in London 1794. He complains that Sunday Schools have existed there for nine years and no single instance of moral improvement has occurred to distinguish any of the Sunday School children from others and that he (the author), and his friends believed that the Sunday School violated the morality of the Sabbath, and the commandments of man are taught in connection with pure Christianity. This sentiment I fully endorse.

As to Sunday Schools being a divine institution I think ought to be fully settled in every intelligent mind, when the principle is applied as presented in the treatise, seeing that what God designed that men should do, he has so forcibly enjoined, and that this as well as all other human institutions is so extremely destitute of any support from the scriptures. And even admitting for the sake of argument, that we are justified in employing it as a help to extend the doctrine of the Bible as understood by the Brethren, it is worthy of serious consideration whether more would not be lost than gained. If we were strong enough to have our own schools in every neighborhood and control them in our own way, we might wield an influence over our own children and as many as would patronize us from other families, but here is the difficulty, and the danger, there are but few localities where this is the case, then what is the alternative? Why we must associate with other denominations, and we must meet them upon equal privileges in the selection of books, and giving instructions, &c., and then what is the consequence? It is that we lose instead of gaining, the children of others will most assuredly not, sacrifice the priviliges of fashion and other indulgences that they are taught to regard as innocent, and conform to the usages of these peculiar people, for so long as they can believe that they can be saved without making these sacrifices they are not going to make them, and this is not all for our own children seeing that we virtually recognize them as acceptable worshippers by uniting with them in devotion, will naturally incline to shun the cross and sympathize with them and their religion more or less. So every time we assimilate with them, the advantage accrues to them in the accession of numbers and our cause suffers loss. This is the inevitable consequence, and we cannot avoid it, and if we adopt the Sunday School system generally, we cannot possibly avoid assimilation more or less, and the final result will be that having employed the Sunday School as a "help," we will have to employ all the helps of corrupted Christianity, inordinate indulgence in the fashions and superfluities, with the mourners bench exercise corrupted to keep up our fraternity in name, and then the principle is lost, we must persevere in our exclusive practices, or abandon our peculiarities there is no alternative that I can see.

The better way as it appears to me is to keep the text constantly before the mind. Is it from heaven or of men seeing that our heavenly Father has in all his acknowledged institutions so faithfully instructed and "called us unto fellowship with his Son Jesus Christ," as in the observance of the Holy Sabbath the passover baptism, the Lord's Supper, feet washing, the holy kiss, to which we may add the doctrine of peace, self-denial, taking up the cross, &c., and forwarned us of the danger of adding to or taking from, or alowing any innovations whatever. Stand still in the way and ask for the old paths and walk therein, and the promise is sure, that we shall find rest unto our souls, oh the glorious prospect the grand consummation.

In victory death is swallowed up,
All danger passed away;
No more to drink of sorrows cup.
We live in endless day.

My head thou wilt annoint with oil,
My cup will overrun;
I'll rest from all my care and toil,
The work assigned is done.

(*Concluded.*)

GOLDEN WEDDING.

It was our happy privilege, recently, to mingle in one of the extraordinary and uncommon scenes of the present day and times; being what is sometimes called a "Golden wedding," but more properly a "Family Reunion," which was celebrated May 22nd 1873 at the house, and in the family of our aged brother and Father-in-law, Samuel Meyers residing 3 miles north of McVeytown, Mifflin county, Pa.: whose family consists of ten children, six sons and four daughters, all of whom are still living and were personally represented with their companions on the above occasion.

The meeting at the old homestead was a scene of much joyful interest and feeling on the part of all. The aged parents who apparently are almost ready to depart this life, and pass over, were once more, on the earth, permitted to take by the hand sons and daughters; from whom they were separated by long distance and time; some residing in Ill., some in Ind., others in Ohio, while the remainder in Pa.

With tears of joy, the aged father and weeping sons and daughters meet, and greet each other with the deeply comprehensive expression, "we are all here yet." It made our heart throb with joyful emotion to hear these loving words fall from aged and trembling lips; expressive of so much gratitude to the great preserver of all things.

The history of the family is as peculiar as the circumstances that brought about the reunion. The father, whose age is nearly 76 years, and the mother 5 years less, were married 50 years 2 months and a few days. The father moved to the valley, or place where he now resides, 3 years before marriage, which took place March 27, 1823. The mothers maiden name was Elizabeth Sholenberger, born and raised in Pfoutzes Valley, Juniata county, Pa. The father was raised in Lost Creek Valley, same county. Moved to Mifflin county in 1820, where they have lived ever since, without any move except from an old log house a few yards away, into the large brick building in which he and his son Reuben F. Meyers now resides; and what is most remarkable there has never a death occurred in the house. Two of the sons are ministers and one a deacon, also two of the sons-in-law are ministers and one a deacon. The remainder of the family are all members of the Church except two sons and one son-in-law. There are 59 grand-children living and but few deaths have occurred; showing a remarkable longevity, and a strong tenacity to life; as a peculiar characteristic of the family.

The order of arrangement for the occasion was excellent, and of a strictly religious character. At about ten o'clock the family and a few guests assembled in the large room, seated and furnished for the occasion. Elder Joseph R. Hanawalt and wife, were seated at the head or first; after him the father and mother, then the children, with their companions according to age, beginning at the eldest, after this the guests which made in all about 30, besides, some of the grandchildren.

The services were then opened by the aged and gray haired father, who rose before his honored family and guests, leaning upon his staff and with trembling emotion delivered a free and complimentary address, followed by reading an appropriate passage from the Bible, and singing of a hymn, which was followed by a season of fervent thanksgiving and prayer, by Elder Hanawalt; after which privilege was given to sons and sons in-law, to address the meeting: James R. Lane, who was the oldest son-in-law spoke first, followed by P. S. Myers and myself, briefly, all of which assumed an air of elegance, and a truly religious character. A deep feeling of gratitude formed the chief element of the whole affair. After the family compliments were all offered, then rose to the floor an old neighbor, Mr. Gabriel Dunmire, who furnished the guests with a historical account of the father's early settlement in the Valley, and many complimentary remarks, which was done with much feeling and respect, who was followed by the old family physician, Dr. Rothrock of McVeytown, who did much credit to himself and the family by his very appropriate remarks and laudible address. Then our much respected Bro. J. R. Hanawalt closed this exercise by a short but touching address to all, in a very becoming and Christian manner. The scene closed by singing and prayer, after which the company of guests were conducted to an adjoining room and seated in order around a table richly ladened with the good gifts of the earth, when all were made happy in the partaking of these refreshments and in pleasant converse with each other. A move was set on motion by Mr. Dunmire and Dr. Rothrock to present the father and mother each with an easy rocking-chair, as a token of the high regard all had for them, which was soon put into effect, and a sufficient amount was raised for that purpose.

The distance of travel, counting for one person, in coming to the place would be about 11272 miles and and whole expense about $240.00. The occasion seemed to be highly appreciated by both of the parents, and afforded a season of refreshing to both of their souls that we hope will be pleasantly remembered while they live, and was a scene of much joy and pleasure to all who participated in it, while we trust that God was honored in all that was said and done.

GEO. BRUMBAUGH.

UNLAWFUL INTERCOURSE.

Ephraim hath mixed himself among the people. Ephraim is a cake not turned. Strangers hath devoured him and he knoweth it not. Moses 7: 8.9.

The tenor of the above charge against Ephraim can hardly be mistaken. It is that strangers hath devoured him and he knoweth it not, that is, by familiarity with strangers to God, he had become initiated into their ways and practices and consequently had brought the displeasure of God upon him, and so interceptibly had this evil crept upon him that he even knew it not. So dangerous a thing is it to have familiarity or unlawful intercourse with strangers to God or enemies to his cause, and yet how common a thing it is in the Old Testament to hear complaints against Israel for their too great familiarities with the heathen, and shall we, who are called Christians, make no difference in the choice of our company or connections between the pious and profane or between the formalist and the real Christian? We find that the primitive Christians did make this distinction and St. Paul asks: "what fellowship hath righteousness with unrighteousness and what communion hath light with darkness and what concord hath Christ with Belial?" Should we not therefore take upon us this part of the cross of Christ in this day of degeneracy, and neither abet nor encourage either by our presence or support, and of the popular and fashionable schemes of religion of the present day lest we thereby treat with too much familiarity or hold an unlawful intercourse with those who, though profess to serve God and say that they are of the circumcision, yet their circumcision has become uncircumcision and they are, in reality, enemies to God and to the cause of his Christ, enemies too, more dangerous to the souls of men than the heathen or infidel, for from the latter we fly as from an adder. Sanctity and bearing the name of Christians, are considered as proper examples to go by and therefore lead others to imitate their conduct, principal trait of which is pride and covetousness. I therefore, consider such professors of Christianity to be equally avoided as a heathen or infidel by those who live in the life and power of religion. "Wherefore come out from among them and be ye separate saith the Lord, and touch not the unclean thing, and I will receive you and will be a father unto you and ye shall be my sons and daughters saith the Lord Almighty.

A PILGRIM.

A WORD TO OUR YOUNG BRETHREN AND SISTERS.

Now these things have I spoken unto you that you should not be offended.—John 16: 1.

These words were spoken by Jesus to His disciples after He had told them that the world would persecute them. He had been warning them of this persecution and telling them that when it came, they should not be offended at Him or His doctrine, and it applies to His followers to-day just as well as it did then. So when the world persecutes and hates us, and makes us the filth thereof, we should not be offended, but take fresh courage and try to live nearer Jesus whom it hated before it did us.

My dear young brethren and sisters, I know some of the trials and persecutions which young Christians have to pass through, but let us ever look to Jesus who is able to keep us from becoming offended at the narrow way which leadeth unto life. Many, in our day, are becoming offended on account of pride and worldly lusts, and leaving the narrow way. But hear the Apostle on the subject; "Love not the world, neither the things in the world, if any man love the world the love of the Father is not in Him." Then how careful we should be that we do not let the vain and transient things of this world occupy our time and talent. So my brethren and sisters, when we go astray from the fold of Christ, and we are admonished by our brethren, let us not become offended, but go to Jesus on our bended knees, in our closets, and ask Him to give us oil in our vessels that our lamps may burn brighter, and that we may be a light to the world. There are a great many temptations and worldly things to draw us from our Savior, but He has conquered all these things before us, and will not suffer us to be tempted above what we are able to bear, if we will go to Him and ask for help, for He is a present help in time of trouble.

BY A SISTER.

A LEAF FROM MY KNOWLEDGE DRAWER.

Christ says; "Do not kill." A Christian will obey Christ, therefore a Christian will not kill.

Jesus says; "If my Kingdom were of this world, then would my servants fight." But his Kingdom is not of this world, hence it follows that his servants will not fight.

If the Old Testament had been written by the Christians, it would not have been acknowledged and received by the Jews. But the Jews do acknowledge and receive it, therefore it was not written by the Christians.

The Old Testament was first written in the Hebrew language, and afterwards translated into the Greek about 300 years before the birth of Christ.

The backward action in baptism was invented about 1480 years after the death of Christ.

No two truths ever contradict each other. The Bible is truth, whatever contradicts the Bible is not truth.

Christ told his disciples that they ought to wash one anothers feet. The disciples did what they ought to do, therefore they washed one anothers feet.

The apostles practiced christian baptism in their day, but single immersion was not invented till long after the death of the apostles. Therefore single immersion is not christian baptism.—*J. H. Moore.*

PUTTING OUT A PIPE.

The late Rev. Thomas Collins was a model tract-distributor, being instant in season and out of season. He often traveled in smoking-cars, in order to have a wider field for doing good. In his interesting memoir recently published, are recorded some incidents of one of his journeys.

"In the train I presented a New Testament to a soldier; he received it gladly, and I was pleased to see that he caught the meaning at once when I called it a "sword."

"A cooper got in at an early station, and, without an apology, lighted his pipe. After a little introductory talk, I submitted for his consideration whether the cost of that cloudy gratification would not send a child to school; and whether that would not be a better outlay as it would confer a benefit that would last forever?"

"He said:—'I never thought of that, but is true. So out goes the pipe, and here's for the child.'

"Do you mean so? Will you give up the practice?"

"'T be sure I will, and send the young un to school.'

"I am so glad to have put your pipe out. Will you oblige me by the gift of the cast-off thing?"

"'Certainly sir, here it is.' So with joy I brought the trophy home."

Reader, are you a tobacco user? If so, would not the money you spend on cigars and tobacco go a great way toward increasing the comfort of your family? Will you not "put your pipe out" for their sake?

HE that makes but one step up stairs though he is much nearer to the top of the house, yet has stepped from the ground, and is delivered from the foulness of that. So in the first step of prayer: "God be merciful to me a sinner."

FORBEARANCE is a domestic jewel.

WORKING FOR OTHERS.

That men and women are not placed in the world for their own welfare or their own interest alone, is a fact which we are prone to overlook. We should work, not only for ourselves, but for others also. Everybody should work. Do we know for what great work we are placed in the world? Is it not to prepare ourselves for a state of immortality? Yes, this is the work that is required of us, and this is the work in which we should assist each other. Do not construe this language in such a manner as to make me say that we are not required to labor for the sustenance of the body for without this we could not labor for the salvation of the soul. I simply mean, that if the support of this tenement of clay would be the only work which we have to perform, our existence would be a blank of no importance whatever. Indeed, I doubt very much whether we would have any existence at all. The salvation of the soul, then, is our life work. Have you ever thought of this, my young friends? If you have not, will you please think of it now? Will you not be so kind to yourself as to not only think, but also act upon it now? Will you now, while you are yet living, act upon it yourself and strive to get others to do the same, that it may be said of you, when you are gone, that you did not live for yourself alone but that you assisted others in starting toward the bright home of Saints?

Do you not feel that if you take this course in life, your prospect in the end will be cheering, and that the otherwise dark cloud of futurity will beam radiant light? Ah, yes, and then those dear friends whom you leave behind will not mourn as they would for those for whom there is no hope, but would be animated and cheered with the thought that you have gone to a better world and that by being good and faithful in the cause of their Savior they may join their loved ones in the eternal regions of glory. Let each one, then, instead of working against others by evil speaking, work for others by giving words of comfort and consolation, always exhorting to a life of holiness. It is true that our life may be blotted over with many errors, but when we know this we should remember that "to err is human, but to love divine." Then let the divine institution of love reign in every breast, and then this earth will become more like Heaven, thus bringing about, to a certain extent, an answer to the beautiful petition, "Thy will be done on earth as it is in Heaven. Then, let every reader of the PILGRIM labor for this end in order that the world may become both wiser and better, and we may see the beautiful approaching of God's kingdom, for which the earnest appeal of God's holy people is daily ascending, as it were, upon a spiritual telegraph wire, to the regions of bliss.

MOLLIE E. UMBAUGH.
Collamer, Ind.

ASK thy purse what thou shalt buy.

THE CONSOLATION OF ISRAEL.

"Waiting for the consolation of Israel." Luke—2: 25.

Several glorious titles of Christ have been considered, out of each of which much comfort flows to believers. It is comfortable to a wounded soul to regard him as a physician; comfortable to a condemned and unworthy soul to look upon him under the idea of mercy. The loveliness, the desirableness and the glory of Christ are all so many springs of consolation. In the context you have an account of Simeon's prophecy concerning Christ, and in the text a description of the person and character of Simeon himself, he was a just and devout man; and "he waited for the consolation of Israel." That the consolation of Israel is a phrase descriptive of Jesus Christ is beyond all doubt, if you consult verse 26, where Simeon is satisfied by receiving Christ into his arms, the consolation for which he had so long waited for, as all the believers of the the times which preceded the incarnation of Christ waited for that blessed day. Simeon and others that waited with him were sensible that the time of the promise was come, which could not but raise a general expectation of him, but Simeon's faith was confirmed by a particular revelation, ver. 26, that he should see Christ before he saw death, which could not but greatly raise his expectations to look out for him, whose coming would be the greatest consolation to the whole Israel of God.

Jesus Christ is the only consolation of believers, and none besides them, so speaks the apostles; "for we are the circumcision, which worship God in the spirit, and rejoice in Christ Jesus and have no confidence in the flesh." Phil. 3: 3. Those that worship God in the spirit are sincere believers; to such sincere believers Christ is consolation. "Our rejoicing is in Christ Jesus," and they have no consolation in anything besides him; nothing in the world can give them comfort without Christ. The Gospel is good tidings of great joy, but that which makes it to be so is Jesus Christ, whom it reveals to us. Several things here require attention. What is meant by consolations that Christ, and he only is consolation to believers? 1st, Jesus Christ brings whatsoever is precious to the souls of believers. Is pardon desired by a person condemned? This Christ brings to all believers, "and this is his name whereby he shall be called, the Lord our righteousness." Jer.—23: 6. This cannot but give strong consolation; righteousness is the foundation of peace and joy in the Holy Ghost. Rom. 14: 17. "The work of righteousness shall be peace, and the effect of righteousness, quietness and assurance forever," Isa. 32: 17. Come to a dejected soul laboring under the burden of guilt, and say, cheer up; I bring you good tidings, such an estate has fallen to you, or such a trouble is ended. Alas, this will not reach the heart, if you can bring me, says he, good news from heaven that my sins are forgiven and God is reconciled how soon should I be comforted! And therefore, as one well observes, this was the usual receipt with which Christ cured the souls of men and women when he was here on earth. Son, daughter, "be of good cheer thy sins are forgiven thee." Are the hopes and expectations of heaven and glory cheering? Yes, nothing is if this be not, we "rejoice in hope of the glory of God." Rom. 5: 2 Christ brings to the souls of men all the solid grounds and foundations upon which they build their expectations of glory. "Christ in you the hope of glory." Col.—1: 27. 2nd. Jesus Christ removes from believers whatever is uncomfortable, therein relieving them against all their affliction and sorrow. Is sin a burden and trouble to believers? Christ, and none but him, removes that burden. "O wretched man that I am, who shall deliver me from the body of this death; I thank God through Jesus Christ our Lord." Rom.—7: 24, 25. The satisfaction of his blood, Eph. 5: 2. The sanctification of his spirit, 1 John 5: 6, his perfect deliverance of his people from the very being of sin at last. Eph. 5: 26, 27. This relieves at present and removes finally the matter and ground of all their troubles and sorrows for sin. Do the temptations of satan burden believers? Temptation is an enemy under the walls, it greatly endangers and therefore cannot but greatly afflict the souls of believers, but Christ brings the only relief against temptations. The intercession of Christ is a singular relief at present. "But I have prayed for thee that they faith fail not." Luke 22: 32, and the promises of Christ are a full relief for the future. "The God of peace shall bruise satan under your feet shortly." Rom. 16: 20. Is spiritual desertion and the hiding of God's face the ground of affliction and distress to believers? "Thou didst hide thy face, and I was troubled." Psa. 30: 7. Christ brings to believers substantial consolation against the troubles of desertion, he himself was deserted of God for a time, that they might not be deserted forever in him also the promises are made to believers, that notwithstanding God may desert them for a time, yet the union between him and them shall not be dissolved. Heb 3: 5; Jer. 32: 40. Though he forsake them for a season in respect to the manifestation of his favor, yet he will return again and comfort them. Isa. 54: 7. Though satan pull hard yet he will never be able to pluck them out of his father's hand. John 10: 28, 29. Are outward afflictions the ground of dejection and trouble? How do our hearts fail and our spirits sink under the many smarting rods of God upon us, but our relief and consolation under them all is in Christ; for the rod that afflicts us is in the hand of Christ that loveth us. As many as I love I rebuke and chasten. Rev. 3: 19, his design in affliction is our profit. Heb. 12: 10. That design of his for our good being accomplished. Rom. 8: 28, and after that no more afflictions for ever. "God shall wipe away all tears from their eyes." Rev. 21: 4.

MYSTERY OF GRACE.

KNOW WHAT YOU TEACH.

The great want of the ministry is deeper Christian experience. You may feel the need of more enlarged study. You may be conscious that wider reading, and travel and experience would enable you to light up your sermons with apter illustrations. But there is no lack by which you will feel so crippled as by the conviction that you do not yourself know what you desire to teach others. A pastor said to his people, in a discourse on the Sabbath after his installation, "I shal point you higher than I have been myself." Point them! Yes; but your flock will not go for your "pointing them;" they must be led. The "shepherd goeth before them and leadeth them out." You can not make a sinner feel that the most momentous thing conceivable is for him to save his soul, unless your own heart has been penetrated with the awful realities of the future world. You can say nothing of redeeming love that will melt them, unless your own heart has first been melted. In the drama of common life it may be possible to "assume a virtue though you have it not;" but in winning souls you cannot buy with counterfeit coin. Your power will depend upon your speaking things which your own eyes have seen, and your own heart has felt. This is all I really cared to say, because I so deeply feel that here is the secret of the Lord, here is the hiding of power.

But on this point, brother beloved, I charge you with all my soul:—Sit at Jesus' feet for your sermons. Do not stand on the outside of truth and try to look in; but get inside the truth and try to look outward. Your ministry will hang on you like a leaden weight if your own experience of the truth does not lay upon you a sweet necessity to preach to others. But you will wear it as a garment of joy when you can say, "The love of Christ constraineth me." The Master knew that human resources are futile for this work, and so he said to his disciples, "Tarry ye at Jerusalem until ye be endued with power from on high." There are many qualifications which you are very earnestly and laboriously to seek in order to be a good minister of Jesus Christ; but the one thing you can not do without is the endowment of the Holy Spirit.

"If thy presence go not with me," said Moses, "carry me not hence." And he said, "My presence shall go with thee, and I will give thee rest." —*Advance.*

Youth's Department

Selected by Cora Brumbaugh.

LITTLE MARY'S WISH.

"I have seen the first robin of spring, mother dear,
And have heard the brown darling sing;
You said, "Hear it and wish, and I'will surely come true;"
So I've wished such a beautiful thing!

I thought I would like to ask something for *you*;
But I couldn't think what there could be
That you'd want while you had all these beautiful things;
Besides you have papa and me!

So I wished for a ladder; so long, that 'twould stand
One end by our own cottage door,
And the other go up past the moon and the stars,
And lean against Heaven's white floor.

Then I'd get out to put on my pretty white dress,
With my sash and my darling new shoes,
And I'd find some white roses to take up to God—
The most beautiful ones I could choose.

And you and dear papa would sit on the ground
And kiss me, and tell me 'Good by;'
Then I'd go up the lader far out of your sight,
Till I came to the door in the sky!

I wonder if God keeps the door fastened 'Tight?
But if *one* little crack I could see,
I would whisper, 'Please, God, let this little girl in;
She's as tired as she can be!

She came all alone from the earth to the sky,
For she's always been wanting to see
The gardens of Heaven with their robins and flowers,
Please, God, is there room for me?

And then, when the angels had opened the door,
God would say, 'Bring the little child here;'
But he'd speak it so softly I'd not be afraid,
And he'd smile just like you, mother dear!

He would put his kind arms round you dear little girl,
And I'd ask him to send down for you,
And papa, and cousin, and all that I love—
O dear! don't you wish 'twould come true!"

The next spring time, when the robins came home
They sang over grass and flowers
That grew where the foot of the ladder stood,
Whose top reached the heavenly bowers.

And the parents had dressed the pale still child
For her flight to the summer land,
In a fair white robe with one snow white rose
Folded tight in her pulseless hand

And now at the foot of the ladder they sit,
Looking upward with quiet tears,
Till the beckoning hand and the fluttering robe
Of the child at the top appears.

JEM'S ANGEL.

Jem was cold and hungry and miserable. It had rained all night, and toward morning a sharp north-east wind began to blow, freezing the rain as it fell. Jem's bed was a pretty hard one—a pile of straw partially held in place by what had once been some lengths of blue jean, and covered by the remnants of an old calico quilt. Once Jem had thought himself quite well off, but then that was when Bob was alive. Old Lottie, who was a kind soul if she did get drunk, pitied the poor homeless boys and gave them the privilege of sleeping in her garret at three cents a night. In the morning they went out often without breakfast, to do anything they could find to do—run of errands, sweep crossings, hold a gentleman's horse for a minute, anything that was not begging.

Bob had splendid dreams of some day becoming a newsboy. The time was always coming—alas, it never came!—when such an amount of surplus funds would be left over after the days expenses, that Bob would enter at once upon his career, and then good-bye to hunger and cold and the ills of life. It would take but a few days for Bob to make profits enough to set Jem up in trade too, and then wouldn't they lead a jolly life? Bob's imagination even saw a little cottage in the country and old Lottie in it, cured of her love of strong drink, and peace and plenty everywhere. Jem believed in Bob devoutly. It never occurred to him that such glorious plans *could* fail. Bob had always taken care of him, and always would, of course. He was so much bigger and stronger and then he was so cheery. There was never a time so dark that he couldn't see something bright just ahead.

Poor Jem! all that light was gone now. Bob was very tired one night, and the next morning he didn't even know Jem, but kept talking about the green fields, though it was in the depth of winter, and the little baby sister who died before Jem could remember. Old Lottie didn't go out that day; she had a few pennies in her pocket, and she did all she could for the dying boy, but it was no use. He smiled once before he died, on the wretched little boy at his side, sobbing with cold and terror, and said, "Cheer up, Jem; it'll all come right."

The overseers of the poor took Bob away and Jem was left cold and hungry and miserable.

The sun shone out from a wintry sky that morning after the cold rain. Jem went out. He didn't know where he was going and he didn't care. He just wanted to be where Bob was. Bob was his heaven. He wandered on. Once he stopped and looked wistfully at a stall; there was hot coffee and rolls and great slices of bread, but he didn't say anything. The man at the stall saw him. "Poor little chap," said he, and threw him a thick slice of rye bread. He felt better after that, still he couldn't see how it was to come right, as Bob had said; but then Bob always knew.

He had got a long way from the garret by this time, but he was very cold. Two little boys, warmly clad ran a long ahead of him. One said, "I'm 'fraid we're late," and then they turned in at a church door. As they disappeared the chorus, "Yes, Jesus loves me," came ringing out. Jem stood looking in, and wondering what it meant. The singing went on, and then a sudden longing filled his aching heart to learn *who* it was that loved the little boys and girls in there so much. He pushed the door open and entered. A great stove, bright and glowing stood right by the door; he slipped behind it and no one saw him. Pretty soon they sang again. This time it was, "I am so glad that Jesus loves me." Jem was in a maze of wonder and delight. It was all beginning to come right; he knew it would but he didn't expect it so soon. Finally the warmth stole into him and he slept.

When he woke a gentleman was talking. Jem rose to his feet and listened. A great card was hanging where all could see it, and though Jem could not read, he knew that the gentleman was talking about the words on the card: "He shall give his angels charge over thee." Jem didn't know what that meant, but he listened, and the gentleman spoke very simply. "Is there anything in all the world to be afraid of, dear children? Why, think! God gives an angel—a great, strong, powerful angel—the charge of you, that means the care of you. He sees that you are not able to take care of yourselves, and so he giveth each one of you an angel to go with you and take care of you. He is with you every day, and at night, when you lie down to sleep, your angel watches over you, and keeps you from harm." Jem heard with his heart in his throat. Why, this was just what he wanted, now that Bob was gone. He didn't know who God was, or what an angel might be, but felt pretty sure by this time that Jesus of whom they sang, and the good God who sent the angel, and even the angel himself, were all one and the same good being who took care of everybody in the world, and so would take care of him. Bob must have known all about it, and that was why he said it would all come right.

They sang again, and then the children went away. Jem wanted to make quite sure. He must ask the kind gentleman about it, so as to know where to find God. Nearly all had gone before the gentleman came. He saw the eager face of the ragged boy before he reached him, and stopped.

"Please, tell me," began Jem, "where is the man what takes care of little boys as hasn't got any Bob."

"It is the good God, who takes care of everybody, my poor boy," said the gentleman kindly. "But what has become of Bob?"

"I do' no; they took him off an' put him in the ground; he said it 'ud all come right, but I was 'fraid till you said as how God 'ud send an angel; say, mister, be you an angel?"

"No, my boy," said the gentleman in a husky voice, "I am not an angel, but perhaps God has sent me to you for all that. He takes care of you all the time, and it is he who sent you here to-day."

"Yes, I guess he did. I was so cold an' hungry, an' I didn't know what to do, 'cause Bob's gone and wont never come back. But I ain't 'fraid now. I'll go home an' tell old Lottie. God'll send a angel to go long with me, an' it'll all come right. Bob said so. Thank you, sir, for tellin' me 'bout it."

The brave little fellow started to go out, but Mr. Brown stopped him to learn where he lived, and the next day sought out the child who had taught him such a lesson of trust. Old Lottie wasn't drunk, and told him how friendless the poor lad was; how his father died of hard drink, and his mother a gentle lady, struggled a little and then died, leaving her boys too young to know the name of mother. Mr. Brown's eyes grew moist as she told of Bob's devotion to his little Jem, and when she ended, he took the child by the hand and went out.

Jem never forgot, in the happy, prosperous days that followed, the lesson of trust he learned that morning in the care of the dear Father, and Mr. Brown's faith is strengthened every day by his simple assurance that every thing will somehow and some time "come right."

WHAT AILED OLIVER.

"Get up little boy. You are lying in bed too long; breakfast will soon be ready. The canary bird has taken his bath, and is now singing a sweet song. Get up, get up, or I shall throw this pillow at you!"

That is what sister Charlotte said to Oliver Reed one frosty morning in November. He was a good little fellow; but he had one fault—he was too fond of lying in bed in the morning.

"Don't throw the pillow at me!" cried Oliver; "I'll promise to get up in five minutes."

"If you would be 'healthy, wealthy, and wise,' you must rise early, little boy," said Charlotte.

When Oliver came down to the breakfast table, his father said, "How is this, Oliver? You are late again."

Oliver hung his head; and Charlotte said, "I woke him in good season, sir; but he went off to sleep again the minute I left the room, though he promised to be up in five minutes."

"I went to sleep and forgot all about it," said Oliver.

"Come here, my boy, and let me feel your pulse," said his father. "I should not wonder if Oliver were suffering from a disease which is very common at this time."

Oliver gave his hand to his father, who, after feeling his pulse, said: "Yes, it is as I thought. Poor Oliver has Slack's disease. Take him up to bed again. Put his breakfast by the side of his bed; and when he feels strong enough he can eat it. He may stay at home from school to-day."

The little boy wondered what Slack's disease could be; but he went up stairs with his sister, and he was put to bed. He could not sleep, however. He heard children playing out of doors; he heard Ponto barking and Tommy, the canary bird, sing a sweet song.

Then Oliver called his sister, and said; "Charlotte, what is Slack's disease? Is it very dangerous?"

"I rather think not," said Charlotte. "You dear little simpleton, don't you know what father meant? He meant you were troubled with laziness; that's all."

Oliver saw that a trick had been played on him. He jumped out of bed, dressed, and ate his breakfast, and ran off to school, where he arrived just in season.

Since that day, Oliver has been the first one up in the house. He is no longer troubled with Slack's disease.—*Nursery.*

THE PRECIOUS LITTLE PLANT.

Two little girls, Bridget and Walburgia, went to the neighboring town, each carrying on their head a basket of fruit to sell for money enough to buy the family dinner. Bridget murmured and fretted all the way, but Walburgia only joked and laughed. At last Bridget got out of all patience and said vexedly:

"How can you go on laughing so? Your basket is as heavy as mine, and you are not a bit stronger. I don't understand it."

"Oh, it is easy enough to understand," replied Walburgia.

"How so?"

"I have a certain plant that I put on the top of my load and it makes it so light that I can hardly feel it. Why don't you do so too?"

"Indeed! it must be a very precious little plant. I wish I could lighten my load with it. Where does it grow? tell me. What do you call it?"

"It grows wherever you plant it, and give it a chance to take root, and there is no telling the relief it gives. Its name is patience!"—*H*[illegible]

Men do less than they ought, unless they do all they can.

Censure is the tax men pay to the public for being eminent.

Correspondence.

A Reporter is wanted from every Church in the brotherhood to send us Church news, Obituaries, Announcements, or anything that will be of general interest. To insure insertion, the writers name must accompany each communication. Our Invitation is not personal but general—please respond to our call

SHIPPENSBURG PA., May 30 '73.

Dear Pilgrim:—On last Saturday eve., I had the pleasure of being with brother John Stamy and his kind family. Our acquaintance was an agreeable one, and our first visit, one that will be remembered with pleasure.

On Sabbath morning I accompanied him to church at Milltown, some eight miles distant. The meeting was largely attended. Sermon by brother Stamy, followed by brother Keller, subject, baptism. Two souls were added to the fold. At this place a Discussion was held some years ago between the Brethren and Campbellites. The discussion did not result in a general change of sentiment, yet our Brethren lost nothing, while several of the Campbellites have since united with the Brethren

On Wednesday last, (May 28.) the brethren met at the Foglesanger M. H to hold their Lovefeast. Brethren Keller, Hollinger, Stouffer, Stamy, and an other brother whose name I cannot recall, was the ministerial force from abroad. The meeting was well attended, and an interest manifested. The order during the evening exercises was good, although the house was crowded and uncomfortably warm. The next morning Bro. Stouffer discoursed from the words, "Our Father who art in Heaven," followed by brethren Keller and Stamy. The meeting was a good one, and we have it to say, it was good to be there.

Since here at school, I have formed the acquaintance of most of the brethren of this little congregation and can truly say, I feel at home among them. Bro. Eckerman is the Elder, assisted by brethren John and D. M. Foglesanger and —— Mahn. Through the kindness of the brethren here I get to church nearly every Sabbath, and in this respect I am much better suited at this school than I could be at some others. I am still having some hopes, however, that some plan may be devised by which a Brethren's school may be started in the East. A school of this kind would suit me and all of our brethren and sisters much better. I hope that our brethren may keep thinking about this matter. Things that go into effect so hastily, sometimes do not terminate so well, so let us keep thinking, and when the time comes that we *can* do something, we will be the better prepared for the work. The only obstacle in the way *now*, is a lack of funds, and when I look at the wealth in the Church, it does not seem that that ought to be in the way. But perhaps I cannot see, I only hope it is not the *love* of money that is in the way.

J. B. B.

MEXICO, IND., May 25th, 1873.

Dear Pilgrim:—By your permission I will try and make you somewhat acquainted with this part of the Brotherhood, generally known as the Mexico Church, Ind. The Church has seven ministers, two of which are Elders, about ten Deacons and about 365 members in all. They have a large brick Church house near Mexico, one Church house near Walleytown, and are building a third house not far from Chili.

The church is in a prosperous condition, although the accessions are not so numerous as in some of the churches I see represented in the PILGRIM, owing probably to the cause that the brethren do not indulge in any series of meetings, no more than their regular meetings. They do not seem to think much of what they call protracted meetings, and probably fear to indulge such would be drifting too far from shore, but the apostle saith, "forsake not the assembling of yourselves together as the manner of some is." He does not say regular or call meetings and for our part we do not see but it would be right, and have a tendency to good to have, say a few days meetings for the awakening of those that are slumbering in their sins, and for the encouragement of those that are already traveling on the narrow way.

We, of course, when we sow do not expect for all the seed to mature, as we find some fell on stony ground and sprung up but for the want of depth of earth it withered away. Maybe if such were cultivated and watered with a few extra showers from the pure fountain and told of the "hope which is laid up in heaven for them whereof they have heard before in the word of truth of the Gospel," Col. 1: 5. "They might become *rooted* and built up in Christ and established in the faith," "and awake to everlasting life."

As I have so far deviated from the subject I will not return again, but say, finally brethren whatsoever things are true, whatsoever things are honest, whatsoever things are just, whatsoever things are pure, whatsoever things are lovely, whatsoever things are of good report, if there be any virtue, and if there be any praise, think over these things. Phil. 2: 8. Those thing which ye have both learned, and received, and heard, do; and the God of peace be with you all. 4: 9.

Think the PILGRIM ought to be in every house of both saint and sinner. Take it brethren for yourselves and children to read.

J. B. LAIR.

A MISSION.

Ministerial labor for Bristolville, Trumble Co., Ohio, as agreed upon at the North Eastern District council of Ohio.

All congregations from which ministers go should pay their expenses to Warren and home again, and the brethren of Bristol to pay from Warren to Bristol and return to Warren. Bro. David Byers says he will make all failures right in defraying expenses.

ARRANGEMENT.

Lewis Glass,	May 25.
George Irvin	June 22.
George Worst	July 20.
Josiah Keim	Aug. 17.
P. J. Brown	Sept. 14.
A. M. Dickey or Sadler,	Oct. 12.
J. B. Shoemaker	Nov. 9.
Joseph Bollinger	Dec. 7.
David M. Witmer	Jan. 4.
Mich'l Shrantz or J Mohler	Feb 1.
David Byers	March 1.
———	April—
———	May—

The above is the best that could be arrived at and brother Worst's name was used without his consent, and if not satisfactory, please inform Bro D. Byers in time. We had not enough to fill two appointments.

All of the above appointments have three meetings, by going the day before. For any information wanted previous to going, please address John Strow, Bristolville, Trumble Co., Ohio.

WM. SADLER.

Raleigh Church District, W. Va. We the Brethren met in church council, in May 1873, and considering the necessity of having a meeting house to worship in, it was resolved that we will build one, though we feel our inability within ourselves to do so. It was also resolved that we petition the Brotherhood generally for help and would thankfully receive aid from any arm of the Church. Any person aiding us, can do so by registered letter, bank draft or express, directed to Wm. H. Baily or C. P. Spangler, Raleigh C. H., W. Va. By order of the Church.

Asa Spangler, C. S.
Wm H. Bailey, S. C.
C. P. Spangler.
John W. Gray.
Peter Snuffer.

ANNOUNCEMENTS.

Please announce that we, the brethren and sisters of the Desmoines Valley Church, expect, the Lord willing, to hold our Lovefeast on the 28th and 29th days of June, 1873, at Elkhart, Polk Co., Iowa, about 16 miles northeast of Demoines City. The general invitation is given, and especially to the ministering brethren to be with us.

S. M. GOUGHNOUR.

Please announce that our Communion will be held in our Meeting house in the Spring Creek Congregation, 14 miles S. E. of Warsaw, on the 20th. day of June next. All are invited.

DANIEL MILLER.

Pierceton, Ind.

Eds. Pilgrim:—Please announce Communion Meetings which were arranged at the District Meeting of North-eastern Il., and to all of which meetings we are requested to invite our beloved brethren and sisters and especially the ministering brethren. They are as follows:

Arrangements will be made to con

The Weekly Pilgrim.

JAMES CREEK, PA., June 10, 1873.

☞ How to send money.—All sums over $1.00, should be sent either in a check, draft or postal order. If neither of these can be obtained, have the letter registered.

☞ When Money is sent, *always* send with it the name and address of those who paid it. Write the names and post office as plainly as possible.

☞ Every subscriber for 1873, gets a *Pilgrim Almanac* Free.

OUR ANNUAL CONFERENCE.

We have now returned from our Conference, and no doubt our patrons who had not the pleasure of being there will be anxious to hear something about it, and we are glad that we can inform our readers that we are prepared to meet their reasonable expectations. In this No. we will not give the deliberations of the Conference but simply the outside and preparatory part of it, and even in this, we feel to be as brief as possible. Our Conference is getting to be entirely too big a thing, attended with more labor and cost than what is justified by the ends accomplished, and if we continue to encourage its growing prominence as a place for a grand social and brotherly association of our brethren and sisters, its original design and true character may be measureably lost. This meeting, as now held, seems to have a double character. First the "Brethren's Association" and second, the "Brethren's Council." The characteristics of both of these may be very good and conducive to the growth and prosperity of the Church, but whether the two should be combined and both be held at the same time and place, might be another question—and in fact is now a subject of serious thought in the minds of many of our brethren. That there should be but one leading object or design in our Annual Conference is evident to every thinking mind, but when we go to these meetings and there see the thousands of anxious brethren and sisters present to hear the proceedings of this body, it is against the characteristics of our religion to deny them of this privilege. Therefore it behooves us to get into some plan by which the information there obtained, can be had at home. This can only be done by giving a fair and correct report of their business transactions through our periodicals. This has now been granted with a, perhaps, necessary restriction and we are now prepared to give a report from which as much satisfaction of the proceedings of the meeting can be learned by reading it as was obtained by those who were present.

On Monday morning (June 2.) we with a number of others took the train at our station, where we met a pretty fair delegation from the Eastern Churches, but not as large as we expected on account of a large number having gone up on Friday and Saturday previous. Our company was enlarged at almost every station, so that by the time we reached Bridgeport we numbered about 300. At this place we were necessitated to lay over some four hours with no very desirable accommodations. After being there a short time and learning fully our situation, it was moved that some religious services be held, there being a number of ministers present. The move was favorably received and we soon found a suitable, shady location where there was a temporary stand made, using logs and rocks for seats, which by the way seem to be one of the characteristics of the place.

Bro. D. Keller opened the exercises by lining a hymn, some appropriate remarks and prayer. The exercises were continued by John Gotwals, L. F. Good, J. R. Lane, George Brumbaugh and others. The time, though of a considerable length, was pleasantly and we trust profitably spent. Bridgeport is the present terminus of our line of road and also a point on the Connellsville road. At the regular time the train from the South came along when we all got aboard for Dale City. The train was already pretty well filled and by the addition of our company it was slightly overloaded and in consequence, had a very slow ride. The road from this point to Dale City passes through an extremely rugged country, but the scenery is grand and makes the trip extremely interesting to educated and nature appreciating minds. After a pleasant ride we came to Dale City, the place of our destination. Here we were met by brother Shoemaker and taken to his home where we were well cared for during the meeting. The attendance of this Conference was larger than the two previous years but not as large as on some former occasions. The accommodations were very good and all were entertained as well as could be reasonably expected under the circumstances. The Conference was held in a large barn which is now vacated on account of being within the borough limits. It was well seated and accommodated a large number of people. The eating tent was made of boards, 160x40 feet and seated 750 persons at a time and generally took from three to four tables to accommodate the multitude.

The eating arrangement was especially good, from the fact that they had the right man in the right place. The provisions were in abundance and a surplus of several thousand loaves, so that all were cared for and none turned away empty.

The facilities for having the word preached, was also good, and a large number of sermons delivered during the meeting in the town and surrounding vicinity, which we hope may have a christianizing effect upon the community.

The Conference deliberations were very similar to that of former occasions, and the queries generally were such as had been discussed in former meetings. Some of those who made themselves prominent as speakers became unduly boisterous at times, but on the whole, it was about as good as could be expected especially while we have among us those who have not yet learned that the greatest victory we can achieve is to conquer ourselves. But notwithstanding our seeming difficulties, the meeting was a good one and hope it may have a salutary effect upon the general brotherhood. The meeting and being together of the brethren and sisters was the most congenial feature of the conference and was beautifully expressed by the clerk of the meeting, in the closing remarks of which we have a full report and will be published in the close of the proceedings of the meeting.

During the meeting, we had the pleasure of meeting and forming the acquaintance of many of our patrons and friends and on account of our time being largely taken up in a business relation we could not give our friends that attention that we would have been pleased to do under more favorable circumstances, but for this, we hope all will make due allowance and feel assured that all favors are highly and duly appreciated.

On Thursday A. M., the business part of the meeting closed and our labors ceased. The afternoon we spent pleasantly in taking a view of the town and making a few calls. Friday morning we took the train homeward bound, with a number of others, and after a pleasant ride landed safely home where we found our work about three days behind time. This we will either make up, or lose to run it in at the close of the year. Hoping that all our dear brethren and sisters have safely reached the place of destination and have been greatly benefitted by what they saw and heard we close for the present, expecting, the Lord willing, next week to commence a full report of the proceedings of the Conference.

CONFERENCE REPORT.

For a number of years our brethren and sisters have been calling for a full and correct report of the proceedings of our Annual Conference. Heretofore, this could not be had, but to this meeting we took with us a competent short hand reporter with the determination to give our readers just as much of the proceedings as would be allowed. The subject was before the meeting and the report was granted with a restriction which will be noticed hereafter. We have now a full and correct report of the meeting, including the opening address of the Moderator with all the discussions and the concluding remarks of the Clerk, so that those who remained at home can have as complete a knowledge of the business part of the meeting as those who were present. This cost us money and we hope to be remunerated, in part, by our agents and friends making a determined effort to increase our circulation. 100 or 500 names can be had if our friends will go to work at once. The report will commence next week and be continued until published. The PILGRIM will be sent from No. 21 (or next week) to the end of the year on the following terms. Single copy 80 cents. 5 copies 3.75, 10 copies, 7.00, 15 copies, 10,50 and 20 copies 11.25. Now brethren and sisters, think of it. Many of you have spent, twenty, thirty and some fifty dollars to have the benefits of this meeting. We offer to give nearly or quite the same information for 80 cents. There is scarcely a member in the whole Brotherhood but what would take the PILGRIM the remainder of the year if they were informed of this report. We have now 500 single subscribers. One half of these can send us one name at 80 cts. if they will try. Please try. How many clubs of ten, fifteen and twenty can we have? Go to work at once and let us see what can be done when there is a determined effort made. Those that have not got the money now, we will wait them until after harvest or during the year. In making this offer, we want our agents to take only such as they would not be afraid to trust themselves. As an extra inducement we will send each subscriber, a PILGRIM Almanac FREE as long as we can supply them. We will issue a large extra edition commencing with the "Report" so that all new subscribers can have the proceedings complete. Remember, this report will give all the queries, their discussions and answers. Everybody that has any interest in the proceedings of our A. M. will want to read this report. Give them an opportunity by asking them to subscribe for the PILGRIM. We can still supply some twenty volumes complete at 1.50.

PILGRIM ALMANAC FOR 1874.

All those who have any corrections to make in our ministerial list should do so at once or as soon as possible. Please examine it and wherever you see a mistake, correct it and send it to us. Also give us the names and address of those which were not in last year and those that have been elected within the past year. We also wish reading matter for its columns. All those who wish to assist us will please do so as soon as possible.

MONEY LIST.

Joseph Utz	$4.70	Jno Showalter	3.00
J W Fitzgerald	6.00	Jno A Sell	2.00
H Tallem	3.00	A S Snyder	80
Addison Baker	8.50	Susan Koontz	80
George Wolf	6.00	Josiah Keim	80
Ed. Raile	2.50	D C Moomaw	2.00
J B Lahr	1.00	Sam Chambers	75
J S Becke[illegible]	1.15	B F Moomaw	5.0

AIR-BRAKE.—The Franklin Institute committee of science witnessed a series of experiments with the Westinghouse air-brake, on the train on the Pennsylvania railroad this afternoon, (the 20th) operated from the engine. A train going at the rate of thirty miles an hour was stoped in sixteen seconds, moving 503 feet after the brake was applied. Operated from the center car, it was stopped in fifteen seconds, within 515 feet. Acting automatically, by severing, the train was stopped in twelve seconds within 367 feet. When going forty miles an hour, the brake was applied by severing the engine from the train, and a stoppage was effected in ten seconds, within 316 feet. Various other experiments were made, which were altogether successful.

POSTAL CARDS.—The demand for postal cards is still increasing. Up to date orders received at the Post-office Department aggregate over 22,000,000; prior to the 1st inst. orders for over 12,000,000 were received. The average daily orders since the 1st inst. have been about 1,050,000 This morning orders for 1,499,000 were received. All of the large cities have sent for their second or third supply. The third order from New York was received to day, and is for 1,000,000. Heretofore there has been some tardiness in the production of cards, but to day the manufacturers notified the Post-office Department that they now have three cutters in operation, which cut a little less than 500,000 daily. They state they will add another cutter this week, and three more later, and that an additional printing press will be started as soon as they can supply enough paper to manufacture 650,000 daily.—*Washington Star, May 21.*

AMERICAN WORKING PEOPLE.—The *Scientific American* foots up the whole number of working people in the United States at 12,505,923. The number of inhabitants of the country is 38,558,371, so that the active workers constitute very nearly one-third of the population, the ratio having considerably increased since the census of 1860, at which time it barely exceeded one quarter. 10,669,136 are males, and 1,836,487 females. Between the ages of ten and fifteen years the males outnumber the females in a ratio of nearly three to one; between sixteen and fifty-nine years the ratio increases to nearly six to one; while at ages above sixty years there are more than twelve times as many men at work as there are women. These figures apply to men and women in actual outside employment. It will be noticed as the women grow older their numbers in proportion to the men decrease. This is accounted for by their marrying, abandoning their employments, and settling down to household.

HUNTINGDON & BROAD TOP RAIL ROAD

On and after March 23d, 1873, Trains will run on this road daily (Sundays excepted) as follows:

Trains from Huntingdon South. *Trains from Mt. Dal's moving North*

MAIL. A. M.	EXPS. P. M.	STATIONS.	MAIL. P. M.	EXP'S A. M.
LE 7 45	5 50	Huntingdon,	AR 4 00	AR 8 25
7 50	5 55	Long Siding	3 55	8 20
8 10	6 10	McConnelstown	3 45	8 10
8 17	6 20	Pleasant Grove	3 35	8 03
8 30	6 35	MARKLESBURG	3 20	7 45
8 45	6 50	Coffee Run	3 07	7 32
8 53	7 00	Rough & Ready	2 57	7 23
9 05	7 10	Cove	2 47	7 11
9 08	7 13	Fishers Summit	2 45	7 10
9 20	7 28	Saxton	2 27	6 51
9 40	7 50	Riddlesburg	2 10	6 35
9 47	8 00	Hopewell	2 02	6 22
10 02	8 15	Piper's Run	1 47	6 05
10 17	8 32	Tatesville	1 32	5 48
10 30	8 45	Everett	1 20	5 35
10 35	8 50	Mount Dallas	1 15	5 30
11 08	9 20	Bedford	12 44	5 00

SHOUP'S RUN BRANCH.

LE 9 25 LE	Saxton.	AR 2 15 AR	
9 40	Coalmont.	2 00	
9 45	Crawford.	1 55	
AR 9 55 AR	Dudley	LE 1 45 LE	

Broad Top City from Dudley 2 miles by stage.

Time of Penna. R. R. Trains at Huntingdon.

***Mail No. 2 makes connection at Huntingdon with Mail going East on Pennsylvania Railroad at 4.15 p. m., and West at 5.45 p. m. Mail No. 1 leaves Huntingdon at 7.40 a. m. on arrival of Pacific Express West.

Trains on this road connect with trains on Bedford & Bridgeport, and Cumberland & Pennsylvania Railroads.

G. F. GAGE, Supt.

The Weekly Pilgrim.

Published by J. B. Brumbaugh, & Co.

Edited by H. B. & Geo. Brumbaugh.

CORRESPONDING EDITORS.

D. P. Sayler, Double Pipe Creek, Md.

Leonard Furry, New Enterprise, Pa.

The *Pilgrim* is a Christian Periodical, devoted to religion and moral reform. It will advocate in the spirit of *love* and *liberty*, the principles of true Christianity, labor for the promotion of peace among the people of God, for the encouragement of the saints and for the conversion of sinners, avoiding those things which tend toward disunion or sectional feelings.

TERMS.

Single copy, Book paper,	$1.50
Eleven copies, [eleventh for Agt.]	$15.00

Any number above that at the same rate.

Address,

H. B. BRUMBAUGH.

James Creek,

Huntingdon county Pa.

The Weekly Pilgrim.

"REMOVE NOT THE ANCIENT LANDMARKS WHICH OUR FATHERS HAVE SET."

VOL. 4. JAMES CREEK, PENNSYLVANIA, JUNE 17, 1873. NO. 21

POETRY.

Selected by A. B. B.

MY CREED.

BY PHEBE CAREY.

I hold that Christian grace abounds
Where charity is seen; that when
We climb to heaven, 'tis on the rounds
Of love to men.

I hold all else, named piety,
A selfish scheme, a vain pretense,
Where centre is not, can there be
Circumference?

This I moreover hold, and dare
Affirm where'er my rhyme may go;
Whatever things be sweet or fair,
Love makes them so.

Whether it be the lullabies
That charm to rest the nursling bird,
Or that sweet confidence of sighs
And blushes made without a word.

Whether the dazzling and the flush
Of softly sumptuous garden bowers,
Or by some cabin door, a bush
Of ragged flowers.

'Tis not the wide phylactery,
Nor stubborn fast, nor stated prayers,
That makes us saints; we judge the tree
By what it bears.

And when a man can live apart
From works, on theologic trust,
I know the blood about his heart
Is dry as dust.

ORIGINAL ESSAYS.

IS IGNORANCE BLISS?

It may seem strange that I should take a subject of this kind, especially the affirmative, but from general observation, this is the conclusion that has been forced upon me. I argue from the fact that when a thing is full or complete, capacity is exhausted and all above fullness has a tendency of destroying our happiness.

In pursuit of perfect bliss we may ransack the world from center to circumference and nowhere will such perfect happiness be found as is realized among the poor where education is generally limited, the fact is, large intelligence and forced poverty is a most unfortunate composition, and invariably causes sorrow and vexation of spirit. The most contented family I ever saw were day laborers and and, by judicious economy, make their ends meet at the end of the year. Had this family had their minds opened to the inexhaustible mines of wealth that lie hidden behind the charming curtain termed knowledge, their condition would be quite otherwise. To them, "ignorance was bliss." And to-day, thousands are contented and happy because they know no better, and to gather and weigh all this with that afforded by worldly wisdom the balance would be strongly in favor of the conclusion I have come to, that "ignorance is bliss."

Knowledge is a prolific tree and bears much fruit that is intended to make us happy, but there is a principle connected with it that destroys our relish for enjoying it. It is so much like the Eden apple that I cannot help but notice the similarity. It is always something to be desired, yet never obtained, ever reaching and grasping after a glorious bubble which when seized, like the Sodomite apple, burst into ashes. Knowledge gives birth to a child called ambition and it is one of the most restless and unhappy spirits that ever had an existence in the world. It is all glory, glory, and its cravings are so exceedingly rapacious that it cannot be satiated. The more it is fed the greater becomes its capacities for devouring. So completely did this principle overcome a king of old that after conquering nation after nation, he went out on a mountain and wept bitterly because there were no more worlds to conquer. Such is the nature of that principle which is awakened by a general knowledge of the sciences as now taught.

I have affirmed that "ignorance is bliss" but in doing this I have not asserted the quality of bliss it affords. Bliss has different qualities and degrees. One kind is such as the hungry cow enjoys when first turned into a field of good pasture. It is full and complete. Her capacity of enjoyment would not allow her more, but, it is only animal and for the present, not knowing that it may be a step towards the slaughter house and death. *Such* ignorance is bliss and is a very fair representation of all the bliss that ignorance affords. We see hundreds and thousands of people who are happy simply because they have sufficient to satisfy their animal wants; and when they seat themselves around the festive board, their feelings and aspirations are not very unlike the cow when grazing the new grown clover. Such bliss is not what we are living and striving for, it is from beneath; ours is higher, purer and more lasting. It elevates the spiritual by casting the sensual down.

Brethren and sisters, let us examine the character of our enjoyment, and see from whence it is. We are creatures of circumstances, and are surrounded by many different elements which seek assimilation, and will get it, and will mould our lives according to their qualities or characteristics. We are tending somewhere. Blissful ignorance will lead us downward, while wisdom with its thorn will elevate us to be assimilated with the high intelligences above.

Knowledge is objectionable and dangerous only when unseasoned with that wisdom which is from above. It is like salt that has lost its savor; or, still worse, it is dangerous—a mighty weapon of destruction and death when devoted to a wrong cause. Ignorance is bliss because its capacities are less than its enjoyments. Knowledge is grasping and unsatisfied, because its capacities are large and unfilled.

The aspirations generated by knowledge are different in their tendancies, while one runs for worldly ambition, the other yearns after those heavenly graces which characterizes the truly devoted christian. This is owing to the character of the person, and the influences by which he is surrounded. If an educated man is surrounded by christian influences, the chances are that the power of his information obtained will be exerted in favor of religion and the cause of Christ. Hence the great necessity of watching over the influences that surround our children while in pursuit of this knowledge. Money and education are two great powers in the world. No christian parent would think of sending his son to a place where he knew a bad and dishonest influence would be thrown around him, in order that he could make money and thus become rich. He would naturally conclude that it would be dangerous, and that the gain in dollars and cents would not balance the loss of character sustained.. A loss of character is a great forfeit to pay for the sake of perishable wealth, but let me assure you, it is not greater than may be sustained by sending our children to such schools where an influence may be thrown around them that may ultimately destroy the soul. This is one of the strong arguments that ignorance is bliss and can only be successfully refuted by affording our children facilities for obtaining knowledge without being thrown into the ungodly influences that are brought to bear against them at many of our popular institutions of learning. When will it come to pass that a wise man will hear, and will increase in learning; and a man of understanding shall attain to wise counsels.

LIFE AT HOME.

It is practicable to make home so delightful that children will have no disposition to wander from it or prefer any other place; it is possible to make it so attractive that it shall not only firmly hold its own loved ones, but shall draw others into its cheerful circle. Let the house, all day long, be the scene of pleasant looks, pleasant words, kind and affectionate acts; let the table be the happy meeting place of a merry group, and not a dead board, where a silent, if not sullen, company of animals come to feed; let the meal be the time when a cheerful laugh is heard and good things are said, let the sitting room at evening, be the place where a smiling company settle themselves to books or games till the round of good night kisses are in order; let there be some music in the household, music not kept like silks and satins to show to company, but music in which father and mother and sister and brother join; let the young companions be welcomed, and made for a time a part of the group, so that daughters shall not deem it necessary to seek the obscurity of back parlors with intimate friends, or to drive father and mother to distant apartments; in a word, let the home be surrounded by an air of cozy and cheerful good-nature; then children will not be exhorted to love it—you will not be able to tempt them away from it.—*Dr. Adams.*

The idle should not be classed among the living; they are a sort of dead men, not fit to be buried.

PROCEEDINGS OF THE ANNUAL MEETING OF THE BRETHREN, HELD AT DALE CITY, PA., JUNE 3rd, 1873.

The meeting convened about 8 o'clock in the morning in a large barn, which was fitted up for the occasion with accommodations for perhaps 2000 persons. The building is situated at the north-west end of the town, and was filled to its utmost capacity by the brethren and sisters assembled from all parts of the Union.

Previous to the entrance of the Standing Committee, the interval was occupied in singing in English and German, in which the entire congregation united.

The Standing Committee entered the room, and the Moderator, H. D. Davy then addressed the meeting as follows:

While assembled on this occasion, let us try to remember that the eye of God is upon us, and that we engage in the worship of Him with that degree of solemnity and becoming reverence that may meet his approbation. We name the 253rd number of this collection, "I love thy kingdom, Lord," &c.

After singing this hymn the Moderator said: I trust brethren and sisters in the Lord, that we have tried to appreciate the sentiments contained in the rhymes of the poet, and now, on the occasion for which we are assembled, let us have before our eyes the important thought of the salvation of souls; and in order that that may be accomplished, we must turn our attention and fix our hearts upon the God of our salvation to endow us with wisdom from on high; that wisdom which comes from above, which is first pure, &c. Then as we need that wisdom and God has in store a reservation for us all, we should try to come before Him with a meek and lowly heart, and a contrite spirit, and, as one man, unite our voices with our hearts together in solemn prayer, that He may come right down here amongst us this day, and exercise his power around and over us, and so influence us that all that we may say or do may be consistent with His divine will.

Let us try to realize what we have cost; nothing more nor less than the suffering and death, the groanings and agonizings of the Son of God, who has left the shining courts of Heaven and came down and suffered and died, and spilled his blood that we may be heirs of God. And now, with God before us as the object of all worship, let us unite in prayer.

Elder John Wise then read the 13th chapter of the Acts of the Apostles, and the officers of the meeting were announced as follows;

Moderator—Bro. D. Davy.
Assistant—Bro. D. P. Saylor.
Clerk—Bro. J. Quinter.
Assistant—Bro. John Wise.

Bro. Saylor stated the object of the meeting. The Brotherhood is apportioned out into Districts with authority to do business of a local character. A great many churches and some Districts prefer to send their matters to the Annual Meeting, to be submitted to the decision of the Brethren sent by the different districts to represent them in the Standing Committee; hence the necessity for this committee to hold private sessions for the purpose of examining the letters addressed to them on the different subjects, a great many of which come to them in the form of unanswered queries to which they are expected to frame an answer before submitting them to the meeting for the approval or disapproval of the entire body.

Some further explanations were given by the Moderator, who concluded by urging upon the members the importance of preserving order and maintaining a spirit of Christian unity and feeling.

The first query presented was from the Western Maryland District, as follows:

Is it consistent for brethren to have their lives insured, and how to proceed with those brethren who have their lives insured?

Answer—Concluded to send this query to the Annual Meeting, with the decision that it is inconsistent for brethren to do so.

The answer to the above query, as furnished by the District, was passed.

2nd What Scripture shall we name as an answer to the following question: "How shall those officers among us be installed whose duty it is to serve tables and to attend to the wants and necessities of the poor members?"

Answer—Acts VI, 6.

A protracted and somewhat animated discussion followed the question as to the disposition of this query, which was participated in by some of the brethren, the tenor of the remarks being about as follows:

Bro. Joseph Arnold. The persons referred to are doubtless what we term Deacons, and there is no authority in the Gospel for laying hands on them at their reception.

John Wise. Give us some other Scripture to show how they are installed.

Jos Arnold. I do not know that I am prepared to give any other answer at present.

P. Nead. The Church has authority to say in what manner they should be installed, and every brother and sister is acquainted with the manner, namely with hand and kiss.

D. P. Sayler. When we have the Word as plain as "thus saith the Lord" let us not omit it.

Jesse Roop. This subject has agitated our church very much and inasmuch as the Western District of Maryland has under consideration the same subject, I feel it necessary to say something about it. There can scarcely be two opinions about it in the way the question is brought up. It is simply asked "what answer we shall give,"&c., and I apprehend we can give no other answer than that furnished in both these districts of Maryland. (Eastern and Western) If the question came up as to whether it is right or wrong, I might use different arguments and there might appear to be two sides to the question. It may be said that those persons refered to in that portion of God's word are not called deacons, neither does the query say they are. It styles them in their true character. They were to serve tables and attend to the necessities of the poor, and yet we have a mode of installation which some think is not precisely correct. The question we are called on to settle is, is that answer correct?

E. Slifer. There can be no two opinions in reference to the answer, under the artful manner in which the question is framed. No deacon in our district desires a change. Our oldest deacons are opposed to it. Those persons we hold and call deacons are not the persons refered to in the chapter and verse. The deacons are the creatures of the church, and it defined and laid down their duties at length in the year 1835 at their Annual Meeting, in reference to which you will find that they are a different class of officers. Our deacons have no autherity to preach the word or baptize. Those named there did both. Our church has laid down the duties of the deacons and the order of their installation, and with this I am satisfied, hoping the matter will be passed by without further argument.

S. Z. Sharp. I am not satisfied—It think that inasmuch as Scripture has been demanded, the Church which proposes to be governed by the Holy Scriptures must be very cautious in this matter.

We announce to the world that we are governed by the New Testament and if we shirk our duty in this respect, we are violating the principles laid down for ourselves. If we say that we have no Scriptural answer for this question, then we say we do not go according to Scripture. If there is a Scriptural answer, why shall we not give it? If we have one to give and fail to give it, we only stultify ourselves. The brother who spake, said that years ago the Annual Meeting defined the duties of deacons. That does not answer this question, for the question does not ask for a definition of the duties of the deacons, it simply asks for a Scriptural answer to the question. If it was thought necessary at Jerusalem to have a bishop we who profess to follow the primitive Christians, either do not have such a body, or we have a body different from those and install them in a different manner—one we originated ourselves.

If there is a Scriptural mode of installation, I hope we will adopt it. I have read all the minutes ever published upon this subject, and they define how the Church says, but I have not yet found that they point us to what Jesus Christ or his apostles said. We want to know what the primitive church did, or were instructed to do. We therefore appeal again, that you give us some proper Scriptural authority, and ask that we be not put off in a careless or indifferent manner, but that we receive some satisfaction.

H. Myers. My idea of this question you will find in 1st Timothy, I think near the last chapter, where it is not permitted to lay hands upon any man suddenly. In that same letter Paul wrote to the bishops, explaining that the next class of persons to them were the deacons; and if I understand that aright, it refers to the preachers. Now why should we lay hands upon the table servers, and not on the preachers?

My idea is that the apostles did not at first understand all.

J. S. Holsinger. Is it the duty of this meeting to tell the church what answers to give to every question they may ask? If so, we might continue the session all the year.

J. Roop. Our object is just the reverse. This question did not originate in the east of Maryland, as I understand it. While it is true, as brother Saylor says, no one there is dissatisfied; it is because there is a disposition to forbear. There are brethren there who have ever felt conscientious, and whose object in framing the question as it was framed, honestly, is to have all controversy allayed upon the matter; and we hope the answer may be affirmed by the church; yet the church has the privilege to say what the order shall be in installing.

It is true, that those, the apostles named, had other duties; but that does not affect the question. One of the brothers has told us, that our brethren who serve tables, have other duties too. I think that the brethren's consciences should be respected and regarded; and I claim that the church may answer this question affirmatively, and yet not interfere with the practice of the Brethren. I would therefore propose, instead of tabling this question, that it be taken home and considered by the church as to whether this will confirm or reject this answer; and if accepted, to decide also how it shall be approved.

Jno. Knisley. If we refer to that scripture, or give it as an answer some of our churches may install their visiting brethren by laying on of hands, and others not. We want one order and not two. These things have before caused trouble, and we don't want it hereafter. Some of the churches believe that the deacons should have hands laid on them and this answer will allow of it.

Sturgis. This subject came up years ago, and was settled satisfactorily at that time. But we do not blame the church for inquiring, to know what is the true literal meaning of the scriptural command. The circumstances in the apostolic time were different from now. I will now read a passage of scripture, that applies to the authority the church has according to the necessities of the age in which we live. The Holy Spirit saw, that in future ages different practices would be required; hence the apostle offered the instruction you will find in the 4th chapter of Philippians. In instructing the church he says, "Finally Brethren, whatsoever things are true, whatsoever things are just, whatsoever things are lovely, whatsoever things are of good report, if there be any virtue, if there be any praise think on these things." Therefore the church—the true church—has got up an order here, that is not contrary to the mission; it is just and right that we should select such as we now need and have; and until it can be shown that the office spoken of corresponded with that we now have, we have no right to speak of that installation. I would refer the question back, and if it is not what is wanted, it can come up to next Annual Meeting.

D. Gibbon. Brethren it is the light we want. We have learned from the law of the Lord that we should sanctify him in the heart, and be ready to give the answer to those who would inquire of us.

We know of nothing we may answer such individuals as make inquiry concerning the ordinations of these officers. Should we accept the custom and give that as a reason? I left all connections to unite with a society which has followed the Scriptures. It has been said that there were none dissatisfied, where this originated. It must certainly be a mistake. I, as one, after finding the brotherhood, this was the first to which I took exceptions, and under the present circumstances I would be anxious to be able to give an answer to those who would inquire of me. I also have read the decisions of the Annual Meeting, which are recorded in the Brethren's Encyclopedia, but that not being satisfactory to my mind, and feeling, too, that there may be others that would unite with us who would have no more light or knowledge than ourselves.

It has been said that they were ministers in the second degree, and that they preached the Gospel; but that they preached the Gospel afterwards does not say that they were set apart for this special purpose; for we find that one of these seven afterwards practiced polygamy, and to the church at Pergamos—it was said afterwards that their deeds God hated.

J. Brindle. I think that we apply this command to the wrong answer. Who wait on the table of the Lord, or those who break bread for the communion? I understand it was our Elders, and our Bishops.

J. Arnold. I am satisfied with the remarks of Bro. Sturgis except in one thing and that is that these dissatisfied brethren let it lay over till another meeting and by that time prepare themselves to prove who these seven brethren were, whether what is called deacons or some other class in some other office.

C. Forney. The question demands a true answer, for which purpose consider the necessity for the election of those appointed, which was the neglect of the widows in the daily ministration. We are bound to come down to the idea that they did serve tables daily. Paul said it was not meet to leave the word of God and serve tables. Let us submit that scripture as an answer. If the brethren consider that it would not be deemed advisable to serve tables and preach the Gospel, let them say so and let them remain there as table servers until thought worthy or necessity dictate a farther move.

J. S. Flory. Let the scripture answer stand, and the church continue to install as they have ever done. Let it be amended so as to say that the scripture answer is right so far as the officers referred to are concerned.

J. Wise. I don't know as I can throw very much light on the question, but I would wish to call the attention of the young brethren to the language of the "Acts of the Apostles." The language used in the Acts 6: 3, is: "Wherefore Brethren, look ye out from among you seven men of honest report and wisdom, whom we may appoint *over* this business." I don't say "to do this business," but whom we may appoint OVER this business to superintend it, and to direct how it should be done. In the Church we have others appointed to do the work that is necessary to be done, serving the tables, &c.; we have men appointed who are ordained by the imposition of hands, and we have men appointed to do the business without the imposition of hands, consequently those who are appointed to look *over* the business, are appointed in the manner prescribed in the 62nd chapter of Acts. This is my understanding of the subject, and if it will enable the young Brethren to answer those who ask regarding it, I am satisfied, and I hope they will examine into the phraseology of the text.

H. D. Davy. I have waited some time, and listened to the remarks of our brethren; and when our young brethren come to us as fathers in Israel, and ask us questions as touching our duty toward them and the church, I feel a great responsibility, and feel disposed to give all the assistance in my power. Almost 40 years ago, when I united with the Brethren, as a young brother from Maryland said, "that was the first thing I stumbled upon." I soon got into conversation with older brethren, who took a great deal of pains to instruct me. Now, as I told you this morning, different views will come up on different portions of the Scriptures. They had one view and I another, and they undertook to reconcile my mind to that, to the point, and they did it fully to my satisfaction.

A portion of the church 100 years ago understood that it was the office of deacon; for they had got the idea from a closer examination that it was the first installment—the first laying on of hands on bishops. Now this investigation caused different opinions to be presented to the meeting. Some supposed it was the visiting brethren that had hands laid on them, and others took the position that it was the first installed that had the hands laid on them. A portion of those seven men were ministers. Take them from the ministers and put them to the tables, they thought it would not harmonize with the teachings of the scriptures. Now go down into the tent, and you have an illustration. Here we have a man appointed to oversee the tables. Does he serve the tables? No. Does he oversee? Yes. But when he hears of suffering and want, he does his duty, and attends to seeing that their wants are supplied.

This discussion seemed to satisfy the church, until of late years, when young brethren came into the church. Serving is one thing and overseeing is another.

D. Longanecker. The apostles were appointed by Jesus Christ. They were not to serve tables, and they appointed bishops under them.

John Metzger. The apostles would call them helps, and Paul again says, "Lay hands suddenly on no man."

H. D. Davy. It has been proposed to let the matter stand as it is; let it be deferred, that is, not let this query stand, but let the custom stand as it is, for another year, and let us examine the matter thoroughly, so that we may have oneness of practice, theory, and feeling among us.

P. Nead. I am not going to make many remarks. Those seven brethren, on whom hands were laid, I understand to be evangelists, and mind you, they were to have common stock in that day of the apostles, and these seven teachers were to oversee the common stock.

J. Steel. I must say publicly and openly, that I feel perfectly satisfied with the view of brother Davy and Wise.

J. Garst. We wish the union of the Church. Once we felt as our younger brother, but after close examination relative to the query and answer, we concur with our old brethren, and are satisfied that there was a different class of officers who were called deacons.

— Hady. By giving the scripture explanation, this matter could go on the minutes and never need come up again.

— ——. We have had two classes, overseers and table servers; had we not better make use of different names to separate these characters?

A suggestion was made by one of the brethren that the question be withdrawn by those who presented it.

D. P. Sayler. We can assume no such responsibility.

H. R. Holsinger. We have no plain scripture before us that these persons were selected and appointed over this matter that required supervision. If the bishop, by virtue of his office, is to oversee the church why give a second appointment, and then lay hands on him and retain him as a bishop? And if these are the ministers to serve at the tables, why does the apostle say afterwards, "who will give ourselves continually to prayer and to the ministry of the word?" Then those men are to be appointed, and those bishops to look after those widows and serve those tables, and those who appointed and laid hands on them were to stay at home. Those persons that compose the Church and have the oversight of it to observed that it required other officers inferior to them to look after those widows. It was a question of looking after those widows and serving the tables, and now the superior officers of the church go to work and select with the counsel of the church, men qualified for this business, and appointed them to the duties of the offices, that they may not be required to serve the tables but give themselves continually to the ministry. Because our deacons are appointed to this duty it is not expected that they do all the work, but the deacons are appointed over the work as the Scriptures says. I do not see what objection we could possibly have simply to refer the interrogators to the very passage of Scripture and ask, as a people who understand God's word, to point us to some other Scripture that will answer the purpose. If there is another passage that authorizes the appointment of deacons, then point it out, but do not evade the question. Why not stick to the plain letter of God's word here? I do not say you must give the answer, but I ask that we have a Scriptural answer, as we have these officers and the people wonder where you get the authority. The duties specified are precisely like the duties of our deacons, and the people think they have got that from the 6th chapter of the Acts and they may pass by and not ordain them by laying on of hands and accuse us from deviating from the plain letter of the Scripture. If there is another passage that will give you the plain Scripture for establishing deacons in the manner you have then point us to that Scripture and I will be satisfied, even if half as good as the 6th chapter of Acts. I see no occasion for evading this question. If you cannot follow it, let us do so who have the plain language of God to authorize it. I cannot see why you should read us any part of God's word in that way. Deviate from the plain literal explanation and you can make anything out of it.

P. Neal. We have no common stock in our day. The bishop had the oversight of the matter and the deacons attended to the widows.

A brother objected to the use of the word *crude*, as used by brother Holsinger.

Bro. Sharp. In our church we lay a part of the funds together for the support of the needy. I was always under the impression, that was the common stock of the Church. I ask for information.

P. Neal. It seems there were wealthy brethren who threw all that they had into a common stock which belonged then to one brother as much as to another. No such custom now in the church, every brother throws in his mite for the benefit of the poor.

Bro. Berkey. If the installment is not right why not make a change?

Bro Sayler. We have no knowledge of any ordination by the imposition of hands till after they sold their possessions and laid the price down at the apostles feet. There was then a murmuring of the Grecians against the Hebrews that their widows were neglected in the daily ministration, implying that they had a ministration and some one to administer the things concerning this association. The apostles did not take time to investigate this national dispute but called the church together and asked them to choose seven men &c. just as now when the church is called on to send a committee to a certain place to investigate certain matters. They laid their hands on them but did not invest us with that authority. They saw fit and proper to lay hands on these seven, and when that was settled their visit ceased, and we find Stephen advocating the cause of Christ and sealing the testimony to the truth with his blood. Philip going down to Samaria preaching and baptizing, Nicholas in Minor Asia having got up a scheme in the church and showing that he was liable to err as well as we are. There is no similarity between those seven and our deacons who come in under the head of helps to the church and we install them according to the order laid down by the church.

J. Wise It is manifest to every careful reader of the Acts that there must have been persons to attend to the distribution of the common stock. Brother Sayler has alluded to it, that they sold their possessions and laid the money down at the apostles feet. There were young men there on that occasion to attend to business that the apostles did not attend to; and it is certainly very manifest that the circumstances would produce the necessity of persons to the distribution of the goods of the Church when placed at the disposition of the Church at that time; and to my mind it is very clear that there were persons appointed by the Church for this work, to attend to this distribution prior to the appointment of these seven in the 6th chapter of the Acts of the apostles; and there was dissatisfaction in regard to the manner in which these persons distributed the stock of the Church, the murmurings of part of the Grecians against the Hebrews, that their widows were neglected in the daily ministration. Who neglected it? Did the apostles neglect it? That was not their business; but the simple fact of complaint being made, I infer it was made to the apostles, and to show that it was not their business, they appointed subordinate officers to attend to the business. Those seven men were to see that the daily ministration was equal; that there was none neglected, that all were satisfied and supplied out of the funds of the church, and their duty then being discharged, everything being set in order, they would have time, of course to contend for the faith; said Stephen did so, as brother Sayler says, full of the Holy Ghost and wisdom contend for the faith, and his arguments were so potent that they could not be withstood and he had to seal his faith with his own life. There were certainly persons appointed before the seven. When the dispute was settled and until there was another dispute arose there was no necessity for the appointment. Our helps in the church have the oversight in the church in bearing the provisions to the table, they call on others to assist perhaps, but never in our experience do I remember when the visiting brethren did not come to see and ask what they were to do, knowing that they were subordinate to the overseer of the charge. In this case there was reason for the complaint, not because the apostles were not discharging their duties, but because the minor servants could not do what was necessary for them to do; consequently seven men were appointed for this business, and I want to see the Scriptures to answer the question, to show a passage authorizing a form for the appointment of the brethren we have appointed.

D. Weimer. If it is not out of place I would like to say a few words. We understand by the language of the Apostle that there was a ministration, and if there was such a thing as a ministration, there must have been administrators before the seven were appointed to oversee this administration.

Moderator.—The clerk has the answer ready to read.

Answer as read by the clerk:

Inasmuch as it is not certain that the seven persons on whom hands were laid according to Acts 6th chapter, 6th verse are to perform the precise work as our visiting brethren are to do, and if they were not, then the manner of installation may differ, and the manner of installing our visiting brethren may be sought for in the general principles of the Apostles and not in any one passage, and so the answer of our brethren may be given.

The next paper was offered by the representative of Western Maryland.

Inasmuch as the scriptures lay every disciple under the obligation to answer from the scriptures every scriptural question with regard to any and every part of our faith and practice, therefore, we, the brethren of Brownsville church, inquire of the Western district Council of Maryland what scripture we shall bring as an answer to the question, "How shall those officers among us be installed, whose duty it is to serve the tables and to look after the general interests of the poor members."

By agreement, the answer given to previous question was adopted to this one.

Query 2nd. Is it not sufficient and according to the Gospel to ask the candidate for baptism, while in the water, the question, "Dost thou believe that Jesus Christ is the Son of God, instead of the words of the formula, found in the minutes of 1858, Article 41?

The answer of one of the congregation of this district was, "It is sufficient and according to the Gospel," but it was not approved by the District Meeting; yet the majority said, send the question with their answer, together with the decision of the District Meeting, to the Annual Meeting for its determination.

Quinter. Here is a disposition to change the regular order among us from asking three questions to asking one question. Supposing that the church that has got up that question and brought it here to be granted their wish; then the next thing will be to come up, may not that question be asked out of the water? why did you not think of that? that would be wiser, why did you not think of that? Philip asked the question whether he did not believe. We are sure he asked it out of the water. Then we may go on here, in a house and elsewhere. Thus you see the question will be agitated unnecessarily. As regards the renouncing of the world do we not do it? I suggest that there be no change; but that the demand of this question did not warrant us in making any change.

Naff. I think that to ask that one question and not the others would be entirely out of place.

S. Z. Sharp. While I agree with brother Quinter's remarks there is one thing entirely omitted and that is that the religion of Jesus Christ requires obedience to his commands, while we might have faith in him that did not imply obedience to him. It is necessary that we take the candidate into the church that he may avoid the world. Unless that condition is announced and agreed to by the candidate, I don't see how we are going to follow the command of our Lord, and I think the original order should be retained.

Wise. I propose that this question be tabled.

Sayler. I will just say that those brethren who advocated this question, bring up their arguments.

Moderator. Brother Sayler calls for the argument for the opposite side. If it is not given we will put the question, on passage that the brotherhood may know that this meeting desires no change. If you table it you would not give it that privilege. If I understand the duty of this meeting and its privileges, most assuredly our clerk has the privilege of putting questions into proper shape, and of forming an answer which is very short. If you simply table it here, so far as the authority of this meeting is concerned the brotherhood will know nothing about it. If brother Quinter don't want to put it on the minutes in its simple form, this meeting has the right to do it.

Holsinger. It appears on that that was the intention. The District Meeting sustained the conclusion of this one congregation, and there should be some expression that the brotherhood may know that we go on as before.

Lane. I hope that this question will go on the minutes, that in the future, when these old gray-headed brethren are gone, the young generation will know that in this year, 1875, the question came up and was settled.

Question with answer read by the clerk.

Is it not sufficient and according to the Gospel to ask the candidate for baptism, while in the water, the only question, "Dost thou believe that Jesus Christ is the Son of God," instead of the words of the formula, found in the minutes of 1858, article 41. Answer. We think one question is not sufficient and therefore make no change in our present practice.

Passed without objection.

DISTRICT OF WESTERN PENN'A.

Jos. Berkey. We have the question but it has not been forwarded to myself nor to my colleague. At our District Meeting last year, we had a question which should have been forwarded to this Annual meeting, therefore I refer to it now. While there is a difference of practice among the Brotherhood, in proceedings with members who trespass in a congregation in which they have not their membership, some trying the case in the congregation where the offence

The Weekly Pilgrim.

JAMES CREEK, PA., June 17, 1873.

☞ How to send money.—All sums over $1.50, should be sent either in a check, draft or postal order. If neither of these can be obtained, have the letter registered.

☞ When Money is sent, *always* send with it the name and address of those who paid it. Write the names and post office as plainly as possible.

☞ Every subscriber for 1873, gets a *Pilgrim Almanac* Free.

OUR PERIODICALS.

At our late Conference our periodicals were made the subject of some consideration and from what we could learn of the deliberations of the Standing Committee, some of the old fathers favored the idea of consolidating and running the thing as a Church institution. This would be a new departure and we are inclined to think that the result might not be as satisfactory as may be anticipated. Time and again there has been attempts made to have the Church take charge of a Brethren's school, but it was "no go." After repeated trials and failures, an individual district took charge of the affair and started a school and the result is, a complete failure. The friends of education have become disgusted with the school business as a Church institution and are now turning their efforts towards a private enterprise and the result will be, a success, and that in a short time too. Now if the Church wishes to go back on the publishing business we of course will submit, but wiser heads than ours, predict the same result. It is a notable fact that there is not a self-sustaining Church paper in the United States. It is only by a liberal system of donating that they are sustained. Are our brethren willing, in addition to paying for their paper, to donate liberally towards sustaining a Church paper, and are they compelled to patronize a periodical that they do not wish? The great probability after all is, that the paper published as a private enterprise would get the patrons. If we wish a successful division in the Church, get up a Church paper and thus deny freedom of expression and the end will be accomplished. There is an element in the Church that only needs the spark to make it burn, therefore every possible effort ought to be made towards unity. To accomplish this, conciliatory means must be used.

We do not doubt the purity of the motives that gave rise to this move, but sometimes we act before our plans are matured. We do not see how a move of this kind could better the matter as we are all to be subject to the Church, and it has just as much power over us as individuals in an individual enterprise as it would have if our business was made the Churches business. The only advantage we can see would be to fill the position with better men. This would be possible, but even the best of men would be liable to err and might possibly commit as grievous faults as our present editors. The better plan for the present would be, for those who think we do not conduct our papers as we should, to come forward, as fathers in Israel, and teach us how to do better. We think we are always willing and humble enough to take instruction and advice. It is a fact worthy of note that those who object most to our work, are the ones that contribute least. Brethren, if you have the welfare of Zion at heart, let us hear from you. We have never, as yet, refused a single article of good sound doctrine. If you wish a good and readable paper, go to work and write for us. Our chief business is to select and prepare matter. You do the writing and we will prepare it for the press, but do not object to contraversial writings and then go to work and do the same things yourselves and insist on having them published simply because *you* wrote it. We have been placed in just such a position and submitted our judgment to accommodate such as stand as fathers in the Church. When you meet an occasional sentiment to which you cannot assent, think of the difficulties under which we labor and we think that you, will be prepared, to make some allowance for us. That we have too many periodicals among us is evident and we are favorable to consolidation. The Church ought, and will support two good weeklies, one monthly and a juvenile paper. To this number we ought to come and remain for the present. If any others are anxious to enter the field they should buy out some of the present publishers. This could be done as we suppose, any of us would sell at a fair price, not because we are discouraged or have a desire to abandon the cause, but because every addititional periodical has a tendency to curtail the prosperity of those already published.

In conclusion, we believe that, notwithstanding we have erred, we have been doing a good work and have made many an isolated home glad on the reception of the messages of salvation as delivered to them through the weekly calls of the Pilgrim. Brethren and sisters, labor and pray for us that our work may go forth sanctified by the spirit and produce fruit to the honor and glory of God.

CONFERENCE REPORT.

For a number of years our brethren and sisters have been calling for a full and correct report of the proceedings of our Annual Conference. Heretofore, this could not be had, but to this meeting we took with us a competent short hand reporter with the determination to give our readers just as much of the proceedings as would be allowed. The subject was before the meeting and the report was granted with a restriction which will be noticed hereafter. We have now a full and correct report of the meeting, including the opening address of the Moderator with all the discussions and the concluding remarks of the Clerk, so that those who remained at home can have as complete a knowledge of the business part of the meeting as those who were present. This cost us money and we hope to be remunerated, in part, by our agents and friends making a determined effort to increase our circulation. 400 or 500 names can be had if our friends will go to work at once. The report will commence this week and be continued until published. The Pilgrim will be sent from No. 21 (or this week) to the end of the year on the following terms: Single copy 80 cents. 5 copies 3.75. 10 copies, 7.00, 15 copies 10.50 and 20 copies 14.25. Now brethren and sisters, think of it. Many of you have spent, twenty, thirty and some fifty dollars to have the benefits of this meeting. We offer to give nearly or quite the same information for 80 cents. There is scarcely a member in the whole Brotherhood but what would take the Pilgrim the remainder of the year if they were informed of this report. We have now 500 single subscribers. One half of these can send us one name at 80 cts. if they will try. Please try. How many clubs of ten, fifteen and twenty can we have? Go to work at once and let us see what can be done when there is a determined effort made. Those that have not got the money now, we will wait them until after harvest or during the year. In making this offer, we want our agents to take only such as they would not be afraid to trust themselves. As an extra inducement we will send each subscriber, a Pilgrim Almanac Free as long as we can supply them. We will issue a large extra edition commencing with the "Report" so that all new subscribers can have the proceedings complete. Remember, this report will give all the queries, their discussions and answers. Every body that has any interest in the proceedings of our A. M. will want to read this report. Give them an opportunity by asking them to subscribe for the Pilgrim. We can still supply some twenty volumes complete at 1.50.

Warriorsmark Lovefeast.

On Saturday morning, June 14th, we, according to arrangement, took leave of our office to attend a Lovefeast with our brethren of Warriorsmark, Pa. For want of connection, we were detained in Huntingdon until evening, when we took the train for Tyrone and there made a direct connection with the Bald Eagle road.—At Bald Eagle station, we were met with a conveyance, and in a very short time we crossed the ridge, a distance of two miles, and arrived at the church just as they were preparing to commence feet washing, when we found present, beside the resident ministers, Stephen Hildebrand and Wright. The house was well filled, and the best of order maintained during the exercises, which were not as long as usual, on such occasions, on account of the number of communicants not being so large, but interesting, and, we trust, profitable to both communicants and spectators. After the exercises, we were kindly entertained at the house of our old sister Becks, whose greatest joy see us to be to administer to the wants of the brethren and sisters and all others who place themselves under her roof.

On Sabbath morning we again met for public preaching, when it fell to our lot to address a very large and interesting congregation, followed by a few appropriate remarks by Eld. Grabill Myers. The meeting was a pleasant one and we have seldom seen such a general interest manifested in so large a congregation.

At 3 o'clock, p. m., services were again held, when the congregation was entertained with a very able discourse from, "Who is on the Lord's side?" by Bro. Stephen Hildebrand, followed with some remarks by Bro. —— Wright. The congregation throughout the meeting seemed well entertained and we hope by the blessing of the Lord, good may result therefrom.

This congregation is not large, but the members are kind and sociable and make those feel at home who visit them. The speakers are Eld. Grabill Myers, Samuel Cox, Wm. H. Quinn and Conrad Imler.

On Sabbath evening we spent a pleasant time at brother —— Nearhood's, where we remained for the night. Next morning we started homeward bound—spent a short time in Tyrone with Bro. Quinn and by evening arrived safely home, for which God be praised.

KEEP US SUPPLIED.

Sometime ago we seemed to have an over abundance of copy and intimated something of that kind. Since then our supply has not been so abundant, and in consequence, we are getting short. Please notice this and keep us well supplied with good original articles. Short essays are preferable to long ones and let them be as free from personal ideas as possible. Those who have the time and ability should write for the instruction and comfort of those who have not.

Now is the time to subscribe for the Pilgrim. Only 80 cents from April to end of the year.

THOUGHTS IN A GRAVEYARD.

BY LOVINA H. BURKET.

Dear angel cherub, thou art gone,
How peaceful is thy rest;
Thy loving parents need not mourn,
For thou art gone to rest.

Thou wast too beautiful for earth,
A blossom bright and fair—
A bud that faded at its birth,
To bloom more brightly there.

How like an angel was thy face,
Clothed in the robe of death;
This earth was not thy resting place,
Though thou wast born to wealth.

The valley clods will hold thee fast,
From view thy form is hid;
Soon thou will be with things of past,
Beneath that coffin lid.

With tearful eyes, your parents turn,
To leave this mournful place;
Their loving child from them was torn,
Cold, cold in death's embrace.

But they may meet that angel one,
In *Heaven*, where all is bright;
Then, loving parents, do not mourn,
But seek that world of light.

For O, that bright and better world,
If we, its portals see;
The glorious news has been unfurled,
Like children we must be.

So innocent and pure and good,
Like that dear child of clay;
Believe in Him whose cleansing blood,
Will wash our sins away.

OUR PRIVILEGES.

Things the angels desire to look into.—1 Pet. 1: 12.

Peter, in the first part of this verse, refers those whom he addressed to the prophets and then endeavored to impress them with the value of the Gospel, and the privileges they enjoy, by a comparison of their situation with that of the prophets. They prophecied concerning the glorious future, but *you*, says Peter, are enjoying the benefit of those predictions. *You* are permitted to see clearly the truth which these holy men themselves saw only obscurely, and thus in many ways you are favored above those holy men

After having shown them the value of the Gospel and the privileges they enjoyed by referring to the prophets, he makes the idea still more impressive by referring to the angels. *You* enjoy "things which angels desire to look into." If angels, the inhabitants of the skies, are concerned in reference to things which you now enjoy, should you not feel that your privileges are great, in that you are now partakers of these things.

The things which angels desired to look into are the same as those which the prophets so much desired to understand—the great things concerning the suffering and death of the Redeemer, and the effects that would follow from the presentation of the Gospel, which has now become the power of God unto salvation. Even Simeon, that good old saint, waited patiently for the fulfillment of the revelation, that should see this great salvation, and then breathed a heartfelt prayer that he might depart. So were angels interested in the coming of the Messiah. They were John's messengers when he was preparing the way; an angel conveyed to Mary the intelligence that she should become the mother of the Redeemer; an angel warned the parents of danger, directed them in the way they should go, so as to refute the design of Herod in destroying him; in short they had a desire to look upon these things, and contemplated them with interest. They sensibly feel the condition of man, a fallen creature, tempted, suffering dying and exposed to eternal death.

But what is it that causes the angels to be interested in these things, and what leads them from heaven to earth? There are many things that might interest them, and the incarnation of the Son of God, and the fact that sinners may be pardoned, through the atonement, are considerations that might attract their attention, and call forth a desire to know. But whatever may be the cause, we know that they are interested in the plan of redemption, and this fact should call forth the inquiry, why are not we who are directly concerned, be more interested in the plan of our redemption? If it excited such a deep interest among the inhabitants of the realms above, should it not cause a much deeper interest among us whose hopes depend entirely upon it? The plan of our redemption is revealed to us clearly, and we enjoy the privilege of accepting it as the means for saving our souls.

Reader, you enjoy a glorious privilege. Life and death are before you. One or the other is awaiting you, and which will you choose? It is our privilege to obtain everlasting life and eternal happiness, yet how many are traveling on that broad way that leads to destruction. Are not the angels astonished at the indifference with which man treats the plan of redemption. They are interested in it although they would be happy if they did not understand it. Our *all* depends upon it, yet how very indifferent we are. How wonderful it is that even personal interests will not prompt us to "look into these things." All other subjects of the most trivial and insignificant nature will engage our attention but this great work, the working out of the soul's salvation, is by thousands and millions entirely neglected. Oh what a privilege to be left unenjoyed. Reader think of these things.

There is another class again who give the subject some attention but make it only a secondary matter. The things of this life concern them more and thus they attend to the things that pertain to their eternal interest when it suits them, or when other things do not seem to conflict. It is to be feared that those of us who claim to be looking into these things, are not improving the privileges we enjoy. We are too much engrossed with the things of this life to appreciate them and thus neglect our christian duties and those means of grace so bountifully bestowed unto us.

Brethren and sisters will it not be well for us to see to these things; whether the privileges we have is a source of enjoyment, whether we love the service of Jesus; whether we are willing to make a sacrifice of the things of this life for his sake; whether we are willing if necessary, to sacrifice our own ease and comfort in order to attend to the duties that are devolving upon us as Christians. If so, then indeed may we feel and appreciate the privileges granted unto us. May God help us all to look more and more into those things that pertain to our eternal interest.

J. B. B.

A WORD ON BAPTISM.

Baptism is a command of the New Testament. And all professors of religion in general consider Baptism as a duty, and ought to be attended to in some way or other. Baptism is a positive institution, and therefore we must have some plain precept or example to direct us, both with respect to the persons who are to be baptized and the manner in which the ordinance must be administered. If we proceed in an ordinance without authority from the scripture, God will reject our services with those who hath required this at your hands. "In vain do ye worship me; teaching for doctrines the commandments of men." Baptism is an ordinance peculiar to the gospel dispensation, and therefore the rule of our duty must be sought in the New Testament and not in the Old. It is one thing to maintain that circumstances is not absolutely necessary to the essence of baptism, and another to go about to represent it as rediculous and foolish, or as shameful and indecent, when it was the way which our blessed Savior exemplified, and was the way by which the ancient christians did receive their baptism. It's a great want of prudence as well as of honesty to refuse to grant to an adversary what is certainly true, and may be proved so; "And it came to pass, in those days, that Jesus came from Nazareth of Galilee and was baptized of John in Jordon; and straightway coming up out of the water, he saw the heavens opened and the spirit, like a dove, descending upon Him," and as in the case of Philip and the Eunuch, "and they went down both into the water, both Philip and the Eunuch, and he baptized him." Now it would be very unnatural to suppose that they went down into the water, merely that Philip might take up a little water in his hand to pour on the Eunuch. Baptism is immersion, and was administered in an ancient time according to the force and meaning of the word. Anciently, those who were baptized were immersed and buried in the water, to represent their death to sin, and then did rise up again out of the water, to signify their entrance upon a new life. And to these customs, the apostle alludes Rom. 5: 2-6; also 6 :3-4 there is an allusion to the manner of baptism which is by immersion. The various instances of baptism as recorded in the New Testament, in their view amply provide the principles thus laid down. We refer our readers to the inspired oracles, and say that those baptised by John, confessed their sins. Matt. 3: 6 the Lord Jesus Christ gave the command to teach and baptize: Matt. 28: 19, Mark 16: 15, 16. At the day of Pentecost they who gladly received the word were baptized; and they afterward continued steadfastly in the apostles doctrines and fellowship, Acts 24: 41, 42, 47. At Samarea, those who believed were baptized, both men and women, Acts 8: 12. Cornelius and his friends heard Peter received the Holy Ghost, and were baptized, Acts 10: 44, 48. Infants are therefore excepted because they cannot perform the duties or observe the ordinance of our holy and spiritual religion. Believers and believers only, who have been convinced by the word and spirit of God that they are in a sinful and dangerous condition—are fit subjects for this holy ordinance.

In the present age there are not a few persons who deny the perpetuity of the ordinance of baptism. There is no intimation that the law of baptism was designed to be restricted to any nation, or limited to any period of time. It is a general law without any restriction, except that which refers to character. "He that believeth," a divine law must continue obligatory until it is repealed by divine authority. There is no intimation in the scriptures that the law of baptism has been repealed, and therefore there is no reason to suppose its obligation has ceased.

Baptism answers all the purposes at this day which it answered in the first age of christianity; and these are as needful now as they were then. No reason can be assigned for the observance of the ordinance in the apostle's days which will not apply in all its force to believers in every age of the christian church.

The above considerations afford incontestible proof of the perpetuity of christian baptism, and shows that its observance is as obligatory at present as it was in the days of the apostles; and that it will continue to be as obligatory until the consummation of all things. It being thus evident from the scriptures that baptism is designed by the Head of the church to be coexistent with the gospel system as a constituent part of it and co-extensive with repentance towards God, and faith toward the Lord Jesus Christ; it is manifestly a great error to imag ing the obligation to baptism has ceased. There is not the slightest foundation for such opinion. Against it, there is the strongest evidence. Should this fall into the hands of any who dispute this statement, we would entreat them, seriously, to consider whether they are not, through their mistaken opinions, regarding the perpetuity of water baptism, doing great dishonor to the Saviour by disobeying his command, and to the Holy Spirit by rejecting his written will in setting aside what the scripture so plainly teach to be binding on all believers to the end of the world. This is one of the many texts given for our instruction, showing us what the design of baptism is and what it will accomplish when done in the name of the Lord with a full purpose of heart which can be testified to by many living witnesses, and gives us the answer of a good conscience toward God.

A Reader of the Pilgrim.

PRAYER.

The duty of prayer is urged by every consideration. None but God can provide for us, none but he can forgive and guide and support us. None but he can bring us into Heaven. He is ever ready to hear us. The humble, he sends not away empty; those who ask, receive, and those who seek find. How natural and proper then is prayer? How strange that any can live and not pour out their desires to God! How strange that any are willing to go to eternity with the sad reflection, "I have gone through this world, spent my probation, wasted my strength and am dying, and have never prayed." How awful will be the reflection of the soul through all eternity? I was offered eternal life, but I never asked for it. I lived from day to day, and from year to year in God's world, breathed his air, rioted in his beneficence, forgot his goodness, and never once asked him to save my soul!" Who will be to blame if the prayerless soul is lost.

Susie A. Coffman.

A Right Spirit.—On one occasion a minister found it necessary to punish his little daughter. But Mary climbed into his lap, and throwing her arms around his neck, said, "Papa, I do love you." "Why do you love me, my child?" the father asked. "Because you try to make me good, papa." It is in this spirit that God's people should accept the chastisements he sends, remembering it is in love he rebukes and chastens; not for his pleasure.

He that is good, will infallibly become better, and he that is bad, will as certainly become worse; for vice, virtue, and time, are three things that never stand still.

Youth's Department

LITTLE BARBARA'S HYMN.

A mother stood by her spinning wheel,
Winding the yarn on an ancient reel;
As she counted the threads in the twilight dim;
She murmured the words of a quaint old hymn:
"Whether we sleep or whether we wake,
We are his who gave his life for our sake."

Little Barbara, watching the spinning-wheel,
And keeping time with her toe and heel
To the hum of the thread and her mother's song,
Sang in her own sweet voice, ere long,
"Whether we sleep or whether we wake,
We are his who gave his life for our sake."

That night, in her dreams, as she sleeping lay,
Over and over the scenes of the day,
Came back, till she seemed to hear again
The hum of the thread and the quaint old strain,
"Whether we sleep or whether we wake,
We are his who gave his life for our sake."

Next morning with bounding heart and feet,
Little Barbara walked in the crowded street;
And up to her lips, as she passed along,
Rose the tender words of her mother's song:
"Whether we sleep or whether we wake,
We are his who gave our life for his sake."

A wanderer sat on a wayside stone,
Weary and sighing, sick and alone;
But he raised his head with a look of cheer,
As the gentle tones fell on his ear;
"Whether we sleep or whether we wake,
We are his who gave his life for our sake."

Toiling all day in a crowded room
A worker stood at her noisy loom,
A voice came up through the ceaseless din,
These words at the window floated in:
"Whether we sleep, or whether we wake,
We are his who gave his life for our sake.'

A mourner sat by her loved one's bier,
The sun seemed darkened, the world was drear;
But her sobs were stilled, and her cheek grew dry,
As she listened to *Barbara* passing by;
"Whether we sleep, or whether we wake,
We are his who gave his life for our sake"

A sufferer lay on his bed of pain;
With burning brow and throbbing brain;
The notes of the child were heard once more,
As she chanted low at his open door;
"Whether we sleep, or whether we wake,
We are his who gave his life for our sake."

Once and again as the day passed by,
And the shades of the evening time drew nigh,
Like the voice of a friend or the carol of birds,
Came back to his thoughts those loving words:
"Whether we sleep, or whether we wake,
We are his who gave his life for our sake."

Alike in all hearts, as the years went on,
The infant voice rose up anon,
In the grateful birds that cheered their way
Of the hymn little Barbara sang that day:
"Whether we sleep, or whether we wake,
We are his who gave his life for our sake."

Perhaps when the labor of life is done,
And they lay down their burdens one by one,
Forgetting forever these days of pain,
They will take up together the sweet refrain:
"Whether we sleep, or whether we wake,
We are his who gave his life for our sake."

ABOUT SUSPENDERS.

When I was a well grown boy, being away from home for a vacation, I very naturally broke one of my suspenders. I immediately took possession of an extra pair that my father was using for another purpose, without so much as saying "by your leave.' When he discovered it, he bade me return them to their former use. He then added: "I do not like to have you take possession of my things in this arbitrary way. It has already bred a bad habit in you. But I know that you need suspenders, and you shall have them when you are willing to ask for them."

But I had long cultivated a false independence, and refused to ask properly for things I needed. I had fixed on a way of my own for getting helped at the table, and instead of asking for things with an expression of thanks, I had resolved that a statement of my wants, as "I would like some butter," was as far as I could bring myself to go.

I would not, therefore, ask for the suspenders, and contented myself with the remaining one. I assure you, it was a great annoyance to me to have my pants hung on in that lop-sided manner, and a great grief to my father that I should be so obstinate.

About five weeks after this, my father had a plain talk with me about my folly, his anxiety to give me what I needed, and the wretched habit I was strengthening. He told me it would prevent my getting things from God; for they could only be had by asking for them. I frankly told him I hated to give in after I had held out so long. He only said, it was easier than when he had held out longer.

Still, I was not ready. And as my one suspender was tearing off the top of my trowsers, I changed it over to the other button. Father said I could not be allowed to tear my clothes in that manner, and sent me to get a tow string for another suspender. It cut my shoulder so bad for a week, that I brought myself to say, when he had given me some money for another purpose, "I am sick of wearing these old strings, and I think it high time I had some decent suspenders. Can't I take this money and get some?"

He simply said, "You know you can have them when you frankly and squarely ask for them. But you know that this hinting in a roundabout way is not what is required."

Then I got mad and declared it was a mean shame, that I was an abused boy, and other sputterings of wrath, that were in accordance with my state of temper.

About this time it became necessary to buy me a new suit of clothes. And I gave myself and my father the immense chagrin of trying them on before the dealer, with these old strings over my back. I tried my best to conceal them, but it was with doubtless success. I felt like the boy with the fox under his cloak. I tried to keep my face straight, but it gnawed my very vitals.

Finally, I went to father when he was asleep, and said, "Father?"

He opened his eyes, and said, "Well?"

"I would like some suspenders," said I.

He paused a moment, and then said, "I think you might have phrased that request better, but you will find a pair in that upper drawer."

I went to it, and took out a nice new pair, that had been lying there nearly all the time that had been sawing my shoulder with those old strings. I felt heartily ashamed of myself. He had the thing I wanted all ready provided, was anxious I should enjoy it, grieved over my loss of comfort and temper, while I was keeping him and myself out of a pleasure.

I have since learned that God has blessings already provided—all sorts of suspenders. He yearns to give them to us, is sorry for our toiling and hurts; but we go on sawing our shoulders, tearing our tempers, losing infinite blessings, bearing infinite burdens, and grieving our Father, all because we will not ask for suspenders.—*Zion's Herald.*

ANNOUNCEMENTS.

Please announce that we, the brethren and sisters of the Desmoines Valley Church, expect, the Lord willing, to hold our Lovefeast on the 28th and 29th days of June, 1873, at Elkhart, Polk Co., Iowa, about 16 miles north-east of Demoines City. The general invitation is given, and especially to the ministering brethren to be with us.

S. M. Goughnour.

Please announce that our Communion will be held in our Meeting house in the Spring Creek Congregation, 14 miles S. E. of Warsaw, on the 20th. day of June next. All are invited.

Daniel Miller.

Pierceton, Ind.

Eds. Pilgrim:—Please announce Communion Meetings which were arranged at the District Meeting of North-eastern O., and to all of which meetings we are requested to invite our beloved brethren and sisters and especially the ministering brethren. They are as follows:

Arrangements will be made to convey those that come by Railroad to the above named places by the Brethren and further directions will be given.

Josiah Keim.
B. B. Bollinger.

Please announce that the Richland Church, Richland county, Ohio, will, the Lord willing, hold a Lovefeast at Bro. John Kendell's seven miles North-west of Mansfield on the 21st and 22nd of June. A general invitation is given.

J. C. McMullen.

Dear Pilgrim.—Please say that we, the members of Springfield district, Ind., intend, the Lord willing, to hold a Love Feast on Saturday, June 28th, at Bro. Christian Weaver, one and one-half miles from Brimfield. A general invitation is given to all, especially to ministers, to be with us.

J. Holdin.

QUERY.

Dear Pilgrim: Please give us a little light on the 3rd chapter and 10th verse of 2nd Peter.

A. B.

Query.—Will some of the readers of the Pilgrim be so kind as to give an explanation of Mark 13: 14, 29?

J. D., ——— .

Bro. Editor: Will you or some of the brethren give an explanation of Luke 9: 27? Who were they that should not taste of death, &c?

Z. Henricks.

OUR REPORT.

Some of our readers may object to our report on account of the names being omitted but this was the restriction laid upon us by A. M., and we shall not take the liberty to violate. Those who read it for the sake of truth can arrive at the same conclusions as well without the names as with them and perhaps better.

THE ALTOONA CHURCH.—The time will be soon here that the churches composing the Middle District of Pa., are to report the amount they are willing to give towards building a Church in Altoona. The more we learn of the place, the more necessary it seems that a house should be built there. Some of the churches have reported quite favorably and if all do something near their duty the move will be a success. Go to work at once and report before the 1st of July, to George Brumbaugh, Grafton, Huntingdon Co., Pa.

BOOK NOTICES.

In this department we will notice such NEW BOOKS, as may be sent us by publishers, that are in harmony with the character of our work. A. B. Brumbaugh, M. D., Huntingdon Pa., literary editor, to whom all books must be sent.

THE UNDEVELOPED WEST; *Or, Five Years in the Territories; Being a Complete History of that Vast Region between the Mississippi and the Pacific, its Resources, Climate, Inhabitants, Natural Curiosities, Etc., Etc. Life and Adventure on the Prairies, Mountains, and the Pacific Coast. With two hundred and forty illustrations from original sketches and photographic views of the scenery, cities, lands, mines, people, and curiosities of the great west. By J. H. Beadle.*

We have just received some specimen pages of the above work. It is written in such an entertaining style that it cannot fail to be of general interest. It is now being published by the National Publishing Company, Philadelphia, Pa.; Chicago, Ill.; Cincinnati, O., and St. Louis, Mo. As soon as issued we will give a full description of the work.

THE HOME AND GARDEN.—We have just received the first six numbers of this interesting monthly. The first volume of *The Home and Garden* was published in 1860 61 and was highly prized by us. At the close of the volume it was suspended until the beginning of the present year. It now comes in its old and familiar dress and is as readable as ever. We give it a hearty welcome and hope our home may be benefited from its monthly visits. It is just the thing for our mothers and daughters to read. Published by M. J. Lawrence, Cleveland, Ohio, at 50 cents per year.

UNDERGROUND.—We desire to call the attention to that very interesting, useful and entertaining book published by J. B. Burr & Hyde of Hartford, Conn.—UNDERGROUND OR LIFE BELOW THE SURFACE.—Advertised in another column.

The object of this volume is to describe underground life in its varied phases; and the author has so well succeeded that he has given us a work at once valuable for the fact and information it contains, and fascinating in the manner in which these facts, interspersed with lively incidents in the lives of miners, etc., are set forth.

Those who have any interest in the mineral products upon which we are so dependent should not fail to purchase and read this book, and we are confident they will be abundantly repaid. It is a vast storehouse of information. See advertisement.

A. B. B.

MARRIED.

YOUNG—LANDIS.—At the residence of the brides' parents, by J. Anglemyer, Daniel Young to Lucy Landis, both of Elkhart Co., Ind.

DIED.

SHMUCK.—In the Nettle Creek Church, Wayne Co., Ind., our old friend Jacob Smuck, aged 88 years, and 15 days. His wife died two years before him, aged 88 years and 2 months. He was the father of eleven children, all of whom are living. He leaves many grand-children and friends to mourn their loss.

He was a member of the Presbyterian Church for 65 years, and before his death said he was going where he was waiting to go this long time. He was a native of York Co., Pa., and his funeral was preached by the Brethren.

Our Father dear, you have stayed with us many years, it was hard to part with you, but it is the Lord's doings and we will meekly submit to His will and humbly hope it will not be long until we will meet in that better land where we shall part no more.

A. H. SNOWBERGER.

(*Visitor* and *Companion*, please copy.)

SHAVER.—In the Lower Linville Creek Church, Rockingham Co., Va., June 2d '73, brother George B. Shaver, aged 82 years, 11 months, and 5 days. Funeral services by the brethren from the words, "Set thy house in order, for thou shalt die and not live."—2 Kings, 20:1.

BURKHOLDER.—In the Union Center Congregation, Elkhart Co., Ind. Susannah Burkholder, daughter of J. and C. Burkholder, aged 20 years, 3 months and 14 days. Disease, Quick Consumption.

LYDIA ANGLEMYER

EARNEST.—Near Ritchy, Newton Co. Mo., May 27 '73, of disease of the heart, sister Caroline, wife of Henry S. Earnest aged 34 years, 3 months and 17 days.

The deceased had been a member of the Church of the Brethren since she was 18 years of age. She leaves a husband, six children and a large number of friends to mourn their loss.

JOHN G. SNYDER.

MONEY LIST.

H. P. Hochstetler	2,00	W. P. Workman,	1,50
Daniel Miller,	1,50	C. Butterbaugh,	10,00
J. P. Conver,	3,00	E. J. Beeghly,	6,00
G. J. for S. R. & B. F.	2,50	John Dale,	1,50
		C. Swinehart,	80
Simon Oaks;	1,50	D. B. Arnold,	1,25
Jno. Nicholson,	4,50	J. D. Trostle,	80
D. Negley,	6,00	H. Garst,	1,50
C. Bluuch,	1,50	D. B. Sturgis,	80
Dorace C. Brown	1,50	J. H. Moore,	11,00
Jacob Mohler,	30	D. B. Stutzman,	80
Jos. A. Murray,	1,50	D. Hildebrand,	2,00
Jacob Mohler,	80	Martha M. Fritz,	80

Trine Immersion

TRACED

TO THE APOSTLES.

The SECOND EDITION is now ready for delivery. The work has been carefully revised, corrected and enlarged.

Put up in a neat pamphlet form, with good paper cover, and will be sent, post-paid, on the following terms: One copy, 25 cts; Five copies, $1 10; Ten copies, $2 00. 25 copies, $4.50; 50 copies, $8 50; 100 copies, $16 00.

Address, J. H. MOORE,
Urbana, Champaign Co., Ill.

Oct 22.

DYMOND ON WAR.

An Inquiry into the Accordancy of War, with the Principles of Christianity, and an examination of the Philosophical reasoning by which it is defended. With observations on some of the causes of war and on some of its effects. By Jonathan Dymond Sent from this office, post-paid, for 50 cts.

TUNE BOOK.

The Brethren's Tune and Hymn Book, is a compilation of Sacred Music adapted to all the hymns in the Brethren's New Hymn Book. It contains over 350 pages, printed on good paper and neatly bound. We will send it to any address, post paid at $1.25 per copy

GIVEN AWAY.

A FINE GERMAN CHROMO.

We send an elegant chromo, mounted and ready for framing, free to every agent for

UNDERGROUND

OR,

LIFE BELOW THE SURFACE.

BY THOS. W. KNOX.

942 Pages Octavo. 130 Fine Engravings.

Relates Incidents and Accidents beyond the Light of Day; Startling Adventures in all parts of the World. Mines and Mode of Working them; Under-currents of Society; Gambling and its *Horrors*; Caverns and their Mysteries; The Dark Ways of Wickedness; Prisons and their Secrets; Down in the Depths of the Sea; Strange Stories of the Detection of Crime.

The book treats of experience with brigands; nights in opium dens and gambling hells; life in prison; Stories of exiles; adventures among Indians; journey through Sewers and Catacombs; accidents in mines; pirates and piracy; tortures of the inquisition; wonderful burglaries; underworld of the great cities, etc., etc.

AGENTS WANTED

for this work. Exclusive territory is given. Agents can make $100 a week in selling this book. Send for circulars and terms to agents

J. B BURR & HYDE,

HARTFORD, CONN., or CHICAGO, ILL.

TRACTS.

"ANXIOUS BENCH RELIGION EXAMINED," BY ELDER J. S. FLORY. A SYNOPSIS OF CONTENTS. An address to the reader: The peculiarities that attend this type of religion. The feelings there experienced not imaginary but real. The key that unlocks the wonderful mystery. The causes by which feelings are excited. How the momentary feelings called "Experimental religion" are brought about, and then concludes by giving that form of doctrine as taught by Jesus Christ and recorded by his faithful witnesses.

COUNTERFEIT DETECTER
OR
BAPTISM—MUCH IN LITTLE.

This work is now ready for distribution, and the importance of the subject will speak for it a large demand. It is a short treatise on baptism in tract form intended for general distribution, and is set forth in such a plain and logical manner that a wayfaring man though a fool, cannot err therein. Either of the above tracts sent postpaid on the following terms: Two copies, 10 cts, 10 copies 40 cents, 25 copies 70 cents, 50 copies $1.00, 100 copies $1.50.

Trine Immersion.

A discussion on Trine Immersion, by letter between Elder B. F. Moomaw and Dr. J. J. Jackson, to which is annexed a Treatise on the Lord's Supper, and on the necessity, character and evidences of the new birth, also a dialogue on the doctrine of non-resistance, by Elder B. F. Moomaw. Single copy 50 cents.

THE HELPING HAND.

Containing several hundred Valuable Receipts for cooking well at a moderate expense, making Dyes, Coloring, Cleaning and Cementing. This book also points out in plain language, free from Doctors' terms the diseases of men, women and children, and the latest and most approved means used for their cure, to which is added a description of the Medicinal Roots and Herbs, and how they are to be used in the cure of diseases.

This is a work of considerable importance and we offer it to our readers as being a valuable accession to every household. Send from this office to any address, post-paid, for 25 cents.

1870 1873

DR. FAHRNEY'S

Blood Cleanser or Panacea.

A tonic and purge, for Blood Diseases. Great reputation. Many testimonials. Many ministering brethren use and recommend it. Ask or send for the "Health Messenger." Use only the "*Panacea*" prepared at Chicago, Ills., and by

Dr. P. Fahrney's Brothers & Co.,

Feb. 3-pd. *Waynesboro, Franklin Co., Pa*

New Hymn Books, English.

TURKEY MOROCCO.

One copy, postpaid,	$1.00
Per Dozen,	11.25

PLAIN ARABESQUE.

One Copy, post-paid,	75
Per Dozen, "	8.50

Ger'n & English, Plain Sheep.

One Copy, post-paid,	$1.00
Per Dozen	11.25
Arabesque Plain,	1.00
Turkey Morocco,	1.25
Single German, post paid	50
Per Dozen,	5.50

HUNTINGDON & BROAD TOP RAIL ROAD

On and after June 15th, 1873, Trains will run on this road daily (Sun excepted) as follows:

Trains from Huntingdon South. *Trains from Mt. Dal's moving North.*

MAIL. A. M.	EXP. P. M.	STATIONS.	MAIL. P. M.	EXP'S A. M.
7 45	5 50	Huntingdon,	AR 6 10	AR 8 25
7 50	6 05	Long Siding	6 05	8 20
8 10	6 15	McConnelstown	5 50	8 10
8 17	6 23	Pleasant Grove	5 40	8 03
8 30	6 38	Marklesburg	5 25	7 45
8 45	6 50	Coffee Run	5 11	7 32
8 55	6 58	Rough & Ready	5 05	7 21
9 05	7 05	Cove	4 50	7 13
9 08	7 10	Fishers Summit	4 52	7 10
9 23	7 25	Saxton	4 40	6 53
9 40	7 50	Riddlesburg	4 20	6 35
9 47	7 58	Hopewell	4 15	6 22
10 02	8 12	Piper's Run	4 00	6 05
10 20	8 30	Tatesville	3 47	5 48
10 30	8 40	Everett	3 38	5 35
10 35	8 45	Mount Dallas	3 30	5 30
11 08	9 20	Bedford	3 00	5 00

SHOUP'S RUN BRANCH.

A. M.	P. M.		P. M.	A. M.
LE 9 25	LE 7 35	Saxton.	AR 4 25	AR 6 45
9 40	7 50	Coalmont.	4 10	6 30
9 45	7 55	Crawford.	4 05	6 25
AR 9 55	AR 8 05	Dudley	LE 3 35	LE 6 15

Broad Top City from Dudley 2 miles by stage.

Time of Penna. R. R. Trains at Huntingdon.

*** Mail No. 2 makes connection at Huntingdon with Mail going East on Pennsylvania Railroad at 4.15 p. m., and West at 5.45 p. m. Mail No. 1 leaves Huntingdon at 7.40 a. m. on arrival of Pacific Express West.

Trains on this road connect with trains on Bedford & Bridgeport, and Cumberland & Pennsylvania Railroads.

G. F. GAGE, Supt.

The Weekly Pilgrim.

Published by J. B. Brumbaugh, & Co.

Edited by H. B. & Geo. Brumbaugh.

CORRESPONDING EDITORS.

D. P. Sayler, Double Pipe Creek, Md.

Leonard Furry, New Enterprise, Pa.

The *Pilgrim* is a Christian Periodical, devoted to religion and moral reform. It will advocate in the spirit of *love* and *liberty*, the principles of true Christianity, labor for the promotion of peace among the people of God, for the encouragement of the saints and for the conversion of sinners, avoiding those things which tend toward disunion or sectional feelings.

TERMS.

Single copy, Book paper,	$1.50
Eleven copies, [eleventh for Agt.]	$15.00

Any number above that at the same rate.

Address,

H. B. BRUMBAUGH,
James Creek,
Huntingdon county Pa.

The Weekly Pilgrim.

"REMOVE NOT THE ANCIENT LANDMARKS WHICH OUR FATHERS HAVE SET."

VOL. 4. JAMES CREEK, PENNSYLVANIA, JUNE 24, 1873. NO. 25

REPORT OF ANNUAL MEETING CONTINUED.

(*Continued from page 188.*)

in a congregation in which they have not their membership, some trying the case in the congregation where the trespass was committed, while others would try it in the congregation where the trespasser lived. The answer we give is, that the offender be tried in the congregation where the offence was committed.

NORTH EASTERN OHIO DISTRICT.

QUERY 5. Is is right to gather or boil sugar water on the Sabbath, or Lord's day?

Answer. Best not to do so.

An amendment was proposed: "Members should not do so." Another amendment proposed: "Not right to do so."

The first answer was announced to be passed; but there was a difference of opinion among the brethren, and considerable confusion prevailed, and the question was reconsidered.

——. In case of a sudden freeze, when the pots are likely to burst, would you let it stand there if the crop was likely to be lost?

——. Turn the crocks up on Saturday evening.

——. The Savior never has said we should not not take care of property on the Sabbath day, when loss was likely to be suffered.

——. A very strong prejudice against us exists, that the 'Dunkerd' Brethren do not regard the Sabbath, and I want to show that if individual Brethren will do it that we, as a body, do not approve of it.

——. Say it is wrong.

Brown. This is not the only thing about which there is a prejudice against the Dunkards in the world; and for my part I say I don't care for the combined prejudice of the world, unless the gospel is against. If we are going to be governed by the Bible, let us have proof from it. Now I'm not afraid to take the broad position, that there is not one word of gospel from Matthew to Revelation requiring us to keep any day for the Sabbath; but for the sake of harmony, and according to the law, we keep the Sabbath-day; and the apostle has enjoined that no man shall judge us with regard to meats, drinks, &c. I don't believe in making laws, where God has made none. I believe in keeping the day, as far as we can, without suffering loss. I don't think it is good to go too far in this decision, but I believe that the first answer is the best.

Quinter. Do we understand you to teach that we have no authority for keeping any particular day.

Knisley. Does not the apostle Paul say we shall not neglect the assembling of ourselves together? We have our Sabbath for assembling to worship. I have gone to meeting in the West when the brethren were in the sugar camps. Our answer should be they shall not do so.

Brown. If you brethren in the West cannot govern your churches by the gospel, you cannot do it by making laws where there is none.

Steel. I would not deem it a matter of conscience to attend to anything that is a necessity, on returning from meeting, because the gospel does not bind me to do so, and I would not wish this body to enjoin bondage when there is no thus saith the Lord.

Nead. I understood brother Brown to say that the Saviour furnished a precedent for taking care of property on Sunday. Where is the passage?

Brown. The Saviour was accused by the Pharisees for unlawful things according to that law the brethren mean to bind on us now, for allowing the desciples to pluck the ears of corn and eat, and he asked them the question "if any one of you have an oxe or an ass that is fallen into a pit on the Sabbath day, will he not straightway pull it out?" That would not have been unlawful under the Jewish law. Sugar water would be as valuable as an ox, and as good when saved.

Moomaw. We are taught to remember the Sabbath Day to keep it holy. God made all things in six days and rested on the seventh from all that He had made, and it is enjoined on the children of God in all ages of the world. We are not ignorant of the fact that the Sabbath has been superseded, and instead of the seventh the first is now set apart as the one out of seven in which there shall be no work done. This is accepted by the common consent of almost the entire christian world. So far as the precedent given by the Saviour, I take the position that does not change the matter; we find it was only where animal life was suffering that this violation is admitted. The desciples were hungered when they passed through the corn, and to stay their appetite were permitted to take the ears of corn and rub them and eat. I am mortified to hear the brethren advocating the propriety of violating this holy and sacred institution which comes to us by the strongest testimony in the power of language to convey and thereby put a weapon in the hands of those opposed to us, that we disregard the Holy Scriptures and the Sabbath of the Lord. I then shall favor the answer that it is entirely wrong to do so, in every sense of the expression; and I will venture further by way of encouraging those who are so fearful. I live where tobacco—which requires the most nice attention—is raised. If we fail in planting in season we may fail altogether in getting a crop, and some persons yield to the temptation and plant on Sunday, while others will not suffer themselves to do so. I have heard it remarked that those who obey the commandments of the Lord are more successful than those who are not willing to trust Him. Before I professed faith in the Lord Jesus Christ, I had a quantity of hay cut down on Saturday, and on Sunday hired a help to turn the hay, notwithstanding it was spoiled, as it invariably was for years afterwards, and I have looked on it as a chastisement for the violation of this institution. Put your trust in the Lord, and if you lose your crops He is able to supply it a thousand fold, spiritually if not temporally, and the time will come when we will have no temptation to violate His holy word.

Metzger. I want no such idea to go out from this meeting that we sanction the boiling of sugar water on Sunday. I have preached against doing any servile labor on Sunday, and claim that this is such, and am not afraid to preach it at home and abroad. I have made a great deal of sugar, and never could see much to be gained by this. If we gather our water on Saturday evening and boil until towards midnight, then close up during Sunday the buckets will about run full by Monday morning. Very little would thus be lost, and if so it is only the dust of this world. We are laboring for Heaven and heavenly things, instead of Time and timely things. The Lord has given us six days to labor and will bless our labor Let us not rob him of the one day.

Adjourned.

TUESDAY AFTERNOON SESSION.

The same subject under consideration.

Wise. The propriety of devoting one day in seven to the service of God has been fully shown, but I must express my astonishment in regard to the advocates of the answer attached to the question, that the brethren bad best not do so. Why is it best not to do it if it is not wrong? It must be either right or wrong. If right, it is well to do it; if wrong, best not do it, and we determine the right or wrong of the matter and decide in favor of the amendment, "it is not right for brethren to do so." If right permit it. If wrong prohibit it. We think it unnecessary to adduce any scripture quotations in regard to this, but I perhaps may give one. The Lord Jesus says, "let your light so shine before men" that they may see in us what will prompt them to glorify God. Do we consider that to gather and boil sugar water on Sunday will induce other people to glorify God? Once more, "abstain from every appearance of evil." Let me illustrate. In our country there are large sugar groves, called by our Yankee friends, "sugar bush," and one of our meeting houses is erected in one of these localities; the day for public preaching chances to be a good day for "sap," and the members gather and boil their sugar, and the preacher having no hesitation to do the same, goes into his sugar camp and spends the day there; some of our friends in the vicinity who regard it as christian like to dedicate one day in seven to the service of God, go to the place of worship and lo! the preacher and members are not there. What kind of appearance is that? But, says one, go to meeting first, and after that go home and gather the sugar water; I don't think that betters the case very much. I once heard of a minister cutting wheat after coming home from church on Sunday, and it seems to me that had the appearance of evil—that it was not letting his light shine so that God would be glorified by it. Better to devote the day entirely to the service of God, and thus honor Him and glorify His name. Hence I am in favor of the amendment that it is wrong.

Steel. I would rather let my hay spoil than do any thing of the kind. The injunction laid on the church by the apostle in Acts 5: 5, the answer.

Brown. I am conscientious in this matter. I would like for some of the brethren to give us an explanation of the 16th verse of 2nd Corinthians. If I have not misunderstood the Apostle, he has certainly given us the right to discriminate for ourselves in regard to the Sabbath day.

Sturgis. The Christian church from the days of the Savior were divided in sentiment as to whether they should keep the seventh day or the first. This question which agitated the church for 300 years was finally settled by the council of Nice, and from that day to the present time the christian churches, with a few exceptions, keep the first instead of the seventh. The Apostle did not fully decide the question then because the church was young and in its troubles. The idea is to show that it has been almost unanimously agreed since the third century, to keep the first day as the Lord's day. The day on which the Lord arose, and on which he appeared to John in the isle of Patmos. If it is good and right to keep the Sabbath let us try not to have it evil spoken of.

Passed.

QUERY 1st.—We request District and Annual Meetings, that no report be published of the proceedings of our Annual Meetings by our brethren, further than the queries and answers?

Answer. The brethren in the Southern District of Indiana ask that Annual Meeting stop the publishing of reports further than the queries and answers. Inasmuch as the publishing of the report in the C. F. C. and PILGRIM has not been promotive of peace in the Brotherhood, will it not be best, and make the labor of the Annual Meeting more successful to have no report published except the authorized Minutes, and that this go forth to the public as the expression of the meeting on all subjects brought before it.

SOUTHERN DISTRICT OF MISSOURI.

We desire in this way to call your attention to the matter of reporting the proceedings of Annual *Meetings*, as by brethren Holsinger and Brumbaugh, as injuring and spreading disorder among us. We now refer more especially to their published reports on the subject of feet washing. In their report on this subject, of 1872, they misrepresented the general sentiment of the meeting. The PILGRIM says, "it could be seen that the sentiment of the meeting was largely in favor of the single mode." Brother Holsinger says—in alluding to a certain amendment offered leaving the mode of feet washing subject to the choice of each church,—that only one man (Sayler) objected, leaving the impression that brother Sayler, of all present, alone presented any objection, see page 326, but that it is known that these papers do not properly or truthfully represent the facts in the case as seen by the vote of the Elders on Monday of the General Meeting when 89 voted for the double against 16 for the single mode, which may be assumed as a fair representation of the General Council. You will not have failed to have noticed brother Holsinger's allusion to the counsel of Elders, under the head of Editorial Correspondence, page, 377. We now proceed to lay before you one of the recent results of these reports. In attending to the duties assigned the committee at the last Annual Meeting to visit the Spring River Valley and Cedar County churches, they found among the causes of existing trouble was that of the mode of feet washing. Those favoring the single mode produced these numbers of the C. F. C., and PILGRIM, and in opposition to the minutes of the Annual Meeting, and refused to acquiesce in the action of the meeting, alleging that according to the said reports, the practice of the single mode would in a few years become general. This conclusion is the fair influence of the said report. Instead then of these reports having a wholesome effect in promoting peace among us, they supported a spirit of insubordination to the practice of the Brotherhood. However serious this charge may be looked upon, it is nevertheless true. Taking into consideration brethren Holsinger and Brumbaugh's reasons for publishing their views, with the proceedings of the Annual Meeting, the character of said reports and results, we submit to you the necessity of having reports of Annual Meetings discontinued in the form adopted by these brethren, as detrimental to the peace and good order of the church; or, if the report must be allowed, we suggest that the Annual Meeting, in justice to itself, require said report to be read before the General Conference and by it approved.

In conclusion we yet feel like stating to you a matter of grief to us, by brother Holsinger's allusion to the Missouri Salem College appeal which he says, applies language too offensive to be worthy of an inquiry. We have no desire to revive such a rule, but he publishes that the brethren sent matter too offensive to be countenanced by the meeting, an assumption entirely his own, and he has refused any qualification of said language in his paper when asked to do so, in justice to us. By what right brother Holsinger assumes the liberty he does is unknown to us, and as is our right, we come before you with our statement, and submit to you an evidence that your love for the Brotherhood will direct your labors to promote peace and good will throughout the entire church.

Answer. *Whereas*, The C. F. C. and PILGRIM have published articles with reference to decisions of questions by Annual meeting, differing from the sentiment expressed by said decision, and communications from others, and even from those who are not members of the church, and even of expelled members, reflecting seriously upon the character of the Annual Meeting.

Therefore, *Resolved*, That they be required to make acknowledgement for this offense, and that they be further required to promise to be more guarded in the future in this respect, and advised to publish nothing of the proceedings of the Annual Meeting beyond the questions and answers asked.

H. R. Holsinger. There is, of course but one point that it would seem in place for me to discuss, as whether I shall be requested to make the acknowledgement desired in this answer or not is not for me to discuss, that remains for this meeting to decide. These documents, I presume, were all read in your hearing. I have to say in regard to them, and especially in regard to this long letter, that I have had some correspondence with one of the active persons, and I think the one that wrote it. I was requested last year to publish an article from these parties, and perhaps if I had this letter would not have been before you. The whole matter is backed up by the opposition to education. You all remember, who were present at last meeting, the vehement assertions made in regard to Salem College by those very parties, and because the Annual Meeting saw proper to place its disapprobation upon that movement by tabling the matter, and because I took the liberty to say so, now I am to be brought before this council. You remember that the A. M. of last year decided that it was out of place, and a resolution passed requestioning us not to publish it, and that a motion was made and seconded to require the brethren of that district to make an apology for an assertion proved to be entirely unfounded and untrue, when brethren from the immediate vicinity of Salem College, and the elders of adjoining congregations stood up and said they were unfounded, and so far as Salem College was concerned, untrue, and I had a resolution passed that I was not to publish it and it was inserted because of its falsity and offensiveness. This is the way the matter originated and is backed up. My position has always been that we ought not to pass any resolution or make any decision, unless we expect to live up to it. We want to know what is done at these meetings, and the reasons for doing it, and the Brotherhood wants to know the reason, and all we ask is to give them the same information you give to this body. The brethren at home want to know the reasons as well as you. Why don't this meeting simply pass a resolution without discussions? Because we by discussion get at the truth of the matter, and see the propriety of the decision. This is one of the reasons why I would prefer that a decision of this kind should not be made.

John Wise. We have not in our possession all of the copies of these papers, to which reference is made in the complaint, but I have here an article published in the C. F. C. Jan. 10th, 1873, that is referred to in the answer, "publishing an article written by expelled members that very unfavorably assailed the Christian character of the Annual Meeting."—Reads it.

"Brother Henry, I have obligated myself to do for you what I could, and I try to do so. I have six subscribers for you including our own. I can recommend the C. F. C., and do believe that it contains as much as all the others taken together; and we hope that you will not fear the gates of hell prevailing against the true church, that has the apostles and the prophets for its foundation, and Jesus Christ for its chief corner stone. Gates of hell is a metaphorical expression, representing counsels of men, that are placing yokes upon the disciples' neck, that our fathers and we were not able to bear; as much as to say, we are not going to submit to having such yokes put upon the necks of the disciples; but we will hearken to the Mighty Counsellor, the Prince of Peace, saying, "Come unto me all ye that labor and are heavy laden," &c. It is generally understood that unconverted sinners are the subjects, but this is an indirect application. He had reference to those that were laden and burdened with the traditions and commandments of men. "Come unto me, my yoke is easy and my burden is light."

Brother Holsinger, we do believe that there are hundreds of disciples that are weary of the heavy yoke, and would much rather bear the easy yoke of Jesus; but they fear the gates of hell, that are opposing the counsel of God.

S. A. LEEDY."

Shuler's Mills, O.

Moderator. The writer of that article, as I well know, was expelled from the church 15 years ago and there were eight accusations brought against him, four of which he acknowledged to, and from that time to this he has been a railer against the Church. This is a railing heresy. The wise man says "In the multitude of counsellors there is safety." This meeting is the council of the Brethren, and for an expelled member to call it the gates of hell three times in one item, and for a brother to publish it, is what wounded our feelings. Bro. Holsinger once published another article from that man, and I informed him that he was not a brother; so I did this time, and hence have nothing since by way of publication so harsh as this. Brother Brumbaugh published a letter in the proceedings of the new organization in the State of Missouri, in which he says he was pleased to know there was little difference, so little that he hoped upon examination and investigation the difficulty might be settled. This wounded these brethren, saying there was but little difference, and then giving the title congregational, which seprates them and us as far as the East is from the West is separated. We sympathise with these brethren who are young and inexperienced and have a good deal to learn, and we want to check this, so that they may be more careful hereafter, not publish heretical doctrine opposed to the doctrine of the Church. Recollect your brethren love you, and we believe you love us, and for this reason we talk to you thus face to face, and we want discussions as mild as is necessary to accomplish the object. Now you have facts called for as touching Leedy.

As touching the report of the Annual Meeting last year, I want to say a little to my brethren. When they had given the report with the remarks we made, as well as they could remember, what wounded the feelings of the brethren was that they threw in their own opinion, which was, that the brethren were in favor of the single mode. When I passed the motion I tried to be as careful as possible. I felt my responsibility, and did not want to pass an answer when I discovered that there were many heads shaken. I have never done that to my recollection, and their saying that the large majority was in favor of the single mode, and that there was but a single voice opposed it, threw something upon me that stung pretty smart, but I can bear a good deal, and I can bear that too.

I calculated that I would have about as good an opportunity to get the expression of the audience by facing them, as to sit back to back and now we come up in love, with one another to talk these things over kindly and lovingly, so that good may be accomplished in the name of the Holy Child Jesus.

H. B. Brumbaugh. No doubt this meeting will expect that I should have something to say, in regard to this matter: and I can truly say that I am sorry that I should have done anything that should have been detrimental to the cause that I have been endeavoring to advocate. I have ever endeavored to learn obedience to the church, and I think, if I know myself, this is my disposition.

In regard to inserting that report, I have just this to say: In making that head note refered to, I cannot now remember what I said, but when speaking of the small difference between that report and the manner in which we conduct our exercises, in regard to the ordinances of the house of God, I said that there seemed to be such a very small difference that I hoped that after due investigation the matter could be reconciled. In that I had no reference to the general character and principles of the church as an organization, but simply in regard to the manner in which they performed the ordinances in the meeting of which we gave the report.

As the brother has said, we are young. We confess this, and that we have not perhaps the experience that we should have, and therefore subject to err, like others.

We acknowledge, that after we had been informed of the trouble they have in regard to this organization, we were sorry that we published the report. At the time we published the letter, we were not aware of the circumstances by which that organization was surrounded, and the feeling that existed between them and the brethren at that place. If we had been, we would not have given the report.

In regard to our report with reference to the subject of Feet washing, we simply gave our views, and not the views of the church, just like any other brother would do, under similar circumstances. In regard to the mode of Feet-washing, we ever maintained a neutral position, and all we ever said in favor of the single mode was for the sake of union in the church, and on account of the liberal principles which we claim to have.

We desire to be liberal and to work for the general good of the church, and in order that we may be kept together, and we thought it hard that for such a small difference as was represented in the mode of Feet-washing, a portion of our body should be separated. As to the private letters, we confess we were misinformed. As to casting any reflections upon the conduct of brother Davy, we would say, we would be very sorry to do any such thing, because if we know ourself, we love and respect our aged brother and would be very sorry to do or say anything to hurt his feelings.

It is true we heard many expressions at the meeting in regard to the subject of Feet-washing, and upon those we based our opinion. Perhaps we did not have as much conversation with the brethren in favor of the double mode, as we had with those in favor of the single mode, and that may account for our impression, because the sentiment we came in contact with, was largely in favor of the single mode.

In regard to making an acknowledgement, we shall not do it until called upon, and if the Brotherhood sees fit to call upon us to make an acknowledgement we shall certainly do it. I will just add a few words in regard to giving a report of our meeting.

We believe that, as a general thing, those who are opposed to this report, are those at the meeting, those brethren who have the facilities for attending the meeting—they are present, and hear all, and are satisfied with what they hear; but the call is from those who cannot hear the decision and arguments of this meeting—they call upon us for a report of the decisions of these meetings, and when they come to subscribe to our periodicals, the question asked is, are you going to give a report of the Annual Meeting? Do we not infer from this that it is the general wish and expression of the Brotherhood that they shall have a report of the meeting? Now if these brethren and sisters say we shall not give a report, we shall not do it, but we would have you understand this, that, although we would be cut off from this, there are others here who are reporting, and if it is not published in our periodicals, it will be in some others, and be spread broadcast throughout the world; and thus, if half the world is allowed to have the advantages of the discussions of this meeting, why is it that our brethren and sisters who are so anxious to know what passes here, should be debarred from this privilege?

H. R. Holsinger. I have an explanation to make in regard to the publication of the article read to you. It does occur occasionally that we get an article for publication from persons with whom we have no personal acquaintance. Here we have a letter from a Leedy, a name that stands quite high in the Brotherhood. Now, then, we read this article, not knowing, not caring, whether the man be a Jew, Heathen or Christian; but we read it endeavoring to learn whether it sets forth sentiments of truth, and when we find by inspection that the article sets forth truth, we publish it. Now, then, it occurred in this case, that a power is censured, and some of our brethren here think it reflects upon this meeting, while I thought it was going with power for the Pope of Rome. Did not know that this man was opposed to the Brotherhood; did not know that this man was going for the Annual Council, but supposed from the manner in which he writes that he was going for the Pope of Rome.—"Persons that would institute, instead of the Gospel, traditions of their own." Now it may be possible, that, if this man had specified certain things, and I had known that he was an expelled member of our church, I might have thought that he was going to censure our Annual Meeting, and then it would have gone into the waste basket, but I could not see that he was censuring our Annual Meeting. Let us see how it is. "Gates of hell is a metaphorical expression, representing councils of men." Is this a council of men? Does it apply? I had no right to suppose that it did, unless I knew him to be a railer of the Brotherhood. You may prove that he is such, you can't prove that I knew it, no matter if you sent me forty letters. I examined this letter for the truth part of it, and my assistant editor takes it up and he examined it, and thinks it sets forth the truth, and he has no idea that it aims at our Church.

To tell the truth, brethren, I had before my mind the Roman Catholic Church, and I did not know at the time that this man was not a brother; but here are persons, well acquainted with this man, and knowing him to be a railer and the particular things that he is driving at, it seems to hurt them. As far as I am concerned, it don't hurt me, and I don't know as it had any reference to the Annual Meeting. These are the facts in the case. We want to be liberal. All the writers of the *Companion* are not members of our Church. Some are members of other denominations, and write very excellent articles. Some are the Brethren's children who write and are not members of the church, and write good articles. We examine, and reject or accept it. A man of very high standing in our church may write an article and we decide upon its merits, and if it is not fit for publication, we throw it in the the waste basket, just as quick as any other.

Now, if it is proven that that has reference to our Annual Meeting, and in this Annual Meeting we are going to take such a thing upon ourselves, then perhaps I had better make an acknowledgment. If these things are not true, then they have reference, as I thought they had to the Roman Catholic Church, and I am not called upon to make any acknowledgment. I would say that I know it to be a fact.

Moderator — Brethren, Metzgar, Garber, Miller, Quinter, and many others that are here, bear testimony that they know that this was one of the things why he was put out of the church; that he was always complaining. One reason was because he opposed the counsels of the Annual Meeting.

Holsinger—We don't doubt Brother Davy's assertion, but what has that to do with the question under consideration? Suppose the man was a Heathen or a Publican, what has that to do with the question. Who he is, is not essential in regard to the publication of the sentiment.

Sturgis. I am very sorry that these matters are before us.

As an editor it does appear to me, that any man or woman, reading that communication should know that there was no danger of the Pope of Rome exercising the authority over our Brethren. Our papers should go forth for the education and instruction and warning of our members. I don't want to throw the insinuation that Brother Henry did not think what he says, but I think there was a want of carefulness. It showed that the brother was prying into the church. Some of my friends wrote to me censuring me for my course at the Annual meeting, because I advocated the doctrine and practice of the Brethren; they told me they were going to set up a new order. Some of my dear friends and relatives have gone into that new order, claiming that most of the members of the Annual meeting had set up over the heads of the majority of the Annual Meeting. I have written letters day and night, and convinced them that without the Annual Meeting we would go into fragments. Some of them yielded; others have gone into factions.

Now, then, every editor, and every brother that reads should look closely into the words, and every thing that would throw a fire brand into the Brotherhood should be thrown away.

I believe it would be better to do so; if we cannot avoid this other extreme, better have no papers at all? I say under existing circumstances it is well enough, at least, to admonish our Editors. They have been told by the Annual Meeting in 1870, that they should publish nothing which conflicts with the direct order of the Church, and if they did so, it would be looked into. Hence we claim that there is one paper published that we have no trouble with. But what is the consequence? Something strange and new. Expressions that they gave of the Annual Meeting seem to be taken for the proceedings here. I conclude then, it is better to suppress any further publication. It has been told to me by a few young brethren and sisters that they regard that it is only a few. The majority of the members don't want the thing passed so; this is what it is doing, if we don't suppress it. It has been intimated here that they want to know how we came to those conclusions, in order to be satisfied; though that only goes to prove that they wont obey, and be satisfied. And the Annual Meeting has really been assailed; there is no question about it. Whether Henry meant it or not, it has been declared by an enemy that has assailed me publicly and privately that he was driving at the Annual Meeting; when he calls it the gates of hell. Hence, while I have every confidence in the brethren who published it, I say there is a wrong done that cannot be easily healed. We think now we should suppress any publication, only that which passed the meeting.

To be Continued.

THE WELCOME HOME.

SELECTED BY KATE BARNIZER.

How sweet will be the welcome home
When this short life is o'er,
When pain and sorrow, care and grief
Shall dwell with us no more;
Then we that bright and heavenly land,
With spirit eyes shall see,
And join the holy angel band
In praise dear Lord of thee.

CHORUS:
The welcome home, the welcome home,
The Christian's welcome home.

Lord, grant my frail and wayward bark,
May anchor sure and fast,
Beside the shining gates of pearl,
Where I may rest at last.
When once within, my soul shall know,
No hunger, thirst, or pain;
No sickness, sorrow, care or death
Shall visit me again.

CHO.
The welcome, &c.

O may I live while here below,
In view of that blest day,
When God's bright angels shall come down,
To bear my soul away.
When I shall walk the golden streets,
In garments white and pure;
And sing an endless song to him,
Who made my soul secure.

CHO.

ORIGINAL ESSAYS.

TYPES AND PROPHECY.

A type has been defined to be an action or occurrence in which one event, person or circumstance is intended to represent another similar to it in certain respects, but of more importance and generally future. The Scriptures describe a type as "a shadow of good things to come."—Heb. 10: 1. Shadows are not exact resemblances, but give only a dark outline; yet with sufficient distinctness to convey some general idea of the body, especially when afterward we have the body with which to compare them. One distinction between a prophecy and a type is that a prophecy is a prediction by something said—a type is usually furnished by something done and presented to our sight.

The first revelation to fallen man contained a prophetic declaration of mercy which was an outline of the whole plan; or it may be compared to a seed which contains within itself the elements of the future plant. The first recorded act of acceptable worship, after the fall was connected with a type, expressed by an action that the first prophecy had declared by words,—The first prophecy, that "The seed of the woman should bruise the serpents head," intimated that the Messiah should triumph though not without suffering to Himself. Abel's sacrifice of a lamb seems to have shadowed forth that which was the great purpose of the Messiah's coming,—the putting away sin by the sacrifice of Himself—the substitution of an innocent for a guilty being. We can scarcely suppose that the act of approaching God by slaying an innocent animal could have been suggested to any pious mind as in itself an acceptable mode of worship, but it is immediately seen how, as a divine appointment in reference to the Messiah, it was suited to impress on sinful man that the ways of sin is death—that more than repentance is necessary to forgiveness, that "without shedding of blood is no remission;" Heb. 9: 22, while from the impossibility of the blood of a lamb taking away sin, such a mode of sacrifice was calculated to direct the offerer to look forward to the sacrifice of that lamb whose merits alone could give value to such an offering, and we know from Heb. 17: that "by faith Abel offered unto God a more excellent sacrifice than Cain, by which he obtained witness that he was righteous, God testifying of His gifts," indeed, "sacrifice appears to have been ordained as a standing memorial of the death introduced by sin and of that death which was to be suffered by the Redeemer." For illustration, we have an example of the insufficiency of repentance alone, however sincere and deep, 2 Samuel, 10: 17, and God's acceptance of sacrifice as the divinely appointed means of removing his anger, is remarkably seen in 2 Samuel 54: 25, as compared with Chron. 21: 26-27. The Lord answered David's prayer from Heaven by fire upon the altar of burnt-offering, and commanded the angel to put up his sword again into the sheath. Thus is the anger of God turned away from penitent sinners by the sacrifice of Christ. The Levitical law is throughout, a shadow of good things to come, Col. 2: 17, but particularly observe the services on the great day of atonement, Heb. 10: 1, Lev. 16 chapter as explained Heb. 9th chapter—God came to dwell among them, and he dwelt upon a mercy seat, "and there I will meet with thee and I will commune with thee from above the mercy seat." Ex. 25: 22, and all their worship was directed thither, but they were not to approach even the mercy-seat but, thro' the mediation of an High Priest; nor might the high priest himself come into the holy place, where God was supposed to have his special residence without the blood of sacrifices; which blood is expressly declared to have been for an atonement because of the uncleanness of the children of Israel, and because of their transgressions and their sins: Lev. 16: 16. and 17: 11. "It is the blood that maketh an atonement for the soul." Heb. 9: 22.

To be Continued.

THE WAY.

I have thought of writing a few lines for the readers of the PILGRIM, of which I have been a reader for about one year, and I have received a great deal of good instruction from it, and as I desire to uphold the good cause I will endeavor to present a few thoughts, and as it is necessary to have a foundation before we build I will direct your attention to the 6th verse of the 14th chapter of St John. "Jesus saith unto him, I am the way, the truth and the life, no man cometh unto the Father but by me."

This is a plain passage delivered by Christ himself to Thomas and for a noble purpose, I have no doubt, and as we believe that all Scripture was given by inspiration of God and is good for doctrine, we will, in the first place, try to show you what a way means. In a temporal sense we understand it to be a road or a way leading from place to place, but the way spoken of in our text, is the way that leads from earth to heaven. Then in order that we find this end it becomes necessary that we first get in the way and then be careful and follow him in all things whatsoever he commands us, for he says: "I am the way." He also says, "I am the door, by me if any man enter in he shall be saved," John 10: 9. We will endeavor to give you our understanding of entering in at the door. In the first place, you must believe that he is, and that he is a rewarder of those who diligently seek him. Then in the next place, you must go to work, and how? says one. Well, I will say according to his word. I will give you Peter's way, when they said to him and the rest of the apostles, "What shall we do? Peter said unto them, repent and be baptized every one of you in the name of Jesus Christ for the remission of sins and ye shall receive the gift of the Holy Ghost, Acts, 2: 41. Then they that gladly received his word were baptized, and the same day there were added unto them about three thousand. It seems that these came in at the door and they did not tarry but went to work, and that according to the directions of Peter. And we have the account of them traveling in this way; "and they continued steadfastly in the apostles doctrine in breaking bread and prayers," &c. I think if the people would receive the words of the apostles in this our day as they did in that day and age of the world, there would not be so much difference in professors, and we believe that the Scripture is the same to us in this day and generation as it was then. I will give you another evidence of entering in, which you will find in Romans, 6th chapter, 3rd verse. Know ye not that so many of us as were baptized into Jesus Christ were baptized into his death." 5th verse. "For if we have been planted together in the likeness of his death, we shall be also in the likeness of his resurrection." Let us endeavor to take Christ for our way and follow his examples and commands and let us show to the world that we possess what we profess. Let them see the fruit of righteousness. Let us feed the hungry, clothe the naked, and visit the sick and show mercy. Visit the fatherless and widows in their afflictions and keep ourselves unspotted from the world. Let us make him the way in all things, in the Lord's Supper, the Communion, Feet Washing, the Holy Kiss in prayer and in love.

GODFREY H. SHAFER.

THE RICH YOUNG MAN.

I suppose that all have read about the rich young man who came to Christ to know what he must do to inherit eternal life. Jesus spoke to him of the commandments and asked him if he knew them. He said all these have I kept from my youth up. But what did he then tell him he should do? He told him to go and sell all that he had and give to the poor, but oh, how sorrowful he looked when he thought that he must part with all his possessions, for he was very rich. It seems that he would rather keep his riches and be lost, at last, than to give them up and have eternal life, for we have no account of him ever doing as the Lord told him to do, and how many in this our day look sorrowful when they are called upon (out of their abundance), to give something for the support of others, they are ready to make many excuses and say, "my crops did not do so well last year, I don't think I will have anything to spare." Who gave you what you have got? Who gave health and strength to prepare your soil and sow your grain? Who sent you the early and latter rain to make the earth bring forth? The giver of all good has given them to you, and are you now unwilling to restore to him part of what he has so bountifully bestowed upon you? You have enough to support your families, enough to sell to pay your taxes and some still left to put in the bank. Do you not know the Lord will provide for you? He has promised to provide for all those who put their trust in him. Do not do as the rich man who had no room to bestow his goods, do not go pulling down your barns and building greater ones that you may have room, methinks you can find plenty of places to store them away where they will do much good. Perhaps across the way, lives a poor widow who has two or three little children to look to her for support, take some of your goods there and store them away in her house. And perhaps, a little farther on, there lives an aged couple who have battled long with the cares of this life, who are now disabled for any further service by age and affliction, take some of your goods there. You would cause the widows heart to sing for joy, the fatherless children to praise you, the aged ones would bless you and, best of all, the Lord would reward you. If you do make some sacrifice what of it. If you give without making any sacrifice I fear it may do but little good. You know the Lord loves a cheerful giver, for the good book says: the poor you have always with you. You can do them good if you will. Let us all be intent upon doing something for our fellow creatures—let us forget the sacrifices we are trying to make to help others, and we shall have a two-fold reward, we shall have the sweet consciousness of having done a benevolent act, and also be strengthened by it. Let us not say, in reply to every appeal that is addressed to our feelings, depart in peace, be ye warmed and filled, but let us hasten to their relief and do all we can for them and then we can only say we have done that which was our duty to do.

M. C. K.

Parnassus, Va.

PARTING.

This world is not our home. Soon will come our time of parting, that we part from our native home and country for the far West. Yes, we part from our parents, sisters and brothers and many, very many that have been dear unto us from our childhood up. Near and dear has been many of the associates I have had from quite young to this period, yet I am willing to forsake all these for the satisfaction and interest of those that are dearer to me than all earth, and willing to dwell and be contented in any distant land that would be to the pleasure and interest of my beloved companion and the future welfare of the dear ones that the Lord has given us.

The separation, I hope, will cause us to strive the more earnestly to gain that better country where all may meet to part no more. Oh that glorious abode, that blissful time when this world of parting, sin and troubles of all kinds, will have an end. How earnestly may be our desire to get rid of sin and trouble, and to do more good for our Creator and fellow man; yet how, oh how little is done! Oh, let us often examine ourselves, and strive, with all power and might to overcome our sinful nature and the tempter, and be better prepared for the indwelling of the Spirit of the Lord. Often do I wonder; shall I escape the doom of the foolish virgins? If so, Oh Lord hasten the glorious meeting when we all may dwell together in love and unity. Oh, that blessed, that happy day, when sin is known no more. Oh, perfect love, when shall we possess it, where no unkind word is spoken, where no hard thought is known. Oh, the unspeakable joys of that place! May we be more heavenly minded, and set our affections more to things above. This world is all confusion and vexation of spirit. What murmering, unthankfulness and dissatisfaction is among the human family at this time. Let us be more prayerful, more zealous in the cause of Christ and as we part here, may our souls prayer be; Lord help us to meet above where all is joy and holy love. As I leave our church here, my earnest desire is, may we all meet in those glorious regions of love. May each one of us know the great duty that rests upon us is the prayer of your weak sister in Christ.

SUSANNAH M. HUTCHINSON.

Oak Hill, Va.

Youth's Department.

SWEET BABY SLEEP.

SELECTED BY C. C.

Sweet baby, sleep, what ails my dear,
 What ails my darling thus to cry;
Be still my child, and lend thine ear,
 To hear me sing thy lullaby.
My pretty babe forbear to weep,
 Be still, my dear, sweet baby sleep:

Whilst thus thy lullaby I sing,
 For the great blessings ripened be.
Thine eldest brother is a king,
 And hast a kingdom bought for thee;
Sweet baby, then forbear to weep,
 Be still my babe, sweet baby sleep.

A little infant once was he,
 And strength in weakness then was laid;
Upon His Virgin mother's knee,
 That power to thee might be conveyed.
Sweet baby, then forbear to weep,
 Be still my babe, sweet baby, sleep;

Within a manger laid the Lord,
 Where oxen lay and asses fed,
Warm rooms, we do to thee afford,
 An easy cradle or a bed.
Sweet baby, then forbear to weep,
 Be still my babe, sweet baby sleep.

Thou hast yet more to perfect this,
 A promise and an earnest got,
Of gaining everlasting bliss,
 Though thou, my babe, perceiv'st it not.
Sweet baby, then forbear to weep,
 Be still my babe, sweet baby, sleep.

DO BOYS EVER THINK?

This may seem a strange question, to ask whether *boys* ever think, and some of our little girls may wonder why they were not included in so important a question. I sometimes write from force of circumstances and every day, little boys may be seen doing things so thoughtlessly that it becomes a question whether they *ever* think. Of course all little boys think somehow, but the question is, do they think right.

Boys, and girls too, should always remember that their parents are their best friends and that all they do for them is intended for their special good. Have you ever thought of this? A mother's love, by our Savior, was considered the strongest and the only love that would bear comparison with His own. But notwithstanding this strong love that your parents bear towards you, how often do you think you know best, and do the very things that they wish you not to do? Now boys, how is it, do you think? If you do, you think wrong, because you think against your best interests, because to disobey your parents is the first step on the broad way that leads to dishonor and death.

Again, when we see boys, on Sunday, out hunting, robbing birds nests and stealing apples, can we help but ask, "do boys ever think?" Will such a course ever end well? No, my dear young friends, it will lead you in the wrong direction, away from your father's house, away from all that is right and good and worst of all, away from Jesus, your best friend, who has said, "first of all seek the Kingdom," with the promise, if you do so "all things shall be added." If you are inclined to think, there is nothing that you can think about that will give you so much enjoyment, as obedience to parents and love to Jesus. But how is it with boys who allow themselves to indulge in bad habits, such as drinking strong drinks and smoking and chewing tobacco? Do they think? Let us see By spending 6¼ cents per day in this filthy habit you spend in one year $22,81 cents, and in 25 years, at a reasonable interest, over $2.000. In doing this, do you ever think? Have you ever tried to think how much benefit you are a going to derive from this habit? If you have, the following, I suppose would be the result of your calculations: First, an expenditure of a fortune for which I receive dyspepsia, headache, pains in the back, pains in the side, pains in the legs and pains all over. In addition to all this, I am made a slave to be only liberated in death which is promised at the expiration of half my days. Is it possible that boys do think and still continue to indulge in those habits which produce such unfortunate results? If you have not, will you not do it now, because it may save you from many snares that satan has set for you and lead you to that liberty which Jesus offers and which will make you free indeed.

UNCLE HENRY.

A CHILD'S SACRIFICE.

"My little children, let us not love in word, neither in tongue; but in deed and truth."

A child had a beautiful canary, which sang to him from early morning. The mother of the child was ill—so ill that the song of the little bird, which to the boy was delicious, disturbed and distressed her so that she could scarcely bare to hear it.

He put it in a room far away, but the bird's notes reached the sick bed, and caused pain to her long feverish days.

One morning, as the child stood holding his mother's hand, he saw that when his pet sung, an expression of pain passed over her dear face.—She had never yet told him that she could not bear the noise, but she did so now:

"It is no music to me," she said, as he asked her if the notes were not pretty. He looked at her in wonder.

"And do you really dislike the sound?"

"Indeed I do," she said.

The child full of love to his mother, left the room. The golden feathers of the pretty canary were glistening in the sunshine, and he was telling forth his loveliest notes; but they had ceased to please the boy. They were no longer pretty or soothing to him, and taking the cage in his hand he left the house. When he returned he told his mother that the bird would disturb her rest no more, for he had given it to his little cousin.

"But you loved it so," she said, "how could you part with the canary?"

"I loved the canary, mother," he replied, "but I loved you more. I could not really love any living thing that gave you pain. It would not be true love if I did."—*The Quiver.*

FREELY FORGIVE

It is very easy for us to say we will forgive those who injure us, but it is quite another thing to put it in practice. Many people forgive very much as the little school-girl did to whom her teacher said, "Mary, if a naughty girl should hurt you, you would forgive her like a good little girl, wouldn't you?"

"Yes, ma'am," she said, "if I could not catch her?"

Another little Sunday-school scholar had a notion of forgiveness very much like hers. His lesson had been upon this subject, and his teacher asked him if, in view of what he had been studying he could forgive those who wronged him.

"Could you," said the teacher, "forgive a boy for instance, who had struck you?"

"Y-e-s, sir,' said the lad slowly, after thinking a little, "I could—I guess I could;" and then added, in a husky tone, "I know I could if he were bigger than I am!"

These little folks put us in mind of an old gentleman who had a quarrel with a neighbor, and thinking he was about to die, sent for the neighbor, that difficulty might be settled before he died. "I can't bear," said he, "to leave this world while there is any bad feeling between us. But, mind you," he said with all the energy his feeble voice could assume, "if I get well, the old grudge stands!"

Ah, that is not like the teaching of Jesus. The enemy is not only to be forgiven, but treated like a friend.—True forgiveness empties the heart of all remembrance of old grudges and hate, and fills it with kindness and love.

He who has struck his colors to the power of an evil habit, has surrendered himself to an enemy, bound by no articles of faith, and from whom he can expect only the vilest treatment.

The Weekly Pilgrim.

JAMES CREEK, PA., June 24, 1873.

☞ How to send money.--All sums over $1.50, should be sent either in a check, draft or postal order. If neither of these can be obtained, have the letter registered.

☞ When Money is sent, *always* send with it the name and address of those who paid it. Write the names and post office as plainly as possible.

☞ Every subscriber for 1873, gets a *Pilgrim Almanac* Free.

LET THE WORK GO ON.

In every enterprise, to have success, there must be some one to lead, and especially is this the case in getting up subscriptions. At the very liberal terms on which we now offer to send the Pilgrim from A. M., to end of the year, there is but little difficulty to get subscribers if there is some one to present the matter to the people.—Some of our agents and friends have been doing this with success. In the several last mails we received lists ranging from 12 to 15, with the promise of sending still more in a few days. This shows what can be done when an effort is made. Will not others go and do likewise? Please make the effort. We need it for our own encouragement, and feel assured that so small an amount of money cannot be spent for a better purpose. While we offer the report of our Annual Conference as an inducement, we wish it understood that independent of it we expect to make the Pilgrim fully worth the price asked for it. We have issued some 400 extra copies beginning with the report, so that all can be supplied with back Nos. from A. M. Do not forget our very liberal terms: Single copies, 80; 10 copies $7 25; 15 copies, $10 50; 20 copies, $14 25. Let every one that is interested in having the truth freely disseminated, go to work and see how easily 400 new subscribers can be raised from A. M., to end of the year. Nearly 100 is already received and the work is only commenced.

AN EXPLANATION.

An explanation has been asked of us on the following scripture: (See Matt. 8: 11, 12:

This is part of the consultation that took place between Jesus and the Centurian, and the object evidently was to give encouragement to the stranger and a warning to the unbelieving Jews. Those coming from the East and West are the Gentile nation, including the Centurian spoken to, and was the fulfillment of the prophecies concerning the salvation which was to be for all nations.

The "children of the kingdom" has reference to the Jews as a nation and people. They shall be rejected for their unbelief and hardness of heart, and shall finally be cast out of the Kingdom of Christ, or the true church of God, and in their place, believers of the Gentile nations, from the East and from the West shall come in and take their seats with Abraham, Isaac and Jacob. This may be our happy lot if we are willing to undergo the grafting in process and be as fruitful branches of the true vine stock, Jesus Christ.

Catharine Shidler.—The Helping hand was sent. If not received by this time, let us know, and we will send it again.

J. M. P.—M. J. G's Pilgrim was paid to No. 23, 1873, and is now paid to No. 24, '74. You did not give us Jno. Shelleberger's address, please send it and we will furnish him all back Nos. Your name is in type and we cannot see how your paper can fail to come.

Geo. W. C.—The $125 was received. The Pilgrim is paid to July 23, '73; due us 65 cts.

Crowded Out.—Notes of travel by Eld. J. S. Flory, also, some other correspondence, and just as we are ready to go to press, we have received the "Missouri Committee Report." All will be attended to next week.

Good News.—Some of the last mails are bringing us quite encouraging news in regard to the welfare and prosperity of the Church. In places their has been quite a number of additions to the church, and the good work appears to be on the increase.

DIED.

KOOK.—In Noble Co., Ind., June 4, 1873, sister Caroline, wife of brother I. Kook, aged 39 years, 8 mos. and 18 days. Funeral services by Elder Truly and others.

Our dear sister died in a full hope of a home in that bright world beyond this life of trouble and care. She leaves a kind husband, children and friends to mourn their loss.

BETHKA.—In the Springfield Church, Noble Co., Ind., May 26, 1873, aged 60 years and 9 months.

Sister Bethka was born August 27, 1812, in the town of Broad Oak, Germany, and was married August 27, 1837, and emigrated to America in 1854. She leaves a husband to mourn his loss, but we hope, her gain. Funeral by C. Weaver and the writer.

Joseph Est.

(*Visitor* and *Companion* please copy.)

DEETER.—In the Newton District, Miami Co., Ohio, June 8, 1873, sister Elizabeth Deeter aged 63 years, 2 mos., and 28 days.

She was followed to the grave by a large concourse of friends and relatives.

Mary A. Ross.

KOCHENDARFER.—In the Yellow Creek Church, Bedford Co., Pa., June 15, 1873, sister Caroline, wife of Samuel Kochendarfer, and daughter of Samuel Snider dec'd., aged 31 years, 11 mos. and 19 days. Disease, Diptheria. Funeral by the Brethren, from 2 Timothy, 4: 7, 8, to a large concourse of people. She left a sorrowful husband and 3 children to mourn their loss, 2 having previously died.

MONEY LIST.

Wm. H. Quinn	$1 50	H. F. Nair	2 75
Jacob Musselman	75	D. P. Sayler	50
J. H. Tawzer	1 50	Geo. Maurer	60
Elizabeth Hoofstetler	1 50	H. F. Nair	1 25
J. C. Sidebottom	1 50	D. H. Bonebrake	13 75
J. W. Gibb	10 00	S. M. Pretzman	5 50
		Jos. Zahn	1 50

Correspondence.

A Reporter is wanted from every Church in the brotherhood to send us Church news, Obituaries, Announcements, or anything that will be of general interest. To insure insertion, the writers name must accompany each communication. Our Invitation is not personal but general—please respond to our call.

REPORT OF OUR MISSION TO CRAWFORD CO., PA.

As it is known by the Middle District of Pa., that by the approval of that district, John W. Brumbaugh and myself were sent, after repeated calls, to Crawford Co., Pa., on a mission of preaching. Having now returned from that mission, according to request, I will try to give a brief report of the same, partly by notes and partly from memory.

After attending a Communion at Snake Spring Valley, Pa., I started, May 31, from Bedford to Dale City, the place of A. M., where my colleage met me. After enjoying the pleasures and success of our A. M., with the delights of associating with brethren and sisters from a distance whom we had known before, with the addition of forming pleasurable acquaintances with many that we did not know before, we felt revived; though with somewhat impaired health, yet encouraged, we set out June 5th, in the evening train on the Connellsville Railroad to Pittsburg, arrived safely at 1 30 a. m., had some sleep, and refreshment in the morning. June 6, started on the Pittsburg and Erie Railroad at 7 15 a. m., came to Linesville 12 30 p. m., were met there by our dear friend A. J. Williams, (now brother), who, after kindly caring for a dinner, took us to his house, 7 miles distant, where his kind family were ready to receive us. As Railroad travelling is subject to uncertainty of time, he saw proper to make no appointment till next evening, June 7, Saturday. He however had made arrangement to have the United Presbyterian Church as long as we would stay for meeting, being the nearest to his residence, 1½ mile off. Met with a respectable congregation in the evening, preached from 2 Cor. 1: 2-3, to a very attentive audience. As Mr. Williams had fully made up his mind to be received into the Church by the ordinance of Christian baptism the next day, it was publicly announced that a sermon would be preached on the mode, formula and position in the performance of Christian baptism as we understand it from the Gospel. June 8, Sabbath, met at 10 a. m., with a large congregation, said to be the largest ever met there with the exception of the Dedication of that church. Preached from the Commission as recorded in Matt. 28 latter part. Bro. J. W. B. spoke on the prerequisites to baptism, I followed on the mode, form and position as understood by us from the word of God, with an earnest appeal to search for themselves. At the close of the meeting we went to the water near by, where brother Williams made the solemn vow of allegiance to King Emanuel, the Prince of Peace, the Author of eternal salvation, in the presence of God and before many witnesses. Inasmuch as baptism had never been performed in the manner we performed it, it was undoubtedly a novelty to the large concourse witnessing the solemn scene. However great solemnity was manifested by the spectators as far as I observed, and we have reason to believe that it made solemn and we hope lasting impressions on many. Meeting again in the afternoon, but the meetings being too close together, many came a considerable distance, the meeting was not as large as in the forenoon. Preached from Heb. 2, "How shall we escape if we neglect so great salvation." Respectable audience and good attention. The evenings being short, the people busy and we debilitated, we concluded to have no appointment 'till Tuesday evening, as some thought that as much good could be done by preaching privately from house to house. We had numbers of invitations, many more than we could attend to in the time we stayed with them. We omit the names of those we visited as it would swell this report beyond the limit we wish to give it. We fondly hope that none will consider themselves slighted when we do not particularize, suffice it to say that kindness, love, benevolence and Christian courtesy was shown to us wherever we were, much beyond what we merited, and we are thoroughly convinced that God is there, and that He may, thro' the ministers' faithful charge and strenuous efforts, by the guidance of the Holy Spirit in His own time, gather a numerous church there. I can see nothing to the contrary, many are aroused, awakened and in search of the one thing needful. Brethren, pray for that part of God's moral Vineyard, have ministers sent there to preach the word, expound the truth as it is in Jesus that the hungering, starving souls in that community may be richly fed with the Bread of Life. A heavy rain on Tuesday evening prevented our meeting. Wednesday evening, by earnest request, we met again, the last time for public worship, in a school-house, near brother W's,—only half a days notice, yet the house was well filled and we had a blessed meeting, with earnest requests for more preaching and a longer stay, or at least a promise to visit them again, which we did conditionally.

Mrs. Williams showed us especial kindness, sociability and Christian courtesy, and accompanied us in our visits as much as the state of her health would permit. May the Lord reward her and bless her labors of love as she seems in trouble and in an unreconciled condition. May the Church, in her united prayers, remember her, implore God's divine aid in convincing and enlightening her to become reconciled to God by the *word of reconciliation*. And may the Church in her prayers, remember also our beloved brother Andrew J. Williams, the first fruit of Crawford Co., in his isolated condition, that he may be a light to the world, a bright star in the constellation, his house a house of prayer, his family a family of peace, and that his kind wife may yet become a mother in Israel, and that blessings may flow from his residence to influence that community to partake largely of the waters from the wells of salvation.

Thursday June 12, Bro. W., his wife and his brother Joseph accompanied us to Meadville, 7 miles distant, where at 4 p. m., took the train to Franklin, took the Allegheny Valley Railroad to A. Junction, thence to Butler,—came to friend J. H. Graham's, who formerly lived a close neighbor, his wife being a sister in the Church. This being a place where the Brethren never preached before, Saturday evening, June 14, an appointment previously being made in the Presbyterian Church, where we met entire strangers except the Graham family, a Methodist Communion meeting not far off at the time, and not being known generally, consequently the congregation not very large, chiefly members of that church. I tried to preach from the words, "Take heed unto thyself and unto the doctrine, continue in them," &c., had very good attention,—hope solemn impressions were made. As our order of holding meetings was strange to them we briefly defined our order, as kneeling posture in prayer, the audience cherished and confirmed to it. Next day Lord's day, their Sabbath school being at 9:30 a. m., we made the appointment at 11, being requested by the Supt. to address the scholars we made an effort to do so briefly. We opened the meeting at the appointed time, brother Brumbaugh read the 14th chapter of John, spoke chiefly on the beginning of the chapter. The exercises seemed to be appreciated by the audience as strict attention was paid to the word spoken. Requests were made for more meetings, but a meeting near by in the U. P. Church in the afternoon, we thought best to make no appointment, and the evenings being so short, neither of us well, the church 2½ miles from our house, and had to start very early on our journey homeward we preferred to have no meeting. However we regretted it afterwards when we heard that the Methodists had no meeting, and only being known to a great many that day of our meetings, which many desired to attend, had we made the appointment it was thought that the house would have been filled, as the Brethren never preached there. But may all be for the better if only the Brethren will attend that place again, for solemn appeals were made to come again and preach for us. June 16 we took the train at Butler and came home safely that evening found all well, God's name be praised, for his mercy endureth forever. Amen.

LEONARD FURRY.

New Enterprise, Pa.

TO N. V. K.

Dear and much respected sister in the Lord, your kind and interesting letter of the — came duly to hand. I was much pleased to hear from you, yet I felt sorry that you are so much afflicted. But it being the will of the Lord, suffer it to be so. We shall glorify God in our bodies and spirits which are his, and if in the arrangement of God it is so decreed that you shall glorify him in your body by suffering in the flesh, let it be so. He will always give you grace sufficient to bear, and to endure faithful to the end. And when you will come with those who have come up out of great tribulation, and have with them washed your robe in the blood of the Lamb, and with them have a crown on your head, and a palm of victory in your hand; it may be needful for us, as it was for St. John, to ask who IS THIS? Then dear sister you will forget that you ever suffered in the flesh. To this end the Lord bless you, and sustain you, and give you grace sufficient for all your trials, and never suffer you to be tried above that you are able to bear, but with every trial make way for your escape. I pray for you in Jesus name. Amen.

Now in reference to your question, I will say it is easier to ask than to answer them. So in this I may differ in my views from yours, and from brethren much wiser than I am, but if so, I ask forbearance. Your question is "A new commandment I give unto you," and "by this shall all men know that ye are my disciples if ye have love one to another." "What was this new commandment? Was it that of Feet washing?"

This scripture is recorded by St. John, 13: 34, 35.

In answer I will say, that some hold that the "new commandment" is, that we love one another, and this is the view that I formerly held; others hold that feet washing is the new commandment; and I have heard some affirm that it is the supper. But neither of these will stand the test of Scripture, for to love our neighbor as ourselves was a commandment long ago, and the Scripture testimony that our neighbor means our brother, is abundant and conclusive. So to love our brethren was not a new commandment at the time the Savior uttered the words in question. Neither was feetwashing as a religious observance, altogether new at that time. For God himself had commanded the observance of feet washing, as a religious institution in the earliest days of organizing services among men on earth. See Exo. 3: 17–21, and 40: 30–33. So neither loving one another, nor washing feet could not be called a new commandment. Nor could the supper be called altogether new, for there was some similarity between it and the Passover supper, or the feast of the Passover. It is true that the similarity in this is but a trace, masticating is the only feature altogether similar. Yet it is evident that neither of these observed in their isolation could be termed a new commandment.

We observe that when Jesus began to wash his disciples feet, and coming to Peter he objected to having his washed; but Jesus said unto him, What I do thou knowest not now; but thou shalt know hereafter?" Here Peter is notified that something new would be instituted. No doubt he had known the law that commanded the priest to wash his feet before he serves at the altar, and no doubt had often seen it observed in that way, but for the priest or Master to wash the disciples feet, religiously he knew nothing of. St. Paul, speaking of the priesthood, says: If perfection were by the Levitical priesthood, what further need was there that another priest should rise after the order of Melchisedec, and not be called after the order of Aaron? For the priesthood being changed, there is made of necessity a change also of the law." See Heb. 7th chapter. So Jesus is made a priest, not after the law of a carnal commandment, but after the power of an endless life; has power, and of necessity must change the law, and so has changed the feast of the Passover to that of the Lord's supper, and the slaying, and offering the Paschal lamb, to the breaking bread, and giving the cup or wine the fruit of the vine as representatives of the sacrifice of himself in his broken body, and shed blood once for all; and changing the law of the priest, washing his own hands and feet before serving at the alter, into washing one anothers feet before eating the Lord's supper, and partaking of the bread and wine as emblematical of his body and blood, broken and shed for the sins of the world. Now they are combined as they are given and connected in the Scriptures with the declaration, "If ye know these things, happy are ye if ye do them," evidently, is a "new commandment" never before so combined, so commanded, nor so observed. And now only so observed by the Brethren who are the Lord's chosen few and faithful followers.

Love, the binding bond must be in it all, and if this principle is manifest in us, all men will know that we are his disciples, when we do love one another; and to know this there must be a token given, and he says: "By this shall all men know," &c. The expression "By this," implies more than is expressed, and I believe "By this" the kiss of love is implied. The kiss is a token of love, and its observance as such, is enjoined by the apostles in their writings to the churches five times. We may give signs and tokens by which we may know that we love each other; but these are private and all men cannot know it; but when the member of the body, the church, are seated at the table of the Lord in the observance of the "new commandment," and salute one another, all men can see it and know that we are His disciples because we gave them the token by which they can know i.

God's people always had bands and cords by which they were bound together, and which their enemies always strove to break asunder. The Psalmist said, "The kings of the earth set themselves, and the rulers take council together, against the Lord, and against his anointed, saying, Let us break these cords asunder, and let us cast away these cords from us." Of these bands and cords none are so largely and conspicuously set forth in the word of God as that of His people saluting one another. Jacob said come near and kiss me my son, and he came near and kissed him, Jacob kissed Rachel, Laban embraced and kissed Jacob, Laban kissed his sons and daughters, Esau embraced and kissed Jacob, Joseph kissed all his brethren, Moses kissed his father-in-law. Aaron kissed Moses, Naomi kissed her daughter-in-law, Orpha kissed her mother-in-law, Samuel kissed Saul when he anointed him, David and Jonathan kissed one another, David kissed Absalom, Absalom kissed those to whom he gave his hand. Elisha said, let me kiss my father and mother. I could continue my reference to a great length, but let this suffice to sustain our faith that "By this" the kiss is meant.

My answer to your question, "what was this new commandment?" is this, the ordinance of washing one anothers feet, the eating of the Lord's supper; and the partaking of the broken body, and shed blood of Christ, connected and combined in one service, is the "new commandment," and is what is meant when he says, "If ye know these things happy are ye if ye do them." And, "By this," the kiss is meant as the token by which all men may know that we are his disciples. In christian love I remain your brother, D. P. SAYLER.

Dear Pilgrim: Let me give you a little church news. I left home June 9th, to attend brother John Knisley's Communion meeting. June 10th, we met at their church to hold the above named meeting. An unusual large congregation met. The number of ministers was not very large, yet enough. We had a feast of fat things indeed, and refreshing to the soul.—Six were added to the fold by baptism, and many more felt the strivings of the Spirit. The church held a choice for a minister. The lot fell upon brother William G. Cook, son-in-law of brother John Hoover, who was called from this church recently by death. Brother Cook is a worthy young brother, and we hope the blessing of God will rest upon him.

From here I went to Huntington congregation, to their Communion meeting. This church is in its infancy yet. We commenced meeting at 3 P. M., with good attendance and good order, we had a very pleasant one indeed, and a soul-refreshing feast, and the most rejoicing I ever saw.—Here ten were added to the fold by baptism, and seven more applicants which were baptized the next day.

Sabbath morning, June 15, we went to Antioch. Here again the attendance was large, and much interest manifested, and ten more were added to the fold by baptism, and the church was richly refreshed, and I think all felt much better than they have for some time before, and as the Lord came near, we hope we will all come closer to Him. JESSE CALVERT.

Milford, Ind.

HAMILTON, Mo., June 12th, 1873.

Brother H. B. Brumbaugh, please publish the following contributions received to aid in building a meeting house:

Jacob D. Rosenberger,	$2 00
James Creek, Pa., H. B. Brumbaugh,	6 00
Spring Run, Pa. J.R. Hanawalt	10 00
Dry Valley, Pa., Jacob Mohler	11 30
Brush Creek, Md., D. Gibbon & C. Cronise,	6 30
New Enterprise, Pa., Leonard Fury,	27 25
Total,	$62 85

We have written to all our dear brethren who have manifested a desire to assist us, as above, and would again return our warmest thanks for their liberality and kindness. The above amount is all we have received as yet, and unless we receive more aid from the Brethren and friends, the work will not be accomplished very soon. In Christian affection your brethren, GEO. WITWER; W. B. SELL; DAN'L B. SELL.

New French Religious Sect.

The existence of a religious sect called "Derbists," whose adherents are mostly recruited in the two departments of the Drome and the Ardeche, was scarcely known to the great majority of the Frenchmen until a soldier belonging to this body was tried by court martial a few days ago, for insubordination. The tenets of this sect are principally embodied in the doctrine that human life is absolutely sacred, and that the professino of arms is in itself a crime. In obedience to this teaching a young man who had been sent to join his regiment, refused to carry arms, declaring that he was ready to submit to any punishment, even that of death, rather than repudiate his principles. The colonel had no alternative but to send him before a court martial for breach of discipline; and in the course of the trial the schoolmaster, who had been called as witness, stated that although he had done all in his power to eradicate these ideas, the prisoner held fast to his original purpose. When he told him that, in the event of a battle, he would always be able to fire in the air, the young man declared that he would not do that because it would be an act of treachery towards the government, and that he preferred stating the case to his superiors when called upon to join the army. On similar grounds he refused to purchase a substitute; and in reply to the warning of his schoolmaster that he would render himself liable to be shot for insubordination, he avowed his readiness "to add another to the three millions of martyrs who have already died for their faith." His behavior at the trial was most exemplary, and when questioned by the President of the Court, he confessed thet he had disobeyed the military laws, but had acted in conformity with those of the Gospel.

REMARKABLE FRESHET.—The *Omaha Republican* publishes the report of Captain Moore, of the regular army, who recently returned from a scout in the Republican Valley, whither he had gone with a command of sixty men, by order of General Ord, for the purpose of patrolling the valley and learning the disposition of the Indians. The Cap. mentions an extraordinary flood which overtook his command. While at Blackwood Creek, at about 9 P. M., on the 31st of May, being in the valley of Blackwood, a sudden and devastating freshet came rushing down the valley, carrying away, like corks, men, tents, horses, and army wagons. This valley is between forty and fifty miles in length, and from a mile to a mile and a half wide. Its whole space during the freshet was one raging torrent, six or seven feet deep. Six men and twenty-six horses were drowned by the calamity, and most of the men whose lives were preserved saved themselves from death by catching the limbs of the trees as they swept away, and thus reached the tops of the trees, where, when the dawn of the next day broke, they were still perched. Eleven men were saved by clinging to the top of an army wagon which had stuck to a log on the ground. Five of the bodies of the drowned men were recovered. What is curious about this freshet is, as Captain Moore reports, that there was no apparent cause for this occurrence, as for five days previous there had been no rain, and he is unable to say whence the water came.

HUNTINGDON & BROAD TOP RAIL ROAD

On and after June 15th, 1873, Trains will run on this road daily (Sun excepted) as follows:

Trains from Huntingdon South. *Trains from Mt. Dallas moving North.*

MAIL A. M.	EXP'S P. M.	STATIONS.	MAIL P. M.	EXP'S A. M.
7 45	5 50	Huntingdon,	AR 6 10	AR [illegible]
7 50	6 05	Long Siding	6 05	8 [illegible]
8 10	6 15	McConnelstown	5 50	8 [illegible]
8 17	6 23	Pleasant Grove	5 40	8 [illegible]
8 30	6 35	Marklesburg	5 25	7 45
8 45	6 50	Coffee Run	5 11	7 [illegible]
8 55	6 58	Rough & Ready	5 03	7 [illegible]
9 05	7 05	Cove	4 56	7 [illegible]
9 08	7 10	Fishers Summit	4 52	7 10
9 22	7 25	Saxton	4 40	6 53
9 40	7 50	Riddlesburg	4 20	6 35
9 47	7 58	Hopewell	4 13	6 [illegible]
10 02	8 12	Piper's Run	4 00	6 01
10 20	8 30	Tatesville	3 47	5 45
10 30	8 40	Everett	3 35	5 35
10 35	8 45	Mount Dallas	3 30	5 [illegible]
11 05	9 20	Bedford	3 00	5 [illegible]

SHOUP'S RUN BRANCH.

A. M.	P. M.		P. M.	A. M.
LE 9 25	LE 7 35	Saxton.	AR 4 25	AR 6 [illegible]
9 40	7 50	Coalmont.	4 10	6 [illegible]
9 45	7 55	Crawford.	4 05	6 [illegible]
AR 9 55	AR 8 05	Dudley	LE 3 55	LE 6 15

Bro'd Top City from Dudley 2 miles by stage.

Time of Penna. R. R. Trains at Huntingdon.

***Mail No. 2 makes connection at Huntingdon with Mail going East on Pennsylvania Railroad at 4.15 p. m., and West at 5.45 p. m. Mail No. 1 leaves Huntingdon at 7.40 a. m. on arrival of Pacific Express West.

Trains on this road connect with trains on Bedford & Bridgeport, and Cumberland & Pennsylvania Railroads.

G. F. GAGE, Supt.

The Weekly Pilgrim.

Published by J. B. Brumbaugh, & Co.

Edited by H. B. & Geo. Brumbaugh.

CORRESPONDING EDITORS.

D. P. Sayler, Double Pipe Creek, Md.

Leonard Furry, New Enterprise, Pa.

The *Pilgrim* is a Christian Periodical, devoted to religion and moral reform. It will advocate in the spirit of *love* and *liberty*, the principles of true Christianity, labor for the promotion of peace among the people of God, for the encouragement of the saints and for the conversion of sinners, avoiding those things which tend toward disunion or sectional feelings.

TERMS.

Single copy, Book paper,	$1.[illegible]
Eleven copies, [eleventh for Agt.]	$15.[illegible]

Any number above that at the same rate.

Address.

H. B. BRUMBAUGH.
James Creek,
Huntingdon county Pa.

The Weekly Pilgrim.

"REMOVE NOT THE ANCIENT LANDMARKS WHICH OUR FATHERS HAVE SET."

VOL. 4. JAMES CREEK, PENNSYLVANIA, JULY 1, 1873. NO. 26.

REPORT OF ANNUAL MEETING CONTINUED.

(*Continued from page 195.*)

Whereas the C. F. C. and PILGRIM have published articles with reference to decisions of questions at A. M., differing from the sentiment expressed by said decisions, and communications from others, even from those who are not members of the church, and even of an expelled member, reflecting seriously upon the question of the character of the A. M., therefore,

Resolved, that they be required to make acknowledgment for this offence, and that they further be required to promise to be more guarded in the future in this respect, and to publish nothing of the proceedings of the Annual Meeting beyond the questions and answers as passed.

Sharp. I think that it embodies too much. While there may be a general consent to the first part, I think that the last part would hardly be acceptable to the Brotherhood. I don't know what the sentiment of the Brotherhood is, as regards the first part, but as for the last part, I think it is asking too much, and for the reason, if these Brethren do not publish these proceedings, there are others who are not Brethren, and from the remarks of the Brethren, I have heard that there is such a demand for these proceedings, that, if they cannot be obtained from the periodicals of the Brethren, they will be obtained from other periodicals, not from the Brethren. We cannot stem that tide, we think it would be unwise to prohibit them. Would it not be wise that they first be read at the Annual Meeting before publication, that would certainly be satisfactory to the Brethren and would also give satisfaction to the Brotherhood. If such a plan could be adopted, I think it is worthy of our effort. I should like to see that divided into two halves; first in reference to the acknowledgment, and second, in reference to the publishing of the proceedings. While the paper may be lost by one query, it may be sustained for the other. Therefore I think it would be unwise to take them together. And still another difficulty, I fear we are getting into. Inasmuch as there is such a great demand for the proceedings, the Brotherhood want them, would it not be better to have a church organ, and if the world publishes these proceedings, would it not be better to have a church organ, to which we can refer, as an authority. You may say "we have the minutes as authority," but it seems from the demands for these proceedings, that they do not supply the want that is generally felt.

Do not let us assume so much authority as to suppress it altogether. I am sure the remedy would be tenfold worse than the disease.

Slifer. Those are my views exactly. Two years ago at our Annual Meeting in Berks county, there was a reporter from Philadelphia. He gave the general history of our church, and the report pleased many of our members. Many of our members contributed to have that article republished, I subscribed to it myself. We should not be ashamed of our doctrine when it is truthfully reported, whether by papers from ourselves or anywhere else. Let us send out our views broadcast, that the world may see their truthfulness. We should of course call our editors to account if they publish anything untruthful, but I hope they will not be called to give an account when they give the public a truthful account of our proceedings.

Moderator. As brother Sharp has suggested, something of the kind may be necessary—perhaps so. I have travelled much among the brethren, though, and while I hear a few say they are in favor of the idea, I hear many say they are not in favor of it, as it is now conducted; but for the good of our editors, suppose I suggest a thought. Bring up a query from your church, to your District Meeting, and then to the Yearly Meeting, and then see whether the Yearly Meeting will grant the report to be read at the close of the meeting, and have have the sanction of the meeting before its publication. Something of this kind I think might help you, but as it is now, to my knowledge, I know it is not wholesome to the church, therefore we would advise to stop it at present, until we can see a better way to accomplish the object under consideration.

Holsinger. There have been remarks made that perhaps require a little explanation and correction. The proposition to have the report of the proceedings of this meeting read before this meeting, and inspected by this meeting, before publication is simply preposterous. It is an impossibility. Here we are getting the proceedings of this meeting, its queries and answers, and its speeches, all written out, and to read it all to this meeting would take as long as to hear it in the first place. We have three days work of consideration, and then three days considering that consideration, and then publish it! Why it is altogether out of the question, and cannot be done.

Evidently the object of this proposition is to cut off the publication entirely, for it is proposing an impossibility. So far as the decisions of this meeting are concerned, they are considered and finally passed, and are ready for publication by authority of the meeting; but as to the proceedings, the query is raised and the appeal is made to suppress their publication altogether—that is what brother Sturgis wants.

(Sturgis—I said, "better have none unless we can suppress these extremes.")

Bro. Sturgis has one paper with which he has no trouble, but a few aspirants have come in, and they have created this trouble. Now this very paper to which he refers, had its fiery ordeal to go through twenty years ago, and Bro. Sturgis has forgotten it. Now, when we seem to have gotten under headway—sailing along for a time without any trouble, and a spirit of enterprise and learning has seized the Brotherhood, our day of trial comes, and we have to pass through the ordeal. Twenty-three years ago, as you know, the *Visitor* had to undergo the same persecution, and the same power that wanted to crush the *Visitor*, is now trying to crush us. It is the liberty of the press that is assailed—the question does not simply aim at the report of the proceedings, but is an attempt to strike at the freedom of the Press. My Bro. Davy says he did not learn that the Brotherhood wanted the proceedings published. Unfortunately, I suppose, he did not travel among those persons who read the *Companion*, for we *know* the sentiment of a large majority of our readers, and that they want the report. Brother Davy may travel among those who do not read our paper, and they are, to a man, opposed to publishing the proceedings, and some of them would perhaps oppose the printing of the Bible. The very same element of opposition that opposes our publishing the proceedings of this meeting, this is the element that opposed the printing of the Bible, and the general dissemination of knowledge. I know that not all do this, but it originates from the same feeling.

What harm can there be in publishing the proceedings? How many strangers are there in this congregation, from all parts of the country, who hear all the discussions that take place? Our paper circulates principally among the Brethren, and our readers ask the privilege of knowing what was done here, what speeches were made, and what resolutions were passed. But my brother would say, "No, suppress it, keep them in the dark." If ignorance is Christianity, then my brother Sturgis right, but if we want our absent brethren to act intelligently, I say, give them the facts, and let them be convinced from the heart, of the truth and propriety of the decisions. Then we will go right along and have no trouble. But if you make the decisions, and fail to give any reasons for them, they seem to be without support,

This very day we have had questions under consideration upon which we largely differed. Perhaps if we had gone from man to man, and asked the views of the members privately, the decision would be greatly different to what it now is. That is the way to get the true sentiment of the church, give them our reasons for deciding thus and so, and not say, "Here the Annual Meeting has made this decision, and you have got to submit to it." I believe that every one of us, who loves to be convinced, who loves to go to the Annual Meeting, has, as his primary object, to learn the reasons for the decisions. We spend some fifty thousand dollars for holding this Annual Meeting, and all we get for it is the satisfaction we have of hearing the discussions. Now for the simple sum of from two to three hundred dollars, we propose to give the same satisfaction to the thousands who don't come to this meeting. We have a great many subscribers who are not even able to pay the subscription price of the paper, and to every one of these we bring forth the news that was imparted to us at this Annual Meeting. How much does it cost you to come from Iowa, Kansas, Missouri, to this meeting? Some of you it has cost $75 or $100.

Now for the paltry sum of $1.50, we give you the same satisfaction, and as some of the brethren suggest a great deal more satisfaction. We could perhaps give you a great deal more satisfaction than you enjoy here, for nothing at all. Now, then, the question naturally arises, "why not allow this publication?" Let us sift it down and see what is the reason for this opposition. What are the brethren afraid of? Is not the same sentiment thrown out here before this mixed multitude, that will be thrown out to the readers of our periodicals? Will we publish anything that was not decided here, or that was not spoken here? If this congregation has the privilege of listening to it here, why shall not our members who cannot afford to come here, have the privilege of reading it? What is the reason? Because it makes confusion! Those brethren in Missouri are opposed to the periodicals, opposed to schools, opposed to general knowledge. Why? Because it causes a disturbance and confusion! So did Salem College cause a confusion—Oh, a wonderful disturbance. If it creates confusion to read it, will it not create confusion to hear it, especially to hear these members make these contradictory speeches face to face? Certainly, for here you can gather additional impression from the expression of our features. If it is an evil to allow brethren to know the reasons for the decisions of the body, let the meeting convene in a room with closed doors, and then come to us and say, "We, the elders, we, the bishops, we, the men of God have made this decision, and you have got to submit to it, whether you understand it or not; the law has been passed." If that is not right, then let us go to work and give all the information we can to our fellow members, and endeavor to convince them that what we have done is right, and that it is in accordance with God's word and sound logic.

Sturgis.—I want the brother to be disabused of the idea that I have proposed the thought of suppressing the publication. It is only if the editors cannot be subject as other brethren are subject, to the church, and the general brotherhood, then, I say, it is better to suppress it. That idea is all I intended to convey. I am not an advocate of ignorance at all; I want education and knowledge everywhere, just as much as brother Henry does.

——. It is altogether out of the question to prohibit the publication. Should they misrepresent, let them be required to make acknowledgment, but do not take away the liberty that belongs to them.

Moderator. Inasmuch as my name was mentioned, I would say, that I have been among many brethren, that read the *Companion*, and I think that I have a pretty fair chance to know what the sentiments of those brethren are. While brother Henry thinks I do not travel much among people who read the *Companion*, I would say that I am no respector of the brotherhood, and travel just as much among the young brethren as I do among the old, and perhaps more. I think we will now stop this discussion and put the question to its passage.

Bushby. I cannot give my consent to this answer. In my travels in Minesota, Iowa and Illinois, I think four-fifths of the members are for having the proceedings of Annual Meeting published in our periodicals. My brother from the Northern District of Indiana is here with only $16 in his pocket. They could not collect anything for him because the brethren will not let us know what is done at the Annual Meeting.

C. Forney. In the outskirts of Kansas and Nebraska, we find some of the Brethren that esteem these reports very highly, and many of the young people are ready to be received into the church just from the information received there. It is very natural for people to want to know the reason, and on what grounds a transaction has taken place in Annual Counsel.

——. In my travels in the far west I find that there is a great request for the proceedings of these meetings, and Brethren have told me with tears in their eyes how they desired this, and I have not found a single individual in all my travels who did not want them published. I will oppose the passage of that resolution.

Sayler. I am one that wishes that answer somewhat modified. There are some things in it I would wish to stand, but there are also some little things which I wish to see changed. I simply rise in answer to the last Brethren who have been testifying to the vast demand, particularly among the western people, to know all about the proceedings of the meeting. I am glad to hear it. But I was sent on a journey last fall, and if there ever was anything denounced in unmeasured terms it was the minutes. I am glad to hear so favorable a change reported in the West, to hear that they have begun to think favorably of the meeting. I say again there are some things I would wish to see modified, and there are also some things I would like to see stand, and I propose we adjourn.

A Bro. Let us take the counsel of Bro. Davy, pass the decision as now given and give directions to all the churches to take counsel at home next Spring, and then at the District Meeting, and come to the Annual Meeting prepared to say what they wish in the matter.

Holsinger. If this council take it upon them to say that Leedy had reference to this council, then I am willing to acknowledge that it was wrong to publish it. Why not do so with the proceedings of the Annual Meeting? If wrong why not make us account for it; but I don't want you to prescribe me before, and cut off the liberty of the members. Must we be dumb to unrighteousness in the church, and close our eyes against wrong? No, never, if I publish what is not true bring me to account, but do not prescribe me beforehand. When we must do that I am going to quit preaching, and will never publish a paper where I must be prescribed. If I err I want to be corrected.

Metzger. Some of our old brethren have very good ideas, but are not educated and I am afraid the order of the church would suffer if what every one is said is published. They can all get the minutes and the Scriptures are open, and it seems to me as if it was more a feeling of curiosity than anything else.

A Bro. I believe we are all too strenuous, we should be very careful that we don't censure. So long as our periodicals comes up to their true colors we have no trouble with them. I say, by the experiment of publishing the truth. Two men can hardly tell the same story here, and it is pretty hard to carry it a thousand miles and then tell it.

Wise. There have been intimations that those who oppose this general report are opposed to education. I am a friend of education, but improper education is injurious, and only that education which promotes God's glory and peace and harmony on earth, should be supported by us. We have heard different brethren say that there is an almost universal demand for the general report, in their country, and my brother Sayler says, he is glad to know that the decisions of A. M., are beginning to be respected, but some of the bitter opponents of these meeting are the advocates of the general report, and it is not unusual to hear them say when they get them, "Ah! I guess that old fogy gets his own!" "That's right, let them have it, right and left." That is the result of these general reports where they are so much in demand. Instead of promoting harmony, union, and respect for the church they conduce to the contrary. The general report of the speeches of the Annual Meeting is like that of our speeches in legislative halls, and is according to the political opinions of those who read them, applauded or condemned. I am opposed to anything that would create sectional feeling in our beloved Brotherhood. If we can embrace one another and feel that we are all brethren, and respect one another with that due christian respect, our meeting would be productive of better consequences.

——. I can corroborate the statement of Bro. Wise, as to the slang thrown out in the reading of the reported speeches.

Holsinger. The reason why the report is required more than the minutes of the meeting is because it gives the whys and the wherefores. The minutes are but a law and duty. They were asked to day to point to the word of the Lord, and did not do it. But the argument presented may help the Brotherhood to come to a conclusion. If I could be made believe it is an injury to our beloved Brotherhood, I would not publish them. It costs me more than if I would not publish it. I must labor and go to expense in order to give satisfaction. I do it because the brethren want to know what is done. It is the only way we can keep our brethren together, and if we cannot give the "thus saith the Lord," let us give the next best thing, which is sound reason.

Wise. It has been asserted that I used sophistry. Sophistry is unfair reason, and an allusion to the light minded portion of this congregation has been made, to support that declaration. I spoke of members of the church. I spoke of those who profess to be brethren, and if the publication of a report will make them so light minded that they will speak disrespectfully of their own brethren, I say, *put it down.* I am here to declare, and I think I am ready to substantiate the declaration, that is those who read the Christian Family *Companion*, and those who read the report furnished. I speak that which I do know and declare that which I have seen and heard. There are about as many cases as there were instances that fell under my observation of persons who opposed the general order of the church, as of those among whom these sentiments prevailed. As I said before, I would like to see something done to restrain that influence if possible, that might produce some happy result to the cause of the general order of our brotherhood; nay, I will say more, the teachings of our New Testament. Humiliation will be respected more. I would like to see something brought about to benefit those persons and not encourage them in their wickedness, and if this is sophistry or unfair reasoning, brother Henry is entitled to his position.

WEDNESDAY MORNING SESSION.

After devotional exercises, the unfinished matter of last evening was taken up.

Moderator. Sometimes in a moment of excitement we utter language that we do not design shall convey the idea received by the audience. I was informed that my reference to Northern Indiana yesterday evening conveyed the idea to some that all Northern Indiana was alluded to, and I wish to disabuse the minds of my brethren in regard to the matter. We have some worthy brethren and sisters in Northern Indiana that stand as firm as I for the doctrine of Jesus Christ as inculcated in the Gospel, and taught by the Brethren. I hope the explanation will be sufficient.—Some also called in question the truthfulness of the remarks in regard to calling old brethren by the name of "old fogies." It is a fact, and I am not the only one that heard the remark, and would refer to brother Jacob Troxel.

The assertion was corroborated by the brother referred to and several others.

Answer to previous question, as read by the Clerk. There may be a synopsis of the reasons given as a basis for decisions, but no names of speakers to be used, and those who publish shall be responsible to Annual Meeting for their report.

Passed.

WHEREAS, The C. F. C., and PILGRIM have published articles, with reference to the decisions of queries at Annual Meetings diverting from the sentiment as expressed by said decisions, and communications published from others, even from those who are not members of the church, and even from expelled members, reflecting seriously on the christian character of the Annual Meeting, therefore,

Resolved, That they be requested to make acknowledgments for this offense, and they be further requested to promise to be guarded in the future in this respect.

Passed.

Brumbaugh. As far as I am concerned, it has always been my desire and wish to labor for the church and for the glory of God, and therefore, if we have come short of this duty, as this counsel said we have, or that we have made a mistake, we make the acknowledgement for that mistake, and accept the advice which has been given us. We would have our dear brethren and sisters understand that we are yet young in experience, and that our position is a very critical and responsible one. We are often brought into close quarters, and it is a hard matter for us to decide, and on account of these things we sometimes make the mistakes we have made; therefore, when we are willing to subject ourselves to the decision of our brethren, we hope they will feel themselves under responsibility to stand by us and give us all the advice we need. It is certainly understood that we ask the pardon of the Church for the wrong we have done.

Holsinger. You have me linked with another party, while I think the aim and object is exclusively at me. When I say a thing because I believe it, I am too sensitive in taking it back, unless convinced it was an error. I am not conscious at the present time of ever having published anything in regard to the proceedings of the Annual Meeting that differed from the decisions made. If that can be pointed out to me, I will make the acknowledgement. In regard to the other matter, I will take it all back, provided this Annual Meeting will say that that letter referred to them. I did not publish it myself. Brother Beer gave it to the printer and had it published, and I am not sure that I would have done it. After this explanation I would desire no more. If it has created confusion and dissatisfaction and wounded the feelings of the brethren, I am sorry that it was published. I intend to avoid publishing anything that is injurious, or that I regard as slanderous on our Brotherhood, for I think I love the church of God.

Moderator. If Bro. Henry has been linked with another party the standing committee has not done it. We have taken the papers as they came to our hands, and so acted upon them, and are not accountable. We concluded that the churches and Districts from which they came had examined the number of the paper they referred to, giving the day and date. We might have called for it on our part.

Brumbaugh. If not out of order I would like to have a fair understanding in regard to this report. We have a full report of this meeting and wish to know whether we are at liberty to publish it, without giving the names of the speakers.

——. There is no objections to a true report if the names and their own comments are left out.

Holsinger. When we look upon the actions of our lives as having been offensive or causing any one pain we always feel regret and sorrow for having unnecessarily wounded the feelings of any of our fellow-men, much more our fellow-members in Christ, and on the present occasion, to any of my brethren whom I have wounded and injured I ask their pardon. If I did publish as the proceedings of the meeting, or even gave as my own views at the time, in regard to those proceedings, on the subject of double or single feetwashing, my acknowledgment will cover that. If I did it I say that it was wrong. There are no other brethren here willing to say that it was so.

Moderator. The report will show for itself as will show this afternoon.

Whereas, Bro. Henry Holsinger has committed great offense to the Brethren in their present Annual Meeting, by pursuing the course pursued, when complaints had been presented from various places and Districts, and when an humble and meek explanation was expected, Bro. H., before the whole congregation, made remarks which gave offense to the brethren, and were to the dishonor of the Brotherhood, such a spirit manifested by a minister of the Gospel, we consider also contrary to the Gospel and the profession and character of our Brotherhood.

2nd. He declared that a brother— and the occasion on which he made the remark, shows that he was a brother of some eminence.—would suppress the printing of the Bible, with no testimony before him warranting him to make such a declaration, we consider the charge a dishonor to the Brotherhood.

3rd. In speaking against the brethren in warm and strong language, and alluding to the business done on the morning which pertained to a point which had given the brethren much trouble, but which was settled quite as satisfactorily as expected and we felt pleasantly over it, he said, alluding to the elders, they were asked to give the word of the Lord and refused to do it. We consider this remark injurious to the feelings of the elders.

4th. In saying that one of the brethren used sophistry in his speech we consider a great violation of Christian courtesy and brotherly love.

5th. In declaring he would never submit to the restraint under consideration, plainly shows a spirit of disobedience to the Church.

The offenses were not confined to the Elders, but extending to the congregation, the impropriety grieved a large number of the members, as their strong feelings expressed after the meeting closed, plainly indicated.— Now, in view of the foregoing consideration, we require a very humble acknowledgement, and an assurance that his course in the future be more respectful to the ministers and Elders, and more in accordance with the meekness and brotherly love inculcated in the gospel.

Moderator. I would only say myself that as the business was transacted yesterday afternoon, pretty sharp words were used; the feeling seemed to be manifest to us, we were driven to do something to satisfy this assembly, to satisfy the Brotherhood present, and to vindicate the honor of the Brotherhood, hence we felt our duty as a representative of the Brotherhood of the different states, to do our duty in the matter, and to satisfy the brethren and sisters, is the reason we have got this matter before you.

Sharp. I would like to say one word. Perhaps these restrictions are very good, and may tend to make us more cautious and inculcate that christian spirit, but I would say, show no partiality. I suppose I shall not be compelled to refer to any one individual, but others have heard the remarks as well as I have, and I should be far better pleased if the criticisms that are made would include others besides brother Holsinger, and that it would be more just.

——The remarks reflected very unfavorably on the Standing Committee, and the meeting in general. He said he was ashamed of what brother Wise said. We want brother H. to feel that there are a great number of brethren here, come from a distance, and while he is ashamed, many more were ashamed of what he said. It very unfavorably reflected on brother Wise, and those old gray headed brethren that are contending earnestly for the faith. We want a hearty acknowledgement, as many of us are about his age in the ministry and as lay members.

Workman. I have been badly wounded by seeing our Elders stigmatized, and advise every brother and sister to be careful. Brother ——— drew tears to my eyes by the spirit he manifested, but my mind was carried back to the days of Core, Dathan and Abiram when they opposed Moses with his hoary head, or to Jeroboam, who took counsel of the younger in preference to the aged, with such serious consequences. We want this meeting to understand that we appreciate the counsel of these old brethren, and intend to support them as long as their counsel is in harmony with the word of the Lord. The people of God have been deceived before, and may be hereafter. Let us wait a little. Our time will come by and by, and we will realize what our elder brethren feel now. Let me make this strong appeal, brethren, be careful.

——. Let the spirit of love be amongst us, and let us treat others as we would be treated ourselves. Love is the lever power that moves the world. To ask the pardon of those we have wronged will gain their approbation and we will be exalted instead of humbled.

Holsinger. A brother that has taken his seat, has given me a good lesson and it is possible that he needs one. I have from a child loved the society of the aged brethren; but in reading the Bible, I learn that great men are not always wise, and that the aged do not always understand judgment. Men whom I have regarded as wise, whose gray hairs should have been an honor before men, and a glory upon their old heads, have gone down, and so far denied Jesus Christ as to be lost to Christianity. Three or four men who occupied positions in this standing committee have fallen as low as men could fall in the world. I looked up to them as saints, and now they deny the Christ that died to save. I look now only to the men's conduct, in order to revere him. I take issue with an old man when I cannot agree with his opinions. I take God's word and make that the man of my counsel, and agree with the old brethren when they stand up for the word of God. It seems to me you are taking a course you are not justified in taking. Why not bring me before my own congregation? Why must I be brought before this meeting from year to year? If the spirit I manifest is not of the spirit of Christ I ask your forgiveness. I hope to get into the spirit of Christ, and would like to do his will. I think the man who would try to suppress the publication of the Bible has been a member of the standing committee. This spirit of ignorance and superstition is going to drag every one like him out of the church. If that is a mistake I will make acknowledgement. I have a little advantage over you in knowing these things, who wrote it, and who printed it, and it seems to me it came from that source.

In speaking of the apostolic manner of installation I alluded to a matter before us, and a brother standing beside me, an elder in the church, said they evidently did shirk that matter. I have to bear it because I alluded to it. I believe I should not have used the word sophistry, nor do I think Bro. Wise should have taken it up so hard. I did not mean false doctrine. If you had reason from my remarks, to think I had reference to this standing committee I take it all back. I had reference to those parties that did say it, and not to the standing Committee. If the decisions are according to Scripture, they ought to point to the Scripture, they ought to direct these questions to it. Did you do it brethren? If not you cannot expect an acknowledgment from me. The District Meeting that brought it here answered the question and gave the Scripture, and this meeting refused to let that stand. If the District Meeting had not given an answer then I would have used the word fail.

—— If we leave it go with that broad assertion, it will show that we refused to give Scripture answer. If we could have agreed on the officers we would not have differed.

Moderator. Brother Holsinger said he wondered why he must be arraigned before the Annual Meeting so often. In answer I would say that his words and actions yesterday were offensive to many of our older brethren, and this is why we have to try the matter here.

Slifer. Yesterday when I discovered a disposition to lay the question of the Deacons on the table, I used the word shirk, without any intention. Brother Holsinger used the word evade. I acknowledged that is an answer, but did not insist on any change whatever.

Passed.

Holsinger. The brethren say they could not agree that these offenses were the same, and if that is the way then my assertions were out of order. I acknowledge that was wrong and am sorry it occurred and hope the brethren will forgive me for it.

Slifer. I accept brother Holsinger's apology.

ANSWER OF STANDING COMMITTEE.

Now, in view of the foregoing consideration, we require a very humble acknowledgement of brother Holsinger for his offense, and an assurance that his course in the future shall be more respectful to the church and elders, and more in accordance with the meekness and brotherly love inculcated in the Gospel. (A number of voices called for its passage and it was passed.)

Holsinger. Brethren, all the assurance I can give you is my word. By the grace of God I will try to serve my Master to the best of my ability, and have all the respect toward my brethren that my faith and confidence in their soundness and ability will warrant, regarding God, at all times, as the Sovereign and Judge, before whom you and I must appear.

To be Continued.

POETRY.

A FAREWELL.

The time is swiftly rolling on,
  When I must faint and die,
My body to the dust return,
  And there forgotten lie.

Let persecution rage around,
  And antichrists appear
My silent dust beneath the ground,
  Shall no disturbance hear.

Through heat and cold I often went,
  Through sorrow and distress,
To call on sinners to repent,
  And seek the Savior's face.

My brother preachers, boldly speak,
  Who stand on Zion's walls,
Confirm the strong, revive the weak,
  And often sinners call.

May Zion's sons in peace be found,
  And put their foes to flight,
While I am sleeping under ground,
  May you in love unite.

My brethren all, I bid adieu,
  Your fellowship I love
In time I'll never more see you,
  But soon we'll meet above.

My little babes are near my heart,
  For nature seems to bind
So strong it grieves me to depart,
  And leave them all behind.

Dear Lord a Father to them be,
  And shield them from all harm,
That they may know and worship thee
  And dwell upon thy arm.

My loving wife, my bosom friend,
  The object of my love,
The time's been sweet on earth with
  thee,
  My sweet and harmless dove.

My dearest love don't weep for me;
  Neither lament nor mourn,
I trust I shall with Jesus be,
  While you are left alone.

I never shall return to thee,
  Don't let this grieve thy heart,
But you can quickly come to me;
  When we shall part no more.

JOHN KNISLEY.

ORIGINAL ESSAYS.

ON PRIDE.

"God resisteth the proud, but giveth grace unto the humble."—James 4 : 6.

That pride is an abomination in the sight of God, cannot be gainsayed by any who believe in the scripture of Divine truth. "Every one that is proud in heart is an abomination to the Lord; though hand join in hand, he shall not be unpunished," Prov. 16 : 5. "A high look and a proud heart, and the plowing of the wicked is sin." Prov. 21 : 4. "Be clothed with humility; for God resisteth the proud, and giveth grace to the humble." Pet 5 ; 5. Seeing, then, that God looks upon the proud with abhorrence, and he cannot possibly expect any aid from him, yet it is so necessary for their future welfare.—That the Atheist, the Deist and Infidel indulge in pride and walk in gaudy show, delight in the vain and giddy fashions of this wicked world, seems not so strange to me, for they do not profess Christianity, neither do they believe in God's revealed will, much less in the gospel of our Lord Jesus Christ, which teaches humility almost on every page. But why it is that the mass of believers who profess Christianity, do even exceed Infidels in following the giddy and abominable fashions prevalent in our day, is a matter of surprise to me; for I cannot see how such indulgence can be reconciled with a life of Christianity. Hence we must come to the conclusion that the so called Christianity is at a very low ebb; for nineteenth of the Christian professors belong to these popular churches, who feel no restraint upon their pride whatever. Can the Prince of Peace delight in the worship at the shrine of fashion? Is it possible to conceive the idea of His presence where devotees to the god of this world meet in their devotions? Will God dwell with them in their worship when meeting in His house, decorated and adorned with superfluity in order to make a show and attract the gay, uplifted in heart who indulge in pride and think themselves gods in human form; but alas, alas, so disguised by the horrible fashions of the day, head dress and hunchbacked, that from a distance you hardly know them to be human beings? Impossible, when God's own Son saith, "that whatsoever is highly esteemed among men is an abomination in the sight of God." God only dwelleth with the humble, and delights in the worship of the lowly. The meek shall inherit the earth; but "he searcheth the proud in imagination in their hearts." Pride is reigning in the high and fashionable churches without controversy, and God cannot be there is clear to every intelligent mind that has experienced true and undefiled religion; and that the heart can be humble when external grandeur and display is manifested, is devoid of truth and down right sophistry. An humble heart abhors what God abhors; resists what He resists; loves what God loves, and consequently His external appearance is plain, modest and his whole deportment in life is "clothed with humility," he has learned that of Jesus, and tries to follow His example. But the solemn question comes up here, is pride confined only to those fashionable and popular churches? Here let us pause for a moment; let us seriously reflect and take the matter home to our own fire-sides, to our own church, who professes to be separated from the world, and be a peculiar people. To our sorrow, we see the rapidity of pride, the dreadful monster entering the Church stealthily, cunningly and in the beautiful garb of forbearance and christian courtesy. Would pride approach in the form of a wolf, it would be more clearly seen, and more easily guarded against. But here he comes in the form of a more refined worship, mingled up with a little wisdom of this world, theoretical and educational discourses are admired listened to with pleasure, and if prolonged, with patience; while on the other hand, plain Scriptural discourses are received with reluctance, if prolonged, with impatience, and not unfrequently causes the half of the congregation to sleep. Brethren, Sisters, is it not so? Seeing then that we are drifting rapidly into the stream of popular Christianity, who is to blame? I say, the laity, the members who desire to have it so; dissatisfied with the plain and simple discourses of primitive Christians, they wanted something more refined, discoveries of mens' own making—void of Scriptural quotation—hence thereby stimulating our young ministers to acquire a polished education in order to deliver their discourses in rhetorical, flowry phrases, pleasing to the outward sense, but very seldom touch the heart. Do not think me too severe. I appeal to you, brethren and sisters. Is it not the truth? Have I not observed it when it was known that brother so was to preach? Did I not see many flock to the church that otherwise would have staid at home, members not excepted? Have I not heard expressed that a wonderful sermon was delivered, the best ever delivered there, when perhaps not a half dozen passages of Scripture were quoted in the sermon?

Brethren and sisters, can you not see the drift. Soon, soon we must have an educated ministry, and of consequence also a salaried one. If by God's help we cannot check pride in the Church by raising our voice against it publicly and privately, her glory will depart, the candle stick be removed and God's presence be withdrawn, and we are undone forever. As the ministry degenerates, so nonconformity to the Word degenerates. Can we distinguish brethren and sisters from the world? I am sorry to say that in many localities we cannot by their outward appearance, though we are happy to know that there are still many to stand by the old landmark. Be it known that where ministerial labor is flowing into popularity, there you can see the evidence of pride, the fruits of such a ministry; to see brethren and even ministers, and also dear sisters dressing like the world, though they may not come fully up with the mode and changing of the world, yet come half ways, causes my heart to bleed, and prompts my soul to pity them, because I see that pride occupies a seat in their hearts and prevents the Holy Spirit to possess it, which is so indespensible for our christian journey. I appeal again to you, my dear members, be clothed with humility. Humble yourselves, therefore, under the mighty hand of God, that he may exalt you in due time. For He that shall come will come and will not tarry; the just shall live by faith. May God enable us to become more humble every day, is the prayer of your unworthy servant. Farewell.

LEONARD FURRY.

TYPES AND PROPHECY.

Continued from page 199.

Of typical persons who were not declared to be such till the persons of whom they were types appeared, Adam deserves to be first mentioned, for in respect of his being the author of sin and death to all his posterity, he is said by the apostle, Rom. 5 ; 14, to be by contrast, "the type or figure of him (Christ) who was to come," for the purpose of being the author of righteousness and life to mankind, hence Christ is called, 1 Cor. 15 : 45, the last Adam. Adam was likewise a type of Christ in this respect, that Eve, who was an image of the church, was formed of a rib taken from Adam's side while he was in deep sleep, for this transaction prefigured the formation of the church, the Lambs wife, by the breaking of Christ's side on the cross while he slept the sleep of death as the apostle insinuateth, Eph. 5 : 32. Joseph was a types of Christ in many respects, and was a bright example in every relation and period of life. At the age of 17 years he appears uncorrupted by the wickedness of his brethren or the partiality of his father's discountenancy, the sin of the former, and prompt in his obedience to the latter: Gen. 37 : 2-3. Though unjustly sold as a slave, he is represented as strictly faithful to his master, abhorring youthful lust, though exposed to the strongest temptation. Afflicted and persecuted, yet finding, even when confined as a criminal, opportunity for doing good, Gen. 38 ; 22, 40 ; 7, &c., and though flattered by a king, disowning his own power to interpret Pharaoh's dream, and boldly avowing before this heathen and despotic monarch, the power of God. Ch. 41 ; 16. At the age of 30 years he is suddenly raised to the right hand of Pharaoh, yet is unseduced by the splendor of his situation, being guided by the spirit, he becomes a pattern to rulers, of industry, prudence and justice, Ch. 35 46-48. As a courtier, he shows the strictest regard to truth, with true nobleness of mind avowing the disreputable employment of his connections. As a brother, he exhibits unabated affection, not only to Benjamin, but to those who had hated him even unto death; for his apparent harshness arose from his anxiety to bring them to repentance, and when he had accomplished this, his whole conduct to them was marked by peculiar tenderness, and the most studied attention to their feelings and welfare. As a son, though lord of Egypt, he manifests the most affectionate respect for his aged parent, who was now dependant upon him. As a father, his piety appears in the names he gave his children, and his earnest desire for God's blessing upon them in bringing them to Jacob's dying bed. For 80 years he lived in the midst of the greatest worldly grandeur, surrounded with every temptation to worldliness and idolatry; but his dying breath testified how entirely his heart and treasure was in God's promises.

Next is Joshua, who was of Joseph's posterity, and was a type of Christ. Joshua and Jesus are the same name, the one Hebrew, the other Greek; and therefore in the New Testament, originally written in Greek, Joshua is called Jesus. Acts 7; 45, "which also our fathers brought in with Jesus," that is Joshua, Heb. 4; 8. "If Jesus, (that is Joshua) had given them rest, he would not have spoken of another day." (Edwards on Redemption.) The triumphs through faith of the Israelites under Joshua, may be considered as typical of the final triumph of the Church and of every Christian, thro' Jesus, the Captain of our salvation, 'the author and finisher of our faith." God wonderfully gave his people possession of the land of Canaan, conquering its former inhabitants and the mighty giants, as Christ conquered the devil. He first conquered the great kings on the Eastern side of Jordan, and then divided the river Jordan, as before he had done the Red sea; causing the walls of Jericho to fall down at the sound of the trumpets of the priests. That sound signified the sound of the Gospel. By the preaching of Gospel ministers, the walls of the accursed city, Jericho will fall, signifying the walls of Satan's kingdom. After this, he wonderfully destroyed the mighty host of the Amorites, under the five kings, causing the sun and moon to stand still, to help the people against their enemies, at the prayer of the typical Jesus; plainly intimating that God would make the whole course of nature to be subservient to the work of redemption, and that everything should give place to the welfare of God's people. Thus did the Lord show His great love to his people, that he would make the course of nature to give place to their happiness and prosperity. At the same time the Lord fought as the captain of their host, Josh. 5: 14-15, and cast down great hail stones upon their enemies, by which more were slain than by the sword of Israel; and after this God gave the people a mighty victory over a yet greater army in the northern part of the land, gathered together as at the waters of Merom, as the sand of the sea-shore. Josh. 11; 4, &c.

D. NEELY.

THE BURIAL.

One thing alone is wanting, that the manner of the Jews in burying may be observed—a bier to lay the body on to bear it to the sepulcher. There has been no time to get one, or it is felt that the distance is so short that it is not needed. But that body has the best bier of all, the hands of true affection, to lift it up and carry it across to the new tomb which waits to receive it. The feet let us assign to Joseph, the body to Nicodemus, and that regal head with those closed eyes, over which the shadows of the resurrection are already flitting, let us lay on the breast of the beloved disciple. The brief path from the cross to the sepulcher is soon traversed. In silence and in deep sorrow they bear their sacred burden, and lay it gently down upon its clean, cold, rocky bed. The last look of the dead is taken. The buriers reverently withdraw, the stone is rolled to the mouth of the sepulcher; separated from the living, Jesus rests with the dead. The burial is over now, and we might depart; but let us linger a little longer, and bestow a parting look upon the burying ground. "In the place where He was crucified there was a garden, and in that garden a sepulcher." Plant yourself before that sepulcher, and look around. This is no place for graves; here rise around you no memorials of the dead. You see but a single sepulcher, and that sepulcher in a garden. Strange mingling this of opposites, the garden of life and growth and beauty, circling the sepulcher of death, corruption and decay. Miniature of the strange world we live in. What garden of it has not its own grave? Your path may, for a time, be through flowers and fragrance; follow it far enough, it leads ever to a grave. But this sepulcher in this garden suggests other and happier thoughts. It was in a garden once of old—in Eden—that death had his first summons given, to find there his first prey; it is in a garden here at Calvary that the last enemy of mankind has the death blow given to him—that the great conqueror is in his turn overcome. Upon that stone which they rolled to the mouth of the sepulcher let us engrave the words, "O death, where is thy sting? O grave, where is thy victory? Thanks be to God, which giveth us the victory through our Lord Jesus Christ." What a change it has made in the character and aspect of the grave, that our Savior himself once lay in it! He has stripped it of its terrors, and to many a weary one given it an attractive rather than a repulsive look. "I heard a voice from Heaven saying"—it needed a voice from Heaven to assure of the truth—"Blessed are the dead which die in the Lord." To such the grave is indeed, a bed of blessed rest. Buried with *Jesus*, they repose till the hour of the great awakening cometh, when with Him they shall rise to that newness of life over which no shadow of death shall ever pass.—*Hanna.*

KIND words are among the brightest flowers of earth. They help to convert the humblest home into a paradise. Therefore use them, especially around the fireside. Children, try the power of kind and loving words, not only when visiting among your friends, but when at home.

Youth's Department.

OUR OBJECT.

In my last, the question was, "do boys ever think?" and the conclusion was that they should not only think, but think aright. Everything that God made was pronounced good and therefore of some practical use. Every tree and every herb that grows is intended for some purpose, and even every animal and the smallest insects have their allotted work to perform and places to fill.

If this is so, can it be expected that little boys and girls, who are made so much better than the trees of the forest or the little insects that fill the world, have nothing to do but eat and drink, sleep and play? No, my dear young reader, we all have a work to do, a design to fulfil, and unless we do this, we disappoint the design of God, who made us, and make the world worse for our being in it. This life is only a preparatory state, and all we do should be directly or indirectly for our future good. This disposition is born within us, and we are always willing to labor ever so hard a few hours or days, if we have the assurance that in the future we may receive some enjoyment from that labor. It is no strange thing for us some times to labor for weeks in order that we may enjoy ourselves for a day or even a few hours. Is not this strange, especially when it is known that of this expected enjoyment we may be sadly disappointed, as thousands are every day? In thinking over things, I have often been made to wonder why it is that our young people are willing to make such sacrifices for these uncertain and short pleasures, and yet are unwilling to make a very small sacrifice for joys which are sure, complete and lasting. Then, have an object in view, and let that be for your best interest, both for this time and the time to come. This you can do by ever striving to do good. This is the object for which you were made and for which you are spared every day. There is no way that you can be so happy as by being and doing good. It will not only make yourself happy, but it will help to make all those about you happy. Then, as one who loves you, I would say, think of the object for which you were made and then try and not disappoint God by not fulfilling it. Jesus has come into the world, suffered and died that you might be made happy and live forever; but to have all this he asks of you a small sacrifice or labor. If your father or mother would promise you, by laboring one hour, a whole week of continued enjoyment, would you not gladly accept the offer? I know you would; every one of you would be glad for just such an offer. Now Jesus offers us a thousand times better than this. He offers, if we are willing to labor in His vinyard a few years, ten fold blessings in this time, and in the world to come, eternal life. In the life to come, we are to live in a city that its streets are paved with gold. The glory of God is so great in it there is no need of a sun; there is no night there, and people never die. Now, to enjoy all this, and have a mansion in that city should be the great object of all your labor, and may I not hope it will? If not, you will sustain a great loss, and make yourself forever miserable. This you do not wish to do, neither do you expect it, but do not be deceived, God is not mocked, if you serve the flesh, you must reap corruption, and this will, in the end, produce death.

MAKING CHARACTER.

So many people seem to forget that character grows. That it is not something to be put on, ready made, with manhood or womanhood; but day by day here a little and there a little, grows with the growth and strengthens with the strength, until, good or bad, it becomes almost a coat of mail. Look at the model man of business—prompt, reliable, conscientious, cool and cautious, yet clear headed and energetic. When do you suppose he developed all these admirable qualities? When he was a boy. Let me see the way in which a boy of ten gets up in the morning, works, plays, studies, and I will tell you just about what kind of a man he will make. The boy that is late at the breakfast table, late at school, who never quite does anything at the right time, stands a poor chance to be a prompt man. The boy who half washes his face, half does his chores, half learns his lessons, will never make a *thorough* man. The boy who neglects his duties, be they ever so small, and then excuses himself by saying, "O, I forgot! I didn't think!" will never be a *reliable* man. And the boy who finds pleasure in the pain and suffering of weaker things, will never be a noble, generous, kindly man; a *gentle* man.

And what about the girls? A girl who is peevish and pettish and careless of the comfort of others, who is untidy in her ways, and thinks it does not matter what she says or does at home, or how rude and uncourteous she may be to the dear ones there, is sure to grow into such a womanhood as, I am sorry to say, we have already too much of; the womanhood that scorns the old-fashioned virtues of industry and thrift and skilful handiwork, of love, and gentleness, and brave self-sacrifice, of the charity that thinketh no evil, that seeketh not her own, and that never faileth. She will never be a lady in the old Saxon meaning of the word, "*hlafdig*," *a loaf giver.*—*Little Corporal.*

The Weekly Pilgrim.

JAMES CREEK, PA., June 24, 1873.

☞ How to send money.—All sums over $1.50, should be sent either in a check, draft or postal order. If neither of these can be obtained, have the letter registered.

☞ When Money is sent, *always* send with it the name and address of those who paid it. Write the names and post office as plainly as possible.

☞ Every subscriber for 1873, gets a *Pilgrim Almanac* Free.

WHY NOT GIVE THE NAMES?

Some of our readers are asking, why not give the names in the report of A. M? We answer; because we have promised to be subject to Annual Meeting and it has said, we shall not give the names of the speakers, as will be seen in the report. When the decisions of that body become so insignificant that we cannot conscientiously assent to them we will denounce the whole affair. There is no propriety in the Church spending its thousands, to hold these meetings and then go home and disregard its proceedings and do as we please. The Report, as far as we have heard, is giving very general satisfaction, and goes far to confute the position that a few of our prominent brethren took, that it was only the refractory or disloyal part of the Brotherhood that desired a report of the meeting. This is a great mistake, as we know of some as good and loyal churches as there are in the Brotherhood that would vote almost unanimously for the report, and on the strength of it we have received almost 1-0 new subscribers, and those largely from churches that we know have a good standing.

As to the names, we cannot see but what the Report is quite as good without the names as it would be with them, but if we had our preference we would make every man responsible for the expression of his sentiments. It might intimidate some but others, it might make more careful. But in this we have submitted our judgment hoping that it may all be for the better in the end.

WHO WAS DAVID'S MOTHER?

The answer of this question was given by Wm. Neffsinger in No. 12, page 95 of current volume, but as it is of late, becoming quite a question in the Sabbath School and by the young generally, we will give it again. By referring to 1 Chron. 15 19 you will find that Zeruiah and Abigail were David's sisters. Then turn to 2 Samuel 17,25 and we there find that the mother of Zeruiah and Abigail, David's sisters, was Nahash.

MISSING NUMBERS.

All missing Nos. can be supplied if called for. Some 300 new subscribers can be supplied with back Nos. from A. M., containing the full report at 80 cents. *PILGRIM Almanac* free to every subscriber.

DIED.

MOHR.—In the Logan Church, Logan Co. Ohio, Monday May 5th '73, our old sister Mohr, aged 75 years, 5 months and—days. She suffered much but bore it with christian fortitude. Funeral preached by the brethren, elder Jos. N. Hauffman, Michael Stronger and the writer.

BRINZER.—Also on Sunday June 15th, '73, Michael Brinzer, aged 23 years, 5 months and eleven days.

He was a son of Joseph and Catharine Brinzer and was married to Susan, daughter of brother John and sister Maria Forry. They lived together 5 months and 6 days. The young man met with a serious accident. He was kicked in the face and head by a horse, from which he suffered seven weeks to the hour. Funeral preached by elder Joseph Hauffman and the writer.

J. L. Frantz.

HENDRICKS.—Near Altoona, Polk Co., Iowa, June 12, '73, Susannah W. Hendricks, aged 74 years, and 11 months. Funeral service by brother Geo. R. Baker of Altoona, from John 1; 2.

Thirty years ago my father departed this life, and went home to the mansions above. Now mother too has gone to meet and embrace him, and soon, soon more of the family may be called and the question that concerns us, should be, who will be next? The subject of this notice was baptized 45 years ago and was ever faithful to the cause she espoused.

D. W. Hendricks.

STUTZMAN.—In Muscatine Co., Iowa, June 19 '73, Bro. John Stutzman, aged 33 years. Funeral preached by brother S. Musselman from Tipton, Iowa.

MYERS.—In the Spring Run Congregation, near McVeytown, Mifflin Co., Pa., June 23, '73, sister Elizabeth, wife of brother Reuben T. Myers, aged 31 years, 4 months and 8 days.

Thus an affectionate wife and mother has been separated from a kind husband and dear children, but we trust that those who are left behind will continue looking unto Jesus in their bereavement. She was a dear aunt, and has always been regarded as one that was respected and beloved by all who knew her. Often we have mingled together, sometimes in prayer and song, but now when we meet, this one we'll greet never again in our throng.

She called for the Elders of the church, a few days before she died, and was anointed which gave her great peace of mind. She was a faithful sister in Christ and finally fell asleep in Jesus. Funeral occasion improved by Elders S. Z. Sharp and J. R. Hanawalt, from John 11; 25-26, to a large audience.

Serena Myers.

Correspondence.

For the Pilgrim.

NOTES OF TRAVEL.

BY J. S. FLORY.

Our Communion meeting came off the 17th and 18th of May. Next morning, the 19th, in company with brother W. H. Baily, of Raleigh co., we set out, horse back, on a mission of love to the churches in the northern part of this State. The first night, we put up at friend Edward Duncan's, in Nicholas county; 20th, arrived at Sutton, Braxton county, meeting at night in the Court House; 21st at 11 a. m., meeting at S. H., near brother Bosley's, Bulltown, also at 4 p. m., at same place; 22nd set out for Upsher county, was met on the way by brother L. Fitgerald, who piloted us to his house. After partaking of some refreshments, went to brother John Fitzgerald's, had meeting at 5 p. m., also at night. Early next morning three were baptized.—At 12 p. m., arrived at brother D. Miller's,—owing to a misunderstanding there were no appointments for us at that point—went on and arrived at brother John Kisers, Barbour county, at night. Next day, 24th, at 10 a. m., meeting at the Brethren's new meeting house near Bealington, dined at friend and sister Betty Lathim's; at 4 p. m., meeting again at meeting house; went home with brother W. P. Wilson; 25th meeting at meeting house again at 11 a. m., home, with friend W. Corley; at 4 p. m., meeting at brother J. K. Scott's, Randolph county. Brother Baily had meeting at 4 p. m., near brother J. Kiser's, and from there took another route into Randolph county; 26th had another meeting at brother Scott's at 10 a. m., and at 4 p. m., at the Brethren's meeting house, home, with brother Solomon Gainor; 27th at 10 a. m., meeting again at B. meeting house, home, with brother J. Kiser; at 4 p. m., meeting at friend Gaut's, next morning meeting at same place, home, with brother Solomon Wilson. My horse having got slightly foundered, brother S. Gainer kindly let me have one of his for the time being; 29th at 10 a. m., meeting near brother S. Wilson's, after dinner hurried on to Corinth, meeting at 4 p. m., at brother Israel Gainer's, where I again met with brother Baily. He had attended four meetings on Leading Creek, in Randolph county, home with Eld. I. Auvil, of Shiloh congregation, next morning in company with brother Auvil and brother Wm. Shafer, we set out for Eld. Solomon Bucklew's, Preston county, W. Va., where we arrived about 4 p. m., meeting at night in school house, home with friend and sister Cassady. Next morning, 31st, walked to Rollsburg, 4 miles, on the B. & O. R. R., about noon left on the Fast Line for Cumberland, there to Dale City, where we arrived about 6 p. m, preached at night in the Brethren's meeting house. June 1st, had the pleasure of hearing brother D. P. Sayler preach in the forenoon and brother Enoch Eby in the afternoon, at the Brethren's meeting house. In company with brother Auvil, was taken to Berkley's Mills, preaching at night in Brethren's meeting house, all night with brother Berkley, who next morning took us back to place of A. M. At 11 a. m., preached in the barn, where the council was held; p. m., went in company with Eld Jno. Knisely and other brethren to assist in baptising a son of brother Berkley, who was dangerously ill. He was taken from his sick bed and hauled to the water, where he was baptized, also another at the same time. After having returned to the house we were informed there was another applicant for baptism arrived, we went to the water in company with a few of the brethren and sisters and baptized him. June the 3rd, the Annual Council commenced. Thursday at noon, just after the meeting closed, we took the parting hand of many dear ones, and soon was on our way to Cumberland, where we expected to meet the rest of our company, who had gone down on the morning train. We were behind time, missed connections, so our company was gone. At midnight we took the Fast Line, and next morning at 8 o'clock we arrived at brother Solomon Bucklew's. Our company was gone to attend a meeting at Red Oak school house, at which point we arrived before service was over.—Meeting at 4 p. m., at Petroleum school house; home, with brother Kiser. June the 7th at 10 a. m., meeting at Shiloh meeting house; home with brother W. Shafer; at 4 p. m., meeting at brother Yager's, near Corinth; home, with brother Israel Gainer's; 8th, Sunday, at 9 a. m., meeting at Sugar Creek meeting house; home, with brother Sol. Wilson; at 3 p. m., meeting at Brethren's meeting house near Bealington. Seven precious souls came forward for baptism, four of whom went "straightway" down into the water; home with brother Yager. Early next morning we went with a number of dear brothers and sisters on the bank of the river and led three young souls into the baptismal waters and then said farewell.

In the bounds of this congregation were spent a good portion of our labors of love. There was evidently a strong attachment one to another by the ties of christian love; with them we had often met to sing and pray together and now here by the waterside we knelt to pray the last time, and when the parting moment came, we could not help but think of Paul's parting from his brethren at Miletus, just before he went aboard the ship. We immediately set out on our way, took dinner with brother D. Miller, Upshur county, who accompanied us to our appointment at the Widow Tenney's at 4 p. m. Meeting next morning at the same place, two baptized. Brother Baily went on in the morning and filled the appointment at Indian Camp at 10 a. m.; 4 p. m., we met him there, had another meeting; home with brother Laurence Fitzgerald; 11th set out early, heavy rain all day, meeting at 3 p. m., at brother J. D. Armstrong's, Braxton county, home with brother Basley; 12th set out early, stopped at noon for refreshments and repose at Mr. Benj. Skidmore's, at Sutton, whose kindness to us is worthy of notice.—Notwithstanding we were entire strangers, he administered to our wants free of charge. May the Lord abundantly bless him. At night put up at house of public entertainment. Next day travelled all day, and arrived at brother H. Comer's, Fayette county. Meeting next morning at the school house, after which brother Baily left us for home. At 4 p. m., had meeting at friend Wood's next day, Sunday, the 15th meeting at the S. House, one baptized. Then set out, in company with brother A. Evans, for home, where we arrived before night, and found all in good health, thanks to God our Heavenly Father for his good mercies. Was absent just 4 weeks, attended 33 meetings in this State, and baptized 14, from the age of 80 down to the teens, mostly were young persons.—and now, dear brothers, sisters and friends, it is impossible for me to express the gratitude I feel toward you all who so kindly and willingly done what you could for me—always more than I deserved. The Lord will surely bless you; to Him be all the glory.

THE MISSOURI COMMITTEE.

Many of the brethren and sisters will remember that the Standing Committee of our A. M. of 1872, appointed the following brethren: Wm. Gish,

Isaac Hershey, Christian Holler of Kansas, Enoch Eby of Ill., and John Harshey of Mo., to act as a committee to settle difficulties, and to put into proper order the Spring River Church, Jasper Co., Mo., also for the Cedar Creek Church, Jasper Co., Mo., and for other churches in Mo. The first and the last mentioned brother failing to meet at the time and place appointed, brother Addison Harper of Mo., and brother Michael Forney of Ill., being present, were by agreement taken to fill the places of the two absent brethren. Soon after the committee had done the work for which they were appointed, a report of the same was written out and sent to the PILGRIM office for publication, and not appearing for several months, it was inquired after by one of the committee by private letter. Again some four or five weeks elapsed until an answer by private letter, came from the Editor informing us that he perceived by the letter of inquiry, that we failed to receive a letter from him to us, written in due time after his reception of our report, in which he had stated, and now stated it again, that the publishing of our report was objected to on account of it being too personal, not only objected to by the Editor and publisher of the PILGRIM, but by a number of old brethren to whom it was shown at a Communion, stating though that if the committee insisted upon its publication they would publish it, but would rather not. The committee living in three different States, and would require some length of time, and considerable writing to exchange views as to giving it another form less objectionable on account of personalities, and the Editor failing to point out what persons were named who should not have been named in his judgment, and some of the committee having been written to by members of different churches in other States for a copy of the proceedings of said committee, and their requests complied with, it was thought by the writer (John Harshey), that it would circulate itself without any further trouble to any one, in its true character. But it being made to appear to those assembled at our District Meeting, (Southern District of Mo.,) that incorrect reports have gone forth even into other States as to the character of the work done. Reports circulated by letter written by the parties dealt with, as well as by incautious brethren from other States passing through the localities of those brethren dealt with, or upon meeting with them, in their travels elsewhere, and believing what those pleased to tell them, the report has gone abroad, and may be still going, that they were disfellowshipped for no other cause than for their refusing to wash feet *otherwise* than what is called the single mode. Hence the District Meeting requested that a correct report be published in all of our periodicals as touching the reasons of their excommunication.

It being ascertained by the committee as testified to by a number of members, that a majority of the members of the Spring River Valley Branch of the Church, were favorable to practicing the general order of the Brotherhood in carrying out and practicing the ordinances of the house of God, the following charges were found:

1st Against the ministry for not allowing the church the liberty to vote herself into the unity of faith and practice.

2d. Interfering with the unity of faith and practice of the church in endeavoring to set aside the salutation of the kiss between the Supper and Communion.

3d. In disturbing the peace and unity of the church by teaching that a bonnet or handkerchief upon the head of the sister would fill the measure of the Gospel as taught by Paul, and consequently sisters often appearing in meeting without the proper covering.

4th. Sisters telling the Elders that hoops were profitable and advantageous to them in certain conditions in life, and the Elder saying he believed it, and that the church ought to bear with such, and by so saying kept trouble in the church while hoops were fashionable.

5th. Preaching publicly the restoration, and one minister saying before a congregation, while preaching a funeral where the deceased belonged only to the Odd-fellows, that the deceased would, till the winding up of God's dispensation of grace, shout praises to God, subjecting the brethren to ridicule and contempt by some of their neighbors needlessly.

6th That the churches influence, as being opposed to secret societies, was damaged in those parts by some of the ministers being so very intimate with Masons as to go into a joint note with them to borrow money to enable the Masons to build a lodge on top of a business room in which the brethren seemed to take great interest, near their own dwellings and upon ground owned by them, and sold to others, knowing at the time of sale, that a lodge was to be erected thereon, and by a ministering brother being permitted to be in the Lodge as a spectator when the Lodge was in session, also by having connected themselves with a Building Association, strictly known as the Freemason's and Oddfellow's Building Association.

7th. Speaking disrespectfully of the decisions of Annual Meeting.

The above charges having been admitted and proven, the committee decided that in all the above charges there was either ignorant or wilful guilt resting upon the ministry, and that they should confess it and promise to do so no more, or they could no longer be continued as elders and teachers in the Brotherhood. To this they answered, very decidedly, they had no acknowledgment or promise to make. They were then asked whether they did not intend to submit to the general order of the Church, or the decisions of A. M., to which they emphatically declared they would not. Whereupon the committee's decision was, that as they would not acknowledge to their above guilt and be counseled by the general body or church, they could no longer be continued as members in fellowship in the church with all that sided or went with them.

The committee's decision was endorsed by 17 against 10. Now, in short, we also testify that the same spirit of disobedience to general council existed in all that were elsewhere disfellowshipped.

Isaac Hershey,
Christian Holler,
John Harshey,
Michael Forney,
Committee.

N. B. Brother Harper only acted with the committee in Cedar Co., and in Jasper, before the decision was read out and accepted by the church, he asked the committee to erase his name, with which request they complied.

Visitor, *Companion* and *Vindicator*, please copy.

A LETTER TO MY BROTHER AND FAMILY.

Dear brother John and family: In answer to your letter dated Feb. 26, I will try and explain to you why I felt dissatisfied with the church that you and I had joined. In the first place, I had no desire to join any church, nor to become a Christian. This may sound very strange, but I did not feel at that time that I was a sinner or that I had any need of a Savior, and I think, if I had felt my lost condition and my great mountains of sin as I did since, and knew what I since learned, I should not have joined that church at all. But you, no doubt, remember as well as myself, that we were persuaded to go to catechism and that altogether against my will. I finally went for the sake of keeping peace in the family, but never experienced the least change of heart, and consequently, was not able to renounce the world, the devil and all his works, and hold out faithful unto the end as we were obliged to promise before God and the Church at the time we were initiated. I never realized what a great sin I had committed then. As I had not yet been born of the spirit, it was impossible to live up to my promise and, for my part, I cannot see but what the majority of the church members go with the world, hand in hand, as far as worldly pleasures and fashions are concerned, and I could tell you of a great many things in which I think they do not go according to the Scripture. After I searched the Scripture for myself, I found that I could not stand at the day of judgment as I was, and felt it my duty to become a new being and follow my Savior in all things as far as God gave me power to do. I knew that I had not been born of water nor of the spirit, and that old things had not become new. I also knew that our Savior had been baptized in the river Jordan and that he done so to fulfill all righteousness and for an example for us to do as He had done and I read that He was humble and meek and washed his disciples feet and taught them to do unto one another as He done unto them. We read that they eat the Lord's Supper in the evening and took the Sacraments also in the evening and not in the morning, and further, James, a disciple of Christ, told his brethren to annoint the sick with oil in the name of the Lord, see 5th chapter 14th verse, also the 12th verse about swearing and yet look at some of those preachers, they think it is all right to swear when it is necessary according to law, and of course do not forbid the members to swear. Read the 5th chapter and 19th verse of Matthew, and also the 2d chapter 10th verse in James, and a great many more places I could point out if I had space but we are told to search the Scriptures for in them we think we have eternal life.

Again, our pastor often read to us these words, "Go ye into all the world and teach all nations, he that believeth and is baptized shall be saved." &c., but I don't remember that he read that passage of Scripture to us that reads something like this; "Teaching them to observe all things whatsoever I have commanded you, and lo, I am with you always even unto the end of the world." This, most positively forbade them to teach and enjoin upon the nation the observance of anything Christ had not taught or commanded. If reason, revelation or the principle of civil law can determine anything, this point is determined, and yet our pastor taught us that infant baptism was right but could not point it out to us in the Bible. Do you remember the time that I asked him to show me in the Bible that infants were to be baptized, and do you remember what kind of an answer he gave us? He acknowledged that it did not just say so but it meant that they should be baptized. It is a pity that Jesus came into the world to tell us what to do to be saved and then forgot part of it. It just seems to me as though some think that Jesus did not give the right instructions and that they are going to make it right, at least to suit their own notions. Now let me tell you, the secret of all this is, they are too proud and headstrong to obey Christ's whole law. Did you ever read what St. John tells us in the last chapter of Rev., the 18th and 19th? Please read it. That tells us what the consequences are of adding to, or taking from the words of God. I often wonder that people are not afraid to add to it, when we have such plain words to tell us what the results will be. I think the Scriptures are an all sufficient guide for our salvation, but to say that this and that is not necessary to do when we know that Christ commanded it Himself, is hazardous in the extreme. I think that as soon as we once feel our sins and the great value of our souls, and see on what condition we can be saved and become an heir of heaven, then nothing can be too great a sacrifice, even if we were to lose all, even our lives, it would be a small loss to be compared to the loss of our never dying souls. Oh, can it be possible that people are so ignorant in this enlightened country where we all have our Bibles, and besides, hear so much preaching and a great many more ways of hearing the truth, and yet for all this, think that we can go with the world as long as we are in it, and at last reach that Heavenly shore. I cannot believe that we can serve two masters, because we are plainly taught that we cannot do so and yet so many are in reality serving the devil all the time, and I am afraid he is the one that will pay them for their faithful laboring, unless they renounce him altogether before the eleventh hour, and serve a better master the rest of their days. I suppose by this time you will think that I am a Dunkard, and so I am. I am not ashamed to own it. I would be very foolish to be ashamed to tell that I belong to a church that is not afraid nor ashamed to keep the whole law.

From your sister,

L[illegible]NA MA[illegible]

ORIGIN OF NEWSPAPERS.—Mankind are indebted to Queen Elizabeth and Lord Burleigh for the first newspaper, which was entitled the *English Mercurie.* The earliest number is still in the British Museum library, and bears the date of July 23, 1588. During the Civil Wars, periodical papers, the champions of the two parties, were very extensively circulated, and were edited by such writers as Needham, Birkenhead, and L'Estrange, all men of considerable ability.

In the reign of Anne there was but one daily paper, the *Daily Courant.* The first provincial journal in England was the *Orange Postman*, started in 1700, at the price of a penny, but a halfpenny was not refused.—The earliest Scottish newspaper appeared under the auspices of Cromwell, in 1652.

THE RIGHT KIND OF RELIGION.—We want a religion that not only bears on the sinfulness of sin, but on the unreality of lying—a religion that banishes all small measures from the counter, small baskets from the stalls, pebbles from cotton bags and from sugar, chicory from coffee, alum from bread, lard from butter, strychnine from wine, and water from milk cans; that will not put all the big strawberries and peaches on top, and all the bad ones at the bottom, and sell more bottles of wine than there are baskets grown.

IN the Presbyterian Assembly at Baltimore, a proposition was introduced and debated to omit all titles such as D. D., LL. D., etc., in the official rolls of the church, and though no action was taken at the time, except to refer it to a committee, it is believed the proposition will be finally adopted. This a step in the right direction, and it is to be hoped that other bodies religious and secular, will lose no time in following the example.—*Pittsburgh Dispatch.*

THE first Methodist Conference in America was held in Philadelphia, on the 14th, 15th and 16th of July, 1773. The place where it met is still standing, old St. George's Church. It is proposed to have a Centennial Celebration on the same dates of this year, 1873, and in the same old Church.

BOOK NOTICES.

The *Centennial* is a neat and interesting monthly, published by H. W. Crotzer, Philadelphia, in the interest and to prepare the minds of the American people for the great Centennial Exhibition, to be held at Philadelphia, in the year 1876, or the one hundredth year of American independence.—Mailed to subscribers free of postage at $1,00 per year.

Mischief Brewing and the *Strawberry Girl* are among the prettiest Chromos now offered to the people, and can be had free by subscribing for two first class journals, the *Hearth and Home* and the *American Agriculturist*, that should grace the homes of every family.

HEARTH & HOME, weekly, $3.00; AMERICAN AGRICULTURIST, monthly, $1.50. Orange Judd & Co., N. Y.

THE DARK SIDE of New York and its criminal classes from Fifth Avenue down to the Five Points, or a complete history of New York, is an interesting work, to be published in 20 parts and issued semi-monthly at 10 cents per number, and can be had at all news stores in the United States. The first number is before us. It is printed in excellent style, on good paper and is complete with interest.

GOOD BOOKS.

A large number of our patrons are receiving our books as noticed below, as premiums, and express themselves highly pleased with them. Others who are not agents, have enquired whether we keep them for sale. We have now made arrangements with Mr. Wells to furnish any of their publications post paid at publishers prices. Orders for books must be accompanied with the cash, and plain directions for sending them.

How to read Character, Illus. Price,	$1.25
Combe's Moral Philosophy,	1.75
Constitution of Man. Combe,	1.75
Education. By Spurzheim,	1.50
Memory—How to Improve it,	1.50
Mental Science, Lectures on,	1.50
Self-Culture and Perfection,	1.50
Combe's Physiology, Illus.	1.75
Food and Diet. By Pereira,	1.75
Natural Laws of Man,	.75
Hereditary Descent,	1.50
Combe on Infancy,	1.50
Sober and Temperate Life,	.50
Children in Health—Disease,	1.75
The Science of Human Life,	3.50
Fruit Culture for the Million,	1.00
Saving and Wasting,	1.50
Ways of Life—Right Way,	1.00
Footprints of Life.	1.25
Conversion of St. Paul,	1.00

Life at Home; or, The Family and its Members. A work which should be found in every family. $1.50. Extra gilt, $2.00.

Hand-book for Home Improvement: comprising "How to Write," "How to Talk," "How to Behave," and "How to do Business," in one vol. 2.25.

Man, in Genesis and in Geology; or, the Biblical Account of Man's Creation, tested by Scientific Theories of his Origin and Antiquity. One vol. 12mo, $1.00.

Man and Woman: Considered in their Relations to each Other and to the World. 12mo, Fancy cloth, Price $1 00.

Hopes and Helps for the Young of both sexes, Relating to the Formation of Character. Choice of Avocation, Health, Conversation, Social Affection Courtship and Marriage. Muslin, $1.50.

The Emphatic Diaglott; or The New Testament in Greek and English. Containing the Original Greek Text of the New Testament, with an Interlineary Word for-word English Translation. Price, $4.00; extra fine binding, $5.00.

Trine Immersion

TRACED

TO THE APOSTLES.

The SECOND EDITION is now ready for delivery. The work has been carefully revised, corrected and enlarged.

Put up in a neat pamphlet form, with good paper cover, and will be sent, postpaid, on the following terms: One copy, 25 cts; Five copies, $1.10; Ten copies, $2.00. 25 copies, $4.50; 50 copies, $8.50; 100 copies, $16 00.

Address, J. H. MOORE,
Urbana, Champaign co., Ill.

Oct 22.

DYMOND ON WAR.

An inquiry into the Accordancy of War, with the Principles of Christianity, and an examination of the Philosophical reasoning by which it is defended. With observations on some of the causes of war and on some of its effects. By Jonathan Dymond. Sent from this office, post-paid, for 50 cts.

TUNE BOOK.

The Brethren's Tune and Hymn Book, is a compilation of Sacred Music adapted to all the hymns in the Brethren's New Hymn Book. It contains over 350 pages, printed on good paper and neatly bound. We will send it to any address, post paid at $1.25 per copy.

GIVEN AWAY.

A FINE GERMAN CHROMO.

We send an elegant chromo, mounted and ready for framing, free to every agent for

UNDERGROUND

or,

LIFE BELOW THE SURFACE.

BY THOS. W. KNOX.

942 Pages Octavo. 130 Fine Engravings.

Relates Incidents and Accidents beyond the Light of Day; Startling Adventures in all parts of the World; Mines and Mode of Working them; Under-currents of Society; Gambling and its Horrors; Caverns and their Mysteries; The Dark Ways of Wickedness; Prisons and their Secrets; Down in the Depths of the Sea; Strange Stories of the Detection of Crime.

The book treats of experience with brigands; nights in opium dens and gambling hells; life in prison; Stories of exiles; adventures among Indians; journey through Sewers and Catacombs; accidents in mines; pirates and piracy; tortures of the inquisition; wonderful burglaries; underworld of the great cities, etc., etc.

AGENTS WANTED

for this work. Exclusive territory is given. Agents can make $100 a week in selling this book. Send for circulars and terms to agents.

J. B BURR & HYDE,

HARTFORD, CONN., or CHICAGO, ILL

TRACTS.

"ANXIOUS BENCH RELIGION EXAMINIED," BY ELDER J. S. FLORY. A SYNOPSIS OF CONTENTS. An address to the reader: The peculiarities that attend this type of religion. The feelings there experienced not imaginary but real. The key that unlocks the wonderful mystery. The causes by which feelings are excited. How the momentary feelings called "Experimental religion" are brought about, and then concludes by giving that form of doctrine as taught by Jesus Christ and recorded by his faithful witnesses.

COUNTERFEIT DETECTER

or

BAPTISM—MUCH IN LITTLE.

This work is now ready for distribution, and the importance of the subject will speak for it a large demand. It is a short treatise on baptism in tract form intended for general distribution, and is set forth in such a plain and logical manner that a wayfaring man though a fool, cannot err therein. Either of the above tracts sent postpaid on the following terms: Two copies, 10 cts, 10 copies 40 cents, 25 copies 70 cents, 50 copies $1.00, 100 copies $1.50.

Trine Immersion.

A discussion on Trine Immersion, by letter between Elder B. F. Moomaw and Dr. J. J. Jackson, to which is annexed a Treatise on the Lord's Supper, and on the necessity, character and evidences of the new birth, also a dialogue on the doctrine of non-resistance, by Elder B. F Moomaw. Single copy 50 cents.

THE HELPING HAND.

Containing several hundred Valuable Receipts for cooking well at a moderate expense, making Dyes, Coloring, Cleaning and Cementing. This book also points out in plain language, free from Doctors' terms the diseases of men, women and children, and the latest and most approved means used for their cure, to which is added a description of the Medicinal Roots and Herbs, and how they are to be used in the cure of diseases.

This is a work of considerable importance and we offer it to our readers as being a valuable accession to every household. Send from this office to any address, postpaid, for 25 cents.

1870 1873

DR. FAHRNEY'S

Blood Cleanser or Panacea.

A tonic and purge, for Blood Diseases. Great reputation. Many testimonials. Many ministering brethren use and recommend it. Ask or send for the "Health Messenger." Use only the "*Panacea*" prepared at Chicago, Ills., and by

Dr. P. Fahrney's Brothers & Co.,

Feb. 3-pd. *Waynesboro, Franklin Co., Pa*

New Hymn Books, English.

TURKEY MOROCCO.

One copy, postpaid,	$1.00
Per Dozen,	11.25

PLAIN ARABESQUE.

One Copy, post-paid,	.75
Per Dozen,	8.50

Ger'n & English, Plain Sheep.

One Copy, post-paid,	$1.00
Per Dozen	11.25
Arabesque Plain,	1.00
Turkey Morocco,	1.25
Single German, post paid	.50
Per Dozen,	5.50

HUNTINGDON & BROAD TOP RAIL ROAD

On and after June 15th, 1873, Trains will run on this road daily (Sunday excepted) as follows:

Trains from Huntingdon South. *Trains from Mt. Dallas moving North.*

MAIL A. M.	EXP'S. P. M.	STATIONS.	MAIL. P. M.	EXP'S A. M
7 45	5 50	Huntingdon,	AR 6 10	AR 8 25
7 50	6 05	Long Siding	6 05	8 20
8 10	6 15	McConnelstown	5 50	8 11
8 17	6 23	Pleasant Grove	5 40	8 02
8 30	6 38	MARKLESBURG	5 25	7 45
8 45	6 50	Coffee Run	5 11	7 32
8 55	6 58	Rough & Ready	5 03	7 23
9 05	7 05	Cove	4 50	7 14
9 08	7 10	Fishers Summit	4 52	7 10
9 23	7 20	Saxton	4 40	6 51
9 40	7 50	Riddlesburg	4 20	6 35
9 47	7 58	Hopewell	4 15	6 22
10 03	8 12	Piper's Run	4 00	6 05
10 20	8 30	Tatesville	3 47	5 48
10 30	8 40	Everett	3 35	5 35
10 35	8 45	Mount Dallas	3 30	5 30
11 08	9 20	Bedford	3 00	5 00

SHOUP'S RUN BRANCH.

A. M.	P. M.		P. M.	A. M.
LE 9 25	LE 7 35	Saxton.	AR 4 25	AR 6 45
9 40	7 50	Coalmont.	4 10	6 30
9 45	7 55	Crawford.	4 05	6 25
AR 9 55	AR 8 05	Dudley	LE 3 35	LE 6 15

Broad Top City from Dudley 2 miles by stage.

Time of Penna. R. R. Trains at Huntingdon.

***Mail No. 2 makes connection at Huntingdon with Mail going East on Pennsylvania Railroad at 4.15 p. m., and West at 5.45 p. m. Mail No. 1 leaves Huntingdon at 7 40 a. m. on arrival of Pacific Express West.

Trains on this road connect with trains on Bedford & Bridgeport, and Cumberland & Pennsylvania Railroads.

G. F. GAGE, Supt.

The Weekly Pilgrim.

Published by J. B. Brumbaugh, & Co.

Edited by H. B. & Geo. Brumbaugh.

CORRESPONDING EDITORS.

D. P. Sayler, Double Pipe Creek, Md.

Leonard Furry, New Enterprise, Pa.

The *Pilgrim* is a Christian Periodical, devoted to religion and moral reform. It will advocate in the spirit of *love* and *liberty*, the principles of true Christianity, labor for the promotion of peace among the people of God, for the encouragement of the saints and for the conversion of sinners, avoiding those things which tend toward disunion or sectional feelings.

TERMS.

Single copy, Book paper,	$1.50
Eleven copies, [eleventh for Agt.]	$15.00

Any number above that at the same rate.

Address,

H. B. BRUMBAUGH.

James Creek,

Huntingdon county Pa.

The Weekly Pilgrim.

"REMOVE NOT THE ANCIENT LANDMARKS WHICH OUR FATHERS HAVE SET."

VOL. 4. JAMES CREEK, PENNSYLVANIA, JULY 8, 1873. NO. 27.

REPORT OF ANNUAL MEETING CONTINUED.

(*Continued from page 203.*)

EASTERN DISTRICT OF PENNA.

QUERY.—Is it according to the Gospel or is it conforming to the world when brethren subscribe for railroad stock?

Considered that there is no Scripture forbidding it, but inasmuch as it brings us into associations in which we are liable to violate our christian principles, we would advise brethren not to engage in it.

Proposed to amend by saying "no direct Scripture."

Passed with the amendment.

——. If that implies more than one, then it would be necessary to have more than one in every church.

Wise. The question did not say ordained elders, it says house-keepers.

Moderator. The explanation is called for, I will explain. Two brethren living in the same church, in the second degree, in the ministry, have the oversight of the church, hence these two brethren will look upon themselves as being housekeepers. If they work together, they will work harmoniously, but if they don't there will be trouble. In that case the church would have to decide the matter.

——. Proposed an amendment that where there is a division, or where it does not work well, the church should call for help to regulate that. Passed.

SOUTH WESTERN OHIO.

QUERY.—Is it agreeable with the Gospel or the old order of the Brethren, for members to have musical instruments in their houses, such as an organ, or a fiddle, to amuse themselves playing on them, or for the amusement of the youngsters, to play the organ, and that on the Lord's day and after their return from the house of worship? If considered agreeable, we want the "thus saith the Lord" for it.

Referred to the standing committee for an answer.

THE BRETHREN IN COUNCIL ASSEMBLED.

Would it not be advisable to pass a resolution, that when any one of the members, or of the members' children die, that at the same time they should not neglect to inform all the speakers in their own district if possible, and at the same time have the privilege to send for any other brethren in their districts?

ANSWER. We think it is advisable to inform all the ministers in the church or congregation in which a death occurs, and whoever may be called by the deceased before his death, or the family of which he was a member, to officiate on the occasion.

Sayler. If there is a death the family have the right to send for who they please, and the A. M., should not take any note of it.

Wise. To avoid jealousy was the design, and therefore it would be best, where convenient, to inform all, but let the family have the choice.

——. We would like to have it passed, to avoid the jealousy it has occasioned under certain circumstances, where it can be avoided.

Moderator. In some churches when a death occurs, they will send off twenty-five miles for a preacher, and the brethren living in the congregation are not called on.

——. It is a local matter, and they should settle it among themselves, without bothering the other brethren. Let their own district correct their members.

——. It concerns the whole Brotherhood. Sometimes the ministers do not hear of a death. By this proviso they are at liberty to attend.

Quinter. I always approved of respecting our brethren at home, but I don't want it to pass from this meeting in that shape. Table it and let every district attend to their local concerns at home.

——. I think the brethren ought to be above having their jealousy aroused so easily. As long as we feed this thing it will be kept up.—Table it.

Sharp. I move to send it back to the district and let them dispose of it at home.

Agreed to.

As the Annual Meeting has given the liberty to hold Sabbath Schools, if held according to the gospel, this District Meeting asks the Annual Meeting to give the order called for.

ANSWER. This query is designed to be answered by the answer given to query 14, Minutes of 1868; and, in addition to said answer, we would say that our Sabbath Schools should be held as all our meetings should be held, to the glory of God: 1st Cor. 10, 31. And as the object of the Sabbath School is to teach our children Christianity, Sabbath school teachers should observe the admonition given by Paul, to parents, in which he admonishes them to bring up the children in the nurture and admonition of the Lord. Eph. 6:4.

Moderator. When this query came before our District Meeting and the request was to give the Gospel order for holding Sabbath Schools, I said that inasmuch as the Yearly Meeting had given the authority for holding Sabbath Schools, to send it up to them and let them give the Gospel order for it, as that was called for in the query, and then it was transcribed and put in the present form.

Minutes of 1868, Query 14 read.

McGarvey. There is or might be a great deal said concerning the Sabbath Schools. Properly conducted it is a good institution. When our meetings are conducted in Gospel order our brethren and all that go there as teachers are in order. If so it would be a good thing; but we tolerate teachers to take our classes who don't look like our members, and don't believe the doctrine, and we train up our children after their examples, or get some man to deliver an oration in favor of the Sabbath School who has on his fine cravat, cuffs and gold buttons, and claim the Sabbath School as a good institution, and the means of converting the children. This is not Gospel order. When we have a teacher he should be governed by the Gospel order or it is worse than no school.

Passed.

QUERY.—This District Meeting requests the Annual Meeting of 1873, to reconsider article 15, 1868, touching the propriety of brethren going on stands to preach.

Ans. We can give no better answer than that given in Minutes of 1866, Art. 32.

——. We want nothing but Gospel authority on the question, and a union among the Brotherhood.

——. It is a matter of conscience, as I understand it. I am not conscientious, but my brother here is conscientious. We go to meeting, how are we to preach?

——. You stay down with the brethren that are too conscientious to go up.

——. I would certainly go up or stay down to avoid a showing difference. If I understand the teachings of the scripture it is more safe to keep down. We want unity of practice, and we beg you to consider this sensibly.

Sayler. So far as I read the Testament it is silent on that subject. We learn that the apostle spoke from the stairs, showing that he had his head above the multitude. Solomon dedicated the temple kneeling on a pulpit made for that purpose and God answered that prayer and accepted it. When Jerusalem was rebuilt and the law read by Ezra the priest in the streets, there was a pulpit built large enough to hold thirteen men besides Ezra, and God was pleased with that again; then I don't see where the brethren get their objection to seeing a brother raised up to a position where it can be heard. If I thought the position I occupied had anything to do with my humility I would have the brethren cut a hole in the floor several feet lower than the congregation; but it is not necessary to get down on the floor to lay at the feet of Jesus. The mind is the index of humility and not the body. Half of the meetinghouses in the Brotherhood have an elevation for the speaker, then why be restricted.

Neal. "In the audience of all the people, he said, beware of the scribes," &c.

Sharp. We are aware that Paul did not hesitate to elevate himself a few inches above his audience. If it be necessary, like Paul, to go up on the stairs, or on the top of a high mountain as Jesus Christ did, when the audience was so large, we should do it. I hope no brother will condemn the practice laid down by the Savior himself.

Sturgis. Peter went up on the house top to pray and God heard his prayer. He does not regard it as an exalted position if the heart is right before God. "The time has come when men shall not worship God at Jerusalem or on his mountain, but in spirit and in truth. The spirit of the Lord is liberty, let us exercise it and not restrain our brethren.

——. If we love those high places and have no other idea than just to have a prominent place, it is wrong for us as it was for the Pharisees; but if not our love for the place then it is not wrong.

——. Josiah put down the high places of worship, and was approved of God for doing so. Ezra learned the idea of erecting a stand from Babylon, while in captivity. I am not conscientious. I have been up. When my brother goes up I feel like going up with him, but would like union. If it is not right our proceedings will make it right. I never feel as good up as when I stay down.

Wise. Brethren that don't like to go up had better remain down when we can with any degree of propriety whatever, and that difficulty will be obviated. I don't like a division unless under peculiar circumstances.

Passed.

NORTHERN DISTRICT OF INDIANA.

QUERY.—Since the word of God commands us to preach the Gospel to every creature, will this District Meeting ask the Annual Meeting to appoint a committee of five, to draft and present a plan to the Annual Meeting of 1874, for the successful carrying out of the Gospel into all portions of our country, where there are any brethren.

Sturgis. Such a question came up in 1859, and the Annual Meeting did appoint a committee which drafted a plan that was accepted in some of the Southern States, but on account of the war it never was presented till 1868, when it passed the meeting and is on the minutes, which we believed sufficient, but the brethren having concluded it best to come here and wake up your minds on the subject, it is before us. It appears that it has not been extensively carried out. It appears that they had not the minutes where it came from, and I told them I would have it in all the papers so that those who do not get the minutes can see it.

——. The decision was that every church hold counsel with their own members and see what they would do and report at the District Meeting. It came up at our District Meeting, but was neglected and not brought to the Annual Meeting.

Sturgis. I would advise brethren that no decision of the Annual Meeting will ever execute itself. It is expected that the churches will put it in force.

Quinter. Moved that it be sent back to the church from whence it came and that they be cited to the Minutes as they stand.

Passed.

What is the duty of the committee sent by Annual Meeting to adjust existing difficulties in the Church? Is it not to hear the case in question, with the evidence, and then to form their decision according to the evidence and the Gospel, irrespective of former transactions of the Church or any other committee whatever, and submit it to the Church for its acceptance or rejection.

Ans. Yes.—Referred back.

Adjourned.

AFTERNOON SESSION.

An address was delivered by Dan'l Hill of Ohio, a member of the Society of Friends, on the subject of "Peace," which was interesting, and received with approbation by the audience.

MIDDLE DISTRICT OF INDIANA.

QUERY.—This District requests the Annual Meeting to reconsider Art. 10th minutes of 1868, concerning the advancing brethren in the ministry from the first to the second degree; what is the consent and established order in so doing? Are they received with hand and kiss?

Considered that the proper way to receive them is with hand and kiss.

Re-adopted.

When churches, or individuals, call for committees, shall the party calling for the committee pay the expenses of said committee, or shall the committee say which party shall pay the expenses?

Answer. We think the committee should say who shall pay the expenses.

Passed.

Is it agreeable to the Gospel or the old order of the Brethren for members to have musical instruments in their houses, such as organs, or a fiddle to amuse themselves playing on them or for the amusement of the youngsters, to play the organ, and that on the Lord's Day, and after return from the house of worship?

Answer. It is unauthorized by the Gospel and clearly opposed to the order of the old Brethren and the doctrine of self denial, and not calculated to promote vital christianity.

Longanecker. There are two things in that query; one is whether we shall play on them on the Sabbath, and the other is whether it is wrong to have them at all under any circumstances.

Holsinger. To have a fiddle or other musical instrument for the purpose of amusement, I would be opposed to it, but to cut off musical instruments entirely, I could not consent that it would be agreeable to the Gospel.

Steel. We are to sing with the Spirit and with the understanding also, and I believe it would be a blessing to our church, if the brethren would dispense entirely with the use of musical instruments. If we have them in our houses, it will not be long before we have them in our meeting houses. I would like to know what is meant by sounding brass and a tinkling cymbal.

Passed.

QUERY.—Will this District Meeting, petition the Annual Meeting to grant the right to the districts at their meetings to appoint if necessary, committees to investigate, and settle matters of difficulty, that may exist within the bounds of the district, such selection to be made of brethren residing in the limits of the district when such difficulties may exist, except in cases in which a majority of the churches composing the district are involved?

Ans. We think it best to make no change from our present practice of selecting committees. Passed without objection.

QUERY.—Since the District Meeting of Middle Indiana, last year had under consideration the orphan's home, or a home for orphan children, the meeting expressing itself favorable, but laid it over for further consideration, will not this meeting take into consideration the propriety of erecting a home for orphan children, and members who are a church charge?

Ans. This meeting approves of erecting an asylum for the benefit of the orphan children of the brethren, and all that may be considered subjects for such an institution, but it deserves the decision of the Annual Meeting, and therefore we send the query with its answer for prayerful consideration.

Answer (from the standing committee)—This meeting does not see the propriety of adopting such measures at present; but if the Middle District of Indiana desires to do so, we will not oppose them.

——. I don't believe in such a plan at all. If it starts at one place it may follow along like many other things, which we are now sorry to see. Let each church take charge of its own members, which are a charge to the church.

——. And may be that may be agreeable to many of the citizens of Indiana.

——. I think it would be better to refer it back to the District Meeting.

Wise—The answer says this Annual Meeting does not see the propriety of passing it, but will not oppose it. The next Annual Meeting may view it differently.

Holsinger. I would suggest, that instead of passing this answer, we bid the project God speed. I am favorable to any measure that looks toward the elevation, improvement, and benefit of our fellow-beings; and I am opposed to anything, and shall always give my voice and vote in opposition to everything, that has a downward tendency; and therefore to act consistently with my principles, I would favor this measure. Certainly the motive that originated this plan must have been good; and if this Annual Meeting does not approve of the plan, and does not see the propriety, or necessity of the plan, let them not object to it. And if it is not objectionable, I think they should bid the brethren God-speed, when they undertake such a noble work as this. Where is there a more laudible enterprise in all our land, than to build up an institution of this kind? It is our duty to provide for the wants of the poor.

——. I think our brethren have always provided for the poor and have an order adopted for that purpose.

The passage of the resolution was called for and it was declared passed.

QUERY.—Is it right, and according to the Gospel, to have different styles of hymn-books and to annex the names of those who composed them to the index?

Ans. This meeting desires a good substantial hymn-book, and not a different style as at present; and as to the names of those who composed the hymns being printed, we think it is not necessary.

Sharp. I am led to believe that we often attach the words "Is it in accordance with the Gospel?" to carry a query through. Now I do not believe that the Gospel says anything about hymn books; but the term is often attached merely to give strength to the measure. I hope we will be a little more considerate, and things that are so trifling will not be brought before the body, when questions of greater importance ought to be considered. I hope that the meeting will table that measure. It was moved and seconded to table that question, and it was tabled.

SOUTHERN INDIANA.

Southern Indiana asks the Annual Meeting to adopt a plan to have the different papers the brethren are publishing to be consolidated in one, and if they cannot be consolidated, let the Annual Meeting establish a paper under its own control.

Ans. We recommend the editors to arrange this matter before next Annual Meeting, and if they do not do so, then let the Annual Meeting act in the matter.

Holsinger. Perhaps a few words may be in place and to advantage upon this subject. I am altogether in favor of a consolidation, and am also in favor of the Annual Meeting taking charge of a paper. I would however not like very well for the Annual Meeting to monopolize the publishing business altogether,—but I should be satisfied to pass that answer, if it would not be for the threatening part of it—giving us only one year's time to make the arrangements. I do not know that those arrangements can be made, by the present proprietors of our publications, and I think the best plan would be for the Annual Meeting simply to buy out all the present publishers, and then continue to publish the papers, and I now say that I am ready to sell out at a fair price. If my price does not suit you, I will appoint a man and you appoint a man, and let those two appoint a third, and whatever they say I will take.

I am tired of the business. The time was when I was exceedingly zealous and exceedingly fond of my business, but the crosses I have had to bear, and the labors and difficulties I have had to endure, have completely satisfied me, and I am ready at any time to turn it over into the hands of the Annual Meeting. But, as I say, I do not believe it would be good for the meeting to monopolize the business. None of the churches that pursued such a course prospered in the business; but for a time it might do very well, to have but one publishing house. I think that in this way a great many publications may be brought forth with great advantage to the church. At present, the publishing being divided, it has a tendency to seperate us somewhat:—We have our friends, and the other papers have their friends, and the tendency is towards division; especially when either of the papers would take a radical stand on opposite sides of a question. Another reason for having one house is, that some of our present publishing houses are poor—I know that is the case with our establishment. We need books, tracts, Sunday school papers—we need to publish a number of small books for Sunday school purposes; for you heard to day that the brethren do not want to have just any book thrown into our Sunday schools. We have several books now ready for publication, but we have not the type to print them with. But we think that the Annual Meeting could command the means to secure the publication. Brother Beer's book on the Passover has been ready for over a year, but we have not the means to publish it. We have a work that has been published in the Pious Youth, and which would make an excellent Sunday school book, if we had the means to publish it. Let the Annual Meeting take the matter in hands, and appoint Editors of the different departments, and have a regular publishing house, and I believe the plan would work remarkably well. The only fear that I have is, that after a while this meeting would run the thing too exclusively. I would not like to see any enterprising brother cut off from the privilege of commencing a publication for himself. But I think there would be no contingency of this nature for many years to come. I will do precisely what I said; but I would not vote in favor of the present question because of that one clause, that if we do not consolidate within one year, then the Annual Meeting will commence a publication of its own. Rather than that, I will sell to this meeting. If you pass the resolution, I want you to take my paper off my hands. I do not want another paper started in addition to those we have at present.

——. Certainly, if the A. M., sees cause for starting a publication, no individual power can stop the Annual Meeting from doing so.

Forney. In regard to the brethren of this Annual Meeting publishing a paper, I am fearful that it will lead to the very same trouble we have now to contend with. In order to carry on this house properly, Editors must be appointed, and if our Editors do not keep within bounds they must be considered as all the disobedient members, and if the church has it in hands, it will be more difficult to reach the matter than it is now. I do not know that we can do better than to table the matter, and bring our present Editors to account whenever they become out of order.

Brumbaugh. It certainly places us in a very unpleasant position. We of course expect to publish a paper. If this Annual Meeting will say to us that if they stop our papers, they will not see us lose by it. I am satisfied, the nature of this decision is such, that it would seem to discourage us from meeting our expenses: and I would say, with brother Holsinger, that if such a decision is made, I am ready to sell out.

Kurtz. If this resolution is to pass I am also ready to sell.

Quinter. There must be a pretty extensive feeling that there is something wanting in our periodicals. I feel satisfied of that myself. If the wealth and intelligence of our Brotherhood was more properly directed, we could produce something that would do more good, both in and out of the Church. On that account considerable has been said about consolidation and other courses to be pursued.

But few of you have a full appreciation of the amount of labor and care and of the duties which will be thrown upon the Annual Meeting if they publish a paper. However this matter has been brought forward for suggestion on the part of us all. That being the case, I think it is well enough to have been brought forward. Brethren Holsinger, Kurtz and Brumbaugh need not take alarm that this will go into immediate operation and injure their business. We would like the talents of our church more concentrated.

Many voices here called for the tabling of the question, and it was tabled.

Query. Is it right to put a brother into office to serve as deacon or minister, who does not conform to the order of the church or allow them to serve in any church business at District meetings or Yearly meetings? And would it not be best for brethren that officiate when an election is going on to instruct the church not to give their voice for any that do not conform to the order?

Answer. We advise the brethren to be very careful in giving power, or office, to brethren who do not conform to the order.

Sayler spoke of the manner of installment of officers, and stated that no difficulty would arise where the elders of the church are careful to ask the proper questions at installation as laid down in the order passed in 1845.

Holsinger. The question arises here, what is the order? Shall a member be received as a deacon, if he had been found drunk or guilty of any other crime?

——I think it refers to non-conformity with the world.

Holsinger. If his character be not a good one, if he has not the qualifications required according to the apostle Paul, and it is to this that the query refers, then I say pass it; but if it has reference to the cut of his clothes, &c., I think it is objectionable.

——, The order of the church is to observe plainness and humility.

Sayler. That is certainly the general order, and when he presents himself for installment, I think he should conform to that order.

Passed without objection.

NORTHERN ILLINOIS.

Query. What is to be done in case one one of the members of the church pleads guilty of the act of fornication? Is it the duty of the housekeeper of said church to take the voice of every member present, whether such a one is only to be excommunicated or put in avoidance; or is it the duty of such housekeeper to put the avoidance upon such a member at once, according to I Cor. chap. 5.?

Answer. An elder has no right to either expel from the church, or put a member in avoidance, without the counsel of the church.

Passed without objection.

Query. Do the brethren not think it proper to exert their influence against the admission into the church, of the new hymn book with notes?

Answer. We advise all districts to keep them out of the church in public worship.

——, I want to know why we cannot use them.

——, I think it is necessary for some one to have the notes to start the tune properly.

Sharp. I want to know what is meant by "the new hymn book."

——, It means the Tune and Hymn book—the Brethren's hymn book with notes.

Sharp. We understand that that hymn book was authorized by this body—all the hymns in it. I am speaking of the hymns alone. They were published by brother Kurtz—were subjected to a committee of inspection, and afterwards adopted. Then, some of the brethren, thought that if they had notes in connection with the hymns, it would be an advantage. If these are the books referred to, I understand the question.

——, The Brethren's Tune and Hymn book is the one refered to.

Sharp. Then, if any brother does not wish to use that book, should he not have the libery of using a book that has no notes in it? We would not suppose that a brother here would rob him of that privilege. But on the other hand, where some member can lead in the singing, provided he has some hing to guide him, it is questionable whether we should cut him off from the privilege o using the tunes we all sing. It simply comes to this point: you may sing the tune, but you must not look upon certain characters which tell you how to sing it—you must sing from memory. The query narrows down to this. The book does not present any new tunes, tunes that we do not sing, nor does the query say that we shall not sing new tunes. The only objection seems to be that the Tune and Hymn book contains a certain musical alphabet by which we can spell out the tune, and afterwards read or sing it. Now shall we rob the members of the church from singing a tune which we have been in the habit of singing, just because we have the aid of certain characters which we understand? I don't use that book myself, but I want to have charity for those who need it.

Sayler. I do not know that the objection is against singing from the book because of the notes being in it, but I have heard other objections. When the Tune and Hymn book was introduced among us, we made no objection against individual members buying the book; but, as we did not sing in our church by lining, the church has bought hymn books, and scattered them around through the Meeting-houses. I objected to introduce the Tune Book in that way, and perhaps the same objection I had against it may be the cause of this matter being brought up here.

I considered that the publication of that book was an infringement upon the right of brother Quinter to his Hymn Book, hence I made no objection against members buying them, for their own private use. It is the general use of the book in the church that I object to. It is very well known that if the publishers had published the tunes, without the hymns, there would not have been any sale for them; but they took the hymns of brother Quinters' book, and put tunes to them, thus infringing upon his right. I like the book, but I think it should have been gotten up with a different kind of understanding. That is my objection.

Enoch Eby. Since this comes from our District, I will say that the sentiment of the body I represent, for I am not here to express my own sentiment, is, that the matter of using Tune books will result in choir singing. I have no experience of them, as we do not use them, but this is a prevailing opinion. On this ground, that by such a practice we will lose our simplicity in worship, this matter has been presented. It is not intended to prohibit members from having the books in their houses, but to keep them out of the house of public worship.

Metzgar. I agree with what the brother has said.

Brown. I wonder whether you would object to our using them at Sabbath school?

Sayler. My objection was that it interfered with the sale of brother Quinter's books.

Brown. I have a little personal interest in this matter. I was authorized to get some books for the Sabbath-school, and if you are going to stop me, I want to know before I purchase them.

Moderator. Since these books have got among the brethren, I have seen it come to just as brother Eby has related—the young people sit in the middle of the church in a choir, and the old brethren sit around the outside and don't sing; therefore I think we had better be on our guard in regard to this matter.

Holsinger. I feel almost like apologizing to this congregation for appearing before you so often; but you will observe that all the questions I speak upon are, directly or indirectly, aimed at me or some of my measures; therefore I hope I am excusable for appearing before you so often. It happens that I am the publisher of the Tune and Hymn book, and it was my impression that I had liberty and authority from this body to publish that book. I got it and had it passed, and it is entered on the minutes, and you will find it so when you examine it. That is my impression.

Now, in regard to the infringement, I think certainly it is a little strange that brother Quinter should hold still so long and allow the Annual Meeting to give me the permission to publish it without objection. I do not like insinuations of infringement thrown out upon me at all. I never felt the least compunction for infringing upon brother Quinter's publication; and I suppose I have sold as many of brother Quinter's hymn books—perhaps more than he has sold himself—except those he has sold to me at wholesale prices; and I have been extensively engaged in selling his hymn books at starvation prices. I am willing that brother Quinter should make a statement of his profits and losses.

Again, in regard to the danger of getting to choirs, I would say, that I am opposed to choir singing; but I saw no more choir singing when the Tune and Hymn Books did not exist than I ever saw when they did exist. As to stopping old brethren from singing, it was for the very purpose of keeping the old tunes in existence, and not allowing them to be supplanted, that we have introduced this Tune Book. I am not aware that a single one of our old popular tunes has been omitted, as I was very particular in getting all he old tunes. I believe in congregational singing, and I have been annoyed considerably in going to church when tunes were sung that were new, and in the singing of which we could not join; and I know just how one feels under those circumstances. The object in view in getting up this book, was to prevent this and choir singing. You can never learn to sing a new tune unless you practice it, and as the brethren are not generally in favor of singing schools, we come together and have exercises before the regular exercises begin. If we go there and take up a book and begin to sing, and find the tune strange, we find the sentiment new; and how are we going to bring our hearts into harmony with this sentiment, and to lay our offering of devotion before God, when we have to think of the tune at the same time? But when you have learned the hymn, you can sing with the spirit and with the understanding also. Every tune you sing here is in our Tune and Hymn Book. It is for the purpose of aiding us in devotional exercises that the book was introduced, and not for the purpose of introducing new tunes.

Quinter. Brother Holsinger asks why I did not make any objection to the book in earlier days. I never objected to the book. At the Yearly Meeting in Iowa, when brother Holsinger asked the Annual Meeting to give him some liberty, I believe the meeting made no objection, if brother Holsinger printed the book. He had a part of the book on the stand at the time. I examined it and said, "Brother Henry will you print all the hymns?" He said, "I think not." Therefore, I expected, of course, it would be a book with some of the hymns in it, and tunes it. When it came out it had all the hymns in, except eight or ten. I wrote immediately to Cincinnati, to business men—for I know there is an honorable way to do business—who knew the nature of business of this kind, and they said if the parties had used the book I got up, to add notes to it, they ought to have consulted me. So I passed the matter and never mentioned it to, I think, as many as three persons. Brother Henry knows that I have said nothing, and have nothing to do with bringing this here.—As he said he was surprised that I have said nothing, it was because I did not want to have trouble. Brethren wrote to me from Maryland intimating it to be an infringement, but I never thought it exactly an infringement, except an infringement upon Christian courtesy.

Moderator. I want to say in regard to brother Henry saying that he had got consent of the Annual Meeting, for the publication of this book, that it is a mistake. It is not on the minutes. You that were there recollect. He had a plan laid, pretty deeply, too, and as I was watching the congregation, as I frequently do, when they were talking; the brethren asked me how I discovered that when I was attending to something else. When it was nearly ready to pass, I said "No! I discover something in it that you have not seen." Then I brought that out and showed it to the brethren. Then No! it could'nt pass. It did not pass. It was not by consent of the meeting. It was the object, no doubt, to get the consent of the meeting; but it is not on the minutes.

——. I recollect it. He asked the Yearly Meeting to grant him the privilege to get up this book; but, if I'm not mistaken, it was answered him that if he got one up, he did it on his own responsibility.

Several brethren corroborated this statement.

The query and answer were re-read.

Holsinger. I would ask that you defer this until to-morrow morning, and then we will bring the documents to show in support of our statement.

Cries of "Pass it, pass it!"

Miller arose, and spoke of his regret; that the matter should have come to this point—that they had no trouble about the books in his district—always left the Tune Books at home.

To be Continued.

POETRY.

THE LAST GATHERING

Ocean and earth restore
  All that your arms entomb!
From every distant shore,
  Come to the gathering—come!

Sages of days gone by,
  Long mouldering in the tomb,
Haste to the realms in light,
  Come to the gathering—come!

Warrior with laurelled brow,
  Who fixed a nation's doom,
Come to the judgment now,
  Come to the gathering—come!

Maiden with lips of rose,
  And brow of parian stone,
Haste from thy long repose,
  Come to the gathering—come!

Bright was thy dark eye's gleam,
  Fair was thy cheek of bloom,
Again these charms shall beam!
  Come to the gathering—come!

Mourner with tearful eye,
  Haste to thy long sought home,
A peaceful rest is nigh!
  Come to the gathering—come!

Loved ones of days gone by,
  Haste from the grave's cold gloom;
Again we meet on high!
  Come to the gathering—come!

Ocean and earth restore
  All that your arms entomb!
Myriads from every shore,
  Come to the gathering—come!

ORIGINAL ESSAYS.

For the Pilgrim.

"LET LOVE BE WITHOUT DISSIMULATION."—ROM. 12: 9.

Dear readers of the PILGRIM. The Holy Spirit, in the Apostle's days, saw the necessity of this important exhortation, even among the believers in Christ; hence the inspired Apostle's warning to the church of Rome. He being well acquainted with human nature and a man of much experience undoubtedly saw the fatal consequences of dissimulation. The signification of this term is closely allied to hypocrisy; it is a feigned love, or counterfeit love; a flattering social appearance with a heart full of deceit; or in a more refined sense is often thoughtfully exercised for the sake of giving popularity and esteem among our fellow-men; hence, impure, not real, nor for the sole good of man, neither for the sake of Christ. "Let us not be desirous of vain glory," but whatsoever we do, do it heartily, as to the Lord, and not unto men. We may deceive men, but we cannot dissemble before the Lord, for he knoweth the thoughts of our hearts. Paul, in this connection, after exhorting the members of Christ's body to exercise faithfully in their different gifts given them in their ministration, brings the matter right home to themselves, as a consequence to promote and maintain an unfeigned love amongst them, saith "He that giveth, let him do it with simplicity; he that ruleth, with diligence; he that showeth mercy, with cheerfulness." Let love be without dissimulation. The minister of God may be guilty of this deceitful crime—if I am allowed to use that term—and certainly will be if any other motive prompts him to preach than the love to God and the salvation of men. If worldly honor, if the unrighteous mamon, if self-examination, or to gain the applause of men causes you to forsake your homes and preach a gospel; I say a gospel, for you must in a measure preach your own gospel, if you want to please men or succeed in any of the aforementioned motives. But to preach the Gospel and to be a servant of Christ and to have pure love to God and the love of souls at heart, is quite a different thing, for men will not be pleased to hear their sins denounced and held before their face, yet this is love without dissimulation. It is presumptuous, and the very height of folly to believe that this is pure love, to be so liberal as to assent to every form of worship and to admit it to be right, however far it may differ from the true worship of God established by Jesus Christ the great head of the Church, as revealed in the Gospel. Hence, let us stand firm, and hold upon the platform of the Gospel, and earnestly contend for the faith once delivered to the Saints, if we have to endure the frowns and derisions of a deceitful world, under the garb of Christianity. Remember the Apostle Paul, after being shamefully treated at Phillippi, he says: "We were bold in our God to speak unto you the Gospel of God without much contention. For our exhortation was not of deceit nor, of uncleanness, nor in guile; but as we were allowed of God to be put in trust of the Gospel, even so we spake; not as pleasing men but of God, which trieth our hearts. For neither at any time used we flattering words, nor a cloak of covetousness; God is witness, nor of men sought we glory." Is not this commendable? May it not with propriety be called "the end of the commandment, charity out of a pure heart and of a good conscience, and of faith unfeigned?" Let us copy after it, and have love without dissimulation. But brethren and sisters, this important injunction is not only for the ministers or his only reference to ministerial labors, but also embraces many other things, and even effects our every day actions in life, and hence is indispensable to be guarded against, and ever to be kept in memory, that whatever we say, do or design to do, that it be done in uprightness and out of pure love, and not by flattery or through vain deceit. Dissimulation is a sin which often times causes wonderful mischief when brought to light, which certainly it will be one time or other. Excessive flattery never promises much good, but often does much harm; therefore, let us avoid extremes on either side, be moderate. "Let your moderation be known among all men," For the Lord is at hand. Men sometimes appear very sociable; pretend to be very friendly, flattering and enticing, but beware of such, for there may be poison on their lips. Though we hope better things from members of the church, yet to our sorrow we see things sometimes that shows cunning craftiness, in order to deceive or to take advantage of his fellow-men, if not brother or sister. How necessary the admonition of our text. Beware of formal invitation. I am fearful too much of this kind is in vogue. If your love is not sincere, and your heart wishes not to have the association of your neighbor, for God's sake do not invite him, lest you dissimulate. Mean whatever you say, and say whatever you mean, and no man will be deceived by you. If you give to the poor, do it with a cheerful heart, not grudgingly or boastingly, but in simplicity and out of love to God. Visit the sick, clothe the naked, feed the hungry, entertain the strangers, give alms to the poor, encourage the depressed, lift up those that are stricken down, and comfort the feeble-minded and the God of peace will be with you, and will cause His blessing, like a mighty river to flow from your habitation. Yea, love will reign there and abide with you forever. Enrobed with the righteousness of Christ, your soul shall be joyful in your God; for He hath clothed you with the garment of Salvation. Violence you need not fear, wasting or destruction will be removed from thy borders. The sun shall be no more thy light by day; neither for brightness shall the moon give light unto thee; but the Lord shall be unto thee an everlasting light, and thy God thy glory. And the days of thy mourning shall be ended. Finally, brethren and sisters, show yourselves in your true colors and do not deceive the community with useless display or glittering colors, nor with popular demonstrations, neither with flattering tongues or deceitful lips; but pray God to keep you pure in the love of God, strong in faith and above all things have love without dissimulation.

Now, I beseech you, brethren and sisters, suffer the word of exhortation, for I have raised my voice against feigned love and hypocrisy in milder terms. And I hope for our every benefit. Now the God of peace, that brought again from the dead our Lord Jesus Christ, that Great Shepherd of the sheep, through the blood of the everlasting covenant, make you perfect in every good work, to do His will, working in you that which is well-pleasing in His sight, through Jesus Christ, to whom be glory, forever and ever. Amen.

Yours in weakness,
LEONARD FREY.

New Enterprise.

Life is the time to serve the Lord.

For the PILGRIM.

FOLLOW JESUS.

BY MARY E. GOOD.

How many of us are following in the foot steps of Jesus? And are we trying to do all God has required of us? Christ says if we neglect one of His commands we are guilty of all. What a great meaning these few words contain; how often I think of it. If God's word is to judge us at the last day, as He has said it will, should it not cause us to fear lest we come short. His sayings are sure. How awful would be the thought that one of us who have set out on that narrow way should come short of our duty, and be cast off forever where nothing but remorse and sorrow would be our portion! Let us follow Jesus in the way, and though we meet with troubles and trials on the way, it will make our crown the brighter. Only those who faithfully bear the cross may ever hope to win the crown.

Just think what Christ did for us. He gave His precious blood so freely shed for you and I. Oh! that blood-stained cross. Was there ever love like His? Think what He had to endure for our sakes. We owe every day of our lives to His service. We can do nothing of ourselves, but must look to Jesus for every day of our lives. Some are prostrated upon beds of affliction, others are called from time to eternity without a moment's warning, unprepared.

We who are spared with health and surrounded with every thing calculated to make life comfortable and happy should not be forgetful of the one thing most needful, not set our affections on the things of this earth for soon they will fade away; they are all transitory, of short duration. Soon we, like they will have to perish.—Then let us be up and doing our duty; following Jesus, that lovely example. May we be like Him, and strive to be a light to the world.

Many of us are youthful, our journey just begun, and we will have many troubles and trials to meet, the finger of scorn may sometimes be pointed at us, but let us endure it all for Jesus' sake, and not forget to pray. Let us adorn our-selves with that adornment that becometh the true follower of Christ, not trying to decorate our bodies with the foolish things of this world, to grieve our old brethren and sisters and one above who sees all our actions, as is the custom of some of our members to do. We cannot serve God and mammon, will love one and hate the other. We are all soldiers under one captain.—Thus let us be known by Him by our uniform and wherever we go, take Jesus with us. We need no better companion. Not one day, when we assemble ourselves together in public worship, be plain and modest in our dress, and again when we go out into the world, have our bodies so decorated as though God was not seeing us. Is this a Christian spirit? No, it is far from it. He sees us everywhere. The eye that never sleeps. He knows our every thought before they are found within. Jesus has prepared a home for us and we all desire to go there, but we have a work to perform. How anxious we are here on earth to secure a home, and yet we have such a short time to stay. Let us secure a home in Heaven where we can dwell forevermore with the pure and holy, where there will be nothing to mar our enjoyment.

Many of us communed a short time ago, and perhaps for the last time. I know we will never all meet as we there did, until we surround the table of the Lord in nobler scenes above. I hope the last Communion will long be remembered by us all. O, could we have more such delightful seasons! I know we would be greatly benefited. Let us resolve to live nearer to God as this may have been our last. Let us try to live every day of our lives as if it were our last,—if we stood close on the brink of eternity, that when we are called away it will be a pleasure for us to go, where nothing will disturb our peace and joy, where we can meet those who have gone before and washed their robes white in the blood of the Lamb.

Waynesboro, Pa.

WE ARE PASSING AWAY.

Nothing strikes the mind more forcibly than the thought, 'we are passing away.' Whence our origin, and whence our destiny? This mighty earth has echoed to the tread of teeming millions, that one day dwelt upon her expansive bosom, but their very graves have been forgotten for ages. Countless generations have sprung into existence and labored, thought, studied and died. Huge piles of sculptered marble and chiseled granite remains yet in the Eastern world as relics of modern antiquity. Their manners, customs, religions and laws, to a limited extent, have been preserved on tablets of marble or bronze, but the inhabitants of that era, who flourished for a brief season in the power and strength of manhood, long since yielded to the stern mandate of death, and crumbled again to dust. They have passed away. We have their history through the lapse of near six thousand years to substantiate our position. The irreversable decree of death has reigned coextensive with the human family. It is the great leveler of mankind. It knocks audibly at the door of innocence, at the barriers of vigorous manhood, at the palace of old age. All are summoned at his potent will. Respect for rank ceases. The haughty monarch on his glittering throne endowed with regal power, the orator who holds entranced senates spellbound with the thunderings of his eloquence, the aristocratic and wealthy of all lands, and even the poor beggar are all brought to a common level—the grave. There all present the same stern, rigid, cheerless aspect. Whether high or low, rich or poor, saint or sinner, wise or unwise, all present the same appearance and are alike food for worms. W.

BY-AND-BY.

"By-and-by" is the chant of life, swelling out like an anthem from every form of beauty or of might, and the human heart by night and day, beats time to its responsive measure.

It is the key note of the Christian's anticipations of his future heaven. It gives wings to his faith, on which it flies and mounts upward to that house "not made with hands, eternal in the heavens"—surveys the jasper walls; charmed and overpowered by its beauty, its majesty and the transcendant glory of its beautified angelic inhabitants, his whole nature breathes out the precious tho't —"by-and-by" this glorious palace is to be my eternal home.

Patient Hope, in the hour of affliction and distress, when the world seems dreary and happiness merely a mental delusion, rests its hope for the future upon the blessed assurance that "by and by" the weary soul shall rest in that land, where falls no blight.

The faithful mother gazes upon her smiling infant, regarding it as a jewel dropped from the skies, more precious than the sparkling gems of Golconda, and who can tell her oft-repeated "by-and-bys," as, with an anxious heart and bounding pulse, she watches the sleeping beauty?

In her bright and loving anticipations, she sees the time when it will become a brilliant youth, then a leading, influential man in the cause of right, scattering blessings on every hand and rendering her happy in her declining years, and, in a ripe old age, when his earthly mission is fully accomplished, with his honors thick upon him, pass from earth an angel, to dwell with her and the elder angels of the heavenly world. "By-and-by" are words of life and power to the dilligent in every good cause which he may espouse, enabling him to anticipate the full fruition of his ardent hopes, as a just reward of his active labor, but they are words ending in the bitterness of death to him who neglects a duty which shou'd be performed to-day in response to his favorite motto of "by-and-by," having accomplished no good, and descending to an unhonored grave, unwept save for his guilty folly.—*Christian Advocate.*

Youth's Department.

GET UP EARLY.

Get up early! time is precious—
Waste it not in bed;
Get up early! while the dewdrops
O'er the fields are spread;
Get up early! when the red sun
First begins to rise;
Get up early! when the darkness
Fades from earth and skies:

Get up early! it is sinful
To be wasting time;
Get up early! while the dear birds
Sing their morning chime:
Get up early! while the flowers
Blush upon the sod;
Get up early! while all nature;
Blesses nature's God.

TO OUR YOUNG READERS.

We were just trying to think what we would get for our young readers this week. We have many things that might amuse you but perhaps you have enough of that at home. Our object is to give you something better, something that will interest you and at the same time enable you to learn of God and fa'l in love with Jesus, your best friend. Those of you who have learned to read the Bible no doubt have been made to wonder why Jesus was willing to forsake His Father in Heaven and come down into the world to suffer and die. But if you read carefully, you will soon learn that it was all because He loved us. This is what we wish to impress upon your minds, hoping that when you once learn that Jesus loved you enough to suffer and die for you, that you might be saved and made happy, we can persuade you to love Him enough to try to please Him by becoming good and obeying Him. There are many ways of becoming and doing good which we will talk about at some other time. We give for your entertainment this week, first, "Follow your Guide." We hope you will read this carefully as in it is taught a very wholesome lesson, one that it will be well for you not to forget. Jesus should be your guide and has opened up a "way" for you and now asks you to walk in it. This way is called the "Good old way" and none but the good are allowed to walk in it. Therefore you must first become good by learning to become humble and obedient, and then follow your guide and we can promise you a happy life, a pleasant journey and glorious end.

FOLLOW YOUR GUIDE

The people of Iceland live in regions we would scarcely think could be traversed by man or beast. The mountains on the island are mostly volcanoes, which for ages have poured out over the country vast floods of boiling lava, which has cooled in every variety of form, making great masses of rock tumbled together in the wildest confusion. Here will be a chasm seemingly without bottom. Here the dark crust of cooled lava will be too thin to bear the traveller. There a mass of ice and snow on a mountain side will tumble over the path, ready at a breath to fall upon, and crush and bury the traveller forever. The loose stones, which are started by his foot steps, often roll down the sides of awful precipices, plunging from depth to depth till the sound dies away. Oh how fearful the fate of one who makes a misstep in traversing these paths!

But the guides pass over them as firmly and unconcernedly as we walk our good roads at home. And there is but one course for travellers, and that is to follow their guide, follow him blindly and implicitly.

It would not answer for one to say, "This path is not so blocked up with lava as that. It is pleasanter to walk in. I wish to examine these little creeping plants and flowers that grow on the edge of the cliff. I will go this way."

What do you think would be the result? It would not be long before you would hear a fearful fall, and a despairing cry of "lost, lost."

Just so, dear children, it will be with those who will not follow the heavenly guide. We are all passing over a way in life more dangerous than Iceland roads. We are all the time in danger of falling into sin that will ruin our souls. They look pleasanter than the right path, but the end is death. Our guide has given us a book to teach us the way. So plain is it that nobody need make a false step. Jesus has gone the way before us, and we have but lovingly to follow his footsteps and we shall all reach the blessed home in safety and exceeding joy.—*Child's World.*

DECEPTION.

Never deceive for the sake of foolish jest, or to excite laughter of a few companions at the expense of a friend. Be anxious, when you relate anything, to tell it just as it occurred. Never variate in the least degree. The reason why our ears are so often saluted by false reports is because people, in telling real things, add a little to them, and as they pass through a dozen mouths, the original stories are turned into something entirely different. So, when you attempt to tell anything that you have seen with your own eyes relate it correctly in every particular, and as you grow older, you will reap the advantage of this course.

Youth and old age have too little sympathy for each other. If the young would remember that they may be old and the old would remember that they have been young they would be happier.

The Weekly Pilgrim.

JAMES CREEK, PA., July 8, 1873.

☞ How to send money.—All sums over $1.50, should be sent either in a check, draft or postal order. If neither of these can be obtained, have the letter registered.

☞ When Money is sent, *always* send with it the name and address of those who paid it. Write the names and post office as plainly as possible.

☞ Every subscriber for 1873, gets a *Pilgrim Almanac* Free.

BAPTISM.

Not long since, we had sent us a sermon, delivered by some nameless person, on the subject of baptism, or, rather on the mode of baptism. We are not informed of the design of the sender, but we suppose it is considered, by him, a masterly production. We shall not burden our columns in publishing it, but wish to notice a few of the arguments used, and, perhaps, make a few extracts.

His first point is to determine the meaning of the word *baptism*. After stigmatizing Baptists in general for going back to the ages of ignorance and heathen darkness to determine the meaning of the word *baptidzo*, he says: "Both sides have ransacked all Lexicons and writers of Grecian literature with about equal success; the one claiming that *baptidzo* always means to immerse, while the others have found that it sometimes means wash, cleanse and sprinkle, as well as immerse." But, as he can make no point here, for the sake of argument he will admit that it did mean immerse before the time of Christ, as used by Greek writers. Now follows the sound logic:

"There was no such a thing as Christian baptism before the time of Christ, consequently there could have been no word in use to express it. Words are but signs of our ideas. And surely the name of the thing cannot exist before the thing itself. The child must be born before it is named. Now you might just as well hunt in your old Greek Lexicon for a word to express your idea of a railroad, a telegraph, a daguerreotype, as to expect to find a word to express Christian baptism. Now the ancients knew nothing about railroads, telegraphs, photographs, &c., and consequently they had no need of any word to express them. But when any new thing is discovered and brought before you, you give it a name just as Adam gave names to the animals as they were brought before him.

Thus it has always been when anything new comes up, you either coin a new word to express it, or give some new meaning to a word already in use. How many words we use every day that have taken on new meanings! Who does not know that *pastor* once meant a keeper of sheep and nothing else? Now it means one who has the oversight of the church. So the word *minister* originally meant one who served another a slave; now it means a preacher of the Gospel. So whatever the word baptidzo meant as used by the Greek writers, it does not necessarily follow that when it is picked up by Christ and his apostles and introduced into the Christian family of words, that it was not itself christened and received a new meaning, when made to do a new service. And here we dismiss the whole discussion as it pertains to Lexicons and heathen writers, and come to Christ and his apostles and learn from them the Christian use of the word.

Is not this a strong theory? Most certainly words are signs of ideas, but it should be remembered that words cannot convey ideas unless they have a fixed or established meaning. Would it not have been a ridiculous blunder, if when the press was invented, because there was no such thing before, they had named it a horse or stone! If there had been no word to convey the idea of the actions of a press, the next best thing would have been to *coin* a new word, but as the same action was performed by a number of other machines differently constructed, there was no necessity of coining a new word, because there was a word in use that conveyed the idea of the action, hence it was called a "press," and to distinguish it from other presses used for different purposes, the word "printing" was affixed to it, thus designating its specific use. Just so in Christian baptism. We will admit that it was a new ordinance introduced by God as an initiatory rite to be used in inducting subjects into the Kingdom of Peace. This rite was to signify a death, burial, resurrection and also purification.—Water was an element used for purifying or cleansing, plunging a subject into it was a figure of death and burial, and taking from it again very beautifully represented a resurrection. It also harmonized with being "born again," and "regeneration," hence, immersion in water was adopted by God as the initiatory rite of His kingdom. The next thing is to give it a name. This must be a word, and as words convey ideas, there must be a word used to convey the idea of this action. Now, if there is no word to convey the idea of this action, there must be one coined. But as the action of plunging or immersing things in the water for their cleansing was almost as old as the creation itself, it had an established word to convey the idea of that action, and that word was *baptidzo*, or *bapto*, hence this word is adopted as the name of this rite without the least necessity for a change of meaning. The word conveys the idea of the action alone, without any reference to the intention or result of the action. It has been asked, time and again, if immersion was not intended, why use a word that conveys that idea? Why not have coined a new word, or else used one that would fairly convey the idea that was intended? Either would have been more logical and convenient than to make use of a word that conveyed a different idea, and then change its meaning, especially when the very words were in use that conveyed the idea clearly, that our friend is laboring to attach to this solemn and important rite. In accepting this word as the name of this new rite or sacrament, there is no change of meaning about it. The action is the same, and all the sophistry in the world cannot change it. It is the intention of the action that is changed. A man may be immersed, or baptized, to take his life, to cleanse his body, or as the initiatory rite of the Church of Christ. The same word conveys the idea of these actions fairly, but the intentions are quite different, and must be determined by the attending circumstances. Our friend says: "Minister originally meant one who served another; *now it means a preacher of the Gospel*." Is he not still a minister? What is a preacher of the Gospel? Is he not still a minister? If not, he is no preacher of the Gospel. There is no change of meaning here. The word minister conveys the idea of the action of a preacher of the Gospel as fairly and correctly as it does that of a slave or servant. Both are servants; one ministers to our bodily and the other to our spiritual wants. The only possible change of meaning is in the intention of the action. So, whatever the word *baptidzo* meant as used by the Greek writers, it *necessarily* means yet. It is truly astonishing that a man pretending to be a preacher of the Gospel, would make use of such shallow reasoning before an intelligent congregation. We shall now leave this subject and notice some others that are equally illogical.

Next is introduced John's baptism, and labors to show that in Jordan means at Jordan, or in between the first and second banks, something that no travelers seem to know anything about, except a few *preachers*, who are so prejudiced against water baptism that they can make an ideal Jordan just to suit their taste. We will give another extract:

"But as we wish to be very charitable we will allow that en here means in, and then we ask how far were they in? Up to their ankles, or knees, or loins? And, suppose en puts them in up to their loins, that does not put them under—en only fixes the place and has nothing to do with the mode of baptism. Did they kneel in the water along the shore, or wade out into the water and John take his hand and dip up the water and sprinkle or pour it upon them, or did he dip them backwards once or thrice? Who knows, and who is wise above what is written, and who will add to the word of the Lord and say they were immersed!

Why not just as well say, who will *add* to the word of the Lord and *say* they were sprinkled? This would truly be adding to the word of the Lord, from the fact that it must be admitted that *baptidzo* does not convey the idea of sprinkling but that of immersion, overwhelming or plunging. We are justifiable in saying they were immersed, because we have them *in* the water, and Jesus "went up straightway *out of the water*." If the Saviour was *in* the water, so were the others that were baptized. Then they were all in the water, and there were *baptized* or immersed as is clearly signified by the word used to express the idea of the action.

Again in speaking of Christ's baptism we have the following:

Did he stand or kneel, and did John sprinkle, or pour the water on him, or did he dip him forwards or backwards? Who knows? Who is so bold as to say he was immersed? And it is a matter of very little importance which way it was done, for Christ's baptism was not Christian baptism, and hence the folly of Christians talking about following Christ in baptism. * * * He was formally iniated into the Jewish church when he was eight days old, and he lived and died a member of the Jewish church.

Christ was inducted into the Jewish priesthood when he was thirty years old by a ceremonial washing, as all the Jewish priests before him were.

If Christ's baptism was not Christian baptism, then there is no such a thing and we might as well discard the whole plan of salvation. John was a man *sent from* God and not from the Jewish Church. His preaching and baptism was from God, having for its design a preparing of a material or people for the new kingdom of peace which was being ushered into the world, of which Christ was to be King. In Christ submitting to this God-ordained rite, He fulfilled part of the "all righteousness" and became our examplifier in entering "the way" and thus could, with propriety, say, "follow me."

If Jesus lived and died a member of the Jewish Church, so did His apostles and we have no Christian Church.

In setting up a kingdom there must of necessity, first be subjects before there can be a king. These subjects were prepared by the Baptist and Christ, when He came, assumed by right, the Kingship, hence the Kingdom or Church of Christ. But that Christ, in receiving John's baptism, was inducted into the Jewish priesthood is a freak of modern theology. The Jewish Church at that time, must have been burdened with an exceedingly great number of priests, as we have every reason to believe that Christ's baptism was in all respects, similar to that of all others that were received during the Baptist's administration, and if John's baptism, as administered to Christ, made Him a Jewish priest, it also made priests of all others that were baptized.

Next week we will notice some of the household baptisms.

FOR SUNDAY SCHOOLS.

We are frequently asked for papers to distribute in Sunday schools, and as we have on hand a large number of odd copies of the Pilgrim, we will send them for Sunday school distribution at the following rates: 50 copies post paid, 35 cents, 100 copies, 70 cents, 200 copies, $1.25. Nos. of different issues will be sent. This offer is less than the postage and cost of paper, but we do it, hoping it may be for the good of the schools and may be used as a means of spreading our doctrine and introducing the Pilgrim. Superintendents and friends of Sunday schools will please notice this offer.

QUERY.

Will some brother or sister please give an explanation on the parable of the laborers in the vineyard, recorded in the twentieth chapter of Matt.

S. C. Miller.

EXPLANATION OF LUKE 9 27.

Dear Editor: If you find the following correct, please publish it, if not, give us some light on the subject.

"But I tell you of a truth, there be some standing here which shall not taste of death till they see the Kingdom of God."

Those who should not taste of death till they saw the Kingdom, were his apostles, eleven of the twelve, for Judas by transgression fell.

"Kingdom of God" here means the Holy Spirit which the apostles received on the day of Pentecost. Acts 2; 4.

A PILGRIM.

MARRIED.

MCKINLY—FLOWERS.—At the residence of the brides' father, on the 25th of June '73, Mr Henry McKinley to sister Rebecca Flowers.

JOHN WISE.

HALL—DARRAH.—In Winamac, Pulaski Co., Ind., at the house of the brides' parents, May 22, '73, Mr. David Hall and sister Margaret M Darrah.

D. R. FREEMAN.

DIED.

COFFMAN.—In the South English River Church, Keokuk Co., Iowa, June 15, '73, Joseph D., youngest son of Benjamin F. and Anna Coffman, aged 3 months and 8 days. Funeral services by the Brethren. Scripture selected, 1st chapter of the 1st Epistle of Peter, 24th verse.

(*Visitor*, please copy.)

STUCKMYERS.—In the same district near North English, Iowa Co., Iowa, June 21, '73, sister Rhoda, wife of Benj. Stuckmyers, aged 28 years, 4 months and 7 days. Disease Consumption.

She had been ailing for some time, but on the evening of her death went to bed as usual. Sometime in the night her husband awoke and found his companion a corpse. Her spirit had taken up its abode, as we believe, in the Paradise of God. How forcibly are we again reminded to be at all times prepared to die, or prepared to meet our God in peace. She leaves a sorrowing husband, five children and a number of relations to mourn their loss. The funeral services were attended to by Eld. Jacob Bower in the Christian Church, in the town of North English, to a large and sympathizing concourse of people.

D F. FLORY.

Visitor, please copy.

MOYER.—In the Lower Miami Church, Montgomery Co., Ohio, June 22, sister Christinna Moyer, aged 79 years, 6 mos. and 1 day. Funeral improved by Peter Neal and David Bowman.

Sister Moyer was born December 22 1793 in West Virginia. *Her* maiden name was Beaver. When about 12 years old her parents moved to Preble Co., Ohio, where she was united in marriage to Michael Moyer, who preceded her to the Heavenly home about 13 *years*. They lived and toiled about 40 years to make home comfortable. Though they had no children of their own, they gave homes and raised six homeless children, to whom they filled the place of kind and affectionate parents, all of whom are still living, and can rise up and call them blessed. They were kind and benevolent in the true sense of the word, never turning the unfortunate or hungry away empty, but always administered to their wants. She joined the church over fifty years ago, and lived a consistent Christian. Her afflictions were protracted and severe but through it all she kept her heart stayed on Jesus and her eyes on Heaven. When death came she was ready and now rests from her labors, and her works do follow her.

DANIEL BOCK.

BOYER.—In the Union District, Marshall Co., Ind., June 26, '73, John, son of brother George Boyer, aged about twelve years.

This boy left home to go fishing—as they live near a small lake—and waded in to fish, and went in a little too far. He sank down into the sand nearly to his knees and could not get out, his head got under water and there he was found drowned, standing upright in the water. Truly this was a solemn occasion and should be a warning to boys, and to us all. Funeral occasion improved by brethren Adam Appleman and Wm. G. Cook, from Matthew 24: 44.

A. APPLEMAN.

KINSEY.—On the 15th of June, sister Emma Kinsey, only daughter and only child of brother Gabriel G., and sister Amanda Mumbard, fell asleep in Jesus, in the 23d year of her age. Disease, inflamation of the stomach. Funeral services by the Brethren, to an unusually large congregation, indicating the very high esteem in which she was held by her acquaintances, all seeming to marvel at this mysterious providence, and doubtless if they could have had their choice would have willed it otherwise, and are only reconciled by the knowledge that it is God, and hence we are still.

She left besides a large circle of friends, the lonely father and mother, and a youthful husband, to whom she had only been married seventeen days, to mourn their loss, to whom our tenderest sympathies are awarded with the earnest exhortation to be always ready to meet her in that land where they are not married nor given in marriage, and where there is no more death and where sorrow and sighing flee away.

B. F. MOOMAW.

By the request of her parents.

(*Visitor* and *C. F. C.* requested to copy.)

Correspondence.

EPISTOLARY.

Dear Pilgrim:—I seat myself this pleasant day to write a few lines for your excellent volume. It has been a long time since I wrote for the "papers." When at our late Annual Meeting at Dale City, Pa., I met many acquaintances I love so much. My heart was made glad when I could again meet and talk with those I love. I think it may be the last A. M. I shall ever attend. My health is poor. I have been sick all Spring and am not much batter yet. I came home from the A. M. very much fatigued, but I can say "the will of the Lord be done." O, how many I saw there whom I shall never see any more in this world! A great many said to me "Why don't you write more for the papers?" Some said they were so glad to hear from me. One sister said she always looked for my name first when she got the papers, but she had not seen it for a long time. Now dear sisters, you may see my name once more, if the Editor of the PILGRIM thinks my article worth printing.

I have very poor health and am quite feeble, which makes me think I shall not live long. I think, when I look back over my life, I have lived a long time,—a little more than forty seven years. Oh! how have I spent my days? I think if I had my blooming days to live over again, and know what I now do, I would spend my time very differently. Yes' so it is young friends; it may be so with you when you get old and think you must soon die and go to God, there to see all you have ever done pass in open review before you. Oh! think before you get old. It will save you from "a thousand snares to mind religion young." Yes it fits us for "declining years, and for the awful tomb." I think I will soon go home to dwell with God forever. Oh! how good God has been to me, to spare me so long, so that I may be ready to meet him at his coming. My dear sisters, when we have been from home for a while, how glad we are to return again O, will we be so glad and feel ready when our time comes to go home to our Father's house where there are many mansions. There we shall see all God's children. We shall see our dear friends, some of my children are there, father, mother, and many more dear ones. Who has not some friends there that they would like to see? I think we should forsake our sins for Christ's sake. O, how much he has done for us to save our poor souls! Yes, he gave himself for us; cannot we do his will and good pleasure that we may all be saved? God gave his only son to save us from hell. Oh, sisters let us love God more and serve him better, let us follow Christ that we poor weak creatures, may be saved in Heaven to praise God forever. I know if we will love God with our whole heart we will serve him better. If we are not saved, it will be our own fault, and not Christ's, He has done all things well. When we read the Scriptures, we can find many good lessons to teach us how to live right, and by living right, we may die right. "If God so clothe the grass, which today is in the field, and to-morrow is cast into the oven, will he not much more clothe you, O ye of little faith?" O, yes, when we feel how little our faith is, no wonder we are so cold in love to God If we had the faith in God we should have, our love would burn as a fire within us. Then we would believe in him and trust in him. God wants us to believe in him, trust him, love his word, feel that we are his. I often wonder at myself that I have so little faith in God. Without him we can do nothing. Dear sisters, let us see what kind of faith we have. Is it a living or a dead faith? We should have a faith that works by love,—love to God and to mankind; then we will have power to overcome evil with good This is the victory that overcomes the world, even our faith. I fear when death comes, we will feel that we have not lived as we should have done, and as we will wish we had done.

Christ says "I am the true vine and my Father is the husbandman." Now if we do not bear fruit, we will wither and be cast into the fire and be burned. "Every branch that beareth fruit he purgeth it that it may bring forth more fruit." Now, sisters, if we were purged from all our sins we could do more to glorify God's holy name. "I am the vine ye are the branches, he that abideth in me and I in him, the same bringeth forth much fruit, for without me ye can do nothing." If we are the branches let us bear much fruit, that we may abide in him, and he in us. O, sisters, let us bring forth much fruit to the honor and glory of God. Christ is the vine and we are the branches. When we see our grape vines and see the tender branches, I wonder if we are so closely connected to Christ as those tender branches are to the vine. If not, may God graft us in, so we may bear fruit, and enjoy in the end everlasting life. Sisters, pray for me that I may be one of the branches. Farewell.

NANCY WISE.

Scenery Hill, Pa.

H. B. Brumbaugh. Dear brother: Our health this Spring has been only middling good but we are still trying to do something in the Lord's Vineyard, or trying to follow the "old landmarks." Our dear old bishop, Samuel Lidy, has gone to rest and left a vacancy in the church.

We had a Lovefeast on the 13th of June and held a choice for a speaker. The lot fell upon Caleb Secrist, a very worthy young brother that has been a member of the church for only two years. Truly the Lord's ways are not man's ways. Yours in love,

S. S. CRESSWELL.

Dear Editors: Will you please answer the following question? Who was the young man referred to in Mark 14; 51, "and there followed him a certain young man, having a linen cloth cast about his naked body; and the young man laid hold on him, and he left the linen cloth and fled from them naked." WM. J. DEACON.

Oakland, Va.

ANSWER. We are not prepared to say who he was, neither do we know of any way of ascertaining It is supposed that he resided near the garden and that he was acquainted with Jesus. On hearing the tumult and being concerned about the welfare of Jesus, he hastily arose from his bed without taking time to dress himself, threw over him the linen, and went forth to offer his assistance, but when the men that had taken Jesus saw him, supposing him to be one of the disciples, laid hold on him, or his garment, which being loose, enabled him to escape, but left him naked. If anybody knows more about the young man, we shall be glad to hear from them.

Dear Editors: We wish to learn through the PILGRIM whether there are any brethren residing in Pulaski Co., Ind. If there are any in the above or adjoining counties, please give us your name and address *soon* through the PILGRIM or address Addison Baker, Carthage, Jasper Co.' Mo.

NOTE. We are sending PILGRIMS to Pulaskiville and Winamac of the above county. At the first office, address, Andrew Browsher, and the last, D. R. Freeman.

TO THE CHURCHES OF MID. DIST. OF PA.—As is known by the churches of Mid Pa, by resolution of the District Conference, each Church was to report to me, before the 1st of July, how much they would be willing to give towards building a Church in Altoona Pa. Therefore, thirteen have reported, and as I was not to report to the investigating Committee until all Churches were heard from, I hope that those who have not yet reported, will do so immediately. Adress George Brumbaugh, Grafton, Huntingdon Co. Pa.

MONEY LIST.

Jno J England	$0.80	Geo Kinney	3.20
Wm Book	75	Lewis Workman	3.00
J B Diehl	50	Sarah Hoffman	25
M. Brumbaugh	1.70	S C Miller	1.50
W N Clemmer	75	Jacob Troxel	2.50
S Musselman	50	Jacob P Lerew	1.60
Wm Leedy	3 20	Jos Hanse	80
E A Whitter	1.50	W H Carrier	1.80
D W Hendricks	1.00	S S Cresswell	1.80
J L Frantz	8.00	Lewis Funk	80
R Maugens	80	S S Cresswell	1.50
Jos Drury	2.00	H J Brubaker	80
Henry Ebie	1.30	Dan E Brubaker	85
M Beshor	3.20	Fannie H Keim	1.30

BOOK NOTICES.

In this department we will notice such NEW BOOKS, as may be sent us by publishers, that are in harmony with the character of our work. A. B. Brumbaugh, M. D., Huntingdon Pa., literary editor, to whom all books must be sent.

How to Acquire and Preserve Health.

H. N. McKinney & Co., No. 16 N. 7th St., Philadelphia, Pa., are the publishers of this important book, written by Dr. C. W. Gleason well known throughout the country, having acquired a distinguished reputation as a popular Lecturer. His sanitary teachings are valuable and safe. Grievious errors are committed daily by all, consequent upon our ignorance in regard to proper food and the function of digestion. The writer says: Human beings are not strong and healthy in proportion to the amount of food they eat. Over-eating is one of the greatest evils of civilized life. * * * All gluttons are torpid, feeble and indolent." No minister can interest and edify a congregation "with their stomachs full of all manner of unclean things, pork, cabbage and baked beans and strong coffee for breakfast, and cold ham, turkey, gristle, &c. for dinner, when brains and nervous energies are fully taxed to digest what they have eaten and where mental and moral natures are overwhelmed with stupidity and lethargy." No man can eat unwholesome food and spend much of his time in profound mental labor without causing serious derangement, and disease of the organs of digestion.

On clothing he says. "All the clothing worn by human beings should be suspended upon the shoulders, and never upon the waist. It is simply impossible for any one to wear the clothing loose (as it should always be worn) when fastened around the waist, for the reason that its own weight will cause it to drag down until it becomes so tight that it can drag down no further." He suggests a well adjusted underwaist for women, and we bear testimony that such a course would relieve much of the wretchedness among women, and relieve much pain and distress.

Received through Messrs. Lippincott & Co., Publishers, Philada., and Wm. Lewis, Huntingdon, Pa. It is sold by subscription. Address as above. A. B. B.

In West Tennessee there is a sect of professing Christians known as Thomasites, whose distinguishing belief is the annihilation of the wicked after Christ shall make his second personal advent to reign over the earth a thousand years. This second coming they suppose will take place in about seven years from this date. This sect is an offshoot from the Campbellites or Christian Disciples.

St. Louis has a Church of Christian Fellowship. It is Congregational, but exceedingly free, as will be seen by the following statement of faith: "We believe in the sovereignty of God, the sinfulness of man, the divine nature and mission of Jesus, the dependence of the soul upon the Divine Spirit, the inheritance of immortality, and our duty to openly teach the truth as it was taught by our Lord. We accept the Scriptures as containing the revelations of God, and we look for the constant illumination of every prayerful soul. We accept baptism and the Lord's Supper as ordinances adapted to assist our spiritual growth."

HUNTINGDON & BROAD TOP RAIL ROAD

On and after June 29th, 1873, Trains will run on this road daily (Sun excepted) as follows:

Trains from Huntingdon South. *Trains from Mt. Dallas moving North.*

ACCM P. M.	EXP A. M.	STATIONS.	EXP'S P. M.	ACCM A. M.
5 30	8 10	Huntingdon,	AR 6 05	AR 9 25
6 00	8 20	Long Siding	6 00	8 20
6 11	8 30	McConnelstown	5 48	8 13
6 19	8 38	Pleasant Grove	5 40	8 00
6 32	8 50	MARKLESBURG	5 25	7 45
6 43	9 02	Coffee Run	5 12	7 35
6 50	9 09	Rough & Ready	5 05	7 27
7 00	9 17	Cove	4 58	7 18
7 05	9 20	Fishers Summit	4 53	7 13
7 20	9 40	Saxton	4 40	7 02
7 35	9 55	Riddlesburg	4 18	6 45
7 43	10 05	Hopewell	4 11	6 28
7 53	10 15	Piper's Run	3 59	6 24
8 10	10 28	Tatesville	3 45	6 10
8 20	10 40	Everett	3 35	5 58
8 30	10 50	Mount Dallas	3 30	5 53
8 55	11 15	Bedford	3 05	5 30

SHOUP'S RUN BRANCH.

A. M.	P. M.		P. M.	A. M.
LE 9 50	LE 7 30	Saxton.	AR 4 25	AR 6 50
10 05	7 45	Coalmont.	4 10	6 35
10 10	7 50	Crawford.	4 05	6 30
AR 10 20	AR 8 00	Dudley	LE 3 55	LE 6 20

Broad Top City from Dudley 2 miles by stage.

Time of Penna. R. R. Trains at Huntingdon.

*** Mail No. 2 makes connection at Huntingdon with Mail going East on Pennsylvania Railroad at 4.15 p. m., and West at 5.45 p. m. Mail No. 1 leaves Huntingdon at 7.40 a. m. on arrival of Pacific Express West.

Trains on this road connect with trains on Bedford & Bridgeport, and Cumberland & Pennsylvania Railroads.

G. F. GAGE, Supt.

The Weekly Pilgrim.

Published by J. B. Brumbaugh, & Co.

Edited by H. B. & Geo. Brumbaugh.

CORRESPONDING EDITORS.

D. P. Sayler, Double Pipe Creek, Md.

Leonard Furry, New Enterprise, Pa.

The *Pilgrim* is a Christian Periodical, devoted to religion and moral reform. It will advocate in the spirit of *love* and *liberty*, the principles of true Christianity, labor for the promotion of peace among the people of God, for the encouragement of the saints and for the conversion of sinners, avoiding those things which tend toward disunion or sectional feelings.

TERMS.

Single copy, Book paper,	$1.50
Eleven copies, [eleventh for Agt.]	$15.00

Any number above that at the same rate.

Address,

H. B. BRUMBAUGH.

James Creek,

Huntingdon county Pa.

The Weekly Pilgrim.

"REMOVE NOT THE ANCIENT LANDMARKS WHICH OUR FATHERS HAVE SET."

VOL. 4. JAMES CREEK, PENNSYLVANIA, JULY 15, 1873. NO. 28.

REPORT OF ANNUAL MEETING CONTINUED.

(*Continued from page 211.*)

Query. Inasmuch as that part of the instruction for holding the Annual Meeting, recommended for trial to the Annual Meeting of 1866, which recommends that no boarding tent shall be put up for the purpose of feeding and entertaining a mixed multitude, and also that part which recommends that there be no meeting in the building where the Annual Meeting convenes, do not seem satisfactory, would it not be well for the A. M. to reconsider, and so amend that part of the instructions as to give the committee of arrangements leave to feed and entertain the multitude as seems most convenient for them, and also to select the places for holding meetings for public worship?

Answer. Yes.

Sayler. I suppose, if you pass this and burden yourselves in this way, we have no objections—we will travel to you.

Brown. If they want to do that in the West, and God has given the means with which to do it, I say, God bless them.

Eby. Ever since this resolution was adopted, the place of A. M. has violated the rule; the rule has been violated here. A large tent has been put up, and preaching has been conducted here; and when the Annual Meeting violates its own rules, it is no wonder that the members at home fall back on us and try to hold us responsible.

Metzger. We want to have the privilege of welcoming our brethren; and we have hungry souls out in Illinois, and we want the privilege of hearing you preach to us. This query came from the Southern district of Illinois, but I think Illinois is a unit on that matter.

Moderator. The question is, to reconsider a portion of our previous minutes. I would only say that, when the meeting was held at Price's, in Franklin county, a good many of the old brethren went four or five miles away before they got anything to eat. It cost a little more than $4,000. The next year, in the state of Maryland, it cost about $2,000, and all satisfactory. Every one was fed that came, and I heard no complaint at all. Preaching went on through the neighborhood, and some fifty odd meetings, brother Sayler says, were held in that neighborhood. Now if you see fit to hold them in this way, and pay the expenses, I am inclined to think you will drive a good many old people from the tables. That has been done here. The young people rush in before us, and take the seats that were designed for us.

Metzger. You see it is in the minutes not to erect a tent to feed a mixed multitude, and you have seen the rule violated from year to year, and the brethren think it cannot be avoided. Now if it cannot be avoided, let us not have it on the minutes and transgress it. When we get the brethren out west, we want them to preach. The people will come to our neighborhood probably on Friday or Saturday, expecting to hear preaching at the place of meeting; and they will be disappointed. We would like to have arrangements made for the brethren that visit us, to preach where it will do the most good.

Holsinger. The difficulty arises, as I understand it, principally on account of the restrictions relating to preaching, &c.

Sturgis. I am in favor of passing the query.

Metzger. It is possible that some may think that the passage of this resolution might warrant the conclusion that we would spread the news broad-cast over the land, that we will feed a mixed multitude; but nothing is farther from the intention. Do not deprive us of our privileges though; and trust us to make the proper use of them.

Moderator. Let the minutes be allowed to stand as they are, but give brother John the privilege to have it as he pleases.

——. That will satisfy us if you place it on the minutes, so that our brethren from a distance can see that we are not transgressing the minutes.

——. I would not like it to go out that we will feed all who come, but simply to leave it to the committee to do as best they can. We have never had a meeting there; and Springfield is only 25 miles from that place, and people may come from there and also from St. Louis, and press us so that we cannot work at all.

Sayler. I have been at many yearly meetings, and I have lain on hard boards; but I won't do it again; and I think that a multitude has no business to crowd in on our business. I have attended yearly meetings where, when an individual came in who did not belong to the church, he was told to go out. That is the way we held our first meetings; and we want to get back to the old way, and hold them as we have a right to hold them, if I understand the gospel.

Preaching at the place of meeting, has been the cause of breaking up that custom. We used to meet on Friday and Saturday, and on Sunday we gave the people preaching; and the word only went out on Saturday afternoon, that there would be preaching on Sunday. It is the spirit of insubordination on the part of some of the members that has caused us to hold them as we now do. It has occurred that the crowd has forced us to leave the place and go into a private house, to hold the meeting and do the business. It got so bad that we had to entreat churches to take the meeting, and it will get back to that again. I will preach to you a week, at any other time, but when it comes to conference meeting, I want that to be a church meeting.

——. We did not understand that our minutes prohibited the erection of a tent, except for a mixed multitude; and we gave it in the papers in that way, and we were not troubled with the outsiders.

Minutes left unchanged.

Query. A brother brings a claim against a sister's husband, and requests the sister to pay it, which she refused to do. Then the brother or brethren got up a query to cover said case and sent it to the Annual Meeting; and through the influence of the query a committee was sent; and through the influence of the committee and some other brethren, the sister was prevailed to settle it by giving her notes, and the other brother for security, and the security brother was compelled to pay said claim; and the sister's husband says he will pay the claim if the brother or brethren that got up said query will prove what is contained therein. Should not the brother or brethren be required to prove said query?

Answer. Inasmuch as this case had been virtually settled by a committee chosen by the Annual Meeting to settle it, we consider it inexpedient to open the subject again, and we think they should not again consider it, but that it should be returned to the place in which it originated.

Moderator. I presume there are very few here that know the nature of the case well enough to understand the matter as it is here presented. I would just say, that brethren John Wise, John Metzger and myself were the committee referred to in the investigation of that matter. Some other parties went to the parties to settle; and accomplished a settlement. As to our influencing the settlement, I do not think we did that, but it was settled, and the parties were satisfied; and now it comes up here for a rehearing. If it must be brought to life, I suppose we can do it.

Several of the brethren called for the return of the query, and the answer was passed without objection.

Query. Inasmuch as oftentimes the innocent party must call for a committee, and bear all the expenses, would it not be more just for the committee to decide who shall pay the expenses?

Answer. We think the committee should decide.

Moderator. Was there a question like this passed to-day, brethren?

Several voices. Yes, yes.

One brother suggested, that the present query differed from the former one, by the insertion of the words, "Innocent party," and that it would be better on that account to have this query passed separately. The suggestion was adopted and the answer passed.

Query. Would it not be well for this meeting to give an expression for a brother to attach to his publications such titles as "The Brethren's Tune and Hymn Book," and "The Brethren's Almanac;" conveying and leaving the impression thereby that the brethren have sanctioned them officially?

Answer. We think it is wrong to use the name. "Brethren's Tune and Hymn Book," or "Almanac."

Many voices. "Table it," and some voices, "Pass it." The demand for the tabling of the resolution was repeated.

Holsinger. I have just a few words to say in regard to it. I want just to point you to this one thing: what objection has the meeting to calling a book the "Brethren's Tune Book," or "The Brethren's Almanac?" or to call a printing establishment "The Brethren's Publishing House," or what objection have you to the name "Brethren's Hymn Book?"

I am asking what objection this meeting can have to it? What is the name of this body? This body has never yet recognized to be called the 'brethren;' they call themselves German Baptists, and I would like to know where we infringe upon the name of German Baptists, when we use the term 'brethren?' We are not infringing upon the German Baptist church.

——. I would just say, that the word 'brethren's' is a plural noun, in the possessive case. Now, if you will prove that this property belongs to the church, then I have nothing more to say.

Holsinger. Well, the Brethren patronized it—it is published in the interests of the Brethren and for the good of the Brethren.

Tabled.

SOUTHERN DISTRICT OF ILLINOIS.

Query. Would it not be good for the Brotherhood to buy a good, durable tent and have it transported from place to place, wherever needed, for the accommodation of the Annual Meeting?

Ans.—This District Meeting thinks it would be good for the brotherhood to have such a tent, and hereby requests the Annual Meeting of 1873 to pass it, if they approve of it, to solicit donations from all the churches of the brotherhood as each feels willing to give; and that said donations be sent to some brother appointed by the Annual Meeting to receive them, before the 1st of September, 1873, and to provide that, if such donations exceed the cost of the tent, then such surplus to be used in spreading the gospel or otherwise forwarding the cause of the Master; and also, that two brethren be appointed to procure such a tent, and have it in readiness for the Annual Meeting of 1874, and keep it thereafter constantly under their control for the accommodation of the Annual Meeting.

——. I would think it would be inconsistent to have such a tent, and yet say in the minutes that we shall have no tent.

——. The minutes read, "A tent for the feeding of a mixed multitude."

Moore. We considered the question carefully. We can procure a tent at a very reasonable rate, of very durable material, and that can be transported from place to place with perfect safety; and perhaps the amount that you now have to pay for the erection of a tent for one year will purchase a tent that can be used for ten years. We have investigated the matter very carefully, and corresponded with parties who are engaged in the manufacture of tents.

A description of the tent was given by Jacob Berky also the manner of putting it up. Another brother stated that a tent 30x60 at St. Louis, would cost about $300, and brother Wolf of Ill., spoke at some length, urging the proposition and showing the advantages to be derived from a tent of this kind.

Sayler. I am quite sure that, if we are going to have meetings in the future, as we have them now, we should certainly have such a tent; and I was about to make this proposition: that as the brethren in the West have asked for the privilege of getting the world together, and as they have to prepare for it, that they buy the tent; and I feel quite certain in my mind that when the brethren come there, and see it, they will not let you get into any difficulty. The meeting will probably convene before the obligation becomes due.

——. I love to see the brethren so careful. We have only made the request of the Annual Meeting, that if others will not take the tent, the brethren will take it. We don't want to urge you to do it. All you have to do is just to allow us the liberty. Here is a brother who says Ohio will help. We think Iowa, Missouri and Kansas will help.

——. I know Nebraska will be willing to help.

The passage of the answer being called for the question was put as follows:

"Shall we grant them the answer or shall we let them go on?

Metzgar. I want to make a proposition. I hear the brethren in Indiana like the idea. Some say the brethren in Ohio will assist; and I have heard some remarks about Pennsylvania and other parts. My proposal is, that every church, or district, that feels like donating can report how much their church will throw in; and do this before the 1st of August. Do not send money, but just how much each church will donate to get the tent. Then, in case we see that we can raise enough, by the 15th of Sept. we want it sent in. We can report it through our periodicals.

Brown. That is just what I was about to suggest. I think we ought not to do anything until we have the money or the promise of it.

Moderator. Let this meeting grant them the privilege to go on, and make their arrangements, and let it go on the minutes, and let it so be understood.

Metzgar. I would suggest that you send your letters to brother Daniel Vaniman; he is our clerk.

Brown. I would suggest also that you have it published in the periodicals.

Moderator. Does this meeting say, "Grant them the privilege"?

The brethren—Yes.

Moderator. And not let it go on the minutes?

A Brother—Why not?

Moderator. There is no necessity for it.

Adjourned.

THURSDAY.

MORNING SESSION, JUNE 5th, 1873.

QUERY.—A man who was living in adultery after making full confession to the brethren, of his standing, was received into the church, and afterwards obtained a letter of full membership from said church and moved into another church, which church then rejected him by the decision of the Annual Meeting of 1850, article 12. Would it be according to the gospel and the decision of A. M., if the brethren, that received him made acknowledgment to the man and also to the Church?

Ans. Considered that the brethren that received him make acknowledgment to the church, and to the man, and give him the reason for receiving him.

Amendment proposed as follows:

That the church be requested to make acknowledgment to the man in case he asks it.

Passed with the amendment.

QUERY.—Whereas the signs of the times and the public sentiment at large indicate a favorable reception of the doctrine of peace, should not the brethren advocate that doctrine, by preaching and tracts, more than before?

Ans We believe they should.

Laid on the table.

APPLICATION FOR ANNUAL MEETING.

Southern District of Ill.

Resolved that the district renew its request for the Annual Meeting in 1874.

Adopted.

QUERY.—Will the Annual Meeting of 1873 reconsider article 10th of the minutes of 1872, and define "Put them away," according to scripture? (This refers to likenesses).

Ans. This Annual Meeting understands the phrase 'Put them away' to mean put them out of sight.

On the question of reconsidering there were cries of "yes" and "no."

Sturgis. These Annual Meetings do not execute themselves. If you see the pictures not put away, why not do it yourselves. Let good enough alone, and if they do not put them away deal with them. I have never believed that any brother or sister worshipped these pictures. If they have the picture of an old father or mother that they want to see once in a while I am not the man to say keep it away. Some will not consent to such stringent means because they have something in their house you don't want them to use.

——. Confine your argument to the question, and if there is any scripture to tell how far to put them away, give the brethren the scriptures and they will obey.

——. The gospel teaches me to abstain from all appearance of evil, and if this is an evil then destroy it. It is a hard matter to go half way in this thing. A friend gave one to my daughter, and when I discovered that she had it, I asked liberty to burn it. If it is no evil then bring them out and show them to whom you please.

Forney. I think it is not necessary to debate the question. Let every brother and sister examine the scriptures, and if the brethren harmonize the matter it will be for the better.

Tabled.

QUERY.—Inasmuch as query 11 of 1872 is not headed, will not the Annual Meeting devise some plan to have it enforced thro'-out the whole brotherhood? We, the brethren of Kansas and Nebraska, ask the standing committee to answer.

Ans. In case the church permits its members to take illegal interest in opposition to the decision of Annual Meeting of 1872, article 11, the aggrieved members may apply to the Annual Meeting for a committee to set in order the things that are wanting.

Question deferred from yesterday taken up. Do brethren not think it proper to exert their influence against the admission into the church, of the new hymn book, with notes.

Answer. We advise all Districts and churches to keep them out of the church in public worship.

Holsinger. In 1869, this Annual Meeting was held in Virginia, and at that meeting there was a request made which reads as follows: "What does this District think of the propriety of requiring brethren who shall hereafter write and publish books to submit them to a committee appointed by the yearly meeting for examination and approval before they offer them to the public?" Answer. We do think it advisable for brethren to do so."

I appealed to the Annual Meeting of 1870 for a committee to investigate the book—"The Brethren's Tune and Hymn Book." At the same time a similar request was made by one of the Districts of Indiana, asking the A. M., to appoint a committee to publish a tune and hymn book for the same purpose, and the request was tabled, so I read in my report of the proceedings of the A. M. But then when my appeal came up for the appointment of a similar committee, instead of granting me the committee, this A. M., passed the following:—"Resolved, That the Brethren's Tune and Hymn Book, supposed to be published by brother Holsinger, be ruled out under the instructions of Art. 47, minutes of last A. M." A brother presented a book to be examined and asked for a committee, who examined the book. This restricted one Publishing business. I could not get a Committee and the thing was held in check. Then I said to the A. M., if you will not give me a committee, relieve me of the restrictions. They did it, and gave me liberty to publish the Tune book. They took hold of the publishing business, and granted me license in this single case. Since that time, notwithstanding this act, a number have gone on and published books without asking for a committee. That matter you don't find on the minutes of the A. M. Precisely as the case yesterday evening.

Brown. For the very reason that choir singing and instrumental music by machinery instead of the human heart, were making encroachments upon us, and the round note system was coming in, and to do away with these things we looked upon it as necessary to have the Tune book published, with the character notes, so that we could all use them. It seems to me this thing is brought up as a kind of target to shoot at brother Holsinger, and if we carry it too far it will naturally array the younger class against the older. Let us try to get along in peace and harmony. I move that the matter be entirely dismissed.

——. Let them learn the tunes at home, but not bring the note book into the church.

Brown. It seems to me this is driving at anything that looks like a little advancement.

——. Let us not be too hard on the tune and hymn book.

Sayler. I opposed the introduction into the church for the reason that I considered it an infringment on the copy-right of brother Quinter. Another reason is that it is a new thing, which some of us cannot use.

Holsinger. The first hymn book ever printed by the Brethren had the notes in it, of which I will raise you up fifty witnesses here in this congregation. Where is your new thing?

Sturgis. I intended to buy these books for my children and grandchildren, but on going to church I want them to take the hymn book and leave the note book at home, and then both books will be patronized.

Passed.

Query. Inasmuch as there are constant additions to the church and the ministry of young brethren, who are desirous to learn the proceedings of the A. M., would it not be advisable to publish in pamphlet form, all the Minutes of Annual Meeting, since last date, which is inclosed in the Encyclopedia, including those not published previous to said date, and have said pamphlet arranged so as to admit subsequent Minutes?

Answer. Approved of and recommended.

Proposed to postpone and go on the minutes for further consideration.

Passed.

Query. Is it right for brethren to solemnize marriage in cases where parents have been divorced, and the second parties living?

Answer. No.

Passed.

Query. Inasmuch as there are differences of opinion among the brethren as to the nature of offenses that should be settled between the parties immediately concerned, or that may be brought direct to the church, it is desired that this meeting define so as to bring about more unanimity of action.

Answer. All offenses that are directly against a brother or sister, should be settled according to Matt., 18; but such as are of a general nature, affecting the whole body, said body must be concerned in the settlement of its own account. In case a brother neglects or refuses to go according to the 18th of Matt., then the church should send brethren to investigate and report to the church according to Matt., 18.

Passed.

Query. Pursuant to a call for a special meeting of the District Counsel of the Southern district of Iowa, to be held in Monroe congregation, Feb. 20th, 1873, for the purpose of devising ways and means to send two brethren to preach the Gospel in districts where there are no members, and the people desire to have the brethren preach. A small number of members having assembled from Jefferson and Monroe, after some deliberation, a vote was taken, and the following resolution that two brethren be chosen for said purpose, to be furnished with whatever means may be contributed, and sent to such places as may seem to them and to this meeting the most for the advancement of the cause of the Lord.

Lost.

2nd. *Resolved,* That this meeting request the delegates at next A. M., to present the following query to said meeting for its consideration: "Is it according to the gospel for Counsel Districts to select brethren from amongst their ministry and send them to preach the gospel in places where there are no ministering brethren, and where people desire the brethren to preach, and to pay the traveling expenses of such brethren?"

Answer. It is according to the Gospel, we believe, and the decisions of A. M. See Minutes, 1868, Art. 21st.

Passed.

COMMITTEES APPOINTED.

1st. Inasmuch as the letter of the Spring Creek Church, Lebanon Co., Pa., calls for assistance to settle difficulties in said Church, we appoint them the following committee: D. Garlock, C. Bomberger, Samuel Harley.

2nd. A request from the Upper Deer Creek Church, Cass Co., Ind., the following brethren selected: Joseph McCarthy, John E. Shively and Gottleib Keller.

3rd. A request for a committee to go to Indian Creek Church, Montgomery Co., Pa., Moses Miller, D. P. Sayler, Dan'l Keller, J. G. Glock, Jacob Price.

4th. Committee to visit Saymons and Antioch Churches, Huntington Co., Ind., H. D. Davy, Danl. Brower and J. Wise.

5th. Astoria Church, Fulton Co., Ill., H. D. Davy, R. H. Miller, John Metzgar, Enoch Eby.

6th. YellowCreekChurch, Bedford Co., Pa., Isaac Meyers, Jacob Price and J. G. Glock.

8th. Black River Congregation, Van Buren Co., Mich., Jacob Berky, H. D. Davy and D. B. Sturgis.

8th. Waterloo Church, Iowa, H. Strickler, Peter Forney, Abram Stehmy and Thos. Sayder.

Passed.

Bro. Sayler proposed a resolution of thanks to the railroad companies, for the facilities afforded in getting to the meeting; to be entered on the minutes and noticed by the editors.

Passed.

Bro. D. P. Sayler was appointed a committee to make arrangements for next A. M., with the Baltimore and Ohio R. R., and all its branches.

Bro. H. D. Davy, was appointed a committee to make arrangements with the Pittsburgh, Fort Wayne & Chicago R. R. and Panhandle R. R.

Bro. J. S. Flory to make arrangements with the Chespeake & Ohio R. R.

Bro. J. B. Beechly, with the O. & M. R. R., from Columbus to Cincinnati & St. Louis.

Bro. H. R. Holsinger, Penn'a Cen. and Pittsburgh & Connellsville R. R.

Recommended that the housekeepers of all the churches lay the question of procuring a tent for next Annual Meeting before the churches, whether they will do anything toward it or not, and report to Bro. J. Metzgar, Cerro Gordo, Illinois.

Concluding remarks by Bro. Jas. Quinter:

Beloved Brethren, The time for seperation has come. Many of us from different parts of the Brotherhood have been permitted to assemble together, and no doubt you have enjoyed yourselves together. Perhaps my Brother Holsinger exaggerated the thought when he said that more good was done outside of the congregation than in, nevertheless our meeting together on occasions of this kind, I do regard as a benefit to the Church. To see our young brethren and sisters, and the older ones meet and mingle among us and with us; and if there is a difference in the attainments of grace, among us, if the elder have improved their seasons, and if we have grown in grace as we ought to have grown, and have got a little more grace, in coming in contact with others. I think there is a disposition in the grace of God, to go into others that come in contact with good. When a good and bad person come together there my be a tendency in the evil to go out into the good, as well as the good into the evil, and as good is stronger than evil, if we as Christians enjoy the grace of God as we should, the power of grace is stronger than the courage of sin, and if there is any change it ought to be in favor of the bad. Hence, I say the mingling thus together, if there is any better or worse among us, I think the worse are made better, in being thrown in this way. If we feel as we ought to feel, we who are older, and those who claim to be a little wiser and better, if we have made this attainment, then in coming in contact with others it may be presumed that they are nothing the worse.

Mingling then together, from all parts of the Brotherhood, I believe is promotive of the spirit of love that characterizes our Brotherhood; hence I am glad to have another oportunity, and although it is true that the cloud is sometimes great, over us, I like to see my brethren and sisters coming together on occasions like this. It shows an attachment to the Church and Brotherhood. I hope we all will go home profited by this intercourse with one anothe. I hope our our young brethren and sisters may have less prejudice against the elder than they have ever had, and that the elder may go away with less prejudice against the younger than some may have had; and upon the whole, that this meeting has been a blessing to us.

In conclusion, let me entreat you to remember our principles and our profession, the grand characteristics of our brotherhood, and the characteristics of the Gospel; and do not forget that among these characteristics are love, meekness, humility and that brotherly love, and particularly, above all, holiness which is characteristic of the Brotherhood.

It is perhaps out of season to talk now, but I wish to give expression to the bent of my mind. I am sorry as we all are to leave; and this indicates that it has been good to be together.

We have gone through a great many kinds of labor, and there is no kind of labor that seems to us more arduous, than the labors of this meeting. We would rather go and preach than feel the labors of these meetings, knowing how much some brethren require of us, and the dissatisfaction and difficulties in securing an answer when there is none to give, which make the labors of these meetings exceedingly arduous. But the time will come, when all our labors will be over, and a season of uninterrupted rest, peace and joy will be our portion forever.

Adjourned.

The Conference was then closed by the offering of a fervant prayer to God in behalf of the deliberations of the meeting and for the present and future welfare of Zion. It closed on Thursday at 12 M. when the Congregation began to make preparations for starting homeward.

As a list of the delegates from different districts, was omitted in the beginning of the report, we now give it, thinking it may be of general interest.

DELEGATES.

Pennsylvania District.

Eastern—D. Garlach, J. Reiner.
Middle—Jacob Price, J. Spanogle.
Western—Jno. Wise, John Berkey.

Maryland District.

Eastern—J. D. Trostle, D. P. Sayler.
Western—D. Long.

Virginia District.

No. 1—B. F. Moomaw, J. Brubaker.
" 2—J. Wise, Solomon Garber.
" 3—Martin Cosner.

Tennessee District.

H. Garst, S. Z. Sharp.

Ohio District.

N. E—J. Garver, J. B. Shoemaker.
N. W—H. D. Davy, J. Kurtz.
S. W—J. Brilheart, J. Brown.

Indiana District.

N—D. B. Sturgis, J. Berkey.
Middle—J. Barker.
Southern—Jos. McCarty.

Illinois District.

Northern—Enoch Eby.
Southern—J. Metzgar, D. Wolf.

Iowa District.

Northern—H. Strickler.
Middle—R. Badger.
Southern—Christ Harden.

THE MYSTERY OF GODLINESS.

Without controversy, great is the mystery of Godliness. God was manifest in the flesh, justified in the spirit, seen of angels, preached unto the Gentiles, believed on in the world, received up into glory.—1 Tim. 3; 16.

From the reading of this part of Paul's writings, it appears that true godliness was a great mystery at that time, and is yet to some. Many perhaps came to the conclusion, had they lived when Christ and the apostles were upon the earth, with the infallible proofs the Savior showed that He was the Son of God, and the apostles, how they were "endued with power from on high," yet there was but few, that is, comparatively speaking, that believed on Him. This may seem strange to some, in this nineteenth century, but I do think if they would reflect rightly upon the subject and become willing to be led by the plain word of God, the mystery in a great many points, would soon reveal itself.

I, for my part, believe that the world is growing darker and darker every day in true godliness, and I sometimes fear it is getting too much in the Church, but Oh, my brethren and sisters, let us use all the power that is within us, by the help of God, to strive lawfully, for short of that, we will not receive the crown. If we believe that we are in the latter time,—I do, for we see so much of the spirit which Paul speaks of in the 4th chapter of 1st Timothy. And we are taught "as it was in the days of Noah, so shall it be at the coming of the Son of Man." By this, I must believe that the world is getting worse, if not, there would be no danger of the world coming to an end. If the world is getting wiser, as there are many contend, there is no danger. No doubt the world is getting wiser in worldly affairs, but not spiritually. Then, if we believe this, it is no mystery to us that true godliness is a mystery to so many. But I do think, even since God gave the promise to our first parents that He would put enmity between the serpent and the woman, and between thy seed and her seed, it was a mystery, but that mystery was solved. God was in Christ Jesus—reconciled the world unto Himself sending His Son into the world, bringing life and immortality to light through the Gospel. We will admit that there are mysteries to our mind, for the Holy Ghost overshadowed her, and that is about all we know. Still He was made known in the flesh by being born of the Virgin Mary, justified by the spirit upon that memorable day when our beloved Savior came to John to be baptized, when the spirit bore testimony that He was the son in whom He was well pleased. John 10; 32 33. Rom. 1; 4, and declared to be the Son of God with power according to the spirit of holiness by the resurrection from the dead. 1st Peter 3; 18. For Christ also once suffered for sins, the just for the unjust that he might bring us to God, being put to death in the flesh but quickened by the spirit, seen of angels when they rolled back the stone in the morning of the resurrection. And also 1 Peter 1; 12, speaking what the angel desired to look into and preached unto Gentiles. Paul was called to preach to the Gentiles, for in the 2d chapter of Timothy 2d verse, we read where he was ordained a preacher and a teacher of the Gentiles, also in Eph. 3; 8, where he speaks to the Gentiles the unsearchable riches of Christ. Many other passages we might cite you to where he was to preach to the Gentiles. He came to His own and his own received Him not, but as many as received Him to them He gave power to become the sons of God. It appears there were still some few that accepted Him, therefore He was believed on, and at last when He had accomplished the everlasting plan of salvation, He was received up into glory. He has now gone into Heaven and is on the right hand of God, angels, authorities and powers being made subject unto Him.

A PILGRIM.

THE passionate are like men standing on their heads; they see all things the wrong way.—*Plato.*

POETRY.

COME UNTO ME.

With tearful eyes I look around,
Life seems a dark and stormy sea:
Yet 'midst the gloom I hear a sound,
A heavenly whisper, "Come to Me."

It tells me of a place of rest;
It tells me where my soul may flee;
Oh! to the weary, faint opprest,
How sweet the bidding, "Come to Me."

When the poor heart with anguish learns
That earthly props resigned must be,
And from each broken cistern turns,
It hears the accents, "Come to Me."

When against sin I strive in vain,
And cannot from its yoke set free,
Sinking beneath the heavy chain,
The words arrest me, "Come to Me."

When nature shudders, loath to part
From all I love, enjoy and, see;
When a faint chill steals o'er my heart,
A sweet voice utters, "Come to Me."

Come, for all else must fade and die;
Earth is no resting-place for thee;
Heavenward direct thy weeping eye!
I am thy portion, "Come to Me."

Oh, voice of mercy! voice of love!
In death's last fearful agony;
Support me, cheer me from above,
And gently whisper, "Come to Me."

ORIGINAL ESSAYS.

THE CHRISTIAN'S HARVEST.

Say ye not there are yet four months, and then cometh the harvest? *Behold*, I say unto you lift up your eyes, and look on the fields, for they are white already for the harvest.—John 4:35.

Christ previous to the utterance of this expressive language, had been exhibiting a remarkable zeal to God's glory. The disciples had not conceived of the importance of His mission, and when He told them He had meat to eat that they knew not of, they failed to comprehend the import, and concluded that some one had given Him to eat while they were gone to the city to procure meat. Jesus perceiving their limited knowledge of the nature of His mission, teaches them in the following clear, concise language: "My meat is to do the will of Him that sent me, and to finish His work."

This language, no doubt, gave them an idea of the importance of His mission, but still they wondered why He should refuse to take food after having taken none for so long, and being so weary with the journey. They thought He should not neglect to take food although His mission was an important one; but Christ's whole purpose was to glorify God, and as a special opportunity was presented for the accomplishment of His purpose, He improved it to the exclusion of every other consideration. This was the nature of Christ's work; it was always of first importance,—His highest purpose. But the disciples did not appear to have this high ideal of the Christian work; therefore says Jesus to them in the language of the text, "Say not ye, there are yet four months, and then cometh the harvest."

In this Jesus teaches the immediate results of our efforts to glorify God. The time from the sowing the seed to the harvest in Judea was four months, and the husbandman could not expect to reap the fruits of his labor until that time had expired. But not so with the Christian when he sows the Gospel seed, it may bring forth fruit immediately, and this is the idea that Christ conveys to His disciples. He had just been preaching to a Samaritan woman and now already many of the Samaritans were coming to hear Him. This thought certainly adds importance to the Christian labor. We do not, like the farmer, have to wait a time before we can expect to reap the fruits of our labors. The results may be immediate, and what joy and comfort this realization affords us? Christian reader, does not the fruits of righteousness strengthen and invigorate the soul? Ah, yes, they are truly joy and peace in the Holy Ghost. If then we are laboring for God, we may at any time lift up our eyes and look on the fields to see if they are not already white to harvest.

From these considerations we may learn lessons that afford much comfort and consolation to the Christian heart. We may learn first, in view of the fact, that the results of our labors may be immediate, that there is much encouragement to labor for God. Reader, have you ever thought seriously of the Christian's work and the results of his labors? Are you interested in the work? Is it your meat to do your Master's will? It is to be feared that in view of the great encouragement we have to labor for Christ, many are too much concerned about the things of this life, and many of the seasons for unplanting the precious seeds of truth are left pass by unimproved. We, perhaps, like the disciples, are more concerned about the meat that sustains the body than that which enlivens and strengthens the soul. And why a feeling of this kind? Is not the soul more important? How much we become interested in the things that tend to enhance our pecuniary interest. We can then make the greatest sacrifices of ease and comfort,—the inclemency of the weather is then no obstacle; we can leave our homes to attend to these things on days that are entirely too bad to go to church. A feeling of this kind is prevalent, and what is there to encourage it? It may be a long time before we can realize the benefits of our labor and then they are only transient and will perish with the using thereof. But if we labor for Christ and the salvation of souls, we may immediately realize that which the world knows not of,—that inward consciousness of right,—that strength of soul that enables us to see and feel that the fields are already white for the harvest; and then we will not feel so much concerned about the things of this life. The salvation of our soul and that of others will be our highest purpose.

There is another thought that is worthy of our consideration that we will notice briefly. When there are indications that the Gospel is effectual, and that the harvest is ready to be gathered, even then we may overlook opportunities for doing good. A conversation with a single person on a religious subject may create a deep interest throughout an entire community. Christ's conversation with the Samaritan woman at the well, created the deep interest that was felt through that city. So we should improve every opportunity to labor for the salvation of souls. We may sometimes conclude that it is of no use to talk to certain individuals on the subject of religion—they may not apparently have a definite purpose in view, or their standing in life may not be such as to exert an influence. But these things should not be considered when we are laboring for the salvation of souls. Christ's conversation with a single woman ripened a whole field, and so may we, christian reader, by conversing with a single individual mature and ripen a whole community, ready to be gathered into the garner of the Lord.

The result of neglecting to do our duty, is another important consideration. What will be the final result if we become so much engrossed with the things of this life and neglect to reap when the fields are ripe to harvest. What could the farmer expect after having sown the seed, and then when the harvest comes he should neglect to reap it. Certainly starvation would be the result. So it will be with you, dear reader, if you neglect your Christian duties. Every one will have to give an account of their doing in this life, and how empty, how destitute will be the condition of those who have failed to glorify God by laboring for the advancement of His Kingdom. There will be no reward for those; only those who reap will receive wages unto eternal life. Reader, think of this. Thousands of Christian professors, it is to be feared, are to-day neglecting to reap unto eternal life, and are only laying up treasures on earth. How bitter indeed will be their disappointment when they, too late, learn that a man cannot lay up treasures on earth and in Heaven too. John tells us "If any man love the world, the love of the Father is not in him."

Let us be careful then, dear reader, to employ all our time and talent in the service of the Lord, and then when the great day of final accounts comes, we will be rich through Him that hath loved us. O, the riches of God's glory! May we all look forward with joyful anticipation to the time when we shall share with all God's chosen ones the unsearchable riches of our Heavenly home.

J. B. B.

Perfection is the point for which all should steadily aim.

WISE WORDS FOR MOTHERS.

My heart is often grieved to see the little children of some of the families of my friends growing up to be very troublesome, not only to themselves, but to all with whom they associate. Now what should be done? Many mothers are, to all appearance losing control over their little ones, though they are not aware of it. Their desire is to govern them well; but they fail, because they yield to their whining and fretfulness. They wear a yoke that they will not be able to break, till death shall sever it.

Mother, when you once refuse your little ones something that they cry for, do not yield to them, because they kick, or attempt to strike you to obtain it. Rather make them feel the weight of the rod, so strenuously urged by Solomon. Many mothers are afraid to use the rod. God wisely intends that all parents should govern the children that He has given them, as they are accountable to Him for their well being. The temper of your little ones is soured, for all future life, by whining and fretting at every little thing. Why do you allow it? Break that stubborn will. Never threaten, unless you finish, sacrifice your own feelings for their eternal good. A few days of firm training will soon subdue them. Let your discipline be strict. Give a command, and see it obeyed promptly, without their first saying "I don't want to," or, "I won't."

Let them feel that you will be obeyed, and that it will be at their peril to disobey. The loving hearts of many mothers will shrink from such measures, which they will regard as harsh; but your child will soon be trained to obedience, and you will have no farther trouble. When they arrive at maturity they will rise up and bless you, because they have been well governed. And then they will know how to govern their own children. Remember to pray often with and for your children. A mother's sincere prayers will shield them from temptation, and promote their eternal salvation. M. A. H.—*Christian Observer.*

A CHEERFUL HOME.

A single bitter word may disquiet an entire family for a whole day. One surly glance casts a gloom over the household; while a smile like a gleam of sunshine may light up the darkest and weariest hours. Like unexpected flowers which spring up along our path, full of freshness, fragrance, and beauty, so do kind words and gentle acts, sweet dispositions make glad the home where peace and blessing dwell. No matter how humble the abode, if it be thus garnished with grace and sweetened with kind 'he Educated, as a rule, live ger and to better purpose than the earned; the wealthy longer than poor; the good longer than the and vicious; then get wisdom, knowledge, get understanding, educated; get riches, but get it estly, and give liberally to God's r, the extension of His Kingdom building up of His Zion, but ve all, seek the riches of l's grace, the wealth of His love, incomprehensible abundance of "Things he has prepared for those t love Him" —be good and you ll be eternally happy.—*A. B. umbaugh, M. D.*

THE WAY TO LIVE.

Ten minutes of weak ripening will nge a brave heart into the depths of happiness as suddenly as a thunder-m will overcast a clear summer sky. only way to live is to cast away ables and contentions, which cannot cured by fretting. A thing that one belongs to the past. In justice he requirements of the present, and sibilites of the future, you cannot back and make yourself wretched r things which cannot be undone.

The Lord's Day.—A gentleman o had been using the boat of omas Mann, a pious waterman on Thames, asked him if he did not ke seven days in a week. "No, " replied Thomas, "that would be ing what does not belong to me. e Lord's day is not mine; and refore I never work on that day."

Nothing teaches patience like a den. You may go round and tch the opening bud from day to , but it takes its own time, and cannot urge it on faster than it l. If forced, it is only torn to ces. All the best results of a den, like those of life, are slow regularly progressive.

t is not the bee's touching on the vers that gathers honey, but her ding for a time upon them, and wing out the sweet. It is not he t reads most, but he that medi-s most on divine truth, that will ve the choicest, wisest, strongest istian.—*Bishop Hall.*

When Joseph's brethren were leav- him to return home, he kindly and ely said to them: "See that ye fall out by the way." How comfortably pleasantly would brothers and sis- , friends and neighbors, live to- ner if they were to remember and ow this excellent advice.

Lay your finger on your pulse, I know that at every stroke some rtal passes to his Maker; some ow-being crosses the river of death; l if we think of it we may well nder that it should be so long be- e our time comes.

Youth's Department.

DON'T LET MOTHER DO IT.

Daughter, don't let mother do it!
Do not let her slave and toil
While you sit, a useless idler,
Fearing your soft hands to soil.
Don't you see the heavy burdens,
Daily she is wont to bear,
Bring the lines upon her forehead—
Sprinkle silver in the hair?

Daughter, don't let mother do it!
Do not let her bake and broil
Through the long, bright summer hours,
Share with her the hardy toil.
See, her eye has lost its brightness,
Faded from the cheek the glow,
And the step that once was buoyant
Now is feeble, weak and slow.

Daughter, don't let mother do it!
She has cared for you so long,
Is it right the weak and feeble
Should be toiling for the strong?
Waken from your listless langour.
Seek her side to cheer and bless,
And your grief will be less bitter
When the sods above her press.

Daughter, don't let mother do it;
You will never, never know
What were home without a mother
Till that mother lieth low—
Low beneath the budding daisies,
Free from earthly care and pain—
To the home so sad without her,
Never to return again.

THE YOUNG.

I would speak affectionately to you who are in the bloom of your days, and conjure you, "if there be any virtue and it there be any praise," to "remember your Creator in the days of your youth." Whilst you are yet strangers to the seductions of an ensnaring world. I would warn you against the evils which will gird you round when you go forth from the peaceful asylums of your childhood and mix, as you unavoidably must, with those who lie in wait to destoy the unwary. I would tell you that there is no happiness only in the fear of the Almighty; that if you would so pass through life as not to tremble and quail at the approach of death, make it your morning evening prayer that the Holy Spirt may take hold of your souls, and lead you so to love the Lord Jesus in sincerity, that you may not be allured from the holiness of religion by any of the devices of a wicked generation. You read of a monarch who wept as his countless army passed before him, staggered by the thought, that yet a few years and those stirring hosts would lie motionless in the silent grave. Might not a christian minister weep over you as he gazes on the freshness of your days, and considers that it is but too impossible, that you may hereafter give ear to the scorner and seducer. Thus might the buds of early promise be nipped; and it might come to pass that you, the children, it may be, of pious parents, over whose infancy a godly father may have watched, and whose opening hours may have been guarded by the tender solicitudes of a righteous mother, would entail on yourselves a heritage of shame, and go down at the judgment into the pit of the unbeliever and the profligate. Let this warning be remembered by you all; it is simple enough for the youngest, it is important enough for the eldest. You cannot begin too soon to serve the Lord, but you may easily put it off too long; and the thing which will be least regretted when you come to die is, that you gave the first days of existence to the preparation for heaven.—*Melville*

THE BOY TO BE TRUSTED.

"What book is that?" inquired a merchant one day of a youth from the country, who, while searching his bag for a letter of recommendation, had let a book fall on the floor.

"My Bible, sir."

"Your Bible! What are you going to do with it here in the city?"

"Read it, sir. I promised my mother I would read it every day; and I shall do it sir!"

The firm tone and flashing eye told the merchant that he had a boy of principle and grit before him. He felt that a boy who loved his Bible after this fashion could be trusted. He hired him, found him true and trusty, kept him many years as a clerk, and finally made him his partner.

In this fact you see a merchant taking it for granted that a boy who loved his Bible after this fashion could be trusted. He was right. Mark the point, and tell me if you find a Bible-hating boy who can be trusted. Isn't it a fact that boys who hate the Bible are not trustworthy? If, therefore, you wish to be true, trusty, and trusted, you must love your Bible. With the Bible as the rule and guide of your life, every duty will be performed in a manner well pleasing to God, and of necessity well pleasing to men.—*S. S. Messenger.*

Hold on, Boys.—Hold on to your tongue when you are just ready to swear, lie, or speak harshly, or say any improper words.

Hold on to your name at all times, for it is more valuable to you than gold, high places, or fashionable attire.

Hold on to the truth, for it will serve you well and do you good thro'-out eternity.

Hold on to virtue; it is above all price to you in all times and all places.

Hold on to your good character, for it is, and always will be, your best wealth.

Hold on to your temper when you are angry, excited, or imposed upon.

In the awful mystery of human life, it is a consolation sometimes to believe that our misfortunes, perhaps even our sins, are permitted to be instruments of our education for immortality.

The Weekly Pilgrim.

JAMES CREEK, PA., July 15, 1873.

☞ HOW TO send money.—All sums over $1.50, should be sent either in a check, draft or postal order. If neither of these can be obtained, have the letter registered.

☞ WHEN MONEY is sent, *always* send with it the name and address of those who paid it. Write the names and post office as plainly as possible.

☞ EVERY subscriber for 1873, gets a *Pilgrim Almanac* FREE.

OUR DEFENSE.

No matter how slow and reluctant we may feel in meeting charges brought against us, it sometimes becomes necessary, in order to vindicate our position. But in doing it, we shall maintain the spirit and forbearance of true Christianity, and come out manly and openly. We are disgusted with this unbrotherly way of throwing daggers under a mask. If we are guilty of any misdemeanor, say so, if not, let us know who are, that we need not feel ourselves implicated.

The *Vindicator* of July, under the head, "Our Mind on Reporting" implicates us or "our weeklies" (and as we have only two, we must be included) with transcending our authority or violating the descisions of A. M. Of this, we plead, "not guilty." In regard to the Report, the decision was, There may be a synopsis of the discussions given without giving the names of the speakers. We understand the synopsis business very well, and knew it gave us more liberties than we cared about using, as it might be the ground work of bringing against our report, the same charge of last year, that of unfairness or partiality. Giving a synopsis of a man's argument is equivalent to abridging or cutting it down, which may be done indefinitely, or to suit our taste or judgment of the force and bearing of the argument. In using this liberty we might have sifted some of the arguments until there would have been nothing left and thus, have been charged of partiality. For this reason we informed A. M. that we were prepared to give a full report of the meeting, and wished to know whether we would be allowed to publish it providing we omitted the names. The answer by several of the old brethren on the stand was: "There will be no objection to the report if the names are left out." This answer was not countermanded and we expressed ourselves satisfied and there was nothing more said.

In our report, as given by our reporter, we tried to do justice to all the speakers by giving their sentiments on the subject discussed as clearly as possible, omitting only such parts or points as had no bearing on the subject, thus after all, only giving a synopsis of the discussions, as it should be remembered that in giving a synopsis of an argument, we are not allowed to omit anything that will destroy its force. Therefore we claim that our report is in harmony with the liberties given by A. *M.*, and that henceforth brother Kinsey will be more definite in his criticisms.

As to the propriety of having a report, we had but little to say, as it costs us more than what it brings us in. We felt quite willing to submit it to the Church or A. M., and the result was, the report was called for. It is the voice of the Church that wants a report, but our brother says, "That is no reason we should have them." How is this, dear brother, are we to hear the voice of the Church or your opinion? It is true, some very good brethren fear the result of these things, but they should remember that others, equally good, see the propriety of them. There is no possible wrong about the report; if there be a wrong about it, it is in the speakers. Therefore it would seem the part of wisdom in us to labor to remove the cause of the evil by getting them right, instead of encouraging them by hiding their inconsistencies. It should be remembered that truth will not lose by investigation, and where the spirit of Christ is there is liberty. These who are on the side of right have nothing to fear, but reporting will cerrtainly have a tendency of putting there on their guard who are in the habit of talking for the mere sake of argument. The only true road to reformation is to make men responsible for their conduct.—This is done by reporting what they say, and we hope that henceforth our brethren will come up to our A. M., with their tongues bridled and their souls filled with the Spirit of Truth. Then our reports can go forth as a vindication of truth and an honor to God. As to reports being a new or strange thing, it is a mistake. In the councils of the Jewish Chruch, they had their scribes to report the proceedings, and what do our brethren mean when they pray that our ministers' tongues may be as the pen of a ready writer? In conclusion, be careful not to stigmatize others with causing divisions, when you may be equally guilty of the same crime.—Charity thinketh no ill to his neighbor.

In *Companion* No. 27, under "Companion please copy" we get another bluff that is so much like the petty jealousies of children, that we discard it altogether. Such things are a disgrace to our common cause and would much better become men of less pretentions Truly great men have condescended to small things; very small.

Correspondence.

Dear Pilgrim: I am always anxious, and much pleased to hear from the Church through our PILGRIM and we believe all our brethren and sisters are interested in the cause of Zion. Then it becomes the duty of those who can, to write the Church news of every Church district in the Brotherhood. By this, brethren and sisters, we can hear many encouraging words, which may make us more strong to go forth in the good work. In this arm of the church things pertaining to the church are progressing, and our prayer to Almighty God is, that they may so continue to the honor of our Father in Heaven. Yesterday the brethren and sisters were called upon to initiate one more precious soul into the fold by baptism. The subject was Bro. Henry Whitesell. He has been quite feeble in health for some time. We pray God to give him strength physically and, mentally, that he may abide in the truth and prove himself a worthy workman.

A sad accident occurred June 26, John, son of Bro. George Boyer, aged twelve years, went to a lake near home to fish, and as was a custom he waded into the water, there being no boat at command, and by chance, came upon a soft bottom and being in water as is supposed, above his shoulders, sank immediately down into it over his head and was found standing in the mire with his head only about four inches beneath the surface, in mire almost to his knees. Oh! what must have been the thot's of that sorrow stricken father when he found his loving son buried in this watery grave. We hope God will give him fortitude to withstand all.

Our Sabbath school is doing a noble work. Though much more good might be done, if the brethren and sisters were more firmly united upon this subject of so much importance. It, indeed and in truth, would be a good help to the cause of Zion if carried out in the glory and honor of God. I do sincerely hope the day is not far distant when there will not be a dissenting voice to the cause. Oh brethren, the responsibility of raising our children in the nurture and admonition of the Lord. I ask, is not a well conducted Sabbath school a good school to bring us to Christ? How much good might be done if we would only go at the work with firmness and earnestness. Can we do too much for the cause of true Christianity? I answer, NO.

Then let us employ more time and work more in the cause. There should not be one particle of labor diminished in the other duties of the Church. Some may say we will have too much to do. Fear not brethren and sisters, of doing too much labor for the Lord. But rather fear of doing too little. Some cannot see the good in a Sabbath school. Perhaps they have never attended one conducted by the Brethren as was our experience in this arm of the Church. No Sabbath schools, are very encouraging when first commenced. Our first attempt met with some opposition, but since they have seen the good work doing its duty, they believe the cause a good one. There is no good work but has its abuses. Look at the good work of religion and see how much it is abused by some classes of individuals. Brethren organize more Sabbath schools and work for the advancement of God's Kingdom, and pray earnestly to him for aid, and you will succeed in doing much good. I will give you a condensed report of our school, by request of our Secretary, for the past fourteen sessions.

Attendance of officers,	70.
Teachers,	90.
Scholars,	8.20.
Spectators	2.64.
No. of verses recited,	25.98.
Total attendance,	12.00.

Average attendance at erach school 90.

Brethren and sisters, I hope my weak effort has not offended one soul, but that it may be for the good of the cause of my Master. I ask the prayers of my brethren and sisters in the great work and field of labor, assigned me by the Church, for I feel without their prayers, and the aid and assistance of God, I can do but little. Brethren pray more, and may God's choicest blessings rest on the Church, that we may keep united in the strong union of love is the prayers of your unworthy Bro.

WM. G. COOK.

Plymouth, Ind.

Dear Bro., D. C. Moomaw:—This beautiful Sabbath evening, when nature hath clothed herself in such beautiful colors, when all the sweet influences conveyed by the glorious sunshine, the balmy air, the music of Nature's sweetest songsters, and more than all, the peaceful quiet of the Lord's day, touch our spirits with that power that makes us, for awhile, forget our cares and troubles, and lifts us above the world and its selfishness; in this frame of mind, how natural is it for us to think of the past, and its mercies; of the future, and its hopes, of the loved ones who have gone before, and loved ones who are separated from us only by hills and vales. Thus we have been thinking of you, and wondering how you prosper in the battles of life.

Yesterday evening we partook of those sacred emblems which the Lord instituted "to show forth His death till he comes," and the services were conducted with such holy reverences, and sincerity, on the part of the brethren and sisters, that I wondered how the unprejudiced looker on could help saying and feeling in his heart, "surely these are the people of God." It was entirely new to me, but it was something which I had often longed for, and which I sincerely and heartily enjoyed.

Father returned from the A. M., last night, which he reports to have been very interesting and harmonious, except a little difficulty, as usual, with our brethren of the type. Let us hear from you soon. How is your health, and your courage? As for ourselves, we are are all well; I am still—thanks to the Lord—progressing slowly towards health, and I can tell you with the authority of experience, that though our troubles and sufferings are multiplied above the average that falls to human lot, yet the comforts we receive, and the supernatural strength, and help which ıeu follows the gold-paved streets, ea of glass mingled with fire, the ers, harping with their harps, the ic song of triumph sung by the tless myriads of the ransomed of ɔamb, the crowning of the victors the fadeless crown, and the final entation to our Father, by the rious Lord, of those who *con-* ·*d* with Him in His tribulation, who washed their robes and made white in His own precious blood. am still enjoying the approving s of an affectionate Master. My h is steadily improving, and I resumed the important work of aching the unsearchable riches of Gospel." May the Lord of the yard grant that I shall not lay it again till He comes to reckon His servants, or until, as a sheaf ripe, I shall be gathered unto fathers in Israel. May He fully re you to perfect soundness, ically and spiritually, and enable to consecrate a requisite portion ich priceless gifts to the conver- of your deluded fellow-creatures, of the physical and spiritual gos-

ive us the pleasure of a visit soon, write often. Our usual greetings l the household.

Your brother,
D. C. MOOMAW.
lacksburg, Va.

Notes of Travel.

BY J. S. FLORY.

OMAHA, Neb. June 28, 1873.

aving had a very kind invitation liberal offer to accompany a party en to take a look at the Great Valley, and the much talked of itory of Colorado, and believing weeks of recreation being nec- y for my health, I left home the 23rd and arrived at Hun- ton at night, and owing to the our train was behind time we d to make connection with the nboat for Cincinnati. Had to in over until morning when we by boat to Siotaville, thence by to Hamlin, Ohio, and thence to innati, where we arrived at 6:20 . Was kindly entertained at d McIlvains until 5:32 p. m., n we left on the O. & M. R. R., St. Louis. Next morning at day- we passed through some fine try in Ill., harvesting was going wheat crops looked fine indeed. 7:10 a. m., arrived at St. Louis, at 8:30 on the N. M. R. R., ar- l at Kansas city, 8.30 p. m., left :30 for Council Bluffs, next morn- in passing up the Missouri River ms we noticed quite a variation he corn crop some looked as gh it was just planted, some just some two feet high and some s high as an ordinary man's head. ved at Council Bluffs, at 9 o'clock . Three other trains arrived after which owing to the travel- crowds made the place a place usiness indeed. All passengers and gage had to be changed here to transfer company's cars which all across their magnificent iron ge to the other side of the Mis- i river and delivered us into the of Omaha, were we remained un- -day. We took a stroll early in morning about the back part of the city which stands upon the bluff. We visited the public school-house which cost one hundred thousand dollars. A collegiate education can here be obtained under the free school system without any extra cost. From the front veranda of the buil- ding, we had a grand view. The city of Omaha in the main lay be- low our feet, the waters of the Mo., which were very high, and numerous islands were spread out before us for miles in width. Just opposite, we could have a full view of Council Bluffs, which is an important place. The great R. R. bridge, like a web, spans the river to our right, to our left, far away we can see the winding sheet of waters coming down, upon which the sun is shining in splendor. The city is beautifully interspersed with green trees, the bluffs have fine natural groves with resident houses scattered through them. Council Bluffs is on the west border of Iowa, and Omaha on the east border of Nebraska, and is noted for the joint, over-land trains to California, and the west used to lay in their supplies, and do yet, even many who go by rail lay in a good lot of commissary stores to avoid those big bills along the line. At Omaha we had our first sight of the Chinese. Will be off for the Platt Valley this p. m. More anon.

Dear Pilgrim: Let me give you a little church news. I left home June 18,—went to Chicago, and on the 19, left Chicago for Pontiac, Livingston Co., Ill; thence north to Cornell, where I met our dear brother Keelin Heck- man and went home with him, found all well. Here I thought, what joy there will be when we will meet in Heaven! As I had not seen the sister for some time, and knowing her from a child, our meeting was a joyful one. I enjoyed myself very much with the Br., and family. The brother is a speaker in the first degree and one of the chil- dren a member, though young, being the oldest daughter. On the 20th, I went to their Communion with brother Heckman and family. The Lovefeast was at brother Adam Youngs'. This church is called the Vermilion Dis trict, is yet in its infancy and is growing. May God help it to prosper. Lovefeast commenced at 10 a. m. Here I met Elder Rufus Gish and brother Jacob J. Kindig, and other beloved members from Woodford Co., Ill. Had a feast of fat things. A choice for deacon was held and Bro Jonathan Swihart ordained. Had very good order. Meeting at the same place the 21st, and in the evening at a school-house. Next day at the same place at 10 a. m. In the afternoon at 3 o'clock in Cornell, and in the even- ing at the same place. Here there was three applicants for baptism, two of brother David Heckman's daughters, and one of brother Paul Dale's, all young. May God help them to live faithful till death is our prayer. Bap- tized them on Monday morning, and then took my leave from them and went to Woodford Co., stopped off at Benson, where I met our brother J. J. Kindig, a minister in the second degree,—went home with him found all well. From here I visited brother Henry Kindig, thence, friend Wm. Irons, stayed till evening and then taken to meeting by friend Iron's fam- ily. Had a very good meeting. Next morning, the 25th, I went back to friend Wm. Irons, and was taken by him to friend John Coley's, and by friend Coley to brother Andrew Rud- dell, where I remained over night, en- joyed myself very much with the Bro. and sister and their kind daughter, their only child. I hope she will soon become a member of the Church. On the 26th, I, with brother Ruddell and sister and daughter visited some of our old acquaintances, and among whom was old father Coley. the father-in-law to bro, Ruddell, he being in his 75th year and out of the church, but prom- ised us he would not wait much lon- ger. May the good Lord help him to carry out his promise, for he cannot stay much longer. The old mother is a very kind sister, and said it would give her much happiness if her hus- and would come in before they would have to separate. The same evening I went back to brother Andrew Rud- dell's, stayed until next day, thence was brought by friend Briand Coley to his house, remained until evening and then to meeting by friend Coley. Had very good order and attention, went home with brother Rufus Gish. Next day brother Gish to me to broth- er George Gish, where I stayed until evening and then went to the church again, where we had another meeting. Home with brother John Woods, a very kind family. Next day being Sabbath, I went with brother Woods and family to Sabbath School. Had a very good school, two hundred an fifteen being present, and the members told me they have had five hundred. All appear to take an interest in the school, and I think it is well conduc- ted. At 11 o'clock we had meeting at the same place, being in the Brethren's church, and in the afternoon meeting at five o'clock. Here four made appli- cation for baptism. On Monday morn- ing the 30th, met at 8 o'clock on the banks of Panther Creek, "where prayer was wont to be made." Quite a num- ber of members and others met with us. Baptism was administered, and here we took the parting hand. Went home with brother J. J. Kindig and from there to Benson with Bro. Kin- dig. Here our young lambs met us to bid me farewell. Took the 1 o'clock train and got to Plymouth on the 1st day of July. At 3 o'clock I arrived at home when a call was made to visit a sick man some four miles distant. I baptized him.

So the good Lord is still adding such as shall be saved. O, brethren let us not be idle, but do all we can, by the help of God, to get poor sinners to turn to God, and hide multitudes of sins.

May God bless all is my prayer.

JOHN ENSLEY.

DIED.

HANAWALT.—In the Spring Run Con- gregation, Mifflin Co., Pa., May 25, 1873, sister Barbara, wife of George Hanawalt, aged 30 years, 8 months and 23 days.

The deceased, after a severe and pro- tracted illness, departed with resignation and composure, leaving a husband and 8 small children, and a very large circle of relatives, including an aged mother, to mourn their loss.

HOFFMAN.—In Cedar Co., Iowa, June 28, sister Elizabeth, wife of Samuel Hoff- man, formerly from Somerset Co. Pa., aged 70 years. Funeral preached by brother S. Musselman.

Obituaries, &c., crowded out.

BOOK NOTICES.

DIGESTION AND DYSPEPSIA.—A Complete Explanation of the Physiology of the Digestive Processes, with the Symptoms and Treatment of Dyspepsia and other Disorders of the Digestive Organs. Illustrated. By R. T. Trall, M. D. Bound in Muslin, price $1.00. Ready July 19th.

This Book will constitute by far the best work on the subject ever published. With fifty Illustrations; showing with all possible fulness every process of Digestion, and giving all the causes and directions for treatment of Dyspepsia, a disorder which, in its various forms, is the cause of nearly all the diseases from which the human race is suffering.

The Work is sure to meet with a large sale, and orders should be sent in at once.

Address S. R. WELLS, Publisher,
389 Broadway, N. Y.

GENERAL INTELLIGENCE.

THE New York *Daily Graphic* has agreed to provide the two skillful aeronauts, John Wise and W. H. Donaldson, with all the aeronautic appliances for crossing the Atlantic Ocean, at an expense of 10,000, reserving the right to name certain persons who shall accompany them, and the exclusive right to publish the particulars of the voyage as soon as they shall land in Europe.

This will certainly be a daring exploit, and cannot be contemplated with any other than very serious apprehensions. The aeronauts, however, have made some very long and daring flights across land, and if across land, why not across water? Prof. Wise made the trip from St. Louis to New York, a distance of 1000 miles in nineteen hours, and on other occasions has made trips of greater or less distance, by appointment from east to west. The result of such an exploit cannot be of any practical utility, but may aid largely in scientific investigation.

A VERY destructive tornado occured in the lake regions, Wis., recently. Reports from that region say that vessles were wrecked and many persons drowned. The course of the tornado from northwest to southeast was about five miles in width, and in this track everything—crops buildings and fences were leveled. Its course extended through Missouri, Ohio, Indiana, Kentucky and Tennessee, and the reports all agree in describing it as the most destructive tornado that ever visited the West and Southwest in many years. The pecuniary loss is supposed to reach millions of dollars, aside from the loss of life and incalculable personal suffering entailed.

Two fatal cases of cholera in Jersey City are reported. The disease continues its course at Cincinnati, Memphis, and Nashville, but with a decreased rate of mortality.

Sick Headache.

Dear Brethren and sisters, having witnessed much suffering from SICK HEADACHE, we now offer a Speedy and *Sure Cure* for the same. It is pleasant to take and can be sent by mail.

Address with stamp.

DRS. WRIGHTSMAN & FLORY.
July. 8-4t. South Bend, Ind.

GOOD BOOKS.

A large number of our patrons are receiving our books as noticed below, as premiums, and express themselves highly pleased with them. Others who are not agents, have enquired whether we keep them for sale. We have now made arrangements with Mr. Wells to furnish any of their publications post paid at publishers prices. Orders for books must be accompanied with the cash, and plain directions for sending them.

How to read Character, illus.	Price, $1.25
Combe's Moral Philosophy,	1.75
Constitution of Man. Combe,	1.75
Education. By Spurzheim,	1.50
Memory—How to Improve it,	.1.50
Mental Science, Lectures on,	1.50
Self-Culture and Perfection,	1.50
Combe's Physiology, Illus.	1.75
Food and Diet. By Pereira,	1.75
Natural Laws of Man,	.75
Hereditary Descent,	1.50
Combe on Infancy,	1.50
Sober and Temperate Life,	.50
Children in Health—Disease,	1.75
The Science of Human Life,	3.50
Fruit Culture for the Million,	1.00
Saving and Wasting,	1.50
Ways of Life—Right Way,	1.00
Footprints of Life,	1.25
Conversion of St. Paul,	1.00

Life at Home; or, The Family and its Members. A work which should be found in every family. $1.50. Extra gilt, $2.00.

Hand-book for Home Improvement: comprising "How to Write," "How to Talk," "How to Behave," and "How to do Business," in one vol. 2.25.

Man, in Genesis and in Geology; or, the Biblical Account of Man's Creation, tested by Scientific Theories of his Origin and Antiquity. One vol. 12mo, $1.00.

Man and Woman: Considered in their Relations to each Other and to the World. 12mo, Fancy cloth, Price $1.00.

Hopes and Helps for the Young of both sexes, Relating to the Formation of Character. Choice of Avocation, Health, Conversation, Social Affection Courtship and Marriage. Muslin, $1.50.

The Emphatic, Diaglott; or The New Testament in Greek and English. Containing the Original Greek Text of the New Testament, with an Interlineary Word for-word English Translation. Price, $4.00; extra fine binding, $5.00.

Trine Immersion

TRACED

TO THE APOSTLES.

The SECOND EDITION is now ready for delivery. The work has been carefully revised, corrected and enlarged.

Put up in a neat pamphlet form, with good paper cover, and will be sent, post-paid, on the following terms: One copy, 25 cts; Five copies, $1.10; Ten copies, $2.00. 25 copies, $4.50; 50 copies, $8.50; 100 copies, $16.00.

Address, J. H. MOORE,
Urbana, Champaign co., Ill.
Oct 22.

DYMOND ON WAR.

An inquiry into the Accordancy of War, with the Principles of Christianity, and an examination of the Philosophical reasoning by which it is defended. With observations on some of the causes of war and on some of its effects. By Jonathan Dymond Sent from this office, post-paid, for 50 cts!

TUNE BOOK.

The Brethren's Tune and Hymn Book, is a compilation of Sacred Music adapted to all the hymns in the Brethren's New Hymn Book. It contains over 350 pages, printed on good paper and neatly bound. We will send it to any address, post paid at $1.25 per copy.

GIVEN AWAY.

A FINE GERMAN CHROMO.

We send an elegant chromo, mounted and ready for framing, free to every agent for

UNDERGROUND

or,

LIFE BELOW THE SURFACE.

BY THOS. W. KNOX.

942 Pages Octavo. 130 Fine Engravings.

Relates Incidents and Accidents beyond the Light of Day; Startling Adventures in all parts of the World Mines and Mode of Working them; Under-currents of Society; Gambling and its *Horrors*; Caverns and their Mysteries; The Dark Ways of Wickedness; Prisons and their Secrets; Down in the Depths of the Sea; Strange Stories of the Detection of Crime.

The book treats of experience with brigands; nights in opium dens and gambling hells; life in prison; Stories of exiles; adventures among Indians; journey through Sewers and Catacombs; accidents in mines; pirates and piracy; tortures of the inquisition; wonderful burglaries; underworld of the great cities, etc., etc.

AGENTS WANTED

for this work. Exclusive territory is given. Agents can make $100 a week in selling this book. Send for circulars and terms to agents.

J. B BURR & HYDE,

HARTFORD, CONN., OR CHICAGO, ILL

TRACTS.

"ANXIOUS BENCH RELIGION EXAMINIED," BY ELDER J. S. FLORY. A SYNOPSIS OF CONTENTS. An address to the reader: The peculiarities that attend this type of religion. The feelings there experienced not imaginary but real. The key that unlocks the wonderful mystery. The causes by which feelings are excited. How the momentary feelings called "Experimental religion" are brought about, and then concludes by giving that form of doctrine as taught by Jesus Christ and recorded by his faithful witnesses.

COUNTERFEIT DETECTER
or
BAPTISM—MUCH IN LITTLE.

This work is now ready for distribution, and the importance of the subject will speak for it a large demand. It is a short treatise on baptism in tract form intended for general distribution, and is set forth in such a plain and logical manner that a wayfaring man though a fool, cannot err therein. Either of the above tracts sent postpaid on the following terms: Two copies, 10 cts, 10 copies 40 cents, 25 copies 70 cents, 50 copies $1.00, 100 copies $1.50.

$133 33/100 worth Sunday School books for $100 from any or all Publishers. Send for Circulars. J. C. BLAIR, S. S. Book-Store, Huntingdon, Pa.

Trine Immersion.

A discussion on Trine Immersion, by letter between Elder B. F. Moomaw and Dr. J. J. Jackson, to which is annexed a Treatise on the Lord's Supper, and on the necessity, character and evidences of the new birth, also a dialogue on the doctrine of non-resistance, by Elder B. F Moomaw. Single copy 50 cents.

$5 to $20 per day! [illegible] Portland, Maine

THE HELPING HAND.

Containing several hundred Valuable Receipts for cooking well at a moderate expense, making Dyes, Coloring, Cleaning and Cementing. This book also points out in plain language, free from Doctors' terms the diseases of men, women and children, and the latest and most approved means used for their cure, to which is added a description of the Medicinal Roots and Herbs, and how they are to be used in the cure of diseases.

This is a work of considerable importance and we offer it to our readers as being a valuable accession to every household. Send from this office to any address, postpaid, for 25 cents.

1870 1873

DR. FAHRNEY'S

Blood Cleanser or Panacea.

A tonic and purge, for Blood Diseases. Great reputation. Many testimonials. Many ministering brethren use and recommend it. Ask or send for the "Health Messenger." Use only the "*Panacea*" prepared at Chicago, Ills., and by

Dr. P. Fahrney's Brothers & Co.,
Feb. 3-pd. *Waynesboro, Franklin Co., Pa*

New Hymn Books, English.

TURKEY MOROCCO.

One copy, postpaid,	$1.00
Per Dozen,	11.25

PLAIN ARABESQUE.

One Copy, post-paid,	75
Per Dozen, "	8.50

Ger'n & English, Plain Sheep.

One Copy, post-paid,	$1.00
Per Dozen	11.25
Arabesque Plain,	1.00
Turkey Morocco,	1.25
Single German, post paid	50
Per Dozen,	5.50

HUNTINGDON & BROAD TOP RAIL ROAD

On and after June 20th, 1873, Trains will run on this road daily (Sun excepted) as follows:

Trains from Huntingdon South. *Trains from Mt. Dallas moving North.*

ACCM P. M.	EXPS. A. M.	STATIONS.	EXP'S P. M.	ACCM. A. M.
5 50	8 10	Huntingdon,	AR 6 05	AR 8 25
6 00	8 20	Long Siding	6 00	8 20
6 11	8 30	McConnelstown	5 48	8 09
6 19	8 38	Pleasant Grove	5 40	8 00
6 32	8 50	MARKLESBURG	5 25	7 45
6 43	9 02	Coffee Run	5 12	7 35
6 50	9 09	Rough & Ready	5 05	7 27
7 00	9 17	Cove	4 56	7 18
7 03	9 20	Fishers Summit	4 53	7 15
7 20	9 40	Saxton	4 40	7 00
7 35	9 55	Riddlesburg	4 18	6 45
7 43	10 05	Hopewell	4 11	6 38
7 55	10 15	Piper's Run	3 50	6 24
8 10	10 28	Tatesville	3 45	6 10
8 20	10 40	Everett	3 35	5 58
8 30	10 50	Mount Dallas	3 30	5 55
8 55	11 15	Bedford	3 05	5 30

SHOUP'S RUN BRANCH.

A. M.	P. M.		P. M.	A. M.
LE 9 50	LE 7 30	Saxton.	AR 4 25	AR 6 58
10 05	7 45	Coalmont.	4 10	6 35
10 10	7 50	Crawford.	4 05	6 30
AR 10 20	AR 8 00	Dudley	LE 3 55	LE 6 20

Bro'd Top City from Dudley 2 miles by stage.

Time of Penna. R. R. Trains at Huntingdon

*** Mail No. 2 makes connection at Huntingdon with Mail going East on Pennsylvania Railroad at 4.15 p. m., and West at 5.45 p. m. Mail No. 1 leaves Huntingdon at 7.40 a. m. on arrival of Pacific Express West.

Trains on this road connect with trains on Bedford & Bridgeport, and Cumberland & Pennsylvania Railroads.

G. F. GAGE, Supt.

The Weekly Pilgrim.

Published by J. B. Brumbaugh, & Co.
Edited by H. B. & Geo. Brumbaugh.
CORRESPONDING EDITORS.
D. P. Sayler, Double Pipe Creek, Md.
Leonard Furry, New Enterprise, Pa.

The *Pilgrim* is a Christian Periodical, devoted to religion and moral reform. It will advocate in the spirit of *love* and *liberty*, the principles of true Christianity, labor for the promotion of peace among the people of God, for the encouragement of the saints and for the conversion of sinners, avoiding those things which tend toward disunion or sectional feelings.

TERMS.

Single copy, Book paper,	$1.50
Eleven copies, [eleventh for Agt.]	15.00

Any number above that at the same rate.

Address,
H. B. BRUMBAUGH.
James Creek,
Huntingdon county Pa.

The Weekly Pilgrim.

"REMOVE NOT THE ANCIENT LANDMARKS WHICH OUR FATHERS HAVE SET."

VOL. 4. JAMES CREEK, PENNSYLVANIA, JULY 22, 1873. NO. 29.

POETRY.

SELECTED BY D. M. HOLSINGER.

"NOTHING BUT LEAVES."

Mark 11:13

BY MARY E. B. TOURTILOTTE.

When across Judea's mountain,
Broke the moon in silver sheen,
Where a fig-tree by the wayside
Stood with shining leaves so green;
Came our Savior faint and thirsty,
Seeking fruit and finding none,
For his earnest search discovered—
Nothing there but leaves alone

After fruitless quest he turned
From the barren tree away,
Saying, let no fruit be gathered
Off thy branches here this day.
And another morn beheld it
Drooping, all its verdure fled,
Blighted, neath that fearful sentence
Dry and withered, crisp and dead,

Thus when Jesus comes in judgment,
With the trumpet's awful sound,
Will his dread displeasure wither
Those with whom no fruit is found:
And are we for whom he suffered—
Pain and anguish, grief and shame,
In our life and conduct bearing—
Fruit to glorify his name,

Oft my wayward steps have wandered
From the strait and narrow way,
Yet I love thee, dear Redeemer,
Guide me that no more I stray;
Lay thy welcome burden on me,
Cheerfully thy yoke *I* take,
And thy cross I'll bear it gladly,
Joyfully for thy dear sake.

Here I bring my heart my Savior,
Lay it humbly on thy shrine,
And with love and trust unshrinking,
Place, by faith my hand in thine;
Crying guide me now and ever,
Be my future what it may,
If thy blessed hand but lead me,
It will end in perfect day.

Clouds of woe may gather round me,
Dark and drear my path may be,
Grief may crush, and sorrow wound me,
Only keep me close to thee.
And forbid that when thou comest—
Claiming fruit from all thine own,
I should wither 'neath the sentence,
"NOTHING HERE BUT LEAVES ALONE."

ORIGINAL ESSAYS.

PREACH THE WORD.

Preach the word, be instant in season, out of season, reprove, rebuke, exhort with all long-suffering and doctrine. For the time will come when they will not endure sound doctrine, but after their own lusts shall they heap to themselves teachers, having itching ears.—2 Tim 4; 2-3.

It is not my purpose, in placing the above Scripture at the head of this article, to attempt to make it any plainer, but to call the attention of the reader to the prediction therein contained, and then to ask himself or herself, if the prediction is not being fulfilled in our time, if indeed it has not been often fulfilled heretofore.

"Sound doctrine" appears to become stale to many persons who attend preaching, and many more do now absent themselves from preaching, because, as they say, the preacher runs in the same old channel that he first started in, forgetting on their part, that it is his. the preachers duty, to "preach the word." Others think the preacher is too severe and sarcastic, forgetting again that it is his duty to "reprove and rebuke." Hence many will not attend preaching unless some one can entertain them by their eloquence, or in some peculiar way present, shall I say the truth, or only a part of it? Perhaps the latter manner of expressing the idea, is the more correct one; and then if I apprehend the matter aright, the prediction is fully verified that their lust is gratified, and they have then the "itching" of their "ears" abated for the time at least, ready to have the process repeated again when opportunity affords. But is such preaching and such hearing acceptable with God? All will say, that is another question. This is the question that should most concern us. I have been led into this train of thought in consequence of what I have been recently reading, and of some preaching I have recently heard. Both writers and preachers were making efforts to combat *erroneous preaching*, which is one of the requirements of these degenerate times, demanding something new, that some men's and some women's ears might be tickled, or in other words have the itching of their ears abated.

Such preaching might be comparatively harmless, were they to confine themselves to vain philosophy, but when they lay their hands upon the word of God, and say that such and such portions is not binding upon us, or that it is not correctly translated, especially when it conflicts with their peculiar dogmas, or even go so far as to say that it conflicts with other Scripture, and hence it should not be regarded, then indeed we should be on our guard, and learn to appreciate such portions of Scripture as is found at the head of this article, and others of a similar import, which abound in God's word.

But to come to the point specifically, has been recently deemed proper by some in their disposition, as I must think, to gratify this "*itching ear*" class of hearers,—to lay violent hands upon the Lord's prayer itself. That prayer that we all have been taught in our infancy to lisp, by religious, and even irreligious mothers,—that prayer that the Son of God Himself taught His disciples, when asked to be taught how to pray. It is this undermining of "*sound doctrine*," to which I more particularly alluded to above that those writers and preachers were combatting. What do they say about the Lord's prayer, do you ask? Why they say it does not bind us to use it, it was only enjoined upon the disciples *The Savior only washed his disciples feet*, and none other, hence that only binds them also, and we are exempt. So it would appear at first thought, but how does it look when the light of God's word is reflected upon the subject?

In His commission to His disciples His last words were, "Teaching them to observe all things whatsoever I have commanded you, and lo, I am with you alway, even unto the end of the world." Behold the value of God's word, and the great necessity of preaching it. But say they, it is inconsistent with the teaching of James. The Savior says "Lead us not into temptation," and James says, "God tempts no one, nor can He be tempted." There is no contradiction here, but suppose there was, who should we hear, James in preference to Christ? Every Christian will say, No, for we are not followers of James but of Christ. But I said there was no contradiction The Lord's prayer says, "Lead us not into temptation," James says "God does not tempt any man," nor does Christ say he does, but he does say by implecation, that the Father tempted him. Matt. 4, 1. "Then was Jesus led up of the Spirit into the wilderness to be tempted of the devil." So says Matthew. Knowing his sore trial, he could with propriety teach his disciples to ask their Heavenly Father to exempt them from such fiery trials. The next objection to the Lord's prayer is, that we are required to say "Thy Kingdom come, thy will be done in earth as it is in Heaven." They say His Kingdom has come in earth, hence we should not pray for that we already enjoy. But is it as fully established here as in Heaven? That is the point we are to aim at, then we see the necessity of the petition. Now turn to the Scripture at the head of this article and repeat it, and I imagine you will perceive the value of the Word and the necessity of having it preached.

EMANUEL SLIFER.

PROFANITY.

We are emphatically in the age of profanity, and it seems to us that we are on the topmost current. One can not go through the streets anywhere without having his ears offended by the vilest of words, and his reverence shocked by the most profane use of sacred names. Nor does it come from the old or middle-aged alone, for it is a fact as alarming as it is true, that the younger portion of the community are the most proficient in the degrading habit. Boys have an idea that it is smart to swear, that it makes them manly; there never was a greater mistake in the world. Men, even those who swear themselves, are disgusted with profanity in a young man because they know how, of all bad habits, this clings the most closely and increases with years. It is the most insiduous of habits, growing on one so insensibly that almost before he is aware he become an accomplished curser.

THE WAY TO LIVE.—Ten minutes of weak ripening will plunge a brave heart into the depths of unhappiness as suddenly as a thunderstorm will overcast a clear summer sky.—The only way to live is to cast away troubles and contentions, which cannot be cured by fretting. A thing that is done belongs to the past. In justice to the requirements of the present, and the possibilities of the future, you cannot look back and make yourself wretched over things which cannot be undone.

HE that has no resources of mind is more to be pitied than he who is in want of necessaries for the body; and to be obliged to beg our daily happiness from others bespeaks a more lamentable poverty than that of him who begs his daily bread.

—There is a strong tendency in us all to believe what we desire to be true, and to draw those conclusions to which our inclinations lean.

AN APPEAL

TO THE BRETHREN OF THE FIRST DISTRICT OF VA.

Beloved Brethren: I have thought for some time past of addressing an appeal to you relative to the "Resolutions" we adopted at our District meeting, and as buried thoughts are not of much practical value, we now will send them out through the columns of the PILGRIM.

In these Resolutions we recognized the importance of combining our efforts to more effectually spread the doctrine of the Brethren. We also resolved to appoint a committee of one Deacon to act as our agent in carrying forward this work.

It will be readily admitted that we, as a body, are doing comparatively little in propagating the Gospel. The work rests exclusively on the ministry, unaided by the church. As we are justly opposed to a hireling ministry it becomes a subject of interest how to utilize the power of our lay brethren, and in these "Resolutions" we secured in part the adoption of measures to make that power available. We hope brethren our "Resolves" were adopted with the determined purpose to execute them. Remember good intentions alone will accomplish nothing.

Now much depends on the wisdom of the appointment of the committee whether it will be a success or a failure. In my opinion he should be possessed of the following qualifications:

1st. He should be steadfast in the faith.

2nd. He should be a brother of energetic character and zeal. Brethren have different talents. Some are most excellent in one department of their official duties, while they are utterly disqualified for other services. An active worker, who will not be afraid to stir up the pure minds of the brethren frequently to the importance of casting in their monthly contributions, will accomplish more than a dozen brethren who are indifferent whether anything is done or not. Let such a one be appointed in every congregation, and let him remember that the amount of work he performs will be reported at our next D. M., and that it will be a just measure of the interest he feels in the cause of the conversion of sinners.

At every church meeting throughout the year the subject should be presented to the members and our ministers should advocate the virtue of liberality and press its claims on the church. If this is neglected and the committeeman is incompetent for his task, then that congregation will report "nothing done" next year to the shame and mortification of every lover of Jesus. The brethren also should think this a golden opportunity to help their hard worked preachers, and should cast in abundantly of the means that their Lord has committed to their trust. It is simply ridiculous for a truly converted soul to be content with the contribution of a few odd dimes or quarters to a work fraught with such momentous results. The amount of wealth in the hands of the brethren composing this District would justify the expectation of the contribution of hundreds of dollars and the distribution of thousands of books and pamphlets, preaching the doctrine of the Gospel, and if such a report is made next year, how gladly will it be hailed and welcomed by every lover of the holy cause. We look forward to that report with the most intense solicitude even at this early day, trembling between hope and fear; hope that the work will be a grand success and will reflect credit on the spiritual character of our churches; and fear, that, through negligence, we suffer the stigma and odium of indifference to fall with their blighting effects upon us.

The Elders should make the selection of books with the greatest prudence and foresight. In my opinion books of controversy should be rejected, or if selected, they should be distributed with much caution. I do not wish to be understood as not appreciating the labors of the champions of our cause, who meet the Goliaths of the sects in the fields of debate, but the records of these contests are more efficient in other fields of our mission. Neither should books or pamphlets which are waging aggressive warfare, that is those that are merely attacks on the errors of others, be selected. These are very useful in their sphere but we do not consider this their sphere or field of labor.

Our literature that presents the pure doctrines of the Gospel, that treats of the ordinances and practices of the church, of the apostolical, primitive church as it is represented by the Brethren is that that is particularly suited to the demands of this movement. Without disparaging the labors of others I will suggest that "*Nead's Theology*" will meet our demands as fully as any work within our reach. While it is not considered a work of great demonstrative power and erudition, yet it will meet the requirements of the uneducated most effectually. "Moore's Primitive Baptism" should be disseminated by the hundreds of thousands. It presents the great subject of baptism with such force and ability that much good will result from a general distribution of them. "Trine Immersion" by B. F. Moomaw should also be liberally distributed. It has one objectional feature, however, that will render it inapplicable, measurably, to our wants, and that is, the first part is of a controversial character. Notwithstanding the treatises on the New Birth, on Non resistance, and on the Lord's Supper are of such value that they should not be lost on account of our objection to his discussion on Immersion. There are other writings of value that should be selected. Winchester's Dialogues should be reproduced and a compilation of testimonies, in favor of our practice and in accordance with the Gospel, from the writings of the Fathers would be a work of value. For the present, we might safely risk a few dollars with our Editors for the free distribution of odd numbers of our periodicals. They can be had for postage, doubtless, and they would be glad, no doubt, to rid their offices of all such accumulations in that way.

Again we should offer a premium of a small compensation for the best defense of the various ordinances of the church, such for instance as a defence of Feetwashing, of the Holy Kiss, of Non conformity to the world, of Non-resistance, of Anointing the sick, of wearing the Covering for the Head, of the Lord's Supper, of the Apostolical doctrine of the relation of the Church to the State, &c. A work on this latter subject is of special importance at this time, to define our position on that subject, it should treat:

1st. On the design of governments.

2nd. How far the church is permitted to claim their protection.

3d. The limits of the jurisdiction of both bodies.

These are to be received as simple suggestions. Each of the foregoing should be written so as to be published in pamphlet form, and sent to the secretary of the D. M., B. F. Moomaw, in case the proposed premium is offered. We will not suggest the amount of the premium. Any congregation can advertise the offer and it will be placed to their credit in the annual report.

The publication of these treatise should be deferred until they are examined by competent brethren at our next D. M., and those that are received then, will be considered as the property of the District, and published and distributed at its expense.

The writings of the brethren that I have recommended should be purchased at cost, as the authors have doubtless sold enough to liquidate expenses. No brother should desire to make a speculation out of our association. Vigilant eyes will be watching its interests, and swift retribution will be visited on any brother that will be tempted to try it.

In conclusion, brethren, let us get about the work in earnest. Can we not have an exhibition next year that will show the Brotherhood that we mean business! Let us not embarrass the movement by groundless fears that it is something new, and consequently should be opposed. It may be new to us, but it was not new to the Apostle Paul. He wrote to his brother "by all means to bring the parchments." Parchments were "the skins of certain animals prepared and rendered fit for writing on," and no doubt exists in my mind that those he alludes to contained the writings of the Evangelists and of other brethren, much of which has doubtless been lost. Hence we should make haste to redeem the time already lost, and revive a practice based on such high and unequivocal authority.

If our brethren editors or others feel interested in the business, and can help us with their counsels, this will be their assurance that such help will be acceptable.

Your brother,

D. C. MOOMAW.

Blacksburg, Va.

WHAT ARE YOU DOING?

Yes, my dear friends, what are you doing just now, when almost everybody and every insect is so full of business and of life? Are you who are blessed with means and privileges, doing anything that will improve your minds and affections, anything that will make you feel you are living to be useful in time, and glorious in eternity; anything that will cause the world to feel sad when you are numbered no more with the living? We came not into the world to idle our time away and not be profitable in some way. We are all born to fill some station in life. Let us consider what Christ did for us and what we are doing for Him, and we shall no doubt find ourselves wanting in the discharge of our duty. Look around you, there are your dearest relatives; your friends and neighbors, over whom you have much influence. Are there none of them vulgar and profane? None living lives of idleness, vice and crime? If there are, what are you doing to reclaim and restore them to usefulness and good society, that they may be blessed and God bless you? What answer does your conscience give to these inquiries? If you are not engaged in the service of the Lord, it is time for you to shake off the deadning spell and do something worthy the ambition of immortal spirits that you may be blessed in time and glorious in eternity. The world extends her joys and pleasures to all who desire them, but the joys and pleasures which the world can afford us are of short duration. But the happiness which the Christian experiences, and the joy which animates his heart, are of a durable nature and will reach beyond the gloomy grave. Then, why not be a Christian? why tarry so long? Do you expect to come with less difficulty by waiting awhile? You may be deceived, your destruction may be sudden, it may overtake you by surprise. You now, put far off, the evil day. Thus you will continue to do, 'till death shall come upon you in all its terrors. Wholly unprepared, you will hear the dreadful summons. As it was with the inhabitants of Sodom and Gomorrah, so it will be with you, they were eating and drinking, marrying and giving in marriage and knew not, till the Lord rained upon them brimstone and fire out of Heaven and destroyed them all. Then the best time to make the start is Now, for it is appointed unto man once to die. Knowing this to be a fact, how necessary that we prepare for the solemn change, so that our spirits may go to Him who called us hence. Who among us would not be willing to part with all the vanities of this world for a home in Heaven? Sinner, we ask you to make the start, and you will have Jesus, your best friend, to strengthen and cheer you as you are making your way to Heaven and immortal glory. O, what an animating thought that we can have the privilege of all once meeting again beyond this vale of tears if we love and obey the Lord.

"O blessed day! O glorious hope!
My soul rejoices at the thought,
When in that holy, happy land,
We'll take no more the parting hand."

MOLLIE UMBAUGH.

Collamer, Ind.

HARVEST.

"Six days thou shalt work, but on the seventh day thou shalt rest: in earing time and harvest thou shalt rest." Exo. 34: 21.

Harvest is now at hand and we are in the midst of it, but probably before this will appear in print, it will be past. God has blessed us with a plentiful harvest. He has always blessed us with more than we deserve. This alone should cause us to present unto him a living sacrifice which is our reasonable service.

But in thinking of the present harvest, the mind is carried to the future, when the angel will cry to him that sat on the cloud, "Thrust in thy sickle and reap, for the time is come for thee to reap: for the harvest of the earth is ripe." That will be an important harvest to all of us. We will constitute the fruit of that harvest, we will not then be the reapers as is the case in the present one. The Savior, in the parable, calls the harvest the end of the world, and the reapers are the angels. But we have much to do with sowing the seed, and the growth of it, as well as the preparing of the ground. So then we have an important part to perform. If the farmer neglects any one of these, he will not reap a good harvest.

The seed must be pure. We must be born of that incorruptible seed the word of God. Then will we be good seed or the children of the Kingdom. So then it belongs to us to know what seed we are born of. If the farmer sows seed that does not suit the soil or climate, or is not pure, the loss is not so great but that he can endure it, but he will change his seed the next time. Not so in the harvest of the end of the world. Then let us see well to what seed we are born. Now is the time to judge the seed. We have the detector, the word of God. We must be born of the spirit, which is the word. The Savior said "the words that I have spoken they are spirit and they are life." If the spirit that we are born of don't lead in a strict obedience to that word, we have not the spirit of Christ, and are not the good seed or the children of the kingdom. There is no seed but good seed and tares. The devil sows the tares. Whatever that incorruptible seed, the word of God does not teach, will produce tares if it is sown.

Let us be careful that we don't accept of tares, for they come from the evil one. So then, dear brethren, and sisters, let us watch and pray for the harvest is near at hand, at least with some of us. It would be a lamentable thing if we would have soon to say, "The harvest is past, the summer is ended and we are not saved." But if we are the children of the kingdom (not of the world,) our lot will be a happy one. As God commanded the children of Israel to rest in earing time and in harvest, so we will rest. What a glorious rest! "There remaineth a rest for the people of God." Let us labor for that rest.

H. BEELMAN.

Dillsburg, Pa.

TYPES AND SHADOWS.
SENNACHERIB.

The object of the Mosaic dispensation was to show man's need of a Savior. This is remarkably shown in the miracles of Moses, so frequently inflicting death as the punishment of sin, the typical nature of which may be further noticed in the all wise and often mysterious dispensations of Providence. In a time when king Hesekiah reigned over Judah, Sennacherib, that great king, of Asyria and head of the greatest monarchy then in the world, came up against all the fenced cities of Judah. After he had conquered most of the neighboring countries, he sent Rabshaker, the captain of his host, against Jerusalem, who, in a very proud and scornful manner, insulted Hesekiah and his people, as being sure of victory; and the people were trembling for fear, like lambs before a lion, having sent a blasphemous letter to Hesekiah, which he opened and spreading before the Lord, in the temple, with prayer and tears, entreating him for assistance against the Asyrians, whereupon the prophet Isaiah assured him that God will deliver him and defend that city, as a token of which he gave them this sign: "That the earth for two years successively, should bring forth food of itself from the roots of the old stocks, without their plowing or sowing; and then the third year they should sow and reap and plant vineyards and eat the fruit of them."—2 Kings 19: 29. This is mentioned as a type of what is promised in verses 30 and 31st. "And the remnants that is escaped of the house of Judah, shall yet again take root downward, and bear fruit upward, for out of Jerusalem shall go forth a remnant, and they that escape out of Mount Zion. The zeal of the Lord of hosts shall do this.

The corn springing again after it had been cut off with the sickle, and bringing forth another crop from the roots, represents the church reviving again and flowing like a plant after it had seemingly been cut down past recovery, when the enemies of the church have done their utmost and seem to have gained their point, and have overthrown the Church, so that its being is scarcely visible, but is like a living root hid under ground. There is in it a secret life that will cause it to flourish again, and to take root downward and bear fruit upward. This was now fulfilled, the king of Asyria had already carried captive the ten tribes; and Sennacherib had also taken all the fenced cities of Judah and ravaged the country round about: Jerusalem only remained and Rabshakeh had in his own imagination, already swallowed that up, but God wrought a wonderful deliverance. He sent an angel that, in one night, smote 185,000 in the enemies camp. This great deliverance of Judah from Sennacherib is, like the redemption of the Israelites from the bondage of Egypt, and the deliverance of the Jews the Babylonish captivity,—typical of salvation by Christ: prefiguring the greater and more important deliverance of mankind from the captivity of sin, and their introduction into the heavenly Canaan.

D. NEGLEY.

REMINISCENCE.

Bro. Brumbaughs:—Seeing an article published in No. 23, present volume, written by bro. B. F. Moomaw that should not have appeared without some modification as therein are sentiments expressed transcending the restrictions laid on you editors, again and again at our Annual Meeting. Why the dear bro., who assists in making these decisions sends articles conflicting with said decisions, is a mystery to me. I allude to Sunday Schools. Had he only reference to the abuses of said schools we would not have objected. Will the abuse of a thing make void the good of it? Then we must quit preaching.—But I understand him, in the first place, to class Sunday Schools *indiscriminately* with *Freemasonry.*

The minutes of A. M. in 1868, Art. 14, reads as follows: "*We advise* that where the nature of the case will admit *for brethren to hold Sabbath School* &c., to which I say Amen, and think it is according to Scripture.—See also Art 1st. minutes of 1857 and 1862.

We need not hunt in a corrupted church for the origin of Sabbath Schools, but go back to the days of the Savior. The Jews had their Synagogues—Sabbath Schools—to which they resorted on the Sabbath in order to read the Scriptures, and to have them expounded to the people, and Christ went there, read the Scriptures and taught them on the Sabbath again and again. If the origin is not from Heaven, Christ taught an institution that was of man, and we have a right to follow his example; for no other Sabbath School we would sanction but where the Scripture is read and expounded in its true meaning, and from such a school no evil results can be the consequence. And in such a manner the brethren in Annual Council advised it to be conducted. Bear with me for consistency is a jewel.

Yours in love.

LEONARD FURRY.

New Enterprise, Pa.

ADDITION TO A NOTICE.

By request, I write in addition to that which has been properly written and published, in regard to Mary Noffsinger, who died April 12th, 1873.—

Her maiden name was Ridder. She was born in Ashe county near New River, North Carolina, emigrated with her parents to this county in her young days; was married to Daniel Noffsinger, who died six years ago at the age of seventy-five years; and as no notice has been given of his death we will give it here. He was born in Westmoreland county, near Greensburg, Pa. He also came to this county in his young days, became a member of the church the same day his wife did, and was for years a minister in the church, and in his last years a Bishop. His disease was Apoplexy. From the time of the attack, he lived about three hours. Funeral services by brethren, A. Arbaugh and D. Bowman.

I will now state what the friends particularly desire to know in regard to the old sisters disease. It was a peculiar one. Many people are living who never heard of the like. It was Contraction or Stricture of the Esophagus, the organ through which the food passes to the stomach. For four months it gradually enlarged, impairing, and finally altogether destroying the power to swallow anything, producing death ultimately by starvation.

These parents raised ten children, five sons and five daughters, who are all living yet, the oldest 59 years old, Six are members of the church, one a minister, and one a deacon. We hope the Lord will help, that through the instrumentality of the Gospel, the others may be drawn to Christ before it is too late.

(Visitor please copy.)

ELD. DAVID MURRAY.

Dayton, Ohio.

A LETTER TO A SISTER.

Dear Sister:—Being alone to-day and looking over the columns of the PILGRIM, I saw your name signed to such a hearty admonition to repentance, and to the pressing onward of the Christian, I felt aroused to drop a few lines to you, as we are admonished to exhort one another. Now, as speaking to you on the subject, how are we to press onward? We read where brethren were admonished to leave off the first works, such as laying on of hands &c., and to go on to perfection. We are told to be perfect in good works. I open the Bible and see what good works are. Read St. Luke's Gospel, the 6th chapter, from the 27 to the end of the 49 verse. Heeding these words of love from our dear Redeemer, (as you have described Him to us), will prepare us for the separation which the chapter above named speaks of. Men separate us from their company as evil doers, and speak evil of us for Christ's sake, and we may rejoice, for great is our reward, remembering that this life is but a journey to that land where we shall enjoy all things with joy unspeakable and full of glory. Dear sister, as I intend to go to Canada if it is the Lord's will, to my brother, we may, in all probability, never see each other again in this world. Oh, may we be found faithful loving the Lord above all, who is the creator and preserver of all things, that He may, through mercy, be for us when all men are against us, and gather us home where parting shall not be known, is my prayer.

ELIZA FIKE.

Nankin, Ohio.

Men blush less for their crimes than for their weakness and vanity.

A memory well stored with Scripture, and sanctified by grace, is the best library.

Grace thrives by frequent meditation on portions of God's word. "Let the word of God dwell in you richly."

All politeness is owing to liberty.—We polish one another and rub off the corners and rough corners and rough sides by a sort of amicable collision.

CLOSET PRAYER.

This article inserted in the *Presbyterian* and from the pen of Henrick Johnson, D. D., is richly worth perusal, and we insert it hoping that it may be beneficial to our readers. The writer we think sets forth the subject in the proper light. There is certainly a growing tendency to be too formal in our worship, while individual prayer, that which brings us into direct communion with God is too much neglected. We are commanded to pray *in secret*, and this direct communion with our God is the great antagonistic power against the evils of this life; it should therefore be habitual and frequent:

Every soul needs a closet. True prayer will find one. It is the instinct of the heart thirsting for God. It is the command of the Master—Enter thy chamber. It is the way trodden by Jesus. "When he had sent the multitudes away, he went up into a mountain apart to pray." "He withdrew himself into the wilderness and prayed." "He continued all night in prayer to God." "Sit ye here while I go and pray yonder."

"Cold mountains and the midnight air
Witnessed the fervor of his prayer."

Men are professing to follow Jesus who never think of following him into these solitudes. Men are professing to follow Jesus who, alas! have never found, or at least kept, a closet. The tendency of the age is to outwardness in Christian life—to activities, works, push, stir, doing. God forbid that we should depreciate any true Christian activity. But there is a morbid externalism, which may cut off the very springs and sources of our piety, and leave us smitten with dry rot. The good works may not be done with the spirit of ostentation and with noise of trumpets to be seen of men;" but they may be done in such forgetfulness and neglect of inner life, personal holiness, communion with God, as to rob them, however arduous, and however selfdenying, of all their efficacy and spiritual power.

There is no blast of trumpets in this duty; it attracts no notice, makes no noise. The closet is a still, hidden place, not seen of men; and its duties are secrets with God. But he who thinks he can accomplish very much for God without this source of supply, has yet to learn the very alphabet of Christian efficiency. The closet is where a believer replenishes his stock. It is the secret place where the culture of personal holiness goes on. He enters in, and opens the sources of his heart, and asks God to flood them with his spirit. He shuts the door and communes in spirit with Jesus. He leans upon that bosom, weeps his tears there, sobs out his sorrow for sin, gets his "Go in peace" from his forgiving Lord, washes in his blood again, strengthens his faith, catches something more of his Lord's spirit, fortifies his soul, deepens and widens his spiritual experience of grace power; and when he opens that door and comes forth, he is something better, stronger, purer, humbler for that talk with God in the secrecy of an inner chamber.

Hence the unspeakable, indispensible value of frequent solitude for communion with God; not simply for hurried, ejaculatory, or silent petition, but for thoughtful and even protracted prayer, with posture of devotion and audible expression. Mount, desert, closet, still hour, to what uses have these been ordained! How grand spirits have been erected for heroic work by them! What solemn and precious baptisms they have furnished! What preparations for labor and sacrifice and victory! Jacob at the ford Jabbok, Elijah on the mount, Elisha in the chamber with the dead child, "the door shut on them twain," Daniel in the den of beasts, Jeremiah in the court of the prison, Jonah in the belly of hell, Jesus in Gethsemane; it was the closet, the still hour, the talk face to face with God alone, that gave all these their lofty moods, their might with men, their spiritual victories. It is there the soul touches the unfailing fountain of spiritual supply. There the mountain tops are reached that pierce the clouds and bring down fatness.

We have activities enough; the church never so bristled with good works. The busy hum of our ecclesiastical machinery is heard all over the land. Alas! what meagre and inadequate results. The activities have been with too great self-sufficiency, and without the sufficiency that is of God. Our works need to be vitalized and surcharged with power from on high. The channels of that power are broken hearts. Hearts get broken in the closet; and there and then they pull down the power. Surely it is the voice of the Master to every disciple this day, "Enter into thy closet and shut thy door."

CHRIST.

An aged Chistian was very near the end of his journey. Like Jacob of old, he leaned as it were on the top of his staff, and conversed with children and friends. Length of days, wealth, position, and a loving family had made his life what the world would call a success. A merchant for half a century, failure had never been written against his name. His word was as good as another's bond.

After the active business hours of life's day were over, he spent the eventide in his pleasant home, with his favorite books and papers about him, and cared for by loving hearts and tender hands. Respected of men, and blessed in his household, who shall say, as men count profit and loss, that life to him was not a success.

And yet listen to the testimony of his last hours. "This life is a blank without Christ," were the words spoken to a Christian friend, who stood by his bedside. Resting for a moment on the hilltop, and looking back over the pleasant path that had led him thither, he ascribed all the blessings of the way to Jesus his Lord.—For nearly fifty years an earnest disciple of the Master, he could say as his eyes grew dim and strength failed, "What have I in heaven but Thee, and what is there to be desired beside Thee." What now to him are the houses and lands and stocks? Is not his Redeemer everlasting riches? Did He not tell of the many mansions in his Father's Kingdom, prepared for the faithful? What to him in this solemn hour, is the respect and trust of men if the Lord shall only say to his waiting soul, "Well done good and faithful servant."

What indeed, in comparison, are children beloved, and friends however dear, if Jesus the conqueror of death, makes the valley light with his presence?

O, to pass from life into the shadows of the grave without Him, the Christ, would be utter emptiness and void. The soul reaching there for help, finds that the deeds and titles, notes and bonds, which certify earthly possessions are worth no more than so many blanks.

But to this dying believer the world was not a blank, for Christ, the brightness of the Father's glory, filled it with his all sufficient presence.

So, as all earthly scenes vanished and faded away in the mists of death, a look of glad surprise, as if the spirit had caught a glimpse of the glories beyond the river, was impressed on the countenance of the departing saint. "Let me die the death of the righteous."

GENERAL INTELLIGENCE.

THE prospects for the Altona Church is pretty fair. All that is needed is a little more liberality on the part of those who think they can do nothing.

GEORGE WINANT of York Springs, Adams Co., Pa., has lately been elected to the ministry in the Upper Conawago Church.

THE PRESBYTERIANS of Huntingdon, Pa., have voted free pews in their new Church, soon to be completed at that place. This is a move in the right direction and, no doubt, will insure larger congregations than would otherwise be had.

ELD. J. S. FLORY is now on a trip through the West. Colorado seems to be *the place* where they are locating a colony. He seems to be enjoying the trip hugely and, no doubt, is keeping his eyes open. The last account we had of him, he was at the Teller House in Central City, Col.

J. B. of Springfield District, Ind., says: "Our Spring Lovefeast came off on the 28th of June, and as I saw Christ's children drawing near and the multitude of spectators my heart was made glad. It was a rich feast, thus to meet together with brethren and sisters in the Lord and to partake of the broken body of our divine Master. We feel especially thankful to the ministering brethren who came and labored for us."

FROM an exchange we are informed of a very destructive storm occuring lately in the neighborhood of Covington and Dayton Ohio. It is reported as the most terrible that ever occurred in the country, destroying thousands of dollars worth of grain, which was yet ungathered and millions worth of property. Will be glad if some of our readers will send us a true acount of it.

ELD. JOHN KNISLEY of Union Church, Ind., after sending his greetings to the household of faith, says: "Our harvest is good. Wheat is very well filled but not all cut yet, (July 11.) The last of June and the first few days of July were very wet and the wheat badly blown down which makes it hard to cut, and much will be left on the field. Everything seems to be in a prosperous condition and the health of the neighborhood is good."

CONTEMPLATED PERSECUTIONS OF THE CHINESE.—San Francisco has done a very contemptible thing in legalizing the persecution of the Chinese. The object is to drive them out of the city. To this end it is ordered that when a Chinese offender, or one charged with an offense, is incarcerated in jail, his que be shaved off; that a special tax of $60 per annum be levied upon Chinese laundries; and finally that the Chinese dead shall not be removed for interment in their native land. The tax they could and would bear, but as the other two measures involve, to the Chinese mind, perpetual dishonor in this world and perdition in the next, they are effective in driving out these harmless and valuable laborers. This is a cowardly persecution of laborers.

A terrible earthquake occurred June 29th in the neighborhood of Verona producing the most disastrous results, and causing great loss of life and property. Upwards of one hundred persons perished.

The shocks were of the most violent character, and producing the greatest alarm at Verona and the surrounding country for miles. On the first warning of the disaster the people left their houses with the greatest haste and ran into the streets. Others forsook the city and fled to the country for safety. Buildings were shaken to their foundations and many fell into ruins, burying their occupants in the pile or crushing and killing those who happened to be in the streets beneath. Many fine buildings have thus been destroyed, the loss of which it is at present impossible to estimate.

THE progress of Romanism in England is becoming so rapid as should excite alarm among Anglo American Protestants. The following list of distinguished converts from the Protestant faith would indicate the classes of society in which that faith is in least easy keeping, Dr. Maning, Archbishop of Westminster; the Marquis of Bute: the Earls of Oxford, Kingsborough, Denbigh, Dunraven, Granard, Pembroke, Buchan; Miss Gladstone, sister of the Right Hon. W. E. Gladstone; Miss Stanly, sister of the Dean of Westminster; and the Rev. W. H. Wilberforce, brother of the present Bishop of Winchester. It is said that there are two hundred Roman Catholic priests who were at one time clergyman of the church of England.

Not only these, but the Queen has it is said recently appointed Cardinal Cullen and Archbishop Manning to the intimate political relation of members of the Privy Council. They hold office during the life of the sovereign. The Catholics of Doublin also demand a University to be conducted entirely on Catholic principle, and to receive the patronage and emoluments of the government.

PROGRESS OF METHODISM IN NEW YORK.—At a late meeting of the Methodist Preacher's Association, the most noteworthy part of the proceedings was the reading of some statistics concerning the progress of Methodism in New York city from the time it began its work here in 1766 down to 1870, contrasting its condition with that of other denominations and its ratio of increase to population. In 1768 the First Methodist Episcopal church in America was built in John street, New York, on the site of the church which now stands there. The population in that year was 18,000. In 1790 the Forsyth street church was built, and in 1800 what is now known as the Seventh street church was erected. From that time onward Methodism grew apace. But its golden period was from 1835 to 1860. Its relation to the population between 1768 and 1870 shows an increase of Methodism up to 1860 and a considerable decline from then to 1870. Statistics of other denominations showed that the Baptists had in 1870 thirty-eight churches or one to every 24,000 of the inhabitants. The Methodists and Roman Catholics have about the same proportion, while the Presbyterians have one for every 18,000, and the Episcopalians one for every 13,000.

Youth's Department.

SPEAK GENTLY.

It is not so much what you say
 As the manner in which you say it;
It is not so much the language you use
 As the tones in which you convey it.

"Come here!" I sharply said,
 And the baby cowered and wept;
"Come here!" I cooed, and he looked and smiled,
 And straight to my lap he crept.

The words may be mild and fair,
 Or the tones may pierce like a dart;
The words may be soft as the summer air,
 Or the tones may break the heart.

For words but come from the mind,
 And grow by study and art;
But the tones leap forth from the inner self,
 And reveal the state of the heart.

Whether you know it or not,
 Whether you mean or care,
Gentleness, kindness, love and hate,
 Envy and anger are there.

ABOUT HARVEST.

It is so extremely warm, that we did hope "Uncle Henry" would be around with something good for our young readers, but we suppose as harvest only comes once a year, he is so busy engaged in laying in store for himself and little ones, that he has not time to write. This is all right and we can easily excuse him, as he no doubt thinks that editors have as much time to write as he has. Well, this may be so, but we have so many things to attend to and think about, that it is hard for us to collect our thoughts enough to write an article unless we compose it of the many jots that are now popping into our mind as we pass along.

Twelve months ago we were in the midst of harvest, just as we now are, but it seems to us we hear many say, "but with us things are greatly changed. Last harvest, Willie Eddie, Susie and Nellie, were happy and jolly prattlers in our little groups, but long ago they have sickened and died and our homes are now all quiet and never so sad." Yes they are gone. You see, the Lord's harvest is ripening all the time. They were little sheaves, fully ripe and therefore were gathered. You are now growing and perhaps ripening for the harvest. The Lord's reapers are out because the Master says, "see, the harvest is already here, thrust in your sickles and reap."

But you ask, "Does he not reap any until they are ripe?" No, not one. They must all be ripe, but the trouble is, some are worth nothing when they are ripe. Little boys and girls are all expected to bring good fruit, but some become naughty by being disobedient to parents, tell stories and finally steal. Then it is that they are reported unfruitful, but he says, spare a little while longer and then if they bear not fruit, cut them down. After this is done and still no fruit, then they are ripe for the reaper and will be cut down because they will not bear fruit. Are there any such among our readers? If there are, look out for the reaper because you will surely be cut down and cast away. The ground cannot be cumbered with things that will not be of any use. The good die because they have lived their time of usefulness and the bad die, because they have wasted their time and will never become useful.

Just across the way there is a public house having on it the usual sign "Hotel." This formerly meant a whiskey shop or a place where boys are trained for the penitentiary or gallows, but we are glad to say, in this case, it is a place to entertain strangers—but this is not what we intended saying. The other day some little boys undertook to spell this sign, and as it is not divided into syllables they commenced spelling; h-o-t, hot, e-l, el hot-el, and strange as it may appear, one of them supplied another h, and pronounced it hot-hel. That boy had learned something from the character of that sign. It does convey ideas and some that are not very pleasant either.

Some time ago a father passed in and out of a door over which this sign was placed until he became a drunkard, when he abused and ill-treated the wife of his bosom, a son learning from his fathers conduct, became angry and shot his father. That father is now dead, the son is sent to prison for life, while a widowed mother and disgraced children are left to mourn their sad fate. Such, dear young friends are the fruits of evil doing. They were ripe for the harvest, but not fit to be gathered into the Lord's garner. Then, prepare yourselves for the harvest. It will and must come, and it will be good or bad, just as you make it.

NOW.

If we were to give you a motto to go through life with, one that would stand you for warning and counsel in any strait in which you might find yourselves, we would give it in this one word, "Now."

Dont' waste your time and your strength and your opportunities by always meaning to do something—*do it!* Only weakness comes of indecision. Why, some people have so accustomed themselves to dawdling along from one thing to another that it realy seems impossible for them to squarely make up their minds to anything. They never quite know what they mean to do next. Their only pleasure seems to consist in putting things off as long as possible, and then dragging slowly through them, rather than to begin anything else.

Don't live a single hour of your life without doing exactly what is to be done in it, and going straight through it from beginning to end, Work, play, study whatever it is, take hold at once, and finish up squarely and cleanly, and then to the next, without letting any moments drop out between. It is wonderful to see how many hours these people contrive to make of a day; it is as if they picked up the moments that the dawdlers lost; and if you ever find yourself where you have so many things pressing that you hardly know how to begin, let me tell you a secret; Take hold of the very first one that comes to hand, and you find the rest all fall into file and follow like a company of well drilled soldiers; and though work may be hard to meet when it charges in a squad, it is easily vanquished when brought into line. You may have seen the anecdote of the man who was asked how he accomplished so much in life. "My father taught me," was the reply, "when I had anything to do to go and do it." There is the secret—the magic word, "Now!"

THOU GOD SEEST ME.

A little girl who had been disobedient, was reproved by her mother for bad behavior, and reminded that God saw her when she was naughty, and that He did not love disobedient children. She was told, too, that it was said in the Bible, "Children obey your parents."

"God cant' see me because the blind is down," said the little offender, imagining that because the blind was drawn down inside the house, it being evening, therefore the eye of God could not be on her.

This was the idea of a child scarcely three years of age, but I fear there are some other boys and girls, two or three times as old, who sometimes when they are doing that which they know is wrong conceal themselves somewhere or other, thinking that no one is looking at them.

They forget it is written in the Bible, "Can any hide himself in secret places that I cannot see him? saith the Lord." Endeavor to recollect that you are continually in the presence of Almighty God, and bear in mind that short but important text which every little reader has heard. "Thou God seest me." wherever you go, it will, I doubt not, keep you from doing that which is wrong when you are placed in temptation.

Our duties are like the circles of a whirlpool, and the innermost circle is home. The road to home happiness is over the stepping-stones which lie above the brook of daily discomforts.

In youth, prepare for old age.

The Weekly Pilgrim.

JAMES CREEK, PA., July 22. 1873.

BAPTISM.

CONTINUED.

In our last, we promised to next notice "indoor baptism," on the passages of scripture that is claimed as being favorable to such baptisms, but shall first notice the case of the Eunuch. We wish it understood that we do not review this sermon on account of its merits, but because it contains the arguments generally used against immersion.

The first argument in this case is, that the country through which they were passing was a desert and therefore, not a sufficient amount of water to immerse. Such arguments, at once show a great want of testimony against baptism by immersion. With God there is no impossibilities and men seek after them, only when they wish to have an excuse for disobedience. If immersion was as agreeable to the carnal mind as is sprinkling, the validity of it, never would have been made a question. It is the cross they wish to avoid. He now asks; "And where did the Ethiopian get his idea of baptism? The record does not show that Philip said a word to him about baptism,"claiming that he (the Eunuch) got it from the passage which he had been reading from Isaiah. Is this not strange that Philip in preaching Christ, should say nothing about baptism? Does not the word say; "then Philip opened his mouth and began at the same Scripture, and preached unto him Jesus?" If Philip or any other man could have preached Jesus or the plan of salvation to enquiring sinners without saying a word about baptism, then we will yield the argument in this case. If we have reasonable objections against baptism or immersion, why not produce them and avoid such miserable sophistry? To think of Philip preaching Jesus without saying a word about baptism is extremely ridiculous and shows a lack of honesty of purpose.

In speaking of "into" and "out of" we have the following:

"But as we wish to be very liberal, we will allow you your "into" and "out of," and will only remind you that into is not under; and remember, it is not said, that the Eunuch was any farther in than Philip. If eis puts the Eunuch under it must put Philip under also; for it applies equally to both. "They both went down into, eis, the water;" and there is no more proof that the Eunuch was under the water than that Philip was."

That is certainly very liberal to grant such admissions, but to inform Baptists that "into is not under" is quite a favor. Such bits of wisdom indicate extreme shrewdness. We do not suppose that immersionists ever thought of such shallow reasoning. We do not claim into, eis, puts them under the water, but it puts them both in the water and in a position ready for baptism. But he says: "There is no more proof that the Eunuch was under the water than that Philip was, but the record says: "and they went down, both Philip and the Eunuch; and he (Philip) *baptized* (immersed) *him*." Such reasoning is equivalent to saying, "there is no more proof that the Eunuch was baptized than that Philip was," But the record is too plain to admit of such reasoning, therefore we dismiss it as illogical and void of truth.

We will now notice some of his In Door Baptisms. We will first notice that of Cornelius. This is taken, because the place where they were baptized is not designated. The record says, "And he commanded them to be baptized in the name of the Lord." Peter did not even baptize them but commanded those who were with him to baptize them, without saying anything about the place where the ceremony was to be performed. In common parlance, if I was commanded to wash something no matter where I was, at the time the command was given, I would go to a place where it could be done after the usual manner of washing. Just so, it is altogether reasonable to suppose, did they who were to baptize (immerse) those on whom the Holy Ghost had fallen. If this could have been performed in the house, we have no objections to offer. Independent of the meaning of the term *baptized*, this circumstance gives nothing in favor of either mode but when, in connection with it, we consider the fact that baptized means immersed, the whole weight of the argument is thrown on our side.

The baptism of the Jailor is also claimed as an indoor baptism. After the usual explanation of the inner and outer prison and the Jailor's house, all being under the same roof, he speaks of the impossibility of Paul, in the midnight hour, taking them away off to some river "among the mountains of snowy Thrace," for the sake of immersing them. This says he, would not have been the easy yoke and light burden of which our, Savior speaks. On the same hypothesis it might be argued that it was real ugly and ungrateful of our Savior to allow his followers to be buffetted and persecuted as they were, and even Paul, on the present occasion, to be cast into prison and his feet placed in the stocks. Such a process is certainly attended with much more mental and physical suffering than simply to be immersed. Yet we find to them the yoke was so easy that they were made to sing praises to God. Such arguments seem very trifling, yet they are the best they have to offer.

Without noticing the argument any further, we will review the record as it stands as found in Acts 16: 9-34. From the 19 to the 25 ver. we have the account of their apprehension, beaten with stripes, given in charge of the Jailor and placed in the stocks in the inner prison, 25 verse, Paul and Silas sang praises to God.

26. The earthquake, opening of doors and loosening of the prisoners bands.

27. The keeper is awakened and seeing the doors open, thinks of destroying himself.

28. Paul seeing that it was all the providence of God, calls upon him to do himself no harm

29. The keeper calls to some members of the family, for a light and then went in and fell down before Paul and Silas.

30 Makes the important query, how "to be saved."

31. The answer given, "Believe on the Lord Jesus Christ."

32. They preached unto him and all that were in his house, the word of the Lord.

33. He (the jailor) took them and washed their stripes, and was baptized, and all his house. Now, from the record, we come to the following rational conclusion; At the beginning of the narrative, the jailor and family was in one part of the house and Paul and Silas in another part of the same house, or the innermost prison.

After the miraculous intervention of God, the Jailor procures a light and goes to Paul and Silas and enquires for the way of salvation (29 30 verses).

The Jailor then takes Paul and Silas out of the prison into his own part of the house and there they (Paul and Silas) spake unto him, and all that were in his house, the word of the Lord. (31, 32).

The Jailor then took them (Paul and Silas) and by them, were baptized also, and all those of his house, to whom they preached the word of the Lord. (33.)

In the above, it is not said where he took them, but the next verse (34) says: *and when they brought them into his house*. This is *bonafide* evidence that they were taken out of the house, and as the record says they were baptized, equivalent to immersed, they were undoubtedly taken to a place where it could be performed according to the established formula, as given by God and practiced by Christ and His followers.

After a careful reading of the passages referred to, it must be seen by every candid mind that men are hard put too for evidence to prop up a groundless cause. There is not a single passage in the New Testament to prove that baptism was ever performed in a house, or in doors, and if there was, it would not, by any means, prove that they were not immersed. Our space is too limited to follow the subject further at present, but will conclude in our next by noticing, who are subjects for baptism.

ANNUAL MEETING REPORT.

In last weeks issue, we concluded our report of the proceedings, and from the general expression, so far, and the demand for it, we conclude that it is giving general satisfaction. Notwithstanding our circulation has been increased a little over 200 since the A. M., we are still prepared to accommodate several hundred more with the numbers containing the report. We will now send the PILGRIM to the end of the year, from the time the subscriptions are received, with all the numbers containing the report of A. M., for 75 cents, or we can still supply some twenty subscribers with complete sets at $1.50. Keep the good work moving. Harvest is now about over and very few will refuse to give 75 cents for so much good reading matter. Agents sending to the amount of $5.00 and over, can deduct 10 per cent for the trouble, or divide it among the subscribers as they see proper.

HYMN BOOKS.

As our patrons are becoming impatient, we must make an explanation. Some three weeks before Annual Meeting we ordered a lot of Hymn Books, but none came. At A. M, we saw brother Quinter and, if we remember rightly, he promised to attend to it on his return——but just now, we are informed that the books have arrived, and all orders will be filled forthwith. Please excuse the delay, as we done the best we could, and, no doubt, Bro. Quinter did the same.

ANNOUNCEMENT.

Please publish through the PILGRIM that the Church of the Cerro Gorda district, Ill., have their Communion Meeting on the 27 and 28 of September 1873, and also the District Council Meeting of Southern Ill, will be held at the same place on Monday 29. It is desired that the churches of Southern Ill be fully represented, and a hearty invitation is given, especially to the ministering brethren to be with us on the occasion.

These coming by Rail-road will stop off at Cerro Gorda. By order of the Church.

JOHN METZGAR
JOSEPH HENRICKS.

MONEY LIST.

Daul Eller	$0.80	A Lichtenw'r's	2.10
Wm. Angle	6.75	Jacob Gault	2.25
L. C. Oaks	2.40	A J Correll	9.30
H. F. Nair	2.25	Daul Keller	4.25
Saml Chambers	2.60	S C Showelter	.50
Isaac B. Trostle	1.50	S E Miller	1.00
T. M. Kauffman	1.50		

Correspondence.

Notes of Travel.

BY J. S. FLORY.

CHEYENNE, WYOMING TERRITORY, July 2, '73.

June 28, I wrote from Omaha; left there by the U. P. R. R. at 2 p. m., and arrived at Grand Island, a town 155 miles west of Omaha. At 9 o'clock p. m., next day, Sunday, went to the Episcopalian Church. The minister wore a large white robe that extended to the floor. The ceremonies were tedious, the *lecture* good, but short, the money feature prominent, the display of fashion and meek righteousness not lacking in any wise. A. M. attended Sunday School at the Baptist Church, which was lively, and would be called by many, spirited. At the close of the school a Methodist minister held forth for a while after their ordinary manner. The society in most respects, we concluded, was about the same as in the East. At 7:30 p. m., we were again aboard the train, and at 9 o'clock were at Gibbon, 29 miles further West, where, next morning, we procured a spring-wagon and buggy sufficient for the party to take a look at the country. We went about ten miles north of the R. R., found some fine lands, plenty of which is open for homestead claims, some within five and six miles of the R. R. At noon we stopped by a stream and done good service to our lunch which we had carried with us, after which we took a stroll over the prairies that looked like the illimitable ocean. With a glass we could see timber at a distance. There were signs of rain, so we turned our course for town. One of our party got a shot at an Antelope, another, killed a few Plover—came in all right except a slight wetting by a shower. Owing to a heavy rain the train was delayed 12 hours, so we did not leave Gibbon until July 1st at 8 o'clock, when we set out and passed over some fine country, and some not very attractive, where we saw numerous Antelopes, and Prairie dogs skipping about, and thousands of cattle grazing.

The Platte river is a wide sluggish stream, the bridge across the north fork is over a mile in length. Sydney, 414 miles west of Omaha, is a beautiful spot, at which point quite a number of U. S. soldiers are stationed. At 2 o'clock at night we arrived at this point, 516 miles west of Omaha. Here is the Junction of a R. R. running to Colorado, and is quite a stirring town, a number of Troops are stationed here also. From this point we can see the snow-capped mountains. The air is pure and bracing. It is very healthy here. We expect to be off in a short time for Colorado, so no more at this time.

GREEN CITY, WELD CO, COLORADO. July 3, '73.

Having leisure, I will pen a few lines from this locality. We left Cheyenne yesterday at 2 p. m., and traveled for 50 miles due South, in this Territory, parallel with the snowy range of mountains, the tops of which are covered with perpetual snows. Our travel, to near the town of Greely, was through a rugged and almost barren region, but the moment we were ushered across the irrigating canal, near Greely, we were much surprised at the contrast. I remarked it was like jumping from a desert into a garden. Beautiful fields of wheat, oats, &c., lay upon our right and left, and we halted at the depot and found ourselves in a flourishing town situated on the waters of the south Platte. Here we were met, according to previous arrangement, by Mr. J. A. Pace, and T. M. Barnar of this place, who kindly took us to the town of Evans, three miles distant, where we remained until this morning, when we were brought in conveyances, to this town, 27 miles from Evans.

As the agricultural interests of this Territory depend, in a great measure, upon irrigation, I will give you some details touching the subject. The water has to be conveyed from the river by canals around at the base of the bluffs or high lands and from the main canal, latteral canals are made that conduct the water to the farms, and small ditches carry it over the farms and gardens as it is needed. There are rains in the Spring that generally give the crops a good start, then two to four lettings on of water generally are sufficient to insure a crop. The soil is composed of coarse sand and loam, and at first appearance looks as though it was unproductive, and nothing but actual observation could have persuaded me it was so productive as it is. This country is laid down on our "school-day" Geography, as a great desert and at first sight it has that appearance, but now it is proven that much of it is susceptible of being made the most productive and valuable lands in the West. Irrigation is yet in its infancy but it has practically proven to be a success. As a proof we mention some instances how sections improve and towns spring up where irrigation is available. The town of Greely is only three years old and contains 1800 inhabitants and a prosperous community surrounding it. Evans, three miles distant, is a town of 600 inhabitants and seems to be flourishing. This town, Green City, is only 11 months old and contains about 25 houses, some of them spacious residences, and a population of 300. A more energetic and prosperous colony I think will be hard to find. What they have done has been accomplished under some disadvantages unknown to other colonies one of which is, they had all their lumber to haul 27 miles, being situated that distance from the Railroad, but will have one soon. They have also, in the few months mentioned, constructed a main canal 17 miles long, (have yet 6 miles to construct), at a cost of 12 to 15 thousand dollars. There is one fill on the canal 740 ft long, 25 feet high, base 100 feet wide, and 25 feet wide at the top, with a plank flume the entire length. This fill alone could not be made for less than $3,000. The canal will inclose about 10,000 acres. This colony bids fair to be very prosperous. How can it be otherwise, where there is manifest such an energetic spirit as is here, and controlled by such men as Mr. Pace and *Mr.* Barnar, of Va., Dr. White of Md., and others.

As to the great productiveness of the soil there is no doubt. Reliable statistics show that one hundred and fifty tons of beets have been raised to the acre. The average yield of wheat, in the Territory, is 27 bushels to the acre, 75 to 90 per acre have been raised, oats about the same, weighing 45 pounds to the measured bushel, cabbage 60 pound to the head, squashes 150 to 200 pounds apiece. Grass yields enormous crops. It is not so good for corn, but yet good corn can be raised. The elevation here is about 5,000 feet higher than at Omaha. As a stock country, it is hard to surpass; for dairy business it is excellent indeed. As one remarked here "the crowning glory of Colorado is its healthiness of climate," which must be enjoyed in order to have a proper idea of its beauty and exhilarating influence. There is but little sickness here. I have been creditably informed that in one of those colonies of 9,000 inhabitants, there were but two deaths in the last twelve months, and they were invalids when they came here. Many invalids that come here are now enjoying good health. The country is fast settling up and in every respect improving more rapidly than any other Territory in the bounds of the N. American Continent. The mineral resources of Colorado are immense, and there being so many working in the mines gives an excellent market for everything raised here. As to the society here, it is good, and well deserves the term, first class. In this respect, many who come here are surprised. The majority are persons of refinement and religiously inclined, sociable and courteous. Politics are seldom mentioned. King alcohol has a poor show here, in this town, such a thing as a saloon or dram-shop is not known, a drunken man is seldom seen. In matters of education, but few sections of country have more flattering prospects than Colorado, a large majority of the public lands being reserved for educational purposes. Teachers must pass a critical examination before they can teach. With all the good reports I had heard of this Territory, I must say I was more favorably impressed than I expected.

WINAMAC, IND., June 27, '73.

Dear brethren of the Pilgrim:—I now drop you a few lines, agreeably to your wishes, in regard to church news. We, the brethren and sisters of the Winamac district, held our Communion meeting on the 14 of June, commencing at 10 a. m., and continued next day till noon. We believe that many good impressions were made by the preaching of the word and the practicing of the ordinances of the Lord's house.

The following ministering brethren were with us: John Knisley, A. Appleman, A. Eisenhour and W. G. Cook from Union District. David Rupel from Pine Creek and J. S. Snowberger of Monticello, all of Ind. The brethren labored zealously for our every good and we were much built up, for which we tender our grateful acknowledgements. We also held a choice for one speaker and one deacon which resulted as follows: Benjamin Bowsher was called to the ministry, and Jacob Bookover to the deaconship, and your unworthy servant was forwarded to the eldership.

Yours in Christ,
D. R. FREEMAN.

MEMORIUM.

In memory of Christian Miller, whose obituary notice appeared in PILGRIM, No. 17. By the request of some of her friends, I will try and give a sketch of her life. She was born in 1793, in Hampshire Co., of late, Mineral Co., W. Va. She was the daughter of Elder Daniel Arnold and was married to Abraham Miller and moved to Augusta Co, Va., and there raised a family of 11 children, 10 are yet living. She left 67 grandchildren, 53 living, and 29 great-grand-children, 27 living, numbering 107 in all. She was a widow 26 years to the day, and was a member about 57 years. Her late illness was protracted, which she bore with patience and resignation. She was not known to murmur, and would smile at the thought of the time when the change would come. She enjoyed the esteem of all, and died as she lived, without an enemy, with a bright hope of a better world.

S. N. WINE.

Dear Pilgrim:—On June 29 and 29 the brethren of the Desmoines Valley Church, celebrated the Lord's Supper. We had a good meeting, and have reason to believe that the Lord was with us. Three souls were added to the church by baptism, and we think that many more were seriously impressed with the necessity of regeneration and "holiness of life." But how apt our carnal minds are to wait "for a more convenient season." The brethren also held a choice for one minister and two deacons. The lot fell upon brother Samuel Gouchnour for minister, and brethren John Mathias and Jacob Eshleman for deacons.

Yours in love,
D. E. BRUBAKER.

DIED.

SLAGLE.—On June 22, '73, near Pemberton, Shelby Co, O., Elnora, youngest daughter of John W. and Mary C. Slagle, aged 5 mos. and 21 days. Funeral preached by the Rev. Ferguson, from St. Luke 18: 16.

NICHOLAS TRAPP.

FIKE.—In the Mexico Church, Ind., on the 29th of June, 1873, sister *Barbara*, wife of Bro. Jacob Fike, aged 58 years, 1 mos. and 19 days.

She leaves a husband and many friends to mourn their loss. Funeral by J. Fisher and others from 2: 29 chap. [illegible] to a large concourse of people.

J. H. L[illegible]

SNYDER.—In Union Church, Marshall Co., Ind., July 9, '73, Catharine, wife of Adam Snyder, aged 20 years, 8 months and 1 day. She leaves a husband and many kind friends to mourn their loss. She was married about one year. Funeral by the writer.

JOHN KNISLEY.

BOWMAN.—In the Cooks Creek Congregation, near Harrisonburg, May 30, '73, the well known and aged brother John Bowman. On Sunday June 1st, his remains were taken to the graveyard near the meeting-house, and committed to the tomb. The occasion was improved by brethren Isaac Long and others from [illegible] to a large and attentive congregation.

He leaves a large number of children, grand-children and great grand-children, and many sympathizing friends, who mourn the loss of a father, a grand and brother. He [illegible] example worthy of imitation. He was in his [illegible] year.

S. N. WINE.

BOOK NOTICES.

In this department we will notice such NEW BOOKS, as may be sent us by publishers, that are in harmony with the character of our work. A. B. Brumbaugh, M. D., Huntingdon Pa., literary editor.

GERMAN BOOKS.

As is well known, our Church the Brethren was, and still is, largely of the German element, yet, of late years, the German language is rapidly being displaced by the English. This is much regretted by a large number of our people who think, and rightly too, that the language should be retained. The trouble consisted in not having it taught in our public schools. We are glad to learn that of late, public sentiment has been changed in favor of the German and is now being substituted for some of the other languages and even in the great seats of learning the question of substituting it for that of Greek has been gravely discussed.

Another impediment in the way of study of German was a want of proper rudimentary text books. This want is now fully supplied in Ahn's Rudimentary German Series, published by Mr. Steiger, which consists of the following books:

AHN'S First German Book. By Dr. P. Henn. Exercises in reading, writing, spelling, translation, and conversation. Printed in bold type, and containing a very large amount of German Script. Designed for the two lowest grades.) Boards $0.25.

AHN'S Second German Book. By Dr. P. Henn. (Exercises in writing, reading, translation, and conversation. Containing much German Script. A sequel to the First German Book. With Paradigms and Vocabularies of all German and English words occurring in both these books.) Boards $0.45.

These two books together form:

AHN'S Rudiments of the German Language. By Dr. P. Henn. (With vocabularies. Edition of 1873.) Boards $0.65.

Key to AHN'S Rudiments of the German Language. By Dr. P. Henn. Boards $0.25.

We have received and given the above works a very careful examination and have no hesitancy in pronouncing them the best of their class that ever came under our notice. They lead the scholar so gradually, and the words and sentences used are so simple and familiar that it makes the study of German both easy and pleasant, even without the aid of a teacher. Mr. Steiger publishes a number of other German works which, for the accommodation of our patrons, we will notice when received. Any of the books will be sent at the annexed prices by addressing, E. STEIGER,
Nos. 22 & 24, Frankfort Street, N. Y.

TWICE CROWNED, is the title of a book published by Claxton Remson & Co. of Philadelphia, giving in detail, in the form of a story, many incidents in the reign of Queen Mary sometimes called "Bloody Mary." The story opens during the closing months of the peaceful reign of King Edward VI of England; gives details of the fate of the martyr, Lady Jane Grey—the ten days of royalty—followed by that of Queen Mary with its cruelties, persecutions and martyrdoms; the dark fiendish plottings of Gardenier and Bonner, bearing the sacred titles of Bishop yet the "master spirits" of those dark days and that reign of terror; and the commencement of the reign of Queen Elizabeth.

The *Twice Crowned Queen* was Lettice Kenworthy, daughter of the lodge keeper of the Earl of Carrington; first crowned "May Queen," and again, four years afterward, amidst the "fires of Smithfield" her second crowning, this time with the crown of glory.

Let the young of America beware and know where they stand—for simple Gospel Truth or dark corrupting error, which? And as they read these historical facts may they cherish more devoutly the blessings they enjoy, and rejoice in the liberty wherewith Christ has made us free." Price $1.50.

INFANT DIET.—A paper read before the Health Association of the city of New York, by A. Jacobi, M. D., Clinical Professor of Diseases of Children, College of Physicians and Surgeons, New York.

There are few subjects upon which parents so greatly need more knowledge and careful, serious, thought than that of infant Diet. We advise every parent, and every person entrusted with the care of infants to procure and carefully read this little book. Published by G. P. Putnam's Sons, New York. For sale at the PILGRIM Office. Price 12 mo paper, 50 cts.

GOOD BOOKS.

A large number of our patrons are receiving our books as noticed below, as premiums, and express themselves highly pleased with them. Others who are not agents, have enquired whether we keep them for sale. We have now made arrangements with Mr. Well's to furnish any of their publications post paid at publishers prices. Orders for books must be accompanied with the cash, and plain directions for sending them.

How to read Character, Illus.	Price, $1.25
Combe's Moral Philosophy,	1.75
Constitution of Man. Combe,	1.75
Education. By Spurzheim.	1.50
Memory—How to Improve it,	1.50
Mental Science, Lectures on,	1.50
Self-Culture and Perfection.	1.50
Combe's Physiology, Illus.	1.75
Food and Diet. By Pereira,	1.75
Natural Laws of Man,	.75
Hereditary Descent,	1.50
Combe on Infancy,	1.50
Sober and Temperate Life.	.50
Children in Health—Disease,	1.75
The Science of Human Life,	3.50
Fruit Culture for the Million,	1.00
Saving and Wasting.	1.50
Ways of Life—Right Way,	1.00
Footprints of Life.	1.25
Conversion of St. Paul,	1.00

Hand-book for Home Improvement: comprising "How to Write," "How to Talk," "How to Behave," and "How to do Business," in one vol. 2.25.

Trine Immersion

TRACED

TO THE APOSTLES.

The SECOND EDITION is now ready for delivery. The work has been carefully revised, corrected and enlarged.

Put up in a neat pamphlet form, with good paper cover, and will be sent, post-paid, on the following terms: One copy, 25 cts; Five copies, $1.10; Ten copies, $2.00. 25 copies, $4.50; 50 copies, $8.50; 100 copies, $16.00.

Address, J. H. MOORE.
Urbana, Champaign co., Ill.

Oct 22.

DYMOND ON WAR.

An inquiry into the Accordancy of War, with the Principles of Christianity, and an examination of the Philosophical reasoning by which it is defended. With observations on some of the causes of war and on some of its effects. By Jonathan Dymond. Sent from this office, post paid, for 50 cts.

TUNE BOOK.

The Brethren's Tune and Hymn Book, is a compilation of Sacred Music adapted to all the hymns in the Brethren's New Hymn Book. It contains over 350 pages, printed on good paper and neatly bound. We will send it to any address, post paid at $1.25 per copy.

GIVEN AWAY.

A FINE GERMAN CHROMO.

We send an elegant chromo, mounted and ready for framing, free to every agent for

UNDERGROUND

OR,

LIFE BELOW THE SURFACE.

BY THOS. W. KNOX.

942 Pages Octavo. 130 Fine Engravings.

Relates Incidents and Accidents beyond the Light of Day; Startling Adventures in all parts of the World; Mines and Mode of Working them; Under-currents of Society; Gambling and its *Horrors*; Caverns and their Mysteries; The Dark Ways of Wickedness; Prisons and their Secrets; Down in the Depths of the Sea; Strange Stories of the Detection of Crime.

The book treats of experience with brigands; nights in opium dens and gambling hells; life in prison; Stories of exiles; adventures among Indians; journey through Sewers and Catacombs; accidents in mines; pirates and piracy; tortures of the inquisition; wonderful burglaries; underworld of the great cities, etc., etc.

AGENTS WANTED

for this work. Exclusive territory is given. Agents can make $100 a week in selling this book. Send for circulars and terms to agents.

J. B BURR & HYDE,

HARTFORD, CONN., OR CHICAGO, ILL.

TRACTS.

"ANXIOUS BENCH RELIGION EXAMINED," BY ELDER J. S. FLORY. A SYNOPSIS OF CONTENTS. An address to the reader: The peculiarities that attend this type of religion. The feelings there experienced not imaginary but real. The key that unlocks the wonderful mystery. The causes by which feelings are excited. How the momentary feelings called "Experimental religion" are brought about, and then concludes by giving that form of doctrine as taught by Jesus Christ and recorded by his faithful witnesses.

COUNTERFEIT DETECTER

or

BAPTISM—MUCH IN LITTLE.

This work is now ready for distribution, and the importance of the subject will speak for it a large demand. It is a short treatise on baptism in tract form intended for general distribution, and is set forth in such a plain and logical manner that a wayfaring man though a fool, cannot err therein. Either of the above tracts sent postpaid on the following terms: Two copies, 10 cts, 10 copies 40 cents. 25 copies 70 cents. 50 copies $1.00, 100 copies $1.50.

Trine Immersion.

A discussion on Trine Immersion, by letter between Elder B. F. Moomaw and Dr. J. J. Jackson, to which is annexed a Treatise on the Lord's Supper, and on the necessity, character and evidences of the new birth, also a dialogue on the doctrine of non-resistance, by Elder B. F. Moomaw. Single copy 50 cents.

THE HELPING HAND.

Containing several hundred Valuable Receipts for cooking well at a moderate expense, making Dyes, Coloring, Cleaning and Cementing. This book also points out in plain language, free from Doctors' terms the diseases of men, women and children, and the latest and most approved means used for their cure, to which is added a description of the Medicinal Roots and Herbs, and how they are to be used in the cure of diseases.

This is a work of considerable importance and we offer it to our readers as being a valuable accession to every household. Send from this office to any address, post-paid, for 25 cents.

1870 1873

DR. FAHRNEY'S

Blood Cleanser or Panacea.

A tonic and purge, for Blood Diseases. Great reputation. Many testimonials. Many ministering brethren use and recommend it. Ask or send for the "Health Messenger." Use only the "*Panacea*" prepared at Chicago, Ills., and by

Dr. P. Fahrney's Brothers & Co.,

Feb. 3-pd. *Waynesboro, Franklin Co., Pa.*

New Hymn Books, English.

TURKEY MOROCCO.

One copy, postpaid,	$1.00
Per Dozen,	11.25

PLAIN ARABESQUE.

One Copy, post-paid,	75
Per Dozen, "	8.50

Ger'n & English, Plain Sheep.

One Copy, post-paid,	$1.00
Per Dozen	11.25
Arabesque Plain,	1.00
Turkey Morocco,	1.25
Single German, post paid	50
Per Dozen,	5.50

HUNTINGDON & BROAD TOP RAIL ROAD

On and after July 17th, 1873, Trains will run on this road daily (Sun excepted) as follows:

Trains from Huntingdon South. *Trains from Mt. Dal's moving North.*

ACCM P.M.	EXPS. A. M.	STATIONS.	EXP'S P. M.	ACCM. A. M
6 05	8 15	Huntingdon,	AR 6 00	AR 8 30
6 10	8 25	Long Siding	5 55	8 25
6 20	8 30	McConnelstown	5 45	8 15
6 27	8 37	Pleasant Grove	5 38	8 11
6 40	8 50	MARKLESBURG	5 25	7 58
6 50	9 00	Coffee Run	5 15	7 48
6 57	9 08	Rough & Ready	5 08	7 41
7 05	9 15	Cove	5 00	7 33
7 08	9 18	Fishers Summit	4 57	7 33
7 25	9 35	Saxton	4 45	7 15
7 40	9 50	Riddlesburg	4 25	6 55
7 48	9 56	Hopewell	4 18	6 48
8 00	10 15	Piper's Run	4 05	6 35
8 15	10 26	Tatesville	3 50	6 20
8 25	10 35	Everett	3 38	6 08
8 35	10 45	Mount Dallas	3 35	6 05
9 00	11 10	Bedford	3 10	5 30

SHOUP'S RUN BRANCH.

A. M.	P. M.		P. M.	A. M.
LE 9 45	LE 7 30	Saxton.	AR 4 35	AR 7 05
10 00	7 45	Coalmont.	4 20	6 50
10 05	7 50	Crawford.	4 15	6 45
AR 10 35	AR 8 00	Dudley	LE 4 05	LE 6 35

Bro'd Top City from Dudley 2 miles by stage.

Time of Penna. R. R. Trains at Huntingdon.

_ Mail No. 2 makes connection at Huntingdon with Mail going East on Pennsylvania Railroad at 4.15 p. m., and West at 5.45 p. m. Mail No. 1 leaves Huntingdon at 7.40 a. m. on arrival of Pacific Express West.

Trains on this road connect with trains on Bedford & Bridgeport, and Cumberland & Pennsylvania Railroads.

G. F. GAGE, Supt.

The Weekly Pilgrim.

Published by J. B. Brumbaugh, & Co.

Edited by H. B. & Geo. Brumbaugh.

CORRESPONDING EDITORS.

D. P. Sayler, Double Pipe Creek, Md.

Leonard Furry, New Enterprise, Pa.

The *Pilgrim* is a Christian Periodical, devoted to religion and moral reform. It will advocate in the spirit of *love* and *liberty*, the principles of true Christianity, labor for the promotion of peace among the people of God, for the encouragement of the saints and for the conversion of sinners, avoiding those things which tend toward disunion or sectional feelings.

TERMS.

Single copy, Book paper,	$1.50
Eleven copies, (eleventh for Agt.)	$15.00

Any number above that at the same rate.

Address.

H. B. BRUMBAUGH.
James Creek,
Huntingdon county Pa.

The Weekly Pilgrim.

"REMOVE NOT THE ANCIENT LANDMARKS WHICH OUR FATHERS HAVE SET."

VOL. 4. JAMES CREEK, PENNSYLVANIA, JULY 29, 1873. NO. 30.

POETRY.

HOME OF GOD'S CHILDREN

Where, where is the home of God's children?
Oh say, will you please tell me where?
For we know it's a home of great beauty,
And free from all sorrow and care?

Is it on a green isle in the ocean,
Beneath blue and unclouded skies;
And far from dark scenes of trouble,
That the home of God's children lies?

Or is it in some faraway valley,
Unmarked by the foot-steps of care;
And surrounded by high purple mountains,
That will not let death enter there?

Or perhaps by the side of still waters,
Where birds sing, and sweet flowers bloom;
In a land yet unseen by a mortal,
Is it there—that beautiful home?

We would know, for our two little treasures
Have been called by our Father away,
To dwell in the home of God's children,
While we here in loneliness stay.

We oft grieve that they so soon have left us,
And our home is so lonely and drear,
Since we catch not the sound of their foot-steps,
Nor their sweet childish voices we hear.

Oh yes, now we know, it is with Jesus,
He calls them as lambs to His fold;
It is there—the bright home of God's children,
In a region of glory untold.

And we know that our dear little children
Are among the bright things in that land,
And in safety are kept by the Shepherd
And fed by His bountiful hand.

It is not on an isle in the ocean,
No, nor yet in a vale far away,
But it is by the side of still waters
And Jesus is with them to stay.

Far away in the storm-clouds of sorrow,
From sickness, temptation and care—
For each in His own home of glory,
He's prepared a bright dwelling place there.

And it is by the side of life's river,
Where pastures and bright flowers grow,
That He leads our Mamie and Charlie,
And they are quite happy we know.

They are free from the fruits of transgression,
From sorrow, vexation and pain,
And we pray Thee, Oh Jesus, to help us
To meet them in glory again.

And there a small family united,
We will gather around Thy white throne,
To praise and adore Thee our Savior,
In the home of God's children—sweet home.

* * *

Ringgold, Md.

ORIGINAL ESSAYS.

THE ANOINTING OF JESUS.

There is, I believe, not a point of duty in preaching the Gospel by the Brethren, more neglected than the anointing of Jesus. That He was anointed by a woman at Bethany, six days before His death, is evident from the Scriptures.—See Jno. 12. And that the Son of God commanded it to be preached, as a memorial to her, is twice recorded. Why is it not done when the Savior says it shall be done? Matthew and Mark say, "A woman came to Jesus, having an alabaster box of very precious ointment, and poured it on His head, as He sat at meat."—But it appears that some took indignation, thought it to be a waste, and that it would be more profitable to have it sold, and the money appropriated to the support of the poor. But saith the Savior, "Why trouble ye the woman? for she hath wrought a good work upon me. For ye have the poor always with you; but one ye have not always, For in that she hath poured this ointment on my body, she did it for my burial. Verily I say unto you, wheresoever this Gospel shall be preached in the whole world, there shall also this, that this woman hath done, be told for a memorial of her."—Matt. 26; 13 Mark 14: 9. Turn to John Chap. 21, and you will find this woman to be Mary, the sister of Lazarus, whom Jesus had raised up from the dead. It was that Mary who sat at the feet of Jesus, so attentively listening unto His wholesome discourses while her sister Martha was concerned with many things, and requested Him to tell her to assist. But Jesus saith, "Martha, Martha, thou art careful and troubled about many things; But *one thing is needful*: and Mary hath chosen that good part which shall not be taken from her." Behold that pious sister! How deeply her love was rooted toward her lovely Savior! She even forgot temporal service, and Jesus recommended it as a good part, and the only thing needful.

Let our sisters learn a lesson who are concerned so much in serving when entertaining visitors. Do not be superfluous in furnishing your tables, thereby only throwing out temptations for intemperance. Let us all guard against unnecessary cares of worldly things, lest we might neglect the one thing needful. Mary, by being so much attached to her Master, as seen at the death of Lazarus, her brother, when she met Jesus she fell down at His feet saying, "Lord if thou hadst been here, my brother had not died." Jesus evinced to the world that He loved her, and regarded her as a woman of extraordinary merit. The Jews likewise, regarded this family as a notable one, because they wept with Mary when they came to comfort them; Jesus saw them weeping. O what a tender feeling our lovely Savior has! He "groaned in the spirit, and was troubled, yea, "*Jesus wept*." Connecting together all these circumstances of natural attachment, and Divine principles of Holy love, we come to the conclusion that Mary, through influences from Heaven, was moved, with the costly odorous Spikenard to anoint the Lord of life and glory; anticipating the embalming of His body for His burial, which otherwise could not have been done, as we shall soon notice. Solomon in his songs alluded to this act so nobly executed by the foreknowledge of God.—Cant. 1, 2, 3. "Let him kiss me with the kisses of my mouth: thy love is better than wine, because of the savor of thy good ointments, thy name is an ointment poured forth; therefore do the Virgins love thee." We read "the house was filled with the odor of the ointment." O, the glorious act of the godly woman, worthy to be spoken of in all the land, where the Gospel is preached, as a *memorial* to her. "For she hath done what she could do; She is come aforehand to anoint my body to the burying."—Mark 14; 8

Brethren you know that Christ died on the cross according to Scripture.—Now as the type of Christ, the Paschal Lamb in Egypt, had to be slain between evening, at the going down of the sun, so Jesus the antetype, had to expire at the precise time in the day, which we presume 3 o'clock according to our reckoning. The next day being the Sabbath, time would not then admit to embalm his body for his burial, hence Joseph and Nicodemus took him hastily from the cross and laid him into a sepulcher near by, or near at hand; and the women that followed, returned and prepared spices and ointment, but rested on the Sabbath day according to the commandment.—See Luke 23: 56.

But alas, alas! their design was prevented through the interposition of God who raised him from the dead, early the first day of the week before the holy women could embalm him. Had it not been for the foresight of pious Mary, the body of Jesus, the anointed of God, inorder to introduce the Gospel, the glad tidings of man's salvation and the substitute for sinners, would not have had the honor of being anointed. Inasmuch then as it appears to be needful to embalm His body for His burial, as shown by His own declaration; consequently we conclude that had Christ's body remained without burial, the whole fabric of God's arrangement would be destroyed.—This may be a strange idea to some, hence I will give a reason for this expression. It is clearly prophesied by David and the Savior that He was to be buried. If this prophecy had failed, it would have proved God's inability to accomplish His design, and in consequence man's reliance on His promises would be lost, yea, lost forever! Hence we see that it is doubly important to often speak of the noble act of Mary, the sister of Martha and Lazarus, according to the injunction of our Master, "Wheresoever we preach the Gospel as a memorial of her.

Brethren let us consider it as a part of the Gospel, as it truly is. Nor non-embalming, we may reasonably conclude, might have prevented the resurrection of the Lord Jesus Christ, which is the crowning point of our religion, and without it our faith would be in vain, and our hope among all men most miserable. Hence I exhort, I admonish, preach the word, and do not forget that this part also belongs to the word.

In conclusion I would say to the dear readers of the PILGRIM who have no just claim to be called the adopted children of God, be cautious, reflect upon your condition. Your day of grace may be closed any moment and if you die unreconciled to God, you cannot expect to meet His approbation; your doom will be banishment from the presence of the Lord forever. Hence come to Jesus, obey His commandments, secure the one thing needful speedily, and continue faithful unto the end, and I assure you it will be well with you, and that good part will never be taken from you. May we all live a life devoted to God and His holy service, until the Lord will take us home to meet together in the blessed climes of immortality to forever bask in the smiles of a reconciled God, is the prayer of your unworthy brother.

LEONARD FURRY.

TYPES.
(Continued.)

Having said thus much concerning persons who in their natural characters, actions and fortunes are declared to have been types of future persons and events, it remains to speak of events happening to the ancient church and people of God, which by the circumstances wherewith they were accompanied, are shown to have been typical of greater events that were to happen to the people of God under the gospel dispensation. Now concerning these, we have two observations to make. The first is that the things respecting the ancient people of God, which prefigured the greater things to happen to the people of God under the gospel dispensation, were in some instances foretold before they happened to the ancient people. Our second observation is that the predictions of these figurative events were also predictions of the event which they prefigured of this double sense of prophecy. Various instances might be given, suffice it however, to mention one instance only: namely, the deliverance of the Jews from the Babylonish captivity and their restoration to the land of Canaan. These, though natural events, prefigured the much greater and more important deliverance of mankind from the captivity of sin, and their introduction into the heavenly Canaan, for in the writings of the Evangelists passages of the prophecies, which foretold the deliverance from Babylon, are applied to that greater deliverance, for example, Isaiah 40: 2,3, is said by Matt. 3: 3, and by our Lord himself, Matt. 11: 10, to have been fulfilled by John the Baptist preaching in the wilderness of Judea; yet these verses in their first and literal meaning, evidently relate to the return of the Jews from Babylon, for Isaiah in the end of chapter 39, having foretold that all the riches of his palaces, which Hezekiah had shown to the messengers of the king of Babylon, should be carried away to Babylon, and that his sons should be carried thither captives, and made Eunuchs in the palace of the king of Babylon. The prophet in this 40th chapter mitigates the severity of that prediction, by foretelling that while the Jews were oppressed with the miseries of their captivity, God would order his prophets who were among them to comfort his people by assuring them that their captivity would at length come to an end, because considering their sufferings as a sufficient punishment for their sins as a nation, he would pardon and restore them to their own land, 2 verse. "Speak ye comfortably to Jerusalem, and cry unto her that her warfare is accomplished, that her iniquity is pardoned, for she hath received of the Lord's hand double for all her sins." The people in Babylon being thus assured that they were to be brought back to Judea, the first tho't, as B. South observes, which would occur to the captives, would be the difficulty and danger of their passing through the deserts of Arabia, where the nearest way from Babylon to Jerusalem lay. Wherefore the prophets in Babylon, to remove the fears of the people, were ordered to assure them that by whatsoever road they should return, it would be made commodious for their safe passage, and this assurance the prophets would give them in language taken from the custom of the Eastern princes, who, when they were about to march with their armies through difficult roads, sent pioneers before them to widen the narrow passes, to fill up the hollows, to level the heights and to smooth the rough ways through which they were to march. Verse 34, "The voice of one crying in the wilderness, prepare ye the way of the Lord, make straight in the desert an high way for our God; every valley shall be exalted and every mountain and hill shall be brought low; the crooked shall be made straight, and the rough places plain." By these images the prophets intimated that God was to march from Babylon at the head of his people to protect them during their journey, and to bring them safely into Judea. These things are more plainly expressed, Isaiah 52: 12, "Ye shall not go out with haste nor by flight; for the Lord will go before you, and the God of Israel will be your reward." But although this whole prophecy in its first and literal meaning, evidently relates to the deliverance of the Jews from Babylon, the application of the above cited passage to the preaching of John the Baptist by the Evangelist Matthew, and by our Lord himself, showeth plainly that the prophecies concerning the deliverance of the people of God from the Babylonish captivity, had a second and higher meaning, of which the literal sense was the sign. By foretelling the deliverance of the Jews from Babylon, these prophecies foretold the deliverance of mankind from the infinitely worse bondage of sin. Moreover the command to the prophets in Babylon to comfort God's people by announcing that their sins were pardoned, and that they were soon to be bro't back to their own land, was a command to the ministers of the gospel in every age to comfort penitent believers by assuring them that their sins shall be pardoned, and that Christ will bring them safely into the heavenly country, (of which the restoration of the Jews to Canaan was an emblem and pledge,) because he hath successfully removed all obstacles out of their way. The preparation of the way of the Lord among the Jews by the preaching of John the Baptist, was fully expressed by the voice of one crying in the wilderness. The Jewish Church, to which John was sent to announce the coming of the Messiah, was at that time in a barren and desert condition, unfit, without reformation, for the reception of her king. It was in this desert country, destitute at that time of all religious cultivation, in true piety and good works unfruitful, that John was sent to prepare the way of the Lord by preaching repentance. A series of prophecies delivered probably toward the close of the reign of Hezekiah, from chap. 40 to 66 of Isaiah. This portion of the prophet's prediction constitutes the most elegant part, not merely of his writings, but of the whole Old Testament. The chief subject is the restoration of the Church. These prophecies are introduced with a promise of the restoration of the kingdom, and the return from the captivity in Babylon. The redemption from Babylon is employed as a type to shadow out a redemption of infinitely higher nature: the prophet so connecting these two events as scarcely ever to treat of the former without introducing some allusion to the latter.

D. NEELEY.

LED BY THE SPIRIT.

For as many as are led by the spirit of God, they are the sons of God. Rom. 8: 14.

As all Scripture is given by inspiration of God, and is profitable &c., I thought to pen down a few thoughts upon the above.

1st. Led or leading.
2d. The spirit and its unity.
3d. The sons of God.

Now rationally speaking, when anything is led, there must be a leader, and it cannot be led unless it becomes subject to the leader, either by persuasion or by being overpowered. Lead means to guide or go before. Now to define this more fully, we will take a horse or a colt from the pasture; his master bridles him, but not being accustomed to leading he attempts to run the opposite direction, but as soon as he is overpowered or subdued he becomes subject, then he can be led. Now when we see our depraved selves, the awful calamity that is awaiting us, and that we are nothing of ourselves, then we feel the need of a leader, but before we are ready to be led we will require some knowledge of the leader. "But no man hath seen God at any time, the only begotten Son which is in the bosom of the Father he hath declared him." John 1: 18. Now let us hear the Son, "God is a spirit, and they that worship him must worship him in spirit and in truth." John 4: 24. The apostle confirms the same and says, "Now the Lord is that spirit," 2 Cor. 3: 17. Then if we are led by that spirit we will be led in the service of God, led to do what that spirit dictates unto us, led to follow Christ in the way, as Paul says, "walk in the spirit and ye shall not fulfill the lust of the flesh." "But if ye be led by the spirit ye are not under the law." Now we must be in possession of the spirit of Christ. "If any man have not the spirit of Christ he is none of his." Rom. 8: 9. Those two spirits are very closely connected. "I and my Father are one." John 10: 30. "I am in the Father, and the Father in me." John 14: 10. The apostle says, "But he that is joined unto the Lord is one spirit." 1 Cor. 6: 17. Then we can be joined in spirit. The Savior's reasoning concerning man and wife is similar to this, "And they twain shall be one flesh," not one in body, not one in person, but united in the bonds of love, joined in heart. Christ in his prayer, for the apostles prayed for the unity, says, "That they all may be one; as thou, Father art in me, and I in thee, that they also may be one in us: that the world may believe that thou hast sent me. And the glory which thou gavest me I have given them; that they may be one even as we are one." John 17: 21-22. Then we would understand that we are to be perfectly joined together, of the same mind, same judgment, and speak the same thing; become entirely submissive, subject to the Church and to the gospel, and Paul-like, "do all things without murmuring and disputing." Then we are fit subjects to commune. Then what is Communion? Paul says, "For we being many are one bread, and one body; for we are all partakers of that one bread." 1 Cor. 10 17. We do not understand Paul to mean that that bread should be in one lump, but composed of the same material, composed of many grains of wheat, combined together so we cannot distinguish one from the other; they all resemble each other. In the previous verse he speaks of the cup of blessing which is composed of the juice of many grapes, all resembling each other, but combined, united, in one body. Now when we are thus united, when that oneness exists, and we resemble each other in outward appearance, we then have a union, and there can be a Communion. John says, "Beloved we now are the sons of God, and it doth not yet appear what we shall be, but we know that when he shall appear we shall be like him for we shall see him as he is." 1 John 3: 2. And Paul says, "For I reckon that the sufferings of this present time are not to be compared with the glory which shall be revealed in us, for the earnest expectation of the creature waiteth for the manifestation of the sons of God."—Rom. 8: 18-19.

S. N. WISE.

God is always inviting you to His throne. He says: "*Let* me hear thy voice; come near unto me, that I may bless thee."

Deeds are fruits, words are but leaves.

THE CHRISTIAN WARFARE.

The Christian life is a warfare, and if the victory is to be won, it requires a valiantness, because our foe is a mighty one. He has had long and constant drilling. He has won many a victory, and when he failed it was of small importance to him, except in the few battles which he fought with our Captain IMMANUEL. But now our captain has given us our orders and has, Himself, gone before. Then ho! ye fellow-soldiers of the cross, wake ye up and to your arms. Carnal weapons, of the most deadly sort, are too weak for us. To trust in them would be to lean upon a broken reed which pierces the weary soul. But ah, we have the weapon of warfare which is "mighty through God to the pulling down of strongholds, casting down imaginations and every high thing that exalteth itself against the knowledge of God, and bringing into captivity every thought to the obedience of Christ." Such a weapon is the sword of the Spirit. We want none of your two edged swords, but something sharper, which pierces even to the dividing asunder of joint and marrow, of soul and spirit, and which discerneth the thoughts and intents of the heart. Not Solomons' sword, which affrighted the harlot to the inevitable confession, but that sharp sword which "goeth out of his mouth, that with it he should smite the nations." Then, onward ye soldiers of the cross, and let your watchword be the "rod of iron" which shrinketh not nor stretcheth not: it bendeth not nor wasteth not, and with it he shall rule the nations, and treadeth the vinepress of the fierceness and wrath of Almighty God. "Put ye on the whole armor of God, the girdle of truth, the breast-plate of righteousness, the preparation of the Gospel of peace, the shield of faith, the helmet of salvation, the sword of the spirit, praying always with all prayer and supplication in the spirit." C. C. ROOT.

Mirabile, Mo.

LOVE.

Dear brethren and sisters, I fear there is not as much love in the Church as there should be. Surely there is not one who has tasted the sweets of redeeming love who would be unwilling to give up everything for the pearl of great price, the blessing of perfect love. O, ye that are convinced of the necessity of being holy, and still feel your hearts to be cold and hard, all that you can do is to just give your whole selves to Jesus, just as you are, and He will soften and purify your hearts and fill you with His perfect love. Dear brethren and sisters, our Savior has manifested His love toward us in many ways. First he sent His only begotten Son to die on the cross, all for the love of this sinful world. I feel thankful this evening that God had so much love for me that He opened my eyes and showed me my awful condition, and pardoned my sins before it was forever too late. I feel sorry to think that there is so many that will not hear the loving words of the Savior when He says, "Come unto Me, all ye that are weary and heavy laden, and I will give you rest."

Dear brethren, I think many more would enlist under the blessed banner of our Savior, if they could follow all the fashions and maxims of the world, but dear friends, remember you cannot take any of your enjoyments along when the rider comes on the pale horse and seizes you. Remember there is no repentance in the grave, no pardon offered to the dead. Sinner, stop before it is forever too late. AMANDA ANDERSON.

Shepherdstown, Pa.

WE SEEK A CITY TO COME.

For here we have no continuing city, but we seek one to come."

How true this is, that we have no abiding city here. When we look around us and see the great works of art, and how soon all must be dissolved, yes, very soon shall the great splendor and vain pomp of this world be cast down. Often do our minds recur to the great Celestial City, where sin and sorrow never molest. Oh, to see the vanities of this sinful world, it causes us to wish for the glorious event when we shall see the New Jerusalem descending and the King of glory seated on His throne to dwell with His saints a thousand years when the meek shall inherit the earth, and, be no sin nor sorrow to mar their sweet fellowship and peace on earth. They shall come up to the Holy City to worship every year. Oh, that glorious Millenium! Shall we be so happy as to dwell with the King during this period? Shall we arise to meet Him in the air? Oh, what a meeting that will be! Sweet to think that we shall drop this mortality and put on immortality; to be free from sin and temptation and meet together in the Holy City. We can there see the faces of all our dear ones on earth, in that glorious meeting. May we, as a dear family of Christ, reign with Him where all is harmony and love. Brethren and sisters, let us be more engaged in prayer and meditation. It is this that sets our affections above. Let us, each day, pray for wisdom to show us the path of duty, strive to know our own misgivings, pray for more faith that we may desire the sweet hour of prayer.'

"Till from Mount Pisgah's lofty height
I'll view my home and take my flight,
This robe of flesh I'll drop and rise,
To seize the everlasting prize."

S. M. HUTCHISON.

Center View, Mo.

A God-like man is the only goodly man; a Christ-like nature brought into the soul doth only denominate a man a true Christian.

UNCONSCIOUS INFLUENCE

It is said that among the high Alps at certain seasons the traveler is told to proceed very quietly, for on the slopes overhead the snow hangs so evenly balanced that the sound of a voice, or the report of a gun, may destroy the equilibrium and bring down an immense avalanche that will overwhelm everything in ruin in its downward path. And so about our way, there may be a soul in the very crisis of its mortal history, trembling between life and death, and a mere touch or shadow may determine its destiny. A young lady who was deeply impress with the truth, and was ready, under a conviction of sin, to ask, "what must I do to be saved?" had all her solemn impressions dissipated by the unseemly jesting of a member of the church by her side as she passed out of the sanctuary. Her irreverent and worldly spirit cast a repellant shadow on that young lady not far from the kingdom of God. How important that we should always and everywhere walk worthy of our high calling as Christians?

Let us remember that we are always casting the shadow of our real life upon some one; that somebody is following us, as John followed Peter into the sepulchre. Happy if we when all the influences of life flow back and meet us at the judgment, we can lift up clean hands and spotless robes and say, "I am pure from the blood of all men!" Happy then to hear even one soul saying to us out of the great multitude, that following the shadow of our Christian life and devotion, he found Jesus and Heaven.—*Christian.*

"HE SHALL SIT AS A REFINER."

Mal. iii. 3.

This beautiful allusion of the prophet finds a very striking illustration in the process of preparing our precious metals for the mint. After several preparatory steps, the bullion is taken to the refiner, where it is put into a cup, and melted under a blast of atmospheric air. The oxygen of the air uniting with its impurities, forms a litherage, or scum which is absorbed by a preparation put into the cup for that purpose, or carried over the edge of the cup by the blast. This is called cupellation, and immediately on its termination the beautiful phenomena of brightening is seen. Just as the last trace of alloy clears from the silver a peculiar bright and vivid flash seems to cover the whole bath, and for an instant every brick in the arch of the furnace above is perfectly reflected as from a mirror. So to the individual as well as to the Church, the coming of Christ is ever as a refiner of silver. He comes in his word, by the illumination of his spirit, eliminate the base metals of error and superstition.

He comes in the mysteriousness of our new spiritual life with a vitality that throws off the old man with his deeds, and clothes us with the new man. "Sitting" is indicative of the carefulness and importance of the operation. So Christ superintends this work of grace in us with matchless skill. Brother, it may seem the heat is too intense or too protracted, but the refiner knows. It is not to punish us, or to note the quantity of dross that is carried off, that we are tried in this fiery trial, but that his own image may shine forth in our hearts and lives.—*Rev. D. G. Strong.*

BUILDING CHARACTER.

SELECTED.

There is a structure which every body is building, young and old, each for himself. It it is called *Character*, and every act of life is a stone. If day by day we be careful to build our lives with pure noble upright deeds, at the end will stand a fair temple, honored by God and man. But as one leak will sink a ship, and one flaw break a chain, so one mean, dishonorable, untruthful act or word will forever leave its impress and work its influence on our character. Then let the several deeds unite to form a day and one by one the days grow into noble years, and the years, as they slowly pass, will raise at last a beautiful edifice, enduring forever to our praise.

H. BEELMAN.

PRAYER.

Nothing can destroy a real prayer: its flight to the throne is swift and certain. God will not fail you, though you fail yourself. Though you faint, he fainteth not, neither is weary.—Lift up your cry, and he will lift up his hand. Go to your knees, you are stronger there; resort to your chamber, and it shall be to you none other than the gate of heaven. Tell your God your grief; heavy to you, it will be light enough to Him. Dilemmas will all be plain to his wisdom, and difficulties will vanish before his strength.—Oh, tell it not in Gath that Israel cannot trust in God; Publish it not in the streets of Askelon that trouble can dismay those who lean upon the Eternal arm. With Jehovah in the van, O hosts of Israel, dare ye fear? The Lord of hosts is with us, the God of Jacob is our refuge. What man's heart shall quail, or what soul shall faint? Lift up the hands that hang down and confirm the feeble knees. Say unto the feeble in heart, "Be strong; fear not. God is with you; he will help you, and that right early."—*Christian.*

LIFE AND ITS OBJECT.

Our short life should not give us much concern. My mind is like a piece of ground which being overrun with weeds which no diligence can render quite clean, no care keep them from appearing again, even after they have been plucked away. Surely so it fares with me and my sinful anxieties. They are ever springing up anew and troubling me and nothing will utterly and entirely destroy them, till the ground be turned up by the plow of death and left fallow till the resurrection. Yet that I be not fallen and unfaithful in the work of the Lord, let the busy hand of faith be ever plucking up the base weeds of unbelief.

Again, why am I so much concerned about a world I am so soon to leave? Were my possessions to fall on this side of Jordan, and I, to inhabit here forever, what more could I do than I have done, and am doing? Yet I am but a stranger, a sojourner and a pilgrim; here to-night but gone to-morrow to return no more, yea this night what dare I boast of to-morrow, not knowing what the silent watches of the night may bring forth. And if not of a day, far less of many, may I boast. It is but a look and I have lost sight of this world eternally. Why then set my heart on that which shall one time or other so terribly deceive me. A few moments, and my eternal state is begun and I am in the world of spirits, and dashed out of the roll of the sons of men, yea out of the remembrance of all my nearest relations. Should I then be over careful of what entertainment I meet with by the way. If I may make a happy journey I ought to think more on my home than on my usage by the way. Surely one should be ready to think that men carried their riches to eternity with them, yea, and more welcome on that account, or why these unwearied endeavors and perpetual bereavings of rest to obtain them? O, folly that I concern myself with moments and neglect eternity, fear that I should be distressed about a day which scarce has dawned till done, and dwell not with joy in ages to come, faithlessness that I should doubt the promise, yea the appendix to the promise for salvation from sin and eternal life, is the promise.

Now though my whole life were one scene of affliction, yet the very shortness of it, might sweeten it tho' it be a vapor, a shadow, a wind that passeth away, surely the attending calamities can be of no longer continuance than that duration upon which they attend. Nothing can pass from this world to that but my disembodied immortality. I see that my concern turns on a wrong hinge and my case terminates on a trifle. All my concern should be, not to provide for the few moments of this life, but to improve for endless eternity, and that care which I expend on the vanities of time and how to be possessed of them, I should lay out in piety on the treasures of glory and to prepare for the divine possession. Well may I commit to him the bearing of my charges, by the way, who has adopted me for His son and made me an heir of His kingdom.

A PILGRIM.

SELF DENIAL

Self denial is an important lesson that all should learn. If we do not learn it in youth we may grow up to be very unhappy men and women. It is rather hard sometimes, to control our own selfish desires, but we will find by so doing that we accomplish a great many good things.

Have you ever noticed the difference among your playmates, between one who tries to make everything pleasant and he who does not?

On the other hand notice a child that is of a selfish disposition and does not try to cultivate a generous one; such a one will indulge in sin and folly more and more as he grows older, and will finally become miserable himself. No little children will go to such, expecting to find a place in their affection, for their very selfishness will cause every one to turn from them, feeling that in their hearts there is no warmth.

We all like good generous people. Then let us try to cultivate generosity, which we may do by first practicing self denial. May we ever remember this important theme, for a great deal of the trouble in after life is the consequence of its neglect. Would we were all wise enough to know that a good hearted, self-denying, generous person exerts an influence that will live throughout time and to all eternity.

THE SYMPATHY OF CHRIST.

No softer blows the southern breeze in spring, than breathes the sympathetic life of Christ among the cruel crags of human selfishness and hate. No name so utters from its every letter the tender tones of sympathy; as the name of Jesus. In this respect as in all his life, he towers above all competing lives, as Mount Blanc above his fellows. As he lived and moved in Palestine, Christ was in the simplest and completest sense of the term, a sympathetic man. There was nothing false or forced about his sympathy. Honest, and as if instinctively, it broke forth from his heart on every occasion. From the bridal party of Cana to the bier of Nain, it flowed through all grades of want and woe like a crystal brook through a hundred thirsty fields. No two words ever written or any other, considered among all their surroundings, reveal so much of this as those sister words forever associated with the sorrowing sister: "Jesus wept." But a man sits on the throne today. As the God man lived on earth, so the man God lives in heaven. His human sympathy that beat in his heart here, in like manner throbs there. He is the same human friend of humanity now, that he was in the kitchen of Mary and Martha. With the same sympathy with which he met the widow at the gate of Nain, he meets the bereaving widow at the gate of grief, giving now as then, the true sympathy of a perfect man. A human heart is on the mediatorial throne. If he considers mortal pains and common griefs in Judea once, he regards them in America now. Believe it my brother, believe it, my sister, eighteen centuries have built no stone wall between the Redeemer and his redeemed. "Jesus Christ" of Nazareth "is the same yesterday, to day, and forever."

Religious News.

THE Baltimore papers state that two young men of great promise, who have been studying for the Episcopal ministry, have applied to the Rev. Dr. Fuller to study for the Baptist pulpit under his direction. They addressed the Eutaw Place Baptist church two successive Wednesday evenings, and were received for baptism.

A HEBREW Theological Seminary is the latest step in the way of education. Obviously it is a want of the country and the age. As the number of Jews is great, and increasing in wealth and influence, it is natural that they should desire a ministry of culture and learning. There are more Jews in New York than in Jerusalem.

THE Pope has publicly expressed his great regret that the clergy of his Church attended the funeral of the Italian statesman Ratazzi. He said: "The priests showed themselves greater courtiers than ministers of God." But the priests are beginning to do as they please, whether the Pope likes it or not. It is hard to keep his sheep from jumping over the fence.

THE great sensation of the day, is Prof. Wise's trip to Europe in a balloon. The preparations will soon be completed and the trip will be attempted some time during next month. The Domestic Sewing Machine Co., sends one of their machines along, with the understanding that it is to be used as ballast if needed. This seems to be a dangerous experiment but those concerned are sanguine in their expectations. They take with them, bedding, provisions, writing tables and everything necessary to give a correct report of their trip, also a boat for their use, in case they should drop into the ocean.

IN England and Scotland they have what they call the established Church. This Church and its ministers are supported by taxation the same as our civil government. This, to the other denominations, is becoming burthensome as they, in addition to supporting their ministry are compelled to pay their full quota towards supporting the Established or Episcopal Church. On the 6th of May a motion was presented to the House of Commons against it but was lost by a vote of 356 against 51 in favor.

THE following statement was made, under oath, by a Roman Catholic priest on Ward's Island, New York, on the 9th day of July 1873.

"I believe I have divine authority to secure Protestant children from their Protestant mothers and MAKE them Catholics. I deny the right of the Protestant minister to do the same."

This is showing the Catholic color pretty clearly. The proselyting spirit is unabated and it will be well for our parents to be on their guard. The *New York Observer* makes the following remarks: "Will you place your son or daughter in a Roman Catholic school, or one in which by any possibility the influence of a Roman Catholic may be brought to bear upon the youthful mind? What can you expect but that your unsuspecting child will be seduced into the Church that does not hesitate to avow such an infamous system as this priest professes? Your child may not admit to you her apostasy. She will be taught to conceal and deny it if necessary. But she will be ruined by such influences as this shameless priest employs, and you are to be held responsible before God for the destruction of your own child."

REV Edward O. Forney of the Norristown Pa. Reformed Church has toppled over into Catholicism.

Our Church Paper gives the following apt comparison: "A good old German Prince once wanted a safe coachman. Of those who were bro't before him for the place, he inquired how near to a terrible precipice they could safely drive, and keep the carriage from tumbling over. One could go within a yard. Others could do it better still—say within a foot. An expert could drive within an inch or two. One more quiet than the rest, said he never yet tried how near he could go, since his aim was always to keep as far as possible from danger. He was employed to do the driving for a Prince, who valued his own neck and safety. That is the spirin which we are to treat this Romanizing tendency. We once thought we ought to be also of those who, with profound skill tried to drive very near the verge, so that looking down into the dangerous chasm, they could see the horrible depths of sin below. Now after seeing others of such boasted skill, topp ing over and tumbling in one after another, we have come to the conclusion that it is safer to keep away from the dangerous gulf."

Just so, the men are not so much to blame as the Church. Mercersburg has long, been playing the foolhardy, experiment of trying how close they could drive, to Catholicism, thinking that they might thereby get some of them to ride in their coach, but the results prove it to be a failure, as some of their best passengers stepped over into the Catholic coach. It should be remembered that when men offer to go half way towards meeting the devil they always lose, as he keeps *good* coaches. That new "Confession of Faith" is a close drive, very close, and no wonder there is an occasional tippling over.

Youth's Department.

EARLY PIETY.

Amongst those things that have most influence over the minds of men are profit and pleasure. While recommending early piety to you, think not that I wish to render you poor or unhappy; far from it. I rather wish you to be truly rich and truly happy, not merely for the little span in which the earthly pleasures or riches are enjoyed, but forever and ever. Where is that treasure to be found that will enrich you for eternity? Not amidst the wealth of this world. Man knows not the price thereof, neither is it found in the land of the living. The depth saith, it is not in me, it cannot be had for gold. Where are they that, but a few years back, possessed pleasure and honors, parks and palaces, and crowns and kingdoms. All vanished from the world. While entreating you to pursue more solid good, I would recount to you some of the advantages of religion of youth. Early piety is comparatively easy. The total corruption of man's heart is such, that at every period of life there are difficulties in turning to God. At any time it is needful to strive to enter the strait gate, but it is much easier to turn to God in our youth than it is in later years. The heart is not so much hardened as it is by a longer life in sin and folly. The mind is not so hard to instruct as it is when prejudices have so darkened all its faculties as almost to exclude the heavenly light when sin has long reigned triumphantly, when satan has long led the sinner captive. It is hard to escape from this tyranny, and many have experienced this. The Scriptures confirm the doctrine of the difficulty of conversion late in life. "Can the Ethiopian change his skin or the leopard his spots?" "Then may ye also do good that are accustomed to do evil." In this sense, we may apply, with propriety, the words of Nicodemus: "Can a man be born when he is old?" When is it that disease is most easily checked? Not when it has laid fast hold on the vitals, but when its first symptoms appear. When is it that the mistaken traveler may most easily forsake the wrong and return to the right path? Not when he has traveled for miles in a wrong direction, but when he enters that way. Were you rushing down a steep hill, when might you easily stop? Not when you had nearly reached the bottom, but when you began to descend, so as the poet says:

'Tis easier work if you begin,
To serve the Lord betimes;
While sinners that grow old in sin,
Grow hardened in their crimes.

In another view, early religion is comparatively easy. There is reason to believe that God will sooner hear your prayers for mercy and grant more peace and pardon if you turn to him at once, than if you refuse from time to time to heed his calls. If you delay to comply with the means of grace it may lead you through scenes of doubt and pain and fear which but for these refusals you would have never known.

Early religion has frequently to surmount many discouragements which may render it more acceptable to him, who tries, in various ways, the faith of his disciples. It is pleasing to him to see his young followers overcoming the world and pressing on to heaven in spite of all that is done to hinder them. Young persons are most apt to be pleased with the follies and vanities of a sinful world, its theatres, novels, romances and other time-wasting and sinful pleasures, having frequently more charms for them than for those of riper years, and by them, its laugh is often more dreaded. Thus, those who will be seriously religious must not always expect to escape ridicule. It is one of satan's grand weapons when his servants cannot persuade others out of serving God, they try to laugh them out of it, so that we need not be surprised if we hear the true christian ridiculed.

Another advantage of early religion is, that its possessors avoid the evil of an entirely unprofitable life. When Paul sent one sinner who had been a dishonest fugitive slave, back to his master Philemon, he spoke of him as one that had been unprofitable but was now profitable to the apostle himself and to his former employer. It is, my young friends, an awful fact that while destitute of early religion, you answer none of the ends of your creation, you are unprofitable to God for you bring him no glory. You are unprofitable to the world around you; your associates are not encouraged by your example to follow the way of peace, but by your negligence and folly, are hardened in their sin. You are unprofitable to your dearest friends, if they are the friends of God—instead of cheering them by your piety, your religion is their grief and sorrow and if they are unacquainted with the Gospel, instead of trying to lead them to seek its blessings, you go along with them to destruction. You are unprofitable to yourself, for alas, while negligent of obeying God you are adding sin upon sin and are making the heavy load of your transgressions heavier, are filling up the measures of your iniquities and thus you are heaping up wrath against the day of wrath. O wretched youth, and would you live a cumberer of the ground, useless as the thistle, lonely as the deadly nightshade, and in the sight of God, more hateful than the poisonous serpent. Were it even certain that God would spare you to repent at some future time, yet thro' mere delay, how many barren and worse than useless years would you pass. The late convert loses much peace and joy, much holiness and happiness and many opportunities of serving God, and much of that grace of which even the youngest never obtain enough.

Grow in grace is a work of time. An infant does not, in an hour, obtain the strength and vigor, the comeliness and stature of manhood. Though an infant has all the parts of the future man, he has them in a weaker state. The new convert compared with the confirmed Christian, is like an infant. He is in Christ, yet but a little child. He is possessed of the same disposition as the more confirmed Christian, but in a weaker state, and by the growth of years, graces are brought nearer to perfection. So universally is this the case that even the apostle Paul, not long before his martyrdom, after being almost thirty years a Christian and an apostle, still declared that "forgetting the things that were behind he reached unto those that were before," and asserted that he was not perfect. O, how much of divine grace must they lose whose best years slide away before the work of life is begun. Those years that might be beneficial to themselves are but a dismal blank, are years marked with the stains of ingratitude and sin. Should you delay obeying the Gospel you will lose much grace here, and then may expect to lose much glory hereafter, and even a pardoned penitent at last you might have to utter such a wish as the celebrated Earl of Rochester is said to have uttered. He wished he had been a crawling leper in a ditch, a link boy or a beggar, or had lived in a dungeon rather than to dishonor God as he had done. But my young friends, reverse this scene. Imagine religion to be your early choice, Jesus chosen as your Lord and prize, as your salvation, and God adored as your helper, and O, how changed do all things appear! Then would you, in some humble measure, glorify His dear name who bought you with His precious blood, then would you recommend His Gospel and display the influence of his love; then, though you would feel yourself an unprofitable servant, an unworthy creature, yet your five talents, or two or one would be employed for the honor of your loving Lord. Early religion would cause you to glorify God, His name would be honored by you, His will done in you, His glory promoted in your life and advanced by your example. Then, too, would you be profitable to your dearest friends. Are they pious? How they would rejoice over you, and lay down their heads more calmly in the dust when leaving a beloved child to fill up the place in the Church of Christ below, when they depart to that above. O my young friends, if you have parents whose prayers have long ascended to God in your behalf, gladden their hearts by choosing their God for yours. Let them say over you, "This my son, or this my daughter was dead and is alive again, was lost and is found." But perhaps you reply, my parents and friends are altogether unacquainted with religion they live careless of the service of God, and have taught me to do the same. Alas, if this be the case it is a lamentable one, yet perhaps youthful piety might render you profitable to them. Do you love them, and can you bear the thought of soon losing them forever, or of meeting them only in that miserable world where affection never enters? Yet this must be, if you and they make light of Jesus and salvation, much as you may love each other now. All that love will be forgotten if you should together be banished to everlasting darkness and despair, and would you not save them from that dreadful ruin? O, would you remember your Creator in the days of your youth, perhaps it might lead them to think of those things which belong to their everlasting peace. Then also, would you be profitable to others, the ministers of the Gospel might be gladdened by you, the Church of Christ delighted in you and the angels of Heaven rejoice over you.

Continued next week.

A wounded reputation is seldom cured.

The Weekly Pilgrim.

JAMES CREEK, PA., July 29. 1873.

☞ How to send money.--All sums over $1.50, should be sent either in a check, draft or postal order. If neither of these can be obtained, have the letter registered.

☞ When Money is sent, *always* send with it the name and address of those who paid it. Write the names and post office as plainly as possible.

☞ Every subscriber for 1873, gets a *Pilgrim Almanac* Free.

BAPTISM.

Continued.

SUBJECTS FOR BAPTISM.

About this there should be no question, as the design of it admits of none. Baptism is a sacrament for the remission of actual sins, and where there is no sin, no sacrament is needed. In the death, or fall of Adam all died, or were made subjects of sin, but in the death of Christ, all were made alive, or the original sin atoned for, hence there is now, no sin imputed to the world but that of actual transgression. Therefore all children born into the world are in a reconciled condition, have no actual sins and need no sacrament for sin, and therefore are not subjects for baptism. But the adult who has grown to years of discretion, does not, while living in sin, stand in covenant relation with God, hence the necessity of a sacrament to bring him into that relation. To become subjects for this sacrament there are two essential requisites, that of faith and repentance, or repentance and faith. The two are so inseparably connected that it is difficult to determine which comes first. In the law of reconciliation there is a provision made for actual sins but there can be no actual sin until there is an actual transgression or violation of law, and that law cannot be violated until the person is capable of understanding it. Hence, an actual sinner is one who violates a known law. It is by the law of Christ that we become cognizant of sin and learn that we are sinners. A faith in that law brings us to repentance, and genuine repentance makes us fit subjects for the sacrament of baptism. Therefore we very rationally conclude that none are fit subjects for baptism, but such as have faith in the Lord Jesus Christ, and repent of their sins.

The first instance of baptism on record is that of John's. In these baptisms we have faith and repentance, and that enforced by works or fruits. A simple confession was not sufficient, but it was said to them, "Bring forth, therefore fruit meet for repentance." From these baptisms were excluded all such as were not able to make a confession of faith and give visible signs that it was sincere.

In giving the great commission, we have; "He that believeth and is baptized shall be saved." The Commission was, "Go ye * * preach the gospel to every creature," and the conditions of that preaching was, "He that believeth and is baptized shall be saved." None but believers are or can be included in this commission as subjects for baptism as they must be believers and how can infants believe; who are not capable of understanding the law? In every recorded case of baptism that we have in the New Testament, they were believers, and we are prepared to prove it. But says one, we have household baptisms and in them there must have been children. We will briefly notice those cases. First is that of the Jailor. If this record proves anything, it proves entirely too much and is only used because there is really nothing better. But we will quote from the narrative, Acts 16, 32. "And he spake unto him the word of the Lord, *and to all that were in the house*." Now, *the all*, here referred to are the same that were baptized, and they were such as could have the word of the Lord spoken to them, they must have been such as were capable of believing. Again in the 34th verse we have "*believing in God with all his house*." Therefore, in the record we have nothing but believers as subjects for baptism.

And the household baptism is claimed in the case of Lydia, but the circumstance does not indicate where they were baptized, or that there were any children belonged to it, but the circumstanstantial evidences are rather strong against. Lydia was of Thyatira and notable as being connected with the dyeing-works of that place. She was a Jewish proselyte and there is not a particle of evidence of her being married or having children. The baptism occurred during the time that they, Paul and Silas, and some woman were at the river-side where they had resorted to pray and baptize. The narration says; "And we sat down and spake unto the women that resorted thither." These were all women that could be spoken to, and of the number was Lydia's household as it follows directly after, "And when she was baptized and her household," so that in all the household baptisms that can be produced, in not a single case, can it be proven or infered, that there was an infant included. How strange then that men will contend for that for, which there is not an iota of evidence within the lids of the Bible.

To be Continued.

Copy Wanted.—Our contributors will please supply us with some good original essays as we could make use of some just now. Those who have the time and talent should make use of it in laboring for the up-building of Zion.

SAD NEWS.

Under this head Bro. J. R. Royer says," Eld John Zug died on yesterday (July 20,) his funeral will be on the 23. He was of the Tulpahocken Church—hope some brother will give a report of his ministerial labor &c."

As Eld, Zug was extensively known in the brotherhood we will be pleased to have some one send his obituary with any other information that may be of general interest to our readers.

FOR SUNDAY SCHOOLS.

We are frequently asked for papers to distribute in Sunday schools, and as we have on hand a large number of odd copies of the Pilgrim, we will send them for Sunday school distribution at the following rates: 50 copies post paid, 40 cents, 100 copies, 75 cents, 200 copies, $1.50. Nos. of different issues will be sent. This offer is less than the postage and cost of paper, but we do it, hoping it may be for the good of the schools and may be used as a means of spreading our doctrine and introducing the Pilgrim. Superintendents, and friends of Sunday schools will please notice this offer:

Correspondence.

Notes of Travel.

BY J. S. FLORY.

Dear Pilgrim: I last wrote from Green City this Territory. On the morning of July 4th, having procured teams, blankets and an outfit of commissary stores, we set out, with nine others, for a trip down the Platte Valley. Travelled all day and at night camped out on the broad plains the ground for our bed, and the starry heavens over our heads. We may sleep out in this country with impunity, as the night air is pure and healthy. Next day we travelled on, passed Fort Morgan, and about noon arrived at the Old American Ranch, where we found a few settlers. Here we camped and after dinner went across the Platte river, which we had to do by wading. It was a novel undertaking, the course we waded was near or quite a mile in width and in places 4 feet deep, but we all arrived safely to shore, viewed the site for a colony town and took up claims. We found this section the most favorable of any we visited for agricultural purposes. There being a large scope of tillable lands that can be easily irrigated, and of surpassing beauty and productiveness. A Rail road is now in course of construction that runs along the Platte No rail road lands for speculators to get hold of, but all open to those that want to homestead or pre'empt. On our return we again waded the river and next day at 2 p. m. set out on our return. July 7th arrived at Green City. Had a meeting. A colony organization was effected, to be called Beaver Colony. An irrigating Canal company was also gotten up that water might be gotten at once into those valuable lands. July 8th, we returned to Evans and at 5 p. m. took the train for Denver City, the capitol of Colorado, where we arrived about night. Denver is quite a thriving city, beautifully laid out, a place of much wealth and business, and centre to which hundreds of invalids go and thence to the various springs and pleasure resorts of the mountains. In the morning, in company with D. B. Cady, passenger agt. of the U. P. R. R., J. F. Randolph, passenger agt., of the Illinois Central R. R., Dr. G. W. Butler, of Frederick City, Md., and Mr. A. Vines of Ind., we had the pleasure, through the courtesy of H. H. Given, superintendent of the Colorado Central R. R., of taking a free ride to Golden City, and thence up Clear Creek Canon to Black Hawk and Central City. Golden City is a thriving place, situated in a beautiful valley among the foot hills of the Rocky mountains. From Golden City, we went up on the narrow guage rail road, which runs up a deep gorge among the mountains: in some places the grade is an ascent of 211 feet to the mile, and winds up the creek like the trail of a huge serpent, nowhere is the road over 200 yards in a straight line. The scenery brought to view while passing up this canon, is said to be in beauty and sublimity unsurpassed by any in the world. It is truly terrible and sublime on either side, the mountains are piled up one upon another; and some places perpendicular, so that there is barely room for the narrow road to be constructed, and the creek comes down in rushing madness over rocks and through gorges. The mountains are in many places bare, in others studded over with the cedar, fir and pine.

The magnificence of the scenery was such, that we were impressed with the thought, truly there is a God of power beyond our comprehension, and the more we see and learn of Him as manifest in nature and revelation, the more we feel to adore, revere and fear Him. Truly it is a fearful thing to fall into the hands of such a living God, who hath spoken these mountains, valleys, and all other things into existence by the word of his power and might.

In passing up this canon we noticed quite a number of gold miners at work, delving into the mountain sides like quadrupeds after the shining ore, and also tearing up the bed of the stream, working in gravel, stone and water, all for that, the love of which is the root of all evil, while in a great measure the one thing needful—the riches of God's grace—is neglected. Black Hawk and Central City, are two small mining towns, in close proximity one to another, wedged in between the mountains. Numerous quartz mills and smelting furnaces are in operation. Rich silver mines are also in operation here, some of which contain three to four thousand dollars worth of silver to the ton of quartz. At the Teller Hotel we got a first-class meal. From the roof of the house we had a fine view of the surrounding mines and mountains. This town is located 8,300 feet above the ocean, several thousand feet higher than Denver City. We had, from Denver, a fine view of this range of mountains which looked grand and imposing with the background of snow clad ridges and peaks. The most prominent peaks are Pike's peak, 13,300 feet high, Long's, 14,000, Mt. Lincoln, 16,100.

Not far from Central City are the

Idaho Springs, and other places of resort for travellers and invalids. The climate here is cool, dry and bracing. We expect in a short time to return to Denver and then set out homeward bound. Our visit to the mountains and gold and silver mines, so far, has been pleasant and instructive.

Dear Pilgrim:—We ask the liberty of having a sketch of our trip and what we learned at A. M. &c., published in your columns. I have remained silent for some time but will now resume my pen again. Many brethren and sisters at A. M. wished to know the cause of our silence, but we have no particular cause.

In company with mother I left home on Friday p. m., via. Martinsburg. Remained over night with bro. G. W. Brumbaugh at Clover Creek. Saturday morning crossed Tussey's mountain to Cove Station, met a number of brethren and sisters on the train. Became rather tired of our lengthy wait of four hours and a half at Bridgeport. Never having gone the route, there was much that attracted my attention. Reached Dale City about 6 p. m., Saturday, June 31st. Found a number of brethren and sisters at the depot and among others bro. Hol-inger and Annie who escorted me to their home. After taking supper at the large boarding tent, we attended divine services at the Brethren's church. Sermon by bro. J. S. Flory from Rev. 3; 18. "I counsel of thee" &c. Sabbath morning sermon by bro D. P. Sayler to a very large congregation from the text found in Ephe. 2: 20. This was the first opportunity of hearing bro. S. although I have read many of his articles in our periodicals. At 3 p. m. attended the address of the S. S. We had rather expected to see the Sunday School in session, but the brethren tho't it best to have some one address the whole congregation. We are glad to know that Sabbath Schools are becoming something of interest among us.—Trust the brethren and sisters will manifest a greater interest in the good cause. I do not have the privilege of attending a S. S. conducted by the brethren, but hope the day is not far distant when we shall have one in our midst. Sabbath at 4 p. m., had the pleasure of listening to the sermon delivered by bro Enoch Eby from Isaiah 45—19 inclusive Also had the pleasure of forming his acquaintance during the meeting. Sabbath eve., for the first time, we had the good pleasure of hearing bro. John Wise from Rev. 4 latter clause of first verse. Exhortation by bro. Spanogle. I shall not soon forget the interesting conversation we had with bro. Wise while waiting for the train at the depot I felt myself much benefitted thereby. Many thanks to the dear brother for his instructions. Monday p. m. we were addressed by bro. Buckalew and Peter Nead. Neglected to note the text and it has passed from my memory. Monday eve. sermon by brethren Major and D. B. Sturgis from Jno 6: 27. Dear brethren and sisters, let us labor more faithfully for that meat "which endureth unto eternal life." On Tuesday eve. we were delighted to hear that bro. S. Z. Sharp would address us. Having been a student under his care, I still desired to receive instructions from him. Text John 12: 47, 48. I felt very much benefitted, although very tired from over exertion. Also had the pleasure of meeting sister S. She still has our thanks for past kindness shown us. Wednesday eve. sermon by bro. D. Longenecker and J. I. Cover.—Text 1. John 4: 1. Thursday eve. sermon by bro. Garst and Pence of Tennessee. After services heard many regrets that the brethren were so brief, but we suppose the ministering brethren as well as others felt weary. Friday eve bro. S. Z. Sharp spoke again from 1. Tim. 4: 8, followed by bro. Reidenbour. This was the last sermon we had in Dale City. Could not attend all the sermons, but attended those at the church. Other brethren spoke whom we had a great desire to hear, but it was impossible to attend all the sermons, as they were delivered at different places at the same time. Neither did I have an opportunity of hearing all the decisions. Think part of what I did hear would, perhaps, have better been omitted. On Saturday morning I in company with bro. G. and sister Myers, bro. Sharp and others, started on our homeward journey. Reached James Creek 3 p. m. where I remained with the PILGRIM family until Monday morning. Attended services there on Sabbath eve. in the Lutheran church.

After leaving James Creek, stopped at Huntingdon. Bro. A. B. B. of that place, has our thanks for kindness shown to us while there. On Monday eve., came to Tyrone and stopped with bro. Quinn. Found them well and very busy. Reached home on Tuesday.

The trip was one of delight to me. The privilege of attending the meeting was a greater pleasure; also enjoyed the society of the brethren and sisters and friends. Had the pleasure of meeting with many with whom I was acquainted, and also formed the acquaintance of many others of whom I had often heard. But we are confident that we shall not all meet again on this side of the grave. Perhaps some have already passed to the other shore.—Let us all labor faithfully to the end that we may obtain the crown of life.

E. R. STIFLER.

Hollidaysburg, Pa.

LIBERTY, Bedford Co., Va.

Dear Pilgrim: I wish you to change my address to Liberty, Va. I am living here at this time and find more brethren and sisters here than I expected. There are about 30, and seven were baptized on yesterday. Preaching by J. Moomaw of Roanoak Co., Va. There are two other small societies of member started up in this county, (Bedford, Va.) One at Falling Creek and the other at Skinnerl's School house, where we had two first class sermons by brother Moomaw. All admitted that there could not be anything said against them. The doctrine of the Brethren is well received in this vicinity by all that heard it. We look for good success in this Co., and pray that the good work may go forward that has now commenced in the old county of Bedford. Slavery is no more in the way, as it once was.

I believe, one opposition after another will be removed until a great reformation will take place and God will reign and rule in his own appointed way. This we are taught in the New Testament in which Christ lives, and if he continues to live in it, it will finally gain, and the world come under the true government of peace. The good that has been appointed, must come to pass at the appointed time, but we must not add to nor diminish from the old landmarks which our fathers have set. Do not forget it, brethren and sisters. Ever look to our Heavenly Father for all needful blessing, as he is the author and giver of all that is good. Let us pray and trust in his grace.

S. W. OVERSTREET.

Lovefeast at Jacob Malott's.

On the 8th of June, according to previous arrangements, we met with the brethren and sisters of Sidling Hill, Bedford Co., Pa., to participate with them in a Communion Meeting, and this being the first meeting of the kind ever held in this part of the country, the people flocked together from far and near, to hear and see, what these people would have to say and do. The meeting was held in the barn of friend Jacob Malott's, whose kindness and hospitality, we fondly hope heaven may bless, and the brethren not forget. In the afternoon, at the time appointed for service, a large collection of people were present, to hear the preached word. Elders Jacob Steel, Henry Clapper, David Clapper, Nicholas Martin, G. Horman, G. Bricker, A. Rowland, D. Young and D. Miller were the ministers present. The brethren also had an election for two deacons and one speaker, the lot fell upon Absalom Malott for speaker and James Take, and —— Correll for deacons, who are efficient for the charge. The meeting seemed to be much appreciated by both members, and hearers. We believe there were many honest hearted people present, who if they can be permitted to enjoy an unhindered view of the Sun of Righteousness, will soon learn the fact that there is no other name given under heaven whereby we can be saved but the name of Jesus." The good conduct of the people, and the order of the meeting, was certainly commendable. About one hundred communed, two added to the church. Meeting closed at noon on the 9th.

D. F. GOOD.

Waynesboro, Pa.

ANNOUNCEMENTS.

Please announce that the Cedar Creek Church, Anderson Co., Kansas, have appointed a Lovefeast on the 16th and 17th of August, '73 to commence at 2 o'clock p. m., at the house of Jacob Eighlaltz. A general invitation is given, especially to the ministering brethren. If any come by railroad, stop off at Garnett. The place of meeting is about 7 miles North-west of Garnett. Conveyance will be in attendance. By order of the Church. B. A. RADSELL.

Please publish through the PILGRIM that the Church of the Cerro Gorda district, Ill., have their Communion Meeting on the 27 and 28 of September 1873, and also the District Council Meeting of Southern Ill, will be held at the same place on Monday 29. It is desired that the churches of Southern Ill be fully represented, and a hearty invitation is given, especially to the ministering brethren to be with us on the occasion.

Those coming by railroad will stop off at Cerro Gorda. By order of the Church.

JOHN METZGAR
JOSEPH HENRICKS.

Please announce through the PILGRIM, that the brethren of Whitesville Church, Andrew Co., Mo., intend holding their Lovefeast, the Lord willing, on the 20th, of September. We heartily invite all members that have a desire to be with us. Preaching to commence at one o'clock. Place of meeting, two miles North-east of Whitesville. B. BASHORE.

DIED.

RIGGLE.—In Stanislaus Co., Cal., June 2, 1873, Jesse, son of brother Eliphas and sister Sarah Riggle, aged 2 years, 3 mos. and 8 days. Funeral by the brethren.

RIGGLE.—In the same family, on the 12th July, 1873, Charlie Riggle, aged 8 yrs. 5 mos. and 9 days. PETER S. GARMAN.

(*Visitor* and C. F. C. please copy.)

ELLIS.—In the Coldwater Church, Iowa, June 19, 1873, sister Susan, wife of Bro. Benjamin Ellis, aged 57 years, less one month, had nine children, (six are now living) and eleven grand children, a husband and many friends to mourn their loss; but not as those who have no hope. Funeral occasion improved by Eld. Benj. Beeghly of Waterloo, from Rev. 14: 13., to a large collection of friends and relatives.

The above died almost without any warning, as it is said by those present, that in fifteen minutes from the time she was taken sick she passed away without a struggle. Disease supposed to be heart affection. Another solemn warning to us all, and more especially to those of her children, who have not yet confessed Christ by obeying his commands.

MOSS.—Also in the same Church, and near the same place, June 24, sister Moriah, widow of Bro. David Moss, (who died over two years ago at this place,) aged 85 years, 8 mos. and 6 days. Funeral attended by a large concourse of relatives and friends, and the occasion improved by Eld W. J. H. Bauman from first epistle Peter, 1: 24.

Our beloved sister leaves a number of near relatives and three orphan boys to mourn their loss. She called for the Elders and was anointed in the name of the Lord shortly before her departure. She expressed a willingness to go, with a full assurance of obtaining the crown that is promised to the people of God. J. F. EIKENBERRY.

Visitor and *Companion* please copy.

CLAAR.—In bound of the Yellow Creek Church, Blair Co., Pa., July 18, 1873, sister Margaret, wife of Bro. John Claar, aged 41 yrs., 3 mos. Disease, Typhoid fever.

She left a sorrowful husband and 6 children to mourn their loss. She, at her request, was anointed sometime previous to her death. Funeral by the brethren from Rev. 14: 15.

BAKER.—Also in the same Church, near Bloomfield, Blair Co., Pa., June 20, 1873, sister Leah, wife of bro. Frederick Baker, daughter of bro. Samuel Hollinger, aged 33 years, 9 months, and 15 days. Disease Continuemen fever.

She leaves a sorrowful husband and 3 children to mourn their loss. She also requested to be anointed, but alas! till the brethren came it was too late. She was a consistent sister and devoted herself to the Lord in her young days. May others follow her example. Occasion improved by the brethren Matt. 24; 44, to a very large concourse of people. Thus our church in a few days lost two dear sisters, but hope the Church triumphant gained in order to swell the victorious Song in Heaven in honor to God and the Lamb. May these solemn occasions be sanctified to the conversion of members to fill their places in the Church militant, is the prayer of your unworthy correspondent. LEONARD FURRY.

BOOK NOTICES.

In this department we will notice such NEW BOOKS, *as may be sent us by publishers, that are in harmony with the character of our work. A. B. Brumbaugh, M. D., Huntingdon Pa., literary editor.*

BOOKS RECEIVED.

FROM HURD AND HOUGHTON 13 Astor Place New York.—The Riverside Press Cambridge Mass.

PROTECTION AGAINST FIRE &c., with practical suggestions for the security of life and property. By Joseph Bird. cloth 12 mo. $1.50.

HOMES AND HOSPITALS, or two Phases of Woman Work as exhibited in the labors of Amy Dutton and Agnes E. Jones. 12 mo. cloth $1.50.

THE GIFT OF THE KNEES or the Ministry of Prayer, the Ministry of Power. 18 mo. cloth $1.25.

THE PROPHET OF THE HIGHEST, or The Mission of John the Baptist, by Nahum Gale D D Frontispiece. 16 mo. cloth. $1 00.

THE MINISTRY WE NEED, by Seth Sweetser, D. D. 16 mo. cloth, 85 cents. For sale by Wm. Lewis, Huntingdon, Pa.

G. P. PUTMAN'S SONS Issue an attractive list of New Publications for the season of of 1873.—"Woods' Prose and Poetical Works," People's Edition, "More Worlds Than One." The creed of the Philosopher and the hope of the Christian. "All Around the World, &c., &c., 200 Illustrations. Also "The Great Problem," doubtless a very valuable work. Their "Handy Work Series," already comprising eleven volumes on subjects of special interest, would be a valuable addition to any collection. We shall again call attention to these, by their Titles & also to their "Series of Popular Manuals," all of Scientific importance and embodying the latest resources.

HURD & HOUGHTON announce among their latest publications a new book by Mary Clemmer Ames —OUTLINES of Men women and Things.

THE WRITINGS OF THE CAREY SISTERS, which are so universally admired.

J. B. Lippincott & Co., the celebrated Philadelphia publishers announce among their recent publications some of the most valuable and desirable works —*A New Dictionary of Poetical* Quotations, by S. Austin Allibone, LL. D., whose name at once gives character to the work.

ANTIQUITY OF MAN, by Sir Charles Lyell Bart. M. A., F. R. S. etc. new edition.

THE GLORY OF THE HOUSE of Israel, by Frederick Strauss. *A New Theology* by H. B. Browning M. A.

CHOLERA by Dr. Hartshorne, which is a matter of considerable interest at this time.

A. B. B.

LIPPINCOTTS' MAGAZINE is a *finely* Illustrated Monthly of Literature and science. Terms $4.00 yearly. Specimen numbers mailed, postage paid, to any address on receipt of 20 cents. New Volume commences with July No.

The August number of *Lippincott's Magazine*, contains the second portion of "The New Hyperion," a record of a journey from Paris to Marly by way of the Rhine. The illustrations to this serial are from the pencil of Gustave Dore, and are profusely scattered through the text, giving pictorial form to many of the most notable incidents and striking passages. The same number presents, among a variety of contributions, the seventh and eighth chapters of Miss *Howitt's* description of life and scenery in the Tyrol, an article on deer-parks by Reginald Wynford, an account of a visit to the interior of Japan, a paper on the fruits and flowers of the tropics by Mrs. Fannie R. Feudge, and charming poems complete,—A very attractive number.

J. B. LIPPINCOTT & Co., Publishers, 715 & 717 Market Street, Philadelphia Pa.

HUNTINGDON & BROAD TOP RAIL ROAD

On and after July 17th, 1873, Trains will run on this road daily (Sun excepted) as follows:

Trains from Huntingdon South. *Trains from Mt. Dall's moving North.*

ACCM. P. M.	EXP'S. A. M.	STATIONS.	EXP'S P. M.	ACCM. A. M.
6 05	8 15	Huntingdon,	AR6 00	AR8 30
6 10	8 23	Long Siding	5 55	8 25
6 20	8 30	McConnellstown	5 45	8 18
6 27	8 37	Pleasant Grove	5 38	8 11
6 40	8 50	Marklesburg	5 25	7 58
6 50	9 00	Coffee Run	5 15	7 48
6 57	9 08	Rough & Ready	5 08	7 40
7 05	9 15	Cove	5 00	7 31
7 08	9 18	Fishers Summit	4 57	7 30
7 25	9 35	Saxton	4 45	7 15
7 40	9 50	Riddlesburg	4 25	6 51
7 48	9 58	Hopewell	4 18	6 43
8 00	10 15	Piper's Run	4 05	6 35
8 15	10 26	Tatesville	3 56	6 24
8 25	10 37	Everett	3 38	6 04
8 35	10 45	Mount Dallas	3 35	6 01
9 00	11 10	Bedford	3 10	5 30

SHOUP'S RUN BRANCH.

A. M.	P. M.		P. M.	A. M.
LE 9 45	LE 7 30	Saxton.	AR4 35	AR 7 05
10 00	7 45	Coalmont.	4 20	6 50
10 05	7 50	Crawford.	4 15	6 45
AR10 35	AR8 00	Dudley	LE4 05	LE 6 35

Broad Top City from Dudley 2 miles by stage.

Time of Penna. R. R. Trains at Huntingdon

***Mail No. 2 makes connection at Huntingdon with Mail going East on Pennsylvania Railroad at 4.15 p. m., and West at 5.45 p. m. Mail No. 1 leaves Huntingdon at 7.40 a. m. on arrival of Pacific Express West.

Trains on this road connect with trains on Bedford & Bridgeport, and Cumberland & Pennsylvania Railroads.

G. F. GAGE, Supt.

The Weekly Pilgrim.

Published by J. B. Brumbaugh, & Co.

Edited by H. B. & Geo. Brumbaugh.

CORRESPONDING EDITORS.

D. P. Sayler, Double Pipe Creek, Md.

Leonard Furry, New Enterprise, Pa.

The *Pilgrim* is a Christian Periodical, devoted to religion and moral reform. It will advocate in the spirit of *love* and *liberty*, the principles of true Christianity, labor for the promotion of peace among the people of God, for the encouragement of the saints and for the conversion of sinners, avoiding those things which tend toward disunion or sectional feelings.

TERMS.

Single copy, Book paper, $1.50
Eleven copies, [eleventh for Agt.] $15.00
Any number above that at the same rate.

Address.

H. B. BRUMBAUGH.
James Creek,
Huntingdon county Pa.

The Weekly Pilgrim.

"REMOVE NOT THE ANCIENT LANDMARKS WHICH OUR FATHERS HAVE SET."

VOL. 4. JAMES CREEK, PENNSYLVANIA, AUGUST 5, 1873. NO. 31.

POETRY.

HOW BEAUTIFUL.

BY LOVINE H. BURKET.

When God in his own wise decree,
Had formed the earth, sky and sea;
The sun to give us light by day—
To drive from us dull thoughts away.

The stars all to their places hie,
To brighten up the dark blue sky;
Oh that our deeds on earth might be,
Like stars to shine o'er land and sea.

For while we sit and wandering gaze,
We soon forget those weary days;
Enraptured with the beauties there,
We think of Heaven, bright and fair.

All, all is beautiful and grand,
And governed by a powerful hand;
While nature's works are grand and true,
I love its beauties to pursue.

The moon sends forth her misty light,
To cheer the earth at dead of night—
Has never yet forgot to shine,
On land and sea—on shrub and vine.

All these are beautiful and good,
Because they emanate from God;
And if we love him—serve him too,
We all, his glory yet shall know.

Willmore, Pa.

ORIGINAL ESSAYS.

ORIGIN OF SABBATH SCHOOL OPPOSITION.

In this article the *origin* of Sabbath School opposition will be considered:

1. *Conscience.* — Many brethren claim to be conscientious in their opposition to Sunday Schools, and we are willing to admit that some are truly so. To admit this, however, is not to justify their course, much less is it to say that they are right. Yet we would speak to this class with great kindness, believing that when the clearer light of the more excellent way shines about them, they, like Saul of Tarsus, will cease to persecute the Lord's cause, and will, instead, become chosen vessels to carry forward the very work which they now condemn and oppose. The writer has heard brethren testify to this fact in connection with their own personal experience and observation. When the Brethren's Sunday School was first started in this neighborhood, they looked upon it with distrust, feared it would result in evil, and hence opposed it. But by and by, as they became better acquainted with the design and workings of the school their fears vanished, and with "confusion of face" they had to acknowledge that, ignorantly and blindly, they had opposed what God had been pleased to bless and to make a means of grace and an agent of great good in the community. We then find that conscience itself, the soundest pillar in the platform of Sabbath School opposition, sometimes rests upon a very sandy foundation, viz:

2. *Prejudice.*—This word is derived from two Latin words, one of which means *before* and the other *judgment*; hence the word means, premature judgment; or, an opinion formed before the facts in the case have been properly examined and considered. Prejudice is, perhaps, the most prolific source of erroneous conclusions and wrong opinions. It gets such a deep hold upon the mind that it seems to transmit itself. People seem to inherit wrong notions, just as they inherit bad traits of disposition, and they are both about equally difficult to get rid of. "To divest one's self of some prejudices," says Greville, "is like taking off the skin." Some people believe just what their ancestors did. The father's creed becomes the son's Bible, no matter how little truth there is in it. May we not trace some of the opposition to Sabbath Schools to this source? Then, again, some seem to look with distrust upon anything that certain other people do. Because Sabbath Schools are held by certain religious sects who don't obey the gospel in all points as we understand it, therefore, Sabbath Schools are wrong! What a silly notion! As well condemn (if this be the ground of condemnation) singing, prayer, public worship and a thousand other things that we hold sacred,—for *they* have them all.—Others there are who look only at the *abuse* of things. They see the Sunday School as we see the moon—only on one side,—with this difference, however, we see the moon on the bright side, while they see the Sunday School only on the shady side. This is because they don't look at it through the clear light of truth, but somewhat as we look at the sun—through smoked glass or some other colored medium. Consequently their ideas on this subject form a very tangled web of thought, full of dust and dead flies. And no marvel: for if we abstain from the use of everything that may be abused, we must do nothing, speak nothing, think nothing—and even then fail in our laudable undertaking. An argument of this kind against Sunday Schools can certainly rest upon no better foundation than that of another source of opposition, viz:

3. *Ignorance.*—This may seem a harsh term to some who oppose Sabbath Schools, but, as it underlies the above topic, our essay would lack an essential head did we not speak of it here in its logical order. Does ignorance underlie prejudice? We think so. To judge before we hear the evidence and weigh the fact is, to judge ignorantly; it is to pre-judge; it is prejudice. But, it may be asked, of what truths are those that oppose Sunday Schools ignorant? We answer: they seem to be—yea we know they are—ignorant of the sweet consciousness, which many feel, that Christ meets and blesses his children in the Sabbath School, making the hour spent there very often the pleasantest, happiest, most cheerful and most edifying hour of the day. Some Sunday School lessons afford more Bible knowledge, and fully as much spiritual food, as many of the *time-*honored, random sermons that we hear from those who deem study and preparation of no consequence, and are, withal, opposed to such innovations as Sunday Schools, Bible classes, religious papers, backed benches, &c.

Again, the opposers of Sunday Schools seem to be ignorant of the spiritual wants of the young, and the sad neglect of parents to supply those wants. Every child has a mind and heart as well as a body, and it has no more right to claim meat and drink for the latter than it has to receive mental and spiritual food for the former. True, it is the duty of parents to give their own children religious instruction at home, but it is equally true that this is one of those duties "more honored in the breach than in the observance;" and, it is also true that some children have no parents, or, if they have parents, the latter are irreligious, and, consequently, not very efficient teachers of righteousness. It is not true that every mother is a Eunice any more than that every boy grows up a Timothy. Nearly all mothers provide for the physical wants of their little ones; but how few provide for the wants of the mental and moral natures! They guide the little feet in safe paths, but let the the thoughts run wild; they give warnings in regard to the well, the highway and other dangerous places, but little or nothing is said about the pitfalls of satan and the broad road that leads to destruction. They serve plentifully every good drink and viand, except the bread and water of life; and discuss every garment and decoration more than the spotless robe of innocence decorated with the ornament of a meek and quiet spirit. Of these and many other things the opposers of Sabbath Schools seem to be ignorant, and to this ignorance we trace much of their opposition. But let us admit that they know all these evils to exist and yet offer no assistance in correcting them. We must then trace their conduct to the fundamental source of unworthiness, and we find that the ultimate origin of their opposition is—

4. *Selfishness.*—A certain writer says that—

"He who will not give
Some portion of his ease, his blood, his wealth,
For others' good, is a poor, frozen churl."

If it be true that the Sunday School is "for others' good," as we claim it is, then it is to be feared that there are a good many "poor frozen churls" even in the hot months of July and August. "No man liveth to himself alone," seems to be the motto of but few, even on the Sabbath day. Some even join the church, not for spiritual benefits, but for temporal advantages. Thousands live merely for self and selfish ends. It is true that among these thousands may be found a few who attend Sunday Schools through selfish motives, but the great majority will be indifferent to a cause that requires so much devotion and self-denial, with so little prospect of temporal reward, as does the cause of Sabbath Schools. When opposition to a good work springs from such a source as base selfishness, it is not out of place to quote, for the benefit of the individual who opposes, these lines of the poet:

The wretch concentres all in SELF,
And doubly dying, shall go down
To the vile dust from whence he sprung,
Unwept, unhonored and unsung.

J. ZUCK, JR.

Mercersburg, Pa.

OUR GREAT EXEMPLAR.

There appears to be a natural disposition in man to copy after something, and when any work is to be performed that is new to us, or that we have but a limited knowledge of, we feel the necessity of having a model from which to copy. We may have a definite explanation as to how the work is to be performed, but an explanation in abstract terms is not so intelligible as an example of something similar. And so it is with reference to everything in this life, we learn more from example than precept. When we read the laws of our country we form a limited idea of the penalty that will result from disobedience, but our minds are still more fully impressed with the suffering and unhappiness that is occasioned from disobedience, when we have an example before us. Who has visited the solitary dens of a penitentiary that has not been more forcibly impressed with the severity of a violated law? The very sad, forlorn appearance of the inmates make impressions on the mind that are indelible. Go too, to the scaffold, and witness the execution of the murderer. You may read again, and again the death sentence, but the terribleness of that sentence is not stamped on the mind as when the example is before you. Examples then always convey ideas most intelligibly, and consequently, we are more easily led by example than precept. Hence God taught man the plan of salvation principally by example.

It was by example that God taught man the law which forbids sin. The first law was that given to our first parents when placed in that paridisiacal home. The penalty of that law was death—a death from which none could deliver us, but God's own Son. There was then no arm to save, no eye to pity, and in this condition man would ever had to remain, had not God's own Son consented to bear the penalty. There are many examples on record illustrating the penalty of sin, but there are none that so forcibly illustrates it as the coming of God's Son into the world to suffer the penalty of a violated law. What an example of suffering! What must have been the feelings of those disciples as they accompanied their Lord to the most secluded spot in that ever memorable garden, and there beheld His suffering! Oh how those deep groans must have wounded their hearts! How deeply astounded they must have been as they saw the large drops of blood ooze from His pallid forehead, and trickle down to the ground! And as they gazed upon that lovely form being nailed to the cross, what must have been their impressions? It was one of the most striking examples of the awfulness of the penalty of sin, and one too that made impressions that can never be erased.

O, sinner will not this example of suffering reach your heart and make you feel your indebtedness to God and the awful consequences of disobedience? Jesus suffered the penalty that you might be redeemed from the curse of a broken law, and if after this great sacrifice having been made, you are disobedient, *you* must suffer the penalty. And how great that penalty!—death, eternal death—banishment from the presence of God and be in torment forever.

When God was about opening up the way of eternal life, He not only gave us an example of the penalty of sin, but also how His law should be obeyed, and how the powers of darkness could be overcome. Hence "the Word was made flesh and dwelt among men." Jesus now stands before the world as our great example. Saith He, "I am the *way*, the truth, and the life; if any man would come unto Me, let him take up his cross daily and follow *Me*." By this we understand that we are to imitate Him, and when we view His life we certainly have before us a perfect model. What an example of obedience! How resigned He was to the will of His Father! When He was about partaking of that bitter cup, how that touching appeal was fraught with simple resignation. "O, Father, if it be possible, let this cup pass from Me; nevertheless not *my* will but *thine* be done."

Dear Christian friends, we have in this an unparalleled example of simple resignation and obedience, and are we endeavoring to imitate His example? Jesus said shortly before He ascended to those anxious inquiring disciples, "In this world ye shall have tribulation." We have no doubt, brethren and sisters, all have experienced the veracity of this declaration. We have had our trials, our afflictions, and sometimes the cup has been indeed a bitter one, but it is God's design that we shall endure trials, afflictions, and even persecutions in this life; and as He has promised to be with us, and not suffer us to be tempted above that which we can bear, we should be resigned to His will, and, like Jesus, be willing to drink the bitter cup to the very dregs. The fact that we have to suffer for righteousness sake should only teach us obedience. Christ learned obedience through the things which He suffered, and when "He was reviled, He reviled not again; when He suffered He threatened not, but committed Himself to Him that judgeth righteously." Think of the things Jesus suffered that He might be an example. He was accused of being a seditious man, charged with being a deceiver, accused of performing miracles through Beelzebub the prince of devils, and finally condemned as a blasphemer against God. All these things were done in a way that would most affect the delicate and tender sensibilities of man; yet He never expressed a desire that they should be punished. These things which He endured only taught Him obedience to His Heavenly Father, and set the world an example of endurance, resignation and obedience.

Christ is also our example in baptism. We find Him when He was about entering on His public duties, at the river Jordan, demanding baptism at the hands of His forerunner John. John thinking himself unworthy, Jesus saith unto him, "Suffer it *to be so* now, for thus it becometh us to fulfill all righteousness." Then John baptized Him and as they "went up straightway out of the water," the spirit of God lit upon Him in the shape of a dove, and a voice from Heaven proclaimed the fact that He was from heaven, and that He was well pleased with the act. Now why was Jesus baptized? Not that He was a sinner, but to show that He approved of the act of baptism, and also give us an example of *where* and *how* to baptize. Jesus commands us to walk in His foot-steps," and by this we understand we are to follow Him very closely,—do just as He did. Now how did He do in baptism? Where was He baptized? Was it done in the house of worship? Was it done by sprinkling a little water on His head? It is not my purpose at this time to argue the subject of baptism at length, but merely to present a few thoughts for the benefit of those who *honestly* and *sincerely* desire to take Jesus as their example and follow in His foot-steps. We ask the reader to seriously consider this matter. Jesus was baptized *in the river of Jordan*. In this, we have, without doubt, an example of the *place* for baptism. It was done *in the water*, and those who are baptized anywhere else but in the water, are certainly not following the foot-steps of Jesus. After the baptism of Jesus, His forerunner John still continued to perform this sacred rite, and the next account we have of him, was in Enon, near Salem. There he was baptizing, and why did he resort to that place? "*Because there was much water there.*" It is evident from the language, that much water was required to perform baptism. Now Jesus did not Himself baptize, but His disciples. They were commissioned to perform this work, and were taught by example *where* and *how* to do it. Philip, who baptized the Eunuch, was taught where to perform baptism, and we have conclusive evidence of his idea of the place. In the 8th chapter of Acts, we have an account of this circumstance. Philip preached unto the Eunuch Jesus, and as he did this, the subject of baptism must have been presented, for "as they went on their way, they came to a certain water, and the Eunuch said, see *here* is water, what doth hinder me to be baptized?" After he was interrogated in reference to his faith, "the chariot was commanded to stand still; and they went both *into the water*, both Philip and the Eunuch, and he baptized him." In this we have a very striking illustration of Philip's idea of the place for baptism. It was *in the water*, corresponding precisely with the example of Jesus. By following up the record in reference to the subject of baptism we do not find a single instance in which it was ever performed in a house. John baptized *in* Jordan, and near Salem because there was much water there. Jesus was baptized *in* Jordan, and Philip went down *into* the water to baptize the Eunuch, and *thus* we have the place, wherever it is at all designated. I am aware that Pedobaptists try hard to prove that the baptism of the Jailor, Lydia and her household, &c., was performed in the house, but as the contrary has been conclusively proven elsewhere in our columns, I do not refer to these baptisms again.

J. B. B.

(To be Continued.)

PERMANENT HOME OF THE RIGHTEOUS.

For here we have no continuing city, but we seek one to come." Heb. 13: 14.

This is a truth, not only abundantly taught in the Scripture, but also seen by daily observation. Man is passing away, and in his best estate is but vanity. If he lives till his fourscore years, it is only as a moment compared to eternity. But how few, Oh! how few, live to that age! "He cometh forth as a flower, and is cut down; he fleeth also as a shadow, and abideth not." He is compared in this present life, "to a vapor that appeareth for a little time, and then vanisheth away." Were death the end of man's existence and no future life to be realized in which his eternal destiny is involved, when the deeds of this present life will be made manifest and be rewarded accordingly; it would not be so important how we live here, and we might say with the sumptuous man, "eat, drink and be merry." But the word of God saith, "Say to the righteous that it shall be well with them: for they shall eat the fruit of their doings. Wo unto the wicked it shall be ill with them: for the reward of their hands shall be given them." Hence, to the righteous the above subject is a consolation, and one of the greatest incentives to live a holy life, devoted to Jesus and his service, for therein he secures the promise of a better state of existence in that city which is to come, and the one that will abide forever. It brings him the bright, cheering, soul's reviving, yea, blessed hope of immortality; in which the faithful of all ages have lived and died; and made strong to endure wonderful afflictions, floods of sufferings and aggravated pains of death. Where is the christian, the child of God who would desire to live always here? Would he not feel to say to himself and to his godly associates, "Arise, let us depart; for this is not our rest; because it is polluted." Abraham by faith sojourned in the land of promise, in a strange country, dwelling in tabernacles with Isaac and Jacob, heirs with him of the same promise. They were contented though they had no princely pallaces to live in, neither everything else congenial to their carnal nature; and why? because they knew that this earth was not their permanent home; their minds were centered and fixed upon a better abode, their affections directed to God in whom they trusted, their citizenship in heaven; "For they looked for a city which hath foundations, whose builder and maker is God." So many of his descendants died in faith, confessed that they were strangers and pilgrims on the earth, they knew that they had no continuing city here; hence their actions declared plainly that they sought a country; they desired a better country, wherefore God is not ashamed to be called their God: for he hath prepared for them a city." Paul saith in behalf of believers, while reproving the enemies of the cross of Christ, (formal or carnal Christians), "Whose end is destruction, whose God is their belly, and whose glory is their shame, who mind earthly things. (A standing warning to inconsistent members.) "For our conversation, (or more properly, as some tender it) our citizenship is in heaven. Certainly our mind and affections should be centered on that elevated, glorious and blessed region from whence John saw the Holy City, the Heavenly Jerusalem, the final abode of the righteous, the city which is to come, descending down from God out of heaven, so magnificently adorned, as the everlasting dwelling place of men, where God will dwell and wipe away all their tears. That we have no continuing city here is a most glorious truth imaginable for that man, and for that woman, who obeys the word of God and walketh blameless, and whose conduct and deportment characterizes him or her to be a Christian indeed. Truly sad were our condition to bear all the ills of life that this flesh of ours is heir to perpetually, but we brethren and sisters, "receiving a kingdom which cannot be moved; let us have grace, whereby we may serve God acceptably, with reverence and Godly fear." For our God is a consuming fire. Hence, the text, no continuing city here is not so pleasing to the unconverted, as slavery to sin, and servants to satan, under the control of the carnal mind, they live in fear and terror of approaching death all the time, unless lulled into a sleep of security by the prince of darkness or their eyes blinded by the God of this world. O, sinner, ponder well the day or moment when your God, whom you daily offend, will bring a period to your existence. You build upon wood, hay and stubble, very inflamable materials, consequently fearful and terrible. "For behold, the day cometh, that shall burn as an oven; and all the proud, yea, and all that do wickedly shall be as stubble; and the day that cometh shall burn them up, saith the Lord of hosts. But unto you that fear my name, shall the Sun of righteousness shine with healing in his wings." Behold the great contrast!

"We've no abiding city here!
This may distress the worldly mind,
But should not cost a saint a tear!
Who hopes a better rest to find."

Ho ye careless, ye that reject the counsel of God against yourself in despising the offers of mercy and slight the invitations, rolling like a mighty stream echoing and re-echoing from one end of the earth to the other through the Apocalyptic trumpet of the Gospel. Hear the word of the Lord concerning the doom of the rebellious; "The earth mourneth and languishes, Lebanon is ashamed and hewn down; Sharon is like a wilderness; and Bashan and Carmal shake off their fruit. Now will I rise, saith the Lord; now will I be exalted; now will I lift up myself, ye shall conceive chaff, ye shall bring forth stubble; your breath as fire shall devour you. And the people shall bear the burning of lime; as thorns cut up shall they be burnt in the fire. Hear, ye that are afar off, what I have done; and ye that are near acknowledge my might. The sinners in Zion are afraid; fearfulness hath surprised the hypocrites. Who among us shall dwell with the devouring fire? Who among us shall dwell with everlasting burnings? Isa. 33. Such threatenings, expressed by the strongest language almost possible, should strike terror into every heart and cause him to examine his own case without delay. Since we have here no continuing city, brethren, sisters, have we an assurance that if our earthly house of this tabernacle be dissolved, that we have that building of God that house eternal in the heavens? Let us earnestly seek the city which is to come. Let us labor to bring others along.

"Take your companions by the hand,
And all your children in a band."

O, children, sons and daughters of pious parents, think, how painful, how dreadful it will be to see fathers and mothers, grand-fathers and grandmothers and brothers and sisters in the Kingdom of God, the happy abode in the city of God with the blessed in Heaven: and ye yourselves cast out: there will be weeping and gnashing of teeth. Therefore turn to God that ye may live. Farewell

LEONARD FURRY.

THERE would not be half the difficulty in doing right, but for the frequent occurrence of cases where the lesser virtues are on the side of wrong.

GREATNESS stands upon a precipice, and if prosperity carry a man ever so little beyond his poise, it overbears and dashes him to pieces.

THE ORIGIN OF BACKWARD BAPTISM.

J. H. Moore; Dear Brother:—Please let me have a little information in regard to the *Origin of Backward Baptism.* By reading the PILGRIM I understand you to say that this method is not yet 400 years old, having been invented since the commencement of the Reformation. Please let me know by whose writings it can be proven. In our neighborhood we have a number of that persuasion, with whom I occasionally come in contact, and I should be able to give unmistakable answers.

Yours fraternally,
ELD. WM. HERTZLER.

REMARKS.—Dear Brother, I prefer to make some remarks in regard to your query, through the PILGRIM, that the same answer may adapt itself to quite a number of other questions that are presented to me I will not answer your question in full, I have not time at present, but will present a few remarks that will likely give satisfaction. I will refer you to the last page of my work on "*Trine Immersion Traced to the Apostles,*" which contains a few extracts taken from the writings of Robinson and Judson from which I gain a part of my information respecting the *modern* origin of Backward Baptism. By referring to the works from which these extracts were taken it is really surprising to see how much testimony these Baptist writers give against their own practice.

I have been thinking of writing a work on the origin of the *Backward Immersion*, but it seems hardly necessary at present. My work on the "*Origin and History of Single Immersion*" will give you about all the information on the invention of Backward Baptism that any one needs to put to flight all the cases of backward immersion in America, or anywheres else. I have repeatedly asked of the learned Baptist for just one case of backward immersion before the year 1522, and have not yet found the man who can refer me to one single instance before this time. This work will likely be published some time the coming winter, it will probably contain a few chapters on the origin of Backward Immersion. The above remarks will answer several other questions that have been presented to me by other parties.

The *Historical Chart of Baptism* will be published as soon as the financial arrangements can be made. My work on "Trine Immersion" is going off quite rapidly, and it is altogether likely that I will soon have to publish a third edition. Several churches are buying them by the dozens to distribute through the country.

Respectfully your brother,
J. H. MOORE.

COME TO CHRIST.

Why should I come says the sinner? Because you are a sinner and should come for pardon. Perhaps you do not feel that you are a sinner, at least, you think you are no worse than others, but better than many. You are no drunkard, thief or adulterer, but keep the Sabbath, read the Bible and attend the house of God. But have you indeed obeyed all the commandments, never broke any of them, always been true, chaste, sober, honest, forgiving, kind; never indulged in pride, malice, anger, deceit or lust? God requires purity of heart as well as of outward conduct, and he knows all our thoughts. Have you then never cherished the thought of sin in your heart, though you have feared outwardly to commit it? The first and chief command is, to love the Lord our God with all our mind and strength. Have you always done this; always been thankful for his mercies; always carefully read his word in order to obey it; always tried to please Him, loved to pray to Him, taken delight in His day, His people, His worship; always striven to be "holy as he is holy," to make known his truth, to induce others to love Him, and endeavored, in all things, to glorify Him? If you have always done this, you have still just only done your duty, and have nothing to boast of. But you have not done it. Conscience tells you so. You know you have sinned thousands of times. You know you have sought your own and have not been prompted by a desire to please God. You have lived for yourself; you have sought man's approval, but God has not been in all your thoughts. The Bible tells us, "If a man says he hath no sin, he deceiveth himself, there is none righteous, no, not one. All have sinned, and come short of the glory of God." O my fellow-sinner, is it not true of thee? The God in whose hand thy breath is, and whose are all thy ways, thou hast not glorified. You are a sinner, guilt, enormous guilt hangs upon you. In God's book, all your sins are written down, you cannot get rid of them. Were you to labor for thousands of years, you could not atone for the past, all you could do would only be your duty. Paying to-day's debt, still leaves yesterday's where it was, and were you to give all you posses, or suffer torture and death, it would not take away sin. The past cannot be recalled, but there is forgiveness, free, full, eternal for the guilty. Jesus has pardon for thee, sinner, purchased with His own blood. Come for it. Come to Jesus Christ for he is both able and willing to give it.

D. WAGAMAN.

SPEAK KINDLY.—When thou goest forth in the morning speak kindly to those around thee; it will lighten the cares and labors of the day, and make the household and all its affairs more harmoniously. When thou returnest at night speak kindly, for it may be, in God's Providence that, before another day dawn, loved ones, of those about thee, may have finished the measure of life allotted for this world, and gone where no restitution can be made and no forgiveness asked. Speak kindly ever.—wherever thou goest wherever thou tarriest; for kind words ever drop sweetly like honey from the honey-comb. A. B. B.

CHRIST'S LAMENTATION OVER JERUSALEM.

No sooner had Christ reached the height of intrepid vehemence at which we have just beheld Him, than he gave way to a burst of tenderness, and changed the language of invective for that of lamentation. At one moment he is dealing out the arrows of a stern and lacerating oratory, and the next, he is melted into tears, and can find no words but those of anguish and regret. Indeed it is a transition more exquisitely beautiful than can be found in the most admired specimen of human eloquence; and we feel that there must have passed a change over the countenance, and the whole bearing of the Savior, which imagination cannot catch, and which if it could, the painter could not fix. There must have risen before him the imagery of a wrath and a wretchedness, such as had yet never overtaken any nation of the earth. And the people that should be thus signalled out were his countryman, his kinsman after the flesh, over whom his heart yearned, and whom he had affectionately labored to convince of danger, and conduct to safety. He was too pure a being, and he loved with too abiding and disinterested a love, to harbor any feeling allied with revenge; and, therefore, though it was for rejecting himself that those whom he addressed were about to be punished, he could not contemplate the punishment but with bitterness and anguish.

And hence the rapid and thrilling change from the preacher of wrath to the mourner over suffering. Hence the sudden laying aside of all his awful vehemence, and the breaking into pathetic and heart-touching expressions. Oh, you feel that the Redeemer must have been subdued, as it were, and mastered by the view of the misery which he saw coming on Judea, and by the remembrance of all he had done to avert it from the land, ere he could have passed thus instantaneously from indignant rebuke to exquisite tenderness. And it cannot, we think, be without mingled emotions of awe and delight, that you mark the transition from the herald of vengeance to the sympathizer with the wretched. Just as you are shrinking from the fierce and withering denunciations, almost scathed by the fiery eloquence which glares and flashes with the anger of the Lord—just as you are expecting a new burst of threatening, a further and wilder malediction from the voice which seems to shake the magnificent temple—there is heard the sound as of one who is struggling with sorrow; and in a tone of rich plaintiveness, in accents musical in their sadness, and betraying the agony of a stricken spirit, there fall upon you these touching and penetrating words, "O Jerusalem, Jerusalem, how often would I have gathered thy children together, even as a hen gathereth her chickens under her wings, and ye would not."—*Melville.*

FINDING FAULT WITH PROVIDENCE.

There is reason in finding fault if there is either hope of thereby amending the fault or of uttering useful warning. Applied to the actions of our fellowmen, adverse criticism is sometimes legitimate. But when the matter complained of lies out of the reach of human interference or control, the language of complaint strikes past all intermediate agents to the Most High. He who accuses, accuses God.

But among the things that are above and beyond our determination, one is obviously the weather. It is God who "causes his sun to rise" and "sendeth rain." It makes no difference, as to the present question, whether we conceive of the action of Divine providence as direct and particular, or as limited to the institution of general laws. In either case, the weather is what it is by the appointment of God. And what is more common? We read, the other day, a paragraph in a daily paper which spoke of "execrable weather"—weather, that is, worthy to be execrated, or cursed. Would not a cursing of the weather be dangerously near to cursing our Maker?

This is a matter on which many Christians, it is to be feared, do not sufficiently reflect. They fall too easily into the fashions of speech that are common, without sufficiently considering what they are saying. We may wish the weather were different, and may express that wish in a proper manner. But when we allow ourselves to be impatient and to "charge God foolishly," it is but too plain that He "is not in all our thoughts."—*Examiner.*

GENERAL INTELLIGENCE.

PARTS of Iowa and Wisconsin were visited by a tornado on Sunday night, 12th inst. At Cedar Rapids, Iowa, it was accompanied by thunder and lightning and rain. The lightning was so continuous and vivid that a person could almost read without any other light.

IN parts of Fond du Lac, Wis., all kinds of grain are so badly cut up that no attempt will be made to harvest it. The hail came in ragged chunks half as large as a man's hand. Windows on the south side of houses were all broken; many lambs and other young stock were killed, leaves stripped from trees and fences torn down.

THE earthquake in Italy, on June 27, was extraordinary. The solid earth seemed for a time converted into a liquid one, and houses were tossed about like ships at sea. There were fourteen movements, seven forward and seven backward, each occupying a second, as regular as the beat of the clock. Many persons were killed at Bellimo, and many injured.

THE Cholera is reported to be very bad in the northern part of Alaxander county, Ill., and about fifty-five miles from Cairo. It is said that from the 10th to the 14th inst. there had been thirty cases, twenty proving fatal. The neighborhood is said to be almost without an inhabitant, every one having gone to the hills. The crops have been left to take care of themselves.

CHOLERA IN INDIANA—Mount Vernon, in the southwest corner of Indiana, has suffered severely from the cholera. In five days, thirty deaths have occurred. More than half the population have left the town, many hundreds of them coming to Evansville. Others are preparing to leave unless a favorable change takes place immediately. No business has been transacted there for several days, and the place has a deserted and gloomy appearance.—Physicians have arrived from the surrounding towns and are rendering all the assistance in their power. Among the deaths on the 20th, were Dr. Matzedorf, a young German physician, who since the appearance of the epidemic has been most active in behalf of the sick and dying; one man with his two daughters died, the last but one of a family of ten who died of the scourge.

There is a move being made to petition the Middle District of Pa., to build a Church in some city or town, every year. This move, if successful, will be one among the best ever made by the Church. Of course, much will depend upon the action of the District in regard to the proposed Church at Altoona. At last account, out of 23 churches only 14 had reported. The majority of those reported have done very well and if the unreported part would do proportionately well, the committee could proceed at once. It is an undeniable fact that our Church has not yet learned to be liberal in the way of providing means for the success of the cause. Our possessions are too much *ours* and not enough the Lord's. We forget that all we have is from the Lord and that he has the power to give or withhold as seemeth good in His sight. Taking this view, why not give liberally with the assurance that the Lord can and will restore tenfold. We hope that not a Church in our district will feel that it has done its duty without doing something towards this very much called for move. Brethren and sisters, let us give liberally, and see if the Lord will not bless our store. Let us get in earnest and plant a Church in every town where there seems to be an opening.

EMIGRATION OF MENNONITES.—The party of commissioners representing the Mennonites of Russia, who, early in June, went to the North west on a tour of inspection, have recently decided not to settle in a body at any given point, but propose to divide and locate in different sections, to be chosen hereafter. They believe this plan will result in advantage to themselves, enabling them to assimilate more readily with other communities, and affording better opportunities for obtaining a knowledge of the people, customs and government of the country. Each of the agents now here represents different communities of Mennonites or Lutherans of from 200 to 2,000 families. Besides the Mennonites of Russia, there are many German Lutherans represented by these commissioners, and this visit is but the preliminary step in one of the grandest emigration schemes on record—there are no less than 300,000 Protestants in Russia and Prussia who are contemplating a removal to this country, after the reception of the reports submitted by the gentlemen now here. The Mennonites are of Protestant belief, and in some respects resemble the Quakers. They never bear arms, use profane language, or engage in lawsuits. They are exclusively a farming people, are very intelligent, and, as a class, are wealthy.—*N. Y. Ob.*

SUICIDE seems to become more prevalent every year. In looking over the morning paper we notice some twelve cases for the day before. The causes, seemingly, are different, but when fully tested prove to be the same—that of disappointment. Some for love, want of means, financial failures, crime, and not a few on account of proving untrue in positions of trust, who, rather than be detected, in their crime, and their own life. There seems to be two general causes for the growing frequency of suicide. First, the fastness and extravagance of the age. The standard of living is becoming so high that but few can fully reach it, others in the attempt become bankrupt and to end their shame, commit suicide, while still others have betrayed most sacred positions of trust and when the facts are about to be revealed, rather than meet the disgrace of themselves and families they rashly lay hold on their own lives. But another cause is, the growing infidelity of the age. This infidelity is, perhaps, more liberal than radical. God may not be altogether rejected, but He is being made so liberal in His judgments that almost anything is made an excuse for religion, and no crime is beyond His leniency, or to be more plain, God does not mean what he says. When such a faith becomes established there is no way to determine just how much He does mean. If His mercy will reach the saintly hypocrite, why not sincere suicidism.

Youth's Department.

EARLY PIETY.

Concluded.

Perhaps, if spared for future years, you may become a parent, and what a blessing it would be to your family to train them up in the way of peace.—God might reward your exertions by their conversion. They might act the same part to their children, and they again to theirs, and thus religion beginning in your early conversion, might flow on in your family for ages to come. Think not that this is an improbable case, it has often been realized. In addition to the blessings I have mentioned, it is the happiness of the real Christian, that all events in life are designed as blessings to him, all are for our good, and all will end in glory. even afflictions are blessings in disguise, for "Whom the Lord loveth He chasteneth, and scourgeth every son whom He loveth. All things work together for good to them that love God." Our light affliction, which is but for a moment, worketh for us a far more exceeding weight of glory.

The Christian often finds the path to heaven most secure when beset with thorns, and the sea of life safest, when most storms; afflictions, to the children of God, prove the best of mercies — The smiles of the world might allure them to ruin, but its frowns urge them towards heaven. The Martyr's flames have often preceeded the flame of heavenly joy. The crown of thorns has been the forerunner of a crown of glory, and they have drank the bitterest dregs of grief's most bitter cup, who shall hereafter rejoice evermore. It has been said that on board a ship, in the midst of a violent storm, when the Mariners were in distress and alarm, a little boy remained composed, and being asked the cause of his composure, answered: "My father is at the helm." So may the Christian say in every time of trouble, my heavenly Father is at the helm, and He will steer me safe through every storm, or when He pleases say to the tempest "peace be still."

One great advantage of early religion is, that it prepares the soul for every possible event. If you would make an early escape from all the dangers by which you are exposed by sin, and obtain an early title to the mansions in heaven, although God may grant you long life, an early knowledge will secure you that protection, and that which will make your life one of peace and happiness. But, perhaps, God designs only a few more months for you, and, if so, though it might be pleasant to live, it will be more pleasant to die. Possessed of an interest in the blood of Christ, you will find the shortest life the shortest path to heaven. Early death would be early blessedness. The world might lament your early, and in their view, untimely departure, while you rejoice in having gained a home in the paradise of God. They who arrive there before they have passed the short span of twenty-five years in this world, will never wish to come back and pass an other twenty-five here.

Let me relate a litte history relative to this. Some years ago, in a village there lived a thoughtless girl.—Her name was Mary, and like most around her, she knew not God, and lived in the sinful pleasures of the world. Soon after she had completed her thirteenth year, a young woman, who had chosen the better part, persuaded Mary to accompany her to hear a sermon. The place of preaching was the cottage of an humble Christian, one of the Lord's poor. The subject was "The carnal mind is enmity with God." Mary listened, the Lord opened her heart; she felt the power of divine truth, and obeyed the same, and was made an heir of heaven. A few months afterwards she took sick and then the Lord was her support; she found promises sweeter, and sweeter, that there were enjoyments in His Word that none knew only those who realize them. At length she entered into rest before she had spent eighteen years on earth.

So my young friends, how much the grace of God may do for those who embrace religion in early life, even in a short time. On Mary's thirteenth birth-day, she was thoughtless and careless and on her eighteenth could arrive a saint in glory. Within the short space of something more than four years, she was enabled to forsake the world, to find a Savior, to profess His Gospel, to honor her profession, to languish calmly through months of sickness, to conquer death, and doubtless land in Heaven. In that short time, she found the Lord, finished His will, and went to rest. How blessed was early piety to her. She might have said, like many others, I am not yet fourteen, surely hereafter will be soon enough for me, and had she reasoned thus, and put off, though but a few years, her inquiry for salvation, God, it seems, by early death would have put it off forever. Delay not then to accept that blessing which is the source of every other blessing. Your life is as uncertain as hers.

G. W. BRICKER.

Claylick, Pa.

HE that hath tasted the bitterness of sin will fear to commit it; and he that hath felt the sweetness of mercy will fear to offend it.—*Charnock.*

THE TRUTH A WITNESS.

At a certain place in a certain town not far from here, two boys, Peter and John, who were brothers, had a feeling of malice in their hearts toward Harry, one of their associates, and about of the same age, because Harry said some hard words, as they called them, a good while ago. So Peter and John agreed to take spite out of Harry, at some conveuient time, and did so by beating him with their fists until he was quite bruised. They did this, as they said, because Harry had said bad words about them.

When they left Harry go, he went home and told his father what happened who felt very sorry, but tho't perhaps Harry gave occasion for the treatment. So when Harry's father asked him, why Peter and John abused him, he told his father, they said I called them names and used bad words, and I did not. So the father of Harry took him over to see Peter and John and their father about the matter. When the father of Peter and John heard what happened, he was also sorry, but supposed that Harry must have given occasion for the treatment. He asked Harry whether he did not do or say something during the day that made the boys cross, not supposing his two good boys had cherished a spiteful feeling for a long time toward Harry. Then Peter and John were called and asked about the matter. The two boys confessed they had hit Harry, and that for using hard names and saying bad words, and the boys both testifying the same thing, would let poor Harry father an untruth. But Harry made a manly appeal to the boys by saying, "What did I say, or what did I do to-day?" Then Peter and John replied, "Oh, you did not say or do anything to us to-day out of the way, but a long time ago,"and now for the first time, Harry found out what they really abused him for, quite to the astonishment of all,—a thing that should have been buried and forgotten long ago. So notwithstanding Peter and John testifying that what Harry said to his father was true, yet they were punished for keeping malice in their hearts and avenging themselves on Harry. Harry got clear, we notice, by the two boys testifying to what he said was true. When Harry and his father were returning home, he said to his father, "Father, if I had not told the truth, I could not have proved it." Boys and girls, always tell the truth, because the truth has always a witness.

D. F. GOOD.

THOU canst not do one good thing, nor overcome the weakest enemy, nor take one step in the way to heaven, without Christ.—*Romaine.*

DON'T LET YOUR LIFE BE A FAILURE.

Few sadder sentences fall from the lips than this:"My life has been a failure." And the saddest part is, that the failure can rarely be retrieved, because the convicton to most people, comes too late—Comes in the feebleness of old age when the brain is weak, and habit strong; comes after strength and true work and self diciplice is gone. Says Rev. W. H. Murry: "Society is full of failures that need never have been made; full of men who have never succeeded; full of women who in the first half of their days did nothing but eat and sleep and simper, and in the last half have done nothing but perpetuate their follies and weakness. The world is full, I say, of such people; full of men of every trade and profession, who do not amount to anything; and I do not speak irreverently, and I trust not without due charity, without making due allowance for the inevitable in life, when I say that God and thoughtful men are weary of their presence. Every boy ought to improve on his father; every girl grow into a noble, gentler, more self denying womanhood than the mother. No reproduction of former types will give the world the perfect type. I know not where the melennium is, as measured by distance of time; but I do know and so do you, that it is a great way off as measured by human growth and expansion. We have no such men and women yet, no age has ever had any, as shall stand on the earth in that age of peace that will not come until men are worthy of it."

Young men!—young women! don't let your lives be failures. Make the best of what God has given you. Let your gratitude to him for life and its noble endowments, be expected in full devotion of will and tho't, and strength, to whatever work he brings in his wise providence to your hands. And remember that it is only good and useful work that he provides. Shun work—work that harms your neighbor in any way, as you would the deadliest thing. No true success ever comes from evil work. It may bring a harvest of golden apples, and purple grapes: but the apples will be like those of Sodom, full of bitter ashes, and the grapes sour.—*Arthur's, Home Magazine.*

THERE is no reason to fear that the religion which is developed in sunshine will shrivel and die in the darkness; that the plant which thrived in the conservatory will perish in the storm-blast.

WORK while you can, for the night cometh when no man can work.

The Weekly Pilgrim.

JAMES CREEK, PA., Aug. 5, 1873.

☞ How to send money.—All sums over $1.50, should be sent either in a check, draft or postal order. If neither of these can be obtained, have the letter registered.

☞ When Money is sent, *always* send with it the name and address of those who paid it. Write the names and post office as plainly as possible.

☞ Every subscriber for 1873, gets a *Pilgrim Almanac* Free.

BAPTISM.

Continued.

SUBJECTS FOR BAPTISM.

The fact is, there is not one parent out of ten who have their children baptized, can give the least reason for so doing except that their minister says it is a duty that should not be neglected. Thus parents are blindly led into a thing for which there is no foundation, and then delude their children by a false hope, the crime of which, may not be realized until after they are brought up before the judgment bar of God.

Ministers of the Gospel have no more right to baptize infants than idiots or Hottentot heathen. Salvation is a personal matter and parents or no one else has the right to choose the religion of their children by proselyting them while they are yet unconscious infants. Baptism is a sacrament instituted by God for the remission of actual sins. Therefore it is a matter for their own choosing and not that of another. If they after becoming cognizant of being sinners, repent of these sins and have faith in Jesus Christ, as the mediator for sins, they are then fit subjects for baptism and come under the power of the commission; "He that believeth and is baptized shall be saved." It is passing strange that a single one, of general intelligence, should risk their salvation on such a groundless foundation, yet thousands do it against better light and judgement. We are glad however to know that a large number are not willing to die without the assurance that they have been born again, and are baptized upon a living faith in Christ,

A case of this kind came under our notice a few years ago. He was a man that had passed his three score and ten—had been told by his parents that he was baptized when he was a child, and with an ever accusing conscience, he labored to make himself believe that all was well, and succeeded well enough while in the enjoyment of health, but when sickness came and life's cords, one after another, began to snap assunder, his anchor (hope) would not reach bottom, and while lingering upon his bed of sickness and death, his mind became troubled and the power of truth came flashing in upon him so powerfully that while alone, he was frequently heard to say; "he that believeth and is baptized shall be saved." In conversing with him, he said; I now believe, but am not baptized. They tell me that I was baptized but I know nothing of it." In his dreams, he sat by the water side, a man came along of whom he requested to be baptized, the answer was; "If thou believest thou mayest." He was then taken down and buried with Christ in baptism and then went on his way rejoicing, but on getting awake it was all a dream, and still unwilling to surrender altogether to the power of converting truth. After a few months of fighting against wrong teaching, he gained the victory and we were called upon to come and baptize him. My elder brother and I went and found him in bed and very low, but the spirit was willing, and after a season of prayer, he was taken out of his bed, taken to the water and there baptized upon a living faith in Jesus.

After his return, he was so cheered and felt so invigorated, that he sat in his chair for several hours. His cup seemed now to be full and he was ready to depart. After another season of prayer, we took our leave of him to meet no more until we reach the other shore, as we in a few weeks got the intelligence that he had fallen asleep in Jesus with a blessed hope of immortality.

Oh, how we wish all that are thus deluded might have the advantage of such an experience before their dying hour.

In conclusion, we would say, do not be deceived. Cursed are they that make flesh their arm. Your salvation depends not on another, but on yourself. If you believe and are baptized, the promise is, you shall be saved. Believers, and believers only are fit subjects for baptism, and he that teaches otherwise, has not a thus saith the Lord for it, because there is not a single passage in the New Testament in favor of anything but believer's baptism.

OUR LARGEST LIST.

There was a number of our agents wishing to know where our largest list goes. We would have given the information sooner but it did not seem to be fully determined, as some of our prominent lists in a short time, were considerably changed. Cerro Gordo, Ill, at present is 15 ahead of all others, numbering 60 names. This we call good for one office, and if our other periodicals have a corresponding circulation, speaks well of the community, showing that they are a reading people. We have agents that sent us larger numbers of subscribers, but not at one office. Such lists are encouraging and show that our brethren and sisters are interested in the cause of religion. All of our agents done quite well and a number are still at work and not without success. One since A. M., has added 20 names to his list, another 19, others smaller numbers, but have added materially to our list. This morning, a brother sends us 7, which he says he gathered in a few hours, and thinks if all would make a similar effort, our circulation might be doubled. We wish the effort might be made. We can still supply a considerable number with all the papers containing the report of A. M., and the remainder of the year for 75 cents. Let the work continue, all such favors are highly appreciated.

POSTAL CARDS.

Postage, in a business of some magnitude, is a matter of considerable importance and a cheaper system of postage has long been desired. This, we now have in the "Postal Cards." To us, they are a saving institution and could be used by our agents and readers, in many instances, to advantage. In gathering subscribers, if you do not wish to send the money until you can get more, give your postmaster one cent and get a card, and on this you can send the name as well as in a letter and save four cents. If Nos. are missing or you have any short business transaction, a postal card will answer just as well as a letter. They can be had now at almost any post office, and cost one cent each whether you get a single one or a thousand. A penny saved is two pennies made.

MISSING NUMBERS.

Some of our readers complain of not getting all of their papers. For this, we are sorry as we know how vexing it is to miss our weekly paper, especially if we are interested in them. We observe as much care as possible in sending them properly, but the postal department is not as perfect as it should be, and some of them are lost by the way. To remedy the disappointment as far as possible, we will send all that are missing if informed of the numbers. In calling for the lost papers, always give the number instead of the date.

Bro. J. H. Moore informs us that he intends soon to have published several works which are now in course of preparation. Bro. Moore is a good writer, and will give nothing to the Brotherhood and the public but what is strictly orthodox. His works will be announced when ready for distribution.

BOOKS.

We have, now on hands, a good assortment of Hymn Books, also the Brethren's Tune Books. Those in want of either can be supplied at once.

LITERARY NOTICES.

Protection Against Fire, by Joseph Bird, Hurd and Houghton, Cambridge, Mass. This book is by an author who is the greatest authority upon fires, and their prevention in the country—a practical man, who has been forty years collecting the material here used, experimenting upon the suggestions and advice here given. His warnings have been repeatedly given through the journals and in public talks, so that he has come to be recognized as authority upon this subject. Mr. Bird's principle seems to be that the only practical way to stop a fire is in its incipiency,—"An ounce of prevention is better than a pound of cure."—The book is very readable, graphic and animated in style, and discusses an important subject in a manner calculated to arrest the attention of any one. Price, $1.50.

The Ministry we Need, by Seth Sweetser, D. D. Hurd and Houghton. This little book will be found interesting by all Christians, but has a special adaptation to the wants of those who are in the ministry, or liable to be called into it. "The harvest truly is great but the laborers are few."—Price 75cts.

For sale by Wm. Lewis, Huntingdon, Pa.

Harper's Monthly for August is received and as usual, complete with interesting reading. Among the leading and most instructive papers are "The little Laborers of New York City." This embraces ten pages and is of rare interest. It is astonishing to learn what a vast amount of labor is performed by the "little hands" in our large cities. "The Telegraph" is instructive and should be read by every body. Also "Madame De Sevigne and Her Contemporaries, *Hawii-nei*," "John Blake's Name Sake," "Ten years among the Rowing Men," "Signers of the Declaration" and a number of others, are papers that will be read with much interest. Published by Harper & Brothers, New York, at $4.00 per year.

Scribner for August leads off with "Nantucket" giving a very lively description of this once renowned place, followed by "Normady Picturesque," The "Compas Stone," "Modern scepticism," "Mount Shasta," "Beyond the Portals," "Home and Society," "Culture and Progress," and a large amount of other interesting and instructive reading. Published by Scribner & Co. New York at $1.00 per year.

The Phrenological Journal, our old favorite, comes as ever filled with information none can afford to do without. There is nothing in which we should exercise so much care as supplying our families with unexceptional reading. The crimes of the late murderers, Walworth and Stoddard are both traced to low and trashy Novel reading. Clean your houses of such trash and supply your children with high toned Magazines among which there are none better than the *Phrenological Journal*.—Published by S. R. Wells, New York, at $3.00 per year.

FOR SUNDAY SCHOOLS.

We are frequently asked for papers to distribute in Sunday schools, and as we have on hand a large number of odd copies of the Pilgrim, we will send them for Sunday school distribution at the following rates: 50 copies post paid, 40 cents, 100 copies, 75 cents 200 copies, $1.50. Nos. of different issues will be sent. This offer is less than the postage and cost of paper, but we do it, hoping it may be for the good of the schools and may be used as a means of spreading our doctrine and introducing the Pilgrim. Superintendents and friends of Sunday schools will please notice this offer:

MONEY LIST.

Sarah. *Barnhart*	3.25	Daniel *Brower*	1.50
C. Secrist	.80	John I. Garber	.50
George Worst	.80	W. C. T. all right	2.50
B. B. Bollinger	1.55	S. J Garber	0.51
R. M. ——	1.50	Dr. Solomon	1.35
Samuel Ryman	1.50	A. P. N. ——	6.00
John A. *Myers*	3.75	G. W. Bricker	.35

Correspondence.

LETTER TO E. R. S.

Dearly beloved sister:

O, what a goodly heritage is mine! Truly my lines have fallen to me in pleasant places. So were my tho'ts when I received your kind, encouraging, and sympathizing letter, and am prompted with feelings of Christian fellowship and affection to pen a few lines this beautiful morning, to let you know that I am still on praying ground and pleading terms with my heavenly Master, am still blessed with a reasonable degree of health, food and raiment. I feel that I ought to be content. Although I have passed through a sad ordeal, yet I feel that I am highly favored, for I am daily surrounded with blessings more than can be numbered, from the hand of our Heavenly Father, who heareth the cries of the needy, for not a sparrow shall fall to the ground without His notice. In His promises I have hope, faith and confidence, knowing that what He does is well done, for His purposes are all wise. Amid all these blessings, I have often to think of departed days, of years that have gone by, of the loved ones that have passed away with the days and years never more to return. I still feel the sad vacancy that has been caused by the hand of death, that never can be filled, save by the love of Christ,(but I have not fully attained to that as yet.) Sometimes I feel a desire to depart, to leave this world and be at rest, but all the days of my appointed time will I wait with patience, until my change shall come

Dear sister, I am living in the blessed anticipation of that glorious change which is awaiting us, when these mortal bodies shall put on immortality, and this corruptible shall put on incorruption, when the soul shall burst the prison house of death and mount on golden wings to meet the Lord in glory. Dear sister, may we be the happy participants of that glorious event, that we may behold the King in His beauty, may behold those that have come up out of great tribulation, and have had their robes washed and made white in the blood of the Lamb. My earnest desire and prayer to God is, that we may not be of the number that shall call to the rocks and mountains to fall on them and conceal them from the face of Him that sitteth upon the Throne, but that we may range the blessed fields, assemble on the banks of the River, and sing hallelujahs forever and ever.

When I commenced I was at a loss to know what to write, but my prayer was that I might write something that would be pleasing in the sight of God, something that would leave a lasting and pleasing impression on your mind, something that may encourage you on your way to the Holy Hill of Zion, something that may have a tendency to encourage both of us, (and all who may read these imperfect lines,) to strive to raise the Gospel-standard higher, to strive more fully to unfurl the banner, the blood-stained banner of the Prince of Peace, that we may be enabled to die more to the world and worldly pursuits, and come nearer to the wounded side of our blessed Redeemer. O, sister dear, if all professing Christians would strive more earnestly to keep the Gospel-armor bright, they would have less time to decorate their dying bodies with all the useless articles of fashion. Beware of the allurements of the goddess of fashion, for methinks, she, like alcohol, has a tendency to send many down the broad road of eternal ruin. My desire is to retain the old landmarks that together, we may strive to improve our talents that when our Master comes, we may hear the welcome plaudit, "Well done good and faithful servant, thou hast been faithful over a few things, enter into the joy of thy Lord."

Bro. Jacob Conner expects to attend the Annual Meeting, I hope if you are there you may become acquainted with him, [We did have the pleasure of meeting him. E. R. S.] My health is much better than it was a year ago. I would like to see you very much, perhaps, the Lord willing, it may happen sometime. Write soon again, for it is a great pleasure to know that you still remember me. Pray for me that I may still try to press upward and onward that when I am done with time and timely things, I may be so happy as to meet my loved ones on the shore of everlasting deliverance, and I hope to meet you there. Please accept my warmest thanks and best wishes. From your weak sister in the Lord. H. HOLLOWARSH.

Pottstown, Pa.

Notes of Travel.

BY J. S. FLORY.

Fairfield. Iowa, July, 19, 1873.

Dear Pilgrim:—I last wrote from Central City, Col. We returned to Denver City the 9th, and the 10th at 9 a. m., set out for Omaha, Neb, where we arrived next evening at 2:30, and left Council Bluffs at 4 p. m., and at 2:30, next morning, arrived at this place, from whence we went to Washington, and thence to Keokuk co., Iowa, where our parents and many other relatives and friends live. Had three meetings with the brethren in their meeting house near South English. Our time being limited, we had to set out homeward bound this morning and arrived here just before noon and have to tarry until 5:40 p. m. when we expect to be again on our way by rail. The crops in this State are abundant. The wheat harvest just now fairly coming, will be a great one.—Corn and other crops are also promising. I notice there is much of the old, crop of corn on hand. It is not likely there will ever be a famine in these United States while there is an Iowa to pour into the "Lap of plenty" her millions of bushels of grain. This State is improving in many respects very rapidly. One noticeable feature in her general appearance, is her groves of timber, which makes her begin to look like a timbered country, all the result of a well directed policy of her many thrifty farmers, in planting trees around and about their premises. When first I visited these wide extended prairies, they were almost an entire unbroken landscape of natural scenery; now they are in appearance, like a garden blossoming in richness and beauty, teeming with an enterprising population. The fulfillment of of that poetic prophet who, long ago, said,

> "I hear the tread of the pioneer,
> Where soon shall roll a human sea."

The weather is extremely warm and unpleasant. This town is the county seat of Jefferson co., and a thriving place of business, situated on the I. B. & W. R. R. and also the Chicago R. I. and Pacific R. R. railroad passes through it.

Yours truly.

Home, July 21, 1873.

I last wrote at Fairfield, Iowa, at which place I left the evening of the 16th at 5:30 a. m., one hour late, consequently missed the Cincinatti train. So I had to lay over 6 hours. Arrived at Cincinatti at 11 o'clock at night—had to lay over all day at Cincinatti, or until 4 p m., when I left, aboard the elegant steamer "Fleetwood" arrived at Huntington next day at 10 a. m, left in a few minutes, aboard the cars, and at 4 p. m. arrived at home and found all well. Truly the Lord blessed us abundantly, and we still are the recipients of His great mercies.

Dear Editors:—The *Weekly Pilgrim* continues to make its ever welcome visits to our home, and to fully realize the joy its messages give us, would be to be placed in our position. Those who live in a neighborhood where the Brethren are numerous and have the advantage of attending church every Sabbath, have no idea how hungry we, who live away out here in the prairie, isolated from kindred spirits, become for the Bread of Life. But we feel to thank God that though we as yet have no minister of the Gospel to preach for us, we have a *Pilgrim* who comes to see us every week, and gives us several good sermons with much good news from the general Brotherhood. Brethren and sisters, how we wish you would all write more. It does our souls good to hear of the welfare and prosperity of our beloved Zion. In our isolated condition, we sometimes are made to think that we are only "a few" but when we read of the large congregations and the many entering the Fold of Jesus, we take courage and thank the Lord. There are many things that transpire in the Eastern churches that would be of much interest to us in the far West. Then, for the sake of us and the many like circumstanced, let us have the news of the Kingdom. Yours in hope of eternal life. S. R. F——

ANSWER TO QUERY.

Jno. 10: 9.

"I am the door: by me if any man enter in, he shall be saved, and shall go in and out and find pasture."

I am not in the habit of unraveling mysteries, but will give my views, in short on the above Scripture.

"Shall go" in signifies,entering into the Church of Christ on earth by repentance, faith and baptism.

"Out" is leaving the Church Militant and entering the Church triumphant, which will be a change from mortality to immortality, a pasture so rich to the soul that it can not be compared to the pastures as enjoyed by the world, a pasture that will never be parched and burned by the sun, but will be fresh to the soul as a river of water.

JAMES L. FITZGERALD.

ANNOUNCEMENTS.

Please publish through the PILGRIM that the Church of the Cerro Gorda district, Ill., have their Communion Meeting on the 27 and 28 of September 1873, and also the District Council Meeting of Southern Ill, will be held at the same place on Monday 29. It is desired that the churches of Southern Ill be fully represented, and a hearty invitation is given, especially to the ministering brethren to be with us on the occasion.

Those coming by railroad will stop off at Cerro Gorda. By order of the Church. JOHN METZGAR
JOSEPH HENRICKS.

Cedar Creek Church, Anderson Co., Kansas, 16th and 17th of August, 1873.

Whitesville Church, Andrew Co., Mo., Sept. 20, and 21.

MARRIED.

BROWN—KEPHART.—At the house of the undersigned, Thursday July 24, '73, Mr. George S. Brown, of Brownsville, Md., to Miss. Laura O. Kephart, of the city of Altoona, Pa.

WM H. QUINN.

DIED.

HOOVER.—In the Clover Creek Congregation, Blair Co., Pa., July 10, '73, Bro. Jacob P. Hoover, aged 69 years, 5 mos. and 14 days. Funeral services by Eld's Jacob Miller and Daniel Holsinger from Rev. 16: 15.

Brother Hoover had been a very consistent member, and up to the time of his death had served in the office of deacon for many years, with much credit to himself and benefit to the Church. He was a good and wise counsellor, and was always ready to do his duty. The neighborhood has lost one of its best citizens, and the church a strong post. He was taken away very suddenly. He had been complaining for a few days but did not think it to be serious, and on Wednesday morning he told his companion that he would go to the mill that day. So he went to the stable and fed his horses and returned to the house to partake of breakfast, and soon after he had eaten, he told his wife that he felt sick, she should make him some tea and he would lie down. She stirred the fire and then went up to his room where she found him lying on the bed dying, and expired before any other person could be called in the house. On Friday the 18th, his remains were conveyed to the family graveyard, followed by a very large concourse of neighbors and friends to mourn their loss.

T. B. MADDOCKS.

SNELL.—In the Sugar Creek Congregation, Allen Co., Ohio, July 16, '73, sister Mary, widow of Joseph Snell deceased, formerly of Rockingham Co., Va., aged 79 years and 29 days. Funeral service by the Brethren from 2 Cor. 5: 1.

DANIEL BROWER.

BROWN.—In the Blue River District, near Columbia City Ind., on the 1st of July '74, after a short and severe illness, Elon, son of brother Daniel and sister Rebecca Brown, aged 15 years, 11 mos. and 21 days. Funeral services by Eld's David Barr and Joseph Zeigler, from James 10: 17.

A dutiful son, affectionate brother, and faithful friend. His loss is deeply mourned, not only by his parents and relatives, but also by a large circle of friends and neighbors who greatly sympathize with the bereaved.

EZRA ZUMBRUN.

A YEAR WITHOUT A SUMMER.

The following is a brief abstract of the weather during the year, known as the year without a Summer:

January was mild, so much so as to render fires almost needless in parlors. December previous was very cold. February was not very cold, with the exception of a few days it was like its predecessor. March was cold and boisterous during the first part of it; the remainder was mild. A great freshet on the Ohio and Kentucky rivers caused great loss of property. May was more remarkable for frowns than smiles. Buds and flowers were frozen, ice formed half an inch thick; corn was killed and the fields were again and again planted until deemed to late. June was the coldest ever known in this latitude. Frost, ice and snow were common. Almost every green thing was killed. Fruit was nearly all destroyed. Snow fell to the depth of ten inches in Vermont, several in Maine and three in Central New York, and also in Massachusetts. Considerable damage was done at New Orleans in consequence of the rapid rise in the river, the suburbs were covered with water, and the roads were only passable in boats. July was accompanied by frost and ice; on the fifth, ice was formed of the thickness of window glass, thro'. out New England, New York, and some parts of Pa. Indian corn was nearly all destroyed. August was more cheerless if possible than the Summer months already passed. Ice was formed half an inch thick. Indian corn was so frozen that the greater part was cut down and dried for fodder. Almost every green thing was destroyed both in this country and Europe. Papers received from England stated that it would be remembered by the present generation, that the year 1816 was a year in which there was no Summer. Very little corn ripened in New England and the middle States. Farmers supplied themselves from the corn produced in 1815 for the seed of the Spring of 1817. It sold for from four to five dollars per bushel. September furnished about two weeks of the mildest weather of the season. Soon after the middle it became very cold and frosty, and ice formed a quarter of an inch thick. October produced more than its share of cold weather. November was cold and blustering. Enough snow fell to make good sleighing. December was quite mild and comfortable. The above is a brief summary of the cold Summer of 1816 as it was called in order to distinguish it from the cold season.

The winter was mild. Frost and ice were common in every month of the year. Very little vegetation matured in the Eastern and Middle States.—The sun's rays seemed to be destitute of heat through the summer; all nature seemed to be clad in a sable hue, and men exhibited no little anxiety concerning the future of this life. The average wholesale price of flour during that year, in the Philadelphia market, was thirteen dollars per barrel. The average price of wheat in England was ninety-seven shilling per quarter.—*Farmer's Cabinet, Amherst, N. H.*

HUNTINGDON & BROAD TOP RAIL ROAD

On and after July 17th, 1873, Trains will run on this road daily (Sun excepted) as follows:

Trains from Huntingdon South. *Trains from Mt. Dallas moving North.*

ACCM P.M.	EXP'S A.M.	STATIONS.	EXP'S P.M.	ACCM A.M.
6 05	8 15	Huntingdon,	AR6 00	AR8 30
6 10	8 25	Long Siding	5 55	8 25
6 20	8 30	McConnelstown	5 45	8 15
6 27	8 37	Pleasant Grove	5 38	8 11
6 40	8 50	MARKLESBURG	5 25	7 58
6 50	9 00	Coffee Run	5 15	7 48
6 57	9 08	Rough & Ready	5 08	7 40
7 05	9 15	Cove	5 00	7 31
7 08	9 18	Fishers Summit	4 57	7 30
7 25	9 35	Saxton	4 45	7 15
7 40	9 50	Riddlesburg	4 25	6 55
7 48	9 58	Hopewell	4 18	6 48
8 00	10 15	Piper's Run	4 05	6 35
8 15	10 26	Tatesville	3 50	6 20
8 25	10 35	Everett	3 38	6 08
8 35	10 45	Mount Dallas	3 35	6 05
9 00	11 10	Bedford	3 10	5 30

SHOUP'S RUN BRANCH.

A. M.	P. M.		P. M.	A. M.
LE 9 45	LE 7 30	Saxton.	AR4 35	AR 7 05
10 00	7 45	Coalmont.	4 20	6 50
10 05	7 50	Crawford.	4 15	6 45
AR10 35	AR8 00	Dudley	LE4 05	LE 6 35

Bro'd Top City from Dudley 2 miles by stage.

Time of Penna. R. R. Trains at Huntingdon.

***Mail No. 2 makes connection at Huntingdon with Mail going East on Pennsylvania Railroad at 4.15 p. m., and West at 5.45 p. m. Mail No. 1 leaves Huntingdon at 7.40 a. m. on arrival of Pacific Express West.

Trains on this road connect with trains on Bedford & Bridgeport, and Cumberland & Pennsylvania Railroads.

G. F. GAGE, Supt.

The Weekly Pilgrim.

Published by J. B. Brumbaugh, & Co

Edited by H. B. & Geo. Brumbaugh.

CORRESPONDING EDITORS.

D. P. *Sayler*, Double Pipe Creek, Md.

Leonard Furry, New Enterprise, Pa.

The *Pilgrim* is a Christian Periodical, devoted to religion and moral reform. It will advocate in the spirit of *love* and *liberty*, the principles of true Christianity, labor for the promotion of peace among the people of God, for the encouragement of the saints and for the conversion of sinners, avoiding those things which tend toward disunion or sectional feelings.

TERMS.

Single copy, Book paper,	$1.50
Eleven copies, (eleventh for Agt.)	$15.00

Any number above that at the same rate.

Address,

H. B. BRUMBAUGH.

James Creek,

Huntingdon county Pa.

The Weekly Pilgrim.

"REMOVE NOT THE ANCIENT LANDMARKS WHICH OUR FATHERS HAVE SET."

VOL. 4. JAMES CREEK, PENNSYLVANIA, AUGUST 12, 1873. NO. 32.

POETRY.

Let Every one Sweep Before His Own Door.

(A Paraphrase.)

Do ye heed the homely adage, handed down from days of yore,
"Ere you sweep your neighbor's dwelling, clear the rubbish from your door."
Let no filth, no rust there gather—leave no traces of decay,
Pluck up every weed unsightly, brush the fallen leaves away.

If we faithfully have labored thus to keep without, within,
Plucked up envy, evil-speaking, malice, each besetting sin,
Weeds that by the sacred portals of the inner temple grow,
Poisonous weeds the heart defiling, bearing bitterness and woe,

Then, perchance, we may have leisure o'er our neighbor watch to keep,
All the work assigned us finished, we before his door may sweep;
Show him where the mosses clinging—tokens ever of decay—
Where the thistles, thickly springing, daily must be cleared away.

But, alas! our work neglecting, oft we mount the judgment seat,
With his failings, his omissions, we our weary brother greet;
In some hidden nook forgotten, searching with a careful eye,
We the springing weeds discover—some slight blemish there descry.

For his slothfulness, his blindness, we our brother harshly chide,
Glorying in our strength and wisdom, we condemn him in our pride;
Ask not why he has neglected thus before his door to sweep,
Why grown careless, he has slumbered, failed his garden plot to keep.

On the judgment seat still sitting, we no helping hand extend
To assist our weaker brother his short comings to amend;
For his weariness, his faltering, we no sweet compassion show,
From our store no cordial bring him, no encouragement bestow.

But, while busied with our neighbor, urging him to ceaseless care,
Calling to the thoughtless idlers, to their labor to repair,
Lo! unseen the dust has gathered, weeds are growing where of yore
Flowerets rare and sweet were blooming, when we swept before our door.

Ah! how easy o'er our brother, faithful ward and watch to keep,
But alas! before our dwelling hard indeed to daily sweep;
Harder than to share the conflict, "by the stuff" at home to stay,
Easier far to sit in judgment than to humbly watch and pray.

ORIGINAL ESSAYS.

A DEFENSE.

Dear Pilgrim: I feel called upon to take some notice of the article that appears in your last issue under "Reminiscence," by way of defence of your prerogatives and of my own consistency and the correctness of the principle, contained in the essays written by me and published in the current volume.

That you, as editors, have violated any order of the Annual Meeting, I fail to discover; upon this point, I therefore, in your behalf, plead not guilty. In the meantime, however, in the exercise of a fair proportion of charity towards my dear brother, I award to him the most profound sincerity, and believe that he is impelled by the full belief that he is warranted by the statutes in making the allegation. I think that he is mistaken, notwithstanding, here then is the issue, the point to be settled. We will then, with becoming deference, to him as a wise exponent of questions, appeal to the "law and the testimony," "What sayest the law, how readest thou."

See minutes of A. M. of 1869, Art. 1, Sec. 4. This article covers the whole ground as I opine upon this question. Note particularly in this review what is written in italics.

Section 4th, In reference to controvertial articles published in our religious papers, "we council and advise our Brethren Quinter and Kurtz and H. R. Holsinger, to publish nothing in their periodicals that disputes the practice *of the precepts and ordinances of the Gospel as handed down to us from Christ and the Apostles through and by the forefathers of the Church.*

Has Sunday Schools been handed down to us from Christ and the apostles *through the forefathers of the Church?* We negative the question, and assign our reasons, and will, presently pay our respects to the argument on the affirmative side of the question as advanced by brother F.

The first act of council on record upon Sunday Schools took place in 1838, eighteen hundred and thirty-eight years after Christ, and one hundred and thirty years after the organization of the Church in America. What was the sentiment of this council? Minutes of 1838, Art. 10.

Whether it be right for members to take part in Sunday Schools, class meeting *and the like,* considered most advisable to take *no part in such like things.*

In this decision, these old fathers of the Church must have been in beautiful harmony, as it appears to have settled the question for a period of nineteen years, until convention of Annual Council in 1857. Here it comes up again, but in a different form. See Art. 11.

"How is it considered for brethren to have Sabbath Schools conducted by the brethren?

Ans. Inasmuch as we are commanded to bring up our children in the nurture and admonition of the Lord, we know of no scripture which condemns Sabbath Schools." &c.

In answer to the quotation here given, we refer to our notes in the Essay as appears in the PILGRIM of June 10th, current volume. The argument in the next sentence, "we know of no scripture condemning Sabbath Schools," reminds us of Luther. When a scripture was demanded of him to justify the elevation of the host, he gravely remarked that he knew of no scripture forbidding it, a very unsafe ground upon which to establish a religious practice, I would say, and doubtless my brethren in the main, will endorse the sentiment. It will not fail to strike the notice of all who examine the acts of council upon this subject, that the prevailing opinion has been throughout that these schools, to be of utility to the cause of the Church, should be absolutely under the control of the brethren. If this was practicable in all cases we could not object so much, but as this is not the case, I am fully satisfied that the tendency for good and the promotion of vital Christianity is doubtful, to say the least of it, and with all the proof, is clear that the institution has not been handed down to us through and by the forefathers of the Church, therefore you stand exonerated from the charge preferred against you of transcending your privileges in this case, and I think you can consider yourself honorably discharged.

To the imputation of inconsistency, my answer is, that viewing the subject abstractly I acknowledge the appropriateness of the insinuation, all of us are, or appear to be, more or less inconsistent, therefore "consistency is a jewel," but as to the establishing and sustaining the great principle underlying the series of essays including Sunday Schools written by me, which is that all institutions that are from heaven are so fully and clearly authenticated in the scriptures, so unmistakably set forth that they do not admit of the possibility of being mistaken and that those that are of men are so extremely destitute of support from that source that all strict constructionists of the divine code cannot fail to see from whence they are. That I am, in this respect, not guilty I plead, and looking at this subject from this standpoint I necessarily arrive to the same conclusion that, whatever it may be, if not divinely authorized, it is of men and, in this respect, must be of the same class. If I have not maintained the truth of my position throughout these essays, then I am at fault, but such argument as this; "I think it is according to the scriptures and therefore say amen," and its conneccions, can not overthrow a super structure that is so well fortified. I would say then, to my dear brother that, if I have spoken evil bear witness of the evil, but if well please do not lay your hand on my mouth. We ask again, does the questioning the propriety and utility of Sunday Schools dispute the practice of the precepts and ordinances of the Gospel as handed down by Christ and the apostles? If there is a precept for Sunday Schools in the history of our blessed Christianity, then it is an ordinance from heaven, but that it has been ordained by heaven I confess I cannot find testimony to satisfy my mind, and it appears, that it was never suggested to the mind of the Church for 1838 years and then considered of such questionable propriety that it was "considered most advisable to take no part in such like things." And nineteen years after this, in the researches of the friends of the invention, the wonderful discovery was made that if there was no Scripture to support it there was none that condemned it. So much then for the proof that Sunday Schools is an "ordinance handed down by Christ and the Apostles." But my dear brother Furry, in his zeal to defend a special favorite, puts on his spectacles, deeply colored with the tincture of partiality, and partly by the influence of the rays of respect for Scriptural truth and partly by the shade of Sunday School glasses *thinks* he sees divine authority for them, but presently with an effort superhuman he leaps over a period of 1830 years, and then finds the Jews and even Christ in the synagogues reading the Scriptures and expounding them to the people, and beholds a Sabbath School. What a pity that my brother was not aware that if he had just came down to Virginia, Maryland, Tennessee, Ohio, Indiana or wherever the brethren have churches organized, and even in Pennsylvania, and perhaps at New Enterprise, the Sabbath Schools, such as are now in question, could not be found. Such Sabbath Schools as those referred to in the synagogues, where the Scriptures are read and expounded, could have been enjoyed everywhere. But romance apart, and returning to sober reality, let us examine these Jewish and early Christian Sabbath Schools.

Math. 13: 54. "He taught them in their synagogues insomuch that they were astonished and said "whence has this man this wisdom and these mighty words?" No modern Sunday School here. Mark 6: 2. "And when the Sabbath day was come he began to teach in the synagogues and many hearing him were astonished saying from whence hath this man these things and what wisdom is this that is given unto him that even such mighty works are wrought by his hand." This looks to me like the way we hold our Sunday Schools in Virginia; preaching the word.

Mat. 4: 23. "And Jesus went about all Galilee teaching in their synagogues, and preaching the Gospel of the kingdom, &c. Mark 1: 39, "And he preached in their synagogues throughout all Galilee and cast out devils. Luke 4: 44, "And he preached in the synagogues of Galilee." Acts 9: 20, "And straightway he, Paul, preached Christ in the synagogues, that he is the Son of God. 13: 5 "And when they were in Salamis they preached the Word of God in the synagogues of the Jews; and they had John to their minister." 15: 21, "For Moses of old time hath in every city them that preach him, being read in the synagogues every Sabbath day." Paul and his company came to Antioch, they went into the synagogue on the Sabbath day and after the reading of the law and the Prophets, the rulers of the synagogues sent unto them saying: "Ye men and brethren if ye have any word of Exhortation for the people say on. Then Paul stood up and beckoning with his hand said, men of Israel and ye that fear God give audience," and he preached an eloquent sermon, and when the Jews were gone out of the synagogue the Gentiles besought that these words might be preached to them the next Sabbath. Acts, 13 chap. 14: 1. "And in Iconium, the apostles spake in the synagogue, so that many believed, Jews and Greeks." And coming to Thessalonica where there was a synagogue, Paul as his manner was, went in unto them and three Sabbath days reasoned with them out of the Scriptures preaching Christ unto them. Acts 17. 1.

How abundantly do these Scriptures exemplify the reading of the Scriptures to an intelligent audience, but surely it requires a great stretch of the imagination to see in them a shade of testimony in favor of Sun. Schools of modern type, or in other words a degree of supernatural wisdom, which was not possessed by the forefathers through whom the precepts and ordinances of the Gospel was handed down to us.

Outside of my own investigations in determining the legality of Church usages, whether in our own or others, when I come in contact with men of acknowledged ability, and large experience and deep research into the mines of Gospel truth, seeing them fail to produce a single testimony from the Scriptures to sustain such usages, I am more and more confirmed that they are of men and not from heaven, and all that I ask in the case in question is that my brethren who differ with me, will consider it in the broad daylight of divine revelation; look at the dangers of being unequally yoked with unbelievers, and thereby having our good manners corrupted and drawn more and more into the current of corrupted Christianity. I have not jumped rashly at my conclusions, it is the result of much thought and careful observation, therefore my mind is pretty well settled; but I am aware that we may look at any subject from different standpoints and honestly arrive at different conclusions and therefore should exercise the most extensive charity toward each other. To suppose that we must see alike in every particular, in matters of policy, is a weakness too palpable to be indulged where there is a reasonable degree of intelligence, and to undertake to compel others to see and act as we do, is an exhibition of the spirit of intolerance altogether contrary to the spirit of our beloved profession. All will understand from these premises that I entertain no unkind feeling toward those who differ with me; far be it from me to allow myself to indulge such a thing for a single moment, and if there is anything in this treatise that would appear personal, be assured it is not so intended. I can stand the severest test of my opinions in the way of argument, but under personalities I confess I am sensitive, and therefore I strictly guard against the use of personalities, and in conclusion, if there is anything in this communication that involves the privileges of the press, I, and I alone am responsible, and avow myself a lover of the Church and its usages as handed down to us from Christ and the apostles through the forefathers of the Church.

Fraternally yours,
B. F. MOOMAW.

Bonsacks, Va.

OUR GREAT EXEMPLAR.

(Continued.)

The place for baptism we think should be evident from the examples before us, to every honest seeker after truth, and we shall now refer briefly to the mode.

First, we appeal to reason. O come let us reason together! If any other than immersion was the mode, would it have been necessary to resort to a place where there was much water? Would Christ have went down into the water to be baptized? Would Philip and the Eunuch both have went down into the water if immersion had not been the mode? If water was as repulsive to Philip and the Eunuch as it, apparently is to the people of this day, they surely would not have went into it, unless it was an imperative duty,—unless it was requisite to the performance of baptism. It does seem to us that our own reasoning, our own judgment, should teach us in reference to this subject.

As to the meaning of the word baptize, the most eminent linguists of ancient and modern times, define it as meaning to immerse, and we might cite to many of these as evidence, but for the present we will only refer to a couple examples in Holy Writ that conveys the meaning Christ attached to it very clearly. When Nicodemus came unto Jesus in the solitary hours of the night to enquire more fully concerning His doctrine, He taught him in reference to baptism. "Verily, verily I say unto thee, except a man be born again He cannot see the Kingdom of God." In this Christ evidently referred to the change that must take place in every regenerated soul. The carnal nature, the spirit of evil must be crucified, and the heart changed by the agency of the Holy Spirit. But Nicodemus failed to comprehend the import of Christ's teaching. Then He says, "Verily, verily, I say unto thee, except a man be born of *water* and the spirit he cannot enter into the Kingdom of God." In the first instance Jesus taught him in reference to the subject of regeneration, and lastly He taught in connection with it, the external evidence of regeneration. Now by water, Christ evidently signified baptism, and we are to be *born* of water before we can enter the Kingdom of God. How are we to be born of water? What relation must the subject sustain to the water in order to resemble a natural birth? Certainly there must be an application of the subject to the element, and not the element to the subject; and further, anything short of an immersion can not at all resemble a birth. Jesus, in order to go through the birth literally, and give us an example, descended into Jordan's flowing stream, and this idea He taught the Jewish ruler by this very apt and impressive comparison. Again the apostle's idea of Christ's meaning of baptism is indeed very evident. From Paul's writings to the Romans, we have the following: "Know ye not, that so many of us as were baptized into Jesus Christ were baptized into His death? Therefore we are buried with Him by baptism into death," &c. Here the apostle compares it to a burial, and he certainly knew how to baptize. I have in my possession, a copy of Barne's notes, and as he is a commentator of considerable note, I will quote his comments upon this passage: "It is altogether probable that the apostle in this place had allusion to the custom of baptism by immersion; this can not be proven so as to be liable to no objections, but I presume this is the idea that would strike the minds of the great mass of *unprejudiced* readers." Just so, and if our desires are to follow the example of Jesus with an unprejudiced mind, this would be our conclusion with reference to all these passages, but in this instance there is really no room left for even the prejudiced mind to cavil with the truth. What would you think, dear reader, of sprinkling a little ground over a dead body and calling it buried! The idea is simply preposterous, and we must certainly conclude that immersion was Paul's idea of baptism.

By reference to 1st Peter, 3: 21, we glean very clearly Peter's idea of baptism. He alludes to the circumstance of Noah and his family being saved by water, and then uses the following simile: "The like figure wher unto baptism doth now save us, (not the putting away of the filth of the flesh, but the answer of a good conscience towards God,) by the resurrection of Jesus Christ." Now Peter certainly alludes to baptism as essential to our salvation, and what is his idea in reference to the mode? The parenthetical clause shows very clearly that he had in view an immersion, because the mere sprinkling of a little water on the forehead would not have conveyed the idea of cleansing. But the action in baptism that Peter had in view did convey the idea of putting away the filth and therefore, for fear some might be mistaken as to its true design, he made a clear, concise explanation. It is not to put away the filth of the flesh, "but the answer of a good conscience toward God." Again, the Jews and Gentiles, those whom he was addressing, were in the habit of bathing frequently in water, for the cleanliness of their bodies, and Peter was fearful that they might become confused as to the true design. If any other than immersion had been the mode Peter had in view, it is certainly evident to all that this explanation would not have been needed.

From these considerations, dear reader, it does seem to us that the way of our great exemplar in baptism is clear, and that we should not err therein. And we would urge you to lay by every preconceived opinion you may have and seriously consider the subject. It is important. The declaration of Jesus is positive, "Except ye be *born* of water and the spirit you cannot enter into the Kingdom of God." If, then, by being *born* of water Jesus meant immersion, what will be your condition if you are not immersed? Will it not according to the language of Jesus, debar you from an entrance into His Kingdom? Oh, this is an important thought! It is a question upon which hangs our eternal destiny, and may God prompt you to solve it so as to meet divine acceptance before it is too late.

Jesus also gave us an example of how to meet and overcome temptations. Shortly after he had given us the example of baptism, He was led by the spirit into the wilderness to meet and combat with Satan. This conflict every child of God will have. Following the example of Jesus in baptism will not free us from the power of Satan. It is then that he often presents his most powerful temptations. How often does he prompt us to make a show of our religion; how often does he prompt us to disobey God's Word; how often does he take us upon the mountain and show us the kingdoms of this world and the glory of them; how often does he offer us these things if we would only worship him. But thanks be to God we have the power to overcome all these temptations, and Jesus as our example. And how did he overcome this great enemy of souls? Simply by making use of the Word of God. "It is written," said Jesus, and thus He gained the victory. So we may, reader, if in time of temptation, we use "the sword of the spirit which is the word of God."

In conclusion, let me intreat you to follow the example of Jesus. Ask God to give you strength to overcome the enemy of souls, and finish the work He has given you to do, in a manner that will meet His approbation. Jesus is our exemplar in this. He prayed frequently to His heavenly Father, and if it was necessary for Him to pray frequently, how much more necessary is it for us. He would spend hours, and even nights in prayer, that He might be able to withstand the enemy of souls and accomplish the work for which He came. How can we, poor, needy, dependent creatures expect to gain the victory, and accomplish our work without frequent prayer to God?

Christ also gave us an example of perseverance and devotion to the great cause of Christianity. "My meat is to do the will of Him that sent Me, and to finish His work," was His language, and never did He allow anything to deter Him from the great work He had to accomplish until on the cross He cried, "It is finished." He said to the people on one occasion, "Seek ye first the Kingdom of God and His righteousness and all these things shall be added unto you." This is His language to us to-day. We should follow His example in this, that we make the service of God our highest purpose and all other things only secondary. May God help us all to be more careful to follow Jesus the great Exemplar. J. B. B.

"JESUS WEPT."

Oh, what blessed tears were those! Who could have witnessed them unmoved! But why did He weep, what was it that so deeply affected Him, and caused the bitter tear to flow? We read where He in several instances wept, but on this occasion he was at the grave of Lazarus. It appears that He had a particular regard for this little family of Bethany, Mary, Martha, and their brother Lazarus. Often, when weary from traveling from place to place, He would resort to their home, and there rest secluded from the busy scenes of life, when every attention that kind hearts could suggest, and liberal hands bestow, were freely imparted to their divine Guest. At the time Lazarus was taken sick, Jesus was not in the immediate vicinity, was, no doubt, away on His mission, doing good to the children of men, but the sisters sent unto Him, saying, "Lord, behold he whom Thou lovest is sick." They, at this time especially desired His presence and sympathy, for they well knew that Jesus loved them and would share their sorrow, and, perhaps, would heal their brother. But in the meantime, for the record says, "He remained still two days in the place where He was," Lazarus died. This was a severe affliction for the lonely sisters, and especially so in the absence of their Lord, for they thought if He had been present he would not have died. Jesus hearing of his death came to Bethany to the scene of *mourning*, and when the joyful intelligence was conveyed to Martha that He was coming, she arose quickly and went out to meet Him and said unto Him, "Lord, if Thou hadst been here my brother had not died." She then went and called Mary, and when the sorrow-stricken sister came into His presence, she repeated the same words, and when He saw her weeping and those who accompanied her, He also wept with them. The deep, pungent grief of those bereaved sisters could not be witnessed by the tender compassion of Jesus unmoved, and there, around the tomb of their beloved dead, He lifted up His voice and wept. Oh, how He must have loved them!

Since then, many have gone unto the grave to weep there, and many sad hearts have returned from the spot that contained the lifeless forms of those who were near and dear, but the same Jesus who mingled His tears with the bereaved ones of Bethany, is ever near to comfort the disconsolate, and His divine compassion reaches unto all conditions of life. It is hard, very hard, to have our loved ones taken from us by the cold, ruthless hand of death, yet if we, like the sisters of Lazarus, can look forward with bright anticipations to a happy reunion beyond this vale of tears, the glorious thought should calm our sorrows and dry our tears. Jesus loved this little family dearly, but in order to test their affection for Him, and that He might have an opportunity of displaying His power by raising him from the dead, He saw fit, in His wise judgment, to take from them their only brother. Thus it is often in this life, those who are near by nature's ties are called away in order to draw the affections heavenward,—away from these earthly scenes, and although the heart may seem broken, and bitter tears flow, yet it is God who has seen fit to wound, and He will heal the broken-hearted, and His name be glorified thereby. He is a God of love and *great mercy*, and does not afflict His children willingly no more than would a kind earthly father grieve his child, but chastens it that his commands and precepts may be obeyed.

Dear sinner, Jesus loves you too, and would have you come unto Him and live. He has long been waiting for your return, and still stands with outstretched arms to receive you. Then why grieve Him so, why resist the tender pleadings of His love? He has called you time after time, and yet you linger in the paths of sin. Oh, why do you treat your *best friend* with such indifference? He gently knocks at the door of your hearts for admittance, and yet you refuse to let the heavenly stranger in. Soon, very soon, He may knock for the *last time*. He says in His Word, "My spirit shall *not always* strive with man." Sinner, Jesus loves you and weeps over your ingratitude. W. A. C.

Pilgrim Office.

START RIGHT AGAIN.

In these days when religious teachers seek to place themselves before Christ, in the hearts of the willing and simple minded, and when converts are manufactured by electricity by scores, and when so many doubts arise about the power of the Christian religion because of tyrannical and over-reaching religionists, and because foreign bigots are in the ascendency, it is well for us to settle down on the first principles, which are to believe first, that God exists and has made all things, and see that he is merciful and has provided a remedy for all sin. Grounded in these it will not be difficult for us to find our way to the Father after self-trust and faith in others have departed. And the conditions of this remedy which is centered in love can then be realized. Abiding in this love which makes it impossible from its very nature for us to wrong Him for whom it exists, we can ride triumphantly over the scorn, suspicion and contempt even of those whom we respect, whose disapprobation is by far the most cutting. Then we are prepared to work out our own salvation, which is as I believe to become settled in the first principles, and then to work out the rest with our own brains, hanging, in the meantime, our consciences on what we thus work out. Trust not in men or princes (very good men) for they damn and send to hell many who will wear crowns of rejoicing in heaven. "See that no man takes thy crown;" if he takes your conscience and you do everything because he thinks it right, then to him by right belongs your crown of rejoicing. "See that *no man takes thy crown*."—*Christian Cynosure.*

HE RISETH FROM SUPPER.

This expression of John the Apostle, signifies rising from a meal prepared, made ready to eat, but not eaten. Rising from a place where a meal was, and is eaten, as having been on a table, the proper phraseology would be, riseth from the table.—a meal or supper set down to, by any one, and eaten; it is impossible to rise up from that meal, or supper, because, in rising up and leaving, the person leaving, has eaten it, and taken it with him. Any religionists holding the idea of Jesus having eaten supper, to which he had set down because of the expression, "He riseth from supper" is a perversion of proper Bible phraseology; and misdirects the disciple of Jesus in his inquiries after Bible truths. D. F. Good.

ENCOURAGING NEWS.

Gilboa, Putnam, Co., O.

Dear Pilgrim:—Under the kind providence of God, we are happy to inform you that the little colony of humble followers of the meek Savior located in the west branch of the Rome Congregation are passing through a season of peace, happiness and prosperity. Cordial love and a oneness of effort seem to pervade, which results, as such labors always do, in constant accessions to our number. We have had 18 accessions within 15 months by baptism, and six by letter. Several have made application while the prospect is yet encouraging for continued accessions. May the Lord yet favor us with His blessing, for, in casting an eye over our field of labor, we see it ripening ready to harvest, but are sad to know that though the harvest is so great yet "the laborers are few."

I. J. Rosenberger.

SINS AGAINST THE BODY.

BY MRS. AMELIA E. BARR.

It is the duty of every one to be acquainted with the conditions on which alone he can have "a sound mind in a sound body;" and if some little trouble is involved in the pursuance of these conditions, "the game is worth the candle," since it is very certain that the mind must ask permission of the body to be healthy, happy and successful.

Marital, the ancient epigrammist, says: "*to be* is not called Life, but to *be well*;" and Cicero in his second book "De Officiis," gives us the true canon of a rational hygiene—"Preserve health by attention to the body, by temperance in living, and by refraining from sensuality."

Attention to the body is both positive and negative; we sin against it both by omission and commission. But the first of all its requirements are pure air to breathe. The merest tyro in hygienic matters, knows that air deficient in oxygen, and surcharged with carbonic acid gas from breathing lungs, cannot either properly purify the blood, evolve heat, or develop vital force; and that, under such circumstances, the unpurified blood is sent coursing through heart, arteries and veins, becoming more and more vitiated at every revolution; until, if continued, typhus, cholera, or dysentary supervene.

I do not think that the neglect in this matter is as persistent and criminal as it was a few years ago. The line upon line and precept upon precept of hygienic reformers have done good. The homes of both rich and poor are improved, and the mass of people are more sensitive to their rights in this respect. The neglect of this first law of health is chiefly remarkable in churches, theatres, halls of public amusement, etc. There, the amount of vitiated air is largely increased by the gas illumination; and before the close of any ordinary play or opera, it is very probable that at least one-eighth part of all the air in the building has already passed thro' our neighbor's lungs. Thus we constantly witness the most fastidious individuals, who would scruple to eat what their neighbor's hand had touched, inhale without objection, the breath issuing from his nostrils.

Dr. Franklin used to take what he calls an *air bath* every morning. He argued that the skin was a breathing organ, and should not only be kept clean, but should also be exposed to the embraces of the pure air, at least five or ten minutes every twenty four hours; combined with a cold sponging and the use of a coarse towel, there can be no doubt of its excellence. Southern hygienists advise a *sun bath* as equally good, provided the head be sheltered.

Cleanliness is next to godliness. If a man cannot pray, he can wash; and there is no doubt but what

> "From the body's purity, the mind
> Receives a secret, sympathetic aid,"

and, as good George Herbert says, "the mind's sweetness will bear its operation upon the body." There is even something unnatural and unbelievable in a dirty Christian.

The want of physical exercise is another sin against the body. Tens of thousands suffer from exercising the brain too much and the muscular system too little. "Where the stimulus is, there flows the blood;" and if the blood is healthy, there is activity of nutrition, perfection of development, vigor of function. But exercise, to be really healthy, should be of such a kind as to set the whole frame in motion, rouse to action the nervous centres, and briog every part alternately into activity.

In all exercise, however, the importance of *mental* stimulus is very great, for it is comparatively valueless, unless the idea of taking it for health is lost in the interest of the occasion. The felon at his task has plenty of exercise, but it has not the good influence of the row on the river, the walk with a friend, the holiday in the woods.

The love of children for recreation, shows what Nature thinks about it, and to the aged it is no less important; for if judiciously used, it will retard, if not prevent, "that second childishness and mere oblivion," which too often clouds the last days of human life.

The hygienic laws regarding food do not need "twelve tables;" they are few and simple, and easily enforced by sensible men and women. First, it must be understood that oily, fatty elements, heat the body, glutinous or plastic elements nourish it. The first then fortify the system against cold; the second repair the waste of the tissues, and give strength to the muscles and nervous system. Climate and circumstances must, therefore, vastly alter cases in their use, and a man's own reason is the only adviser needed.

Whatever food is eaten, it should never be eaten very hot; it should be thoroughly masticated; it should be simple in character and cooking; it should only be eaten in quantities commensurate with the wants of the system. Man is an omniverous animal, and may eat almost anything, if he does not exceed; whereas rigid vegetarians, by excess in quantities, may induce serious and distressing consequences.

The sense of hunger is the natural index as to both time and quantity, but the digestive organs should certainly be allowed to dispose of one meal before they are cumbered with another. People in active life cannot be quite regular; excessive labor may demand an earlier meal one day than is necessary another—a large margin in these things is left for discretion. But little children and old persons should, in all dietary matters, make order their first law.

No laws are so obvious as those of diet, none are so flagrantly broken. And this, in spite of knowledge, and in spite of certain punishment; for, though we oppress nature with apparent impunity for years, she will, at last, present her bill to a broken constitution.

As a rule, pure water is the best of all drinks, but very little fluid ought to be taken during meals. Hot, watery soups before a solid dinner, dilute the gastric juices, and tea and coffee in large quantities have the same effect. But, when drinks are taken as stimulants, they come under the severest condemnation. If taken to increase the vital force, the extra exertion made under their influence, is made at the expense of the constitution; and the oftener it is repeated, the more permanent the debility, which is its certain re-action. In no case can stimulants be a substitute for solid nourishing food.

But the organs and functions of animal life need something beside air, exercise and food. They must have periods of complete rest. By protracted effort, the eye, the ear, the brain, etc., all lose their sensibility. Then sleep is to organic life what food is to animal life. All that food is to the blood, sleep is to the sensation, thought and muscular activity.

When the system is perfectly healthy, sleep suspends all the powers of animal life; not the slightest consciousness exists. Such sleep is the surest guarantee of longevity. The continued action of the mind on any subject, will make the sleep dreamy and unrefreshing. Sluggish drowsiness relaxes the solids, and induces languor and debility, while excessive wakefulness weakens the brain and the whole system. Nothing is so excellent for soul and body, as a good solid bar of sleep between day and day, provided it be taken in a room thoroughly ventilated, and on a sensibly hard bed; for when a person feels such an enormity as a feather bed a necessity, he is in a very bad physiological condition, and the sooner he gets out of it the better.

Something must be said on the influence of the mind and the *Will* upon hygienic conditions. The Will, is indeed the guardian of the body's interests. Thus, though the food, when once within the stomach, is beyond control, the Will has the power of selecting the quality and quantity of it. Again, though respiration is an involuntary act, the Will can promote its efficiency by selecting pure air, or accelerating it by exercise. The will, then, is a kind of sentinel over the organic functions.

I have already mentioned the good influence of mental stimulus in physical exercise, and every one knows how vehemently mental excitement disturb organic functions. Grief, anger, fear, disappointment, throw the body into sudden tumultuous mutiny. But though for an hour or two there may be confusion and panic, a Will under thorough discipline will speedily recover its sudden surprise, and regain its equanimity.

The self-command of soldiers and statesmen, shows the power that can be acquired by the Will over the body, and the advantage of such a discipline in a hygienic point of view, can hardly be over estimated. Under control like this, the ills of life are only like the transient sorrows of childhood—

> "Burs on youth's glittering raiment hem."

When the sympathy between the nervous system of organic life and the mind maintains this delightful character—which is the natural result of observing the laws of health, —then and only then, a man may be said to have "a sound mind in a sound body."—*Science of Health.*

FULLY DEVELOPED CHRISITANS.

Our religion is intended to make us symmetrical Christians, fully developed throughout. Too many men consult taste, aptitude, facility, or opportunity in their heart progress, and thus fail of moral rounding out. One is full of personal activity, but he cares nothing for prayer meetings or religious conferences. Another is zealous for all meetings, but has no earnestness in Christain work. A third is active and devotional, but is niggardly in the use of his money. Others have their specialties in which they excel, but their failings, which amount to a blemish of character. Of course, it is better when one is good in any department than if he failed in all. But how impressive is the life which is full and thorough! It speaks of one who is "complete in Him," and who is going toward perfection in the Christian graces.

THE story is told of a woman who freely used her tongue to the scandal of others, and made confession to the priest of what she had done. He gave her a ripe thistle top, and told her to go out in various directions and scatter the seeds, one by one. Wondering at the penance, she obeyed, and then returned and told her confessor. To her amazement, he bade her go back and gather the scattered seeds; and when she objected that it would be impossible, he replied that it would be still more difficult to gather up and destroy all the evil reports which she had circulated about others. Any thoughtless careless child can scatter a handful of thistle seeds before the wind in a moment, but the strongest and wisest men cannot gather them again.

PRAYER! What battles has it not fought! what victories has it not won! what burdens has it not carried! what wounds has it not healed! what griefs has it not assuaged! It is the wealth of poverty; the refuge of affliction; the strength of weakness; the light of darkness. It is the oratory that gives power to the pulpit; it is the hand that strikes down satan, and breaks the fetters of sin; it turns the scales of fate more than the edge of the sword, the craft of statesmen, or the weight of sceptres; it has arrested the wing of time, turned aside the very scythe of death, and discharged heaven's frowning and darkest cloud in a shower of blessings.—*Guthrie.*

THE promotion, or else degeneracy of man, is as perpetual the apparent course of the solar and lunar orbs.—Either upward and more and more resplendent in glory, more and more fervent in warmth, stronger and stronger in power, or else downward, the lower the faster in his course to coldness, darkness, despair and finally that night "in which no man can work." Except if happily he should at some period of his life call upon his sun to stand still upon Gibeon, and his moon in the valley of Ajalon until he avenge himself of his enemies, as it is "written in the book of Jasper."—*C. C. Root.*

GENERAL INTELLIGENCE.

THE Cholera still prevails in different parts of the country and is generally traced to some local causes.—Cleanliness, it is said, is next to godliness, and we are sure it is an important auxiliary to health and a safeguard against Cholera. In some of the western towns it was reported as being very bad but now subsiding.

—The following is said to be an approximately correct classification of the adherents of the various churches among English-speaking people: Protestant Episcopalians, 12,500,000; Presbyterians, 11,500,000; Baptists, 10.500,000; Congregationalists, 7,500,000; Methodists, 15,000,000; Roman Catholics, 10,000,000—57,000,000 of Protestants, against 10,000,000 of Roman Catholics.

GREAT FIRE IN BALTIMORE.—The "City of Monuments" has had its turn at a severe conflagration. About ten blocks have been partly burned; between three and four of these totally. The section destroyed was chiefly occupied by small stores and factories, and for the most part, except on the eastern and northern limits with common class residences. The loss is estimated from $600,000 to $800,000.

GERMAN CHURCH ORGANIZED.—The *Advance* states that on June 20, a German church of thirty-one members was organized near Fontenelle, Nebraska, as a result of the labors of Rev. Mr. Mollenbeck, who was appointed last fall the first German Congregational missionary for Nebraska. This church includes a German evangelical colony from the little duchy of Lippe-Detmold, all of one faith, old neighbors and friends in the fatherland, and now in their new homes anxious to lift up their influence against German infidelity and formalism. By united voice on the day of church organization they asked that Mr. Mollenbeck be installed as their pastor, pledging him the first year, for a part of his time only, out of their poverty, $250 towards his support.

CURE FOR BEE STINGS.—A correspondent of the British Gardener's Magazine writes: "on the 15th of April last a young man, employed near bees, had the misfortune of being stung. No remedy being near at hand, I remembered Mr. Gordon's note on the cure of bee stings, at page 491 of the *Gardeners Magazine* for 1872. I recommended him to apply the common soil to the wound as described by Mr. Gordon, and it immediately relieved the pain and prevented the swelling. Such a receipt is more valuable than gold to all who have anything to do with bees. I formerly used common blue for bee stings, but common soil is preferable.

—A correspondent writing about the recent earthquake in the north of Italy, says; "The effects of the earthquake at the village of St. Pi do Feltota were terrible. It was the fete of St Peter, the patron saint of the place. The church was gaily decorated and was crowded with worshipers when, without a moment's warning, an undulation swept beneath the village and down came the roof and the walls of the church, burying its living contents. Those nearest to the door were able to escape, but of the remainder thirty eight were killed on the spot—eighteen men and twenty women—and a great many were seriously hurt. The priest officiating had his arm broken. Two others, assisting, escaped. The entire village was one scene of fallen and falling houses.—*Advent Times.*

From a recently published statement, it appears that the average life of the Jew in London is forty-nine years, while of the Christian it is only thirty-seven years. Of a given number of Christians, only one quarter will, as a general rule, live to be sixty years, while among Jews, one quarter live to be at least seventy-one. Among children, fourteen per cent, of the Christian population die between one year and five years of age, while only ten per cent of the Jewish children. In Prussia it requires fifty-one years for the Christian population to double itself, and only forty-one years for the Jewish.

Youth's Department.

OH! LITTLE CHILD.

Oh! little child, lie still and sleep,
  Jesus is near,
  Thou needst not fear;
No one need fear whom God doth keep,
  By day or night;
Then lie thee down in slumber deep,
  Till morning light.

Oh! little child, thou need'st not wake:
  Though round thy bed
  Are dangers spread,
Thy Savior care for thee will take,
  Jesus is strong,
And angels watch thee, for His sake,
  The whole night long.

Oh! little child, lie still and rest;
  He sweetly sleeps
  Whom Jesus keeps,
And in the morning wake so blest
  His child to be:
Love every one, but love Him best,
  He first loved thee.

Oh! little child, when thou must die,
  Fear nothing then,
  But say Amen
To God's command, and quiet lie
  In His kind hand,
Till He shall say, "Dear child come fly
  To heaven's bright land."

NO MOTHER.

A few days ago, a little girl, one of my Sabbath school scholars not yet seven years old whose mother died two years ago, came to my house to visit me. She is a pleasant lovely little girl. As she sat by me, I talked to her, telling her about Jesus, and the beautiful angels; about the happiness of Heaven and how we ought to love and obey God, and that he would take all those who loved him to live with him above; and as I was thus talking, the tears began to trickle from her eyes, and she began to sob aloud. When I asked her why she cried, after wiping the tears from her eyes, she said, "When you talk that way, it makes me think of my mother, then I have to cry."

Whether this little girl's mother was a good woman, a christian, I do not know; but I told her that if we loved God, and did what he commands us, we should again meet all our dear friends who are good, and obedient to God while they were in this world. She said she loved Jesus, and would try to be a good girl.

My young friends, have we not all some dear friends, a mother a father, a brother or sister, or some other dear ones who have died, and who we believe gone to live with the angels in Heaven? I can say I believe I have some very dear friends there; and often, like the little girl, when I think of them, tears will come into my eyes.

Suppose those dear friends who have loved Jesus, and lived holy lives could speak to us, and tell us how happy they are, would it not encourage us to try more than we ever have to live obedient to God, that we might also, when we die, be taken to that happy place? And suppose those who have been wicked and disobedient while they lived, could speak to us, and tell us of the terrible punishment with suffering, would it not fill us with terror and trembling? and would we not pray to God, day and night to help us to overcome all wickedness and sin, and make our hearts pure and clean from all that is hateful in his sight, that we may escape that dreadful punishment?

When these die who have been good, and obedient to God, they are glad that they can now go home, and be happy; they are only sorry that they did not do more for Jesus; but when the wicked die, and know that they are the enemies of God, their hearts are filled with terror, and O, how sorry they are that they did not obey God; and often they say "O, if I only had my life to live over again, how different it would be;" or "Oh, that God would let me live just a few days longer, that I might make peace with him and be prepared to die."

My dear little readers, I hope you will often think of God, of your dear Savior who died for you, and often think of your dear friends who have died; and if you think they are gone to that blessed place in Heaven, try to live so that you may meet them there. Live so that when you die, you may rejoice that you have loved and served the Lord, and that you are now going to meet your dear friends and be forever happy. Love and serve God all the days that he lets you live, then you need not wish that you had your time to live over again.—*Herald of Truth.*

AN HOUR A DAY.

There was a lad who, at fourteen, was apprenticed to a soap-dealer. One of his resolutions was to read an hour a day, or at least at that rate; and he had an old silver watch, left him by his uncle, which he timed his reading by. He stayed seven years with his master, and it was said when he was twenty-one he knew as much as the young squire did. Now, let us see how much time he had to read in, seven years, at the rate of an hour a day. It would be two thousand five hundred and fifty-five hours, which at the rate of eight hours a day, would be equal to three hundred and ten days, equal to forty-five weeks—nearly a year's reading. That time spent in treasuring up useful knowledge would pile up a very large store. Try what you can do. Begin now. In after years you will look back upon the task as the most pleasant and profitable you ever performed.

Little minds are too much hurt by little things. Great minds perceive them all, and are not touched by them.

A small unkindness is a great offence.

The Weekly Pilgrim.

JAMES CREEK, PA., Aug. 12, 1873.

☞ How to send money.—All sums over $1.50, should be sent either in a check, draft or postal order. If neither of these can be obtained, have the letter registered.

☞ When Money is sent, *always* send with it the name and address of those who paid it. Write the names and post office as plainly as possible.

☞ Every subscriber for 1873, gets a *Pilgrim Almanac* Free.

SUNDAY SCHOOLS.

Some of our brethren are getting a little lively on the Sunday School question, but the discussions are so well seasoned that the best of feelings will be maintained. The subject, undoubtedly will bear investigation and is not without its sides.

The first thing to be considered is whether the question is to be discussed in its widest sense, or as conducted by the Brethren. Preaching, though at first, divinely authorized, if now investigated as a whole, would not be found having divine sanction resting upon it, therefore we must confine our investigations to the original intent and not its abuses. Because the original intent of preaching is shamefully subverted, is no reason that preaching should be abandoned, but rather that much greater efforts should be made in the right to counteract the evil.—Because other churches have introduced Sunday Schools and substituted them into nurseries in which to proselyte the young into their respective churches, is no reason that we should not make use of the same day in teaching our children the Scriptures, and thus bring them up in the nurture and fear of the Lord. It does not matter what this work is called, as they can be as essentially different from the popular Sabbath School of the day, as is the preaching of the true Gospel from Mormanism or infidelity.

Bro. Furry is discussing the merits of Sunday Schools as held by the Brethren, while brother Moomaw was seemingly investigating the original Sunday Schools as an institution, which, we think, are materially different, and is so considered by brother Moomaw, as he says, "If this were practical in all cases, we could not object so much," (meaning schools under the control of the Brethren.) Again in brother Moomaw's investigations, under the caption of "Whence is it?" he has not committed himself from the fact that he has not told us that everything originally apostolic is yet resting under divine sanction, nor that everything invented by or through the wisdom of men is necessarily evil. There are many things now practical and assented to by good Christians, that cannot possibly be traced so far back as the apostles. Where, in the Scriptures, have we our precedent for having Hymn books and singing several hymns in connection with preaching, or from whence are our Church houses that are now being erected everywhere throughout the Brotherhood? These are of men, or fully as much so as teaching our children the Scriptures on the Sabbath day, yet we believe they have a divine sanction and are efficient means of grace. That brother Moomaw can maintain his position that Sunday Schools as now accepted is a modern institution, none can deny, but whether he will condemn it for its lack of age is for him yet to say, and we would be pleased to have his disposition of such things as are now considered good and yet are without a direct precedent in the Scriptures.

If we are to have any more on the subject of Sunday Schools, let it be, as held by the Brethren. There are a large number of our churches that have had them introduced and can speak from experience. Let us have some of the results or conclusions.—What kind of an influence have they exerted, and how conducted? If evil, let us have it, and in what way the evil was done. If good, let us also have it, showing in what way the good was accomplished. Such reports would form a very good base upon which to found our conclusions. If on a whole, good seems to be the result, we know the Church will not oppose them, as we are willing and anxious to avail ourselves of every means of grace.

Annual meeting *allows* but does not *enforce* Sunday Schools. It stands as an institution of merit and the more of that, is found in its favor, the more fully will it be sanctioned, hence we believe that it is altogether proper fo Bro. Moomaw to investigate and file his objections and Bro. Furry and others, their advantages, but please stick to the subject and not to the persons discussing it.

SABBATH MUSINGS.

God said, "Six days shalt thou labor but on the seventh, thou shalt rest from all thy labors." In harmony with this divine command, we have daily went forth from the first day of the week until the last, as the harvest was plenteous but the laborers few. The evening of the sixth came and with it a consciousness that we had endeavored to do our duty. With a calm and hopeful feeling we dismissed the labors of the past and turned our thoughts towards the approaching rest. Oh, how sweet is rest to the weary! The sun in all its loveliness, sank behind the green hills and it was night. Soon the curtain of darkness was drawn around a busy world and thousands laid them down, soon to be unconscious in the arms of sleep, there to await the coming of the blessed Sabbath morn. It came, but not to all. During the night, the sickle of death was doing its work, because it is harvest:—sheaves are ripening some to be gathered into the garner of the Lord while others are to be cast into the fire. But to us it came, not because of our merit but the love of God. If ever nature in harvest time put on her beautiful garments it was this morning. Everything seemed to rejoice in the goodness of God, and if the green hills, the growing corn, and a balmy, rustling breeze had a voice, it would be, "Oh, come and let us go up to the house of the Lord." Why not? Has not Jesus promised to meet His children and there feed them on the pastures of love? If God has given us six days for to labor for the sustenance of the body, will we rob Him of the seventh, or rather rob ourselves of the blessings it affords? We know not what others done, but our seat was in the Sanctuary where we met Jesus, and like a disciple of old, we were made to feel: "And did not our hearts burn within us as He talked with us?" It causes us to rejoice, when we think of the thousands, of a like precious faith, who, to-day, were represented in the congregations of the saints, and the many ministrations of the words of life that were put forth. Talk of power, there is much of it in the world. Hosts may go forth in battle array, and with terrible instruments of war, cause the earth to tremble, but a competing army comes with greater power, and they are cut down as the stubble—the mighty become as water, their proud banners are trampled beneath the enemies feet and their glory laid in the dust. Not so with the army of the saints that have been, this day, fighting for Jesus. If the weakest saint, on his knees, causes the devil to tremble, what must have been the magnitude of that power as exhibited to-day by the camp of the righteous in falling at a throne of grace and there pleading in behalf of sinners? Brethren and sisters, we feel that we are weak—that we are only a few, but it is because our spiritual eyes are closed to the power that is around and for us. If, like Elijah's servant, our eyes could be opened, we too could look around us and see the horseman and chariots. After all, there are more for us than there be against us. All that is lacking, is a little more faith. Do not be discouraged, we shall reap if we faint not. Only believe, and then stand still and see the salvation of God.

But how we are digressing—we intended telling you that after returning from church we took our paper and pencil and went out on a hill that overlooks the surrounding neighborhood, with the intention of noting down such thoughts as might be presented, and now you have them, mixed and confused, just as are sometimes presented when alone and without any particular subject bearing upon the mind. To us, the penning them was a sweet pastime, and hope they may present to you, dear reader, thoughts worthy of contemplation.

BOOKS &c. FOR SUNDAY SCHOOLS.

We are having quite a number of inquiries in regard to furnishing suitable books and papers for Sabbath schools, showing that there is a growing demand for something of this kind. To answer inquiries, we will just say that there are as yet, no books published by the brethren suitable for a Sabbath school Library, We could select and supply you with books very cheaply, but a large majority of books now published for this purpose are so trashy that we cannot recommend them as proper for our children to read. The best schools among the Brethren do not use them and they are also being discarded by some of the best schools of other denominations, the fact is, fifty per cent of all the books published for this purpose are not only worthless but decidedly injurious to the young and should be guarded against as cautiously as novels and other light reading. But that children should have some simple but substantial, reading to illustrate Bible truths, is evident from the many calls that are made upon us for something of this kind. To meet this want, we have now under contemplation, to publish for another year, a monthly in parts, one for each week, to be made up principally of Bible lessons especially adapted to the wants of the young. This publication must be put at such low figures that all schools and those having families can afford to take it, and we believe that we are prepared to do that. Those brethren and sisters who are interested in having something interesting and good for our Sunday Schools, will please correspond with us as we will be pleased to have the co-operation of all and any suggestions as to the nature and form of the work, will be thankfully received.

Bro. Root, under "arrears," calls attention to an important subject. He knows, as well as do all our readers, that we have been very liberal with all our patrons and therefore does not wish to have us imposed upon, or our liberality undervalued. The best way for our readers to manifest their gratitude, is not to disappoint our trust. We have ever been willing to accommodate our readers by giving them their own time during the year, but because we do this, none should put off payment until the last moment. When we offer to wait you we mean, until you can get the money, but when you get it brethren, you ought to pay us, so if you have it ready please send it along, if not we will try and wait you a little longer.

Correspondence.

THE COMMISSION.

Dear brethren: My mind has, for some time, been engaged in study concerning the Commission of our Savior, Matt. 28: 19, "Go ye therefore and teach all nations, baptizing them," &c. When I consider how they are taught and receive the truths of the Gospel, I have been made to wander whether we as a body, are doing our duty when we stay at home and let so many precious souls die without a true knowledge of Jesus, who died for them as well as for us, and who are calling continually for some to come and preach the Gospel to them. Mark says, "Go and preach the Gospel to every creature," and when we look over our country we see so many places where the truth has never been preached, and there are also heathen lands where man worships idols, and knows nothing about the true God. To them, other denominations are sending Missionaries to teach them, and we believe that we preach and practice the truths of the Bible, and this being the case other doctrine must be ,in part, wrong, hence will we stand still and see the poor heathen led astray and live and die without making an effort to save them? But we need not go to Asia or Africa, or to heathen countries to find heathen, but we can find them in abundance in America, and why is it, brethren, when we have a civilized government and are protected in preaching the gospel anywhere, that we do not go and preach more than we do? We have our Brotherhood divided into small districts, and from three to five and six preachers in a district, have meeting once in a week, or once in two weeks, and all the preachers sit behind the table while one or two preaches, and so we cannot preach a sermon more in less than four, six or eight weeks, and the Savior, when He sent out the preachers, He sent them two and two, and told them to go from city to city and teach the people the word of God. It appears to me if we had a desire, as Paul had, for the salvation of the people, there would not be so many in our country who never heard the Brethren preach, or the Bible explained in its purity. Here are our cities and villages right around us, and perhaps we have never preached there. Why is it, brethren? Are those souls not worth as much as others, or will we suffer them to go to destruction without a warning from us, and at the day of judgment rise up and testify against us for not doing our duty in warning them? I very much fear we will have to answer for some of this. Should there not be a move made to have the gospel spread more? I answer, yes. If we would take the money we spend unnecessarily for vain and foolish things, and give it for this purpose, I believe we would receive a rich reward at the day of reckoning. I very much fear, brethren, the reason we do not send more preachers to convert the people is, that we are too covetous, and grasp the mighty dollar too tightly. Perhaps we have not yet read "that the love of money is the root of all evil." Truly, the Savior says, "The harvest is great and the laborers few," but I believe the laborers are plenty were they only sent out. The Church calls them to the work, but when they are called then there is nothing more done. Will we not, brethren, give a little of what the Lord has given us for the support of His cause? If not, I fear the love of God is faint in us, for if we have this world's goods and see our brother in want, or our friends, and we shut up the bowels of compassion, how dwelleth the love of God in us, and I am certain we can see numbers in need of the Bread of Life, and we might be the cause, or help of their salvation, did we do our duty. Yet, we stand back and look on and see so many dragged into ruin without lending a helping hand. Will we not make an offering of a little of this world for the Lord, when God has made such a great offering for us, even that of His own dear Son? O, what love! Brethren, let us pray for more love and more of that spirit that will lead us into all truth. My brethren who are young with me in the ministry, let us devote our time and service more to the Lord, and study that we may show ourselves workman that need not be ashamed of our Lord's work, rightly dividing the word of God, and be faithful laborers in the Vineyard of the Lord, not hiding our Lord's money or laying it up in a napkin. Remember God has given us a talent for which we are held accountable. Brethren, pray for us, that we may be able, by the help of the Lord, to accomplish much, laboring for the salvation of souls. What I have written is in love, may it be received in love is my prayer.

ADAM APPELMAN.

Plymouth, Ind.

ON REPORTING.

Dear Pilgrim:—The time has now come when the Brotherhood throughout may, and should say what are their sentiments in regard to the great question, whether we shall,or shall not have a full report of Annual Meetings. All should, by some means, express their feelings upon this matter. And now, as the established Gospel order is, to settle a question of a local character, in the congregation which it concerns, by the individual voice of its members comprising that body, why should not a question of so general a nature, the entire Brotherhood directly and equally concerned, be settled upon the same principles? This can easily be done by next A. M. This would be the Republican not the (Episcopal)form of government which we preach and practice as Apostolic.

Meanwhile this question should be carefully and prayerfully considered. The result of the past reports, carefully,scrutinizingly observed, and the various results, in the different parts of the Brotherhood, should be reported through our periodicals as they occur, whether they be good or bad. Now as to whether this reporting is a new thing as already intimated by the brother of the *Vindicator*, I would only say, I am in possession of a similar report. The first meeting of this kind ever held by the Brethren was in year A.D.53,held at Jerusalem, as recorded in Acts, 15th chapter. There Simon it appears rose up after much disputing, and his speech is given verbatim. The next speakers names given are Barnabas and Paul, and after they had held their peace James answered and said: "Men and brethren. hearken unto me.' Then he spoke lengthily and even referred to what Simon had already said and so on. And after his speech it seems it was passed and the decision written out and sent to the churches. So dear brethren and sisters, I conclude that giving those reports is not a new thing but strictly Apostolic. So when ever we seem to see bad results of those late reports, let us be cautious that we give just judgment, and prosecute not the innocent, and acquit the guilty, and see whether it is truly the illegitimacy of the reports, or the disposition of the character in which we see the result.

C. C. ROOT

LONGMOUNT, Boulder Co., Col. }
July, 25, 1873. }

Bro. Brumbaugh:—As there are so many brethren and friends wishing to hear from me, since I am in this territory, and as it is out of my power to give all a private letter, I thought, as it is requested that I should write through the PILGRIM, I will therefore pen these few lines.

In the first place, I will say that it seems rather lonely, as there is no organization of the Brethren here. I find however, three brethren and one sister here in Boulder Co., but know of no others here except at Trindad,in the southern part of the State. I find many kind friends who are anxious to hear the doctrine of the Brethren. They listened with much interest to the story of the man of sorrows. I also find many skeptics and many who have been made to doubt, because of the corrupt conduct of those who have professed to be the followers of the lowly Jesus, and more especially those who come here professing to be preachers. Brethren, here is a wide field for you to use your talents and means for a good purpose. I feel as if the brethren could do much good here if they were settled down and would preach the doctrine in its native simplicity, and then live it out in every day life. This must be done if they ever expect to do anything that will be to the honor of God.—The last few years of my life, and especially the last year, has shown to me more fully than ever, that pride and vanity have taken hold of the church as it were by the forelock, and if, not soon checked must inevitably lead to ruin. Oh! brethren all who are called to watch over the interests of the flock of God, do we discharge our duty in trying to reclaim the wandering sheep? My heart has been sorely pained to see that the world has bought so many away from the simplicity that is in Christ. When the midnight cry is heard, and their lamps are gone out, then their trouble will come.—"The harvest is passed, the summer is ended, and we are not saved."

Now as many wish to know something of the climate &c., of this country, I will say that the climate is very good, especially for weak lungs or Asthma, if the disease has not made too great inroads upon the vitals already. But if diseases are of very long standing, or have made much progress in their work of destruction, it is altogether vain to look for health in Colorado. Persons in advanced stages of these maladies will live longer in the states than here. If men, in the states, would live as they do when they come here, they will find their health improving very nearly, or quite upon the same ratio as here. If, on coming here, instead of fine drinks and highly seasoned food, strong Coffee, Tea, &c., you drink the pure water that comes rushing down through the canyons and gulches of the Rocky Mountains, and use wild beef, and take plenty of exercise in the open air, you will improve. This is a good farming country for small grain if you have plenty of water with which to irrigate.

Yours in love.

A. HUTCHISON.

ARREARS.

I wish to say to those who subscribed to me for the PILGRIM, and who have not paid for the present volume, that I desire to settle up with all the subscribers and the editors in due time to encourage the editors to give all such as need it, time on the next volume. Expecting to travel considerable during our fall communion season, I would be pleased to find all such that I may meet prepared for said settlement. And now as my canvassed territory is at least one hundred and sixty miles in length east and west, and as I shall not likely see them all, I could wish they would all be represented by their names in the PILGRIM money list, or otherwise by the first of November. Fraternally yours,

C. C. ROOT.

LAST NOTICE.

As the time has now come that we must have our copy for an *Almanac* for 1874, we once more call upon our brethren to help us to make it as complete as possible.

First. Please examine the ministerial list and note mistakes, also make a note of all the ministers that are not in our list and send them to us with their address.

Second. All those that have their District Meeting appointed for 1874, send us a notice of them, and we will have them inserted.

Third. We wish some good copy for all its pages. Those that feel like aiding us will please prepare it at once and send it along. Biographies or anything of standing merit will be admitted.

Fourth. The cover or outside pages will be used for advertisements. Any person having anything that they wish before the public can have a space at the following rates:

1 column.	$25.00
[illegible] "	14.00
[illegible] "	8.00
[illegible] "	5.00
1-16 "	3.00

Dear Pilgrim: Please announce that we, the Brethren of the Milmine District Piatt Co., Ill., intend, the Lord willing, to have our Communion the 25th of September. Meeting to commence at 10 o'clock, in the morning. It is hoped that inasmuch as the brethren of Cerro Gordo district have appointed their Communion on the 27th of the same month, and the Council Meeting of the Southern District of Ill., to be at the same place a few days later, that brethren expecting to attend these meetings will arrange so as to be in time to attend our Communion also. Those coming by railroad will stop at Cerro Gordo. All are invited. By order of the Church.

DANIEL MOHLER.

Announcements, &c., crowded out.

NEWS ITEMS.

The great balloon excitement now prevailing has one good thing about it at least, it turns attention from things terrestrial to things celestial.

Mr. Green's Nassau balloon, which made the memorable voyage from London to Weilburg, Germany—a distance of 500 miles—was fifty feet in diameter by sixty feet long; contained 85,000 cubic feet of gas, and could raise 4,000 pounds, including its own weight.

The new trade dollar is to contain 378 grains of pure silver, and weigh 420 grains, Troy. Of late years, silver has greatly depreciated in value, the supply being greater than the demand; and so, to get rid of our superfluous bullion, the new dollar will be coined, and sent to seek a market in China, where, as is anticipated, it will be as acceptable as the old Spanish and Mexican dollars.

The telegraph is to be utilized in the good work of furnishing the true time every day at 12 noon, The Observatory at Washington being the regulator, the noon instant is to be indicated by it to New York and thence to the principal stations over the country. This will be of immense value to railroads and many branches of business, as well as of interest to all.

The burning of the forests on Long Island is a great misfortune in every way, and entails immense losses in some cases upon those who can ill afford them. Besides the vast quantity of timber and growing wood that has been destroyed, farm-houses have been consumed, two small villages have been burned, and three children perished in the flames. Patchogue would have been burned but for the energetic precautions of her people in building counting fires to head off the column of advancing flame. Such wholesale destruction of property and life seems needless and wicked.

LITERARY NOTICES.

THE BATH, It's History and uses in Health and Disease. By R. T. Trall, M. D., Author of "The Hydropathic Encyclopedia," "Hygienic Hand-book," "Cook Book," "Watercure for the Million," etc.

We have had the pleasure of examining this work, and have no hesitancy in pronouncing it No. 1, on the subject which it treats. It treats on every imaginable use of water for health and its restoration, with illustrations of all the different baths and how used, in fact it is just the work that is needed and should be read by all who desire to enjoy good health.

Published by S. R. Wells, 389 Broadway, New York. In paper cover 25 cents, muslin 50 cents. We can furnish our readers this valuable work, post paid, at the above rates.

The Most Attractive Subscription Book Published this Year.

IN SEARCH OF

THE CASTAWAYS:

A Romantic Narrative of the Loss of Captain Grant of the Brig "Britannia," and of the Adventures of his Children and Friends in his Discovery and Rescue. Embracing the Description of a Voyage Round the World.

By JULES VERNE,

Author of "Twenty Thousand Leagues under the Sea," etc. 170 Fine Engravings; 620 Pages. Price $3.50.

Agents Wanted. For descriptive circulars, terms, territory, etc., address

J. B. LIPPINCOTT & Co.,

Aug 12 3t. Publishers, Philadelphia.

GOOD BOOKS.

A large number of our patrons are receiving our books as noticed below, as premiums, and express themselves highly pleased with them. Others who are not agents, have enquired whether we keep them for sale. We have now made arrangements with Mr. Wells to furnish any of their publications post paid at publishers prices. Orders for books must be accompanied with the cash, and plain directions for sending them.

How to read Character, Illus.	Price, $1.25
Combe's Moral Philosophy,	1.75
Constitution of Man. Combe,	1.75
Education. By Spurzheim,	1.50
Memory—How to Improve it,	1.50
Mental Science, Lectures on,	1.50
Self-Culture and Perfection,	1.50
Combe's Physiology, Illus.	1.75
Food and Diet. By Pereira,	1.75
Natural Laws of Man,	.75
Hereditary Descent,	1.50
Combe on Infancy,	1.50
Sober and Temperate Life,	.50
Children in Health—Disease,	1.75
The Science of Human Life,	3.50
Fruit Culture for the Million,	1.00
Saving and Wasting,	1.50
Ways of Life—Right Way,	1.00
Footprints of Life,	1.25
Conversion of St. Paul,	1.00

Hand-book for Home Improvement: comprising "How to Write," "How to Talk," How to Behave," and "How to do Business," in one vol. 2.25.

Man, in Genesis and in Geology; or, the Biblical Account of Man's Creation, tested by Scientific Theories of his Origin and Antiquity. One vol. 12mo, $1.00.

Man and Woman: Considered in their Relations to each Other and to the World. 12mo, Fancy cloth, Price $1.00.

Hopes and Helps for the Young of both sexes, Relating to the Formation of Character. Choice of Avocation, Health, Conversation, Social Affection Courtship and Marriage. Muslin, $1.50.

Sick Headache.

Dear Brethren and sisters, having witnessed much suffering from SICK HEADACHE, we now offer a Speedy and *Sure Cure* for the same. It is pleasant to take and can be sent by mail.

Address with stamp.

DRS. WRIGHTSMAN & FLORY.

July 8. 4t. South Bend, Ind.

Trine Immersion

TRACED

TO THE APOSTLES.

The SECOND EDITION is now ready for delivery. The work has been carefully revised, corrected and enlarged.

Put up in a neat pamphlet form, with good paper cover, and will be sent, post-paid, on the following terms: One copy, 25 cts: Five copies, $1.10; Ten copies, $2.00. 25 copies, $4.50; 50 copies, $8.50; 100 copies, $16.00.

Address, J. H. MOORE,

Urbana, Champaign co., Ill.

Oct 22

DYMOND ON WAR.

An inquiry into the Accordancy of War, with the Principles of Christianity, and an examination of the Philosophical reasoning by which it is defended. With observations on some of the causes of war and on some of its effects. By Jonathan Dymond Sent from this office, post-paid, for 50 cts

TUNE BOOK.

The Brethren's Tune and Hymn Book, is a compilation of Sacred Music adapted to all the hymns in the Brethren's New Hymn Book. It contains over 350 pages, printed on good paper and neatly bound. We will send it to any address, post paid at $1.25 per copy.

GIVEN AWAY.

A FINE GERMAN CHROMO.

We send an elegant chromo, mounted and ready for framing, free to every agent for

UNDERGROUND

or,

LIFE BELOW THE SURFACE.

BY THOS. W. KNOX.

942 Pages Octavo. 130 Fine Engravings.

Relates Incidents and Accidents beyond the Light of Day; Startling Adventures in all parts of the World; Mines and Mode of Working them; Under-currents of Society; Gambling and its *Horrors*; Caverns and their Mysteries; The Dark Ways of Wickedness; Prisons and their Secrets; Down in the Depths of the Sea; Strange Stories of the Detection of Crime.

The book treats of experience with brigands; nights in opium dens and gambling hells; life in prison; Stories of exiles; adventures among Indians; journey through Sewers and Catacombs; accidents in mines: pirates and piracy; tortures of the inquisition; wonderful burglaries; underworld of the great cities, etc., etc.

AGENTS WANTED

for this work. Exclusive territory is given. Agents can make $100 a week in selling this book. Send for circulars and terms to agents.

J. B. BURR & HYDE,

HARTFORD, CONN., or CHICAGO, ILL.

TRACTS.

"ANXIOUS BENCH RELIGION EXAMINED," BY ELDER J. S. FLORY. A SYNOPSIS OF CONTENTS. An address to the reader: The peculiarities that attend this type of religion. The feelings there experienced not imaginary but real. The key that unlocks the wonderful mystery. The causes by which feelings are excited. How the momentary feelings called "Experimental religion" are brought about, and then concludes by giving that form of doctrine as taught by Jesus Christ and recorded by his faithful witnesses.

COUNTERFEIT DETECTER

or

BAPTISM—MUCH IN LITTLE.

This work is now ready for distribution, and the importance of the subject will speak for it a large demand. It is a short treatise on baptism in tract form intended for general distribution, and is set forth in such a plain and logical manner that a wayfaring man though a fool, cannot err therein. Either of the above tracts sent postpaid on the following terms: Two copies, 10 cts, 10 copies 40 cents, 25 copies 70 cents, 50 copies $1.00, 100 copies $1.50.

$133 33/100 worth Sunday School Books for $100 from any or all Publishers. Send for Circulars, J. C. BLAIR, S. S. Book-Store, Huntingdon, Pa.

Trine Immersion.

A discussion on Trine Immersion, by letter between Elder B. F. Moomaw and Dr. J. J. Jackson, to which is annexed a Treatise on the Lord's Supper, and on the necessity, character and evidences of the new birth, also a dialogue on the doctrine of non-resistance, by Elder B. F. Moomaw. Single copy 50 cents.

$5 to $20 per day! Agents wanted! All classes of working people, of either sex, young or old, make more money at work for us in their spare moments or all the time than at anything else. Particulars free. Address G. Stinson & Co., Portland, Maine.

THE HELPING HAND.

Containing several hundred Valuable Receipts for cooking well at a moderate expense, making Dyes, Coloring, Cleaning and Cementing. This book also points out in plain language, free from Doctors' terms the diseases of men, women and children, and the latest and most approved means used for their cure, to which is added a description of the Medicinal Roots and Herbs, and how they are to be used in the cure of diseases.

This is a work of considerable importance and we offer it to our readers as being a valuable accession to every household. Send from this office to any address, post-paid, for 25 cents.

1870 1873

DR. FAHRNEY'S

Blood Cleanser or Panacea.

A tonic and purge, for Blood Diseases, Great reputation. Many testimonials. Many ministering brethren use and recommend it. Ask or send for the "Health Messenger." Use only the "*Panacea*" prepared at Chicago, Ills., and by

Dr. P. Fahrney's Brothers & Co.,

Feb. 3-pd. *Waynesboro, Franklin Co., Pa*

New Hymn Books, English.

TURKEY MOROCCO.

One copy, postpaid,	$1.00
Per Dozen,	11.25

PLAIN ARABESQUE.

One Copy, post-paid,	75
Per Dozen, "	8.50

Ger'n & English, Plain Sheep.

One Copy, post-paid,	$1.00
Per Dozen	11.25
Arabesque Plain,	1.00
Turkey Morocco,	1.25
Single German, post paid	50
Per Dozen,	5.50

HUNTINGDON & BROAD TOP RAIL ROAD

On and after July 17th, 1873, Trains will run on this road daily (Sunday excepted) as follows:

Trains from Huntingdon South. *Trains from Mt. Dallas moving North.*

ACCM. P. M.	EXP. A. M.	STATIONS.	EXP'S. P. M.	ACCM. A. M.
6 05	8 15	Huntingdon,	AR5 00	AR8 20
6 10	8 25	Long Siding	5 55	8 25
6 20	8 30	McConnelstown	5 45	8 18
6 27	8 37	Pleasant Grove	5 38	8 11
6 40	8 50	MARKLESBURG	5 25	7 58
6 50	9 00	Coffee Run	5 15	7 48
6 57	9 08	Rough & Ready	5 08	7 41
7 05	9 15	Cove	5 00	7 34
7 08	9 18	Fishers Summit	4 57	7 30
7 25	9 35	Saxton	4 45	7 15
7 40	9 50	Riddlesburg	4 25	6 55
7 48	9 58	Hopewell	4 18	6 48
8 00	10 15	Piper's Run	4 05	6 35
8 15	10 26	Tatesville	3 50	6 20
8 25	10 35	Everett	3 38	6 08
8 35	10 45	Mount Dallas	3 35	6 05
9 00	11 10	Bedford	3 10	5 30

SHOUP'S RUN BRANCH.

A. M.	P. M.		P. M.	A. M.
LE 9 45	LE 7 30	Saxton.	AR4 35	AR 7 05
10 00	7 45	Coalmont.	4 20	6 50
10 05	7 50	Crawford.	4 15	6 45
AR10 35	AR8 00	Dudley	LE4 05	LE 6 35

Broad Top City from Dudley 2 miles by stage.

Time of Penna. R. R. Trains at Huntingdon.

*, *Mail No. 2 makes connection at Huntingdon with Mail going East on Pennsylvania Railroad at 4.15 p. m., and West at 5.45 p. m. Mail No. 1 leaves Huntingdon at 7.40 a. m. on arrival of Pacific Express West.

Trains on this road connect with trains on Bedford & Bridgeport, and Cumberland & Pennsylvania Railroads.

G. F. GAGE, Supt.

The Weekly Pilgrim.

Published by J. B. Brumbaugh, & Co.

Edited by H. B. & Geo. Brumbaugh.

CORRESPONDING EDITORS.

D. P. Sayler, Double Pipe Creek, Md.

Leonard Furry, New Enterprise, Pa.

The *Pilgrim* is a Christian Periodical, devoted to religion and moral reform. It will advocate in the spirit of *love* and *liberty*, the principles of true Christianity, labor for the promotion of peace among the people of God, for the encouragement of the saints and for the conversion of sinners, avoiding those things which tend toward disunion or sectional feelings.

TERMS.

Single copy, Book paper,	$1.50
Eleven copies, [eleventh for Agt.]	$15.00

Any number above that at the same rate.

Address,

H. B. BRUMBAUGH,

James Creek,

Huntingdon county Pa.

The Weekly Pilgrim.

"REMOVE NOT THE ANCIENT LANDMARKS WHICH OUR FATHERS HAVE SET."

VOL. 4. JAMES CREEK, PENNSYLVANIA, AUGUST 19, 1873. NO. 33.

POETRY.

WAITING.

I am waiting, calmly waiting,
Till the Master bids me come
To the glory of His presence,
To the gladness of his home.

Long, the way my feet have trodden,
Dark oftimes my path has been,
Heavy burdens I have carried,
But the heaviest was sin.

Calmly, in the quiet evening
Of life's long eventful day,
I with folded hands am waiting
Till the shadows flee away.

Never more by active service,
Shall I honor my dear Lord;
But perhaps by patient waiting,
May as well fulfill His Word.

Mercies more than I can number,
From a loving Father's hand,
Have been scattered in my pathway,
Even in a desert land.

Often by the cooling fountain
He my weary feet hath led;
Never has my God forgotten
To supply my "daily bread."

Still the best is all before me;
Very soon these bands of clay
Shall dissolve, and my freed spirit
Rise to bright and perfect day.

Then, in my Redeemer's presence,
With the friends who early died,
I shall taste the bliss of Heaven,
And be fully satisfied.

—*Christian Observer.*

ORIGINAL ESSAYS.

ENERGY INDISPENSIBLE FOR THE ATTAINMENT OF OUR SOUL'S SALVATION.

"Wherefore gird up the loins of your mind, be sober, and hope unto the end for the grace that is to be brought unto you at the revelation of Jesus Christ." 1 Peter 1: 13.

Jesus Christ, in the night of His betrayal, said unto this apostle, "Simon, Simon, behold satan hath desired to have you, that he may sift you as wheat, but I have prayed for thee that thy faith fail not; and when thou art converted, strengthen thy brethren." This the holy apostle Peter was now doing in writing letters to the believers scattered through the different countries encouraging them in their trials, and directing their minds beyond this time, where trials shall end in victory, and temptations, endured by faith, shall bring forth rejoicing with joy unspeakable and full of glory; their faith swallowed up in vision, ending in the salvation of their souls—things the angels desired to look into. "Wherefore," in view of these great and precious promises he would say, "gird up the loins of your minds." Meaning by a metaphor derived from the custom of the Orientals, and indeed the ancient world in general, of girding the long, flowing robes about the loins, or engaging in any active exertion, that you should gird up the loins of your mind, engage with activity in working out your salvation; or in other words, keep your minds and affections continually disencumbered and prepared to run the race set before you, by casting aside all carnal prejudices, and abandoning all anxious cares about the things of this life, and whatever might prevent you from understanding, embracing, and obeying the Word of truth.

Brethren and sisters, remember energy on our part, is very necessary in securing the precious jewels, the pearl of great price, the glorious inheritance which is incorruptible, undefiled, and that fadeth not away; the crown of life, the blessings of heaven, the joys of the saints, and the associates of the holy angels, with God and the Lamb in glory. "The kingdom of heaven suffereth violence, and the violent take it by force." "Strive to enter in at the strait gate." The exhortation to Timothy was, "Thou therefore endure hardship as a good soldier of Jesus Christ." "And if a man also strive for masteries, yet is he not crowned except he strive lawfully." Hence it requires not only striving, but also a lawful one, that is, according to the directions given by the great Head of the Church. The Christian's journey is represented to us in the similitude of a race to be run which requires the most strenuous effort that can be put into exercise to win the prize. We are commanded to "lay aside every weight, and the sin which doth so easily beset us, and run with patience the race that is set before us, looking unto Jesus the author and finisher of our faith." These passages show that it requires muscular power; mind, soul and body must be brought into requisition on the part of man. "But I keep under my body, and bring it into subjection; lest that by any means when I have preached to others, I myself should be cast away." (Paul.) Hence, the phrase gird up the loins of your mind is a very appropriate admonition of the apostle Peter.

In connection with this he adds, "Be sober." Sobriety is a virtue truly becoming a Christian. One of the most important characteristics in a Christian man and woman is lacking where soberness is wanting. The Greek term used here is *Nyphontes*, denoting serious sober-mindedness. See 1 Thess. 5: 6, also 2 Tim. 4: 5. In the former, the term is translated, watch and be sober; in the latter, "But watch thou in all things." Hence, to be sober, in the the text under consideration, on our part, requires great care and watchfulness in many things. Sobriety as defined by Webster, means, first, habitual soberness or temperance in the use of spirituous liquors: as when we say a man of sobriety. Secondly, freedom from intoxication. Thirdly, Habitual freedom from enthusiasm, inordinate passion, or overheated imagination; calmness, coolness. Fourthly, "Seriousness, gravity without sadness or melancholy." "Mirth makes man not mad, nor sobriety sad." In order to be sober we must guard against extremes of any kind, or excess in anything, in short to be temperate in all things. Dear brethren we have a conflict here, a battle to fight, and this combat is against three principle enemies; against our own corrupt nature, against an ungodly world, and against the devil; hence our armor must be bright, our equipment of the very best kind, and our armory well filled; for we know not how long the fight will last; our warfare may be a protracted one.

In the Grecian games, one of their important exercises was running foot-races and at the end of the race was set up a prize, and the first that came out received that prize, and as many did run at the same time, of course, one only could obtain the prize. Another exercise was boxing, for which the victor received a certain crown, and as those gymnastics had to be well trained before they were admitted, and consequently well up to avoid the strokes they often beat the air. Now the apostle Paul contrasts the Christian's race and warfare with those Grecian ones in a striking manner. The uncertainty of theirs, and the certainty of the Christians. "Know ye not that they which run a race run all, but one receiveth the prize? So run, that ye may obtain. And every man that striveth for the mastery is temperate in all things. Now they do it to obtain a corruptible crown; but we an incorruptible. I therefore run, not as uncertainly; so fight I, not as one that beateth the air.' If they were temperate in all things, or sober, for that which passeth away, shall we not, brethren and sisters, be sober and temperate in all things for that which abideth forever and ever?

"And hope to the end is also an important point in our text. Hope is an indispensable Christian grace to the final perseverance of the saints. Where hope is lost, labor will cease. In a natural point of view for instance, if the farmer would not hope to realize a crop in putting out his seed, he would certainly not labor to cultivate his field and sow his seed: but hope causes him to do it yet he may fail in realizing his expectation. The nature of the Christian's hope is confidence in God, and a firm reliance of his promises and an assurance of realizing the same providing they do their part. Such a hope cheers them up in adversities, in afflictions and under severe trials. It points to the future, to the life to come, hence, it affords joy. "Rejoicing in hope, patient in tribulation; continuing instant in prayer." The thought of the child of God in his hope is, that he will be relieved from all the ills of this life in the future world, and there be clothed with immortality; therefore we may call it a lively, blessed, joyous, cheering, soul-reviving, and soul-sustaining hope. It maketh not ashamed: because the love of God is shed abroad in his heart, by the Holy Ghost which is given him. O, who would not be a child of God! Come sinner, ye that are careless, unconcerned and dilatory in this important work. Perhaps some of you are fearful, distrusting the sustaining power of Almighty God. Hope in God, confide in His promises, and trust in His faithfulness; do your part and I will assure you that God will do His through Jesus Christ our Lord.

Brethren and sisters, be constant, be steadfast; we have strong consolation, I mean, we that have fled for refuge to lay hold on the hope set before us; "which hope we have as an anchor of the soul, both sure and steadfast, and which entereth into that within the vale." "Hope to the end, for the grace that is to be brought to you at the revelation of Jesus Christ." The object of our hope is to realize grace—which means favor—in the day when the Lord Jesus Christ shall be again revealed. This grace alluded to in our text, is brought unto every child of God that continues faithful in obedience to God, and walketh in all His commandments blameless. It is secured for Him through the meritorious atonement made by Him, who is to bring it at His revelation. It is a final, eternal life, the crowning point of our religion, the finishing stroke of our redemption; it is the final adoption to wit, the redemption of the body. They that have the first fruits of the spirit, even do groan, waiting for that important event.

Glorious things of thee is spoken!
City of the living God;
Zion's children, band unbroken,
Strive to enter, linger not.

Dear children, members of Christ's body: does it not stimulate our drooping spirits and arouse it to activity in view of these precious promises? Happy is that man and that woman that realizes them, Brethren, sisters, household of the same family, regenerated by the same Father; redeemed by the same Savior; received by Him as His brethren and sisters by adoption. Can we not wholly devote ourselves to His service by trying to imitate Him and copy our walk according to His example? Yes we can, by daily dying to sin and live unto righteousness. O, let us be humble, separated from the world, consecrated to God and sanctified by His word. True we cannot obtain these things by our own strength, but we must set our mind and our will to this work, rely on God, depend on his strength; hence, on our part it requires, watchfulness and prayer to God daily, that we enter not into temptation. Hear the conclusion of the matter in Paul's language, "Work out your own salvation with fear and trembling, for it is God that worketh in you both to will and to do of His own pleasure." Phil. 2: 3. "Wherefore gird up the loins of your mind, and be sober, and hope to the end for the grace that is to be brought unto you at the revelation of Jesus Christ." "He that endureth to the end shall be saved." "Be thou faithful unto death and ye shall receive the crown of life." Wherefore my beloved, let us be steadfast, unmovable, always abounding in the work of the Lord; Forasmuch as we know that our labor is not in vain in the Lord.

LEONARD FURRY.

SANCTIFIED AFFLICTIONS.

In a time of famine in the land of Israel, Elimelech with his wife Naomi and his two sons Mahlon and Chilion, went to sojourn in the land of Moab. One of the sons there married Ruth, and the other married Orpah. The father and sons all died, leaving the three women widows and childless.—At the end of ten years, Naomi having heard that there was plenty again in Judah, set out to return to her own land, and both her daughters-in-law followed her a part of the way, "And Naomi said unto her two daughters-in-law, Go, return each to her mother's house; the Lord deal kindly with you, as ye have dealt with the dead and with me, the Lord grant that ye may find rest, each of you, in the house of her husband. Then she kissed them, and they lifted up their voice and wept. And they said unto her, Surely we will return with thee unto thy people."—Ruth 1: 1–10. Naomi entreated them again to return, "And they lifted up their voice, and wept again: and Orpah kissed her mother-in-law; but Ruth clave unto her. And she said, Behold, thy sister-in-law is gone back unto her people, and unto her gods: return thou after thy sister-in-law. And Ruth said, Entreat me not to leave thee, or return from following after thee: for whither thou goest, I will go; and where thou lodgest, I will lodge: thy people shall be my people, and thy God my God: Where thou diest, will I die, and there will I be buried: the Lord do so to me, and more also, if aught but death part thee and me. Orpah wept but returned unto her people and unto her god's.—Ruth loved Naomi for her piety. Her decision seems to have been founded not merely on natural affection, but on religious conviction. Her own declaration, "Thy God shall be my God," implied a direct renunciation of Idolatry. The testimony of Boaz shows this. "The Lord recompense thy work, and a full reward be given thee of the Lord God of Israel."—Chap. 2: 12.

Naomi and Ruth having arrived at Bethlehem just at the beginning of harvest an All-wise Providence who guideth the steps of his faithful servants, conducted Ruth to the fields of Boaz, "A mighty man of wealth, of the family of Elimeleth," to glean or gather ears of grain after the reapers. He who led Ruth to this spot, directed the foot-steps of Boaz also the same way. Observing among the gleaners a female he said unto his servant that was set over the reapers, "Whose damsel ,is this?" When he found that this was the young Moabite who had shown such friendship to Naomi, the heart of Boaz was moved, and he immediately encouraged her in the tenderest manner to glean in no other field. Ruth who was surprised at such generosity, in one to whom she was utterly unknown "bowed herself to the ground" and poured out the effusions of a grateful heart. The noble minded Boaz cheered her by his approbation of her dutiful conduct, and by the uttering of this expressive prayer, "The Lord recompense thy work, and a full reward be given thee of the Lord God of Israel under whose wings thou art come to trust." When Ruth returned in the evening to Naomi, and informed her of all that had happened and in whose field she had gleaned, Naomi saw immediately that the divine hand was bringing about good for them.—"Blessed," says she, "be he of the Lord, who hath not left off his kindness to the living and the dead."

The remainining part of this history is intimately connected with two remarkable statutes in the Israelitish Code. The one was that if the elder branch of a family sold any part of his land, the next of kin had a right to redeem it, and if he refused to do so, the privilege descended to the next in succession. The other law was, that if the elder branch died leaving a widow without children, the next kinsman would marry her, and raise seed to his brother. Naomi knew well the obligation of these precepts, and as she was too old to think of a husband, [Chap. 1: 12.] she transferred her right to Ruth. The Almighty blessed this marriage of Boaz, to Ruth, with a son, to whom was given the name of Obed. This child Naomi took and laid in her bosom and became its nurse.—When Naomi returned from the land of Moab, a disconsolate and destitute widow, her affliction appeared so severe in her own estimation, that she said to the Bethlehemites, who were all moved about them, and they said, "is this Naomi," and she said unto them, "Call me not Naomi [pleasant or beautiful] call me Mara [bitter] for the Almighty hath dealt very hardly with me."

We here notice the providence of God over individuals. The wonders of that Providence appears in the means by which God brought about the conversion of Ruth, and her admission into the family of the Messiah, through the famine in Israel, Elimelech's misfortunes, his son marrying a Moabitess, and her son's affliction in becoming a widow; thus does he overrule evil and afflictions for good.—Psalm 119: 71. Thus were the latter days of Naomi better than the beginning, and the evening of her life compensated for all the afflictive providences. The crosses and distresses which she had experienced in the land of Moab. The dutiful conduct and unshaken faith of Ruth, were abundantly rewarded by the God of Israel, for whom she had renounced all things, and is on record as an example of piety, for the instruction of all generations. On her was bestowed the honor of being the great grand mother of David, and consequently of him who was the hope of Israel, and the redeemer of the human race. Well therefore may we adopt the pious exclamation of Bishop Hall: "O the sure and bountiful payments of the Almighty; who ever came under his wing in vain? Who ever lost by trusting in him? Who ever forsook the Moab of this world for the true Israel, and did not at least rejoice in the change?"

D. NEGLEY.

METHODISM FIFTY YEARS AGO AND NOW.

Alike all other human institutions, liable to yearly amendments, to devolve from generation to generation, and to be entrusted as a whole, into the hands or bishoprick of a few men, has Methodism shared the inevitable fate of degeneracy. It is said of Elder Axley of that persuasion, who had his day of activity in Church; about fifty years ago and upward, that he once presided at a quarterly meeting at the house of a widow Conoway in Blount Co. Tenn. After preaching on Saturday, he announced the order of the meeting for the Sabbath. Lovefeast in the morning, he gave them to understand who were to be admitted and who were not. No rings, no ruffles, no bows on the bonnets &c. Sunday morning came and brought the membership generally. Mr. Axley stood at the door to judge who were proper subjects for admittance as they came in. There was a good sister with a bow on her bonnet. No admittance. The preachers, "continues the biographer, fortified every position by giving book, chapter, and verse. No rhetorical speech making, but plain exposition of Bible truths. Mr. Axley as a neighbor was not surpassed by any. At house raising and log rolling he was put forward as leader, and could plan and have more work done in a day than any other man in the country. As a farmer he was no sloven. Everything was convenient. A tool for every work, and a place for every tool. Nothing was out of place and nothing lost. Here we have an example of Methodism fifty years ago.

Methodism claims for herself great advancement and success in the past fifty years, notwithstanding all her natural conflicts and spiritual persecutions; and through the wise counsels of her episcopacy, great moral improvements; but no degeneracy.

Now my brethren and sisters in Christ, if all the impnovments upon rings, ruffles, and bows upon bonnets which Paris with all the fashion inventing world could contrive and invent in the last fifty years can have been episcopated as legitimate advancements or as moral improvements upon the adorument of the women in modest apparrel, with shamefacedness and sobriety, for which Mr, Axley contended for but fifty years ago; and if those delicate effeminate hands with diamond mounted rings, and carried on persons clad in the finest broadcloth that can be obtained, which deal out to those silkey, and gold ornamented, and artificial decorated communicants the Holy Emblems, I say if they are more like the hands of the old fishermen or tent maers than were those of the house raising and log rollers, then the claims of improvements are just, if not, degeneracy was a reasonable term. But now let us look around us and then back fifty years; or even less and ah, we see that the Methodists are not alone in this respect, and perhaps not the farthest gone in this wild career. But let a hint suffice the wise.

C. C. ROOT.

SUNDAY SCHOOLS OF MEN.

The more this subject is ventilated the more thoroughly, are we convinced that it is not from Heaven. Seeing that its advocates in their determinate zeal to defend, become so nervous, unable to produce a single precept from the Bible, or a single precedent in the history of the Church in the primitive and purer ages are forced to adopt and apply the unchristian and uncourteous epithets to those that differ from them of "prejudice" "ignorance," "selfishness," a spirit certainly not obtained from the school of Christ, but from some school of human invention, and counterpart to the spirit possessed by the Ephesians, when Paul declared, "that they be no gods which are made with hands," &c., they were full of wrath, and cried out saying, "Great is Diana of the Ephesians," causing great confusion, catching Paul's companions they rush into the Theatre, and when Paul would have gone in, doubtless to reason with them, as his manner was from the Scriptures, the disciples aware of the danger, suffered him not, and, others of his friends, chief men of Asia, desired him not to adventure himself into the theatre. And when Alexander would have made his defense, they perceiving that he was a Jew, and opposed to such idols, to sustain their ungodly cause, "all with one voice about the space of two hours cried out, great is Diana of the Ephesians." This was, doubtless, in their minds an overwhelming argument, but not so convincing to the mind of Paul and his companions, and therefore, would be likely to expose them to the epithets, "prejudice," "ignorance" and "selfishness." But so sanguine were these Ephesians that they would say that Paul and his brethren were ignorant of the "sweet consciousness" enjoyed in the worship of the great Diana. They, like some of modern date, needed no divine revelation, for their image had fallen down directly from Jupiter. Acts 19.

We, from this history, may learn another profitable lesson which is that it is vain to try to meet such with Bible argument; that nothing short of legal interference will meet the case. But I speak not of these things because a strange thing had happened unto me, for I have been accustomed to hear continually the appellation "Ignorance," "Prejudice," and "Selfishness," applied to the brethren who contended for the faith once delivered to the saints, before and ever since my connection with the fraternity. Ignorance in some of its aspects it is true, is bad enough, but nevertheless adopting the language of brother Quinter upon a certain occasion, I would say, that there are some things even worse than ignorance." An *ignoramus* for instance. "An ignorant person. *A vain pretender to knowledge.*" Webster's second definition.

The Rulers, Elders, and Scribes, &c., perceiving that Peter and John were unlearned and ignorant men, seeing their boldness they marvelled. "And they took knowledge of them, that they had been with Jesus." Acts 4: 5, 6, 13. They were ignorant as to the rudiments of the world, but had taken upon them the yoke of Christ and learned of Him. They had not learned from corrupted Christianity, nor from men of any stamp, nor yet from Jupiter, but by the revelation of Jesus Christ, here they planted their banner, and like Paul, determined to know nothing but Jesus Christ and Him crucified; determined to know none other as their ruler and governor, he having been crucified notwithstanding. Upon this platform I desire to stand, and by grace expect to stand, until evidence and argument from these premises outweighing that in the side of the scale I now occupy is produced, I will then at once change my position, but the construction of my mind will never allow me to change because *some junior*, or senior shall say I see the good effects, or "I feel a sweet consciousness" that I am acceptably in the service of the Master. Were I thus easily convinced I might long since have been anything, and everything from Paganism, Judaism, Mahommedanism, Catholicism, all the various forms of Protestantism down to Mormonism, Freemasonry and all its kindred secret associations. They all being in sympathy with these sentiments forming their conclusions from these premises.

Seeing the danger to which the children of men would be exposed, the Apostle Paul gives the following very suitable warning: "Beware, lest any man spoil you through philosophy and *vain deceit* after the *traditions of men*, after the *rudiments of the world and not* after Christ." Col. 2: 13.

I have merely noticed briefly the form and spirit of the attack of the premises I occupy upon this question, simply alluding to the assertions. Arguments there has none been adduced, when arguments are presented from the Scriptures, establishing the fact that Sunday schools are from Heaven, and not of men, I will not only willingly, but gladly change my position for it is extremely pleasant, with me to be on the popular side of any question, with my brethren.

B. F. MOOMAW.

Bonsacks, Va.

GO ONWARD.

Dear brethren and sisters, we should not grow weary nor faint in our mind, but press on in the narrow way, try with all our minds to follow the example of our Master, as sincere and obedient children, through evil report as well as good report; endeavor to grow in grace and in the knowledge of the truth, day by day, as it is in Christ Jesus. Strive to become humble, meek and lowly in heart and mind and to die unto all self, to become altogether nothing in ourselves, poor, needy creatures, depending alone upon the help and grace of God who will abundantly bestow all needful knowledge, wisdom and instruction. He will help us to walk uprightly in his sight. O, should we not then strive with all our heart, mind and will to leave all self, to die daily and grow in grace, wisdom and strength, to deny all worldly lusts and pleasures, to abstain from every appearance of evil, so that our minds may be placed on heavenly things? There remaineth a rest to the people of God, who soweth not after the flesh but after the spirit, and seek nothing but the will of God, die daily unto sin and all unrighteousness; are no more conformed to the world with its unfruitful works of darkness, but who are transformed by the renewing of their minds that they may prove what is that good, acceptable and perfect will of God.

The grace of God, that bringeth salvation, hath appeared unto all men, teaching them to deny themselves of all ungodly and wordly lusts, to live godly, righteously in this present world, for we are not of the world, even as Christ, whom we, serve and honor, was not of the world but of the Father. We are not born of corruptible seed but of incorruptible, of the word of God which liveth and abideth forever, therefore we bring forth the fruit of the spirit. We sow in tears that we may *reap* in joy. O, let us then, all try to depart from all iniquity, bringing forth the fruits of the spirit, love one another as Christ loved us, for by this we may know that we are His disciples. How much more happiness would be felt in the heart if we would practice more love towards each other; if more would be constrained to turn from their evil ways; if the Church would make greater progress in the conversion of souls, and if she would exercise, daily, more of that pure and heavenly love. I pray the Lord to give us more of that pure love that we may manifest it among the members and to the whole human family.

A. H. BAUN.

Ashland, Ohio.

TROUBLE.

Trouble is more frequently made than sent. If every person would take the world as it is—its joys and sorrows—and yield at once an humble reconciliation to what is unavoidable, there would be far more happiness, and infinitely less misery than there is. Six thousand years, experience ought to convince mankind that there are clouds here as well as sunshine, and the man who starts life with the expectation that everything before him will be smooth and uninterrupted, is a dreamer who knows nothing of the world's realities. Wealth cannot shield us from disappointment and affliction, and poverty is not as heavy on the heart as the cares brought on by the possession of uncounted riches.

We cannot keep death away from our door, no matter how faithfully we may guard its portal: nor can we so control the mind and disposition of others that the most tender ties and associations are not at times snapped asunder. Let us take matters as they come, and try to be content. If we are prosperous, we should rejoice and give God the praise. If we fail in our enterprise and find our plans of business dwarfed and thwarted, let us submit coolly to the visitation, and try again with renewed hope and effort. There is no use lamenting, when lamentations will do no good—or shedding tears, when they only tend to heighten our sorrows. The grave will soon cover our troubles, and there is a happy life beyond, which we can make our own, no matter how the world treats us.

CHRIST THE RISEN SAVIOR.

Continued from page 131.

The Lord now speaks to us in every part of Scripture as far as it respects our dispensation, and suits our case with as much authority as He did to Israel from Mount Sinai, but with words of mercy and grace instead of terror and dismay. For if Christ be risen from the dead, then is His atonement accepted. He died for our sins and rose again for our justification. He was arrested for our debt and cast into the grave or prison. But as full payment had been made He was speedily liberated. Having overcome the sharpness of death He hath opened the Kingdom of Heaven to all believers. The foundation of our hopes are now surely laid, the way of access to a throne of grace is now made manifest, for the risen Savior is also ascended into the Heavens to appear in the presence of God for us and is able to save to the uttermost all those that come to God by Him seeing He liveth to make intercession for them.

The resurrection of Christ assures us that all power in heaven and earth are given to Him, and that He is made head over all things. To His Church, He both died and rose again that He might be the Lord both of the living and dead. Angels, principalities and powers are made subject to Him. He is King of Kings and Lord of Lords, all nature obeys Him. All the treasures of wisdom and knowledge are hid up in Him. He has unsearchable riches and invincible power. The fulness of the spirit resides in Him. All the fulness of the god-head dwells in Him bodily. He has become the author of eternal salvation to all them that obey Him, and He must reign till all His enemies are made His footstool. It is therefore no light matter that we are considering, yet saith Jehovah, I have set my king upon my holy hill of Zion. Kiss the Son lest he be angry and ye perish. Every individual must either bow to the sceptre of His grace or be broken in pieces by the iron rod of His omnipotent indignation.

We are also taught that true Christians are conformed to Christ in His death, resurrection and ascension. By motives and grace derived from their crucified and risen Redeemer, they die to their former hopes, pleasures and pursuits, their sensibility to temporal things is deadened, carnal self love, the main spring of their activity in past times is broken, they are crucified with Christ nevertheless they live, yet

Continued next week.

WAR OPPOSED TO CHRISTIAN RELIGION.

Who can calmly reflect with subdued and unbiased judgment, the following commands of the Bible, and not be convinced that peace is one of the vital principals of the Christian religion, and that, war cannot be tolerated among a christian people, viz: "Thou shalt not kill." "Be at peace with one another." "Avenge not ourselves, but rather give place unto wrath, for it is written, vengeance is mine; I will repay, saith the Lord." "Love your enemies, bless them that curse you, and despitefully use you and persecute you, that ye may be the children of your Father which is in Heaven."

"Resist not evil; but whoever shall smite thee on thy right cheek, turn to him the other also." "Let all bitterness, and wrath, and anger and clamor and evil speaking, be put away from you, and be kind one to another, tender hearted, forgiving one another, even as God for Christ's sake, hath forgiven you." "And when his disciples, James and John, saw this, they said, Lord, wilt thou that we command fire to come down from Heaven and consume them as Elias did? But he turned and rebuked them, and said, "Ye know not what manner of spirit ye are of. For the Son of man is not come to destroy men's lives, but to save them. And they went to another village.

"In this the children of God are manifest, and the children of the devil; whosoever doeth not righteousness is not of God, neither he that loveth not his brother. For this is the message that ye have heard from the beginning, that we should love one another, not as Cain, who was of that wicked one and slew his brother. And wherefore slew he him? Because his own works were evil, and his brother's righteous."

Marvel not my brethren, if the world hate you. We know that we have passed from death unto life, because we love the brethren. He that loveth not his brother, abideth in death. Whosoever hateth his brother is a murderer; and ye know no murderer hath eternal life abiding in him." From whence come wars and fightings among you? come they not hence from your lusts which war in your members?" Follow peace with all men, and holiness, without which no man shall see the Lord."

If my kingdom were of this world, then would my servants fight," lead a peaceable life in all godliness." "The fruits of the Spirit are love, joy, peace," &c. "Thou shalt love thy neighbor as thyself," and the parable of the good Samaritan makes every human being our neigbor. "God is love; and he that dwelleth in love dwelleth in God, and God in him." Be kindly affectioned one toward another with brotherly love, in honor preferring one another." "Bless them that persecute you, bless and curse not." Therefore, if thine enemy hunger, feed him; if he thirst give him drink; for in so doing thou shalt heap coals of fire on his head."

"Be not overcome of evil, but overcome evil with good." Love worketh no ill to his neighbor." Is it love to an enemy to kill him? is it love to prepare to kill him? and yet the supporter and advocate of war doeth all this. Then how can the love of God dwell in him?

The Bible aboundeth with principles of peace. It cherishes and encourages all those virtues which lead to peace, and condemns everything which tends to war, and the use of outward instrumentalities as weapons of war and defense.—*Messenger of peace.*

INSINCERITY IN SPEECH.

Say what you think, rather than what you imagine other people expect you to say. Or if you feel, as we often may, that we had better not, or not then say what we think, say nothing. At any rate believe that it is a genuine promotion of the health of society to let our words be honestly ours. Affect no sentiments which you do not own. I do not of course refer to those phrases of courtesy which are universally current and understood, as when a man sets his signiture to the statement that he is an obedient servant to one whom perhaps he has just been declining to serve. Nor do I mean that we are expected to give utterance to each sentiment which arises in our hearts. That would be selfish. But do not, especially in religion, affect feelings which are alien to you. It is incalculable what wanton harm is done by this. We can see it when a man more honest than others, ventures to put some criticism, which has risen in many minds, into words; or, Luther-like, to question some empty dictum which has been long tacitly permitted to exist. By a touch he can thus free many a mind. He simply makes bold to open the door and let himself out; and lo! he has provided an exit for a grateful stream of prisoners who follow him, and then see that after all they might as well have delivered themselves.—*Leisure Hour.*

One reason why christianity has so little success in the world is because professing Christians subordinate to so many other considerations. Local residence, occupation, friendship, marriage are settled, and the question of religion goes for little or nothing. It is compromised, and a compromise is next to a surrender. Were it the ruling principle with Christians, it would be on the sure way to the world's throne though it might be through suffering.

BIBLE promises are like the beams of the sun, which shine as freely in at the window of the poor man's cottage as at the rich man's pallace.

GENERAL INTELLIGENCE.

S. E. MILLER wishes to know if there are Brethren living in Jewell Co., Kansas. Who can give the desired information?

THE CHURCH at Coffee Run, James Creek Congregation, will be put under course of erection this week and will be pushed along as rapidly as possible. It is expected to be completed early in the Fall.

PROF. WISE, who proposes to cross the ocean in a balloon, grounds his expected success on the theory that at a certain altitude there is a steady and rapid current of air setting from West to East. He says that out of 446 aerial voyages he has made, 414 have carried him Eastward.

THE TIME for political strife has come and dupes are getting to work with a good will. King "politic" has become a tyrant and those desiring the honor of small offices can expect to do large barking for them. Let all true Christians be careful not to perjure their souls, dishonor their profession and sell the Lord of life and glory for a mess of pottage.

A BROTHER of Cerrogordo, Ill., whose name we cannot now remember, wishes to know why his communication was not published. This informs him that it was placed with other copy, for preparation, but by some means part of it was lost, hence its non-appearance. Please write again, and we will endeavor to be more careful in the future.

SOME TIME ago, our old and respected brother Samuel Brumbaugh of Saxton, Pa., met with a serious accident, having his shoulder dislocated and an arm broken. After the first shock was over, his condition seemed to be hopeful and it was tho't that he would soon get well again, but of late, we are informed that there is a change for the worse, and it is feared that his case is doubtful.

ONE of the largest and best buildings now in course of erection, in West Huntingdon, is the *Weekly Pilgrim* Office. It is a double, three story brick, with basement under the whole house. The one part is intended for the dwelling and the other for press room, store room, sanctum, stationary room, private office and type room. The press room will be in the basement, connected with the type room by an elevator. The store room will be on the first floor, 18x43 making one of the best rooms in that part of the town. The sanctum, stationary and private office will be on the second floor, having a side entrance from the cross or 14th street, and the type room will be on the third floor. The whole building will be heated from the basement by a modern "heater," making it the best and most convenient publishing house outside of the large cities.—*Exchange.*

BEAVER COLONY—COLORADO.

The town of Beaver, Weld Co., Colorado, has just been laid out, and a settlement commenced there called "Beaver Colony." It is situated on the North side of the South Platte River in the North E. part of Col., about one hundred miles East of the Rocky mountains and immediately on the line of Rail-road now building from Julesburg on the Union Pacific Rail-road to Denver, the capital of the Territory, which road it is expected will be in running order this coming Fall. Beaver will doubtless be an important point on the road as a depot and eating station, and at no distant day be a county seat, as Weld Co. will eventually be cut up into at least three counties. Surrounding Beaver, it is said by those who should know, there is the largest body of choice agricultural lands to be found in the Territory. Easily watered by irrigating, canals carrying an abundance of water from the Platte River. The matter of irrigation, to my mind, was such that I thought of it with much disfavor until by personal observation I was otherwise impressed. The more abundant yield of superior crops has satisfied me that farming by irrigation in Colorado pays well. The fine dry and healthy climate must be first enjoyed before anything like a just idea of their advantages can be had. Owing to the extensive mining region not far off, thronged with miners, the market for farm products must continue one of the best. Now is the time for the homeless, or any one who desires it, to get homes in that section of country, as it will be rapidly taken up either by preemption or homesteads. Any one going there can secure 320 acres of choice bottom land, and have thousands of acres of range for stock. One hundred and sixty acres can be had under the pre-emption bill to which a good title can be had in six months by paying $1.25 per acre. The party then can, if he wishes, sell it readily for $5 per acre. Whether he sells or not, he can then go and take another lot of 160 acres as a homestead which he gets free by living on it five years. Any one can file on both claims soon after arriving there. The prospects are now good for a settlement of Brethren to commence there early next Spring with a speaker or speakers.

We do not desire to over persuade any one, but would say to those contemplating a removal, we would be glad to have you help build up a flourishing settlement, and if members of the church, help disseminate by word and deed the principles of a true Christianity to a community in that part of the world. This is one of the most successful ways of prosecuting the missionary work to the evangelizing of the world. Other incentives than worldly considerations should prompt us in our change from place to place. The world is large, sin reigns throughout the bounds of civilization, souls are precious everywhere in the sight of God, —His proffered mercy is boundless and free,—from sea to sea, may the CRUCIFIED be preached, His Gospel be believed and practical Christianity, such as exemplified the character and life of our Lord and Master, be the *rule* rather than the exception.

J. S. FLORY.

Orchard View, W. Va.

Youth's Department.

TO A CHILD.

Never, my child, forget to pray
Whate'er the business of the day ;
If happy dreams have blessed thy sleep,
If startling fears have made thee weep,
With holy thoughts begin the day,
And ne'er my child forget to pray.

Pray Him by whom the birds are fed,
To give to thee thy daily bread ;
If wealth His bounty should bestow,
Praise Him from whom all blessings flow ;
If he who gave should take away,
O ne'er my child, forget to pray.

The time will come when thou wilt miss
A father's and a mother's kiss ;
And then, my child, perchance you'll see
Some who in prayer ne'er bend the knee ;
From such examples turn away
And ne'er my child, forget to pray.

THE YOUNG NAZARENE.

The story of the child Jesus is so interesting and full of encouragement that it never grows old. Our young readers cannot do better than to make His life a constant subject of study. But the question may be, how came it to pass that he was called a Nazarene. I will try and tell you. Because Adam and Eve ate of the forbidden fruit they became sinners and felt very miserable. On account of this disobedience they for the first time learned that they were subjects of death and already began to feel its affects. In addition to this, were to be driven out of the beautiful garden which God had prepared for them. They were now to go out in the plains and till the land with their own hands with the knowledge that among their good seed sown, should spring up with it, thorns and thistles. This seemed very hard after living so happily in Eden. To give them some hope, God told the serpent (the tempter)in the persence of the woman, that the seed of the woman shall bruise the serpents head. This is the way we generally hear it quoted or said, but by turning to the third chapter of Genesis 15th verse, you will find that it reads a little differently. God says, speaking of the seed of the woman, "It shall bruise thy head and thou shalt bruise his heel." This was the first promise that Jesus should come, and was afar off, but in every generation after that, the promise was renewed and made plainer. These promises were made through good men that we read of in the Bible, called prophets.

Now because these were good men, all they said must come true. One of them, in telling about Christ and the time He should come, said he was to be called a Nazarene. By reading the history of Jesus, you will learn how this was fulfilled.

The account says He was born in Bethlehem, a village or town of Judea. Some say he was born in a manger, but the account does not say so. It says he was born and laid in a manger. Somewhere in the Bible, it says he was born or brought forth under an apple tree. I will not now tell you where that place is but propose to our Sunday school teachers that they let this be one of the questions to be answered at the next school. No matter how strange the question may appear, it can be found in the Bible, and I hope that none of my young readers will give it up until they find it.

But this is not telling how he came to be called a Nazarene. When Jesus was born it was noised abroad that he was to be king. This reached the ears of King Herod and he became fearful that he might lose his position and to avoid this, he commanded that all the male children of two years and under should be destroyed, thinking that among the number surely this new king would be destroyed, but an angel told his father in a dream that he should take the young child (Jesus) and flee to Egypt, so that when the wicked Herod was destroying the innocent children, the young king was safe with his mother over in Egypt. After Herod's death he was again commanded to return to the land of Israel but when he got into Egypt and heard that Herod's son reigned in his stead, he concluded to turn into Galilee and and dwelt in a city called Nazareth. This was done, the Scriptures tell us, that it might be fulfilled which was spoken by the prophets, He shall be called a Nazarene. He was called a Nazarene then, because He dwelt a short time in Nazareth. This city had rather a bad reputation for you remember that some time afterward it was asked, "Can there anything good come out of Nazareth?" Yes, there was one good thing come from there and that was the humble Nazarene, Jesus, the King of righteousness and the Savior of the world. If it had been a city of bad reputation prior to this, the fact of the young Nazarene living there a short time caused it to be a place of note. Just so it is with a wicked and sinful heart. No matter how bad a reputation a sinner may have, if he admits Jesus into his heart a short time, it will be changed and gain as great a reputation for being good as it had for being evil before.

You, dear young friends, have an influence and how well it would be for you if the society in which you associate would always be made better on account of your presence. There are many places that need young Nazarenes to step in and improve their reputation. Study well the character of the young Nazarene and then strive to imitate His example. At twelve years of age, He was at His Father's business. Some of you are much older and are still in the emp'oy of satan whom to serve is sin and death.

UNCLE HENRY.

CHRIST BLESSES LITTLE CHILDREN.

MATT. 19; MARK 10; LUKE 18.

Our Lord came into the world to bless and save not only adults, but also children, and he loved them very tenderly. This he displayed in the following circumstance; Pious Jews were in the habit of begging the blessing of distinguished teachers and priests, on their children. As the people recognized Christ as a teacher who had come from God, some pious mothers once brought their children to Jesus, that he might bless them, by laying his hand upon them, and praying for them. As it was evening and Jesus had been employed all day in teaching and healing the sick, his disciples thought that he required rest, and rebuked those who bro't their children. The parents could very easily have presumed, though falsely, that either their request was improper, or that Jesus, who was kindness itself, did not love children. But when he observed this conduct of his disciples, he was displeased,and said, "Suffer little children to come unto me, and forbid them not, for of such is the kingdom of heaven. Verily! I say unto you, he that receiveth the kingdom of heaven not as a little child, shall by no means enter therein." And he took them up in his arms and blessed them.

Here we read of parents bringing their children to Jesus Christ. Your parents also bring you to Jesus, when they send you to school, or to receive religious instruction: for there Christ has his servants who receive you in his name.

You should whilst yet young, belong to the kingdom of God. Remember your Redeemer and Maker in your youth, then at an early age you will be saved.

Many in early youth have had hands laid on them in the name of the Lord Jesus, and they were blessed, but all did not retain the blessing, because they did not persevere in good. The blessing departs from all who do not carefully preserve it.

Our children thou dost claim,
And mark them out for thine,
Ten thousand blessings to thy name,
For goodness so divine.

Our offspring still thy care,
Shall own their fathers' God,
To latest times thy blessings share,
And sound thy praise abroad.

MATT. 18: 14. Even so it is the will of your father that is in heaven, that one of these little ones should perish.

WATCH YOURSELF.

"When I was a school-boy," said an old man, "we had a schoolmaster who had an odd way of catching boys. One day he called out to us, 'Boys, I must have close attention to your books. The first one of you that sees another boy idle, I want you to inform me, and I will attend to his case.' 'Ah,' thought I to myself, 'there's Joe Simmons, that I don't like. I'll watch him, and if I see him look off his book, I'll tell.' It was not long before I saw Joe look off his book, and immediately I informed the master. 'Indeed,' said he, 'and how did you know that he was idle?' 'I saw him,' said I. 'You did; and were your eyes on your book when you saw him?' I was caught, and I never watched for the boys again.—*Little Christian.*

TWO SOMEBODYS.

I know somebody who always appears to be miserable, and this is the way she contrives to be so: thinking always about herself; constantly wishing for that she has not got; idling her time; fretting and grumbling.

I know somebody who is much happier, and this is the way she contrives to be so: thinking of others; satisfied with what her Heavenly Father has best judged for her; working, caring for somebody else besides herself, and thinking how she can make others happy.

My little "Somebody," which kind of a "somebody," are you.—*Little Christian.*

"READ—TRY."

There was once a very little boy who used to ask his mother a great many questions, and how do you think she answered him? "Read, and you will know," said she, and then she would give him books, where he found all he wished to know.

Sometimes, too, this little boy used to wish that he could do this difficult thing, and instead of discouraging him, this good mother would say one little word, and that word was "try." The little boy was Sir William Jones, afterwards one of the most learned men that ever lived.

LET us not love those things much which we are not sure to live long to love, nor to have long if we should.

As love without esteem is volatile and capricious, esteem without love is languid and cold.

The Weekly Pilgrim.

JAMES CREEK, PA., Aug. 19, 1873.

☞ How to send money.--All sums over $1.50, should be sent either in a check, draft or postal order. If neither of these can be obtained, have the letter registered.

☞ When Money is sent, *always* send with it the name and address of those who paid it. Write the names and post office as plainly as possible.

☞ Every subscriber for 1873, gets a *Pilgrim Almanac* Free.

A SHORT VISIT.

At different times we promised to make a visit to the brethren living in the vicinity of the Cross Roads Meeting house, Clover Creek congregation, but never could see a way of going until last Saturday, being informed of that being the regular time of holding services at that place on Sunday. Wishing those remaining at home to have an opportunity of attending Church, we left our horse and took the morning train south on Broad Top for Cove Station, where we got aboard the hack and in three hours reached Fredricksburg, a distance of about five miles. This may seem like slow travel and it was too, as I walked the same road coming home in one and a half hours, but then we had no load, which we suppose made the difference.

We arrived at Bro. J. W. Brumbaugh's in time for dinner, but as sister J. W. B. was helping to prepare a dinner at her sons, we were taken there, where we were well cared for. After dinner, we called upon bro. G. W. Brumbaugh, and found him in his, or rather, their Foundry, Bro. J. L. Wineland being a partner. They do the general run of work done at foundries of similar capacities, but their principle work is manufacturing plows. They are making a plow at this place that gives very general satisfaction wherever tried, and the demand for them is so great that they cannot keep up with the orders. The great secret of a good plow lies in the moldboard. If this is so shaped that the inclined plane is not too steep and the pressure against it equal there is an important point of excellence gained. In this they claim that they have succeeded, and we think, justly too, as the draft is light and the plow cleans readily. They have also invented a draft rod with a spring attached which is an important addition, greatly saving it from danger of breaking when striking a rock or solid body. On the whole, they manufacture a No. 1. plow and we would advise those who want a good machine in that line to give them a trial. Address Brumbaugh and Wineland Clover Creek. Pa.

In the P. M. Bro J. W. B. took us up to Bro. Daniel Diehl's who resides near the C. R. Church where we were kindly received. In the evening there was an appointment in the Church which we filled. Here we met Eld. D. M. Holsinger also John Replogle, minister in the Yellow Creek Congregation. After preaching we were kindly cared for in the house of Bro. Diehl. Sabbath morning there was public preaching again at the same house, and again we tried to exercise in the ministration of the word, and was followed with some interesting remarks in German by Eld. Jacob Miller of the Yellow Creek Congregation. As the brethren here have Sunday school, and met at 3. P. M. we were invited to be with them and address the School which we agreed to do. We were then taken to the home of Bro. Simon Snider where we were refreshed with the good things of this life and enjoyed a short but pleasant season in the society of the family, Bro. S. B. Furry, Keifer and others. We enjoy such occasions and could wish them to happen more frequent.

At the appointed hour we met in Sunday school capacity where we met a large number of young men, ladies and children, also a number of parents some whose heads were quite gray. That, brethren and sisters is what means success in Sunday schools.

Gray hairs indicates age which commands respect and means order. Notwithstanding the attendance was large for the occasion, the order was quite good and almost all participated in the exercises. After the regular business of the School was done, we made a short address to the scholars and friends, which was received with marked attention, and we hope that some of the ideas dropped at random may have made impressions that may result in good. S. B. Furry is superintendent and Daniel Diehl and D. Burket assistants. The name of the other officers we have not got. Spent the night at Eld. J. W. Brumbaugh's and early on Monday morning made for Cove Station, where we got aboard for home. On the train we met our esteemed brother and fellow laborer in the ministry, S. A. More of Yellow Creek Congregation, and had a short but interesting talk—Marklesburg—and we are off —home—all well.

THE COLORADO COLONY.

On another page, the attention of our readers are called to the building up a Colony in Colorado. This is an enterprise that we have often thought of, and look upon it as being a move in the right direction. The idea of leaving home, brethren and sisters, relations and friends, to emigrate to the distant west, in a strange land sparsely settled with strangers, is by no means cheering or pleasant and under such circumstances, none will be induced to go but such as are under the stern necessity of bettering their condition in life, though it should be a land flowing with milk and honey. The time has come that we are beginning to live socially, and we hope spiritually too, and in forming our locations, we are about as careful that these wants can be enjoyed as we are that our bodies can be sustained. By going as a Colony, taking with us friends and neighbors, and especially brethren and sisters of a like precious faith, our prospects are very much changed, so much so that even a strange land appears as a home. The idea of some 30 or 40 families of brethren and sisters forming a community away out in the promising fields of Colorado is so congenial to our mind that we almost feel like pulling up stakes and going along especially since we learned that our esteemed brother J. S. Flory is to be one of the number. We hope that Beaver Colony may be a success and that many of our brethren and sisters, now seeking homes, may take advantage of this very desirable opportunity, and that by another year the *Pilgrim* may have a goodly representation in this new field.

AN EXPLANATION.

By reading brethren Moomaw's and Mussleman's articles of this issue, it will be seen that they take exceptions to brother Zuck's "Origin of opposition to Sunday schools" or more especially to the spirit which it manifests. At the time the article was placed on the hook we did not give it a very careful examination, as we were always rather favorably impressed, with brother Zuck's writings. That some of the expressions in the article referred to are rather strong and savored with a seemingly unchristain spirit we admit, but we believe that the protesting brethren have accepted it in a stronger sense than was intended by the writer. In reading articles or a subject having two sides there should always be an allowance made for the excess of force used on one side to meet a corresponding excess on the other side which may be real or anticipated. When Bro. Moomaw proves that Sunday schools, as an institution, is of men, he as virtually condemns its friends, as Bro. Zuck condemns those who oppose them, and we all know there are some very good brethren that are favorable to Sunday schools and also that they have the sanction of A. M. Both sides are represented by good brethren and to condemn either is not good, not proper, not charitable, and is not called for in the discussion of the subject. As said before, we have no objections to having the subject thoroughly examined. To do this, there is no necessity of controverting or being personal. For our part, we are favorable to Sunday schools as held by the Brethren and whose only reading book is the Bible. Precepts for teaching our children the Scriptures are as old as the Bible and we anticipate no trouble in proving that parents are under the most sacred obligations to either teach them or have them taught, but this may be done at home as well as in the Sunday School, but Sunday Schools have this advantage in their favor, they may reach cases that cannot be reached by parental training, and our desires for doing good should by no means, be confined to the family circle. Christ came to save sinners and we are justifiable in making use of any means that will accomplish this great end, without stepping outside of the "landmarks" or the spirit of the Gospel. Our good brother Musselman seems to think we stepped outside of our limits in admitting Bro. Zuck's production, but we hope not, especially when we make due allowance for the pointed and pungent style of some writers. Because we believe in Sunday Schools, does not cause us to love any the less those who differ from us, but hope, if any more feel like writing they will confine themselves to the subject. This must be done to insure insertion.

ATTENTION.

Last year when we made a call for copy &c. for our Almanac, the responses were so slow that we could scarcely get ready, but after it was too late we had copy in abundance, it even continued to come in long after the Almanac was published. Now we hope our brethren will not do the same thing this year. If you go right to work and prepare something for us, which we hope you will, it can be admitted; if there is any delay, it will be too late as the work must soon be commenced. See in our other notice what is wanted.

LAST NOTICE.

As the time has now come that we must have our copy for an *Almanac* for 1874, we once more call upon our brethren to help us to make it as complete as possible.

First. Please examine the ministerial list and note mistakes, also make a note of all the ministers that are not in our list and send them to us with their address.

Second. All those that have their District Meeting appointed for 1874, send us a notice of them, and we will have them inserted.

Third. We wish some good copy to fill its pages. Those that feel like aiding us will please prepare it at *once* and send it along. Biographies or anything of standing merit will be admitted.

Fourth. The cover or outside pages will be used for advertisements. Any person having anything that they wish before the public can have a space at the following rates:

1 column,	$25.00
½ "	14.00
¼ "	8.00
⅛ "	5.00
1-10 "	3.00

Correspondence.

Beloved brother of the PILGRIM—No. 31, again was welcomed by us as usual, and on delivering unto us his first address, headed "Origin of Sabbath School Opposition," all concluded that the PILGRIM, with his beautiful motto, stepped a little out of his proper Christian element, in spreading an essay through the world and Brotherhood rather harsh against a great number of God's people, and all such that are not in favor, or in other words opposed to Sabbath School. The writer, in said article, speaks very hard and I think in a very unbecoming way and manner against a great number of faithful servants of Christ, and of our dear old brethren and sisters in the Lord. I for one am not in favor of S. S., and am at no time afraid nor ashamed to tell any one so. Also I am well acquainted with a great many faithful brethren and friends, old and young, East and West, brethren standing as strong pillars in Christ's Church, that are not in favor of the cause, as I do not believe it profitable to enter into any controversy, I will not at present give my reasons for the same, but I think I could produce sufficient, lawful and good reasons for saying so. The writer, in said production, is looking at all such brethren and sisters as "not having the clear light of the excellent way," and that such are indeed "persecuting the Lord's cause." This is saying too much. Where is the spirit of Christ manifested in such an expression as this? If the writer is a man of the world, then I have no more to say, and will be still, only I am somewhat surprised that the PILGRIM makes himself a medium for the same, condemning all such brethren, and all that are opposed to S. S. This includes a great many East and West, and perhaps the majority throughout the Brotherhood, which we know walk in the light of the Gospel, sound in the faith, have stood firm as good soldiers of the cross, and as strong and powerful pillars upon the platform of Christ, have done a great deal of good in the cause of Christ and for the welfare of Zion, in its primitive order, have labored day and night, faithfully, in watching over the flock, in preaching the Word, in prayer to God for the welfare of the Church, spend and be spent for the promulgation of true religion, until the present day. Thro' them the word was spread, the churches prospered in number and in reality of religion, they oppose all new inventions and "innovations" &c. Now then, one will have the boldness to attack such, and will look at them to be "in darkness, prejudiced, ignorant and selfish," "being only guided by the fathers creed," "of a silly notion," "would as well condemn singing, praying, and public worship,"—as "looking unto the Gospel of Christ as through a colored medium," that is through prejudice, ignorance and selfwill, &c., and their mind in Scripture were like "a tangled web of thought, full of dust and dead flies, and as persecuting the Lord's cause." Brethren, this will not do. Further, in the 3d and 4th paragraph such are regarded as ignorant, if so, they are then not enlightened by the power of the spirit, and compared unto a frozen churl, *i. e.* rude, surly, ill-bred, unfeeling, selfish,&c. The whole manufacture bears the spirit of contempt, derision and scorn, against such that are not in favor, or opposed to S. S., and this includes a great number of faithful servants of Christ. In my time I took close and particular notice of S. S., even among the Brethren as well as others, and I fail to see any *real* good fruit resulting out of it, but rather harm, and therefore I am not in favor of the cause, but not through prejudice, selfwill, or fathers creed, let it be considered a silly notion, &c., I am not ashamed nor afraid to let every one know it. As the question is in dispute, I will not give my reasons for it, because I do not love controversies or disputes among the Brethren, but if brethren do write articles for the press, it should be done in love and in the spirit of love.

Your brother,
S. C. MUSSELMAN.

Dear Brother Brumbaugh: This evening, I feel to drop a few ideas for the PILGRIM and its readers. We all have a work to do and can do something for the cause of Christ either by actions, talking or writing, but we should be careful how we do it. There is a possibility of talking or writing too much or not to the purpose. Our great object in life should be to convert sinners and teach them to look to the Truth as the power of God unto salvation. There are many in our day that cannot or rather will not endure sound doctrine, neither do they love to hear the truth preached as it does not move in harmony with the carnal mind.

Dear brethren, when I look around me it seems as if popular religion was becoming the order of the day, and many in making loud professions do it from the lips only, as their actions speak them far away. I heard a man preach to-day from: "How shall we escape if we neglect so great a salvation?" The discourse was very proper until near the close when he said, "It was not only a great salvation because of its author; its freedom and its great power, but because of its unity. Notwithstanding we have many different denominations, yet they are all christians all being born of the same spirit." How strange it is that men will contend for and preach things that are so antagonistic to truth and sound reason. Do not men know that those who are born of the same spirit will teach the same thing? The Scriptures teach us of the *one spirit* which teaches the same thing. To suppose that this spirit will teach me one thing and my brother something directly the reverse is to deny its power altogether. Again, there is but *one faith*. This faith is the result of the teaching of the one spirit. Then, how can all these different faiths be the result of the teachings of one spirit. Truly, the time has come that Paul speaks of when they will not endure sound doctrine.

When I compare the religion of the world, as now held forth, with the religion of Christ, the true principles as set forth in His life and character seems to be possessed by the few only. Pride and corruption are dragging its thousands down to destruction in spite of all the warnings that can be given. Tell some men that they must be born of water and the spirit and they will make light of it. Cannot endure it. Brethren, let us be steadfast and study well to show ourselves approved of God, as workmen that need not to be ashamed, rightly dividing the word of truth. Our labor will be short and the time will soon come that we can lay or armor by and go to our reward. Then let us labor the more earnestly for the salvation that delivereth from sin so that we may appear before God without condemnation.

BENJAMIN DANNER.

ANNOUNCEMENT.

A Communion meeting has been appointed in the Otter Creek Church to be held 3 miles south west of Virdin, Macoupin co., Ill., on the 10 & 11 of Sept. Preaching to commence at 10 A. M.

By order of the Church
DANIEL VANIMAN.

Please announce that we the members of the Yellow Creek Church, Bedford Co., Pa., intend, the Lord willing, to hold a Communion Meeting in the Snowberger Meetinghouse, near New Enterprise, on Thursday the 2d day of October next, commencing at 4 o'clock, p. m. A general invitation is extended especially to ministers.

By order of the Church.
LEONARD FURRY.

Please announce that the brethren of the Fawn River Congregation, Lagrange Co., Ind., intend, the Lord willing, to hold their Communion meeting on the 4th and 5th of Oct. An invitation is given to all. Those coming by rail road will stop off at Lima, where conveyance will be had to place of meeting, which will be at the Brethren's new Meetinghouse.

By order of the church,
ISAIAH HORNER.

Bro. Brumbaugh: Please announce through the PILGRIM, that the brethren comprising the Grasshopper Valley Church, Jefferson Co., Kansas, intend holding their Lovefeast, the Lord willing, in their Meetinghouse in the town of Osawkee, on the 4th and 5th of Oct. A general invitation is given, especially to ministering brethren. Meeting to commence at 10 o'clock, a. m. By order of the Church.

A. PEARSOLL.

Please announce through the PILGRIM, that we, the brethren of the Dunnings Creek Congregation, Pa., will hold a Lovefeast, the Lord willing, on Friday the 3d day of Oct., commencing at 4 o'clock, p. m. Meeting to continue over Sunday. A hearty invitation is given to all to be with us, especially ministering brethren. By order of the Church.

J. B. MILLER.

Please announce that we intend to hold our Communion meeting on the 4th and 5th of Oct. 1873, in the Stone Church, Marshall Co., Iowa. Several others expected to follow in rotation after ours. Those ministers in Indiana wishing to be with us or any others will please remember the time.

ELD. JOHN MURRAY.

Cerro Gordo, Piatt Co., Ill., Sept. 27 and 28.

District Meeting for Southern Ill., at the same place on Sept. 29.

Cedar Creek Church, Anderson Co., Kansas, 16th and 17th of August, 1873.

Whitesville Church, Andrew Co., Mo., Sept. 20, and 21.

In the Cerro Gordo district, Ill., Sept. 27 and 28, 1873.

MARRIED.

SELL—HAGEY.—By Eld. J. W. Brumbaugh, at his residence, Aug. 7, 1873, Bro. Lewis Sell of Bedford Co., and sister Hettie Hagey of Blair Co., all of Penna.

DIED.

BLACKBURN.—Near New Paris, Bedford Co., Pa., Aug. 1, 1873, friend Wm. Blackburn, aged 79 yrs., 9 mos. and 9 days. Funeral sermon on the 10th inst., by J. S. Holsinger, from Job 14: 1, 2.

S. H. FURRY.

EBERLY.—In Pattonville, Bedford Co., Pa., Aug. 5, 1873, sister Eberly, her maiden name was Deardorf, aged 81 years, 9 mos. and 11 days. Disease, old and worn out, which ended suddenly, as is supposed by a stroke of palsy.

Her husband preceded her some years ago, about the same age. This family is noted for their heartiness, as they raised 9 children and never had a physician in their house. She was a consistent member and mother in Israel, and maintained her strength of mind to the last. Occasion improved from Heb. 13: 14, by the brethren to a large audience.

LEONARD FURRY.

MOREHOUS.—In Solomon's Creek Congregation, of consumption, July 29, '73, sister Mary Etta Morehous, aged 19 yrs. 3 mos. and 23 days.

She suffered extremely for some time which she bore with Christian patience and desired that the time would come to leave this world of trouble and go to rest. Text, Rev. 7: 14, 15.

JESSE CALVERT.

BROWN.—In Jefferson Co., Kan., June 4, 1873, our much beloved sister and mother-in-law, Anna, wife of Jacob C. Brown, aged 64 years, 11 mos. and 4 days. She leaves a sorrowing husband and children and a large circle of friends to mourn their loss but we believe that their loss is her eternal gain.

A. PEARSOLL.

EWING.—In the west branch of Rome Congregation, Putnam Co., O., May 27, 1873, Wm. Ewing, aged 81 years and 11 days. Text, Eccl. 12: 5.

He was for many years a member of the Lutheran church, then of the Methodist, but spent about 8 years of his life previous to his death in faithful service in the church of the Old Brethren. A kind and faithful companion and sister, children and friends are left to mourn their loss.

I. J. ROSENBERGER.

FLUCK.—In the Yellow Creek Congregation, Bedford Co., Pa., Aug. 3, 1873 Emma, daughter of friend Samuel and sister Rosanna Fluck, aged 4 months and 12 days. Funeral services by S. A. Moore and Rev. Shoemaker of the Reformed Church.

SMITH.—In the same county, August 8, Daniel Smith, at the advanced age of 97 years. Funeral by S. A. Moore.

WEST.—In the same Congregation, Aug. 8, sister Lizzie West, aged 19 years, 4 mos. and 1 day. Funeral by the brethren.

Bro. S. A. Moore, says, that the deceased was a lady of excellent morals and approved conduct. Some time ago she became ill and during her sickness she became penitent, with a strong desire to make her peace with God. Three weeks prior to her death she called for brother Moore to visit her who found her quite low but strong in faith and with a determined purpose to serve the Lord. In this condition she requested to be baptized. She was then taken in a buggy to the water, and there, in the presence of some brethren and sisters and friends, buried through a living faith, with Christ in holy baptism. A short time before her death she requested that religious services should be held in her room, which was complied with to her great enjoyment. She died in a full hope of a blessed immortality and we trust has now gone to her reward.

The Post office department has been called upon to decide whether or not living honey bees are to be considered mailable matter. It appears that a Massachusetts man has invented a little cage within the prescribed limits as to size and weight, into which he can pack a queen and seven other bees, and he wants to send bees in this way through the post office. The postmaster and clerks object, and the question has been referred to the Postmaster General for decision.

LITERATURE.

A. B. Brumbaugh, Huntingdon, Pa. Literary Editor.

SCRIBNER & CO., publishers of *Scribner's Monthly Magazine*, which is such a universal favorite, announce the commencement of a new Illustrated Monthly Magazine for boys and girls, for early in the present fall. It is to be edited by Mrs. Mary Mapes Dodge, the late popular editor of the children's department of the *Hearth and Home.* We bespeak for this enterprise a generous reception, and will hail with pleasure this new candidate for juvenile favor. Children need plenty of reading matter suited to their age and wants, and happy the editor that can so conduct a juvenile magazine that it shall meet the want properly.

Homes and Hospitals; or Two Phases of Woman's work, as exhibited in the labors of Amy Dutton and Agnes E. Jones. Published by Hurd and Houghton, Cambridge, Mass. This book is a record of the ministrations of these two brave English-women, who following in the foot-steps of Florence Nightengale, the champion of trained hospital nursing, devoted themselves to the care of the sick and needy; Miss Dutton going from house to house caring for the distressed in their homes and ministering to them: while Miss Jones concentrated her whole time and entire energies to hospital work. The book is one of deep interest to all Christian workers, but specially to those whose field of self-denying labor lies among the poor and suffering, the forlorn and vicious, and is calculated to give them clearer views, and a better understanding of their duties, and teach them how properly to direct their efforts. Price $1.50.

The Prophet of the Highest, or the Ministry of John the Baptist, (Hurd and Houghton.) This is a narrative of the life and work of John the Baptist, in the form of a story. It is an interesting little book, vigorous and animated in style, and it is to be hoped may tend to do good by having the reader pattern after the virtues of this great teacher and forerunner of the True Light. Price $1.00.

The Weekly Pilgrim.

Published by J. B. Brumbaugh, & Co.

Edited by H. B. & Geo. Brumbaugh.

CORRESPONDING EDITORS.

D. P. Sayler, Double Pipe Creek, Md.

Leonard Furry, New Enterprise, Pa.

The *Pilgrim* is a Christian Periodical, devoted to religion and moral reform. It will advocate in the spirit of *love* and *liberty*, the principles of true Christianity, labor for the promotion of peace among the people of God, for the encouragement of the saints and for the conversion of sinners, avoiding those things which tend toward disunion or sectional feelings.

TERMS.

Single copy, Book paper,	$1.50
Eleven copies, [eleventh for Agt.]	$15.00

Any number above that at the same rate.

Address,

H. B. BRUMBAUGH.
James Creek,
Huntingdon county Pa.

The Weekly Pilgrim.

"REMOVE NOT THE ANCIENT LANDMARKS WHICH OUR FATHERS HAVE SET."

VOL. 4. JAMES CREEK, PENNSYLVANIA, AUGUST 26, 1873. NO. 34

POETRY.

TAKE ME IN.

The dark night has come down on the plain,
'The shepherd has gathered his sheep
In the fold, where tempests nor rain,
Can ne'er trouble their safe-guarded sleep.

While the ninety and nine are all there,
Calmly resting within the fold,
Take your crook, good Herdsman, go forth,
There is one straying out in the cold.

Oh! haste, then good shepherd and find,
'Tis weary with toil and alarms,
'Tis famishing, foot-sore and faint,
Then please carry it home in your arms.

Ah, that lost one still wandering away
In the storm and darkness to die,
Alone, without comfort or cheer,
Dear Lord and lovely Savior, is I.

There is many a wand'rer to-night
Far out on the tempest-swept world,
With no landmark or light to cheer,
Struggling on through the darkness and cold.

Yes, many a dear lost one still strays
'Mid the wild delusion of sin,
And many a weary one prays
"To thy fold, dearest Lord, take me in."

E. W Putman.

ORIGINAL ESSAYS.

THE HIDDEN MANNA.

To him that overcometh will I give to eat of the hidden manna, and I will give him a white stone, and in the stone a new name written, which no man knoweth saving he that receiveth it." Rev. 2: 17.

The above is a part of the message which John was to deliver to the church at Pergamos. This church though faithful in the main, yet the great Searcher of hearts found a few things against her, which after having pointed out, and signified his displeasure against, he exhorts her to repentance, and threatens her with his divine judgments if she persists in error. Then follows the language of our text, wherein is couched a precious promise to those who would heed the divine admonition, and who would overcome or resist those errors which he so much detested.

The great fault of the Pergamos church was, that they tolerated some false doctrine, which is compared to the doctrine of Balaam, who taught Balak to cast a stumbling block before the children of Israel, to eat things sacrificed unto idols, and to commit fornication. The teachings and practice of this ancient heretical sect, the Nicolaitanes was certainly similar to the insidious policy of Balaam, for the Holy Spirit after having told this church what were the teachings of Balaam, says, "*So hast thou also them* that hold the doctrine of the Nicolaitans, which thing I hate. Balaam corrupted the children of Israel by his wicked stratagem so these Nicolaitans were corrupting the Christian church by their impure teachings and corrupt practice.

In the account we have of Balaam in Numbers 22, 23, 24 there is no mention made of this advice given by him to Balak; yet the careful reader can perceive that it was Baalam's desire to grant Balak's request, for the angel with the drawn sword told him that his way was perverse before the Lord. Num. 22: 31. It seems clear then, that though Balaam blessed Israel, he did it against his will, being compelled by a divine impulse.

Mortified and disappointed, as he no doubt was, at being thus forcibly held back from honor and wealth, for Peter says, "He loved the wages of unrighteousness." 2 Peter 2: 15. He coveted the rewards of Balak. He seems to have been determined upon revenge. And knowing the holy character of Israel's God, he knew that to compass their ruin, would only be, to seduce them into idolatry, and uncleanness. In this last device this treacherous foe was successful; they were invulnerable until they sinned, their sins drew down upon them the fierce anger of the Lord, and he chastened them very sore. Here we may profitably pause for reflection. Though the righteous are dear to God as the apple of his eye, (See Deut. 32: 10; Psalms 17: 8; Zech. 2: 8.) And though nothing can separate us from the love of God which is in Christ Jesus our Lord, (Rom. 8: 35, 38, 39.) Nor, pluck us out of our Redeemer's hand, (John 10: 28,) yet we may separate ourselves from our divine protector. So long as we abide in him, and his words abide in us, we are in possession of a power which the combined power of earth and hell may not overthrow, for we have at our command, heaven's defense the assurance being given that we may ask what we will and it shall be done unto us. John 15: 7. But if we abide not in him, then will we be cast forth as a branch and be withered. Perseverance of the saints depends upon their own faithfulness. God will remain faithful to us, if we remain faithful to him, but he will not force us against our wills.

But to return to our subject. It is asserted by the father's that the Nicolaitans were a branch of the Gnostics, and that their lives were profligate and vicious. This may be inferred from the manner in which St. John compares their teachings, with the instructions given by Balaam, and which had the same demoralizing effect upon the Christians that Balaam's council had upon the Israelites. To eat things sacrificed unto idols, and to commit fornication seems to have been a part of the practice of these Nicolaitans. Their object evidently was to gain converts to their doctrine, and therefore they taught that it was not sinful to indulge the passions; and that it was no harm to partake of an idol sacrifice. Perhaps they told these Christians that if their hearts were right, it mattered little what their outward conduct was. That they might have faith in Jesus, and yet approach an idol altar. Faith was all that was necessary, and if only they had faith, their conduct was of little consequence. They no doubt taught that they might mingle with those heathens in their festivities, and associate with them in their pleasures, and yet preserve their hearts pure toward God. The dogma that if the heart is right, all is right, does not appear to be a new theory. By such insidious teachings, they no doubt drew many into their ranks; for man is ever desirous to retain as much of carnality as he possibly can, and yet reach heaven. Therefore many unwary Christians were induced to unite with this sect; being persuaded that they could gain heaven, and yet enjoy the pleasures of sense and escape persecution.

The partaking of an idol sacrifice having become the test to which Christians must submit, if they would escape the rigors of the Roman law, many weak, and unstable Christians, through fear of torture and death, or from love of pleasure, seem to have given heed to these false teachers, and were trying to make their way to heaven over a less thorny and rugged path, than that marked out to them by the great Head of the Church. But what does he say of their conduct? How does he approve of their efforts in trying to avoid the cross? Does he not tell them that he hates this thing, and that unless they repent he will fight against them with the sword of his mouth?

It would seem that the situation of the Pergamos church was peculiarly trying. Their beloved pastor, the faithful Antipas had, a short time before the reception of this message, been torn from them, and put to death in a most cruel and painful manner; and from verse 13 we may infer that the inhabitants of this city were particularly wicked, and depraved, and then in addition to the wickedness from without, with which they had to contend, perverse teachers had come into the fold, and were drawing away the affections of the Christians from the simplicity of the truth. Truly this church had fightings without and fears within.

Their great Master was well acquainted with their circumstances, he knew how much they had to overcome, and he knew that their victory would be likely to cost them the loss of all things on earth, and even life itself; and yet he urges them on to action, he holds up before them a glorious promise, but not a promise of earthly felicity, no, no, he will give them the hidden manna and the white stone, which no man knoweth, saving he that receiveth it.

Ancient Israel, during their long journey of forty years in the wilderness were nourished with food prepared by God, expressly for them, food which the rest of the world knew nothing of. Each day a supply sufficient for their wants was given them. Thus were they nourished by the divine hand, while traversing a desert waste, until they gained their promised possessions.

When Israel first beheld this substance like hoar frost, lay round about their camp, they were astonished, and asked, "What is it? for they knew not what it was." Moses answered, "This is the bread which the Lord hath given you to eat." This substance was afterwards called manna by the Israelites. David calls it angels food, Psalms 78: 25. Israel means a prince of God, or one who

KNEEL WHEN WE PRAY.

Kneeling in prayer is *scriptural.* Elijah, David, Daniel, and hosts of holy men and women of the Bible bowed their knees in prayer. And, above all, Christ our Lord, who is our pattern, knelt. "And he was withdrawn from them about a stone's cast, and *kneeled down and prayed.*" Therefore, "Oh, let *us* worship and *bow down*; let *us kneel* before the Lord our Maker."

Kneeling in prayer is *rational.* It is the position that expresses dependence and want. Are we not altogether dependent on God, and do we not need anything? It betokens humility, submission, and earnest entreaty. Does it not behoove sinners to approach the Most High and Lofty One, before whose majestic and holy presence angels vail their faces—humbly and submissively, and in all sincerity implore pardon and salvation.

Kneeling in prayer is most *natural* and *appropriately expressive.* Does not kneeling come very natural in time of great affliction and danger, even to impenitent and godless men? Have not hundreds fallen upon their knees, and called for help when in imminent danger upon the great deep? Yea, we know that such men dropped upon their knees even during a hailstorm and implored Heaven to spare them. The uncivilized nations of the earth are led by this instinct of nature, to kneel and prostrate themselves when they appear in the presence of their superiors. And this attitude is so beautifully and appropriately expressive of prayer, that it needs no explanation to any one in order to understand what it means. Seeing one upon his knees, with folded hands and uplifted eyes, the wildest savage at once understands the meaning, and even he feels some chord of his rude nature touched.

How, then, shall one find a shadow of excuse for a habit in prayer which our pen revolts to notice; to *sit lazily* upon the seat, and lay one's head cozily upon the back of the seat in front, while the minister, and perhaps a few earnest Christians are upon their knees imploring God to have mercy upon such wretches! And oh! tell it not among the heathen that hundreds and thousands of professing Christians in various denominations of this blessed land, adhere stubbornly to this disgraceful, God-defying habit! To our mind there is nothing more disgusting and revolting than to see a member of the church, one who professes to *follow Jesus*, too proud or too lazy to kneel in prayer in public worship! And we have no words to express our astonishment at a ministry too effeminate to venture one earnest rebuke of such public irreverence toward God, and abuse of reason and nature in the house of the Lord!—*Advent Times.*

RULES FOR PREACHING.

1. Do not discover too much of your plan in a sermon,
2. Do not pass anything until you have cleared it of the brain.
3. Use your natural tone.
4. Do not clog your memory too much.
5. Be sure you eye God; His glory and the good of souls; having the day before mastered yourself and manpleasing.
6. See that you speak slowly.
7. Look to your affections that they are not forced.
8. Preach, speaking and talking to the people—look on them.
9. Take heed of overwording anything
10. Be sure you make the people understand what you wish of them.
11. Take no Scripture slightly; trouble not many open metaphors.
13. Be sure you feed yourself; or it will do little good, and you none.
14. Take these four candles to find out what to say: 1st. The Scripture unbiassed. 2d. The thoughts and experiences of good men. 3d. Your own experience. 4th. The condition of the people.
15. Break off anywhere rather than jumble things together, and tire the weakest of your flock.
16. Never pass over any point of truth if you have aught to say upon it.
17. Let your doctrine, etc., be about spiritual things.
18. Beware of forms; nor be tied to one way. Divide observationally, textually, and doctrinally.
19. Be always on the subject next to your heart.
20. Be sure to extricate any godly point you speak out of any doctrine.
21. Let there be no affected looks, etc.
22. Never mind the people but think of yourself and God.
23. Do not think that your earnestness can prevail; but it is the force of spiritual reason. The Holy Ghost of the power.
24. Do not think your hearers can receive as you conceive.
25. Let there be something in every sermon to draw sinners to Christ.
26. Take heed that your comparisons be not ridiculous, and yet homely.
27. Study every Scripture beforehand.
28. Take heed of bolting truth, of extravagances, needless heads, digressions, etc.
29. Shun apologies, for they always stink. "I'm unwell," etc.—*Baptist Union.*

GENERAL INTELLIGENCE.

A number of Jewish citizens have addressed a petition to Mayor Medill, of Chicago asking protection from the disturbance of their Sabbath, beginning on Friday and Saturday evening by prohibiting the carrying on of trade in the vicinity of their places of worship. No action has yet been taken on the petition.

THE annual retail sale of intoxicating liquors in this country, is $700,000,000; and according to the best authority, it burdens the Republic with 800,000 paupers, at an annual cost of $100,000,000. The cost of crime, from intemperance, is $40,000,000; the waste of grain, fruit, etc., $50,000,000. The loss of productive industry to the country, through wasted time and talent of tiplers and drunkards, is $225,000,000; the support of insane, idiots and disabled, is $100,000,000; wages or value of time of time of manufacturers, dealers, clerks and employes in the traffic, is $300,000,000; wasting our country's resources annually, $1,500,000,000; and adds to the Government revenue only $10,000,000.

HOW A DEBT WAS LIFTED.—A church in Wisconsin was embarrassed by a debt of $10,000. A crisis came and it must be paid. To have raised this in the usual way would have been simply impossible. But this plan was hit upon: Let one cent a day for five hundred days be a share, to be paid weekly, monthly, or quarterly, as convenient. Every child can take at least one share. The poorest can save and lay by two, three, or five cents a day. Some will take ten shares, some twenty, and a few a hundred. If a thousand persons—and there was as many as that in the congregation—take an average of two shares each—that is, save and give two cents a day each, for five hundred days, the $10,000 will be reached. This was presented and explained from the pulpit. Early in the week canvassers went to work, and in a short time, to the great surprise and delight of all, the full amount was subscribed.—*Advance.*

A late letter from the Holy land informs us of the discovery of an teresting and important item of history at Nablous, the ancient Sychem. At this place reside the remnant of the Samaritans, who for 2,000 years have had no dealings with the Jews and in whose synagogue is to be found the Samaritan copy of the Pentateuch. In this synagogue a missionary of the English Missionary Society has discovered a record kept by the priests of events that had occurred reaching back to hundreds of years before the time of Christ. Arguing that the commotion created by the visit of the Savior to Schechem would arouse the anger of the priest and provoke him to make an appropriate entry on this ancient register, the Missionary, Mr. El Kary, ascertained the name of the priest in office about the time of Christ, and examined the record. He was rewarded by discovering an entry to this effect: "the nineteenth year of my priesthood, and the 4,281st year of the world, Jesus of Nazareth, the son of Mary, was crucified at Jerusalem." Mr. El Kary is engaged in making a thorough examination of the ancient recrd.

A BAPTIST AT THE WHIPPING POST.—The first recorded instance of public punishment for disregarding the old order of the General Court of Massachusetts which decreed the use of secular force for openly opposing the baptism of infants, occurred in the year 1644, when, we are told, a poor man by the name of Painter, having a child born would not suffer his wife to carry it to be baptized. He was complained of to the Court, and *enjoined* by them to suffer his child to be baptized. But poor Painter had the misfortune to dissent both from the Church and court. He told them that infant baptism was an anti-Christian ordinance, for which he was tied up and whipped. Governor Winthrop tells us he belonged to Hingham, and says he was whipped "for reproaching the Lord's ordinance." Mr. Backus judiciously inquires, "did not they who whipt this poor conscientious man, reproach infant sprinkling by taking such methods to support it, more than Painter did?

THE DEFECTIONS OF ROME.

IN NORRISTOWN, PA.

The following, written by a correspondent of Norristown, Pa., we clip from the *New York Observer.* It shows clearly what Mercersburg is doing for Catholicism, and also how near the Rev. Higbee himself approaches it.

About the first of July the citizens of this place were startled by the announcement that Rev. E. O. Forney of the Church of the Ascension (German Reformed) had resigned his charge (not to the Classis, but to the consistory or trustees,) and had gone over to the Roman Catholic Church. Mr. Forney is a young unmarried man, but a few years in the ministry, this being his second charge, and it supposed his objective point is the *Catholic* priesthood. As will be anticipated by the reader, he is a graduate of the Mercersburg school of theology. A few years ago a previous pastor of the Norristown Church, Rev. Mr. Ermantrout, went over to Rome, as also, more recently, Rev. George Dering Wolff, who had also been its pastor. Thus this church seems to have been a nursery to those in transit to the papacy. Mr. Wolff first, and Mr. Forney since, made their submission to Rome at a Jesuit college or monastery in the upper part of this (Montgomery) county. Since going over, Mr. Wolff has become the editor of the *Catholic Standard*, and that journal came out with an historical account of the progress of Mr. Forney, as well as himself, in travelling straight along the road from Mercersburg to Rome. His article was a convincing argument that the current theology of Mercersburg has its objective rest in the bosom of the Roman Church, As might be supposed, this paper flung the question of Mercersburg theology and Mr. Forney's defection into the public arena through the local press, and much has been written on the Protestant side.

Thus the matter stood after a month's discussion, when, on Sun-by last, (Aug. 3,) Rev. E. E. Higbee, President of Mercersburg College (by a previous engagement with the late pastor) came to fill the pulpit, which is still vacant. Mr. Higbee preached from the text (Romans viii. 12), "*Therefore, brethren, we are debtors not to the flesh to live after the flesh.*" The Reverend gentleman read all the prayers of the morning services, facing an altar in the rear, which was beautifully decked with a wreath or bouquet of flowers, very artistically commingled with green leaves and vines. During the whole service, except in the sermon and the *...and act of pronouncing absolution*, the preacher's or rather priest's, back was turned to the people; and I could not help thinking that if there had been a crucifix where the altar stood, the unities of time and place would have been greatly improved! The sermon was mysticism mystified. He opened by describing man as a composite being, of flesh, mind and spirit, but incapable, without a struggle through the agency of God's mysterious grace through the Church; or till as children, we learn through the "*sacrament*" of the rod, to receive the mystery of redemption; until then, though made in the image of God, we are in bondage. After thus describing the bondage of humanity, he referred to "the seed of the woman who did not conquer the enemy till endued by baptism, and by fasting in the wilderness, and wrestling in the garden, and finally on the glorious morn of Easter he obtained the victory." "Thus not by moral, social or political reform, are we encouraged to hope, but by the Son of Mary," and the officers of the church. There is one baptism by which we are "inserted" into this Christ who conquered the weaknesses of the flesh, and thus makes us partakers of the life to come."

In closing, the Professor referred to the trials of the church in loosing its pastor by a defection to Rome, comparing them to those of Paul at Philippi, Iconium and Lystra, and exclaimed—"Suppose your pastor has left you? What then? are you not left? Suppose five, six or a dozen persons have gone to Rome? To their imputed testimony, that Mercersburg led them there, we offer the evidence of hundreds of our ministers who have not gone over." He urged great charity and forbearance toward the lost pastor, and those others who, from supposed convictions of duty, go to Rome.

In all his closing remarks, which were often personal and apologetic, he never so much as *hinted* at the corruption, errors, or heresies of the Roman Church. The occasion seemed to demand this, but his tongue was silent.

Youth's Department.

THE LITTLE LABORERS OF NEW YORK CITY.

As Uncle Henry is not around with a paper for our young readers this week, we will make an extract from the *Harpers' Monthly* of the number of little laborers employed in the different factories in New York. It is really astonishing to learn how many little boys and girls are employed in the factories, and our young readers will, no doubt, be pleased to learn something in reference to them. The father of poor children is often compelled to put his little ones to work very early, and in many instances is indifferent to their natural and mental growth, and believes his children should pass through the same hard experience which he had himself. This being the father's mind, the wages of his children are the most important, and their education much neglected. In Great Britian the children are also employed in the factories and a few years ago the evils of infant workers increased to an alarming extent. Hundreds of thousands of children were found growing up without any education, except the knowledge of a small branch of factory labor, in which they were engaged, without any development of body, their little forms being bent and rickety, and their growth stinted by premature labor. At last a number of reformers and philanthropists determined to put a stop to this overlabor of factory children, and after considerable effort, laws were made to protect these children and provide in part, for their education. This same evil, the overlabor of children in the factories, was also felt in the New England States, and soon laws were made to protect and provide for their education. In Massachusetts a child under the age of ten years could be employed in any factory. Children between the age of ten and fifteen years were not allowed to be employed unless they had attended a day school at least "three months of the year preceeding," and if this amount of education was not secured, the employer was obliged to dismiss the child.

In New York it is difficult to obtain any information in reference to the children employed in the factories. The employers are jealous of one another, and suspect sinister motives on the part of persons making inquiries.

"It is estimated on trustworthy grounds that over 100,000 children are at work in the factories of New York and the neighboring districts while from 15,000 to 20,000 are "floaters," drifting from one factory to another. Of these the envelope factories employ about 8,000 children, one quarter of whom are under fifteen years of age. The average earnings of the little workers are $3 per week. The ventillation in these factories is generally good. The gold-leaf factories employ a large number of children, though the exact statistics of the number cannot be given. This occupation requires much skill and delicacy of touch; it is not severe but demands constant attention. The outside air is carefully excluded from these factories, owing to the fragile nature of the material used. The girls employed are mostly over fifteen years of age. The burnishing of gold, silver and china-ware is mostly done by girls, some of whom are under thirteen years of age. Singularly enough, it is said that men in this business require to wear breast-plates, in order to prevent injury from the steel instruments employed, while the girls who labor at it sit at long tables, their undefended breasts pressing against the handles of the frame. Paper-collar factories are a very important branch of children's labor. Fully 8000 from twelve to sixteen years of age are employed in it. A girl can count and box 18,000 collars in a day of ten hours.

Paper-box factories, embracing all sorts and sizes, from a match to a work box, employ at least 10,000 children. These become very expert, and often invent new patterns. The material being cheap, the children are permitted to take home enough to do extra work, and are thus, in fact, excluded from night schools.

In regard to factories for making artificial flowers it is extremely difficult to obtain trustworthy information, as access to the shops is rigidly refused. After dinner considerable investigation; it seems to us that from 10,000 to 12,000 children are engaged in them, of whom nearly 8000 are under twelve years of age. Many are only five and seven years of age. The latter are employed preparing and cutting feathers for coloring. Employers claim this to be a healthy business, but, judging from the pale and sickly countenances of the girls, we doubt the assertion.

Another important industry employing children in the city is the manufacture of tobacco. The tobacco factories contain fully 10,000 children of whom 500 at least are under fifteen years. The youngest child we saw employed in them was four years of age. He was engaged in stripping tobacco, and his average earnings were about one dollar per week. Many laborers work all their lives in these factories. We saw persons as old as eighty years in them. A man seventy years of age told us he had spent thirty years in one factory. His two sons had entered the factory with him at the age of ten and twelve years, and were now at work as men in the same shop. Another, the foreman, and general workshop manager had entered that factory thirty-five years ago, when a boy ten years of age. In some of these factories, boys under fifteen years are employed in dusky cellars and basements, preparing, brining, and sweetening the weed preliminary to "stemming." The under-ground life in these damp cavernous places tends to keep the little workers stunted in body and mind. Other boys from ten to twelve years were squatting on the floors whetting the knives of the cutting machines with a mixture of rum and water applied with a sponge. The rapidity with which the girls work is wonderful. A girl of sixteen years can cut up thirteen gross of packages of chewing tobacco in tin foil, and twenty-two gross in paper in one day. Girls and boys from twelve to sixteen earn in this business from four to five dollars per week. Some little girls only eight years of age earn three dollars per week. The fact is that these children are often able to perform the same amount of this light labor as adults, while they only receive a portion of the pay given to older laborers. Thus the children who ought to be in school are made to deprive older laborers of their employment and remuneration.

Still another branch absorbs a great number of children—the twine factories. No accurate estimate can be obtained of the number of little laborers in these, but it is known to be very large. In one up-town factory alone, 200 children, mostly girls, are employed. This work is dangerous. The "hackling machines" are generally tended by boys from ten to fifteen years of age. Their attention must be riveted on the machinery, and can not relax for a moment, or the danger to life or limb is iminent. The "twisting machines," attended to by girls, are equally dangerous. Many have lost their fingers, or joints of them, that were caught in the twine. Only great presence of mind has saved many of these girls from losing the whole hand. We know in one instance, in a single night school in New York, five factory girls who had each lost a finger or thumb. It is evident that strict legislation is needed here, as it has been in England, to protect these young workers from dangerous machinery. The air of these twine factories is filled with floating particles of cotton and flax, and must be exceedingly unhealthful.

It will be seen that these condensed statistics what an immense population of children in this city are the little slaves of capital. How intense and wearing is their daily toil, and how much of their health and education is sacrificed in these early years and premature labor! The evil in New York is evidently enormous, and most threatening to our future. These children, stunted in body and mind, are growing up to be our voters and legislators. There are already over 90,000 persons in New York who can not read or write. These little overworked operatives will swell this ignorant throng. Fortunately this great abuse has not escaped the attention of humane men.

IF we work upon marble it will perish; if we work upon brass, time will crumble it into dust; but if we work upon immortal minds—if we imbue them with principles, with the just fear of God and our fellow-men—we engrave on those tablets something which will brighten to all eternity.

HAPPINESS consists in making others happy.

The Weekly Pilgrim.

JAMES CREEK, PA., Aug. 26, 1873.

☞ How to send money.—All sums over $1.50, should be sent either in a check, draft or postal order. If neither of these can be obtained, have the letter registered.

☞ When Money is sent, *always* send with it the name and address of those who paid it. Write the names and post office as plainly as possible.

☞ Every subscriber for 1873, gets a *Pilgrim Almanac* Free.

TO OUR CONTRIBUTORS.

We have thought for some time that a few suggestions to those who contribute to our columns might not be out of place, and in doing so, we hope none will become intimidated, and discontinue their efforts to write. There are a number of our brethren who have very good ideas that cannot express them in writing according to any form, that is, they cannot construct their sentences properly, neither can they punctuate and spell correctly. When we come to prepare their manuscript for the hands of the printer, it often requires a great deal of remoddling, and even then, comes through the press in rather a crude state. Much of our literature would not bear the inspection of the grammarian, but in most instances, the ideas are expressed so as to be intelligible, and are the means, we trust, of converting souls to God, and giving energy and vitality to our blessed Zion. Let then, none be discourrged on account of their literary defects. Send us your ideas and we will freely put them in the best shape we can. Our labors as editors and publishers, are greatly augmented by the general deficiency of education in the Brotherhood, and we hope these things may suggest to the minds of the brethren and sisters the importance of securing so much of an education, at least, as will enable them to express their ideas clearly and intelligibly. The importance of this ability can scarcely be over estimated, and we hope in the not far distant future, that the truth which we so earnestly desire to propogate through the medium of the press, may be increased in brilliancy and power, by being expressed in clear, concise tho't, and that the work of those who labor in the capacity of editors and publishers, may be greatly facilitated.

There are just two things however, which if our contributors would observe, that would greatly diminish our labor.

1st. *Do not use more words than are needed to convey your ideas.* Some communications are so full of words that we can scarcely find the ideas, and thus gives us a good deal of trouble and loss of time. You know there is always a delay and loss of time, when we have to hunt after a thing when we want to use it. We do not want a display of words in our paper,—nothing but sound, solid, pointed truth. Please then do not be careful about that matter.

2. *Be careful in the use of quotations.* Do not quote more than is relevant to the subject, and quote it correctly. Some of our contributers quote more Scripture than is needed, and then in quoting express it partially in their own language. This is very annoying, and to this we wish to direct special attention. Do not trust your memory in making quotations, turn to chapter and verse and quote the precise language, and punctuate and spell just as you find it there. By so doing you will save us much labor, and your articles will come out more correctly. Then, too, when you wish to give the reference, always put it at the *end* of the quotation and not at the beginning.

Example.—" But Paul cried with a loud voice, saying, Do thyself no harm: for we are all here."—Acts 16: 28.

Now brethren and sisters, we would not call your attention to these things, if it were not just as easy to do it right as wrong, and at the same time save us so much labor. We would like to make a little advancement towards accuracy in the construction of our literature, and we hope you will do all you can to lighten our labors.

In conclusion we would say, let us hear from you all, more frequently. Do the very best you can and we will be satisfied. When you write to us business letters, do not forget to note anything that might be of interest to our readers. Under the head of " General Intelligence," we have room for all such little items and will be gladly received.

Again when writing on any subject upon which there is a difference of opinion, be careful that you do not throw too much irony in your communication. Base all your conclusions on the Truth, which, accompanied by a meek and lowly spirit, such as should characterize all Christians, will certainly be " mighty through God, to the pulling down of strong holds." If our brethren are in error in reference to any subject, and are fortifying themselves against us, let us storm them with the Word of God. It is the weapon of our warfare and one word of truth, if accompanied by the proper spirit, may shatter the foundation of the grossest error.

J. B. B.

SUBJECTS.

As a general thing, writers prefer to choose their own subjects and it is right that they should do so, but sometimes we get to running hobbies and the more weighty matters are neglected. On this account we will make choice of a few subjects which we kindly ask our contributors to make use of for some future articles for the Pilgrim.

1st. What is religion, and how obtained? If not obtainable, how is it practiced?

2. What is conversion, and at what time or how far must the sinner go to be converted?

3. What is regeneration, and what is essential to be truly regenerated or born of God?

4. How can we use our money for Jesus and the advancement of His cause, most advantageously? We have all learned too well, how to use it for our own gratification, and the advancement of satan's kingdom, therefore we want our brethren and sisters to suggest or point out some of the ways that it can and should be used in accomplishing good.

We do not give these as a number of queries to be answered for our own information, but as subjects for separate and distinct articles, for the general good of our readers, and we will be glad to hear from all who feel to treat them with a view of accomplishing good. At the same time, all are at liberty and invited to write on any subject that they may deem most profitable to the general reader. We want our Pilgrim to be a pilgrim indeed, going forth filled with Bible truths, (the power of God unto salvation,) and the consolation of the saints.

OUR ALMANAC.

A good Almanac has become a household necessity, and the people are so accustomed to having one that they would scarcely know how to keep house without it. We are now preparing to give to the Brotherhood one that will meet every want of a Christian family. The plan will be the same as that of last year, but we hope to make it much better in contents, especially the Ministerial List. On this, we are determined to spare no pains, and will do everything in our power to make it as complete and correct as possible. We have already added some 200 names not published last year, and made a large number of corrections.

In making it full and complete, much depends on our readers. If every one will feel interested and send us all unpublished names, our object will be attained. This, we think, all should be, when it is taken into consideration that it is a *free* gift. The paper for the cover will be heavier than that of last year, thus making it more serviceable. We are being pretty well supplied in everything except District Meetings. These should all be sent in immediately, as it would be a convenience to have them published. There is also room yet for some more good copy. Anything to be inserted must be sent in within 15 days.

BOOKS.

We have orders for a number of books of which we have none on hand. We have now sent for them, and will fill all orders as soon as our supply is received. Of the Tune Book and Hymn Books we have a good supply, and can fill orders promptly.

Trine Immersion Traced to the Apostles, is one of the most valuable works of the kind ever published on the subject, and should not only be read by every member in the Brotherhood, but should be bought and distributed by the thousands. We have now made arrangements with brother Moore to keep it for sale at our office, and will be pleased to fill all orders now sent us.

PERSONAL.

John Clapper. All right—book sent.

E. P. L. Dow. The subscriptions make $4.50. You sent $5.00, what is the extra 25 cents intended for?

A Number of good essays are now on hands and will be forthcoming.—Among these are, " Youthful Instruction," " A Proposed Compromise," "The Necessity and Advantage of Reading and Writing," and a number of others that will be of interest to our readers. Having these essays on hand, we feel that we can send the Pilgrim on its mission, the coming week, laden with good things. This we would always desire to do, but sometimes we have not the variety of good, healthful food that we should have, to convey to our readers. This want we hope we will not have to experience so much in the future.

LAST NOTICE.

As the time has now come that we must have our copy for an *Almanac* for 1874, we once more call upon our brethren to help us to make it as complete as possible.

First. Please examine the ministerial list and note mistakes, also make a note of all the ministers that are not in our list and send them to us with their address.

Second. All those that have their District Meeting appointed for 1874, send us a notice of them, and we will have them inserted.

Third. We wish some good copy to fill its pages. Those that feel like aiding us will please prepare it at *once* and send it along. Biographies or anything of standing merit will be admitted.

Fourth. The cover or outside pages will be used for advertisements. Any person having anything that they wish before the public can have a space at the following rates:

1 column,	$25.00
½ "	14.00
¼ "	8.00
⅛ "	5.00
1-16 "	3.00

MONEY LIST.

Sarah Barnhart	$3.25	J Eichenbrode	50
C Secrist	80	J S Baker	50
Geo. Worst	80	Jas Oxenrider	1.00
B B Bollinger	1.25	M Emma Rohrer	3.00
R M——	1.50	Cyrus Stoner	2.25
Saml Hyman	1.50	B F Shultz	50
Jno A Myers	3.75	G R Baker	3.00
Daniel Brower	1.50	D B Teeter	80
John J Garber	80	John Clapper	7.13
Wm. C Teeter	2.50	Esther Grater	1.21
S J Garber	6.60	E P L Dow	5.00
Dr. Solomon	1.25	Wm H Carrier	1.50
A P N——	6.00	J Newcomer	75
G W Bricker	75	J Zook	85
D Mahon	75	J Wareham	2.50

Correspondence.

Editors Weekly Pilgrim: —Being prevented from attending A. M. this year, on account of sickness in my family, I felt to appreciate particularly, the new feature in our publications, viz., a full report. All that is lost now by not being at the A. M. is the exquisite sensation of meetings and greetings of those whom we so dearly love, and have met so often that it has almost become a necessity, like the meetings of Israel at Jerusalem in ancient days.

I have read with great interest again and again the "Deacon Question" as it used to be termed a quarter of a century ago, and I came to the conclusion that it might do no harm to throw in my mite as common stock and let the reader take the same for what it is worth.

Some thirty odd years ago the question sprung up "Ought not the deacons have hands laid on at their installment like those seven in Acts?" This was agitated more or less till the year 1849, when brethren were requested to prayerfully investigate the matter so as to be ready by next A. M. to give a decision and have the matter settled forever.

In this interim certain brethren ascertained that neither of those seven were ever called "deacons," and that consequently theirs must have been a different office, though not named. The conclusion was, that there must have been "Table Servants," like the brethren reasoned this year. Then looking at the qualifications set forth that those "Seven" should possess which are afterwards described by Paul, that Elders or Bishops should possess, the conclusion was that those seven were the first Bishops, who at the same time constituted a committee to set in order that was wanting at Jerusalem in the Church. This being accomplished, they were at liberty to go abroad and preach the Gospel, which we find them doing with great effect. Another consideration presented itself viz: that Christ personally called the twelve, like any other potentate or king calls or nominates his own cabinet and delegated no power to any one to do this for Him, as the calling of Saul of Tarsus, especially proves.

Another idea sprung up; that as God at first created Adam and Eve perfect or complete, man and woman, but they being created, produced children, who had to be brought up to man and womanhood by degrees. In like manner when Christ created his Church, they were complete or perfect, on the day of Pentecost from whence they started out and brought forth children as Paul abundantly sets forth. The office of "Apostle" becoming extinct with their death, there must of necessity be a begining of such as may fill their places. Their outward "sign" then is the laying on of hands, and the means used to qualify them fully is prayer for the gift of the Holy Ghost, or power and wisdom.

It is a remarkable fact that there were no brethren present from Pennsylvania, Maryland, or Virginia, at the A. M. in 1850 near Dayton, Ohio, where Bro. Hoke presented the conclusions that himself and others had come to with the reasonings, arguments, and scriptural references. While he was reading it brethren took notes, and all agreed that those "Seven" must have been the first ordained Elders or Bishops, and as the question lay settled apparently till now, I suppose that manuscript of Hokes, must be in existence yet, and would probably give much satisfaction if it were put to press and brought forth in our periodicals. I am of the opinion Bro. H. Kurtz knows all about it, I think he gave a short extract once of the same.

Thus Bro, Ed's, I have given some of what I recollect yet of the above query. You are at liberty to do what you please with the same.

Yours in love,
F. P. Loer.

Bloomingdale, Mich.

My dear brethren and sisters: —According to promise, I will now write to you through the columns of this good paper. Having for sometime been very anxious to visit my dear relatives and brethren and sisters in Christ, in Botetourt County, Va., I took the train here at Sewel depot the 8th of July at three oclock p.m. for White Sulpher Springs in Greenbrier Co., stopped a few moments, then on to Covington Alleghany Co., stopped 20 minutes for supper, then 14 miles to Clifton, and then same evening, a distance of 100 miles where I was met by friends who took me to my dear afflicted sister whom I had not seen for many years and where I spent many pleasant, hours with her and her dear children, she being a widow and very sickly. Her health has been very bad for some time, but I found her and left her rejoicing in hope of a glorious immortality beyond the cold grave. I had some of our *Pilgrims* with me, she read them through again and again having never saw them before. I had only two with me, I think the *Pilgrim* would do a great deal of good in her neighborhood. I promised to send it to her, she is very anxious for the paper. I enclose her name and address, send her the paper, and I will send you the money. (The paper is sent, Ed.) On the 13th I visited some more of my relatives, two sisters and their families. On the 14th preaching by the brethren where I enjoyed myself very much with dear old brethren and sisters whom I never expect to see again in this world of sorrow. Oh how pleasantly the hours passed away while singing praises to God and hearing the Gospel preached in all its purity. On Monday the 15th, on to Fincastle, spent the day with old acquaintances met with some of my relatives. Took the stage at 2 p. m. for Amsterdam, stopped a few minutes, then on to Bro. Peter Niningers, the beloved old brother who visited me when I lived in Mercer, twenty years ago. I shall never forget him and the kind brethren that were with him at that time. I took supper with him and the dear sister, his wife, and his son. I would have been pleased to have stayed all night with them but my sister who lives a short distance, in Troutville, sent for me and I very reluctantly had to leave them. Went to my sisters, spent one day and two nights, then my brotherinlaw took me to visit another sister, stayed over night, had a season of joy, found her strong in the faith. She was anxious for the *Pilgrim*. I told her she ought to take it so that she could hear from the churches and brethren, as she has not the pleasure of attending meeting. A great many sisters are deprived of that privilege. It often makes my heart ache to see them hungering and thirsting after the Gospel, and while so many of us are blessed with that great privilege. But dear sisters, don't be discouraged. I hope the Lord will send a laborer into his vineyard for the Savior says: "blessed are they that hunger and thirst after righteousness for they shall be filled. On the 19th, returned to Troutsville and enjoyed the pleasure of visiting many of the brethren and sisters and acquaintances near Amsterdam. In that vicinity I was gladly received and kindly cared for. Left there in company with my brotherinlaw, a Baptist minister, and came to Fincastle, spent a few hours with some acquaintances and friends, then, same day, went on to the Run and neighborhood where I was born and raised. It made me feel sad indeed when I saw the old farm and the beautiful trees where I spent my childhood days with my brothers and sisters some of whom are now trying the realities of another world. Spent a few days with friends, then on to Craigs Creek to visit another sister, spent a few days with her, then in company with herself, her son, and a young lady, went to Clifton Depot a distance of twenty miles, remained with my dear afflicted sister until 4th of Aug. then bid her farewell, with a very faint hope of ever seeing her again in this world, but a strong hope, if faithful, of meeting in a better world where parting is no more. Took the train at Clifton Depot on the 4th for Covington. At Sewel Depot I got off and found my son waiting for me, took a little refreshment, and then ferried the river and went two miles to Bro. J. S. Flory's where I was kindly received, and took dinner. Arrived safely home same evning and found all well.

Your unworthy sister,
Nancy Crouse.

ANNOUNCEMENTS.

Our Communion Meeting will be held in the Clover Creek, Congregation, Blair Co., Pa. on the 30th of Sept., and 1st day of Oct. The usual invitation is extended.

J. W. Brumbaugh.

There will be a Communion Meeting at the residence of Bro. Morgan Workman, three miles east of Loudonsville, Sept., 6th 1873, on the P. Ft. W. & C. R. R. The brethren are invited and especially ministers.

E. P. L. Dow.

The Brethren of the Black River Branch, Medina Co., Ohio, have appointed a Communion Meeting on the 3d of October, in their Meeting-house in Chatham. All are invited, and especially ministering brethren.

Jos. Rittenhouse.

We, the brethren of the Logan Church, Logan Co., Ohio, have appointed a Lovefeast on the 9th day of October, usual invitation to all. Those coming from the East will stop off at Bellfountain, and those coming from the South at West Liberty, and those coming from the West stop off at DeGraff.

J. L. Frantz.

Please announce through the Pilgrim that we, the Brethren of the Mohecan Church, Wayne Co. Ohio, intend, the Lord willing, to hold their Love Feast on the 29th of Sept., '73, commencing at 10 o'clock a. m. A cordial invitation is given to all the brethren and sisters to share our hospitalities. By order of the church.

Geo. Worst.

The Lord willing, there will be a Lovefeast in the Mill Creek Congregation, Adams Co., Ill., near Liberty, in the 6th and 7th of September.

Also on the 13th and 14th Sept., in the same district, in Pike Co., near Barry at the house of the undersigned. Brethren and sisters from a distance are heartily invited, especially ministers. John Clingingsmith.

Otter Creek Church, 3 miles south west of Virdin, Macoupin Co., Ill., Sept. 10, 11.

Yellow Creek Church, Snowberger Meetinghouse, Bedford Co., Pa., on Thursday, Oct. 2, at 4 o'clock, p. m.

Fawn River Congregation, Lagrange Co., Ind., on the 4th and 5th of Oct.

Grasshopper Valley Church, Jefferson Co., Kan., Meetinghouse in the town Osawkee, Oct. 4 and 5.

Dunnings Creek Congregation, Pa., on Friday, Oct. 3.

Stone Church, Marshall Co, Iowa, on the 4th and 5th of Oct.

Our Lovefeasts of Maryland, will be held as follows:

Sam's Creek, Oct. 11, commence 1½ p. m.
Monocacy, " 17.
Meadow Branch, " 21, com. 1½ p. m.
Beaver Dam, " 23.

The usual invitation is extended.

E. W. Stoner.

Cerro Gorda, Piatt Co., Ill., Sept. 27 and 28.

District Meeting for Southern Ill., at the same place on Sept. 29.

Cedar Creek Church, Anderson Co., Kansas. 16th and 17th of August, 1873.

Whitesville Church, Andrew Co., Mo., Sept. 20, and 21.

In the Cerro Gorda district, Ill., Sept. 27 and 28, 1873.

MARRIED.

KLEPSER—WINELAND.—At the residence of the undersigned, Aug. 17, '73, Mr. David M. Klepfer, to Miss. Hannah Wineland, all of Fredericksburg, Blair Co., Pa.

GUYER.—HETRICK.—Also by the same, July 27, '73, Mr. Daniel S. Guyer, and Miss Lizzie Hetrick, all of New Enterprise, *Bedford* Co., Pa.,

S. A. Moore.

KEIM—HILL.—At the residence of the brides' parents, on the 10th of August, '73, Bro. Josiah Keim, to sister Sarah Hill.

W. A. Murray.

DIED.

MILLER.—On the 26th of July, 1873, infant daughter of brother John and sister Catharine Miller, aged 4 weeks and 5 days. Funeral by the writer and M. Swenger, from Luke 18: 16.

J. L. Frantz.

Obituaries crowded out.

Errata.—In my notes of travel in No. 29 of Pilgrim, where it reads in figures, 9.000, it should be 1500. And where it reads a large majority of the land is for school purposes, it should be a good proportion.

J. S. Flory.

LITERATURE.

A. B. Brumbaugh, Huntingdon, Pa.
Literary Editor.

The Undeveloped West or Five Years in the Territories, by J. H. Beadle.

The National Publishing Co., of Philadelphia, has just issued one of the most remarkable, and attractive books of the century. It is well known to every one that, far beyond the Mississippi, and stretching over half the continent, is a vast region which we vaguely term "The Great West"—a region abounding in the most wonderful natural formations, rich in precious mineral deposits, and offering the greatest attractions to the settler and the tourist. Though so often spoken of, it is almost an "unknown land."

Mr. Beadle went into this region for the avowed purpose of seeing and describing it, and his journeyings and observations were all governed by a fixed purpose, that of discovering and making known the actual character, condition and resources of the country visited by him. He first traversed the States of Iowa, Minnesota, Nebraska and Kansas, examining the lands, and living and conversing with the people of those sections. For five years he kept moving from point to point, exploring the Territories, and the great and rich States of the Pacific Coast, encountering strange people and innumerable hardships and braving many dangers in his wanderings among the savages. He visited the rich mines of Colorado, Utah, Nevada and Idaho; passed into California and Oregon, and there enjoyed peculiar advantages for seeing and investigating the resources and curiosities of those remarkable States. He spent considerable time in New Mexico, Arizona and Texas, and in his account of his observations and discoveries in those strange and deeply interesting portions of our country will commend this book to the careful consideration of the scholar, as well as to all who seek practical information or amusement. His only companions in his travels in Arizona were Indian guides, and for weeks during his explorations in that Territory he never saw the face of a white man.

To prospective emigrants and settlers in the "Far West," this history of that vast region will prove an invaluable assistance, supplying as it does, a want long felt of a full, authentic and reliable guide to climate, soil, products, distances, localities, means of travel, etc. It may be relied upon, and we recommend our brethren and all those "going west" with the view of locating, to obtain all the reliable information relative to the country that is possible, and the established reputation of the author of this work adds to its value as a reliable source of such information. It is comprised in one large octavo volume of 823 pages, and illustrated with 240 fine engravings of the scenery, lands, mines, people and curiosities of the Great West, and a new map of region described.

It is sold by subscription only and agents are wanted everywhere.

Books Received.—From National Publishing Co., Philadelphia, *The Undeveloped West*, or Five Years in the Territories.—Beadle.

J. H. Butler & Co., Philad'a. *New American Spellers and Readers*. One set of each—6 books. *Mitchell's New Geographies*, Primary, Intermediate and Physical.

From James Vick, Rochester, N. Y., A pair of beautiful flower *Chromos*. Flora's Jewels and Autumnal Flowers.

The Weekly Pilgrim.

Published by J. B. Brumbaugh, & Co.
Edited by H. B. & Geo. Brumbaugh.
CORRESPONDING EDITORS.
D. P. Sayler, Double Pipe Creek, Md.
Leonard Furry, New Enterprise, Pa.

The *Pilgrim* is a Christian Periodical, devoted to religion and moral reform. It will advocate in the spirit of *love* and *liberty*, the principles of true Christianity, labor for the promotion of peace among the people of God, for the encouragement of the saints and for the conversion of sinners, avoiding those things which tend toward disunion or sectional feelings.

TERMS.

Single copy, Book paper,	$1.50
Eleven copies, [eleventh for Agt.]	$15.00

Any number above that at the same rate.

Address,
H. B. BRUMBAUGH,
James Creek,
Huntingdon county Pa.

The Weekly Pilgrim.

"REMOVE NOT THE ANCIENT LANDMARKS WHICH OUR FATHERS HAVE SET."

VOL. 4. JAMES CREEK, PENNSYLVANIA, SEPTEMBER 2, 1873. NO. 35

POETRY.

For the PILGRIM.

INVOCATION TO THE FISHERMAN.

"Come ye after me, and I will make you to become fishers of men."—Mark 1:17.

Come fisherman, come to these whirlpools of error,
Come, cast ye your nets for the famishing ones:
For many are dashed on the wild reefs of terror,
And many sunk down neath the dark waves of sin.

Niagara's rapids! less potent their rushing,
Than these wild waves of fashion on which we are tost,
All the well-springs of love, from the tender heart gushing,
With the dark, chilling waters, are mingled and lost.

Then, come, with your calm words of sweet consolation;
We tire of this strife, of this turmoil and care,
We weary of gaud and the world's dissipation,
Is there room for us there? Is there room for us there?

Yes, come with your broad nets of love and salvation,
And cast in these cesspools of darkness and sin;
From these depths of despair and the soul's desolation,
O gather us in! come and gather us in!

At shrines where we worship frivolity enters,
With gew-gaw and glitter, the spirit to win;
At the Sacrament, oftimes, idolatry centers:
To your Love-feast of purity, gather us in.

ORIGINAL ESSAYS.

THE NECESSITY AND ADVANTAGE OF READING AND WRITING.

"Search the Scriptures, for in them ye think ye have eternal life, and they are they which testify of me."

The above portion of the Holy Scriptures comprehends and implies both the necessity and the advantage of reading and writing. And further, it implies the condition of those who do not search the Scriptures.

There are two distinct elementary operations in the mind when the creature is in the act of doing what Jesus says in the text. The first is the selection of the object to be sought for, and the second is a conclusion as to the proper manner of searching. This or a similar division is indispensibly essential to a correct conception of the gulf which the word "search" is designed to overleap or bridge. Every soul is continually making a selection of something. There is a certain degree or kind of mental consciousness while every one of these selections is made. Even the little infant when it begins to walk soon learns to select, when left alone, the different directions in which it walks, and as its power of determining which way to go increases, so the reason and necessity of exercising that power also increases. When it begins to talk, of course at first, like walking—it is at random, the reason of its operation are very indistinct, and as the fond mother would fain, with her hands, set one foot before the other to make it walk at once as she desires, so she would with her fingers gladly guide its little tongue to make it utter the sentiments of its little heart as she wants to hear them. But soon, by reason of nature and the help of nature's God, it selects in its mind from the many sounds it has heard, those which approximate a representation of its thoughts. As with the first attempts at walking and talking, so with thinking, it is at random. That is, in the judgment of finite man there is no reason or order or truth in it. The thinking of little children is something. God has created it. He has told man to name it for his convenience and benefit, which has been done in the same manner that a certain animal was named horse. But in regard to the material nature of man, the child grows up into manhood or womanhood, and as it does so, its selection of objects becomes more and more reasonable and definite. By and by, the place where "two ways met" is reached,—the point where temporal things end and eternal ones begin,—the position where the soul becomes conscious, though the best selections of earthly objects has been made—that without a Savior it is forever lost, eternal death and eternal life are presented to view as two principal objects, one of which *must* be chosen. Happy is he who has made the latter his choice, and having done so, happier is he if he searches for that object in the right place and in the right way. The Jews thought they had eternal life in the Scriptures, but really they had it not. They only thought so. For this very reason they were told to search the Scriptures—that they might be enlightened and converted to God,—that they might by this searching and wandering in the dark see and come to the light. The tyro or raw student, who is induced by some influence or other to become master of any one science, must, in order to reach any degree of proficiency, apply either intentionally or accidentally all his knowledge of other sciences to aid him in searching a particular one, so the soul that comes to God employs all its powers intently to become proficient in the service of the Master. Faith in God and in the Lord Jesus Christ, is the only sure foundation that will endure forever; it is the position above all other positions. Money, education, knowledge, ability and all other things that are worthy, are positions, but none of them is equal in importance to that of a genuine faith in God. "Without faith it is impossible to please God" Faith manifests itself by works. Reading the Word of God, therefore is the evidence of faith in it, and it must first be written before it can be read. The art of writing therefore is a prominent agency by which God's word is transmitted to men. As vessels are indispensible to carry water from the fountain to satisfy the temporal wants of man, so the art of writing is indispensible to carry the living water from the eternal fountain to supply the wants of the soul. As the idea of pure water is preserved by carrying it in clean vessels from the fountain, so the idea of the truth is preserved by writing it correctly. The moral condition of those who do not search, is like the physical condition of those who drink water that has, after flowing from the fountain, been carried in polluted earthen vessels, and who will not go to the fountain that they may believe there is pure water. Search the Scriptures.

J. B. GARVER.

YOUTHFUL INSTRUCTION AN ADVANTAGE.

"And that from a child thou hast known the Holy Scriptures, which are able to make thee wise unto salvation through faith which is in Christ Jesus."—1 Tim. 3:15.

That this early instruction, Timothy received, was of great benefit to him as a young minister of the Gospel, is evident from the recommendations the apostle Paul gives him to the Church, and that it was according to Scripture and condusive to his salvation is equally plain from the exhortation of the same apostle: "*But continue thou in the things which thou hast learned and hast been assured of*, knowing of whom thou hast learned them." That faith and holy teachings he possessed, as is intimated, was owing to his instructions while young, instilled into his mind, first by his grand-mother Lois, and by his mother Eunice.

Now Brethren, we all know that not every child has a grand-mother *Lois*, nor a mother *Eunice*, in which dwells that unfeigned faith to teach him in the ways of salvation, neither has every child a pious father to bring him up in the nurture and admonition of the Lord. Yes, to our sorrow, we often see brethren and sisters suffering their children to run wild, without restraint on their part, desecrating the Sabbath by being in mischief all that holy day. Is it not much better then, for pious, faithful brethren and sisters to collect such children together, not interfering with our public preaching, on Sabbath afternoon or in the morning, to have devotional exercises, reading of Scripture, and expounding the same in its true import, and trying to impress the same upon their tender minds, the necessity of obeying God in all His requirements as He revealed Himself therein, and the great advantages of the early acceptance thereof? Every unbiased mind will certainly have to answer in the affirmative. It is said if we adopt Sunday schools for our help, we will have to employ all the help of corrupted Christianity, &c. With equal propriety, we may say, we have adopted the building of Meeting-houses for our help, consequently we will have to employ all the help of a corrupted Christianity to conduct our exercises, because the building of Meeting-houses has its origin in man, we have it not from the fathers of the Church, nor from the apostles, neither from Christ, hence no divine institution. Wonderful idea! But can the proper use of the same, the one equal with the other, not receive the divine sanction? Certainly they can.

Brethren, do not understand me to advocate Sabbath schools as generally conducted by the mass of professors, or even a mixed up school. If the brethren cannot have it under their own control and conducted according to Scripture, they had much better be dispensed with, and as such do exist among the Brethren, I fear some have resulted in evil, being too much assimilated to the customs of corrupted Christianity. Hence my voice cries strongly in favor of such, to have them rooted out, for from these arises the brethren's opposition and prejudice against the schools in general. But I cannot see any valid reason, where there are two brethren at least, well posted in Scripture, strong in faith and well established in the principles of the Church, why they cannot, in the neighborhood where they live, organize a school, or if the term suits you better, a *nursery* for the education of the youth in the principles of the Gospel as understood by the Brethren. Gather in the Brethren's children first, then the outcast and all others that are willing to come. Teach nothing but what corresponds with the truth, and especially do admonish them against pride and the corruptions that is in the world through lust. I contend there is a similarity between the synagogue and a properly conducted Sabbath school. For in the former they came together with their families to hear the law read and expounded by those who understood it. So in a properly conducted Sabbath school, the Gospel is read, appropriate remarks made thereon, and if a speaker comes, the invitation is given to give a word of exhortation. The only difference I can see is, that this school is chiefly to supply the wants of the neglected youth, the intention is alike, for the highest good. The thought that a school conducted upon such principles is a desecration of the Sabbath, appears to me simply preposterous. Hence I advocate no other but what the Annual Council recommends in the last decision, 1868, query 15,—Answer. *We advise* that where the nature of the case will admit of it, *for the Brethren to hold Sabbath schools*, &c. To be properly understood, I say again, *I solemnly protest* against Sabbath school as generally conducted by modern Christianity, but am strongly in favor of making every proper, *evangelical* effort to have our children well instructed in the Word of God, and the principles of the Christian religion, as early impressions will not be easily forgotten as the writer can testify.

LEONARD FURRY.

WHEN your temptations let you alone, let not your God alone; but lay up prayers and the blessings of a constant devotion against the day of trial. —*Jeremiah Taylor*.

TEACHING.

"It is written in the prophets and they shall be all taught of God."—John 6: 45

In the subject before us, the idea of teaching presents itself to the mind and we readily admit that what we know, has been imparted to us through the channel of teaching. The Prophets have written upon the subject, and the idea is exhibited in lessons to us every day of life. But those lessons are not all from that source, which will give us an eternal benefit. The idea of teaching at once presupposes a teacher and that gives us two characters; teacher and pupil. Then if we are pupils, are we willing to be taught of God, as was written by the prophets? And what are we taught? From common observation, we would think that God had a variety of ways in teaching us godliness for one goes for Paul, another for Apollos, another for Cephas, and a very few for Christ.

At the present day, God teaches the people by His messengers, and the text book is the Gospel, which shows us the way of salvation clearly. Now if we have a little talent, and have made the proper use of it, from the privilege we enjoy in this land of free schools, it will not take us long to decide, when a man presents himself to us in the character of a teacher, whether he is sent of God or not. For whomsoever the Lord sends to teach or preach, will preach God's word, and that is clearly written out in the Gospel. And who of us cannot tell what is Gospel and what is not? Christ said to His disciples, "Go ye therefore, and teach all nations. Teach them to observe all things whatsoever I have commanded you; and, lo, I am with you always even unto the end of the world."—Matt. 28: 19, 20.

This brings the messenger of God into close quarters, for the observing man or woman will readily detect him, if he teaches not the "all things" and set him down as an imposter. This we should do, but strange it is, that the close observing are so few and men are permitted to go forth and proclaim what they call Gospel, and it is gulped down by the masses of the community. Astonishing to behold! I do believe that the so called Christianity is as corrupt now as it was in the days when the Savior tabernacled in the flesh; when He told the Jews that they made the Word of God of none effect through their tradition. Traditions are abundantly taught from the pulpit, and the press in this our day; therefore it becomes very necessary for those who desire to enjoy the benefit of salvation to be on their guard, that they be not deceived with this army of imposters, who are teaching the near cut to Heaven. Paul says, though an angel from Heaven preach to you any other Gospel than that which we have preached let him be accursed. Then the truly responsible position of the true messenger of God is set forth by Paul in the following language: "To wit, that God was in Christ, reconciling the world unto himself, not imputing their trespasses unto them; and hath committed unto us the word of reconciliation. Now then we are embassadors for Christ, as though God did beseech you by us; we pray you in Christ's stead, be ye reconciled to God."—2 Cor. 5: 19, 20. Now if we profess to have received our embassy from the Court of Heaven, or in other words sent out by the Church of the living God, the pillar and ground of the truth, and teach not the "all things" commanded by Jesus, we will be branded as liars, and forfeit our inheritance in the kingdom of heaven.

If we were to go on and particularize, our essay would become too lengthy. Christ says: "He that entereth not into the fold by the door, but climbeth up some other way the same is a thief and a robber. Then the idea of a door or a way is presented to us by which we may enter in, and if we enter not in we are on the outside, and those who were outside of Noah's ark, were drowned; which is a representation of the ark of safety to us, and we must enter into it. And how are we to enter? With our sins we cannot enter. Then how are we to get our sins cancelled? John the harbinger's proclamation is the beginning of the Gospel, and he preached the baptism of repentance for the remission of sins. Peter, who was chosen by the Lord, preached repentance and baptism for the remission of sins, and promised the gift of the Holy Ghost. Paul tells us the teaching he received from Ananias was, "Arise and be baptized and wash away thy sins, calling on the name of the Lord." Here are three testimonies from three inspired persons, teaching the same doctrine, and Christ says, "In the mouth of two or three witnesses, shall every word be established." Again, Paul says, when writing to the Gallatians, "Brethren, as many of you as have been baptized, into Jesus Christ, have put on Christ." Then if such have put on Christ, of course they are in Him, and let me assure you, dear reader, whoever you are, if you are in Christ, you are safe; you are well fortified; the wall around you is more precious than gold.

The first step then, is, Repentance, Faith, and Baptism, which is the initiatory rite into the fold. Then the duties begin which connects themselves with the Christian religion, and are plainly set forth in the Gospel. For instance, go with us to the night in which He was betrayed, for there he for us all a pattern laid. He sent two of His disciples to prepare a commemorative supper, but before they ate it, He washed His disciples feet to show forth a cleansing. Although they before had been washed in baptism, they now only need wash their feet, and would be fit recipients to partake of the sober repast and solemn emblems of His broken body and shed blood, when done with a sincere motive, and not Judas-like. Then in the same night, he said, "Watch and pray that ye enter not into temptation; for the spirit is willing but the flesh is weak." Afterward the apostles said, "Greet one another, with an Holy Kiss," which is a token of love. Oh that we had more of the love of God shed abroad in our hearts, and that love for one another is our prayer.

GEO. WORST.

New Pittsburg, O.

THE AGENTS OF SABBATH SCHOOL OPPOSITION.

Under this head we will speak of three characters, the well wisher, the sluggard, and the grumbler.

The well wisher.—Opposition, in its mildest form comes from those who are friendly to a measure, but who will go no farther than merely to *wish* it well. Their heart is not in the work, and if they have any faith in it, it must be that dear faith which says to the destitute, "Depart in peace, be ye warmed and filled," without giving as much as a mite of wool or a morsel of bread. In this case, what the tongue says, sounds very friendly, but unless it be accompanied by some effort to mitigate his sufferings, the cold hungry beggar, would look upon it as the basest mockery, and the one that uttered it would be regarded as anything but a friend. Those who pursue such a course, deny in deed, what they profess in word, and are in reality the enemies of the cross of Christ. In somewhat the same light we look upon those who profess to be friendly to Sabbath Schools, but who fold their arms, stand aloof and neglect every opportunity to help along with the good work. Do they not essentially oppose the cause? True, they *wish* it well, but it is to be feared that they encourage less by their good wishes than they discourage by their conduct. They claim to be neutral, but their influence falls to the side of the opposers of the cause. Others are led by that influence to assume the same or a worse position and every accession to the neutral ranks is a reinforcement against the cause. If one of these neutral well-wishers were to see a child on the street in danger of being run over by a passing train, would he fold his hands and *wish* that it might escape, while at the same time he might easily save it by a little exertion? If such were his conduct, we imagine that he would be looked upon as being as much of an enemy to that child as if, instead of wishing it well, he had wished it ill. Well, we claim that there are hundreds and thousands of children on our streets and highways, in narrow lanes and dark alleys who are in great danger of being trodden down by the lusts of sin; and we claim, too, that it is the object of the Sunday School to rescue these children, a work so important that no true Christian can consistently stand idly by and merely wish it well. Some brethren are so neutral on the Sunday School question that they do not even wish it success, yet they claim not to be opposed to the Sunday School. They say, "If it be of God it will prosper; if not, it will go down." Well, brother, let us see about this. It is certainly not true that everything that is of God prospers *in specific cases*, neither is it true that everything that goes down is not of God. The Church itself languishes in some places; in other places it has "gone down." Is it therefore not of God? It is just the same way with the Sabbath School; it may go down in certain sections, and yet the cause itself be all that we claim it to be. Both Church and Sabbath School, as well as every other good cause, go down just as soon as men refuse to be instruments in the hands of God to keep them up, no sooner, no later. God does not work independently of man in these matters. No brother; He does not work independently of what even you, one man, may do or neglect to do. If there is a Brethren's School in your section do not stand idly by and console yourself with the thought that it has your good wishes. Let it also have the prayers of your heart, the labor of your hands and the best thoughts of your mind. There are times when a cause will suffer more by our cold neglect than it would at other times from our active opposition. Does your Sabbath School languish, struggling between life and death? If so, now is the time for you to improve that resting talent. Dig up the napkin that contains it and away to the rescue! If you can do no more, put on a cheerful countenance and go to the school, go every Sunday. Your friendly presence and smile of approval will revive more than one weary heart and may save the school. Do you refuse to render a service so small to a cause that you can *wish* God-speed? If so, you are to be pitied for your apparent indifference to what God requires at your hand.

J. ZUCK, JR.

Mercersburg, Pa.

A PROPOSED COMPROMISE.

Whereas there has, of late, rather a spirited controversy sprang up in the PILGRIM about Sunday schools, some writing against and others in favor of them, some of the former allege that they are not from Heaven, meaning, I suppose, that we have no authority in the Gospel, *which is from Heaven*, for Sunday Schools. Now I would propose a compromise. In the first place, I will state that we, here in the Yellow Creek Church, Bedford Co., Pa., have had, during the Summer months for seven or eight years, a little meeting on each Sunday afternoon, which we have called Sunday School, to distinguish it from our regular forenoon meetings, which meetings are controlled by the Brethren. We meet together, old and young, with our children, and also invite all, children and adults to attend it. This meeting we conduct as follows: We open by singing and prayer, the same as our forenoon meetings, then, having formed the children, and all adults who are willing, into classes, we then read a chapter from the New Testament, (we have also a spelling class for such as cannot read,) then we ask them some simple questions from said chapter, which they will answer if they can, but if they cannot, we try to answer them for them. We also extend the liberty to all who wish to ask questions, which we will answer if we can, and then sometimes we talk to them a little in a simple way. We try to teach them good morals, and exhort them to be orderly when they go to meeting, telling them that God will love and bless them if they will be good, &c. Then we distribute to the children tickets, whereon are printed short passages from the Bible, then we close by singing and prayer and dismiss. We also encourage them to read the Bible at home and commit as much of it to memory as they can.

Now for all this, I think we have authority. We have authority for assembling ourselves together, and certainly our children should have the same privilege, as the lambs need food as well as the sheep, and we have authority for singing, praying, reading, teaching and exhorting, and we are also commanded to bring up our children in the nurture and admonition of the Lord. But the latter may be objected to on the ground that it should be done by the parents at home, which I admit, but it may be a great help to the parents to have their children instructed and admonished at these little meetings, and besides, there are some children who do not have pious and God-fearing parents, who impart unto them the admonitions and instructions which they require, and some of which they receive at these meetings. But we have no Sunday School celebrations, no exhibitions, nor picnics connected with them.

Now as I have proposed a compromise, I would suggest, as the term Sunday School is not in the Bible, and is therefore said not to be from Heaven, to drop the same and call our Sunday afternoon meetings simply Children's Meetings, or something similar. But it may be said, should we not on the same ground drop the terms, Annual Meeting, Standing Committee, Delegates, District Meetings, Visiting Brethren, and other terms which we make use of, which are not in the Bible, and consequently may be said not to be from Heaven. For my part, I have no objections to using these terms, neither could I see any wrong in using the term Sunday School, but merely for the sake of a compromise I would be willing to drop it, but I would be very sorry to have these little meetings discontinued, which I know by experience to have done much good.

DANIEL SNOWBERGER.

New Enterprise, Pa.

ONE LORD, ONE FAITH, ONE BAPTISM.

This portion of Holy Writ is enough within itself, to convince every candid mind, if looked at in its proper light, that God has but one way of worship that meets His approbation. The apostle declares that there is but one faith, and Christ the Author of it. Under the Jewish law, or the law given by Moses, there was but one form of worship, and that alone pleased God; "for the law was given by Moses, but grace and truth came by Jesus Christ."

Then the law of Christ has established union and without union there could be but little peace. God has given unto us a law, through Christ, that will create a union amongst the true believers of His Kingdom. This Kingdom is on earth, though not of the world, and has a law and subjects.—These subjects are entitled to the privileges of this Kingdom, and if not subject to the law, then they are not of that Kingdom; they must surely belong to another one. Then there is but one faith, one way to get to heaven. If there is more than one way, I have never learned where it is.

Brethren, do we possess the one Faith or way spoken of by Paul? If we do, we have found the one way that leads from a sin-cursed world to the bright world above. There are many faiths afloat in the world, and who is the author of them? Is God? Is Paul or some other one? We think God the author of the one, and Paul an advocate of it, and depraved short-sighted creatures the authors of faiths. It would look not much like union in the house of God if all the different ways of worship were of God; for says one, I am sent to teach that none but adults are entitled to baptism, and that by immersion. But another says, I am sent to teach that all are entitled to baptism, young and old, the infant as well as the gray headed father, and this can be accomplished by sprinkling or pouring. Stop says a third, you are both wrong; there is no need of either, we can be saved without baptism. All that is necessary is to be born of the Spirit. In comes a fourth, and says it is all human invention, we will all be saved for Christ died for all, and consequently all will be saved.—Stop says a fifth, you are all wrong, you have not that one faith for you are contradicting each other. What, God send a man to teach that baptism by immersion is the proper mode, and another that sprinkling is right; another that pouring is right, that immersion is wrong; another, that neither of the former are necessary, all claiming to be the followers of Christ!

Brethren what do you think of it? Kind reader, what do you say about it? What kind of a oneness would you call such a mixture? There is but one faith, and the Christian has that faith. Will the Word of God, which is the sword of the spirit, teach me that baptism by trine immersion is right, and another that it is not? Does the Holy Spirit teach me that the Lord's Supper is not the bread and cup, and another that it is? If we thus contradict each other, and fight and quarrel over these plain commandments of God, can we all be led by the Holy Spirit, that was sent to guide the believer into all truth? I think not. Somebody is wrong as sure as men contend for so many ways. The Christians are to speak the same thing; all to have the same judgment, all to see eye to eye, all to glorify God by the same mind and same mouth, all walking by the same rule. These are the principles of the doctrine of Christ, and without them, we are not true believers. Man may think he has the one faith, and still is short of it. It suits the carnal nature to believe a part of God's Word and reject the other. What a different state of things there would be if all professors were bound together by the bonds of true religion. Let us take a glance at the state of affairs. How different it is now from that of the time of the apostles. You see fine houses, gilded seats, in which the hearers receive from the polished minister, that which tickleth their ears, receiving large salaries, &c How different from the persecuted and bonded apostles, driven to and fro, stoned, mocked, and even put to death, just because they contended for the one faith. O, ye who cry peace, when there is no peace, remember that God will call you to judgment, there to give a strict account of your ways. Some will say, all are right and then condemn us, because we contend for the good old way. Brethren, one and all, contend for the one Lord, one faith, one baptism.

BENJAMIN BASHORE.

Whitesville, Mo.

Pleasures waste the spirits more than pains; therefore the latter can be endured longer and in greater degree than the former.

Certain books seem to have been written not to give instruction, but to indicate that the author knew something.

BELIEVE THE GOSPEL.

The time is fulfilled, and the kingdom of God is at hand, repent ye and believe the Gospel.—Mark 1: 15.

These words came from the lips of the Savior after His temptations in the wilderness. And as Jesus elsewhere said, "The words I speak are not mine, but the Father's who sent me." And as God said, I will put my words into his mouth and he shall teach the people whatsoever I command him. We suppose it was the command of God he taught. The Gospel, which Jesus commands people to believe, is the good news or glad tidings of great joy to all mankind, which Jesus came to accomplish, and angels desired to look into. These glad tidings was long predicted before Christ said the kingdom of God is at hand. And Christ said, "The kingdom of God is within you." This then, methinks, must be the new birth, the change of heart, which causes those who have experienced it no more to look upon things as temporal and according to the flesh, but as eternal and according to the spirit; but Alas! Alas! there are four births spoken of in the first chapter of John's gospel, and only one which will produce the new creature in Christ Jesus. And for the dense smoke which arose from the bottomless pit (when opened by the star that fell from heaven, See Rev. 9th chap.,) or in other words, those who have been born of any of the births spoken of above, excepting the one which is of God, have so mystified the air or polluted the Gospel light with false and every wind of doctrine that thousands scarcely know their right hand from their left in spiritual matters. Yet like the worshipers of Baal, might be made to cut themselves with knives and lancets till the blood would gush over them in their zeal, which is not according to knowledge. O what a work then to preach the Gospel of Christ in its simplicity and purity.

In the early ages of Christianity, the evangelists had only to convince the Jews that this Jesus, whom they preached, was that identical person predicted by their own prophets and foretold by their own Scriptures, to be their only Messiah and Savior, and to persuade the Gentiles that their gods were no gods, but dumb idols, that could neither hear, speak, walk nor talk, but that there was a true and a living God of which they (the Gentiles), had some faint idea of, although unknown to them in His true light, and they were ready to accept the truth, but now-a-days the true evangelist must needs teach those who think they are enlightened and have the religion of Jesus Christ in their hearts that they must undergo a change, (that even Nicodemus a ruler of the Jews could not comprehend), before they can even see into the mystery of godliness. Now then in what light must we view the world in while in an unconverted state, but as sheep having no shepherd who think they have the light of Christ in them, yet are walking on the barren mountains of sin and folly, not subject to the law of God, neither indeed can be under such circumstances. How then is this new birth and great change to be brought about? We answer, we have something to do with it ourselves, namely: God who is the author and finisher of our faith, has given us talents more or less which we will term reasoning powers. And by the right exercise of these, the grace of God, which bringeth salvation will appear and teach us that denying all ungodliness and worldly lusts we should live soberly, righteously and godly in this present world. Now if we occupy the talent God has given us, we will inquire whence we originated, what we are and where we are hastening to, and thus we may learn both by experience and the Word of God, that we have no abiding city here, and that by nature we are fallen creatures and in an unsaved and deplorable condition. In order to extricate ourselves from this unhappy condition, we will begin to inquire, "What must we do to be saved?" Without faith it is impossible to please God, and we may do well to consider how the fall of man was brought about, and by a careful examination we will learn that our mother Eve doubted the word of God, and finally disbelieved it, and believed the word of the serpent and acted out the principles of her unbelief. So we must believe that God is, and that he is a rewarder of all those that diligently seek Him, and that He so loved the world that He gave His only begotten Son that whosoever might believe on Him should not perish, but might have everlasting life. By living out the principles of our faith, we will be made the sons and daughters of God, by faith in Christ, and if we henceforth suffer ourselves to be led by none other than the spirit of Christ, striving to grow in grace and in a greater knowledge of God and of Jesus Christ, whom he has sent, counting all things but as dung, so that we may win him and keep the faith, we conclude that there is laid up for us a crown of righteousness which the Lord, the righteous Judge will give to us in that great day and not to us only but to all them that love his appearing. Amen.

D. BOSSERMAN.

"Beware of the wounds of the wounded souls. Oppress not to the utmost a single heart, for a solitary sigh has power to overset a whole world."

GENERAL INTELLIGENCE

THE A. MEETING TENT, it should be remembered, to be a success, should be attended to at once. All those who intend to do anything towards it should report to Daniel Vanimen, Box 53, Virden, McCoupin Co., Ill. The tent, 80x220 feet, will cost $1800,00.

THE EDITOR of *Our Church Paper* treats the departure of the Rev. Forney very calmly, and prefers the quiet let him go system to that of throwing curses after him and making a fuss generally. Just so. He is only a man and not a very great one. O, what (?)

THERE is a move on the wing of starting a school for the Brethren in Pa., on the co-operative plan, location not determined. The plan is something like the following: Let the necessary funds be divided in shares of $5000 each, with the privilege of taking as many shares as desired. Those who are friendly to the cause will then report to a properly appointed person, the number of shares they wish to take. When there is a sufficient amount raised to insure success, there will be an election held by the share-holders, each one having as many votes as he has shares, for a board of directors whose duty it shall be to locate and erect the necessary buildings, determine on the teachers, and put the school in operation. Who says success?

THE FOLLOWING views of Advent theology is from an exchange, and is accepted by the *Advent Christian Times* as being courteous, candid and appreciated.

"The leading points of doctrine held by the Adventists are that man is wholly mortal; that he is unconscious in death; that there will be a resurrection of all men, just and unjust, that Christ's second coming is a literal one, and it is near, but the exact time is not certain; that the earth is not to be burned up, but purified by fire, and will be the future abode of the righteous."

That man is wholly mortal, unconscious in death, and then can be resurrected, kind of confuses our ideas. It seems quite rational for mortal things to be unconscious, but for them to be resurrected and again receive their identity, is beyond our ordinary way of comprehending things.

THE PROBATION SYSTEM.—The Methodist Churches South, have abandoned the "probation system," and Rev. Dr Edwards makes the following report of the success attending the change;—"The transaction was easy and without any friction. Pastors became more careful and guarded in receiving members. The fruits of our revivals were gathered in with caution and with solemn and impressive ceremonies, and the result has been that a comparatively small percentage of their additons to the church is lost. The experiment has proved perfectly satisfactory. I have never heard, to my recollection, a soitary preacher or layman express any regret that the probation system was abolished in our branch of the great Methodist family; but, on the contrary in interchanging views with pastors or people, have everywhere heard unqualified gratification expressed at the change." *New York Observer.*

AN interesting Conference, largely composed of converted Indians was recently held in Dakota. About one hundred and fifty delegates were present, some of whom had travelled five hundred miles. Nine churches, under the care of the American Board, have one thousand members, seven ordained Indian ministers, fifty elders, deacons, etc. Last year they contributed about $1,000, and seventy-nine converts were made. The report as to the temporal condition of the Indians is hopeful. About one-third of the delegates to the Conference were Indians who had been arrested and imprisoned for supposed complicity with the Minnesota massacre of 1862, and who were converted in the revival which followed.

ON SABBATH last, Aug. 24, the last remains of Rev. Devolt Fouse, of the Reformed Church, Huntingdon Co., Pa., were laid in their last resting place by a deeply sympathizing congregation of members and friends. He was a man of more than ordinary activity and zeal in the cause in which he spent his life to build up. He labored in the ministry some 32 years, and in that time built up some eight respectable congregations, four in Woodcock Valley, and the others, in Morrison's Cove, Blair Co. Notwithstanding he had the oversight of so many charges, it is said that he failed to meet only one or two of his appointments. He was a man of considerable influence in his Church, plain and humble in appearance, and greatly beloved by his flock. The funeral was the largest ever attended in the community, and the religious exercises were conducted by the Revs. Kiefer, Cort, Sangaree and Sykes.

A GERMAN correspondent gives the following account of the social and moral results of the late war: "According to what I observed and learned by friends, the late war, tho' so glorious in victories, has done great injury to the population of Germany on the whole, for Materialism, Raticnalism, infidelity, and immorality, are vastly increasing. Even the Prussian army, formerly distinguished for excellent discipline and moral superiority compared with other armies, is now getting corrupted, and losing its strength and valor. I am afraid that the very same sins that ruined France will ruin Germany, unless the whole nation earnestly seek to serve God, instead of their own lusts. The best of the people see the corruption that increases, and mourn for their people and country, and pray for a fresh outpouring of the Holy Spirit, and a general regeneration of the nation. It is the old truth ever again. The conquerer loses in the end, and ruins himself by accepting and imitating the same follies and sinful practices of the nation he trod down. So it was with the Medes, Persians, Greeks, Romans, and I fear so it will be with the most civilized nations of the present time."

EMIGRATION OF MENONITES.

On Friday last, a delegation of nearly a hundred Menonites, from the Crimea, arrived in this city on their way to the West to make arrangements for an extensive emigration to this country. They are from the villages of Friedensleig ("Stone of Peace") and Bruderfield (Brother's Field") in the Crimea, five miles from the shore of the Black Sea. It is now five weeks since they left Russia, journeying to this country by way of Feodesso, Odessa, Berlin and Hamburg. They are essentially German, speaking the language of Fatherland. They emigrated a long time ago to Russia on account of their religious principles, one of which is they cannot perform any military service. Representatives of this sect are found in the Netherlands, Germany, Russia, Switzerland, France and America. The whole valley of the Vistula is scattered over with them. In the Crimea they have their own church schools, which their children are obliged to attend from the age of six to fourteen years. They have also their higher schools, up to the grade necessary for teachers of the children's schools. They are nearly all agriculturists. In settling on the steppes of Southern Russia every colony planted forest and fruit trees, and now every house is surrounded by an orchard, with a piece of woods in the vicinity.

By a Russian edict of the 4th of June, 1871, they, with all the colonies in Russia, were allowed to choose between emigration, or, not having emigrated at the end of ten years, to become subject to all the laws and obligations of ordinary Russian subjects. The Canadian Government held out inducements to the Menonites to settle in Canada, promising them complete immunity from military service; but the people refused, saying that if they were obliged to emigrate they would prefer to come to the United States. This advance guard is principally composed of young men, with their families. They held religious services at Castle Garden on Sunday last. The Rev. Mr. Neumann, of Brooklyn, with whom they had previously been in correspondence, and who has taken a warm interest in them, preached.

A deputation representing forty thousand Menonites has been in America some time, searching for suitable lands on which to establish a colony. They have visited Colorado, Minnesota, Texas and Illinois. They have not yet determined where to locate the colony, but will decide upon their return to Russia, and they hope to send out a company of at least five thousand Menonites in May next.—*New York Observer.*

SIR WM. Blackstone declares that all human laws derive their binding force solely from their divine original, and must command what is right and prohibit what is wrong; and no law is valid if contrary to God's law. And he does not regulate nor license crime, but prohibits it, as in the commandments, saying, "Thou shalt not kill; thou shalt not steal." Therefore, all enactments that license, regulate or permit the traffic in intoxicating beverages are wrong, because they are at variance with Divine law, which is, "Wo unto him that giveth his neighbor drink, that puttest thy bottle to him, and makest him drunken also."

Youth's Department.

THE GOOD SHEPHERD.

My dear young readers, I have not the privilege of talking to you as often as I could wish or expected to do, but I see you are not forgotten, as every week there is some provision for you through the PILGRIM. I love to talk to my young friends and would feel much encouraged if I could have the assurance that my effort in writing for you was interesting and instructive.

You no doubt have heard the often used expression: "The fodder is placed too high for the lambs." You perhaps understand it as well as I can explain. If in feeding, the racks containing the fodder are placed so high that the sheep can just reach it, the lambs will be too small to get any. Therefore, the good shepherd places the rack and feed quite low so that all can reach it, the older ones by bending down a little, and the younger ones, by stretching up. My object is to feed the lambs of the flock of PILGRIM readers, therefore I wish to be as low and simple as possible. "Feed my lambs" is the command of our dear shepherd Jesus Christ. You are the lambs of the flock and Jesus, the good shepherd, to keep you within the fold, has commanded that you be fed and cared for. But so soon as you refuse to hear the Shepherds voice and refuse his food, you will begin to stray away in search of other food which belongs to the enemy, and the more you eat of it, the wilder, more disobedient and sinful you become, and if not found and taken back by the Good Shepherd you will get lost in the wilderness and be devoured by the wolves (bad men).

Dear reader, where are you to-day? Are you in the Good Shepherds fold, or are you out on the barren mountains of sin? You can tell this by where you are feeding. If you are in the fold, you are feeding on the Good Shepherds food. A very important part of this food is, obedience to parents I hope my young readers are feeding largely on this very good pasture, as there is nothing in the world that will make you so good as this. The Good Shepherd promises that you may live long on the earth. It will not only make you to enjoy a long life, but it will make you good, useful and happy. Disobedience is the first step outside the fold and just as sure as you are disobedient to your parents, so sure are you outside of the fold and when you get out, you begin to grow wicked, become bold and learn bad things. This you do not wish to do because it is dangerous and will end in death. It will not only make you wicked and miserable in this world but you will thus offend the Good Shepherd and in the world to come, he will not own you as his lambs, but will cast you into outward darkness where there will be weeping and gnashing of teeth. Would not this be very dreadful, especially when Jesus has done so much to save you? By disobedience, which is sin, we were all driven out of God's fold and became as stray sheep, wandering in the mountains without a Shepherd, but God pitied us so much that he sent his own Son, the Good Shepherd, after us to gather us in again. In seeking to save us it became necessary for him to suffer much, and finally to be nailed to the cross and there to die that we might be saved. This is what is called the cost of our salvation and it was paid freely. In this salvation, all little children are included when he says: "Suffer little children to come unto me and forbid them not, for such is the Kingdom of Heaven." Then when you are born into the world, you are all lambs of the flock of Jesus, and if you die while you are thus young, good and obedient, you die in the fold and will be happy in the world to come. But as we grow up in the world, become actual sinners and stray away from the Good Shepherd's fold, and are no more the lambs of his flock, therefore it is said of us "we must be born again" or return again into the fold. I may talk of this in my next.

UNCLE HENRY.

LOSING ALL.

A few years ago a merchant failed in business, and went home in great agitation. "what is the matter?" asked his wife. "I am ruined; I am beggared. I have lost my all!" he exclaimed, pressing his hand against his forehead as if his brain was in a whirl.

"Ah!" said his wife; "I am left." "All pappa!" said his eldest boy; here I am." "I too pappa," said his little girl, running up and putting her arm around his neck. "I's not lost pappa," repeated Eddie. "And you have your health left," "And your two hands to work with pappa" said the eldest; "and I can help you." "And your two feet, pappa, to carry you about." "And your two eyes to see with, pappa," said little Eddie.

"And you have God's promises," said grandmother, "and a good God," said his wife. "And Heaven to go to," said his little girl. "And Jesus who comes to fetch us there," said his eldest.

"God forgive me!" said the poor merchant, bursting into tears. "I have not lost my all. What are the few thousands, which I called my all, to these most precious things which God has left me?" And he clasped his family to his bosom and kissed his wife and children with a thankful heart.

Ah! no, there are things more precious than gold or bank stocks, valuable as these may be in their place. When the Central America was foundering at sea, bags and purses of gold were strewn about the deck as worthless as the merest rubbish.

"Life life!" was the prayer. To some of the wretched survivors, water, water!" was the prayer. "Bread bread!"—it was worth its weight in gold, if gold could have bought it.

The loss of property must not cloud the mind with a wicked forgetfulness of the greater blessings which are left behind. No man should despair; for no man has lost his all until he has lost his integrity, lost the mercy of God, and lost his hope of Heaven at last.—*Our Paper.*

A TEACHER in one of our city public schools says she can almost invariably select from her pupils those who read the newspapers at home; such are sure to exhibit a better acquaintance with geography, orthography, and the true meaning of words.

The Weekly Pilgrim.

JAMES CREEK, PA., Sept. 2, 1873.

☞ How to send money.—All sums over $1.50, should be sent either in a check, draft or postal order. If neither of these can be obtained, have the letter registered.

☞ When Money is sent, *always* send with it the name and address of those who paid it. Write the names and post office as plainly as possible.

☞ Every subscriber for 1873, gets a *Pilgrim Almanac* Free.

DODGING THE QUESTION.

A good brother accuses us of dodging the question relative to Sabbath Schools. We say, nay good father, not so. Our position on this question has been, candid and straightforward. As to the Sabbath school as an institution, we are opposed. But when properly conducted as some of our brethren and others try to conduct them, we are *decidedly* in favor. The whole taken together, makes too large a dose for us, we cannot swallow it. To send our children to schools where this "any thing-will-do" doctrine is taught, and then send them home with a tale called religious, about "Edie May" "The Drunkards Daughter" "The Little Orphan" and hundreds of others that never existed except in the mind of some visionary money grabber, is a monstrous sham and should be so considered by every intelligent Christian parent. Sabbath schools may have done much good in disseminating religious instruction, but they have done more in establishing sectarian bigotry and still more (pardon the expression) in making novel readers. We are not in market to be sold or bought against or in favor of any side, neither do we intend to ride the rail, but speak with truth and soberness that which we think becometh sound doctrine. To do this, there is no necessity of calling any, ignorant, prejudiced or enemies. These are expressions that we sometimes use thoughtlessly without anticipating their full force of meaning and greatly depreciate our character as a body. We sometimes forget that when we speak disrespectfully of, and injure one of our brethren or sisters we mar the body of Christ of which we are all members. Then brethren and sisters, let us not become excited about our little differencies, but let us manifest the spirit of kindness and brotherly love that characterized the whole life and deportment of our blessed Master. If we would all do this, how much more agreeable it would be all around. We would not need to consume the midnight oil in determining whether or not to publish this or that brother's article, because charity thinketh no ill of his neighbor much less of a brother or sister in Christ. Our productions would accomplish much more good, our blessed cause would be honored and the Pilgrim would become a mighty power for good in the world. Then, because we are not so radical as some others, do not not think we are trying to dodge questions, but laboring to keep in the bonds of peace and brotherly union, remembering that it hath been said, "Blessed are the peacemakers; for the shall be called the children of God."

TO THE SCATTERED MEMBERS.

From the general character of our contributions, you may think that we have too many Martha's and not enough Mary's, that we are too careful about the many things, and not enough mindful of the one thing needful. This may be so, but we hope soon, to somewhat change the character of our reading by being able to give more practical reading better adapted to the spiritual wants of those who have not the advantage of the daily and weekly ministration. We often think of our scattered ones who stand isolated from that sweet communion realized by the assimilation of kindred spirits. The appeal "pray for us" is treasured up and in our private, as well as public devotions we think of you. That the Pilgrim visits are appreciated, encourages us to a greater effort in supplying you with that spiritual food which, to the soul, is more than meat and drink. When you say that the fountain of God's mercy is ever flowing, you are right. It is a glorious faith to believe and realize that God is everywhere present, and that He regardeth not numbers so much as a broken heart and a contrite spirit. Wherever there is a heart to pray, there is a temple for worship and a God to hear. Your hopes for Heaven can be as sure-founded, and your prospects as bright for Heaven and eternal deliverance as though you were surrounded by an encampment of saints. You, no doubt, often think of the advantages that these enjoy who are surrounded by those of a like precious faith, but they may be more imaginary than real. God is our all sufficient good, and the more we learn to associate with Him, the less we care for the association of earth and the house, in which we live. Paul felt, to be absent from the body, was to be present with the Lord. Though we live in the flesh, contaminated with sin and surrounded by the influences of carnality, yet it is possible to become so dead to them all that the imprisoned spirit may soar aloft and hold sweet communion with God and like, with Paul, it will be a question whether we were in the body or whether we were of out it.

Books. We call the attention of our readers to our book notices under the head of "Literature." These are all books sent us by the different publishers for review, and you can feel assured that it is not our purpose to flatter, but only give such notices as we think the merits of the works deserve, and notice only such books as will be safe and advantageous for ourselves and our children to read. We have now made arrangements with a number of publishing firms and can supply our readers with any book desired at publishers prices.

Our Agents and patrons will please make arrangements to settle up their old accounts as soon as possible as the year is growing short and our bills are getting long. One of our agents gathered up almost 70 subscribers, and says he has, as yet, only got between $7,00 and $8,00. This looks a little slow, but perhaps it is for a want of opportunity. Please do not forget us.

Historical Chart of Baptism by brother J. H. Moore is received and presents a beautiful and novel appearance. The workmanship is well executed, and the arrangement very good, being the result, no doubt, of considerable thought, research and planning, giving, at one view, an abridged history of baptism for the first four centuries of the Christian era. Bro. Moore has given the subject of baptism long and careful study and therefore knows whereof he speaks. For price of Chart &c., see advertisement on last page.

Webster's Unabridged Dictionary.—It has now stood the test of time, and received in approval not only that popular verdict, which in the United States has called for over fifty million copies of the Webster series, but the thorough endorsement of our best scholars, as put forth individually, and in the pages of the authoritative periodicals. It is not only, to quote Professor Stowe, "in many respects the greatest literary work which America has ever produced," but it is in many respects the greatest literary work produced in any nation or age.—*New York Mail.*

ANNOUNCEMENTS.

Please announce through the Pilgrim, that we expect, the Lord willing, to hold our Lovefeast in the Coldwater Church, in the new stone Meetinghouse, on the 8th and 9th of October, and we extend the usual invitation to all and especially the laboring brethren. Our railroad station is Greene, about a half mile from the Church.

John F. Eikenberry.

Please publish that the brethren of Hopewell District, expect to have their Communion on Friday the 4th of October, commencing at 4 o'clock, p. m. Preaching next day and on Sunday. The usual invitation is extended, especially to ministering brethren. Eld. Jacob Steel.

Otter Creek Church, 3 miles south west of Virden, Macoupin Co., Ill., Sept. 10, 11.

Yellow Creek Church, Snowberger Meetinghouse, Bedford Co., Pa., on Thursday, Oct. 2, at 4 o'clock, p. m.

Fawn River Congregation, Lagrange Co., Ind., on the 4th and 5th of Oct.

Grasshopper Valley Church, Jefferson Co., Kan., Meetinghouse in the town Oskaloosa, Oct. 4 and 5.

Dunnings Creek Congregation, Pa., on Friday, Oct. 3.

Stone Church, Marshall Co., Iowa, on the 4th and 5th of Oct.

Our Lovefeasts of Maryland, will be held as follows:

Sam's Creek,	Oct. 11,	commence 1½ p. m.
Monocacy,	" 17.	
Meadow Branch,	" 21,	com. 1½ p. m.
Beaver Dam,	" 25.	

The usual invitation is extended.

E. W. Stoner.

Cerro Gordo, Piatt Co., Ill., Sept. 27 and 28.

District Meeting for Southern Ill., at the same place on Sept. 29.

Cedar Creek Church, Anderson Co., Kansas, 16th and 17th of August, 1873.

Whitesville Church, Andrew Co., Mo., Sept. 20, and 21

In the Cerro Gordo district, Ill., Sept. 27 and 28, 1873.

Clover Creek, *Blair* Co., Pa., on the 30th day of Sept. and 1st of Oct.

At the residence of Morgan Workman, near Loudonville, Sept. 6, '73.

Black River Branch, Medina Co. Ohio, October 3.

Logan Church, Logan Co., Ohio, Oct. 2.

Mohecan Church, Wayne Co., Ohio, 20th September, '73.

Mill Creek Congregation, Adams Co., Ill., 6th and 7th of September.

Also in Pike Co., near Barry, September 13 and 14.

Correspondence.

A Reporter is wanted from every Church in the brotherhood to send us Church news, Obituaries, Announcements, or anything that will be of general interest. To insure insertion, the writers name must accompany each communication. Our Invitation is not personal but general—please respond to our call.

Dear Pilgrim:—To criticise or find fault with the actions or doings of our friends whom we dearly love, seems to be very ungenerous and hard, especially when we are aware that all of us are subject to do wrong and act sometimes inconsistently, but whatever is done out of love is with the design of doing good, and if received in that spirit, will effect good and bring the parties concerned in closer intimacy and firmer friendship.

With these thoughts before our mind, we go back some 18 or 20 years and attend an Annual Meeting where the question came up, whether it was right for brethren to write for the Gospel Visitor under a fictitious name. It was decided that writers should give their real names or at least the initials of their names. In course of time, we got nearly all the writers proper names, their modesty had left them, and conscience acquiesced. Thus we become acquainted with each other, though hundreds of miles apart, friendship was formed, and when we occasionally met at A. M., we enjoyed each others presence largely. True our blunders and shortcomings in our communications were in the possession of our readers with our name, so we strove to do better, and many did much better, and some real good. It is also true there was some sharp cutting sometimes, but what of that, so that we did not fall out by the way, and if we did, that we became reconciled and we did.

Now the above being true, is it not very strange to restrict the Reporters at the last A. M. from giving the names of the speakers? I would have concluded at once that it was an affected modesty, but the thought that this reporting the talks of the Brethren had been strenuously opposed formerly and now granted without restrictions, that would be giving too much at once. Where there are many heads to be fitted it requires many sizes and shapes. It is not strange at all that there are differences among a body of people of over 100,000 souls, especially considering that this number is more than double to what it was 20 years ago, many coming in from all other denominations in the land, year by year, with the determination to do nothing but what is directed by the Word of God, and therefore often oppose that where the Word is silent; but the unction from above would teach forbearance. But that unction will never be found where there is selfwill and want of charity. "To be easily entreated" is a virtue that all of us should try, by all means to come in possession of. It produces such sweet feelings, whereas selfwill creates a perfect hell in the breast of him that is in possession thereof. Now I trust we shall not only have no opposition to give the names of the speakers in their proper place next year, but also that we will all strive to lay aside selfish whims and prejudices which are entertained yet more or less by those that came from Babylon to build up the "Holy City."

F. P. LOEHR.

Bloomingdale, Mich.

HE CALLS US

Dear Brethren and Sisters.—When meditating upon the times, the following lines came to my mind: "O, that there were such an heart in them that they would fear me, and keep all my commandments always, that it might be well with them, and with their children forever."—Deut. 5: 27.

So God's word is to us to-day brethren. Oh, that there were such an heart in them, should be our constant desire and prayer, and to have this desire fulfilled we should cry aloud to the dying sons and daughters of men, that we may thus clear ourselves as watchmen on the walls of Zion. These were the words of the prophet to the Baalites. The children of Israel were commanded to keep the whole law and to observe all that was commanded them, but their hearts were moved from God and he became displeased with them, in the wilderness, and overthrew them because they had zeal for God but not according to knowledge. They were ignorant of God's righteousness and went about to establish their own righteousness, not submitting themselves to the righteousness of God. Therefore they entered not in because of unbelief

Dear reader, how is it with you? Are you safe, or are you justifying yourself in your unregenerated condition? Think a moment is it not God that wants you to hear him when he calls you by the loud soundings of the Gospel? Does he not call upon you to obey all the commandments of the Lord Jesus Christ blameless? How are you spending your time. Have you your children around you and speaking to them of the love of God, and trying to impress upon their minds the one thing needful that there may be such an heart within to fear God, and that it may be well with them forever? It is our duty to talk with them in the house, at their outgoings and their incomings that we may teach them to seek the Kingdom of Heaven and its righteousness, first, that we may all have the hope of that inheritance with the saints in light. My love to all the household of faith.

JACOB J. KINDIG.

Woodford Ill.

Dear Pilgrim:—In No. 31, of present volume, I find an article written by brother J. Zuck, headed, "Origin of Sabbath School Opposition," which I am sorry has found its way into the columns of the PILGRIM. As a friend of the cause, and a lover of vital godliness, I am firmly impressed with the conviction that the essay referred to will tend to greatly impede the success of many schools now in their infancy, as the manner and language employed in relation to those of the Brotherhood who do not see as others do on the subject, will only tend to embitter their feelings against the institution instead of making them more favorable towards it. Such pointed assertions are uncourteous and quite out of place, especially when they are without a single "thus saith the Lord" for them. Some of the assertions used do not savor the spirit of Christ, and will, no doubt, grieve many of the old veterans of Christ and arouse to action the spirit of opposition to Sabbath School, which every careful Bible reader knows is not altogether groundless. I thank God for the carefulness which some of our brethren exercise in relation to this question, as, by it, I have learned many practical lessons. I think I know in part what it is to disciple brethren's and other children, and feel that if the important charge was left entirely in the hands of novices, the cause might soon fall into disrepute. In these things we should be careful and not overstep or go beyond our bound, not affecting wisdom over our fellows as knowledge unseasoned with grace is a great misfortune.

D. F. GOOD.

Waynesboro, Pa.

PYRMONT, IND.,
August 10, '73.

Dear Editors:—As you solicit Church news from all districts, I will give you a few sketches of news from our new organization, called the Fairview district, Tippecanoe Co. Ind. This is a new organization from the west end of the Northfork. Wildcat Dist. the church line being the county line between Tippecanoe and Carroll county.

About twelve months ago we mutually agreed to divide, and form a new district, and since that time we have built a new meeting house called the Fairview Church, had a Communion on the 20th of June. We also held an election for two deacons and two ministers which resulted in electing brthren Robert Atchison and Joseph Zahn for ministers, and brethren Adam Sensenbaugh and John Mohler for deacons. I hope the good Lord will enable them and us all to work together in love and union, hoping the good work of the Lord may still roll on according to his holy and divine will, that we may finally all be brought together on the flowery banks of eternal deliverance where parting will be no more.

SAMUEL ULERY.

Dear Pilgrim:—I notice that the subject of dress is much treated of in our periodicals, and I think it is all right. I noticed recently that a sister complained that the sisters' cross in dress is heavier than that of the brethren. I, for my part, do not feel to complain. There is not a plainer command in the Scripture than non-conformity to the world, and if there is a more marked distinction in the sisters apparel, I feel to rejoice that we are in the right, rather than complain.

A YOUNG SISTER.

MARRIED.

LYONS—MOUR.—By the undersigned, at his residence, Aug. 18, 1873. Mr. B. F. Lyons of New Enterprise, Pa., to Miss Hannah Mour of Hollidaysburg, Pa.

IMLER—HOOVER.—Aug. 21, by the same, at his residence, Mr. Thomas Imler of New Enterprise, Bedford Co., Pa., to Miss Susan Hoover of Woodbury, Pa.

DIED.

KAYLOR.—In the Logan Church, Logan Co., Ohio, June 20, 1873, sister Laura Rebecca Kaylor, aged 19 years and 10 months. Funeral conducted by brethren Jos N. Kauffman, M. Savonger and the writer from Matt. 24: 42-43-44, to a large audience.

The subject of this notice was one of a serious nature. Her disease was Consumption. About 3 weeks before she died she sent for the brethren and wanted to be received in the church by baptism. She was very weak, not able to walk. She was hauled ¾ of a mile to the stream, and then seated on a chair and carried in a stream and then placed on her knees and baptized with ease. Dear young people, take warning.

J. L. FRANTZ.

MICHAEL.—In the Middle Fork Church, Clinton Co., Ind., August 2, '73, sister Hannah, wife of brother John Michael, aged 44 years, 6 months and 21 days, leaving ten children, all living, and 6 grand-children, a husband and many near relatives and friends to mourn their loss. On Sunday the 3d, she was conveyed to the Brethren's graveyard by a very large crowd of people, more than ever was seen at this place. Occasion improved by Eld. Isaac Billheimer, from Matt. 21: 42.

J. N. CRIPE.

STEEL.—In the Hopewell Congregation, Bedford Co., Pa., Aug. 22, 1873, Bro. Wm. P. Steel, son of brother Samuel and sister Phebe Steel, and grandson of Eld. Jacob Steel, aged 19 years, 2 mos. and 3 days. Funeral occasion improved by the brethren to a large and attentive Congregation.

S. A. MOORE.

SMITH.—In Jefferson Co., Iowa, March 20, 1873, of Typhoid fever, Catharine, wife of Samuel Smith and daughter of brother John and Margaret Fishel, aged 35 years, 8 months, and 19 days, leaving a husband and four children to mourn their loss. Funeral preached by brother Peter Lutz.

SNOOK.—In the same place, Sarah, wife of Jacob Snook, aged 70 years and 3 months. The cause of her death was palsy. Mother Snook was a member of the Methodist church. Funeral by Bro. Peter Lutz.

PRIEST.—In the same place, Malinda S., daughter of Wm. and Ruth Priest, on the 30th of July, 1873, aged 11 years, 4 mos. and 26 days.

The subject of this notice met her death in a most shocking manner, she was making a fire, and to make it burn, poured coal oil on out of a can, when it caught, the can bursted, and the burning oil flew all over her and burned her so badly, that she died next day. Funeral preached by brother Peter Lutz.

DAVID B. TEETER.

KLEIN.—In Fairview, Frederick Co., Md., Aug. 21, 1873, friend Frederick Ernest Klein, aged 82 yrs., 10 mos. and 13 days. Funeral sermon by Elder J. D. Trostle, from these words: "Set thine house in order; for thou shalt die and not live."

PHEBUS.—In New Market, Frederick Co., Md., Aug. 8, 1873, brother Emanuel, son of brother Peter and sister Emeline Phebus, aged 18 years, 5 mos. and 7 days. Occasion improved from Rev. 14: 13, by the brethren.

The subject of this notice was one worthy of regard; when visited by the brethren, they inquired how long he had been considering the importance of being adopted into the Father's family, he answered, "For several years, ever since E. W. Stoner was here (which was nearly two years), and preached from the words, "The like figure whereunto baptism, doth also now save us." Although but a youth he had read the truths of the Gospel, and very much enjoyed the society of the brethren and sisters. He was afflicted with disease of the intestines during the Summer, which he bore with Christian patience; never complained of being sick too long nor desired to get well. On the morning of the 7th his mother inquired of him if he was still satisfied to depart unto the Lord? He remarked that there was nothing more for him to do but requested her to send for brother ——, that they anoint me with oil in the name of the Lord. Thirty-five hours after he was annointed he expired. How pleasant to see those die who fall asleep in Jesus.

D. GIBBONS.

LITERATURE.

A. B. Brumbaugh, Huntingdon, Pa. Literary Editor.

MAGAZINES FOR SEPTEMBER.—*Lippincott's* for September is an attractive number. It contains an unusually entertaining paper on "English Court Festivities;" and an article on "The Patrons of Husbandry." The New Hyperion continues with increasing interest. The concluding paper on Fruits and Flowers of the Tropics gives an accurate and striking description of the marvelous vegetation of Oriental countries, also a sketch of Eastern Travel, &c. Among many very interesting articles we name Our Home in the Tyrol which is continued with illustrations; and how they keep a hotel in Turkey, gives a very entertaining picture of life and manners in the East, as observed in the native Khans and at the great hotels in Constantinople and Cairo. These are a few of the leading articles in this really interesting and attractive number of this popular monthly.

Scribner's Monthly has increased its circulation eleven thousand during the past year, and the increase has been a steady one from month to month. The September number is fully up to its standard. A Cruise among the Azores is of special interest, as also the paper on Central Park. Arthur Bonnicastle and Bret Harte's story continued with absorbing interest. The Birds of the Poets illustrated is exceedingly attractive. Among the many interesting articles will be found the Liberty of Protestantism in reply to a former article under same title; also Modern Skepticism. This is an unusually attractive number.

HARPER for September, continues Gen. Sherman's tour through the East which will be read by the many, with much interest as it reveals many curious facts in regard to the "Ancient land." With the helps that are now within reach of the intelligent reader a man in his chamber can learn more of the world and its history in ten months than can be learned in travelling in ten years. Take for example, this No. of Harper. First, we are led through the strange and curious remains of the Ancient Europe. Next, we are taken into the great City of New York, and there introduced into the wonders of the Deaf and Dumb Asylum. We have not only a written description but the whole thing is put before our eyes with such familiar and life-like illustration that the reader can scope the whole thing as correctly as if he were there and indeed he can know more about it than thousands who go there. Then we are taken to Florence there to see the Protestant Cemetery, from there to Copenhagen and take a look at the old Castle, and then around through Africa, in fact every part of the known world with their facts and fancies are presented to the reader through its pages, and no man can afford to sit down in stupid idleness when he can receive a world of useful information by sending $5.00 to Harper & Brothers, New York, and get their excellent Magazine.

A. S. BARNE'S & Co., New York, announce a new Quarterly—*The International Review* to be edited by Prof John M. Leavitt, The object of the work will be to discuss with the best ability of our country the great questions of the age—literary, scientific, social, national, religious. It will be solid, fearless, progressive; and a medium of communication for representative thinkers of the age. About sixty of the best writers and most valued authors of Europe and America have been secured as regular contributors. The first number will be issued about January 1st, 1873. Subscription price $5.00, for the year.

BOOKS RECEIVED.—*History of the Bible—Illustrated*—by Wm. Smith, L. L. D., author of Dictionary of the Bible. National Publishing Co.

CHOLERA.—Its nature, prevention and treatment, by Henry Hartshorne, A. M., M. D. Lippincott & Co.

LIPPINCOTT'S MAGAZINE from January to July, 1878, being all the No's of Vol. XI and the first No. of Vol. XII. Yearly, $4.00.

HUNTINGDON & BROAD TOP RAIL ROAD

On and after Aug 14th, 1873, Trains will run on this road daily (Sun excepted) as follows:

Trains from Huntingdon South. *Trains from Mt. Dal's moving North.*

EXPS. P.M.	MAIL. A.M.	STATIONS.	MAIL. P.M.	EXP'S A.M.
6 15	7 45	Huntingdon.	AR6 50	AR9 20
6 20	7 50	Long Siding	6 45	9 15
6 35	8 00	McConnelstown	6 35	9 05
6 40	8 05	Pleasant Grove	6 20	8 58
6 51	8 20	MARKLESBURG	6 15	8 45
7 01	8 35	Coffee Run	6 05	8 35
7 08	8 41	Rough & Ready	5 58	8 29
7 15	8 50	Cove	5 49	8 20
7 18	8 53	Fishers Summit	5 46	8 17
7 35	9 10	Saxton	5 35	8 05
7 50	9 25	Riddlesburg	5 15	7 45
7 55	9 32	Hopewell	5 10	7 39
8 10	9 45	Piper's Run	4 58	7 26
8 21	9 57	Tatesville	4 43	7 12
8 32	10 07	Everett	4 33	7 03
8 40	10 15	Mount Dallas	4 30	7 00
9 00	10 35	Bedford	4 05	6 35

SHOUP'S RUN BRANCH.

A. M.	P. M.		P. M.	A. M.
LE 9 20	LE 7 40	Saxton.	AR5 25	AR 7 55
9 35	7 55	Coalmont.	5 10	7 40
9 40	8 00	Crawford.	5 05	7 35
AR 9 50	AR8 10	Dudley	LE4 55	LE 7 25

Bro'd Top City from Dudley 2 miles by stage.

Time of Penna. R. R. Trains at Huntingdon.

***Mail No. 2 makes connection at Huntingdon with Mail going East on Pennsylvania Railroad at 4.15 p. m., and West at 5.45 p. m. Mail No. 1 leaves Huntingdon at 7.40 a. m. on arrival of Pacific Express West.

Trains on this road connect with trains on Bedford & Bridgeport, and Cumberland & Pennsylvania Railroads.

G. F. GAGE, Supt.

The Weekly Pilgrim.

Published by J. B. Brumbaugh, & Co.

Edited by H. B. & Geo. Brumbaugh.

CORRESPONDING EDITORS.

D. P. Sayler, Double Pipe Creek, Md.

Leonard Furry, New Enterprise, Pa.

The *Pilgrim* is a Christian Periodical, devoted to religion and moral reform. It will advocate in the spirit of *love* and *liberty*, the principles of true Christianity, labor for the promotion of peace among the people of God, for the encouragement of the saints and for the conversion of sinners, avoiding those things which tend toward disunion or sectional feelings.

TERMS.

Single copy, Book paper, $1.50
Eleven copies, [eleventh for Agt.] $15.00
Any number above that at the same rate.
Address.

H. B. BRUMBAUGH.
James Creek,
Huntingdon county Pa.

The Weekly Pilgrim.

"REMOVE NOT THE ANCIENT LANDMARKS WHICH OUR FATHERS HAVE SET."

VOL. 4. JAMES CREEK, PENNSYLVANIA, SEPTEMBER 9, 1873. NO. 36

POETRY.

THE FAITHFUL FRIEND.

SELECTED BY C. S. C.

When the cup of our pleasure is mingled with gall,
And the tears of our anguish like rain drops descend;
It is sweet to remember and know through them all,
There is still ever living a Savior and friend.

Though the skies may be darkened, and stars be obscured,
And the gloom of midnight encircle the heart,
Yet we still in our sadness by Christ are assured,
That the joy of his presence shall never depart.

When the wild waves were tossing the ship on the sea,
And the tempest was sweeping, and danger was nigh,
There were heard mid the waters of rough Galilee,
Sweetest words of the Savior, "Fear not, it is I!"

All along through the desert so barren and drear,
Where its sands are so scorching and burdens oppress;
He that walked in the furnace is felt to be near,
Even there He is ready His loved ones to bless.

When we come to the river, the river of death,
Though in weakness we shudder, yet Jesus is there;
We can feel through us thrilling His life-giving breath,
And the hope that it wakens soon conquers despair.

O soon when we stand on the bright shining shore,
Will the tears of our sorrow be all wiped away;
And with storms and with tempests to trouble no more,
We will walk in the light of the Lord as our day.

ORIGINAL ESSAYS.

GETTING RELIGION.

The phrase *getting religion* has become very common and is much used in our day; sinners are invited to come to what is called the *Anxious Bench*, and get religion, and many convicted sinners, with a desire to obtain pardon of their sins, being taught by their spiritual advisers, that there they can obtain the blessing which they seek, come to the said bench, and there exercise in leaping and all manner of contortions, in prayer and calling upon the Lord till they fancy that they are *through*, as they call it, and have obtained the desired blessing; some getting through sooner than others, and some linger at the bench a long time and cannot get through; the preacher sometimes, as though he was getting impatient, tells them that they are through and did not know it. And this is, I believe, what is called *getting religion*, and, if I am not mistaken, they then believe their sins pardoned, and consequently feel happy.

Now if the Apostle Peter had answered those who, on the day of Pentecost inquired what they should do: "*Come to the anxious bench and get religion every one of you in the name of Jesus Christ for the remission of sins*;" or if Paul had answered the jailor, when he inquired what he must do to be saved: "*Come to the anxious bench and get religion and thou shalt be saved, and thy house*," then those said advisers and those who are so advised, would have good ground for the course they pursue. But as the Apostles gave quite different answers to those inquiries, we must also, in order to obtain the pardon of our sins, pursue a different course.

I will now explain what religion is, or what the word implies, though I would deem this entirely superfluous, (as any school boy should know this) were the word not so much misapplied. James says: "Pure religion and undefiled before God and the Father is this: "To visit the fatherless and widows in their afflictions, *and* to keep himself unspotted from the world." James 1: 27. Now this implies practice, and not something that we obtain. The word in Greek is *Threskia*, which is defined by Grove; *religion, worship, divine service*, and as a secondary meaning; *superstition, false religion*. Luther has rendered it *Gottesdienst*, which is in english, *divine service*.

Now to say that we obtain, or as it is commonly expressed, get religion, would be equivolent to saying we get divine service, or we get worship. How would this sound? or would there be any sense or propriety in such an expression? I trow not.

I think I am understood that *religion* is something that we cannot get or obtain, but something that we must practice. If we serve God with a pure motive and according to his directions, we practice pure and undefiled religion. But there is also an impure and false religion, such as the Mohammedan and the Pagan religion, which is practiced by millions of the human race, and there may also be, and doubtless are, thousands and perhaps millions, who profess to practice the Christian religion, and yet do not practice it according to his revealed will, this also impure and defiled. To such the words of the Savior, which he spake to the Scribes and Pharisees would apply: "Ye hypocrites, well did Esaias prophesy of you, saying, this people draweth nigh unto me with their mouth, and honoreth me with their lips, but their heart is far from me. But in vain do they worship me, teaching for doctrines the commandments of men." Matt. 15: 7, 8, 9.

Then I would advise all who desire to have a knowledge of the true meaning of the word of God, not to misapply the terms found in the Gospel, but read and search the Scriptures carefully and sincerely try to ascertain what God requires of us and practice accordingly. If we do this we have the promise of receiving, not that imaginary thing, which is by many called religion, but the Holy Spirit who shall lead us into all truth, and, being led by that spirit we have the assurance that we are the children of God. See Rom. 8: 14.

DANIEL SNOWBERGER.

New Enterprise, Pa.

REGENERATION, WHAT IS IT?

The term regeneration in its simple meaning is reproduction, the act of forming into a new and better state. Born again is synonymous, and to be born is to be produced or brought into life; so born again is made use of by the sacred writers, to signify that spiritual life infused by the spirit and grace of God, called the new birth.

Man brought forth into natural life is said to be born, so man brought into spiritual life is born again, or begotten again. Now as man, by actual sinning against God, becomes estranged or alienated from Him; consequently dead to good works he loses his relationship to God by doing evil; he is represented in the word of God to be a child of wrath, dead in sins, and in order to become a child of God—alive to righteousness, he must be born again, regenerated. This cannot be effected in any other way but by introducing the power of God. Hence the necessity of the preaching of the Gospel. The Gospel of Christ is the power of God unto salvation to all them that believe. Herein lies the necessity on the part of man of believing and accepting the truth of the Gospel of Christ. "My words they are spirit and they are life."—Jesus.

By the reception of the word of God then new life is infused into the soul by the grace of God; that change by which the will and natural enmity of man to God and his law is subdued, and a principle of supreme love to God and his law, or holy affections are implanted in the heart. This is an internal work and produced by the will and power of God, but will be made manifest externally in man by submission and obedience to all the requirements of the Gospel. "Of His own will begat He us with the word of truth, that we should be a kind of first-fruits of his creatures."—James. "For in Christ Jesus I have begotten you through the Gospel."—Paul. "Being born again not of corruptible seed, but of incorruptible, by the word of God which liveth and abideth forever."—Peter. Three inspired and infallible witnesses to prove my position. Hence to claim a new birth and reject Christian baptism is erroneous, and he that trusts in it is deceived. To say a man is regenerated who opposeth feet-washing and the Lord's Supper as commanded in the Gospel is absurd and shows a shallow conception of the the theological term regeneration.

A genuine new birth necessitates the word and spirit to co-operate, hence, whatever is commanded in the word of God for man to do, must be obeyed. Inasmuch then as the Author of salvation, the Great Head of the Church, Jesus Christ our exemplar connected water with a new birth, no honest believer will undertake to separate it. "Except a man be born of water and of the

CONNECTION.

Ignorant mortals are rash in their conclusions on the conduct of Providence, being blind in their views and impatient under woes. But to compose my combating thoughts, and make me wait the issue of all things with patience, let me look into some remarkable Scripture narrative, and see the fair sunshine of kindness, after the storms of trouble and clouds of indignation are gone.

First, then, let me look into that which befel the friend of God. Think what joy filled the patriarch's breast, when promised a son in his old age, and how this joy was increased when the promised seed was born, circumcised, and grew up to be a pretty boy, the joy of both his parents. But look again and see the amazing temptation, and scene that ensues. The promised seed must be sacrificed, and that by the hand of a most affectionate father, yet see his aged joints tremble all the way to Mount Moriah, to offer up his beloved Isaac, as it were, resigning the promise again to God, trusting that He would make it out some other way, though it were by raising him from the dead. Now let us view the beginning of the trial of his faith. How dark and gloomy, how opposite to reason, affection and religion. But let us connect the latter end with the beginning, and all at once it is beautiful and bright. There his faith is true, here it triumphed; there God commands, here He commends His obedience; there He requires, here He restores Isaac. The voice of God at first, seems to strike at His former promise, here it confirms all with new promises. Enlarged blessings and this glorious name superadded, the father of the faithful, Abraham comes home full of gladness and gratitude. And we have the divine account to teach us to wait the end before we draw our conclusions of God's providential way.

The second is, the account of Joseph. In the first part of the scene, see his young heart ready to burst and break with bitter anguish. Hear his many but fruitless supplications to his cruel brethren. How melting are his cries, while his hard-hearted brethren draw him out of the pit to sell him for a slave. Nothing can save him. Compassionate Reuben is not within reach of his cry. The price is agreed upon, the money is paid, and away he must go, and neither his parting importunities, his piercing cries, nor pitying back looks can move them to relent. Moreover after a little advancement in Egypt, he is thrown from the liberty of a servant into confinement of a prison. This at first sight is a melancholy scene. But if we look to the sufferings of a tender hearted father, it is heightened to the highest pitch. All his sons and daughters gather around the grey headed mourner to comfort him, but in vain, for still he thinks he sees the wild beasts tearing his beloved Joseph to pieces, who screams out for help. But none to help is near, and then he is like to faint thro' the excess of sorrow. Now this is the first part of the providence which indeed, has a very dejecting aspect, and if we had never heard more of the matter, we would have concluded them both very miserable. But let us see how the connection stands. Jacob who had mourned many years is at last overflowed with tides of joy. Joseph, the lost, the long lamented Joseph, is still alive; the youth that was sold into Egypt as a servant. All Egypt is at his service. He who had his feet hurt with fetters, may now bind princes at his pleasure, and teach senators wisdom. He who lately drudged about in a dungeon to attend prisoners, becomes a father to a king, his brothers who envied him for his dreams, which bred their envy, he whose life they so little valued saves the lives of thousands, and at his whose supplications his brethren would not hear. All the land of Egypt is governed, the long separated relations meet and melt in kindness on one another's necks.

We have a similar instance. The great Apostle Paul, and by his own observation too, in his epistle to the Philippians, this great man after his singular conversion, preacheth Christ in many trials and sufferings, till at length he returns to Jerusalem. There by the enraged and unbelieving Jews he is set upon, and would have been slain had not the Roman captain rescued him. But he is so persecuted with their cruel rage, and underhand dealings, that he is compelled to appeal to a heathen emperor. Now the great apostle of the Gentiles, to the grief of the church, is a prisoner. Hence, says he, "I Paul the prisoner of Jesus Christ." He is a long time confined in Judah, then sent to Rome, where, though ship-wrecked in his passages, he arrives and is kept two years a prisoner. But says he to the Philippians, "I would ye should understand brethren, that the things which have happened unto me have fallen out rather unto the furtherance of the Gospel, so that my bonds in Christ are manifest in the palace and in all other places; and many of the brethren in the Lord waxing confident by my bonds are are much more bold to speak the word without fear."

How noble the connection. Paul intends to visit Rome at his own expense to preach the Gospel, but providence, at the emperor's expense, brings him to make converts, not only in the royal palace. The Jews think they have succeeded to their wish when they have thus got rid of a pestilent fellow, and a ring-leader of the sect of Nazarenes, but they could not have fallen upon a better method to spread his doctrine. From appearance his success must end when his imprisonment begins. But it is quite the reverse, not only Paul persists in preaching the Gospel, but the brethren wax bold. What reason then have I to complain on the first part of the providence. While the outer wheel is only seen should I not wait till the inner wheel turns round and I can read plainly the last connection, and what though that should be reserved for eternity, there every providence shall be completed to mine everlasting comfort.

A Pilgrim.

GENERAL INTELLIGENCE

Bro. E. Slifer of Burketsvill Md., under date of Aug. 28, says:

On the 12th day of Aug. 1878, in the morning abount 2 o'clock, our country was visited with a very destructive hail-storm, destroying cornfields, gardens, and thousands of panes of window glass. It extended over a scope of coutry 20 miles in length and from 1 to 2 miles in breadth, and in the immediate vicinity of our village, our streams were very much swollen, and additional damage done by the fall of seven inches of water during twenty-four hours after the hail-storm."

High Church People becoming Catholics.—Of four persons lately received into the Roman Catholic Church in Boston and vicinity, says the *Congregationalist*, one was Mr. Richard Bliss, connected with the Agassiz Museum in Cambridge and for several years a member of the Episcopal church; another Miss Libby of Boston, a member of the very high Episcopal church of the Messiah; a third a Mr. Ward, a member of the church of England; and the fourth Rev. C. R. Brainard, formerly rector of the Episcopal church in Quincy. Those who are fond of looking up antecedents, will be struck by the similarity in these cases. Prof. Wharton has written lately on "Ways to Rome." Is one of them here indicated?—*N. Y. Observer.*

A Terrible accident occurred near Lemont on the Chicago and Alton Rail road by a freight train coming in collision with a south express passenger. The coal train was running at the rate of 20 miles per hour and the express at about 30, neither engine seeing each other until it was too late to reverse, a fact accounted for by a turn in the road and partly by a dense fog. The two trains came together with fearful force. Being on the curve, however, each engine left the track and passed eachother, that attached to the coal train striking the baggage car a few feet from the end, breaking the coupling between it and the smoking car, which the engine struck fair in the end and with such force as to throw the forward end in the air, so that the engine ran under it, tearing the floor completely out and hurling the fifty or sixty unfortunates who were in the car in a struggling mass to the lower end where there was no chance to escape, and then ensued a scene of horrors which cannot adequately be described. The smokestack and dome of the engine were knocked off by the collision, and the broken timbers of the smoking car penetrated the boiler, letting loose a dense volume of hot steam, which poured into the car, blinding and scalding the inmates who with shrieks struggled vainly to extricate themselves, but their condition was such as would not admit of help and six had to perish outright, while several others died soon after and still others will follow The cause is attributed to the carelessness of the conductor and engineer of the coal train, whose orders were to lay over at Lemont until the passenger arrived.

CHRISTIANS IN RUSSIA.

While in Calcutta in 1869 we formed a very pleasant acquaintance with a missionary of the English Church, Rev. James Long, who had spent the most of a long life of Christian labors in India. A man of learning, strictly evangelical in his views, and having a truly catholic heart, he was ready for every good word and work. On his return to his native land he made a visit to Russia, notices of which we have seen from time to time in our foreign papers. We have just received the following, which he communicated to the *Missionary Intelligencer* of the Society with which he is connected:

"The laity of the Russian Church are beginning to take an interest in works of benevolence and religion. I have become acquainted, during my residence in Petersburg, with various interesting illustrations of this. One Madam ——, the wife of a General high in the Russian service, took me one day to visit an institution founded by her for the education of girls and affording aid to poor women. She held a mother's meeting, in which, while the women worked, she expounded to them with great zeal and efficiency the epistle for the Sunday. She has been frequently in England. I visited two of the prisons with a Russian lady who expounds the Scriptures to female prisoners. I went to one of the worst houses in Petersburg, the nest of thieves and the vilest characters, where a few years ago the skeletons had been dug up of persons who had been murdered there at night and then buried on the premises; yet two Russian ladies pay weekly visits to this place, give religious instruction, and are endeavoring to form a ragged school on the premises. The system of district visiting is being introduced into various parishes in Petersburg. I met one lady of high rank, who, when in England, engaged herself as a district visitor in a parish in order to learn our system. I know another case of one who devotes herself to translating books from the English into Russian. Among the books translated is the Missing Link."

It is gratifying always to receive assurances that even in those churches that are most given up to error and formalism the spirit of God is moving upon the hearts of some, and that there are those who truly devote themselves to the service of the Master. "Grace be within them that love our Lord Jesus Christ in sincerity."—*N. Y. Observer.*

Youth's Department.

HOW TO ENTER THE FOLD.

In my last I was telling you about the Good Shepherd and his fold and about the danger of getting out of it. By this, I suppose you understand that you are in the fold. This depends on how good you are and how much you are able to do. The Bible says that he that knoweth to do good and doeth it not, to him it is sin. Now, no doubt, some of you are old enough to know to do good and have not done it, therefore you have become sinners and as no sinners can be in the good Shepherds fold, you must be on the outside, and to be there, is very dangerous, just as much so as it would be for a lamb or a sheep to be outside of the sheep-fold in a country where there are bears and wolves. Jesus is a good Shepherd and wants you to do nothing but what is easy. He says, "My yoke is easy and my burden is light." But when he tells us that we must be good and obedient and we refuse to do it we grieve him and he finally casts us outside or rather by becoming bad we go out ourselves. We begin to feel like the young man we read of in the Bible. He thought he knew a great deal and was able to care for himself. He thought it was too small to remain at home and do what his father told him. He, at last, begged of his father to give him his share and he would go out and set up for himself. You remember how he went off to a far country where he got among bad people and soon wasted all that his father gave him. Then it was that he became in want and got so hungry that he would have been glad to eat with the hogs that he was feeding, but his money was all gone and therefore no person would give him anything. Just so you will feel after you have become disobedient, learned to sin and strayed away from the fold of Jesus; but will you do like this lost son did? When he found that he was lost and away from his father's house, he repented of his folly and determined to go back again. Now this is what I want you to do. Some of you have grown to years of understanding, to a time that there is more required of you than to simply obey your parents. There is something that tells you that you are sinners, that you have went away from your father's house, that you are in a lost and undone condition, without hope and God in the world. This you learn from reading the Scriptures and hearing them preached. From the same source you learn that Jesus is callingyou and the kind invitation is, "Come to me." To do this you must make a full resolve to forsake your former sins. This is what is called repentance. But this alone did not take the prodigal son back to his father's house, but he had to do something more, he had to return and enter his father's house as a stranger, as one that was lost and had no right there whatever. So you must do. By sinning you died to all that belonged to you as a son or daughter and to again become a child you must be born again. This means a conversion or change of mind, with a determination to do whatever Jesus commands you, it is to stop doing evil and learn to do good. But as God wants us to be known as the sheep of his fold, he has given us a sign that all who see it may know that we have now been made willing to return into his fold and be his sons and daughters. This sign is water baptism. He says, "Repent and be baptized for the remission of your sins," or, "ye must be born again." By being baptized in water, or buried in baptism you go through the sign of a death and by coming out again you come through the sign of a resurrection or birth. You are now born of water, after which it is said ye shall receive the gift of the Holy Ghost or be born of the Spirit. This Spirit will lead you into all truth which will make you wise unto salvation. This is the plan the Bible gives for you to get back again into the Good Shepherd's fold, and I hope that not one of my readers who are conscious of being sinners will feel safe for a moment until they have returned to the fold of Jesus and thus become his adopted children.

I have now tried to be as plain and simple as I could and hope you will understand what I have written. I feel a deep concern for your salvation and now advise you not to put it off till it is too late.

UNCLE HENRY.

A SCAR ON THE SOUL.

One of my most pleasant memories of early Sabbath school days is of a lad who for a short time was my pupil. My acquaintance with him began thus:

Being in the country in the summer, the first Sunday of my stay I went to a different church from that attended by the family with whom I sojourned. We came from a distance and in the same carriage. Knowing it was communion at the church which my friend attended, to save them trouble of calling for me after the morning service I walked to the place where the horse and wagon were fastened under an elm-tree behind the church, intending to sit there until they should join me. Only two other vehicles were there, in one of which sat a boy whom I observed to be assiduously driving off flies from the horse, saying as he did so, "Poor Ned! poor Ned! next Sunday we'll have a new net. Pa won't forget to buy one this week, 'cause I'll help him to remember." His back was toward me, so he was unaware of my presence; but his kind words and acts so attracted me that I resolved upon further acquaintance. I walked back and forth a few times before taking my seat in the wagon, and soon had an opportunity to observe the pleasing face and gentlemanly bearing of the little fellow. Presently I said,—

Your horse has a kind little master, I perceive."

"That's because father and mother think so much of Ned," replied the boy, modestly. "Besides, I don't like to see him so tormented by the flies. You see he has stood it all the time I was at church, and now I have come to help him."

"Then you were at church during the first service?"

"O yes, ma'am and I went to Sunday school at nine o'clock."

"I should think you would be tired being confined so long. Why not run about a little? Wouldn't you like to?

"Yes ma'am but then poor Ned would be so pestered. I'd rather stay.

"Then your father and mother did not bid you to?"

"No ma'am; but somehow I'd feel better to do so.?

Kind little fellow! I said to myself; and then asked.

"What are you going to do this afternoon?"

"I'm going to read to blind Samuel."

"That will keep you confined, too."

"Yes but I'll have my dinner first, and a little time to run about in the orchard, too," he replied.

"Suppose you let me go in your place?"

"O, but I promised," said the boy, quickly, and looking up earnestly.

"I could excuse you in some way."

"Please ma'am I don't see how, because I'm not sick."

"But why be so particular, as long as Samul is not neglected."

"I can't explain it very well ma'am replied the boy, looking a little troubled,—perhaps feeling a little disappointed in his new friend who seemed apparently desirous to lead him astray,—"I can't explain it but it wouldn't be reading to him, besides, he would be disappointed not to see me; but that wouldn't be the worst of it."

"What would be the worst of it?"

"Well ma'am as you ask me, I'll tell you what my father and mother taught me that to break my promise even in a small thing is a sin, and every sin leaves a scar upon the soul."

I now commended the little fellow warmly, and told him that my questions were merely to enable me to become better acquainted with him.

"O I am so glad!" said the child with a breath of relief; because I was beginning to like you."

"And could you not have liked me otherwise?"

"No ma'am; not if you wished me to do wrong," replied the child candidly.

Noble boy! his nice sense of right and honor increased with his years. He lived to become a fine and high principled young man, possessing a remarkable influence over others for good; his quiet example, and firm but unostentatious adherence to what was good and right giving weight to his words. He died early but lived long enough to make his mark on many souls, some of whom became converted through his instrumentality.

How true the word about the "scar upon the soul!" Yes, every sin even though subsequently repented of, leaves a disfiguring mark, as unsightly to the eye of God as a scar upon the face would appear to us.—*S. S. Times.*

HOW YOUNG MEN FAIL.

"There is Alfred Sutton home again with his wife to live on the old folks," said one neighbor to another. "It seems hard after all his father has done to fit him for business, and the capital he has invested to start him so fairly. It is surprising he has turned out so poorly. He is a steady young man, no bad habits as far as I know; he had a good education and was always considered smart: but he doesn't succeed in anything. I am told he has tried a number of different sorts of business, and sunk money every time. What can be the trouble with Alfred, I should like to know, for I don't want to have my boy to take his turn."

"Alfred is smart enough said the other, "and has education enough but he lacks the one element of success. He never want's to give a dollars worth of work for a dollar of money, and there is no other way for a man to make his fortune. He must dig if he would get gold. All the men that have succeeded honestly or dishonestly, in making money, have had to work for it, the sharpers sometimes the hardest of all. Alfred wished to set his train in motion, and a smashup was the result. Teach your boy friend Archer, to work with a will when he does work. Give him play enough to make him healthy and happy, but let him learn early that work is the business of life. Patient, selfdenying work is the price of success. Ease and indolence eat away not capital only but worse still, all a man's nerve and power. Present gratification tends to put off duty until to morrow or next week' and so the golden moments slip by. It is getting to be a rare thing for the sons of rich men to die rich. Too often they squander in a half score of years what their fathers were a life-time in accumulating. I wish I could ring it in the ear of every aspiring young man that work, hard work, of head and hands, is the price of success."—*Country Gentleman.*

LITERATURE.

A. B. Brumbaugh, Huntingdon, Pa. Literary Editor.

RECENT AND COMING PUBLICATIONS.—Claxton, Remsen & Haffelfinger, Philadelphia, have just issued a new edition of "*Rollins Ancient History*," in 4 volumes Octavo. Prices $9, $11 and $16, according to binding. There are still many thousands of persons who should read this reliable history who have never yet done so.

Also, "*Burton's Anatomy of Melancholy*," new edition with engraved title and frontispiece, 8 vo. Price $2 75 and $3.50.

Also, "*The Virginia Housewife*" or Methodical Cook, 12mo $1.00. This same house announce "An Appeal to the Reverend Clergymen of the U. S. on behalf of the Primal of God for Mankind."

J. B. LIPPINCOTT & Co., announce a new edition of "*Berkeley's Principles of Human Knowledge*," with notes and comments from various sources, making it the most complete edition of this Philosophical Classic yet issued.

This same house have recently issued "*Work, Play, and Profit*, or Gardening for Young Folks, &c." Illustrated, 12mo. cloth $1.25.

Also, "*Thoughts on Life and Character*," by S. P. Herron, 12mo. cloth $1.50.

Also "*The Record of a Happy Life*," &c. Portrait, cloth $1.25.

Also nearly ready, "Philadelphia and its Environs," &c. A very valuable and interesting book for all those who may visit the "City of Brotherly Love." Price 50 cts.

Also the "*Spiritual Delusion*," its methods teachings and effects; the philosophy and phenomena critically examined, 12mo. fine cloth $1.50.

"FLORA'S JEWELS," &c.—*Chromos.*—JAMES VICK, Rochester, N. Y., the celebrated Seedsman and Florist, is the publisher of several beautiful Chromos, of flowers. The first, issued for the Spring of 1871, shows 31 varieties of flowers; and that for Autumn 16 varieties of Lilies. The Spring chromo for 1872 exhibits 41 varieties of flowers; and that for Autumn 30 varieties of Hyacinths, Tulips, Narcissus, &c. The Spring chromo for 1873 is a most beautiful picture. It consists of a statute of "Flora" the mythological goddess of flowers, supporting a vase containing about 50 varieties, of natural size and color, while all around, as though they had just dropped down, almost hiding the pedestal is a profusion of equally beautiful flowers, making on the whole an elegant picture. The size of these chromos is 19x24 inches, and the price unmounted is only 75 cts.; mounted on cloth, $1 25, or framed in a beautiful walnut and gilt frame, $3.00.

COMMENTARY ON THE NEW TESTAMENT, designed for Christian Workers. By Rev. Lyman Abbott. No. 1. Matthew, chapters 1-8 New York; A. S. Barnes & Co. 111 & 113 William Street. 25 cents per number sent by mail post paid.

We have had the pleasure of examining No. 1, Vol. 1, of this New Commentary embracing the first seven chapters of Matthew, and are much pleased with the general character of the work. Its purpose is to avoid criticisms and give such an exposition of the sacred Text as will or can be readily understood by the mass of readers. The notes are profuse and comprehensive and less objectionable than that we have heretofore read. There are a few views presented from which we dissent, but on the whole we consider it a valuable addition to sacred literature, and advise our readers to send 25 cts. for No. 1 and examine it for yourselves. See extract on another page.

THE MOUTH OF GOLD.—A series of Dramatic sketches, illustrating the life and times of Chrysostom. By Edwin Johnson. Published by A. S. Barnes & Co., New York. Price $1.00.

This is decidedly a work for cultured minds, and to such it will be intensely interesting. We have taken advantage of our leisure moments in reading its pages, and it has not only proven to be a pleasant pastime, but interesting and instructive. The work is written in blank verse, elegant in diction and elegantly bound.

BOOKS RECEIVED.—From J. B. Lippincott & Co., through Wm. Lewis, Huntingdon, Pa.—"THINKERS AND THINKING," by J. L. Garretson, M. D., (John Darby.) If this book proves to be as good as "Odd Hours of a Physician" by this same author, we shall not hesitate to give it a warm commendation. Price, extra cloth, $1.50.

The Weekly Pilgrim.

Published by J. B. Brumbaugh, & Co.

Edited by H. B. & Geo. Brumbaugh.

CORRESPONDING EDITORS.

D. P. Sayler, Double Pipe Creek, Md.

Leonard Furry, New Enterprise, Pa.

The *Pilgrim* is a Christian Periodical, devoted to religion and moral reform. It will advocate in the spirit of *love* and *liberty*, the principles of true Christianity, labor for the promotion of peace among the people of God, for the encouragement of the saints and for the conversion of sinners, avoiding those things which tend toward disunion or sectional feelings.

TERMS.

Single copy, Book paper,	$1.50
Eleven copies, [eleventh for Agt.]	$15.00

Any number above that at the same rate.

Address,

H. B. BRUMBAUGH.

James Creek,

Huntingdon county Pa.

The Weekly Pilgrim.

"REMOVE NOT THE ANCIENT LANDMARKS WHICH OUR FATHERS HAVE SET."

VOL. 4. JAMES CREEK, PENNSYLVANIA, SEPTEMBER 16, 1873. NO. 37

POETRY.

WILLIE.

BY LOVINA H. BURKHART.

Willie, thou art gone to God,
You fell beneath that chastning rod;
So young, too fair on earth to stay,
So God has taken him away.
Dear Willie, loved so well while here,
Your death caused many a bitter tear;
Your life was very brief on earth,
Your voice is hushed from joy and mirth.

But you have joined that angel throng,
You were too pure to do one wrong;
You've joined that bright angelic band,
Cherubic legions fill that land.
Yes, Willie, you are happy there,
You'll always be an angel fair,
You beckon your dear parents come,
To meet you in that better home.

Dear parents, mourn not for your child,
Just look and see those youths so wild;
Go staggering home along the street,
Their loving parents there to meet.
Your child will never share their fate
He's living in that high estate,
Where only angels ever dwell;
Dear Willie, now, a long farewell.

Wilmore, Pa.

[Selected by Hannah Hollowbush.]

I'LL PRAY.

BY MRS. MARY JANE PHILLIPS.

When the day-star gilds the eastern sky,
And along the earth soft shadows lie;
Ere breaks the sun's first cheering ray,
I'll kneel and to my Savior pray.

When the noontide sun, with fervid light,
Dispels the shades of the darksome night;
Stealing from earthly cares away,
I'll kneel and to my Savior pray.

When the wearied sun sinks down to rest,
And daylight fades away in the west,
And twilight draws her curtains gray,
Again I'll kneel, again I'll pray.

When I awake at the midnight hour,
In gratitude to the all-wise Power,
That keeps me safe both night and day,
I, to my Savior, God, will pray.

When sorrows rise and my heart is sad,
When life hath lost all the charms it had,
And trouble o'er me holds its sway,
Ah! *then I'll kneel and humbly pray.*

ORIGINAL ESSAYS.

RELIGION, WHAT IS IT? HOW OBTAINED?

"What is religion, and how is it obtained? If not obtainable, how is it practical?"

Dear editor and readers of the PILGRIM, having some time ago despaired in my ability to write, I laid down my pen to write no more for the public eye; but seeing the above subject proposed, by the editor, as a subject for brethren to write on, I feel this morning to give it a few thoughts and if they do not come up to the editor's standard he need not publish them. There are three heads, or points in the subject as proposed, but I will consider them in their order as they are proposed.

First. *What is Religion?* Religion is a word, a form of speech by which we express the same thing as by Godliness. To be God-like, or Christianity; To be Christ-like. The meaning of the word as defined by Webster and others is, a binding together; a union; a connection. Webster defines from the latin *religo*, to bind anew, *re* and *ligo* to bind. This rendering makes the word very expressive. When applied to man it conveys the idea that he is bound to God; that he is in union and connection with Him; and as the word means to *re, bind* it implies that he at one time was bound to, and was in union and connection with God, which we all once were; for, "All things are of God, who hath reconciled us to himself by Jesus Christ, to wit, that God was in Christ, reconciling the world unto himself, not imputing their trespasses unto them." Thus by this act of God, in which man was neutral, He bound, and brought into union and connection with himself all mankind; or as the text has it "the world." But man, by actual transgression of God's law, breaks the band of union and connection with Him; and hence, the words of reconciliation are given that he may be *re-bound* to God.

Religion then is a divine principle and power of God in the soul which binds it to him; and brings it in union and connection with Him. The terms *binding*, *union*, and *connection* are expressive of *attachment*, of *oneness*, of *sameness*, and of perfect *similarity*. To illustrate these, let us suppose two streams of water flowing together and forming but one stream after their junction. Here is a perfect union, a complete connection. So perfect and complete that the waters of the two head streams can neither be separated nor distinguished. So religion brings the soul in union and connection with God, that His "Spirit bears witness with our spirit that we are the children of God. So complete will the Spirit of God, and our spirit be assimilated, that the two bear witness one to the other that they are one and the same.

How is the Spirit of God known? First, It was exhibited to man in the life and character of His servant David, of whom God said, "He is a man after my own heart." Was his a sinless heart? No! David often and sometimes grieviously sinned. In what then was it God-like? Simply in this, that he never justified an error by blaming others, but always, on conviction, frankly acknowledged the sin. Hear him: "I acknowledge my transgressions; and my sin is ever before me. Against thee, thee only, have I sinned, and done this great evil in thy sight. Behold, I was shapen in iniquity; and in sin did my mother conceive me." "But David spake unto the Lord, when he saw the angel that smote the people, and said, Lo I have sinned, and have done wickedly: but these sheep, what have they done? Let thine hand, I pray thee, be against me, and against my father's house;" are specimens which God claims to be after His own heart; and are striking contrasts with that of Saul who in the face of a manifest disobedience of God's word could boastingly say to Samuel, "Blessed be thou of the Lord: I have performed the commandment of the Lord."

2. The Spirit of God has been more fully exhibited in the life and character of His Son our Lord Jesus Christ among men while on earth. In the Gospel it may be read and understood by all. He says, "I am meek and lowly in heart," like David, (*his type*) but more fully developed. Meekness and lowliness of heart are characteristics of the Spirit of God; and these traits of character proceeding from no other source wherever found, are evidences of the "Spirit of God bearing witness with our spirit, that we are the children of God." Meekness is the evidence of that charity which suffereth long, and is kind; that envieth not, and is not puffed up; and doth not behave itself unseemly, seeketh not her own, is not easily provoked, thinketh no evil. Rejoiceth not in iniquity, but rejoiceth in the truth; Beareth all things, endureth all things." Where the Jews said unto Jesus, "Say we not well that thou art a Samaritan, and hast a devil?" Jesus simply and mildly said. "I have not a devil; but I honor my Father, and ye do dishonor me." But He did no sin, neither was guile found in His mouth. Who, when He was reviled, reviled not again; when He suffered, He threatened not; but committed himself to Him that judgeth righteously." But when on the cross, He prayed, "Father forgive them, for they know not what they do." Lowliness of heart is associated with meekness and long-suffering. And Christians are bid to walk worthy of the vocation wherewith they are called. "With all lowliness and meekness, with long-suffering, forbearing one another in love; endeavoring to keep the unity of the Spirit in the bond of peace." And, "Let this mind be in you, which was also in Christ Jesus. Who made Himself of no reputation, and took upon Him the form of a servant, and was made in the likeness of men." He said, "My meet is to do the will of Him that sent me, and to promote His work."

This, dear reader, is the fruit of the Spirit of God as exhibited to men in the lives lived by these His servants and Son while among men on earth. And in whom that selfsame spirit works to will, and to do the same things, is an evidence that the soul is *bound* to God, and is in *union* and *connection* with Him, and has religion secured, "and how obtained." Having already referred to the truth, that "All things are of God, who hath reconciled us to Himself by Jesus Christ, and hath given to us the ministry or word of reconciliation in the Gospel, which is the power of God unto salvation, it is revealed how to obtain it, and is so *plain, simple*, and easy to be understood, that looking to it none can err therein. "But there were false prophets also among the people, even as there shall be false teachers among you, who privily shall bring in damnable heresies, even denying the Lord that bought them, and bringing upon themselves swift destruction. And many shall follow their pernicious ways, by reason of whom the way of truth shall be evil spoken of, and through covetousness shall they with feigned words make merchandise of you, whose judgment now of a long time lingereth not, and their damnation slumbereth not."—2 Peter, 2 1-3.

These merchandisers and perverters of truth have come upon us, and have so mystified the truth that it is needful that one teach them which be the first principles in the oracles, or word of God. Man must be born again saith Jesus. And to be born again he must repent from dead works, which is to repent from sin, for to sin is to die. The wages of sin is death. Repenting from sin, is to reform, and to abstain from sin; and with sorrow and contrition of heart, confess it to God. Ceasing to do evil, and learning to do well: and the wicked to forsake his way, and the unrighteous his thoughts, is repenting from dead works.

2. Faith in God, which consists not in a mere belief in Him as the Creator of all things, but also that He was in Christ by whom the world may be reconciled to Him; which embraces faith in the resurrection from the dead, and of eternal judgment.

3. Such are to be baptized, immersed, into water in the name of the Father, and of the Son, and of the Holy Ghost; which is for salvation, and for the answer of a good conscience toward God by the resurrection of Jesus Christ from the dead, (Mark 16: 16,) (1 Peter, 3: 21,) and for the remission of sins, and the gift of the Holy Ghost. (Acts 2: 37-39).

This is the New Testament Scripture way of obtaining the religion which *binds* the soul to God, and brings it in union and connection with Him. But men have sought out many inventions; these however, are cisterns that hold no water, and as walls plastered with untempered mortar.

Third. "*If not obtainable, how is it practiced?*" I do not understand this proposition; it negatives the whole subject, for if religion is not obtainable, there can be no religious practice. Hence I conclude the language does not express the writer's meaning, and if so it evidences that even editors who criticise the language of others are themselves subject to error. I assume the liberty to change the phraseology to read, And if obtainable, "how is it practiced." (We shaped our proposition thus because many of our brethren object to the term "getting religion" and think it to be a thing to be practiced rather than obtained.—Ed.)

The declaration of the Son of God that man must be born again, and the testimony of the apostle that some in his day were born again, and had purified their souls, is evidence sufficient that religion is obtainable. But if obtainable, how is it practiced. We have seen that to obtain religion man must believe, repent, and be baptized for the remission of sins, and he shall receive the Holy Ghost; and Jesus says, He shall lead him into all truth, and bring to his remembrance all things He had commanded them. Now the fruit of the Spirit is love, joy, peace, long-suffering, gentleness, goodness, faith, meekness, temperance; against *these* there is no law."

These being the *fruits* of the Spirit, wherever that Spirit bears witness with our spirit, the same fruits will be produced. But as no man can serve two masters, the children of God must not be unequally yoked together with unbelievers, but must come out from among them, and be separate from them in all their religious exercises; must have no part with them in any of their amusements, such as pic nics and religious festivals of whatever name they may be; they must take no part with them in their fairs and gambling associations, whether they be church or county fairs; they all originate from the same source, and the Savior, long ago, drove these fathers out of the temple as a set of thieves and robbers. The child of God must not touch any of these unclean things; he must not be conformed to the world in any such like things, but must be transformed from them, having had his mind renewed by the Spirit, in his repentance, faith and baptism; he must prove to the world what is the good, acceptable, and perfect will of God; which is ever your sanctification." But to be holy, Christians must forsake all unholiness. If they have any lawful business matter pertaining to this life to transact with unbelievers, they must transact with dispatch, and according to truth and righteousness that the Christian light may so shine that the good works may be seen by all. If the Spirit bears witness with our spirit that we are the children of God; we must not pattern after the unholy, and unbelieving in any of their sinful practices, their style, and change in fashion; they must not be like them in any of their sinful habits. But they must let the light of their profession be seen in their lives wherever they are or go. Children of God must be, and are, a praying people, they must pray much in secret, they must pray when they retire to bed at night, and when they rise from it in the morning. They must eat their daily food with thanksgiving and with prayer, in such a way that all that are at the table may see it, hear it, and know it; and if they be heads of families they must have stated times for family prayer. In short, brethren must pray everywhere, lifting up holy hands, without wrath and doubting. In like manner also that women adorn themselves in modest apparel, with shame-facedness and sobriety; not with braided hair, or gold, or pearls, or costly array; but which becometh women professing godliness with good works." But let her be sure that she be decently *covered because of the angels.* But as Christians do not use their Meetinghouse for a dwelling, nor a barn; even so let not the sisters use for a religious cover when in the house, the covering made and used for service, and protection, and shelter from sun and storm; but a decent cover made for the express purpose, so when she comes in the dwelling, or the house of worship, and lays aside her *weather shelter cover* (as her usual manner when coming into our houses is) and she will not be uncovered in time of prayer to dishonor her head and grieve the angels.

D. P. SAYLER.

EVIDENCE OR EFFECT OF REGENERATION.

Regeneration infuses a new life, that is, a spiritual life into the soul, whereby it is enabled to perform spiritual action to live a life devoted to God. By the willing reception of God's Word, he will be a partaker of His Divine nature, hence that creature delights in the law of God after the inward man. Whatever God demands of him in His Word, that he will do with pleasure. That God-like principle, love, is so deeply implanted into his soul that nothing will be a burden or too heavy a task for him to do if God requires it of him, even to the losing of his own life for *Jesus' sake.* Love to God and love to man are the distinguished characteristics of a truly regenerated man. He that loveth not knoweth not God, for God is love. It is impossible to be born of God and not know Him, and to love Him in the sense the Scripture teaches without knowing Him is equally so, and the evidence of loving Him is *keeping His commandments.* "For this is the love of God that we keep His commandments, and His commandments are not grievous." Likewise the wisdom of knowing Him is keeping His commandments, "He that saith I know Him, and keepeth not His commandments, *is a liar*, and the truth is not in him." This connects knowledge and love together as the assurance of being born of Him and the keeping of His commandments, the consequent effect of both. Hence for a man to say he knoweth and loveth God, and doubts the essentials of any command of God enjoined upon man to be observed, is a double evidence of an illegal birth; being born of blood, or of the will of the flesh, or the will of man. Again, do we allege by the Word of God, that it is vain for a man to claim regeneration without loving his brother; "for every one that loveth him that begat, loveth him also that is begotten of him." "If a man say, I love God and hateth his brother, *he is a liar*, for he that loveth not his brother whom he hath seen, how can he love God whom he hath not seen?" If a man loves his brother, he will not suffer him to be in want, if he does, it shows a want of loving God. "But whoso hath this world's goods and seeth his brother have need, and shutteth up his bowels of compassion from him, how dwelleth the love of God in him?" Brethren, "let us not love in word, neither in tongue, but in deed and in truth." If a man be truly born of God, that compassionate principle that is in God must pervade his soul entire to bring forth continued actions of benevolence towards his fellow-men, no difference whether he be a friend to him or an enemy; whether he has done good to him or evil. Love your enemies, do good to them that hate you, are as positive commands as any in the Word of God by which he is born. God, through the death of His Son, reconciled us to Himself while we were enemies to Him. O love divine, how great to behold! Astonishing! Truly becoming an Almighty Being, whose will is that none should perish but that all should come to Him through repentance and live forever. Can it be possible for any that are born of God to see a lost and a ruined world, although their enemies, suffering and famishing for the want of the Bread of Life more extensively distributed among them when they have the means so abundantly at command.

Brethren and sisters, let us make a stronger effort to evangelize the world, especially our immediate country and fatherland, lest unbelievers may have sufficient reasons to doubt our regeneration. Abstinence from sin is also an evidence, for "whatever is born of God doth not commit sin, for his seed remaineth in him, and he cannot sin because he is born of God." God's seed, which is His Word, being the origin of the change in man which formed him a new creature, remains in him, a power of God conferred upon man that he, on his part, is able to maintain; that he cannot sin willingly or presumptuously is the meaning of the apostle, "For as many as received Him, to them gave He power to become the *sons of God*, even to them that believe on His name." This is the internal witness of them that are born of God and that he hath passed from death unto life. "We know that we have passed from death unto life because we love the Brethren." Love unfeigned, and that one that is the fulfilling of the *whole law* is the legitimate fruits of regeneration; a holy principle wrought of God into the heart, the inward part of man, but externally manifested to the world by deeds of love, benevolence, meekness, self-denial, goodness, temperance, patience, Christian forbearance and courtesy, peace, holiness, godliness, hope and faith which endues him to openly confess to the world by action that he believes the whole Word of God by observing the cardinal ordinances, baptism, Feet-washing, the Lord's Supper, the Communion, the salutation of the kiss and the anointing of the sick as instituted by the Great Head of the Church. Such are the evidences and effects of regeneration. More Anon.

LEONARD FURRY.

LOVE ONE ANOTHER.

It is easy to love our friends. We can do this without the love of God. It requires no effort. But when we have the love of God shed abroad in our heart, we love our enemies, and do good to those that hate us; and pray for those who despitefully use us.

That person is to be pitied who dares to profess religion, but does not love his enemies. "If thine enemy hunger, feed him; if he thirst, give him drink." Let us look at our Great Exampler.—Christ died for the ungodly. This includes His enemies. Love led our Savior unto the garden of Gethsemane, where he sweat great drops of blood! "His soul was exceedingly sorrowful, even unto death!" Saying unto His disciples, "Tarry ye here, and watch with me."

He went a little farther, fell on his face, and prayed, saying: "O, my Father, if it be possible, let this cup pass from me;" and instantly exclaimed: "nevertheless not my will but thine be done." As He returned to His disciples He found them asleep. He went away the second time and prayed; repeated the same petition, and enduring incomprehensible agony! As He returned again, he found them asleep. Did He reprove them for having so little sympathy for Him? Did He accuse them of being only partially saved and possessed with sleepy devils? No, no. To one who had declared, he would die with Him before He would deny Him, Jesus said: "What! could ye not watch with me one hour?" but added the apology; "The Spirit indeed is willing, but the flesh is weak." Jesus left them and went away the third time and prayed. As He returned He found them asleep! But there are no reproaches for their want of sympathy. He said unto them, "Sleep on now, and take your rest."

The Son of man was betrayed into the hands of sinners, and nailed to the cross. Even then He thinks of the dying thief, who cries; "Remember me," and answers, "This day shalt thou be with me in Paradise." Nor does He forget His cruel murderers, but pleads, "Father, forgive them, for they know not what they do." There was no spirit of revenge there.

God is represented in the Holy Scriptures as being love. "God is love; and He that dwelleth in love dwelleth in God; and God in him." While we are commanded to love our enemies we ought also to love one another. If one of God's little ones, a brother or a sister, has got into darkness and temptation, it should be our first business to pray with and for him, and with one united faith, hold on to God, until the power of the enemy is broken. "The Kingdom of heaven suffereth violence, and the violent take it by force."

How is it with you? If men hate you, and persecute you, and say all manner of evil against you, can you rejoice in that day? Can you forgive them, love and pray for them? If not let me say to you hasten to your closet, and there plead with God, for more of the Spirit of Jesus, until you feel a burning love for their immortal souls.

Although you may feel as many times as did David, when he complained of his slanderous enemies, that, "The mouth of the wicked and the mouth of the deceitful are opened against me: they have spoken against me with a lying tongue. They compass me about also with words of hatred, and fought against me without a cause."

Then give yourself unto prayer. Let the inconsistency of others lead you to search well your own hearts. Be very careful what you say with *reference to them*. Command your tongue to be silent. It is not your work to sit in judgment. O there are wonderful mysteries in this great salvation. No wonder angels desired to look into it.

While it is the consolation of the Christian that God knows his heart, should it not be the terror of the hypocrite that his false dealing is seen by the eye of Jehovah?

The Spirit of God searcheth all things. If you have any hatred towards any one, you cannot hide it from God. His all-searching eye will behold it, and in reality you are none of His.

"If a man say I love God, and hate his brother, he is a liar, for he that loveth not his brother whom he hath seen, how can he love God whom he hath not seen?" This is impossible. For unless we love one another, God will not dwell in our hearts, neither is His love perfect in us. But there are various ways in which we may manifest our love to the children of men. We may speak kindly to the erring. We may feed the hungry and clothe the naked.

"Whoso hath this world's goods, and seeth his brother have need, and shutteth up his bowels of compassion from him, how dwelleth the love of God in him?"

O, think of the love God has manifested toward us. When there was no eye to pity, he gave His Son to suffer and die for us.—*Earnest Christian.*

SABBATH EVENING.

Sabbath Eve., the day is closing, another Sabbath, sweet day of rest is about over, and soon will be numbered with the things of the past. Thus one Sabbath after another is ushered in and passes away, until ere long, we shall enjoy their sacred influence no longer,—our Sabbath's in this world will be passed. But have we spent this day, this sacred day of rest to our own benefit and to the honor and glory of God? This is a question of momentous importance to us. Can we, in this evening hour, review the day that has so rapidly passed by, and say, we have spent its sacred hours laboring in the service of Jesus,—working for the advancement of His cause, and the upbuilding of the Redeemer's Kingdom? If so, we can rest with the sweet consciousness of having done our duty, and the approving smile of God resting upon us. But if we have spent this Sabbath, the day which our Savior set apart as a day of rest, and commanded His followers in clear, concise language to "remember and keep holy," unprofitably, not appreciating its hallowed influence, surely we will have come far short of performing our duty, and have incurred the displeasure of God. It is a season of rest, a day when we should lay aside the cares and vexations of life, and spend it in laboring for the interests of the immortal soul.

W. A. C.

LOOK TO JESUS.

Look to Jesus to be made like him. He is the model of a Christian. "His nature and his name is love." He is meek, loving, pure and good. It is not the will of God that you be like some one else, but it is his will that you be like Jesus. "Let this mind be in you which was in Christ Jesus." It is not essential either to your salvation or usefulness that the capacity and gifts of another be yours, but that you have the mind of Christ.

Look to Jesus in the day of temptation and trial. you have left the service of satan. He hates you for it. He will do all he can to overthrow you. His stratagems are cunningly devised. He is the "accuser of the brethren." when the waves of discouragement roll around you, he will say, "where now is is your God?" But look to Jesus He has overcome the devil. He will give you power over him. Is the day of trial upon you? Do storms of sorrow fall?—Look to Jesus "He is the fulness of the Godhead bodily." He is mighty to save. His eye is on you. You have a friend "who sticketh closer than a brother. Trust in and obey him and all will be well. Look to Jesus.—*M. N. Downing.*

Selected by W. S. JONES.

MOSES RESISTING TEMPTATION.

'And the daughter of Pharaoh came down to wash herself at the river; and her maidens walked along by the river's side, and when she saw the ark among the flags, she sent her maid to fetch it. And when she had opened it, she saw the child; and behold the babe wept.—Exodus 2: 5, 6. By faith, Moses, when he was come to years, refused to be called the son of Pharaoh's daughter; chosing rather to suffer affliction with the people of God, than to enjoy the pleasures of sin for a season.—Heb. 11: 24, 25.'

A princess and her maidens gay
Were bathing in the Nile one day;
Just where the little flags met the tide,
A willowy basket they descried
That little ark a mother's love
Of twisted osiers neatly wove;
And many a prayer and pious thought
She breathed while at her task she wrought.

Without, within, 'twas lined and sealed,
The mother's priceless gem to shield
From sun and wind and rushing wave,
And from Nile's greedy god† to save.
The princess from the river drew
The ark—aside the covering threw;
Behold a Hebrew babe appears,
A loving babe, bedewed with tears.

Compassion touched the lady's breast;
She hushed his infant fears to rest,
Called him her son, gave him a name,
And Egypt's heir the boy became.
Son of a princess!—on the child
A court with all its splendor smiled—
A court corrupt—a king and throne
Sustained by gods of wood and stone.

From Israel's faith to Egypt's sin,
These idols sure the child will win!
Example will his youth betray,
To walk in pleasure's dangerous way.
Mark with what ease, what skill divine
High heaven works out its fixed design:
A faithful nurse the princess sought—
Quick was the child's own mother brought.

From her he learned in youth's first spring,
The wonders wrought by Israel's king,
Learned to deplore his brethren's woes,
And scorn the horrors of their foes.
With purpose firm, in man-hood's prime
He left the gilded halls of crime,
Power, wealth, and honors all laid down,
Nor stopped to catch the falling crown.

On Horeb's mount, in Jethro's tent,
Long years of peaceful toil he spent;
Hallowing the throng of daily cares
With holy thoughts and heavenly prayers.
A Shepherd's staff and seat of stone
Outweighed the scepter and the throne
With conscience pure, and soul serene,
No roof is low, no station mean.

Behold a pattern, bright and high,
To fire the youthful Christian's eye;
Go, mark it well; then ask within,
Have I this holy dread of sin?
No golden bribes, no courtly pride
Could lure this heavenly youth aside;
From scenes of guilty pomp he fled,
In peace the lonely hills to tread.

"How in his place should I have done?
As Pharoah's or as Jethro's son?
Embraced temptation's gilded bait,
Or shared the exile's bitter fate?
'E'en now I hear the still small voice
That whispers, Make the Lord your choice:
E'en now the God that Moses saw,
Strives from the world my heart to draw.

"Oh Thou whose grace when asked is given
To lift the soul from earth to heaven.
Lead me where living waters flow,
And let me with thy lilies grow."

†The ancient Egyptians worshipped the crocodile as a living god.

THE blossom can not tell what becomes of its odor, and no man can tell what becomes of his influence and example, that roll away from him and go beyond his ken on their mission.

RIGHT AND REPUTATION.

Most men possessed of any character or influence, have sometimes to choose between right and reputation.—Two courses are open before them. To go in one of them will be to gain position, win respect, and acquire influence. To go in the other will be to sacrifice friends, forsake honor, and imperil worldly prospects. And at the parting of these ways, some stand hesitating until the hour of decision is past, while others promptly choose their course, whether for evil or good. An honorable reputation is a precious treasure. A good name is better than great riches. It is the result of long and faithful labor, the fruit of a lifetime's work. It wins attention and respect, and gives to its possessor influence and position. As a means of good it becomes a sacred trust, to be guarded with unceasing vigilance.—But it is an uncertain possession and may pass away like a dream. A single indiscreet word or act may sully or ruin a reputation that has been built up through many years; and no man has a right thus to waste his reputation, or from mere willfulness and wantonness imperil his good name. No man can afford to defy public opinion when public opinion is right; no man can afford to defy it unless it is clearly wrong. No man has a right to do as he pleases, regardless of the commonsense judgment of mankind. Men are to respect the feelings and wishes of others, and every man is bound to please his neighbor, for his good and his edification. When we say what we like, others will answer with something we do not like. If we move according to the law of selfishness and willfulness, others will do likewise, and that to our disadvantage.

There is, however, for the Christian, a higher law than the law of expediency; a loftier principle than the care of personal repute. High above the standards of public opinion and public propriety, rises the Christian's banner, on which is blazoned, "Holiness unto the Lord." Conscience is more stringent in her rules than society; and, in following the word of God, the Christian will keep his *inner* life more pure and spotless than the world will ask that his outward conduct shall be. He walks before God, and the consciousness that his fellowship is with the Heavenly Father, gives to his whole existence an elevation which the world can never comprehend. The world's rebuke to such a man is for his fidelity rather than for his sin. They ask him to come down to their level, and to agree with their lower standard of propriety and morality. And failing in their efforts to degrade him from his high estate, they, like Potiphar's wife, accuse him of the very crimes they had vainly tried to induce him to commit.

It is then that the Christian must choose betwen right and reputation.—He cannot satisfy the world's demands. No matter what concessions he makes, its exactions increase from day to day. Each compliance is the basis of a new demand, and Satan is satisfied with nothing less than the whole. Somewhere this compliance must stop, and when it stops, reputation must suffer, and hurricanes of abuse and reproach may be expected. And the best place, the surest, and the easiest place to stop the whole, is at the beginning.

A Christian man can well defy public opinion in a righteous cause; he can brave public scorn, if he is sustained by a conscience void of offence towards God and man. Character is more than reputation, and what a man *is*, is of more importance than what he is said to be.

He who has given himself to the Lord, has not held back his reputation. Though he would not willingly do anything that should bring reproach upon his fair name, yet when the great batteries of hell are opened upon the hosts of Emanuel, he expects to smell powder, and to be blackened with the smoke and grime of war. And between Right and Reputation it does not take him long to choose. He has a character written on high of which man can never rob him; he is but a pilgrim here; his life and his honors take hold upon the ages of eternity, and what cares he for the plaudits of a single hour; or of the reproaches that rise like a windy tempest, and die away like the murmur of a passing gale.

Man's judgment is a light thing, and a man's day is very brief. And a world like this, the Christian has but little honor to expect. The only faultless being that ever trod this earth, "made himself of no reputation," was hated without a cause and hung between two thieves. And he marks out for his followers a path of shame and sorrow, of cross bearing and tribulation. And the man who follows Christ has no time to turn back and see what the devil has to say about it. Let him keep on his way, careful of God's honor, and careless of men's reproach, earnest to do right, but indifferent to the clamor of those who impugn his motives, or condemn his acts.

"The Day" will reveal all things. High among the thousand conquerors who shall shine in the light of God in the great Hereafter, will be men of no reputation, who were unhonored and unsung at home, and whose acquaintances were hardly willing to acknowledge that they knew them. But their reward is sure. The book of God's remembrance records acts that never were printed, published, praised, nor acknowledged. The book of life holds names that have been expunged from sectarian church-rolls, yes, that have figured in court writs and jail commitments, in prison records and in death warrants!

"A little while!" ah, how this brief hour will change all questions of reputation, and exalt the followers of right. How hypocrisy shall shrink, and self-exaltation dwindle, before the glance of Him whose eyes are as a flame of fire. A few brief days will tell the story, and we shall see as we are seen, and know as we are known. Let us cling then to the right, no matter how reputation may suffer; and let us "judge nothing before the time, till the Lord come, who shall both bring to light the hidden things of darkness, and manifest the counsels of the hearts."—*The Christian.*

LITTLE BY LITTLE.

They who are willing to serve God by doing little things well, may serve Him always and everywhere; but they who stand waiting for some great thing to do, will probably never find the occasion they seek, and therefore will never serve Him at all. They also overlook a plain Bible truth, namely, that to be faithful in little things is often the best way to our being allowed the use of great things. Those who use one talent well, will often find that God increases the well-used talent.—If we would be strong to any service to which God may call us, let us not overlook the means which He generally uses in giving strength. The grace of to day will not do for to-morrow. The petition which our Lord has put into our lips is this: "Give us day by day our daily bred"; or as it is in the margin, "Give us for the day our daily bread."

Little masteries achieved,
Little wants with care relieved,
Little words with care expressed,
Little wrongs at once confessed,
Little graces meekly worn,
Little slights with patience borne;
These are treasures that shall rise
Far beyond the smiling skies.

—*Church Paper.*

GENERAL INTELLIGENCE.

The Coventry congregation, in the vicinity of Pottstown Pa., have had 20 accessions of members since the 2nd of March.

—A Kansas pastor declined an addition of a hundred dollars to his salary for this reason, among others, that the hardest part of his labor heretofore had been the collection of his salary, and it would kill him to try to collect a hundred dollars more.

THE GREAT GRAPHIC BALLOON is now on exhibition at New York and if no interference comes in the way, is expected to start for Europe on the 10th inst. By our next issue we expect to inform you of the result of one of the most daring undertakings of the present age. It is hoped that the project will be a success.

ELD. J. R. HANAWALT, of McVeytown Pa. informs us that he has just been raised from a bed of sickness. He is well pleased with the idea of reporting the proceedings of A. M. but does not see the propriety of withholding the names of the speakers, thinks that none should be afraid of their arguments if worth anything, and is not in favor of muzzling the press especially when the editors labor to defend the truth.—Yea, verily, Ed.

THE *Herald of Truth* for September is largely filled with matters pertaining to Mennonite emigration from Russia. From it we learn that the Russian brethren are leaving their native land under very great difficulties. The government seems slow to let them go and are throwing in their way every possible difficulty. Officials defer giving them their passes and in some cases they have been compelled to pay as high as eighty dollars in fees to procure them, and after Jan. 1st. 1874 no young man between 20 and 27 years of age will be allowed to go.

BROTHER W. S. JONES of Amsterdam, Va. says: "Cholera is prevailing at Bottetourt Springs. On Aug. 30 four were buried and since then I have learned that seven deaths have occurred there of cholera since yesterday the 30th. There were also some deaths at Biglick and Gishes Mills on the Va. & Tenn. R. R. It was never known among the mountains of Va. before. A man and his family moved from this place to Jonesborro, Tenn. A short time ago he died, when his widow and two children returned on the same line of road, to Gishes Mills, where they all took the cholera and died.

EXTENSIVE ART GALLERY.—Next to the Bible no book is more useful than Webster's Dictionary. The Unabridged is an extensive art-gallery, containing over three thousand engravings, representing almost every animal, insect, reptile, implement, plants, &c, which we know anything about. It is a vast library giving information on almost every mentionable subject. It indeed has been well remarked that it is the most remarkable *compendium of human knowledge* in our language.—*Household Advocate.*

OFF TO LIBERIA.—Rev T. S. Malcom, of Philadelphia, publishes a statement to the effect that preparations are in progress for another expedition to Liberia. Out of more than three thousand applications for passage, a careful selection will be made. The number sent must depend upon the means furnished. Among the worthy freedmen who wish to aid in building up a Christain Republic in Africa there are not less than one thousand in Georgia. One of these is an elder in the Presbyterian church, and another a Baptist preacher. Many of thier friends wish to accompany them. Such men are peculiarly needed in Africa. Firmly planted in Africa, the work will not only be self sustaining, but missionaries will be sent to regions beyond. We ask help from all friends of the freedmen and of Africa. Fifty dollars will pay the passage of an emigrant, and the same sum will secure six months support while clearing land, building houses, and planting a crop.

—There is some alarm breaking out over the prospect of an inundation of Chinese to this country, swamping Christian civilization with the surplus of China's 350,000 heathen people. As a general thing the Christain press entertain little fears of the issue between Christianity and paganism and no doubt their confidence is safe. The fear of getting the "hords" of Asia within point-blank range of missionary effort ought to be the last thing for Christians to entertain. That the tales of their vicious propensities and brutish practices are largely the invention of those who prey upon them is evident enough from the fact that convictious for criminal offenses are less in proportion among them, in courts where every influence is against them than among the "native" population of the Pacific slope. As for their heathen superstitions, the idea that they can prevail in the very stronghold of Protestant Christianity is little complimentary to the latter; and at most, the injury to the Christian world would perhaps not be greater than the enforcement by "Christain" nations of the opium traffic on these same heathens.

The following from *Harpers Weekly* shows very clearly that Romanism is not decaying, notwithstanding the reverses it has had in Europe: But it is not the spiritual but the political power of Rome that is now disturbing the tranquility of Europe and of America. Of the two factions into which the Papal Church has been divided since the Council of Trent, the more liberal has been suppressed. The Jesuits who drove their plowshares over Port Royal and crushed the intelligence of Naples and Florence, rule over the Romish Church. Shorn and maimed, it is still endowed with a terrible energy. It is united pitiless and desperate. By a sudden stratagem it has seized upon the government of France, and laughs at the rage of the people. Its priests have filled Spain, just rising to a better life, with bloodshed and civil disorder. It threatens rebellion and ruin in Germany. It plots the desolation of Italy. In Ireland it has become the center of political strife; and feeble as are its apparent resources, its unity and its vigor, its merciless and destructive policy give to its politicians of the Vatican an extraordinary influence in the affairs of both hemispheres. Yet the press and the public schools are its enemies. The press detects its strategy; the public school lays the foundations of purer morals and a purer faith. The one firmly requires the exclusion of religion from politics, the other makes good citizens even of the least cultivated class of Romanists. To silence or to bribe the press, to close the public schools is the aim of Romanism in Europe and America.

Youth's Department.

SELECTED BY HANNAH HOLLOWBUSH.

THE WAY OF HOLINESS.

O let me seek that path
Where winds of woe,
And storms of sin and wrath,
Can never blow!

The star of heavenly hope
Has ever beamed
Along the way cast up
For the redeemed.

It is a blissful way,
Safe and secure;
Leading to realms of day,
A pathway sure.

All other paths we tread
Through this dark clime,
Must be with fears o'erspread,
With cares of time.

But O! this holy way
The vulture's eye,
And hideous beasts of prey,
Shall ne'er descry!

Then let me seek the path
Where winds of woe,
And bitter storms of wrath,
Can never blow.

MY FATHER'S BUSINESS.

When Jesus was twelve years of age he was taken up to Jerusalem with His parents, as the custom then was, but instead of returning with them He remained behind, conversing with the doctors and lawyers. When He was missed there was a great stir about Him, and after several days He was found. When asked to give an account for His strange conduct, His only answer was, "Know ye not that I must be about My Father's business?" He was not concerned about the other little boys that must have been in so large a company, but He had a work to do and the time had come that it should be commenced. That work was to attend to His Father's business.

Now every little boy and girl has a work to do and that work is to attend to father's and mother's business, or in other words, to obey and try to please them. You perhaps have never thought that all their labor and concern is for your good and comfort, and were it not for their continual care for you, soon you would come to want and be driven about among strangers without a home or anybody to provide food and clothing for you. When you were young and could not care for yourselves, your parents watched over you and spared no pains or labor to make you happy. Now you have grown up and are able to do many little turns for them and thus lighten their labor. This should be your chief delight and should be your greatest joy to be about your fathers' business. You owe this to them first, because of what they done for you, and second, because all they have is expected to be yours if you be good and dutiful children. Your father's business is your business, and the better you attend to it the better it will be for you.

There is nothing that looks so well and speaks so well for children, as to see them kind and respectful to parents. It is a crown of honor and will receive its reward. When I go to your father's house and find you busy in attending to your father's business, I say to myself, that boy will make a good man or that girl will make a useful woman, and do you think I will be mistaken? Not a bit of it. Just as sure as good little trees grow up and make good big trees, so sure will good little boys and girls make good men and women, if you only keep on being and doing good. You see it is attending to father's business and the better that is attended to the more it will prosper and grow. When you do this you should not think you are doing it for father alone, but you are only helping him to gather that which is intended for you. Then, when bad boys and girls try to tempt you and take you away from your work to go into mischief or idleness, tell them that you *cannot* go, that you must attend to your father's business.

UNCLE HENRY.

A LETTER.

Dear young readers of the PILGRIM, I have thought of writing you a letter for some time, as it appears to me that your department is partially neglected. Uncle Henry has been writing you some very good and interesting letters, and I hope you will all read them with interest. I was much pleased with his last letter in which he told you how to enter the fold. Will you not all try to enter the fold? This you can easily do by believing in Jesus, and doing what He says. Now you may not all understand what is meant by believing in Jesus, and I will try to illustrate it to you.

Not long ago I heard a boy say that Harry Boyd was the best boy in the country, and when Harry says a thing, you may be sure he will do it, and he will stand by you through thick and thin. He'll never desert his friends, no difference how much it may be to his disadvantage to do them a favor. Everybody believes in Harry. Now this boy by praising Harry, was unconsciously dwelling on the very traits of our lovely Jesus. He always stood by His friends, and never failed in any of His promises, and therefore everybody ought to believe in Him. If you do not know what believing in Jesus means, just apply to Him what the boy has been saying of his friend, only remember that all this is true of Jesus in a higher sense than it can be of any boy, no difference how good and true he may be.

Jesus is our best friend; He has done more for us than any earthly friend can or will do. And he has promised to stand by us at all times, if we will be good and put our trust in Him.

If you understood what believing in Harry means, you can certainly understand what believing in Jesus means. You trust in Harry; you believe what he says he will do, and just so you will do when you believe in Jesus. You will trust in Him, and believe what He says. This is believing in Jesus, and is just as easy to understand as that you believe in Harry Boyd.

Now as you have been pointed to this lovely Jesus, and also how you may enter into the fold, and be under His kind care and protection, I hope none of our little readers will be so thoughtless as to remain outside. If you do, you are subject to very many dangers, and if you have as much faith in Jesus as you have in Harry you will enter at once. Come then to Jesus, believe what He says, and He will be your best friend—a friend that will stand by you in sickness, in health, life or death, in time and eternity.

A FRIEND OF THE LITTLE FOLKS.

THE BREWER'S DOG.

A gentleman taking an evening walk along the road near Grantown, saw two men supporting a third, who appeared unable to walk. "What is the matter," he inquired, "Why," was the reply, "that poor man has been sadly bitten by the brewer's dog." "Indeed," said I, feeling rather concerned at the disaster. "Yes, sir, and he is not the first by a good many that he has done a mischief to." "Why is that dog not made away with?" "Ah, sir, he ought to have been made away with long ago, but it wants resolution to do it. It is the *strong drink*, sir, *that's* the BREWER'S DOG."

Beware of the dog.

HOPE is a prodigal young heir, and experience is his banker; but his drafts are seldom honored, since there is often a heavy balance against him, because he draws largely on a small capital, and is not yet in possession, and if he were, would die.—*Fuller.*

The Weekly Pilgrim.

JAMES CREEK, PA., Sept. 16. 1873.

MINISTERIAL QUALIFICATIONS.

Continued from page 286.

There are two ways of learning the Scriptures. The one is by memorizing and the other is studying their spiritual import. The first should not be made a hobby at the risk of a sacrificing of the other, which is possible. It should ever be remembered that the letter killeth while the spirit maketh alive. To be able to quote correctly and readily is an important qualification and greatly to be desired, but even in this, there may be extremes to endanger the success of the minister. In memorizing, the power of the mind is wholy concentrated or fixed upon words and their order of connection, and while the mind is thus engaged it is not free to scope ideas. Tho'ts or ideas to be of practical utility, must be linked together as a chain, the same as memorized words. When a man exhausts all of his mind power in running a memorized chain, as soon as he gets to the end of that chain he is done unless he can strike another memorized chain, from the fact that his mind force is exhausted in being concentrated, not on ideas, but words, and has not time to form an orignal chain of thought. Thus is produced a memorized sermon or a sermon of quotations which, no matter how orthodox, falls upon the ear as a dead letter void of the spirit. This is especially so when memorizing is done with great difficulty. To such we would advise, not to labor to memorize at the risk of sacrificing the spiritual import and the power of free thought. If you cannot memorize words, take hold of the ideas they suggest, and of that material, form an original chain that will always be at your command, as your mind can thus be free, and you can make it as you go, it is spirit matter clothed in a natural garb and is conveyed to the mind of the hearer on purely psychological principles. When memorizing can be done readily and be retained so as to be reproduced without a labored effort, the memorized and original chain of thought may be so assimilated as to make a complete whole, in which case, it may reach the hearers with power and effect. But whether memorized or its spiritual import utilized, it is the ministers power and therefore, a full knowledge of it should be considered an important auxillary in successful preaching.

The old adage "Water cannot be drawn from an empty well" is especially applicable in the case of the minister. In order that there may be a ready flow the vessel must be kept full, not only full enough to cause a sickly flow, but there should be a sufficient reserve to form a pressure and the greater that pressure the more freely and with the greater power will flow forth the stream of living water. Our blessed Master is a complete example of this ever abounding fullness. The insects, the tiny plant, the trees, the rocks, hills and mountains, the rivulets, the flowing streams, the great waters and the heavens with all their studded glory was brought into requisition in order to enforce the truths of redemption and salvation. The knowledge that our great Exampler made use of in delivering the plan of salvation, may be embraced under the following general heads: philosophy, psychology, theology, zoology, geography and astronomy.

Some of our brethren may think that these are rather high sounding terms and that they know nothing about them, but this is a mistake as we venture the assertion, that we have not a brother in the ministry that has not a considerable knowledge of all these different branches of learning. Let us define. Philosophy: The science or knowledge of things as they exist and their causes. Psychology: The science or knowledge of the soul. Theology: A knowledge of God. Zoology: A study of the animal world, their classification &c. Geography: A description of the earths surface and Astronomy, a knowledge or description of the heavens. With all these, our Savior was aptly conversant and familiar, and this knowledge is within the reach of every brother that is called to the ministry and to refuse to obtain and make use of it, is to refuse to become fully efficient in this most high and responsible calling. Nature with its causes and effects is an open book written by the finger of God and was the text book of the greatest of all teachers, Jesus. When He wished to demonstrate the nature and growth of the Kingdom of God in the soul, He took up the parable of the mustard seed, the three measures of meal, and the treasure hid in the field. The preacher of the Gospel is beautifully represented in the sower going forth to sow. Regeneration, or the new birth, by the grain of corn planted in the earth, and the end of time by the fig tree casting forth its leaves, in fact, the whole plan of salvation was delivered and enforced through parables of things in nature as they then existed, hence, the necessity of becoming fully conversant with these things in order that we may not only fully understand their nature, causes and effects, but be able to make use of them in enforcing the truths of the Gospel.

In regard to a choice of books treating on the different sciences, we will not suggest as there are many works written by as many authors, and all are sufficiently good to obtain a very fair knowledge of the respective branches they profess to teach. When we are provided with a good knowledge of these things, then it is that we are instruments ready for the Master's use and all that is needed to make us efficient ministers of the Gospel is inspiration. Inspiration, we fear is but vaguely understood. Do not suppose that it is intended to supply the want of knowledge or that it is a creating power. The object of inspiration, is to enable us to make use of the knowledge which we have. That wisdom which cometh down from above, is that power which expands the memory and enables us to grasp that which we know (not that which we do not know) and present such part of it as may be necessary to bring about the desired effect. The day of miracles, is passed the means of knowledge is placed within our reach and it is our privilige to make use of them. We have now given our views of how the material or subject matter may be obtained in order to become efficient in the ministry. If our time will admit we may, in a future number, say something about the mode or manner of preaching in order that it may be made more effectual.

Correspondence.

A Reporter is wanted from every Church in the brotherhood to send us Church news, Obituaries, Announcements, or anything that will be of general interest. To insure insertion, the writers name must accompany each communication. Our Invitation is not personal but general—please respond to our call.

Dear Brother Brumbaugh: I take it for granted that you wish the opinions of the brethren on the different subjects now being discussed in the PILGRIM. I love the paper and the principles that it advocates, but am no scholar and therefore cannot express my ideas as I would wish to. I have been reading the different articles on Sunday Schools, and given the subject some attention, but thus far, I cannot find any thus saith the Lord for them. I fully agree with Bro. B. F. Moomaw's views in PILGRIM of June 10. I have no objections to improvement in the arts and sciences, but God forbid that we should ever undertake to improve or append to the Christian system as laid down by the great Lawgiver. Let those then who have a proper respect for God's perfect law, stand firmly upon it. Though it may seem to be in danger, it is perfectly safe and will not deceive. Like the uncomely rock that lifts its head in the midst of the ocean, covered with the accumulated moss of centuries and has withstood the surging billows of many a storm and still occupies its place, so will you be when you shall have withstood the waves of temptation and the current of popular ideas, and the allurements of modern date. Though the removal of the sands from around may give some disquietude and concern, all will be well, for God hath said, though the stars shall leave their orbits in confusion, the moon mourn in blood, the sun be blown out, the world be enveloped in flames and the heavens pass away, my word shall never fail, while, like the icebergs in the northern seas, though they mount up in columns in appearance like ships, turrets, temples and spires, overlaid with silver and gold as they change their positions to the rays of the sun dazzling to the eye, fascinating to the mind, yea, most magnificent to behold, but presently, when driven into more Southern climes, they lose all their splendor, the burning rays of the Sun falling upon them, down they go, turret after turret, spire after spire, and column after column until all is lost in the sea. So with modern improvements and false principles. Though they are very beautiful while changing their position to suit the age and taste, but when brought into contact with the scrutinizing judgment of Him who has said His word shall judge every man at the last day, then, oh then, what will become of those who have trusted in them? What says the powerful Word? "Depart from me ye workers of iniquity, I never knew you."

Sunday Schools are highly esteemed among men and by the popular religionists of the day, and if we are not careful they may become an abomination in the sight of the Lord. What I have written has not been done for the sake of controversy, but given simply as my views with due respect to those of others.

S. S. CRESSWELL.

Onburg, Pa.

Dear Pilgrim:—I thought I would write you a few lines to let you know something about how we have to labor in this part of the Lord's Vineyard to accomplish the great work.

I left my home August 14, in company with brother George Crouse. We rode 29 miles, reached the Dewford school-house, on the Blue Sulphur Mountain, at half past two o'clock, P. M., where we met with our beloved brethren and sisters. Had quite an interesting meeting, went home with Bro. Poppe, where we were kindly cared for. Next morning set out and rode 39 miles, reached my brother-in-law's, on Anthony Creek, Greenbrier county, where we had meeting Saturday evening, Sunday morning and Sunday evening. We met a large congregation of my old acquaintances. It was quite an interesting time; they seemed to receive the Word with joy. It was the first meeting ever held by the Brethren in that immediate neighborhood. On Monday morning set out and forded

Greenbriar River three times, rode 12 miles and reached friend Kiester's, whose father had been a member of the Brethren for many years, now deceased. He was formerly from Highland Co. Here we met with more of our acquaintances, had one meeting, then rode 5 miles, reached the Brush Church and had quite a good meeting there. Went home with friend Henning, spent the night and was kindly treated. Next morning rode 22 miles, reached my uncles, where we dined. They were very desirous for us to return and have meeting there. We started half past 3 o'clock, rode 16 miles and stayed all night with my cousin. Had meeting next morning at 10 o'clock on Laurel Creek Mountain. Then rode 5 miles, had meeting at the Richison school-house, home next day.

We think truly the Lord stood by us, and blessed our labors. There is a great cry in that section of country for the Gospel.

CHARLES H. MASTERS.

GARNETT, KAN.
Aug. 21, 1873.

Dear Pilgrim:—I now drop you a few lines agreeable to your wishes in regard to church news. We, the brethren and sisters of the Cedar Creek Church, held our Communion meeting on the 16th of August, commencing at 2 p. m., and continued next day until 5 p. m. We had a good meeting, and good order. The people say it was the largest congregation they ever saw in this neighborhood. We have reason to believe that the Lord was with us. Two souls were added to the Church by baptism, and we think that many more were seriously impressed with the necessity of regeneration and holiness of life. The following ministering brethren were with us: Isaac Hearshy, Neosho Falls, Woodson Co., Kan., Jacob Yoder, Nevada, Vernon Co., Mo., Bro. Barnhart of Franklin county, Kansas, and brethren Hoover and Numer of Bourbon Co., and others.

The brethren labored zealously for our every good, and we were much built up, for which we tender our grateful acknowledgements. We also held a choice for deacon. Bro. Jesse Studebaker was advanced to the Eldership, Peter Struble to the second degree in the ministry. John Miller and Christopher Rodabaugh for deacons.

The church has been organized one year, and there has been eight added by baptism, six by letter. We now number 32, and think there are prospects for more. Yours in love.

N. D. HADSELL.

Dear Pilgrim:—I will send you a few items of news for your columns. The Church here at Limestone has not been prospering much within the last twelve months. We received a few members by letter. Our annual church visit has been attended to and the members have expressed themselves to be in union and love, and to remain with the Church as long as it keeps house according to the Gospel.

Our Church meeting was held Aug. 23. Bro. Jos. Bowman of Knob Creek Church, was with us. At this meeting it was concluded by the Church, that the official force was too weak and accordingly took the voice of the members present to see if they were willing to call one to the ministry and one to serve in the office of deacon, and the result was favorable to the move, but as there was no elder present, the Church agreed to appoint another meeting on Saturday, Aug. 30. At this meeting Eld. F. W. Dove was present and brother James Hilbert was called to the ministry and one for deacon whom I shall not name.

The day previous to our first church meeting we had a harvest meeting. Bro. Jesse Crosswhite was with us and preached twice, also next day, evening, and on Sunday.

There has been considerable sickness here in Tennessee during the Summer. The cholera has been very fatal in places but is now abating. The fever and flux is also prevailing in some localities. In the fore part of the season we had plenty of rain, then dry weather until recently, we are having some refreshing showers. H. M. SHERRY.

Freedom, Tenn.

Editor of Pilgrim, According to promise, we will, by your permission, give a little report of some funds that some good liberal hearted brethren contributed to help us to liquidate a debt yet standing against us here in the Monticello Church, on our Meetinghouse, which we now have nearly all paid. The Church by being encouraged by these gifts, made another effort, so that we think that we can get through without much trouble, yet if any would still feel to favor us with a little aid it would be thankfully received—could be sent to the undersigned.

Received from Covington Church, Ohio, S. Mohler,	$ 55.00
Harris Church, Ohio, Henry Smith,	35.00
Yellow Creek Church, Pa., D. Snowberger,	8.50
David Cochenour,	1.50
Snakespring and Hopewell, by A. Snowberger,	6.50
George Clapper,	50
In all	$106.50

For the above, the church feels thankful, as members of the body of the faithful. We hope and pray that we may all be faithful to the end.

In behalf of the Church.

JOHN S. SNOWBERGER.

Monticello, White Co., Ind.

ANNOUNCEMENTS.

The members of Wadams Grove District, Stephenson Co., Ill., have agreed, the Lord willing, to have their Communion meeting on the 11th and 12th of October, commencing at 1 o'clock. Lena, on the Ill. Central Railroad, is the nearest station, two miles from place of meeting. A general invitation to all. By order of the Church. ENOCH EBY.

There will be a Communion meeting, God willing, in the Dry Creek Congregation, Linn Co., Iowa, on the 1st and 2d of November, '73. A cordial invitation is extended to all who wish to be with us, and especially to ministers. JACOB BOCK.

The Brethren of Root River Branch Minn., intend to hold their Lovefeast on the 4th and 5th of October. Those coming by Railroad, will stop off at Lima Springs where they will find conveyance to place of meeting. Brethren from the East coming West are invited to be with us, especially ministering brethren.

There will be a Lovefeast in the middle fork of Wildcat Congregation on the 29th of October, and also the District Meeting of Southern District of Indiana on the 30th and 31st of October. Brethren coming from the North and North east will stop off at Moran, on the Croffertsville R. R. on the 28th of said month. There will be conveyance at Lafayette on the 28th and none after that time. Brethren will be at the Love house on main street. By order of the Church.

ALLEN MOHLER.

Please announce a Communion meeting to be held in Union Center Church, Elkhart Co., Ind., on October 1st, '73. Those coming by Railroad will stop at New Paris.

JOHN ANGLEMYER.

Our Communion Meeting, Aughwick Congregation, will be held on the 7th and 8th of October, commencing at 1 o'clock on the 7th. Trains on the East Broad Top R. R. leaves Mt. Union, at 11:50 a. m., and 5:50 p. m. Stops at Aughwick Mills and Shirleysburg—the latter place is preferable. All are invited to attend.

J. G. GLOCK.

Please announce that, the Lord willing, there will be a Lovefeast in the Monticello Church, White Co., Ind., in the Meeting-house on Pike Creek, 3 miles North-east of Monticello on the 10th of October, commencing at 10 o'clock a. m. Also meeting next day. J. S. SNOWBERGER.

Hamilton Congregation; Caldwell Co Mo., October 4th and 5th.

North Coventry Congregation, near Pottstown, Pa., October 4th and 5th.

Nemishillen Congregation, Stark Co., Ohio, Sept. 27.

Spring Run, Mifflin Co., Pa. on the 5th of October.

(Dry Valley Meeting-house, *Mifflin* Co. Pa., October 3 and 4.

Falling Spring Congregation, Franklin Co., on the 10th of October.

Crooked Creek Church, Johnson Co., Iowa, Sept. 20 21.

Beaver Run, Mineral Co, W. Va., on the 11th and 12th of October.

Limestone Congregation, Wash. Co., Tenn. on the 4th Saturday of September.

James Creek Pa., on the 10 and 11th of October.

Grasshopper Valley Church, Jefferson Co., Kan., Meetinghouse in the town Osawkee, Oct. 4 and 5.

Dunnings Creek Congregation, Pa. on Friday, Oct. 3.

Stone Church, Marshall Co, Iowa, on the 4th and 5th of Oct.

Our Lovefeasts of Maryland, will be held as follows:

Sam's Creek, Oct. 11, commence 1½ p. m.
Monocacy, " 17.
Meadow Branch, " 21, com. 1½ p. m.
Beaver Dam, " 25.

In the Cold Water church, in the new stone meeting house, on the 8th and 9th of October. Nearest railroad station is Green, about a half mile from the church.

In the Hopewell District, Bedford co., Pa. on Friday the 3d of October, commencing at 4 o'clock.

Yellow Creek, Church Snowberger Meetinghouse, Bedford Co., Pa, on Thursday, Oct. 2, at 4 o'clock, p. m.

Cerro Gordo, Piatt Co., Ill., Sept. 27 and 28.

District Meeting for Southern Ill., at the same place on Sept. 29.

Whitesville Church, Andrew Co., Mo., Sept. 20, and 21.

In the Cerro Gordo district, Ill., Sept. 27 and 28, 1873.

Clover Creek, *Blair* Co., Pa., on the 30th day of Sept. and 1st of Oct.

Black River Branch, Medina Co. Ohio, October 3.

Logan Church, Logan Co., Ohio, Oct. 9.

Mohecan Church, Wayne Co., Ohio, 20th September, '73.

Fawn River Congregation, Lagrange Co., Ind., on the 4th and 5th of Oct.

MARRIED.

BRUBAKER—FILBRUN.—At the bride's residence, Sept. 7, 1873, by the undersigned, Nicholas Brubaker (Minister of the Gospel), to Mrs. Elizabeth Filbrun both of Montgomery Co., Ohio.

B. F. DARST.

CESSNA—BURGET.—By the undersigned, Sept. 4th, 1873, near New Enterprise, Bedford Co., Pa., at his residence, Bro. Watson W Cessna to Miss Mary *Burget*, all of Hopewell township. L. FURRY.

FLUKE—FISHEL.—By the same, at the same place, and on the same day. Mr. John R. Fluke to Miss Sarah Fishel of the same place.

DIED.

PATE.—Near Bloomfield, Bedford Co., Pa., Sept. 7, 1873, Nancy, infant daughter of friends Jacob and Rebecca Pate, aged 2 mos. and 28 days. Occasion improved from Math. 18: 1, 2, 3, by the brethren. L. FURRY.

McCONOUGHY.—In the Aughwick branch, Huntingdon Co., Pa., July 3, 1873, George, only son of brother James and sister Jane McConoughy, aged 15 years, 3 mos., and 3 days. Occasion improved by the brethren. A. L. FUNCK.

BEAR.—In the Limestone Church, Washington Co., Tenn, Aug. 9th, 1873, sister Mary, consort of brother David Bear, aged 31 years, 10 mos. and 4 days. Funeral preached on the 24th inst., by brethren Jesse Crosswhite and S. G Arnold. Text, 1 Cor. 15 chapter.

The subject of this notice was formerly of Virginia. Very soon after they came to Tennessee, she and her husband united with the Church, here at Limestone, in 1861. After this they again went back to Virginia, and staid until quite recently. She was a faithful member in the cause of her Master. It was said that she was ready to go. We hope our loss is her eternal gain.

HENRY M. SHERRY.

SHOEMAKER.—In the Maple Grove Congregation, Ashland Co., Ohio, Aug. 12, 1873, sister Catharine, wife of Bro. Isaac Shoemaker, aged 41 years and 7 mos. Funeral service by the writer and others, from John 19: 30, "It is finished."

This sister had been a faithful member of the Church for over 20 years having joined when young, and remained faithful, until it pleased the good Lord to remove her from amongst us by death, which was very sudden. She leaves a husband and 4 dear children to mourn their loss.

D. N. WORKMAN.

(*Companion* please copy.)

FORD.—In the Winamac Congregation, Ind., Aug. 20, 1873, brother Benjamin Ford, aged 76 years, 3 mos. and 5 days.

He had been a member of the Church about two years, and before he died he called for the Elders and was anointed with oil in the name of the Lord, having an evidence behind him that he has gone home to that bright world of eternal glory.

MONEY LIST.

Andrew Spanogle	1.00
Wm. H. Myers	.25
S. E. Long	.35
John N. Cripe	.25
Wm. Myers	3.00
Simon Mixel	1.50
B. Ellis	3.00
D. B. Teeter	8.75
Mary Tesenloet	1.50
Samuel Lutz sr.	3.00
A. E. Shoemaker	11.20
Jacob J. Kindig	.60
J. P. Noffziger	2.40
A. L. Funk	1.00
Mollie E. Houck	1.00
W. M. Foglesanger	.25
Jacob Bock (overlooked)	1.50
J. R. Foglesanger	.80
George Ober	1.50
D. R. Freeman	6.00

LITERATURE.

A. B. Brumbaugh, Huntingdon, Pa. Literary Editor.

J. H. BUTLER & Co., Philadelphia, Pa., the celebrated SCHOOL BOOK publishers, have recently issued a very complete series of Spellers and Readers—"The New American Series." Nine years experience in teaching has enabled us to properly appreciate a good text book. We call these excellent. The Spellers comprise two books primary and pronouncing, while the Readers comprise five books, which are graduated from sentences composed of the simplest words for beginners, carefully up through the series to the complete selections for advanced students. Every book in the series bears evidence of careful preparation with taste and ability. The matter is well selected, and written, and is of such a character that it is at once attractive and instructive. The engravings are superior to those of any other series. The price of the books of this series is lower than that of any other series, though of superior execution and binding. Their adoption by the State of Vermont, in the cities of Philadelphia and New York, besides hundreds of other cities and towns is another evidence of their merit.

BIBLE HISTORY, Illustrated,—*A Very Valuable Religious Work.*

The great and growing interest which has been manifested of late years in the study of the Sacred Scriptures, by persons of all religious denominations, has led to the preparation of a number of volumes to facilitate such a course of study. The best of these is *The Illustrated History of the Bible*, by Dr. Wm. Smith, LL. D., of England, which has just been issued by the Nations' Publishing Co., of Philadelphia.

No one who has tried to study the Sacred Narrative can fail to be aware that his greatest need is a clear, and comprehensive explanation of the historical portion of the Bible. As a matter of course, such an explanation should proceed only from one whose acknowledged abilities as a writer, and whose profound knowledge of the ancient languages and history, entitle his statements and opinions to unqualified belief. Such a man is Dr. Wm. Smith; the fame of whose learning and intimate knowledge of sacred and classical history is worldwide. There is, perhaps, no more profound Biblical and Oriental scholar now living, and in addition to this distinction he enjoys the rare honor of possessing the perfect confidence of all religious denominations, by all of whom he is regarded as a thoroughly reliable, conscientious, and impartial writer. His "Dictionary of the Bible," reached the enormous sale of over 2 0,000 copies in the United States alone.

The work before us is written in a clear, forcible and brilliant style, and abounds in that particular kind of information which the great mass of Bible readers most need. Few, even constant readers of the Bible, know what a world of romance, beauty, stirring interest and profound dramatic action there is in the Holy Book. This history fully develops these, and carries us from the creation of the world to the death of John the Evangelist, with an interest that never flags.

To this magnificent work of Dr. Smith, is added a lucid and complete history of the Jews, from the taking of Jerusalem by Titus to the present day, abridged from Dean Milman's celebrated History of the Jews. The story of the terrible siege of Jerusalem by Titus, the destruction of the Temple the dispersion of the Jews, their wanderings over the face of the earth, and their persecutions and sufferings in strange lands, form an attractive close to this splendid volume. No one can rightly understand the prophecies relating to the Jews, and the utterances of our blessed Lord concerning them, if ignorant of this portion of their history, for it is here that we must read the fulfilment of those prophecies.

The work is comprised in one large, handsome octavo volume, of 1105 pages, and illustrated with over 250 fine engravings, maps, etc. It is the most valuable religious work of the day, and will have an extensive sale. It is emphatically a great book, and the price is very low, considering its size and value. It is sold by subscription only, and agents are wanted in every county.

MITCHELL'S GEOGRAPHIES have been kept fully up to the times and form the standard series of America. It is composed of six books, and judging from those we have been permitted to examine,—Primary Intermediate, and Physical—they are entitled to the reputation.

This house publishes many valuable text books. D. W. Proctor, Esq., of this place is the agent who will supply catalogues, terms for introduction or books.

New Hymn Books, English.

TURKEY MOROCCO.

One copy, postpaid,	$1.00
Per Dozen,	11.25

PLAIN ARABESQE.

One Copy, post-paid,	75
Per Dozen, "	8.50

Ger'n & English, Plain Sheep.

One Copy, post-paid,	$1.00
Per Dozen	11.25
Arabesque Plain,	1.00
Turkey Morocco,	1.25
Single German, post paid	50
Per Dozen,	5.50

HUNTINGDON & BROAD TOP RAIL ROAD

On and after Aug 14th, 1873, Trains will run on this road daily (Sun excepted) as follows:

Trains from Huntingdon South. *Trains from Mt. Dal's moving North.*

EXPS. P.M.	MAIL. A. M.	STATIONS.	MAIL. P. M.	EXP'S A. M
6 15	7 45	Huntingdon,	AR6 50	AR9 20
6 20	7 50	Long Siding	6 45	9 15
6 35	8 00	McConnelstown	6 35	9 05
6 40	8 05	Pleasant Grove	6 29	8 58
6 51	8 20	MARKLESBURG	6 15	8 43
7 01	8 35	Coffee Run	6 05	8 35
7 08	8 41	Rough & Ready	5 58	8 29
7 15	8 50	Cove	5 49	8 20
7 18	8 53	Fishers Summit	5 46	8 17
7 35	9 10	Saxton	5 35	8 05
7 50	9 25	Riddlesburg	5 15	7 45
7 55	9 32	Hopewell	5 10	7 38
8 10	9 45	Piper's Run	4 58	7 26
8 21	9 57	Tatesville	4 44	7 12
8 32	10 07	Everett	4 33	7 03
8 40	10 15	Mount Dallas	4 30	7 00
9 00	10 35	Bedford	4 05	6 35

SHOUP'S RUN BRANCH.

A. M.	P. M.		P. M.	A. M.
LE 9 20	LE 7 40	Saxton.	AR5 25	AR 7 55
9 35	7 55	Coalmont.	5 10	7 40
9 40	8 00	Crawford.	5 05	7 35
AR 9 50	AR8 10	Dudley	LE4 55	LE 7 25

Bro'd Top City from Dudley 2 miles by stage.

Time of Penna. R. R. Trains at Huntingdon.

***Mail No. 2 makes connection at Huntingdon with Mail going East on Pennsylvania Railroad at 4.15 p. m., and West at 5.45 p. m. Mail No. 1 leaves Huntingdon at 7.40 a. m. on arrival of Pacific Express West.

Trains on this road connect with trains on Bedford & Bridgeport, and Cumberland & Pennsylvania Railroads.

G. F. GAGE, Supt.

The Weekly Pilgrim.

Published by J. B. Brumbaugh, & Co.

Edited by H. B. & Geo. Brumbaugh.

CORRESPONDING EDITORS.

D. P. Sayler, Double Pipe Creek, Md.

Leonard Furry, New Enterprise, Pa.

The *Pilgrim* is a Christian Periodical, devoted to religion and moral reform. It wil advocate in the spirit of *love* and *liberty*, the principles of true Christianity, labor for the promotion of peace among the people of God, for the encouragement of the saints and for the conversion of sinners, avoiding those things which tend toward disunion or sectional feelings.

TERMS.

Single copy, Book paper,	$1.50
Eleven copies, [eleventh for Agt.]	$15.00

Any number above that at the same rate,

Address.

H. B. BRUMBAUGH.

James Creek,

Huntingdon county Pa.

The Weekly Pilgrim.

"REMOVE NOT THE ANCIENT LANDMARKS WHICH OUR FATHERS HAVE SET."

VOL. 4. JAMES CREEK, PENNSYLVANIA, SEPTEMBER 23, 1873. NO. 38

POETRY.

I WOULD LOVE THEE MORE.

Lord! I fain would love thee more,
Learn thy precepts, do thy will;
Seek thy dealings to adore,
Trust thy wisdom and be still.

I believe thy love to me,
Seen in all thy wondrous ways:
Shall my heart as marble be,
Cold and silent in thy praise?

Oft I say "for *me* he died,"
Yet my sinking spirit grieves;
Let my foes in darkness hide
For I know my Savior lives.

Lives! His weakest one to bless;
Lives! the burden of my song:
Lives! a fount of blessedness;
Lives! to love me all day long!

Once I wept my thorny road,
Once I mourned my weary feet;
Now He takes my lightest load,
And He makes my service sweet.

Lo! the hand I pierced, I see,
Opens wide my Father's door;
And on high to plead for me,
Jesus lives forevermore.

From "*Gift of the Knees*" Hurd and Houghton, Cambridge, Mass.

WHERE DID CAIN GET A WIFE?

Published by the American Tract Society and translated from the German, by Daniel Snowberger, New Enterprise, Pa.

A dialogue between a preacher and his unbelieving neighbors, Hans and Kunz.

Kunz. Mr. Preacher, the Bible contradicts itself. First it says: Adam and Eve were the first people that God created, and they had two sons, Cain and Abel, one of which slew the other. And then comes up at once: Cain went into another land and there took a wife. There must therefore, already have been other lands and other people besides Adam, Eve and Cain. And consequently it cannot be true that Adam and Eve were the first people.

Hans Men, now-a-days become still more and more enlightened, Mr. Preacher! And therefore they do not so blindly believe what is said unto them, but they examine everything closely. Hence they cannot accept of anything as it stands in the Bible.

Preacher. Sirs, you severely accuse the Bible. I hope, nevertheless, that you possess so much feeling of righteousness, as to permit the accused to defend itself. Well then, neighbor Kunz, will you be so kind as to read to us the passage from the Bible concerning Cain?

Kunz. I think, Mr. Preacher! you are, no doubt, already acquainted therewith.

Preacher. Very good! But I wish that you and neighbor Hans might also become acquainted with it. Please read what is written in Genesis 4:19 17.

Kunz. Well if you wish it! Here stands: "And Cain went out from the presence of the Lord and dwelt in the land of Nod, on the East of Eden. And Cain knew his wife, and she conceived and bare Enoch; and he builded a city and called the name of the city after his son Enoch."

Preacher. Now where is it written that Cain went into another land and in that other land took a wife?

Kunz. Why this must surely stand here.

Preacher. Search now with all diligence, you will not find it. You see, neighbor Hans! Thus it stands with the much boasted searching and examining now-a-days. We examine so carefully that we do not even go to the trouble to open the Bible to see what is written therein.

Kunz. But still it is here written: Cain went and dwelt in the land of Nod. So then there was already a land there, and people must already have dwelt in that land.

Preacher. A wrong conclusion, neighbor. The land of Nod and all other lands, were, of course, there so soon as God had created the world, but from this it does not follow that there were already people dwelling therein. Then please observe: Nod signifies in Hebrew, flight or banishment. So then it is evident, that this land (Nod), which was, till now, uninhabited and unknown, received, through Cain's flight, its first inhabitants as well as its name. When, for instance, we read in the history of America, "The Dutch navigator Hudson, was the first white man that landed in the mouth of the Hudson River, where New York now stands".—we at once suppose, as was truly the case, that this river was named after him. Or, when we read; "The Pilgrim Fathers, who in 1821, sailed from England to America in the "Mayflower," landed in Plymouth, in the State of Massachusetts," we do not conclude that there did already exist, before their arrival, a city and a State of that name: but we come to the conclusion that the founding of the city of Plymouth and the State of Massachusetts followed their arrival. Just so did Cain make the land of Nod an inhabited and definitely named country.

Kunz. Suppose this were so, it still remains for you to show where Cain got his wife.

Preacher. Please first tell me, is it written that he took a wife in the land of Nod?

Kunz. To be sure this is not written, but, "And Cain knew his wife."

Preacher. Therefore not, "He took a wife," but, "He knew his wife." She was then already his wife, whom he, when he fled from the presence of the Lord, brought with him to the land of his banishment. For the wife must go with the husband. So it has always been.

Kunz. Very well, but where did he get a wife? This is a nut, Mr. Preacher, that you will not crack.

Preacher. Oh, if only your hearts had no harder shell than this nut, I would rejoice, for this is not hard to crack. Will you be so kind as to read the 3d and 4th verses of the 5th chapter of Genesis?

Kunz. Here stands: "And Adam lived a hundred and thirty years, and begat a son in his own likeness, after his image, and called his name Seth; and the days of Adam, after he had begotten Seth, were eight hundred years, and he begat sons and daughters?

Hans. What! does this stand in the Bible? Had Adam other sons besides Cain, Abel and Seth, and daughters also?

Preacher. To be sure he had. And so there is much in the Bible, wherewith you men, notwithstanding all your enlightenment, are yet unacquainted.

Kunz. I cannot see how with this, the knot is untied. You do not mean that Cain married a daughter of Adam—his own natural sister?

Preacher. Who else? Why should he not do this?

Kunz. Why this is against all morality, and I should suppose it would also be against the Bible.

Preacher. The Bible is the source of all genuine morality. Where in the world would you obtain rules of morality that would be everywhere valid and binding, if not in the Bible? Philosophers never agree; whatever the Bible, for instance in the Decalogue, teaches as our duty, is so clear that every one understands it alike, and so illuminating, that every one acknowledges it as right and salutary, even those who transgress it. Now as regards the marriage between blood relations, the Bible teaches us that it is sinful now, but in that early day it was not.

Kunz. How could that be sinful now which was not sin then?

Preacher. There is nothing sinful but that which is contrary to the commandments of God. But at that time God had given no commandment herein, and for wise purposes. For he would, as Paul says in his discourse at Athens, that "Of one blood all nations of men should dwell upon the face of the earth."—Acts 17: 26. But if this is to come to pass, all men must descend from one pair, and the children of this one pair must intermarry. Otherwise this could not be. The great idea of the fraternization of all men, which is now-a-days boasted of as a discovery of reason and enlightenment, is nothing but an old Bible doctrine, which at the time it was first preached upon earth, appeared unto the wise Greeks and Romans, as quite foolish and absurd. And our modern enlightened ones would lead us back again into the ancient Pagan blindness. If we would permit them they would make us forget the great truth, that all men are brethren. For this doctrine is undermined, if we rob it of its only foundation and support whereon it rests, namely the descent of all men from one pair.

Hans. I must acknowledge, I had never thought of this. I see very well that there can more be said in favor of the Bible than I had supposed. But you are not done yet, Mr. Preacher, you must explain unto us yet how Cain could build a city when there were so few people in the world.

Preacher. Well this was such a city as we have hundreds here in

America, * a city that is composed of ten or twelve, or even three or four houses, and occupied by so many families. You have travelled about a great deal neighbor Hans, have you not met with such towns?

Hans. Enough more than I desired. It has happened already that I have passed through such a town and inquired where the town was, which was said to be situated here, and then I was told the few cabins that I had scarcely noticed, this was the town.

Kunz. But whence came these, be they only three or four families who inhabited the city of Enoch?

Preacher. From the posterity of Cain, the Bible tells us, that men, in that ancient time lived many hundred years. From this we may safely conclude that their vital and generative powers were stronger and more durable than that of the people of the present day, and that we, therefore, when we are told of so many of the ancient fathers; understand from this a great number of children. So it could, in a few decades, come to pass that the posterity of one man could populate a considerable city.

I believe, dear neighbors, I have complied with your wishes and answered your queries. So I allow myself the modest petition to you, that you would now begin to read the dear Bible attentively through in its connections. For I discover anew, that the greater part of the opponents of the Bible, do either not read it all, or only superficially with preconceived unfavorable opinions, and without earnestly endeavoring to understand it aright. So then men generally read things therefrom which are not therein. You see I only desire that you actually do that which you yourselves said was important and necessary, viz. to examine everything closely.

* Such a small collection of houses would not be called a city in America. (Translator.)

MYSTERIES CONNECTED WITH REGENERATION.

Inasmuch then, as Regeneration is produced from seed divine, conceived into the heart of him who is regenerated and is an internal work, wrought in man by cooperation of God's spirit, no man, especially no carnal minded one, can comprehend the mode of operation which brings forth the new man in Christ Jesus. Nicodemus, though a ruler of the Jews, even after Jesus had illustrated that important change effected by earthly things, said: "*How can these things be?*" "Jesus answered," (in order to humble him and show him his ignorance emphatically asks:) "Art thou a master in Israel, and knowest not these things?" I fear, many who would be masters or teachers in Israel, in this day are as ignorant, or perhaps more so, than this notable ruler, or else they would not teach commandments of men instead of the commandments of God. And why so? because either self-interest or inexperience of the power of God, through want of a genuine conversion, being born of man, converted by man, consequently imbibed his doctrine, and is just as zealous to cleave to it, and defend it as the child of God is to defend the word of God. And indeed his zeal will induce him to go beyond the bounds of a true Christian, for the deceptive doctrine he imbibed does not put him under the same restriction.

The word of God, by which the child of God is born, restricts fighting with carnal weapons. "For the weapons of our warfare are not carnal, but mighty through God to the pulling down of strongholds; casting down imaginations, and every high things that exalteth itself against the knowledge of God, and bringing into captivity every thought to the obedience of Christ." Paul. But popular religion, or man-teachers, defend their doctrine, use the most powerful and deadly instruments that can be invented to kill their fellow men, and if needs be, their brother, in order to subdue him to their cherished doctrine; and if not successful for want of power, sooner than succumb, lay down their life, seal their faith with their blood. Hence, zeal is no distinctive mark of one that is born of God. For instance, did we not see in the late Rebellion brethren in the same faith fighting against one another, killing by wholesale both sides, calling fervently upon their God for success, and if killed, preached to heaven; hence fearless of death, if heaven be their portion. Sure signs of being born of man whose god is the god of this world.

By the foregoing remarks, I endeavored to show how man can be led astray, deceived, blinded and through deceitful workers influenced to lay down their lives for a false religion. Hence the greatest mystery of a proper regeneration lies on the part of the unregenerate. "The natural man receiveth not the things of the Spirit of God; for they are foolishness unto him, neither can he know them, because they are spiritually discerned."—Paul. John the loving disciple referring to the love of God by which they are called the sons of God, says, "Therefore the world knoweth us not, because it knew him not." The Savior on a certain occasion, said, "I thank thee, O Father, Lord of heaven and earth, because thou hast hid these things from the wise and prudent, and hast revealed them unto babes." New born babes are those that are born of God, such that have received the Lord Jesus Christ as their Savior, that obtained power from him to become the sons of God, even those that believe in His name." His name is the Word of God, consequently they do all what His Word demands; and this seems foolishness to the unconverted.

This new birth, in a certain measure, is mysterious even to them that are born again. The Savior compares it to the wind. "The wind bloweth where it listeth, and thou heareth the sound thereof, but canst not know whence it cometh, and whither it goeth: so is every one that is born of the Spirit." Now we feel the wind but cannot see it, we do not know where it commences, neither do we know where it ends. A storm may rage some distance from us, we hear it roar, the sound is perceptible, it may be in a short little circuit, and every place surrounding very calm, no man knoweth the cause of it nor where it started, nor where it ends, but the effects can be seen where it rages; and we also know that its power comes from above, God is the author and the moving cause of it. So is he that is born of the Spirit. He cannot see that Spirit which moves him to act, but he feels its operations. He knows that it comes from above, because by Divine impulse, he is moved to forsake sin and all unrighteousness, become obedient to the word of God, and the effect thereof is seen by a holy life and a godly conversation. But where that commences and ends he does not know, for he is yet too imperfect to see it; the changes and vicissitudes and temptations he has to pass through is not revealed to him but he knoweth that if he endureth to the end, that he will be called to another Regeneration more glorious, the Renovation of the body, of which we will treat in our next.

L. FURRY.

NEARING DELIVERANCE.

"For now is our salvation nearer than when we first believed."

The Bible contains many interesting and soul cheering subjects but there are none so inexpressibly sweet and overflowing as that of nearing deliverance. Every step we take, every breath we breathe, brings us nearer and still nearer. In every age, in every clime the same happy, holy thought has seized the aching and care worn heart and bid it look up and hope on because deliverance is on the wing, and soon will lift the mysterious vail that now hides the desired haven.

Just now we think of the man of patience. He had been blessed to a fullness, all that earth could afford, to make life pleasant and enjoyable was his, but still he was flesh or clothed in flesh, contaminated with sin and susceptible to its influences. Satan came along and strips him bare, first his earthly possessions, then his children, and lastly touches his flesh and wraps him in pain and anguish from the crown of his head to the soles of his feet. Every possible source of earthly pleasure was now cut off, and his condition seems to be a sad one indeed, but above and beyond all this, shone the bright star of hope. He saw the joy that earth affords, one after another taken away, but as these failed away, he was impressed with the truth of approaching dissolution. These pains and aches could not always last. He knew that the end was approaching, and with that, deliverance. All at once the blessed truth breaks into his soul and the happy exclamation was "I know that my Redeemer liveth" and if He liveth, what then? Ah, it was everything. It was resurrection, it was redemption, still more, yes, it was nearing deliverance, a foretaste of pleasures evermore. David, Israel's sweet singer, at different times in his eventful life, had the curtain drawn aside and his heart was made to leap for joy when the great deliverance was unfolded to his view. Good old Simeon was so powerfully enraptured at the glorious spectacle that he became impatient and wished to tarry no longer. The fullness of his brightest hopes had now been realized, he asked nothing more but "Now Lord let thy servant depart in peace, for mine eyes have seen thy salvation." The Lord's Christ was to him an eternal deliverance from the throes of this death, a passport from death to life, and as soon as his eyes beheld him, the sting of death was removed and he embraced the monster as fondly as men receive their most welcome friends. Deliverance was so very near that he beheld it in all its fullness. Kindred feelings to these were enjoyed by the chosen few that were made witnesses to this great deliverance, especially was this their happy lot near the close of their eventful lives, but perhaps to none of them was this great deliverance so vividly shown as to the apostle Paul. He became so dead to the world and the flesh that it was altogether immaterial to him whether he was in the body or out of it. When he consulted his own choice, it was to be absent from the body and present with the Lord. And when he considered the work whereunto he was called, he was quite willing to remain, not only willing to remain, but to die daily if he could be the means of saving others. He was very willing to be cursed for his brethren's sake, that is, be crucified as was his Redeemer. What cared he for this tenement of clay, let it go, let it dissolve for we know if this earthly house were dissolved we have a building of God, a house not made with hands eternal in the heavens. He was fully aware of the approaching dissolution of his body but instead of, being a terror to him, it was his greatest joy, because he ever groaned to be delivered from the body of this death. Salvation was the only star in his horizon and his eyes became so fixed on it that he could see nothing but Christ and him crucified. If any seemed to be growing weary on the way, he introduced to them the subject of nearing deliverance. "For now is our salvation nearer than when we first believed."

No waiting or lagging now, the heat and burden of the day will soon be over, fight on, the battle will soon be won, remember the crown is not at the beginning nor in the middle but at the end of the race. Such was the character and disposition of the author of our text. He not only taught by precept but his whole life was a living example of what he taught.

If the hope of deliverance was so unspeakably glorious to those who lived and died eighteen hundred years ago, should it not be equally our joy to know that deliverance is nearing? Yea, verily, and it does us good even now to realize the blessed assurance that to-day there are thousands filled with the same hope and are now groaning to be released from this body of death. What are the thoughts, of the old sainted pilgrim as he sits in his lonely chair? Once I was young but now am old, yet the Lord hath never forsaken me, but where are they of my household? Where my brothers and sisters, the companions of my youth, and where, the partner of my joys and sorrows? All gone, gone and I am still left, but time is passing, to-day and to-morrow are only short periods, but when past, will be two days nearer home, nearer the companions of my earthly joys, nearer, perhaps, a dear son or daughter whose eyes I reluctantly closed in death, nearer the one who stood by me in my thickest trouble, nearer the haven of rest, and above all, nearer my Redeemer who died and now liveth for *me*. Yes for *me* he suffered, for *me* he died, for *me* eternal deliverance is approaching.

Not long since, we visited the home of an old saint whose husband had gone to his reward. For a number of years she has been confined to her room, and to look at her condition from a natural standpoint we would suppose her lot to be far from agreeable, but go to that old mother and you will be surprised to learn the fullness of joy she realizes. No fretting no murmuring there, all is peace and expectation. Ask her how she feels, the answer is, "Oh, I am quite well and have much to be thankful for. I am often alone but seldom feel lonely, as Jesus, my best friend, often stands by me." She is a living example of the patience of Jesus, and is only waiting the invitation to leave this body of clay and go home. She fully realizes the truth of old brother Paul's nearing deliverance. For now is my salvation nearer than when I first believed, a few more risings and settings of the sun, perhaps another dropping of the leaves and then the Master will come. Oh for such an abiding faith, how my soul longs for the time when these eyes, now befogged by the world's gaudy show, will be more fully opened to the joys that are in store for the saints.

Brethren and sisters let us awake to the redemption that is approaching. If we are awake and alive to the holy profession which we have made, we are most certainly approaching deliverance. As age grows upon us let us not feel that we are growing old, but only maturing, only getting ready for the Master. Let us therefore walk the more courageously and put on the whole armor of light. Stand fast in the liberty wherewith Christ has made us free, ever pressing onward and upward for the prize which will be given us when deliverance comes.

H. B. B.

LOVE AND LABOR.

Feeling somewhat lonely this morning, I thought I would write a few lines for the PILGRIM to encourage my dear sisters. I love to read communications written by our own, the weaker sex. There are a great many of us too neglectful about writing for our periodicals. We should all try and do our part. I always think there are others who are more capable of writing than I am, and I presume it is the case with many others. This is why there is a lack of duty performed by the sisters, but this should not discourage us, for all that is lacking is energy, and a good will, and if we desire to do good, such little trifles will be no hindrance to us.

We find it hard to live a Christian life among so much wickedness, for there is so much of it going on at the present day, but this should make us feel more humble, for this life is fleeting and we know not how long we may stay here. Dear sisters, we have many trials, troubles and temptations to encounter, and many obstructions cast in our pathway. We are often looked upon with contempt because we do not follow the frivolous fashions of the world, but this should make our faith much stronger. We should never get discouraged at such things. Let us not care for what the world may say about us. Let us be on our guard for the eyes of the Lord are over the righteous, and His ears are open to their prayers; trust in the Lord at all times ye righteous, for nothing shall separate you from that eternal love, which for you, poured out on Calvary the precious blood of Jesus. Let us love one another more and labor as dear children of God. Let us not be idle and say we can't do anything, we have no talent, we can't write for the press, or we can't sing or pray. Let us try and do the best we can.

Do you remember reading the parable spoken by our Lord concerning the talents? We can compare this parable to ourselves. Our Lord was on earth once, He gave us talents and is gone with the intention of coming again to see how we improve our talent. But we did not all get the same amount of talents. Some of us have five, some two, some only one. If we have but one, let us try to improve it and gain more to it, so when the Lord comes He will find us faithful servants.

CHARLOTTE J. MASTERS.

LABOR FOR THE MEAT WHICH ENDURETH.

Labor not for the meat which perisheth, but for that which endureth unto everlasting life.—John 6: 27.

There seems to be a natural tendendy to overestimate the value of pecuniary effort, or that by which our natural wants are supplied. The Savior warned those who were following Him merely that they might partake of the loaves and be filled of this error, and says, "Labor not for the meat which perisheth." By the term meat, as used in the Scriptures, is not meant merely flesh but food in general, and the providing of food is one of the most important considerations of this life. The Savior does not mean that we shall not labor at all for the support of our natural wants, but merely directs the attention of those whom He addressed to the greater importance of laboring for the food which strengthens and supports the soul. It is certainly not wrong to provide for our natural wants. The apostle in writing to the Thessalonians, tells them that those who do not work should not eat; and again it is said that he that will not provide for his house is worse than an infidel, and hath denied the faith. From these allusions it is evident that it is our duty to labor for our sustenance. But while we thus labor we should always keep in view the more important labor, the effort to obtain that spiritual food that will strengthen and invigorate the soul.

When taking a view of the manner in which men perform their labor, and the zeal they manifest in their work, it appears that laboring for this spiritual food is only a secondary matter. We think more of what we shall eat or drink, and labor harder to obtain it than we do for that life giving, life sustaining food that nourishes and keeps alive the inner man. This is not in harmony with the teaching of Jesus when He says, "Therefore take no thought saying, what shall we eat? or what shall we drink? or wherewithal shall we be clothed?" We are first to seek the Kingdom of God and His righteousness, and then food and raiment, and the things that we need will be supplied. God never withdraws Himself from those who put their trust in Him. He keeps them as the apple of His eye, as the sheep of His pasture, and why should we manifest so much concern about these things? Take therefore not so much thought about how you shall supply your natural wants, but seek rather the supply of your spiritual wants.

But what is it that supplies our spiritual wants? What is this meat which endureth? Jesus says, "My words, they are spirit, and they are life." We understand then, that the words of Jesus, the Gospel which He delivered to men, will nourish and strengthen the soul, it is to the weak and weary soul what food is to the weary and fatigued body. We must labor to make an application of this word to the governing of our lives, obey its teachings, inculcate its principles, and then indeed will the soul become strong and healthy. We should be induced to labor for this supply from the consideration of the exceeding great value of the soul. The soul is of more value than the whole world; it is so valuable that there is nothing that can be given in exchange for it. But valuable as it is, if the means for its salvation are not applied, if the word of God is not obeyed, it will die. "The soul that sinneth, it shall die." Disobedience is sin, and if we continue disobedient to the plan for our redemption, the soul must evidently die to the joys and glories that are held in reservation for those who are laboring for the meat which endureth forever.

May we not then, in view of the great value of the soul, and the comparative insignificance of the body be induced to give ourselves less concern in reference to the perishable things of this life, and seek more after the things that pertain to our eternal happiness. Fear not the destruction of the body, but rather fear the destruction of the soul, that immortal principle which must exist forever, either in a state of wretchedness, or everlasting bliss.

"Never is a wise man better employed, never is he more busy, than when in silence, he contemplates the greatness of God and the beauty of his works; or when he withdraws from society, for the purpose of performing some important service to the rest of mankind; for he that is well employed in such studies, though he may seem to do nothing at all, does greater things than any other in affairs both human and divine."—Seneca.

From "*Thinkers and Thinking.*"

IT is the mind that makes the body rich; and as the sun breaks through the darkest clouds, so honor gleams in the meanest habits.

THE labor of the body relieves us from the fatigues of the mind; and this it is which forms the happiness of the poor.

He is the greatest prince who can govern his own passions.

Pride cannot bear reproof, but humility bows before it.

Begin with modesty, if you would end in honor.

ALONE WITH GOD.

Christian life in our day is full of activity. It finds pleasure in planning, giving, and working for the growth of Christ's cause. Meetings for prayer are multiplied in time of revival, and every evening and often hours of the day are devoted to mutual and quickening effort. Associations and conventions of various kinds are held almost weekly, whose chief object is to stir Christian hearts to more earnest and more constant labor for the Master. Young converts are full of zeal to win others to Jesus; and young men spend all their spare moments in carrying out good plans of Christian labor. An increasing multitude ask in the spirit of the converted Saul, "Lord, what wilt thou have me to do," and hold themselves ready for sacrifice or service. This spirit of consecration gives joy to all Christians who recognize it, and inspires confident hopes in the aggressive movements of the church.

But it conceals also a great peril: All Christian power springs from communion with God, and from the indwelling of divine grace. One can do good to others only as his own heart pulsates with love to Jesus, and has a present experience of his love. We can impart only what we receive. Any stream will run dry, unless fed from unfailing springs. And Christian labor will be fruitless, and Christian zeal be like sounding brass, unless the soul waits daily on God, and finds new strength in prayer and in study of his Word.

Jesus, when he forsaw especial difficulties in His way, was wont to go apart by Himself to pray. He made His own soul strong by communing with the Father. He received new quickening by the fuller inflow of divine life. The example of the Master is law to the servant. "They that wait upon the Lord shall renew their strength." If one would have a warm heart, he must find it at the mercy-seat. If he would be wise to win souls, he must have a rich and fresh experience of the truths of the Bible in his daily life. If he would have power with his fellow men, he must wrestle and prevail with God like Jacob at Peniel. There is reason to fear that much Christian activity is wasted, from lack of the preparation which gives success. Solitude with God should go before intercourse with men. The closet is preliminary to the prayer-meeting.

It is even the more important for the inquirer and the young convert to be alone with God. Depth of conviction, a strong grasp of the promises, firmness of purpose in the new life, are born of direct intercourse with God. He knows the needs of the heart better than the wisest pastor. He can guide the troubled soul more surely than any Christian friend. Solitude with God is an imperative need of the awakened sinner, for help cometh only from him. In the great revival, predicted by Zachariah, when the spirit of grace and of supplication was to be poured out, it is written, the land shall mourn, every family apart."

There is danger, in a time of a religious awakening, of too many meetings, as of too few. It may be hard to know the right medium. But it is certain Christians need to be much alone with God, and with his Word, to receive power for successful labor. It is equally certain that awakened and burdened souls need to be more with God than with men. Their help comes only from him, and they will find it soonest when cut off from reliance on any human helper. Many of our revivals leave weak converts, because they have leaned on secondary agencies instead of on the living God. And they leave Christians with little of permanent spiritual gain, because their fervor has been kindled by meeting together instead of waiting alone on God.

If the activity, which is one of the most hopeful features of our age, can be joined with a love for solitude with God; the Christian life will be rich in fruits, and Christian labor will have signal success.—*Selected.*

WHERE IS YOUR FAITH?

Professors of Christianity and preachers of the Gospel sometimes complain that the church is cold, the ministry indifferent, and especially that sinners are hardened, and that the preaching of the Gospel does not produce the effect that it did in days gone by. And then they will begin to unpack their mouldy bread, and tell over what good times they had ten, twenty, thirty or forty years ago; but it is all past now—men are hardened, and will not hear and believe the truth.

Is this the way you talk and feel? If so I have a word to say to you. God has not changed during the last twenty or forty years. He is the same yesterday, to-day and forever. Jesus Christ has not changed, for He changeth not. The Holy Ghost has not changed, nor has it left the world, for it was sent to abide with the Church forever. The Gospel has not changed. No matter how much you may have mangled it, distorted it, revamped it, and improved it with your new notions, pet theories, and vain imaginations= the Gospel and the Bible remain the same. The heart is still deceitful, the flesh is corrupt, and its lusts, desires, works, and fruits, are just the same now that they were when Cain killed Abel, when Lot was vexed in Sodom, when the Jews rejected Christ and crucified the Lord of glory. Sin has not changed,—it is still vile, hateful, polluting, accursed of God and a curse to man.

Now what is the matter? With the same God, the same Christ, the same spirit, the same Bible, the same Gospel, the same promises, the same sinners, and the same wrath to shun and heaven to gain, what is the reason there is not the same result? It may be true that the people where you choose to dwell and labor, who build churches and pay salaries, are some of them Gospel-hardened. But Christ has never bidden his servants to spend their whole lives preaching a rejected message to a rebellious people. He says, "Go ye into all the world," and somewhere in the backwoods, the highways, the by ways, or in the lanes and streets of the city, are hungry, starving souls, waiting for the sweet compulsion which shall bring them in to fill the vacant seats of the marriage of the Lamb, and as ready to hear the Gospel call, as other sinners have been in years gone by. And with the fields whitening, the harvest great, and the laborers few, you cannot urge the hardness of men's hearts as a sufficient reason for a fruitless ministry.

The reason is, you are back slidden yourself. It is needless to mince the matter. You complain that others do not feel under your exhortations or your preaching; the trouble is, you do not feel yourself. You talk of the hardness of sinner's hearts;—the fact is, your heart is hard. You complain of carelessless and worldliness when you are careless and worldly yourself. Christ is just as near today as he was twenty or thirty years ago. And if he is not as near, and as dear, and as precious to you to-day as at any time in your life, you are simply backslidden from Him.

Ah, my brother, this will never do! Get near the Lord, bury your old experience,—it is dead, and mouldy, and rank. Go to God's word for fresh bread. Burn up your old sermons. Hide yourself in your closet and draw near to God. Get your own heart broken and then other hearts will break. Put away your whining, and cant, and make believe sympathy; your heavenly tones, and all your tricks to raise a smile or draw a tear, and come down to the solid hard-pan of solemn fact. Do not pretend to be what you know you ought to be, but be content to own up just what you are. Tell the people that you are dead and buried, worldly and stupid, lukewarm, dumb and blind. Tell them the truth; and tell them, worst of all, that you don't feel half so ashamed or so bad about it as you ought to. Get down to the bottom of the hill where you belong, and then God can use you and exalt you.

Away with the doubts and cavils of unbelief. God lives, and souls perish! If you will be His servant, and endure His cross, and obey His commandments, and do His work, He will lead you through trials, toils, hunger, cold and nakedness, it may be, but He will crown your labors with a blessing; and preserve you blameless till He shall appear.

Put away whining, grumbling, envying others or complaining at your lot. Turn to God. Your congregations are as large as you will want to answer for in the day of judgment. Your one talent is quite enough for you till you dig up the old mouldy napkin and get it out and use it; and as for reputation, and bodily comforts, you are ten times as well off as your Master was,—so now, what more do you want? What more can you ask for?—*The Christian.*

GENERAL INTELLIGENCE.

THE BAPTIST CHURCH claims that they are taking the lead in Chicago, They have a membership of 5,428. The Episcopalians 3,728 and the Methodists 3943. Chicago boasts of 212 churches as places of worship.

OUR MINISTRIAL List for the 1874 Almanac promises to be a very great improvement on that of 1873. Look out for the largest and best Almanac ever published by the church. Free to every subscriber to the PILGRIM for 1874.

ANTI-TOBACCO REVIVAL.—Last week, at a Methodist Camp Meeting in Conn. the Rev. D. W. C. House gave a sound surmon on tobacco, at the close of which over 20 Ministers come forward and voluntarily foreswore the use of tobacco from henceforth and forever. We know of some other ministers that would be benefited by taking a similar pledge.

A BROTHER of the Manor Church Md. under date of Sept. 13 says: Last Sunday Bro. Zook of Franklin Co. Pa. was with us. Two young men were baptized, and four weeks previous to this a young woman entered the fold.

Slowly sinners leave the world and its pleasures to become the followers of Christ, but we are glad to see them come if only one or two at a time.

AVERAGE WEALTH of the churches in the United States.

"The Baptist churches average about $3,042; the Methodists, $3,273 the Presbyterians come next, at $7,083; Congregational $9,234; Uniuersalist, $9,436; Episcopal, $14,036; Roman Catholic, $16,023; Unitarian $20,266; Dutch Reformed or Reformed Church of the United States, as they now call themselves, $22135 the Jewish very naturaly representing great wealth with their metropolitan syungogues, staod at $33,919, at the head of the list.

THE CHRISTIAN ADVENT TIMES Publishing Co. are liquidating a debt of $4,000 by gratuitous funds from its patrons in cash and pledges. Last week there was over $800 sent in pledges besides a considerable amount of cash. That looks like business and throws the Altoona church move quite in the shade. If some of our contributors would give us several good articles on our proposed subject, "How to spend money for Jesus, it might be a help to the cause.

Brethren wake up. Are there none that understand this subject well enough to write on it? perhaps some of our sisters understand it better.

Since the Rebellion, the Presbyterian Church is divided. There has been numerous attempts made to effect a union, but so far there has been but little accomplished. The following opinion is expressed by the Philadelphia Presbyterian.

"The general feeling growing now rapidly at the North is, that the stretched out hand, which no friendly hand from the other side grasps, had better be returned to its place."

A RELIGIOUS MOVEMENT.—Of late there has been a religious movement in Norway. It has been looked upon as the uprising of the people for liberty and justice and goes far to show the tyranical spirit of some of our protestant churches when they become invested with power. Prior to 1845, Norway was an absolute Lutheran monarchy and to be anything but a Lutheran was to be put in jail, and even yet in Norway no one can hold any office whatever under government who is not a member of the Lutheran Church, and has not taken the sacrament; and if any man holding office, no matter whether the highest or the lowest, were to join any other sect or body, he must at once relinquish his appointments.

Such regulations are felt to be extremely tyranical but this is still not the worst part of it. Between the ages of fifteen and nineteen, every young person must be confirmed and take the sacrament according to the usages of the Lutheran Church. If not confirmed before the age of nineteen, he or she is liable to be put to jail. To get from under this yoke of oppression, in the name of religion, the people have called a meeting represented by delegates from all parts of the kingdom and after discussing these and other questions, they voted by large majorities to have them abolished. This same devilish intolerance was by the same sect, meted out to our brethren before they left Germany and emigrated to America.

THERE are those who profess to see indications of a general outbreak in Mohammedan countries against the Christians. Persecutions have been a little more numerous and a little more severe of late, and the increasing friendliness of Mohammedan potentates—the Sultan and the Khedive, for example—is looked upon as ominous for their Christian subjects. All these powers become less formidable in military and naval forces, it is not unlikely that they will be less and less inclined to brook the presence among them as deniers of their faith. It has never been through good will that they have granted toleration, and it wants but the frown of Europe to be turned away, to let their hatred loose.

Youth's Department.

TRUE COURAGE.

There is a great deal said these days about true courage and is considered a great honor for big people to possess and act it out. This spirit by example and precept, takes hold of the young and they too wish to show themselves boys and girls of pluck and courage. This is very proper as nothing good or great can be accomplished without the exercise of more or less true courage. But the trouble is, so few know what true courage is and on this account, it is so badly taught to the young that but few ever learn to practice its virtues.

Not long since, I dropped into a hotel where is sold that ugly stuff sometimes called "wild-fire" or more properly whiskey. Soon a half dozen young men come in, when the leader walked up to the bar and offered to treat the crowd. One after another, answered to the call and stepped up and swallowed down the liquid fire until it came to the one furthest back in the crowd. He shook his head and said that he did not wish any. Several called out: "Come along Harry, this is a treat and the rest of us have all drank, don't you stand back and play the dunce."

This was a sharp cut, but it only brought the man out of him and he said, in a determined tone: "I don't drink neither would I, if a thousand were to call me a dunce."

At this positive denial they all commenced to jeer and laugh at him calling him baby, dunce, coward, and every mean name they could think of, and then one much less than he walked up and bantered for a fight, calling him all kind of abusive names, but he stood firm and calmly said: "I do not wish to fight."

In the room was a man of considerable age, no doubt a father, and should have been possessed of wisdom but evidently he was not, for instead of applauding the boy for his noble conduct, he called out: "You young fool, why do you not knock him down? If you were my boy and would show yourself such a coward, I would thrash you."

The boys reply was: "My father's dying request was that I should not lie, steal, swear, fight nor drink whiskey. I promised, and by God's help, sir, I shall live it out."

The man was confused and had no answer to make. The little bully did not banter any more for fight, but with the crowd, quietly marched out.

Now, my young reader, who was it that had true courage? I know you will all say it was the boy who dared to do right. Just so. The greatest courage that any person can possibly have is to do right. The leader of that crowd was a gross young sinner. The young men that drank with him were cowards because they knew it was wrong and was afraid to do right, and the old man was not only a sinner and coward, but he was extremely foolish in justifying a cowardly act. True courage consists in boldly standing for the right, such courage will always end in a victory. Had the boy been a coward, he would have drank with his companions rather than endured their scoffs, but then he would have broken his promise and thus not only committed a sin, but took his first step in the downward course which might have ended in a drunkard's grave. This young man was a soldier that a widowed mother could well be proud of. Such courage will fight him through every temptation, prepare him for every event of life and give him a character that will open good positions for him, in short, it will make a man of him. He was no coward because he refused to drink and fight, but it was a brave struggle against wrong. By the help of such courage he avoided the first step in sin, and by the exercising of such courage, my young readers, you may escape any snare that the devil can place in your way. Don't forget it, true courage is to *do right*. When you are tempted to do wrong, remember that it is cowardice pleading with you. Courage says, no, I must not do it because it would not be right. Lying, chewing, smoking, stealing, drinking, swearing and fighting belong to cowards and sinners, and just so soon as you do any of these things, you take one step away from the right path and cause a black spot on your character.

UNCLE HENRY.

NEVER TELL A LIE.

All liars shall have their part in the lake of fire. Never lie because Satan is the father of lies and liars. A false witness will utter lies A deceitful witness speaketh lies. (Prov. xiv; 5,25.) He that speaketh lies shall perish. (Prov. xix; 9. To deceive any one is to lie. You can act a lie, and the wrong is just as great as to speak one. Do you put your trust in Jesus? Then remember, to lie, to laugh at a lie or in any way to deceive or be pleased with deception, is to dishonor him who shed his precious blood for the salvation of your soul: and yet God's Word says, "I write unto you, little children, that you sin not, but if any man sin we have an advocate with the Father, even Jesus Christ the righteous, and if we confess our sins, he is faithful and just to forgive our sins."

If you are not one of God's dear children, and sometimes tell an untruth do not trust in your promises to do better; just so sure as you expect to in your own strength, overcome this terrible habit, just so sure will you fail. Go to Christ, dear boy or girl, Go to Christ. He can, and He only will help you, and fill you with the spirit of truth, that you may speak the truth from the heart.

OBEDIENCE.

"I wish I could mind God as my little dog minds me," said a little boy looking thoughtfully on his shaggy friend; "he always looks so pleased to mind, and I don't."

What a painful truth did this child speak. Shall the poor little dog thus readily obey his master, and we rebel against God, who is our Creator, our Preserver, our Father, our Savior, and the bountiful Giver of every good?

The dog had been kindly treated by his young master, his wants had been supplied, and he did not forget it.

Little children, and grown-up children too, are daily receiving favors from the kind hand that supplies all our wants, and yet how often we forget our obligation to Him, and refuse to obey him. Let us try in time to come, to remember with greatful hearts the blessings that our Heavenly Father is so constantly bestowing, and obey him cheerfully.

A LESSON OF GRATITUDE.

A gentleman was once making inquiries in Russia about the method of catching bears in that country. He was told that to entrap them, a pit was dug several feet deep, and after covering it over with turf, leaves, etc, some food was placed on the top. The bear, if tempted by the bait easily fell into the snare.

"But he added, "if four or five happen to get in together, they all get out again."

"How is that?" asked the gentleman.

"They form a sort of ladder by stepping on each other's shoulders and thus make their escape.

"But how does the bottom one get out?"

"Ah! these bears, though not possessing a mind and soul such as God has given us, yet can feel gratitude; and they won't forget the one who had been the chief means of procuring their liberty. Scampering off, they fetch the branch of a tree, which they let down to their poor brother, enabling him speedily to join them in the freedom in which they rejoice."

Sensible bears, we would say, are a great deal better than some people that we hear about, who never help anybody but themselves.—*The Carrier's Dove.*

The Weekly Pilgrim.

JAMES CREEK, PA., Sept. 23, 1873.

☞ How to send money.—All sums over $1.50, should be sent either in a check, draft or postal order. If neither of these can be obtained, have the letter registered.

☞ When Money is sent, *always* send with it the name and address of those who paid it. Write the names and post office as plainly as possible.

☞ Every subscriber for 1873, gets a *Pilgrim Almanac* Free.

IS CONSCIENCE A CORRECT MORAL GUIDE.

Conscience is that faculty or power of mind which enables us to decide between right or wrong, according to the knowledge we have about the subject upon which we wish to make a decision. Therefore, in examining the subject of conscience, it should ever be remembered that knowledge is the basis; the source from which it emanates, and that without knowledge there could be no conscience. This is fully demonstrated from the fact that our conscience neither excuses nor accuses us in regard to things of which we have no knowledge. We meet with such occurrences in our every-day life. We sometimes speak inadvertently of a neighbor or friend. We do it with a good conscience because there was no evil intent in it, and we do not anticipate any bad to result from it, but perhaps, the next day we are informed, that our friend is offended at what we told him. Our conscience now reproves us sharply, for the very thing we done yesterday, with an approving conscience. The act is not changed, but we have had an addition to our knowledge, and that changed the state of the conscience, and to-day it decides directly the reverse of what it did on yesterday. A man comes into my office and begs alms; just a few minutes prior to his coming, I am informed that he loves his dram, and wishes the money to take it across the way and spend it for whiskey. With a good conscience, I refuse to give him alms because my knowledge tells me that it is wrong to give a man a weapon to kill himself with. After he is gone, a neighbor comes in and tells me that I was wrongly informed, and assures me that the man is strictly temperate but met with a sad misfortune, and is altogether worthy of my charities. I meet the poor man again, and with an approving conscience, tender to him alms. Is my conscience changed? Not at all. My knowledge is changed, and on the strength of that change my conscience changes the decision. I felt just as good when I withheld as when I gave, because, in both cases I done it through a sense of duty. Again, we will take the case of the savage. Some of them are brought up to believe that the white man is their worst enemy, and that the more of them they murder and destroy, the happier will be their condition in the spiritual hunting grounds after death. Imbued with this knowledge, he kills the white man with as good a conscience as we could have in saving a man from death and eternal ruin. In both cases, conscience is based upon knowledge and duty. These illustrations, we think, set forth very clearly, the nature of conscience and prepare us to answer the questions as presented: "Is conscience a correct moral guide? We answer that it is correct just so far as our knowledge is correct in regard to what true morality is, and not a particle farther. If we have a thorough knowledge of good morality our conscience will check or decide against every violation, but if we have only a partial knowledge of morality our conscience will guide us only in that part which we know. Therefore, we come to this conclusion: Conscience always dictates right according to the knowledge we have, but that right (in our estimation) may be wrong from the fact that the knowledge upon which we based our conscience, was wrong. This is a clearly established fact from the illustrations which we gave. It should be remembered that we are brought up surrounded by different circumstances, and that true morality is very differently understood, hence good morality is often grossly violated and that too with a good conscience. This does not prove that those who violate, are necessarily bad or have an evil conscience, but that they are wrongly taught, that they are deficient in knowledge. To make conscience a guide in such cases would be right in principle, but wrong and unsafe in practice, *i. e.* it would produce bad results.

Just now the question presents itself, what is conscience? Is it a guide at all? Not a bit of it. We will illustrate again. I am traveling along a familiar road, but my mind is so absorbed in my business that, without noticing it, I take a wrong road. My conscience never says a word about it. Something occurs to divert my mind from its course and I look around me, things appear strange, and my knowledge tells me that I have taken a wrong road. This knowledge produces a sensation of sorrow or disappointment, I feel badly. This feeling or sensation is my conscience, and knows no more about the road I wish to travel than do the trees by the wayside, and as a guide, it does not answer my purpose nearly so well, because, when I looked at them they told me I was wrong, but conscience remained quiet until it was informed of the mistake, and then it made me feel badly, and to get rid of that feeling, my knowledge dictated, better go back. Now, it is very evident in this case, that conscience was no guide but a sensation or feeling that served as a stay or check and enabled me, from the knowledge I had of the road, to form a rational decision.

Conscience then, properly defined, is that power or principle that affords us pleasure when we do right, according to the knowledge we have, and, pain when we do wrong, and is no guide morally or spiritually. Conscience is right, is good and its warnings should be heeded if the knowledge from which it emanated was good.

Paul, while earnestly persecuting the Church, was acting strictly in harmony with his knowledge, and said, "I have lived in all good conscience before God until this day."—Acts 23: 1. His conscience or feeling was good, his principle was good because he was actively engaged in what his knowledge told him was his duty, but the practice and result was bad. Now if conscience had been a guide to right it would have checked Paul in his mad career, but it did just the contrary, it approved every act he done. It afforded him sensations of pleasure, but as soon as he received other knowledge, his conscience or feelings were changed, and even to think of what he had been doing, gave him sensations of pain. That he was deeply conscientious before he was converted, is plainly shown in his writings. In Acts 26: 9, he says: "I verily thought with myself, that I ought to do many things contrary to the name of Jesus of Nazareth." Again, in speaking of Israel, he says: "For I bear them record, that they have a zeal of God, but not according to knowledge. Israel was zealous and had a good conscience and they obeyed its voice, yet it was all wrong—because it was not according to knowledge. Just so it is with thousands to day, they live and die with a good conscience, yet the result of their whole life is a series of wrongs from beginning to end, from the fact that they were wrongly taught, their knowledge was deficient. Such act in good faith and may receive their reward on principle. But there are thousands who, unlike Paul, refuse knowledge, and fight against the promptings of conscience, until it becomes seared as with a hot iron. Such are wrong, both in principle and action or practice and will come under condemnation because he that knoweth to do good and doeth it not to him it *is* sin.

In conclusion, if you wish to do right and feel right, search the Scriptures, the fountain source of all knowledge, and obey them. By so doing you will enjoy a conscience void of offence. After all, the Scriptures are our only safe-guide, and he that putteth his trust in them shall not be made ashamed.

SUNDAY SCHOOLS.

When we first admitted the subject of Sunday schools into our columns, we thought our brethren could discuss it without getting into personal controversies, but it seems not. There is a little too much spirit, fire or zeal somewhere and if not checked, will go far beyond its intended limits. First comes reviews, then defenses, then apologies, then reviews of review until the subject is lost in a personal controversy. Brethren these things ought not so to be and for the present, we have concluded to suspend the discussion unless a more charitable spirit is manifested and personalities avoided, therefore those who have written either in the shape of reviews, amendments or apologies, will please excuse us for their nonappearance. From the general views as expressed, we believe that the Brethren, as a body, are in favor of Sunday schools if they can be properly conducted. The great question now seems to be, to know how this can be done, and we know of no plan that pleases us so well as that given by brother Snowberger and practiced in their school at New Enterprise, Pa. Other brethren may have just as good schools, and perhaps better, but as we have not had the pleasure of giving them a personal visit, or having a written form of their manner of conducting them, we can not judge of their merits.

In justice to brother Zuck, we will say, he has written an apology, or rather a vindication of his position, and assures us that it was by no means his intention to hurt or wound the feelings of any of the brethren.

As we remarked before, some of our brethren are entirely too sensitive on questions that do not exactly correspond with their manner of thinking.—We must learn forbearance towards eachother and have respect for the conscience of others as well as our own, but above all, let us have respect for our children and see that we stand not in the way of having them taught the Scriptures.

ATTENTION—PLEASE.

We have, standing out on our books, nearly $1,000. Of this we do not complain as we promised to wait on those who did not have the money when subscribing. We have now patiently waited nine months, and as we have some payments to make, and badly need some money, we now ask every reader who yet owes us for subscription &c. to pay us, if possible, between this and the 11th of October. Now brethren and sisters, let us see how much you can oblige us by sending or having it sent right along. Those who pay to agents, don't wait for them to ask for it, but oblige them and us by attending to it at once. We wish it understood that all who can and will pay us between this and the time specified will confer us a *special favor*.

Correspondence.

Dear Pilgrim:—Perhaps a few words from the Aughwick Congregation will be acceptable to you.

On Saturday eve., August 26th, I boarded the Westward Pa., Central mail train at Mt. Union, and arrived at Mapleton, a village three miles distant, in due time. Nothing worthy of notice came under my observation during this short car ride except the usual thought of the pleasantness of the trip which is embraced by *Jack's Narrows*, giving a good view of the beautiful scenery which particularly characterizes the banks of the "blue Juniata" at this point.

My chief object being the fulfillment of an engagement to preach on Sunday at Ladds Grove, the name of a school-house about eight miles up Hares Valley, I pursued my journey on foot about four miles, when the day was far spent, and being weary and only a short distance from a brother's house, I turned aside and abode with him during the night. I thought it must be a heart of stone that could not relish such a privilege under such circumstances. I would advise any one who has an aversion to lodging with poor people in humble cottages in the mountains, to start on foot on a gratuitous fifteen mile preaching journey late in the day, and have only one place to feel welcome.

In the morning the brother kindly offered me a seat on his wagon which I accepted gladly with his family. After arriving at the place appointed and engaging in singing several hymns with the assembly, we were not a little surprised and gratified to be joined by brother A. L. Funck, who preached to us from Acts 3d chapter on the subject of repentance. His remarks, in my judgment, were made to bear upon the essential points, and what was still more important and rare, I think they were tolerably well received.

After services returned with Bro. James Dougherty and family, accompanied by sister Hettie Doll and two lady friends, to his house, dined with him, thought and talked of many things, among which was the sad intelligence that a neighbor's child, a girl seven years old, while carrying a dish down stairs, fell, breaking the dish and falling on it, cut the large blood-vessel in the neck, and expired in five minutes.

I left them, committing them to God's care, and started on my way homeward again on foot. I reached home at five o'clock considerably fatigued, fully convinced that my good things were not in this life.

Two other meetings were attended by the brethren at the same hour at different points. Of their propriety the people who attended and God are the judges. God willing, I will write you again next week.

Yours Fraternally.

J. B. Garver.

Dear Brethren:—I have just been reading in Pilgrim No. 35, Editors address "to the scattered members," which brought a few things to my mind which I thought to pen for your columns if agreeable. Editors think to change the character of the reading, and give more practical reading matter. So be it. Let us have more matter relating to the one thing needful, and to the fundamental principles of our faith, or, if that is sufficiently established, which it is no doubt with every member (but perhaps not with every reader,) let us have exhortations relating directly to our spiritual duty, as well as our temporal duty towards our fellow-men, or upon such subjects as set forth in No. 34 of Pilgrim. But whatever we do, let it be done in and through the spirit of love and brotherly kindness, consistent with our profession of peace.

I love the Pilgrim, and always love to read every column in its pages, but I regret to say that there has been recently some matter that has wounded the conscience of some of its readers, and have not savored very much of that charity that thinketh no ill, in fact we doubt if such language would emanate from an humble Christian heart. And also think that if the writer would respect and love the Brotherhood as he does his pet cause, he never would have used such epithets as he did in derision of a part of the Brotherhood

Come, dear brethren and sisters, let us "Awake to righteousness and sin not, for some have not the knowledge of God, I speak this to your shame."—1 Cor. 15 : 34. "See that ye walk circumspectly, not as fools, but as wise, redeeming the time because the days are evil, wherefore be ye not unwise, but understanding what the will of the Lord is."—Eph. 5 : 15-17.

Now brethren, let us prove all things and hold fast only to that which is good. In conclusion, if there is anything herein that seems to be personal, be assured that it is not meant so to be. But if one side is to be fully represented, allow the other to be heard also, but that we may all labor together for the good of souls, for the prosperity and the praise of God, is the desire of your weak brother. J. B. Lair.

Mexico, Ind.

Springfield, Ohio, Sept. 1, 1873.

Mr. Brumbaugh. Dear Sir: If my request is not out of place, I would like if you would favor us with an explanation on the subject of conscience, through the Pilgrim.—The question has been asked in our Sunday School, "Is conscience a correct moral guide?" and the majority of the leading members of our Sunday School, are of the opinion that it is not, and that it is a creature of education and consequently would be as apt to direct us in the wrong way, as in the right. But when I consider the teachings of the Scriptures, and my own convictions, in regard to the principle of conscience, I am led to believe that such is not the case. I believe that if we would live in strict obedience to the voice of conscience, that our deviations from the path of duty, would be much less than they are, and we would be better qualified to receive and appreciate the truths of the Scriptures. It is said of Paul, when brought before the council, that he said, "Men and brethren, I have lived in all good conscience before God until this day.—Acts 23 : 1. It appears that Paul in this case, did not hesitate to accept the testimony of his conscience, as correct, and again Paul says: "For our rejoicing is this, the testimony of our conscience, that in simplicity and godly sincerity, not with fleshly wisdom, but by the grace of God, we have had our conversation in the world, and more abundantly to youward."—2d Cor. 1 : 12. By considering these, and other corresponding passages, I am inclined to think, and I am fully satisfied in my own mind, that it is only by neglecting and refusing to obey the dictates of conscience, and indulging in the sinful lusts of the flesh, that we deviate from the path of right.

Inasmuch as my education is very limited, I am not able to express my ideas in regard to the principle of conscience so as to be rightly understood, and for this reason I hope you will favor us with an explanation on the principle of conscience and its tendencies. I have yet much to learn, and will gladly receive all the information that I can get that will enable me more clearly to understand the Scriptures. David Benton.

For answer see editorial page.

Dear Brethren: I have often tho't of penning a few lines ever since I have been taking the Pilgrim. I have not been taking it long, but long enough to be pleased with it, and like it too well to give it up, would not be without it for anything, especially now, as I am lying on my bed sick and cannot be with the brethren and sisters at Salem Meeting-house where they are holding a Lovefeast, commencing to-day, the 6th at one o'clock, but thanks be to God, I have this hope that while their prayers are ascending to Heaven, they will not forget the absent ones.

E. V. Hausenfluck.

Waterlick, Va.

DIED.

ETTER.—Same District, Aug. 10, Eld. Wm. Etter, aged 72 years, 5 mos., and 23 days.

Bro. E. labored zealously in the ministry until some years ago, he lost his sight, but had it partially restored, and since then has been in feeble health, and could not attend the meetings regularly, but the one at the meetinghouse near his place, where his seat was very seldom vacant. A few days before his death he was afflicted with gravel, from which he suffered much until relieved by death. But we trust his affliction which was but for a moment, has worked for him a far more exceeding and eternal weight of glory. Occasion improved by Eld. William Boyer and Joseph Oype.

BENNETT.—On Sept. 3, 1873, brother James Y. Bennert, aged 51 years, 9 mos. and 8 days.

Brother James was a minister in the second degree, and labored with your unworthy servant, as a co-laborer in the Winamac Congregation about four years. He contended earnestly for a conformity to the old order of the Brethren. He leaves a wife and six children to mourn the loss of a kind husband and father. Funeral preached by Bros. John Knisley, Adam Appleman and the writer, to an attentive congregation. D. R. Freeman.

FOGLESANGER.—In the Ridge District, July 25th, Jacob Foglesanger, aged 74 years, 8 mos. and 23 days.

The subject of this notice was afflicted for many years, though not seriously, until a few days previous to his death. He was only absent from the table three meals before he died. His departure, although not unlooked for, was sudden when it came, but we fondly hope, that what the church has lost on earth, it has gained in heaven. Funeral services by Eld. Daniel Keller and John F. Stamy.

RINEHART.—In the Black Swamp District, Sandusky Co., Ohio, Bro. Jacob Rinehart, aged 69 years, 1 month and 13 days. Funeral occasion improved from 2 Timothy, 4 : 6, 7, 8, by the writer.

Noah Henricks.

ANNOUNCEMENTS.

Please announce that the brethren and sisters of Solomon's Creek Congregation have appointed a Communion Meeting to be held at their Meeting-house 3 miles North-east of Milford, September 26, '73, to commence at 4 p. m. The usual invitation to the brethren and sisters is extended. Jesse Calvert.

The Lord willing, we will have our Lovefeast at the Free Spring Meeting-house, Juniata Co., Pa., on the 27th of Sept., commencing at 1 o'clock p. m. Preaching on the 28th in the forenoon. Place of meeting about three miles South-east of Mifflin Station, and about the same distance North-east of Thompsontown. M. Bashoar.

Hamilton Congregation; Caldwell Co Mo., October 4th and 5th.

North Coventry Congregation, near Pottstown, Pa., October 4th and 5th.

Nemishillen Congregation, Stark Co, Ohio, Sept. 27.

Spring Run, Mifflin Co., Pa. on the 5th of October.

Dry Valley Meeting-house, Mifflin Co. Pa., October 3 and 4.

Falling Spring Congregation, Franklin Co., on the 10th of October.

Beaver Run, Mineral Co., W. Va., on the 11th and 12th of October.

Limestone Congregation, Wash. Co., Tenn. on the 4th Saturday of September.

James Creek Pa., on the 10 and 11th of October.

Grasshopper Valley Church, Jefferson Co., Kan., Meetinghouse in the town Osawkee, Oct. 4 and 5.

Dunnings Creek Congregation, Pa., on Friday, Oct. 3.

Stone Church, Marshall Co, Iowa, on the 4th and 5th of Oct.

Our Lovefeasts of Maryland, will be held as follows:

Sam's Creek,	Oct. 11,	commence 1½ p. m.
Monocacy,	" 17.	
Meadow Branch,	" 21,	com. 1½ p. m.
Beaver Dam,	" 25.	

In the Cold Water church, in the new stone meeting house, on the 8th and 9th of October. Nearest railroad station is Green, about a half mile from the church.

In the Hopewell District, Bedford co., Pa. on Friday the 3d of October, commencing at 4 o'clock.

Yellow Creek, Church Snowberger Meetinghouse, Bedford Co., Pa., on Thursday, Oct. 2, at 4 o'clock, p. m.

Cerro Gordo, Piatt Co., Ill., Sept. 27 and 28.

District Meeting for Southern Ill., at the same place on Sept. 29.

In the Cerro Gordo district, Ill., Sept. 27 and 28, 1873.

Clover Creek, Blair Co., Pa, on the 30th day of Sept. and 1st of Oct.

Black River Branch, Medina Co. Ohio, October 3.

Logan Church, Logan Co., Ohio, Oct. 9.

Mohecan Church, Wayne Co., Ohio, 20th September, '73.

Fawn River Congregation, Lagrange Co., Ind., on the 4th and 5th of Oct.

Waddams Grove, Stephenson Co., Ill., October 11 and 12.

Dry Creek, Lynn Co., Iowa, on the 1st and 2d of November.

Root River Branch, Minn. 4th and 5th of October

Middle Fork of Wild Cat Congregation, Ind., on the 29th of October, and District Meeting of Southern District on the 30th and 31st.

Union Center Church, Elkhart Co., Ind., October 1st.

Aughwick Congregation, Huntingdon Co., Pa., on the 7th and 8th of October, commencing at 1 o'clock p. m., on the 7th.

Monticello Church, White Co., Ind., on the 10th of October.

LITERATURE.

A. H. Brumbaugh, Huntingdon, Pa. Literary Editor.

"THINKERS AND THINKING." By James E. Garrettson, M. D., (John Darby,) author of "Odd Hours of a Physician."—J. B. Lippincott & Co. Publishers.

This is a really meritorious book. Its theme is of life, and man's relation with life; its text "Life! no query: What is life? What is it to live? What is it to get the most out of living?" Its search is for that which thinkers and thinking yield, Truth,—the truth of life and of living: It is a book for thinkers; written in that very pleasing style of the author's late work "Odd Hours of a Physician" which was so greatly appreciated, never wearying the reader with wordy detail, but dropping the thought leaving the thinker to clothe it, and passing to the truth adduced. The author sketches pleasantly the various schools of Philosophy, himself a practical philosopher of the most healthful character. It would be difficult to follow him through this book without gaining the conviction that confusions lie in ignorance, and not in facts. It promises to become quite popular, and will meet with warm acceptance by all true thinkers. Send to this office, or to Wm. Lewis Huntingdon Pa., and obtain a copy. Price in extra cloth $1.50.

THE GIFT OF THE KNEES, or the Ministry of Prayer, the Ministry of Power.—Hurd & Houghton, Cambridge, Mass.

The objects of this volume is not so much to bring forward new arguments in favor of prayer, as to exalt its mission and power as vital every-day necessity to the living Christian Prayer is the sustaining breath of the Christian life,—the Key that unlocks the great treasure-house of the Father, from which flows all the bounties of His all-bountiful hand. How few of those professing the christian name, really possess the faith to enable them to comprehend the full meaning of, and receive with confidence the Savior's words: "All things whatsoever ye shall ask in prayer believing, ye shall receive." Few christians could read this book without arriving at a deeper conviction as to the efficiency of daily, earnest prayer, and the necessity of carrying it even into their every-day life. Send to this office, or to Wm. Lewis Huntingdon, Pa., and secure a copy of the book. Price $1.25.

BOOKS RECEIVED.—"THE ANCIENT HEBREWS, with an Introductory Essay concerning the World before the Flood. By Abraham Mills, A. M. A. S. Barnes & Co., New York. Price $1.75 sent by mail.

From CLAXTON, REMSON & HAFFELFINGER, Philadelphia, Pa.:

DICTIONARY OF SHAKESPERIAN QUOTATIONS. One vol. cloth gilt $2.50.

GREAT TRUTHS BY GREAT AUTHORS. One vol. Octavo. Fine cloth, price $2.00.

HOMO *versus* DARWIN, 12mo., cloth $1.00.

CHILDREN *with the* POETS. By Harriet B. McKeever. 12mo., cloth, $1.50.

PLAIN EDUCATIONAL TALKS, WITH TEACHERS. By A. N. Raub, A. M. 12mo. cloth, $1.50.

VULGARISMS AND OTHER ERRORS OF SPEECH. 16mo. cloth, $1.25.

THE CHRISTIAN SABBATH VINDICATED and the Sabbath in its political aspect. By Ienotus. Price $1.50.

CHRISTIAN HOUSEHOLD.—Whispers to a Bride. By Mrs. L. Phelps. 16mo. $1.00.

PRIESTHOOD AND CLERGY, *Unknown to Christianity*, &c. 12mo. cloth, 75 cts.

THE LAST PASSOVER.—A harmony of the Evangelists, &c. By J. R. Whitney. 16mo. $1.00.

FAIRMOUNT PARK, Philadelphia, Pa. By Chas. S. Keyser. Fine cloth $1.00.

HUNTINGDON & BROAD TOP RAIL ROAD

On and after Aug 14th, 1873, Trains will run on this road daily (Sun excepted) as follows:

Trains from Huntingdon South. *Trains from Mt. Dal's moving North.*

EXP'S P.M.	MAIL A.M.	STATIONS.	MAIL P.M.	EXP'S A.M.
6 15	7 45	Huntingdon,	AR6 50	AR9 20
6 20	7 50	Long Siding	6 45	9 15
6 35	8 00	McConnelstown	6 35	9 15
6 40	8 05	Pleasant Grove	6 29	8 58
6 51	8 20	MARKLESBURG	6 15	8 43
7 01	8 35	Coffee Run	6 05	8 35
7 08	8 41	Rough & Ready	5 58	8 29
7 15	8 50	Cove	5 49	8 20
7 18	8 53	Fishers Summit	5 40	8 17
7 35	9 10	Saxton	5 35	8 05
7 50	9 25	Riddlesburg	5 15	7 45
7 55	9 32	Hopewell	5 10	7 38
8 10	9 45	Piper's *Run*	4 58	7 26
8 21	9 57	Tatesville	4 43	7 12
8 32	10 07	Everett	4 33	7 03
8 40	10 15	Mount Dallas	4 30	7 00
9 00	10 35	Bedford	4 05	6 35

SHOUP'S RUN BRANCH.

A. M.	P. M.		P. M.	A. M.
LE 9 20	LE 7 40	Saxton.	AR5 25	AR 7 55
9 35	7 55	Coalmont.	5 10	7 40
9 40	8 00	Crawford.	5 05	7 35
AR 9 50	AR8 10	Dudley	LE4 55	LE 7 25

Bro'd Top City from Dudley 2 miles by stage.

Time of Penna. R. R. Trains at Huntingdon.

. Mail No. 2 makes connection at Huntingdon with Mail going East on Pennsylvania Railroad at 4.15 p. m., and West at 5.45 p. m. Mail No. 1 leaves Huntingdon at 7.40 a. m. on arrival of Pacific Express West.

Trains on this road connect with trains on Bedford & Bridgeport, and Cumberland & Pennsylvania Railroads.

G. F. GAGE, Supt.

The Weekly Pilgrim.

Published by J. B. Brumbaugh, & Co.

Edited by H. B. & Geo. Brumbaugh.

CORRESPONDING EDITORS.

D. P. Sayler, Double Pipe Creek, Md.

Leonard Furry, New Enterprise, Pa.

The *Pilgrim* is a Christian Periodical, devoted to religion and moral reform. It will advocate in the spirit of *love* and *liberty*, the principles of true Christianity, labor for the promotion of peace among the people of God, for the encouragement of the saints and for the conversion of sinners, avoiding those things which tend toward disunion or sectional feelings.

TERMS.

Single copy, Book paper,	$1.50
Eleven copies, [eleventh for Agt.]	$15.00

Any number above that at the same rate,

Address.

H. B. BRUMBAUGH.
James Creek,
Huntingdon county Pa.

The Weekly Pilgrim.

"REMOVE NOT THE ANCIENT LANDMARKS WHICH OUR FATHERS HAVE SET."

VOL. 4. JAMES CREEK, PENNSYLVANIA, SEPTEMBER 30, 1873. NO. 39

POETRY.

Selected by HANNAH HOLLOWBUSH.

THE INQUIRY.

Tell me, ye winged wind,
That round my pathway roar.
Do ye not know some spot
Where mortals weep no more?
Some lone and pleasant dell,
Some valley in the west,
Where, free from toil and pain,
The weary soul may rest?
The loud wind dwindled to a whisper low,
And sighed for pity as it answered "No!"

Tell me, thou mighty deep,
Whose billows round me play,
Knowest thou some favored spot,
Some island far away,
Where weary man may find
The bliss for which he sighs,
Where sorrow never lives,
And friendship never dies?
The loud waves rolling in perpetual flow,
Stopped for awhile, and sighed, to answer "No."

And thou, serenest moon,
That with such holy face,
Dost look upon the earth
Asleep in night's embrace;
Tell me, in all thy round
Hast thou not seen some spot
Where miserable man
Might find a happier lot?
Behind a cloud the moon withdrew in woe.
And a voice sweet, but sad, responded "No!"

Tell me, my secret soul,
Oh! tell me, Hope and Faith,
Is there no resting place
From sorrow, sin, and death:
Is there no happy spot
Where mortals may be bless'd,
Where grief may find a balm,
And weariness a rest?
Faith, Hope and Love best boons to mortals given,
Waved their bright wings, and whispe'd—
"Yes, in Heaven."

Selected by E. R. STIFLER.

NO ROOM FOR JESUS.

O, plodding life! crowded so full
Of earthly toil and care!
The body's daily need receives
The first and last concern, and leaves
No room for Jesus there.

O, busy brain! by night and day
Working, with patience rare,
Problems of worldly loss or gain,
Thinking till thought becomes a pain!
No room for Jesus there.

O, throbbing heart! so quick to feel
In others' woes a share,
Yet human loves each power enthrall,
And sordid treasures fill it all!
No room for Jesus there.

O, sinful soul! thus to debase
The being God doth spare!
Blood-bought, thou art no more thine own;
Heart, brain, life, all, are His alone;
Make room for Jesus there:—

Lest soon the bitter day shall come,
When vain will be thy power
To find in Jesus' heart a place;
Forever closed the door of grace,
Thou'lt gain no entrance there.

ORIGINAL ESSAYS.

THE OPENING OF THE FOURTH SEAL.

For the information of the readers of the PILGRIM who may not have easy access to ancient history of the world, I will transcribe for its pages a chapter from S. G. Goodrich's History of the Nations, Vol. II, page 802, 803, chapter ccc4xii, A. D. 526.

The reign of Iostioican was marked also by great calamities. The superstitious people were appalled by the appearance of comets of prodigious magnitude. Earthquakes and pestilence added their real scourges to these terrors. In 529, an earthquake at Antioch destroyed two hundred and fifty thousand persons. In 531, the ancient and noble city of Berytus was shaken to the earth. Constantinople suffered severely, and a part of the Church of St. Sophia was thrown down.

In 542, a terrible plague, which originated in Egypt, swept over the whole known world, and continued its ravages more than fifty years. It is said there was not a spot upon the earth, even to the mountain tops, that was not visited by this dreadful scourge. During three months, the mortality at Constantinople was from five to ten thousand daily. Many districts in Asia, dispopulated by this visitation, have remained waste to the present day. As this is the most wide spread and destructive pestilence that ever visited the earth, as far as we are able to learn from history, we subjoin the description of it furnished by Procopius, who resided at Constantinoble, who was an eye-witness of this terrible calamity, and, from his connection with the Byzantine government, possessed the means of learning all that could be known of its origin, progress and effects. The account of this writer is as follows:

At this time (A. D. 542) arose a pestilence which almost destroyed the whole world, attacking all nations and tribes of men, and sparing neither sex nor age. No diversity of climate, latitude, diet, habits, or mode of life obstructed the progress of the pestilence, all varieties of mankind fell prostrate before its sweeping march. Some countries were ravaged in Summer, others laid waste in Winter. It first arose in Egypt, among the inhabitants of Pelusium, from whence proceeding in two separate routes, ravaged Alexandria and the rest of Egypt on one hand, and on the other, extended into Palestine, from which country it spread over the entire world, advancing with uniform rapidity thro'out the whole of its progress. It did not suddenly exhaust its venom in any spot, but proceeded with regular steps, and continued in every place along its route a certain space of time, marching thus deliberately to the very extremities of the earth, as though determined that not the most remote corner of the Universe should escape its ravaging search. Not even an island, a cavern or a mountain top was spared. If any spot was passed over lightly on its first visit, the pestilence was sure to return and fall with fatal malignity upon the people whom it had first spared, not leaving them till it had swept the full proportion. It always began on the sea coasts, and spread into the interior.

In its second year, about the middle of Spring, it reached Constantinople, where I happened to be at the time. The plague brake out in this manner; Multitudes of diabolical spectres were seen, bearing the shape of some human figure. Whoever met one of these spectres seemed to be struck on some part of his body, and was on the instant taken sick. At first, the persons who saw these spectres, attempted, by prayers and devotions, to free themselves from their attacks, but all in vain, for in the very temples to which they ran for succor, they fell down dead. Then they shut themselves up in their houses, and if their friends called at the door, they refused to see them; not the loudest knocking would be answered, for every one feared that some demon was in pursuit of him. Some were attacked in another way: they fancied in their sleep that they beheld these apparitions, or heard voices crying that they were numbered with the dead, and straightway they were attacked by the pestilence. Others neither saw the spectres nor dreamed of them, but felt the disease approach in a fever on awakening from sleep, some were seized walking, others while they were about their occupations; they did not change color, nor feel a violent heat or inflamation, but from morning till evening, the fever wore so mild a character, that neither the patient nor physician was alarmed. But on the first or second day, or not long after, swellings arose in the abdomen, under the arms, behind the ears, and on the thighs. These particulars were common to all who were attacked by the plague, but there were diversities in the action of the disease, owing either to the different habits of the body in different individuals, or to the sovereign power of Him who sent the calamity. Some fell into a heavy lethargy, others were seized with a furious madness. In their lethargy, they seemed to have forgotten everything like persons buried in eternal sleep; and, unless attendants were constantly at hand to supply them with food, they died of starvation. In their madness, they never slept, but were continually frightened with apparitions and fears of being murdered; they uttered horrid cries, and ran hither and thither, to save themselves by flight. If the sufferings of the sick were dreadful, those of their friends were hardly less so, for they were disheartened with the labor and anxiety of watching over the miserable patients.

The disease was not propagated by contagion, for neither physician nor other persons caught it by touching the bodies of those infected, and multitudes who nursed the sick and buried the dead, escaped its attacks, while others, who were in no way exposed, took it and died. In their delirious ravings, they rolled themselves on the ground, threw themselves from the house-tops and plunged into the sea, not from thirst, but impelled by an ungovernable fury. Many unattended, perished from hunger. Those who escaped from lethargy and delirium were carried off by excruciating pains in the swellings.

The physicians, ignorant of the

nature of the disorder, imagined the cause to lie in the swellings, and therefore dissected their tumors in the bodies of those who had died, to discover the secret of the malady. They found them to consist of coals, or black lumps, containing so malignant a poison, that many of them died immediately from the effects of it. Some found their bodies covered with black pustules, these died within an hour. Many were killed by sudden vomitings of blood. Some, after living in great extremity, and being given over by their physicians, recovered, to the astonishment of every one; others, who seemed quite safe, assured of recovery, unexpectedly died. Human skill and human wisdom seemed utterly at fault, for all things were at contradiction. If one man was helped by the use of the bath, another was killed by it. If some perished in an extraordinary manner, others escaped wonderfully. No remedy for the disorder, no preventive against it, could be found. When a man took the inspection, it seemed by chance; when he escaped, it happened he knew not how. Children born of infected mothers were sure to die.

The plague prevailed four months at Constantinople, and during three months it raged terribly. At first, the number of deaths was but little above the ordinary proportion; but as the epidemic grew more active, they increased to five thousand a day, and afterward to ten thousand a day, and even more. At first, every one buried those of his own household, and such dead bodies as were found here and there; but afterward everything was left to chance, and disorder, for servants were left without masters, and masters without servants. Houses were left desolate, and the tenants remained unburied. All the tombs in the city being filled with bodies, men were sent into the fields in the neighborhood to bury the dead there; but the number of the corpses increasing more and more, they became tired of digging graves, and piled up the bodies in the towers of the city wall, by taking off the roofs and throwing in the bodies, till the towers were full, when the roofs were replaced. A foul air was thus driven by the winds over the city, and added to the infection.

No funeral offices were performed over the dead; people thought it sufficient, if they were able to carry them to the shore, cast them by loads into boats, and let the waves transport them wherever chance might direct. All factions and dissensions were hushed in the city; people assisted one another and buried one another without thinking of their enmities. Vicious and abandoned men, struck with horror at the awful death which menaced them, became suddenly penitent and devout; yet, as the danger passed away, and their fears abated, they returned to their old ways and surpassed their old deeds in iniquity: so that it might be said, and not without truth, that the pestilence, either by chance or the will of Providence, had spared the very worst of mankind."

Were these fifty years the period of time of the opening the fourth seal of the seven sealed book? "And when he opened the fourth seal, * * I looked, and behold a pale horse: and his name that sat on him was Death, and Hell followed with him. And power was given him over the fourth part of the earth, to kill with sword, and with hunger, and with death, and with the beasts of the earth."—Rev. 4: 7, 8.

D. P. SAYLER.

REFORMATION.

I have often thought that if a desire to do the divine will, which the importance of the subject should at all times inspire, was sincerely and fervently indulged in by mankind, there would be no great difficulty in convincing one another of the important doctrines relating to the kingdom of Christ. Neither would it consist with the wisdom and goodness of God, to permit such to continue in any errors fatal to their own salvation, nor in their tendency to their fellow-heirs.

I would not be understood as inculcating the idea that in the present imperfect state, entire uniformity in either faith or practice is to be expected. The true christian unity is not comprehended in the adoptions of any precise creed, or a test in christian love. This however, is not a mere name, nor that kind of charitable disposition, as some men reckon charity which overlooks the faults of others. It is, to use the language of the Apostle, a drinking together in the same spirit, or a sitting together in heavenly places in Christ Jesus.

But, although perfection of knowledge is not the lot of humanity, and therefore perfect unity of faith is not to be expected in the present state of being, a perfection ofdesire to know and do the Divine will is not only to be expected, but is absolutely necessary and indispensible. Nothing less than this perfection of desire can properly be called sincerity, and nothing less than this will be acceptable to the Divine Being, who requires the devotion of the whole heart.

And as this perfect desire to know and perform the will of God, is what is most necessary, so unhappily, it is what is most wanting among the professors of the holy name of Christ, and the want of this all important disposition is, to me, the strongest proof of the degeneracy of the present age. Was this desire prevalent in the minds of Christian professors, how different would be the aspect of things among them. We should not see them indulging in practices adverse to their high and holy profession merely because they were sanctioned by custom or participated in by others whom they had been induced to consider wiser and better than themselves, but despising the world's dread laugh, or the censure of singularity, they would take a firm stand, on Christian principles, in opposition to the current of custom; alike unconcerned with regard to the popular praise or popular odium. This is the only way in which reformation can ever be accomplished, or true Christian principle advanced. Each for himself, must submit to take up the cross and deny himself of whatever is contrary to the laws and precepts of Jesus Christ.

It is altogether futile to suppose, that, at any period, mankind will all be convinced of the truth and make a move for reformation. It is only by every one acting firmly, according to the light with which God has favored him, that we need ever expect this blessed work to progress in the world. The little stone which the prophet Daniel saw in divine vision, cut out of the mountain without hand's gradually grew till it become a great mountain, and filled the whole earth.

May the Lord in his infinite goodness, hasten this period and strengthen the little that remains that is ready to die, that the nations may yet come to his light, and kings to the brightness of his rising.

The principle inculcated in this communication, I recommend to the serious consideration of every one. The path of duty is easy and plain. There is a law which writes in the heart—ever present with us to direct us in what is right and if every person would come to the full resolution always to do right, whatever it might subject him to as regards the loss of interest in this world, a good name among men, or denial of anything that belongs to self, we should soon see a great change for the better on the earth.

Where there is a want of this disposition of heart, there is a want of everything which pertains to true righteousness before God, but whoever attains to it, will insure the saving of his soul, which is more than all this world. Therefore, if our right eye, foot or hand cause us to offend it is better for us to part with it at once, however painful it may be to flesh and blood, than to delay it through any earthly consideration whatever, for what shall it profit a man if he gain the whole world and lose his own soul.

J. N.

Cearfoss, Md.

PRIDE.

The following is copied from the *Religious Telescope*, and is from the pen of bishop J. Weaver. The paper was sent us by one who knows, and the subject is so well treated that we gladly give it room in our columns with the hope that it may have a tendency to check that unclean spirit which is becoming too prominent in our own Church. We are aware of the general cry of "old fogyism" but its from the devil and makes it the more necessary that we should continue to show our colors and stand for Jesus.

And now abideth pride, fashion extravagance, these three; but the greatest of these is pride—simply because it is the root of the whole matter. Destroy the root and the tree will die. It is hardly worth while to waste ammunition in shooting at fashion and extravagance as long as the root is alive. Most persons say it does not matter how people dress, pride is in the heart. Very true, but straws show which way the wind blows. Plain exterior may cover a proud heart; but depend upon it, a fashionable exterior seldom if ever covers up a plain heart. Some rules work two ways and some will not.—A lady once asked a minister whether a person might not be fond of dress and ornaments without being proud? He replied, "When you see the fox's tail peeping out of the hole you may be sure the fox is within." Jewelry, and costly and fashionable clothing, may all be innocent things in their places but when hung upon a human form they give most conclusive evidence of a proud heart.

But is it possible that a man can be found at this advanced age of refinement that dares to speak or write a word against pride, and its consequences? The large majority of that class of men died and were handsomely buried some time ago. Now, the pulpits have nearly all shut down on that style of preaching. The fact is we have passed that age, and are living in better times. Our fathers and mothers were far behind the times. They were good enough in their way, but dear me, they would not do now. They wore plain clothes, worshipped in plain churches and sung oldfashioned hymns. They talked and acted like some old pilgrims that were looking for a better country; and when they left the world they stuck to it to the very last, that they were going to a city where there is no night. And it is my deliberate opinion that a vast majority of them went just where they said they were going.

But they are nearly all out of the way now, and the people have a mind to try a different route. We can be christians now and do as we like. Yes indeed. We can have fine churches, cushioned seats costly carpets, a fashionable preacher, and have all our fiddling and singing done to order. Why, in some of our modern churches the majority of the choir are not even members of the church;—and they do sing so sweetly,—perfectly delightful. The music rolls over the heads of the congregation like the sound of many waters. Not a word can be heard; but the sound is glorious. Sometimes one sings all alone for a little while, then two and pretty soon the whole choir will chime in, until the whole house is filled with the most transporting sound. Now if this is not singing with the spirit, and with the understanding also, then what is? that's the question. I know it is a little risky to speak out against pride at this day because the church is full of it. It is of no use to deny it. And hundreds who occupy the pulpit, whose duty it is to point out these evils plainly, are like dumb dogs; they don't even bark at it. They just let it go, and go it does with a vengeance. And in proportion as pride gains in the church, spiritual power dies out. They will not, cannot dwell together, for they are eternal oposites.

It is a sin and a shame for men and women professing christianity to spend money the way they do to gratify a proud heart, when ten out of every twelve of the human race are yet unsaved, and eight out of every twelve have not as much as heard the Gospel of Christ. There are many evils in the land, and in the church but I doubt if any evil is doing more harm than pride. It has stolen into the church by degrees and now rules with a rod of iron. Churches that were once noted for plainness, and whose law still stands against pride and fashion are practically powerless on the subject. It seems that nearly all creation is kept busy in furnishing fashions enough to satisfy the cravings of the depraved heart. An old scotch preacher is reported to have said in a sermon at Aberdeen, "Ye people of Aberdeen get your fashions from Glasgow, and Glasgow from Edinburg, and Edinburg from London, and London from Paris, and Paris from the devil." Now I cannot say that we get our fashions by that route but I am tolerably certain that they originate from the same head-quarters.

The religion of Christ is pure, peaceable, gentle, easy to be entreated, and full of mercy. All Christains are baptized with one spirit, into one body. They mind not high things, but condescend to men of low estate. Their highest ambition is to honor God with all they have and are. They are not puffed up not conformed to this world, but transformed by the renewing of their minds. There is no such thing in heaven nor earth as a proud Christain; there never was, nor never can be. Pride is of the devil—it originated with him; and he is managing it most successfully in destroying souls. But who is to blame for this state of things in the church? First, and mostly the pulpit is to blame. Men who profess to be called of God to lead the people to Heaven, have ceased to rebuke this soul-destroying heaven-provoking spirit. But why? First for a living, then for popularity Esau sold his birthright for a dinner of greens. That was a costly morsel for him. But now, men sell out "cheap for cash or produce." Churches that were once powerful for good are now well nigh lost in forms and fashions. We may shut our eyes and wink and whine, and cry old fogy, and grandfather, and Moses and Aaron, and all that, but the fact is before us, pride, fashion, and extravagance are eating the very life out of many of the heretofore best congregations in the land. The world is running crazy. The rich lead the way, because they can, while the poor strain every nerve to keep in sight; and and the devil laughs to see them rush on. Pride "thrust Nebuchadnezzer out of men's society, Saul out of his kingdom, Adam out of paradise, and Lucifer out of heaven." And it will shut many more out of heaven, who are now prominent in the church. Neither death nor the grave will change the moral character of any one. The same spirit that controlled in life, will cling to the soul in death, and enter with it into eternity. The angels of God would shrink from the society of many a fasionable christian of this day. A few such souls in heaven would ruin everything. Among the first thing they would propose would be a change of fashion. Those pure white robes that the saints wear would not suit their taste at all. In life they care little about Christ and spiritual things, and they would care no more for them in heaven than on earth. If there were two heavens, one where Jesus is all in all, and the other with a Paris in it, I presume the road to the Paris heaven would be crowded with fashionable Christians. "Ma" said a little girl, "If I should die and go to heaven, should I wear my *moire antique* dress?" No my love, we can scarcely suppose we shall wear the same attire of this world in the next.' "Then tell me ma, how the angels would know I belonged to the best society?" In the views of that little girl we have illustrated the spirit of many a would-be Christian of this day. "If ye then be risen with Christ, seek those things which are above, where Christ sitteth on the right hand of God. Set your affections on things above, not on things on the earth. For ye are dead, and your life is hid with Christ in God.

Contentment is happiness.

A LETTER FROM ABROAD.

Hamburg, Germany, May 1st., '73.

My dear Father and Sarah:—We left New York on Friday at one o'clock April 18th. We took the steamer the 17th at one o'clock; it rained so hard and was such a storm, that we did not leave until the next morning. As soon as we got fairly out to sea, we all took sick. I the first, then Lannie, then Olive and Howard. We lay on benches on the deck all day. At night we dragged ourselves to our beds, but were too sick to undress. The next day Lannie and myself lay in bed all day. Olive and Howard went on deck and remained there most of the day. Howard got well enough to take care of the rest of us, and Olive got better soon; but Lannie and myself were sick all the way over but two days. We were out twelve days and all that time we did not land. We stopped out at sea about one mile, at Plymouth England, where they sent a little steamer to take the mails, and some passengers, and then we landed in the channel, at Cherbourg, France, where they again sent out a little steamer to take the mails and forty passengers, that were going into France. We stopped at Plymouth England, on Monday morning at six, at Cherbourg France in the evening at five o'clock. Then we came into the German sea where it was fearfully stormy. We came out of the German sea into the Elbe River at ten o'clock yesterday morning. We came up the river about twenty miles where we were transferred from the steamer Silex, to a river steamer that brought us to Hamburg, so we were out nearly thirteen days. Oh you do not know how thankful we were when we could set our feet on land once more. The continual motion of the steamer for a long time, seeing nothing but water and once in a while a sailing boat or a steamer, is more tiresome than I can tell, especially when one is sick all the time, and has no appetite. I never want to cross the sea again but once, and that is to go home to America. Coming up the Elbe River yesterday, we saw some strange looking villages. The houses are only one story high, and the roofs run up to a point. They looked so strange to us. But we also saw some beautiful castles and lovely gardens. We landed here at Hamburg at about three o'clock. The city looked very strange to us. The streets are so narrow and the houses so high. Some years ago part of the city was burned down and has been built up since, and is more in the modern style. It is a very clean city, and is really a beautiful city; but the customs, and money—and everything is so different, that we have a great deal to learn. The people can generally understand English, but my German they cannot understand. When I speak to them in German, they do not know what I mean, or what language I speak. The hotel we stopped at, is a very nice place; everything is so clean, and we like the cooking very much. We expect to be here a few days yet, and then we expect to go to Berlin and stay there a few days. Then we go to Dresden, where we expect to stay 6 months, and commence to learn German. We can already read the signs in the streets. We have great appetites. We can scarcely get enough to eat. There was one woman died on the steamer coming over. She died on Sunday evening at eight o'clock. The same night at two o'clock they lowered her into the sea, but we did not know it till the next morning. She was in the steerage passage.

Now I want you to write to me soon, I am so anxious to hear from you. We all feel quite well since we got on land. Direct your letter to Dresden Germany. The children join me in love to you both. The boys are enjoying themselves so much.

From your daughter,
NANCY L. SPROGLE.

WHO ARE THE ELECT?

Dear Pilgrim:—Whilst meditating on the goodness of God, the subject of election came to mind, and as I often heard people say a part was to be saved and a part lost, and that God designed it to be so from the beginning, for He knew all things, and the thought presented itself, how could God be just? Why not save all? While thus engaged, my mind ran in this way: Can I not say or do something to remove such doubts? And these words came flashing thro' my mind: all they that do and keep the commandments elect themselves heirs of the kingdom, none need to be lost, none will be lost but such as refuse to elect themselves by keeping the commandments. When I look at election in this light I feel to exclaim with the poet:

"Ride on, ride on blest Jesus,
Ride on thy crown is glorious;
Over sin, death and hell,
Thou wilt make us victorious."

MARY BURNS.

HOW TO PRAY ARIGHT.

"When ye stand praying, forgive if ye have ought against any." This duty may be inferred from that petition in the Lord's Prayer, which says, "Forgive us our debts, as we forgive our debtors." But the practical exercise of the duty is here intensified by the injunction not to use an unimpressive generality, but in time of prayer to set specially before the view the case of the individual then offending against us. Only thus it is, that to any real or effective result we fulfil the part enjoined. Christians too frequently hold by the generality and omit the specialty. But when desiring to use Christ's prayer after Christ's manner, they must adopt His own explanation of the way in which they are to employ it.

O, blessed Lord Christ, who hast taught us that unless we forgive, we cannot be forgiven, forbid that our prayer for pardon should ever be rendered void by our slackness to bestow pardon on others; and help us to forgive those who have offended us, as freely as we ask forgiveness from Thee for ourselves.

What is my duty in all perplexities? Humbly to wait on the Lord and to seek his guidance step by step.—*Rowland Hill.*

GENERAL INTELLIGENCE

A party of Mormon emigrants, who recently arrived in Paris on their way to America, have been warned by the Prefect of Police that if they attempt to hold their religious exercises in public they will be expelled from the city.

THE Yellow Fever has been raging with terrible fatality in some of the Southern cities. At Shreveport, Louisiana, it is reported that there was an average of 40 deaths per day, the population only being 4,000. The city was so panic stricken that the dead could scarcely be buried, while many of the sick were uncared for.

THE *Daily Graphic* Atlantic Balloon Enterprise proved a failure in the first attempts, but Mr. W. H. Donaldson, the brave balloonist, has determined to reconstruct it and hopes to be able to make a successful voyage to Europe in a few weeks. In the meantime the *Graphic* Co., have now commenced a silk balloon of smaller dimensions, but with every improvement that modern science can suggest, and are determined to show the world that they meant business.

A strong argument newly illustrated, for the observance of the Sunday laws demanding cessation from labor has just been mentioned. The fact on which it is based we can not vouch for, for we have not inquired into it. It is said that most railway accidents occur near the end of the week, when the powers of the overworked and weary employes begin to fail and give signs of need of rest. This is asserted by the Chicago *Mail*. Hence it is inferred that there is a strong argument based on the nature of man for Sabbath observance.

NERVOUSNESS.—What is the cause of nervousness? Can it be cured?

ANSWER.—Nervousness sometimes comes from the constitutional temperament. One who has a strongly marked Mental Temperament, and not quite enough of the Vital Temperament, if he or she overwork or study too much, or have care and anxiety arising from unfavorable conditions, or large Cautiousness, will become nervous, as it is called. The way to cure it is to avoid tea, coffee, spices, alcoholic liquors, tobacco and opium; to live on simple, plain diet, retire early, and sleep abundantly, and avoid subjects and people whose tendency is to irritate and excite.
—*Phrenological Journal.*

FINANCIAL CRASH.—One of the greatest crashes that perhaps ever occured in the United States, happened in New York on the 19th and 20th inst., 50 prominent houses have been closed, and the end is not yet, as many others must immediately follow.

The cause is wholly attributed to the wrong policy of our men of means, of investing in rail road bonds with the hope of realizing large gains. The result is, their boasted bonds are now worthless bits of paper, and their money spent in wild railroad schemes set on foot by visionary men who saw the beginning more plainly than the end. Those of our brethren who preferred railroad bonds to good titles for the Kingdom, will perhaps, think of our proposed subject, "How to spend money for Jesus," of which none of our readers seem to know enough about to give us an article on it.

BRO. DAVID BROWER, of Salem, Oregon, says: "I have exchanged my farm near South English, Iowa, for a farm seven miles east of Salem Oregon. This is the county-seat of Marion Co., and also the capital of the State. I expect to move on the farm about the 22d of Sept. Our crops are very good here in the valley, such as wheat, rye, oats and grass. Vegetables and fruit we have in abundance. The health is good. The ark of the Lord is moving slowly, but I believe a good feeling exists among the brethren generally. We have meeting about every Sunday but the laborers are few while the harvest is great. We would be glad if some laboring brethren, sound in the faith, would come to our assistance. We would also be glad to have lay members come over and help us carry on the great work of the Lord."

THE following, we extract from a Catholic Journal and goes to show how awfully depraved the human heart may become. Such a thing would seem to be beyond the credulity of an idiot, yet there are thousands who are otherwise intelligent, that will snap at such baits.

"'The Rev. Father Lewis, of Clifton, Staten Island, New York., received last week a large supply of the miraculous water from the grotto of Lourdes. Any one writing to him and enclosing an offering will receive by express a flask of the precious water. The offerings will be employed towards defraying the expenses of the freight from Europe, custom house, bottles, labels, packing, etc., etc. Whatever is over and above will be given to the sanctuary of the Lourdes, or to some other charity. In using the water it is customary that the parties seeking to be benefited should make a Novena in honor of Our Lady of the Immaculate conception, and during the Novena receive the Holy Sacraments if possible. Father Lewis begs us to state that, farther than this, he has no time to answer the very many letters he has on the subject, but would advise all who can do so to read the beautiful book, "Our Lady of Lourdes,' by H. Lassere."

THE CHURCH OF THE BRETHREN.—Dedication of the Church of the Brethren took place, yesterday on Marshall street, below Girard avenue. It was formerly called the Church of Christ, and is composed of what are known as Dunkards. This sect emigrated from Germany to Germantown, in 1717, and, on December 23, 1723, were first organized with a charter. They have no written creed or confession of faith. Their place of worship in this city was formerly on Crown street, below Callowhill, which was sold last Autumn, and they commenced in October the erection of the building which was dedicated yesterday. It is a neat brick structure, 42 by 65 feet, the cost of which, including the ground, was $20,500.

The audience room will seat about four hundred persons, and is fitted up with stained pine pews and neat gas fixtures. The pastors of the church are Revs. Jacob Spanogle and C. Custer. Among those participating in the services yesterday were Rev. Jacob Riner, of Montgomery county; Jesse Calvert of Indiana, and Grabill Myers, of Blair county, Pa. There is a comfortable lecture room in the basement of the church, and there are 150 scholars in the Sunday school, with an average attendance of 100.—*Ex.*

SCIENCE AND THE BIBLE.

The thing to be lamented is that the moment men of science get hold of a fact they instantly begin to see it in opposition to God's Word. But the vaunted "fact" of Tuesday often takes another shape on Wednesday, and on Thursday is found to be no fact at all. The truth is that geology, as a science, consists mainly of probable guesses. That "field of peat," says Sir Charles Lyell, "has probably been 7,000 years in course of formation." "No," replies a friend of his own, in a published criticism, "I think it quite possible that it has only been 700 years in growing." A piece of pottery is found in the valley of the Nile, and a geologist immediately argues that it must have lain there more than 20,000 years. But an antiquarian soon points out marks upon which show it to be less than 2,000 years old. Yet it is upon guesses of this kind, which do not amount to a tenth part of a proof, that the Lyells, Owens and Colensos venture boldly to assert that it is clear that Moses knew nothing whatever of the subject on which he was writing.

Just in the same spirit de Bunsen and his followers unhesitatingly assert that the growth of languages proves that the world must be more than 20,000 years old. We refer them to the confusion of tongues described by Moses, which at once dissipates their dream. "Oh! but that was a miracle," they reply, "and we have made up our minds never to believe a miracle." Very well, gentleman, there we must leave you; for men who make up their minds before inquiring are not acting like reasonable beings. A dozen other little juntos are now at work in the same laudable fashion. One set was not quite certain that a man was "developed" out of an ape. Well, and what was the ape "developed" out of? They do not know. Our comfort in all this is that this influenza will wear itself out like the Tractarian, or like the infidel fashion of the days of Bolingbroke. Men have been striving to get rid of the Bible and its inconvenient morality for nearly these 2,000 years; but they were never farther off from their end than they are at present.
—*The Christian.*

Youth's Department.

SEEKING THE KINGDOM OF HEAVEN.

A farewell essay read before the Brethren's Sabbath School at Waynesboro, Pa., on Sabbath August 23d, 1873, by brother J. Zuck, Jr.

It has always been my desire to do what I could while connected with this Sabbath School, and I desire to cast in my mite to-day, by reading a few thoughts which you may consider my farewell address to the school. My subject is "Seeking" based upon these words of Jesus; "Seek first the kingdom of Heaven."

Seeking means searching, trying to find out, trying to obtain. It implies the existence of desire. We may know that a thing is lost, and this, too, is implied in the word, but unless we desire to obtain it, we will not search for it. The great business of life is seeking for something or other, and this is all right if we seek the proper things. But here we are very liable to fail. Many seek wealth, and when they obtain it, they put it to no good use; others seek fame and power, only to abuse them; some we are glad to know, seek the Kingdom of Heaven, but how few seek *first* the Kingdom of Heaven? The number is very small, and yet there is no reason why it should not be very large. There are many reasons why we should enter the Lord's vinyard in the morning of life, but no one, that I can think of, why we should neglect doing so until the eleventh or twelfth hour and run the risk of dying in the meantime or of becoming too old to be of any use after we are in. Death bed repentance *may* win Heaven—remember where there is a may a "may not" is implied—but youthful piety has promise both of the life that now is and also of that which is to come. Seek *first* the Kingdom of Heaven. This gives the time to seek.

Let us next inquire *where* we shall seek the Kingdom of Heaven.

Boys you won't find it on the streets

and street corners after night. "The prince of the power of the air" is very apt to set up his kingdom at such places—it is a kingdom of darkness, blacker than the blackest night and if you are not very careful he will call you into his service. He is very cunning and deceitful and perhaps you are not as wise as you think you are. Beware, the paths of sin may seem very smooth and easy at first, but you will find them very crooked and dangerous before you go very far.

You have perhaps heard the story of the silly little fly that a big wicked spider coaxed up his winding stair. He told the innocent little fly that he had a fine parlor, a splendid bed a grand mirror and many other nice things, all of which it should enjoy if it would only come and dine with him The ugly spider! He had no such thing. His fine parlor was nothing but a miserable black den, where he would kill his innocent little visitors, and then laugh at their foolishness for believing his polished lies.

Well, boys and girls, let me tell you that the bad man is a big ugly black spider and that you are a silly little fly, whenever you think or say or do anything that he wants you to do. Don't forget this. Every bad thought takes you one step nearer his den; a vulgar or profane word will take you another; a disobedient act toward your parents will take you two or three and a quarrel with brother, sister, or a playmate will take you as many more. You are now pretty close to the cunning spider. Beware that he does not grab you and pull you into his den. If he does, you may never come out alive. His den is full of the bones of his victims! Every murderer that is hanged, every one who dies a drunkard's death, all who go down to the grave in disgrace, all these have been in the spiders den. Many of the spiders victims are put in prison and some are chained. You may see some of these poor deluded creatures at Chambersburg in the County prison, and others in the penitentiary at Philadelphia. All these were once innocent little flies but they have been in the spider's den so long that they have lost their innocence and look almost as ugly as the spider himself.

In other words, all these bad men and women were once boys and girls like you, and perhaps some of them had just as good and kind parents and friends as you have, and thought themselves just as "sharp and cute" as you do. But the spider was too cunning for them; beware that he does not prove too cunning for you. He seeks you day and night, and he often leads you quite near his den without your knowing it. But you can know it; he has three signs, hurry up. Look out for them. On the first you will see these words: "Bad thoughts" This sign hangs just outside the door. The second hangs inside near the door. On it you will see: Bad words." The third sign hangs some distance up the stairway, and contains the words: "Bad actions." You may read all these signs from the outside, if the door is open, but I would not advise you to stay long enough to read them all; as soon as you see the first, it is time to run. Run before you get tangled up in the spider's web, it may be too late afterward. As soon as you are old enough to read these three signs, you are old enough to be tempted, you are old enough to yield to sin; and in my opinion, you are old enough to give your hearts to the Lord, to become the disciples of Jesus, Christians. Seek *first* the Kingdom of Heaven. This is the only safe course. You will find a knowledge of this Kingdom and of the proper way to seek and find it, in the Holy Scriptures, and these we are all commanded to search. *This is just what you are doing here in the Sabbath School.* Here you can *get help.* This help would be very highly prized by you, if you could only appreciate the worth of what you are seeking, or *ought* to be seeking. It is a goodly pearl worth more than all the world. This being the case, how earnest we should be in our search.

You have heard of children losing themselves on the mountains. How soon the whole neighborhood is aroused in behalf of the little wanderer! A few years ago a child was lost on the mountains near my home, and though I was a hundred miles away, I soon got the news. How eagerly the people turned out to hunt the absent child! Men and boys searched the mountains from morning till evening, and from evening till morning, and so on for several days, but all in vain. All the mothers in the neighborhood made the grief of the bereaved mother their own grief. How rejoiced all would have felt had some one brought the news that the lost was found, and all was well. But this news never came. Months after, some of the bleached bones of the unfortunate child were found far back in the mountains, and near them, some gathered moss and sticks with which the lost child had perhaps built a little play-house to amuse itself in its last hours of loneliness and distress.

Now is it not true that many children are lost upon the dark mountains of sin, and others are losing themselves every day? They are getting farther and farther from home, and it is to be feared that their fate may be as sad, and perhaps much sadder, than that of the lost child. Yet how indifferent we are—we who ought to be seeking them. This thought is for the older members—the believing members of the school—and I would to God that I could present it right forcibly to the thousands of professed Christians who stand aloof from the Sabbath School and take no interest in the spiritual welfare of children.

And now a few more words to the older members of the school. It has been about a year since I become acquainted with you and the work that you are trying to carry on. In view of the sad negligence of some, and the sadder conduct of a few others,—all of whom ought to be here helping you along, in view of this, I think you have done well and that you are yet doing well. Some people are too apt to embrace every wind of doctrine, while some are in the other extreme and will not believe anything until they must. They must be educated into the thing, and education is a growth—a very slow growth too, with some people. The trouble is you can not get them under the educating influence. Could this be done their musty notions would very often disappear like darkness before the rising sun. Like Thomas, they doubt, like him they must see with their own eyes and feel with their own hands, but, unlike him, they will not go where they can have these tangible evidences. In the case of opposition to a good work like the Sabbath School, these things are very disheartening, but I don't think that this is just cause for abandoning the work. During the short time that I have been knocking—and I might add, parenthetically,—being knocked around in the world, I have found that many disheartening things must be met and overcome if we would be true to our sense of duty. It is disheartening to some people to be persecuted and evil spoken of for righteousness' sake—so disheartening that they break their solemn vows and backslide. Is this right? Certainly not, for Christ says to such; "Rejoice and be exceeding glad," and He assigns this reason; "for great is your reward in Heaven." I think it would not be out of place to apply this same language to the faithful Sabbath School worker. There is no temporal reward—not as the "temporal" is generally applied, at least. It is a work of love and self-denial. Selfishness and self-interest—in the baser sense—should have neither part nor lot in the matter. It should be the mission of the Sabbath School worker to impart and receive spiritual culture—heart culture—and at the same time honor God by winning souls to Christ. If he labors for this end, surely he ought to rejoice and be exceeding glad in the very face of discouragements, for great is his reward in Heaven.

The efficiency of a Sabbath School depends very much upon the efficiency of its teachers. A failure here is a failure that impairs the whole school. An indifferent teacher will make an indifferent class, and a few such classes will make an indifferent school. Teachers should be prompt and regular on attendance, and zealous in the discharge of duty while with their classes, remembering that their work is the noblest in which they can engage.

Let me entreat you to stand by your Superintendent and second all praiseworthy efforts to promote the welfare of the school. He needs and has a right to expect hearty cooperation. You have placed him in a position of great responsibility, and one that has, no doubt, been very embarrassing. Don't desert him when help is most needed, for it is a work for Christ and the good of souls. Be punctual, earnest, prayerful. It would be looked upon as cowardly for a company of soldiers to choose one of their number to be their captain and then disobey his orders and run away when the fight commences It would even be tho't unbecoming for a private to merely question the propriety of a command. But in this I am sure your Supt. don't want the comparison to hold good. He will cheerfully accord you the right to question, and will as cheerfully adopt your suggestions, if they would bring about an improvement. But let me entreat you to make those suggestions to him first, not to others until necessary, which will seldom happen.

I leave you, my Christian friends, in the hope that at least some of you have enough interest in my spiritual welfare to remember me occasionally at a throne of grace, while I am far far away, trying by a course of study to better fit myself for the duties of life. Pray that I may become less selfish, less self-willed, more devoted to the Lord and better qualified to discharge all the duties of life. This I ask as the most precious boon that you as honest-hearted Christians could grant. God be thanked for the prayers of pious friends. We all need such prayers—especially we who expose ourselves to influences that draw powerfully into channels that it is not our wish to enter. What these influences are some of you who have always been near those of your own faith, can not fully realize. Pray that I may withstand them.

And now in conclusion, let me express a hope that you may all prosper both temporally and spiritually with a prosperity that the Lord can smile upon and approve; that we may all do something to promote the welfare of our fellow-men and that in the end we may be found faithful and accounted worthy to inherit eternal life and wear a crown of rejoicing evermore.

As a Sabbath School, I now bid you an affectionate farewell.

The Weekly Pilgrim.

JAMES CREEK, PA., Sept. 30, 1873.

☞ How to send money.—All sums over $1.50, should be sent either in a check, draft or postal order. If neither of these can be obtained, have the letter registered.

☞ When Money is sent, *always* send with it the name and address of those who paid it. Write the names and post office as plainly as possible.

☞ Every subscriber for 1874, gets a *Pilgrim Almanac* Free.

GET READY.

The time is now approaching when we will send out our prospectus for the coming year, and we hope our agents and friends will be in readiness to receive it and go to work at once. When we have in view any work we generally give it some forethought, in order that we may accomplish it most successfully, and so it should be with our agents who expect to work for us this Fall. You should look over your respective fields of operation and take a view of the material with which you expect to work. Think of all who might possibly be induced to take the Pilgrim the coming year, and how and where you can approach them so as to best accomplish your purpose. There is a great deal in the place and manner in which you solicit subscribers for a paper. If our agents were to go around among the people when at their work with as much energy as a book agent, or an agent for some patent right, there would probably but few refuse; but this work is generally deferred until Sabbath when they are met at church, and then merely asked whether they do not want to subscribe for the paper. By this method many do not take a church paper that would, if approached at the proper time and manner.

Brethren and sisters, it is important that we all take our church papers, and we should also feel it important that we get as many as possible to take them who do not belong to the church. Every member should have them in order that they may be fed and kept alive by the precious truths of the Gospel. Show me the brother or sister who does not care for our church periodicals, and we will show you one that knows but little about the church, and is dead and inactive. Then too, we should try to get those who are not members to read them in order that we may further the cause of our blessed Master. In view of this it does seem to us that our agents have before them a very important work this Fall, and one too, that should have considerable forethought. It may not pay in dollars and cents, but there is a time coming in which you may feel that you are richly rewarded. Every effort that is made, in true faith, for the advancement of the Redeemer's Kingdom will have its reward, if not in this life in the world to come, and the more we thus labor, the richer and greater will be our treasures in Heaven. We hope then, that this work may receive the earnest attention of our brethren and sisters, that you may prepare yourselves to make a greater effort to circulate our periodicals the coming year than you have ever done heretofore. Wake up, the time is drawing near to commence the work, set everything in readiness and then go at it with a will. Try to arrange your other work so as to have some time to devote entirely to this purpose. Visit our brethren, sisters and friends at their homes, and urge your claims upon them the same as you would if introducing some farming implement, and we feel assured that much can be accomplished. There is no reason why the circulation of the Pilgrim should not be doubled the coming year, and from the letters we are receiving from our brethren and sisters, our prospects for a large increase are flattering, and all that is needed is energy and perseverance to double its present circulation. Then kind patrons, please get ready for a long pull, a strong pull, and a pull altogether. J. B. B.

LONG EVENINGS.

The summer will soon be past and, with it, will end the busy season for many of our readers which will give more leisure for reading and writing. The long evenings are approaching which afford those pleasant little seasons in family circles, in fact, they are the Sabbaths of the days and are made to good account in Christian families in reading and obtaining useful and religious knowledge. The time has come that people will read which makes it the more important that we place within their reach, a sound and religious literature. This is what we wish to do and therefore, solicit the co-operation of all such as are interested in the welfare of Zion. Brethren and sisters, awake to the great work and make use of the talents God gave you in converting and saving the children of men. Many who have the time and ability to write, are apparently indifferent to the power they might exert for good, while others waste their time in writing long letters of complaints against what is written. This is not the way to improve the character of our reading, but get to work and supply us with so much good copy, that we will not be necessitated to use the inferior in order to fill our pages. Give us plenty of the good old wine and the new will be to lay over until it gets seasoned. Brethren and sisters, try it once, fill our drawer, and see if the Pilgrim don't come forth, more than ever, filled with spiritual food, meat for the soul.

A number of good essays will be thankfully received at this office.

JAMES CREEK LOVEFEAST.

Our brethren and sisters will please notice that our Lovefeast will be on the 10th and 11th of October, and that all who have a desire to be with us will be heartily welcome. We expect a goodly number of our brethren and sisters from the neighboring churches to be with us, and arrangements will be made accordingly. This invitation is intended to be general, but ministerial visits are always considered special favors. The meeting will commence at 2 o'clock on the 10th and be continued over Sunday. Those coming, will please make arrangements to remain with us until the meeting closes. We will make arrangements for the cars to stop at the Church in the morning and evening of the 10th, both trains, North and South. For the time of trains see schedule in Pilgrim. Those wishing to enter the evening services should come in the morning trains.

GIVE US THE NEWS.

The news of the brotherhood is called for by our readers, and in order that we may be able to give it more fully, different brethren have suggested that we have a reporter in every Church, whose special business it shall be to report every event that may be of interest to the general reader. This is just what we desire and for the coming year we hope to make such arrangements. Who will be our reporters? We would prefer if the churches would appoint their own reporter, and we will see that he gets such a compensation as our abilities will allow. We are willing to accept any suggestions that will improve the usefulness of the Pilgrim.

ATTENTION—PLEASE.

We have, standing out on our books, nearly $1,000. Of this we do not complain as we promised to wait on those who did not have the money when subscribing. We have now patiently waited nine months, and as we have some payments to make, and badly need some money, we now ask every reader who yet owes us for subscription &c. to pay us, if possible, between this and the 15th of October. Now brethren and sisters, let us see how much you can oblige us by sending or having it sent right along. Those who pay to agents, don't wait for them to ask for it, but oblige them and us by attending to it at once. We wish it understood that all who can and will pay us between this and the time specified will confer us a *special favor*.

Change of Address. — David Brower's address is changed from Sublimity to Salem, Marion Co., Oregon.

Several articles of Correspondence came too late for insertion this week,—will appear next.

Correspondence.

A Reporter is wanted from every Church in the brotherhood to send us Church news, Obituaries, Announcements, or anything that will be of general interest. To insure insertion, the writers name must accompany each communication. Our Invitation is not personal but general—please respond to our call.

Dear Pilgrim: It surely affords much gratification to have you say to your readers that my health is about fully restored. It has been steadily improving since last Spring, and I think it is on a better basis than it has been for many years. I have been discharging my ministerial duties regularly this Summer, and hope to be able to continue them unremittingly. I owe my gratitude to God for these mercies, and with His help, I hope to devote my restored health to His service. I hope soon to arrange my temporal affairs so that I can have the time to labor much more than I have heretofore.

For the benefit of those who are similarly afflicted, I will give the remedies I used.

First, I put myself on a strict, hygienic diet, consisting of bread made of unbolted flour, and green fruits of all kinds, canned in the Winter, and baked and stewed in Summer, but never fried in grease. I ate a few vegetables, but none cooked in grease, in fact I repudiated grease in every shape, and butter, and salted meat and pork, and cucumbers, all kinds of pickles, salt and pepper and every other species of condiments. I used eggs and unskimmed milk and buttermilk. I still adhere to this diet and hope to continue it indefinitely, so far as it is practicable. So, when I travel among the Brethren, if they have bread made of unbolted flour, and milk and fruit, they will not fail to gratify my desire as to diet.

For several weeks I took a form of bath called by hygienists, "a fomentation" which did me much good. Apply for instructions how to bathe to Dr. Jackson, Our Home, Livingston Co., N. Y. I would advise any that are afflicted with any disease of the stomach, and most all chronic diseases have their origin there, to go there if their pecuniary affairs will permit it. Also what is very important, I have tried to adhere to the injunction of the apostolic hygienist, St. Paul; "Be temperate in all things."

Our church here held its Communion in August. We were liberally supported by our neighboring ministers and had truly a feast of love. We have had no additions this Summer, but we look hopefully to the future for the time of harvest.

Our Methodist friends have made quite a number of conversions in this vicinity lately. As usual, on such occasions, the forms of admission into the fold were as various as the minds of the applicants. Some were sprinkled, some were poured, and some immersed. In immersing the latter they encountered quite a difficulty in the form of shallow water. But their ingenuity was equal to the emergency. The stream was too shallow to allow the candidate to stand erect and receive the backward dip. Now brethren what do you think was done. The minister directed them to *kneel down* as we do, and then, in the names of the sacred trinity, he immersed them b-a-c-k-w-a-r-d. It is strange what a propensity these single immersionists have to go backward. Right about face brethren and go forward by the divine order. Christ, the founder of our Church, never gave you a precept or precedent for your backward worship, though His enemies are known to have gone backward on several occasions.

I attended a Methodist sacramental meeting recently. They took the Lord's Supper, so called, at about 1 p. m., consisting of a morsel of bread and a sip of wine. It is hard for us to comprehend the meaning of the terms to designate the ordinance as they use them, while we recognize the intelligibility of our pure and good old English. Our only alternative is to relapse, for the occasion, into a kind of a mental and spiritual hallucination. In that happy state we *might* be able to understand how a bit of bread and a sip of wine taken at midday, in a meeting-house, by a company of fashionable men, women and children, Campbellites, Methodists, Presbyterians, Episcopalians, Baptists, Lutherans, Calvanists, Armenians, Rationalists, Spiritualists, &c., *ad infinitum*, can be called the Lord's Supper.

We may be considered mentally and spiritually obtuse, but we choose to remain so rather than to become lost in such a labyrinth of isms and opinions. "Let us be of one mind," is an injunction that has more influence over our actions than the imputation of uncharitableness and self-righteousness which we hear occasionally in whispers designedly audible. Is not that right Bro. Pilgrim? (They all say let him be crucified. Ed)

At some future time I will contribute an item bearing on the famous baptismal controversy. Let this suffice for the present.

Your fellow laborer in the Gospel.
D. C. MOOMAW.

THE ANCIENT LANDMARKS.

Dear Brethren:—The PILGRIM still continues to make its weekly visits to our home, and the oftener I receive it the more I feel impressed to write a few lines for its columns on its beautiful motto, namely, "Remove not the ancient landmarks which your fathers have set." When I look around and see the way things are going on in the Church, my heart is made to feel very sorry. I think any brother or sister with their spiritual eye half open, can readily see to their own satisfaction, that the ancient landmarks have already been removed to a great extent; but some one will perhaps say, in what measure have they been removed? We will notice in the first place, the manner in which we dress and see how it harmonizes with that of our brethren and sisters, we will say, of twenty years ago. Let us look back the short period of twenty years and take a glimpse of the church at that day. Every brother and sister could be recognized by their dress, but how is it in our day and age of the world? Do we not profess to be branches of the same vine that they did in their day, and should not we resemble each other more than we do? If we drift along in the same channel for twenty years in the future, where will we land? I fear the ancient landmarks will scarcely be perceptible. We want to complain of the cross being heavy sometimes, why is it that it seems so heavy to us? Methinks it is all our own fault. We increase its weight to a great extent, by trying to bear the cross of Christ on one shoulder, and the fashions of the world on the other. Remember the words of our Savior, "Ye cannot serve God and mammon," consequently if we serve our Lord and Master, which I hope we are all trying to do, we will have to leave all the vanities of the world, and if we want to follow the fashions of the world, we will have to lay aside religion. For the apostle says, that to whom ye yield yourselves servants to obey, his servants ye are to whom ye obey, whether of sin unto death or of obedience unto righteousness.—Rom. 6:19

Brethren and sisters, let us take up the cross and with a willing mind bear it after Him who bore it up Calvary's hill, and there did not refuse to die for us.

"Take up the cross nor heed the shame,
And let thy foolish pride be still;
Thy Lord did not refuse to die
Upon the cross on Calvary's hill."

A SISTER.

H. B. Brumbaugh, dear brother: Perhaps you are always anxious and ready to hear from the brethren, let the news be much or little.

—The PILGRIM is before me, and among other articles, I have just finished brother D. P. Saylor's on Religion. I generally like the brother's style of presenting his thoughts. They have about them no uncertain sound, but at once tell what kind of mettle they are of. I love to hear a clear and a distinct Gospel tone.

It seems that brother S. has entertained some ideas of laying aside his pen, and not write anymore for the brethren. He is an old soldier, and has fought many long and hard battles, and we can not yet see the propriety of his laying aside his weapons. Peace on earth has not yet been fully established, the enemy is not vanquished, false teachers abound as the waters cover the great deep, false religion is everywhere, and we now need more help in the great cause than ever before.

Christ requires that His servants enlist for *life*, or *during* the *war*—put on the whole armor of God, take the sword of the spirit and fight manfully till the war is over, then the righteous judge will give to all the faithful a crown of life that fadeth not away. As a thought of my own, I suggest that many of our aged brethren, who have both the knowledge and experience to do so, do not generally write enough. The apostle John finished his last roll when he was nearly one hundred years old. Moses continued to write till near the close of his long and eventful life. Solomon gathered his Proverbs when he was well advanced in life. Paul, when ready to lay down his useful life, did not forget to write to his son Timothy. We think brother S. has been on the field too long to now retire amid the din of battle, we need those aged and tried veterans who have long borne the heat and burden of the day, to lead on the destined victorious band, and, when they retire let them fall while in ranks with the faithful, engaged with deadly conflict with the enemy, and then when with sad hearts we bare their bodies from the field to the tomb, we may console our afflictions with the thought that they have fought a *good* fight, they have finished their course, they have kept the faith, and there is laid up for them a crown of righteousness, which the Lord the righteous judge shall give them at that day. J. H. MOORE.

Dear Pilgrim:—On last Sunday I attended meeting four miles South of Mt. Union. The attendance was small. The National Camp Meeting at Newton Hamilton, three miles East of Mt. Union, attracts the attention of nearly all classes of people at present. "Whithersoever the carcass is there will the eagles be gathered together."

On Saturday eve., the Mail train Eastward was already filled to overflowing at Tyrone City. Large crowds were waiting patiently at the station for transportation, but were of course disappointed as the train rushed through as if it were a "fast line," and the disappointed crowds were obliged to walk or wait for the next train. On Sunday our town seemed to be almost entirely deserted. The meeting continued until Thursday. As to the merit or demerit of the affair I cannot say, did not attend. Those who were in attendance (some brethren) should be better qualified than I am, but one thing I am free to assert and prepared to prove, that God will be the final and just judge. In my next, if the Lord will, I intend to give you a description &c., of Mt. Union.

Fraternally yours,
J. B. GARVER.

DIED.

MASTERS.—In Fayette Co., W. Va., Sep. 12, 1873, after a short illness, Ida May, daughter of brother Charles and sister Charlotte Masters, aged 5 months.

Thus dear parents, your little Ida has been called to go on before you, to rest in the bosom of God's love. A bright gem in eternity whom you may meet and greet in the realms of bliss. Labor and live on as pilgrims seeking a better country, abide your time patiently, and the day of deliverance will come to free you too, from this world of sin and sorrow, then in the great resurrection morn children and parents shall all come forth unto eternal life, the hope of that blessed meeting is sweetness even in the greatest of our sorrows. Look up and see the bright golden edge to every cloud of sorrow, affliction and bereavement, which shows God's light and love is just beyond. Lines by the mother:

Farewell my little Ida,
Thou hast from sorrow gone,
Left parents, brothers, sisters,
Deeply thy loss to mourn.

I miss thee, sweet little Ida,
But my loss is your great gain,
This world is naught but trouble,
Temptation, toil and pain.

We will strive to meet thee
When with earth we are done,
And live with thee forever,
'Round God's eternal throne.

J. S. FLORY.

BYRD.—Near Ottobine, in the Beaver Creek District, Rockingham Co., Va., Sept. 14, 1873, sister Catharine, consort of Jacob Byrd, aged 70 years, 5 mos. and 27 days.

Funeral service by Eld. Geo. Wine and others, from Paul's letter to the Philippians 1:21., to a large concourse of people. These words were selected by the deceased, as she bowed in humble submission to the Lord. She leaves a large connection of friends and relations which are scattered over different States. S. N. WINE.

The following deaths occurred in our District, since February last, none of which were noticed in the PILGRIM. By request of the friends I send them for insertion.

Elizabeth, wife of John Hershey, deacon, Feb. 9, 1873, aged 82 years, 11 months.
John Shengle, deacon, Feb. 23, 1873, aged 74 years, 21 mos. and 17 days.
Abraham Kagy, deacon, June 22, '73, aged 55 yrs., 5 mos. and 10 days. The above suffered terribly of cancer, was under treatment of Dr. Metz of Massillon, O.
Susan, wife of Bro. Jos. Summers, July 29, 1873, aged 75 years, 1 mo. and 17 days.
Rebecca, wife of Christian Sollenberger, Aug. 25, 1873, aged 63 years and some months. Apparently in the best of health during the day—she left at evening—apoplexy.
Elizabeth, daughter of friend Joseph Brechner, Aug. 29, '73, aged 1 year and 10 mos.
Samuel Brechner, Sept. 4, 1873, son of the above, aged 3 years and 3 months.
Hiram, son of friend Jacob Hershey, Sept. 11, aged 16 years and some months.
Daniel Edward, son of David Flory, Sept. 16, 1873, aged 1 year and 6 days.

The above were all buried at the Centre Meetinghouse two miles south-west of Louisville, Stark Co., O., Canton District. Services by the Brethren and a few others.
B. B. BOLLINGER.

ANNOUNCEMENTS.

Please say through your worthy paper, that we, the members of the Salamony arm of the church have appointed a Communion meeting on the 28th of October, 1873, at our meeting-house, commencing at 10 o'clock. A general invitation is extended. Those coming by Railroad will stop off at Huntington. There will be conveyance at Huntington the day before to convey members to place of meeting. ELD. S. MURRAY

Hamilton Congregation; Caldwell Co Mo., October 4th and 5th.

North Coventry Congregation, near Pottstown, Pa., October 4th and 5th.

Spring Run, Mifflin Co., Pa. on the 5th of October.

Dry Valley Meeting-house, Mifflin Co. Pa., October 3 and 4.

Falling Spring Congregation, Franklin Co., on the 10th of October.

Beaver Run, Mineral Co, W. Va., on the 11th and 12th of October.

James Creek Pa., on the 10 and 11th of October.

Grasshopper Valley Church, Jefferson Co., Kan., Meetinghouse in the town Osawkee, Oct. 4 and 5.

Dunnings Creek Congregation, Pa., on Friday, Oct. 3.

Stone Church, Marshall Co, Iowa, on the 4th and 5th of Oct.

Our Lovefeasts of Maryland, will be held as follows:

Sam's Creek,	Oct. 11,	commence 1½ p. m.
Monocacy,	" 17.	
Meadow Branch,	" 21,	com. 1½ p. m.
Beaver Dam,	" 25.	

In the Cold Water church, in the new stone meeting house, on the 8th and 9th of October. Nearest railroad station is Green, about a half mile from the church.

In the Hopewell District, Bedford co., Pa. on Friday the 3d of October, commencing at 4 o'clock.

Black River Branch, Medina Co. Ohio, October 3.

Logan Church, Logan Co., Ohio, Oct. 9.

Fawn River Congregation, Lagrange Co., Ind., on the 4th and 5th of Oct.

Wadams Grove, Stephenson Co., Ill., October 11 and 12.

Dry Creek, Lynn Co., Iowa, on the 1st and 2d of November.

Root River Branch, Minn. 4th and 5th of October.

Aughwick Congregation, Huntingdon Co., Pa., on the 7th and 8th of October, commencing at 1 o'clock p. m., on the 7th.

Monticello Church, White Co., Ind., on the 10th of October.

LITERATURE.

A. B. Brumbaugh, Huntingdon, Pa. Literary Editor.

THE LAST PASSOVER.—A harmony of the Evangelists. An account of the closing incidents in the life upon earth of Jesus Christ, Our Passover; Showing the verbal harmony of the four Gospel narratives, arranged by John R. Whitney.—Claxton, Remson & Haffelfinger, Philadelphia 16 mo. Price, $1 00.

In the preparation of this Harmony the author has simply interwoven the different accounts given by the four Evangelists of the same events, so as to give, in their own words, one simple and complete narrative, not even adding a single word or phrase, not even an 'and,' 'but,' 'it' or 'then.'

The author says. "In this arrangement *every word* is recognized as a pearl of price, and every phrase as a thread of gold; and the attempt has been in the spirit of prayer, to so weave all together as to produce a royal fabric where the warp is God's truth and the woof the rich unfoldings of his grace; and the whole is presented as an offering of praise the King of Kings."

This is a very desirable little book. For sale by Wm. Lewis, Huntingdon, Pa., or at this office.

THE ANCIENT HEBREWS; with an introductory essay concerning the world before the flood. By Abraham Mills, A. M.—A. S. Barnes & Co., New York and Chicago. Price $1.75.

Few books can be selected that contain subjects of such deep interest as those, whose pages are devoted to matters pertaining to the Ancients. While this is true in regard to the history of the Grecians, the Romans, and other *profane* nations, it is peculiarly true in regard to the history of the Ancient Hebrews. "Here no darkness or uncertainty veils the mind respecting the *truth* of what is recorded; but everything stands out in bold relief; characters are exhibited as they were; transactions are recorded as they occurred; vice is uniformly detected and punished, and virtue, recognized and rewarded. JEHOVAH himself is the judge; and of the justness of His decisions no question can properly arise."

No books in our library are read with so much interest and profit by ourself and family, as those histories whose narratives relate to subjects contained in the sacred Scriptures. The perusal of this book will afford any of our readers subjects for profitable contemplation.

APPLETON'S JOURNAL.—An Illustrated Weekly, of Literature, Science and Art. Published by D. Appleton & Co., New York. Price 10 cts. per number or $4.00 per year. Monthly parts $4.50 per year. This is a deservedly popular Journal. It gives, in a weekly form, all the features of the best monthly Magazines, while its weekly issues brings it a more frequent visitor to the family than is the case with a monthly periodical. It bears evidence of the same thoroughness, care and ability characterizing the great number of publications—periodicals and books—issued by the Appleton's. The POPULAR SCIENCE MONTHLY published by them at once rose into favor with the intelligent reading public. It should be still more generally known and appreciated. THE NEW AMERICAN ENCYCLOPEDIA, their special work, has taken the lead and become a valued necessity to many thousand "*learners*" throughout the land, and world. They take the lead in Scientific publications. Also in valuable school and text-books.

THE GOSPEL VISITOR, a monthly Magazine devoted to the defence of the Gospel principles and practices, chrisian union, brotherly love and universal charity. Vol. 23 for 1873. Edited by Henry Kurtz and James Quinter; and published at Dayton, O., by H. J. Kurtz Terms $1.25 per year

This is the pioneer periodical of the Brethren and commends itself to them by its consistent advocacy of a pure christianity free from creeds, confessions of faith or ecclesiastical rule. It has lived now over twenty-two years, and its annual volumes neatly bound, as we have them, would form a valuable addition to every brother's library.

DYMOND ON WAR.

An Inquiry into the Accordancy of War, with the Principles of Christianity, and an examination of the Philosophical reasoning by which it is defended. With observations on some of the causes of war and on some of its effects. By Jonathan Dymond Sent from this office, post-paid, for 50 cts.

GOOD BOOKS.

How to read Character, Illus. Price,	$1.25
Combe's Moral Philosophy,	1.75
Constitution of Man. Combe,	1.75
Education. By Spurzheim,	1.50
Memory—How to Improve it,	1.50
Mental Science, Lectures on,	1.50
Self-Culture and Perfection,	1.50
Combe's Physiology, Illus.	1.75
Food and Diet. By Pereira,	1.75

WANTED.

A man to work at the Wagon-making business, who understands the trade, and is capable of running a shop independently. Shop and material furnished. Work plenty both heavy and light. A reasonable chance will be given to a suitable person. A man without a family will be preferred. Apply to or address the undersigned.

GEO. BRUMBAUGH.
Grafton, Huntingdon Co., Pa.

GET THE BEST.

WEBSTER'S Unabridged Dictionary.

10,000 *Words and Meanings not in other Dictionaries.*

3000 Engravings; 1840 Pages Quarto. Price $12.

Webster now is glorious,—it leaves nothing to be desired. [Pres. Raymond, Vassar College.]

Every scholar knows the value of the work. (W. H. Prescott, the Historian.)

Been one of my daily companions. (John L. Motley, the Historian, &c.)

Superior in most respects to any other known to me. (George P. Marsh.)

The best guide of students of our language. (John G. Whittier.)

Excels all others in defining scientific terms. (President Hitchcock.)

Remarkable compendium of human knowledge. (W. S. Clark, Pres. Ag. Col'ge.)

A necessity for every intelligent family, student, teacher and professional man. What library is complete without the best English Dictionary?

ALSO

Webster's Nat'nal Pictorial Dict'nary.

1040 Pages Octavo. 600 Engrv'gs. Price $5.

The work is really a gem of a Dictionary, just the thing for the million.—*American Educational Monthly.*

Published by G. & C. MERRIAM, Springfield, Mass. Sold by all Booksellers.

Trine Immersion TRACED TO THE APOSTLES.

The SECOND EDITION is now ready for delivery. The work has been carefully revised, corrected and enlarged.

Put up in a neat pamphlet form, with good paper cover, and will be sent, post-paid, from this office on the following terms: One copy, 25 cts; Five copies, $1.10; Ten copies, $2.00. 25 copies, $4.50; 50 copies, $8.50; 100 copies, $16.00.

$5 to $20 [illegible]

Historical Charts of Baptism.

A complete key to the history of Trine, and the ORIGIN of Single Immersion. The most interesting, reliable and comprehensive document ever published on the subject. This Chart exhibits the years of the birth and death of the Ancient Fathers, the length of their lives, who of them lived at the same period, and shows how easy it was for them to transmit to each succeeding generation, a correct understanding of the Apostolic method of baptizing. It is 22x28 inches in size, and extends over the first 400 years of the Christian era, exhibiting at a single glance the impossibility of single immersion ever having been the Apostolic method. Single copy, $1.00; Four copies, $3.25. Sent post paid. Address, J. H. MOORE.
Urbana, Champaign Co., Ill.

GIVEN AWAY.

A FINE GERMAN CHROMO.

We send an elegant chromo, mounted and ready for framing, free to every agent for

UNDERGROUND

OR,

LIFE BELOW THE SURFACE.

BY THOS. W. KNOX.

942 Pages Octavo. 130 Fine Engravings.

Relates Incidents and Accidents beyond the Light of Day; Startling Adventures in all parts of the World Mines and Mode of Working them; Under-currents of Society; Gambling and its *Horrors*; Caverns and their Mysteries; The Dark Ways of Wickedness; Prisons and their Secrets; Down in the Depths of the Sea; Strange Stories of the Detection of Crime.

The book treats of experience with brigands; nights in opium dens and gambling hells; life in prison; Stories of exiles; adventures among Indians; journey through Sewers and Catacombs; accidents in mines; pirates and piracy; tortures of the inquisition; wonderful burglaries; underworld of the great cities, etc., etc.

AGENTS WANTED

for this work. Exclusive territory is given. Agents can make $100 a week in selling this book. Send for circulars and terms to agents.

J. B BURR & HYDE,

HARTFORD, CONN., OR CHICAGO, ILL

TRACTS.

"ANXIOUS BENCH RELIGION EXAMINIED," BY ELDER J. S. FLORY. A SYNOPSIS OF CONTENTS. An address to the reader: The peculiarities that attend this type of religion. The feelings there experienced not imaginary but real. The key that unlocks the wonderful mystery. The causes by which feelings are excited. How the momentary feelings called "Experimental religion" are brought about, and then concludes by giving that form of doctrine as taught by Jesus Christ and recorded by his faithful witnesses.

COUNTERFEIT DETECTER

OF

BAPTISM—MUCH IN LITTLE.

This work is now ready for distribution, and the importance of the subject will speak for it a large demand. It is a short treatise on baptism in tract form intended for general distribution, and is set forth in such a plain and logical manner that a wayfaring man though a fool, cannot err therein. Either of the above tracts sent postpaid on the following terms: Two copies, 10 cts, 10 copies 40 cents, 25 copies 70 cents, 50 copies $1.00, 100 copies $1.50.

Trine Immersion.

A discussion on Trine Immersion, by letter between Elder B. F. Moomaw and Dr. J. J. Jackson, to which is annexed a Treatise on the Lord's Supper, and on the necessity, character and evidences of the new birth, also a dialogue on the doctrine of non-resistance, by Elder B. F Moomaw. Single copy 50 cents.

THE HELPING HAND.

Containing several hundred Valuable Receipts for cooking well at a moderate expense, making Dyes, Coloring, Cleaning and Cementing. This book also points out in plain language, free from Doctors' terms the diseases of men, women and children, and the latest and most approved means used for their cure, to which is added a description of the Medicinal Roots and Herbs, and how they are to be used in the cure of diseases.

This is a work of considerable importance and we offer it to our readers as being a valuable accession to every household. Send from this office to any address, post-paid, for 25 cents.

TUNE BOOK.

The Brethren's Tune and Hymn Book, is a compilation of Sacred Music adapted to all the hymns in the Brethren's New Hymn Book. It contains over 350 pages, printed on good paper and neatly bound. We will send it to any address, post paid at $1.25 per copy.

1870 1873

DR. FAHRNEY'S Blood Cleanser or Panacea.

A tonic and purge, for Blood Diseases. Great reputation. Many testimonials. Many ministering brethren use and recommend it. Ask or send for the "Health Messenger." Use only the "*Panacea*" prepared at Chicago, Ills., and by

Dr. P. Fahrney's Brothers & Co.,
Feb. 3-pd. *Waynesboro, Franklin Co., Pa*

New Hymn Books, English.

TURKEY MOROCCO.

One copy, postpaid,	$1.00
Per Dozen,	11.25

PLAIN ARABESQUE.

One Copy, post-paid,	75
Per Dozen, "	8.50

Ger'n & English, Plain Sheep.

One Copy, post-paid,	$1.00
Per Dozen	11.25
Arabesque Plain,	1.00
Turkey Morocco,	1.25
Single German, post paid	58
Per Dozen,	5.50

HUNTINGDON & BROAD TOP RAIL ROAD

On and after Aug 14th, 1873, Trains will run on this road daily (Sun excepted) as follows:

Trains from Huntingdon South. *Trains from Mt. Dal's moving North.*

EXPS. P. M.	MAIL. A. M.	STATIONS.	MAIL. P. M.	EXP'S A. M
6 15	7 45	Huntingdon,	AR6 50	AR9 20
6 20	7 50	Long Siding	6 45	9 15
6 35	8 00	McConnelstown	6 35	9 05
6 40	8 05	Pleasant Grove	6 20	8 58
6 51	8 20	MARKLESBURG	6 15	8 45
7 01	8 35	Coffee Run	6 05	8 35
7 08	8 41	Rough & Ready	5 58	8 29
7 15	8 50	Cove	5 40	8 20
7 18	8 53	Fishers Summit	5 46	8 17
7 35	9 10	Saxton	5 35	8 05
7 50	9 25	Riddlesburg	5 15	7 45
7 55	9 32	Hopewell	5 10	7 38
8 10	9 45	Piper's Run	4 58	7 26
8 21	0 57	Tatesville	4 43	7 12
8 32	10 07	Everett	4 33	7 03
8 40	10 15	Mount Dallas	4 30	7 00
9 00	10 35	Bedford	4 05	6 35

SHOUP'S RUN BRANCH.

A. M.	P. M.		P. M.	A. M.
LE 9 20	LE 7 40	Saxton.	AR5 25	AR 7 55
9 35	7 55	Coalmont.	5 10	7 40
9 40	8 00	Crawford.	5 05	7 35
AR 9 50	AR8 10	Dudley	LE4 55	LE 7 25

Bro'd Top City from Dudley 2 miles by stage.

Time of Penna. R. R. Trains at Huntingdon

*$_*$*Mail No. 2 makes connection at Huntingdon with Mail going East on Pennsylvania Railroad at 4.15 p. m., and West at 5.45 p. m. Mail No. 1 leaves Huntingdon at 7.40 a. m. on arrival of Pacific Express West.

Trains on this road connect with trains on Bedford & Bridgeport, and Cumberland & Pennsylvania Railroads.

G. F. GAGE, Supt.

The Weekly Pilgrim.

Published by J. B. Brumbaugh, & Co.

Edited by H. B. & Geo. Brumbaugh.

CORRESPONDING EDITORS.

D. P. Sayler, Double Pipe Creek, Md.

Leonard Furry, New Enterprise, Pa.

The *Pilgrim* is a Christian Periodical, devoted to religion and moral reform. It will advocate in the spirit of *love* and *liberty*, the principles of true Christianity, labor for the promotion of peace among the people of God, for the encouragement of the saints and for the conversion of sinners, avoiding those things which tend toward disunion or sectional feelings.

TERMS.

Single copy, Book paper,	$1.50
Eleven copies, [eleventh for Agt.]	$15.00

Any number above that at the same rate, Address,

H. B. BRUMBAUGH.
James Creek,
Huntingdon county Pa.

The Weekly Pilgrim.

"REMOVE NOT THE ANCIENT LANDMARKS WHICH OUR FATHERS HAVE SET."

VOL. 4. JAMES CREEK, PENNSYLVANIA, OCTOBER 7, 1873. NO. 40

POETRY.

For the Pilgrim

LONGING FOR HOME.

BY WESLEY.

I am longing for the coming,
Of the snowy-vestured band,
That will bear my weary spirit,
To the sinless, summer land.
As I tread the narrow causeway,
Through this thorny vale, I dream
Of the joys that ever brighten,
Where the pearly waters gleam.

Where the flowers, by the river,
Fling their fragrance to the gale,
Where the ransomed of the Father,
The rich odor, may inhale,
While a strain, unknown to mortals,
Wakes the echo's of the shore,
As it sweeps its glassy surface,
In the happy evermore.

I am waiting for the signal
That shall speak my full release,
And present my welcome passport
To the realms of perfect peace,
Yea, and when my lagging sandals,
All the dusty way have trod,
I shall sing amongst the angels,
By the golden throne of God.

I am longing to be going.
Yet my Father's kind command,
Bids me tarry mid the shadows
Of this misty lower land.
When my pilgrimage is ended,
I shall stem the turbid flood;
And recline upon the bosom
Of the spotless Son of God.

Selected by E. R. STIFLER.

PRAISE THE LORD.

BY CATHARINE MITCHELL.

Come to the blessed Jesus,
And rest within his arms;
Then you will fear no evil,
Nor shrink at earth's alarms.
Come, tread the shining pathway,
Protected by his grace;
It were worth a life of trial
To see his gracious face.

Sing to the great Redeemer,
Who formed the wondrous plan,
And left his heavenly kingdom
To ransom fallen man.
This world is fair to look on,
And mountain, sea and land,
All bear the solemn impress
Of an Almighty hand.

On all creation's altars
A sweet oblation lies,
And earth's unnumbered voices
Send praises to the skies.
The birds of varied plumage
That soar on wings above,
Join in the choral anthem,
To sing a song of love.

Each flower by the wayside
Lifts up its blooming head,
And breathes an odorous perfume
O'er field and valley bed.
The winds that sway the tree-tops,
And kiss the dancing brook,
Sigh with soft gentle murmurs
Through every shady nook.

All speak in glowing language
Notes gladsome or profound;
Then why should man be silent,
When nature's tongues resound?
Chant then the loud hosanna,
And swell the vocal songs,
To worship God, our Savior;
All praise to Him belongs.

ORIGINAL ESSAYS.

For the PILGRIM.

REGENERATION OF THE BODY.

In our former articles we have treated of the regeneration of the soul. In this, we propose to say something of the regeneration of the body. We have shown in our first essay that the primary meaning of the term is reproduction; bringing again into existence or to life. The necessity of a regeneration of the body presupposeth this body to die and to return to corruption which is plain, and we all know it by experience. But the same body shall be renewed and come forth. A renewed life is only revealed to us in the Scriptures. Through the atonement of Christ we all are reconciled to God as His children, but by committing sin we incur God's wrath, hence we become enemies to God, the soul defiled, the mind impure, controlled by the prince of darkness, under his power, and in consequence we act in opposition to the will of God. But by accepting God at His bidding and born of the water and of the spirit, we are adopted as God's children spiritually, the soul cleansed through the efficacy of Christ's redeemed blood, the mind renewed, the body still the same corruptible mortal.

The tabernacle in which the immortal soul dwells must be dissolved, die and turn to corruption before it will be clothed with immortality. The Savior compares the moral change in man to seed sown in the ground, "Except it die it abideth alone, but if it die, it bringeth forth much fruit."—John 12: 24. So the carnal mind must die, the old sinful man crucified, buried again, rise to a new life before fruits unto holiness will be manifested, and this moral change is called *regeneration*. Titus 3: 5. Even so does the change in this physical body bear equal relation to same comparison. "Thou fool, that which thou sowest is not quickened except it die."—1 Cor. 15: 36. Hence the redemption of the body is called an adoption. "They that had the first fruits of the spirit," in the days of primitive Christianity, did "groan within themselves, waiting for that adoption."—Rom. 8: 23. Now as the physical change bears the same relation to the moral one, we understand the Savior to use the same term, *regeneration*, to signify the renewing of the body in Matt. 19 28, the two only places we find it in the Bible.

The Greek term used is *Paligenesia*. Grove defines the term, 1. A new birth, 2 regeneration, 3 renovation, 4 change for the better, 5 resurrection, 6 existence after death, &c. A. Campbell and the revised translation use the term in the latter place, *renovation*. It certainly will take place "When the Son of Man shall sit in the throne of His glory," and when the disciples, who have forsaken all and have followed Him "shall sit upon twelve thrones judging the twelve tribes of Israel." O, the glorious resurrection "when mortality shall be swallowed up of life," the ground-work of our faith, the anchor of our hope, and the eternal rock on which we will land and abide forever. Christ, the first fruits of the resurrection, burst the bars of death and triumphantly arose from the dead, and thereby obtained the victory over death, hell and the grave.

Brethren and sisters, let us be encouraged to persevere in our holy calling; there are great things before us, exceeding great and precious promises, for he that endureth to the end shall inherit all things. May we be revived in our spirits to put forth strenuous efforts in improving our time in the spread of the Gospel when we see so many famishing for the want of the Bread of Life dispersed among them. Let us remember we are citizens of a spiritual kingdom which had a small beginning, and is yet very small compared to the kingdom of this world, but finally is to swallow up all other kingdoms, and shall stand forever. Therefore let us labor for its enlargement with all our might for our days are few. Let that blessed change be ever bearing on our mind, anxiously waiting for that blessed hope of the glorious appearing of the great God and our Savior, the Lord Jesus Christ, who then will regenerate our vile body that it may be fashioned like unto His glorious body, according to the working whereby He is able even to subdue all things unto Himself, for we shall be like Him, for we shall see Him as He is."

O, the happy change, from corruption to incorruption, from mortality to immortality, when the sayings that is written shall come to pass, "Death is swallowed up in victory. O death, where is thy sting? O grave, where is thy victory? Thanks be to God which giveth us the victory through our Lord Jesus Christ."

Therefore my friendly readers, let us be born of God, show forth the fruits of regeneration as the adopted spiritual children of God, walk in all the commandments of God blameless, still try to go on to perfection till God takes us home, seals our perfection in death through Christ's atoning blood, in order to realize the final adoption, even the redemption of our bodies.

LEONARD FURRY.

LIFE!—That which a man has, and has had,—the past, the living present, the future,—the oneness. Not alone to have come; not alone to breathe; not alone the play of muscles and the twitch of nerves;—but the doing, the evolution, the work performed, the destiny accomplished, pleasure made, evil avoided, the gloriousness of creation correlated into ourselves, and given forth by us."—From "*Thinkers and Thinking.*"

DON'T.—Don't scold. It is a violation of christian principle.

Don't tell lies. It is a detestable sin and leads to ruin.

Don't speak evil of your neighbor. It is a violation of God's law.

Don't smoke, chew or snuff tobacco. It is an offence to thy brethren. —*A. B. B.*

IT is not the hasty reading, but serious meditating upon holy and heavenly truths, that makes them prove sweet and profitable to the soul. It is not the bee's touching on the flowers that gathers honey, but her abiding for a time upon them and drawing out the sweet. It is not he that reads most, but he that meditates most on divine truth, that will prove the choicest, wisest, strongest Christian.

I am the way, the truth and the life, and no man cometh unto the Father but by me.—*Jesus.*

THE "CAP" CONTROVERSY.

As the question of wearing the "cap," as a covering for the sister's head in seasons of devotion, is creating a feeling of discord in the peaceful bosom of the Church, whatever will aid in clearing away the mists and stilling the tempest will, I presume, be acceptable. I propose to give for that purpose, a couple of paraphrases of the Scripture which alludes to the controverted subject, and, for the convenience of the reader, I will place each verse opposite to each. Where the interpretation is accepted alike by all parties the mark of equality (=) will indicate it.

1 Cor. Chapter XI.

Ver. 3rd. But I would have you know that the (spiritual) head of every (converted) man is Christ and the (spiritual) head of every (converted) woman is man, and the (spiritual) head of Christ is God. (*God is over all.*)	Ver. 3. =
V. 4. Every man praying or prophesying with his hat on dishonoreth Christ.	V. 4. =
V. 5. But every woman that prayeth or prophesieth without an artificial covering on the head dishonoreth the man, for that is equivolent to having her hair cut off.	V. 5. But every woman that prayeth or prophesieth with her hair cut off dishonoreth the man, for that is equivolent to having her hair cut off. That is a thing is equal to itself.
V. 6. For if it be shameful for a woman to cut off her hair let her put on an artificial covering, but if she will not wear the artificial covering let her cut off her hair, for it has the same effect in bringing dishonor to her spiritual superior, man.	V. 6. But if it be shameful for woman to cut off her hair let her wear it, but if she will not wear it, then let her cut it off.
V. 7. For a man indeed ought not to wear his hat in his devotions, forasmuch as he is the image and glory of God: but the woman, because she is the glory of man, ought to wear an artificial.	V. 7. For the man indeed ought not to wear his hat in his devotions, forasmuch as he is the image and glory of God, but the woman ought to wear her hair for the same reason, that is, because she is the glory of the man.
Ver. 8. The man was not taken from the side of the woman, but woman was taken from the side of the man.—Gen. 2: 21.	V. 8. =
V. 9. Neither was the man created to be a helpmeet to the woman, but the woman was designed to be a helpmeet to the man.—Gen. 2: 20.	V. 9. =
V. 10. On account of this physical and spiritual dependence the woman ought to have an artificial covering on her head because this token of her dependence and this acceptance of her sphere, will be pleasing to her angels who minister to her spiritual wants.—Heb. 1: 14. Matt. 18: 10.	V. 10. On account of this physical and spiritual dependence the woman ought to wear her hair, because this token of her dependence and acceptance of her sphere will be pleasing to her angels who minister to her spiritual wants.
V. 11. Nevertheless the man and woman are mutually dependent on each other for their temporal and spiritual blessings, through the influence of their Lord who is their advocate with the Father.—1st John 2: 1.	V. 11. =
V. 12. For as the woman at the first issued from the side of man she has become an essential agent in the perpetuation of our species, by the ordinance of God.	V. 12. =
V. 13. You shall judge this simple matter yourselves. Is it proper or modest for a woman to pray unto God without an artificial covering?	V. 13. You shall judge this simple matter yourselves. Is it proper or modest for a woman to pray unto God with her hair cut off?
V. 14. Nature, that is the sexual, social and constitutional difference between man and woman, should teach us that it is shameful and degrading for a man to wear his hair long like a woman's or to apparel himself in any one style like a woman's, even as it is immodest and uncomly for a woman to wear a style of garments that belong to men.	V. 14. =
V. 15. But if a woman suffer her hair to grow long it is an honor to her sex for her hair is given her for a covering, or a visible manifestation of the physical distinction between the sexes.	V. 15. But if a woman suffer her hair to grow long it is an honor to her sex, for her hair is given her for the covering which she is to wear when she prays or prophesies.
V. 16. But if any man is disposed to object to my recommendations and demands a thus saith the Lord or authority from the Gospel, I cannot plead the pre-existence of the custom nor its adoption by the churches that were established by the other apostles but I advocate their adoption because I am the chosen instrument to preach to you Gentiles, and I think I have the mind of Christ.	V. 16. But if there are any that are not disposed to submit to these regulations then let them do as they think right. It is a matter of indifference, let them be persuaded in their own mind and if any think it sinful to pray without an artificial covering let them wear one but if any think it not necessary they are at liberty to pray without it.

The brethren and sisters can read the foregoing paraphrases, as they justly represent the different positions of the contending parties, and if they contribute anything to produce a harmony of thought and action among us I will be more than gratified. In conclusion I will submit a few criticisms on the paraphrases of those who maintain that the hair is the covering alluded to by the Apostle.

Ver. 5th. and 6th. would sound more like the twaddle of an idiot than of an apostle, eminent alike for his depth of learning, his purity of heart, and his highly refined spirit; more like the gibberish of a soothsayer, than of the chosen of the Lord to instruct and enlighten an ignorant and superstitious world.

Ver. 15, would advocate the propriety of a detached covering of hair, something like a modern chignon, I presume, that could be put on when she was at her devotions, for this covering, take notice, is only required at times of worship. Taking that view of it, the apostle would have said nothing of certain specified seasons when the covering was essential.

Ver. 16 is the most incongruous and inconsistent of all the others if the anti-covering advocates are right. Paul has stigmatized the practice of praying uncovered as shameful, unnatural, dishonorable, graceless, &c. He used terms that we commonly apply to persons of lewd and profligate characters.

After such severe strictures and criticisms he is supposed to grow suddenly indifferent about it and to give every member liberty to do as he or she pleases. It is a shame, and it is not, it is dishonorable, and it is not, it is graceful, and it is graceless. It is, and it is not. Now the sum of such logic amounts to this. Evil has no other existence than in the mind of man, that is, if we conceive a thing to be evil it *is* evil, if we conceive a thing to be good it *is* good. If that is our law then repudiate the Bible, God and Christ, and everything else that the Christian holds dear, and embark on the rudderless craft of private opinion; and on the shoreless ocean of speculation, and soon the gloomy maelstrom of infidelity and rationalism will engulf us, and a putrid sea of spiritual filth will send such a horrid stench into the nostrils of the Eternal that nothing but a deluge of fire and brimstone can satiate his righteous vengeance. Brethren let us be one even as Christ and the Father are one.

D. C. Moomaw.

P. S.—I will not impugn the motives of those who differ with me on this subject, but suffer me to relate an incident that occurred here recently. A certain sister, after reading 1 Cor. 11th chapter, concluded that verse 15 was a key to the whole subject, and consequently she refused to wear her cap. She was affectionately admonished by able committees of brethren, but all our efforts failed. Soon she purchased a fine breast pin, and wore it, and then we justly concluded that it was the key to her objection to the cap. She is now with the Methodists. A brother who sympathizes with her opposition to "caps" thinks that it would be more consistent to wear the hair in plaits around the crown of the head. I think both ought to read 1 Pet. 3: 3. 1 Tim. 2: 9.

MY SAVIOR IS WITH ME.

What great consolation it is to know as we pass along through this world, that our Savior is with us, for He has promised to be with us if we do as He has commanded us. How these words cheer and encourage us on our way Zionward! They help us to bear up under our afflictions better than if we were alone. They are as sweet music to our ears, as we sit by the bed-side of our departing friends, to hear them say the Savior is with them. O that we could all have the privilege of hearing these precious words fall from the lips of our friends as they leave the shores of mortality. But there are so many that are not willing to accept of the company of Jesus whilst they are enjoying the blessings of health and the pleasures of this world, and therefore they cannot expect Him to be with them in a dying hour. What a dreadful thing is procrastination. It is one of satan's instruments in procuring subjects for his kingdom. How many a poor soul, is to-day lifting its fruitless cries in the regions of dark despair on account of that thief of time. Many times did the spirit strive with them, but procrastination whispered in their ear and said, it is time enough, you are quite young yet and there is plenty of time, wait for a more convenient season. But that convenient season never came, they kept putting it off until it was forever too late; they perhaps, were snatched away without a moments warning. So it will be with many more if they are ashamed to be found in the company of the followers of Jesus.

My dear sisters, let us all with one mind and heart, ask the Savior to be with us, and let us show by our walk and conduct that He is with us and that we are not ashamed to learn of Him and be meek and lowly in heart. Let us not be ashamed to speak a word for Him whenever an opportunity presents itself. Let us not be ashamed to visit the poor and afflicted in the lonely garret, the dark dungeon, or wherever they may be found. Let us ask the Savior to go with us, and we will be sure to be benefitted by the visit. Many happy seasons have the disciples of Jesus in visiting the sheep of the fold, many deep impressions have been made on such occasions that will last through all eternity. They will have cause to praise and thank God forever more for the privilege and opportunity of visiting such in their affliction, for for we expect to pass through this world but once and let us do all the good we can. Then we shall be permitted to roam over the green fields of Paradise, and walk the golden streets of the New Jerusalem.

Our work will then be done,
Where troubles and trials never come,
We shall sing and praise forevermore,
On that bright and happy shore.

M. C. K.

FEAR NOT I AM WITH THEE.

How often has our hearts been cheered while passing under the heavy rod of affliction by the blessed promise of God, "Fear not I am with thee." He is with us in the hour of trouble to bestow his blessing; he is with us in the dark hour of temptation, and he is with us when danger surrounds us on every hand, always with us, ready to watch over, and comfort us.

Dear brethren and sisters, I am one of Gods most humble children, but as unworthy as I am, I can throw myself at the footstool of His mercy, and trust Him as the sinner's friend. I have been among you but a short time, only about two years since I cast my lot with the people of God. Since that time, I have undergone many trials and temptations. I have like many of you, but few friends among the gay and proud. They seem to think that my plaindress is a disgrace to their society, but I have no desire to mingle with them. I would rather spend my time with the friends of my master.

Then let us, dear Christian friends, heed not the frowns of the cold world or the scornful smiles of the gay and proud for we need not fear while God is our friend.

"He knows what all his children feel;
He knows our feeble frame,
He knows what sore temptations are
For He has felt the same."

When we pass through the valley of the shadow of death he will be with us, to lead us safely over the dark stream to the bright heavenly shore, where we will meet with the loved ones who have gone before to bask in the sunshine of his glory forever.

How sweet the thought that after all of our troubles, trials and persecutions, we shall rest in the bosom of his love, never to suffer again, but above all to see the Savior who has died that we, through him, may live in that blessed land of perfect rest; we shall be free from sorrow, sickness, pain and death, for naught can ever enter there to molest the peace of those made perfect.

It may not be long till some of us are called upon to cross the river. We may now be standing on the very brink of eternity for the angel of death to lay his hand upon us. Then let us try to live nearer to the cross of Christ, so that when he sends his messenger we will be ready, and then we need not fear for he will lay his hand beneath our sinking heads, and bear us safely to the other shore.

Your unworthy sister in Christ.

M. F. H.

Fincastle, Va

A LETTER FROM GERMANY.

Dresden, Germany, May 30, '73.

Dear father and Sarah: I wrote to you a month ago from Hamburg, and am very anxious to hear from you, to know how your health is, and how Sarah is by this time. Hope she is better, and that you are stronger and better since the weather is warmer. We remained at Hamburg three days, then we came to Berlin, the city where the King lives. The country between Hamburg and Berlin is very flat and low. It looks very much like our Western praries. The farms are very large and no fences. The farm houses are all built in clusters, and then the farmers go out any direction to farm. Sometimes there is no house for two miles or more. It does not look near as nice as our country does, with farm houses dotted all over the country. Berlin is a very massive city. It is so solid. So many soldiers there; wherever you look, soldiers everywhere. The women have hard work to do, and the able-bodied men are in the army, or rather walking about with their swords strapped to their sides, and smoking and drinking wine and beer. You never get water at the table for dinner unless you ask for it. Every one has wine or beer before his plate. The dissipation in Germany is fearful. We were at Berlin a few days, then we came to Dresden, where we still are. Dresden is a very pleasant place. There is so much to see here of interest. They claim one hundred and twenty thousand inhabitants. We visited the green vault last week where the jewels of the Kings and nobility are kept, or rather the jewels of the royal family of Saxony. They also have a very valuable gallery of paintings, one of the largest in Europe. So many of the pictures were painted in fourteen and fifteen hundred. We also visited a small town near Hamburg, named Eppendorf, where we saw houses about one thousand years old. We often talk about that; we can scarcely realize that we are in the old world. Yet everything is so different here from what it is in America. We see old and young women pulling small wagons about half as high as our spring wagons at home, and draw coal and wood. Sometimes they have one dog to help them draw, and sometimes two. I do pity the poor women; they are just as much of slaves in this country, as the blacks were in the South, only they are not bought and sold. I hate all the German men, they think a woman has to turn off the sidewalks, but they would not lord it over me if I had them much to deal with.

Olive, Howard and Lannie, have been taking German lessons the last three weeks. They can read a great deal, and speak a great many words; understand almost every word. Lannie writes a nice German hand, better than either of the others.

We expect to stay here two or three weeks longer, then we expect to go to Vienna to the Exposition, where we expect to remain one month. Then we go to Munich, then to Switzerland. We have all been quite well since we came to Germany with the exception of colds. I have so often wished for a good American night to get a good long night of sleep. It is not dark here until nearly ten o'clock, and a little after three o'clock in the morning it is daylight again, and as soon as it is light in the morning, the wagons commence to pass along. Then I can sleep but little. It is now seven o'clock in the afternoon, and with you it is about one at dinner time. We are about four thousand miles from you. When we were on the water, the steamer used to travel about three hundred miles in twenty-four hours, and sometimes more. Then we would turn our watches forward about half an hour every day, then they would be about right.

Some days I feel quite lonely and wish I was at home, then again we are seeing a great many wonderful things. I saw the silver cup Luther used to drink out of. There is a beautiful painting in the gallery of a discussion between Luther and Dr. Knox at Leipsic. Luther was born in a little town not far from here, the name Eisenach. We intend to visit the place week after next. There are some very old churches in this place, one built over one hundred years ago, and a great many forts near the city that were built in the time of war. Saxony has a King; his name is King John, *the Wise*. The Saxony people do not like the Emperor, King Willhelm. He is Emperor over all Germany, and Saxony is part of Germany.

The weather has been very cold, and a great deal of rain eversince we came to Germany. The leaves have not their full growth yet. I took a walk into the country two weeks ago, the rye was then coming out in heads.

It is so hard to get letters from home, we have had but two letters since we are in Germany. We expected to go to Frankfort when we left home, so our letters were directed there, and they neglect to send them to us, therefore we seldom hear from home. It takes three weeks to get our letters. We will have them addressed to the United States Consul at Dresden, and he will send them to us wherever we are. I am so anxious to hear from you, and to know how you are getting along. The children join me in love to you all. May God bless and keep you; hope it is His will that we can meet on earth again. NANCY L. SPROULE.

THE POVERTY OF CHRIST!—How it sweetens and ennobles the poverty of his humble followers. What though men despise our lowly condition and extend their scorn to us. Christ has honored it, has borne its mysteries and looks with loving pity upon those who patiently endure it. He does not require us to bear any thing he has not borne. Are we cramped and harrassed for means to meet our necessities? He wrought a miracle to obtain the quota of the tribute money. Are we condemned to coarse and scanty fare? He plucked green corn to appease his hunger. Are we homeless wanderers among the bright and happy homes of earth's prosperous sons and daughters? "The foxes" of Judea "have holes" in the leafy coverts of her sacred mountains, "and birds of the air had nests" amid her vines and fig trees; but among all the dwellings of her pleasant villages and goodly cities, "the Son of Man had not where to lay His head."

Although homeless on earth, how glorious is His home above, "that house of God not made with hands, eternal in the Heavens." The homes on earth from the lowliest hut to the lordliest palace, are made discordant by sin and darkened by sorrow, while from cottage and hall is heard "the voice of Rachel weeping for her children." But within the pearly gates and jasper walls of the New Jerusalem "is no sin, neither sorrow nor crying, for God shall wipe away the tears from all eyes."

There he is preparing a place for us; and here he is preparing us for that place, leading us by the way that seemeth to him best. "Then let us endure as seeing him who is invisible, for our light affliction, which is but for a moment, worketh for us a far more exceeding and eternal weight of glory." And though we have no treasure on earth, let us diligently strive to "lay up treasures in Heaven, where neither moth nor rust doth corrupt, and where thieves do not break through nor steal."

Is God with us? What more do we want? Omniscience, omnipotence, and infinite love, are all these leading the van? Then we will not fear to follow, though it were into Hades itself; for if Jehovah led the way his saints would be safe even there. Treasure up that direction. Do not think so much of the presence of friends in trouble as the presence of God in trouble. "Fear not." What is the next word? "I am with thee, be not dismayed." What is the next sentence? "I am thy God." The richest consolation you can have is that which is derived from the presence of the Lord.

EMOTION IN RELIGION.

Surface emotion doesn't amount to much and isn't worth much. It comes and goes like the shadows of an April day. But there is a deep and abiding conviction, which is of another character, and has another price.

It seems to me that we want more Christian sensibility, more tenderness, more feeling—or breaking up of the fountains of our heart, like the breaking up of the fountains of the great deep, a melting that shall dissolve all our hardness into tears.

This overflowing sensibility, this tender and weeping state, suits well every relation and duty of our Christian life.

Certainly it fits our return to Christ as those who have wandered away from him into paths of worldliness and forgetfulness. Think of coming back to him to hear him say: "I have somewhat against" carrying in our consciousness the self reproach—"I have not lived so near Jesus as I ought. I have followed him like Peter, afar off." If any of us are passing through an experience, does it not become us to go weeping night and day?

This weeping state suits even the joy of restoration. No one has ever had any very great joy who has not known what it is to weep tears of joy.

Could you come to Jesus and receive a fresh and full forgivness; feel his hand laid upon your head in welcome and benediction; hear him say, "Go in peace, thy sins are forgiven thee" sing that song, "Love I much, I'm much forgiven!" and yet keep the tears back? If you were revolving it in your heart, "O, what compassion my Savior has shown me! Every shadow between my soul and His face has departed. I am in near and constant communion with him once more!" would not your eyes overflow?

Such deep sensibility suits well the offering of earnest prayer. We cannot wrestle with God for great blessings with a heart cool and calm, whose pulses are unquickened, whose tenderness is slumbering.

Especially is this tenderness of heart our indispensable preparation for winning souls. You know what the promise is: "He that goeth forth and weepeth, bearing precious seed, shall doubtless come again with rejoicing bringing his sheaves with him." Tell a man he is in danger of losing his soul and tell him as though it were a fact which you bore philosophically, and not as though it were a grief that were breaking your heart, and you will not move him, except to anger and contempt. You can say anything to a man without offense, which you say through tears. If you fling your arms around his neck he cannot resist you. You cannot go hopefully on an errand of salvation, unless you go tenderly. Loving and longing, don't use cold words.

Pray for this precious grace, or rather for this baptism of all the graces. Bring before your mind all the scenes that stir penitential sorrow, tender joy, love's warm solicitude and the fulness of the heart of Christ.—*Rev. A. L. Stone.*

HE CAME TO HIMSELF.

A marvelous sentence it is. In the Greek the thought is stronger. He returned and entered into his own self-hood, he passed from all surroundings, and lifting the veil, stood face to face with his own spirit—his own wasted, forlorn, degenerated, yet still grandly gifted and immortal self.

"He came to himself." Hitherto he had been a man "Beside himself," out of "his mind," acting without reason—bewitched by the spells of some strong sorcery, moving in the somnambulism of a wild and wretched dream. But that dream is now breaking. It is as if his spirit had returned from the sphere of the disembodied, to look upon the realities of the mortal life. He looked upon himself.

He saw himself as he had been—a fair young child in his mother's arms, a beloved boy, his heart bounding, his eyes flashing in the exuberant life of his father's home—a fair young man rich in money, in friends, in social influences and position, in appliances of mental and moral culture, in sparkling gems of tho't in golden, glorious possibilities entering upon life amid the noble arena of a great commercial city.

He saw himself as he might have been and as he hoped to be—in the full career of successful manhood—his eyes flashing with intellect, and eloquent with genius; walking bravely, grandly, among the multitude—a leader, a benefactor, a successful, honored, triumphant career—a full-grown, majestic man.

He saw himself as he was—a wretched outcast. His brow matted with shaggy hair, his dark eyes sunken and heavy, his face bloated, his eloquent lips swollen, his lofty form bent, and crouching, and covered with tattered rags; shrunken, wasted, famishing, wallowing in the mire wherein unclean beasts wallow, munching the unseemly husk whereon the swine fattened. A beloved son! a spurned menial! a glorious man forlorn, ruined, lost!

He looked into himself, bending under his degrading task, lying down in dreamy rest in the sty and pen. And all this in the midst of God's fair world; the Summer hills all around him waving their palms as brave banners; the winds, as they wrestle even with his tangled locks, shouting their watchwords; the great blue Heaven above thrilling with voices, flashing immortal man to life's brave struggles and grand reward; and yet he a discord among nature's harmonies—a blot on nature's writings—a spirit fallen from life's high places, something meant to be a man, but now only a wreck—a desolation! So he seems to himself.—*Charles Wadsworth.*

GENERAL INTELLIGENCE

ANOTHER fire occurred recently in Chicago. The flames spread rapidly until sixty-four houses were burned, chiefly wooden tenements. The loss is estimated at $125,000, which is largely covered by insurance. A large number of families were thrown out of homes but were properly cared for.

THE German Government has resolved to expel the members of the religious orders of the Redemptorists, Lazarists, Congregations of the Holy Ghost and Sacred Heart, and the occupants of close convents from the country within the coming six months.

GEORGE SMITH, of the *Daily Telegraph*, correspondent in Assyria, has found the King's library at Nineveh, and discovered numerous valuable fragments, particularly the missing portions of the broken tablet containing the history of the deluge, hitherto deciphered in the British Museum.

Between two and three hundred Japenese youths are still in this county in the pursuit of education, notwithstanding so many have been recalled. These men will be agents of civilization and many of them of Christianity when they go home.

They will be if they are not taught creeds and faiths instead of the doctrines of the Bible. True Christianity is indeed a civilizing agency.

The new Jewish year 5634, commenced last Sunday, and the *Jewish Messenger* prays that it may bring every blessing to those that dwell on earth, and imbue their hearts with the proper spirit to act right, so that when they are called upon to close their account here they may have some claim to enjoy happiness hereafter.

ELD. A. J. Correll of Forest City, Mo., says: "We have had a very dry season this Summer. The corn crop will be short but will be sufficient for home consumption. Of wheat, rye and oats, we had a heavy crop and sells at fair prices. As for the church, it appears to be in a good condition, and the ark of the Lord is still moving along. The church within the last three years, has increased nearly four double. To God be the praise."

The troubles of the Roman Catholics in Prussia are endless. The endowments of many parish priests are derived from interest on invested capital and rent of land. It has been pointed out to those who have to make payments from these sources to the parish priests that they expose themselves to be sued if they hand the money to priests appointed by the bishops contrary to the laws, and whose receipts could therefore not be legally recognized. There is only one way to be delivered from Rome, and that is to come out of her and be no more a partaker of her sins.—*N. Y. Observer.*

JEWS IN THIS CITY.—There are more Jews in New York than in Jerusalem, and more than any other city in the world, it is said by those who have studied their present state. Mr. Mingins says of New York, "There are more Germans than in Berlin, more Irishmen than in Dublin, more Catholics than in Rome and more Jews than in Palestine." The census does not give religious statistics, but the number of professing Jews residents of this city, has been approximately estimated by the number of Passover biscuits manufactured for their use. The bakeries produced on the average for the last decade, 800,000 pounds yearly, which at the rate of one pound per day for each adult during the eight days generally observed, would make a number of 100,000 persons. They have an Orphan Asylum to accommodate 250 orphans, a Hospital and a number of charitable societies, among which is the Independent Order of B'nal Berith, and have also established within the last few years a Home for aged and indignant of both sexes managed by ladies.

THE YELLOW FEVER.—Most distressing accounts come from Shreveport, La., concerning the ravages of the Yellow Fever. The number of deaths has been very large, and great suffering has prevailed. Large donations of money are being made throughout the country. The great deficiency is in nurses and physicians. The Howard Association, Masons, Odd Fellows, and other Societies, are doing all they can for the relief of the afflicted. The disease is also epidemic in Memphis, but it is believed that its spread may be checked.

THE Methodists and Baptists down in Charleston, South Carolina, have had a little business set-to, which goes to show that neither party has had the leaven of worldliness quite kneaded out yet. The Baptists had a $60,000 church they couldn't pay for, and sold to the Methodists for $20,000. But before the transfer was made, they saw a chance of escape, and repented of their bargain. But the shrewd Methodists insisted that "business was business," and held them to the letter of the contract, threatening them with a lawsuit for damages if they receded. The Baptists find themselves minus a meeting-house, and the Methodists have got a $60,000 church for a third of its value. It was a sharp business transaction as between brokers, but shows that Southern Christianity needs reconstructing slightly.

THE question whether the Bible shall be read in our common schools is considerably agitated and discussed in some States. In New York a Methodist minister recently preached a sermon on the subject, and at the close of the sermon they really appointed a committee to examine the matter and ascertain whether the Board of Education could with legality suffer the Bible to be taken from the common schools. It does seem strange that there should be any discussion about this matter. Can there be any evil result from the reading of the Bible? The idea is preposterous. It is really a shame that a question of this kind is discussed in a Christian land like ours. There is something at the bottom of this discussion that emanates directly from the adversary, and is hurling thousands to perdition. It is *prejudice.* If men would read the Bible with an unprejudiced mind, a different state of affairs would exist. These sectarian differences would be all wiped out and men would be as the apostle exhorts, "all joined together in the same mind and the same judgment." Then there would be no fears about having the Bible read in school

A Presbyterian minister in giving an account of the contributions of the church on the Pacific coast says: "During the past year the church gave to the boards &c., $13,316, or about $2.28 to each member. The average throughout the church at large is, however, about $3,28 a member."

This looks as if they have a zeal for the cause they are advocating, and are willing to give of their abundance to the advancement of their doctrine. It does seem to us that the zeal manifested by other churches should teach us, as a church, how to labor for the advancement of the true principles of the Bible. The apparent zeal may not be according to godliness, but still it should be an example to us who profess to have a zeal that *is* according to godliness. Why do we not, according to the directions given in divine record, lay by every week for this purpose as the Lord blesses us? There are perhaps many of our members that have given comparatively nothing, perhaps have never given $3,28 for the support of the church. Why is it? Is it not a duty? And if so, will not our negligence, may we not say covetousness, stand against us at the great day of final accounts? These are considerations for us to think of, and it does seem to us that it is high time we as a church learn better how to spend our money so as to meet the approval of God.

Youth's Department.

MY THREE LITTLE TEXTS.

I am very young and little;
I am only just turned two,
And I cannot learn long chapters,
As my elder sisters do.

But I know three little verses
That ma has taught to me,
And I say them every morning
As I stand beside her knee.

The first is, "Thou God seest me."
Is not that a pretty text?
And "Suffer the little children
To come unto me" is the next.

But the last one is the shortest:
It is only "God is love."
How kind He is in sending us
Such sweet verses from above!

He knows that chapters I can't learn,
So I think He sent those three
Short easy texts on purpose
For little one's like me.

THE HIDDEN SERPENT.

Serpents or snakes, notwithstanding their spots, stripes, and pretty colors, are looked upon as ugly things, and there are few but what dread the sight of them. This may be largely the result of training, as there are many other things that we love that are really much uglier. We suppose this is on account of the part it played in the Garden of Eden. Those of you who read the Bible remember how Satan entered the serpent and then approached mother Eve and tempted her to eat the forbidden fruit. Why it was that satan made choice of the serpent, we cannot tell, but the possible reason is on account of its cunninguess. It is said to be the most subtle creature of the field. Because it was cunning and showed its wit among the other creatures of the Garden, satan made choice of it as a mantle or covering to hide his own ugliness, and thus accomplished his designs in deceiving our first parents. Because of its being used for this bad purpose God declared it should no longer walk on its legs but crawl on its belly. Ever since that time, the snake has had a bad reputation and every man's, boy's and girl's hands are raised against it, just as if satan continued to speak from his ugly forked tongue. This, though, is a mistake as satan has got entirely too proud to be a snake any more, but now enters the very prettiest places and things just wherever he can get a hole in which he can creep in order to do some mischief, hence, he is still compared to the snake in the grass, or called the hidden serpent. It is true, he is said to be going about like a roaring lion seeking whom he may devour, but he wears such pretty clothes and makes such fine speeches that no person seems to be afraid of him. This is what makes him the more dangerous.

Not long since a little girl, as she was walking along, noticed a bunch of very beautiful flowers and with joy, she ran to secure the coveted prize, but as she was about to grasp them, she saw in the bunch a large serpent ready to make the fatal stroke, should she attempt to take them. Now what we wish to tell you is that this hidden serpent exists not only among the pretty flowers, but in every forbidden pleasure. Every sin puts on its most beautiful colors, but beneath them lies the hidden serpent. Sin within itself is ugly, hateful, and there is no little boy or girl that would think of touching it, was it not, that it hides its ugliness behind some pretty flower or tempting enjoyments. Many of these things are the devils bait, and if you are not careful to let them alone, you will be caught in his trap. Thousands of our young men are tempted by the sparkling cup. When it is red it is beautiful, and to the taste it is pleasant and sweet, but in the end, it stingeth like an adder and biteth like a serpent. The hidden serpent is in it, but reserves the the bite until the victim is within his grasp. Just so many of our young girls and boys, and old ones too, are bitten by that most deceptive of all flowers, pride. To the eye it is charming and the flesh lusts after it as if there was nothing else half so desirable, but at last the hidden serpent appears for it is declared that those who sow to the flesh, reap corruption, and again; the proud, with all those that forget God shall be cast into hell. Fashions, with all their allurements, are the devils trappings and are used as baits to get you in. He well knows if he can keep your hearts on these things you will have no time to serve God, because he always keeps you busy while in his service. My young friends beware of the hidden serpent.

UNCLE HENRY.

I DON'T CARE.

A few days ago a number of boys were playing in the street and presently a lady came out of the house and called her son, who was among the number, to come and help her do some work in the house. But the boy paid little attention to her call and still kept on playing. After while a younger brother came and told him that his mother was needing him very badly and if he did not come she would punish him. And what do you think was his reply? He really said *I don't care.* Is it possible that a boy will not care for the feelings of his kind mother? Now that mother must have been wounded to think that her son did not care to willingly disobey her, and that he would refuse to assist her when she so much needed him.

"I *don't care!*" Boys and girls, think of what your parents have done for you; how they watched over you in your infancy, how they have provided for you, how they have *cared* for *you.* Surely you must conclude that it is very ungrateful to be so indifferent to their wishes. If you do not care to comply with the wishes of your parents who have done so much for you, what is it that you will care for? If you are careless and indifferent to their wishes, you will be so to every one, your brothers and sisters, your friends, and in fact to everything you do. It is only the boy or girl that *cares* for the opinion of others that is loved and respected. If you do not care for the feelings of others or what they may think of you, it is not likely they will care about you, and if you have no one to care for you how very unhappy you must feel. If then you would be happy and make others happy, you must not be indifferent to the feelings of others, you must care to obey your parents, your teachers, and treat with respect all who may *care* enough for you to advise or instruct you.

"*I don't care,*" has caused much sorrow in the world, and we hope the little readers of the PILGRIM will avoid this feeling of carelessness. The first command of promise is that you be obedient unto your parents, and if you are careless about it you will incur the displeasure of God. Remember boys and girls, that it is this carelessness about your duty to God and man that will be the great lament of many a soul.

YOUR FRIEND.

TELLING A LIE WITH A FINGER.—A little boy for a trick pointed with his finger to the wrong road when a man asked him which way the doctor went. As a result, the man missed the doctor and his litte boy died, because the doctor came too late to take a fish-bone from his throat. At the funeral the minister said the boy was killed by a lie, which another boy told with his finger.

I supposed, says uncle John, that the boy did not know the mischief he did. Of course, no body thinks he meant to kill a little boy when he pointed the wrong way. He only wanted to have a little fun, but it was fun that cost somebody a great deal; and if he ever heard of the results of it, he must have felt guilty of doing a mean and wicked thing. We ought never to trifle with the truth.

A HOUSE uninhabited soon comes to ruin, and a soul uninhabited by the Holy Spirit of God verges faster and faster to destruction.—*Toplady.*

The Weekly Pilgrim.

JAMES CREEK, PA., Oct. 7, 1873.

THE MODE OF PREACHING.

At the close of our treatise on Ministerial Qualifications, we promised to give our readers something on the mode of preaching. This is our present intention, and we have just been informed that theories consist of nice calculations and fine wit, but when we come to practice, we have stubborn facts to deal with. Just so, and the more stubborn these facts are, the more carefully and persistently should we deal with them. Incorrect habits are harder to unlearn than are correct ones to learn, hence it becomes the more necessary to give them our early attention.

After the necessary qualifications, intellectual, successful preaching consists, first in the man. Notwithstanding, many people denounce the science of phrenology yet the first thing they do on seeing a man is to portray his character, and pass their opinion on his disposition. Ask them for the basis of their opinion, and they will tell you that they judged from his appearance. Just so and that is the very way that phrenologists come to their conclusions. Then in a certain sense we are all phrenologists, but ofttimes do not arrive at strictly correct conclusions for want of thorough investigation. Nevertheless, it is a stubborn fact that all will, whether experienced, or inexperienced, form an estimate of the character and ability of others at sight, and very often pretty correctly too. Of all callings, the minister of the Gospel must pass through the most rigid investigation and criticism, hence the great importance of us studying how to appear before our congregations, in order that we may exert the most favorable influence for good. The first point we will notice is that of cleanliness of person and apparel. Some writer says that cleanliness is next to godliness but we would prefer to have it, cleanliness belongs to godliness. A man to enter the stand filthy in person and apparel not only shames himself but he disgraces the place he occupies and the position he fills. This may seem a little severe but we mean all we say in its fullest sense. There is positively no excuse for filthiness as long as God sends us rain, which is intended especially for our purification. Cleanliness is not only a christian virtue, but it is essential for the enjoyment of good health and when it adds to our influence for good its importance is made doubly great.

Tidyness is another essential point in the appearance of the minister. This consists in having the hair and beard nicely combed and the clothes properly adjusted. A neglect of this amounts to carelessness and exerts an unfavorable influence, as a man that is slipshod in his apparel will manifest the same disposition in everything else he undertakes. The apostle says: "Let everything be done decently and in order," and to wear our clothes in a slovenly manner is not in order. In taking this position, we do not wish to be understood as advocating pride, that is quite another thing. Many of our old and most influential brethren were very strict in regard to cleanliness and the order of their apparel, and in this respect, set examples worthy to be followed by some of our young ministers. No matter how plain or cheap the clothing may be, if it is clean and worn in a tidy manner, it looks well and commands respect. Jewish historians say that Christ, our Savior, was exceedingly comely in His person and of more than ordinary taste, having his hair parted in a straight seam on the middle of his head, and wore his clothes strictly in accordance with the Jewish custom of style and cleanliness. If any imagine that slovenliness is humility they are very much mistaken, as religion has a purifying effect on the body as well as the soul. Let us ever remember that our calling is an "*high calling*," and to fill it honorably we must have pure hearts and clean garments.

Another very important feature in successful preaching is that of jesture, which signifies bearing or movement of the body and limbs so as to convey our ideas with greater force. The best possible rule for gesticulation is, *be natural*. It is as natural for man to make gestures as it is to talk, the fact is, men cannot and will not speak without making gestures, more or less. The true minister speaks with his whole body, the feet, the legs, the arms, the hands, the eyes and the head all are aids in enforcing our ideas, but if any of the parts are used out of place, they fail to fill the design, and the gestures then become ludicrous and are out of order. Some of us, through force of wrong habit, have got to doing this, and to break ourselves of it, is exceedingly difficult, yet it can be done if we are determined, and to become efficient, in so great a work is certainly worth an effort. True gestures consists not in stamping the feet, pounding the desk, beating the air, knocking over the lamps and clapping the hands. This may do if we expect to take the devil by storm, but he is accustomed to so much *clitter clatter* that we can scarcely hope for this, yet boisterous speaking and boisterous gestures go together. The apostle Paul, when standing on the stairs, to get attention, gently waived his hand. This silent move of the hand had the designed effect.

Again, we say, be natural, don't be boisterous. Let your jestures be in harmony with the nature of your subject. Every move of the foot, the hand and the eye ought to assist in conveying an idea. If it does not, it is a false gesture and has a tendency to confuse the hearer. This is a fact well worthy of consideration, gestures mean something or they mean nothing. If they have no meaning, better not make any, if they have a meaning, still better not make any than use them out of place. If we, while speaking of the earth and the grave, were to raise our eyes upward, and point towards heaven, it would seem strange indeed, yet it would not really be more out of order than to be continually beating, pounding and clapping the hand when it means nothing at all. Such things, when not in extremes, may be in an animated discourse when the speaker is filled with his subject, in short, the gestures should be the result of the subject. Stand erect on both feet, don't prop yourself with your hands as if you were afraid of falling, present a bold front, look as if you intended saying something, and then say it.

A VISIT TO SOMERSET COUNTY.

On Friday morning of last week we stepped aboard the H. & B. T. Railroad for Somerset Co., and in a short time arrived at Bridgeport, the point at which this road connects with the P. & C. Railroad. Here we had to wait over three hours, which by the way is not one of the most pleasant places to pass the time. The accommodations are rather poor and the surroundings not at all inviting. The train South soon arrived and with it brought a number of others to experience with us the vexations of a long wait at a Railroad Station. A gentleman and lady from Illinois were among the number and they soon evinced their impatience by denouncing the country and railroad. They did not want to get into such a dilemma again and seemed to be surprised that people live in such a country when good level land can be had in the west cheap. Well there may be advantages in some parts of the west, there is no clambering thro' and over hills and mountains, but then it is certainly a good thing that all persons do not think and feel alike in reference to these things. The earth's visage in places, is seemingly marred by these mountains and hills, yet after all, give us the mountains and hills, the infinite mind was at work in their formation, and there is beauty in them that lies too deep for the conceptions of some minds. If any of our readers find it necessary to travel this way, and cannot appreciate natural scenery, we would advise them to provide themselves with plenty of reading matter, as there are over three hours time to spend at this point.

The train arrived on time, and after a short ride we were at Dale City. We soon wended our way to the *Companion* office and found Bro. Beer at his post and very busy. He expected to go to Armstrong county to take part in a discussion to commence on Monday of last week, subject, the Supper. Bro. Holsinger was on a visit to Philadelphia, and the latest intelligence from him was that his daughter, Annie, had cast her lot with the people of God. We were glad to hear of this, and hope she may hold out faithful, become a bright and shining light in the church, so that others may be constrained to follow her in the good resolution she has taken.

On Saturday morning early we went to the station to take the train for Mineral Point, and from thence to Somerset. At the station we had the pleasure of meeting our brother C. G. Lint who was also taking the train. We had not been personally acquainted with brother Lint, but as he had been described to us as a man of large proportions, we were not long in concluding that he was in our presence. He accompanied us as far as Mineral Point, and then directed us to the home of his brother, Daniel Lint, who lives near Somerset. We arrived there and remained with him over the Sabbath. We shall not forget brother Lint and wife for their kindness. We were conveyed by them to the homes of a number of brethren, and thus we formed acquaintances that we shall remember with pleasure. We attended church on Saturday eve., and Sabbath. The preaching was done by a lay member. This was a new feature to us. If it is right for members to preach without being called by the church, and if a good talker is *the* qualification, then we suppose the brother is the "right man in the right place." We don't, however, understand it thus, and we hope those of our brethren who may differ from us, will excuse us for saying so. We are not a David and will not therefore go out against Goliath, but if we were to exercise our feelings in reference to the matter, we would put a stone in the sling and hurl it at the head of this Innovation. We do not by any means wish to insinuate that the brother is not sincere, but it does seem to us that if he will consider properly the nature of the ministry, and the medium through which ministers are to be called, he will not feel to assume so responsible a position. But we do not intend to discuss the matter here. From our knowledge of Holy Writ, we have an opinion in reference to it, but it may not be prudent for our humble self to be too free in expressing it. We hope however our brethren will stand by the "ancient landmarks" as established by Christ the great head of the Church, and followed by the apostles in reference to these things.

On Monday morning we were taken by our aged and much esteemed Bro. Lichty to the home of brother John D. Bear, whose acquaintance we formed while attending school at Millersville last Winter. We were pleased to meet him there and our object in taking a trip to this locality was to spend a few days with him. We had a pleasant time at his home and other places we visited during our stay. All will please accept our thanks for their kindness. Brother John expects to teach this Winter, and we feel assured that those who may employ him will soon find that he is just the man for the position.

On Wednesday morning he accompanied us to Dale City. On the train we had the pleasure of again joining the company of Bro. C. G. Lint. We accompanied him to his home where we spent a pleasant time. Spent the night pleasantly with Bro. Beer. Next morning visited the homes of sister Sallie Beechly and Dr. Forney, where we enjoyed ourself much. At noon started for home where we arrived in the evening. J. B. B.

A VISIT.

On last Saturday Sept. 27, we had the pleasure of a visit from our brother and relative, D. O. Brumbaugh of Neb. It was a long time since we saw brother David, and we were right glad for the opportunity of meeting him. He was formerly a resident of this State, but some years ago, determined to cast his lot out in the land of prairies where he is now doing well, and says he does not regret the change. From his information, Nebraska has many advantages and is destined to become a State of considerable importance. It is level and laid off in sections, half sections and quarter sections with lines and roads all running at right angles. This alone, adds greatly to its appearance. The soil is easily cultivated, productive and has an abundance of grass for grazing and hay. Water can also be had in abundance by digging from 20 to 40 feet. They are also greatly improving the desirableness of the country by planting groves which forms wind breaks and protects the buildings from the storms, but they are not half so fine as our old hills. Hills are ugly things to plow over but when we wish to dodge the storms they are real nice. Let others do as they please, we believe in hills, we can't help it.

Brother David also reports favorably of the people and the Church. Since there, he has been called to the ministry and seems alive to his duty. While with us he preached in our meeting house, and we were pleased with the effort he made. Though young in the calling he manifests a spirit in the work, and by proper care and study will make a useful laborer in the Vineyard of the Lord. He has our best wishes for success both temporally and spiritually. His visit East was partly to see his father Samuel Brumbaugh, who some time ago, met with an accident which it was thought, would take his life, but notwithstanding his age he survived and is nearly well again.

ATTENTION—PLEASE.

We have, standing out on our books, nearly $1,000. Of this we do not complain as we promised to wait on those who did not have the money when subscribing. We have now patiently waited nine months, and as we have some payments to make, and badly need some money, we now ask every reader who yet owes us for subscription &c. to pay us, if possible, between this and the 15th of October. Now brethren and sisters, let us see how much you can oblige us by sending or having it sent right along. Those who pay to agents, don't wait for them to ask for it, but oblige them and us by attending to it at once. We wish it understood that all who can and will pay us between this and the time specified will confer us a *special favor*.

Correspondence.

Dear Pilgrim: Again I will venture a few thoughts.

Mt Union, twenty years ago, when I first came here, was a small village containing about three hundred inhabitants. Since that time it has been steadily increasing. The present population is said to exceed seven hundred, among whom are only three families in which we find members of the German Baptist Church.

The prevailing religious denominations being Methodists, Presbyterians, and United Brethren, and each of them has a stylish meeting-house. Some brethren think we ought to have a meeting-house here, and some think of founding and establishing an institution for the "Training up of the Brethren's children in the nurture and admonition of the Lord." I believe that both of these enterprises have become an actual necessity here. There is no place in the U. S., where these two things could accomplish more real good than at Mt. Union. The mind very naturally inquires, why so? and he who investigates thoroughly will find the following causes.

1. That the town is new and destined shortly to attract considerable of attention from the busy children of this world.

2. That the facilities which Mt. Union and its surroundings afford to the children of light for the interception and overcoming of evil cannot be excelled anywhere else upon the earth.

3. That the power in which man is an agency does not inhere so much in different earthly localities as in the man himself.

In regard to the first proposition, it is only necessary to say that the real age of towns does not depend so much upon the length of the time during which it has existed, as upon its condition with respect to its growth, and that condition with reference to Mt. Union is determined by the fact that there are already surrounding it, extensive manufacturing establishments, and more contemplated. Also three R. R's running into it, and the fourth one strongly contemplated; all of which has been induced by the recent discovery and development of inexhaustible quantities of minerals in this section of Pa., with other natural advantages, such as water-power and navigation, fertile valleys, well adapted to grazing, horticulture, agriculture, which are surrounded by mountains covered with valuable timber, &c.

The mere inklings of arguments which I have given to make clear the truth of the first proposition, will apply to the second. The true spirit of Christianity encourages its advocates to press forward and meet the enemy in his "strong-holds" seeking and saving that which was lost.

Lastly.—If the Brethren select Mt. Union or any other place having equal advantages, whereat to accomplish a useful object, they will find after succeeding, that their success depended mainly upon their constant perseverance. "As a bird that wandereth from her nest, so is a man that wandereth from his place." First select the place, next learn what it is to "wander from it," and finally stay in it. Fraternally,

J. D. G.

Dear Pilgrim: Please give notice in your pages that the Eastern District Meeting of Pa., gave a grant to a church, or as many as may join in the enterprise, to get up a better collection of Hymns that will be more adapted to the general wants of our German Churches, than the new one that has been published of late, by the general council of the A. M. Many of our members in this part are not satisfied with that edition, and therefore have concluded to try and suit our own taste by getting up a new book as an individual enterprise or grant as above, and have appointed a committee of three brethren for that important work, namely; Bro. John Hertzler, Bethel, Berks Co., Pa., Jacob Reinbold, Lancaster Pa. And as several churches of the Middle District of Pa., will concur, we thought it would be expedient to give those a representation in the committee, namely; brother Thomas Gray, York, York Co., Pa. These compose the committee, and are requested to convene on the 24th of October next, in the Spring Creek Church, Dauphin Co., Pa., to commence the work of the contemplated Hymn Book. We call upon all who have favorite Hymns, old ones, or yet in manuscript, good matter for the book, to please send them to one of the members of the committee before the date mentioned. We are desirous of having a good collection, and therefore solicit a liberal contribution, as the book shall come forth German and English, and therefore desire matter in both languages. Written by order of the committee.

WM. HERTZLER.

CHANGE OF ADDRESS.

I expect to leave here with my family for Colorado, Oct. 20, Cincinnati, Oct. 21, Kansas City, on the night of the 22d, and on Monday the 23d, arrive at Julesburg Col. on the morning of the 25th. My address will be Beaver, Weld Co. Colorado, Julesburg P. O. J. S. Flory.

MARRIED.

RENSEL—HARBOLT.—At the residence of the undersigned, brother Samuel M. Rensel of York Co., Pa., to sister Sarah Harbolt of Cumberland Co., Pa.

DAVID NISSLEY.

IMLER—EBERLY.—By H. Hershberger, at his residence in Snake Spring Valley, Bedford Co., Pa., on the 11th of Sept., 1873, Mr. John Imler to sister Henrietta Eberly both of this county.

DIED.

WOLF.—Brother Daniel Wolf of Richland Church, Richland co., Ohio, departed this life, Sept. 12th, 1873, aged 67 yrs. and 23 days. Funeral services by C. Wise and the writer. Text Rev. 14:23. The subject of this notice was born in Cumberland co., Pa., in the year 1806. In the year 1837 he moved to Richland co., Ohio, where he lived a consistent member of the church until he died. He leaves a sorrowing wife and five children to mourn their loss, but we hope their loss is his great gain. J. C. Mc MULLEN.

Visitor and *Vindicator* please copy.

MILLER.—On the 22d of Sept., in the southern end of Morrison Cove, in the bounds of the Snake Spring Valley Congregation, sister Elizabeth Miller, aged 73 years, 1 month, and 20 days. The deceased was the widow of John Miller. Funeral discourse by the brethren from the 4th chapter of 1 Thessalonians last part. HENRY HERSHBERGER.

ANNOUNCEMENTS.

Please announce that the Lord willing, our Communion Meeting will be in the Raccoon Creek Church, Montgomery Co., Ind., at our meeting-house one and a half miles north west of Ladoga, on the 17th day of October. An invitation is extended to all who wish to be with us, and especially ministers. M. FRANTZ.

Middle Fork of Wild Cat Congregation, Ind., on the 29th of October, and District Meeting of Southern District on the 30th and 31st.

Our Lovefeasts of Maryland, will be held as follows:

Sam's Creek, Oct. 11, commence 1½ p. m.
Monocacy, " 17.
Meadow Branch, " 21, com. 1½ p. m.
Beaver Dam, " 23.

Waddams Grove, Stephenson Co. Ills, October 11 and 12.

Dry Creek, Lynn Co., Iowa, on the 1st and 2d of November.

Salamony Church, Huntington Co., Ind. October 28 '73.

Beaver Run, Mineral Co., W. Va., on the 11th and 12th of October.

LITERATURE.

A. B. Brumbaugh, Huntingdon, Pa. Literary Editor.

MAGAZINES—October.

Nearly every paper of interest and merit, of the present time, is first given to the public through some one of the leading monthly magazines. Many of the finest records of travel, and of the most popular books, in serial form find their way to the real listening ear, admiring mind and appreciating taste, through the same medium. Politics, Science, Literature, Art, Religion, —all have their leaders, agitators and champions, and their mediums of communication; and those who do not avail themselves of the opportunities afforded through these channels fail to enjoy some of the richest intellectual feasts, and obtain the most valuable information.

The low price at which these periodicals are offered in clubbing with the PILGRIM and other papers brings them within the reach of all.

HARPER for October is filled with its usual variety of interesting and valuable articles. The leading paper "A Lady's Experience," is specially suggestive for woman. This magazine is now in its 47th volume and is still increasing in public favor. Subscription price $4 00 per year. Harper & Bro's, New York.

LIPPINCOTT'S for October presents rare attractions, and has an excellent table of contents. This magazine is a younger applicant for public favor. It is the most finely executed magazine in the country, and one of which Pennsylvanians can justly feel proud. $4.00 per annum. J. B. Lippincott & Co., Philadelphia, Pa.

SCRIBNER for October is a capital number, and replete with attractive articles. The Scribners seem determined to make their monthly the successful rival of all competitors for excellence. We are pleased with its growth and progress. This number closes the 6th volume, and the new volume will open with new features and great attractions. $4.00 per annum. Scribner and Co., New York.

PHRENOLOGICAL JOURNAL for October comes forth laden with good things. It is the champion of Progress and liberty of thought; and its pages are always fresh and exceedingly entertaining. $3.00 per annum. S. R. Wells, New York.

REPUBLIC.—This Journal has already become the recognized exponent of correct political principles. We like its tone. It discusses with ability the great political issues of the day. $2.00 per annum. The Republic Pub. Co., Washington, D. C.

SANITARIAN.—We have received a No. or two of this new monthly devoted to Sanitary Science in its various phases, and especially as related to the preservation of human life. A valuable periodical. $3.00 per annum. A. S. Barnes & Co., New York.

J. B. LIPPINCOTT & Co. have recently added to their list of valuable publications the first volume of a new and revised edition of "PRESCOTT'S WORKS," to be completed in fifteen volumes.

They are the publishers of the SUNDAY MAGAZINE, a profusely illustrated monthly of recreation and instruction. It has a high aim, and a good prospectus for 1874. $2.75 per. annum. Specimen Nos. mailed for 20 cents.

SCRIBNER'S announce the appearance of their new Boy's and Girl's magazine—"*St. Nicholas*," in October. Don't fail to please the children by commencing with the first No. $3.00 per annum. It will be sent with the PILGRIM at $4.00 for both.

HUNTINGDON & BROAD TOP RAIL ROAD

On and after Aug 14th, 1873, Trains will run on this road daily (Sun excepted) as follows:

Trains from Huntingdon South. *Trains from Mt. Dal's moving North.*

EXP'S. P. M.	MAIL. A. M.	STATIONS.	MAIL. P. M.	EXP'S A. M.
6 15	7 45	Huntingdon,	AR6 50	AR9 20
6 20	7 50	Long Siding	6 45	9 15
6 35	8 00	McConnelstown	6 35	9 05
6 40	8 05	Pleasant Grove	6 29	8 58
6 51	8 20	MARKLESBURG	6 15	8 45
7 01	8 35	Coffee Run	6 05	8 35
7 08	8 41	Rough & Ready	5 58	8 29
7 15	8 50	Cove	5 40	8 20
7 18	8 53	Fishers Summit	5 46	8 17
7 35	9 10	Saxton	5 35	8 05
7 50	9 25	Riddlesburg	5 15	7 45
7 55	9 32	Hopewell	5 10	7 39
8 10	9 45	Piper's Run	4 58	7 26
8 21	9 57	Tatesville	4 43	7 12
8 32	10 07	Everett	4 33	7 03
8 40	10 15	Mount Dallas	4 30	7 00
9 00	10 35	Bedford	4 05	6 35

SHOUP'S RUN BRANCH.

A. M.	P. M.		P. M.	A. M.
LE 9 20	LE 7 40	Saxton.	AR5 25	AR 7 55
9 35	7 55	Coalmont.	5 10	7 40
9 40	8 00	Crawford.	5 05	7 35
AR 9 50	AR8 10	Dudley	LE4 55	LE 7 25

Broad Top City from Dudley 2 miles by stage.

Time of Penna. R. R. Trains at Huntingdon.

*** Mail No. 2 makes connection at Huntingdon with Mail going East on Pennsylvania Railroad at 4.15 p. m., and West at 5.45 p. m. Mail No. 1 leaves Huntingdon at 7.40 a. m. on arrival of Pacific Express West.

Trains on this road connect with trains on Bedford & Bridgeport, and Cumberland & Pennsylvania Railroads.

G. F. GAGE, Supt.

The Weekly Pilgrim.

Published by J. B. Brumbaugh, & Co.
Edited by H. B. & Geo. Brumbaugh.
CORRESPONDING EDITORS.
D. P. Sayler, Double Pipe Creek, Md.
Leonard Furry, New Enterprise, Pa.

The *Pilgrim* is a Christian Periodical, devoted to religion and moral reform. It will advocate in the spirit of *love* and *liberty*, the principles of true Christianity, labor for the promotion of peace among the people of God, for the encouragement of the saints and for the conversion of sinners, avoiding those things which tend toward disunion or sectional feelings.

TERMS.

Single copy, Book paper,	$1.50
Eleven copies, [eleventh for Agt.]	$15.00

Any number above that at the same rate.

Address,
H. B. BRUMBAUGH.
James Creek,
Huntingdon county Pa.

The Weekly Pilgrim.

"REMOVE NOT THE ANCIENT LANDMARKS WHICH OUR FATHERS HAVE SET."

VOL. 4. JAMES CREEK, PENNSYLVANIA, OCTOBER 14, 1873. NO. 41

POETRY.

EVENING BY EVENING.

Good night, ye gems of beauty,
Good night, thou gently blue;
On quiet bed I lay me,
And bid farewell to you.
Good night, ye wakeful woodlands,
Good night, ye sleeping flowers,
Amid whose smiles and odors
I've passed day's wayward hours.
Good night, ye star-tipt mountains,
Old friends, the tried and true;
Good night, ye wandering waters;
Ocean, good night to you.
Good night to all, but not to Thee,
My God, who ever art with me.

Good night, dear faces round me,
Night's hours will swiftly run;
And we shall say, good morning,
At the ascending sun.
The farewell hour is coming,
The last good night is near,
When I shall part in silence
From those who love me here.
Then, all my farewells over,
Just passing out of sight,
Unweeping and untrembling,
I'll look my last good night.
Good night to all, but not to Thee,
My God, who ever art with me.

Yet not good night forever;
For He who is my day
Will wake me soon;—I see Him,
Already on His way.
No, not good night forever;
I shall but sleep in Him,
Who shall arouse me early,
While yet the dawn is dim—
Who shall arouse me early,
And bid this flesh arise,
In glorious resurrection,
To meet Him in the skies.
Good night to all, but not to Thee,
My God, who ever art with me.

I see Him, lo, He cometh!
Himself the morning light,
To bring the dawn of gladness,
The dawn that knows no night.
O Bridegroom of the morning!
Bright bringer of the day,
Put on thy fair adorning,
Thy beautiful array.
Lord Jesus, star of evening,
Yet star of morning too;
Earth's uncreated splendor,
Rise on our longing view.
Good night to all, but not to Thee,
My God, who ever art with me.

ORIGINAL ESSAYS.

THE ONES FOR WHOM WE SHOULD WEEP.

"Weep not for me, but weep for yourselves, and for your children." (St. Luke xxiii: 28.)

When they led the Son of God away to crucify Him, a great company of men, and of women followed Him; and it appears the women bewailed and lamented Him. But He turned unto them and said: "Daughters of Jerusalem *weep not for me*." Sensitive people, and especially women are easily moved to tears on hearing of, or seeing a scene of suffering or distress endured by some one, and it is readily understood why these daughters of Jerusalem should weep while they beheld the innocent and meek Jesus, who had never done harm to any one, and who had never spoken a harsh or unkind word while among men on earth, so used, and so ill-treated. But why is it that so few, if any now weep on hearing the account of his suffering read, or talked of. It has been, and still is a source of grief to many pious and good people that they cannot weep on such occasions. For the comfort and relief of all such, I will here say, that no human being can possibly take any part in the suffering of the Messiah. His sufferings were such as only God in the flesh could bear, or endure. And as they were all of an expiatory nature, no man can take part in them. Again, the sufferings of Christ are not a cause of sorrow to man, but are a cause of rejoicing to a lost world, for which He suffered alone; bearing in His body our sins on the tree, hence His suffering is no cause for men to weep. But for themselves, and for their children they must, and do weep.

In reference to the suffering of Christ poets sing, and Christians use unguarded expressions, in these songs and prayers: such as, "Give me to feel thy agonies;" "One drop of thy sad cup afford." Expressions like these are very inconsiderate and improper. One drop of that cup he so earnestly prayed his Father, if it were His will to remove, or take from him, would sink the soul into inextricable ruin, while the agonies he endured when his sweat fell like great drops of blood to the ground, would annihilate the human family. He suffered alone, because His sufferings were to make an atonement for the sins of the world. "Of the people there were none with Him, and in the work of redemption he had no helper." And for Him He will have none to weep.

But weep for yourselves, and for your children. Weeping when produced by ardent and holy desire, is a weapon most powerful in its effect; there is nothing that can awaken the latent sympathies in man so powerfully as heart-felt weeping; and when it is mixed with heart-felt prayer at a throne of grace, will move Jehovah in mercy to the weeper. Weeping is characteristic of God's people in all ages of the world, and Christianity. The patriarchs wept, the prophets wept, the Savior wept, the apostles wept, and God's people still weep. And so profitable and good it is to weep that the prophet felt like weeping much. He says, "Oh that my head were waters, and mine eyes a fountain of tears, that I might weep day and night for the slain of the daughter of my people."—Jer. ix.

"And they that sow in tears shall reap in joy. He that goeth forth and weepeth, bearing the precious seed, shall doubtless come again with rejoicing, bringing his sheaves with him." Psa. cxxvi: 5, 6. And Jesus says: "Blessed are ye that weep now, for ye shall laugh."—Luke 6: 21. Thus it is good to weep; the cause for our weeping must be good, or the effect will be lost. Tears are not always a true index to profitable weeping. Some persons weep and shed bitter tears of wrath; these I consider tears of sin, and of shame to the weeper. These Jesus loving daughters of Jerusalem must not weep for the cause they were weeping.

When the woman which was a sinner stood at His feet behind Him weeping, and washed His feet with her tears, &c., he forbid her not; but said to Simon, her sins which are many are forgiven her; for she loved much. This woman wept over her own degredation and sins, and obtained the forgiveness of all her many sins for which she wept. But these daughters of Jerusalem wept of sympathy; they felt for Jesus in His sufferings, which the Father could not remove from Him, hence He must endure it to save the souls of the children of men from eternal death; and the weeping and tears will be useless. They must not so weep for him, but should weep for themselves and for their children. And so Christ-loving women should weep. I think Christ-loving men should also weep, but as Jesus addressed Himself to women, I will confine myself to them in this article.

Mothers often feel grieved because of their own imperfections and shortcomings, and weep bitter tears of sorrow over it; but are more frequently overwhelmed with sorrow when they think of these children God has given them, and upon whom they bestowed so much care and concern, and prayed so often for, and over them, should feel so little interest in their own salvation. Not unfrequently while seated at the Lord's table contemplating their Savior, whose suffering, crucifixion, and death they are about showing forth in breaking the bread, a noise and disorder is heard about the door among the unregenerate; her heart throbs in her breast at the thought, my children may be among them. Mothers weep, not for Jesus, but for yourself, and for your children. And let your tears not be in secret, like your alms and prayers must be, but let them be seen flowing freely by those for whom they are shed; the effect will be powerful in breaking down hard hearts.

Young women, sisters, daughters of the church who have no children to weep for, have brothers and sisters to weep over; and perhaps even an unconverted father or mother may be the subject for their weeping. When these contemplate the vanities of the unregenerated, and knowing that these brothers and sisters have made this their companions and associates, and knowing too that evil communications corrupt good manners, their hearts are filled with sorrow, and weeping is the result. To these let me say, do not suppress your weeping, do not restrain your tears in the thought that some one might think you were unhappy in your religion. Let your tears flow freely, and let all know why and for whom they are shed. Your tears are precious, they are put in God's bottle, they are in His book, don't fear to shed them, first for yourselves, and then for your parents, brothers, sisters, and friends; mingle them well with your prayers, and you will prevail with God in your and their behalf.

"Weep for the lost! Thy Savior wept
O'er Salem's hapless doom;
He wept to think their day was past,
And come their night of gloom."

D. P. SAYLER.

A HOUSE uninhabited soon comes to ruin, and a soul uninhabited by the Holy Spirit of God verges faster and faster to destruction.—*Toplady.*

NON-RESISTANCE.

"Let every soul be subject unto the higher powers. For there is now power but of God: the powers that be are ordained of God. Whosoever therefore resisteth the power, resisteth the ordinances of God: and they that resist shall receive to themselves damnation. For rulers are not a terror to good works, but to the evil. Wilt thou then not be afraid of the power? do that which is good, and thou shalt have praise of the same: For he is the minister of God to thee for good. But if thou do that which is evil, be afraid; for he beareth not the sword in vain.—Rom. 13: 1-4.

It is thought by many that this passage of Scripture permits a Christian to bear arms, provided he is commanded to do so, by the government or the "higher powers." At the same time there are many that will admit, that we have ample proof to show that it is wrong to kill our fellow man in an individual combat. And there are others, who would not have it wrong even then, if they were in self-defence.

If we consider the subject under this hypothesis, we must notice how it may be lengthened out, and where will it land us. If we have the right to break this one command,—"Do not kill"—because it is the call of our country, have we not with equal propriety, from the same theory, a right to pass by other commands as well as this one? For instance, if the government would command us to worship idols, shall we not obey that call too? Let us suppose that we are under the control of king Nebuchadnezzar, and he sits up an idol, and sends forth a decree, that all nations, kingdoms, tongues, and dominions, must fall down and worship it, must we obey? "Shall we obey man or God? Judge ye."

And again, suppose we were under the government of Rome. "Who sat upon her seven hills and ruled the world," and the command would come from her tribunal, that all in her domain, shall worship that one church and no other; and fall upon those heretics, as they termed them, (but in reality the saints), and "put them to death by fire at the stake." Would it be our duty to obey that command? It's the call of your country. Come drink of the blood of the saints, for it would not do for you to be one of those saints yourself. That would be disobeying the "higher powers." O what folly and vain imagination! The fallacy of such reasoning is evident to every mind and is enough to convince any unprejudiced mind. Could I only picture to you the amount of blood shed by martyrs, caused by the government commanding them to do that which is not in accordance with the Gospel. If I were to say that two-thirds of them suffered for this cause, I do not think that I would be far out of the way.

We have now considered the subject by reasoning alone. Now to the law and prophets; let us not read truth with one eye closed. Let us read it with its connections. It is true that we must be subject to the "higher powers," but I do not understand that we should do that which conflicts with the laws of God. The government at all times, gives us the privilege to submit ourselves by obedience or death, and if we have done either, we have paid the debt, just as much so, as did the Lord when He gave Himself into the hands of the Jews. But if laws do not conflict with the laws of God, we should obey every call, "paying tribute to whom tribute belong, and honor to whom honor belong;" for it seems that the Lord designs that they shall try us at times. By these trials we are purified and for that reason they are called, the ministers of God; because they administer just such things as God would have us undergo.

Wilt thou then not be afraid of the power? "Do that which is good and thou shalt have praise of the same."—Rom. 13: 3. Well may we not fear, when we do that which is good. We have then performed our duty toward man and God, and if fallible man calls us to do more, we can say why need we fear thou hast not power to destroy the soul.

"But if thou do that which is evil, be afraid. For he beareth not the sword in vain." 4th verse. What is meant by the phrase to do that which is evil? I understand it means to disobey the laws, and commands of God. Such as the following: "Thou shalt not commit adultry. Thou shalt not kill. Thou shalt not steal. Thou shalt not bear false witness. Thou shalt not covet."—Rom. 13: 9. Well may we fear, while we stand in the way, of Him that beareth not the sword in vain; when we have not done our duty toward man and God, for He hath power to destroy the body; and while engaged in sin, he "hath power to destroy both soul and body."

"For we wrestle not against flesh and blood, but against principalities, against powers, against the rulers of the darkness of this world, against spiritual wickedness in high places." —Eph. 6: 12. The above is so plain, that I will occupy but little space in commenting upon it, as it can be plainly seen, that there would be no reason for us to wrestle against principalities, powers, and rulers, without a cause. And the cause is simply this: they call for us at times, to perform that which is wrong, and put us in a strait between the laws of God and man. But let us ever bear in mind, that man has not the power to inflict the punishment upon us for disobeying *his* laws that God hath.

We will now notice the actions of the apostles, and see if they obey the laws of man, when they conflict with the laws of God. "And when they had called the apostles, and beaten them, they commanded that they should not speak in the name of Jesus, and let them go. And they departed from the presence of the council, rejoicing that they were counted worthy to suffer shame for His name. And daily in the temple, and in every house, they ceased not to teach and preach Jesus Christ."—Acts 5: 40, 42. Little did they adhere to this command, for it was just reverse to that of God recorded by St. Matt. 28: 19. They remembered the mission of their heavenly Father.

We will now refer the reader, to the example of our Savior, and as He taught more lessons of non-resistance by action, than word, we will only repeat one sentence He spake while teaching this important doctrine: "Put up thy sword again into his place: for all they that take the sword, shall perish with the sword." —Matt. 26: 52. Sword, in the last of this sentence, I understand to be that sword that came forth out of the mouth of the Son of man, (The Word,) of which we have a symbol in Rev. 1: 16.

The question may arise, what should we do if some vile persons would fall upon us for some evil design? I have no other answer than this: We would have to let them stone Stephen to death, and the remainder take to flight like sheep.

Then is there no fighting for us to do? There is. And He has given us a complete armor to fight with, and we have it minutely described in the sixth chapter of Ephesians. And when thus armed, we are told that we "shall be able to quench all the fiery darts of the wicked," and I believe that we can stand, and bid defiance to all imperfect laws of man, to call us from our religious duties; For I am persuaded that neither death nor life, nor angels, nor principalities, nor powers, nor things present, nor things to come. Nor heigth nor depth nor any other creature, shall be able to separate us from the love of God which is in Christ Jesus our Lord."—Rom. 8: 38.

J. A. MYERS.

Millersburg, Iowa.

WANTING.

Thou art weighed in the balances, and art found wanting.—Daniel 5: 27

Were we to consult taste, fancy or pleasure, our pen would have nothing to do with this subject.

Touching upon this solemn subject, places the cross so heavily upon our shoulders that it makes writing at this time, quite a task. "*Weighed in the balances and found wanting.*" How sublime! Aliens to God, aye, *Christians*, how many might we find bearing this honorable appellation, who would faint at the idea of being weighed, for fear of being found wanting. If we are not too delicate, let us look at the state of depraved humanity as it exists in this enlightened age, an age noted for its progress, an age remarkable for its wisdom, admitted to excel all others, both financially and commercially. What do we find? A world stained with pollution and crime. Shall we weigh it in a balance? No. God has weighed us and found us wanting. He has found us wanting in faith, in purity and in energy. He has found us to be a very complaining people. We have complained more to Him than ever the Hebrews did to Moses. Actions speak louder than words, and is it not to be feared that our actions tell, too frequently, that we are complaining? I think they do. I occasionally, while on my pilgrimage, meet those who give no words of comfort, but to the contrary, complain and fret about their wretched lot in life. No one sees half so much trouble, no one ever suffered so great temptations, with them all is clouds, no sunshine, just because they always looked on the dark side. Are they Christains? This is a question I will not answer. After the Lord has weighed them in a balance we shall learn.

It is a great pity that any one should lack any good thing, because that individual that is wanting in any of the religious virtues, is, as the apostle says, after giving us a list of essential rules several religious virtues, "blind and cannot see afar off." Knowledge is virtue, and it is one of which the apostle strongly recommends.

But a glimpse only, brings to view so many of the sins of ignorance, that we are forced to take up the prophetic wail that might be heard in every land and nation: "My people are destroyed for lack of knowledge." May we not safely attribute the slow progress of Christ's blessed, though suffering cause to a want of knowledge?

Three years have elapsed since the writer, then a mere youth, recommended and urged the organization of a Sabbath School in a congregation that numbered one hundred or more members. Did you organize? We did not. And may I tell the reason? There being but One whom I fear, with a considerable degree of reluctancy, I shall. It was not because of a want of knowledge, not that those who opposed the good work were too ignorant to teach or conduct a Sabbath School, but they were those that lacked self-confidence. They were aware too, that the labors of those who conduct Sabbath Schools are attended with great self-denial, hence a life of pleasure and ease. "Who of us are able to conduct a Sabbath School?" Dead silence could echo none, but too many unanimated eyes, dimmed with disinterestness did. What has been the result? Why the weak have grown still weaker by inaction. They have gained no strength by irresolution. Nearing manhood and womanhood are those of their own families, in whose care they would shudder to place the cause of One in whom they have failed to find that implicit faith and the altogether loveliness, which must be found in well conducted Sabbath Schools. Thou art weighed in the balance and art found wanting.

Trusting the few ideas already advanced, will cause, at least, some serious thinking,—we want no other—we shall now endeavor to ascertain whether we are not found wanting many good things by never seriously considering our individual responsibility to God. We are addressed, or rather warned by the text heading this essay, in the singular number.

We are apt to run about making a great fuss about some being too fast, others too slow, and when the fussing is done that is about the end of it. This is not the way to progress; I know no better way to retrogress. I believe in, and would strongly recommend the old adage: "Be sure you are right and then go ahead." There is no telling how much one will accomplish by being right--right in the estimation of God. We will take Webster's place awhile and try to define that man or woman who is right in the estimation of God. 1. One full of the Holy Ghost. 2. One who, regardless of the opinions of men, will assimilate himself unto Christ by acquiring and retaining a holy character, and by doing whatever good in the world he is most capable of performing. 3. One who attributes all the good he may do, or ever has done, to the inspiration of God. 4. One who looks upon his flesh as a bundle of crucified lusts, living only to breathe the air that animates a higher life, a life which not only angels love to admire, but one that God Himself will receive from, and send communications unto, concerning His great work which must, if accepted, be performed in the spirit and fear of God alone.

Such an one need not fear to be weighed in the balance of eternal truth, for in such a soul there is more real worth than in the whole world. And will God give this priceless inheritage to every earnest inquirer of Divine Truth? He will if you are willing to give up all for Christ, perform every known duty, and make no reserve for yourself.

THE IMPORTANCE OF THE CHURCH.

Husbands love your wives, even as Christ also loved the Church, and gave himself for it; that he might sanctify and cleanse it with the washing of water by the word, that he might present it to himself a glorious Church, not having, spot, or wrinkle, or any such thing; but that it should be holy and without blemish.—Eph. 5: 25-27.

In this Scripture the Apostle wishes to impress the mind with the nature of the love that should exist between man and wife, and from the simile used, we have the idea of the exceeding great importance of the Church of Christ. Some persons look upon the Church as a very insignificant institution, and of very little importance, but such persons have surely never thought of the value that Christ, the great head of the Church, and the apostles put upon it.

Its importance is shown in what Christ has done for the Church. *He died for it.* He loved it enough to leave the shining courts of Heaven, come down to this world and die on Calvary's rugged cross in order that it might be established. Does this look as if it was an insignificant institution? Surely those who look at it in this light have never learned that they need a Savior, and that he is to be found alone in the Church. There are others again, who look upon it as an institution of some importance, yet do not appreciate it as they should. We should *love* the Church. This love is made apparent in various ways, and among these, there is none more evident and unmistakable than a *concern* for the Church. If we are indifferent to what the church does, it is a sure sign that we do not love it. There are those who scarcely ever attend the Church meetings, and know but little of its proceedings. Surely such persons have never fully learned of its importance, and consequently have not the proper love for it.

In this life the importance of a thing is estimated by its value, or the price paid for it. The larger the sum of money we pay for a thing, the greater value or importance do we attach to it. Now Christ gave a large price for the Church. He bought it with His own precious blood. Although the Church is not perfect, and indeed it cannot be while its subjects have the world, the flesh and the devil to contend with, yet He loves it and will finally cleanse it, and "present it to Himself a glorious Church." If we then judge the value of the Church, as we do other things, by what is paid for them, we must certainly consider it an important object, and one too, to which our attention should be constantly directed. There is nothing that has cost so much, and consequently there is nothing of so much importance, and that should so constantly demand our attention.

The importance of the Church is further seen from another standpoint. In Tim. 3: 15, the apostle in giving Timothy directions how to conduct himself in the Church, calls it the pillar and ground of the truth. Its importance is here shown by what it does. The truth is here represented as a building supported by one pillar, and that pillar is the Church. This is a very beautiful figure of the importance of the Church. Remove the Church and the grand edifice of truth must fall to the ground.

But the importance of the Church is still made more apparent from a consideration of what truth is. Jesus answered the question on one occasion very definitely, but when Pilate interrogated him in reference to it, he answered him more indirectly in these words: "Sanctify them through thy truth, *thy word is truth.*" God's word is the truth, and is supported alone by the Church. In view of this does it not seem important that we uphold the Church, which is the pillar and ground work of the truth, the Gospel to all the world, going forth sharper than any two-edged sword, conquering and subduing the world.

Then dear Christian reader, let us be live, active members; let us look upon it as something that must prosper, and that its prosperity depends upon us. If the Church fails the truth must suffer; that word which became flesh and dwelt among men, in order that the great sin might be canceled will be crucified afresh, for every feeling of coldness or indifference towards the Church is virtually dishonoring Christ. He loves the Church as a true and devoted husband loves his wife, and as the Church is to be the bride, "the Lamb's wife," when He comes again, does it not seem important that we honor it with our whole soul, body and mind. Then indeed will we see the Church come forth "Bright as the sun, and fair as the moon," and by it the truth will be supported and carried into all the world.

J. B. B.

YOU ASK TOO MUCH OF THE MINISTERS.

Dear brethren and sisters, I have been thinking for some time of writing a few lines under the above heading. The minister is often called away from home to attend appointments, and must leave his family that is as near and dear to him as yours is to you, not knowing, in many instances, how they are to get along during his absence. He must leave his work undone or hire some one to do it, and be absent three or four weeks at a time. Then in addition to this he must pay his own traveling expenses, lose his time, and then when he returns, pay the man who has done his work, all out of his own pocket. The burden is all on the minister, and this is entirely too much. Did the Lord intend that the minister should feed the flock and receive nothing in return? Verily no. Our just and merciful Savior does not ask one of the body to bear all the burden and the rest go free.

When the minister's grain goes to mill the toll dish is dipped into it the same as others. When his wool goes to the carding machine, he must pay the customary price for carding. When the tax gatherer comes around he has to pay the same per cent as other people. When he hires a man to work for him in his absence he must pay the customary price, and get nothing for his time. *Too much.* And when he gets the members together and asks them for a little help, they think that is too much. You soon hear the cry, *preaching for money.* Ask them to bear half your expenses and they say it is *too much.* Ask them to pay one fourth of your expenses and still it is too much.

Just so the minister can say when you want him to come and preach, that you ask too much. When you ask him to write out a note of his travels, it is too much. The minister is frequently asked by the brethren and sisters to write to them and let them know how he is getting along. It takes time and money to write and answer every individual letter. I have felt the burden brethren, and speak from sad experience, and have good reasons to say that you ask too much of your minister. Place yourselves in their stead a little while, and when they ask for a little help, you will not say that they ask too much.

WILLIAM BAILEY

HOW TO BE MISERABLE.

Never extend to your fellow-man, in the hour of need, a helping hand. Sit idly down and allow your tho'ts to dwell upon "the might have been." When a friend offends you in word or deed, mope it out in mulish pout. To allow self and all its sensual gratifications to predominate over your better virtues, and mistrust all around you.

Now is this the way to live? Is this the way to pass away the life that has been bestowed on us by our beneficient Creator? Can we, leading such a life as this, prepare for the great beyond? The echo of my heart answers me back, "No, no!"

Then let us be up and doing; let not the golden hours pass unheedingly by. Dwell not too earnestly upon the past; for yesterday we were, to-day we are, and to-morrow we hope to be.—*Sel.*

THE fountain sends forth pure, sparkling water because the head from whence it flows, is pure. So love emanates from the heart that has been purified by "obeying the truth." The fountain head from whence it flows being pure, a continual stream of love will issue, shedding an influence all around that will alleviate our sorrows, quell our fears and perfect us in the school of God's love, light and liberty.—*J. S. Flory.*

TYPES.

Continued.

It is somewhat a remarkable circumstance that Christ our passover was sacrificed for us, and our deliverance from the bondage of sin completed in the same month, and on the same day of the month, that the Israelites were delivered from the bondage of Egypt. The Israelites went out of Egypt, and Christ was put to death on the 15th day of the 1st month, Nisan, (March or April). Man did not intend this coincidence, (compare Matt. 29: 5, with Acts 13: 27;) but here is evidently an adaptation by God of this part of the history of His chosen people to the times of the Gospel. So also their passing from Egypt through the red sea, the wilderness and the river Jordan, to the promised land is a lively representation of a Christian's pilgrimage through life to that rest which remaineth for the people of God.

The great subject of revelation which was to be fully unfolded, in the New Testament, was the mediatorial character of Christ. This consists in His being a King, a prophet and a priest and in each of the points he was typified by Moses as King. Christ rules over His Church, and so Moses was a type of Him, in being appointed the ruler and leader of the Israelites as prophet. Christ has given laws to the Church, and so Moses was a type of Him, in being a lawgiver to the Israelites. As Priest, Christ, by shedding His own blood, has made a covenant between God and man, and is now interceding for His Church at the right hand of God, and so also Moses was a type of Him:

1st. In being commanded to ratify the covenant made between God and the Israelites, by the sprinkling of blood, (Exodus 24: 8.) which act reminded them of their unfitness as sinners to enter into any covenant with God except through an appointed atonement.

2. In His powerful intercessions, (Ex. 15: 25, 32: 11,) by which many blessings were obtained, and the wrath of God was turned away from his people, compare Ex. 12: 46. which gives an account of the paschal lamb, or as it is called in verse 27, the "sacrifice of the Lord's passover," with John 19 36, and 1 Cor. 5: 7, 8. Observe how the blood of the victim was made the means of preservation from the wrath of God, and how by partaking of its flesh they were strengthened for their journey.

The manna was a type. Compare Ex. 16: 15, with 1 Cor. 10: 3, and John 6: 31-49-58. Its spiritual significance, we are taught, was the type of Christ, the living spiritual bread, with which God feeds his redeemed and spiritual people in their passage thro' the wilderness of this world to the true Canaan of everlasting rest.

The smitten rock was a type. Compare Ex. 17: 6, with 1 Cor. 10: 4, John 7: 37. "They drank of that spiritual rock that followed them, and that rock was Christ." The true rock stands revealed in the presence of the whole world, and we hear him saying: "If any man thirst, let him come unto me and drink."

The ark and mercy-seat, which covered it, was a symbol of God's presence. Compare Ex. 25: 17-22 "And there will I meet with thee, and I will commune with thee from above the mercy-seat," &c., with Heb. 4: 14-16 10: 19. "Seeing then that we have a great high-priest that is passed into the heavens, Jesus, the Son of God, let us therefore come boldly unto the throne of grace, having boldness to enter into the holiest by his blood."

The daily sacrifice and burning of incense shadowed forth the sacrifice and intercession of Christ. Compare Rev. 8: 3, Luke 2: 10, with Ex. 29, 42, 30: 7. As to the use we may make of these types, let us remember that under temptation we have a great Mediator; under a sense of sin, we are called to behold the very paschal lamb who was offered for us. In His name, let us not fear to come boldly to a mercy seat, and let our hearts be filled with His wonderful condescension in having tabernacled in our nature, praying that the same mind may be in us which was in Him. A day did not pass but the whole congregation were reminded of their constant need of an atoning sacrifice, and invited by faith to partake of its blessing. Let this teach us to live a life of faith in Christ our Savior; esteeming, as Moses did, the reproach of Christ, greater riches than anything that this world can give.

This is to apply the types to their right use, and shows how the Jewish and Christian dispensations mutually illustrate and confirm each other, the sacrifices and ceremonies of the law preparing for the atonement of Christ; and that atonement reflecting a dignity and glory upon them, by manifesting their nature and completing their design.

D. NEILY.

ARE YOU CHRIST'S?

The Apostle closes a burning climax with the exalting word, "For ye are Christ's and Christ is God's." Are you Christ's? Many talk about him commendingly or the contrary. Who feels that he is his? That is entire dispossession of yourself. All unrenewed people have a fancy that they are their own They can do what they will with themselves. They can employ their affections, their time, their money, their brains, or what they please. If they owe allegiance to any person it is to those of their own household, or to human beings to whom they are indebted, not to Christ. They may have a blind thought of something due to God, but only in the sense of not violating any voice of conscience in themselves that is, not opposing their better self. Any thought of personal allegiance to Christ, they do not entertain any affection for him, any solicitation for his guidance, any conference as to the direction of their affairs, or the bestowment of their means, or time or words, they do not for a moment entertain. They write books about him, and never ask him to help them in the compositon. They prepare sermons even, on him and never employ his aid in the preparation. They rush into business without any consciousness that all their success must come from him. They engage in their professions and pleasures, unmindful of him by whom are all things. Be ye not like unto them. Do not disregard Christ. Ye are Christ's. Do you show it by frequent interviews with him? You consult your partner; consult this Chief Partner. You even ask information of your clerks, workmen, servants. How much more of your Lord and Master. You seek wisdom of the thermometer and barometer. How much more of him who maketh winds and weather. You ask advice of your wife how to spend your gains. How much more of him who alone has given you anything to spend.

"Ye are Christ,s" implies complete absorption in him. He is all in all. He is your breath, your thought, your love, your wisdom, your business, your pleasure your other and greater self. You think his thoughts, feel his feelings, live his life. You are not your own, you are dead, and your life is hid with Christ in God. So live, so love. Then will you have perpetual peace and power. Then will nothing trouble you above your ability to bear. Then will you go forward cheerfully on the path of life, absorbing to yourself all that is good repelling all that is bad, serene of soul, dwelling in the Heavens. All are yours, because you are Christ's and Christ is God's. Here and hereafter, life and death time and eternity finite and infinity, creature and Creator, man, angel devil even to conquer, Heaven to enjoy, hell to subdue and shun, all are yours, for "Ye are Christ's, and Christ is God's!"—*Zion's Herald.*

USE YOUR OWN TALENT.

Use your own gift—don't try to imitate others. Saul's armour would not fit you. You have not proved it. Down yonder street, where the factory lifts its tall chimneys to the skies, an operative has caught his arm in the hurrying wheels and severed an artery. A hundred men crowd around him in helpless, dumb despair. If only there were a phisician near! If we had only remedies and surgical instruments to staunch the red tide that ebbs so fast! But before the surgeon can be summoned he will bleed to death without an effort made to save him. Stop! out of the crowd a smoke-begrimed artisan steps. He stoops over the wounded man, and places his thumb with the pressure of an iron vice upon the gushing fountain from which the blood was spouting. It was a simple thing, but it saved his life. That man had no medical skill. He possessed no surgical instruments. But God gave him a hand and he used it. Brother, is there a soul near you dying? Away with Saul's armor! "Put it off!" But use the sling and smooth stones of your own God-given opportunities.

THE DUTIES OF A MOTHER.

By the quiet fireside of a home, the true mother, in the midst of her children, is sowing as in vases of earth, the seeds of plants that sometimes give to Heaven the fragrance of blossoms and whose fruit shall be as a rosary of angelic deeds, the noblest offering she can make, through the ever-ascending and expanding souls of her children to her Maker. Every word that she utters goes from heart to heart with a power of which she little dreams. Philosophers tell us in their speculations, that we cannot lift a finger without moving the distant spheres. Solemn is the tho't that every word that falls from her lips, every expression of her countenance, even in the sheltered walk and retirement of home, may leave an indelible impression on young souls around her, and form, as it were an underlying strain of that education which peoples Heaven.—*Exchange.*

GENERAL INTELLIGENCE.

THE Baptists are discussing the question as to whether all the members should be allowed to vote at their church meetings. The objection to all voting is the incapability on the part of some to know how to vote.

The *Presbyterian Weekly* says—"It is rumored at Lancaster that Prof. D. M. Wolf, of Franklin and Marshall College, while interfering with some hazing sophomores, on Saturday night, was stabbed in the abdomen, and dangerously wounded."

Pretty bad sophomores, those. If they have been preparing for the ministry, we suppose their intentions are changed now.

A BROTHER of Mercersburg Franklin Co., Pa., says the agent missed sending his name, and that he can't do without the PILGRIM any longer. This is the precise language of a number of others who have *tried* to do without the PILGRIM. We hope all will take warning from these experiences, and not attempt to be without it the coming year. Our agents should also be on the alert that they do not miss sending the name of any one who desires to be a subscriber.

The criminal code of Nebraska, which went into effect on the 1st of September, contains this provision against swearing—"If any person of the age of fourteen years and upward shall profanely curse or damn, or profanely swear by the name of God Jesus Christ, or the Holy Ghost, every such person shall, for each offence be be fined not less than twenty-five cents, nor more than one dollar."

This is a very commendable law, but the penalty is not very heavy. If such a law was to be established in Pa., it is likely some persons would lose a good many twenty-five cent pieces.

A French paper has the following in reference to their people:

"What is taking place in France is likewise taking place in Belgium. On all sides an effort is being made to make the population fanatical. In some of the most ignorant places they even go so far as to sell small bits of the straw, as 'coming from the dark prison in which our Holy Father the Pope is groaning,' and hearts are melted or exasperated by the thought of this unhappy one, shut up in his prison, lying upon straw, and without doubt also deprived more or less of food."

If this were so the Pope would have a pretty hard time of it, but he is really living in a magnificent palace, amid the greatest luxuries of life. This is a fair specimen of the wickedness and deception of men, and also of how grossly superstitious they will become.

THE Baptists of Georgia have resolved to raise $350,000 as an additional endowment to a university located at Macon. This is certainly a pretty good sum to be raised in one State, and if the membership is not large it will certainly pull pretty heavy on the pockets of some. If the Baptists of Georgia alone, can raise $350,000, ought not the Brethren of all the States in the Union raise enough funds to build one institution of learning. We as a people are by no means poor, and as it is now generally acknowledged that we should have a school especially adapted to the church, it does seem strange that a more strenuous effort is not made. Is it not probable that we love our money too much, and that we all appreciate it more than we do knowledge. If this be so, then indeed it is an evil, and the sooner we get rid of this feeling the better. The *love* of money is the root of all evil.

Youth's Department.

WHAT IS LIFE?

A little crib beside the bed,
A little face above the spread;
A little frock behind the door,
A little shoe upon the floor,
A little lad with dark-brown hair,
A little blue-eyed face, and fair,
A little lane that leads to school,
A little, blithsome, winsome maid,
A little hand within his laid;
A little old-time-fashioned store;
A little family gathering round
A little turf-heaped, tear-dewed mound;
A little added to his soil,
A little rest from hardest toil;
A little silver in his hair.
A little stool and easy chair;
A little night of earth lit gloom,
A little cortege to the tomb.

TO THE YOUNG.

David and Solomon and the other holy and wise men, whose writing were inspired by the Holy Ghost, frequently notice how the works of the Almighty are made to express both His power and His will. They are held out to us to be studied and pondered in our hearts. What we call nature, or the works of God in the creation, is like a large book of pictures in which every one may read the meaning without knowing a letter of the alphabet.

Among the things contained in this large book, let us make choice of a very little creature, and inquire what it is calculated to teach us. The bee is a small insect without reason or knowledge, a fly that lives and moves about for awhile and then perishes, but the whole of its short life is a continued lesson to us, and we will consider how we may best make use of it.

The bee has a wonderful instinct. By instinct we mean that feeling which inclines an animal to do what is right for its preservation or comfort, without its being able to understand why it ought to do so, and without being taught. How much more precious and valuable is reason, which we are endowed with, than the finest instinct of animals; yet very few of us make half as good or constant use of our reason as the beasts do of their instinct. The Lord has been pleased to design that the bee should furnish a great quantity of a very rich and wholesome nourishment for its own use and for us. Honey is very frequently mentioned in Scripture, and of such value was it considered, that the distinguishing character of Canaan, the good land which God chose for His own people Israel, and which is a type of Heaven itself, was a land flowing with milk and honey.

Flowers that so delight the eye by their lovely colors, and charm the smell by their fragrance, are the chief source from which the bee can gather its honey. In a wild state the bees are found in the hollows of rocks and ties, and in the cavities of old walls buildings, but those who keep bees in order to make money from their honey, put them into hives made on purpose for their habitation.

Now no sooner is the bee settled in the hive than it sets about doing its work there. There is no loitering up and down, no resting at ease, or basking in the sun. All is a scene of the greatest activity, and each one goes to work as if the prosperity of the whole hive depended on its exertions.

How few of the youth do this when old enough to know for what purpose they are put into this great habitation, the world. How you love to idle away the precious hours, and make a thousand false and foolish excuses for what you know to be indolence. The little bee goes to work to lay in a store of provisions for the Winter, while it is yet very far distant, and it cannot reason as you can on the value of time, nor understand that if life continues, days of helplessness and sadness must come—days when the flowers will wither, the ground covered with snow, and there will be no possible way of getting a supply if it be neglected while Spring and Summer last. Yet this instinct bids it work, and it works with all its might.

You can well understand what you are told, both by your teachers and by your own reason and conscience. You know that the spring and summer of your life will soon be gone, and that age, should you live to be old, like a dreary Winter, will soon arrive, and that death in the end, will shut you up in the dark tomb. Beyond the tomb you must exist forever upon what you have provided in this world, whether with the blessed, you have laid up for yourself treasures in Heaven, or with the wicked, treasured up unto yourselves wrath against the day of wrath and the revelation of the righteous judgments of God. Knowing this, compare your carelessness and indifference with the diligence and activity of the little bee. Do you think that God will require less from you to whom He has given so much than from this poor insect?

The bee having examined its habitation, goes out in search of proper material to fill it with. It finds in the pleasant garden a thousand lovely flowers and sweet blossoms and upon these it alights, dips its trunk into the cup at the bottom of the flower, takes up a proper quantity of the nourishment, puts it into its little bag and goes on to another flower, and so it proceeds until it is laded with a rich treasure, when it flies away to its hive and carefully lays it up, working busily until it is time to go out for a fresh supply.

Such a garden is the Scriptures. Such flowers blossom in every page, offering you a rich banquet if you will pause to gather it. Oh, that like the bee, you would often alight there, and having read or heard as much as you can bear in mind, take it with you into retirement, meditate upon it, and pray over it until it has nourished your soul, and remains laid up in your memory as a most precious store, to be applied on every needful occasion. Surely the busy must enjoy very much, the warm beams of the sun, the fragrance of the flowers, the freshness of the soft air and it is sweet to hear its pretty humming noise.

I am convinced that if you look attentively at both, you will say that a bee is a more useful and active insect than a butterfly. Though they may be roving among the same flowers at the same time, there is something restless and unmeaning in the motions of a butterfly. I could almost fancy it is only reposing on the flowers for me to admire its beautiful wings. It reminds me of those who do indeed study the Bible and other books, but merely to get credit among men, and to show their talents, not to derive any real benefit from them; and you see the consequence. The butterfly builds no house, lays up no store for the Winter, and therefore as soon as the warm days end, it falls down and dies under the cold breeze.

But how different it is with our little friend, the bee. How wise and discerning is this insect. You may put an artificial flower, made of paper, in the garden and the butterfly will rest upon it, and spread its gay colors in the sun quite contentedly; but not a moment will the bee consent to stay, for there is no honey in that flower. Profit, lasting profit, is the end that this creature has in view. What yields no honey has no charm for it, off it flies to the blossom of the Thyme or the Nettle, or of any lovely looking shrub, whence it can extract its sweet food.

How foolish are they who suppose that an idle life, passed among gay sights and trifling amusements, is happier than that which is devoted to piety and useful knowledge. Will you say that the bee is a melancholy creature? O, look and attend but a moment as she nestles in a sweet blossom, and springs away with her treasure to alight on the leaves of another flower, and bury her little head in it and away again with her bright wings glittering in the sunshine. Poor children you who think religion gloomy, and pity others for being so strict, as you fancy it, I wish you knew how much happier they are than yourselves. What are all your expensive toys, your showy dresses, and your well guilt books of fairy tales and foolish stories? They are but so many paper roses that never yield any nourishment to your minds nor give you material for an eternal store.

To be Continued.

The Weekly Pilgrim.

JAMES CREEK, PA., Oct. 14, 1873.

☞ How to send money.—All sums over $1.50, should be sent either in a check, draft or postal order. If neither of these can be obtained, have the letter registered.

☞ When Money is sent, *always* send with it the name and address of those who paid it. Write the names and post office as plainly as possible.

☞ Every subscriber for 1874, gets a *Pilgrim Almanac* Free.

CLOVER CREEK LOVEFEAST.

Tuesday evening Sept.,30, being the time appointed by the brethren of Clover Creek, Blair Co.,Pa., for their Love feast, we concluded to be with them. After a pleasant ride across Tussey's Mountain, a distance of some 9 miles we arrived at the appointed place for the meeting where we found a goodly number assembled and were at the waterside where prayer was wanted to be made and a believer to be engrafted into Christ by baptism. The exercises commenced at 4 o'clock p. m., where we found the following ministers present: S. R. Zug, of Lancaster Co., Stephen Hildebrand of Conemaugh, J. B. Miller of Alumbank, and Brice Sell of Duncansville Congregation, also the ministers of Yellow Creek and Hopewell congregations. The evening exercises were well attended and the preaching edifying, but not so pleasant to communicants and spectators, had they a better arranged house. The congregation at Clover Creek deserves a better and more conveniently arranged house, and the probability is that they will have one before many more such seasons pass. There are so many advantages in a well arranged house that they cannot be appreciated except by those who have them. This thing of women, especially those having children to care for, sitting on seats without backs, during a two or three hours service, is an act of penance done with exceeding bad grace, the fact is, it is worshiping God under serious difficulties.

The membership present was quite large, and as a consequence, it took a long time to get through with the services, yet, the order in the house, was as good as could be expected under existing circumstances, and the participants of the holy ordinances, no doubt enjoyed a pleasant waiting before the Lord. During the night, we were accommodated with a comfortable resting place in the house of our respected brother J. L. Wineland, a resident minister. In the forenoon at the same place, the congregation was entertained in the German by S. R. Zug, followed by Stephen Hildebrand and others in the English. The congregation was well entertained and we hope the good seed sown will produce an abundant harvest.

After the meeting closed, many of the brethren started toward the Yellow Creek Congregation, where another communion season was to be celebrated on the 3, & 4, but we made our way homeward, though reluctantly, as we much desired to be with our brethren at Yellow Creek, and could we always follow our inclinations, we would have been there, as it is our greatest pleasure to commune with God's people.

McVEYTOWN VISIT.

On Saturday morning, October 4, we took the train at our station with the intention of visiting McVeytown. On entering the cars, we met brother S. R. Zug and wife, brother Marston and wife, and others from Lancaster Co., Pa., on their way homeward, also brother L. Furry, on his way to the McVeytown Meeting. As we had business to attend to at Huntingdon relative to our building, we remained there until the evening train. On our arrival at our stopping place, we made our way for the home of our esteemed brother Abraham Myers, but they were not at home, being on a visit in the West, and as his daughter had already, a number of strangers to entertain, we thought it prudent not to add to her charge, although she had charity enough to receive and entertain us with a grace that would have made us feel at home. We then called upon Bro. Henry Hertzler, who lives just across the way, where we were kindly received, and where we again met our brother, L. Furry, who, whatever his deficiencies may be, is filled brimfull of love for Jesus and the cause, and is an active supporter of the Weekly Pilgrim. At this place, we were hospitably entertained for the night.

On Sabbath morning there was an appointment at or near the station, now called Mattawana. At this meeting there was an excess of ministers, but as we also need an occasional sermon, some of us did well by occupying back seats. The services were opened by George Brumbaugh, and preaching done by L. Furry, J. B. Garver, and closed by John Spanogle. After taking dinner at brother Hertzler's, we noticed a large number of Amish going towards the river for the purpose of performing baptism. Having never seen them perform this rite, we, with a number of others, concluded to witness the ceremony. We did not get there in time to hear or see any of the preliminaries, if they had any, as the last candidate was in the water when we arrived. We were informed that there were eight baptized, but as six of them preferred not to go into the water, they were baptized in the house, which left two to be baptized in the river. They were taken in the river a short distance where the water was about 3 or 4 inches deep, and there kneeled, when the administrator, with his hands, dipped some water and poured on the head of the candidate three times, once at the naming of each person of the godhead. These people are strict conformists, plain and modest in apparel, sober, honest, and generally of good deportment and are said to be good neighbors and citizens. From here, we went to the Spring Run Church house where the Lovefeast was to be held in the evening, but as we have the promise of a local report of the meeting, we will omit the details. The meeting was largely attended, order excellent and the exercises thro'out interesting and edifying, and we can truly say that we enjoyed a feast of fat things to the soul long to be remembered. This Church is under the care of Eld. J. R. Hanawalt, and seems to be in quite a prosperous condition.

THE PILGRIM FOR 1874.

As some subscribers for 1874 are already being received, it becomes necessary that we commence to make our arrangements and set before our readers, some of our prospective improvements. Since our commencement, we have steadily aimed at improvement, and if the opinions of our readers can be accepted as evidence, we have not altogether failed. Whether or not we shall be able to give our readers more interesting reading for the coming year, depends much upon what our contributors will do for us, but that part of the publishing which we have under our control more especially, we expect to improve. One important feature for the coming year, will be better mail facilities, by our removal into our new and commodious office at Huntingdon, which will be completed in some four or five weeks, of which we will speak in another number. Good mail facilities is an important feature in publishing a paper that should not be overlooked, and for this, Huntingdon cannot be excelled, as it is situated along the great thoroughfare of the United States, the Penna. Central R. R. Another important improvement will be the enlargement of the Pilgrim without raising the price. Our present intention is to increase the size 77 inches of surface. This we can scarcely afford to do unless we can largely increase our circulation, but as there has been some complaint that the Pilgrim is too small for the price, we are determined that there shall be no more just cause for such complaint. If our agents and friends will go to work in good time and double our present list, which can easily be done, we can still, by economizing, make our ends meet.

As an additional inducement we will soon have ready for 1874, one of the best Almanacs ever published by the Brethren, to be given *free* to every subscriber. More than this could not reasonably be expected for the small sum of $1.50, but it is hard to tell what we may do should our circulation be largely increased. With our present facilities we can publish a paper, perhaps, a little cheaper than any other company of brethren in the Brotherhood, but we wish to have it understood that we are not holding out these inducements for the sake of competition, as all our periodicals are really too cheap now considering the circulation we have. In due time, our prospectus and Almanac will be ready, when we want three or four hundred new agents, to whom liberal inducements will be given.

MONEY LIST.

George Detrick	$0.00
Joseph Mohler	1.50
D. D. Shively	1.50
Wm. B. Sell	50
Daniel Glick	4.50
J. G. Heckler	25
Jonas Price (all right)	20
John M. Mohler	1.25
J. H. Miller	25
Isaac Bright	1.50
S. N. Wine	3.40
Benjamin Fryfogle	1.50
Jos. D. Snowberger	1.10
Isaac Metsgar	1.50
Thos. B. Maddocks	3.00
Levi Reed	3.50
Thos. D. Lyon, (right)	5.60
Samuel Greenawalt	35
Lizzie F. Miller	1.50
J. H. Brumbaugh	7.65
Andrew Lohr, sr.	1.50
John Zook	7.35
John Billman	1.50
J. H. Garman	1.25
Samuel Hollapeter	80
George Kinney	75
John S. Hanawalt	1.50
Levi Swigart	1.50

MARRIED.

MYERS—NALLEY.—On the 2d day of Oct., 1873, at the residence of Francis Pike, by the undersigned, Mr. Simon Myers to Miss Mary E. Nalley, both of Washington Township, Polk Co., Iowa.

May peace and harmony attend their happy union. D. E. Brubaker.

DIED.

RUSSEL.—In the South Santiam congregation Linn Co., Oregon, June 13th, 1873, our much beloved sister, Ellen Russel, wife of Bro. William Russel, aged 44 years, 9 months, and 12 days.

She leave a sorrowing husband and two children to mourn their loss which we hope is her great gain. Bro. William has lost an affectionate companion, her children a kind mother, but we do hope they will prepare to meet her in the bright world above.—Her disease was consumption, which she bore with Christian fortitude, and oftimes she spoke of her home above. Funeral services by brother David Brower, from John 5: 25, 28 and 29th verses, to a large and attentive concourse of people.

Aaron H. Baltimore.

WHITMAN.—In the limits of the Lower Cumberland Church, York Co., Pa. Sept. 26, 1873, of old age, brother William Whitman, aged 82 years, 3 mos and 8 days. Funeral text "Our light affliction which is but for a moment," &c., by the brethren.

He lived a single life. He has two sisters surviving him. Years ago he retired from his business capacity, submitting himself to the care of his nephew and neice, who also have the care of their frail aged mother, his sister in the flesh and in the Lord. As their hearts are glowing with love and care for their dear old friends, so may it glow for the religion of Jesus Christ.

FLEMING.—In the Lower Conawaga District, Aug. 24th of dropsy, Abraham Fleming, aged 69 years, 2 mos. and 5 days. During his sickness he inclined to the Brethren for refuge, and made very remarkable acknowledgments to them, requesting them to preach his funeral sermon which they did from Psalms xc: 12.
ADAM BEELMAN.

EMMEL.—In the Newton Church, Miami Co., Ohio, July 31st, 1873, sister Catharine Emmel. Also in the same church Sept., 10th, 1873, brother Andrew Emmel, husband of the above named sister. Funeral services of both by the brethren. The subjects of the above notices emigrated to Ohio in the Fall of 1858 where they became members of the church. Their former residence was 15 miles east of Lewistown Mifflin County, Pa. S. MOHLER.

ROWDABUSH.—In the Dunnings Creek Congregation, Bedford Co., Pa., Sept. 1st 1873, Mary Etta, daughter of Jacob and Elizabeth Rowdabush, aged 5 mos. and 12 days. Funeral services by the brethren J. B. MILLER.

Correspondence.

Munich, Baravia, July 18, '73.

My dear father and Sarah: I received your welcome letter, dated June 29, yesterday, and was so glad to hear from you as I never had heard one word from you since I saw you. I am very sorry you are not very well, hope you are feeling better. I am very sorry Sarah is not better than she was when I was there. We hear from home about once a week. Our letters are about four weeks generally coming from Chicago. I wrote to you last from Dresden. We left Dresden on the 7th of June, came up to Rathen, and stayed there over a day, visited the Bastee, where there are mountains of rocks, and which was at one time a great stronghold for robbers in the tenth century. We saw the caves and the places where they hurled people down among the rocks into the ravines. The scenery was very grand. While among the mountains, a thunder storm came up; when we were coming down, we had to take shelter under a large rock. The next day we took the train and came to Bodenbach, where we crossed the line from Saxony to Bohemia, and our baggage was examined here. In the afternoon took the train for, Prague, arrived there in the afternoon or evening. We remained there over Sunday and visited a number of churches, however, all Catholic. The people here are nearly all Catholics—a miserable set of people—lazy, filthy, and very ill looking, and beggars running after you all the time begging. We were really afraid here. Some of the churches are fine. They all have a clock here from which when it strikes, twelve saints come walking out. It is wonderful.

On Sunday evening, at seven, we took the train for Vienna, where we arrived on Monday morning at eight. In this city we spent two weeks and a half. We spent about six days in the exhibition, where we saw people and their finest wares from every part of the world. I cannot begin to tell you what I saw here, the finest machinery, steam plows, and steam wagons. The machinery room alone is one half mile long. It was a great wonder to me. Here they wove from the finest fabric to the heaviest, fine lace, silks, ribbons, velvets, in fact, everything. They also had a great many wax figures with their different costumes, from Sweden, Turkey and Egypt, and the finest fruit I ever saw, from Greece. The center dome is the largest in the world, and is to be left standing after the exhibition is over. It is to last till the last of November. When we first went to Vienna they told us that about one hundred and thirty thousand people visited the Exhibition daily. The last week we were there the crowd was not so great, as the heat was very intense. We could not go out in the heat of the day, on account of the heat. I never felt the heat like it was there. They also had cholera there the first of July. I should think it was not a healthy city as it is not kept neat. The buildings are very large and fine, and is a beautiful city. They number 663,000 inhabitants. There are 12000 Protestants, 10000 Jews, 800 Greeks, and a garrison of 28000. The people are rather a nice looking people—rather fine looking, and it is a fine business city with very fine stores.

We left Vienna June 26, and came up the river Danube to Welk, where we remained over night. Next morning we visited a celebrated Benedictine Abbey, 185 feet above the river, founded in 1089, re-erected 1701, resembling a large palace rather than a monastery. They took us through a number of fine rooms. Our guide was a Monk 75 years old. He told us he saw N—— the first, and seemed to take great pride in telling us. At Welk we took a steamboat, and came up the Danube to Grein, a little town among the hills, where we remained two weeks, and saw German life among the peasants. They seem to be a hard working people and very kind. They looked at us as if we were a show. Americans seldom get into this part of the country, being out of the way of travel. At Grein we took a steamboat again, came to Linz, where we remained two days and visited places of interest.

On last Saturday evening we took the train and came to Salzburg where we remained two days. On Monday we visited the largest salt mines in the world, and Kenig Sea. This sea is six miles long and one and a half wide. Some of the mountains surrounding it, which rise almost perpendicularly from the water, are 800 feet in height. It is sublime. On Tuesday we left Salzburg for Munich. I forgot to tell you Salzburg was a walled city once, a great part of it a natural wall. They also have a great many soldiers there, and it is quite a fine city. The finest church we have seen in Europe we saw at this place. After leaving Salzburg we passed through a beautiful country. It took six hours to come to Munich. We have not yet decided how long we will remain here, this is also a very beautiful city. The streets are very wide and clean, the buildings are very fine and the people generally very nice looking. The weather is much cooler than it had been, it has been very pleasant all day.

We do not know when we will get home, but expect to make that point late in the Fall. John says he is quite lonely at times. Oliver says he is getting along right well. Have you heard of brother Samuel and sister Kate? I have not heard from them since I left America. I often wonder whether Samuel answered that letter I wrote for you when I was there. Oliver and myself both feel quite well, we are much stronger than we were when we left America. We walk a great deal. The boys are very well and growing to be quite large, I think they sometimes get rather tired having nothing to do but sight-seeing. It becomes tiresome at times, especially when it is so hot.

We do not enjoy the German cooking, we much prefer American cooking. We always see rye bread on the table, the poor live on it altogether. I think they don't get much meat in this country, it is very expensive. Of the working class I see a great many taking large pieces of black bread from their pockets and eating it, and they seem to be satisfied. They drink a great deal of beer, the better class drink wine. Water is not very good and they drink but very little.

I would like you to write to me again as soon as you get this, as I am always so anxious to hear from you, if you can only tell me how you are. I hope you will keep well, and that we will be spared to return to America to our dear ones. I hope to see you on my return home. May God bless and keep you well, is the prayer of your daughter. The children join me in love to yourself and Sarah.

From your daughter,
N. L. SPROULE.

Dear Pilgrim: Our Communion Meeting is now past. Once more the brethren and sisters have shown to the world that God has a people on the earth, a people that is not ashamed of His Word. They have witnessed to both small and great, none other things than has been commanded them by the Great Head of the Church. How pleasant to see brethren all agree, all of one mind, all willing to obey God our Heavenly Father in the one way. Yes as pleasant as Solomon's beloved, as beautiful as the rose compared to our beloved. But our feast did not continue long, the vocations of life have called our brethren to their homes. Yesterday the kiss of love and a warm farewell shake of the hand was given. But we meet to part here, brethren and sisters, and when we part, we shall meet, but ah, where and when, will the "again" be? Will it be where we will never sever, as we sometimes sing, or will it be here where sin and sorrow come? But by and by it we fight and labor we will be where we will not labor day after day; it will be in mansions prepared by Jesus. Those mansions are not strewn with saw-dust, and cotton-wool boards for wind breaks. The streets are pure gold, no bleaching wind, no rain, no storm there. O, how many times did our mind center there while the meeting continued! Yes, while others seemed to enjoy life well, our mind was thrown to where the "Sweet by and by" will be fully realized. How vain are the things of this world, how little are they appreciated. The child of God cares not for the giddy show of the frivolous fashions of this dark and benighted world. Brethren, what is this world? What else but a space given to us to prepare for Heaven? It is only a desert of thorns, a quag, a mire, a pit, a world of tears, and a nest of demons with poison under their tongues, ready to hurl you and I down beneath their hatred into hell's dark domain, "where the worm dieth not, and the fire is not quenched." Our Master has warned us to take heed of ourselves lest we become a castaway.

There was a large crowd of spectators, many of which never witnessed the Gospel-show before. I am satisfied that many went away wiser than they came, and no doubt some thought if these people are right, we are wrong, it could not be otherwise. Quite a number of members were present, and behind the table, was able, willing, and ready hearts. A. J. Correll, D. D. Sell, elders, and D. Gibson and S. Blocker, constituted the mouth-piece of the Lord on the occasion. Many solemn impressions were made. Our prayer is that they may be made lasting. One soul was made to rejoice in the act of obedience to the mandates of Heaven. This sister came a distance of thirty miles, (walking part of the way,) to unite with the church. The brethren, we trust, were built up. O may the little army of forty strong, here in Andrew Co., Mo., bow in humble submission to the requirements of the Gospel; may their united strength be for the upbuilding of Zion. To thin the ranks of the enemy, brethren, we must be at our post preaching to the world by our walk and conduct, for actions speak louder than words. If our walk before the world does not correspond with what we profess, better would it be if we would step aside and let others fill our places whom we keep away. O let our chaste conversation at home, (for there is where charity begins,) and abroad be well spoken of. Yes, my brethren, if it takes all we have, if we must sacrifice all for the sake of cultivating the spirit of love, gentleness, meekness, longsuffering, and every principle that Heaven demands of us, let us not be forgetful of these things, and ere long you will see the fruits of your labor. May God help us all to be in the discharge of our duties. S. C. BASHOR.

Whitesville, Mo.

ANNOUNCEMENTS.

There will be a Lovefeast held at Mc Alavey's Fort, Huntingdon Co., Pa., on the evening of the 19 inst. Preaching to commence on the evening of the 18. Those coming by R. R., will stop at Petersburg on the 18, where it is expected there will be conveyances to place of meeting.

Please announce that the brethren of the Welch Run Congregation, Washington Co., Md., intend holding their Lovefeast in the Broadfording Meeting-house, on the 13 and 14 of October, commencing at 1 p. m., and continue next day till noon. A general invitation is given, especially to ministering brethren. C. KEEFER.

Our Lovefeasts of Maryland, will be held as follows:

Monocacy, " 17.
Meadow Branch, " 21. com. 1½ p. m.
Beaver Dam, " 23.

LITERATURE.

A. B. Brumbaugh, Huntingdon, Pa. Literary Editor.

BOSTON JOURNAL OF CHEMISTRY; devoted to the Science of Home Life, the Arts, Agriculture and Medicine. Of the many periodicals coming to our house this is considered the most valuable, useful and practical, and after an acquaintance with it for over eight years, from its origin, we still look forward to its monthly visits with pleasure, and derive profit from each number. Each number is worth much more than the subscription price. We advise every one of our subscribers to try it a year upon our recommendation; and in order to afford them the opportunity we will club with the PILGRIM, and send both for $2.25 for a year. Published by Billings, Clapp & Co., Boston, Mass. $1 00 per year.

THE LITERARY WORLD.—This is a monthly periodical devoted exclusively to literature; and contains careful reviews of the most important, and choice readings from the best new books. Also book notices, literary news, and a list of new American publications for each month. For years we felt the want of just such a periodical, and now feel greatly pleased to know that it has attained to such a position in literary circles, that it is the acknowledged guide in the selection and purchase of new books. Published by S. R. Crocker, Boston, Mass. Price $1.00 per annum.

WEBSTER'S UNABRIDGED DICTIONARY.—The new Illustrated edition of Webster's Dictionary is just the book for everybody. To educated men and women it is indispensable. No student or learner can afford to be without it. The vast amount of various and useful knowledge contained in this ponderous book can be found nowhere else without days and weeks of tedious search. It is a whole library in itself. Next to the Bible it should be valued in every intelligent family.

WEBSTER'S UNABRIDGED ILLUSTRATED.—"Viewed as a whole, we are confident that no other living language has a dictionary which so fully and faithfully sets forth its present condition as this last edition of Webster does that of our written and spoken English tongue."—*Harper's Magazine.*

CHILDREN WITH THE POETS.—By Harriet B. McKeever. This is a carefully compiled volume of beautiful poetry, specially designed "for children between the ages of eight and fourteen" years; but we hesitate not to say that there are those of all ages, through life, who would derive from its pages pleasure, profit and enjoyment. The selections have been made with a view to inspire reverence for holy things and places; to elevate the taste, purify the imagination and improve the mind; and there are thousands of precious youths to whom such a book would be the opening of a new life, and in whose minds many of these poems would wake responsive echoes of love, joy, hope, and lead them to virtue and God.

Give the children plenty of good literature and it will yield abundant returns. If this book contained nothing more than the "*Night before Christmas,*" by Dr. Moore it would be abundantly worth all its costs; but it contains over two hundred charming poems besides, making it a treasury of good things for the young. Published by Claxton, Remsen & Haffelfinger, Philadelphia., and for sale by Wm. Lewis, Huntingdon, Pa., or sent from this office. Price $1.50 to $1.50.

GOOD BOOKS.

How to read Character, Illus. Price,	$1.25
Combe's Moral Philosophy,	1.75
Constitution of Man, Combe,	1.75
Education, By Spurzheim,	1.50
Memory—How to Improve it,	1.50
Mental Science, Lectures on,	1.50
Self-Culture and Perfection,	1.50
Combe's Physiology, Illus.	1.75
Food and Diet By Pereira,	1.75
Marriage. Muslin, $1.50,	
The Science of Human Life,	3.50
Fruit Culture for the Million,	1.00
Saving and Wasting,	1.50
Ways of Life—Right Way,	1.00
Footprints of Life,	1.25
Conversion of St. Paul,	1.00

Man and Woman; Considered in their Relations to each Other and to the World. 12mo, Fancy cloth, Price $1.00.

WANTED.

A man to work at the Wagon-making business, who understands the trade, and is capable of running a shop independently. Shop and material furnished. Work plenty both heavy and light. A reasonable chance will be given to a suitable person. A man without a family will be preferred, Apply to or address the undersigned.

GEO. BRUMBAUGH.
Grafton, Huntingdon Co., Pa.

GET THE BEST.

WEBSTER'S Unabridged Dictionary.

10,000 *Words and Meanings not in other Dictionaries.*

3000 Engravings; 1840 Pages Quarto. Price $12.

Webster now is glorious,—it leaves nothing to be desired. [Pres. Raymond, Vassar College.]

Every scholar knows the value of the work. (W. H. Prescott, the Historian.)

Been one of my daily companions. (John L. Motley, the Historian, &c.)

Superior in most respects to any other known to me. (George P. Marsh.)

The best guide of students of our language. (John G. Whittier.)

Excels all others in defining scientific terms. (President Hitchcock.)

Remarkable compendium of human knowledge. (W. S. Clark, Pres. Ag. Col'ge.)

A necessity for every intelligent family, student, teacher and professional man. What library is complete without the best English Dictionary?

ALSO

Webster's Nat'nal Pictorial Dict'nary.

1040 Pages Octavo. 600 Engrv'gs. Price $5.

The work is really a gem of a Dictionary, just the thing for the million.—*American Educational Monthly.*

Published by G. & C. MERRIAM, Springfield, Mass. Sold by all Booksellers.

Trine Immersion

TRACED

TO THE APOSTLES.

The SECOND EDITION is now ready for delivery. The work has been carefully revised, corrected and enlarged.

Put up in a neat pamphlet form, with good paper cover, and will be sent, post-paid, from this office on the following terms: One copy, 25 cts; Five copies, $1.10; Ten copies, $2.00. 25 copies, $4.50; 50 copies, $8.50; 100 copies, $16.00.

$5 to $20 [illegible]

Historical Charts of Baptism.

A complete key to the history of Trine, and the ORIGIN of Single Immersion. The most interesting, reliable and comprehensive document ever published on the subject. This Chart exhibits the years of the birth and death of the Ancient Fathers, the length of their lives, who of them lived at the same period, and shows how easy it was for them to transmit to each succeeding generation, a correct understanding of the Apostolic method of baptizing. It is 22x28 inches in size, and extends over the first 400 years of the Christian era, exhibiting at a single glance the impossibility of single immersion ever having been the Apostolic method. Single copy, $1.00; Four copies, $3.25. Sent post paid. Address, J. H. MOORE.

Urbana, Champaign Co., Ill.

DYMOND ON WAR.

An inquiry into the Accordancy of War, with the Principles of Christianity, and an examination of the Philosophical reasoning by which it is defended. With observations on some of the causes of war and on some of its effects. By Jonathan Dymond Sent from this office, post-paid, for 50 cts!

GIVEN AWAY.

A FINE GERMAN CHROMO.

We send an elegant chromo, mounted and ready for framing, free to every agent for

UNDERGROUND

OR,

LIFE BELOW THE SURFACE.

BY THOS. W. KNOX.

942 Pages Octavo. 130 Fine Engravings.

Relates Incidents and Accidents beyond the Light of Day; Startling Adventures in all parts of the World. Mines and Mode of Working them; Undercurrents of Society; Gambling and its *Horrors*; Caverns and their Mysteries; The Dark Ways of Wickedness; Prisons and their Secrets; Down in the Depths of the Sea; Strange Stories of the Detection of Crime.

The book treats of experience with brigands; nights in opium dens and gambling hells; life in prison; Stories of exiles; adventures among Indians; journey through Sewers and Catacombs; accidents in mines; pirates and piracy; tortures of the inquisition; wonderful burglaries; underworld of the great cities, etc., etc.

AGENTS WANTED

for this work. Exclusive territory is given. Agents can make $100 a week in selling this book. Send for circulars and terms to agents.

J. B BURR & HYDE,

HARTFORD, CONN., or CHICAGO, ILL

TRACTS.

"ANXIOUS BENCH RELIGION EXAMINED," BY ELDER J. S. FLORY. A SYNOPSIS OF CONTENTS. An address to the reader: The peculiarities that attend this type of religion. The feelings there experienced not imaginary but real. The key that unlocks the wonderful mystery. The causes by which feelings are excited. How the momentary feelings called "Experimental religion" are brought about, and then concludes by giving that form of doctrine as taught by Jesus Christ and recorded by his faithful witnesses.

COUNTERFEIT DETECTER

or

BAPTISM—MUCH IN LITTLE.

This work is now ready for distribution, and the importance of the subject will speak for it a large demand. It is a short treatise on baptism in tract form intended for general distribution, and is set forth in such a plain and logical manner that a wayfaring man though a fool, cannot err therein. Either of the above tracts sent postpaid on the following terms: Two copies, 10 cts, 10 copies 40 cents, 25 copies 70 cents, 50 copies $1.00, 100 copies $1.50.

Trine Immersion.

A discussion on Trine Immersion, by letter between Elder B. F. Moomaw and Dr. J. J. Jackson, to which is annexed a Treatise on the Lord's Supper, and on the necessity, character and evidences of the new birth, also a dialogue on the doctrine of non-resistance, by Elder B. F. Moomaw. Single copy 50 cents.

THE HELPING HAND.

Containing several hundred Valuable Receipts for cooking well at a moderate expense, making Dyes, Coloring, Cleaning and Cementing. This book also points out in plain language, free from Doctors' terms the diseases of men, women and children, and the latest and most approved means used for their cure, to which is added a description of the Medicinal Roots and Herbs, and how they are to be used in the cure of diseases.

This is a work of considerable importance and we offer it to our readers as being a valuable accession to every household. Send from this office to any address, post-paid, for 35 cents.

TUNE BOOK.

The Brethren's Tune and Hymn Book, is a compilation of Sacred Music adapted to all the hymns in the Brethren's New Hymn Book. It contains over 330 pages, printed on good paper and neatly bound. We will send it to any address, post paid at $1.25 per copy.

1870 1873

DR. FAHRNEY'S Blood Cleanser or Panacea.

A tonic and purge, for Blood Diseases. Great reputation. Many testimonials. Many ministering brethren use and recommend it. Ask or send for the "Health Messenger." Use only the "*Panacea*" prepared at Chicago, Ills., and by

Dr. P. Fahrney's Brothers & Co.,
Feb. 3-pd. *Waynesboro, Franklin Co., Pa*

New Hymn Books, English.

TURKEY MOROCCO.

One copy, postpaid,	$1.00
Per Dozen,	11.25

PLAIN ARABESQUE.

One Copy, post-paid,	75
Per Dozen, "	8.00

Ger'n & English, Plain Sheep.

One Copy, post-paid,	$1.00
Per Dozen	11.25
Arabesque Plain,	1.00
Turkey Morocco,	1.25
Single German, post paid	50
Per Dozen,	5.50

HUNTINGDON & BROAD TOP RAIL ROAD

On and after Aug 14th, 1873, Trains will run on this road daily (Sun excepted) as follows:

Trains from Huntingdon South. *Trains from Mt. Dal's moving North.*

EXP'S. P.M.	MAIL. A.M.	STATIONS.	MAIL. P.M.	EXP'S A.M.
6 15	7 45	Huntingdon,	AR6 30	AR9 20
6 20	7 50	Long Siding	6 45	9 15
6 35	8 00	McConnelstown	6 35	9 05
6 40	8 05	Pleasant Grove	6 29	8 58
6 51	8 20	MARKLESBURG	6 15	8 45
7 01	8 35	Coffee Run	6 05	8 35
7 08	8 41	Rough & Ready	5 56	8 29
7 15	8 50	Cove	5 49	8 20
7 18	8 53	Fishers Summit	5 46	8 17
7 35	9 10	Saxton	5 35	8 05
7 50	9 25	Riddlesburg	5 15	7 43
7 55	9 32	Hopewell	5 10	7 38
8 10	9 47	Piper's Run	4 58	7 20
8 21	9 57	Tatesville	4 43	7 12
8 32	10 07	Everett	4 33	7 03
8 40	10 15	Mount Dallas	4 30	7 00
9 00	10 35	Bedford	4 05	6 33

SHOUP'S RUN BRANCH.

A. M.	P. M.		P. M.	A. M.
LE 9 20	LE 7 40	Saxton.	AR5 25	AR 7 55
9 35	7 55	Coalmont.	5 10	7 40
9 40	8 00	Crawford.	5 05	7 35
AR 9 50	AR8 10	Dudley	LE4 55	LE 7 25

Bro'd Top City from Dudley 2 miles by stage.

Time of Penna. R. R. Trains at Huntingdon.

***Mail No. 2 makes connection at Huntingdon with Mail going East on Pennsylvania Railroad at 4.15 p. m., and West at 5.45 p. m. Mail No. 1 leaves Huntingdon at 7.40 a. m. on arrival of Pacific Express West.

Trains on this road connect with trains on Bedford & Bridgeport, and Cumberland & Pennsylvania Railroads.

G. F. GAGE, Supt.

The Weekly Pilgrim.

Published by J. B. Brumbaugh, & Co.

Edited by H. B. & Geo. Brumbaugh.

CORRESPONDING EDITORS.

D. P. Sayler, Double Pipe Creek, Md.

Leonard Furry, New Enterprise, Pa.

The *Pilgrim* is a Christian Periodical, devoted to religion and moral reform. It will advocate in the spirit of *love* and *liberty*, the principles of true Christianity, labor for the promotion of peace among the people of God, for the encouragement of the saints and for the conversion of sinners, avoiding those things which tend toward disunion or sectional feelings.

TERMS.

Single copy, Book paper,	$1.50
Eleven copies, (eleventh for Agt.)	$15.00

Any number above that at the same rate,

Address.

H. B. BRUMBAUGH.
James Creek,
Huntingdon county Pa.

The Weekly Pilgrim.

"REMOVE NOT THE ANCIENT LANDMARKS WHICH OUR FATHERS HAVE SET."

VOL. 4. JAMES CREEK, PENNSYLVANIA, OCTOBER 21, 1873. NO. 42

POETRY.

For the PILGRIM.

THE CHRISTIAN.

BY WESLEY.

Walking in the shadow of the reeking cross,
Counting earthly treasures to my soul but loss,
Following the Master through this nether vale
Though the hosts of darkness fiercely may assail.

Gloom and pain and sadness now my steps attend,
Now a gleam of sunshine does its luster lend;
Weary fluctuations, check my forward course,
Dim the light that gushes from its mighty source.

But the valiant LEADER of the ransomed host,
Lights the glaring beacons on the distant coast;
Lures me by caresses, clasps my trembling hand,
Points to life eternal in the glory land.

Cheered by His blest presence still I follow on,
Battling with reverses, weary, faint and wan;
Leaning on the promise oft in mercy given
If for Him I suffer I shall reign in Heaven.

Though the wiles of satan oft my soul beset,
Fill me with forebodings, sorrow, and regret,
When the sunlight flashes o'er the darkened way,
Basks my soul triumphant in its mellow ray.

By the surging river turbulent and wild,
Free from earthly trammels, God's unsullied child;
Kept by Jesus' power, calmly I shall wait
Till his angels bear me through the golden gate

ORIGINAL ESSAYS.

EXPOSING ERROR.

A great deal of fault is found with the reformers, of the present day, for exposing the errors and corruptions prevalent among professing Christians, not that it is denied, but what evils exist, but by exposing them they say it furnished unbelievers with an occasion to triumph, and contributes to the furtherance of infidelity. I acknowledge that infidelity has more or less prevailed in proportion to the decline of true religion, the probable reason of which is, the votaries of infidelity unjustly charge to the account of Christianity all the bad conduct of its professors. But would this be the case were Christians honest to discountenance in each other every thing prohibited in the Gospel? I think not, for what has the pure Gospel of the Savior to do with the treachery of Judas, the cowardice of Peter, or the bad conduct of modern popes and prelates. But it is with the various sects of religion as with individuals when they depart from the simplicity and purity of the Gospel. They still wish to keep a fair outside, and so long as they succeed in hiding their state from the knowledge of men, they think all is well. Nor is it likely their state will ever be better while they continue in this course, for he that covereth his sins shall not prosper.

There is no sin we are required more carefully to avoid than the leaven of the Pharisees, hypocrisy, and it must be as hateful in the sight of God when found in a community, as in an individual, nor will any man who is acquainted with his Bible and Church history, undertake to say that the most likely way to remedy evils is to conceal them. Why then should he be considered an enemy who like a good surgeon, searches out the part affected, and let the operation be ever so painful, probes it faithfully that he may effect a cure and save the life of the patient. But to view as enemies of religion, those who expose corruption, in the ministers of the present day, is the more extraordinary, seeing these very men who find fault with this course, at the same time admire the honesty and zeal of the ancient worthies spoken of in the Holy Scriptures, who bore their testimony against sin, as well when found in the royal person of a king, as that of an humble peasant, and denounced the judgments of the Lord against the false shepherd's, who instead of feeding, devoured the sheep and clothed themselves with the wool. Nor was this honesty less remarkable in their faithfully recording these things, not even sparing their own foibles which is a trait that distinguishes the Holy Scriptures from human productions, for when a member of a religious body now, undertakes to give to the world a history of the sect to which he belongs, the grand defect which proves the work to be human is the careful avoidance of every circumstance in the narrative, which in the opinion of the narrator, would deform the fair picture he wishes to draw. Thus by a want of true candor, he betrays that weakness and fallibility which in others he is ever so ready to condemn. The extent to which this covering system has been carried by these false friends of religion has proved fatal to the interests of the Redeemer's Kingdom. It was because of this our Savior when on earth found even under the shadow of the Jewish sanctuary the vile broods of serpents, the generations of vipers against whom he pronounced the most awful judgments to be found in the Gospel; nor did this high priest of our profession, like many in this present day, deem it incompatible with the interests of religion, but considered it an important part of the duty of a prophet of the Lord, to unmask these hypocritical pretenders to godliness, and expose their real characters to the world. It was by concealing the evil deeds of the clergy within the walls of cloisters and threatening with tortures and death, any who should dare to call in question the immaculate purity of the church of Rome, which generated and nourished up that monster of ecclesiastical corruption called in Scripture the man of sin, a beast.

Many of the professors of religion at this day do not a little resemble the scribes and pharisees of old, who while they garnished the tombs of the prophets manifested great hostility against Him of whom all the prophets spake, and only because he testified to them that their deeds were evil, nor need any who follow the example of the Savior expect better treatment from those of a similar character, for they in high esteem hold the names of Wickliffe, Luther, Calvin and others, for stemming the tide of corruption, while flowed around them these pharisees Brethren the same spirit which lighted up the fires at Rome and Smithfield, that consumed to ashes the faithful servant of God, David Simpson, that bold champion for truth, when he opposed the corruption of the church of England, did not conceive, as many do, that the interest of religion would be promoted by concealing abuses in his Book a plea for religion and the sacred writings. He laid open abuses and corruptions in all their aggravation, nor was any of the opinion that the course was improper, save the religious body in which the evils existed. Such is the inconsistency of frail man, that while he approves of the method pointed out by Divine wisdom in relation to others, yet when applied to himself, it serves but to awaken his resentment not against his sinful practices, but the one who, like the prophet, Nathan charges home his guilt, by saying, thou art the man.

A PILGRIM.

STRENGTH IN CHRIST.

Although, then, thou seest thyself the most witless and weak, and findest thyself nothing but a prey to the power of darkness, yet know that by believing, the wisdom and strength of Christ are thine. Thou art, and oughtest to find thyself, all weakness, but he is all strength all mightiness itself. Learn to apply his victory, and so it is thine. Be strong, how? In him and the power of his might. But thou wilt say I am often foiled; yea I cannot find that I prevail at all against my enemies but they still against me;—yet rely on Him. He can turn the chase in an instant; still cleave to him when the whole powers of the soul as it were scattered and routed. Rally them by believing. Draw thou unto the standard of Jesus Christ and the day shall be thine; for victory follows that standard and cannot be severed from it. Yea though thou find the smart of divers strokes, yet think that often a wounded soldier hath won the day; believe, and it shall be so with thee. Remember that thy foils, through the wisdom and love of thy God, may be ordered to advance the victory, to humble thee and drive thee from thine own imagined strength to make use of his real strength. And be not hasty. Think not at the very first to conquer. Many a hard conflict must thou resolve upon and often be brought very low, almost to a desperate point, that to thy sense it is past recovery. Then it is his time to step in, even in the midst of their prevailing.—*Leighton.*

A preached gospel by men whose life is such as to destroy all confidence in them is like tendering water in a defiled cup, it disgusts rather than pleases!—*J. S. Flory.*

JESUS ON THE CROSS.

NO. I.

"Father forgive them, for they know not what they do."—St. Luke 23: 34.

I. "THEM"—has reference to:

1. *Judas*—the hypocrite; the covetous disciple; that had the bag, and betrayed his Lord and Master for thirty pieces of silver, that too, like many in these days verify the truth, that the *love* of money is the *root* of all evil.

2. *The Jews*,—who with wicked hands, and false words, and lying tongues, condemn and denounce the Lord.

3. *The Romans*,—who gave His sentence of death; mocked, scoffed, and scourged the Savior, and delivered Him to be crucified, and nailed Him to the cross, and pierced His side.

4. *The Transgressors*,—who railed on Him, with those who wagged their heads as they passed by.

I think the above will include what was directly intended by the Savior by using the word *them*. We simply remark that as it is declared by Jesus Himself, that whatsoever is done to the least of His disciples is done to Him, and as it is possible for us to crucify the Lord afresh, to mock, scoff, and taunt, the Christian; we too, may with propriety be considered among *them*.

II. "THEY DO."

1. They covenant to buy and sell Jesus, that the innocent may be numbered with the transgressors, that His blood may be shed in lieu of the murderer Barabbas's. They also agree upon a *sign* like many similar evil and wicked associations *do* in order to carry out their unholy ends. "Now he that betrayed Him gave them a sign, saying, whomsoever I shall kiss, that same is He; hold Him fast."—Matt. 26: 48, also see verses 3 and 4.

2. They come and seize Him as a thief and a murderer. To have seen that crowd going out to take Jesus would remind us much of the mobs of the city of New York. But as Jesus meets them, He says: "Are ye come out as against a thief with swords and staves to take Me? I sat daily with you teaching in the temple, and ye laid no hold on Me."—Matt. 26: 55.

They now bind Him and take Him to Annas first. "Then the band and the captain and officers of the Jews took Jesus, and bound Him, and led Him away to Annas *first*; for he was father in law to Caiaphas, which was the high priest that same year."—John 18: 12, 13.

3. They now take Him before the high-priest, Caiaphas, and to accuse Him falsely, saying: "This fellow said, I am able to destroy the temple of God, and to build it in three days." Matt. 26: 61. They pronounce Him guilty of death, Caiaphas, who was also Christ's enemy, declared, "Behold, now ye have heard his blasphemy."—Matt. 26: 65. "They answered and said, He is guilty of death. 66th verse.

Now commences a pitiful sight. Reader picture the scene in your minds, that now takes place. Here is God's high priest, with quite a number of priests, scribes, and elders, &c., representing the people of God, the chosen of God, the household of faith, to whom had been committed the oracles of God, and behold what THEY DO. "Then did they spit in His face, and buffeted Him; and others smote Him with the palms of their hands, saying, Prophesy unto us, thou Christ, who is he that smote thee,"—Matt. 26: 67, 68. Luke says: "And the men that held Jesus mocked Him and smote Him, and when they had blindfolded Him, they struck Him on the face, and asked Him, saying, Prophesy, who is it that smote thee? And many other things blasphemously spake they against Him."—Luke 22: 63–65.

4. They next take Him before Pilate the Roman ruler there, at that time. It seems that they had not the power to put Him to death, but must have the sentence ratified by the proper authorities of the land. But Pilate finds no fault in Him. He therefore says unto the Jews, "Take ye Him, and judge Him according to your law. The Jews therefore, said unto him, It is not lawful for us to put any man to death."—John 18, 31. Now here then they desire to have Him tried according to Roman law, and they are prepared with false accusations—accusations quite different from those made before Caiaphas. They say He perverteth the nation and refuses to give tribute to Cesar, and says He Himself is king. "What accusation bring ye against this man?" "They answered and said unto him, If He were not a malefactor, we would not have delivered him unto thee."—John 18: 29, 30. Luke says, "And the whole multitude of them arose, and led Him unto Pilate. And they began to accuse Him, saying, We found this fellow perverting the *nation* (*i. e.* the Roman nation) and forbidding to give tribute to Cesar, saying that He Himself is Christ a king." Luke 23: 1, 2. But still Pilate could find no fault in Him, his mind was less biased than the high priests, "For he knew that for envy they had delivered Him."—Matt. 27: 18. Their rage increases, "And they were the *more fierce*, saying, He stirreth up the people, teaching throughout all Jewery, beginning from Galilee to this place." Luke 23: 5.

5. He is now taken before Herod, who was then in Jerusalem. Pilate having found out that he belonged to his jurisdiction, being a Galilean, sent away to Herod they go with Him, only to augment His reproaches. True Herod was glad at first that Jesus came, but only for self-gratification, for he had heard a great deal about Jesus, and now thought he would see some miracle performed, just to please Him, but in this he was foiled, hence this is what follows: "And Herod with his men of war, set Him at naught, and mocked Him, and arrayed Him in a gorgeous robe, and sent Him again to Pilate."—Luke 23: 11.

6. Again He is brought before Pilate to receive His sentence, to be scourged by him, and to be mocked and abused by the soldiers; soldiers! yes, those men, who know but little refinement, and who always are posted in the way in which torture and insult can be the most successfully administered. They are generally (if they are soldiers long) of a low-lifed, and a degraded disposition. Reader never be a soldier.

"And Pilate gave sentence that it should be as they required."—Luke 23: 24. "Then Pilate therefore took Jesus and scourged Him,"—John 19: 1. Now He gets into the soldiers hands. "Then the soldiers of the governor took Jesus into the common hall, *and gathered unto Him the whole band of soldiers*, And they stripped Him, and put on Him a scarlet robe, and when they had plaited a crown of thorns, they put it upon His head, and a reed in His right hand; and they bowed the knee before Him, and mocked Him saying, Hail, King of the Jews! And they spit upon Him, and took the reed and smote Him on the head. And after that they had mocked Him, they took the robe off from Him, and put His own raiment on Him, and led Him away to crucify Him."—Matt. 27: 27–31.

7. His crucifixion.

They now lead Him away to crucify Him, followed by an immense multitude of people; some rejoicing, others indifferent, while a few are sadly lamenting his fate. And on reaching the spot, I imagine they lay down the cross, that rude piece of timber, they stretch the innocent Lamb of God upon it, but He does not strive nor cry, never draws back His hand whilst the nail was placed upon it to receive those clinching blows that shall pin Him to the cross. Oh! *awful*! SHAMEFUL! SHAMEFUL!! death. He is then raised amid shouts of derision. Oh! the tearing of that sacred flesh as it (the cross) is left down into the hole made to receive it. But it is fastened in the ground.

8. They now all join in general mockery. The soldiers mock Him saying, "If thou be the King of the Jews, save thyself." They also take His garments and gather into a group and divide the spoils, and like soldiers (in general) gamble for His coat,—"cast lots" for it.

Then around come some very lewd fellows. "And they that passed by reviled Him, wagging their heads, and saying, "Thou that destroyest the temple, and buildst it in three days, save thyself. If thou be the Son of God, come down from the cross."—Matt. 27: 39, 40.

A little to the one side stand a set of self-righteous, well dressed priests, who join in the general scene, saying, "He saved others; Himself He cannot save. If He be the King of Israel, let Him now come down from the cross, and we will believe Him."—Matt. 27: 42.

The thief takes occasion to rail on Him, "And one of the malefactors which were hanged, railed on Him saying, If thou be Christ, save thyself and us."—Luke 23: 39.

III. "THEY KNOW NOT."

They were ignorant, of the fact that they were torturing the Son of the living God, the immaculate Lamb, the promised Messiah, their Redeemer and Savior, who was then and there suffering for their sins, and the sins of the whole world.

They know not that He must needs suffer in the way and manner that He did.

They knew not the extent of His suffering—the mental as well as the physical suffering which He endured. They were ignorant that He was made perfect by the things which He suffered," and was opening up a perfect way to glory.

They knew not that He was the first and the last, the beginning and the end, and that in Him was everlasting life. And like Saul, because they did what they did in ignorance, He desired their forgiveness.

IV. FORGIVE THEM.

Here reader is shown the mind of Christ in all its perfection, the mind that every believer in Christ should have, the spirit or disposition that Christians should show toward their enemies.

Why did He ask their forgiveness? Why, but because *reason* could not reach their prejudiced, maddened minds. The first martyr (Stephen) showed a desire that his enemies should be forgiven, and their deeds might not be laid to their charge, which was conclusive evidence that he had learned of Jesus, and was following the Lord in the way.

Jesus desired their forgiveness on account of their ignorance, "for they know not what they do." This forgiving spirit accords well with all His and His apostles' teachings. The Lord's prayer breathes the same spirit as our text.

And not to multiply words we will speedily close. Dear brethren and sisters, old and young, (and especially the young, for they cannot bear reproach perhaps as well as the elder brethren) when you are derided, mocked and persecuted, think of *Jesus on the cross*. Turn and look upon the lovely Savior, surrounded by such a multitude of enemies; and as He looks over them, views their evil and unholy deeds; hears their scornful words of derision and shame, and then with upturned eyes, towards heaven, breathes out in sweet and melting tones the words, "Father forgive them for they know not what they do," and then like the apostles you can be made to rejoice and be exceeding glad that you are counted worthy to suffer with Him.

JOHN ZUCK.

Shady Grove, Pa.

DOING GOOD.

Doing good is a subject of vital importance and should receive our sincere and candid attention, yet how few if any do it justice. There are a great many ways in which we can do good, and to improve all the opportunities which are afforded us, requires us to give the subject very careful thought. We may see many opportunities in which we might have done good, but just in time for them to pass. Therefore we should be watchful and energetic. Watchful that we may consider the circumstances, and energetic in acting out that which we consider our duty to do.

We have all been placed upon the earth for a wise and noble purpose, by a wise, good, and just God, whose end is to glorify Him. In what nobler act can we be engaged or give God more glory than by doing *good*? As he is a wise God we should exercise wisdom and discretion in the performance of those things which tend to give Him honor, as a good God, would have his creatures do Him homage by doing good, and as a just God he demands justice at our hands. Since he has prepared all things well and good, and best adapted to our convenience, He would have of us a repentance, which is nothing less than to do good. As every man is by justice bound to pay his debts, it therefore becomes of us, a duty.

We will consider doing good, a duty or as payment on the debt which we owe to God. As He is continually extending His mercies and kindness toward us, we are to do the same to our fellow creatures as in a measure payment. There is one point which we wish to consider before going farther, and that is, in what condition should we be, to fully discharge our duty? Can a corrupt tree bring forth good fruit? Can one that is in allegiance with a spirit entirely averse to the one which God would have us possess, discharge his duty, or teach of Christ whence all good cometh? No a soul must become regenerated, entirely opposite to his former allegiance, and so long as we adhere to the teachings of the adversary we can produce no good. We must put off the old yoke of sin and put on the new which is easy to bear. Now since we have volunteered in Christ's service, we must bear reproaches for Him as He has borne them for us.

Let us notice the manner in which he came into the world, poorer than the poorest on earth, so much so that his first couch was the manger of a brute. Behold the exceeding love of the son of God! He who inherited all things, permitted himself through love for humanity to occupy the lowest position among men, that the poor and vile might approach Him. Had he come in his original splendor who would have dared to approach unto His presence, for His purity and holiness would have prevented even the most righteous from entering His presence. But he assumed flesh and came and dwelt among men, suffered the infirmites of the flesh and was tempted like unto men that He might bear their infirmities. His whole life was one of continual *doing good* and we as His followers are commanded to imitate His example, and if we do not try to imitate Him we are violating one of the principle commands of God. How can we return good for evil unless we have love for all? And if it were not commanded us to do so, it would be a duty because Jesus loved us. As the life of Christ consisted in continually doing good and loving His enemies, so must our lives be if we desire to do His will, ever having the interest of our fellow beings in view. It is our duty to contribute to their relief as far as lies in our power. We must do them good in word, deed and action, devoting our lives to their interests. In other words: "Live for the happiness of others." In what can we effect so real a happiness as in doing good to others, and having them to adopt the same principle?

How much we can effect by our influence especially, if it be in the cause of Christ. We should try to gain all the influence we can, and by extending it, we may be the means of drawing some precious souls to Christ, and this is the greatest possible good we can do. No temporal contribution can satisfy and make us happy as that contribution to the soul.

Doing good, is also a privilege and the most amiable disposition is the one which acts not merely from a sense of duty, but from option. We should all, I was going to say, try to do good more from privilege than duty, but I fear if we did not consider it a duty and feel under obligations so to do, we would not appreciate it aright. But those who do so from mere option will never lose their reward, and this encourages us; that every *good* deed or word, as well as *evil* done, will be rewarded. Therefore we should live so that as our days decrease may our good works increase, and as death approaches may sin recede.

Yours in Christ.

S. G. KELLER.

HOW TO MAKE THE PROPER USE OF OUR MONEY.

As the editor has given the above as a subject and wishes some one to write on it, I will endeavor, through weakness to do so, hoping the few thoughts I have to offer may tend to our edification.

First, we may give our money to our ministers who are in needy circumstances. They have to ride miles away from home, and whether rain or shine, the poor minister has to go. In the meantime the laity can set at home or go, just as it suits him. Then again when seed and harvest time comes, the minister may be very busy at his work, and at this time he is often called away to preach a funeral, and it is perfectly right that he should go, but the trouble is, his work stops at home, and he is not able to get hands to carry on his work. To such we should give our money instead of giving it to our children, and thus enable them to dress after the foolish fashions of the world. Brethren and sisters, I maintain we might as well dress our own bodies in fashion with the world as our children. Who can show the difference? Money that is spent in such a manner is certainly not spent for the advancement of Christ's Kingdom. We are taught in the Scriptures to bring up our children in the fear and admonition of the Lord. We generally see where brethren follow this rule, their children come into the church at an early age, while others who grant their every desire are pained and grieved to see them stand aloof, and in some instances never come in at all.

In the next place we can help to support the Sunday School. The money that is spent for vanity would be sufficient funds to provide for a Sunday School in every neighborhood where children might be gathered in Christian order, and taught the way in which they should go. If this were done when they arrive at a mature age, they would be more fully prepared to enter the church. Timothy was taught the Scriptures from a child, and so should we teach our children while in their youth. This is the design of the Sunday School, and if properly conducted, not only will the children be benefitted, but the teachers will become more enlightened while *trying* to teach others, and thus may God's name be glorified.

Many are the ways in which we may use our money for the cause of Jesus. We should give to the poor who are destitute of daily bread, and have no clothes and no home. By giving to the poor we lend to the Lord, and will in no wise lose our reward.

Lastly, we can help to build churches, that we may have convenient places to worship in, and that the Gospel may be preached over the whole world. But we should be careful that we do not follow after the world in building them too grand. I fear there is danger of this, and it seems to me that this danger has recently been made apparent. Brethren be careful, the day is fast approaching when we shall have to give an account of our stewardship.

MARY K. ELLIOTT.

Welsh Run, Pa.

TEMPTATIONS.

John Newton says, Satan seldom comes to a Christian with great temptations, or with a temptation to commit a great sin. You bring a green log and a candle together, and they are very safe neighbors; but bring a few shavings and set them alight, and then bring a few small sticks and let them take fire, and the log be in the midst of them, and you will soon get rid of your log. And so it is with little sins. You will be startled with the idea of committing a great sin, and so the devil brings you a little temptation, and leaves you to indulge yourself. "There is no great harm in this," "no great peril in that;" and so by these little chips we first easily light up, and at last the green log is burned. Watch and pray that ye enter not into temptation.

WHEN it is not despicable to be poor, we want fewer things to live in poverty with satisfaction, than to live magnificently with riches.—*St. Evremond.*

It is a pity to see a neat dwelling in which everything seems to dwarf the occupant, in which the occupant is the least circumstance. I have seen men that were only the punctuation of their wealth.

WHENEVER I see a child of God becoming less holy than he was, I know the secret of it—he is clinging less firmly to Christ than he did. Our root must be right, if our fruit is to abound.

IN God's great plan there is nothing small or trivial. The humblest life cost the death of the Son of God. Does it not throw a veil of sanctity around the poorest and most unworthy when we think of the ransom paid for such a life?

SALVATION BY FAITH.

BY WEBSTER D. MOORE.

There is a seeming conflict between us and others on this question. The difference is as to whether we are justified by faith, or faith alone. Those taking the latter position claim that prayer is essential to a Christian life and the gaining of a glorious immortality. *So do we.* Are we then justified by faith *alone?*

Our Savior says: "He that believeth on the Son hath everlasting life." This proves that we can be saved by faith. This is then the question that should concern us: *Have we faith in the Son of God?* This expression of our Savior is similar in construction to that utterance of the apostle Paul: "If children, then heirs." Those who accept of this truth do not ask to have it proven that a child of God is an heir of God. The only point to be determined is whether they are children; for, "if children, then heirs; heirs of God and joint heirs with Christ; if so be we suffer with him, that we may be also glorified together.

Near the close of Christ's ministry on earth he said: "Verily, verily, I say unto you that one of you shall betray me." One of the disciples said: "Lord who is it? Jesus said, "He it is to whom I shall give a sop when I have dipped it." Did his disciples spend time to prove that the one receiving the sop should be the one to betray him? They believed that. They would be more likely to watch and see who should receive the sop.

Let us be concerned about the right matter. There are many expressions to prove that a man can be saved by faith. To write essays on this topic is as useless as an attempt to prove that twice six is twelve. Let us consider the foregoing question: "Have we faith in the Son of God?"

1. "Faith without works is dead." Every seed can produce only one kind of a plant. The species of seed is known by its species of growth. The kind of faith that saves is known by the kind of work it produces. It leads its possessor to abide in Christ—to do His commandments.

Here we are met by this objection: Do not hypocrites keep the commandments of Christ? We are aware that wax fruit often appears like real fruit; that some appear to fast when the heart is not in it. In order to make full proof of our faith we will not rely exclusively upon the external evidence, although we are firmly of the conviction that those who always abound in the work of the Lord have pure hearts. If a tree has thrifty branches, it is safe to conclude, without examination, that it has lively roots. In order, however, to make full proof of our faith, let us examine the internal evidences.

2. Those who believe are not ashamed of Christ. Many hesitate because their faith is weak. To take a stand for Christ demands publicity. They love the approbation of those who seek their own, and not the things that belong to Christ. They are not ashamed of the sentiment that rises against Christ sufficiently to resist it. They will have this proof of faith when they can say:

"I'm not ashamed to own my Lord,
Nor to defend his cause;
Maintain the honor of his word,
The glory of his cross."

The sufficiency of this proof is known by external evidences—*owning Christ before men.* An individual acknowledged to me at one time his desire to become a Christian, but expressed a desire to be immersed where he was not known. He was ashamed to own his Lord before acquaintances. Instead of complying with his desire, I sought to strengthen his faith. In due time he did not care how many witnessed his obedience to Christ. Thus his faith was strengthened, and he became a child of God.

3. Another evidence of saving faith is to disbelieve everything said in opposition to Christ and his word. How many have listened to the Gospel until almost induced to become Christians, and then have turned away because some one has said; It is not essential. How can I be certain that I believe that George Washington was born February 22, 1732? By knowing that I disbelieve every one who speaks differently from that. Christ says "If ye confess me before men, I will confess you before my Father in Heaven." In his commission to the apostles he says: "He that believeth and is baptized shall be saved." How can a person have assurance of faith that is free from objection, who hears the Gospel and then abides by the sayings of those who say: Baptism is a non-essential; you can be saved without it as well as with it; if you will live uprightly before men, you will be saved whether you belong to the church or not. When he disbelieves all this, he may have assurance that he believes as the oracles of God speak, and that it is better to obey God rather than man.

Hence to reiterate, we know that we have faith because,

1. We obey him. "Faith without works is dead." If we concede that faith alone will propel the Christian, and that steam alone will propel the locomotive, we must also concede that neither of them can exist in any degree of importance without something else equally essential.—*their antecedents and consequences.*

2. We are not ashamed of him. "Whosoever believeth in him shall not be ashamed." We are "not ashamed of the Gospel of Christ, for it is the power of God unto salvation to every one that believeth."

3. We do not believe men when they speak differently from him. "Verily, verily, I say unto you, he that heareth my word and believeth on him that sent me hath everlasting life."—John 5:24, also 10 27.
Christian Standard.

GENERAL INTELLIGENCE.

CANADA is having a temperance revival headed by the Bishop of Montreal, who is an earnest advocate of total abstinence.

A Baptist chapel has been completed in the city of Paris, costing $60,000, and seating 600 persons.—The Baptists lead numerically, in Chicago. Their membership is 5,438; the second church numbers 1,217.

It is estimated that the 20,000 members of the congregational churches in Illinois give a little over two cents per week each for five different benevolent objects recommended by the general Association.

THE Secretary of War, it is said, has engaged Mr. James Parton as editor of the original manuscripts of George Washington, which have recently come into the departments possession. Among these papers is the original note-book which Washington used while in command of the army on the field.

THE Yellow Fever has terribly scourged Shreveport, La., nearly depopulating the city, and is still unabated. At last accounts about 400 cases were still under treatment. At Memphis, Tenn., the state of affairs must be deplorable. People die faster than they can be buried. Nine hundred have died since the outbreak of the fever, and still it rages. Hundreds have died unattended. There is a great lack of nurses, and money is urgently asked for and greatly needed.

The yearly meeting of the orthodox Friends held at Richmond, Ind., is now in session. This is the largest yearly meeting of Friends in the world, and its membership has increased 850 in the past year. Last Sunday special services were held, attended by large crowds not connected with the yearly meeting. Wm. Baxter, father of the Indiana Temperance Bill, and Caroline Talbot, who, beside being an eloquent speaker, is a leader in the reformation of fallen women, are present at the meeting.

YELLOW FEVER RAVAGES.—Memphis is suffering terribly from the yellow fever. During the past week there were 240 deaths, of which 146 were from yellow fever, against 68 the week before. The total number of deaths since the disease appeared is 502, nearly all of which occurred in the infected district. The German Bruderbund earnestly appeal to German societies and Germans generally for aid in nursing their sick and burying their dead.

THE jewish ceremony of removing the shoe from the man who refuses to marry his brother's widow was actually performed; as we mentioned a few weeks ago, in Oakland California. Our informant, if we remember correctly, was the *Observer.* But the *Jewish Times* takes Rabbi Wise to task for marrying a man to his brother's widow. The law regulating the former case is explicit, to be found Deut. xxv. 5-11, but as to what tradition has made void, the positive requirements of this law, so as to make compliance a crime, we confess our ignorance, and would be glad to be enlightened.—*Christian Standard.*

The Romish church has met with another check, in Brazil, in asserting her extravagant claims to determine the civil as well as the spiritual status of individuals. The question whether Protestant marriages are dissolved by the conversion of one of the wedded pair to Catholicism has been decided against her. Many Brazilian jurists defended this monstrous assumption, the Catholic bishops sanctioning the re-marriage of converts without regard to their existing wedlock. This state of things has come to an end through the instrumentality of Herr Hermann Haupt who, being in Rio Janeiro, while the post of German Charge d'Affaires in that capital was vacant, called the attention of the Government to the remarriage of two German converts whose protestant husbands were still alive. The Emperor, after consulting the State Council, decided that Protestant marriages are indissoluble except by judicial decree, that the two women had incurred the guilt of bigamy, and that they and the priests who performed the ceremony of marriage had laid themselves open to a criminal prosecution.

AUTHOR OF "HOME SWEET HOME."—In his oration at the dedication of the bust of John Howard Payne in Brooklyn, last week, Hon. Wm. C. Dewitt, in alluding to the authorship of "Home Sweet Home"—said: "Payne never knew what it was to have a home after he was thirteen years old. About this period of his life, his mother, whose love and virtue probably planted within him those sentiments which burst from his soul years after she was gone, and his father, who stood behind the scenes in tears when his boy first trusted himself to the temptations of the stage, went to their long home beyond the grave. From this moment Payne was a wanderer, and despite the tenderness of his heart, and the fascinations of the fair sex, he maintained his celibacy and homelessness until he consummated it by death upon the remote and hoary shores of the Mediterranean. Strange that a wanderer should have sung this song of home. Nevertheless, it was while in London, engaged in writing a drama and when his mind was doubtless dwelling upon his delightful boyhood at East Hampton, that he wrote. "HOME, SWEET HOME." This little poem, like its author, is largely indebted to providential aids for its celebrity. It was not the coinage of many years of meditation, like Gray's "Elegy," nor was it written like our national anthem, amid the scenes it sought to consecrate. Indeed it had been in Payne's possession among his rubbish for a long time before it was brought out at all.

A convention of the Spiritualists was held recently in Chicago, and many of the leading men from all parts of the country were present. During the session a number of speeches were made on various subjects and their radical utterances show very clearly of what spirit they are. Miss Anna Middlebrook, of Connecticut said:

"I stand here to night, as far as the Christian religion is concerned, determined on its destruction. In politics I am a rebel. I avow it boldly. This is a sham republic. With reference to the social problems I am a revolutionist. Why should we in the nineteenth century go eighteen hundred years for our doctrine? Is there not more than we can learn from the living present? If we live up to our philosophy, we will see the time when the mummy creeds of Christianity will be overturned.

Another speaker W. B. Anthony Higgins of Jersey City, said: "We are called Spiritualists. I have another name for our sect. Anti-Christians. (Applause.) To be consistent Spiritualists we must not only change men, but change theories. We have evolved in this country the right to be happy as best we may. Since the Christians have failed to elevate humanity, we must seek that elevation by different paths from those which they have pursued. We have enunciated to the world another form of political liberty— that is, individual liberty—and we are teaching the world that there is no political liberty without individual freedom.

SOME of the difficulties which Mormonism may experience, should they exist long enough, are presented in the following from a letter to the New York *Sun*:

The water of the lake has certainly risen twenty feet since the Mormons first entered the valley. I have seen Saints who tell me that they used to go in swimming at the foot of Black Rock. The rock is now several hundred feet from the shore, and is surrounded by twenty feet of water. If the lake rises in the same proportion for a hundred years the Saints will be drowned out, and Salt Lake City will be sunk as deep as Sodom and Gomorrah. Over twenty years ago the Mormons drove a herd of church cattle over to Church Island, which proved a wonderful grazing ground. They found a ridge extending from the main land to the island covered by barely three feet of water. For years they drove their herds over this ridge.

To-day the ridge is over twenty feet deep, and no beeves have been taken from the island for years. Thousands of wild cattle roam over its valleys and gorges. But one family ever lived there, and that was the family of the church herder. Last year he died, and the island is deserted. At some time the water has filled the whole Salt Lake Valley. A rim or shore line is visible on the side of the mountains thousands of feet above the city. This rim is so plainly defined that a railroad could be built on the side of the range for miles at a stretch without excavating a ton of rock.—*Cynosure*.

Youth's Department.

TO THE YOUNG.

Continued from page 325.

I do not say that you should do nothing but work and study, but I do say that you cannot be happy here nor blessed hereafter, if you make no better use of your valuable time and opportunities, than to gratify your own inclinations, and to obtain the admiration of your fellow creatures for things that a butterfly may perhaps excel you in, or in which at least even if you are skillful and well read, a wise heathen may put you to shame by his superior knowledge. You are Christian children in name, and if you be so in reality, you must do such good works as God has designed that we should perform and walk in them, both old and young.

But we have not yet done with the bee. You will hardly believe that these little insects have in every hive, a queen, to whom they pay the most devoted obedience. They work for her, feed her, take the tenderest care of her young, and will fight and die in her defense. If you rob them of their queen, you reduce them to despair, if you entice her away, you may lead the whole swarm with you wherever you please, they will follow and nothing but death puts an end to their loyal attachment. Here is a beautiful example of submission to parents and teachers, and all that are put in authority over young people, as well as of obedience to the government and the laws. A country disturbed by evil and rebellious spirits, a family of unruly servants and children, or a school where the voice of the teacher is disregarded, and noise and disorder prevails, must be put to shame by a peep into a common bee-hive. We are told in Scripture that God is not the author of confusion, but of peace, and all scenes of disorder and disturbance must be displeasing to Him. Think of the hundreds of bees that inhabit one hive, and how they are crowded together; their delicate cells in the honey-comb, one small entrance to the habitation where the comers and goers must constantly meet and be in danger of disputing the passage, yet who ever hears the little creatures quarreling, or sees them fighting or disturbing one another at their employment. Among them all is order and harmony. They exemplify that excellent rule, "A place for every thing, and everything in its place." And so obliging are they in accommodating and assisting each other, that in this you may find a good example in their conduct. There is no truer happiness than that realized by being in concord. "A house divided against itself cannot stand. If ye bite and devour one another, take heed lest ye be consumed one of another.".

Let us then bear one another's burdens, be helpers together in faith and love, and good works. But we have one Sovereign who has claims on us of a stronger kind than any earthly friend or ruler can have, even the Lord Jesus Christ, who is the head of the Church and the King of His people, who showered the exceeding riches of his love in coming among us to suffer and die for guilty sinners. We are then in duty bound to present unto Him ourselves, our souls, and bodies as a reasonable, holy, lively sacrifice, which he will deign to accept if we yield ourselves freely to his guidance.

But even here alas, how shall we bear a comparison with the poor little bee and its monarchs? Do we show such devotedness to our Lord? Do we work and study for opportunities of doing Him service? Do we deprive ourselves of any indulgence to feed his poor members, and to assist in distributing the Bread of Life among His flock, both those already brought to the fold, and those who are yet wandering without a Shepherd? Are we willing if called on not only to part with our substance, but to hazard our lives in His cause? Preferring death to sin is the thought of being separated from His love, the most unsupportable of all our fears, and alway content to follow where His word leads us. If the ungodly oppose us, endeavoring to drive or to draw us from the path of duty, in all these things the bee may show us what real love and loyalty are capable doing, and if we fall short of such a pattern, what excuse can we make? This is a very serious inquiry, and one at which we ought to pause. We know our duty, and we also know that by neglecting it, we draw down the wrath of the Most High upon us. We feel ourselves continually turning aside from the way of holiness, because our natures are evil and satan tempts us to transgress, but greater is He that is for us than they which be against us, and if we fall or quit the straight path, it is because we do not watch, pray and seek for the help He is so ready to bestow. God teaches the bee to make a right use of what it finds there, and shall He not also teach us, if, like the bee, we fulfill His will. God has made His promise to His believing children, "Thine ears shall hear a word behind thee saying, this is the way, walk ye in it. When ye turn to the right hand, and when ye turn to the left." This is the voice of the Holy Spirit who instructs those who humbly depend on His teaching, warning them from sin and encouraging them to holiness, and many good works you have it in your power to do if your hearts are so inclined. There are many treasures for you to gather, and many may be made rich in spiritual things by your labor, not only from the Word of God, but from all His works, and everything that surrounds you, may you derive valuable instructions and impart it to others.

To do this you must ever pray for grace to improve the time and watch for opportunities of carrying your good wishes into effect. The flower loses no sweetness, though the bee loads herself from its store, and so it is with what I am recommending to you. The riches of God's Word and works are inexhaustible; they will be always sweet and new to you. Every time when you return to gather the good with which they abound, the bee does not, because it was very industrious yesterday, neglect to work to-day, and feast on what it has gathered. No, it knows the value of time too well, and improves every hour. The counsel given to us in Scripture is, "Whatsoever thy hand findeth to do, do it with thy might, for there is no work nor device, nor knowledge nor wisdom, in the grave." The bee labors all Summer that it may in the Winter eat the fruit of its industry, but we rob it of its sweet store, and too often are the harmless creatures put to death, at the same time losing all that they have so toiled to lay up. With the diligent Christian this can never be the case, for thieves cannot break through nor steal. The treasures which are reserved in Heaven for him, and death itself is but the entrance to His eternal inheritance.

Let me hope that a bee will never cross the path of my young readers without awakening a serious thought on the lesson which God has fitted it to teach, and may we all be found with equal diligence and steadiness occupying the stations assigned by His Almighty wisdom and everlasting love.

The Weekly Pilgrim.

JAMES CREEK, PA., Oct. 21, 1873.

☞ How to send money. All sums over $1.50, should be sent either in a check, draft or postal order. If neither of these can be obtained, have the letter registered.

☞ When Money is sent, *always* send with it the name and address of those who paid it. Write the name and post office as plainly as possible.

☞ Every subscriber for 1874, gets a *Pilgrim Almanac* Free.

JAMES CREEK COMMUNION.

In life, we all have our prospective seasons or wants to which we look forward with interest. Our Communion was an event of this kind to us, not only on account of the communion we expected to enjoy with our Divine Master, but also with His children, and we feel that we were not disappointed, as we truly had a good meeting.

Our exercises commenced on the afternoon of the 10, with the following ministerial aid: J. R. Hanawalt, Graball Myers, Jno. Knisley, Leonard Furry, Jacob Steel, A. L. Funk, J. W. Brumbaugh, P. S. Myers, Geo. S. Myers, Geo. Swigart, J. R. Lane, S. A. Moore, J. B. Replogle and D. S. Clapper.

Notwithstanding the large number of speakers present, we had good and interesting preaching and none seemed in the way of others, which often appears to be the case on such occasions.

After the first meeting two persons were initiated into the church by baptism. The evening exercises were largely attended and conducted in such a manner as to inspire the congregation to respectful attention. Quite a number of the members of the surrounding churches communed with us, making the number of communicants much larger than it would otherwise have been.

On Saturday morning we again met for public preaching and had several profitable discourses. For the afternoon there was no appointment made but as there were a large number of people remaining about the church, it was thought prudent to have religious exercises, accordingly it was agreed upon to have a meeting of short discourses, about 10 minutes each, and to see how nearly each one would measure himself we timed them with the following result in minutes: Graball Myers, 5. Jacob Steel, 20. A. L. Funk, 4. S. A. Moore, 6. L. Furry, 4. John Knisley, 8. J. B. Replogle, 3. P. S. Myers, 12. A. L. Funk, 2. Graball Myers, 2. J. R. Hanawalt, 16. The training of children was the topic and proved to be interesting, and we hope, instructive.

We also had very good preaching on Saturday evening, Sunday a. m., and Sunday evening. During the meeting we had a number of calls by brethren and sisters, also the following ministers: L. Furry, P. S. Myers, S. A. Moore, D. S. Clapper, and our esteemed Eld. John Knisley, of Ind., who occupied a seat in our sanctum to-day. Our brother S. W. Bollinger is also with us. He is busily engaged in selling a valuable medicine which we are glad to know is giving general satisfaction where tested.

WANTED.

As we expect to send out our prospectus shortly, we would be much pleased to have a large number of new agents to work for us. There are places where the *Pilgrim* is but partly introduced, and other places again where it is not known at all. Any of our brethren and sisters having acquaintances at such places will confer upon us a *special* favor, by sending us the name of some one whom they think might act as our agent. We will gladly supply any one with prospectus, &c., who will consent to work for us, and we hope our friends will help us to establish agents wherever there is any prospects at all of obtaining subscribers. We are more than ever in earnest in our work, and we hope every one who has the advancement of the cause of Christianity at heart will be willing to give us the helping hand. Let us then have a large number of new, live, active workers. If there are any of our former agents who cannot work for us this year, we hope they will see to getting some one else who is interested in the work, to take their place.

A MISCOUNT.

By a miscount somewhere we failed to have enough papers to supply all of our readers last week. About one hundred of our western subscribers could not be supplied. For this we are very sorry and hope those unsupplied will excuse us, as such mistakes are beyond our control. If any of the number are preserving them for binding and let us know we will try and get the Nos. for them, but hope that none will ask for them but such as are saving them for that purpose.

Send Us a Report.—The Communion season is now about over, and as we are all interested, or should be at least, in the prosperity of our Zion, we hope to hear from the different churches, as they certainly will have something of interest to tell us. Let not some one fail to give us the news.

PERSONAL.

Hattie F. Miller.—R. Ralston's Pilgrim is marked paid on our book. We cannot now say how the oversight occurred in not giving credit in the money list. Our clubbing list will be announced soon, in which *Harper* will be enclosed. We can send you both papers for about the same as *Harper* will cost alone.

S. Musselman. All right. Almanac will be ready for distribution in a few weeks.

J. L. Frantz. The three subscribers you speak of are in the Galley, Huntsville Logan Co., Ohio, and we cannot see how they can possibly be missed in mailing.

Jno. Zook. Correct, thank you, quite satisfactory.

J. H. Biddle. All right. Your name is booked for 1874.

Correspondence.

A Reporter is wanted from every Church in the brotherhood to send us Church news, Obituaries, Announcements, or anything that will be of general interest. To insure insertion, the writers name must accompany each communication. Our Invitation is not personal but general—please respond to our call.

HOTEL LONDRES, PARIS,
Sept., 8, '73.

My dear father and Sarah: I have often thought of writing you, but we have been travelling so much lately, that we have had but little time to write. I think I last wrote you from Munich, from there we went to Insbruck, then to Lindau. Then crossed Lake Constance, to Romanshorn, Switzerland, and to Zurich, where we spent several days. Here I made some inquiries to the name of Longenecker and Eshleman, and they told me the Longenecker's were from near Lake Constance, and the Eshleman's from Zurich, but I did not see any of them. From Zurich we came to Lucerne, then we took the tour of Lake Lucerne to Fluelen, then over the St. Gothard pass to Andermatt, then the Furca pass to the Rhone Glacier, the source of the Rhone River. Then over the Grimsel pass to Lake Rienz and Interlachen. From there to Berne, a very old town, then to Freybourg and Lussan, on Lake Geneva down the Lake to the city Geneva where we spent two very pleasant weeks. We like Switzerland very much, better than we did Germany. On last Friday at five o'clock we left Geneva for Paris, and arrived here in this beautiful city on Saturday at four, after twenty-three hours ride on the cars very tired. This is by far the most beautiful city we have seen in Europe. It is so large we have not seen very much of it, but every part of it we have been in is very fine. The buildings and the streets are the finest I ever saw. We think Philadelphia is beautiful, but it cannot compare with Paris. However we see a number of buildings that were destroyed by the late war, and still more that were burned by the Communes. It seems a shame that they should destroy their own city in that way. We now expect to stay in this city perhaps a month, there is so much to see here. We always hear in America that Paris is such a fearful wicked city, of course we do not know about that, but the people are very nice looking, more so than in any other city we have been in. The streets are very wide and paved very beautifully, it looks to me as if it was cement of some kind.

Last night we had a rain, and this morning I saw the men with large brushes sweeping the water on the sides to run away. A person being in Paris would think it was the best governed city in the world, everything seems to move on like clock work.

We have all been so well all Summer, we are so strong and walk a great deal. Olive often speaks of it, if she visited you she could understand nearly all the German they could talk to her now. Lannie can carry on a conversation in German, and so can Howard, but Lannie speaks it the best of the three. Here they speak French, we get along very nicely as Olive speaks French very well, and the boys are very anxious to learn it. For my part I never expect to learn to speak French. We expect to go to London from here. I do not know what our address will be there, but when I do I will write you again. I would like so much to hear from you but it takes so long to get an answer from America that we will not likely be here long enough to get an answer. John wrote me he paid you a visit on his way to Philadelphia.

We now expect to sail for America early in December, we would like to get home till Christmas. I am beginning to think it very long to get home, however I am much stronger than I was when I left home. Olive is so much stronger. I often wonder how you both are getting along and how your health is. I wrote to Blaus Gander soon after coming to Europe, but have never had an answer. We have had a very hot Summer, but since we came to Paris it has been quite cool. It seems quite Fall like, I see that some of the leaves on the trees in the Park are beginning to color. I think it is quite early for that. It was very hot in Geneva last week, but that is so near Italy, we are now twenty-three hours ride north-west of Geneva. Remember me kindly to Yoder's family. The children join me in love for yourself and Sarah. From your daughter,

N. L. Sprogle.

Dear brethren and readers of the Pilgrim: In No. 39, page 311, Bro. J. H. Moore writes in reference to what I said in No 37, "Having *despaired* in my ability to write, I laid down my pen to write no more for the public eye." I don't know how the word *despair* got into the article, whether I wrote it so by mistake, or whether the printer could not decipher my bad chyrography. I meant to say, *having mistrusted my ability to write*, &c., I thought my reasons justified the conclusions. I wish brother Moore however not to understand me as having laid my weapon down, or my armor off, I still fight *small* battles for the Lord. I had what I thought sufficient reasons to justify me in the conclusion not to write. My reasons I think are known to the Editors of the *Visitor* and *Pilgrim*, to whose columns I had frequently contributed, yet I did write some during the past Winter months, and prepared eleven articles written on eleven different texts or subjects, too long I fear for the columns of our weeklies at one insertion, and I don't like to have my articles cut in twain. I however took them with me to A. M., but none of the Editors asked me for my contributions, and having so little confidence in my ability to write, I did not intrude them on any one. I returned them to their former place in my desk where they now are. So I remained silent until contributions were solicited for the C. F. C., I have contributed some little for its columns, these, however, much against my will and natural inclination, partook too much of a personal and controversial character. This kind of writing is not congenial to my Christian or moral feelings. A reference to my writings in the *Visitor* and *Pilgrim* will show that practical religion, and not controversy, is my part. But I could not see how to avoid personality and controversy in my late writing in the C. F. C. The faith, order, and practice I believe to be the true faith and order the Gospel teaches,—is the same faith and order my fathers' believed and practiced in the church 123 years ago, and has come down in an unbroken line of descent, without a change of name. This *faith* and *order* I not only believe to be that of the Gospel, but deferred it as such, and when it is assailed and denounced by men and women, who by profession would have men believe they believed the same thing, my spirit within me is stirred, and I become terribly aroused, and know no one after the flesh; the mother that gave me birth, and the father who provided me food would be alike subject to *sharp* reproof.

I hope the publishing of articles in our periodicals, written against the order of the Church in any of her practices will forever cease, and the necessity to reply will be avoided. If there is a spirit of insubordination among some members in the Church, and if there be within her folds those who would cause divisions, and to subvert the simplicity that is in Christ, avoid such as says St. Paul, and don't give their heretical views and notions publicity in our church papers, to the grieving and wounding of the brethren who love the church in her faith, order and practice. If there be any who do not so believe, let such seek their associates among those who are of like precious faith with themselves, but suffer them not to corrupt the faith of the lambs of the flock through the medium through which we profess to strengthen their faith.

D. P. SAYLOR.

PILGRIM OFFICE,
Oct 14, '73.

Dear Brethren and Sisters: This morning I am in the PILGRIM Office, where the hands are all busy setting type for the next weeks paper. This is certainly a great satisfaction, that from one place and in so short a time, the good news can be sent broadcast over the land.

I have been looking around in the office, and seeing the care and energy manifested by our dear Bro. editor I do think that all the brethren and sisters should encourage and take the PILGRIM at least, it should be taken by every family, so that our dear children may have the opportunity of reading it. Dear parents, see that your children have implanted into their minds, while young, the true principles of holiness and they will not depart from it. By reading the PILGRIM, our children can learn the practices of the gospel and the Church which will enable them to avoid many of the dangers to which they will be exposed in after life. I do hope that every family of the brotherhood will subscribe for at least, one of our periodicals, and then have a reporter for each Church district. By so doing we could have much more interesting news, and thus become more familiar with the condition of the different churches throughout the brotherhood. Not only may we realize this advantage but it may be the means of converting our children which we should esteem more highly than if we could gain the whole world.

Now dear brethren let us all do something towards enlarging their circulation so that they may have compensation for their labor and enable them to make still further improvements as they intend to do this year. I feel fully persuaded that the more we read and learn of each other the more we will prosper. How glad we feel on entering a house to find one of our periodicals! I soon look over its pages after some familiar name. How good it is that we can thus become acquainted with each other though thousands of miles apart, and instruct each other in those things which are for our eternal good. Brethren and sisters, let us try and get better every day, as we are all nearing the tomb and very soon may pass away.

I have just now, received a letter from my children which gives me much joy to hear that three have been added to the Church since I left home.

Yours truly.
JOHN KNISELY.

REPORT FROM SPRING RUN.

The Lovefeast in Spring Run Congregation, Mifflin Co., Pa., commencing October 5, is now over, and we had a good meeting. The ministerial aid was abundant.

At this meeting a deacon was chosen to the ministry, viz., John S. Hanawalt, and three persons baptized. Since about the first of April, twenty-four have been admitted by baptism and nearly half as many by certificate.

About two hundred communicants were present, and as a few could not be seated at the tables, several strange members, (especially such as had been or expected to be at an other Communion meeting) yielded their seats to as many of this congregation.

A movement is on foot to build a Meeting-house in Matawana which should be a large one, with a gallery so as to accommodate many members, and also a large number of spectators.

The Spring Run Meeting-house should also have a gallery. The want of sufficient room to accommodate the people here is a strong argument in favor of the new M. H. being a large one. Too many are barely large enough at the time of building, and then as the church increases, and the audience gets larger, the house is too small.

S. W. BOLLINGER.
McVeytown, Pa.

Brother Pilgrim: The Coventry Congregation of the Church of the Brethren, held their Lovefeast on Saturday the 4th inst. There were many assembled to partake of the emblems of the broken body and shed blood of our blessed Lord and Master, whom we are trying to serve, for we are not our own, but we are bought with a price.

There were brethren and sisters present from Dauphin, Lebanon, Berks and Montgomery counties. Although the sky was overshadowed with dark clouds, yet all was quiet within. No unruly spectator to mar the solemnity of the occasion. Sometimes a sad feeling would cross our minds when we would think of the dear departed ones who used to sit with us around the table of the Lord, whose loved forms are now hidden away from our sight beneath the cold, cold clods. But we have the hope, the blissful hope, that they are now feasting in the Paradise of God's unchanging love.

Where the anthems of rapture unceasingly roll,
And the smile of the Lord is the feast of the soul.

H. HOLLOWBUSH.
Pottstown, Pa.

Mr. Editor.—In the PILGRIM of the 7th of October, you notice the purchase, by the Methodist, of a Baptist church in Charleston, S. C., at $20 000, which the Baptist claim was worth $60,000, and you close with this uncharitable language, "It was a sharp business transaction as between brokers, but shows that Southern Christianity needs reconstructing slightly," forgetting that the value of property has greatly declined in that unfortunate city and State, under the reconstructing policy persued towards them by the general Government.

Now Mr. Editor, nine-tenths of your readers will understand you as referring to the Southern "Methodist," but this is not correct. The purchase was made by a Negro Methodist church, which belongs to the Northern Methodist church. Why did you not so inform your readers, and let justice be done to a greatly abused church (The Methodist Church South) "though the Heavens fall."

The M. E. Church South needs no "reconstructing slightly," for she is constructed on the broad Scriptural basis of "do justly and love mercy," and return not "railing for railing." It is too much the habit of northern editors to confound the M. E Churches North and South, in the Southern States, and to blame the M. E. Church, South, with things she has nothing to do with.

Believing you would not willingly do injustice to a branch of the Christian Church, and mislead your people, I ask you to insert the above in the PILGRIM.

S. KENNERLY.
Hermitage P. O., Va.

WAYNESBORO, PA.,
October 9, '73.

Dear Brother: I am pained to have you announce the sad intelligence of the death of our very dear brother and Elder Joseph F. Rohrer. He was attending the Lovefeast and Communion Meeting at Marsh Creek, last Friday, took sick, and was bro't to his home near Smithburg, Md., yesterday while our Lovefeast was being held at the Welty Meeting-house, near his home. This evening we have the news of his departure. I cannot realize it! He has been one of our faithful fathers in Israel. He has long and to the last, stood up in defense of the pure Word of God, and faithful vindication of the Christian life that is "not conformed to the world." O what a good record!

Some one will, I trust, communicate a biographical sketch of his life.

Yours in Christ,
D. B. MENTZER.

ANNUAL MEETING TENT.

Ed. of Pilgrim: —Please say to the Brotherhood that the purchasing of a tent is considered a failure for the present, the proposed donations amounting to about four hundred dollars. Only thirty-four churches, out of the many, reported us having considered the matter.

DANIEL VANIMAN.

MARRIED.

SNOWBERGER—RHODES.—At the residence of the undersigned, in New Enterprise, Pa., Sept 30, D. F. Snowberger, and Nancy Rhodes, all of Clover Creek, Pa. S. A. MOORE.

NORRIS—SAYLOR.—At the residence of the brides' parents, Sept. 9th, by George Brumbaugh, Abraham Norris, and sister Kate Saylor, all of Huntingdon Co., Pa.

DIED.

HARLEY.—In the East Coventry church, at the house of her son Rudolph Harley, (deacon) sister Elizabeth Harley, aged 88 years and 2 days.

She was a member of the Coventry church upwards of sixty years and was baptized by Eld. John Price. She lived a widow forty-nine or fifty years. Truly she was a mother in Israel; naturally of an amiable disposition, and this combined with the Christian spirit, made her a lovely wife, a fond mother and a very agreeable sister —She was very tenacious to the old order of the Brethren and had a strong desire to walk in all the commandments of the Lord blameless. The occasion was improved by Elders Kelm and J. R. Price.

H. HOLLOWBUSH.

PERKY.—In Warsaw, Kosciusco Co., Ind., August 5th, '73, brother Daniel Perky, aged 94 years, 9 months and 13 days.

He was immersed two years ago and united with the Brethren. He was annointed with oil before his death. His burial service was held in the Baptist Church in the city, by brethren O. P. Miller and George Cripe from Rev. 14 : 13. Bro. Perkey was quiet and unobtrusive and had, in the course of his daily life, sought and obtained that peace which passeth all understanding. His sufferings he bore with patience and resignation, never murmuring, only expressing a desire that he might die and be at rest. He never sought after wealth or worldly gain, but with heart and hopes stayed on the divine creed, he resigned himself to the keeping of him who doeth all things well. Though a martyr for truth and right, he sustained himself to the last day of his life with unwavering faith and confidence in his Savior.

AGNES E. STONER.

RISH.—In the Logan church, Logan co., Ohio, Sept. 19 '73, our esteemed old sister Rispah M. Rish, aged 76 years, 6 mos and 27 days. She was a consistent member, her seat seldom vacant in the sanctuary. Funeral preached by the writer and M. Swonger from Rev. 14 : 13.

J. L. FRANTZ.

Obituaries crowded out.

LITERATURE.

A. B. Brumbaugh, Huntingdon, Pa. Literary Editor.

THE RIVER OF LIFE is a new collection of popular Music for Sunday Schools by H. S. Perkins & W. W. Bentley, Published by Oliver Ditson & Co. Price 35 cents.

The title of this book is well chosen and suggestive, and clearly connected with that of various hymns, as "By the Crystal River," "Watching on the Shore," "The Shining Ones," "The Water of Life," &c.

The authors seem to have been unusually fortunate in their helpers, having secured contributions of words and music from perhaps forty distinguished writers and composers.

Among the hymns for Infant Classes, we notice:

"Take my hand, dear Jesus,
Let me never stray."

Among those for general purposes:

"My Savior's voice is low and soft,
It's tones are clear and calm."

On the whole, it is fair to conclude that "THE RIVER OF LIFE" is a decided success in its compilation, and can hardly be less so in its sale.

HURD & HOUGHTON, *Cambridge, Mass.*, have in press a new book by Mrs. Clara Erskine Clement—"Painters, Sculptors, Architects, Engravers and their work." Fully illustrated. "The Grammar of Painting and Engraving" by Charles Blanc is also promised for the "Autumn List." "Bianca Cappello," a fine act tragedy, in verse, by Mrs. E. C. Kinney will be ready early in autumn. "The Egyptian Sketch Book," by Charles G. Leland is a lively and humorous description of travel in the East. Mrs. Ames does the children a great favor by collecting the ballads and songs and bits of verse for the children written by the "Carey Sisters" into a volume to be entitled "Ballads for Little Folks." "The work of the Spirit," by Rev. Samuel Cutter is a book of meditation and directions for daily use and will doubtless prove a valuable aid in many families. "Apples of Gold" bound for 1873, will be a treat for the children as it is profusely illustrated. We will supply any of these works as soon as published. Any book published in this or any other country, may be ordered through us at publishers prices.

H. N. MCKINNEY & CO., of Philadelphia, have just issued another book by Harriet B. McKeever—"The House on the Heights." $1 50.

J. B. LIPPINCOTT & CO., have just issued "Out of Sweet Solitude," a book of poems by Eleanor C. Donnelly. Extra cloth; full gilt, $1.50. "Apollos or the way of God" by the Right Rev. A. C. Coxe, D. D., cloth $1.50. The first volume of their new edition of Prescott's Works is "Ferdinand and Isabella" and is edited by J. F. Kirk. Extra cloth, $2.25; sheep $2.75.

WHISPERS TO A BRIDE AND CHRISTIAN HOUSEHOLDS, by Mrs. Lincoln Phelps. With an Appendix containing a History of the Order of Deaconesses 1 vol. cloth, no edges, $1.00. White calf extra gilt, for bridal presents, $3.00.

There are few authors better qualified to perform the delicate task accomplished in writing this gem of a book, than Mrs. Phelps.

The Christian home, the fittest emblem of heaven which earth affords, should be the abode of peace and love, with all minds attuned to harmony, every member a worshipper at the family altar, inscribed to the God of Love and Father of Mercies, with the din of peace hovering over all; this forms a picture as beautiful as it is lovely. Upon every page are thoughts which tend to ennoble and dignify the sacredness of the family relation; and it were a good thing to let those whisperings come to the ears of many a wife, who has nearly forgotten the time when she assumed the bridal vows.

FAIRMOUNT PARK.—Sketches of its scenery, waters, and history By Charles S. Keyser.

"Fairmount Park, at Philadelphia is the most extensive, and in natural advantages the most attractive, among the pleasure grounds of Europe and America. It extends along the Schuylkill River over seven miles, and along the Wissahicken over six miles. It begins at Fairmount and terminates at Chestnut Hill, a distance of nearly fourteen miles, and comprises nearly 3000 acres. We cannot here describe its beauties and attractions. No one going to the "City of Brotherly Love" should fail to visit Fairmount Park, and spend at least one day among its beauties; but those who cannot go will be amply rewarded for the perusal of this little book which gives an accurate description of the Park with fine engravings of its places of interest. Published by Claxton, Remson & Haffelfinger, and for sale by Wm. Lewis, Huntingdon, Pa., or at this office. Price paper 75 cts. Cloth $1.00.

GOOD BOOKS.

How to read Character, illus. Price,	$1.25
Combe's Moral Philosophy,	1.75
Constitution of Man. Combe,	1.75
Education. By Spurzheim,	1.50
Memory—How to Improve it,	1.50
Mental Science, Lectures on,	1.50
Self-Culture and Perfection,	1.50
Combe's Physiology, Illus.	1.75
Food and Diet. By Pereira,	1.75
Marriage. Muslin, $1.50.	
The Science of Human Life,	3.50
Fruit Culture for the Million,	1.00
Saving and Wasting,	1.50
Ways of Life—Right Way,	1.00
Footprints of Life,	1.25
Conversion of St. Paul,	1.00

Man and Woman: Considered in their Relations to each Other and to the World. 12mo, Fancy cloth, Price $1.00.

Hopes and Helps for the Young of both sexes, Relating to the Formation of Character. Choice of Avocation, Health, Conversation, Social Affection Courtship and

Trine Immersion.

A discussion on Trine Immersion, by letter between Elder B. F. Moomaw and Dr. J. J. Jackson, to which is annexed a Treatise on the Lord's Supper, and on the necessity, character and evidences of the new birth, also a dialogue on the doctrine of non-resistance, by Elder B. F Moomaw. Single copy 50 cents.

Historical Charts of Baptism.

A complete key to the history of Trine, and the ORIGIN of Single Immersion. The most interesting, reliable and comprehensive document ever published on the subject. This Chart exhibits the years of the birth and death of the Ancient Fathers, the length of their lives, who of them lived at the same period, and shows how easy it was for them to transmit to each succeeding generation, a correct understanding of the Apostolic method of baptizing. It is 22x28 inches in size, and extends over the first 400 years of the Christian era, exhibiting at a single glance the impossibility of single immersion ever having been the Apostolic method. Single copy, $1.00; Four copies, $3.25. Sent post paid. Address, J. H. MOORE.

Urbana, Champaign Co., Ill.

WANTED.

A man to work at the Wagon-making business, who understands the trade, and is capable of running a shop independently. Shop and material furnished. Work plenty both heavy and light. A reasonable chance will be given to a suitable person. A man without a family will be preferred. Apply to or address the undersigned.

GEO. BRUMBAUGH.
Grafton, Huntingdon Co., Pa.

DYMOND ON WAR.

An inquiry into the Accordancy of War, with the Principles of Christianity, and an examination of the Philosophical reasoning by which it is defended. With observations on some of the causes of war and on some of its effects. By Jonathan Dymond Sent from this office, post paid, for 30 cts.

TUNE BOOK.

The Brethren's Tune and Hymn Book, is a compilation of Sacred Music adapted to all the hymns in the Brethren's New Hymn Book. It contains over 350 pages, printed on good paper and neatly bound. We will send it to any address, post paid at $1.25 per copy.

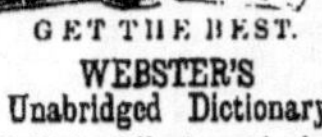

GET THE BEST.

WEBSTER'S Unabridged Dictionary.

10,000 *Words and Meanings not in other Dictionaries.*

3000 Engravings; 1840 Pages Quarto. Price $12.

Webster now is glorious,—it leaves nothing to be desired. [Pres. Raymond, Vassar College.]

Every scholar knows the value of the work. (W. H. Prescott, the Historian.)

Been one of my daily companions. (John L. Motley, the Historian, &c.)

Superior in most respects to any other known to me. (George P. Marsh.)

The best guide of students of our language. (John G. Whittier.)

Excels all others in defining scientific terms. (President Hitchcock.)

Remarkable compendium of human knowledge. (W. S. Clark, Pres. Ag. Col'ge.)

A necessity for every intelligent family, student, teacher and professional man. What library is complete without the best English Dictionary?

ALSO

Webster's Nat'nal Pictorial Dict'nary.

1040 Pages Octavo. 600 Engrv'gs. Price $5.

The work is really a gem of a Dictionary, just the thing for the million.—*American Educational Monthly.*

Published by G. & C. MERRIAM, Springfield, Mass. Sold by all Booksellers.

TRACTS.

"ANXIOUS BENCH RELIGION EXAMINED," BY ELDER J. S. FLORY. A SYNOPSIS OF CONTENTS. An address to the reader; The peculiarities that attend this type of religion. The feelings there experienced not imaginary but real. The key that unlocks the wonderful mystery. The causes by which feelings are excited. How the momentary feelings called "Experimental religion" are brought about, and then concludes by giving that form of doctrine as taught by Jesus Christ and recorded by his faithful witnesses.

COUNTERFEIT DETECTER
OF
BAPTISM—MUCH IN LITTLE.

This work is now ready for distribution, and the importance of the subject will speak for it a large demand. It is a short treatise on baptism in tract form intended for general distribution, and is set forth in such a plain and logical manner that a wayfaring man though a fool, cannot err therein. Either of the above tracts sent postpaid on the following terms: Two copies, 10 cts, 10 copies 40 cents, 25 copies 70 cents, 50 copies $1.00, 100 copies $1.50.

Trine Immersion TRACED TO THE APOSTLES.

The SECOND EDITION is now ready for delivery. The work has been carefully revised, corrected and enlarged.

Put up in a neat pamphlet form, with good paper cover, and will be sent, post-paid, from this office on the following terms: One copy, 25 cts; Five copies, $1.10; Ten copies, $2.00. 25 copies. $4.50; 50 copies, $8.50; 100 copies, $10.00.

THE HELPING HAND.

Containing several hundred Valuable Receipts for cooking well at a moderate expense, making Dyes, Coloring, Cleaning and Cementing. This book also points out in plain language, free from Doctors' terms the diseases of men, women and children, and the latest and most approved means used for their cure, to which is added a description of the Medicinal Roots and Herbs, and how they are to be used in the cure of diseases.

This is a work of considerable importance and we offer it to our readers as being a valuable accession to every household. Send from this office to any address, post-paid, for 25 cents.

1870 1873

DR. FAHRNEY'S Blood Cleanser or Panacea.

A tonic and purge, for Blood Diseases. Great reputation. Many testimonials. Many ministering brethren use and recommend it. Ask or send for the "Health Messenger." Use only the "*Panacea*" prepared at Chicago, Ills., and by

Dr. P. Fahrney's Brothers & Co.,
Feb. 3-pd. *Waynesboro, Franklin Co., Pa*

New Hymn Books, English.

TURKEY MOROCCO.

One copy, postpaid,	$1.00
Per Dozen,	11.25

PLAIN ARABESQUE.

One Copy, post-paid,	75
Per Dozen, "	8.50

Ger'n & English, Plain Sheep.

One Copy, post-paid,	$1.00
Per Dozen	11.25
Arabesque Plain,	1.00
Turkey Morocco,	1.25
Single German, post paid	50
Per Dozen,	5.50

HUNTINGDON & BROAD TOP RAIL ROAD

On and after Aug 14th, 1873, Trains will run on this road daily (Sun excepted) as follows:

Trains from Huntingdon South. *Trains from Mt. Dal's moving North.*

EXPS. P. M.	MAIL. A. M.	STATIONS.	MAIL. P. M.	EXP'S A. M
6 15	7 45	Huntingdon,	AR6 50	AR9 20
6 20	7 50	Long Siding	6 45	9 15
6 35	8 00	McConnelstown	6 35	9 05
6 40	8 05	Pleasant Grove	6 20	8 58
6 51	8 20	MARKLESBURG	6 15	8 45
7 01	8 35	Coffee Run	6 05	8 35
7 08	8 41	Rough & Ready	5 58	8 29
7 15	8 50	Cove	5 49	8 20
7 18	8 53	Fishers Summit	5 40	8 17
7 35	9 10	Saxton	5 35	8 05
7 50	9 25	Riddlesburg	5 15	7 45
7 53	9 32	Hopewell	5 10	7 38
8 10	9 45	Piper's Run	4 58	7 28
8 21	9 57	Tatesville	4 43	7 12
8 32	10 07	Everett	4 33	7 03
8 40	10 15	Mount Dallas	4 30	7 00
9 00	10 35	Bedford	4 05	6 35

SHOUP'S RUN BRANCH.

A. M.	P. M.		P. M.	A. M.
LE 9 20	LE 7 40	Saxton.	AR5 25	AR 7 55
9 35	7 55	Coalmont.	5 10	7 40
9 40	8 00	Crawford.	5 05	7 35
AR 9 50	AR8 10	Dudley	LE4 55	LE 7 25

Bro'd Top City from Dudley 2 miles by stage.

Time of Penna. R. R. Trains at Huntingdon.

*** Mail No. 2 makes connection at Huntingdon with Mail going East on Pennsylvania Railroad at 4.15 p. m., and West at 5.45 p. m. Mail No. 1 leaves Huntingdon at 7.40 a. m. on arrival of Pacific Express West.

Trains on this road connect with trains on Bedford & Bridgeport, and Cumberland & Pennsylvania Railroads.

G. F. GAGE, Supt.

The Weekly Pilgrim.

Published by J. B. Brumbaugh, & Co.
Edited by H. B. & Geo. Brumbaugh.
CORRESPONDING EDITORS.
D. P. Sayler, Double Pipe Creek, Md.
Leonard Furry, New Enterprise, Pa.

The *Pilgrim* is a Christian Periodical, devoted to religion and moral reform. It will advocate in the spirit of *love* and *liberty*, the principles of true Christianity, labor for the promotion of peace among the people of God, for the encouragement of the saints and for the conversion of sinners, avoiding those things which tend toward disunion or sectional feelings.

TERMS.

Single copy, Book paper,	$1.50
Eleven copies, [eleventh for Agt.]	$15.00

Any number above that at the same rate. Address.

H. B. BRUMBAUGH.
James Creek,
Huntingdon county Pa.

The Weekly Pilgrim.

"REMOVE NOT THE ANCIENT LANDMARKS WHICH OUR FATHERS HAVE SET."

VOL. 4. JAMES CREEK, PENNSYLVANIA, OCTOBER 28, 1873. NO. 13

POETRY.

For the PILGRIM.

IT MUST BE SWEET TO DIE.

It must be sweet, in early years, to die,
Like gentle fading flowers;
And pass away without a parting sigh,
To Heaven's blissful bowers.

It must be sweet in early childhood's love,
In gay, harmless infant life,
To leave behind, this world and soar above,
Far from earthly care and strife.

It must be sweet in gentle Spring to die,
Among the early flowers;
As a balmy breeze wafts its sweetness by,
To close young life's earthly hours.

It must be sweet in artless infant years,
To leave all earth's joys behind;
To leave behind its sorrows, joys and fears,
A happier home to find.

O it must be sweet, like a fading star—
To pass in childhood away,
To that beauteous land from earth afar,
Where 'tis everlasting day.

F. W. S.

Antwerp, Mich.

ORIGINAL ESSAYS.

HOW SHALL I INVEST MONEY FOR JESUS?

It is with much reluctance that I attempt to offer a few thoughts to the readers of the PILGRIM upon such a topic. First, on account of my inability to treat it as it should be, and secondly because I know that there are brethren who are better fitted for the task. But to the subject.

That it is allowable and right for the people of God to lay up treasures and accumulate the goods of this world seems clear, and admits of no doubt from the teaching of the Scriptures. But that the people of God have a Gospel right and privilege, either by precept or example, to apply the same accumulated goods in any way, or to any purpose that their fancy or wishes may dictate to them, we greatly doubt. This is far from being the *way* that Jesus points out to us, as we are by Him represented only as *stewards* over the goods, while the Lord is the rightful *proprietor*. So that if we wish to serve our Master acceptably we must necessarily consult His divine *will*, as to *how* we shall dispose of them.

And as money seems to be included as a part of the goods over which we have the stewardship, I think the caption of this article a pertinent one. It is well known that many of our brethren have grown wealthy, and no doubt, legitimately so, in an honorable, upright, straight forward business, and as long as we see them making a faithful disposition of their accumulated goods, we have no cause to censure, but rather feel to justify them. But when we see them follow the example of a money-loving, money-craving, monopolizing world by investing the Lord's goods in Rail road bonds, or place them in the *care* of some wealthy bank, or worse yet, to see them go into the banking business themselves, then our justification ceases and a disposition to reprove such a course takes its place.

I think we ought to consider it one of God's scourges if some of our brethren have met a temporal loss in the late financial panic, on account of non-producing stock, gamblers and reckless speculators. Perhaps a few more such shocks will give us more confidence in the "Lord's securities," and a little less confidence in the wild cat securities that have characterized the late money panic. The Lord tells us that "He that giveth to the poor *lendeth* to the Lord." And when our confidence in that promise is lost, we then lend to the rich, thinking our money is more secure. So when the *bottom* falls out of these earthly securities, let us try the Lord's banks and see whether we will be disappointed.

Do the Brethren know generally how many hundred little congregations are scattered over the West, (and elsewhere for aught I know) that have no houses of worship, save their own private houses and school-houses? And when they wish to hold a Lovefeast they are compelled from the force of circumstances, to build a temporary shed, a tent, or fix up an old saw mill or something of the sort. How easy it would be for some wealthy brethren to lend without interest some of their money for a stated time, to such brethren under the above circumstances. How many prayers would ascend up to the throne of God in behalf of such brethren that would lend their means in this way.

Again how many of our dear brethren and sisters who are toiling day after day without the means necessary to get a fair start in life, that have neither teams, houses, nor land, and yet have families to support. How easy to raise the burden off of such by lending a few hundred dollars for a few years on low interest or no interest at all. My mind just now runs to the benevolent acts of a good old brother that is now across the jordan of death, that had accumulated much worldly goods and lived in Northern Illinois. I know of another old brother who was in very needy circumstances, and perhaps would always have remained so had it not been for the kindness of the rich brother. The rich brother let the poor brother have a farm and stock to raise on the most liberal terms, and the result was the poor brother soon accumulated enough to go west where he was able to buy him a comfortable little home, and though the rich brother is dead, he yet liveth. Such a brother cannot be forgotten. The old brother that was thus favored and who is still living, often repeats the acts of kindness from the rich brother, and even the children of the poor brother rise up to-day and call him blessed; and without doubt the children's children will yet learn the name and the kindness of the rich man.

Thus we have pointed out a few of the ways that we may "invest money for Jesus," but there are many more, too many to point out in one essay. Perhaps some other Bro. or sister will carry the subject farther, or if this should prove acceptable, you may hear more in the future on the same subject from your weak but well wishing brother.

D. E. BRUBAKER.

Iowa Centre, Iowa.

PAST TIME.

We are in a fast age, everything is constantly changing. There is no necessity for a person being drawn back, for the word go or advance is now the ruling element, everything is bustle and speed all around us. Just think for a moment, what wonderful inventions the mechanist bro't to light in the period of the last fifty years, and the artist with his pencil has portraited and decorated the palaces of Kings and Queens. If the vice would only be tolerated with such, but the evil is cropping out and being engrafted in churches, on individuals, &c. Oh! pride stop. I was going to say, if a person at that time, (that is fifty years ago), would have told that generation in the next fifty years, there would be rail roads built, that is, roads by which people, Mdse. &c., will be conveyed from one place to another by steam at the rate of one mile per minute, that person would have been looked upon as being crazy, or accrsted as an idiotic imbecile.

At that age of the world our brethren had to travel hundreds of miles by the wearisome way of horse back, to hold forth the Bread of Life to dying souls, spend half of their time in going from one place to another, whereas now they can travel more comfortable, and meet their appointments at very short notices, which is appreciated by all. Look where you will and you will perceive that every person is trying to advance and move on as fast as the wheels of time can carry them. If we meditate upon the subject of past time, oh what wonderful changes. We can not find words to express our thot's about the matter, and judging the future by the experience of the past, who knows what will be brought about the next fifty years? Things perhaps more marvelous and astonishing than those at present. Language fails to depict the change, and what will become of the Church of the Brethren, (or Church of God, as some frame objection to calling it our Church or Church of the Brethren?) if we don't fortify our ranks a little stronger, I am afraid some of our peculiarities will be lost, because they are just on the brink now,—we are fast following popular churches.

Brethren, you who are placed as watchmen on the walls of Zion, cry aloud lest the enemy will get power of the pulling down of strongholds; arouse, and with a determined zeal fight the battles of the Lord. Press forward with one united effort for the mark, make your calling and election sure, never waver or yield in one point, and I am frank enough to say that at the end of our pilgrimage we will all be united in one family where Christ is at the head. What a glorious consummation that will be! Think about it, meditate upon it, for surely you will not rue it, as it is worth striving for.

C. H. WALKER.

Berlin, Pa.

THE TEACHER.

"Whom shall he teach knowledge? and whom shall he make to understand."—Isa. 28: 9.

The above Scripture has forced itself upon my mind with such vehemence, that I am constrained to comment upon it and hope some poor souls *may* be awakened out of their lethargy. I understand the prophet to have reference to Christ as being the teacher. In different places Christ is spoken of as a teacher. "And it shall come to pass in the last days that the mountain of the Lord's house shall be established in the top of the mountains, and shall be exalted above the hills, and all nations shall flow into it, and many people shall go and say: Come ye, and let us go up into the mountain of the Lord, to the house of the God of Jacob; and he will *teach* us of his ways, and we will walk in his paths."—Isaiah 2: 23. This is the word which Isaiah saw concerning Judah and Jerusalem. Christ, the Lion of the tribe of Judah, is represented as being a teacher. Nicodemus, a ruler of the Jews, acknowledges Him to be a teacher come from God. But now that He has come in form of a teacher, whom shall He teach? In short, I answer, all who will be taught. It is written, "They shall all be taught of God." Sometimes we are told that all does not mean everybody. If this be true, who is able to tell how many are included in the word all. I understand the Savior to mean everybody, or in other words all who are capable of being taught, when He told His disciples to preach the Gospel to every creature, and teach all nations. The reason why so many are in the broad road that leads to destruction, is they are unwilling to come to this teacher. Think not friendly sinner that the Scriptures are too great a mystery for you to understand, for they are the teaching of Christ; by no means. Hear the Savior, "I thank thee Father Lord of Heaven and earth, that thou hast hid these things from the wise and prudent and hast revealed them unto babes." This is sufficient proof to any candid mind that Christ requires no impossibilities of any person. The plan of salvation is so plain that a wayfaring man, though a fool cannot err therein.

But do we find objections to some things required in this teaching? We should not expect God's blessing in observing only a part. He may say to us at His second coming as He did to the Jews at His first coming, "These ought ye to have done, and not to leave the other undone."

Non-essential, is another objection to some of the requirements of the Gospel, as Baptism, the Lord's Supper, Feetwashing, &c. Well let us see how Scripture and such conclusions agree. Ananias said to Paul, "Why tarriest thou, arise and be baptized and wash away thy sins, calling on the name of the Lord.' Thus he thought baptism essential, even to *wash* away his sins. Jesus said to Peter, "If I wash thee not, thou hast no part with me."—John 13. So you see it was necessary for Peter, in order to have a part with Him, to have his feet washed, and we may safely conclude that the washing of Peter's feet, was a prerequisite to a part with him; that is a spiritual part. How can any in the face of these scriptures doubt the essentiality of these things? Oh says one, "faith alone, faith alone is sufficient to save us." But what saith the Scripture? "The word is nigh thee, even in thy mouth, and in thy heart," that is the word of faith which we preach."

That the Word should accompany faith, is fully set forth in this language: Our faith should be in the Word, and if this be so, it is impossible for us to wilfully reject any requirement therein. Faith is the prerequisite to repentance, and repentance the pre-requisite to baptism, and baptism a pre-requisite to remission of sins and gift of the Holy Ghost. These three, must be observed in order, or in other words lawfully, before we have the promise as aforesaid. This is taking "the yoke upon us," and nothing short of this will bring us under the Gospel yoke.

What! says one, a yoke to wear? Yes but it is easy and the burden is light, and by taking the yoke upon us we are then, and only then, prepared to learn of Him. Hear Him: "Take my yoke upon you and learn of me." Hence those are the ones whom He will teach knowledge; having the yoke of Christ upon them, they are willing to be taught of Him, hence will learn of Him meekness and lowliness of heart. Those He will make to understand—all that is necessary, for He will impart to them, He will give them His spirit to guide them into all truth. "Sanctify them through thy truth, thy word is truth."—John 17 chap. So said this teacher. Now in order to obtain sanctification, it is necessary for us to go *through* the truth, not to stop in the middle but go *through*. Now this clearly proves that if we do not go through, that is submit to every precept and example, our sanctification will never be complete. We will become blind, and forget that we were purged from our old sins, but if we, as Paul describes, "Put on the whole armor of God that we may be able to stand: *and having done all to stand*, we must not only have on part of the armor. No. This will never protect us, but we must then do ALL and then we will stand. Though Christian, while in the "valley of humility," had on the whole armour, yet when attacked by Appollyon," he had to fight—do all. Thus if we stand in the King's highway, the way of holiness, Christ will fight. While Christian was contending with his ruthless foe, "He gave him a deadly thrust, which made him give back as one that had received his mortal wound." Perceiving that he made at him again saying, "Nay,' in all these things we are more than conquerors through Him that loved us."—Rom. 8: 37. And then Apolyon spread forth his dragon wings, and left Christian, that he saw him no more. Thus may we put to flight the great dragon or enemy of souls, and only thus.

Let us stand fast in the liberty wherein we are called, for we are not children of the bond-woman, but of the free.

J. M. WELLS.

BE INSTANT.

"Be instant in season and out of season."—2 Tim. 4: 2.

Dear Brother Pilgrim: By the help of God, I wish to pen a few thoughts for your columns from the above heading, for the consideration of those who wish to see eye to eye in the great work of salvation.

1st. We will take Local Option. Perhaps this is out of season, but Paul would say: press on at all events. Now many of the Brethren could or would not go to the polls to vote to put down this traffic which is sending thousands of our fellow-creatures to perdition. But they thought all they were in duty bound to do was to stay at home and pray. We suppose, pray that the great evil might be removed. But we take the ground that they should have gone and voted in favor of a law that would have rebuked the dram seller and waked up the half dead and stupefied drinker. And now to the law and testimonies for the evidence of our assertions. When long ago, God's people sinned, God permitted them to be taken captive and carried to Babylon. There, in their low distress, they hanged their harps on the willows and when their captors required of them mirth and to sing of the songs of Zion, then alas; oh how could they sing in a strange land? But we think there they could pray and did pray for their deliverance and for the restoration of their beautiful house at Jerusalem and the church of the living God. And now what effect had their prayers? Why they caused God to move and soften the heart of Cyrus, king of Persia, so that he gave them an opportunity to rescue themselves from the power of bondage. But now they must embrace the opportunity and take the long and wearisome journey, and then with great affliction, and at the expense of the good will of Sanballet and others, rebuild the house, with the sword in one hand while building with the other. So we think they had something more to do than pray. And we think that the prayers of the righteous has entered the ears of Jehovah, and caused him to move and soften the hearts and minds of those of our fellow-men who hold the reins of government, to give us an opportunity of extricating thousands of our fellow-creatures from a drunkard's grave, and rebuking those who give their neighbor drink, and we should have done it.

2nd. Tobacco and pride are also frequently mentioned in our journals and if there is a cause for mentioning either of them by way of reproof, the accused must be guilty of intemperance which Paul forbids. As a general thing, when intemperance is spoken of it is understood as using too freely the intoxicating bowl, and we will admit that rye, corn, apples, peaches, &c., though very good in their place, yet were never intended to be converted or distilled into spirits and used to the degredation of mankind, but we think when the great orator of the New Testament, speaks of temperance, he means the total abstinence of all unnecessary things and would have us to offer our bodies a living sacrifice wholly and acceptable unto God which, he said, is our reasonable service.

3rd. There is considerable dissatisfaction in the manner of holding our A. M., and no wonder in my opinion, yet it appears almost impossible, taking into consideration the vast number of members in the Brotherhood, that every one willing and able to discuss, to have an opportunity to do so. And indeed I think things belonging to the Church of God, are too solemn, too weighty, too important to be passed by hasty discussions. And are there not many queries brought before A. M., of which by far the majority of members present have no knowledge until brought up for discussion. Now if the weightier matters were postponed for another year, and the queries inserted in the minutes of A. M., and each individual congregation urged to discuss the same in their private councils and also in the district meetings and then send their conclusions to Annual Meeting, would it not be charitable, would it not be brotherly and would it not have a tendency to conciliate many minds? Yea, we think it would, and think something of the kind should be, so as to come nearer the mind of the whole Church. See Acts 15th chap. 22d ver.

4th. There also appears to be some difference of opinion as regards the new commandment, see John 13: 34, 35, which I believe to be the washing of the saints feet for the following reasons: feet-washing, according to Gospel authority, is a new commandment. By Mosaic authority, the means were provided and Aaron and his sons, under penalty of death, must wash both hands and feet and elsewhere, a little water was provided for the weary and respected to wash their own feet. Under the new covenant, Christ washed the disciples feet, teaching a humiliating and leveling system, and is there not one feature in this manner of feetwashing that strongly indicates charity which has a figure of cleansing and which we all need? By this we show to a guilty world that we are willing to condescend to this low act to save those for whom Christ died, showing thereby that we are willing to sustain and help them in working out their soul, salvation. Therefore all men may see and know that we are the disciples of the Lord Jesus Christ when we condescend to the weak things of the world, which God has chosen to confound the things which are mighty.—1 Cor. 1: 27, 28.

"Awake my soul and with thy utmost care,
Thy true condition learn;
What are thy hopes, how sure, how fair,
And what thy great concern."

D. BOSSERMAN.

Gettysburg, Pa.

A LETTER TO SISTER MAGGIE SUTTERFIELD.

Dear Sister: —Your long looked for letter came to hand at last, bearing the sad news of the death of your dear mother and loving sister. Little did I expect to get such news from you, although I often wondered what was wrong that I could not hear from your folks in their new home in Kansas, but your kind letter explains the whole matter. Sad indeed is such a bereavement. As for your dear mother, that was not so much unexpected to me as our dear young sister Catharine.

No doubt you feel sad, as also I do when I call to mind the joys of past associations with your mother and sister. If we have any power of judging in regard to true virtue and piety, I think I can safely say you should not sorrow in such bereavements, you may sorrow in the gloomy loneliness of life, and in the absence of such dear loved ones, but then rejoice, inasmuch as they are released from this earthly tabernacle, and are now enjoying the fruition of a holier tabernacle, a house not made with hands. Yes, I am constrained to believe that those dear sisters have been stripped of mortality, that they might be clothed upon with a bright, glorious, and heavenly body, in which the pure robes of righteousness will ever bespeak their bliss and happiness.

As I have often with them and you, drank deeply of the cup of joy in earthly vessels, while mingling our prayers and tears, our songs and praises around the family altar, in social communion, oh, would I not rather quit this vale of tears, this world of trouble and sorrow, and with them be singing around the throne of God and the Lamb, the blessed songs of deliverance. I call to recollection the happy hours in which we feasted together on heavenly manna, and drank together from the fount of living waters. And ah! I remember well the last farewell tear that was shed, that earnest throbbing of the heart, that last, long sad look of sorrow, and yet filled full of joy, in the blessed hope that if on earth, we meet no more, in Heaven we'll meet on the *ever green shore*.

This teaches us, dear sister, that this is not our home. We are all frail beings, and the great question with us to be solved, is, how shall we live so as to meet those loved ones that are gone before? They have left foot-prints in the sands of their time that we would do well to heed. Pride and fashion are leading the *van*. As to its being the companion of your father's family, I never met it there as I meet it in the world elswhere. Humility and plainness beautifully characterized your mother's household. Ever remember that chastity under which you were brought up. You have now taken the place of a mother, and cannot too carefully guard the young and tender plants given to your care and culture. Be as devoted a mother as your own departed mother was. Let your light shine brighter and brighter unto the perfect day. You have, too, a kind and I trust a devoted husband, and I hope by this time, nearer in the relation by a union of faith. I feel assured his heart is in sympathy with your practice, and that if he loves the blessed Master, all things shall work together for good. I remember your good neighbors, Mr. and Mrs. McFarland. Often have I reflected on the sweet interviews we had together. Hope they are still surviving and leaning closely to the Savior's fold. I wonder if she has forgotten the humble preacher that used to stop and comfort her in her lonely invalid hours. How my heart bounded in the hope of leading a wandering soul to the cooling water that quenches thirsty souls. The narrow way unfolds itself to us mysteriously, and in the imagination of our heart, we close the door and will not let the Master in. I should like to hear from Mrs. McFarland.

Now dear sister, I have no doubt you are lonely; you have no brother or sister near you to fellowship your troubles, but you and all God's dear children have a friend that sticketh closer than a brother. He is near you, yea, within, a secret monitor to teach you, and to lead you into all truth. Obey that loving Teacher; gird about you His armor, and you shall be able to quench all the fiery darts of your foes, and will bring you off more than conqueror. And now may the love of God and the communion of His spirit be with you and all the bereaved of your family, is my prayer.

We are all well, my wife joins me in love to you and your kind husband. Remember me to Mrs. McFarland. Our present address is Adamsboro, Cass Co., Ind.

SAMUEL MYERS.

THE THOUGHT OF DEATH.

It is important that all men should frequently meditate upon death and be ready to meet it, for they know not at what moment they may be called hence. But especially should the sick do so. Sickness is a messenger sent to warn us of its approach.

It is well to think of our death as near at hand, because it tends to draw our hearts away from earth and all its vanities, and fix them upon religion and Heaven. It is calculated to weaken and destroy our sinful passions and desires, and strengthen our Christian graces and holy affections. The man who seldom thinks of death, or always views it as far off will be greatly tempted to forget God and eternity, to live in sin and for this world alone, and to put off religion and all preparation for another world to a future day. This is the cause of the eternal ruin of tens of thousands.

It is useful to meditate upon death as near at hand, because it tends to strip it of its terrors, and prepare us for it. It leads the Christian to set his house in order knowing he must die. He even feels a desire to depart and be with Christ, which he knows to be far better. The fact that a sick person meditates much upon death and prepares himself for it, is no evidence that he certainly must die, and cannot again recover. By no means; he may sincerely repent of all his sins, forgive, and pray to be forgiven, set his house in order, give up the world, and resign himself fully into the hands of God. All this will not cause him to die a moment sooner than the time appointed.

Physicians and friends often make great mistakes, and we have reason to believe do great injury by concealing from the sick their real situation and danger, until they are sinking into the arms of death. To flatter the sick with the belief that they are not in danger and will recover, when it is known to be false, is downright lying, and to lie to a dying man when his immortal soul is at stake, is a crime of which surely no man should desire to be guilty.

We ought not to think of death with that dread and horror which is sometimes manifested by the sick. We can excuse the heathen in view of the gloom which always hangs over their graves, for saying that death is the most dreadful event that can occur, but Christians ought to feel that as life and immortality are brought to light in the Gospel, death is robbed of its sting, and the grave of its victory. The believer dies in the grace of God, the arms of Jesus and the fellowship of the Holy Spirit, and why should he fear?

LANNA E. MILLER.

THE FULLNESS OF CHRIST.

It is only by looking to Jesus alone that we can ever attain comfort, and we can only do this by the power of the Holy Ghost. "None can call Jesus Lord, but by the power of the Holy Ghost." Now this He has promised you, if you will but ask Him, wrestle with Him, and let Him not go until He bless you. He is willing—come without money and without price. He loves to give and to be opportuned. You will never obtain joy and peace by looking within—it is simple and only, Look unto me and be ye saved. "He that believeth in me hath everlasting life." Seek the special influence of the Holy Spirit, and He will take of the things of Christ and show them unto you. Then shall your joy abound, and your peace flow as a river. Keep close to the precious Bible, and God will open to you its rich treasures by the teachings of the Holy Spirit.

Be of good courage. Faith is the gift of God, and God is your Father: and will a father deny his child any good thing? And will a good God, a gracious God, whose name is love, deny you the Holy Spirit, if you ask Him? If he does not answer at once, it is because He loves to hear the pleadings of His child? See in how many instances Christ appeared not to hear when at the very time He designed to grant the petition.

We had better seek Christ sorrowing than to sit down satisfied with a little, and with some vain notion in our heads which brings no fruit to God's glory. Mary sought her Lord sorrowing at the door of the sepulchre, but went away rejoicing to tell the disciples—"The Lord is risen indeed." —*Winslow*.

No thoughtful man's life is uninteresting or barren of marvels. A life real and earnest cannot be devoid of memorable occurrences.—*Spurgeon*.

THE LOVE OF MONEY.

A sister, in last week's issue, notices some of the ways in which we may use our money to advance the cause of Jesus, and while preparing the manuscript, the query arose in my own mind, why is it that so little money is spent for this purpose. There is a cause, and when we wish to remove an evil it is always well to strike at the *cause* first. That the Scriptures plainly teach that we should give of our wealth towards the support of the cause of Christianity is too evident to admit of doubt by those who are Bible readers, and this being so, it is just as much of a duty as any other of the requirements of the Bible.

Why is it then when our money is needed for the furtherance of the Gospel that we do not give it? Why is it that our ministers do not receive the necessary help when they are willing to leave their homes and spend and be spent for the furtherance of the good cause? Why is it there is so much difficulty in raising money to build churches, where it is evident to every one they are needed? Why is it too, that the richest congregations in the Brotherhood are the ones that, as a general thing, do but little, and frequently do nothing at all? To our mind the cause is evident, and I feel free to say that it is nothing more nor less *than the* LOVE *of money*. This is the cause, remove it, and we will soon know how to spend our money for the promotion of the good cause. This may seem like a strong assertion, but the thing is becoming to be too prominent to admit of doubt, and it is certainly high time that every true Christian should go out with might and main to battle against the evil that is now growing amongst us.

The apostle says the *love* of money is the root of *all* evil. From this declaration it is evident that his conclusions were that this undue desire for money was the first cause of every moral evil. What is it that has a greater tendency to debauch the mind with corrupt prejudices, and create unholy desires? It leads us to covet that which does not belong to us, and thus "pierce ourselves with many sorrows." Surely when we think of the result of this unholy desire we should guard against it.

It is really covetousness. Some persons have an idea that by the term covetousness is meant merely the desire to obtain the goods of another, or what does not lawfully belong to them. But this is not really the idea; an undue desire for money in whatever form it may manifest itself, is covetousness. All that we have in the world is the Lord's. He has loaned it to us, and as long as we make use of it as though it were not ours, and so as to meet the design for which He loaned it, then all is well. But it is to be feared that this is not the way in which many look at these things. We look upon the wealth of this world as our own, and make use of it in the gratification of our unholy desires. This is covetousness; it is desiring what does not belong to us; it is robbing God of what belongs to him. There is a time coming, however, when he will demand it of us, and then indeed will there be a dark account to give. Fearful indeed are the denunciations against the covetous or those who do not make a proper use of that which is entrusted to their care, and should cause every soul to shudder.

In 1 Cor. 1: 6, it is ranked with fornication, adultery, idolatry, theft, drunkenness, &c., and none of these, it is said, shall inherit the kingdom of God. Again the apostle in writing to the Collossians says, that covetousness is idolatry. Many more references might be cited to, to show the magnitude of this sin, but let this suffice. Those who have a *love* for money can see clearly the ground upon which they stand, and we would that they consider this matter. It seems to us that it is time there is a reformation in reference to this matter as well as in other things. The cry now is REFORMATION. The Church is becoming proud, &c., and this is all so. We need reformation, but we need it in other things too. Let us have reformation all around, and let us not watch the enemy at one point only, and let him make inroads upon us at other points.

But how are we to determine when we have a love for money? We answer the same as in reference to other things. We can know the tree by the fruits. When persons decorate and adorn the body with useless clothing, it is an evidence that they have a proud heart. When men lie and swear it is an evidence that they have a very wicked heart, and when our whole desire is to lay up money, and are unwilling to give to the support and furtherance of the Gospel, it is an evidence that covetousness exists in the heart.

In 2 Pet. 2: 14, we read of a certain class of individuals whose heart was exercised with covetous practices, and it seems to us there are some at the present time of that description. What think ye? A brother who is *immensely* rich was induced to subscribe for the PILGRIM, but after some time he concluded that he could not pay more than $1.00, and ordered us to stop it when the time was up. Now brethren and sisters, I do not mention this because it is the only instance of a similar nature, nor that we care for the 50 cents, but there is a disposition manifested in these things that does grieve our soul. It is paving the way of more than one soul to perdition, and if we can warn any one of the danger that is lurking unobserved behind them, we shall have accomplished a good work. May God help us all to seriously consider these things, for it is evident that there is too great a love for money in the heart of such persons. Their habits, their ways of doing indicate it in unmistakable language, and are just as devoid of the Christian spirit, as are the proud, the profane, the idolator, the adulterer, &c. There is nothing less than the *love* of money that can engender such close, miserly actions, and this is the root of all these things. Let us then, brethren and sisters, endeavor to root out this evil from amongst us, for it is lurking at the very core of our Christianity and is doing much to impede our progress as a body in the divine life. J. B. B.

Selected by J. D. Bear.

ONE CODE OF MORALS.

It is a good sign of the times that one occasionally hears a woman say "How strange it is that men will not see that there cannot be but one code of morals, and that one for both men and women."

I am always glad to hear it but always feel like answering:

"Yes but it is more strange that women do not make men see it."

This I believe, is one of the things which women must do, if it be done at all. It may seem unfair to lay the blame of this false opinion regarding the morality of men and women at women's doors' I will not say that she was the original cause, but she certainly allows the evil to remain, when it is in her power to remove it.

So long as women receive without demur, as lovers and husbands, men whom they know to be of loose morals, or, rather of no morals; so long as they overlook sins in a man which they would condemn in a women; so long as they laugh at young men's "indiscretions" or carelessly remark, "You can't expect men to see these things as women do, they are different you know;" and worse than all so long as wives say, with a satisfied air, my husband is no worse than other men," just so long will men live on in the old way, cling to the old opinion and remain on the old level, Alas, how low that level is!

If women would demand that men should live as pure and true lives as men demand of women, then would begin the redemption of the world. This I fully believe. But I have little hope of any improvement in morals until women arouse themselves and take a decided stand against immorality, until they refuse, ay, refuse, I know what I am saying, to marry men who do not live strictly pure lives, who cannot reach to them as clean a hand as they expect to receive.

Young women must no longer excuse sins under the name of "wild oats" which young men must of necessity sow; they must no longer draw aside their skirts from the woman who offends, while they reach out a hand to the male offender. Mothers of dissolute sons must no longer sigh, "Oh, if he would only fall in love, and marry some good girl, he might reform." They must rise above such cruel selfishness: selfishness of the worst type. Is this for what our daughters are made? Have they no higher mission than to sacrifice their whole future, that a man may, peradventure, leave his evil ways for a little while?

Away with such blasphemy. Women arise and assert your right to demand as clean a heart and hand at the altar, as you yourselves are expected to carry thither, and accept nothing less.

GENERAL INTELLIGENCE.

The Seventh Day Baptist Anniversaries were held this year in Westerly, R. I., with a large attendance. This body of Christians, numbering 7000 in this country, are raising a memorial fund of $100,000, one half of which is subscribed.

There are 800 Protestant Sunday Schools in France. The Reformed Presbyterian Synod adopted the following on titles: *Resolved*, that wherever the clerk has appended to any member's name the capital letters D. D., he be directed to strike them out." The Theological school of the same body opened this Fall 10 students.

The Illinois Wesleyan Conference met at Kishwaukee last month, Rev. J. M. Snyder, member of the Executive Committee of the National Christian Association, presiding. This Conference raised $1652 for the Wesleyan Publishing House.

The Illinois Conference of the Free Methodist Church was held the first week of the month in Winnebago. This conference numbers 1,346 with 31 preachers. Since its organization in 1861 it has sent out three branches, now grown on distinct bodies: the Michigan, the Minnesota and the Kansas and Missouri Conferences.

The summary of the reports of the American Board for the past year is follows; recipts, $331,000; mission fields 19; station 70; out stations 466 ordained missionaries, 143; female assistants, 199; whole number from this country, 352; native pastors, 104; native teachers, 406; native pupils, 134; churches 197; church members, 9,435; added during the year, 704; training and theological schools, 12; common schools, 496; whole number of pupils, 18,644.

Rev. George Kerry, an English Baptist missionary, writes of a kind of a religious awakening spreading all over Bengal, among both Hindus and Mohammedans: while Rev. R. Bion, of the Dacca Mission, avows his conviction, with regard to the wide region over which his journey extends, that "the number of those who secretly believe in Christ is as great, if not greater, than the number of baptized believers in all our stations put together."

COTTON ON THE PACIFIC.—It is estimated that the cotton crop of California in 1873 will amount to about one thousand bales, of which nearly one half will be exported. Speaking of this crop the San Francisco *Alta* says: "No sales have been made yet, but the price will probably be twenty cents per pound, at which price it will net twice as much per acre as wheat. The picking was commenced two weeks ago, and will be continued until frost, which usually comes in Fresno Co., the middle of the cotton district, about the middle of October. The bolls are beginning to open in the fields, and none of the fields will be caught, before maturing, by the frost, as some were last year. The general opinion of farmers from Merced to Bakersfield is favorable to cotton, and an enlarged area will be planted with it next year."

THE YELLOW FEVER SOUTH.—The latest accounts from Memphis indicate no abatement in the ravages of the yellow fever at that place. As late as last Saturday, citizens continued to leave the place, as the epidemic was spreading to the heart of the city. Eighty deaths were reported during the previous twenty-four hours. Many people who have overtasked themselves in their labors for the sick and are physically exhausted take the fever and die in a comparatively short time. Appeals for assistance for the sick and convalescent are responded to, as the Howard Association acknowledges in a circular it has published. The officer says: "We return our heartfelt thanks to our sister cities and towns for the bounteous aid extended to us in this hour of sadness and distress. From Boston to San Francisco; from Lansing to New Orleans; from almost every hamlet in the land, and even from far off Old England has come such evidences of sympathy as to make our hearts overflow with gratitude, binding us as it does to them with the dearest of ties. The fever still continues its march among us, increasing day by day, taking rich and poor. God only knows when and where it will end. Our receipts for the present are ample to meet our wants and we feel assured that all the aid we need will be forthcoming."

Youth's Department.

MOTHER'S GROWING OLD.

Her step is slow and weary;
  Her hand's unsteady now,
And paler still, and deeper
  The lines upon her brow;
Her meek, blue eye has faded;
  Her hair has lost its gold;
Her once firm voice now falters—
  My mother's growing old.

Her days of strength are over,
  Her earthly joys depart;
But peace and holy beauty
  Are shining in her heart.
The links that bind her spirit
  Relax their trembling hold;
She soon will be an angel—
  Sweet mother's growing old.

My thoughts flow back to childhood,
  When fondled on her knee,
I poured out all my sorrows,
  Or lisped my songs of glee;
But now upon me leaning
  So wearily and cold,
With trembling lips she murmers,
  "Dear child, I'm growing old."

I think of all her counsels,
  So precious to my youth;
How sacredly she taught me
  God's sacred words of truth;
How tenderly she led me
  To Jesus' blessed fold,
Where she will soon be welcomed,
  No longer bowed or old.

The path of daily duty
  Was ever her delight;
She walked by faith and patience,
  And trusted God for sight,
Her hands with useful labor
  Each day their mission told;
Her deeds, like heavenly roses,
  Still bloom, though she is old.

Alas! those hands so skillful,
  Which toiled with loving grace
To make me blessed with comforts,
  And home a happy place,
Those dear hands, pale and wrinkled,
  Are now by time controlled,
They rest in prayerful quiet—
  Dear mother's growing old.

Yet, though her earthly temple
  Fast faileth day by day,
Her soul, with faith increasing,
  Pursues its homeward way:
And when the mists of jordan
  Shall from her sight be rolled,
She'll shine in youth and beauty
  Where spirits ne'er grow old.

O mother, fond and faithful,
  Thou truest earthly friend,
May I be near to soothe thee
  Till all thy struggles end.
And while with sad heart yearning
  Thy form my arms enfold,
I pray in peace to meet thee
  Where saints no more grow old.

"WHAT WILL YOU DO?"

Little boys are often heard to speak of what they would like to be and like to do when they are "men." Perhaps one little boy thinks he will be a farmer, and have plenty of land, to keep horses, cows and sheep, and to raise grain, fruit, and vegetables.

Another may fancy he would like to be a merchant, and live in a large city or town.

Still another chooses to be a doctor, and visit the sick so that the people will be glad to see him if they are ill, and remember him with gratitude when they are well.

All these are very good plans, for all these persuits are necessary to the wellfare of society. We could not do without the farmer, who provides us food, the merchant who sells us clothing, or the physician who is always welcome in the sick room.

But your greatest object should be to do good and tell men about the Savior, that they may believe on him and be saved.

True benevolence leads us to desire the highest happiness of others. And the religion of Jesus Christ is fitted more than all other things to make men happy in this world.

Therefore it is easy to see that people who are benevolent will wish that all mankind may be taught how to gain the favor of God, and how to prepare for eternity. All men know they must soon die, and if they see no brighter world beyond the grave they will shrink from death as from a dreadful foe, and die in hopeless despair. Did you ever my young friend, see a Christian die? Perhaps your own father or mother may have left you, and gone home to Heaven. Perhaps you stood by the bedside and "saw the last struggle, and heard the last groan." It may be your friend died rejoicing in the thought of being so soon with Jesus in that world where there is no sin. How different the scene when a Christian dies from that which is witnessed when the unforgiven sinner resigns his breath.

It is a solemn thing to teach men the way to Heaven, but it is also a great privilege. And if God has forgiven your sins for Jesus' sake, ought you not to show your gratitude to Him by devoting your time, talents, and everything you may possess or acquire to His service? "It is more blessed to give than to receive."—*Cynosure.*

LOAFING.

BY R. M. WOODIN.

In the present generation, many of our young men appear to think a finishing touch to their manners and polish as gentleman can only be attained by frequenting a store or some other public place.

If interrogatated as to their reasons for spending their evenings at stores, they will tell you that such nightly gatherings are planned on the same principle as societies are—a sort of mutual benefit organization.

If the conversation at all times were of a good moral tone, there might be some opportunity for improvement, but the little I have heard of "store talk" has convinced me that the less of it the better, and in my opinion the young man who spends his evenings in stores and bar rooms thinking to be benefitted thereby, is making a great mistake.

A few dollars judiciously invested in good books and papers would furnish any young man with means for pleasant and profitable enjoyment every evening in the year.

There has been and always will be a demand for "brains" and young men possessing good character with plenty of sound and healthful brains, will have a better chance in the world than those young men whose intellect are muddled with the fumes of beer and tobacco.

Loafing is sinful because it is a waste of precious time. Our life is short at the utmost and we can do but little, yet we should "work while the day lasts." It is a poor way to "bury the one talent" in a barroom. Loafing becomes a fixed habit in a short time, and this habit becomes stronger and stronger until people say,—"That fellow is a confirmed loafer."

Look at this subject in whatever light we may, there can be but one conclusion in regard to it in this enlightened age of the world: Loafing is positively disgraceful.—*Young Folk's Rural.*

BROTHERS AND SISTERS.

"My brother is as polite to me as any one else, when I go out with him," said a girl proudly to a companion. What a reflection on his manners at home! A sister will, perhaps, accidentally knock over some of the tools with which her brother is busy. An apology involuntarily rises to her lips, but she stifles it on considering that it is only Jack; and all the satisfaction he is offered for disordered plans is a blunt "oh!" Angry reproaches are sure to follow. "You are real ugly, Jack, to talk so about a thing, you know I didn't mean it," is the equally angry rejoinder. Why did she say so? Two words would have saved all the trouble. Want of politeness is the cause of more quarreling between brothers and sisters than anything else. In their play, children are constantly meeting with little accidents for which they should be taught to apologize. I have seen the cheeks of a child flush with anger, his eyes flash, and a little hand raised to strike the unfortunate breaker of the toy, when, as if by magic, the blow was arrested with these words, 'excuse me, I did not mean to."—*Sel.*

A BLESSING ON CARD-PLAYING.—The Rev. William Romaine was one evening invited to a friend's house to tea, and after the tea things were removed, the lady of the house asked him to play at cards, to which he made no objection. The cards were produced, and when all were ready to commence play, the venerable minister said, "Let us ask the blessing of God."

"Ask the blessing of God!" said the lady, in great surprise: "I never heard of such a thing at a game of cards."

Mr. Romaine then inquired, "O't we to engage in anything on which we cannot ask his blessing?" This gentle reproof put an end to the card-playing.

The Weekly Pilgrim.

JAMES CREEK, PA., Oct. 28, 1873.

☞ How to send money.—All sums over $1.50, should be sent either in a check, draft or postal order. If neither of these can be obtained, have the letter registered.

☞ When Money is sent, *always* send with it the name and address of those who paid it. Write the names and post office as plainly as possible.

☞ Every subscriber for 1874, gets a *Pilgrim Almanac* Free.

MANNOR HILL MEETING.

According to arrangement, we left our home on Saturday morning Oct. 18, to attend a Communion meeting to be held at Mannor Hill, Huntingdon Co. At Huntingdon we expected to meet Eld. J. Spanogle who was to be one of the laborers on the occasion but we were disappointed as we found him not—during the meeting we learned he was unwell, hope he was as time would form a justifiable excuse. We do not wish anybody to be sick, but, we would rather have our brother sick on duty, than to be well and off duty. At Petersburg we were told we would meet brother J. A. Sell of the Duncansville charge but here again we were disappointed, and began to feel as if the laborers would be few in number and in this we were not disappointed, as ourself and Bro. Archy Vandyke were the only ministers present, outside the district in which the meeting was held. The resident ministers were Eld. J. R. Hanawalt and Geo. S. Swigart. At Petersburg we were met with conveyances by brother Budd Harshberger and in company with Bro A. Vandyke, his wife and daughter and several others, were taken to his home, where our wants were amply cared for. The first appointment was made for Saturday evening, when brother Vandyke addressed an attentive congregation from, "Man giveth up the Ghost, and where is he?" The subject was well chosen and proved to be instructive and we hope beneficial to the congregation. For the night, we with a number of others, were kindly cared for, by friend Kocher, of Mannor Hill. On Sunday A. M., we again met in the same house for public preaching, with quite a respectable congregation, after which we with quite a number of others, enjoyed the hospitality of friend Snyder of the same place. In the evening we met for the purpose of participating in the ordinances of the Lord's house, and we truely had a pleasant waiting before Him. The congregation was unusually large, for the place, and the interest manifested, showed that many were anxious to learn of the way that is everywhere spoken against. During the evening it continued raining, and by the time the exercises closed, the weather was very unfavorable, especially to those who had a long distance home, and it was very wet and exceedingly dark. We were among the favored and felt thankful for it. On Monday A. M., was the last appointment. Though it continued to rain, there was a nice little assembly came together, when brother Samuel Powel, who was chosen the day before, was installed to the office of deacon, after which there was public preaching until 1 o'clock, when the meeting closed and the parting hand was given, and from the general expression, many were loath to leave the place where they had been so richly fed with the bread of Heaven, but so it is. With our sweetest enjoyments of earth, the bitter is mixed. We then with a number of brethren and sisters, were taken to the home of brother Hershberger, where we received all the care that kind hearts could suggest or hands perform. As the weather continued to be too disagreeable to drive out, we were all prevailed upon to sojourn until the next morning. This was not according to our program, but there was so much liberality manifest, and the company so good, we consented with a right good grace, and believe, lost nothing by it as the afternoon and evening was spent very pleasantly. On Tuesday morning we were taken to Petersburg and in a short time, were at Huntingdon where we remained till evening, arrived safe at home about 7 o'clock.

This meeting was held in an old Presbyterian Church in Mannor Hill, a small village situated in Stone Valley. The people are sober, enterprising and charitable, and are religiously inclined and largely of Quaker descent. The members are considerably scattered, about 24 in number, and are under the Spring Run charge. They now have two deacons, Budd Hershberger and Samuel Powell, but no minister as yet. It is expected that Bro. Archy Vandyke will move among them again Spring, when it will probably organise, which would seem advisable under present circumstances, as the Spring Run brethren have a long road to travel to fill the appointments.

We had intended to give a short sketch of how the Brethren first started in this valley, but our space will not admit it. From the general impression we think the field to be one of promise, and that by a well directed effort, considerable may be expected of Stone Valley.

OUR APPEAL.

Those of our agents and readers who have heeded our call by sending us our dues will please accept our thanks. Those who have not yet responded will much oblige us by doing so at their earliest convenience, as the time will soon be here to renew for 1874, and all old accounts should be settled before entering your name for the next volume. Those who live a distance from their agent may send it at our risk if enclosed in a plain yellow envelope and properly directed.

OUR ALMANAC & PROSPECTUS.

Next week, we expect to send to all those who have been acting agent for us, the *Pilgrim Almanac* for 1874 and Prospectus, and we hope our agents will get to work at once, and not cease until they have doubled their last years list. Take the Almanac with you and if it gets soiled we will send you another. Remember every subscriber gets one FREE.

☞ If any who have not heretofore been agents for us and wish now to accept it, they will please inform us and we will send an *Almanac* and prospectus *free*.

NEXT WEEK.

For next week we have some interesting correspondence which was crowded out of this No. With the arrangement we are now trying to make, we hope to make the Pilgrim for 1874 more interesting and instructive than any previous volume. Do not forget that it is to be enlarged without raising the price. We are prepared to hold out greater inducements than ever before

CHANGE OF ADDRESS.

Eld. A. J. Correll, from Forest City Mo., to Craig, Holt Co., Mo.

Samuel Myers, from Barnettscreek to Adamsboro, Cass Co., Ind.

Any of our patrons having No's. 31 and 41. will please preserve them as they will be wanted.

MONEY LIST.

Leonard Furry	$13 00	Jno W Wells	5.75
— Crumpacker	1.00	R J Reynolds	1.00
S M Lutz	9.25	S G K	3.00
S A Moore	4.70	Jos H Souder	2.25
R A Snowberger	3.00	Saml Musselman	1.00
A J Williams	1.50	John Dale	2.35
S A Moore	5.00	R S Zook	1.50
J B Replogle	1.00	Nancy Schrantz	40
A Showalter	3.00	Isaac Showalter	1.50
O W Miller	1.50	J S Newcomer	1.25
Wm Strayer	1.50	J H Biddle	1.50
J S Garman	1.50	Archy Vandyke	1.50
D M Foglesanger	1.50	C H Walker	12.00
M McCaughan	1.50	J C McMullen	8.75
J Y Heckler	1.50	S C Satterfield	4 00
David Moore	1.50	Jacob Stever	1.00
G W Fesler	2.40	S Myers	85
Jas Wilders	1.75	D F Good	10.00

Correspondence.

A Reporter is wanted from every Church in the brotherhood to send us Church news, Obituaries, Announcements, or anything that will be of general interest. To insure insertion, the writers name must accompany each communication. Our Invitation is not personal but general—please respond to our call.

CHURCH NEWS.

Fayette Co., W. Va. Oct. 14, '73.

Dear Pilgrim;—My time has been so occupied I have failed to give you any jottings of late. Will now at this midnight hour pen you a few items. Sept. the 13th, attended a Lovefeast with the Brethren in Raleigh Co. The weather was somewhat unfavorable, but we had a happy meeting. The congregation in Raleigh is prospering finely. There has been a number of additions lately, and all seems to be in union. One pleasing feature, we noticed, a good number of the communicants were quite young, and their peaceful happy countenances, gave evidence, they were not ashamed of Jesus or the Gospel order of the church,—all being in order. Sunday morning I had to leave the place of meeting to attend a funeral. Learned there was a good attendance, at 11 a. m., and an unusual good meeting. A few days after, some more were added to the Church by baptism. The afternoon of the 26th of Sept. I went aboard the cars, and speeded my way to Alderson station, in Greenbrier Co. where I was met with a conveyance by Bro. Wm. Probst, and taken to his home. Passing the Blue Sulphur Springs about 9 o'clock at night, a campmeeting was in progress. We called, we saw, and then left next day. Had preaching at a school house, and at night, with the brethren and sisters had quite a blessed communion season, at the home of Bro. Probst. The attendance of spectators was small, owing to the campmeeting near by. "Where the carcass is, the eagles will be gathered together." Next day at 11 a.m., meeting again at the school house, good congregation, one applicant for baptism At 4 p. m., meeting again at Bro. Propst's which was our last appointment, We had expected to meet at the communion meeting, some other laboring brethren, but was disappointed, so we had only one of our colaborers, Bro. C. H. Masters, to assist us. Brethren don't neglect that point, much good might be done there. At night, with others, we walked down to the camp meeting ground. The sermon in the main was good enough, but the disorder that followed was "Confusion worse confounded." The mesmeric influence was of a spasmodic type. From such religion may we ever be delivered. Monday morning Bro. Wm. Probst kindly took me to the station, and at noon arrived at home. Following Friday, Oct. 3d, we had a Communion meeting at Bro. Harrison Conner's near Mt. Cove, this county, had a refreshing season of love with the dear ones of the household of Faith. Preaching next day at 11 a. m., at same place.

Oct. the 11, our Lovefeast came off at our meeting house. There was a large attendance of members present and a crowded house of spectators. Bro. Jas. M. Hutchison from Monroe, Bro. Wm. Baily from Raleigh and Bro. C. H. Masters, were our ministerial help, outside our immediate congregation. We had a feast of good things, indeed. Next morning at 9 o'clock the church met in prayer and devotional exercises when a choice was held for more laborers in the Lord's harvest field. Bro. G. W. Crouse and Bro. Samuel Riner were called and regularly installed into the the ministry. Bro. Henry Sanger to the deacons office and Bro. C. H. Masters and Bro. Joseph Hutchison were advanced to the second degree in the ministry. Public preaching then followed to a large congregation. The exercises were impressive. To many it was the parting hour from us, and we from them, not knowing whether we shall ever meet again on earth, but the hope of meeting on the other shore sweetens the moments of sadness and sorrow. At our meeting two precious souls were added to the number by baptism, and four came out expressing a desire to unite with the church, and others gave evidence they are going to leave the ways of sin and folly, and turn to God hoping for mercy. We shall long remember those meetings as green spots in the desert through which we are passing, traveling to a country where all is peace, love and bliss.

Blessed be God for his goodness.

Truly yours in love

J. S. FLORY.

HOTEL LONDRES, PARIS, }
Sept. 22, 1873. }

My dear father and Sarah:—I have written you but two weeks ago, but I did not then know our address in London, I will now enclose an envelope with our address. I am so anxious to hear from you, having received but one letter from you since we are in Europe. We are all very well and have been all Summer, which we have great reason to be thankful for.

The boys do not seem to learn French as fast as they did the German, they like the German much better. Olive is the only one that speaks French. We like the French people very much, they are very polite, and very neat and clean. We were up on the gate called the Arch of Triumph, where we had a view of the city. There is no use in my trying to describe this immense city. It looks perfectly wonderful to me. I do not know how many miles Paris covers. I used to think Philadelphia was large to look over, but it seemed to me the other day it could be put in Paris and it would not make much impression. We have visited a great many places of interest here. We visited Napoleon's first tomb, and have stood on the spot where Marie Antoinett was beheaded and her husband, Louis XVI, and thousands of others. France has a sad and bloody history. We also visited two suburban towns. Versailes is one hours ride by cars, and is a very interesting place. There is a beautiful Palace there, and the grounds and fountains are very fine. It was the home of Marie Antoinett, Napoleon the first, and many others we take an interest in. We also saw Napoleon's firsts carriage, and Josiphene's and Napoleon III, and many others. We also visited St. Cloud, forty minutes ride by cars. This place was occupied by the Prussians in the late war, and was fired into by the French and destroyed, and afterwards the Prussians set fire to the town and burnt it. We saw the finest water works that we ever saw; it is said to be the finest in the world. We have been in some very fine churches here, and have seen a great deal in Paris. I do not know how long we will stay in Paris yet, but expect to go to London in about two weeks. I do not know how long we may remain in London, but I hope to hear from you while we are there. We have not decided what time we will leave for home, but expect to get home some time in December if our lives are spared.

We have had a good many rainy days since we are in this city, it seems very Fall like, the leaves on the trees have turned quite yellow. The air feels like October weather, but it is cool and very pleasant. As Fall weather comes on I feel that I would like to be at home. I think we are all beginning to feel as if we wish we were there. I do dread crossing the ocean, we were so sea sick coming over and I fear it may be worse late in the Fall. Give my love to Yoder's family and friends. I never had a letter from Gander, I wrote to him. Lots of love for yourself and Sarah, and hope you are both well.

From your daughter,

N. L. SPROGLE.

PYRMONT, IND., }
Oct. 15, 1873. }

Dear Pilgrim:—On last Saturday the 10th, we went to a Communion Meeting in the Monticello Church, White Co., Ind., in a buggy, started before day, took breakfast at Delphi, then proceeded on to the meeting.

The Brethren had already assembled and had commenced the service. Eld. Isaac Bilhimer spoke first, followed by ——Freeman, brother S. Ulery of our District, Fairview, closed. After the close of the meeting it was announced that there were two applicants for baptism. Then it was announced that arrangement had been made by the members to feed the multitude. A sumptuous repast was then partaken of by all present. After dinner went to the water where the holy ordinance of baptism was administered to the two applicants mentioned, one the wife of a young brother lately put to the ministry, and the other a daughter of Eld. Miller of the Palestine District. O the tears of joy that were shed by those brethren! Truly there is more joy over one sinner that repenteth, than over ninety and nine just persons. Bro. Joseph Amich administered the ordinance. In the evening the holy ordinances of the Lord's house were observed; everything went off in good order, and nothing occurred to mar the feelings of any one. On the following morning we listened to farewell discourses by the brethren. Then the time came to part. We were almost led to exclaim,

"O could we stay with friends so kind,
How would it cheer my troubled mind."

I shall not soon forget the friendly associations formed with the Brethren of White Co. Started home about noon in company with Eld. Isaac Bilheimer, arrived there safely at 5 p. m., found my family well for which I feel thankful.

During our brief visit one of our brethren in the North Fork District was consigned to the narrow limits of the tomb, speaking to us in tones that cannot be misunderstood that "we have no continuing city here," but oh, let us seek one to come, eternal in the heavens, where we can ever be with the loved ones that have gone before, that have "washed their robes and made them white in the blood of the Lamb." This is the desire of your unworthy brother,

JOSEPH ZAHN.

Dear Pilgrim:—It may be interesting for you to know that on Sabbath, the 5th day of October, the members of the Mexico Church Ind., met at their commodious church-house, near Mexico, to once more celebrate the sufferings and death of our Lord and Savior, which he endured on that memorable hill of Calvary.

The attendance was large, the whole country was out, besides numbers of members from the adjoining churches. And what made the crowd doubly large, was the running of two excursion trains on the Eel River Valley R. R., which brought in hundreds from other counties that otherwise would not have been there. We cannot say how many were in attendance, but we do know that they numbered in the thousands considerably, neither do we know how many members were in attendance, but think there were over 400 that communed. The meeting commenced promptly at 9 o'clock on Sabbath morning at two places. The sermon in the house was delivered by Eld. A. Shepler from Pipe Creek Church; and out doors by Elder A. Miller, from White Co. The ministers present were Elders Jacob Metzgar, Abram Shepler, ——Mohler, Abram Miller, Myers, Bowser and others.

The preaching was effective, so that one soul was constrained to turn to the Lord and was baptised, and from appearance we should think that others were favorably impressed, so much so that we trust before the lapse of many more such seasons, they will show by their upright walk and holy conversation that it was good for them to be there.

On Monday morning after the multitude had taken breakfast, prayer &c., being offered, the brethren began their farewell addresses. Indeed some were feelingly addressed, and all were made to feel the solemnity of parting, after being together on so solemn an occasion. Some old ones that never expect perhaps to meet again with their brethren and friends on such occasions, while some younger ones have already been called to a country too far distant that they will never meet their friends again in this world.

May God add his blessing to all that has been done and is being done, according to His will, is the prayer of your weak brother,

J. B. LAIR.

Mexico, Ind.

MARRIED.

JOHNSON—DUEISE.—In Fayette Co., W. Va., Oct. 5th, by Eld J. S Flory, sister Henrietta Dueise to Mr. William Johnson all of Fayette Co., W. Va.

SNIDER—REED.—At the residence of John Anglemyer, Sabbath morning, Oct. 5th, 1873, Mr. Joel Snider to Miss Mary Reed both of Elkhart Co., Ind.

MILLER—KAGARICE.—On the 19th of Oct., at the residence of of John S. Berger, near New Enterprise, by the undersigned, Mr. John H. Miller and Miss. Susan E. Kagarice, both of Bedford Co. Pa.

CALLITHAN—GARRETSON.—Also on the same day, by the same, at the residence of L. B. Snowberger, Mr. Daniel Callithan to Miss Margaret Garrettson, all of Bedford Co., Pa.

S. A. MOORE.

SCOTT—LAMBERT.—At my residence, Aug , 7th 1873, Mr. F. M. Scott to Mrs. Mary J. Lambert both of Holt Co. Mo.

A. J. CORNELL.

KNISLEY—ENGYEART.—At the residence of the bride's mother, near James Creek, Huntingdon Co., Pa., Oct. 16, 1873, By Eld. George Brumbaugh, Eld. John Knisley of Marshall Co., Ind. and sister Rebecca Engyeart of Bedford Co, Pa.

DIED.

STROUGH.—August 31st, 1873, Nora Strough, infant daughter of Abraham and Elizabeth Strough, aged 10 months, lacking 1 day. Funeral discourse by the brethren on the first Sunday in September near Craig, at Miller's school house, in Holt Co., Mo.

A. J. CORNELL.

ROHRER.—In the Antietam Arm Oct. 9, Eld. Joseph Rohrer, aged 63 years, 8 months, and 0 days.

Bro. Joseph was absent attending a Lovefeast in Adams Co., Pa., when taken sick. On the fourth day after becoming sick he was taken home with an improved condition of health He continued to improve, and the sickness seemed to promise a speedy recovery, but on the afternoon of the 9th, suddenly the hand of death was laid upon him and in a few minutes breathed his last; even the family were not conscious of it until the spirit had gone.

D. F. GOOD.

P. S. I will give a more detailed account of his sickness and death next week.

D. F. G.

DORR —On the 9th inst., near Shady Grove Annie Clara, daughter of brother H. F. and sister Eliza T. Dorr, aged 1 year, 8 months, and 15 days.

MILLER.—On the 10th inst, near this place Antietam Church, sister Nancy, wife brother John Miller dec'd, aged 70 years, 9 months, and 21 days.

SAYGER.—On the 10th day of Oct. 1873, Cora A., daughter of brother Ira and sister L. J Sayger, aged 7 months, and 6 day. (In the Mexico church) Funeral services by brethren Fisher and John Elkenbury from Mark 10 : 13,14.

J. B. LAIR.

BEILER.—In the Union District, Marshall county Ind., Oct. 1st '73, our much respected friend and brother John H. L., son of our beloved brother Samuel and Mary Beiler, aged 25 years, 5 mos. and 5 days

He leaves father, mother, and two brothers and two sisters to mourn their loss. During his affliction his mind was heaven ward, and he made the necessary arrangements for death. He desired baptism which was done in the name of the Father and Son and Holy Ghost, in which he rejoiced in the Lord and was very happy; he asked those present to sing for him, and then he would sing: "O come angel band." Then called father and mother to his bedside and bade them farewell, also his brothers and sisters, and told them to meet him in heaven He also called his comrades and preached to them that they could hardly endure it. Such a time has never been witnessed by those present. Thus he died, in full assurance of a home in heaven. May we meet him in that blissful land is our prayer. Funeral preached by brother Jesse Calvert, to a very large concourse of people.

A. APPLEMAN.

LITERATURE.

A. B. Brumbaugh, Huntingdon, Pa. Literary Editor.

APPLETON'S JOURNAL, though issued in weekly parts is put up in monthly parts sewed and trimmed. Every third part contains five weekly numbers. Price of parts containing four weekly numbers fifty cents, of those containing five numbers fifty cents. Subscription price $1 50 per annum. The regular subscription price of the weekly numbers is $4.00, and it is one of the cheapest and best periodicals published in the country. We will furnish it with the PILGRIM at $1 75 for both. D. Appleton & Co., New York, Publishers.

POPULAR SCIENCE MONTHLY, conducted by E. L. Youmans, and published by D. Appleton & Co., is a monthly publication containing instructive and attractive articles, original, selected, and illustrated from the leading scientific men of different countries, giving the latest interpretations of natural phenomena, explaining the applications of science to the practical arts and to the operations of domestic life. In its literary character it aims to be popular without being superficial, and commends itself to the intelligent reading classes of the community. Its contributors are men who know their subjects, and who address the new scientific public for the purposes of exposition and explanation. It is a valuable monthly, of about 130 pages, now commencing its fourth volume. We will furnish it with the PILGRIM at $5.50 for both.

PLAIN EDUCATIONAL TALKS with teachers and parents. By A. N. Raub, A. M., (Claxton; Remson & Haffelfinger, Philadelphia, Pa.) This book though not entirely new is still as interesting, valuable and no doubt will prove as fresh to many who should have read it, as though it had just issued from the press. Prof. Raub is a practical teacher and one of our most esteemed educators. Being a "Normal Schoolmate" of ours we had the opportunity, and learned to know his worth, and can appreciate his book, as the production of one who "knows whereof he speaks." There is so much to learn in relation to the training and teaching of children, that has not been learned and that by those who are much concerned, that we advise every parent and teacher to embrace every opportunity to obtain good ideas on this important subject, and such will find this book worthy of careful reading. Price $1.50. For sale at this office.

BOOKS RECEIVED.—From HURD & HOUGHTON, *Riverside Press, Cambridge, Mass.* Outlines of Men, Women and Things. By Mary Clemmer Ames. 16mo. cloth, $1.50.

SONGS from the OLD DRAMATISTS. Collected and edited by Abbe Sage Richardson. 1 vol. small quarto. Cloth gilt, $3.00.

BOARDING-SCHOOL DAYS. By Vieux Moustache, with Illustrations by Nash and Darley. 1 vol. beautifully bound, $1.50.

THE LAST POEMS OF ALICE AND PHEBE CARY, edited by Mary Clemmer Ames. Crown 8vo. cloth, $2.00.

For sale at Wm. Lewis', Huntingdon, Pa., or may be ordered from this office.

POPULAR SCIENCE MONTHLY.—Oct and Nov., 1873, D. Appleton & Co., New York. $5.00 per annum.

Sunday School Books

The Bible & Publication Society

Have determined to make Sunday Schools the following very

LIBERAL OFFER

for the remainder of the Society's

JUBILEE YEAR.

We will sell you for Cash:

$400	worth of	Sunday-school	books for	$300
200	"	"	"	150
134	"	"	"	100
100	"	"	"	75
66	"	"	"	50
34	"	"	"	25

We make this offer *only for the next four months.* It will close February 28, 1874.

We have on hand at the present time an unusually choice assortment of the best Sunday-school Library books, and can make you a selection that I know will please you. Address, B. GRIFFITH, Sec'y.

530 Arch Street,

Co. 28 3t. eow Philadelphia, Pa.

GOOD BOOKS.

How to read Character. Illus. Price,	$1.25
Combe's Moral Philosophy,	1.75
Constitution of Man. Combe,	1.75
Education. By Spurzheim,	1.50
Memory—How to Improve it,	1.50
Mental Science, Lectures on,	1.50
Self-Culture and Perfection,	1.50
Combe's Physiology, Illus.	1.75
Food and Diet. By Pereira,	1.75
Marriage. Muslin, $1.50.	
The Science of Human Life,	3.50
Fruit Culture for the Million,	1.00
Saving and Wasting,	1.50
Ways of Life—Right Way,	1.00
Footprints of Life,	1.25
Conversion of St. Paul,	1.00

Man and Woman: Considered in their Relations to each Other and to the World. 12mo, Fancy cloth, Price $1.00.

Hopes and Helps for the Young of both sexes, Relating to the Formation of Character. Choice of Avocation, Health, Conversation, Social Affection Courtship and

The Emphatic, Diaglott; or The New Testament in Greek and English. Containing the Original Greek Text of the New Testament, with an Interlineary Word-for-word English Translation. Price, $4.00; extra fine binding, $5.00.

Commercial Institute.

Book-keeping and English branches. Thorough instruction. Education for Business. Can take six students more. Homes provided. Good society. Brethren numerous and preach regularly in town and country. For further particulars please write to D. B. MENTZER, Prin., Waynesborough, Franklin Co., Pa.

WANTED.

A man to work at the Wagon-making business, who understands the trade, and is capable of running a shop independently. Shop and material furnished. Work plenty both heavy and light. A reasonable chance will be given to a suitable person. A man without a family will be preferred. Apply to or address the undersigned.

GEO. BRUMBAUGH,
Grafton, Huntingdon Co., Pa.

DYMOND ON WAR.

An inquiry into the Accordancy of War, with the Principles of Christianity, and an examination of the Philosophical reasoning by which it is defended. With observations on some of the causes of war and on some of its effects. By Jonathan Dymond Sent from this office, post paid, for 30 cts!

TUNE BOOK.

The Brethren's Tune and Hymn Book, is a compilation of Sacred Music adapted to all the hymns in the Brethren's New Hymn Book. It contains over 350 pages, printed on good paper and neatly bound. We will send it to any address, post paid at $1.25 per copy.

Trine Immersion.

A discussion on Trine Immersion, by letter between Elder B. F. Moomaw and Dr. J. J. Jackson, to which is annexed a Treatise on the Lord's Supper, and on the necessity, character and evidences of the new birth, also a dialogue on the doctrine of non-resistance, by Elder B. F Moomaw. Single copy 50 cents.

Historical Charts of Baptism.

A complete key to the history of Trine, and the ORIGIN of Single immersion. The most interesting, reliable and comprehensive document ever published on the subject. This Chart exhibits the years of the birth and death of the Ancient Fathers, the length of their lives, who of them lived at the same period, and shows how easy it was for them to transmit to each succeeding generation, a correct understanding of the Apostolic method of baptizing. It is 22x28 inches in size, and extends over the first 400 years of the Christian era, exhibiting at a single glance the impossibility of single immersion ever having been the Apostolic method. Single copy, $1.00; Four copies, $3.25. Sent post paid. Address, J. H. MOORE.

Urbana, Champaign Co., Ill.

GET THE BEST.

WEBSTER'S Unabridged Dictionary.

10,000 *Words and Meanings not in other Dictionaries.*

3000 Engravings; 1840 Pages Quarto. Price $12.

Webster now is glorious,—it leaves nothing to be desired. [Pres. Raymond, Vassar College.]

Every scholar knows the value of the work. (W. H. Prescott, the Historian.)

Been one of my daily companions. (John L. Motley, the Historian, &c.)

Superior in most respects to any other known to me. (George P. Marsh.)

The best guide of students of our language. (John G. Whittier.)

Excels all others in defining scientific terms. (President Hitchcock.)

Remarkable compendium of human knowledge. (W. S. Clark, Pres. Ag. Col'ge.)

A necessity for every intelligent family, student, teacher and professional man. What library is complete without the best English Dictionary?

ALSO

Webster's Nat'nal Pictorial Dict'nary.

1040 Pages Octavo. 600 Engrv'gs. Price $5.

The work is really a gem of a Dictionary, just the thing for the million.—*American Educational Monthly.*

Published by G. & C. MERRIAM, Springfield, Mass. Sold by all Booksellers.

TRACTS.

"ANXIOUS BENCH RELIGION EXAMINED," BY ELDER J. S. FLORY. A SYNOPSIS OF CONTENTS. An address to the reader: The peculiarities that attend this type of religion. The feelings there experienced not imaginary but real. The key that unlocks the wonderful mystery. The causes by which feelings are excited. How the momentary feelings called "Experimental religion" are brought about, and then concludes by giving that form of doctrine as taught by Jesus Christ and recorded by his faithful witnesses.

COUNTERFEIT DETECTED
OR
BAPTISM—MUCH IN LITTLE.

This work is now ready for distribution, and the importance of the subject will speak for it a large demand. It is a short treatise on baptism in tract form intended for general distribution, and is set forth in such a plain and logical manner that a wayfaring man though a fool, cannot err therein. Either of the above tracts sent postpaid on the following terms: Two copies, 10 cts, 10 copies 40 cents, 25 copies 70 cents, 50 copies $1.00, 100 copies $1.50.

Trine Immersion

TRACED

TO THE APOSTLES.

The SECOND EDITION is now ready for delivery. The work has been carefully revised, corrected and enlarged.

Put up in a neat pamphlet form, with good paper cover, and will be sent, post-paid, from this office on the following terms: One copy, 25 cts; Five copies, $1.10; Ten copies, $2.00, 25 copies, $4.50; 50 copies, $8.50; 100 copies, $16.00.

THE HELPING HAND.

Containing several hundred Valuable Receipts for cooking well at a moderate expense, making Dyes, Coloring, Cleaning and Cementing. This book also points out in plain language, free from Doctors' terms the diseases of men, women and children, and the latest and most approved means used for their cure, to which is added a description of the Medicinal Roots and Herbs, and how they are to be used in the cure of diseases.

This is a work of considerable importance and we offer it to our readers as being a valuable accession to every household. Send from this office to any address, post-paid, for 25 cents.

1870 1873

DR. FAHRNEY'S Blood Cleanser or Panacea.

A tonic and purge, for Blood Diseases. Great reputation. Many testimonials. Many ministering brethren use and recommend it. Ask or send for the "Health Messenger." Use only the "*Panacea*" prepared at Chicago, Ills., and by

Dr. P. Fahrney's Brothers & Co.,

Feb. 3-pd. *Waynesboro, Franklin Co., Pa*

New Hymn Books, English.

TURKEY MOROCCO.

One copy, postpaid,	$1.00
Per Dozen,	11.25

PLAIN ARABESQUE.

One Copy, post-paid,	75
Per Dozen, "	8.50

Ger'n & English, Plain Sheep.

One Copy, post-paid,	$1.00
Per Dozen	11.25
Arabesque Plain,	1.00
Turkey Morocco,	1.25
Single German, post paid	50
Per Dozen,	5.50

HUNTINGDON & BROAD TOP RAIL ROAD

On and after Aug 14th, 1873, Trains will run on this road daily (Sun excepted) as follows:

Trains from Huntingdon South. *Trains from Mt. Dal's moving North.*

EXPS. P. M.	MAIL. A. M.	STATIONS.	MAIL. P. M.	EXP'S A. M.
6 15	7 45	Huntingdon,	AR6 50	AR9 20
6 20	7 50	Long Siding	6 45	9 15
6 35	8 00	McConnelstown	6 35	9 05
6 40	8 05	Pleasant Grove	6 29	8 58
6 51	8 20	MARKLESBURG	6 15	8 43
7 01	8 35	Coffee Run	6 05	8 33
7 08	8 41	Rough & Ready	5 58	8 29
7 15	8 50	Cove	5 49	8 20
7 18	8 53	Fishers Summit	5 46	8 17
7 35	9 10	Saxton	5 35	8 05
7 50	9 25	Riddlesburg	5 15	7 45
7 55	9 32	Hopewell	5 10	7 38
8 10	9 45	Piper's Run	4 58	7 26
8 21	9 57	Tatesville	4 41	7 12
8 32	10 07	Everett	4 31	7 03
8 40	10 15	Mount Dallas	4 30	7 00
9 00	10 35	Bedford	4 05	6 35

SHOUP'S RUN BRANCH.

A. M.	P. M.		P. M.	A. M.
LE 9 20	LE 7 40	Saxton.	AR5 25	AR 7 55
9 35	7 55	Coalmont.	5 10	7 40
9 40	8 00	Crawford.	5 05	7 35
AR 9 50	AR8 10	Dudley	LE4 55	LE 7 25

Bro'd Top City from Dudley 2 miles by stage.

Time of Penna. R. R. Trains at Huntingdon.

***Mail No. 2 makes connection at Huntingdon with Mail going East on Pennsylvania Railroad at 4.15 p. m., and West at 5.45 p. m. Mail No. 1 leaves Huntingdon at 7.40 a. m. on arrival of Pacific Express West.

Trains on this road connect with trains on Bedford & Bridgeport, and Cumberland & Pennsylvania Railroads.

G. F. GAGE, Supt.

The Weekly Pilgrim.

Published by J. B. Brumbaugh, & Co.

Edited by H. B. & Geo. Brumbaugh.

CORRESPONDING EDITORS.

D. P. Sayler, Double Pipe Creek, Md.

Leonard Furry, New Enterprise, Pa.

The *Pilgrim* is a Christian Periodical, devoted to religion and moral reform. It will advocate in the spirit of *love* and *liberty*, the principles of true Christianity, labor for the promotion of peace among the people of God, for the encouragement of the saints and for the conversion of sinners, avoiding those things which tend toward disunion of sectional feelings.

TERMS.

Single copy, Book paper,	$1.50
Eleven copies, (eleventh for Agt.)	$15.00

Any number above that at the same rate. Address,

H. B. BRUMBAUGH,
James Creek,
Huntingdon county Pa.

The Weekly Pilgrim.

"REMOVE NOT THE ANCIENT LANDMARKS WHICH OUR FATHERS HAVE SET."

VOL. 4. JAMES CREEK, PENNSYLVANIA, NOVEMBER 4, 1873. NO. 14

POETRY.

YE ARE THE LIGHT OF THE WORLD.

BY WESLEY

The light that disperses the gloom,
That sin has cast over the land;
Relieving the shades of the tomb,
No power can its progress withstand

The radiance that spans the wide seas,
To gather the erring ones in,
That power sufficient displays,
To crush the dark armies of sin.

The light whose effulgence shall bear,
On its wings, the glad tidings of peace,
Till every nation shall hear
And share in its rapturous bliss.

Oh, Zion! thou light of the world,
Illumine the mountain and plain,
Till satan in fury is hurled
From the throne of his infamous reign.

Thy pillars so massive and strong,
Are founded on infinite love,
To thee all the graces belong,
That center in Zion above.

Oh! glorious light of the cross,
From Calvary's summit sent forth;
Consume from our hearts all the dross,
And purge every sin from the earth.

Go forth then all-conquering light,
No shade can thy fleetness oppose,
Till thou hast thy mantle of white,
Thrown over the last of thy foes.

Then earth shall rejoice in thy peace,
And hushed be the voices that weep;
And righteousness cover her face,
As the waves do the face of the deep.

The lion shall cease to devour,
And dwell with the lamb of the fold;
When light in meridian power,
Assumes her eternal control

Then over the dark realms of night,
From heaven's high dome shall be hurled,
The message, LO THIS IS THE LIGHT,
MY CHURCH IS THE LIGHT OF THE WORLD.

From the *New York Observer.*

GATHERING LILIES.

BY MRS. E. H. J. CLEAVELAND.

"My beloved has gone down into his garden to gather lilies."—Solomon's Song 6: 2.

The Lord went down to his garden, one day,
To gather lilies, the Scriptures say,
And set them again in the borders green
That blossom the heavenly hills between

And just as he came in the sweet old song,
Year after year he has passed along,
Seeking the flowers of the 'sons of men,'
Gathering now as he gathered then.

A miser sat by his bag of gold;
Hundreds of times were its contents told.
'I've gathered the fragments, Lord,' said he,
'All for myself, and none for Thee.'

'Go, scatter it all, your shining store
To feed the hungry and clothe the poor;'
These were the words that the dear Lord said;
'I'll gather you, then, for my royal bed'

And as he went on his shining way
He came where another had toiled all day
In the winter's cold and the summer's heat,
Was he for the heavenly garden meet?

'I have builded churches, great and small,
For all persuasions, and given them all
For the worship of Thee,' he pleading cried.
Then the gentle voice of the Lord replied:

'But you have not offered a single prayer,
Nor bowed your head in those temples fair;'
And there stood a tear in his pitying eye
As he looked on the man, but passed him by

Still looking for lilies, he came again
Where another strayed from the haunts of men;
Trembling, he stood before the Lord,
And made this plea, says the holy word

'I had one talent, but I was afraid,
And safe in this napkin it is laid;
There now thou canst take what is just thine own.'
Then the eye of the Master turned to stone,

And he moved his lips these words to say:
'Coward! thy talent I'll take away;
No leaf can bud and no flower can bloom
On thy naked stem in my heavenly home.'

Then he stood where a pure and simple child
Sat humbly down by a savage wild,
And was telling him o'er and o'er again,
How the Lord came down to ransom men:

And a radiant light from his Christ-eyes fell
As he heard her warning of death and hell.
'Lo! here is a flower in my home to set,'
Said he, and his cheeks with tears were wet

'Since thou hast told with thy feeble breath
The way that a soul can be saved from death,
Thy sins, so many, I'll freely hide,'
The Lord, in his loving-kindness, cried,
"And I'll gather you now, O lily fair;
Come up to my garden and blossom there."

ORIGINAL ESSAYS.

CAN A MAN COME TO CHRIST IF HE WILL?

Dear Brethren: I am a reader of the PILGRIM, and though not a member of your Church, I advocate the principles set forth in the columns of your paper. I will venture a few thoughts upon the question, Can a man come to Christ if he will?

The work of the Holy Spirit, in the regeneration and sanctification of sinners, is described as giving life to the soul. Every faculty of the soul is operated upon, and the understanding is illuminated; the will is subdued, and the affections rectified. In this machine there are several wheels. Some think that there is a propelling power to every wheel; one to the understanding, another to the will, and another to the affection; and that every faculty of the soul will be turned some time before it is launched into Eternity. This view of the subject has puzzled the brains of many, and caused them to make a dilligent search, whether the Spirit of God operates first on the understanding or the will. All the wheels in the machinery of human redemption are cog-wheels; they all turn together, and it is impossible for one to turn without the other. That knowledge which is immediately connected with eternal life, is not merely a speculative, but a feeling, an experimental knowledge of the soul in all its faculties. An unconverted man may have sufficient knowledge to write a good body of divinity, but this sort of knowledge will avail him nothing in the day of judgment. It is not connected with life eternal, for it produces neither peace of mind nor holiness of conduct. There are others who cannot compile a penny catechism; but they know the truth and the truth has made them free.

Without due consideration of this view of the subject, a man may ride his horse against the fence all the days of his life. He may say that the chief difficulty, in the way of a sinner coming to Christ, is in the understanding, but if his head were as light as the head of an angel, while his will is contrary to the will of God—while the carnal mind is enmity against God—the difficulty still remains.

But the moment the bars of the lock of the will are drawn back, to his great astonishment he finds himself in the bosom of his dear Redeemer, clasped in the arms of him whose bowels of compassion yearn over him. If any man, under the sound of the Gospel, is so ignorant as not to know God, and the way of salvation through Jesus Christ, it is because he will not come to a knowledge of the truth. The fact is, all the wheels are turning the wrong way, on the pivot of enmity against God. It is true the understanding is darkened: darkness has covered the whole earth and gross darkness the people; but the understanding may say to the will, there would have been more light in the garret had it not been for the smoke that ascended from the furnace of (loving) darkness more than light. It is the steam below that darkens the windows above. Here lies the mischief. Here is the mother of all the evil. The sun shines as bright as ever; the windows of the house are neither few nor small; but who can see in the smoke of unwillingness? The house of our first parents in Paradise was almost as light as heaven itself, until it was darkened by the infernal smoke arising from the furnace of unwillingness, heated by hell-fire in their wills and affections.

Can a man come to Christ if he will? Most certainly. Who is to hinder him? But who can subdue his stubborn will? The Holy Spirit of God.

Now I imagine I see four men endeavoring to raise Lazarus from the grave. The first is rubbing him well with the salt of duties, under the consideration that he can if he will; but there is no hope of accomplishing the object. Well, said the second; I will whip him with the scorpions of threatenings of hell and damnation. I think I will make him feel; but still there was neither life nor feeling. I have a band of music, said the third, that has made many to dance before now. He tries it, but still there is no life. The fourth said, I will go to Jesus, the God of means; He has promised the Holy Spirit to those who ask him; if Jesus, the resurrection and the life, will undertake the work, he will live. I have heard that He raised Jarius's daughter from the dead,—the power of the resurrection dwelleth in Him. Let this consideration encourage every minister of the Gospel. Nothing less than the operation of the Holy Spirit of God can truly convert the most moral individual; and that agency is able to convert the chief of sinners.

O! that all the ministers of the Gospel would believe this, and turn their faces towards the heavenly wind,—the gale which blows from the New Jerusalem,—the glorious promise in the prophecy of Joel—and pray, O breath! breathe upon these slain, that they may live.

Respectfully submitted.

JOHN B. WRIGHTSMAN.

Amsterdam, Va.

He who rejoices in God will never be confounded or ashamed, world without end. It is an abiding joy. If I rejoice in the sun it sets; if in the earth it shall be burned; if in myself, I shall die; but to triumph in One who never fails and never changes, but lasts forever—this is a lasting joy.—*Spurgeon.*

LET BROTHERLY LOVE CONTINUE

HEB. 13: 1.

Every organization of whatever name design, has some distinguishing or badge or word whereby the members are known to each other. And the inference may be deduced, that so the Church has a mark. That mark is stamped on all the teachings of Christ and the apostles, and is quoted by one of the ancient writers, as proof that those who were called Christians were indeed such. That mark I conclude is *love*, for the heathen word in beholding the dealings of Christains with one another said "See how these Christians love." The theme of the beloved disciple, was love. "Love, says he, is of God" He also says, "God is love." And again, "We know that we have passed from death unto life because we love the brethren." Love then we conclude, is to be the ruling spirit of the Christain, for the first fruit mentioned of the spirit is Love.

In reading over the Epistles, we find, one church particularly commended, "The Thessalonians." Paul writes to them, "As touching brotherly love, "Ye need not that I write unto you, for ye yourselves are taught of God to love one another." This church, in all the purity of its actions, became "Ensamples of all that believed in Macedonia and Achia." And when he wrote his second Epistle to them, he said, "We are bound to thank God always for you brethren, as it is meet, that your faith groweth exceedingly, and the love of every one of you all toward each other aboundeth." Here then we have an instance that human nature is capable of this high attribute of God. This church, composed of members redeemed from idolatry, laid firm hold on the principles of Christianity and practiced them daily. What a lesson for us who have had these truths sounded in our ears from our earliest existence, but who alas! practice more in the letter, than in the spirit. Much is said of love, union &c., by professing Christians all over the land, but do we always remember that "Love worketh no ill to his neighbor, therefore love is the fulfilling of the law." The apostle John, in his 1st epistle, 3d chapter, latter half, clearly defines the position of brethren. Let us then turn to the concluding part of the 12th and whole of the 13th chapter of 1st Corinthians, and following Paul's course of argument and see how he makes brotherly love paramount to all other gifts and graces. The most distinctive feature of the Apostolic church was its possession of supernatural gifts. There was the gift of healing, a particular branch of the gift of miracles. The gift of tongues, sometimes supposed to be the knowledge of foreign languages, but we never read of its exercise for the conversion of foreign nations nor indeed foreigners, except on the days of Pentecost. It would seem from the 14th chapter that the individual from some cause, was in sne'an estatic state perhaps, that he uttered words unintelligible to the bystanders, and it would seem indeed, that his own understanding was suspended. This gift must have been highly esteemed on account of its being strange and wonderful, for Paul speaks at some length on it, but concludes that the gift of prophecy, reveals God's will to us more particularly than foretelling future events, more to be desired than that. But he sums up all the spiritual gifts and comparing them with love, says they are as nothing if that essential be lacking, and in conclusion of his argument says, "If any man think himslf to be a prophet or spiritual, let him acknowledge that the things that I write unto you are the commandments of the Lord." And again he said, "Now abideth Faith, Hope, Love, but the greatest of these is Love."

It is not only essential for new converts, for he says Let brotherly love continue." The promise in every case is to him that overcometh. And in the Revelation which John wrote to the Church at Ephesus, occur these words: "I have somewhat against thee because thou hast left thy first love. Remember therefore from whence thou art fallen and repent and do thy first works or else I will come unto the quickly and remove thy candlestick out of his place except thou repent. And to him that *overcometh* will I give to eat of the tree of life which is in the midst of the Paradise of God.

HATTIE F. MILLER.

JESUS WEPT.

JOHN 11: 35.

As I was made to weep a few days ago over a departed sister, I have had some serious thoughts. To day I was by the bedside of one that had perhaps made but little preparation for the future and as she breathed her last, I was made to weep. The thought struck me, why do we weep? The answer was, because Jesus wept. But this is not fully answering the question.— Then I will first notice that Jesus was not the first to weep, and secondly why he wept.

The prophets also wept. We find Isaiah weeping over the spoilings of his people. Isaiah 22: 4. Jeremiah wept over his people. He says, they are foolish; they are wise to do evil, but to do good, they have no knowledge." Then he complains that he cannot weep enough and says, "Oh, that my head were water, and mine eyes a fountain of tears that I might weep day and night." And he tells his people to "give glory to the Lord your God, before he cause darkness. But if ye will not hear it, my soul shall weep in secret places for your pride, and mine eyes shall weep sore and run down with tears." Jer. 4: 22; 9; 1, 13, 15, 19, 17. When we sum it all up, we see that the prophet wept for the downfall and pride of his people.

Then why did he weep? It seems he wept on his way to the grave of Lazarus. Why did he weep? Did he weep because Lazarus had died?— No, for he knew he was going to raise him again. Did he weep becanes he was not present when he died? No, for he heard of his sickness, but he looked around and saw the stubborn Jews weeping, and he remembered the many miracles he had done to show that he was the Son of God, and now I am even going to raise the dead from the dusty bed, and with all this they still will not believe. This is the reason I believe, why Jesus wept. Then the question comes, why do we weep? Do we weep because our friends die? Of course we feel sad, but when we have a hope and remember that it is the Lord's doings, we should not weep so much.

But there is something else to weep for, when we remember the provisions the Lord has made for us, and bids us come to him. He calls us in many ways. He comes and takes from our midst one who has been engaged in his service, telling us. "Be ye also ready." Next he calls a sinner showing that God is no respetor of persons, and also our mortality, but with all this, we see some heedless sinners standing as unconcerned as the stubborn Jews, just as if there will be no hereafter. This causes us to weep.

Brethren and sisters, let us weep a little more for them and ourselves; let us pray a little more, let us pray with a little more zeal, and let our light shine a little brighter that they may see our good works.

Sinners let me say to you, you have no assurance of your life; you are traveling on a dangerous road, you are as it were standing upon slippery rocks while fiery billows roll beneath. All the tears that are shed for you, all the prayers that are offered for you, will not save you unless you render your service to God; your abode will be in everlasting torment. God only wants your obedience. Then dear sinner, think before you die.

"Life is the time to serve the Lord,
The time to insure the great reward"

S. N. WINE.

VALEDICTORY.

J. S. FLORY.

This day my ministerial labors in W. Va., close, for awhile at least, and it may be forever, that is in a personal capacity. I preached my farewell discourse to a crowded house of brethren, sisters and friends; text, last chapter 2 Cor. 11th verse, after which four more precious souls were united to the church by baptism.

I had for a long time considered the propriety or impropriety of severing my personal connection from this field of labor. A peculiar chain of circumstances seemed to force me to the decision I made, and impressions from a higher source than earthly considerations prompted me to this decision. May the Lord's will be done.

I anticipated a severe trial would be my lot, but the realities of that trial was unforeseen in a great measure, for when the time drew near for my departure, I then and then only began to feel what it was to leave the dear ones of the household of faith, and when the hour of separation came it was indeed an hour of sorrow. It was a sad thought to me to leave the congregation where I first was led to know the Lord in the pardon of my sins, as I hope; where I was nurtured with spiritual food; where I was first called to the labor of the holy ministry, and to leave those who imposed such confidence in poor me as to set me with others to feed the flock of Jesus. All these and more were the thoughts that came to my mind, and to this was added the thought what sorrow seems to pervade the souls of those that are to me brothers, sisters, fathers, mothers and children in the faith, and I the cause of that sorrow. O brethren, forgive me for thus leaving you in sorrow, they that sow in tears shall reap in joy. The Lord's ways are not our ways, and it I am recreant in my calling or duty, I hope the Lord will forgive me.

The hope of meeting again, did indeed sweeten the cup of bitterness. In God I put my trust and am willing to do His bidding. If the God of peace remaineth with you, you must prosper. O may the strong arm of His love be around and about you, and though the floods of opposition surge around you, God will comfort you, help you and bless you. May you and my God forgive all my past follies and shortcomings. We will meet again near the grave, nearer eternity, or perchance at the judgment. How shall we meet? Nearer, oh yes, nearer our God, I hope more perfect, more happy, more like Christ, so may it be. Amen.

LET US BE PATIENT.—Let us be patient. As the years wear on towards the deep sunset we are weary at making our near approaches to a reconciliation and real intimacy with God. But do we long for that rest religiously enough to wait for it? stillness is our needed sacrifice. Baffled and broken, the soul must often be, before its immortal strength comes. Humiliation of pride—an utter consciousness of infirmity—to be kept painfully out of our inheritance—all these are the price of conquest. Do not pray for exemption from them but victory by them.—*Huntington*.

A MEMORIAL.

For the encouragement and consolation of the husband, children, friends, and members in general, of the church of Jesus Christ, who feel themselves bereft through the sudden and unexpected departure of sister N D. from our midst.

It is true, we all know this, that this world is not our home; it is not our permanent abiding place, yet we are placed, by our Creator, into this mundane sphere a little season for our mutual benefit, and attachment to one another as probationers for eternity. And if we live in obedience to God's law, we form lovely and peaceful association together: such ties and natural relationship that nothing in this world is able to dissolve. But God, who is the Governor of the Universe, interposes, and for reasons unknown to us, does sometimes very suddenly, by the icy hand of death, snatch asunder the closest, the loveliest and nearest relationship that can be formed; and *where* is the creature that can resist or even may demand of God to know why dost thou thus deal with me? Hence, submission to his will, and willing resignation to his Divine providence in all cases, is acceptable in the sight of God. But we are human, and in consequence our sympathies excite our feelings, and we cannot refrain from weeping, and it is certainly not wrong to do so; for Jesus in his humanity, wept at the grave of Lazarus. "Weep with those that weep," is an apostolic command.

Dear brother, you feel bereft of a devoted wife whom but a few days ago you accompanied to a large meeting; your unworthy Bro. saw her there, cheerful, in reasonable health, apparently bidding fair for a long life. Little did we expect that her mortal remains would be laid beneath the clods of the valley in so short a time; but now she hath left us, we shall see her no more; her sweet voice will be no more heard amongst us here in this vale of tears; the the children's call, the dear and lovely appellation, MOTHER, will receive no response; Silence shall take the room of her ready answers, gloom and solitude occupies her place in your fireside. O, we can compassionate your feeling. Grief, undoubtedly, has stricken your heart and when the unexpected fell-destroyer came, sorrow penetrated your soul, and trouble overwhelmed your feelings and disturbed your mind, we may well imagine. But amidst all these trials, there is a hope that reaches beyond this time. Be of good cheer, persevere in your calling, be faithful unto death; we believe that you can meet her in a better world, for we have a hope that your loss is her eternal gain. If so, you have a gem in heaven, a star added to the constellation of the celestial world. A happy welcome to expect in the church triumphant in heaven, where joy will extinguish sorrow, and gladness shall root up gloom and solitude, death lose its sting, and the grave be swallowed up in victory; faith end in vision, and hope in reality.

And you dear children, you as the tender off-spring of your departed mother, you are now deprived of the further instruction and admonitions of a tender hearted mother. Let her voice be heeded and become fruitful; though she sleepeth, yet she can be heard and obeyed in order to conduce happiness to your undying souls, and minister an entrance into the everlasting kingdom, to meet your dear mother in the embrace of Jesus, with all the redeemed, who are singing the *new song* of redeeming love; gladness and everlasting joy will be upon your head; sorrow and sighing shall flee away. Come to Jesus, unite with your young sister in the service of the Lord. Sustain dear father in his trials, assist him in his devotions, where possible, fill the place of your mother at the family altar, around your fireside, and in the church. By so doing glory will redound upon your head, honor to your name and exaltation to heaven shall be the consequence; and the pleasure of a happy re-union with your mother in the regions of bliss, the final result.

Mother you feel the loss of a daughter, you were loathe to part, but *soon*, SOON your race is run, your journey will be ended; be thou faithful unto death, hope in God, confide in His promises, you shall meet your daughter, happy in eternity. Brothers and sisters, hold fast to that which you have, that no one may rob you of your crown.

"A few more rolling days and years,
Shall bring a period to your tears.
Soon you shall reach that blissful shore,
Where parting will be known no more."

Finally, my brethren, my sisters, let us be of one mind, earnestly contending for the faith once delivered to the Saints, that we may all meet in heaven, never more to part.

LEONARD FURRY.

A MEMORIAL.

SICKNESS AND DEATH OF ELDER JOSEPH F. ROHRER.

On the 3rd of October, in company with his oldest daughter, he repaired toward Marsh Creek, Adams Co., Pa., to attend a Communion meeting to take place, the day following. They remained over night with Elder Joseph Sherly and family near Gettysburg. The meeting convened next day according to appointment, at 1 P. M., and our dear brother was among the number, enjoying himself in meeting with the Marsh Creek brethren. Meeting was opened and our brother Joseph, consented to address the congregation from the second chapter of Philippians and fifth verse. "Let this mind be in you which was also in Christ Jesus." He, in the exposition of this Scripture made some very good and close applications; some soul-stirring appeals in warning the sinner, and also encouraging the faithful on the way to Zion. At the close of his remarks he felt an acute pain in his left arm, to which he was subject, and which seemed to increase in severity, drawing toward his chest and body. After the afternoon service, he went to the house of Bro. J. D. Pfoutz near by. He was deprived from enjoying any further services with us that evening and night. The best medical service was rendered, but notwithstanding he suffered much pain. His wife and son arrived on Monday morning, and remained until Wednesday; he feeling better, and worse by times. On Wednesday, the 8th, they brought him home. He seemed to stand the ride well, only tired. On Thursday the indication of disease seemed to promise a speedy recovery; he rested well. In the afternoon he called for some nourishment, afterward he told his wife and family, he thought he could sleep. The family left the room for some minutes, when his wife returned to see whether he was resting well, when behold! he was just about expiring. He breathed his last apparently without a struggle. The feelings of the bereaved and sorrow-stricken family may be imagined.

On Sabbath, the 11th, his remains were conveyed to their last resting place, at Welty's Meetinghouse, amid a large and sorrowing concourse of friends and people. The funeral cortege consisted of some two hundred carriages, &c.

Thus another of our faithful veterans and standard bearers of the cross, have passed over, while the community has lost one of its worthy and exemplary citizens; and the church one of its devoted members, an Elder and counsellor in Israel, and the family a kind and affectionate husband and father.

To the dear family I would say, we deeply sympathize with you, and may your and our loss be his great gain, and may God who is rich in mercy, grant you grace for the day of trials, and a rich effusion of his spirit for the enjoyment of the Eternal.

D. F. GOOD.

THE LATTER RAIN.

It is very usual in the life of grace for the soul to receive, in after years, a second very remarkable visitation of the Holy Spirit, which may be compared to the latter rain. The latter rain was sent to plump out the wheat, and make it full, mature, ready for the after harvest ripening. So there is a time of special grace granted saints, to prepare them for the glory, to make them completely meet to be partakers of the inheritance of the saints in light.

To some this is given in the form of what is very commonly called a second conversion. "When thou art converted, strengthen thy brethren," was Christs remark to Peter, who was even then a converted man. My brethren, there is a point in grace as much above the ordinary Christian, as the ordinary Christian is above the world ing. Believe me the life of grace is no dead level; it is not a fen country—a vast flat. There are mountains, and there are valleys. There are tribes of Christians who live in the vallys, like the poor Swiss of the Valaise, who live in the midst of the miasma, where fever has its lair, and the frame is languid and enfeebled. Such dwellers in the lowlands of unbelief are forever doubting, fearing, troubled about their interest in Christ, and tossed to and fro, but there are other believers who, by God's grace, have climbed the mountain of full assurance and near communion. Their place is with the eagle in his eyrie, high aloft.

They are like the strong mountaineer, who has trodden the virgin snow, who has breathed the fresh, free air of the Alpine regions, and therefore his sinews are braced, and limbs are vigorous; these are they who do great exploits, being mighty men—men of renown. The saints who dwell on high in the clear atmosphere of faith are rejoicing Christians—holy and devout men, doing service for the Master all over the world, and everywhere conquerers through him that loved them. And I desire, Oh! how earnestly I desire you to be such men. My craving is that all of you, my beloved, who have been watered by the former rain, may also be refreshed by a more than ordinary latter rain, which shall make you more than ordinary Christians, bringing you beyond the blade period and the ear period, into the full corn in the ear.—*Spurgeon.*

SMALL means often accomplish great things. Each of us may do something for others, and true sympathy and loving ministry are never lost.

THE knowledge of evil may help to do good, and assist us to measure its value: every new idea should be to us a new feather in wings that bear upward.

A MUDDY stream, flowing into one clear and sparkling, for a time rolls along by itself. A little further down they unite, and the whole is impure. So youth, untouched by sin, may, for a time, keep its purity in bad company; but a little later, and they mingle.

IT was a saying of Aristotle, that virtue is necessary to the young, comfortable to the aged, serviceable to the poor, ornamental to the rich, honorable to the fortunate, succorous to the unfortunate, ennobling to the slave, and elevating to the noble.

THE SHEPHERD'S VOICE.

There are many voices in these last, perilous times clamoring to be heard, yet there is but one which it is safe to follow, and that is the voice of the Good Shepherd, who said, "My sheep hear my voice, and I know them, and they follow me."—John x: 27. Let us notice some of these voices, and contrast them with the voice of the Good Shepherd, that we who are looking for his immediate coming may learn to distinguish between his voice and that of a stranger, for in these days, if it were possible, the very elect will be deceived.

Spiritualism is lifting up its voice, saying, "Here is the mighty power of God." Beware. "The thief cometh not but for to steal, and to kill, and to destroy." "My sheep know not the voice of strangers," said Jesus.

Again we hear his voice (Matt. vi: 19, saying, "Lay not up for yourselves treasures upon earth;" but who is giving heed to it? There are a few, we trust, but the greater mass are listening to another voice, and grasping the world as never before—heaping up treasures for the last days although the true Voice says, "How hardly shall they that have riches enter into the Kingdom of God!" Let us make to ourselves friends of the mammon of unrighteousness by using it for God and the poor, that when we fail, they may receive us into everlasting habitations. This voice may seem as an idle tale to many, but it proceeds from Him who will judge the world by the word which he has spoken. xii: 48. Who will hear it? "My sheep hear my voice."

Listen again: "How can ye be here which receive honor one of another, and seek not the honor that cometh from God only?" John v: 44. It would seem that many are out of the hearing of this voice, and are listening to the voice of a stranger. While indulging in the vain fashions of the world, bowing at its shrine, seeking its pleasures, and adorning themselves with all the superfluities the wicked one can invent, they do not heed the direction, "Let your adorning be the hidden man of the heart, not the outward adorning of plaiting the hair, or of wearing of gold, or of putting on of apparel, but that of a meek and quiet spirit, which is in the sight of God of great price." 1 Pet. iii: 3. 4. "My sheep hear my voice—they know not the voice of strangers."

When we see the church amalgamate with the world—in "church fairs," "sociables," etc., etc., forgetful of God and mindful of mirth, the attentive ear can hear above the murmur of the throng the voice of the Shepherd, saying: "Come out from among them, and be ye separate, and I will receive you." 2 Cor. vi: 17. "My sheep hear my voice, and they follow me."

When those who profess to be looking for the return of the true Shepherd, habitually absent themselves from the meetings, and yet tax themselves more to attend worldly visits and parties of pleasure than it would be necessary for them to do in order to attend religious services, have we not reason to fear that they have forgotten the Voice which is saying to us; "Forsake not the assembling of yourselves together, as the manner of some is, but exhort one another, and so much the more as ye see the day approaching?" Heb. x: 25. "My sheep hear my voice."

Again, if we join with the vain in foolish talking and jesting, are we not listening to the voice of a stranger more than to the voice of Him who said: "For every idle word that men shall speak, they shall give account thereof in the day of judgment. For by thy words thou shalt be justified, and by thy words thou shalt be condemned."

Once more hear the voice of the Good Shepherd: "If thy brother trespass against thee, go and tell him his fault between thee and him alone." Matt. xviii: 15. "He that hath an ear to hear, let him hear."

To hear this voice effectually, there must be inward stillness and quietness, with full consecration and faith. May the Lord help us to listen to the Shepherd's voice now, that we may be found ready to hear him say in the last day, "Well done."—*Advent Herald.*

GENERAL INTELLIGENCE.

The trial of Edward S. Stokes, for the murder of James Fisk, Jr., in New York City, began October 15. Several days were consumed in getting a jury. The evidence produced thus far is about the same as that given at the other trials. Considerable speculation is had as to the result, and but few expect a verdict of murder in the first degree.

A terrible prairie fire swept over twenty-five miles of country, near the Omaha and South-western railroad, in Saline and Jefferson counties, Nebraska, on Tuesday of last week. Many houses and large quantities of grain were destroyed. At Wilbur ten children were caught in the flames. Three perished on the spot, three others were fatally burned, and the rest terribly scorched. A woman in trying to rescue them received fatal injuries.

THE AUGUST GALE.—The losses caused by the terrible storm in August are summed up thus: One thousand and thirty-two vessels, of which 135 were small fishing schooners, are known to have been destroyed during the 24th and 25th in the neighborhood of the Gulf of St. Lawrence and the Atlantic shores of Novia Scotia, Cape Breton, and New-Foundland. In addition to this large number, over ninety vessels were destroyed by the same storm in its course before reaching Novia Scotia, making a grand total of at least 1, 122 vessels destroyed within a few days. Two hundred and twenty-three lives are definitely reported as lost, and the most moderate estimate of the numerous cases in which whole crews are stated to have been lost, swells this number to nearly 500; while if to this be added the loss of life on land and in the earlier history of the cyclone, the grand total amounts to about 600 lives. The records also show that about 900 buildings were injured or totally destroyed in the same dates by this storm.

RELIGION DEFINED.—A new definition of "Religion" is given by the Rev. J. W. Chadwick in the "Free Religion" Convention last week: he said that the best definition of religion was "Man's sense of of the relations to the powers behind phenomena."

This is something new indeed, and exhibits some of the material of which that convention was composed. If you wish to know whether a man has religion and interrogate him as to whether he has "a sense of his relations to the powers behind phenomena," if he be a man of good judgment, he will tell you you are a lunatic, and it would really strongly indicate it.

UNION COMMUNION.—Referring to the communion service at Dr. Adams church, in which members of the Alliance of all denominations participated, the *Baptist Union* says: "We saw several Baptist ministers present who took the bread and cup with the saints, and gave a good testimony for Christian communion High Churchism received a tremendous blow by this union service. What can proscriptive Episcopalians say in defense of their dogmas when the Dean of Canterbury unites with a Presbyterian ministering the Sacred Supper? How can close communion Baptists persist in exclusiveness when their leading men participate in such a service as this? Surely the Spirit of Christ is dissolving the fetters of sectarianism, and making us all better Christians, whatever may be the fate of customs which have divided us into sects. The influence of that blessed hour in Dr. Adam's church will be most salutary, wide-spread and lasting."

This act on the part of some of the leading men in the Baptist Church shows that either they have no principle at all, or are willing to sacrifice it for the sake of popularity. How any man can claim that immersion only is baptism, and then go and commune with those who are not baptized at all, according to his view, is a question we cannot solve. But "how can close communion Baptists persist in exclusiveness when their head men participate in such service as this?" This is a wonder indeed. It is altogether likely that some of the close communion Baptists are a little more closely allied to Jesus and his word, than to their head men and this solves the mystery as to how they can persist in exclusiveness. They have learned from Him that the Communion is intended only for the Lord's people, and they are those who follow Him in *the* way. That pedobaptists follow Christ in the way is an admission that no true Baptist can make, and when he participates with them in the Communion, he destroys the power of the doctrine that immersion only is Christian baptism. It may seem strange to those who are born of men that Baptists will persist in exclusiveness when some of their leading men have launched out on the sea of popular delusion, but to those who are born of God, it is no strange thing. They do not look to poor, weak, fallible men as a guide. If the spirit of Christ is at work in that convention and its dictates followed, then indeed will the fetters of sectarianism be dissolved. Its office saith Jesus, is to lead us into truth, but whether this spirit is really at work, and whether that grand union Communion will have a salutary and wide spread influence for good is another question.

DESTRUCTION OF WORKS OF ART IN JERUSALEM.—During the recent disgraceful squabble and riot of the monks around Jerusalem there was one incident that should especially pain all lovers of art. This was the destruction of the two pictures by Murillo in the Bethlehem church that fell a victim to ecclesiastical fury. They were true Murillos, and masterpieces; and, what is worse, having been dispatched to the church immediately on their execution, and there retained, it is believed that they have never been ingraved. They were unusually well preserved, too, for, on being placed in the oratory of La Creche, both canvases had been covered with glass to protect them from candlesmoke. One of the subjects was the Nativity, the other the adoration of the Magi. In reading with involuntary indignation and disgust of this barbarious instance of iconoclasm, one is reminded of what Thackeray wrote on the same scene and topic nearly thirty years ago. In his *Journey from Cornhill to Cairo*, speaking of the leading Christian sects in and around Jerusalem, he says, "These three main sects hate each other; their quarrels are interminable; each bribes and intrigues with the heathen lords of the soil to the prejudice of his neighbor. Now it is the Latins that interfere, and allow the common church to go to ruin, because the Greeks purpose to roof it; now the Greeks demolish a monastery on Mount Olivet, and leave the ground to the Turks, rather than allow the Armenians to possess it.— On an other occasion, the Greeks having invaded the Armenian steps which lead to the (socalled) Cave of the Nativity at Bethlehem, the latter asked for permission to destroy the work of the Greeks, and did so. And so round this sacred spot, the center of Christendom, the representatives of the three great sects worship under one roof, and hate each other!" The church of La Creche is, as its name implies, the church of "The Manger" (*i. e.*, the reputed place of the nativity of Christ); and to this spot, and the furious wrangles of which it has been the scene, we may therefore apply the exclamation which Thackeray makes regarding the tomb of Christ: What a place to choose for imposture, good God!—to sully with brutal struggles for self-aggrandizemen or shameful schemes of gain!" The Germans had the grace to try to spare with their bombs the spire of Strawsburg cathedral. Religious fanaticism in the Middle Ages directed itself to the destruction of "pagan art, no matter how beautiful; but in these enlightened days for ecclesiastical fury to take up the barbarious role of destruction, which even savage war discards, is pitiable indeed.—*Lippincotts Magazine*

Youth's Department.

SCHOOL DAYS.

I suppose my little readers are beginning to think that uncle Henry is sick or has forgotten his young charge. I wish to tell you that neither is the case, but there has been so many good things in the PILGRIM of late that I thought I might as well wait awhile, but as the evenings are getting long, my class is doubtless getting larger and therefore will want more good things to read and talk about. School days are now here and my young readers all have the opportunity of going to school and learning to read and write and a great many other things, some perhaps that you should never know or learn. But what I intended to tell you about is the great privilege which you now enjoy over those who were boys and girls thirty or forty years ago. Things were quite different then to what they are now, especially schools. Uncle Henry can well remember when he went to a school house built of round logs and an old fashioned fire place in it something like some of our old wash houses of the present day. Into that a number of large logs were laid and around the poor little shivering schulars gathered, with one side burning and the other freezing. As uncomfortable as the schools were, they lasted only three months, and it was a favored boy that could attend more than half the term.

You may wonder why this was, but you will understand when I tell you that there has been changes in other things beside schools. In those days the farmers had no threshing machines and large separators to thrash out their crops in a few days like they now have but had to tramp it out with horses. To do this, it took nearly all Winter and while this kind of thrashing was going on, it generally took two boys to ride the horses. Uncle Henry was always fond of riding, but this was too much of a good thing and when he got an opportunity of going to school, he capered off with a light heart. So you need not wonder that some of the old uncles do not know so much about Grammar and Geography as some of the young people now do. In those days the young people did not have the many good and pretty books and papers that they now have. You also have many other advantages now that they did not have. I speak of these things to remind you of the great privileges you enjoy, and hope you all will make the best possible use of them. You may not now see all the advantages of a good education, but if you live to become men and women, you will deeply feel the loss of it if you neglect to obtain it. Only a short time ago I heard a man say that he would give two thousand dollars, if he could now have a good education. He was an old man and a minister of the Gospel. He felt that his lack of a good education was a great hindrance in his holy calling.

I just now, think of several young men who when boys, thought it was no use to go to school, but they are now in callings that greatly demand a good education and they now sorely regret that they were so foolish as to waste their golden opportunities. So it may be with you if you neglect the many advantages that you now enjoy.

In conclusion, uncle Henry advises you as one who knows, make good use of your time, go to school every day that you can, and strive to learn as much as possible. You will never, *never* regret it. Remember golden opportunites always run forward, and unless you catch them as they come along they will be forever lost.

UNCLE HENRY.

GRANDMOTHER.

BY ELSIE G——.

For a long time I did not understand it at all. I thought that because grandmothers often were feeble and old-fashioned, they could never really feel as we children do; they needed no particular notice or enjoyment, for it was their nature to sit in rocking-chairs and knit. They seemed quite different from the rest of the world, and not to be especially thought about; that is, by girls who were as full of merry plans as we were.

Grandmother lived with us, as father was her only son. We had a vague idea that she helped mother mend the clothes and knitted all fathers winter stockings, besides some pairs for the church society. We were supposed to love her, of course, and we were never openly rude, for indeed we had been taught to be polite to all aged persons. As for grandmother, she was one of those peaceful souls who never make any trouble, but just go on in their own way so quietly that you hardly know they are in the house. Mother sat with her sometimes, but we girls, in our gay, busy pursuits, rarely thought of such a thing. She seemed to have no part in our existence.

It went on so for some time, till one day I happened at sundown to go into the sitting-room, and there sat grandmother, alone. She had fallen asleep in her chair by the window. The sun was just sinking out of sight, leaving a glory of light as he went, and in this glory I saw grandmother—saw her really for the first time in my life!

She had been reading her Bible, and then, as if there had been no need of reading more, since its treasure already lay shining in her soul, she had turned the book over upon her lap and leaned back to enjoy the evening.

I saw it all in a moment,—her gentleness, her patience, her holiness. Then, while her love and beautiful dignity seemed to fold about me like a bright cloud, the sweet every day lines in her face told me a secret, that even then in the wonderful sunset of life she was, O, how human! So human that she missed old faces and old scenes; so human that she needed a share of what God was giving us,—friends, home interests, little surprises and expectations, loving offices, and, above all, a recognition in the details of our fresh young lives.

Girls! when grandmother woke up, she found us all three stealing into the room; for God had helped me, when I went to tell my sisters about it. Mary only kissed her and asked if she had had a good nap; Susie picked her ball of yarn off the carpet, where it had roiled, and began to wind it, all the while telling her a pleasant bit of news about one of the school-girl's; and I—well, I knelt down at grandmother's feet and just as I was going to cry, I gave her knees a good hard hug, and told her she was a darling.

That's all, girls. But it's been different ever since from what it was before.—*From St. Nicholas for November.*

PROFANITY.

TO THE BOYS OF AMERICA.

DEAR BOYS:—Did You ever see a lovely plant overshadowed and choked by great ungainly weeds, till it had no strength to bud or bloom? Just so the noxious weeds of *Profanity* shadow your character and choke from your heart every sweet blossom of purity and refinement.

I hope there are many among you who never use bad language of any kind, but I want to warn you all against profanity. First it is exceedingly sinful to take the name of God in vain, and how often do we hear the name of our blessed JESUS CHRIST—who died for us—profaned. Any boy has some influence, be it more or less; and if he indulges himself in the use of profane language he places a very bad example before his acquaintances. Besides, this ensnaring practice would surely bring you into bad company and evil companions would lead you to many vices. Vicious boys would soon trace you and flock around you, while the good could find no pleasure in your society. If you have a friend on earth—one who seeks your best interests, you may rest assured that that friend would suffer deep sorrow and humiliation if you were to entangle yourself either with bad associates, or the disgraceful fault of which I have warned you. Every boy should have a certian independence to enable him to stand up for what he knows to be right, no matter who or what resists him. The lack of independence, is the stumbling-block over which very many fall into temptation. Do not be led through the world boys, by a set of loafers, unwerthy to be your leaders. Be independent; have a mind of your own; find where the right is, and uphold it: then you can respect yourself and be respected by others, even by those who desire to lead you astray; while on the other hand, they could not despise you in their hearts, for demeaning yourself in what all know to be wrong.

Putting aside the wickedness of profanity, you cannot be a gentleman in a worldly sense, and use rough or profane language; for this vulgar habit would transform you into an ill bred unmannerly boor, and stamp the unmistakable mark of a nobody upon you, and thus you would be excluded from refined, intelligent society. Who desires to be a *nobody?* Think of this boys, when you are tempted to *swear!* Avoid all slang expressions. They are often the prelude to this vile evil. To those, young or old, who have already formed the habit, I say—"It is never too late to mend." Resolve, at once, that you will prove yourself stronger than the habit. If in a moment of anger or forgetfulness, you fail, do not be discouraged, but try again, and yet again, if need be. Do not despair, I entreat you; but persevere until the hideous monster is trampled under your feet!—*New York Observer*

As travelers in a foreign country make every sight a lesson, so ought we in this our pilgrimage.—*Hall.*

The Weekly Pilgrim.

JAMES CREEK, PA., Nov. 4, 1873.

☞ How to send money.—All sums over $1.50, should be sent either in a check, draft or postal order. If neither of these can be obtained, have the letter registered.

☞ When Money is sent, *always* send with it the name and address of those who paid it. Write the names and post office as plainly as possible.

☞ Every subscriber for 1874, gets a *Pilgrim Almanac* Free.

THE PANIC.

Of late the great theme of conversation is, the panic, *the panic*, and we are commanded to weep with those who weep, and mourn with those that mourn, but at this time, we scarcely know whether to weep or to thank God and take courage. It would be well, just now, to bear in remembrance the sayings of the good old prophet, "The wicked flee when no man pursueth but the righteous are as bold as a lion" and again; "I was young but now I am old, yet have I not seen the the righteous forsaken nor their seed begging for bread"

That the American people had become terribly extravagant is admitted by all, and the more the Lord prospered us as a nation, the more profligate and sinful we became. The goddess of fashion has become the god of the world and millions strew their all at her feet without a sigh of regret, and if a Paul takes the courage to speak against it, the long and deafening cry is; Great is the god of the Ephesians (Fashion). But, says one, what has this to do with the panic? Much in different ways. God works by means and this may be one of the ways of stripping many of the fashionable world of the curse which tempted them into this whirlpool of destruction and give them an opportunity of becoming more sober and reflecting. Desperate diseases require desperate remedies, and if men and women will persist in worshiping gods made with hands, the only remedy is to bereave them by destroying their idols. If extravagance was the cause, the remedy is very evident. Let us cease to be extravagant, and the panic will vanish as the dew before a morning sun. To day, there is more money spent in one month, in sinful extravagance than it would take to feed and clothe all our poor until spring. But Ephraim is joined to his idol and we will be to let him alone, and examine our own situation. The question for us to solve is, what effect will the panic have upon us?

There is a class that, no doubt, will be necessitated to experience some inconveniences during the coming winter. We mean those who were laboring along public lines and public works. But even these, if willing to labor and economize, may be cared for, as, where there is a will, there generally is a way.

Railroad building and manufacturing is a blessing to a country when kept in bounds, but all extremes are dangerous, as these things proved to be. They not only robbed the country of its surplus money but they took from it the motive power. In other words, they monopolized all other kinds of labor. Such inducements were held out by them for labor that farmers and local mechanics could not compete, and as a result they suffered loss, so much so that many of the producers ceased to produce, and became consumers, the fact is, farming did not pay any more especially if it had to be done by hired labor.

The present panic will revolutionize the labor system. The old adage runs: "Ill is the wind that blows nobody any good." We do not make large pretentions in prophesy, but our humble opinion is that, at least, a little of this good will be blown towards farming and local industries, and that eventually, will flow towards all other honest occupations of life. Elevate the producer and we elevate the nation. Starve the mother and the children must suffer. This has been the late policy and the result is before us. Our future policy must be, increase the producers by decreasing the consumers, or feed the mother that the children may grow fat.

There is no necessity for us becoming alarmed, as the panic, to the mass, is more imaginary than real, and what little there is of it, we are helping to make by hoarding up what we should circulate. If all those who have a little surplus money will persist in wrapping it up in a napkin, the result will and must be, hard times. The money is in the country and all we need, is to have it circulated. There never was a better time to invest money in improvements than just now. Produce is plenty and labor and material will be cheap. Such a course will not only benefit the inventor, but will give employment to the laboring class, and thus drive the wolf from their doors during the winter that is now upon us. Our population must be provided for, people will not starve in sight of steaming tables and full storehouses, therefore it will be much better to make arrangements for people to earn their living than to encourage idleness by bestowing to them that for which they can have no opportunities to labor. The circulation of our money, is the only possible remedy for a panic, even, if the government was to issue millions and every one that would receive it would lay it away, the country would be none the better for it. Then let us cease talking panic and go to work. God will help those who help themselves. The one that gained five talents received five more as a bonus, while the one that hid his, had even that taken from him. There is no call for desponding. God is not dead, neither is he sleeping, every storm is followed by a calm and every panic, by its years of prosperity. The wicked flee when no man pursueth, but the righteous will God hold in everlasting remembrance and their seed shall not be found begging bread.

LITERARY NOTICES.

Under the above head we have been noticing such books &c., as are sent us for that purpose. To this, a few good meaning and well disposed brethren take exception, and fearing that there may be others of the same kind, we make an explanation. We have become a reading people, and perhaps, read more good substantial books than any other class of people. On this account we have repeated and numerous queries in regard to books. Our opinion is wanted of certain works, others wish to know where good books can be had, and still others, what kind of books they should read.

Editors are expected to know anything and everything that people are pleased to ask them, and if they fail to give satisfaction, the verdict is, "they have mistaken their calling." Hence, to meet our wants and those of our readers, we have opened a literary column in which we notice and review such books as are sent us by a few of the leading publishing houses. These books are generally of the highest type of morality, and many of them contain just such information as we all should know, the fact is, we do not notice any books that we would hesitate to place before our children. We have been raised among books and therefore claim that our judgment, after examining a book, should have, at least, as much respect as that of those who judge from the titles only. We are aware of the dangerous influence of bad books, and there are none that are more zealous in excluding from our homes and children, books of erroneous or irreligious tendencies than ourself. We are too closely wedded to the sacred cause which we have espoused and the "ancient landmarks," to admit favorable notices of books calculated to lead the enquirer after truth astray.

While a few object to these notices, many commend and consider it quite a favor to be informed of the new and interesting publications. Many of our ministering brethren have went all the way to Philadelphia in order to purchase their books of J. B. Lippincott & Co. Those same books we can furnish, postpaid, as cheaply as they can be purchased in the city unless taken in large quantities. We can also supply books from other publishers at their published prices.

These facts in connection with our notices afford our readers privileges which should not be ignored even by those who do not care to read books. But to avoid every possible excuse for objection, we have determined to enlarge the Pilgrim, thus enabling us to give so much good reading that those who object to book notices will have no time to read them unless they do like it was said of those who objected to the report of A. M., read them first. Brethren, do not be too hard with us. The eighth page we claim for our own use and if, by it we can make a little money to meet the many losses we sustain by careless brethren not paying us our dues, you will not complain.—Please don't.

Prospectus.—Our Almanacs are now ready, and this week we send one containing a prospectus, to each of our agents so far as known to us. We neglected to mark all our agents so that in many cases we could not tell who they were. In such cases we generally sent it to the first one on the list. If we have made mistakes and sent to the wrong ones, we hope they will be kind enough to hand over to the proper person. If any of our agents fail to receive one we hope they will inform us of it immediately and we will send at once. All others who may feel like working for us will be supplied with Almanac and prospectus on application.

Nancy Crouse, The money you sent for your sister's Pilgrim is received, but we cannot remember her name. If you will send her name we will give her credit for the amount sent.

MARRIED.

KAGARICE—OTTO.—At the residence of John S. Brumbaugh, Oct. 23d., 1873, by the undersigned, David E. Kagarice to Miss Mary Otto, all of Bedford Co., Pa.
S. A. Moore.

MOURER—SINGER.—At my residence Oct. 7, 1873. Peter Mourer, near Upton, Franklin Co., Pa., and Sarah E. Singer, near Waynesboro, same county.

BONEBRAKE—WOODS.—Also by the undersigned, at the residence of the bride's son-in-law, Baltimore, Md., Henry Bonebrake, near Waynesboro, Pa., and Mary A. Woods, of Baltimore. All were members of the Church.
J. F. Oller.

DIED.

DOOLY.—In the Yellow Creek Congregation, near New Enterprise, Bedford Co., Pa., Oct. 20, 1873, sister Nancy, wife of Thomas Dooly, daughter of Bro. Daniel Replogle, dec'd., and sister Nancy Replogle, aged 45 years, 7 mos. and 27 days. Her mortal remains were committed to the earth witnessed by a large concourse of people. Occasion improved by the brethren from Thess. 1: 4, latter part.

The subject of this notice was an amiable sister, much attached to the Church, as her seat was never found vacant in the meetings, unless unavoidable reasons. Sudden and unexpected was her departure from the devoted husband and her dear children, of whom 5 are living, one belonging to the Church. May the deep wound struck into their fireside be the means of doubling the seats left vacant in God's church.
Leonard Furry.
(Visitor please copy.)

Correspondence.

Brother Brumbaugh: —Having closed our Communion Meeting on the Merced River, we thought some brethren in the Atlantic States would like to hear from us and our Communion Meetings in California, therefore if these lines will be favored with an insertion in the PILGRIM, the opportunity is offered.

Three meetings were held in a beautiful grove on the bank of the Merced River, five miles from Cressies' Station, on a branch road of the Western Pacific R. R., in Merced Co., Cal., in the San Joaquin Valley. The brethren and friends met on the ground previous to holding the meeting, cleared the ground of the brush and weeds, prepared or erected seats, a stand for preaching, and tent for sleeping for the women, children and aged, the more unincumbered went to barns and houses close by. In preparing the place, the brethren and friends showed a zeal for the blessed cause we profess, worthy of imitation.

Preaching commenced on Friday evening, October third, Saturday 11 o'clock, public preaching, in the afternoon, church council till evening, then preaching, every morning at half past seven, morning worship. Up to this time, Sunday, our labor in preaching the Word was on general principles. Sunday at 11, Trine Immersion was the theme dwelt on, and as the evening drew on, those solemn ordinances were attended to, according to our Lord's direction. At 4 o'clock, public preaching again, on the great theme of the christian passover, from the bondage of sin to the liberty in Christ Jesus, from law to Gospel. That this was not a Jewish institution, for Jesus Christ Himself had instituted it at least 24 hours in advance of the true Jewish time,—that He Himself, as the Lamb of God would expire on a Roman cross for the sin of the world, at the true Jewish time of slaying the lamb.

At five o'clock, Sunday evening, commenced the lecture of self-examination, from 11th chapter of 1st Cor., this done, the supper was all placed on the table, and the members took their seats around it, 7 o'clock Feet-washing commenced. At the reading of the 4th verse of the 13th chapter of St. John, the administrator rose from supper, laid aside his garments and took a towel and girded himself, then poured water into a basin and washed the brothers feet next to him and wiped them with the towel wherewith he was girded. The brother that had his feet washed, washed his next brother's feet, and so on till the last brother at the end of the table had his feet washed, he then washed the feet of the administrator, so every brother washed and wiped his brother's feet and had his feet washed and wiped by his brother. The sisters proceeded in like manner; the salutation accompanied Feet-washing. Then we ate the supper, and as Jesus commanded, so did we, while some were yet eating, the administrator arose, took the unleavened bread, emblematical of Christ's broken body, blessed and brake it, then the brethren brake with one another; in like manner we proceeded with the cup, or emblem of Christ's shed blood,—a hymn was sung and our Communion season closed. The brethren and sisters were made to rejoice, our spiritual life refreshed and strengthened. The very best attention was given by the spectators, who watched every move with profound silence. At the close, some of the spectators were heard to say; "That fills the bill the best of anything we ever saw."

Monday morning, the sun rose beautiful and fair, shining on our little camp ground like it always does in the Summer season in Cal. I thought of Israel's camping at Elim where there were twelve wells and seventy Palm trees; Israel had the type and we the substance.

After morning worship on Monday, 6th of October, the church considered some matters pertaining to the church till 11 o'clock, then public preaching. Between one and two o'clock we went to the river-side where prayer was wont to be made, and baptized one. After dinner we convened again in council, considering the necessity of calling an active, clear-minded, zealous brother to the field of the Gospel, to labor in the different places in California as the church might direct. We have seen the weakness of our present system of preaching the Word, and desire to put forth more Gospel-like effort to send the glad tidings of God's love to a perishing world. Arrangements were made and decided upon for the maintenance of the missionary and family, if he had one. The plan was new to us and was talked over with a good degree of caution, for pride and self-will sometimes clings very closely to those who are called the servants of Jesus Christ. Monday evening was to be our farewell discourse, but at the hour of preaching there came up a shower of rain and disconcerted us for the evening, (an early rain for California.) Tuesday morning we met early on the ground, the sun shone bright, the winds still, the clouds all gone; after singing and prayer to God, thanking Him for His mercy to us, we ate our breakfast together and started for our homes, rejoicing in God and sorry to part with one another.

The cost of the meeting and amount of provision was as follows: 200 lb bread, 230 lb beef, 100 lb pork 440 lb cabbage and sweet potatoes, 100 lb Irish potatoes, 20 lb coffee & tea, 20 of butter, 20 of honey and sugar, pepper and salt to answer the demand, and a cook three days. The contributions by the brethren and friends over reached the cost of the provision $13, which was voted to the preachers to pay their traveling expenses.

I have attended many Communion seasons, but have never witnessed one of more love and zeal on the part of the brethren and friends.

ELD. GEO. WOLF.

Dear Editor of Pilgrim: It was my privilege once in my life to visit your district, and formed during my brief sojourn, the acquaintance of some of the beloved brethren which I shall ever cherish. I first met brother George Brumbaugh at Cross Roads, preaching in the morning, heard a sermon by old brother Geo. Brumbaugh in German. At same place in the afternoon we attended a funeral, the subject a young girl of ten or eleven summers; the bud just nipped as it began to blossom in the parents view, and here I cannot refrain from using a stanza of the poet:

"E'er sin could blight or sorrow fade
Death came with friendly care;
The opening bud to Heaven conveyed,
And bade it blossom there."

On Tuesday morning was solicited by brethren Brumbaugh and Maddocks to attend a Lovefeast in brother James A. Sell's congregation. Bro. Sell, though very young, stands at the head. He much needs the prayers of the church. O that the brethren were more watchful, prayerful and faithful. Stayed over night with brother John H. Stiller whose house consists of six interesting daughters, and what a pity it is that but one has consented to follow Jesus, the way, the truth and the life, while the rest perhaps, have made excuse either to bury their father, or give them good-by which are at home. And he also has six sons, and two have left the ancient landmarks, and have gone in the way of Balaam, the son of Bosor, and after Balak for a reward.

Wednesday we returned to Martinsburg where we had an evening meeting. It is written the Lord can shut and no man can open the door of utterance. Here I made the acquaintance of N. B. Blough, the author of the religious dialogue. Was glad to form his acquaintance, as well as our sister E. R. S., who also contributes to the columns of the PILGRIM. May they consider what they say and the Lord be with them.

Thursday evening we took leave of our dear friends and boarded the cars for Altoona, where we remained over night, next morning, Friday, we took the train for Harrisburg, then changed cars for Hagerstown, tarried all night with our cousin A. Leckilder. Saturday morning we took the train for Brownsville, home, on W. Co. B. R. R.

Our visit was short and hurried, although very pleasant, owing to the contemplated Lovefeast at home, which was appointed on the 11th inst at Brownsville, Washington Co., Md. The weather being very fine, there was a good attendance both of the members and friends generally. The ministers of other congregations present were D. P. Sayler, Hanson Seneseny, David Long, Jacob Trostle, David Rinehart and Jeremiah Brown. The preaching was good and was well received, if strict attention and good order are fair indications.

About eighteen months ago Bro. Geo. D. Bear died, who was for many years the elder of this congregation, and since that time the congregation has been without an elder, but at the recent Lovefeast it was agreed with great unanimity to have Bro. Eman'l Slifer ordained to be elder. His colaborers are Cornelius W. Castle and Eli Yourter. The members of this congregation reside in the southern part of Middletown Valley, Frederick Co., and Pleasant Valley, Washington Co., Md. The principal place of worship of this congregation is Brownsville, within three hundred yards of the Washington Co. branch of the B. & O. Railroad, and about 7 miles east of Harper's Ferry, W. Va. The regular appointment for preaching at Brownsville will be on the 25th of this month, and every two weeks from that time on. We would be pleased to have ministering brethren stop with us when they pass this way. Yours in love.

C. W. CASTLE.

Brownsville, Md.

NOTES OF TRAVEL

J. S. FLORY.

October 20. The day set for our departure has come, and we are on our way with our family, which consists of wife and eight children, for Colorado. The morning was indeed a stormy one, something like 6 inches of snow fell during the night, fruit trees are badly broken, the forest trees are bent near the ground and roads blocked up by fallen trees. Through the snow, we had to make our way seven miles to the Railroad Station. At 12:20 m., we were off all right, aboard the train,—arrived at Huntington at 5:50 p. m. Boat at the wharf awaiting the train, all was bustle and confusion for a time, however, in a little while we were "at home" around a hot stove in the cabin of the Steamer "Exchange," which immediately rounded out and set her head down the beautiful Ohio, for Cincinati. Owing to the extreme low tide of water and dark and rainy night, she struck ground several times and then lay up.

Oct. 21. At daylight the boat was again on her way, the shores are white with snow and it has been snowing all forenoon, the atmosphere is indeed "winterish." As usual, we have a variety of characters on board. A very talkative M. E. minister makes himself agreeable to us. We have aboard a Roman Catholic Priest who looks and acts just like other people. Then we have a fair representation of fashion, folly, and bombastic conceit and selfishness. In their actions, these butterflies of fashion would seem to say, "Wish we could live in a world where we would not necessarily come in contact with plain, humble, modest people" They will get the privilege doubtless by and by, for there is such a world,—to come, however. Also we have to wonder if *they* were ever children, or just born into the world with full grown noses to turn up at every childish wish or whim! One *right we have*, and that is to smile in "our sleeve" at their peculiar sensitiveness.

Oct. 22. Arrived at Cincinati. Last night at 1 o'clock, at the landing, met with brother and cousin Noah Flory and brother Daniel Cline, both of Rockingham Co., Va., who were just on their return from Colorado, were well pleased with their trip, and made a purchase in the town of Beaver, Col. Also met with brother J. K. Holsberry of Barbour Co., W. Va., who is going to accompany us to Col. To-day is pleasant, we are lying over here until this eve. at 5:50, when we expect to leave by the Ohio and Mississippi R. R. for St. Louis. All are well, thank the Lord.

LITERATURE.

J. B. Brumbaugh, Huntingdon, Pa. Literary Editor.

"GREAT TRUTHS BY GREAT AUTHORS."—A Dictionary of Aids to Reflection, &c., from writers of all ages and both Hemispheres, (Claxton, Remson & Haffelfinger, Philad'a.) This work purports to be a collection of "Illustrations of Truths or Things new and Old," and it certainly forms a mine of finest thought of great value to any one. The extracts are remarkable passages from the writings of all the great authors of standard literature, and an arrangement in alphabetical order, with the author's name attached. Such a book must be of special value to speakers who desire to refer to the that's upon a particular subject, of the great and good who have preceded them, without being obliged to spend days and even weeks in weary search through their separate works; and to the young, as furnishing the means of storing their minds with a fund of exalted and ennobling thoughts, by which they can shape their destinies, and lead them to nobler deeds and purer lives Price $2.00 in fine cloth bevelled boards. Sent from this office

ONE of the great dangers attending the use of the various sedatives employed in the nursery is that they tend to produce the *Opium-habit*. These quack medicines owe their soothing and quieting effects to the action of opium, and the infant is by them given a morbid appetite for narcotic stimulants. The offering for sale of such nostrums should be prohibited, as tending to the physical and moral deterioration of the race. In India mothers give to their infants sugar pills containing opium, and the result is a languid, sensual race of hopeless debauchers In the United States the poisonous dose is administered under another name; but the consequences will probably be the same. Popular Science Monthly for October.

OLD AND NEW, for November, is before us, and is the first visit of this interesting monthly. It is conducted by Edward E. Hale, and is now completing its 8th volume. The premiums and inducements for new subscribers are truly wonderful. 1st. A Chromo lithograph "Confidence." 2d. A new book by Mr. Hale, worth $1 50. 3rd. Three numbers free, next before the year begins, or 4th, two handsome engravings instead of Chromo. Besides all the magazine itself is excellent. Will send it with PILGRIM, both for $4.75 including premiums P. B. Perkins, Business Agent, Boston, Mass.

Literary Intelligence.

THE initial chapter of a new serial entitled "A Daughter of Bohemia," by "Christian Reid" (Miss Fisher) contained in *Appleton's Journal* of October 25th. It depicts life in a Southern city, and exhibits all the peculiar powers, and constructive talent which have marked the previous works of this author

THE best photographs of Tennyson, Darwin and Carlyle are taken on the work of a Mrs. Cameron an amateur artist in photography living in the Isle of Night.

THE readers of *Harper's Magazine* for November have the opportunity of welcoming back to the Easy Chair Mr. George William Curtis. Prof. Jas. De Mille commences a new serial—"The Living Link" in the same number.

IN the November *Scribner*, Mr. Froude begins his "Annals of an English Abbey," (illustrated). "Old and New Louisiana," the second paper of "The Great South," is superbly illustrated A paper on Stedman, with portrait, by A. R. Macdonough, and a paper by Stedman, on Mrs. Browning, doubly celebrates the name of that popular critic and poet

THERE seems to be no limit to the editions of Dickens' works A "New Household Edition" in fifty-six elegant volumes and with 550 illustrations by F. O. C. Darley and John Gilbert, &c, on steel, is announced from the "Riverside Press" of Hurd & Houghton.

WE notice by the announcement in the *Phrenological Journal* for November that the second volume of the "New American Cyclopædia" revised edition, now in course of publication by D APPLETON & Co, New York, is now ready. This is a great work, and a large library in itself It will consist of 16 bi-monthly volumes, and is an immense undertaking; but just such an one as will be satisfactorily accomplished by the enterprising house having charge of the project We predict for it an immense circulation and expect to arrange to supply our patrons with the work as issued.

HUNTINGDON & BROAD TOP RAIL ROAD

On and after Aug 14th, 1873, Trains will run on this road daily (Sun excepted) as follows:

Trains from Huntingdon South. *Trains from Mt. Dal's moving North.*

EXPS. P. M.	MAIL. A. M.	STATIONS.	MAIL. P. M.	EXP'S A. M
6 15	7 45	Huntingdon,	AR6 50	AR9 20
6 20	7 50	Long Siding	6 45	9 15
6 35	8 00	McConnelstown	6 35	9 05
6 40	8 05	Pleasant Grove	6 29	8 58
6 51	8 20	MARKLESBURG	6 15	8 45
7 01	8 35	Coffee Run	6 05	8 35
7 08	8 11	Rough & Ready	5 58	8 29
7 15	8 50	Cove	5 49	8 20
7 18	8 53	Fishers Summit	5 46	8 17
7 33	9 10	Saxton	5 35	8 05
7 50	9 25	Riddlesburg	5 15	7 45
7 55	9 32	Hopewell	5 10	7 38
8 10	9 45	Piper's Run	4 58	7 26
8 21	9 57	Tatesville	4 43	7 12
8 32	10 07	Everett	4 33	7 03
8 40	10 15	Mount Dallas	4 30	7 00
9 00	10 35	Bedford	4 05	6 35

SHOUP'S RUN BRANCH.

A. M	P. M		P. M.	A. M.
LE 9 20	LE 7 40	Saxton.	AR5 25	AR 7 55
9 35	7 55	Coalmont.	5 10	7 40
9 40	8 00	Crawford.	5 05	7 35
AR 9 50	AR8 10	Dudley	LE4 55	LE 7 25

Bro'd Top City from Dudley 2 miles by stage.

Time of Penna. R. R. Trains at Huntingdon.

*,*Mail No. 2 makes connection at Huntingdon with Mail going East on Pennsylvania Railroad at 4.15 p. m., and West at 5.45 p. m. Mail No. 1 leaves Huntingdon at 7.40 a. m. on arrival of Pacific Express West.

Trains on this road connect with trains on Bedford & Bridgeport, and Cumberland & Pennsylvania Railroads.

G. F. GAGE, Supt.

The Weekly Pilgrim.

Published by J. B. Brumbaugh, & Co.
Edited by H. B. & Geo. Brumbaugh
CORRESPONDING EDITORS.
D. P. Sayler, Double Pipe Creek, Md.
Leonard Furry, New Enterprise, Pa.

The *Pilgrim* is a Christian Periodical, devoted to religion and moral reform. It will advocate in the spirit of *love* and *liberty*, the principles of true Christianity, labor for the promotion of peace among the people of God, for the encouragement of the saints and for the conversion of sinners, avoiding those things which tend toward disunion or sectional feelings.

TERMS.

Single copy, Book paper,	$1.60
Eleven copies, (eleventh for Agt.)	$15.00

Any number above that at the same rate.

Address,
H. B. BRUMBAUGH.
James Creek,
Huntingdon county Pa.

The Weekly Pilgrim.

"REMOVE NOT THE ANCIENT LANDMARKS WHICH OUR FATHERS HAVE SET."

VOL. 4. JAMES CREEK, PENNSYLVANIA, NOVEMBER 11, 1873. NO. 45.

POETRY.

THE MODEL CHURCH.

SELECTED BY HATTIE F. MILLER.

Well wife, I've found the model church! I worshiped there to-day;
It made me think of good old times, before my hairs were gray.
The meetin'-house was fixed up more than they were years ago;
But then I felt, when I went in, it wasn't built for show.

The sexton didn't seat me 'way back by the door;
He knew I was old and deaf, as well as old and poor,
He must have been a Christian, for he led me boldly through
The long aisle of that crowded church, to find a pleasant pew

I wish you'd heard the singin'; it had the old time ring,
The preacher said with a trumpet voice, "Let all the people sing!"
The tune was Coronation, and the music upward rolled,
Till I thought I heard the angels striking all their harps of gold.

My deafness seemed to melt away, my spirit caught the fire;
I joined my feeble, trembling voice with that melodious choir,
And sang as in my youthful days, "Let angels prostrate fall;
Bring forth the royal diadem, and crown him Lord of all."

I tell you wife, it did me good to sing that hymn once more;
I felt like some wrecked mariner who gets a glimpse of shore,
I almost want to lay aside this weather-beaten form,
And anchor in the blessed port forever from the storm.

The preachin'? Well, I can't just tell all that the preacher said;
I know it wasn't written, I know it wasn't read.
He hadn't time to read it, for the lightnin' of his eye
Went passing 'long from pew to pew, nor passed a sinner by.

The sermon wasn't flowery, 'twas simple Gospel truth:
It fitted poor old men like me; it fitted hopeful youth.
'Twas full of compensation for weary hearts that bleed;
'Twas full of invitations to Christ, and not to creed.

The preacher made sin hideous, in Gentiles and in Jews,
He shot the golden sentences down on the finest pews,
And—though I can't see very well—I saw the falling tear,
That told me hell was some ways off, and heaven very near.

How swift the golden moments fled within that holy place!
How brightly beamed the light of heaven from every happy face!
Again I longed for that sweet time when friend shall meet with friend;
When congregations ne'er break up, and Sabbaths have no end.

I hope to meet that minister—the congregation too—
In the dear home beyond the skies that shine from heaven's blue.
I doubt not I'll remember, beyond life's evening gray,
The happy hour of worship in that model church to-day.

Dear wife, the fight will soon be fought—the victory be won;
The shinin' goal is just ahead, the race is nearly run.
O'er the river we are nearin' they are throngin' to the shore—
To shout our safe arrival where the weary weep no more.

ORIGINAL ESSAYS.

A WONDERFUL QUEEN.

Many kings and queens have lived, reigned and died in this world. In worldly honor and glory they shone for awhile, then passed away. Nations bowed to the will of some whose influence was great indeed. And now Victoria wears the coveted crown of England, and that too with merited praise, for none had a more virtuous and peaceful reign than she, but the queen we now propose to write about is one of quieter power, yields her scepter over a large territory and has more subjects than any that ever lived. Her influence is such as to cause the masses in her domain to bow to her will, and yield to her peculiar whims, whether for good or ill. Some of her edicts are full of absurdities and abominations yet she is obeyed. Her subjects are led by the winning smile she ever wears as the master leads the galley-slave to do his bidding by his frowns. Her tax levy is the most oppressive ever imposed by king, queen, or government, yet it is paid, though often to the sacrifice of comfort, food and drink. The honest gains of the labor are poured in her lap while the children go hungry and naked. The rich lavish out the thousands to her bidding while the beggar is turned hungry from the door, old and young, rich and poor, pay her tribute and in return for their earnest devotion to her desires, she gives torture the most severe, and chastisements the most cutting. The Chinese torture their children by compressing the feet of their children in small wooden shoes, but this queen has ingenious contrivances of springs and cords that torture and compress the human body of her subjects out of its natural shape, thus driving many to immature death, by other inventions, after her bidding, her subjects are forced into the streets, highways, and public places in *indecent* apparel, as if in mockery of God's work in shaping the "human form divine." Her code of laws is a medley of inconsistencies, full of torture, deprivations, poison, rapine and murder. She sends her subjects to her schools of folly and learns them to dance to her music, full of deceit as it is. Crowns them with a crown of ballast doubtless for the purpose of equalizing the power of sense wanting within! The world is ransacked for the benefit of her subjects, her command covers the seas, factories are ever humming in busy work to supply her demands, even the silent dead are not free from her disturbance, their silken tresses and golden curls are wanted, and they are shorn of their locks to please her living subjects. She has no special or fixed laws of policy, but politically is subservient to the wills, wishes and inventions of her agents, of whom she has some in every court and mart in the civilized world. In religion she is wonderfully liberal and full of eccentricities, an open enemy to the religion of Jesus Christ because he dared to reprove her of her sins, consequently she frowns upon those that would follow Him, however often smiles upon them that she might thus gain them to herself, and her ways are so winning that often after they had left her she wins them back to to her "bed and board," and leads them through her dazzling halls and deceitful bowers. She seems to take special delight in thus bringing the story of the *cross* into disrepute and defiling the profession of those that claim to belong to another kingdom. Oh how many has she thus led to cross the threshold of hell! To live for a while under her favor and drink of the cup of her fornication even to the bitter dregs and then pass to her *last reward*—an empty title—Christless, lifeless, and wanting in everything but the fruits of condemnation. Yea, the reward of those that die under her reign is such as devils get and fiends endure. Her subjects are often warned, and invited to rebel against her iron rule, but nay, they love too well; her smiles and her winning ways keep them in allegiance to her will. 'Tis true, a few forsake her and when they go, she sends forth after them a flood of scoffs and jeers by which means others that would go are constrained to remain with her.

Whence cometh this great and wonderful Queen? Where doth she dwell and where are her dominions? She cometh from a low country, born of a dragon, rocked in the cradle of gross darkness, brought up into this world a pampered child of pride, full of rebellion and a heart steeped in iniquity, clothed in "purple and fine linen." she reigns over the world which is her territory. The bounds of her domain are from sea to sea and from pole to pole. Her temple and dwelling place is as large as her dominions. Her name, by the world, is extolled above every name, none so poor but they look up with admiration to her dazzling royalty, none so high but they stoop to her in willing obeisance. Her name is "FASHION." To that name the world sings songs of praise, to that name busy feet dance, and to that name the world bows the knee. To that name devils fasten their chains of allurement; around that name abominations cluster weighty enough to sink a world, and at the sound of that name hell is moved and darkness stirred up. Jesus, the meek and lowly, has declared war against the Queen, and His soldiers fighting for to have those delivered that have been led captive by her. The war is one of fierce contest because of superior numbers offered, and because she too often has her dwelling place *in the camp* of Israel. Oh for the sake of a perishing world let us put her out! Jesus, our captain, has given orders to do so, and shall we not obey him? The forces of Jesus are few in number, but the God of hosts is with them, and eventually Queen *Fashion* must be overcome and her subjects destroyed. Like Korah and all that pertained to him, though claiming a place in Israel—in the church—all the votaries of pride and fashion must go down into the pit. Lord save us from the abominations of pride, fashion and folly!

J. S. FLORY.

GRIM care, anxiety, moroseness, all this rust of life, ought to be scoured off by the oil of mirth. It is better than emery. Every man ought to rub himself with it. A man without mirth is like a wagon without springs, in which every one is caused disagreeably to jolt by every pebble over which it runs.

THE LOVE OF NATURE.

There are many persons who go through the world with their eyes closed to the beauties of nature. This should not be so. We should cultivate a love of the beautiful in nature. How beautiful is the earth with its oceans, its continents, its stupendous mountains, and its variegated scenery! What a vast field of thought does it present to the minds of men in its mineral, vegetable, and animal kingdoms: and when we look abroad at the illimitable worlds which present themselves to us in every direction, we can truly exclaim, in the language of the pious Psalmist, "Day after day uttereth speech, and night after night sheweth forth knowledge." Everything that we can take cognizance of through our senses is teeming with life, and reminds us of our Divine Author. As we behold Him manifested in the beautiful forms of vegetable life, we feel that to know more of His power would be a blessing unto us. We see Him manifested in the animal kingdom, and we are lost in wonder, while our thoughts ascend unto Him to know more of His power. Flowers speak to us of His tenderness and love. The birds warble forth His praises, and all nature proclaims in language that cannot be mistaken, "The hand that made us is Divine." Nature teaches us lessons of utility, beauty, progression and love. Let us call your attention to the seasons, in the annual changes, commencing with Spring.

When the sun starts on his northern tour, the icy chains that have bound the laughing rivulet, the skipping brook, and the leaping cascade, begin to relax, and they go dancing on their joyous glee to fulfill their grand destiny. The crocuses and hyacinths begin to bloom, the buds to swell and burst, the birds to choose their mates and build their nests, and, at last, amid blooming flowers, bursting buds, and singing birds, old gray-haired winter progressively glides into the flowery lap of Spring.

Here, certainly, is progress, use, and beauty all combined. But these infallible signs indicate to the husbandman that the proper time has arrived when he must prepare the soil and sow the seed for the coming crop. Mark, now, how strictly in accordance with the progressive law does the work of growth go on. First the tender blade comes peeping out of the warm bosom of mother earth, and day by day increases in stature. Then see how gracefully the growing corn bows its leaves of green; how majestically it rears its tasseled head on high, and how beautifully, from its girdle, hang out the silken cords! There are many people in the world that are such perfect utilitarians that they see no beauty in all this. They only see so many bushels at harvest time, and so many dollars for their money-bags. But behold with what luxuriousness of beauty nature bedecks herself beneath the strong and fructifying rains of the Summer sun; notice the white and red roses, the blushing petunias, the delicately formed china asters, the crimped-leaved poppies, the majestic tiger lilies; nor would we forget the morning-glories, from whose beauty lingers but an hour; nor would we be unmindful of the tiny flowers whose bright eyes and smiling faces fill our souls with beauty; nor of the sunflower, the hollyhock, and all those of a statelier class; all bloom in beauty and loveliness, covering the earth with delight and making the air redolent with fragrance. How beautiful are all the flowers, and how I love them! It seems, sometimes, as though they were only so many foot-steps of angels scattered over our pathway here to lure us to fairer worlds above, where immortal flowers bloom and never fade.

But Summer grows weary, at last, with the burden of her fruitfulness, and pours the result of all her toil in the gorgeous lap of Autumn. The fields, that all Summer long were green with growing grain, are covered all over with a ripening crown of glory; then again, the woods—

"O, I love to gaze on the grand old woods,
Dressed in their russet, gold and brown,
And one by one to see their tinted leaves
Softly, gently, come falling down.
They seem like glittering rubies bright,
Plucked from some lofty, regal crown,
To richly grace the solemn marriage rite
Of Summer green with Autumn brown!"

Who does not love the Autumn? Those beautiful October days, so dream-like, as though they were especially made for meditation! Everything so still, and the bright rays of the sun are softened by the haze of the atmosphere. The Autumn oftentimes, in its brightness, reminds me of some toil-worn pilgrim, drawing near the end of life's journey after an active life well spent. Just as his steps begin to descend the valley, the radiance of the brighter world breaks around, and a smile lights up his countenance with immortal beauty delightful to behold, ere death draws his curtain over the scene.

In conclusion let me recommend to all to cultivate a love of the beauties of nature, and to study the great book of nature and learn from its mystic pages. Its pages glisten with beautiful extracts from a still grander work, the universe of God. Its poetry is in time with the music of the spheres, and its well-rounded periods and brilliant metaphors are the impulses of that great First Cause. Nature's book was written by God, and its leaves glisten with the choicest treasures of His infinite mind. * * *
—*Phrenological Journal.*

A LEARNED divine one day accosted a simple-hearted Christian busy in his daily toil:

"Well, John, it is a long and hard way to heaven, is it not?"

"O, no, sir," was the ready answer; "it is only three steps."

"Three steps! How is that John?"

"Why sir, nothing is plainer. First, step out of yourselves; second step, into Christ; third, step into heaven."

The astonished minister, years afterwards, acknowledged his indebtedness to that poor rustic for one of his profoundest and most comprehensive lessons in experimental theology.

"SILENCE IS GOLD."—The Arabs, have a proverb which says, "Speech is of silver, but silence is of gold." There is no question concerning the terribly mischievous effects of an evil tongue, and the truth of this proverb can that be questioned; but when silence is too great it leaves one like King Midas, dreary amid all his gold. We can have too much of a good thing. Silence may reign in selfishness or stupidity, as well as in wisdom.

GENERAL INTELLIGENCE

THE Indiana Quakers have yielded to a very sensible change in their discipline. All restrictions in relation to marrying out of the society have been swept away, and Friends in Indiana are not now liable to discipline for doing so.

The following is from an exchange and is an example of how those who do not believe in the true Messiah are constantly being deceived by false Messiahs:

The *New Free Press* of Vienna has just published from the pen of the eastern traveler, Baron de Maltzen, an account of a pretended Messiah who has appeared in Arabia; He "is a Jew of Sana, in Yemen, with fascinating exterior having remarkable brilliant eyes and a melodious voice. After studying the mysteries of the great cabalistic work, the Zoha, he withdrew from men, eventually retired to a desert where he submitted to bodily mortification and self-denial. He soon became distinguished as a worker of miracles, and, as such, attracted the attention of the superstitious, brought various kinds of food, and were pleased that he condescended to accept their offerings. The increase of their flocks and of their households, and even their success in the attack upon hostile troops, were attributed to the power peculiar to this worker of marvelous doings. His reputation has spread far and wide among the Arabian population, and many incredulous stories are circulated about him.

The following is a description by the Rev. Dr. Duff, of Scotland of the relics which the Catholic church claim to have preserved and are now exhibiting to those whom they have succeeded in duping:

Some of the bones of Abraham Isaac, and Jacob! The stone on which the father of the faithful offered his only son! Chips of the brazen serpent! Preserved specimens of the manna in the wilderness! and of the blossoms of Aarons rod!

Descending to gospel times, we have the axe, saw, and hammer of Joseph, the espoused husband of Mary! The camel's hair garment of John the baptist and the linen on which he was beheaded; and the forefinger wanting the nail, the identical forefinger with which he pointed to the blessed Savior, saying "Behold the Lamb of God!" the Holy coat of the redeemer himself; spikes of his thorny crown; and fragments of his cross! a piece of Peters staff and chain, his sword somewhat rusty, the stone on which the cock crew and rags of the sail of his boat when a fisherman on the Lake of Gallilee! part of the Virgin Mary's hair, and girdle, one of her combs and shoes, her spousal ring, and a considerable quantity of her milk! Of other apostles and holy martyrs, we have endless and countless fragments and memorials, in the diversified form of hair heads and skulls, tongues teeth and beards, jaw-bones and shoulder-blades ribs and livers and hearts, legs and toes and slippers, yea, and portions of the very breath of some carefully enclosed in stoppered vials, with one feather out of the wings of the Archangel Gabriel.

MEMPHIS AND THE YELLOW FEVER.—Reports from Memphis to the 28th represent the fever to be slowly abating. On Sunday not more than a dozen new cases were reported. The majority of the cases lately have been of a milder type, and yield more readily to prompt treatment. Drs. White and Blount died on the 26th inst., making eight physicians who have fallen victims to the disease. The colored people are taking the fever and about fifty of them are reported sick. Help will be needed for some time to come for the convellescents and the poorer classes, as the stagnation of all kinds of business will prevent many from supporting themselves who are able and willing to work. The Young Men's Christian Association of this city has received the following telegram from Vincent Coyler, at Memphis: "Out of a population of 2, 509 in the first and second wards, and Chelsea in the city, there have been over 1,000 deaths from the fever. Neighborhoods are deserted. Funerals and sickness on every side. The solemnity is awful—worse than on the battlefields of the war. The enemy is unseen and more fatal. The people are greatly united. Christian and Hebrew, Catholic and Protestant, black and white work together in perfect harmony." The Association has forwarded about $1,500 to the Memphis Relief Committee, and aid has been sent from many quarters Boston, Washington, New York and other cities have subscribed liberally.

Youth's Department.

TO OUR YOUNG PATRONS.

DEAR BOYS AND GIRLS:—The PILGRIM has been coming to some of you, on his weekly visits, for nearly four years and to others not more than ten months. All of you have been receiving his visits frequently and long enough to be acquainted by this time, and we do hope that the acquaintance may be pleasant and profitable to you. The PILGRIM will have to cease making his visits to you unless you give him another invitation. If you have intimate and good friends you never forget to invite them back when they come to visit you, no matter how frequent those visits may be. Now the PILGRIM looks for an invitation only once a year, and as the year is nearly at a close and the time is here that this invitation is looked for, we hope his visits may have been so pleasant and agreeable that all the boys and girls will not forget to invite him back the coming year. We know that some of you like to read the PILGRIM, for your papa's in writing to us have told us so. Not very long ago a father said that he was very well pleased with the PILGRIM, and that his little boy asked him to read the Youth's Department to him, as soon as he received it, and sometimes he could hardly wait until it would come. This little boy will not forget to have the PILGRIM invited back to his home next year, and we hope this will be the feeling of you all. Don't let papa forget to send the invitation. We love to visit your homes and bring along something good for boys and girls to read, and we will feel pretty badly if we do not get an invitation to come back again.

The coming year we will try to make the Youth's Department more interesting than heretofore. Our boys and girls must not be neglected, and we are now prepared to make such selections that will interest and instruct you, and in addition to this we expect to have a larger number of contributors to your department. There are those who delight to talk to boys and girls and from such, we may expect to have occasional talks that will interest you. May we not then come to you another year? Nothing will delight us more than to receive another free invitation, for it is our highest purpose to do you good. PUBLISHER.

WHERE IS YOUR INFLUENCE?

The young readers of the *Pilgrim* may think that Uncle Henry has a great deal to talk about, but after all he does not say half as much as he thinks.

When I look around and see how fast the world is getting to be, especially our young folks, I cannot refrain from feeling concerned. I have of late, given the young considerable attention or thought, because on you and the moulding of your character, depends the welfare of the church. A few years more, and the old fathers who now so earnestly labor and pray for you, will be no more, and you will grow up to take their place, and the great question with me is, will you do it? When I look over a crowd of our young, the query is, who, fifteen or twenty years from this, will be our ministers? It is from among you, dear young friends we expect them to come. Do you ever think of the high and holy calling you may be made to fill? There is much said and written about the glory of high sounding titles, and perhaps some of you may be aspiring after a great name, or position in life. If you are, you may and must be disappointed in the end. Even if you were to be successful and gain a great name, it will bring sorrow and disappointment in the end as it is all vanity and vexation of spirit. A high position in the church is much more to be desired.

The good old apostle Paul says that all *things* are but as filth compared with the glory and honor that is to be found in the Kingdom of Christ. Then, commence now to seek after those riches and that glory. Do not think you are too young. Our blessed King's orders are, "first seek the Kingdom and its righteousness." You have an influence even before you may think of it. Let that be for Jesus and in favor of the church. It often pains me to see some of our young devoting their first years and best part of their life in favor of the devil, and thus help him build up his kingdom and work out their own destruction by inches. Do not think you are without influence and it is your liberty to give it where you will. Where shall it be? Will you give it in favor for Jesus who died to save you, or to satan who seeks to drag you into hell, a place only prepared for himself and his angels? Do not be so unthoughtful, so unjust and so unreasonable as to give your young and best days to the enemy of your soul, and then in your dying hours, throw your wreck, your span of useless life on God's mercy and saving grace. He has no need of you, especially after you have spent the vigor of your life in fighting against him. It is you that needs him. You need him every day, every hour, every moment—every breath you draw is from him. You cannot afford to have such a God angry with you, yet you dare to make him angry, because it is said that God is angry with the sinner every day. Every moment of time you spend, and every influence you give in favor of satan, puts you lower and farther away from God. Then think to whom you are giving your influence. Let it be in favor of God, of the church and of yourself, and you will be happy in time, and in eternity receive everlasting life.

UNCLE HENRY.

THE BEST BOOK IN THE BEST PLACE.

There are many great libraries in the world. Some contain nearly a million books. Some of these books have been great blessings to the world; but there is one book which claims to be before all others, and above them all. It is the Holy Bible. This is truly the best book. As its name means, it is "the Book" —the book of books—God's book. It came from God, and leads to God. It is his gift to all people of every age. It has done more good in the world than all other books that have ever been written.

In the Bible are declared the character, ways and purposes of the God of Providence and grace, and in what relations man stands to his Creator, and to his fellow-man. It answers the questions, Whence came I? What am I? Whither am I going? It is a book of the purest doctrines and the wisest precepts. It is full of light and truth and love. It relates facts, and teaches by examples. It makes known the best way of living, the most comfortable way of dying, and tells of eternal rest in Heaven.

But the principal glory of the Bible is that it reveals the person and work of Christ, and the only way of salvation by faith in him. It is the "word of Christ." The great truth it makes known is, that God so loved the world as to send his son to be the Savior of men.

"This is the record, that God hath given to us eternal life, and this life is in his son." Whosoever believes in him shall be saved. In its invitations and promises Christ is "commended" to sinners as their only hope and refuge. It points to his life as their best example, and to his Cross as the only way to their reconciliation with God and to Heaven; and promises to us the help of the Holy Spirit.

Should not the best book be put into the best place? The Psalmist tells where that is: "Thy word have I hid in mine heart." Psalms cxix. 11. It is well to have the Bible in our houses, and to see it on our tables. It is better still to have it stored in our memories. But best of all to have its truths in our hearts. "I have lived a lonely life," said the shepherd of Salisbury Plain, "and have often had little to eat; but my Bible has been meat, drink, and company to me; and when trouble has come upon me, I do not know what I should have done if I had not had the promises of the Bible for my stay and comfort."

In a time of persecution a Bible was taken from a boy, and burnt before his eyes. "I have got the seven chapters of St. Matthew's Gospel in my heart," said he: "you cannot burn them out." That was a safe place for the truths of the Bible, was it not?

The best book should be in the best place for the best purpose. "That I might not sin against thee." It is the Holy Bible. It shows us that sin is an evil and bitter thing; that it is defiling, deceitful and disgraceful; that God sees and remembers it; that we should confess it, repent of it, and forsake it; and that we should look to our Lord Jesus Christ, whose blood cleanseth from it, and by whose grace alone we can conquer it, and live a life of holiness. Young reader, read your Bible, cherish its truths in your hearts—obey it.—*Little Messengers.*

KISS ME, MAMMA.

"Kiss me, mamma, before I sleep." How simple a boon, yet how soothing to the little suppliant is that soft gentle kiss. The little head sinks contentedly on the pillow, for its peace and happiness within. The bright eyes close, and the rosy lips are revealed in the bright and sunny dreams of innocence.

Yes, kiss it, mamma, for that good-night kiss will linger in memory when the giver lies mouldering in the grave. The memory of a gentle mother's kiss has cheered many a lonely wanderer's pilgrimage and has been the beacon-light to illuminate his desolate heart; for remember, life has many stormy billows to cross, many a rugged path to climb, with thorns to pierce; and we know not what is in store for the little one so sweetly slumbering with no annoying care to disturb its peaceful dreams. The parched and fevered lip will become dewy again, as recollections bear to the sufferer's couch a mother's love—a mother's kiss. Then kiss your little ones ere they sleep; there is a magic power in that kiss which will endure to the end of life.—*Western Recorder.*

Why not strew the path of life with flowers? It requires no stronger efforts than to plant thorns and briers. Is it not strange that we bend all our efforts in cultivating those plants which afford no pleasure, but on the contrary, abridge our happiness, while we suffer to spring up spontaneously, the few stray flowers that occasionally throw a smile along our way? It need not be thus. The few happy men around us should teach us an important lesson. There is no reason in the world why we should not be as happy as they. If we would look on the path of life as a road, we must cultivate ourselves, and go diligently about it. Less frequently would we have cause to mourn over the bitter past, or the dark and cloudy present. If our years have run thus far to waste, let us with care, influence the future and with all care and attention cultivate those fruits and flowers that will yield a harvest of agreeable pleasure.

No summer but it has a winter; he never reaped comfort in his adversity, that sowed it not in his prosperity.

Good management is the secret of success.

The Weekly Pilgrim.

JAMES CREEK, PA., Nov 11, 1873

☞ How to send money.—All sums over $1.50, should be sent either in a check, draft or postal order. If neither of these can be obtained, have the letter registered.

☞ When Money is sent, *always* send with it the name and address of those who paid it. Write the names and post office as plainly as possible.

☞ Every subscriber for 1874, gets a *Pilgrim Almanac* FREE.

WE MEAN BUSINESS.

A brother in writing to us says: "I am glad to hear that you are going to enlarge the PILGRIM, not that it is too small as it is, but this shows prosperity and zeal for the good work of the Lord." Just so, dear brother, we *mean* to prosper in our business. First we are about our Lord's business, and in this more especially do we *mean* to prosper. "Wist ye not that I must be about my Father's business," was the open rebuke of Jesus when his parents sought him and found him so busily engaged in the great work for which his Father sent him. We have a work to do, and does not every one know that we should be about it? We are to work out our soul's salvation, and labor for that of others. This is our business, and if ever we felt in earnest, if ever we felt like "push," it is just now. We are stirred to a more strenuous effort from a consideration of the nature of this work. It is great because it requires self-denial, a continual warfare with the adversary of souls, a race in which the whole structure of the inner man must be brought into exercise. It is important because our eternal interests depend upon it. It is time to work because surrounding circumstances teach us that we are nearing the Jordan of death, soon our Father will call us over, our work will be ended, and then our reward according to our work. If we do not work we have not the promise of a reward; we cannot expect to have part in the unsearchable riches of Christ, and participate in the things that God has prepared for those that love him.

Again we are to labor for the salvation of others, and as the soul is of more value than the whole world, does it not seem important that we be interested in this work? Our object when we embarked in our present vocation, was to open up an avenue through which the souls of men might be reached, and thus enable all the laborers in Christ's Vineyard to perform a work for the Lord; and as we see that our object is, in a degree, being met, we feel encouraged. Ah, yes, we *mean* business, and we hope that every brother and sister will wake up to the importance of this work. It is altogether likely that we are not wide awake to the interests of our heavenly Father, or there would be greater efforts made for the advancement of the Redeemer's Kingdom; our Journals would be filled with thrilling appeals to the sinner, and the prevailing evils now extant in the world, would receive many a thrust from the great spiritual sword "which is mighty through God to the pulling down of strong holds." It is time, my brethren and sisters, that we take hold of this sword and fight, for the enemy is approaching us on every side, and is assuming such an appearance that, if we are not careful, we may not distinguish him from a friend. Then let us be wide awake, live, active, business men, so that the interests of our Lord do not suffer, and when the great day of reckoning comes, we be not found wanting.

Again we *mean* business of a pecuniary nature. It is right that we should follow our callings in life with a fixed purpose, and a determination that at least, opens the way to success; and our contemplated enlargement, and improvements *do* indicate that we are bent on making our business a success. In this, our readers can feel *assured* there is no deception. We *mean* business. Is this not right? Did not the apostle tell the Roman brethren to not be slothful in business? Yes. It is right, and this we think the brother had in view when he commended our proposed enlargement. The paper is really large enough for the price, but we are determined to make it "look like business," hoping that all right thinking brethren and sisters will appreciate our efforts, and in the end we may be paid for it. Shall we be disappointed? Is not our calling a laudable one, and since we are all dependent, to a certain extent, on one another, in whatever vocation we may pursue, is it not our duty to help each other? This mutual dependence should not be overlooked, and as we are determined to do our part, we hope our patrons will do theirs, and then indeed may we expect to be successful. In addition to the enlargement, we give every subscriber an Almanac free. The printing of these Almanacs alone, cost no small sum, say nothing of the labor they cost in getting them ready for the press. Then our rates to agents in addition to all this, surely presents the appearance of business, and the idea of prosperity. We hope then that our patrons will get to work immediately and in earnest. Our list in order to have a proper pecuniary remuneration, should be doubled, and this can easily be done, and from present indications will be done. WAKE UP. The time is here to be at work. We *mean business*.

J. B. B.

OUR ALMANAC.

Our Almanac is now completed and we suppose that before this, all our known agents have received a copy containing a prospectus, and are ready to go to work. As to the merits of our work, we shall not say anything more about it being the best &c., as others may take a notion to say the same thing, which will necessitate one of our statements to be incorrect. To have the best of anything is a laudable ambition, but perhaps it will be most prudent to let others make the decision. All that we shall say about it at present is, that we did the very best we could in putting out a first class Family Almanac, containing all the information about the signs and seasons that we are expected to know. It also contains an interesting table calculated to show the Solar Cycle, Dominical Letter, Golden Number, Epact New year, Shrovetide, Easter, Ascension, Whitsuntide, 1st Sunday in Advent and Christmas, from the year 1816 to 1890 inclusive, and the Centennial Almanac, for 1874. This old prognosticator tells us that Saturn is the ruling planet for 1874. We shall not tell you what it says about the weather, crops &c., but it does say all about them, and is much more convenient to farmers and people generally than barometers, as it gives us the information so much farther ahead, that we have time to prepare things as they come. In addition to this, it contains some very interesting religious and biographical reading, and quite an extensive Ministerial List in alphabetical order, giving the post office and county. Notwithstanding all our exertion and care to have as complete a list as possible, we notice a number of mistakes generally typographical. This happened because we could not read the proof, and the parties failed to decipher our chirography. These errors are of such a character as to produce no inconveniences, but there are others for which we feel more sorry. We notice a few names omitted that we had and should be on the list. Among these we just now remember the name of Christian Custer 475 Franklin street Philadelphia. These are errors over which we had no control as they were not seen until it was too late to correct them.

TAKE ONE FREE.

As an extra inducement for our brethren and friends to take the PILGRIM, we have gone to considerable trouble and expense in publishing a first class family *Almanac* for 1874. They are now ready for distribution and we offer one FREE to every subscriber to the PILGRIM for 1874. They will be sent to subscribers post-paid, as soon as the names are received. Now is the time to subscribe. The PILGRIM for 1874 promises to be better than ever before—will be enlarged and otherwise improved and a *Pilgrim Almanac* FREE, all for the small sum of $1.50. All new names sent in before the 1st of Dec. will get the remaining Nos. *free*. Don't delay but send in your names at once, old and new, and get your Almanacs before the New Year commences.

TO OUR SINGLE SUBSCRIBERS.

We have, on our list, between 500 and 600 single subscribers. Out of this number, we ought to get many agents who would be able to send us good lists for the coming year. On account of the large number, we did not send prospectus to all as we did on former occasions, therefore, we now say to any or as many as think they could get us some subscribers, let us know, and we will send you an Almanac and prospectus forthwith. Send along, brethren, sisters and friends, and see how much can be accomplished by a little effort.

HOW A SISTER PAID FOR THE PILGRIM.

Dear Brethren:—I have now been reading the PILGRIM for two years, and it seems to me I cannot get along without it. Enclosed find $1.50 which I have now saved by laying by the littles that I succeeded in earning in my spare hours. At one time I thought I would be to give up my faithful weekly friend, but when I thought of the many good messages it brought me and the pleasant hours spent in perusing its pages, I determined that I would have it even at a sacrifice of some of the things that now fill my scanty board, but it is said that necessity is the mother of invention, and it was so in my case, as I earned this money by sewing for my neighbors while they were cozily sleeping in their beds. Though it was earned by hard work at late hours, I never gave that much money with a better will. May the Lord bless and prosper you in the good work.

The above is from a sister in W. Va., and speaks for itself. Brethren and sisters, you that are blessed with plenty, take knowledge from this poor sister. Where the love of Jesus reigns supreme in the soul, hard times and poverty will not be a hindrance in subscribing for the PILGRIM.

MARRIED.

MILLER—HOOVER.—At the residence of the bride's parents, near Henrietta, by the undersigned, Nov. 2, 1873, Mr. John W. Miller, of Pattonville, Pa., to Miss Nancy Hoover of Henrietta, Pa.

S. A. MOORE.

DIED.

SANGER.—In the Beaver Creek Congregation, Rockingham Co., Va., October 18, 1873, of typhoid billious fever, after a short illness, our much beloved sister Rebecca F. consort of Bro Samuel F. Sanger and daughter of Eld. Daniel Thomas, dec'd, aged 26 years and 1 day. She leaves a sorrowing husband, 1 child, mother, brothers and sisters and many relatives and friends to mourn their loss, which we hope is her great gain. She bore her affliction with patience and christian fortitude, and spoke of her home and said the separation would not be long. Funeral occasion improved by Eld. Solomon Garber and others, from Rev 14: 12, 13.

S. N. WINE

SKILES.—In the Middlefork Congregation, Clinton Co., Ind., Sept 18, 1873, our much beloved sister Lydia, wife of

Bro. John Skyles, formerly of Augusta Co., Va., aged 65 years, 8 months and 13 days.

She lived with her husband 47 years, less 4 days, and had been a faithful member of the church 45 years, and 25 days, had 8 children, 6 living; 40 grand children, 35 living; and 2 great grand children, living. The loss of our departed sister is sensibly felt by all who knew her. Her seat has hardly ever been vacant in the meetings. She was truly a mother in Israel, always ready and willing to administer to the needy: to say the least in her death the church has lost a faithful and lively member, the afflicted neighbors and friends an often visitor, the children a cheerful mother, and the husband an affectionate wife. Funeral services by Elders Isaac Billheimer and Isaac Cripe.

JOHN N. CRIPE.

EVANS.—In the limits of Lower Cumberland Church, York Co., Pa., Oct. 22, '73, of old age sister Catharine Evans, aged 80 years and 5 days.

An only daughter with whom she lived, remained to mourn her loss. She survived her husband twenty years, and lived and died a faithful sister. Religious exercises by the Brethren. Text, "I go to prepare a place for you."

Please refer to second obituary No. 41, for further information.

A. BEELMAN.

ZELLERS.—In the Clarion Congregation, Clarion Co., Pa., Oct. 23, '73, our beloved brother John Zellers. He was born in Switzerland, July 18, 1775, making him, at the time of his death, 98 years, 3 months and 14 days. Funeral occasion improved by the writer from Romans 4: 7-8, to a very large and attentive congregation.

GEORGE WOOD.

Correspondence.

NOTES OF TRAVEL.

J. S. FLORY.

GREELY, Colorado, Oct. 26, 1873.

I first wrote from Cincinnati, Ohio, which city we left on the 22nd at 6 p. m., arrived at St. Louis next morning at 9 o'clock, crossed the Mississippi river, waited about an hour and a half and then set out for Omaha on the north Mo. St. Jo and Council Bluff R. R., where we arrived next day, the 24th, at ten o'clock. The bustle and confusion at Omaha is greater on the arrival and departure of trains than any point we have ever been in our travels. All baggage is transferred from the east side of the river to the west by the Transfer Company. No baggage is checked farther than to Omaha, so it has all to be reached at that point. The baggage collected by the arrival of some four to six trains, is all transferred at once. When the unloading commences, it is a busy time of hunting baggage of all descriptions out of the heavy laden cars, others taking it up and crying out at the top of their voices the number of the check. Along, a long counter or banister is a crowd of eager watchers with checks in hand, when their number is called, they cry out, "here" or "yes," then, others re-check it, and it is loaded on the waiting train. I was necessarily compelled to stand at the bar for over one hour before I got sight of my baggage. Policemen have a busy time keeping order amid such a hubbub of confusion. Finally the last piece of baggage comes out and soon we hear "All aboard." We then enter a car where we are lucky in getting seats for our party soon after the arrival. There are some peculiarities connected with traveling by rail across the plains not to be found elsewhere. One is the laying in of provisions for the trip, owing to the exorbitant charges for the necessaries of life at the eating stations. The cars were crowded and it seemed as if every one, like ourselves, had their children with them. Boxes and baskets of provisions, rolls of blankets, pots, cups, and other things too tedious to mention were crowded under the seats over head and in the aisle so that it was difficult to pass. At meal time there was a general picnic in the car, making of coffee and tea, running to and fro for water, crying of children, scolding by somebody, and a general hubbub was the order, and never the exception. Taking all in all, we got along remarkably well. At night several inches of snow fell, next day the 25th was a cold day. At 1 p. m., we arrived at Cheyenne, Wyoming Territory, left at 2: 25 on the Denver Road for this place, where we arrived at 5: 30 p. m. In the waiting room of the depot found a good warm stove where we left our family, and sallied out in quest of quarters, found a house to suit us for rent, took it, ordered a cook stove from a hardware store to be put up immediately, thence to the coal yard and ordered a load of coal, had our baggage taken to our house soon, and in *one hour and a half* had our family around our own stove and the cooks at work, and by the time supper was announced, had laid in a supply of commissary stores, furniture &c., &c. All could do ample justice to the meal prepared for all were in excellent health and fine spirits. A good night's rest followed and here we are to day settled down in this beautiful town in this far off territory. Thus in less than a week we have come from amid the mountains of the Alleghaney, traveled through six states, one territory, and landed here near the base of the Rocky mountains. Truly this is a fast age. Our journey was indeed a favorable one, all having good health and no loss of anything, having brought all our goods, 1200 pounds through safely, and at a trifling cost. Never did we feel more thankful to God for his kindness and abundant mercies shown to us than now. Truly He has in His long kindness and tender mercy blessed us far beyond our deserving.

Bro. James K. Holsberry whom I mentioned fell in with us at Cincinati, is still with us, is well and hearty and pleased so far with Colorado.

To-day I attended services at the Baptist Church, the discourse was a good one. In a day or two, I shall, no preventing Providence, go down the Platt to Beaver of which more anon. It is a beautiful day, the snow is nearly all gone, except on the mountains, where it is said it lies "eternally."

Direct the *Pilgrim* and all that write to me, direct to Greely, Weld Co. Colorado.

EPISTOLARY.

A letter to my afflicted sister and all the dear brethren and sisters at a distance. I feel this morning like giving you, through my great weakness, some church news, as I think the church news is always interesting.

In the first place, our Communion meeting was held here on the 11th and 12th of October, in the Brethren's new meetinghouse. We had quite a feast of love together. A number of brethren and sisters from a distance were with us. Our hearts were made to rejoice in the Lord, to see sinners returning and giving their hearts to God while young. Four souls came forward, out of a large crowd, and gave their hands to the minister and their hearts to God. On the Sunday of our communion, they were all baptized but one. One old brother was baptized with the rest of the young ones, aged about 70 years or upwards. In all 6 were baptized, one on the evening of our Lovefeast, and one on Sunday after. Among them was my daughter and her husband, I. C. Joseph Ranger and his wife. Oh, dear brethren and sisters, my heart was made to rejoice to see some of my dear children come and go with me. But then sad to think, some of them stay back while time is so precious and life so uncertain; but dear sisters, we will pray on, and hold out faithful, and I hope the Lord will hear us, and answer our feeble petisions by and by.

Our ministering brethren from a distance were Bros. James Hutchison from Monroe Co., and Wm. Bailey from Raleigh Co. Oh dear brethren and sisters, let us continue in prayer for our laboring brethren who are going forth and discharging their duty so faithfully, in proclaiming the Gospel to a sinful world. My dear afflicted sister, I must tell you how we all felt after our good meeting was over. We had to bid farewell to our much beloved brother J. S. Flory. Yes he preached his farewell sermon last Sabbath, immersed four precious souls, and bade us all farewell for Colorado. He started yesterday, the 20th, with his family. His last words were finally Brethren farewell, farewell sisters, farewell unconverted friends, I hope to meet you all above. He preached a wonderful sermon, the house was crowded and running over, for all could not get in. Yes my dear afflicted sister, I thought of you often and many others of my dear sister, at our good meeting, who are deprived of those privileges that we now enjoy. I thought if only you could be with me at our communion meeting. You know how much we talked of the goodness of God when I was to see you. But pray on sister, I hope the Lord will be with you in all your afflictions, for we know if we are faithful to endure our sufferings and afflictions here, it is for our own good. Then dear sister let us be faithful and soon we shall be released from our trials, troubles, and afflictions here, and hear that welcome voice, "come up higher."

A little more about our good meeting, but not perhaps, exactly in place. There was an election held for a minister and a deacon. We cast our lots and the lot for minister fell on Bro. Samuel Riner and my companion George W. Crouse, and for deacon Bro. Henry Ranger.

My dear brethren and sisters don't forget to pray for us all that the dear brethren may go forth in the discharge of their duty, in tearing down the strongholds of satno, and building up Zion, and that we, the sisters, may be faithful in attending to our duties as the Lord may give us strength; and in trying to bring up our children in the nurture and admonition of the Lord. From your unworthy sister

NANCY CROUSE.

Fayetteville, W. Va.

MAPLE GROVE COMMUNION

This meeting was held on the 1st day of October, at the Meeting-house for the first time. Public preaching commenced near 10 o'clock, to a large congregation. The following ministers were present: J. P. Ebersole, Jacob Garver, Joseph Rittenhouse, J. B. Shoemaker, George Irvin, Gideon Bollinger, bro. Pittinger, Wm. Murray, George Fleck, D. M. Witmer, Henry Killhefner, David Workman, James McMullen, Israel Roop, Bro. Ross, J. B. Mishler, Moses Weaver, Bro. Ellis, John Nicholson, Samuel Garver and a few more.

There was present quite a large number of members and seemed to enjoy themselves well, and better order in the house could not be expected. The good spirit appeared to rule. May the Lord bless all for their good attention.

OWL CREEK COMMUNION.

Was held on the 24th of Oct. Public preaching at 10 o'clock, good congregation and good attention. Evening exercises were well attended and good order in the house, preaching next day at 10 o'clock and in the evening, and the next day, (Sabbath) and evening. Meetings all well attended, except the last, (rained.). Had three meetings in the congregation six miles distant while those at the meeting-house were going on,—in all eight sermons, besides the Communion evening. The following ministers were present: C. Wise, Jos. McMullen, Gideon Bollinger, Wm. Murray, Wm. Sadler, Eli Stoner, James Workman, David Workman, David Ross and four of their own,—had a pleasant time. Some of the Adventist's were present trying to make converts, but so far as we know they failed. They are very strenuous about a fixed day for the Sabbath different from the one recognized throughout the world almost claiming that the mass of the world cannot count seven. They profess to hold to the law but drop the penalty (stoning to death) and when called upon to give thus saith the Lord for their day, they cannot or do not do it. They are a body that claim their existence since 1844, a branch of Millerism. Men generally labor before they rest, and while they claim that we rest first, which cannot be, one must become weary before they can rest, or else they are always in rest. May the Brethren stand fast 'till the Lord gives them their crown, and may a blessing rest upon all that showed respect to God's word and his people.

WM. SADLER.

Nankin, Ohio.

MONEY LIST.

J ? Blauch	$ 3.00	J D Eshleman	10.00
B ?. Flory,	20.00	Jonas Grabill	6 00
Eld. Geo Wolf	5.00	Sam'l Wareham	1.00
Nancy Crouse,	1.50	Sam'l Williams	3.00
Mary Kiser,	1.25	S S Creswell	1.75
Moses Kling,	1 50	G W English	1.50
S C Miller	1.50	C C Root	10.40
J. D Sidebottom	5.00	J Allen	2.00

LITERATURE.

J. B. Brumbaugh, Huntingdon, Pa. Literary Editor.

The eloquent and able paper on "Modern Infidelity" by Prof Christlieb, read before the Evangelical Alliance, is to be published immediately, in a separate volume, by the *Harper's*, and will contain a portrait and memoir of the author.

Jas. R. Osgood & Co., will immediately publish a little book entitled "Sex in Education; or a Fair Chance for the Girls," which will likely make a stir among the advocates of co-education of the sexes. We have never been able to call the attention of our readers to the publications of this old, established publishing house, and their many valuable publications, but we expect to continue to do so in the future. Their editions of the Poets are the finest in the country. The poems of Longfellow, Saxe, Whittier, Howells, Proctor, &c., &c., we believe are published exclusively by this house. Their Red Line editions of the Poets would form excellent holiday gifts. Those of Longfellow, Saxe, Burns and Proctor have been issued recently. They had issued "Child-life in Poetry" and now as a companion to it give us "Child-life in Prose," by John G. Whittier. They have just issued poems by Edmund Clarence Stedman, the "poet whom poets love." We expect next week to give a notice of Whittier's Pennsylvania Pilgrim, which refers to our people it is said, complimentarily, being from a "*Friend's*" stand-point.

Those desirous of forming an acquaintance with the Darwinian Theory can do so best by reading the works of Darwin, and not by the newspaper reports, which are more likely to be a reflection of views taken on the subject by the writer. His works in 6 volumes, published by the Appleton's would be read by a great deal of pleasure and profit by those having a taste for scientific investigation.

We have "Good News for the Children" this week. "St. Nicholas" the beautiful illustrated magazine for boys and girls has come; and it is brim full of instruction, entertainment and delight for all, from grandpa to the baby. We predict that the 30,000 copies issued will "not go half round," for it is so fine, so beautiful, and the publishers will send this, first, and any succeeding No. for 25 cents. The pictures are beautiful, representing incidents in boy and girl life, natural scenery, animals, birds, &c. We could not tell you all it contains, you must see it. See advertisement.

The publishers of *Scribner's Monthly* say, "We intend to publish a Christian Magazine in which there shall be free thought and full expression of the ablest minds. We mean to make Scribner's Monthly the best magazine in the world, and to this end no pains or expense will be spared," and judging from the past, we believe they will make good their promise. The new volume commences with the November number.

Outlines of Men, Women and Things, by Mrs. Mary Clemmer Ames. (Hurd & Houghton, Pubs.) This book is characterized by the fresh, breezy, agreeable style of its gifted author; and the varied and personal character of its topics will give it special interest to every reader. And from the little bitterness of utterance when anything reminds the author of the late war, we like the tone of the book. We will quote the closing passage of "Indian Summer in Virginia." After speaking of the scenes on the Antietam battle-field and the dead who sleep in the long trenches there, she says: "Since that September evening what superlative days have trailed their splendors along these mountain sides! They linger still. As I see the great pines on the mountain tops, dip their needles in the ascending sun I say, 'Another matchless morning! It must be the last!' And when the sun drops down the valley, and its sentinel mountains change from amethyst to amber, and vale and river are flushed with unimaginable hues, "Italy cannot more than mate this sunset! But there cannot be another!" Yet the perfect days have merged into weeks, and still the miracle goes on. It is as if Summer—not the impassioned queen whose ensanguined death we watched upon the mountains yonder; but another Summer, serener, softer than the first—smiled in the very face of Winter, brightening the world ere she leaves it forever."

We are in receipt of some of the finest and best subscription books in the country, from the National Publishing Co., Philadelphia, Pa. and we advise all those who are desirous of engaging in a business wherein they can benefit others while they benefit themselves, to write to this company for canvassing books and terms for their "New Family Bible" which is the best and most perfect in the market; Dr. Wm. Smith's 'Bible History;' 'The Light in the East;' 'Human Science' by O. S. Fowler, the 'Undeveloped West,' by Beadle; &c., &c. We recommend the company to the confidence of agents, feeling assured that they will be liberally and fairly dealt with.

The Weekly Pilgrim.

Published by J. B. Brumbaugh, & Co.

Edited by H. B. & Geo. Brumbaugh.

CORRESPONDING EDITORS.

D. P. Sayler, Double Pipe Creek, Md.

Leonard Furry, New Enterprise, Pa.

The *Pilgrim* is a Christian Periodical, devoted to religion and moral reform. It will advocate in the spirit of *love* and *liberty*, the principles of true Christianity, labor for the promotion of peace among the people of God, for the encouragement of the saints and for the conversion of sinners, avoiding those things which tend toward disunion or sectional feelings.

TERMS.

Single copy, Book paper,	$1.50
Eleven copies, [eleventh for Agt.]	$15.00

Any number above that at the same rate.

Address,

H. B. BRUMBAUGH.
James Creek,
Huntingdon county Pa.

The Weekly Pilgrim.

"REMOVE NOT THE ANCIENT LANDMARKS WHICH OUR FATHERS HAVE SET."

VOL. 4. JAMES CREEK, PENNSYLVANIA, NOVEMBER 18, 1873. NO. 16.

POETRY.

The Son of Man Came to Seek that which Was Lost.

BY WESLEY.

Oh wonderful love, by Messiah displayed,
In leaving a throne whose effulgence ne'er fades,
But through the long lapse of eternity's years,
Will shine in full grandeur as time disappears.

Foregoing the homage of angels above,
The pure, blest oblation of unsullied love,
Foregoing the worship of all heaven's host,
He came down to seek and save that which was lost.

Oh! words of blest import, they shed a bright ray,
O'er the wanderer's path as he plods his lone way,
Transmitting the light to his weary sad heart,
Inviting him from folly's ways to depart.

Estranged from the circle where prayer's soothing balm,
E'er brought to the turbulent soul a sweet calm;
For down the rough channel of dark unbelief,
He's swept 'till he feels the mad fires of grief.

Now seeking repose from the weight of despair,
Which on his sad heart doth incessantly bear;
He turns his wan gaze to the light that is poured,
Upon the deep gloom by the life-giving word:

And battling with satan through mazes obscure,
He hears the glad message of mercy and power,
Though hell's fiendish legions their fury exhaust,
The Son of Man came to save that which was lost.

Now prone on the ground, and with tear-suffused eyes,
His earnest petition ascends to the skies;
And brings the response from the crimson-stained cross,
The Son of Man come to save that which was lost.

From Calvary's crest issues forth the deep tide,
'Twas oped by the spear penetrating his side;
The vilest by faith in its merit may share,
The exquisite glory of heaven's pure air.

And when on the pinions of faith we behold,
The unrivaled beauties of Zion unfold
We'll praise the high power that purged away our dross,
And brought to His Kingdom the souls that were lost.

UNREST AND REST.

A life very full of God's blessing;
A faith only heaven could keep:
A hope well illuming my daytime;
A love keeping watch while I sleep.

So blessed, yet so tired and weary!
The "many things careful about"—
The toiling and spinning of lilies,
The grasshopper burdens without.

So blessed, yet so hardened to blessings!
So troubled, and anxious and tired,
So grieved at the griefs that have hurt me,
I hasten, dear Lord, to thy side.

A bird tired out with its flying,
Yet longing for higher up sky;
A child wearied out with its crying,
Would yet go to its father and cry.

O Father! thou knowest my weakness,
Thou knowest my sins great and small,
Thou knowest for all of the worry,
The child is worth nothing at all.

I bring thee the tangle; I made it,
The tangle of life, Father, see—
It is knotted and twisted and broken,
Oh, straighten it all out for me!

It has grown far too dark here to fix it,
My poor eyes but ache with the strain;
But perhaps up in glory 'tis lighter,
Oh, straighten it, Father, again!

I know that the night is for resting,
The darkness shows heaven above,
That the "soul that is full loatheth honey,"
The hungry soul bitterness loves.

So help me to rest in the night time,
Though clouds hide my heaven and thee,
And when I can't help it "dear Father,
Dear Father," come help it for me.

S. S. Times.

ORIGINAL ESSAYS.

A THRILLING APPEAL TO THE UNCONVERTED.

Prepare to meet thy God. Amos. 4:12.

The words under consideration in the connection they stand, appear to us in the form of a challenge that the Lord God made to the children of Israel. He brought them up under His fostering care, and selected them from out of all other nations and He gave them special privileges by committing to them *His Oracles*, upheld them and brought them out of bondage from a powerful Kingdom by a high and uplifted hand, in order that they should be a peculiar people to serve Him as the only true and living God. But alas! ALAS! they departed from their Lord and worshipped idols, and done all the abominations the nations have wrought whom the Lord has driven from them. Hence He punished them in various ways in order that they should turn to Him and live, but they proved to be a rebellious stubborn people at that time, wholly given to idolatry, and would not hear the voice of the Lord. He saith, "I have overthrown some of you as God overthrew Sodom and Gomorrow, and ye were as a firebrand plucked from the burning, yet have ye not returned unto me." "Therefore this will I do unto thee, O Israel: and because I will do this unto thee, prepare to meet thy God, O Israel." Be ready to withstand judgments and fight against me, if the gods you serve are stronger than I, and let them deliver you when I meet you for destruction. Now let us apply the text, in this sense, to our present time and see in what a sad condition the sinner, I mean the impertinent sinner, stands, while living in disobedience, and rebellion against God. O may the Holy Spirit guide my pen, and indite matter sufficiently important to awaken the unwary, arouse the careless, penetrate the hearts of the unconverted and strike terror into the camp of the wicked, in order to solemnize their every hearts, bring them to conviction that may result in a complete conversion.

My dear friends, consider your condition, the glorious privilege you have. The blessing of the Gospel, which is the power of God unto salvation, is freely offered to you; you are invited to come. *The spirit says come.* You have an inward monitor, an innate principle received from your Creator, endowed with intelligence and sound reasoning on which the Spirit of God operates. *The bride saith come.* The Church of God through her faithful ministers, continually calls you to come. And why will you not come? The door of mercy stands open night and day, to welcome a free admittance into the Church of the living God. But notwithstanding all these favors, all this invitation to partake of the inestimable blessings held out before you, you stand in bold defiance and virtually say: *I will not come.* I appeal to you; bring forth your reasons. Produce your strong arguments. Dare you impeach God with partiality by saying I have not the power? Do you not know that He is no respector of persons? For it is the will of God that all should come to repentance and live. TURN! *O turn*, for why will you die! Think what the Savior hath done for you. Can it not soften your flinty heart when your thoughts are directed to Gethsemane? The bloody sweat, the agonizing groans, the exceeding sorrow that overwhelmed his pure soul. If that is not enough to pervade your heart to commiseration; then look forward a little to Mount Calvary. See Him there accused as a malefactor, as a disturber of nations, as a violator of the law of God. Scourged, mocked, smitten in the face, spit upon, crowned with thorns, betrayed by His friend, forsaken of His God, raised between heaven and earth in order to die a cursed death. Behold Him crying, my God, my God, why hast thou forsaken me? And all these He suffered, to save you and me. O how can you refrain from coming to Jesus. Have you ever, my dear dying friend, seriously reflected on these things? If not, I pray you as a lover of your souls, do so now, remember, I try to impress this important matter upon your minds, when I make this thrilling appeal. Can I make you to understand that every conviction you stifle, and every call you refuse, every invitation you slight, and every opportunity you spurn is adding to your guilt, is signifying that you stand in rebellion to God's laws, defy His holy word, reject His gracious promises and disesteem His Almighty power, and make light of the strenuous in the words of our text by which he challenges you to meet him. "Prepare to meet thy God." Will you refuse, and from time to time persist in refusing to comply with the condition of salvation, when there is nothing to hinder you? Do you not know that you add daily to your own condemnation and your consequent punishment will be an aggravated one? Stand in awe, O sinner, blush in your disobedience; terror will overwhelm your soul, "when the Lord Jesus Christ shall be revealed from heaven with all His mighty angels, in flaming fire, taking vengeance upon all them that know not God, and obey not the Gospel of the Lord Jesus Christ." Will you be able to stand? Are ye prepared to endure His vengeance? Let this text be heeded in the form of a command. "*Prepare to meet thy God.*"

LEONARD FURRY.

* *

NARROW-MINDED men, who have not a thought beyond the sphere of their own outlook, remind one of the Hindo maxim, "The snail sees nothing but its own shell, and thinks it the grandest palace in the universe."

WHAT I HAVE BEEN THINKING

It has been said that society is composed of two classes of persons, the active and the passive. The active are the energetic and enterprising, who work and keep the wheels of progress moving onward, while the passive sit idly by and enjoy the fruit of their labors. If there are any improvements to make or expenses to bear, they either have not the means, or do not seem to feel interested enough to lend a helping hand. Such persons could be very well dispensed with. I think it is the duty of every member of society to cast in their mite and show a good will. If they cannot do much, they can, at least, encourage others and try to prove that they appreciate the benefits that flow from their labors.

In society of a worldly or temporal nature, it does not make so much difference, but when it comes to a society of a spiritual nature, the church, we cannot find room for the passive class. This is a hive that cannot afford to keep drones, we want all workers. If we are not pressing forward, we are going backward,--we cannot stand still. These things have been very forcibly brought to my mind of late, and I determined to take up my pen and write a few of my thoughts on the subject. If we would see the Church thrive and prosper, we must be up and doing, there is no time to sit down and fold our hands. It is true, we cannot all preach, neither would it be profitable, there are many other ways in which we can be doing good and helping to spread the Gospel and enlarge the borders of Christ's Kingdom. There is no true and sincere member of the Church but what desires to see others brought to the knowledge of the truth, and it is their bounden duty, by example and precept, to encourage others to join in with the overtures of mercy, not for the mere purpose of enlarging the church, but from a desire that others may enjoy that future happiness which is promised to those who love and serve God. A hearty love to God and man will create such a desire in the heart of every Christian.

The Brethren are very zealous in teaching and observing the Church ordinances, which I believe is all right, but may we not neglect some command about as plain, and equally as binding as the Church ordinances, for instance the command "Go ye into all the world and preach the Gospel to every creature?" When the Savior says go, does He not mean it? Are the Brethren as strenuous about that command and as zealous in obeying it as they are some others? We believe there is but one true Church, and that it has been in existence ever since Christ founded it, but there is only a very small part of the world that hears the Gospel preached in its primitive purity.

Let us look at other denominations and see what they are doing. They are very zealous in spreading their doctrines far and wide, they spare no pains and make use of all the means they can command, and compass land and sea to make proselytes to their faith. Let us notice the Roman Catholics. They are to be seen in every land and country, their churches, schools and colleges can be seen in almost every city and town. Many of our brethren can remember well when and where the Mormons first took their rise, what an insignificant little band, and how hated and despised they were when they left the East and took up their abode in the far West, but now they are sending missionaries to foreign lands and making converts even in the islands of the ocean.

In looking at other denominations, we condemn their pomp, fashion and style of architecture as not in accordance with the humble teachings of the Savior, and rightly too, but ought we not to feel condemned when we see them spend so much money for show, and we do not spend more for the spreading of the Gospel? Have the Brethren ever sent a missionary to foreign lands? But some will say, charity should commence at home, we have many living in heathen darkness in our own land and country which is all very true, but is there as much as could and should be done at home? There are many calls but few responding to these calls, what will be the excuse in the day of judgment for not more fully obeying this command? It cannot be poverty. I am not much acquainted with the Brethren outside of the bounds of the church I live in, and was not brought up in the faith, but I learn there are many wealthy brethren, and as they are so zealous in contending for the faith, ought they not spend a little more of this world's goods to help to propogate the true doctrines of the Scripture? We know we have no abiding city here, then why should we lay up treasure here? As we do not spend money in adorning ourselves and following the vain amusements of this world, it gives us a chance to lay up wealth which may be a temptation to make an idol of. Complaints are coming from almost every quarter that pride is creeping into the Church, that our young members do not conform to the order of the Brethren, which is lamentable enough as pride is an abomination in the sight of the Lord, but may it not be possible that some of our older ones who have lived all their lives in conformity to the order of the Church as far as dress is concerned, and in consequence of not spending unnecessarily, have become wealthy. I say might it not be possible for them gradually to set their hearts and affections on their property and thus make an idol of it, which is as much abhorred in the sight of the Lord as pride? There is danger of their forgetting that it is the Lord's and that he has lent it to them and will expect it back again with usury, not in the form of dollars and cents, but in the form of souls, redeemed from sin and misery.

I have said that the Brethren condemn the style of architecture displayed in the building of churches by other denominations, if we build our churches plain ought we not to build the more of them? I have sometimes been led to believe from the actions of some brethren when they have met to arrange such matters as the building of a church, that they look at it from a temporal standpoint of view a little too much, they seem to forget that it is giving to the Lord, and their conversation on that subject sounds more like some worldly enterprise which they are rather forced into against their will, than like humble Christians, building a house for the worship of God.

I have noticed that the Brethren will contend very earnestly for the faith, in the way of argument, both publicly and in private conversation, and sometimes I have noticed when it became necessary to contribute a few cents or dollars for the upbuilding of that faith, some of those same brethren were not quite so ready to aid the cause. For instance, when brethren will say their chief aim and whole desire is for the honor and glory of God and the prosperity of Zion, and when they are solicited to assist in building a church or holding a communion, they are not able to give a cent towards the former and very little to the latter, or sometimes when ministering brethren go on a mission of labor and love to other churches and labor with them in word and doctrine, helping to build them up in the most holy faith, and some of the active members knowing their pecuniary circumstances, and that they have families to support, feel it their duty to bear their traveling expenses or allow them some slight remuneration for their time, then it is that the passive ones do not feel that their services are needed nor that they have any duty to perform. A few dollars spent that way will often do a great deal of good, and it is one of the ways of spending money for Jesus. I believe there are many ministering brethren who are fully able and willing to declare the whole council of God, who could do much good by travelling and preaching if their families did not need the labor of their hands.

I notice that when a minister comes from a distance and is noted for being a good speaker, how the brethren and sisters all turn out to hear him, and some who are not very often seen at our regular appointments come then. Then would it not be wisdom in us, and is it not our duty to God and our fellow-creatures to keep them at the work the church has set them apart for, and can we spend our surplus money in any better or nobler cause than sending missionaries out in all the world, scattering the pure seeds of the Gospel, and building churches for the worship of that God whom we believe we are the true worshipers of.

One more thought and I will close. When I read the reports of communions from the different churches, I learn that some of those communions are attended by a greater number of ministers than is necessary to hold the meeting, and I always read that they had a good meeting and all enjoyed themselves well, why should they not? It is about as near Heaven as we can get on earth when Christians meet to worship God and practice the ordinances of his house, it is a foretaste of Heaven and it is no wonder they like to be together, but we are not promised Heaven upon earth, we are to bear trials, crosses and separations here, besides there is a great deal of work to do when we look around and see the broad fields that are ready for the laborer and know that they are few. We feel as though some of those ministers could do more good by scattering out and preaching the Word to many who have never had an opportunity to hear the truth, and who would gladly accept of it if it was presented to them.

And now, brother Brumbaugh, if these few thoughts are worthy of a place in the PILGRIM, please insert them, if not, throw them in your waste basket and you will oblige me.

From your sister,

L. WEAVER.

Brimfield, Ind.

THE PAST COMPARED WITH THE PRESENT.

In the primitive days of Christianity, so great was the persecution of believers that none but those who were real disciples of Christ, or sincere inquirers, came often to their assemblies, and it was easy to distinguish between those that served God, and those who served Him not. But after Constantine embraced Christianity, and it became popular, worldly-minded men took upon them the name of Christians, and became rulers in the Church; and the abomination that maketh desolate was set up, the true humble disciples of Christ were then under the necessity to take the apostles advice; and come out from among them and be separate, in order to be the sons and daughters of the Almighty. And said the Apostle, "What fellowship hath light with darkness, or Christ with Belial?" But these faithful ones were despised and persecuted, and considered as enemies to the cause and church of God, by the body of professing Christians, yet they were the remnant spoken of in Rev. 12: 17; who kept the commandments of God and had the faith of Jesus Christ. The offerings and services of unrenewed and worldly men are not acceptable unto God as may be seen in the case of Cain and the Israelites in the time of Isaiah the prophet. Read Isaiah 1: 11; "To what purpose is the multitude of your sacrifices unto me? saith the Lord: When ye come to appear before me; who hath required this at your hand to tread my courts? Bring no more vain oblations; incense is an abomination unto me; the new moons and Sabbaths, the calling of assemblies, I cannot away with; it is iniquity, even the solemn meeting. Wash you, make you clean; put away the evil of your doings from mine eyes; cease to do evil; learn to do well."

The apostle who recommended to his brethren not to forsake the assembling of themselves together, also besought them by the mercies of God to present their bodies a living sacrifice, holy and acceptable unto God which was their reasonable service. The state of the Pharisees, notwithstanding their zeal for God, and their regular sacrifices, fasting, and prayers, our Savior declared to be worse than the publicans and harlots. And whenever a religion becomes fashionable, and is no longer a cross to put it on, the proud, the covetous, and the worldly will embrace it, attend meetings and conform to its precepts and regulations, for it is a reputable thing, and adds to their respectability. Oh there is the danger.

May the God and Father of our Lord Jesus Christ open the eyes of His dear children to see the necessity of looking to Him continually, and keeping an eye single that their bodies may be full of light.

Our Lord has said, "Ye shall know the tree by its fruits: men do not gather grapes of thorns, nor figs of thistles." And all those who go under a high profession of religion attend meetings, and draw near to the Lord, with their mouth, and honor Him with their lips, while their hearts are far from Him, and filled with covetousness, will find themselves rejected in that day, for Christ will say to them: "Depart from me, ye that work iniquity." But to those who endeavor with a sincere heart, to serve the Lord and watch against every evil thought, words, and action, praying for daily bread, that their souls may be nourished up unto eternal life He will say "come ye blessed of my Father, inherit the kingdom prepared for you from the foundation of the world. But professors in this day, it would seem, believe that they can serve God and mammon, love the world and follow their own wills, and be accepted of God, by going to meeting and attending to some of the outward services of religion. Our blessed Redeemer said, "I come not to my own will, but the will of Him that sent me." "And unless a man deny himself, take up his cross and follow me, he cannot be my disciple." And said the apostle, "Be not deceived, God is not mocked, for whatsoever a man soweth that shall he also reap." The Lord has always had a few faithful ones in every age. When our Savior appeared among men, there was a Simeon, an Anna, a Nathaniel, with others, no doubt, but these few did not save the Jewish people from that destruction, which their wickedness and hardness of heart so justly merited. I often said, O that their calamities and destruction might prove a warning to professors of religion, to the end of time, and lead them to cleave to the ways of true righteousness, that they may escape the miseries that came upon them. O that people would see the necessity there is to turn from blind guides, who will neither enter the true kingdom, nor, let others enter, and go to the Lord to be taught of Him, whose inviting language is "son or daughter give me thy heart;" and if we are so truly wise as to give our hearts to Him, He will sit as a refiner of silver and purify them as gold. And then, and not till then will the offerings of Judah be pleasant unto the Lord.

A PILGRIM.

HOW THE CHURCH SHOULD SPEND HER MONEY

Dear brethren of the Pilgrim: As I notice that you request an article on the proper expenditure of money, I will now try to say something on that subject. That there are many ways in which money can be spent to the honor and glory of God is evident. It is so spent when it is bestowed upon the needy, in order that their physical wants may be supplied. This every true child of God knows, and therefore needs no comment. But there are other ways that seem not to be trodden by the brethren, that ought to enlist our serious attention, and if well considered may be found that money can be spent to the further extension of the Gospel.

Now brethren, I am going to tople over on the missionary subject. That it is both proper and right that the Gospel should be preached to every creature, I only need to refer to the commission as recorded by the Evangelist Matthew, Mark, and Luke. We notice that the command was given by the Lord Jesus, that his Gospel should be preached to every creature. But those whom he had chosen was unlearned and ignorant, and hence they were to tarry at Jerusalem until they were imbued with power from on high.—Luke 24: 49. And when the day of pentecost was fully come they were with one accord in one place.—Acts 2d chapter. Then follows the miraculous gift of the Holy Ghost and the imparting of tongues, and then unlearned as they formerly were, they were now properly qualified to do what the Lord commanded them. The epithet was formerly applied of being poor unlearned fisherman, but God chose this little band of unlearned men to confound the things that was mighty, and so complete was their education that three thousand men of the nations of the earth, were added to Christ's mystical body, the Church, in one day.

Now brethren, we notice that the gift of tongues was essentially necessary to the furtherance of the Gospel while in its infancy, and being thus necessary, it was incorporated by the Lord Jesus Himself. I contend that the Church should not lose any of her qualifying principles, or those things which the Lord gave her, as means to be used for her extension. Jesus said, "Of those which thou gavest to me, I have lost none save the son of perdition, that the Scripture might be fulfilled," the Master lost nothing that was gived to him, but everything answered its end to the fulfilling of the Scripture Jesus is our example, hence it follows that we should not lose anything that was given us. The gift of tongues is not the son of perdition, but the gift of the Holy Ghost. The Holy Ghost is the comforter that is to lead us into all truth. It leads us into the gift of tongues. The injunction of the apostle is that we lose none of these things; hence if everything must be preserved, the gift of tongues should be retained. But when we look around, we discover that the Church, to a certain extent, has lost this power, and the consequence is, she is losing her power that God gave unto her for successfully preaching the Gospel to every creature. The church is hemmed within the shores of America. Over eighteen hundred years have passed away; the gift of tongues annihilated, and most of the nations are sitting in darkness. The apostle would say, "Beloved these things ought not so to be." Right here, brethren, is a chance to spend your money with profit. The command was to tarry until they were imbued with power. There was a house at Jerusalem that was built and dedicated unto the Lord, and the people worshipped there and also received instruction, and I think that it was at this house that the unlearned fishermen were educated and received a proper knowledge of the oriental languages in order that they might preach the Gospel to every creature. Let the church build houses and employ teachers in order that she may again restore that which is lost. Let the church select brethren that are young and full of faith, and let them remain at these places long enough to obtain a proper knowledge of the nations to whom they are to go. Then let them go and preach, saying, "Repent and believe the Gospel." Let us hold up to the nations Jesus Christ and Him crucified. Let them teach them the observance of all things, and this might be done by sending a few to every nation, and then we can have the assurance that we are doing what the Lord commanded us to do.

JOHN W. FITZGERALD.

OUR BARKS ARE SAILING

We are taught in divine truth, that this earth is not our home, and that we are destined for another clime. Our barks are launched upon the waters of time, and in order to become sailors, it is necessary that we should have a good captain, or one who is amply qualified, to instruct us, for when we enter the cooling stream, it is then we covenant with our captain to be true and faithful to the end. There it is that we commence to sail, and Christian sailors, remember that the waves of temptation may round us roll; grasp firmly the rudder, and keep your little ship in the true channel, lest she be dashed against the rocks. Fervent prayer, is requisite to our becoming proficient, in the cause we espouse, keeping in remembrance that each of us must steer our own barks, and also, see that we give a helping hand to those who have not yet set sail, under the banner of King Jesus.

Vain world, under whose banner are you sailing? I fear some are holding to the rudder of worldly fame, whilst others are holding to the root of evil, (money), and others to pride, &c. And, behold, you are all under the banner of the devil, for Christ saith, "They that are not for me, are against me." So you can plainly see that there are but two ways to sail, to misery, or to eternal happiness. Then in the name of Jesus, I beseech you, sail in His bark.

A. M. GOOD.

Waynesboro, Pa.

There is no death: what seems so is transition.

For the PILGRIM, by request.

THURMAN ON THE PASSOVER REVIEWED: ERROR EXPOSED.

Continued from page 355.

But Thurman says, "If they had not intended to eat the passover before the following night, this their reason for not going into the judgment hall, was no reason at all; for one thus defiled had only to be unclean until evening, for he could wash his flesh with water, and when the sun is down he shall be clean, and shall afterwards eat of the holy things." Now we admit the correctness of this law; but we object to his mode of reasoning from it. The Jews were unavoidably liable to become unclean, no difference how careful they might be. To touch a dead body, or even to touch anything that was unclean, caused uncleanness: and for this reason there was a provision in the law, whereby persons thus defiled might become clean again. But had the Jews gone into the judgment hall in the case referred to, their uncleanness would have been willful and without excuse, and not through weakness or accident, and consequently we do not believe their uncleanness could have been removed by the conditions of this law. He also says: "If our Lord came not to destroy the law, but to fulfill, he must have necessarily ate of that passover as enjoined by the law; and if the Son can do nothing of himself, but what he seeth the Father do, he could have instituted no new passover of his own." Now did he not institute Feet-washing and the Communion at the same time he instituted this supper? They certainly were something new, and if he had power to institute these ordinances, why, with the same power, could he not institute the Lord's Supper? As to Christ's fulfilling the law, we believe he had fulfilled this part of the law three times since his baptism; and if three times fulfilling the law was not sufficient we would like to know how many more times would have been sufficient. Concerning the day of the week on which Christ was crucified, and the time he was to remain in the grave, he says, "We are then compelled either to admit that the crucifixion was on Thursday or deny the word of Christ—'So shall the Son of Man be three days and three nights in the heart of the earth?'" The seeming difference between our Lord's prediction of the time he was to be in the grave, and the time during which his body was interred, is very easily obviated, by considering that it was the custom of the orientals to reckon any part of a day of twenty-four hours for a whole day; and to say a thing happened after three days and three nights, was the same as to say that it happened after three days, or on the third day. Compare Esther 4: 16 with 5: 1. Christ being entombed in the closing of Friday, this was counted a day and a night; and Saturday was another day and night; and he rose from the grave on Sunday morning, which was counted another day and night, which, according to the oriental mode of reckoning time, would be three days and three nights. In this, our ex-brother betrays a very limited knowledge of the oriental customs, for the great pretentions he has made to science and literature; but, according to his own words, he is not one of the wise prophets. Speaking concerning the time of Christ's second coming, to judge the world in righteousness, he says, "The wise shall understand," and we all know that he did not understand, for Christ failed to come when he said he would, therefore with his own words he condemns himself as a foolish prophet.

He also says, in speaking concerning the time when the Lord's Supper should be kept, "Those who observe it at any other time than that upon which the passover was to be kept, do appear to charge the apostles with having been remiss in their duty, and then assume the authority to supply their omission." Now, if Christ, the great head of the Church, did not keep this supper on the night the Jews were to eat the passover, as we have clearly shown, why should his followers be restricted to that night in keeping this ordinance? He does not say, "Thou shalt therefore keep this ordinance in his season from year to year, like the passover was to be kept;" but he says, "As often as ye eat this bread, and drink this cup, ye do show the Lord's death till he come." 1 Cor. 11: 26. Hence there is no restriction concerning the time of keeping this supper, but as often as it is done in order, it certainly will be acceptable.

With a few words to those brethren who have been giving ear to this false prophet, and have ceased to celebrate the sufferings and death of their adorable Redeemer, I will bring my article to a close. Under the law of Moses any person that was clean, and was not on a journey, and forbare to keep the passover, was to be cut off from among his people, Num. 9: 13; and Christ said; "Verily, verily, I say unto you, except ye eat the flesh of the Son of Man and drink his blood, ye have no life in you." John 6: 23. Now "If every transgression and disobedience" under the law, "received a just recompense of reward, how shall we escape," says Paul, "if we neglect so great salvation?" Heb. 2: 2-3. We will therefore say with Paul," Brethren, mark them which cause divisions and offenses, contrary to the doctrine which ye have received, and avoid them." Some may think this is taking advantage of Thurman, since he has been excluded from the Brethren, but remember his works have not been excluded, and it is to them we are replying.

B. F. KOONS.

Nettle Creek, Ind.

ATTENDING MEETINGS IN PHILADELPHIA.

It was on a very warm Saturday evening in June, when I arrived, in company with my brother and a cousin, in the great secondary metropolis of America.

I knew there were brethren living in the city, and I knew where some of them lived, but there were some doubtful apprehensions in my mind in regard to the propriety of forcing ourselves upon their hospitalities, having had no customary notices sent ahead—neglectful and behind the "times" in that, so my cousin and I decided to lodge at the "Merchants Hotel." My brother promised to meet us there in the morning and accompany us attending meetings during the day. Upon arriving at the hotel we were apparently very kindly received,—no brethren could have appeared more courteous to us. We soon made a bargain to lodge with them at $3.00 per day apiece. During the evening several finely dressed-to-bacco chewing gentleman talked a good deal of Quakerism to us. They asked us a great many questions. We finally told them that our school teachers used to tell us to be careful not to ask strangers too many questions, and they finally told us they were clothing, boot, shoe &c., merchants, that it was their way of getting acquainted with merchants when they stopped at the "Hotel," and that they always regarded the Quakers as an honest, upright people.

The next morning we went to Crown St. to the Brethren's Sunday School and preaching. There were quite a number of ministering brethren present, had a good meeting I thought,—did not see any of the brethren asleep. In the afternoon my brother told me there was an appointment made for the people to gather to worship God in another street at 2 o'clock, where the celebrated Dr. Chambers would preach, so we went. The house was substantial, large and grand. The preacher was young and adorned with shining, costly attire. The sermon was stiff and cold, I thought. After he was through with his vanity it was announced by the sexton that Chambers was improving in health, and expected to be with his flock in October—that he had sent a letter to be read to his congregation, which was done. In it he made some very touching appeals to his congregation, imploring them to do their duty to one another and to God. I thought the reading of the letter was the best part of the exercise. It was well seasoned with very appropriate Scripture. There was good order, I did not hear any noise except that of the speakers and the musicians during the whole time of the exercises, neither did I see anybody asleep. My brother had often told me if I would go with him to meeting in the city he would give me five dollars for every person I saw asleep during the exercises, also five dollars for every male resident of the city who kept his hat on at any time in the house. As sleeping in meeting in the Brotherhood is indulged in at some places to an alarming extent, I made it part of my business to ascertain the cause of it by going to assemblies called saints and kept awake, and then try to reduce it or banish it altogether from among the Brethren—at least where I am called to preach. I have however, since concluded to make some allowance to those of my brethren who indulge which I would not make to those Philadelphians, and will allow each one that indulges to discover the reason of that allowance himself. If he can't find it let him wake up and keep awake during meeting. In the evening my brother told us there was another place where it was said the Gospel would be preached by a man eighty years of age, named Dr. Wadsworth. I wondered whether, by reason of age his memory and other abilities (if ever he had any) had not become very much impaired. I felt as curious to see and hear the strange (to me) new old famous, so considered preacher as Zaccheus was to see Jesus. We soon found our way to the place appointed. The door-keeper asked us whether we wished to go in. We answered yes, then he bade us follow him. After going half lengthwise through the aisle he opened a door that led to one of the pews under the gallery, the ceiling of which we nearly touched, or rather our heads nearly reached the ceiling while standing upright. After being seated I ventured a half suspicious, half fearful glance at the grand and spacious apartment and at the congregation. The seats were already nearly all comfortably filled, though it was full half an hour before the appointed hour to commence the exercises. I was surprised to see nobody staring at me or anybody else. There seemed to be a solemn silence except an occasional touch of a fan against a fancy ribbon. Feeling myself at least out of iminent danger, I began to scrutinize things nearer at home. In front of me were some Hymn Books in a shelf made for the purpose. I picked up one of the books and looking at the title page saw the words "The Reformed Dutch Church of North America." I read some of the "preface" and found that the compiler complained of their predecessors quite similarly to the manner in which brother Quinter complained of the predecessors of our present Hymn Book. I wondered whether ever our Brotherhood would in all ages of time to come, reform to such an extent and in the same direction as the one I was looking at must have done. I wondered whether reform and pride really and necessarily always had to go together. While my mind was still busily engaged upon these things, the celebrated pastor made his appearance in the dazzling pulpit. His outer garments were coarse and loosely thrown around his body and hanging on his arms, giving him air and appearance much like the pictures of the ancient prophets as we see them in the Bible. His manner seemed to me both natural and simple throughout. His prayer was warm and plaintive as that of a little child, though it seemed to me he asked God to do more than I had ever heard any man ask of Him at one time in so many words. The subject of his discourse to the congregation was the conviction and conversion of sinners to God. He handled it with such a spirit of power that I could not see how any person under the sound of his voice could continue in the indulgence of known sin, until I remembered the passage "Not all that say unto me Lord, Lord, shall enter into the Kingdom of Heaven, but they that do the will of my Father which is in heaven." The sermon was so well jointed, so well composed and seasoned with warmth and many other things essentially necessary to accomplish the work for which it was designed that no one could help but say, "Lord, Lord."

I receded from the threshold of this great modern semi-heathenish temple full of gods, with convictions and apprehensions of the awful judgments of God against spiritual wickedness in high places and against whosoever "maketh a lie." But thanks be to God the only wise and beneficient preserver of all that is worthy, there is a way to escape the wrath of an offended God. There is an avenue that leads to eternal bliss at His right hand. J. B. GARVER.

Mt. Union, Pa.

LIVING SPRINGS.

Go among the mountains, and you will see that it is the living spring that flows away down through the vale. And where it flows, the grass is green, and the flowers bloom, and the cattle drink, and the children linger to dip the foot, and hear the sweet song of the little rills. Yet the spring itself is in no way exhausted by all this. Exhausted? It never will be. It is fed by the drawing sun, by the condensing mountains, by the bountiful clouds, by the great and wide sea. When the sea is empty, and the heavens are dry, the little fountains of the earth will yield no more. Well up without stint, ye springs sent into valleys which run among the hills. Give to every beast of the field, let even the wild asses quench their thirst. Go murmuring into rills of laughter, and rolling into rivers of song, and never be afraid or give one backward look. You have the sun above you, and the hills around you, and the great oceans of the earth behind you, all holding themselves bound and ready to serve you, if you continue to serve others by your flow. Christians let your inner life fed and nourished by the indwelling word of Christ, have not ostentatious, or self-confident, or noisy, but yet natural, continuous outflow and expression.—*The Christian*

"CHRIST LIVETH IN ME."

This no doubt, seems a strange assertion to those unacquainted with the faith and experience of the Christian. Strange and bold as it may seem, it is confirmed by the life of every real Christain, who no longer lives the old life of sin, but the new life of holiness. In Christ, there was undecried inexhaustive intensive life, which he had the power to impart.

Christ lives in the Christian as the origin of his life. Apart from Him there can be no spiritual life. In Him as believers we live and move and have our being. Only a semblance of life and that for a brief period, can be maintained apart from Christ. "As the branch cannot bear fruit except it abide in the vine, no more can ye, except it abide in me" I have seen the pruner go forth in the spring-time to cut off the crooked and useless branches. For a time they seemed to maintain their life, the buds opened into blossoms, and leaves began to appear; but, long before the heat of summer was over, they had withered completely. They had no continuing life when severed from the tree.

Christ lives in the Christian as the result of his faith. The life I live in the flesh, says the apostle, I live by faith in the Son of God. Christ lives in us as we reflect His image. Often the child bears the likeness of a parent. So the Christian bears about the marks of the Lord Jesus. Christ lives in us as the father lives in the child who carries on the business and executes the plans of his father. Christ lives in us as the teacher lives in his pupil. The teacher has a moulding influence, and the pupil reflects the life of his master. Christ lives in us, when we do his will and execute his plans, truly and grand as he lived in the apostles. We can see how he lived in their preaching and in their work in the churches they established, upon and in the great missionary enterprises upon which they embarked. He lives in us by the abiding Comforter, the Holy Spirit; for if a man have not the Spirit of Christ, he is none of his. If Christ live not in you, you have no life that is abiding. If He does, let the glory of your life be manifested. "Herein is my father glorified, that ye bear much fruit; so shall ye be my disciples."

Youth's Department.

GREAT MEN.

Do you want to be a great man? many boys think they would like to be great men when grown up, and sometimes they amuse themselves by fancying all the wonderful things they will do some day. But perhaps it would be better to think how you can become a great man, than what you would do if you were one.

If you want to be a very tall man, and perhaps sometimes you wish that too, how can it be? You will not all at once spring into a tall man. You can only be a tall man if now, while you are a boy, you grow a little every day. So small indeed the difference each day between the growth if you become a tall man, and that of the boy who becomes only a short man that we cannot see you grow any more than the other; yet it is only by this little difference each day and each year that you can become tall instead of short.

In the same way, if you want to be a great and good man, do not expect that something will, by and by, come upon you all at once and make you so. There are instances no doubt in which some unexpected event has changed the whole course of a man's life, or so wrought upon his mind as to bring out powers and feelings which had been hidden and unused before. But for the most part, great men grow out of great boys, and if you wish to be one, you will be much more likely to attain it by being a great and good boy, than by dreaming of great men, and neglecting what you can do now. I do not mean that you must do wonderful things, for such may not come in your path, but do every thing, great or small in a great and noble spirit; not great in pride but great in humility, great in love, great in faith and hope.

Shall I tell you what the greatest man I ever knew did, when he was a boy? He was at school with his eldest brother; and this brother had done something wrong, and the master was going to flog him. Charles did not beg that his brother might be forgiven, for he knew that the charge was just and the punishment certain. He went up to the master and said: Give me the flogging instead, I am stronger than my brother and can bear it better." Do you wonder that such a noble boy became a noble man? You will easily believe me when I tell You that when he was a man he was ever ready to sympathize with every one in distress, and to help them, whether by adding to his hard work or by taking from his earnings more largely than he could well spare. All who knew him loved him, and all who even looked at him seemed to catch something of his happiness if not of his benevolence.

When I said if you want to be a tall man you must grow every day, did not you think to yourself, "But I cannot grow by trying, I cannot make myself grow?" Do not forget that this is just as true of becoming a great man in any sense in which it is worth while to be great. You cannot begin to be a good boy of yourself, as you will find if you try. But then, though you cannot be sure of being tall, for you do not know whether it is God's will to make you so, you can be quite sure of being the best sort of great man, that is a good man, if you really wish it; for God has promised to give the Holy Spirit to those that ask him.

God's Holy Spirit within you will make you good and great. How? By making you like Christ. What is it that most touches our hearts in the anecdote of the little boy I have told you about? Is it not that his love to his brother was something like Christ's love. Christ loved us so much that he died on our behalf. The more by God's Spirit's help we see Christ's wonderful love, the more we shall love him, and the more we shall become like him.—*New York Observer.*

CULTIVATE A PURE EXPRESSION

Every word that falls from the lips, of mothers and sisters especially, should be pure and concise, and simple; not pearls, such as fall from the lips of a princess, but sweet, good words, that little children can gather without fears of soil or after shame, or blame, or any regrets to pain thro' all their life.

Children should be taught the use of good, strong, expressive words—words that mean exactly what they should express in their proper places.

If a child, or young person, has a loose or flung-together way of stringing words when endeavoring to say something, he should be made to try again and see if he can do no better.

It is painful to listen to many girls talk. They begin with "my goodness!" and interlard it with "oh!" and "sakes alive!" and "so sweet!" and "so queenly!" and so many phrases, that one is tempted to believe that they have no training at all, or else their mothers were very foolish women. There is nothing more disgusting than the twaddle of ill-bred girls; one is provoked often into taking a paper and reading, and letting them ripple and gurgle on like brooks that flow, they know not whither.

My heart warms with love for sensible girls and pure boys; and after all, if your girls and boys are not thus, I fear that it is not our fault that this great truth rests in the hands of the women of our land. If we have a noble, useful purpose of life we shall infuse the right spirit in those around us.—*Arthur's Home Magazine.*

The Weekly Pilgrim.

JAMES CREEK, PA., Nov. 18, 1873.

☞ How to send money.—All sums over $1.50, should be sent either in a check, draft or postal order. If neither of these can be obtained, have the letter registered.

☞ When Money is sent, *always* send with it the name and address of those who paid it. Write the names and post office as plainly as possible.

☞ Every subscriber for 1874, gets a *Pilgrim Almanac* Free.

THE DEDICATION.

While living in the world it seems so natural to take after its ways, especially in calling things after their names. When we were yet a boy we remember quite distinctly of church dedications (not among the Brethren) but cannot so well remember of what the ceremony consisted. Dedications are still rife in the world but have undergone many modifications, so much so, that the original definition has become almost absolete and a new one given, which means to beg enough money to cancel the debt.

Some time ago, we attended the dedication of a very stylish Presbyterian Church and according to the nature of things, we expected to see considerable ceremony and hear largely about dedicating the wooden temple to the worship of God, but in this we were disappointed, as there was as little as possible said about these things, and not a word said about money. This we thought to be one of the "new departures." The exercises were commenced as on ordinary occasions when an invited minister or lecturer entertined the audience from the following text: "John Knox." We shall not now tell our readers where this text stands, hoping that you have read your Bible sufficiently to know that it is not in it. He labored much harder to show that John Knox was the Lion of the Reformation, than that Jesus was the Christ, and we have no doubt that some, after the discourse, thought he was the greater of the two. We were pleased with the dedication but tho't the "Knox" a grand fizzle. But this is not what we intended to talk about. We only introduced this to show that our dedication was after a different style. Eld. Grabill Myers opened the discourse and instead of taking for his text "Alexander Mack" he took the "Commission." We confess we thought it a little odd for the ocasion but he insisted upon it that he was right, and before he was through showed that building church houses formed quite a prominent part in the "Go ye." Our good brother always was full of the "commission" and we suppose it will "go" with him to the grave, as even now, limping along with a crutch on each side the holy fire burns within, as brightly as ever. He that endureth unto the end shall obtain the crown.

To be a little more explicit, the brethren of James Creek thought it prudent to build a Church house at Coffee Run, and accordingly got to work and by the first of November it was completed. The house was intended for ordinary meetings and we suppose, for that purpose, will be large enough, although it proved too small on last Sabbath. It is substantially, plainly, and neatly built, and will answer the purpose of worshiping God in very well. Friday Nov. 7, was the time made choice of to hold the first meeting. The following ministers were present during the meeting: Grabill Myers, G. W. Brumbaugh, J. R. Lane, J. L. Wineland, and S. A Moore. Bro. Jno. Wise was to be with us, but for some cause, failed to come. The weather part of the time was unfavorable and the nights quite dark, yet the attendance was on an average, good, and we feel that we had a very good meeting and brethren who labored so faithfully for us, deserve and have our thanks.

SHALL THEY BE REPORTED?

During our late meeting, a number of subjects were discussed in our private "sociables." Among others, was, "Is a brother justifiable in allowing an other brother or sister to defraud him designedly, of his just dues without reporting him to the Church?" There is a principle connected with this question that is worthy of the consideration of every brother and sister. On this subject we have two positive precepts which are sufficiently broad to cover every case. "Thou shalt not defraud." "Thou shalt owe no man." Every debt, no matter how small, voluntarily made, must be met, and every one that refuses to do so is an open violator of both the moral and divine law. Through a false charity, we sometimes forgive debts rather than go to any trouble or cause hard feelings even where the debtor refuses to ask forgivness and is able to pay. This may seem good on the part of the creditor but how is it with the debtor, and is it right so to do?

To illustrate the idea more clearly our "chief speaker" related a case Some years ago he sold a brother an ax. In a year after, the brother moved west and took the ax along but never paid for it. "Now says he, I did not care for the loss but did I do my brother justice by allowing him to take the unpaid ax without reproving him of defrauding, and may I not have laid in his way a temptation which may lead him to greater violations?" * This fairly illustrates the moral of the case. By such charity we not only allow him to commit sin but to remain in sin, as no brother or any body else can stand justified in the sight of God when he is a defrauder or refuses to pay his honest debts. There is possibly, only one way that a debt can remain unpaid and the debtor be justified. That is when the creditor is willing to forgive at the request of the debtor. This annuls the obligation, and both parties may be justified. Of course, inability is an exception always understood.

We are under moral and religious obligations to our brethren and if we cover over their obligations by forgiving debts unasked for and uninformed of it, we become partakers of their sins.

Therefore we very justly conclude that all claiming to be Christians are under sacred obligations to pay their honest debts if it is in their power to do so.

If any neglect or refuse to do so, it is the creditors duty to inform them of their faults, and if they refuse to render satisfaction, they should then be reported to the church.

If this rule was rigidly carried out, it might save the good reputation the Brethren once had, but is now measurably being lost. Brethren and sisters, think of these things and do not allow our good name to come into disrepute by neglecting that which is your duty to do. Remember, it was the small foxes that spoiled the vines, and small sins may destroy your reputation and finaly lead to ruin.

* If this comes to the notice of a brother who has been, for a long time, chopping wood with an unpaid ax, it will be well for him to reflect and turn from the evil of his way, lest he might be tempted to commit a similar sin by not paying for the Pilgrim

MINISTERIAL VISIT.

During our Coffee Run meetings we had the pleasure of welcoming into our Sanctum our genial brother and colaborer S. A. Moore. After passing the usual greetings looking around and transacting a little business it was moved to get aboard the train and run down to Huntingdon to see how the new Pilgrim Office was getting along. But on being informed that the train was an hour behind time we agreed to feel disappointed and return to the office again. On entering we were agreeably surprised in meeting our esteemed brother J. F. Oller of Wayneshoro' Pa. After this meeting our disappointment vanished and were made to feel that all things work together for good. After spending a short but pleasant season together we supped and again started for the train to attend the appointment at Coffee Run. We tried to prevail on Bro. Oller to stop off with us but he said "I go a fishing" and a fishing he did go. Bro. Oller during his stay told us some good things and some that were strange very strange. The good fills our souls with gladness, the strange makes us weep.

A WORD OF CAUTION.

Our brethren and sisters will please not give their names and money for the Pilgrim, to agents of doubtful reputation and who are known, not to pay their debts. Through this neglect, we have lost seriously and have a few agents for the present year who have sent us large lists, but as yet paid nothing. We hope however, they will still be in time and pay us before the year closes. If not, we shall report to the church to which they belong and demand an investigation. If any of our agents have gathered names from different churches and it is inconvenient for them to collect it, let us know, giving the names and addres and we will try and have it collected ourselves, or still better, those who have not yet paid and it is inconvenient to pay the agent, enclose it in a letter and send it to us.

NOTICE.

All those who have subscribed for the Pilgrim under brother George Mourer and have not yet paid, will please hand it to brother Daniel Miller or send it directly to us and much oblige.

Isaac Glery. All righs, names marked paid as reported.

Bro. Samuel Ream, of Yankton, Decotah Territory, says they have been living there for four years and did not hear a sermon preached until two weeks ago. After all this fast, he got a good dose of spirit, but water baptism had nothing to do with being born again. The subject was the "new birth." He also informs us that since last Spring, about 2.000 Germans from Russia settled in their neighborhood.

The Altoona Church Again.—We had thought this enterprise a failure, but from report of Committee in present issue it will be seen that the prospects are getting better and looks towards success. We hope that the appeal made to Middle District of Pa., will not be in vain.

In the obituary of Eld J. F. Rohrer by a wrong figure, his age was made 93 instead of 63 as it should have been.

OUR CONDITIONS.

We are being asked whether our conditions for the coming year will be the same as the present year. In the main, we expect them to be the same, but would say to those who have the means, pay us at the time of subscribing or at the first part of the year. If all that can, will do this, it will enable us to meet our obligations and give a little more time to those who cannot pay cash or at the beginning of the year. All those who have not paid for the present year will be expected to pay before the beginning of the new year. 3t

AGENTS WANTED.

We want a good active agent, to solicit subscribers for the Pilgrim, in every Church in the brotherhood. If there are any that feel to labor for us and are not supplied with prospectus and *Almanac* will please write us and we will send by return mail. Remember, the Pilgrim for the coming year will be enlarged and every subscriber will receive the *Pilgrim Almanac*, handsomely gotten up, containing a "Ministerial List," giving post-office, county and State, with other valuable information free. 5t.

Correspondence.

A Reporter is wanted from every Church in the brotherhood to send us Church news, Obituaries, Announcements, or anything that will be of general interest. To insure insertion, the writers name must accompany each communication. Our Invitation is not personal but general—please respond to our call.

REPORT.

TO THE MIDDLE DISTRICT OF PA.

We the undersigned Committee appointed by said District to view sites for a Church house in the City of Altoona, having this day viewed a number of sites, have found several lots, that we think quite suitable for the erecting of a house for worship, and have made a disposition as follows: The Brethren of Altoona not being able to ascertain what could be raised in consequence of no definite site, we have appointed a purchasing and Building Committee with instructions to make the effort to raise sufficient funds in connection with that subscribed by the District, to purchase one of the sites and build. But if they fail to raise the amount or a sufficient portion to make it safe, to hold the note over until next District meeting. This committee is to report to Bro. Geo. Brumbaugh, Grafton, Huntingdon Co., Pa., who will give publicity and specify a time when the donations shall be paid.

Committee. { SAMUEL COX.
CONRAD IMLER.
R. MCFARLAND.

In our investigations we made it a point to learn the condition of this flourishing city and the feelings of the Brethren residing there, and also the feelings of a number of the citizens, and there seems to be a very great anxiety to have a house built for the worship of God. In connection with this feeling and the solemn injunction, "Go ye into all the world, teach all nations, &c," we make a strong appeal to this District to come to the aid of the churches here so that they may be able to build a house suitable for the worship of God, and that souls may be taught the knowledge of the Lord as revealed in His word. In so doing, you will meet the approbation of God, and discharge a duty that is obligatory on us all. We believe that the Lord has a people here. The sympathies for the Brethren are strong by those who have a slight knowledge of the humble doctrines of Jesus, and the cry from Macedonia (Altoona) is, come and help us. May the God of all grace move upon the hearts of all His dear children to give of abundance to this noble work which may be made effectual in saving perishing souls.

Committee: { JOHN W. BRUMBAUGH
JOHN SPANOGLE,
PETER S. MYERS.

Dear Brother:—I notice in the PILGRIM that you solicit church news from all parts of the Brotherhood. I thought I would give a little from this part of God's moral vineyard, if you think it worthy of room in your valuable paper.

Our Communion meeting came off according to appointment, which was on the 4th and 5th of October. We had a very pleasant time, good preaching and good order all through the meeting. The ministering brethren from a distance were Bros. John Beachly, from Marshall Co., Iowa, Benjamin Ellis, Butler Co., Iowa, Wm. Robey, Pierce Co., Wisconsin, and brother Whetstone from Winona Co., of this State. They all held forth the truth with power, as it is recorded by Christ and his holy apostles, and we cannot help but believe that there was some good impressions made on quite a number and we hope lasty ones too, at least I for one was made to rejoice that the Lord still was with his people, for I believe that he was there with us, for he has promised where two or three are gathered together in his name, that he will be in their midst What better promise do we want? So brethren and sisters, let us all try to hold out faithful unto the end, for if we do, we have the promise of everlasting life, a palm of victory in our hands and a crown of glory on our heads. Glorious promise.

JOSEPH DRURY.

Bristol, Minn.

OUR VISIT TO ALTOONA

Took train at McVeytown, Friday evening for Altoona City. Arrived there about 8 o'clock, met brethren John W. Brumbaugh, John Spanogle and others at the depot awaiting our arrival, when we were soon taken in charge by the brethren. Bro. Spanogle and myself were taken by brother Robert McFarland, where we were kindly cared for. Next morning, met, brother Imler joining us. We were then conducted to the various sites for a meeting-house, found one at each end of the city that would be well suited for that purpose, on the south side of the P. R R; the west part of the city being the business part principally, consulted with several parties relative to the matter, but in consequence of the city and vicinity not having done anything, there could be nothing definite done. We then returned to Bro. McFarland's, held a consultation and decided as per report. Bro. Spanogle took 2 o'clock train for home. In the evening there was an appointment at the Winchrenarian Church, congregation small but very attentive. Lodged with brother McFarland. Sabbath morning, met in the Methodist Church. Bro. Brumbaugh addressed a very attentive audience. Also met there in the evening—house by this time filled, and some outside. After services closed, one came forward requesting to be taken into the church by baptism. Lodged with sister Cuffman, lately from Spring Run.

Now brethren, from present indications, there is every prospect for doing much good at that place, and no means should be left untried nor effort slackened until the end is accomplished, viz. that the Brethren may stand on their own soil where they may be unfettered to proclaim the word of the Lord. Shall the people of Altoona stand up in the judgment and condemn us, not for want of doctrine nor of dollars, but for want of a will to give them? Nay, but shall say, "Blessed is the cheerful giver."

P. S. MYERS.

McVeytown, Pa,

FROM THE MAPLE GROVE CONGREGATION, OHIO.

Inasmuch as I have not seen any report or news from our arm of the church, Maple Grove, Ashland Co., Ohio, and as you still solicit news from the churches, I will try to write a few lines for your valuable paper.

We are still trying to labor for the advancement of the good cause. We built an addition to our meeting-house so as to make it convenient for ho'ding Lovefeasts in, and held the first Lovefeast in it on the first of October which was very interesting, quite a number of speakers and members from the neighboring churches, and also from a distance were with us. Very good order during the exercises and good attention to the preaching. It was a feast of love long to be remembered.

I have taken the PILGRIM for the last two years, and have again subscribed for 1874, still feel to give it our support and welcome it to our home. May God's choicest blessings rest upon it that it may be the means of doing much good is the prayer of your brother in the Lord.

ISAAC L. RUBY.

Nankin, Ohio.

Dear Editor:—Will you please say to the Iowa brethren, there is a call for them to preach in Deleware Co. Iowa. I think that there might be much good done here. The people are anxious to hear the Brethren preach. I have heard some of them say "if they live up to the Bible we will join in with them."

This is as peacable a neighborhood as I ever lived in. I live one and a quarter miles west of Davenport on the St Paul R. Road. Delhi is my station. There is a good school house near by that can be had to hold preaching in. Delhi is my post office. Please brethren come and preach for us.

ELMIRA ARMSTRONG.

Delhi, Iowa.

NOTICE.—There will be a series of meetings held in the Maple Grove Meeting-house, Ashland Co., Ohio, commencing January 3, '74, and perhaps will close on the evening of the 11th. A general invitation is extended to ministering brethren and others to be with us. By order of the church.

WM. SADLER.

Explanation Wanted.

Some brother will please give an explanation through the PILGRIM, on the 9th verse 3d chapter of the first Epistle General of John. "Whosoever is born of God doth not commit sin, for his seed remaineth in him and he cannot sin because he is born of God," more particularly on the phrase, "for his seed remaineth in him and he cannot sin."

J. H. F.

MARRIED.

HAGERMAN—LONG.—By Eld. David Long, Nov. 5, '73, at the residence of Bro. A. Shafer, near St. James' College, Washington Co., Md., Wm. Hagerman and sister Susan Long.

DIED.

EARLY.—In the Honey Creek branch, Allen Co., Ohio, Oct. 22nd, 1873, our esteemed brother Jacob Early, Jr., leaving many friends, an affectionate companion, a sister, and five children to mourn the loss of a kind and affectionate father.

The subject of this notice was only sick 7 days and shortly before his departure he called for the Elders who anointed him according to the instruction of the apostle James. Funeral sermon by the brethren, from 2 Kings 20: 1 to a large collection of brethren and friends. DANIEL BROWER

KEEVER.—In the Monticello Church, White Co., Ind., Oct. 29, 1873, sister Sarah, wife of of brother Thomas Keever, and daughter of Bro. John D. and sister Nancy Hilling, aged 21 years, 9 mos. and 21 days.

She left a sorrowing husband, a deacon, and two little daughters, with many friends and relatives to mourn her, as we would feel untimely death, yet knowing that our Father is all-wise and knows what is for our good and His glory, we say His will be done, having this assurance that we need not sorrow as those that have no hope, for our dear sister, though young in years gave evidence in all her department, that the love of Christ was shed abroad in her heart, and that her life was hid with Christ in God, and when Christ who is our life shall appear, she will also appear with Him in glory. Having this assurance given us by her christian example, we all feel to comfort ourselves with these words. Her mortal remains were laid in the silent grave on the 31st, in the grave-yard at our Meetinghouse according to her desire, when the occasion was improved by the brethren from John 14: 19.

PRICE.—Also in same neighborhood, Ellen Price, wife of Joseph Price, a member of the Methodist church, after a long seige of suffering, on the 4th day of November, 1873.

On the 9th her funeral was largely attended, and the congregation addressed by Rev. Neal, pastor in charge of that order, assisted by one of his brethren Rodger, and the writer

J. S. SNOWBERGER.

SHIVELY.—Okaw Church, Piatt Co., Ill., Sept. 1873, Elisabeth Ann wife of Bro. David D. Shively, and daughter of Bro Martin and sister Susannah Neher, aged 31 years, 4 mos. and 18 days.

She was received into the Church at the age of 16 years, kept house with her now bereaved husband 11 years, 10 mos. and 28 days. Had four children 3 sons and 1 daughter, all living. Funeral services by the brethren.

ISAAC ULERY.

MILLER.—Near South English, in the English River Church District, Keokuk Co., Iowa, Nov. 5th, 1873, sister Polly consort of Bro. George Miller, aged 67 years, 1 mo. and 12 days. Funeral services improved by the brethren from the latter part of the 15th chapter of 1st Cor.

The subject of the above was a member of the Church for forty-five years, the mother of 15 children some of whom are members of the Church of the Brethren. Others have gone before their mother to try the realities of the other world. She was not confined to her bed long and bore her affliction with Christian fortitude. And we hope she will reap the reward of all faithful in the mansions of eternal bliss. And may God in mercy enable the old brother, husband of the deceased, (who is a cripple, not being able to walk without a crutch), to hold out faithful in the good cause of serving Christ, and all the children come into the fold of the Lord, so that all might meet in that better land.

B. F. F.

(*Companion* and *Visitor* please copy.)

MILLER.—In the Manor Church, near Funkstown, Md., Oct. 31, Catharine, wife of Bro. J. G. Miller, aged 64 years, 10 mos. and 4 days.

Her remains were followed to the place of burial, at Beaver Creek, by a large number of sympathizing friends. The occasion was improved from Rev. 4: 13, by Eld. D. Long and Andrew Cost.

BYRD.—In Fightmantown, Washington Co., Md., Oct. 30, Sarah, wife of Samuel Byrd, and daughter of sister E. Palmer, aged 23 years and 5 mos. Funeral services by Bro. Daniel Stouffer, from Gal. 11: 7.

D. E. W.

MONEY LIST.

David B. Teeter,	$6 00
Noah Chrahoof,	.75
Elihu Moore,	11.40
Dire Davis.	1.50
John Boyer,	1 25
Joseph Drury,	2.25
A. J. Kough,	7.00
Jacob Troxel,	22.30
John Bothke,	1.00
S. W. Bollinger,	3.00
John Nail,	1.50
Leonard Wolf,	1.50
Mrs Margaret Sayer,	3.00
Isaac Ulrey,	6,00

LITERATURE.

J. B. Brumbaugh, Huntingdon, Pa.
Literary Editor.

WE have, for several weeks past, in this department of the PILGRIM, regularly announced the forthcoming and recent books of the publishing house of J. B. Lippincott, & Co., of Philadelphia, with their assurance that we would be permitted to give our readers a more extended notice of the books as published and received. We have the pleasure of acknowledging the receipt of their first favor, a pamphlet of 74 pages, 8 vo, containing three stories—"KITTY'S CHOICE: a story of Berrytime," "Leonard Heath's Fortune" and Ballacchi Brothers," by Rebecca Harding Davis. As we do not devote our time to this kind of reading, and do not advise our readers to do so, we leave the details of the merits of this pamphlet if it has any, to those who have the time and the disposition so to do.

WE promised last week to give a notice of "WHITTIER'S PENNSYLVANIA PILGRIM." We have received a handsomely bound copy of the book from the publishers Jas. R. Osgood & Co., Boston, and have read it with much pleasure. Whittier's Poems are never dull, but this story of "Pastinas" the founder of the "Friends" in Pennsylvania has many gems of beauty and truth. This appropriate to the season:—

"And when the miracle of Autumn came,
And all the woods with many colored flame
Of splendor, making Summer's greenness tame,

"Burned, unconsumed, a voice without a sound
Spake to him from each kindled bush around,
And made the strange, new landscape holy ground."

As of truth we quote:—

Enough to know that through the winter's frost
And Summer's heat, no seed of truth is lost.
And every duty pays at last its cost."

The book contains several poems besides. In "The Robin" we read:

"Prayers of love like rain-drops fall.
Tears of pity are cooling dew,
And dear to the heart of our Lord are all
Who suffer like Him in the good they do."

We will supply our patrons with the work at the retail price $1.50. For sale by Wm. Lewis, Huntingdon, Pa.

"THE LIGHT IN THE EAST," is the title of a very valuable religious work just published by the National Publishing Co., of Philadelphia. It issued for the purpose of meeting the want so often expressed in all parts of the country, of a comprehensive religious work suited to all classes and free from sectarian bias. This book supplies that want, and will be found especially valuable to parents and others wishing to instruct the young in the truths of religion, and in this age of skepticism and materialism, it is fortunate that a book so popular in its character, should be devoted, so thoroughly, to the plain, old-fashioned truths of Christianity. The work comprises one large volume of 850 pages, illustrated with over 200 fine engravings. Starting out with the Life of Christ, the work of Rev. John Fleetwood, the book covers an extent of ground, and a range of subjects which make it a valuable history of Christianity from the earliest times. Then follows Lives of the Apostles and Holy Women, Old Testament Characters, Patriarchs and Reformers; a history of the Jews from the earliest times to the beginning of the present century; a comprehensive account of the various religious sects, and a chronological table, the whole containing a vast amount of entertaining and instructive reading which will be eagerly read by all.

The book is sold only by subscription and agents are wanted in every county.

We will interest ourselves in securing agencies for any of our friends or patrons for this work, for Dr. William Smith's Bible History, or one of the best Family Bibles we have ever met with; all published by the National Publishing Company. Their Bible contains many valuable features not found in other Bibles. It is illustrated with over 500 fine engravings, many of them by the celebrated artist Dore. It contains a History of all the existing Religious Denominations. And a valuable feature is its containing the complete Dictionary of the Bible of Dr. Wm. Smith, conceded to be the most comprehensive and valuable ever published. The illustrations show accurately the manners and customs of the period. Biblical Antiquities and Scenery, Natural History, &c. Everything usually contained in first-class family Bibles is contained in this with the addition of the above and many other valuable features besides. It is the cheapest and most finely executed Bible in the market. It is sold by subscription and we are very sure that no one could engage in a *better* business than selling this book. So let some one in every Church, secure the agency and go to work.

DYMOND ON WAR.

An inquiry into the Accordancy of War, with the Principles of Christianity, and an examination of the Philosophical reasoning by which it is defended. With observations on some of the causes of war and on some of its effects. By Jonathan Dymond Sent from this office, post paid, for 50 cts.

GOOD NEWS!!
FOR THE CHILDREN.
St. Nicholas Has Come!!
He is coming every month.

This beautiful New Magazine published by Scribner & Co., with its Pictures, Stories and Talks, is now ready. $3.00 a year. We will send it with the PILGRIM for one year for $4.00. The PILGRIM and Scribner's Monthly, $4.75. The three for $7.00.

TUNE BOOK.

The Brethren's Tune and Hymn Book, is a compilation of Sacred Music adapted to all the hymns in the Brethren's New Hymn Book. It contains over 350 pages, printed on good paper and neatly bound. We will send it to any address, post paid at $1.25 per copy.

Trine Immersion.

A discussion on Trine Immersion, by letter between Elder B. F. Moomaw and Dr. J. J. Jackson, to which is annexed a Treatise on the Lord's Supper, and on the necessity, character and evidences of the new birth, also a dialogue on the doctrine of non-resistance, by Elder B. F Moomaw. Single copy 50 cents.

GOOD BOOKS.

How to read Character, illus. Price,	$1.25
Combe's Moral Philosophy,	1.75
Constitution of Man, Combe,	1.75
Education. By Spurzheim,	1.50
Memory—How to Improve it,	1.50
Mental Science, Lectures on,	1.50
Self-Culture and Perfection,	1.50
Combe's Physiology, Illus.	1.75
Food and Diet. By Pereira,	1.75
Marriage. Muslin, $1.50,	
The Science of Human Life,	3.50
Fruit Culture for the Million,	1.00
Saving and Wasting,	1.50
Ways of Life—Right Way,	1.00
Footprints of Life,	1.25
Conversion of St. Paul,	1.00
Natural Laws of Man,	.75
Hereditary Descent,	1.50
Combe on Infancy,	1.50
Sober and Temperate Life,	.50
Children in Health—Disease,	1.75

Man and Woman: Considered in their Relations to each Other and to the World. 12mo, Fancy cloth, Price $1.00.

Life at Home; or, The Family and its Members. A work which should be found in every family. $1.50. Extra gilt, $2.00.

Hand-book for Home Improvement: comprising "How to Write," "How to Talk," How to Behave," and "How to do Business," in one vol. 2.25.

Man, in Genesis and in Geology; or, the Biblical Account of Man's Creation, tested by Scientific Theories of his Origin and Antiquity. One vol. 12mo, $1.00.

The Emphatic Diaglott; or The New Testament in Greek and English. Containing the Original Greek Text of the New Testament, with an Interlineary Word-for-word English Translation. Price, $4.00; extra fine binding, $5.00.

AGENTS WANTED FOR

BEHIND THE SCENES AT WASHINGTON.

The spiciest and best selling book ever published. It tells all about the great Credit Mobilier Scandal, Senatorial Briberies, Congressional Rings, Lobbies, and the wonderful Sights of the National Capitol. It sells quick. Send for specimen pages and see our very liberal terms to agents. Address NATIONAL PUBLISHING Co., Philadelphia, Pa. Oct. 28-8t.

TRACTS.

"ANXIOUS BENCH RELIGION EXAMINED," BY ELDER J. S. FLORY. A SYNOPSIS OF CONTENTS. An address to the reader: The peculiarities that attend this type of religion. The feelings there experienced not imaginary but real. The key that unlocks the wonderful mystery. The causes by which feelings are excited. How the momentary feelings called "Experimental religion" are brought about, and then concludes by giving that form of doctrine as taught by Jesus Christ and recorded by his faithful witnesses.

COUNTERFEIT DETECTER
or
BAPTISM—MUCH IN LITTLE.

This work is now ready for distribution, and the importance of the subject will speak for it a large demand. It is a short treatise on baptism in tract form intended for general distribution, and is set forth in such a plain and logical manner that a wayfaring man though a fool, cannot err therein. Either of the above tracts sent postpaid on the following terms: Two copies, 10 cts, 10 copies 40 cents, 25 copies 70 cents, 50 copies $1.00, 100 copies $1.50.

THE HELPING HAND.

Containing several hundred Valuable Receipts for cooking well at a moderate expense, making Dyes, Coloring, Cleaning and Cementing. This book also points out in plain language, free from Doctors' terms the diseases of men, women and children, and the latest and most approved means used for their cure, to which is added a description of the Medicinal Roots and Herbs, and how they are to be used in the cure of diseases.

This is a work of considerable importance and we offer it to our readers as being a valuable accession to every household. Send from this office to any address, post-paid, for 25 cents.

FREE TO BOOK AGENTS.

An Elegantly Bound Canvassing Book for the best and cheapest Family Bible ever published, will be sent free of charge to any book agent. It contains Over 600 fine Scripture Illustrations, and agents ar meeting with unprecedented success. Address, stating experience, etc., and we will show you what our agents are doing, NATIONAL PUBLISHING Co., Philad'a. Oct. 28-8t.

Trine Immersion
TRACED
TO THE APOSTLES.

The SECOND EDITION is now ready for delivery. The work has been carefully revised, corrected and enlarged.

Put up in a neat pamphlet form, with good paper cover, and will be sent, post-paid, from this office on the following terms: One copy, 25 cts; Five copies, $1.10; Ten copies, $2.00. 25 copies, $4.50; 50 copies, $8.50; 100 copies, $16.00.

Historical Charts of Baptism.

A complete key to the history of Trine, and the ORIGIN of Single Immersion. The most interesting, reliable and comprehensive document ever published on the subject. This Chart exhibits the years of the birth and death of the Ancient Fathers, the length of their lives, who of them lived at the same period, and shows how easy it was for them to transmit to each succeeding generation, a correct understanding of the Apostolic method of baptizing. It is 22x28 inches in size, and extends over the first 400 years of the Christian era, exhibiting at a single glance the impossibility of single immersion ever having been the Apostolic method. Single copy, $1.00; Four copies, $3.25. Sent post paid. Address, J. H. MOORE, Urbana, Champaign Co., Ill.

1870 1873

DR. FAHRNEY'S
Blood Cleanser or Panacea.

A tonic and purge, for Blood Diseases. Great reputation. Many testimonials. Many ministering brethren use and recommend it. Ask or send for the "Health Messenger." Use only the "*Panacea*" prepared at Chicago, Ills., and by

Dr. P. Fahrney's Brothers & Co.,
Feb. 3-pd. *Waynesboro, Franklin Co., Pa*

New Hymn Books, English.

TURKEY MOROCCO.

One copy, postpaid,	$1.00
Per Dozen,	11.25

PLAIN ARABESQUE.

One Copy, post-paid,	75
Per Dozen, "	8.50

Ger'n & English, Plain Sheep.

One Copy, post-paid,	$1.00
Per Dozen	11.25
Arabesque Plain,	1.00
Turkey Morocco,	1.25
Single German, post paid	50
Per Dozen,	5.50

HUNTINGDON & BROAD TOP RAIL ROAD

On and after Nov. 2nd, 1873, Trains will run on this road daily (Sun excepted) as follows:

Trains from Huntingdon South. *Trains from Mt. Dal's moving North.*

EXP'S. P.M.	MAIL. A. M.	STATIONS.	MAIL. P. M.	EXP'S A. M
5 50	8 05	Huntingdon,	AR4 00	AR9 20
5 55	8 10	Long Siding	3 55	9 15
6 05	8 20	McConnelstown	3 45	9 05
6 10	8 26	Pleasant Grove	3 40	8 58
6 25	8 45	MARKLESBURG	3 25	8 45
6 35	8 55	Coffee Run	3 15	8 35
6 40	9 03	Rough & Ready	3 09	8 29
6 48	9 10	Cove	3 01	8 20
6 51	9 13	Fishers Summit	2 58	8 17
7 10	9 30	Saxton	2 45	8 05
7 25	9 45	Riddlesburg	2 25	7 43
7 31	9 52	Hopewell	2 20	7 38
7 45	10 05	Piper's Run	2 08	7 26
8 00	10 17	Tatesville	1 55	7 13
8 10	10 27	Everett	1 43	7 03
8 15	10 30	Mount Dallas	1 40	7 00
8 35	10 50	Bedford	1 20	6 40

SHOUP'S RUN BRANCH.

A. M.	P. M.		P. M.	A. M.
LE 9 40	LE 7 20	Saxton.	AR2 30	AR 7 50
9 55	7 35	Coalmont.	2 15	7 35
10 00	7 40	Crawford.	2 10	7 30
AR10 10	AR7 50	Dudley	LE2 00	LE 7 20

Bro'd Top City from Dudley 2 miles by stage.

Time of Penna. R. R. Trains at Huntingdon.

***Mail No. 2 makes connection at Huntingdon with Mail going East on Pennsylvania Railroad at 4.15 p. m., and West at 5.45 p. m. Mail No. 1 leaves Huntingdon at 7.40 a. m. on arrival of Pacific Express West.

Trains on this road connect with trains on Bedford & Bridgeport, and Cumberland & Pennsylvania Railroads.

G. F. GAGE, Supt.

The Weekly Pilgrim.

Published by J. B. Brumbaugh, & Co.

Edited by H. B. & Geo. Brumbaugh.

CORRESPONDING EDITORS.

D. P. Sayler, Double Pipe Creek, Md.

Leonard Furry, New Enterprise, Pa

The *Pilgrim* is a Christian Periodical, devoted to religion and moral reform. It will advocate in the spirit of *love* and *liberty*, the principles of true Christianity, labor for the promotion of peace among the people of God, for the encouragement of the saints and for the conversion of sinners, avoiding those things which tend toward disunion or sectional feelings.

TERMS.

Single copy, Book paper,	$1.50
Eleven copies, [eleventh for Agt.]	$15.00

Any number above that at the same rate, Address,

H. B. BRUMBAUGH.
James Creek,
Huntingdon county Pa.

The Weekly Pilgrim.

"REMOVE NOT THE ANCIENT LANDMARKS WHICH OUR FATHERS HAVE SET."

VOL. 4. JAMES CREEK, PENNSYLVANIA, NOVEMBER 25. 1873. NO. 17.

POETRY.

CHOOSE YE.

BY WESLEY.

What will ye, that Heaven imparting,
Misfortune's dark purposes thwarting,
Adversity's presence averting,
May life's azure firmament gild?
Shall gold overburden thy coffers
With all it enchantingly offers—
The transient delight it discovers,
On which, fondest hopes, men may build?

Shall fame lift her canopy o'er thee,
And bear her proud banner before thee,
Whilst millions, in wonder adore thee,
And hail the triumphant approach,
Or power thy progress attending
Whilst low at her shrine thou art bending,
And wide thy dominions extending,
Illumine thy path by her touch?

Shall wisdom pour out all her treasures
And strive to redouble thy pleasures,
As time by his hasty step, measures
The years that roll joyously round?
Now pending thy weak indecision,
Awaiting thy earnest petition,
Behold the great Moral Physician
Whose power confesses no bound.

Shall earth's potent glories combining,
To thee their professions assigning,
Disperse every shade of repining
That e'er may thy happiness mar?
Or wilt thou, earth's riches ignoring,
Thy manifold frailties deploring,
Is Him all thy homage restoring,
Return from thy wandring afar?

Oh choose ye the way of salvation
And dwell in blest anticipation
Of joining the great congregation,
Who bow at the feet of the King,
Then sit by the cross of thy Savior
Enjoying the bliss of His favor,
Assured that thy soul shall forever,
The triumphs of Calvary sing.

Oh then shalt thou joyfully sever,
All sinful attachments forever,
And sit by the banks of the river,
Awaiting thy final release.
And when the loud trumpet is sounding,
The unrenewed millions confounding
Thy soul shall, with ecstacy bounding,
Enjoy the sweet solace of *peace*.

ORIGINAL ESSAYS.

THE LUST OF THE EYE.

Paul says truthfully, "I had not known lust except the law had said thou shalt not covet. The law came to him, and in it he discovered his true condition, and through it he was enabled to escape from the consequences of that condition. When telling what lust is, he says "Lust, when it is conceived, bringeth forth sin, and sin when it is finished bringeth forth death." Therefore in order to obtain (not a genuine conception of lust), but a genuine knowledge of it, the mind must commence its investigations at a correct idea of the death to which the apostle refers, and thus by a deductive method of reasoning comes to the knowledge which Paul had of lust. The first indistinct, unfinished or mystified conception anybody can or ever could have of law, is the circumstance of God saying unto Adam, thou shalt not eat thereof. "In the day thou eatest thereof thou shalt surely die," together with Adam's proceedings and the result to whatever extent it may be developed in the mind.

It is clearly understood that a mere physical death does not embrace the whole province of that result. Furthermore it is clear that a natural or physical death is only a symbol of the real, only a visible or conceivable sign of the invisible and inconceivable. This signature remains stamped upon all flesh, upon those who are under the promise and upon those who are not; but on the former it has no power, while it remains in full force upon the latter. It is therefore an eternal death which the sinner suffers, an eternal destruction which the word death, in a significant sense, bridges or overleaps. In commencing the proposed destruction we soon discover that sin is the cause of death, that lust is the cause of sin, and that the devil is, as he always has been, and always will be, the cause of lust, and consequently the primary cause of all evil.

Sin commences to exist at the conception of lust, and at death—the commencement of eternal misery—it is finished. Sin is a perverted consciousness of disobedience, a condition of the soul which defies the members of the body to work righteousness, a condition which insists upon, and prevails in the transgression of known wholesome laws. All the relations and manifestations which surround it have been briefly summed up in the sentence, "Sin is the transgression of law." It is produced or bro't forth by lust which is a perversion of the senses. The apostle embraces all lust in the language, "lust of the eye and the lust of the flesh." It covers all the ground infected with the dreadful poison. The "lust of the eye" is an unrestrained or ungoverned, injudicious use of the sense of sight. It commences where the appropriate use of this very delicate yet powerful organ ends. This organ is an important avenue leading to the very center of the soul. It is by or through it that much of truth and error, of light and darkness, of sin and righteousness, etc., is forever stamped upon the soul. God has created it for a wise purpose as is the case with all that He has made; a judicious use of it answers that purpose, but a perversion of it thwarts God's design respecting it. Eyes were made to see with, but not to see everything that comes before them in an ungoverned or unrestrained manner. They are very delicate,—they take on physical and spiritual disease readily, when exposed to violations of the laws concerning them, but they are pure and powerful when directed into wholesome paths. As wine, or the elements of which it is composed, was made to make man's face to shine and his heart glad, though if he abuses it a disastrous effect is produced, so God has created light to assist his creatures in coming unto Him. Through the eye which he has created, by the help of light, which he has also created, impressions of material objects are made upon the mind, and thro' these, by the help of other physical organs, impressions are made on the soul which result in the birth of a new creature in Christ Jesus. A correct and practical knowledge of experience is providence in mortals, though man is not the inventor or founder of that providence or God, but he becomes a son of God by permission, by redemption at the first dawn of the knowledge of God in him.

It is by such experience thus a healthy condition of the whole physical organization is suggested and preserved, or injured and destroyed temporally; and likewise the immaterial nature—structure or soul eternally destroyed or saved. When "lust of the eye" is conceived then sin is brought forth in some form. Lust of the eye is an inordinate desire to see anything. This foul affection prevails to an alarming degree at the present day in the world, at two principle points—namely, in short, at the two extremes which hold a position close on either side of the mean which is righteousness, a proper desire to see the things that God designed to be seen. There can be no particular or general rules given to govern the use of the eye, other than those given in the Gospel. Different circumstances must determine or fix different points at which lust begins. Therefore "let every man be fully persuaded in his own mind." Let every man have not "a mind of his own" but the "mind of Christ," and so use the sense of sight to glorify God.

J. B. GARVER.

Mt. Union, Pa.

ONLY TWO.

Only two ways. One broad, the other narrow; one leads to destruction, the other to life; many go by the one, few by the other. Which is your way?

Only two sorts of people. Many sorts in man's opinion,—many societies, classes, sects, and denominations. Only two in God's sight,—the righteous and the wicked, the wheat and the chaff, the living and the dead. Which are you?

Only two deaths—the death of the righteous, and the death of the wicked. Which do you think you will die? Which do you wish to die? Which would it be if you were to die this moment?

Only two sides at the day of judgment—the right hand and the left. Only these two. Those on the right hand will be blessed—"Come, ye blessed of my Father," Those on the left will be cursed—"Depart ye cursed." All must appear before the judgment-seat of Christ, to receive the things done in the body, whether good or bad. What word shall be spoken to you? On which side of the throne will you stand?—*Selected.*

Love of freedom is a prison flower and we do not learn the full value of liberty until we are imprisoned. The true nature of spring is not appreciated until winter is upon us, and the best May songs are written by the fireside.

Witty sayings are as easily lost as the pearls slipping off a broken string but a word of kindness is seldom spoken in vain. It is a seed which, even when dropped by chance, springs up a flower.

THE ADVENT OF CHRIST.

Glory and excellency characterizes itself in the mind of Jehovah when the sublime decree sounded through his self-existant word, "*Let us make man in our own image.*" Beautiful indeed was man as he came from the heart of God, endowed with power and dominion to subdue the earth and rule over every other creature, the Lord God had made upon the earth. Noble as the work of creation is, wonderful is the construction of the earth, the foundation thereof is unfathomable, the corner stone thereof is incomprehensible. It caused the morning stars to sing together, and all the sons of God to shout for joy. If the formation of the earth caused the heavens to sing with joy and shouting, the existence of man, "fearfully and wonderfully made," whom God has pronounced "*very good,*" are called marvelous works, both events highly significant, and nobly displayed the wisdom and power of God. But the incarnation of God's only Son, through whom the world was made, with His redemptive power to restore fallen humanity, far exceeds those events, and compared with them, almost sink into insignificance. Hence then, what appellations shall we use? Where will we find adjectives to describe the greatness, the sublimity and the wondrous mystery in the appearing of "God manifest in the flesh?" Did God really appear incarnate? If the word of Inspiration is to be credited, we can answer this question, if not our efforts are useless, and man's existence is deplorable.

The angel Gabriel, when he visited Mary, the virgin espoused to Joseph, said, "Fear not, for thou hast found favor with God. And behold, thou shalt conceive and bring forth a son, and shall call his name *Jesus*, He shall be great and shall be called the Son of the Highest." Mary said, "How shall this be, seeing I know not a man?" The angel replied, "The Holy Ghost shall come upon thee, and the power of the Highest shall overshadow thee; therefore also that holy thing which shall be born of thee, shall be called the Son of God." More than seven centuries previous, Isaiah propinsied, "For unto us a child is born, unto us a son is given, and his government shall be upon his shoulder, and his name shall be called 'Wonderful Counselor, the Mighty God, the everlasting Father, the *Prince of Peace*.'" Titles alone belonging to Divinity. Inexpressibly wonderful and unexpectedly lowly did the King of glory appear in this world. The people were not prepared for the reception of such a potent personage, whose appearance caused devils to tremble and wicked men to fear. But holy men and women rejoiced that a celestial inhabitant was called down from Heaven, bringing the gladsome news to the humble shepherds, followed suddenly by a multitude of the heavenly host's, praising God and saying, "Glory to God in the Highest, and on earth, peace, good will to men." Prodigies, astonishing even the heathens, bespeaks the greatness of Him who finally is to subdue the world and establish an everlasting Kingdom which shall never be destroyed; and to whom all the angels of God pay homage. Yet He came as a little babe in the poor despised little town of Bethlehem. Behold Him, the Son of God, there wrapped in swaddling clothes lying in a manger, "because there was no room for them in the inn." Oh what wondrous condescension! No space for the convenience of such a crisis. That world spoken into existence by that word now made flesh has not the attention that the least of his creatures have. And why so little noticed by man? So little honored, and yet according to the flesh, descended from the royal house and linenge of David. O, the wonderful works of God! The depths of his wisdom! Who can fathom it? "For he shall grow up as a tender plant, and a root out of dry ground."

The objects of His appearance magnify the event exceedingly. As there are many, we hardly know where to begin in noting the most important to do justice to His Divine attributes. Man, through the magnitude, wisdom, and foreknowledge of God, was made *good*, and for the purpose that he, as his Creator, should receive honor and worship from him, and that man on his part should enjoy him forever. But alas, *alas*! Man fell, through the deception of an opposite power then in existence. He forfeited his right to the tree of life, and lost his divine image and near relationship to his Maker; death was written on his brow, corruption on his body, estrangement upon his soul, enmity on his mind, and eternal punishment on his existence. But God, who is rich in mercy and boundless in love, and whose breath brought life and a living soul into his inanimate body, interposed in behalf of poor fallen man. Hence the Triune God sends his Son, the second person of the Trinity. He willingly disrobed himself of his divine glory, left the enjoyments of the angels, the personal presence of his Father, assumed mortality, came down to this mundane sphere, the theatre of his sufferings, the scene of his trials, and the drama of his death. And for what? Surely to ransom fallible man. O, wondrous love! Amazing condescension! Depth of mercy, exceeding greatness of sympathetic benevolence!

"Amazing pity brought him down.
Redeeming love secures his crown;
In meekness he obedience wrought,
That rose him to the throne of God."

Great was the work of God in the creation of man, but greater in the redemption. And the greatest will be in the general restoration, when the babe of Bethlehem, the wonderful God-man, Jesus Christ, shall have put down all rule, subdued all authority unto himself, and shall have destroyed the last enemy, death, and then shall deliver his Kingdom unto his Father, that God may be all in all.

The wonderful appearance of Jesus Christ manifest in the flesh, is an event highly important, because he was the only efficient sacrifice to atone for the sins of the world. He was selected and slain in the mind of Jehovah before the foundation of the world. Yea, "through the determinate council and foreknowledge of God," he was chosen as the expiatory sacrifice to fully atone Adam's sin transmitted to the children of men for four thousand years. Truly an event fraught with many important objects. The fulfillment of many prophecies was necessarily one grand design in order to establish the Bible as a truth and a revelation from God, also vindicate God in his purposes, and fully demonstrate his veracity. Eve, the mother and progenitress of all the human race, looked for the fulfillment of this promise in her first born son, though she was dreadfully disappointed. Abraham, the father of all the faithful, saw his day, spiritually, and rejoiced in it. Patriarchs and pious kings anticipated his coming with gladness, yet died without the sight. Generations were born and died, and others succeeded them and also passed away without seeing their long expected Messiah. Holy men saw glorious visions of the beauty and the blessings of the Great Redeemer's Kingdom. Daniel was favored with the time of his advent, Micah with the place of his birth, but holy Simeon, who long waited for the consolation of Israel, in his old age was permitted to see the Holy Child in its infancy. O, the old man's soul was filled with gladness, and his heart with overflowing joy. "Lord now lettest thou thy servant depart in peace, for mine eyes have seen thy salvation." O, imagine his greatness; the excitement produced! Elizabeth's son, the forerunner of Jesus, leaped with joy, being filled with the Holy Ghost before he was born. The humble shepherds in the plains of Bethlehem, left their flocks to the mercy of the wild beasts, to behold the wonderful sight. Angels winged their flight through the immensity of space to mingle in the joys of earth, crying, "Glory to God in the Highest, upon earth, peace and good will to men." A peculiar star, prognosticating his birth, drew wise men from the far off East to worship the King of the Jews, and bring precious spices as presents, in order to make their worship more effectual. This noble event is the precursor of many noble objects already accomplished; but the most important are yet to come. The revelation of the will of God to man,—the means of grace therein contained, the glad tidings of man's salvation, in which life and immortality is brought to light, the sufferings of the Son of God and the atonement through his death, the deliverance of the captives from the regions of the dead, the glorious and triumphant resurrection of his body from the grave, by which he secures man's resurrection, and changes from corruption to incorruption, and from mortality to immortality; whereby the grave is swallowed up in victory, and death hath lost its sting. In his prophetic office, he became the leader of his people and the commander of all nations, in humility he exemplified the way to Heaven; mercy, benevolence, goodness, forbearance, holiness, justice, submission, obedience, and love to God and man characterized his life while tabernacling here in the flesh. In his high priestly office, he became himself the victim for the expiation of guilt, not his own, but for the human family, and by his own blood entered into the (sanctum sanctorum) holiest of all once into Heaven itself, to appear in the presence of God for us. He ascended up to Heaven, led captivity captive, and gave gifts to men. He is sitting now upon his mediatorial throne at the right hand of God as a merciful, compassionate High Priest, as an advocate in order to intercede for saints and sinners.

But Oh, what is yet to be accomplished! Behold he shall come again, not as a babe rocked in a manger, but as a *mighty conqueror* in the power of his magesty; crowned as King of Kings and Lord of Lord's. The resurrection of the saints, the destruction of his enemies, the conversion of the Jews, the reign with the saints a thousand years here upon the earth, the final destruction of the devil and his emissaries, the general resurrection and subsequent judgment, the casting of the wicked into the lake of fire, and the reception of the blessed into his Kingdom, are things yet to be accomplished, and truly worthy of a God. Hence we see him humble in his birth, derided in his humanity, rejected in his teachings, mocked in his sufferings, rejoiced in his death, denied in his resurrection, discredited in his ascension, opposed in his second coming, and finally, when he shall reign as King in his royal camp, and to the Holy City with his saints, he will be surrounded by an army of enemies, "the number of whom is as the sand of the sea." ALAS, *alas*! Fire shall fall down from God out of Heaven to devour them. To sum up the whole matter in reference to the importance, magnitude and sublimity of the Savior's advent into this world, we humbly acknowledge it to be inexpressible, and beyond human comprehension.

Brethren and sisters, and all God-fearing friends, let us appreciate the exalted scene and profit thereby, in order that we may become fit subjects to reign with our exalted Savior in his everlasting *Kingdom*. May God prepare us for that glorious reign is the prayer of your weak servant. Amen, yea, Amen.

LEONARD FURRY.

New Enterprise, Pa.

THE TEST OF DISCIPLESHIP.

Therefore, whosoever heareth these sayings of mine, and doeth them, I will liken him unto a wise man, which built his house upon a rock.—Matt. 7: 24.

These words occur in that ever memorable sermon which our Savior delivered upon the Mount. From what we read in the latter part of the 4th chapter of Matthew, we can discover why the Savior went to the mountain. It evidently was that he might have some repose, as his fame was so great, caused by the extraordinary power displayed in his preaching, and also in his ability to heal the people, of all manner of diseases, of which they were afflicted. Repose, was what I apprehend he sought.

His disciples followed Him, and when He arrived at the place contemplated by Him, He seated Himself, and His disciples came to Him, "And He opened His mouth and taught *them*, saying." The question here obtrudes itself upon us. Whom did He address? His disciples only or the multitude, or some, who, no doubt, followed Him? Were it not for the truth taught in the 28th ver. of this 7th chapter of Matt., and several other verses not so plain, I would not hesitate to say that he taught His disciples only.

But this I am constrained to say, He taught His disciples specifically, and the others present incidentally; for I do not think the multitude were present, and I therefore still think His object in repairing to the mountain was to obtain repose. But as His mission to this earth was to do good, both to the souls and bodies of the human family, He could not let this opportunity pass. Hence it is said, "He opened His mouth," from which flowed some of the most sublime truths, to which the human ear was not accustomed to hear. Well may it be said by those present, that they were "astonished at His doctrine."

In this discourse are contained requirements, which none but those who have covenanted with Christ can attend to. To possess the characteristics named by the Savior in this sermon, in the very commencement, presupposes, that the person must have entered into covenant with Him, and thereby possess, himself or herself, with that superabundant amount of grace, which is only attainable after their baptism, at which period they enter into covenant with God.

Now what are those superlative graces indicated in this sermon? "Poverty of Spirit," "Mourning," no doubt on account of sin. "Meekness," "Hungering and thirsting after righteousness," "Merciful dispositions," "Purity of heart," a disposition to be "peace-makers," a willingness to submit to, "Persecution for righteousness." Amidst of all, to rejoice, and be exceeding glad. Why glad? Because, that thereby, you may let "your light so shine, that others seeing your good works may also glorify your Father which is in Heaven." Hence I conclude the language, or precept at the head of this article, was addressed specifically to the disciples then present, and also all other disciples everywhere to be found, and in all ages past, present, and to come.

What then are the tests of discipleship? This sermon is full of tests, and they all revolve in this one grand and comprehensive test: Do the things I require of thee. In the text before us, you will perceive two things to be required of us: "hearing" and "doing," and neither can be done without, "doing" presupposes that we have "heard." The absence of "doing" does not indicate that we have not "heard." Alas, it is but too frequent that we hear but we do not heed. There lies the difficulty, both as respects the child of God, and those who make no profession.

And indeed the latter are most generally more consistent, than the former. I have often heard the latter say, what is the use of my going to preaching, for I know more now than I practice. Whilst that is no excuse for such, yet it reflects upon many who hear continually and do not. We all have a work to do, whether recognized as the children of God, or of those on whom the wrath of God rests. Let every person then see to it, that they attend to their individual case first, and also assist in promoting the interest of other's. I say, first spiritual and then temporal. Also, as much as in us lies, do good to all men. I am much interested, in having all do the works assigned to us. I mean "the works of the Lord, which we are to abound in." I do not mean those works which have no merit. There are works that God commends and others He condemns, even of those that are highly estimated by some people. We must distinguish between those works. There are those compared to "filthy rags," whilst others will have their reward even the giving of a cup of water to a disciple. And even among those of good works, their is danger of doing. One may be substituted for the other, which would be wrong. Suppose a case: say we were at a Communion Meeting, and becoming convicted of sin, wish to attach ourselves to the Church, but do not have the opportunity to be baptized. But being sincere, the Church wishing to secure our membership, say to us, you may have part with us in partaking of the ordinances if you be baptized hereafter. Would that make it right? Not at all. But such is now allowed by liberal Christianity. Yea, they do not care whether they are baptized or not. Let us then hear and afterwards obey in all things, and all things in their proper order. May the Lord be our helper.

EMANUEL SLIFER.

LOOKING TO JESUS.

The bitter storms of adversity may frown upon us, and we may be made to drink out of sorrow's bitter cup; the home of our childhood may be taken from us ruthlessly and without mercy, but that still small voice that on one occasion spoke to the disciples, on the sea, may whisper "Peace be still." Then while leaning on the words of Jesus we may rejoice with exceeding joy, we have a home in Heaven where our joys are not blighted by sorrow.

Looking far down the ages of time, and beholding our ancient fathers' scourgings, oft our hearts are made to exclaim, it is good for us to be afflicted. Who would not wish to suffer for Jesus' sake? These light afflictions will work out for us a far more exceeding amount of glory. Man with the carnal mind cannot believe these things. When his earthly possessions are taken from him, his all is gone; he hath not the Holy Spirit to tell him he will abide with him, even unto the end of the world. Glorious consolation, the time is coming when our mortality will put on immortality, and death will be swallowed up in victory. Then away to sereuer climes where joys are unspeakable and full of glory.

Dear friends, for the sake of the One who has died the ignominious death, whose sufferings were greater than any man could endure, turn to Jesus, where true consolation is found. Often do we see contritions humble sigh, and even tears of sorrow fall for living in open rebellion against the One who says, "My yoke is easy, and my burden light."

Come to Jesus then, whatever may befall you. You may then look beyond this vale of tears, for there is room in Heaven for all they that will come.

C. H. HAWBECKER.

Upton, Pa.

THE STARLESS CROWN

BY J. S. FLORY.

Sometimes we read of a supposed starless crown, in heaven, worn by some of the redeemed. Are there such crowns there? Perchance there are or will be. Can they be crowns of glory? Our influence in leading souls to Jesus adds stars to the crown laid up for us. Shall we ever see mothers there with starless crowns? Oh what a though! Not one child in Heaven with them, their influence too much of a worldly nature in life, and the result, in Heaven a starless crown! Fathers too much engrossed in business to let their light shine, much care had they to see their sons set up in the world, and now saved—perhaps—but solemn thought, a starless crown. Brother, shall I meet thee there with a starless crown? Dear sister, shall we ever see thee wearing a crown without a star? God forbid! Work for Jesus, gather the outcast in, plead with sinners, live out your religion in such a way that others may be attracted to the illuminating light, and then in Heaven, a starry crown shall be your lot. How ready, and with what joy angel-fingers fix those stars in your waiting crown, when it is announced another sinner free in Jesus' love, led there by your influence. Oh! the reward we shall reap for our labors of love if those labors are seasoned with an earnest devotion for the cause of our blessed Master. Happy moment that, when death shall be swallowed up in victory, and we shall be carried on the wings of love to the gates of eternal glory. But ah! the joy "unspeakable and full of glory" we there shall experience when we meet in those realms of bliss with dazzling crowns of untold treasures, that shall ever shine in the same blaze with the halo of light that surrounds the throne of God and the Lamb. Not a *starless* but a STARRY crown may we all have. Amen.

Greely, Colorado.

A YEAR'S TROUBLE

Sometimes I compare the troubles we have to undergo in the course of a year, to a great bundle of fagots, far too large for us to lift. But God does not require us to carry the whole at once. He mercifully unties the bundles, and gives us first one stick which we are able to carry to-day, and then another which we are able to carry to morrow, and so on. This we might easily manage if we would only take the burden appointed for us each day; but we choose to increase our trouble by carrying yesterday's stick over again to day and adding to morrow's burden to our load before we are required to bear it.—*Newton.*

WISDOM is better than rubies; and all the things that may be desired are not to be compared to it.

GENERAL INTELLIGENCE.

THE English District of the Lutheran Synod of Ohio has had a disruption, owing to its persistent opposition to secret societies.

THE colored Baptists of Kentucky have organized a General Association for themselves. They are to meet in Paris, Ky., August 14.

A GREAT revival has occurred recently in the Baptist Church at Brownsville, Tenn. Over 150 conversions had taken place at last reports, and the work was still going on.

AT the dedication of a house of worship by the Methodists, in New Jersey, recently, a gentleman gave $10,000. It certainly was liberal in these days of financial panic.

THE Annual meeting of the Disciples of California, was held near Stockton, commencing Oct. 3d, and continued ten days. The meeting was held in a grove about two miles from Stockton, and the people accommodated in barracks or tents erected for that purpose.

—A pilgrimage to Jerusalem, says the *Christian Standard* is the latest project in this line. The Bishop of Paris is organizing it, and the pilgrims were to leave Marseills about the middle of this month for Alexandria, and thence, *via* of the Isthsmus of Suez, to the Holy City. From there, excursions are to be made to Bethlehem, Jordan, Jericho, and the Dead Sea, etc, and on the return Samaria, Athens, Sicily and other points will be visited. The duration of the whole will not be far from two months and a half.

THE EVANGELICAL ALLIANCE is by many prominent religious periodicals pronounced a great success. It may be by bringing about a moral sociability among professing christians, but further than this we cannot see it. There is but one way that a union of God's people can be effected and that is by building upon the platform of the Gospel. Just so soon as sects are willing to bury their creeds and accept the truths of the Bible, a spiritual union can be brought about and no sooner. Worldly unions may be effected by agreeing to disagree and call each other brethren, but God will not sanction such unions, as it is declared that there is but one Lord, one *faith*, and one baptism.

A NEW DEPARTURE.—Rev. Robt. Reitzel formerly of the German Reformed Church of New York, was expelled from that body on account of low and immoral habits. A large number of the Congregation went with him when they formed a new order and styled themselves "German Protestants." They then went to work and built a house, which was scarcely finished until the new reformer began to preach an exceedingly liberal doctrine, some of his sermons being in direct opposition to the teachings of the Bible, and finally, boldly asserted that he did not believe in the existence of God or Jesus Christ, as the Son of God. His congregation then informed him that he must change his manner of preaching or resign.

"On Sunday morning last, during the course of his sermon, he announced that his views had undergone a change, and not believing in Christianity, he did not desire longer to be known as a Christian minister and his connection with the congregation must terminate.

He then joined in with a german element in harmony with his views, organized a Free Thinkers Club and is now their preacher or rather lecturer.

THE Christian Church has had a marvelous success. In a little over a half century it has grown to a membership of nearly six hundred thousand. This success has been largely owing to the diffusion of papers and books. From the beginning, these people have believed in the potency of the press. They have been earnest and aggressive. Already the Christian church supports more than a half-dozen weekly newspapers, perhaps twice as many magazines, juvenile periodicals, etc., beside a first-class Quarterly Review. They have several well endowed colleges, and a half-score of seminaries and schools.

This shows what the Christian church can do in the way of supporting periodicals, and we think if the church of the Brethren had the zeal they ought to have, there would not be so much talk about too many periodicals. We need them all to propagate our doctrine, and we think it is high time that we cease to complain about the cost, and go to work and endeavor to augment their power to accomplish this end. This may be done by a more general diffusion of them among the people. The power of the press should not be overlooked, and surely a church as wealthy as ours, should not complain of two $1.50 weeklies. The idea is preposterous.

A SCHISM.—The Old School Baptists have been having trouble recently on account of some of their prominent men belonging to secret societies. Some time ago a man who belonged to the Odd Fellows died, and the Rev. Mr. Rose, a minister of some prominence in the Church was called upon to perform the funeral services, and at the grave it was discovered that he belonged to the society himself. The brethren would not then allow him to preach the funeral sermon, and the Rev. Correll, who was also present, took his place. This caused considerable trouble, as the Rev. Rose still continued to preach, and a number of the brethren sided with him. Recently they held their association in the country, known as Pigeon Cove this State, and here the matter came up for settlement. After some discussion it was found that the matter could not be satisfactorily adjusted, and the Rev. Rose and two other ministers with those of the laiety who sympathized with them, making in all about thirty, withdrew, and went to Neadmore, some seven miles distant, and there held their Association. Thus, the matter ended with a division in the Church.

—A remarkable Jew, claiming to be the Messiah, has recently made his appearance in Arabia, where his fame has spread far and wide. He came forth from the desert, where he spent many years mortifying the flesh, and he pretends to work wonders, perform miracles, and give the evidence of his divine mission. He has a melodious voice, remarkable brilliant eyes, and a fascinating appearance. The Bedouins take his offerings, and many of them have already accepted him. Another claimant of Messiahship appeared last year in Australia; met with poor success among the people, and we have not heard of him for some time. We now learn that a female Savior, who claims to be the daughter of God, chosen to suffer for the redemption of her sex, is creating a prodigious sensation in Southern Russia. Her name is Gabacrewicz. She pretends to perform miracles, to raise the dead, make the blind see, and the lame walk. The Government lately shut her up in prison, but they find she cannot thus be crushed out; for the prison has become a place of pilgrimage to multitudes, who declare that she can perform miracles even when incarcerated.—*Commercial*

—The heathen authorities of Duke Town, Old Calabar, have issued a proclamation, commanding a recognition of the Christian Sabbath, as follows: "Henceforth on God's day no market is to be held in any part of Duke Town territory; no sales of strong drink, either native or imported, indoors or verandahs; no work; no play; no devil making; no Egbo processions or palavers, etc. etc. Any person violating the provisions of this proclamation will be subject to heavy Egbo penalties." If the heathen can enforce such laws, Christians may take courage.—*N. Y. Observer*

A DEPARTURE FROM ROME.—The following is taken from the *Italian News*:

An extraordinary scene was witnessed at the Baptist meeting rooms, in the Via Laurina, it being no less than the recantation of Rev Father Paola Cav Grassi, one of the Canons of the Patriarchal Basilica of Santa Maria Maggiore. At the morning service Father Grassi, a man of great erudition, advanced in age, and of benignant and commanding presence, delivered an address in which he said his convictions had led him to leave the church of Rome and join a sect of Christians who worshipped God, not according to the dogmas and superstitions invented by men, but in accordance with the Gospel of Jesus Christ, as set forth in the Holy Scriptures, and taught by the divinely inspired apostles. Rev Jas. Wall delivered an eloquent address on the solemn step taken by Rev. Paola Grassi, and then baptized him by immersion, in the presence of a crowded audience who appeared deeply moved by the impressive ceremony. At the evening service Rev. Paola Grassi read his recantation, which is in the form of a letter addressed to His Eminence Cardinal Patrizi, the Vicar General of the Diocese of Rome.

THE NEW NIAGARA BRIDGE.—The bridge across the Niagara River from Buffalo to Fort Erie is finished the last of the immense trusses being placed in position only a few days ago. These spans or trusses are from 197 to 510 feet in length, are made of iron, and of the pattern known as the pratt truss; these rest on eight piers and two abutments, all built of solid masonry the piers being incased in an armor of half-inch iron plate to protect them from the ice, which forms in great quantities in the river, and with re-enforcements from the lake, makes a very formidable destructive agency. The bridge has two draws, one of which is said to be the largest in the country, it having, an opening of 160 feet. The funds for the building of the bridge, are furnished by a stock company of Canadian and American capitalists and is leased to the Grand Trunk, Great Western Air Line, the Canada Southern and the New York West Shore and Chicago Railroads. There is only one track on the bridge, as when the contract was made, three of the roads now using it, were not thought of in time to alter the plans.—*N. Y. Observer.*

EXTRAORDINARY DARKNESS.

The *London News* of Oct 24th says: "Early yesterday, Woolwich experienced a sudden and almost unexampled visitation of darkness. The morning had been wet and gloomy throughout, but at 1 p. m., the sky was overcast by a dark pall, which seemed to obscure every vestige of light from above. The darkness was not that of a London fog, for vistas of lighted windows could be seen for a long distance. It was rather the darkness of midnight, but there was a reddish tint in the sky like that occasioned by a great fire. The atmosphere was very heavy and opressive, the rain had ceased, and the wind which had been blowing from the south east, entirely abated. The effect was dismal in the extreme. Nervous people encouraged the most dread forebodings: more reasonable ones attributed it to an eclipse of the sun, but found no confirmation of it in the almanac. Fowls went to roost, pigeons and other birds stopped in their flight to seek the nearest shelter, and every living thing seemed impressed by the scene. The period of intense gloom lasted about five minutes, when light gradually broke in from the west and in an hour afterwards there was brilliant sunshine"

Youth's Department.

THE CHANGES.

Well, here we meet again—did I say, meet again? Yes, some of us, but not all. There are a number of parents and little brothers and sisters weeping around little chairs that now sit in the corner unfilled. There is not only a vacancy in little chairs and around the firesides, but in the fond parent's hearts there is a void left that cannot be filled, and before we meet again, some of my young readers that are now so full of life and vigor, and whose cheeks glow with health, may be among those who have made the vacant seats. What changes a short week brings! Only a short time ago, the trees were green with their waving foliage, a week later, and the pretty leaves have changed into scores of the most beautiful shades and tints,—so pretty, so beautiful that we could almost wish that they would remain thus always. But ah, those beautiful colors are signs of decay and betoken an early death—passing away—so much like the change that happens those who die, that it makes us feel sad. In health, we see the ruddy, rosy cheeks, but when sickness comes, they change to a more delicate hue, and in death, to the beautiful lily white.

A few weeks more, and all nature is stripped of its robes of beauty, all looks cold, stern and dead. But still we do not feel so sad after all, because nature has laid aside its old and tattered garments that it may prepare or make ready for prettier ones when spring-time comes again, and the little brothers and sisters that are no more, have only passed over to the evergreen shore, where they are happy, happy evermore, and are awaiting the time that we too shall put upon us our beautiful robes and steer for the other shore.

But why all this, dear children? Because Jesus has come, and because he came to save us from the power of the grave and raise us up from the dead. He loves us all, but he loved children first, I suppose, because he too was a child first. Therefore the Bible tells us that he took them up in his arms and blessed them. But his love continues. When they get old enough to talk and understand the wishes and wants of their parents, he says to them, "Children, obey your parents in the Lord, for this is right,"—and again: "Children, obey your parents in all things, for this is well pleasing unto the Lord."

When you get older and grow in knowledge so that you can comprehend what God requires of you, he says: "But seek ye first the Kingdom of God." If you neglect this, you commence to grow in sin, and he then tells you to "repent and believe the Gospel." If you still refuse all these calls, he concludes by saying: "He that believeth and is baptized shall be saved, he that believeth not, shall be damned." All these conditions he gives us with the expectation that we will accept them, and it is because of this expectation that we look forward with so much confidence and joy.

The hope that we shall live again, dispels the gloom of winter and makes December as pleasant as May. Hoping then, dear young readers, that you have noticed and have taken instruction from the late changes in nature, I leave you with the expectation of having another talk with you before Christmas comes.

UNCLE HENRY.

THE VALUE OF A GOOD NAME

That very wise man Solomon, says, that a good name is rather to be chosen than great riches, but perhaps some of our young readers cannot fully understand how this is. All good boys and girls like to have others speak well of them, and this alone affords great pleasure. There is nothing that will make boys and girls who have a proper regard for themselves, more unhappy than to be assured that their friends do not appreciate them,—that they have done something, which exhibits a trait of character that renders them repulsive to their friends. On the other hand, what an amount of pleasure it gives to be assured that you are loved and respected by your friends. Boys and girls all appreciate money but it is doubtful if any are more pleased on receiving a nice sum, than when they hear some one speak well of them. Not long ago I attended a Sabbath School and on the seat in front of me there were a number of boys ranging, perhaps, from 12 to 14 years old. They recited very creditably and their conduct was admirable. When the exercises were over the usual collection was taken, and one of the boys said he had nothing less than a 15 cent piece, it is most too much for once, but says he, it is for a good cause, I will give it all, and then Mr. M. will think I am liberal. Now this boy had some idea of the value of a good name, and seemingly valued it higher than money. How many of our young friends would give money in order to be thought liberal by their friends? Money is a very good thing, and all boys and girls should be taught its value, but then it is not to be compared with that of a good name. No difference how rich you may be, if you have not a good name you cannot enjoy life. Every feeling of pleasure that we experience in this life arises from good of some kind, and in this consists our happiness. Money alone cannot give us this feeling: it is only when we use it in such a way as to command the respect of others, that it can afford us any pleasure at all.

I hope then all our young readers, will understand that riches alone cannot give enjoyment, while a good name will. You may not have any money, yet your good name may afford you the highest enjoyment this life can afford. The boy that gave his 15 cents to the good cause that he might have the name of being liberal, felt happier than if some one had given him that sum, and so it is, happiness is the most precious boon in this life. This is obtained by doing good, and if we do good then we will have a good name. This is so valuable that money cannot buy it.

YOUNG PILGRIM.

IS YOUR NOTE GOOD?

A Boston lawyer was called on a short time ago by a boy who inquired if he had any waste paper to sell. The lawyer, pulling out a large drawer, exhibited his stock of waste paper.

"Will you give me twenty-five cents for that?"

The boy looked at the paper doubtingly a moment, and offered fifteen.

"Done," said the lawyer, and the paper was quickly transferred to the bag by the boy, whose eyes sparkled as he lifted the weighty mass.

Not till it was safely stowed away did he announce that he had no money.

"No money! How do you expect to buy paper without money?"

Not prepared to state exactly his plan of operations, the boy made no reply.

"Do you consider your note good?" asked the lawyer.

"Yes, sir."

"Very well; if you say your note's good, I'd just as soon have it as the money; but if it isn't good I don't want it."

The boy affirmed that he considered it good; whereupon the lawyer wrote a note for fifteen cents, which the boy signed legibly, and lifting the bag of papers, trudged off.

Soon after dinner the little fellow reappeared, and producing the money, announced that he had come to pay his note.

"Well," said the lawyer, "this is the first time I ever knew a note to be taken up the day it was given. A boy who will do that is entitled to note and money too;" and giving him both, sent him on his way with a smiling face and a happy heart.—*Selected.*

SELF-SACRIFICING DEVOTION OF WOMEN.

Men too often quietly accept a woman's sacrifices as the proper and to-be-expected thing, and scarcely pause to consider their extent and cost. The wife exhausts strength to promote the husband's comfort, and it may be that sometimes he pities her toil and weakness; but it does not occur to him to forego a part of his usual gratification in order to save her health, or to provide her with additional assistance, or to send her away on a vacation tour for needed recruiting of body and mind. It is not that the man is penurious, or cruel; but he does not think about his wife as he expects her to think of him. He is so accustomed to the idea that a wife should be an example of self-sacrificing devotion, that he accepts the fact as a matter of course.

A woman should have the sense and firmness to protect her own health and happiness, and to train her family, husband included, to deny themselves for her, as she is ever ready on fit occasions to deny herself for them. This may be done in a way so quiet and gentle, by little words and methods which, from the first, assume that such is the family spirit, that all will accept the theory, and be gradually perfected in the practice. Wives and mothers often make a great mistake on this point. They take upon themselves all the self-denial of the family, and indulge and pamper the husband and children, until they become selfish and exacting, and require to be deferred to and waited upon to a most unreasonable extent. No woman has a right thus to spoil the other members of the family, and to sacrifice herself. They are not as noble in character, or as happy in their minds, or as well fitted to bless others in their various spheres of life as if they were taught to give as freely as they receive. The husband who does the most for his wife will love her the most, and no children will be so affectionate and pleasant as those who are accustomed to deny themselves in order to assist and please their mother. On the other hand, many a wife has sacrificed her own comfort, for years, to gratify a self-indulgent husband, only to find that she was little appreciated, and that he was increasingly exacting and petulant; while many a mother, also, has slaved for her children, to save them work which would have benefited them in soul and body, only to be treated, in the end, as a convenient drudge to promote their pleasures. We therefore warn all selfishly inclined men, not to be so ready to avail themselves of woman's devotion, as if it was their birthright; and we warn enthusiastic, warm hearted women not to allow a virtue to degenerate into a vice.—*Selected.*

The Weekly Pilgrim.

JAMES CREEK, PA., Nov. 25, 1873

☞ How to send money.—All sums over $1.50, should be sent either in a check, draft or postal order. If neither of these can be obtained, have the letter registered.

☞ When Money is sent, *always* send with it the name and address of those who paid it. Write the names and post office as plainly as possible.

☞ Every subscriber for 1874, gets a *Pilgrim Almanac* Free.

ARE WE ON DUTY?

Placed as we are, in a position which gives us access to almost every channel of religious information, and seeing the unremitting efforts that are being made to convert the world to the prevailing doctrines, dogmas, that are now afloat in the land, the question comes up with all seriousness and force, are we as the church, making the effort that we should to convert it to the religion of Jesus? This question is full of importance and upon its issues, hang the destiny of precious souls. It is a question that involves us all according to our several abilities. There are none exempt, not one. Every living member of the body of Christ forms a part of the grand whole, hence every member has a place to fill and a duty to perform, and just so soon as we can get every member to realize this great truth, so soon will the church be in perfect working order, and ready to put on her strength—for in her is vested all power—and go forth to christianize the world.

When we look around us and see what the professing world is doing, our eyes are greeted with a zeal that should command our highest admiration, but when we consider that that zeal is spent in a wrong direction, it should excite our fears and elicit our sympathies. Brethren and sisters, can we feel at ease, can we rest upon our rusting blades, while countless thousands are being lead down the broad road to ruin? Can we remain unmoved while numbers untold, are crying for the living waters? We may, but it is because we feel not the worth of perishing souls weighing upon us. Ah, could we feel as did our blessed Master, when the whole burden of our sins sank so heavily upon Him. Could we fathom *that* love that constrained Him to drink the cup of our sorrows and feel the pangs of our sins, we would then be able to feel a brother's woe and make haste to deliver him from the way that leadeth to destruction. He had but one object for which he labored while in the world, that sinners might be saved. His, was a life of love, labor, and every opportunity was embraced to do a good deed or convey an important lesson, even when weary, hungry, and thirsty, He could not enjoy the enticing privilege, until He first supplied the children with bread. The burning prostitute finds grace in His presence and is comforted with the touching mercy, "Go sin no more." The Apostles forsook homes, land and people, in order that they might be properly inducted into the great work before them, and Paul, in view of the excellency of the great work, by the space of three years, ceased not to warn every one, night and day, with tears. If such were their zeal may it not well be a question with us, in view of the effort and sacrifices that we are now making, whether we are doing our duty? The question may be, how can we do our duty? We answer, by making use of the means that God has so graciously given us. There is no use of praying for means, as we now have more than we put to good use. There are many ways by which we may enter upon this important work, but in every case it requires a personal effort either directly or indirectly. Every man and woman too, must work out their own salvation, and that is done by aiding some one else to work out theirs. This we can do directly or indirectly owing to in what position God has placed us. If we are not called to preach, we may, by using the means which God has given us, aid some one else to preach. The object of the Church should be, to have the Gospel preached, or the plan of salvation made known. We are not all called to preach, but we *are* all called into the vineyard, and all are expected to work and help to bear each other's burdens. If the minister's burden is too heavy, let some of the lay members take part and thus fulfill the law of Christ. Again, we can all preach, and sometimes loudly too, by our walk and conduct. These things wield a power that should not be overlooked, as there is nothing gained by preaching on Sunday, if the members are engaged all week in tearing down, what they tried to build up.

Another very prominent means of accomplishing good is through the medium of the press. This is an acknowledged power by the Church, and we are glad that the brethren are so fully availing themselves of its advantages. Take from us our Church papers and we, to a very great extent, would become lost to each other. It brings us together, and those that are afar off are made near, not only in distance, but also in a spiritual relationship. Those growing cold and indifferent are warmed up, the hopeful are strengthened, the isolated are visited, to the poor the gospel is preached, and the sinner is invited to a banquet of mercy that is large and free.

Brethren and sisters, these facts have been made evident to you all, and if so, you should not be unmindful of the great privileges thus afforded. Perhaps there is no other way in which you can accomplish more good with so small an amount of money as by sending the Pilgrim to your friends and to the poor. Such gifts are highly appreciated, as we know, by the many grateful acknowledgments that have been made, some asserting that through it they obtained their first convictions, and were thus lead to an investigation of the Bible which resulted in their return to God. There are thousands that might be reached in this way, that cannot be by any other means. In conclusion, we would suggest to those that are full of love for Jesus and are waiting for an opportunity to manifest that love, to think of the propriety of sending the Pilgrim to the hungry and the poor, and thus feed them with the bread of life. The poor both in goods and in spirit, are always with us, and are acceptable subjects for our charities.

THE WEEKLY PILGRIM FOR 1874.

The present year is rapidly drawing to a close and the time has come for us to make preparations for the coming volume. This we have been doing and are now prepared to state our inducements for 1874. Our object has been to improve a little every year. How far we have succeeded in the past, our readers can judge. We have now before us a letter containing $1.50 for 1874. He says: "This will be my fifth year that I have subscribed for the Pilgrim. I am well pleased with it, and think it is getting better and more interesting every year."—We do not suppose that all think as does this brother, but there are many that do think the Pilgrim has improved.

The first thing we present for your consideration is our enlargement which will be an extra addition of reading surface weekly, of between 70 and 80 square inches.—This will add considerably to our expenses and labor and the advantage will all be in favor of our readers, but if our agents all get to work and send us a corresponding increase of subscribers, we may still hold our own.

The second is, our Pilgrim Almanac. This, of course, is no very great inducement but it is certainly worthy of a consideration, as we gave its compilation a large amount of labor and care and we do not hesitate in saying that it is as good an Almanac as ever was published by the church. Each subscriber for 1874 gets one *free*.—They are now ready for delivering, and will be sent as soon as the new lists come in. Therefore all should have their names sent in as soon as possible so that the Almanacs may be delivered. Agents that prefer to deliver the Almanacs to their subscribers themselves can do so by ordering from us, the number they think they can make use of.

Another inducement is, we expect more contributors for our pages. We give just now the name of sister Mattie A. Lear. We hope to give our readers the productions of her pen quite frequently. Eld. D. P. Sayler also informs us that he will write, for the coming year and has already sent us a contribution for the first number. We are glad to make this announcement as he was, in our infancy, one of our chief standbys, and we have learned to look up to him as one among our chief men. We also expect all our old contributors to labor for us and also many more new ones.

Our new location will also give us advantages that we did not have heretofore. Our mail facilities will be much better than at our present location, in fact as good as can be had anywhere, enabling us to send our mail, in safety and with dispatch, in every direction. When all these advantages are duly considered we do not see how more could be expected, especially when the low price asked for our paper, $1.50, is taken into consideration. The fact is, unless our present list is largely increased we will probably lose by the enterprise. We therefore make a strong appeal to every brother and sister, and all others that appreciate our labor, to give us your aid and influence. Do not be satisfied with subscribing for yourself, but try and have every body else to take and read the Pilgrim. Our success will depend largely upon the efforts that our agents may make. You, dear brethren and sisters, have it within your power to double our list. Will you not do it? Go to work at once and present your strong arguments. The cause is a good one, and God will bless the effort. Every family should take one or more religious papers. It will be worth much more to them than fashionable dresses and other follies that destroy both body and soul. Do not let the panic scare anybody as that has now touched bottom and money will soon be as flush as ever. Those that do not have it when subscribing, and are industrious and honest, can pay it at some future time or during the year as heretofore. The Pilgrim is the poor man's friend and never refuses to call at his door when invited. Come one, come all. Send in your names at once and with it do not forget that of your neighbor.

SHALL WE HAVE DISCUSSIONS?

This seems to be the query on the minds of a number of our brethren. While some are favorable to it, others strongly oppose, and a few we are told, think of not taking the Pilgrim any more on account of the Sunday School agitation we had some time ago, but we hope that after duly weighing the matter they will change their minds and not forsake us because they cannot fully agree with all we said and did. We are sorry if we have, in any way, offended our dear brethren whom we love, because we certainly had no such intention. Whatever may be for the good and prosperity of the Church, we desire to do, and wherever we come short of this we wish to have it attributed to our short-sightedness and not to a wilful disposition to deviate from the truth as it is in Christ Jesus.

Some of our brethren may think, if they were in our position they would do everything just right. There may be some that would have done better, but even they would have found it a very difficult matter to please all. Our first and chief object is to please God and if we are successful in doing this, we hope to be able to please our brethren. In trying to do this we do not always please ourselves but sometimes submit our own judgment and accept that of those who have greater age and experience in the divine life. As to discussions, we are opposed to them, believing that they have not a tendency of sanctifying the Lord in the eyes of the people, especially when conducted in the manner and spirit that has been done heretofore, in our periodicals. We only once indulged our contributors in admitting a personal agitation, and hope we may have no occasion to do so again. By this, we do not wish to be understood as closing our columns to a fair, free, and open investigation of the truth, when done in the proper spirit and with a design of coming nearer the "ancient land marks," as set forth in the Law and Testimony, but our design shall be as ever, "forgetting those things which are behind and reaching forward to the things which are before." With the ability that God may give we shall endeavor to labor for those things which will work for peace in the Church, as well as for the comforting of the saints and the saving of the sinner. If we all have that mind within us that was in Christ Jesus, we hope there will be no offence taken or given and that there will be no necessity for a single one to forsake us for the coming year, but that all may invite us back again for 1874.

OUR CONDITIONS.

We are being asked whether our conditions for the coming year will be the same as the present year. In the main, we expect them to be the same, but would say to those who have the means, pay us at the time of subscribing or at the first part of the year. If all that can, will do this, it will enable us to meet our obligations and give a little more time to those who cannot pay cash or at the beginning of the year. All those who have not paid for the present year will be expected to pay before the beginning of the new year. B.

AGENTS WANTED.

We want a good active agent, to solicit subscribers for the PILGRIM, in every Church in the brotherhood. If there are any that feel to labor for us and are not supplied with prospectus and *Almanac* will please write us and we will send by return mail. Remember, the PILGRIM for the coming year will be enlarged and every subscriber will receive the *Pilgrim Almanac*, handsomely gotten up, containing a "Ministerial List," giving post-office, county and State, with other valuable information FREE. B.

THIS week some correspondence, obituaries, &c., is unavoidably crowded out. We are sorry for this, and next week will arrange the make up of our form so as to admit all. We intend to make the giving of church news a specialty the coming year, and earnestly solicit our brethren and sisters to send the news.

ABRAHAM FLORA, your name is marked paid on our book.

ABRAHAM GOOD. The book is sent.

Correspondence.

Items of Travel and Notes by the Wayside.

J. S. FLORY.

GREELY, Weld Co., Col., Nov. 8, '73.

Dear Pilgrim:—By request, I will continue to give, briefly, such items as may be of interest, to at least, a portion of your readers.

Having housed my family in a comfortable habitation in this town, and provided them with present necessities, I set out, the 28th of October, on a trip down the South Platte River. My associates were a gentleman of this town, who took his team, Bro. Holsberry, and a man of the legal profession from Michigan, who was the most eager person to get a shot at a Buffalo I ever saw. After a pleasant ride of 28 miles over fine roads, we put up for the night at Greene City. Next day, in the afternoon, we suddenly and unexpectedly came across a herd of buffalo coming up a ravine from the river. Our legal companion seized his rifle, jumped out of the wagon and gave them chase, but he soon gave up that sport, owing to the fact, he was left far in the rear in a few minutes. We had a hearty laugh at his expense. A few miles farther on, we came to old Fort Morgan, (now abandoned), from which point we could see numerous herds of buffalo ruminating along the distant bluffs. At night we camped at a Stockman's Ranch, having taken with us our own provision and bedding. Next day, about 4 o'clock, we arrived at the site of the proposed town of Beaver. Were just in time to save our claim from being "jumped" a game that certain parties were engaged in. I found a few houses had been put up since my visit in July, our irrigating canal progressing, there being 4 miles of it partially constructed, and steps being taken to push it through to completion as soon as possible. The money panic has delayed the lying of the track of the railroad, so it may be some months yet before the road will be in running order.

Being in the heart of the buffalo range, I had the ambition to try my hand in a hunt. If the Prince of Wales could leave his home in Europe, and come to the far western region to get a shot at one of those huge animals, and the papers of the two Continents should teem with an account of the preparations for the occasion, no marvel if I should have a thought in that direction. Therefore, next morning without much ado other than providing myself with a rifle, and wading the river *barefooted through the ice*, I found myself in the valley where it was expected herds of buffalo would soon make their appearance coming to the river for water. I did not have to wait long, until they could be seen coming over the bluffs, and slowly wending their way towards the river. I got under cover of the bank of the stream and hurried down that I might get in the immediate front of the nearest herd, which contained about 50 head. On they came, I awaiting their approach with considerable interest. As they came near, so that their ponderous forms could be measured with the eye, their piercing eyes be seen, and heavy tread be heard, I confess I felt a little "feverish." The idea of coming face to face with 50 wild buffalo, was duly considered. By the by, just before they arrived at the bank, they made a slight turn, and went plunging over the banks into the river. I selected out a fine fat one, pulled trigger and down came buffalo, shot through and through. The next moment I leveled on a fine cow, but not so lucky this time. She was badly wounded, but went off on a double quick with the rest of the herd. That was my first and last hunt, and I have no reason to complain. Thousands of buffalo are being killed almost daily. Some of these animals will weigh, live weight, near or quite two thousand pounds. Those that are not too old, make as fine beef as I ever ate. The meat can be had in that region, by the ton, at one cent a pound, or hunters will kill them for one dollar apiece. Hundreds of wagon loads of buffalo beef are bro't up into this section and sold at 4 cents per pound, and many car loads of the meat is sent East. After making some little improvement on my claim, I returned home with a good supply of buffalo and antelope meat. The antelope is something smaller than the common deer, they are numerous thro'-out this country.

There is yet much choice land open for pre-emption or homestead in the Platt Valley, but it is being taken up very fast. In July when I was down, I was one among the first that took claims in the neighborhood of Beaver, now about all is entered above that point, and for 20 miles below, on the side of the river that the rail-road runs. But on the opposite side, there are fine bodies of bottom land yet untaken, and farther down on the line of R. R., there are sections very desirable for settlement.

Since my arrival here, we have had the most delightful weather I ever experienced anywhere. True, it is cold at night, but through the day it is moderate and pleasant, the thermometer often being up to 60 degrees in the shade. I almost daily come across persons who come here invalids, and now are hale and hearty, able to work hard and enjoy the fruits of their labor.'

There is a wide field here for labor in the ministry, to the building up of Zion. I can see no reason why a true Gospel preached will not find adherents here as elsewhere. More anon.

A CALL FOR HELP.

H. B. Brumbaugh:—Please give this room in the PILGRIM, so that its readers may have a chance to contribute in the good cause.

We, the members of the Montgomery Congregation, Indiana Co., Pa., are but few in number and generally poor. But I will first give you a sketch of our troubles before the war. We made an attempt to build a meetinghouse, and had received some help from other congregations, but the war coming, and some of our brethren being drafted, we felt it our duty to pay for them to save them from going to war, which soon exhausted us, so that we were not able to build. We then refunded back the help we had received, thinking to build some time when we would become more able. In the year 1862, we commenced it again. The school houses were closed against us, and we had no suitable place to hold meeting. We thought by getting some help we might build a house 40x60 with basement half size. We have it now so that we hold our meetings in it, but not finished, and are in debt between $300 or $400. We have appealed to the Brotherhood at large, through the *Companion* but it appears while some have given liberally, others have not heeded our call at all. We borrowed money the second time in order to come up to promise. We now have it for three months. We have received between $30 and $40 since we made the call in the *C. F. C.*

Now dear brethren and sisters, I deem it not necessary to remind you of charity or its promises, as I feel satisfied that you have all been taught this lesson by our Lord and Savior, and that we all know our duty in this respect, if we are only willing to do it. I would just say this, if all the brethren that may chance to read this appeal, I mean all that have plenty and to spare, would come to our relief by sending us $1.00, others that are not so well blessed with this world's goods 50 cents, and others 25 cents, and others again 10 cents would it not more than relieve us? Now who is the brother that would not relieve the congregation of the brethren in a cause like this, by paying so small an amount?

Dear brethren this begging is in no wise pleasant to me, or any of us, and were we able within ourselves, to pay this debt, I think we would much prefer to pay it ourselves than to ask for help. Any one that may have pity on us, and feel like helping us to pay the above named sum, can do so by sending it by letter to H. Spicher, Hills Dale Indiana Co., Pa.

The above is written by permit of the Church. I will keep a record of all that will be sent and report through the PILGRIM or C. F. C. just as you may desire, at the end of 3 months. This we will do if the Lord will. H. SPICHER.

Visitor please copy.

HURRICANE, Mo., Nov. 12, 1873.

Dear brother Editor:—Having seen a solicitation in the PILGRIM for a reporter in every church district, I thought it might be interesting to some to hear of our little district. The brethren were organized about six months before I came to this place, about two and a half years ago, with eight members. We received since, fourteen by letter, and eight by baptism.

We had our Lovefeast on the 8th of Nov. at the house of Bro. Michael. The congregation was not very large because we could accommodate but few spectators, the house being small, but we had very good attention. Next day and evening we had preaching in a school house close by. Our meetings were all very good, and during our meetings we received one dear young sister by baptism, and two more made application to be received next Sunday. Brethren C. C. Root and John S. Hays were the ministers from other districts.

As I have many acquaintances, I will say to them that I still preach nearly every Sunday, and sometimes during the week.

Yours in love.

ELI METZ.

NOTICE.—There will be a series of meetings held in the Maple Grove Meeting-house, Ashland Co., Ohio, commencing January 3, '74, and perhaps will close on the evening of the 11th. A general invitation is extended to ministering brethren and others to be with us. By order of the church. WM SADLER.

MARRIED.

SNIDER—EBERSOLE.—By the undersigned, at his residence, November 16, 1873, Mr. David R. Snider, of Martinsburg, Blair Co., Pa., to Miss Rosa Ebersole, of Bedford Co., Pa.

S. A. MOORE.

McBRAYER—MURREL.—On Oct. 9, by George Witwer, at his residence in Hamilton, Mo., Mr. Francis M. McBrayer and Miss Dela Jane Murrel, all of Daviess Co., Mo.

WALKER—McCREARY.—On Oct. 30th by the same at his residence, Mr. Rellis Walker and Miss Caroline McCreary all of Daviess Co., Mo. GEO. WITWER.

DIED.

HOSLER.—In Solomon's Creek Church, Oct. 19, 1873, Bro. David Hosler, of typhoid fever aged 53 yrs., 9 mos. and 6 days.

He died in the triumph of a living faith, said he was ready to go, exhorted his friends all to meet him in heaven, and gave a special farewell to each of his family, and asked those of them who belong to the church, to be faithful, and those who did not promised him they would soon. We trust those dear children will not forget what they promised a dying father. He had been a member of the Church for a number of years and was very faithful, was much loved by all who knew him and especially by the Church. Funeral by Yontz, D. Shively and the writer from Job. 14: 10. JESSE CALVERT.

Companion and Visitor please copy.

LITERATURE.

A. B. Brumbaugh, Huntingdon, Pa. Literary Editor.

THE prospects of success, of the "INTERNATIONAL REVIEW," are so favorable that the publishers, A. S. BARNES & Co., of New York, have decided to issue it every two months instead of "quarterly" as we previously announced to our readers. The first number will appear in December.

ROSWELL C. SMITH, the publisher of *Scribner's Monthly* and *St. Nicholas* possesses a remarkable genius for 'pushing things' as may be seen from the premium list of *St. Nicholas* which offers all sorts of attractions up to an education or a trip to Europe. There has been but one voice on the new monthly—that it is a thorough success, in which verdict old and young critics, alike, join.—*Publisher's Weekly.*

WE are in receipt of a beautifully gotten up little book of poems from the press of J. R. DURBORROW & Co., Huntingdon, Pa., printed from large clear type on heavy tinted paper. The title of the book—"THE CROWNING GIFT OF HEAVEN" alludes to God's greatest and best gift to man—His Spotless Son, Man's Redeemer and Savior. The book comprises different poems, the thoughts of each suggested by prominent scenes in the life of Christ—"The Birth of Christ," "Disputing with the Doctors," "At the Tomb of Lazarus," "On Mount Tabor," "His Entry into Jerusalem," "In Gethsemane," "His Arrest," "His Trial," "His Crucifixion," "His Resurrection," "His Ascension." The author J. W. Welch of Alexandria, Pa., is the same whose poems for several weeks past, in the PILGRIM, under the name of Wesley, have been so much admired. Paper 50 cts.; sent postage paid from this office.

THE YOUNG FOLKS' RURAL for November is, we believe, the very best number of this unique journal yet published. No wonder that this periodical is achieving so remarkable a success. It would be a timely and valuable addition to the regular reading matter of every family that does not already receive it, and we would advise an examination of it before making up your list of papers for the coming year. It is $1.50 per year, with two lovely American Landscape chromos "thrown in." Dialogues and declamations are furnished for school and social uses, and cash prizes are given for best "compositions." Sample numbers sent post-paid for ten cents. Address H. N. F. LEWIS, Publisher, Chicago.

"THE LAST POEMS OF ALICE AND PHŒBE CARY," have been gathered by Mrs. Mary Clemmer Ames, and issued in a handsome volume by Hurd & Houghton of New York. This book contains all the literary remains of the Cary sisters, save a volume of poems for children, which we announced a week or two ago and which will soon appear. In the thousands of homes where these poet sisters were known this book will be sure to find appreciative readers. They were the people's favorites, like Burns and Whittier, they loved Nature and delighted in the lessons she taught; they were pure and good, and their songs have been accepted, and have taken deep hold upon the public mind. Thanksgiving day is near at hand, and we have "The Chopper's Child: a story for Thanksgiving Day" opening with this pretty verse:

"The smoke of the Indian Summer
  Darkened and dimbled the rills,
And the ripe corn like a sunset,
  Shimmered along the hills;
Like a gracious, glowing sunset,
  Inlaced with the rainbow light
Of vanishing wings a-trailing
  And trembling out of sight."

Delicately drawn pictures of nature, and poetic gems sparkle all through this volume. For sale by Wm. Lewis, Huntingdon, Pa., or sent from this office. Price $2.00.

HURD & HOUGHTON have also published recently, a collection of poems entitled "Songs from the Old Dramatists" edited by Mrs Abby Sage Richardson, in a beautiful volume on tinted paper, morocco cloth, gilt edges, making a very handsome gift book. Price $3.00 for sale as above.

SOLECISMS AND OTHER ERRORS OF SPEECH—is a title of a most useful little book, containing a large amount of very valuable and useful information in a comparatively small compass. Our thought is, that if many of those who have not enjoyed the advantages of early education, or those whose early habits have established inaccuracies in speech, were to read and carefully consult this little volume they would soon be able to avoid those errors and vulgarisms now entirely too common even among ministers. It ought to be found in every family as a daily companion for learners. Published by Claxton, Remsen & Haffelfinger, Philadelphia. Sent from this office, beautifully bound, for $1.25.

GOOD BOOKS.

How to read Character, illus. Price,	$1.25
Combe's Moral Philosophy,	1.75
Constitution of Man. Combe,	1.75
Education. By Spurzheim,	1.50
Memory—How to Improve it,	1.50
Mental Science, Lectures on,	1.50
Self-Culture and Perfection,	1.50
Combe's Physiology, Illus.	1.75
Food and Diet. By Pereira,	1.75
Marriage. Muslin, $1.50.	
The Science of Human Life,	3.50
Fruit Culture for the Million,	1.00
Saving and Wasting,	1.50
Ways of Life—Right Way,	1.00
Footprints of Life,	1.25
Conversion of St. Paul,	1.00
Natural Laws of Man,	.75
Hereditary Descent,	1.50
Combe on Infancy,	1.50
Sober and Temperate Life,	.50
Children in Health—Disease,	1.75

DYMOND ON WAR.

An inquiry into the Accordancy of War, with the Principles of Christianity, and an examination of the Philosophical reasoning by which it is defended. With observations on some of the causes of war and on some of its effects. By Jonathan Dymond. Sent from this office, post-paid, for 50 cts.

GOOD NEWS!!

FOR THE CHILDREN.

St. Nicholas Has Come!!

He is coming every month.

This beautiful New Magazine published by Scribner & Co, with its Pictures, Stories and Talks, is now ready. $3.00 a year. We will send it with the PILGRIM for one year for $4.00. The PILGRIM and Scribner's Monthly, $4.75. The three for $7.00.

TUNE BOOK.

The Brethren's Tune and Hymn Book, is a compilation of Sacred Music adapted to all the hymns in the Brethren's New Hymn Book. It contains over 350 pages, printed on good paper and neatly bound. We will send it to any address, post paid at $1.25 per copy.

Trine Immersion.

A discussion on Trine Immersion, by letter between Elder B. F. Moomaw and Dr. J. J. Jackson, to which is annexed a Treatise on the *Lord's* Supper, and on the necessity, character and evidences of the new birth, also a dialogue on the doctrine of non-resistance, by Elder B. F. Moomaw. Single copy 50 cents.

Sunday School Books

The Bible & Publication Society

Have determined to make Sunday Schools the following very

LIBERAL OFFER

for the remainder of the Society's

JUBILEE YEAR.

We will sell you for Cash:

$100	worth of	Sunday-school	books for	$300
200	"	"	"	150
133	"	"	"	100
100	"	"	"	75
66	"	"	"	50
33	"	"	"	25

We make this offer *only for the next four months.* It will close February 28, 1874.

We have on hand at the present time an unusually choice assortment of the best Sunday-school Library books, and can make you a selection that I know will please you. Address, B. GRIFFITH, Sec'y.
550 Arch Street,
Oct. 28-31. eow Philadelphia, Pa.

AGENTS WANTED FOR

BEHIND THE SCENES AT WASHINGTON.

The spiciest and best selling book ever published. It tells all about the great Credit Mobilier Scandal, Senatorial Briberies, Congressional Rings, Lobbies, and the wonderful Sights of the National Capitol. It sells quick. Send for specimen pages and see our very liberal terms to agents. Address NATIONAL PUBLISHING Co., Philadelphia, Pa. Oct. 28-81.

TRACTS.

"ANXIOUS BENCH RELIGION EXAMINED," BY ELDER J. S. FLORY. A SYNOPSIS OF CONTENTS. An address to the reader: The peculiarities that attend this type of religion. The feelings there experienced not imaginary but real. The key that unlocks the wonderful mystery. The causes by which feelings are excited. How the momentary feelings called "Experimental religion" are brought about, and then concludes by giving that form of doctrine as taught by Jesus Christ and recorded by his faithful witnesses.

COUNTERFEIT DETECTER
or
BAPTISM—MUCH IN LITTLE.

This work is now ready for distribution, and the importance of the subject will speak for it a large demand. It is a short treatise on baptism in tract form intended for general distribution, and is set forth in such a plain and logical manner that a wayfaring man though a fool, cannot err therein. Either of the above tracts sent postpaid on the following terms: Two copies, 10 cts, 10 copies 40 cents, 25 copies 70 cents, 50 copies $1.00, 100 copies $1.50.

THE HELPING HAND.

Containing several hundred Valuable Receipts for cooking well at a moderate expense, making Dyes, Coloring, Cleaning and Cementing. This book also points out in plain language, free from Doctors' terms the diseases of men, women and children, and the latest and most approved means used for their cure, to which is added a description of the Medicinal Roots and Herbs, and how they are to be used in the cure of diseases.

This is a work of considerable importance and we offer it to our readers as being a valuable accession to every household. Send from this office to any address, postpaid, for 25 cents.

FREE TO BOOK AGENTS.

An Elegantly Bound Canvassing Book for the best and cheapest Family Bible ever published, will be sent free of charge to any book agent. It contains Over 500 fine Scripture Illustrations, and agents are meeting with unprecedented success. Address, stating experience, etc., and we will show you what our agents are doing. NATIONAL PUBLISHING Co., Philad'a. Oct. 28-81.

Trine Immersion

TRACED

TO THE APOSTLES.

The SECOND EDITION is now ready for delivery. The work has been carefully revised, corrected and enlarged.

Put up in a neat pamphlet form, with good paper cover, and will be sent, postpaid, from this office on the following terms: One copy, 25 cts; Five copies, $1.10; Ten copies, $2.00, 25 copies, $4.50; 50 copies, $8.50; 100 copies, $16.00.

Historical Charts of Baptism.

A complete key to the history of Trine, and the ORIGIN of Single Immersion. The most interesting, reliable and comprehensive document ever published on the subject. This Chart exhibits the years of the birth and death of the Ancient Fathers, the length of their lives, who of them lived at the same period, and shows how easy it was for them to transmit to each succeeding generation, a correct understanding of the Apostolic method of baptizing. It is 22x28 inches in size, and extends over the first 400 years of the Christian era, exhibiting at a single glance the impossibility of single immersion ever having been the Apostolic method. Single copy, $1.00; Four copies, $3.25. Sent post paid. Address, J. H. MOORE.
Urbana, Champaign Co., Ill.

1870 1873

DR. FAHRNEY'S

Blood Cleanser or Panacea.

A tonic and purge, for Blood Diseases. Great reputation. Many testimonials. Many ministering brethren use and recommend it. Ask or send for the "Health Messenger." Use only the "*Panacea*" prepared at Chicago, Ills., and by

Dr. P. Fahrney's Brothers & Co.,
Feb. 8-pd. *Waynesboro, Franklin Co., Pa*

New Hymn Books, English.

TURKEY MOROCCO.

One copy, postpaid,	$1.00
Per Dozen,	11.25

PLAIN ARABESQUE.

One Copy, post-paid,	75
Per Dozen, "	8.50

Ger'n & English, Plain Sheep.

One Copy, post-paid,	$1.00
Per Dozen	11.25
Arabesque Plain,	1.00
Turkey Morocco,	1.25
Single German, post paid	50
Per Dozen,	5.50

HUNTINGDON & BROAD TOP RAIL ROAD

On and after Nov. 2nd, 1873, Trains will run on this road daily (Sun excepted) as follows:

Trains from Huntingdon South. *Trains from Mt. Dal's moving North.*

EXPS. P. M.	MAIL. A. M.	STATIONS.	MAIL. P. M.	EXP'S A. M.
5 50	8 05	Huntingdon,	AR4 00	AR9 20
5 55	8 10	Long Siding	3 55	9 15
6 05	8 20	McConnelstown	3 45	9 05
6 10	8 26	Pleasant Grove	3 40	8 58
6 25	8 45	MARKLESBURG	3 25	8 45
6 35	8 55	Coffee Run	3 15	8 35
6 40	9 03	Rough & Ready	3 09	8 29
6 48	9 10	Cove	3 01	8 20
6 51	9 13	Fishers Summit	2 58	8 17
7 10	9 30	Saxton	2 45	8 05
7 25	9 45	Riddlesburg	2 25	7 45
7 33	9 52	Hopewell	2 20	7 38
7 45	10 05	Piper's Run	2 08	7 26
8 00	10 17	Tatesville	1 55	7 12
8 10	10 27	Everett	1 48	7 03
8 15	10 30	Mount Dallas	1 40	7 00
8 35	10 50	Bedford	1 20	6 40

SHOUP'S RUN BRANCH.

A. M.	P. M.		P. M.	A. M.
LE 9 40	LE 7 20	Saxton.	AR2 30	AR 7 50
9 55	7 35	Coalmont.	2 15	7 35
10 00	7 40	Crawford.	2 10	7 30
AR10 10	AR7 50	Dudley	LE2 00	LE 7 20

Bro'd Top City from Dudley 2 miles by stage.

Time of Penna. R. R. Trains at Huntingdon.

***Mail No. 2 makes connection at Huntingdon with Mail going East on Pennsylvania Railroad at 4.15 p. m., and West at 5.45 p. m. Mail No. 1 leaves Huntingdon at 7.40 a. m. on arrival of Pacific Express West.

Trains on this road connect with trains on Bedford & Bridgeport, and Cumberland & Pennsylvania Railroads.

G. F. GAGE, Supt.

The Weekly Pilgrim.

Published by J. B. Brumbaugh, & Co.

Edited by H. B. & Geo. Brumbaugh.

CORRESPONDING EDITORS.

D. P. Sayler, Double Pipe Creek, Md.

Leonard Furry, New Enterprise, Pa.

The *Pilgrim* is a Christian Periodical, devoted to religion and moral reform. It will advocate in the spirit of *love* and *liberty*, the principles of true Christianity, labor for the promotion of peace among the people of God, for the encouragement of the saints and for the conversion of sinners, avoiding those things which tend toward disunion or sectional feelings.

TERMS.

Single copy, Book paper,	$1.50
Eleven copies, [eleventh for Agt.]	$15.00

Any number above that at the same rate.

Address,

H. B. BRUMBAUGH.
James Creek,
Huntingdon county Pa.

The Weekly Pilgrim.

"REMOVE NOT THE ANCIENT LANDMARKS WHICH OUR FATHERS HAVE SET."

VOL. 4. JAMES CREEK, PENNSYLVANIA, DECEMBER 2, 1873. NO. 18.

POETRY.

THE ANGEL SINGERS.

Oh! to my mind comes a fancy,
Of a lovely spot far away,
Blooming in beauty immortal;
Fanned by breezes wafting gently,
Onward bearing the sweet perfume
Of leaves and flowers eternal;
A sweet, fair spot, untouched by gloom,
Where love and joy, forever bloom.

There two angels kneeling gently,
Amid the breeze that's wafting by,
'Neath the pure, softly beaming light,
With hands uplifted fervently;
Mild and beautiful, side by side,
With eyes so sweet and forms so slight.
Pure, Oh pure as the land they've trod,
Are singing anthems to their God.

Pure and gentle as the zephyr,
Floating on that Heavenly shore;
Soft as the azure tinted skies,
More sweet than falls on mortal ear,
The songs of childhood's happy days,
The soul-breathed anthems thrills and dies,
In love, devotion, joy and praise,
To the source from which all blessing flows

The pure breezes waft on gently,
Bearing the balmy fragrance by;
The mellow light glows softly still,
'Mong bright green leaves that lowly sigh,
In beauty 'round the landscape lies,
And still there with heavenly thrill,
Those soft, pure strains of music rise
And charm that quiet Paradise.

Oh, sing on, ye angels, ever!
Away o'er death's gloomy river
Where love and beauty never dies—
Sing on, when thou wilt—together,
Kneeling 'mid the pure light gently;
Oh soft as the glance of thine eyes!
Sweet as the flowers around thee!
Chant, O chant, thy heavenly lay!

F. W. S[illegible].

Antwerp, Mich.

ORIGINAL ESSAYS.

"WITH MY SOUL HAVE I DESIRED THEE IN THE NIGHT."

ISAIAH 26: 9.

From my bed of repose during the night watches when all around seems wrapped in stillness, I can look up through the window and see the shining stars in martial array, and oft the silver moon pours down her lunar light upon my bed. Oft have I thus spent wakeful moments in looking up to the vaulted star specked heavens, and by faith peered beyond where God resides. At such a time when the body is seeking rest from the toils of the day, the mind no longer is harassed by the noise and confusion incident to daylight, but freed from all visible surroundings, it can sweetly or silently commune with God. To me such moments are full of solemn reflection, and often to my mind recurs that passage of Scripture, "Great art thou, O God! great in thy works. When I consider the heavens the work of thy fingers, the moon and the stars which thou hast ordained; what is man that thou art mindful of him? and the Son of Man that thou visitest him?" And quite recently in one of those silent conversations of the mind, the language of the prophet came to me: "With my soul have I desired thee in the night." Then followed a train of thought in substance something like, the following: Why should my soul desire the Lord in the night? Because it is the time of darkness, and the time we desire light, and God is light. The prophet was a servant of God,—he loved God; with his soul he desired him in the night.

The beloved of God are the children of God,—the servants of God. In the noon-day of their religious life and experience, they enjoy the sweet comforts of a Savior's love, having come by faith unto the "perfect day" of illuminating light; but ah! where is the one that does not at times experience a night of spiritual darkness, not death, but only darkness? That darkness is brought about in various ways: sometimes when all seems prosperous, and we move along in the blaze of prosperity, a sudden turn in the road, we come to the reverse of fortune, and such darkness broods over our spirits. In our prosperity we may have almost forgotten God, our desires were earthly, carnally, but now seeing our dependence in God, faith moves our heart and we cry, "My soul desireth thee in the night.

Often when we are living in a happy, joyful, family circle, mother, father, brothers, sisters, children dear, all, all here! We fail to appreciate the goodness of God in thus lighting up our home world with all the stars of a family association. But alas! Death stalks that way, a shining one is cut down. A father, or a mother, or perchance the idolized child of the happy group. The sun of joy goes down, then, oh, then, will not the heart then turn to God for comfort? Then will the soul desire thee, O God, in the night. Again we may pass from the full illuminating glare of God's loving countenance to a state of spiritual darkness, owing to many trials, troubles, and temptations, and the deceitfulness of sin. In those dark hours of distress, the trembling soul, yet beleiving in God, yet loving Jesus will cry out, "With my soul have I desired thee in the night." It is for our good that we have those trials, those seasons of gloom. The child that looks to its parent for shelter and protection may wander away some distance, when the day is bright, but when night comes it draws near, and in midnight darkness it feels only secure while nestling in that bosom where its trust is. So with the child of God, when gloom broods over the soul, then it feels to draw nearer to that bosom, that can shelter from any storm. It is needful our souls desire the Lord in the night, because it is the time of dangers. When natural night spreads her mantle over the city, the robbers come from their lurking places to kill and to steal. And when spiritual darkness broods over our souls, then satan comes with his hosts to try us, bids us murmur at God's dealing with us, or perchance will tell us "curse God and die," or persuade us we are not a child of God, and tell us a "thousand frightful things." But the soul that desires God in the night, shall be safe. Look up, desponding ones, and know daylight will come in all its beauty. Because you have to pass through many a fiery trial, and the smoke of God's chastening rod hide from view the light and joy you once seen and felt, don't suppose God has cast you off. By no means: he careth for you and would have you purified, fit for his use in heaven.

We notice some stars shine brighter than others, and all are brighter, the darker the night. So we cannot all expect to experience the religion of Jesus just in the same measure or degree, and the darker the gloom that pervades the aerial heavens of the soul, the nearer we will cling to the cross; the more our souls will desire God in the night, and brighter to his eye will we appear. We rejoice to see the beloved of God living in the joy and consolation of the light and liberty of a free Gospel, that seems to illumine their pathway with the very fires of heavenly love, and would they might thus go on ever basking in the sunshine of the Holy light; but while we love to see such, we by no means, despise those who have to pass through great tribulation. seasons of gloom and sorrow. Oh may we with our souls desire the Lord in the night, that when the morning cometh,—the bright morning—the glorious morning, we shall be with our God, our Savior, and our all.

J. S. FLORY.

Greely, Col.

A DRUNKARD'S WARNING

Bro. Brumbaugh, I select from the Baltimore *Daily American*, for the PILGRIM, that it may have the widest possible circulation.

A young man entered the barroom of a village tavern, and called for a drink. No, said the landlord, you have too much already. You have had *delirium tremens* once, and I cannot sell you any more. He stepped aside to make room for a couple of young men who had just entered, and the landlord waited upon them very politely. The other had stood by silent and sullen, and when they had finished, he walked up to the landlord, and addressed him: "Six years ago, at their age, I stood where these young men now are. I was a man with fair prospects. Now at the age of twenty-eight, I am a wreck, body and mind. You led me to drink. In this room I formed the habit that has been my ruin. Now, sell me a few glasses more, and your work will be done; I shall soon be out of the way; there is no hope for me. But they can be saved; they may be men again. Do not sell it to them. Sell it to me, and let me die, and the world will be rid of me; but for heaven's sake sell no more to them!" The landlord listened, pale and trembling. Setting down his decanter, he exclaimed! "God helping me, that is the last drop I will ever sell to any one." And he kept his word.

Dear readers of the PILGRIM, take notice, and be timely warned. Is it not a fact known to all, that drunkards are made of small beginnings? *Then never take the first sip*, but you *venders* and *retailers*, tremble at the thought of *selling* or *giving* the unthinking youth the first drink. Remember it is declared by the Lord's prophet, "Woe unto him that giveth his neighbor drink, that puttest thy bottle to *him*, and makest *him* drunken also, that thou mayest look upon their nakedness: Thou art filled with shame for glory: drink thou also, and let thy foreskin be uncovered: the cup of the LORD's right hand shall be turned unto, thee, and shameful spewing *shall be* on thy glory."—Hab. 2: 15, 16.

D. P. SAYLER.

A REPLY

In PILGRIM No. 40, page 314, appears an article from the pen of Bro. D. C. Moomaw, entitled, "The Cap Controversy." In the above named article the brother gives us what he calls a *paraphrase* of several texts of Scripture. To some of these paraphrases we seriously object.

We have no particular liking for controversy, neither do we often engage in it, but as the subject under consideration particularly interests us, we will try, by the help of God, to present a few thoughts upon it.

In paragraph 2d, the brother qualifies head, by the word spiritual, telling us what kind of head. Now brother Paul places no qualifying adjective before head, but simply says, "The head," leaving us to learn from other portions of Scripture what kind of head he means. That he does not mean, as brother M. would have us believe, a spiritual head, we would infer from what he says in Colossians 1:18 "And he is the head of the body, the church." The apostle here does not limit this headship of Christ to a portion of the body, which we think he certainly would if brother M.'s explanation was correct. If it read, "And he is the head of the male portion of the body, the church," then it would harmonize with the brother's views.

But this subject is still made plainer in verse 19 of chapter 2. "And not holding the head, from which all the body by joints and bands having nourishment ministered and knit together, increaseth with the increase of God." Here the apostle defines body more clearly he says: "ALL the body." All the body has the same head. All draw nourishment from the same source.

If Paul had said from which all the male members of the body, etc., then we would conclude that the female had some other spiritual head, and drew spiritual nourishment from some other source, we should then be very glad for brother M's explanation, as it would clearly point out whence we must look for spiritual nourishment, and to whom we must go for spiritual supplies.

Does the brother mean to tell us that man occupies the position of Christ's vicegerent toward woman? We had always thought there was but one man at a time who claims this splendid prerogative over his fellow creatures, and that he resides at Rome. Surely we are not at present prepared to accept of such a species of subordination, but if the brother can prove to us from the sacred oracles, such a heaven's decree, then we will submit, for with Abraham, we know that the Judge of all the earth doeth right. But it is too painful a doctrine to accept upon a mere assertion.

That God has ordained that man is our head in some respects, and to same extent, we freely admit. We are not ignorant of the fact that a part of the sentence which God pronounced against Eve as a punishment for her sins, was that her husband should "rule over her," but we have no more reason to think that punishment extends to spiritual things, than we have to think that man's punishment extends to spiritual things. See Genesis 3:17, 18, 19.

The word head occurs often thro'-out the sacred Scriptures, and it has several significations besides its natural one. We must judge of its meaning, not only from its connections, but from other portions of Scripture.

We do not know the exact state of things in the Corinthian Church at the time the apostle wrote, but it would seem that there existed considerable confusion at that time, and that the different members did not know their proper sphere of action, or a least, did not act in their proper sphere. Hence we have the language of Paul contained in the 11th chapter of his epistle to that church, "But I would have you KNOW." From this language it seems they did not know what he was about to tell them. But in what sense, or to what extent each of these prerogatives of headship is exercised, Paul does not here say, but by reading carefully all he says on this subject, we may perhaps learn his meaning. In verse 8 and 9 he gives reasons for man's priority; then in verse 10, he says, "For this cause," or because of this priority, "ought the woman to have the [token of] power on her head because of the angels."

We understand the apostle's meaning to be something like this: though man does, for certain reasons, occupy a superior position in this world, yet God has bestowed upon woman, or upon those who receive Him, the power to become the daughters of God, even to them that believe on His name. He has given her the power to become spiritually equal with man, and with him to receive the spirit of adoption whereby she too may cry, "Abba Father." He hath also given her power to receive the witness of the spirit with her spirit that she is a child of God. And if children, then heirs; heirs of God and joint-heirs of Jesus Christ. Yes blessed be God, if so be that we suffer with Him, we may all be glorified together, for it is written, "There is neither Jew nor Greek, there is neither bond nor free, there is neither male nor female: for all are one in Christ Jesus."—Gal. 3:28. Here upon our King's highway all temporal distinctions are annihilated. The vallies are filled, and the mountains must be brought down.

The apostle would say, let the woman wear upon her head a token or sign of this great power. Let her show that she appreciates the great privilege which God has bestowed upon her. By this sign she also shows her respect and deference to man whom God has constituted her head in some things.

But what shall this sign be? Paul says it shall be a covering. Some, however, seem to understand from verse 15, that Paul means that the hair shall be this covering. We will try to look at this matter a little. In verse 6, the apostle says, "For if the woman be not covered, let her also be shorn; but if it be a shame for a woman to be shorn or shaven, let her be covered." "Let her ALSO be shorn." Let her likewise, or in like manner be shorn. Surely if language means any thing, we must understand Paul to say that if she will not submit to wear the artificial covering, let her also, or in like manner have her natural covering taken from her. But if this be a shame, a disgrace, "let her be covered," let her wear the artificial covering.

No greater indignity could have been offered to a virtuous lady in Paul's day than to deprive her of her hair, which was at once her glory and her pride, and which she nourished with great fondness. Paul would then say, if she feels it to be such a shame, or disgrace to be deprived of her natural covering, let her wear this artificial covering, for it is just as much out of place for a Christian lady to be without this covering when she prays or prophesies, as it would be for a modest lady of the world to have her hair cut short. See verse 5.

Again if Paul had meant that the hair was the covering which he had so earnestly urged the sisters to wear, he would have said in verse 15, for her hair is given her for THE covering. He would have placed the definite article THE before covering, instead of the indefinite A, showing that the hair was the specific covering to which he had referred. But since he says a covering, his meaning is evident. The hair is certainly a covering, but not that particular covering which Christian women are required to wear as a sign to distinguish them from the women of the world, and also to show that they are betrothed to Christ. Oh my dear sisters, this is indeed a badge of honor! Why then should we be ashamed to wear it? What if the world does look upon it as a silly whim, that does not destroy its importance.

When we look upon those nations upon whom the blessed light of the Gospel has never shone, and contrast the condition of the women of those nations with the condition of the women who bask in the sunlight and liberty of our dear Jesus, then, oh then, we can appreciate what Christianity has done for us! Oh! how our hearts bleed in sympathy for our poor down-trodden sex, when we read of the cruelty and injustice that is done them among barbarious nations, how they are made to bear a double burden, not only their own punishment, (see Genesis 3:16,) but also the burden of manual labor which God designed that man should bear, Gen. 3:19.

However much our modern reformers may boast of what they are doing to elevate our sex, we are content to cling to the dear old Bible. Let its spirit be fully carried out, and it will elevate us to that high position which God designed for us to fill. If Christianity fails to elevate the race, the fault is not in this heaven-born system, but in those who teach and practice it. The scheme is perfect, but sometimes the medium through which it is brought to the children of men, is very imperfect. Oh, let us seek knowledge right from the fountain-head, where truth gushes forth clear as crystal from the throne of God and of the Lamb.

But what kind of covering shall be worn? The apostle does not specify what kind, but simply says a covering. We think we can discover wisdom in this. Paul wrote not merely for the instruction of the Corinthian Church, but for the instruction of all Christians, in all nations, and all ages. Customs are necessarily different among different people and in different ages of the world. Had the apostle designated the kind of covering, there would have been no latitude for adaptation to times and circumstances. In this case it would have been a much greater burden than it now is, for instance had he said, let her wear a veil, instead of saying, let her be covered, for the veil was probably the kind of covering worn by females in his day, and would, no doubt, have been the kind he would have specified had he pointed out the particular kind. Now this would only have increased the difficulty. The next question would be, what is meant by a veil? The veils that are worn in this country at this time are nothing like the veils that were worn in ancient times, and are still worn by the ladies in the Levant. Veils are of different kinds and of different patterns. Some of them not only covered the head, but the face, and the entire person. But Paul only requires that this covering which he speaks of shall cover the head.

The veils that were, and are still worn in the East have a different design from this covering. To a married lady, the veil is the badge which distinguishes and dignifies her in that character, and betokens her alliance to her husband, and her interest in his affections; therefore to deprive her of this is one of the greatest indignities that she can receive.

The covering which is here spoken of, is the badge which distinguishes and dignifies the Christian woman in that character, and betokens her alliance to Christ, and her interest in his affections. Shall we say that she ought to feel it as much of an indignity, as much of a shame to be, without this covering, as an Eastern lady would to be deprived of her veil? Paul made no difference between the married and the virgin, for this covering is to be worn because of the angels, of which we shall try to speak presently.

As the Holy Spirit has not pointed out what kind of covering shall be worn, it is the province of the Church, the next highest authority, to specify the kind. The Church of the present age, in this country has adopted the cap. We admire her wisdom and her judgment, we don't see that she could have chosen anything that would answer the purpose better, that would be more becoming and appropriate. This is a covering for the head, and that is what is required. It is neat, plain and convenient. However if she, in her wisdom, shall ever see that some other covering will answer the purpose better, let her adopt it, and we will cheerfully acquiesce. The Church does not claim infallibility, but as we are required to "hear the Church," and to be subject one to another, will not our refusal to adopt this covering, be an act of disobedience to our dear Lord? And then is it modest for an individual member to prefer their own wisdom to the wisdom of the Church? "Where no counsel is, the people fall; but in the multitude of counsellors there is safety."—Prov. 11: 14. We do think then that we ought, as obedient and Christ-loving children, wear the covering which the Church has adopted.

When shall it be worn? In verse 5, we read, "Every woman that prayeth or prophesieth with her head uncovered, dishonoreth her head." And in verse 10, we read, "For this cause ought the woman to have (the token of) power on her head because of the angels." From the above we understand that this covering has two significations, first, to show her respect to man, therefore when she worships with him she should wear the token of her respect. Secondly, because of the angels; and we understand that the word angel includes the Angel Jehovah That holy Being who led the ranks of Israel through the wilderness, and of whom God gave them this promise, "Behold I send an Angel before thee, to keep thee in the way, and to bring thee into the place which I have prepared. Beware of him, and obey his voice, provoke him not, for he will not pardon your transgressions, for my name is in him."—Exodus 23 : 20, 21, and of whom Isaiah says that, "He led them through the deep as a horse in the wilderness, that they should not stumble.". The Prophet here seems to allude to the dexterity of some of the Eastern nations, and particularly the Arabs in the management of even bad horses. Such is their skill with this animal if one of them be mounted upon a good charger, he can with a wonderful tact, carry, as it were, another horse, (though he may be stiff, feeble, and foundered) along with him. No matter how rough the road, or how beset with dangers, if one of these admirable horsemen have firm hold of the bridle, he will gallantly conduct him through in perfect safety.

The Prophet's figure is natural and grand, showing how gallantly Jehovah led the children of Israel through the Red Sea Though they were weak and feeble, yet he by his Almighty arm, and with an inexpressible vigor, conducted them safely through all the inequalities in the bed of the sea, caused in some instances, by deep cavities, and in others by abrupt intervening rocks.

This beautiful figure will also apply to us. If we but yield up the bridle of our wills into the hands of Jesus, and reign ourselves completely to his guidance, he will bear us safely over all the pitfalls, inequalities and impediments that may intersect our pathway, and will land us upon the mount of deliverance. Though we are all ignorance and weakness, yet he is all wisdom, and strength, and if we place ourselves under his protection, we are safe, no matter how dangerous the road over which we must travel, and no matter how feeble and helpless we are. Paul said," he took pleasure in infirmities, for when he was weak, then was he strong."—2 Cor. 12 : 10. And why? Because these things kept him very dependent upon Jesus, and that dependence kept him very near his precious Savior, therefore he took pleasure in them, because they hedged him in from the world and kept him in in the society of that one in whom he so much delighted.

If then this covering is to be worn as a sign that we are under the conduct and protection of the great God-man, the answer to the question, when shall it be worn? would be whenever we need his guidance and protection. And when do we not need it? Who of us could sustain ourselves for an hour without his help? Who of us could resist the smallest temptation, or bear patiently the slightest insult? Oh how wretched would we be, should this dear Friend, who is a very present help in trouble, withdraw his face from us? We lately received a letter from one who is laboring to build up the Master's cause in the West, the writer said, "I must find a Savior in everything of my life's experience or I have no Savior at all. Oh! I must find him in disappointments in life, in calculations purely secular. I must find him in sorrows and afflictions, in poverty, in all outward conditions, as well as in the services of his house." How perfectly do these words breathe the sentiments of a soul whose dependence is in Jesus, and who has learned that there is no strength in the arm of flesh.

What glorious privileges have we! Jesus, the author and finisher of our faith, is also our leader and protector through life's journey. Now we see him through a glass darkly, or as viewing him through a semi-transparent glass, or through a glass that is cloudy and dull as the ancient glassware; but then we shall see him face to face. O, let us then be faithful a little longer. Every commandment has a deep signification; if we cannot comprehend their full import now, yet if we obey in the letter and try to understand the best we can, the time will soon come when we will no longer know in part, but shall know even as also we are known.

MATTIE A. LEAR.

Urbana, Ill.

HOW TO SPEND MONEY FOR THE LORD.

After seeing the invitation under the above heading, and observing the seeming reluctant respond to the call, I have deliberated upon a plan, and decided to transmit it upon paper. It will no doubt be handed to the readers of the PILGRIM, and must meet their general approval in order to be of any service to them, or the unborn thousands of human beings that must soon fill their places in the duties of this world.

I have only one consolation in the matter of its approval or disapproval and I need no other. Whatever it may merit it will receive. To give a plan with such illustrations showing its practicability and necessity as would be essentially necessary to deeply impress the people to whom it is addressed would occupy more time and space than I am now prepared to fill. Perhaps at some future time I will write more on this subject.

Early in our contemplated plan of using money for Christian benefit, we meet an obstacle that must in some practical way be disposed of. How shall the Church obtain the money, which it must obtain before it can properly discuss the question of its most prudent use. Has any of the brethren money that they would loan. The answer would be, yes, if we are to be safely secured and get our interest. The plan comprehends all these conditions, and will give satisfactory surties for the use of money should it become necessary to borrow.

But some say there is no use of drawing plans for the benefit of Christian influence, for it is progressing, and if each one will do his part, as an individual, all will go well. This is about the view that it is taken by very many persons whose intentions are good, but let us illustrate this proposition: A great military officer moves his army to the field of battle and orders a halt, and addresses his men, here is the enemy in sight. Now if each of you will do your duty, you will surely win, but I am not going to plan this battle or command; you are expected to fight as individuals and take care of yourselves. The fortunes of such a battle would be lost for want of a leader, a plan of battle, &c And so is much of that which is given for Church purposes lost for the want of a well matured plan upon which to devote it.

Our plan comprehends first the necessity of a state council at which each Church within, should be represented. That council to divide the state into as many districts as may be necessary, and each district furnished with one minister, and after assigning each minister to his work, we must ask how is this man to get his living and provide a support for a family? The answer has been already given, work for it. But this proposition is not in perfect keeping with a minister's stern duties. Can a commander of a large army perform all the duties of a common soldier, and command his army successfully? Certainly not, neither can any man devote his time to preaching and find sufficient time to perform the amount of labor necessary for his entire support.

Neither is it in perfect keeping with the principles of Christian duty that a preacher live entirely upon the assessments made upon the Church, and be thus provided with a strong inducement to rear his family in idleness, a vice into which some churches have run to an alarming extent. It then becomes our next object to provide for the common wants of each Minister, the first of which we will call a home, or station, to consist of not more than 30 acres of good land as favorably located as possible with sufficient improvements to render comfortable its inmates. To obtain this let as much of the purchase money be obtained by contribution as possible, and if no part can be thus obtained, let some one who has money to loan make the purchase for the church, in whose interest the property should be used, and to whom it must in all cases belong; they being required to work a gradual reduction of debt until the property should become an absolute accession to the Church. It would be a prudent use of Church money. The amount thus given would provide the Church with a station from which the Gospel could be preached all over a district without incurring any considerable traveling expenses. When a minister becomes restless or unworthy let his place be filled by another. Let the various districts meet once each year and hold a State convention, where a good effort should be made to kindle an interest in the cause of Christian duty. It would only be necessary to send a small amount of help to a minister in time of great urgency of his work, to enable him to live comfortable, and he would be thus freed, in mind, of some of the perplexities connected with getting a living, which often hinder ministers in preaching the Gospel. The duty of improving by the cultivation of trees and plants, those little homes, would afford the family a healthful and useful employment, and afford them part of a living. I might very appropriately add some comment upon the necessity of such a plan here in California, but suffice it to say that within a few miles of us there are people that do not know there is such a Church as the Brethren.

J. H. DUNLAP.

ABOMINATIONS.

For that which is highly esteemed among men, is an abomination in the sight of God —Luke 16: 15.

A round colorless lapelled coat, a plain unfashionable print calico garment, or a plain coarse unbleached muslin cap, are things that are not an abomination to God except when they are highly esteemed among men. "There is nothing unclean of itself, but to him that esteemeth anything to be unclean, to him it is unclean." If the apostle meant inordinate affection, which I believe he does, then everything that can be known or mentioned except God himself, is an abomination with God when it is highly esteemed among men.

Big humps, big lumps and wildernesses of crimps and frills worn as raiment by women, and enormous, hideous masses of hair or bark piled on their heads surmounted by little platts, ornamented with lace ribbon, bird's tails &c., are abominations in the sight of God according to the degree at which they are esteemed or overestimated or "highly esteemed" among men. To be sure, the care and attention that men bestow upon them, and more particularly the manner of that care and attention shows that degree of estimation. Therefore let no one think himself to be somebody because of gay or vile raiment, else he is one who justifies himself before men, but God knows his heart, and his raiment, no matter whether vile or gay is abomination in the sight of God. As it is with raiment, so it is with food, and as it is with food so it is with all that is earthly, transitory, passing away. All these things are meant, by the apostle when he says, "But if thy brother be grieved with thy meat, thou walkest not charitably, that is, if thou continuest to eat it while thy brother continues to be grieved, and of course if thou art aware of such grievance. J. B. GARVER.

GOD'S POWER

Every great work of art tells of the toil of the artist. From bottom to top of the temple there is evidence of the labor of workmen. The hammer, saw, plane, and other implements are in constant use, even to construct the smallest buildings, nor is any work without the use of means. He commanded, and it stood fast. "His power sets fast the mountains," not by daily, yearly or continued labor, but by a word. And while it is good for us to speak of his love, mercy, goodness, it is equally good to "talk of his power."

He that loses his conscience has nothing left that is worth keeping.

The Weekly Pilgrim.

JAMES CREEK, PA., Nov. 25, 1873.

☞ How to send money.--All sums over $1.50, should be sent either in a check, draft or postal order. If neither of these can be obtained, have the letter registered.

☞ When Money is sent, *always* send with it the name and address of those who paid it. Write the names and post office as plainly as possible.

☞ Every subscriber for 1874, gets a *Pilgrim Almanac* Free.

LIBERTY.

If there is one thing that is especially dear to mankind generally, it is liberty, the fact is, it seems to be the great basis of all our actions in life. For it, the world is kept in a continual commotion, and to obtain and enjoy it, there is no sacrifice too great to be withheld. The great watchword is, "Give me liberty or give me death." There may be and is an undue desire for worldly or national liberty, and our zeal may carry us beyond the limit of christian obligation, but there is a liberty that we are justified in obtaining even at a sacrifice of our own life. We mean the liberty that is obtainable through Jesus Christ.

This liberty was purchased for us by an exceeding great price, so great that there was found but one that was able to cancel the great debt, and is free to all, on complying with the conditions on which it is promised. These conditions are faith, repentance, and baptism.

By an intelligent and voluntary compliance with these, we receive an heirship and become the adopted sons and daughters of God. These are rightly considered the primary conditions, and in regard to them there should be no diversity of opinions. But there is a code of secondary conditions that are necessary for our growth and perfection in the divine life, upon which we may slightly differ without affecting our christian character or prospects of reward. That there are no advantages in this, we all readily admit, as the one-mindedness that was to characterize the disciples of Jesus is greatly to be desired, but it is the unavoidable outgrowth of the admixture of the carnal or fleshy, and the spiritual. Notwithstanding we have passed through the regeneration and received the power to become the children of God, yet we are in the flesh, and have its cravings to contend with. Even the apostle Paul, in all his holy zeal, could not be delivered, hence, his judgment, in regard to the minor points of doctrine, was sometimes tainted with this mixture of flesh and spirit as well as some of the other disciples. The circumcision, the eating of flesh, and the keeping of fast days, were things upon which slight differences of opinion were obtained, yet they did not excommunicate each other, nor cease to be disciples. The spirit of nonforbearance was largely developed in the minds of the twelve. When they came across disciples who did not exactly walk with them, they were quite ready to pronounce the ban, but their Master teaches them somewhat different "He that is not against me is *for me*." We desire to impress this idea with power, upon the minds of every brother and sister. We are so apt to undervalue, and even ignore, the zeal of our brethren who slightly differ from us, even if they have as much divine sanction in their favor as have we. Here is where charity and christian forbearance ought to come in. Our established order will not save us, neither will it justify us in ignoring those of our brethren and sisters who may conscientiously differ from us, if they are in the faith, and are laboring for Jesus. The Bible is our order, it is the Brethren's order, and we acknowledge no other, neither is it our purpose to defend any other. The ancient landmarks which we wish to defend are not those set by men but by God as delivered through His Son and established by the Apostles. This is what our brethren preach, and what they expect us to publish. Then let us hear nothing more about "old order" nor "new order" but Christ and Him crucified. If our brethren do not *see* things exactly as we do, let us not rob them of their liberties, or judge them by any order or creed, as in our public preaching we deny *in toto* of having any such thing. We should extend the widest liberties to those who have become the heirs of this great salvation, and not refuse to fellowship them as long they consistently contend for sound doctrine. We should ever remember that ten may be right, and ten thousand wrong, or that ten may differ from ten thousand, and yet, all meet the approbation of God. I may eat flesh and enjoy a full liberty of conscience, my brother may abstain and enjoy equal liberties, but because *we* differ, we should not rob each other of our liberties. The Kingdom of God does not consist in meats and drinks, neither in the technical points in the observing of the ordinances of the Lord's House, but in the spiritual import. Every ordinance has its special design. This design is what we should seek after, that we may realize it, and not lose its power in seeking after the letter. We are not contending for liberalism nor radicalism, but Christianism. With the apostle Paul, let us determine to judge one another no more, but judge this rather, that no man put a stumbling block or an occasion to fall, in his brother's way. Let us exercise forbearance one towards another, and if any of us think we are strong, let us bear the infirmities of the weak, thus following after things which make for peace, and may the God of peace and liberty abide with us all.

SET STAKES.

Some years ago we worked on the farm, and while at that vocation it fell to our lot occasionally to prepare the seed ground ready for the sower. This is done by making furrows a certain distance apart so as to form a gauge to the sower, that the seed may be evenly distributed over the surface. In order that those furrows may be straight, and an equal distance apart, it is necessary to have something to go by as a guide, and this guide consisted in a stake being set at a certain distance from the point from which we started. This stake is removed on every return to the point at which it stood, and placed at a certain distance from the last made furrow, and by this means we are enabled to make straight furrows, and the field is marked or gauged ready to sow.

The stake is set for a point at which to aim in order to make straight furrows, and this principle may be applied in everything we do in life. If we wish to attain success in any undertaking, we must set our stake and keep our eye on it. No matter what our calling may be, this is the principle upon which we must necessarily act. If we wish to enter the calling of a farmer, our purpose generally is to procure a piece of land, provide it with the necessary buildings and raise it to the highest state of cultivation. This in many instances places the stake far ahead of us, so far that we are scarcely able to see it. But then, as we have done when making furrows, if the stake was to far ahead, we would sight to some object in range with it, in order to make the furrow straight, so we may do in this calling, or any other. We can set our stake far ahead, and then sight to something in range with it. For example, we may aim first to have our land paid for, and when we have reached this point, then we may aim to improve it, so as to make it produce bountifully, and then we may aim to put on it the necessary buildings &c., and then we have arrived at the stake we first set. If our labors are not yet ended on earth, we may set another stake and thus keep on until the whole field is marked, or until our time in which to labor is ended.

So it should be in obtaining an education. We should have some object in view for which our knowledge is to be acquired. We should set our stake, and I believe we should set it as far ahead as possible, and then direct all our energies towards the reaching of that point. By this I do not mean that we should aspire to have the name of being educated, or the praise of men; we should set our stake higher than this. God has given us talents that are to be used, and our aim should be to employ these so that when He comes to reckon with us, He may receive His own with usury. This is the point at which we should aim, and if we ever keep our eye firmly fixed upon this point, and strive to reach it until the close of our earthly career, then may we hear the welcome plaudit, "Well done thou good and faithful servant: thou hast been faithful over a few things; I will make thee ruler over many things; enter thou into the joys of thy Lord." The tho't of receiving such an approval from our Divine Master is surely the greatest incentive that can be presented. What is the praise of men, compared with the approval of our blessed Master? Then dear reader, when you are striving to obtain knowledge, be sure that you set your stake above the honor of this world.

We should make *straight* furrows. What crooked unsightly furrows some persons make in this world! They appear to set no stake at which to aim, and thus they ramble up and down through life without accomplishing anything. God has placed us in this world in order that we may honor and glorify Him. It is through us that He expects to sow and reap, and unless we set a stake, unless we have some purpose in view, our furrows will be crooked and unsightly, and thus the design of God, in us will be frustrated.

In our various callings and pursuits in this life if we pursue them with proper motives, we glorify God. All that we do should be done with an eye single to the honor and glory of God, and hence the pursuing of our various callings in life, with the proper object in view, may be as by marks in range with the great central point at which we should all aim—the mark for the prize of our high calling in Christ Jesus. This point, dear reader, is in the distance so far that we cannot fully realize the blessedness of our condition when we arrive there. It is said, "Eye hath not seen, neither hath it entered into the heart of man, the joys that God hath prepared for them that love Him." Of these unseen and unheard of joys we shall all partake when we reach that point. Let us then, endeavor to set our stakes in range with that great central object, and though it may apparently be far off, if we shrink from no duty, and falter at no difficulty, ever keeping our eye on the stake, put our trust in God, our efforts will surely, finally, be crowned with success. May God help us all to set our stakes aright.

J. B. B.

New subscribers to the Pilgrim will, by sending in their names now, receive the remaining numbers of the present volume and an Almanac, all for $1.50.

WHAT SHALL BE THE SUBJECT?

Some of our contributors, who are interested in the great cause which we are laboring to advocate, and who desire to aid us, by writing for our columns, are asking us for subjects. This, we suppose is because they desire that their labors shall be as acceptable as possible. Some time ago, we gave a few general subjects for the consideration of our writers and we believe they all received some attention, but were by no means exhausted, as we thought them sufficiently important to command the attention of a greater number of our contributors, but we have concluded that our brethren and sisters, in this respect, are like ourselves, prefer to choose their own subjects. This we think is altogether right, as we have different gifts and our minds, through the influence of different circumstances are forced into different channels. But we wish to suggest a few ideas in regard to what should be our subject matter.

First we wish it understood that the PILGRIM is gaining a very respectable circulation outside of the membership. For this we have been laboring, and we are glad to know that our expectations are not in vain, not only in this fact, but we have the full assurance that it has been the means of accomplishing good, and of presenting the truth acceptably to the minds of some that could not otherwise be reached. Therefore we wish our writers to bear these facts in mind, and when writing, let the consideration be, how will this appear to the mind of the stranger, and what kind of an influence will it have upon the mind of the honest inquirer after truth? We wish to send the PILGRIM out into the world as a Missionary and want it to carry nothing but *sound doctrine*.

A second design is that it shall be a medium through which the Church can investigate the truth by the comparing of our different views with the Bible, and thus come to that sameness of mind so desirable in the body of Christ. To do this profitably and acceptably, requires much wisdom and christian charity. If these elements are not freely exercised, our investigations will lead to strife, envy and vain debatings. These things brethren and sisters, ought not so to be.

Another very prominent feature in the PILGRIM, is to preach the Gospel, especially to the poor and isolated. In this we have been doing a great and good work as many homes in the distant west and south who have not the privilege of attending meeting, are made to rejoice on the reception of the good news it brings to their doors every week. If our work is made the subject of fervent prayer by any, we believe it is by this class. Truly, to the poor the Gospel is preached, if by no other way, the PILGRIM does it.

Church news has become a great *desideratum* in the Church, so much so that we would scarcely know how to get along without it. In Paul's time he thought it necessary to go around to all the churches he had established "to see how they do." This information, we can now, to a very great extent, get through our periodicals, hence they have become a medium through which we learn of each other's welfare and the general prosperity of the Church.

Having thus set forth some of the designs of our work, it occurs to us that our readers should have a pretty general idea of what should be our subject matter. In short, brethren and sisters, whatsoever worketh for the peace and prosperity of the Church and the salvation of sinners, think of and write as the spirit may move.

A FEW WORDS TO OUR AGENTS.

The time has now come that our agents are getting to work and are asking for information as to how they shall proceed, &c. This is right, as every man should fully understand his business before he undertakes it. We shall always be happy to give our agents any information which may tend to their advantage or convenience.

Our first suggestion is, go to work and gather all the names you possibly can. Those that are prepared, let them pay at the time of subscribing. As many as can, let them pay by the beginning of the New Year. Those who cannot pay by that time, let them pay as soon as they can, or during the year. Do not refuse any that you have good reason to believe will pay during the year. To the worthy poor, members or no members, give it for whatever they feel able to pay. We cannot think of refusing any such who desire to read it, and we believe there are but few but what can pay a little. It is really the duty of the church to see that such are supplied with the PILGRIM and ought to contribute at least, part of it, but if the Church will not do it and there are those who desire to have it, try our liberality and we will do the best we can, but do not send us the name of such as you know to be doubtful pay.

As fast as you gather the names, send them on so that we may get them booked and send them their Almanacs. The money can be sent when you get a sufficient amount collected. At present we would prefer not to receive checks on doubtful banks. Wherever you can get postal orders, send them, if you cannot do this, send it in a registered letter. When agents do this, we allow them to deduct from the amount, the expenses of remitting. All amounts of $1.50 and under, may be sent at our risk if carefully put up and properly addressed.

As a remuneration to agents, we give the eleventh copy free, that is, any person sending us ten subscribers and $15,00 will get the eleventh copy for his trouble. For all names sent over this number, ten per cent off. For the percentage we will give any book or books noticed in our pages or the agents can divide it among themselves or deduct it from the whole amount.

All agents who prefer to distribute the Almanacs themselves can do so by letting us know the number they need. We however, wish it understood that we do not wish our agents to sell any Almanacs or give them to any but actual subscribers.

If you wish special information in regard to special cases, please write us and we will cheerfully give it. In soliciting subscribers, do not forget to inform them that the PILGRIM is to be enlarged and otherwise improved.

Now brethren and sisters, we are trying to do our duty by enlarging and improving our work, and we hope you will all make an effort to give us a corresponding increase of circulation so that we may be remunerated, in part, at least, for the extra labor and cost that will be necessary in order to publish the PILGRIM for the coming year.

SEND FOR ONE FREE

Don't forget it, every subscriber gets a *Pilgrim Almanac* FREE. We have now commenced their distribution and are sending them out by scores. Now is the time, send in your names at once and get the best family Almanac ever published. It is the only complete *Family Almanac* ever published by the Church containing all the signs, the weather, prognostications, the "Hundred year Almanac" and everything else that is needful for a christian family to learn from an Almanac. It also contains a complete ministerial list, giving the name of the county to each address. This is an original feature with us and adds greatly to the value and interest of the list. All that have renewed their subscription, and all new subscribers will receive their Almanacs in a few days, as we are now sending them out as fast as we can get our lists in order.

OUR REMOVAL

For several weeks we have been busily engaged in getting our building completed at Huntingdon where we expect to move as soon as it is ready. Our calculation was to have it ready by the first of November, but on account of unfavorable weather in the after part of the season and the early snap of cold, the work was delayed beyond our expectations. The house is now nearly completed and as soon as it gets sufficiently dry to make it safe, we expect to change locations. It will be noticed in the Almanac that our address is Huntingdon. This we done in order to avoid trouble after our removal. Our contributors and agents will please continue our present address until ordered to have it changed.

SHALL WE HAVE A REPORT OF A. M.

Some of our readers are already anxious to know whether we intend to give a report of A. M. Those who are aware of the course we pursued at last A. M., can feel assured that there will nothing be left undone on our part. The demand is so great for a full report that we cannot see how we could meet the expectation of our readers without giving it, and if A. M. does not take an absolute stand against it our readers need have no fears about not getting the report.

CHANGE OF MAKE UP.—This week our readers will notice a change in the make up of our form. The present arrangement will leave two whole pages for correspondence, obituaries, &c. We hope now our brethren and sisters will send us enough news every week to fill out these two pages. If there is not enough correspondence to fill them, we will put Youth's Department on the last page, but would prefer to have this department some where else, and fill the two last pages entirely with correspondence &c. We have made this arrangement so as to admit all the correspondence that may reach us each week, and that none be crowded out. Now brethren and sisters, please send along the news, and make our PILGRIM more and more interesting.

OUR CONDITIONS.

We are being asked whether our conditions for the coming year will be the same as the present year. In the main, we expect them to be the same, but would say to those who have the means, pay us at the time of subscribing or at the first part of the year. If all that can, will do this, it will enable us to meet our obligations and give a little more time to those who cannot pay cash or at the beginning of the year. All those who have not paid for the present year will be expected to pay before the beginning of the new year. 3t

AGENTS WANTED

We want a good active agent, to solicit subscribers for the PILGRIM, in every Church in the brotherhood. If there are any that feel to labor for us and are not supplied with prospectus and *Almanac* will please write us and we will send by return mail. Remember, the PILGRIM for the coming year will be enlarged and every subscriber will receive the *Pilgrim Almanac*, handsomely gotten up, containing a "Ministerial List," giving post office, county and State, with other valuable information FREE. 5t.

Correspondence.

A Reporter is wanted from every Church in the brotherhood to send us Church news, Obituaries, Announcements, or anything that will be of general interest. To insure insertion, the writers name must accompany each communication. Our invitation is not personal but general—please respond to our call.

THE BETHEL MISSION SCHOOL.

Perhaps some of your readers would be interested in a short sketch of this Sunday school, located in Cincinna ti. The building in which the school meets, is situated quite a distance *down town*, even at the water's edge, where the proud streams come and go, bearing their burdens from city to city. We followed the crowd as strangers do when attending Beecher's church in Brooklyn. After climbing a fatiguing flight of stairs, we found ourselves in what by the hum, might have been mistaken for a bee hive, so busy was each worker. We found seats where we could command a good view of the room—and such a sight as was there presented. Imagine if you can, fourteen hundred children, ranging in age from mere babes to fathers and mothers. The school is composed of the poor of the City, news boys, ragamuffins, &c, regular "Street Arabs" who are induced from various motives to come. At the close of the session, each one receives a ticket, by presenting, which they can obtain food and clothes. A penny collection is also lifted, to defray incidental expenses—if their poverty they cast in their mite, far outweighing the costly offerings of the rich. Rewards are given to each one who induces any of their companions to attend the school, thus making missionaries of every one, and giving them a field of labor. Teachers being absent, I was prevailed on to teach a class of five interesting little girls, and during the brief hours of our intercourse, I became really attached to them, the attachment of sympathy for their forlorn condition. The children are taught to sing God's praises, each one receiving a song paper at the entrance. It does one good to hear with what hearty good will each and every one enters into the service. Their many happy voices in unity with the Organ and the Superintendent's voice, produced a pleasing effect. After the singing came the reading and oral lessons, then more singing and the final prayer, in which the whole school stands, with folded arms and bowed, and repeat "Our Father who art in Heaven" and "Now I lay me"&c.

The main room, side rooms, and galleries, were so densely packed, it seemed almost impossible for another person to find sitting room, and yet I am told that there are as many as twenty five hundred present at times. It is indeed a good and great work; the many can be reached by Gospel influence in this way, that would never be in any other. A good word dropped, may, after many days, bring forth an abundant reward. I came away feeling thankful for the lesson I learned in humanity's needs, and ready to speak a good word for the earnest advocates of truth. May God speed his work. L. H. MILLER.

ANSWER TO QUERY BY J. H. F.

NO 46 PAGE 367.

The scripture referred to, will be found in the 3rd chapter and 9th verse of the first Epistle general of John. By the ability God may give, I will present my views. "Whoever is born of God doth not commit sin." To be brief, there never was a birth, without a conception, but there are different conceptions and different births, John 1:13. We can be born of blood, of the will of man, of the flesh, or of God. The last birth is the one that we now have under consideration. Now the word of God is the seed that causes the conception, and it abideth not alone but dieth. "The letter killeth but the spirit maketh alive." The body is dead because of sin, the former things which he loved he now hateth. The seed, the word of God, has now become the spirit and life. He is now secured as was Noe. See Gen. 7:16. God closed the door and they were all saved from the destruction of the flood. This favor Noe obtained by obeying God, and when he had complied with all the requirements, God closed the door. So if we abide in the doctrine of Christ, we have both the Father and the Son, and that seed that remains within as is like a consuming fire. If we build on that foundation, wood, hay, or stubble, we shall suffer loss, but he himself shall be saved yet so as by fire. So then if we are the Sons of God, the spirit of God is within us, and the body is dead because of sin, so that if we come short of our duty toward God, it is no longer I that do it but the evil that is within the flesh. When God closes the door and we are within, we are of that number of which the apostle writes: "Blessed is the man whose sins are forgiven, and whose iniquities are covered.

But there is another feature to be considered. In the first Epistle of John 1st chapter and 8th verse, it is said: "If we say we have no sin, we deceive ourselves and the truth is not in us." So that as long as we are at home in the body, sin is within us, for there is no man that sinneth not. Kings 8:6. But the seed cannot sin because it is of God, and he has closed the door. He will not forget your labors of love that you have shown towards his name.

I might go on talking about many things, but will let this suffice for the present, knowing that if this will be inserted in the PILGRIM it will appear before my dear brethren, whom I hope if they see any thing wrong, will correct and make it right. Such are some of the things that ought to be taken into consideration in our periodicals. JACOB STEEL.

Dear Pilgrim:—As you are still soliciting Church news, I wil give you some from this part of God's moral vineyard. Our communion season is over, and I will endeavor to give a report of the same, but will commence first with the meeting at Knob Creek Church. Quite a number of members participated in the communion exercises, and good order prevailed throughout the entire congregation. Some were added to the Church by baptism on Saturday. This Church, I am informed, has been in a prosperous condition during the summer that is now passed.

On the second Sunday of Sept. we had a call meeting here in the Limestone Church, and two young persons were added to the Church by baptism. According to arrangement, our Communion meeting was on the fourth Saturday and Sunday of September. There was a pretty large attendance of members, and one soul was added to the Church of the faithful on Saturday. There was good order during the entire meeting.

On the second Saturday of October, mother and I went to a Communion meeting in the Cherokee Church. At this place three persons were added to the Church, two of them husband and wife, and it was said they were nearly 90 years of age. A large crowd was present and good order. There was also preaching on Sabbath.

The Pleasant Valley meeting was on the third Saturday and Sunday of October. There was a large attendance, good order, and some added to the Church. On the fourth Sunday brother Joseph Long, of Md., preached to us at Limestone to a very attentive congregation. We were sorry that he made such a short stay. He came in the morning and left again in the evening. We hope that other brethren in the East will remember us and give us a call, as we will be very glad to have them visit us oftener.

On Thursday morning, Oct. 30th, I started alone, on horseback, for Laurel, Washington Co., Va. I stopped at uncle and brother Christian Wine's for dinner and then on to brother Joseph Wine's, Sullivan Co, Tenn., where I remained all night. I was kindly received and cared for, although his family were unwell. His wife had recently a spell of sickness, and has yet a severe cough and cold. The rest are also severely afflicted with cold and cough. I had expected to have brother Wine accompany me, but as his family was unwell, he could not leave home. On Friday morning I started very early knowing I would have to ride all day alone. I went on through Blountville, the county seat of Sullivan to Bristol where the East Tenn., Va. & Ga., & Atlantic Miss. & Ohio R. Rs. connect. The State line runs through this town. I then went on to Abingdon, the county town of Washington county, Va. As I passed along through this section I saw some very nice farms. From Abingdon I went on to Laurel river, 13 miles distant. Arrived at friend Daniel Rosenbalm's in the evening. Same evening went to Laurel school house to meeting. Here I met with brother Solomon G. Arnold, from Limestone who was on his way back from a Communion meeting in Ashe Co., N. C., and brother Prater from N. C., and the brethren of Laurel. After services had commenced, brother Jesse Crosswhite of Cherokee, and Joseph Ellit of Stony Creek were added to our company. Preaching by brother Prater to an attentive congregation. On Saturday, Nov. 1st, at 11 a. m. preaching again. At 4 p. m. the subject of self-examination was treated by brother Crosswhite. In the evening the members present performed the ordinances as the Savior has commanded. Had a crowded house and good order with a few exceptions. On Sunday the 2nd, at 11 a. m. preaching again by brother Crosswhite to an attentive congregation. At 4 p. m. brother Crosswhite conducted a singing, and after singing we went to friend Henry Mock's, to the funeral of sister Emeline Wright, consort of brother Wm. Wright, of Johnson Co., Tenn. She died from the breaking of an internal abscess. She was a member of the Church over six years. The funeral occasion was improved by brother Crosswhite, from the 23rd Psalm, to a large and attentive audience. From here we went to friend Rosenbalm's, where we remained all night. On the morning of the 3rd I started for home and soon got in company with brother Arnold. We rode together until we got across the Watauga river, Washinton Co., Tenn. Here we separated and I went to brother and cousin John Sherfy's where I met with a kind reception, and was well cared for during the night. In the morning I started on my way home and arrived there in the afternoon. Found all well. Thanks be to God for the manifestation of his goodness in permitting me to meet with my brethren and sisters who came from far and near to commemorate the death and sufferings of our blessed Redeemer, who bled and died on the cross for our sins, and not for ours only, but for the sins of the whole world.

Yours truly,
HENRY M. SHERFY.
Limestone Depot, Tenn.

CRAIG, Holt Co., Mo., Nov. 9, '73.
Dear Pilgrim:—By your permission I will, through your columns, give my opinion of this part of Missouri. From what I have seen of Missouri, Nebraska, Kansas, and the far West in general, I have come to the conclusion that persons can do as well here in Holt Co., Mo., in a temporal point of view as anywhere else in the far western States It is true, it is very cold in the winter, and rather warm in the summer. It does not, however, become so extremely warm in the summer. At present the weather is beautiful, almost like in May. The climate is healthful. The health of the people for the last three years has been remarkably good. Myself and family have never enjoyed better health than we have since we came to this part of Missouri. Taking all into consideration, I have come to the conclusion that a person cannot make a living as easily, and live as pleasantly anywhere in the far west as here. To the brethren and friends who want to move west, I would say, come here, and judge for yourselves. You can get homes here improved or unimproved, at low figures. Tracts of land can be had containing from 40 acres up to as large as any man would want. Brethren and friends, you who have a hard way of making an honest living in the East, come to Missouri. I can assure you it does not take half of the labor to raise a crop here that it does in places in the

East. I have hitherto said but little about the country, and the reason was I wanted to become acquainted with it first. I am now satisfied that this is the place for all working people to come.

A CALL FOR HELP.

I will now change the subject, by telling you our want. We want a house in which to worship the God of Abraham, Isaac and Jacob, and our God in spirit and in truth. Now dear brethren, if there is a house needed anywhere it is here, and as we are few in number and in rather limited circumstances, we are not able to build one ourselves. As the building material is all bought in our cities, and brought from other States, it is high in price. Lumber sells from 3 to 5 dollars per hundred. We only want a small and plain house, but still it will cost more than we are able to pay ourselves. Now brethren and sisters, we do not want to beg money for anything but a good purpose, and will simply ask all who are willing and able to give us $1.00 or 50 cents apiece. If all will do this, I believe the house will be built. Now this is a very small amount that we ask of you, and then only those who are able and willing. Who among us is not able and willing to give this very small amount towards the building of a house for the worship of God? Who is he? Time will tell. I have helped to build and repair seven meeting-houses in my time, and have paid towards the same 175 dollars. Now I am again where there is no meeting house, and am a very poor man as respects this world's goods, but thanks be to God, I am rich in Christ, and humble in spirit. May the blessing of God attend us, and the Holy Spirit rule and overrule our words and actions, so that all we do may be to the honor and glory of His great Name. The will of the Lord be done is the prayer of your weak Bro.

A. J. CORRELL.

P. S. All that wish to send us their mite can do so between this and the 1st of January 1874. We will give the amount received by that time or soon after. If we receive enough so that we can risk to build, we want to commence in the Spring as soon as possible. Money may be sent to any of the following brethren: A. J. Carrell and Isaac Zeigler, Craig, Holt Co., Mo.; Joseph Glick, Joel Glick, and John Miller, Mound City, Holt Co., Mo.; Isaac Wampler, Samuel Glick and Jacob Silvoise, Forest City, Holt Co., Mo. A. J. C.

CHURCH NEWS.

On the 7th of November, I was conveyed, by my wife and son to Huntington, and and there took the train for Ft. Wayne. Here I changed roads and went on the Grand Rapids road to Loudon Station, where brother James Harvey met me and conveyed me to his home where I had some rest and refreshment. Then he took me to a Methodist meetinghouse for preaching. A small congregation in consequence of bad roads and a dark rainy evening. After preaching I was again conveyed to brother Harvey's for a night's rest which I needed very much.

On Saturday the 8th, I was conveyed to brother Henry Smith's where the members of the Cedar Creek District met for church council. Elders John Brown, Shatt, and Christ Weaver, were with us in council. The meeting was opened in order. Then came up the business for the day, which was the dividing of the aforesaid district. As the territory of the district was very large, and meeting places rather inconvenient, after a careful consideration and a good deal of counseling, some in favor of making two, some three, and some four districts, the vote was taken, whether three or four. It carried for four by a large majority. There are four ministers in the district, and they so located that it suits well, and gives territory plenty to each one to make large churches. Brethren Jeremiah and Jacob Gump are both Elders, and the other two are not. So brother Jacob Gump was chosen and appointed to take the oversight of those two districts that have no one in the full ministry. Brother Jeremiah Gump has also charge of two districts besides the one in which he lives. The name of Jacob Gump's district is Cedar Creek; Jeremiah Gump's, White Oak Grove; James Barton's, Cedar Lake, and Harrison Ellson's, Little St. Jo. The meeting closed by singing and prayer. After partaking of a meal, Bro. Ellson conveyed me to a Winebrenerian meetinghouse for preaching. A very comfortable house, where we preached Saturday evening, Sunday and Sunday evening. Notwithstanding the nights were dark, roads bad, and the weather unfavorable, we had large congregations, and good attention, except a few individuals. May the Lord pity them. The other ministers divided and preached in other neighborhoods. We don't believe in a half dozen ministers at one meeting, and at other places people almost starving for the want of preaching.

On Monday morning Brother Jacob Gump took me in his carriage some nine miles to his house, where we had some rest and dinner. Then he took me to the station, and the trains having changed time, I missed all connection, so he took me to Bro. George Gump's. Bro. George took me to Ft. Wayne, a distance of ten miles, where I took the train for Huntington. Here I was met by my son and conveyed home a distance of seven miles. Got home after night. I found all well, thank the Lord. May the Lord bless the brethren and sisters for their kindness shown toward me. My prayer is that they may live in peace, and be a light to the world, so that the Church may prosper and be powerful. SAMUEL MURRAY.

HUTCHISON, Kansas, Nov. 16, 1873.

Dear Brethren.—As I have moved to Kansas, I wish my paper changed to the above address. There are only three members living here in this part of the state that we know of. We hope that some of the Brethren as they pass this way, will stop and preach for us. We have a beautiful country and the climate very favorable, as there is, at this date, some green grass to be seen three or four inches long. We enjoy good health and think the land is as good as in Ill. There is plenty of land here yet for homesteads and preemption and road lands, at very low rates on 16 years time. There is a good opening here for to build up a church. Our neighbors all say, write for some preachers to come and preach for us. We all want preaching. I hope some of the brethren will, at least, come and look at the country for themselves. The town of Hutchison is only two years old and now has about 600 inhabitants, a court house, a school house and a settlement 18 miles west of it. Now dear brethren I am not capable of doing much writing, but I love to read the columns of your excellent paper. M. V. WAMPLER.

CLARENCE, Mich. Nov. 24th, '73.

Kind Brethren:—I have seated myself to drop you a few lines. It is different with me to what it is with most of our brethren. We have not the opportunity to assemble with our people in public worship or in private conversation. We are too far away from where there are any other brethren, but we are happy to say that we had three visits from Brother F. P. Loehr last winter, and had very good meetings, and three obeyed the Gospel and are enrolled with the believers to live and to die. We would be very thankful for some such visits from our ministering brethren. Bro. Loehr has promised to visit us frequently, if his health would permit, but the last he wrote me, it was very poor, but I hope he has regained it, and will come to see us soon. Brethren count my name for the PILGRIM for the coming year. We are will pleased with its visits and would be very lonely without it.

MOSES MOIST.

Dear brother:—It has been a query in my mind, why it is, that the Gospel is so little preached in the German language at the present day, while there are still, connected with the Church, quite a number of persons that have their education in the German language, and who could better understand a discourse delivered in the German than in the English language. JOHN BETHKE

This may be a query of some importance to others. If so, we would be glad to hear their views on the above. [ED.]

EXPLANATION ON 1ST JOHN 3:9

If a man is thoroughly changed or converted to God, God dwelleth in him, or in other words, God through the influence of His holy spirit, His seed, takes possession of the heart, consequently he cannot commit sin, because God lives in him and he in God—he is born of God.

A PILGRIM.

ROBISON'S ECCLESIASTICAL HISTORY.

This Work is now entirely out of print, and copies cannot be purchased from the publishers. I therefore adopt this method of getting the work to examine. If any brother has a copy and will sell it, he will please inform me immediately. The book is very valuable and hence parties owning the work, may not be willing to sell. If they are willing to loan it, they will give me notice to that effect and I will then inform them how to send the work. I will pay for transportation both ways, and also for the use of the book if demanded. Many of those old books are now entirely out of print, and the only way left to get them is to borrow. J. H. MOORE.

Urbana, Champaign Co., Ill.

NOTICE.—There will be a series of meetings held in the Maple Grove Meeting-house, Ashland Co., Ohio, commencing January 3, '74, and perhaps will close on the evening of the 11th. A general invitation is extended to ministering brethren and others to be with us. By order of the church. WM. SADLER.

DIED.

SMALL.—In the Falling Spring Congregation, Sister Elizabeth Small, aged 24 yrs. 6 months and 14 days. She departed this life rejoicing in the Lord. J. ZUCK

SHOWALTER.—Near Crooked Creek, Mcpherson Co., Kansas, Susan F., daughter of friend Amos Showalter, and granddaughter of David and Sarah Moore, aged 4 years, 10 months,—days. She came to her death, July 19, '73, from the bite of a rattle-snake.

Alas how changed that lovely flower,
Which bloomed and cheered my heart;
Fair fleeting comforts of an hour,
How soon we're called to part.

SARAH MOORE

CROILL.—November 2, '73, in Snake Spring Valley Church, Bedford Co., Pa., sister Sarah Croill, aged 25 years, and 11 days. Funeral service by the Brethren from 1st Cor. 15: 51 52

Our dear sister, though young in years, has been a bright example in the church, and in her death has been bereft of a kind sister, and the husband of a kind and affectionate wife. Her last request was that the brethren should pray for her husband, that he too should make preparations to follow her. May those words sink deep in her husband's heart and enable him to enter the fold of Jesus, and follow his dear wife

About a year ago sister Croill, with her husband and uncle, Simon Mixel, moved to Covington, Miami Co., Ohio,—enjoyed the kindness of the brethren and sisters very much at that place, but during the Summer season her health was not so good, and some cholera raging there, they made up their minds to return to the mountains, but sickness and death rages there too. They were only here about two months when our sister took sick and died very suddenly with neuralgia in the stomach.

HENRY HERSHBERGER

MONEY LIST.

Henry Barrick	1.50
Abraham Good	2.00
David Goodyear	3.00
Frederick Huber	.25
John Hamburger	3.00
Sarah Bowman	.25
David Troxel	5.50
D. B. Bonebrake	1.50
Jacob Troxel	7.80
S. M. Kintner	4.75
C. R. Paige	.75
E. Longenecker	3.00
John N. Barnhart	7.50
L. C. Oaks	7.50
John Ahearn	1.75
Henry M. Sherly	4.30
Jacob Eigenbrode	1.50
D. R. Young	.80
Moses Moist	1.50
John Zuck	5.57

LITERATURE.

A. B. Brumbaugh, Huntingdon, Pa. Literary Editor.

In the *December Magazines* we are introduced to a rich feast of good things. It seems to us a marvel that there are still those who seldom taste the palatable, and wholesome food here spread out, monthly, for their enjoyment and profit.

THE ATLANTIC for December completes the 32d. volume and is filled with its usual variety of valuable articles. This periodical for 1874 promises to be quite as varied and attractive as ever before. Many of the best writers in the land are employed on the *Atlantic*, and it discusses with ability the leading questions of the day. To miss a number is to miss a treat.

OLD AND NEW is a new but welcome visitor to our table. The December number closes the 8th volume, and judging from its table of contents, for the volume, we should say its readers must have been well entertained. Here is its motto:

"Gently and without grief the Old shall glide
Into the new; the eternal fear of things,
Like a bright river of the fields of heaven,
Shall journey onward in perpetual peace.

POPULAR SCIENCE MONTHLY has already taken a high place among the leading periodicals of the age. We are all greatly interested in the scientific subjects which it discusses from the stand-points of the leading scientists of the age and time. We confess that we had no idea of the value of this monthly until we had the privilege of perusing its numbers. Herbert Spencer's articles are intensely interesting. Prof Perrier's researches and experiments are of vast importance. Every author is a master of his subject. Illustrated.

SCRIBNER'S for December is we think the best number yet issued of that favorite magazine. The second article on Louisiana, profusely illustrated, opens the number; this is followed by a paper on "Savage Man" with striking illustrations. An interesting sketch, with portrait of Proctor the young English astronomer now in this country.—A poem—"Lake"—A poem by Bret Harte, besides an abundance of interesting matter.

LIPPINCOTT'S for December is an unusually attractive number. It opens with a continuation of "A New Hyperion" illustrated by Dore's characteristic sketches; which is followed by "Sketches of Eastern Travel," "Life at the National Capitol," "The History of the Crisis," a timely and able article on our present financial difficulties. Several poems of merit, and several entertaining articles complete the number and year.—The January number begins a new Volume and rare attractions are promised.

HARPER'S. This is the opening number of a new volume—the 48th—of this well established and sterling periodical. There are several profusely illustrated articles—"The Water Ways of New York" "Around Lake Lemon" &c. &c. Then we have "A Golden Wedding" a poem by H. B. Hudson, illustrated, which will doubtless awaken pleasing memories in the minds of many who are on the declivities of life. It is a capital number. The Harpers' periodicals *Magazine*, *Weekly* and Bazar together give an amount of finely illustrated reading matter in a year that is surprising, and which could not be purchased in books for four times the cost.

ST. NICHOLAS, for December, the second number of Scribner's new Magazine for the young, is as bright and full of good things as the first issue. There are 40 pictures this month. It is a perfect success. Its monthly visits cannot fail to delight and please the children.

THE NURSERY is the name of a monthly magazine for youngest readers published by John L. Shorey, Boston Mass., at $1 60 per year, fully illustrated. This little magazine is worth 25 dollars of tuition at school to a child. With *Pilgrim* $2.50.

IN WOOD'S HOUSEHOLD MAGAZINE for November, the table of contents seem to have been spread for a Thanksgiving feast, and gives evidence of unabated efforts to add to its excellence. It contains an article from the pen of Rev. Robert Colyer of Chicago which is well worth a year's subscription. It is a marvel of cheapness, the price being only $1 00 per year and with the chromo of "Yosemite," 14x20 inches only $1.50. Mag. Chromo & PILGRIM $2.50.

THE PHRENOLOGICAL JOURNAL for November, confirms the oft-repeated opinion of the Press at large, that no one can read that publication without deriving some practical good. It is full of meat for the mind, well served and savory. Witness articles like these: Rev Dr. Blanchard, Pres. of Wheaton University; The Briton, the Inspirational Race; Our Immortality; Growth in Character and Heart; Conversations about faces, with numerous illustrations; Money, Its Functions and Requirements, which our Capitalist should all Read; Application of Art in Dress; Wives who henpeck; Address to Young Men; The Late Panic; Failures in Business; Intemperance. Price 30 cents, $3.00 a year. Write at once to the Publisher, and secure the volumes for 1874, (S. R. Wells, 389 Broadway, New York,) or we will send the PILGRIM and JOURNAL one year to any address at $3.50 per year. Sample copies of the *Phrenological Journal* sent from this office on receipt of 3 cent stamp to pay postage.

THE first number of the *International Review* will have contributions from several of the ablest minds in America and Europe. Let every one who wishes to obtain the freshest views on all subjects, commence with the first number and continue.

HUNTINGDON & BROAD TOP RAIL ROAD

On and after Nov. 2nd, 1873, Trains will run on this road daily (Sun excepted) as follows:

Trains from Huntingdon South. *Trains from Mt. Dal's moving North.*

EXP'S. P. M.	MAIL. A. M.	STATIONS.	MAIL. P. M.	EXP'S A. M
5 50	8 05	Huntingdon.	AR 4 00	AR 9 20
5 55	8 10	Long Siding	3 55	9 15
6 05	8 20	McConnelstown	3 45	9 05
6 10	8 20	Pleasant Grove	3 40	8 58
6 25	8 45	MARKLESBURG	3 25	8 45
6 35	8 55	Coffee Run	3 15	8 35
6 40	9 03	Rough & Ready	3 09	8 29
6 48	9 10	Cove	3 01	8 20
6 51	9 13	Fishers Summit	2 58	8 17
7 10	9 30	Saxton	2 45	8 05
7 25	9 45	Riddlesburg	2 25	7 45
7 30	9 52	Hopewell	2 20	7 36
7 45	10 05	Piper's Run	2 08	7 26
8 00	10 17	Tatesville	1 55	7 12
8 10	10 27	Everett	1 43	7 03
8 15	10 30	Mount Dallas	1 40	7 00
8 25	10 50	Bedford	1 20	6 40

SHOUP'S RUN BRANCH.

A. M.	P. M.		P. M.	A. M.
LE 9 40	LE 7 20	Saxton.	AR 2 30	AR 7 50
9 55	7 35	Coalmont.	2 15	7 35
10 00	7 40	Crawford.	2 10	7 30
AR 10 10	AR 7 50	Dudley	LE 2 00	LE 7 20

Broad Top City from Dudley 2 miles by stage.

Time of Penna. R. R. Trains at Huntingdon.

. Mail No. 2 makes connection at Huntingdon with Mail going East on Pennsylvania Railroad at 4.15 p. m., and West at 5.45 p. m. Mail No. 1 leaves Huntingdon at 7.40 a. m. on arrival of Pacific Express West.

Trains on this road connect with trains on Bedford & Bridgeport, and Cumberland & Pennsylvania Railroads.

G. F. GAGE, Supt.

The Weekly Pilgrim.

Published by J. B. Brumbaugh, & Co.

Edited by H. B. & Geo. Brumbaugh.

CORRESPONDING EDITORS.

D P. Sayler, Double Pipe Creek, Md.

Leonard Furry, New Enterprise, Pa.

The *Pilgrim* is a Christian Periodical, devoted to religion and moral reform. It will advocate in the spirit of *love* and *liberty*, the principles of true Christianity, labor for the promotion of peace among the people of God, for the encouragement of the saints and for the conversion of sinners, avoiding those things which tend toward disunion or sectional feelings.

TERMS.

Single copy, Book paper,	$1.50
Eleven copies, [eleventh for Agt.]	$15.00

Any number above that at the same rate.

Address,

H. B. BRUMBAUGH,
James Creek,
Huntingdon county Pa.

The Weekly Pilgrim.

"REMOVE NOT THE ANCIENT LANDMARKS WHICH OUR FATHERS HAVE SET."

VOL. 4. JAMES CREEK, PENNSYLVANIA, DECEMBER 9, 1873. NO. 49

POETRY.

THE STRAIT GATE.

BY WESLEY

Strait the gate that leads to glory,
  Dimly seen by mortal eye,
Heralds tell a pleasing story
  As the sinner passes by.

Enter in 'tis sweetly ringing,
  Life and power He will impart,
Sighing will be turned to singing,
  If thou yield to Him thy heart.

Enter in, O, why thus standing
  Idly all the sunny day?
See around the threshold bending,
  Lovely forms in bright array.

Prostrate now his grace imploring,
  Seek the narrow way of life;
Thy unworthiness deploring
  Leave the path of sin and strife.

Persevere till faith's keen vision
  Penetrate impending night,—
Strengthened by a firm decision,
  Thou shalt hail celestial light.

Prayer will soon reveal the beauty
  That o'erhangs the pilgrim's way;
'Tis the path of faithful duty
  Ending in eternal day.

Lions fierce thy soul to frighten,
  By the way may hoarsely roar,
But thy hope again shall brighten,
  They are chained by Jesus' power.

Haste thee then, no longer tarry,
  Leave the thorny path of sin:
To the gate thy burden carry,
  And with praises enter in.

Walk the narrow way to Heaven,
  Firm the cross and banners bear,
And when flesh and soul are riven
  Thou shalt sing with Him in air.

Then the golden gate shall open
  To admit thy happy soul;
Then shall culminate thy hoping
  In fruition's joyous roll.

ORIGINAL ESSAYS.

JESUS ON THE CROSS.

NO. III.

"Woman, behold thy son." "Behold thy mother."—John 19: 26-27.

I. THE MOTHER'S CARE FOR HER SON.

1. *His physical culture.* Nothing should be of more vital importance to the mother in the care for her son than his culture. The true mother carefully watches his physical development. The food that is best adapted to such a development is cautiously selected for him. Strong meat is kept from him until he arrives at a proper age to receive it, at first he is only permitted to receive the sincere milk. The mother's delight is in her son's hale and hearty appearance, the rosy cheek, the bright eye, and the strong full muscle. To secure his proper physical culture, he is clad with proper raiment, such as will protect him from the heat in Summer, and the cold in Winter. He is not permitted to walk first, lest he become deformed, thus her never tiring vigilance enables her to successfully care for his physical culture.

2. *His mental culture.* The child is a great learner. The mind is constantly engaged in finding out something. It is a great imitator. The mother knowing this, she directs her son's attention to many different acts performed by her, and to various objects of size and color. The mother is the greatest and most successful, as well as the most persevering of all teachers. Therefore her words should be well chosen of correct language, for she has the foundation of all the arts and sciences to lay. Hence if the child is incorrectly instructed in his first years, he will require much remodeling, and perhaps never be completely exempt from the errors of early instruction. What is put into the first of life, is put into the whole of life. It is more expensive to pull down and rebuild the mental faculties, than the physical structure.

3. *His moral culture.* The mother should be strictly moral in her habits. The son should always be taught by word and example to speak the truth, and to act the truth. He should have no examples of deception to learn from. The virtue of honesty should be highly prized, seeing the great want of it among men and nations. He should be taught to be just—to do that which is fair and right, and that will bear inspection. Many children, as well as many men, do not like to have their word or work examined on account of their improper moral culture.

4. *His spiritual culture.* This division of the subject is of paramount importance. Timothy had the advantage of this early pious culture, from his mother Eunice. Paul says of him, "And that from a *child* thou hast known the holy Scriptures, which are able to make thee wise unto salvation through faith which is in Christ Jesus."—2 Tim. 3: 15. This spiritual culture he received from his mother and grandmother. Paul says, "When I call to remembrance the unfeigned faith that is in thee, which dwelt first in thy grandmother Lois and thy mother Eunice; and I am persuaded that in thee also."—2 Tim. 1: 5. Just here I will remark to all mothers, in your great care for your sons, sow early and continually those spiritual seeds which will grow into a holy and pious life. The garden of the heart is yours to till. How easy cultivated before the thorns and noxious weeds of sin and folly take root therein. Your influence for good in shaping your son's spiritual life, and securing for him a happy end in glory, is of more value than the influence of many preachers in after years. Many pious and good men can testify that the teachings of a pious mother had more influence upon them in bringing them to Christ, than all advice or instruction received elsewhere. Mothers, your care stands first, stands last, and stands high above all others in moulding character and in christianizing the world. "Woman, behold thy son!" Yes, behold him and see what you can make of him by proper care, or suffer him to become by neglect and indifference. "Woman, behold thy son!" is the Lord's command, and is full of weight and power.

5. *Spiritual application.* The elder should care for the younger in the household of faith. The Church is the mother of all her servants—preachers. They have been brought forth (born of her) by her, and it is her highest duty to care for their physical, mental and spiritual wants. It is by her we are led to pastures rich and fair. She gently leads us along step by step, until finally, we shall become perfect men and women in the Kingdom of our Father in glory.

II. THE SON'S CARE FOR HIS MOTHER.

1. *Her physical comforts.* Jesus said unto the disciples whom he loved, "Behold thy mother! And from that hour that disciple took her unto his own home."—John 19: 27. As the mother's first care is to provide for her son, so also it is the son's first duty to supply his mother with the necessaries of life. But how could Jesus with propriety say, "Behold thy mother!"? It is because we are all one family *in Christ.* Having become the sons and daughters of God by adoption, Jesus said unto his disciples on one occasion, "Behold My mother and My brethren! For whosoever shall do the will of My Father in Heaven, the same is My brother, and sister and mother."—Matt. 12: 49-50. No doubt the mother of Jesus had all the benefits that disciple's home could command, fed, clothed and protected by loving and well directed hands, "*own home*" means much.

2. *Her spiritual enjoyments.* The advantage of religious society cannot be over estimated. The Son of God upon the cross knew well by experience what it was to be homeless, and without a place where to lay his head, and also the enjoyment it afforded to be with those that love us. The son's sympathies are such for his mother, as to rejoice when she rejoices, and to weep when she weeps. Around the family altar of that beloved son, this mother could have her spiritual wants daily supplied, such enjoyments as pious and God-fearing mothers delight in.

3. *Spiritual application.* The younger should reverence and respect the elder as well as be in subjection unto them. It teaches us how careful we should be in taking care of those widows who are left and bereaved in this cold and unsympathizing world. "Honor widows that are widows indeed."—1 Tim. 5: 3. The elders also are worthy of our care, "Let the elders that rule well be counted worthy of double honor, especially they who labor in word and doctrine."—1 Tim. 5: 17.

III. JESUS' CARE AND PROVISION FOR ALL HIS PEOPLE.

1. *In time.* Jesus is that good and faithful shepherd that provides well for the lambs of the flock. He ever taught His disciples how they should love one another. In the closing scenes of His life He taught that mutual care that one should have for the other, which is so necessary for the welfare of His much loved kingdom. In calling that disciple's attention to behold his mother, a practical lesson is taught us. He shows us how he wishes us to look

upon the needy and administer unto their wants. The widows are to be cared for, not to be sent to the poor-house, as many are of the so-called Christian denominations, but to be received into *our own home*; there to eat of what we eat, to wear of what we wear, and to share and enjoy of the blessings that God has blessed us with. I fear that the Church is prone to attempt to keep its poor a little *too* cheap. Remember Jesus' provision. He says as ye do it unto the least of these My brethren ye do it unto Me. Would you select or accept the shabbiest house in the community,—one that nobody else wants and give it to Jesus to live in, and there to subsist upon that which will *just* and perhaps poorly keep Him warmed and fed? There are many I kindly ask to think of *their own home*, when making provision for the poor. Remember the rich man had his good things in his lifetime, and Lazarus his evil things. But mark the contrast after death, the one is tormented, while the other is blessed. The rich man was not tormented because he was rich, but because he neglected the poor. Jesus made much more provision, and bestowed much more care upon His people, than we can discuss in this article, yet there is another class that we wish to call the attention of the Church to; viz. those who are called and sent to preach the glad tidings of great joy to all people. Jesus had great care for such. When He was with his disciples, He sent them out to preach the Gospel and to heal the sick, saying, "Take nothing for your journey, neither staves, nor script, neither bread, neither money; neither have two coats apiece."—Luke 9: 3. But just before he was crucified He gave them quite different directions. He called His disciples unto Him and said, "When I sent you without purse, and script, and shoes, *lacked ye anything*? And they said nothing. Then said He unto them, but now he that hath a purse, let him take it, and likewise his script."—Luke 22: 35 36. Now the Church calls and sends its ministers forth, should it not enquire if they *lack anything*? I am very sure that there are many willing servants of the Church, who have been called to the ministration of the Word of God, by the Church, who could and would do much more for the good of Zion, and for the good of precious blood-bought souls if they were not so often *sent empty away*.

We say *sent empty*, because the Church expects the poor brother to do as much labor and to bear his own expense in doing it, as the rich brother who has abundant means at his command. Now brethren, this is contrary to reason, the love of God, the Gospel and the Lord's provision. "*Woman, behold thy son!*" Paul says, "If we have sown unto you spiritual things, is it a great thing if we reap your carnal things? Do ye not know that they which minister about holy things live of the things of the temple? *Even so* hath the Lord *ordained* that they which preach the Gospel should live of the Gospel.—1 Cor. 9: 11, 13, 14. But says one, Paul labored—worked with his own hands, and desired none of these things, &c. True, and so do all of your poor preachers. And upon the same ground you should not call or send any man to preach the Gospel who is not like Paul—*unmarried*. Yet notwithstanding Paul had no family to provide for, he received aid from the Church to carry on his mission. Says he, "I robbed other churches, taking wages of them, to do you service, for that which was lacking to me the brethren, which came from Macedonia supplied."—2 Cor. 8: 9. I will just here remark what an old and faithful servant of the Lord said to me about a year ago, one who has preached the Gospel for about thirty years, says he, "We have some brethren worse than barbarians." And he gave me the testimony. When Paul was cast on the Island of Melitia it is written, "And the barbarous people showed us no little kindness; who also honored us with many honors, and when we departed, *they laded us with such things as were necessary*."—Acts 28: 2, 10. For brethren to ask (and many rich brethren ask it by their actions), their preacher who is in limited circumstances, to study the Scriptures, and to "show thyself approved unto God, a workman that needeth not to be ashamed, rightly dividing the word of truth," to preach the word, to be instant in season and out of season, to visit the sick and to minister unto their spiritual wants, to attend every funeral that he may be called upon to attend, to provide for his own house that he be not worse than an infidel, and in addition to all this, to spend more of his own hard earnings to serve the church than the richest brother in his congregation pays into the church treasury, is asking more than they will be able to give a reason for, when they shall stand before the judgment seat of Christ. "Whoso hath this world's goods, and seeth his brother have need, and shutteth up his bowels of compassion from him, how dwelleth the love of God in him?"—I John 3 17. I am happy however to know, that while the Church as a body, has not been doing as much as it might, there are many brethren in the Church who are very charitable in giving unto their preacher those things that are necessary, and in inquiring if they lack anything. May God forever bless them for their labors of love, for the Lord's cause.

2. *In eternity.* Jesus said unto His disciples, "I go to prepare a place for you." "In My Father's house are many mansions." Rich are the provisions that Jesus has made for all His people in the world to come. He has made these provisions for all those who do His commandments,—*all things*" whatsoever He has said unto them. Glory unspeakable and pleasures that never cease. Great will be the care that He, the Light of the city of God, will bestow upon the saints in the evening of this world, when He shall have gathered them from the East and the West, the North and the South, and have made them to sit down to that rich repast in His Father's Kingdom, and will gird Himself and come forth and serve them.

In conclusion, "Behold the man!" See how wonderfully His mind was engaged for the human family while He was hanging on the cross. He desired the pardon of those who crucified Him, had mercy on him who believed and repented, and made those wise and necessary provisions for the household of faith. "Woman, behold thy son!" "Behold thy mother!"

JOHN ZUCK.

Shady Grove, Pa.

TOO LONG

On this phrase, at the head of this essay, I will make some suggestions, in order to show the importance of the two words, because they may be properly applied to show the imprudence of our conduct, and in this sense, we will now use them. We are so forgetful, hence an occasional reminder may serve as a caution; a word to the wise is sufficient.

When we come to meeting fifteen or twenty minutes after the appointed time we have either slept *too long* or have not arranged our matters the day previous as we should have done, so that in the morning we had too much to do; hence it took us too long to make an early start, to be in time to hear the introduction and prayer, the most important point, to prepare the mind for the solemn services of God. "Seek first the Kingdom of God and His righteousness, &c. When our exhortation to prayer is prolonged to ten or twenty minutes in our public meetings, and a little sermon preached, we have forgotten the injunction of Paul, "I exhort therefore, that first of all, prayers, intercessions, and giving of thanks be made for all men," (I Tim. 5: 1,) and also have violated the instructions of our general council. Hence *too long*, says the audience, we get tired of it, and is anti-Scriptural.

If we continue our prayers to an unusual length in our public meetings, we are likely using vain repetitions, and are not complying with the words of the Savior, "But when ye pray, use no vain repetitions." Therefore it is not only imprudent, but in opposition to the teachings of Christ. I have frequently noticed in public meeting when long prayers are made, that the hearers become very restless and inattentive. When we come together to teach the people the unsearchable riches of Christ, the intention is not to have a meeting of prayer, but of preaching the Gospel of Jesus Christ; hence let us not consume half of that time in singing and prayer. We have our family worship, our social meeting, and other occasions that we should avail ourselves of in singing the beautiful songs of Zion, and offering praises to God. Yes, brethren and sisters, how often could we spend our time better to the honor and glory of God in such a way as in useless talk and vain conversation. But do not understand me to mean that we should have no singing and prayer at our public worship. No, no, singing revives the soul and stirreth up the minds of the hearers from drowsiness and lethargy, and fervent prayer is necessary to draw the blessings of God upon us, and secure His presence and help, so much needed in the solemn assemblies Let your words be few, earnest, and the pure desire of your heart, and for the express purpose then needed; singing, the same way, and depend upon it, God will hear you and grant what ye need without a multiplicity of words, for He knoweth your desires.

Preaching may be too long, when not interesting. A sermon historical if too long, is wearisome, and not calculated to benefit very much. A doctrinal discourse is calculated to instruct and enlighten the mind, and if earnestly and intelligently delivered, may not be so easily too long. Paul at Rome, to the Jews "expounded and testified of the Kingdom of God, persuading them concerning Jesus, both out of the Law of Moses and out of the prophets from morning until evening."—Acts 28: 23. Exhortations are beneficial, and are mostly calculated to arouse the feelings of the hearer. They are very appropriate after a good doctrinal sermon; but if too many words and repetitions are made they may be too long. Finally if the time has expired, and the one that concludes preaches another sermon before prayer, it is out of place, and makes the services too long, and is extremely tedious and wearisome to the audience. To conclude this part we would add: if the speaker is *done*, and continues by repeating again and again what he said before, *too long*, TOO LONG, is the language of the hearer; I am tired, I heard you say that before. And above all, let us avoid repetitions unless it adds strength to the meaning, and guard especially against unnecessary words and meaningless phrases into our discourses.

We will now turn the heading phrase into another direction: For instance when a man or a woman is convinced of their duty they owe to God, and will neglect to do it, we are fearful they are waiting *too long*. Many of our dear young friends who are now in eternity, have undoubtedly thought of preparing themselves but neglected it until death robbed them of that glorious opportunity. Now it is evident they waited too long. When we see numbers living careless and unconcerned in this world, gay in their life, vicious in their habits, foolish in their conduct, proud in their demeanor, strutting about in the height of fashion, as if they could command God to obey them, we are very much afraid that those are waiting *too long* to prepare themselves to meet their God, and we are sure that they have already continued too long in idleness and folly. That old man and that old woman that still waits for a better opportunity to turn to God, has waited too long, and offended God too long already. That soul that is now struggling against the iron grasp of death, seeing the terrors of hell before him with the yawning lake of fire to receive him the next moment, sees too late that he has waited *too long*. Consternation and dreadful disappointment will seize many souls at the day of judgment to see that they have waited *too long*.

LEONARD FURRY.

BE not stingy of kind words and pleasing acts, for such are fragrant gifts, whose perfume will gladden the heart and sweeten the life of all who hear or receive them.

CHARITY.

Nothing is known except by comparison. If I know that my mother has always had more true regard for me than anybody else; if I am fully pursuaded of the truth that she manifests, in reality, more concern for all her children than anybody else ever will, or ever would, if he could, then my soul is about right so far as maternal affections relate to it. But if I am unable to imagine or allow in my mind that other people's mothers are just as affectionate as mine, then I have not charity and don't know what it is.

The father that feels all that a parent can feel of the real wants of his offspring, and supplies them, discharges his parental duties very well. But if he don't see the wants of anybody else's children, he don't see charity. When he sees the wants of others and a remedy in his power, then he sees charity, and at the very point where he applies the remedy he receives the "charity."

The fact of a man being able to deliver a lecture on the nature and power of money is no guaranty that he has any! Neither is the fact of a man being unable to deliver such a lecture a sure guaranty that he has no money. So it is with charity. Different circumstances alter different and similar cases, according to other different and similar mixed cases, and circumstances. If any person is offended at me, because I eat more of the meat-flesh, words or spirit of Christ than he wants to eat, and am consequently larger in Christ than he is, which if he knows, then his offence comes through his own envy, and I walk uncharitably toward him, if he prevails upon me to stop eating, and charitably, if he don't and can't. It will be seen at last by all who thoroughly purge the floor, that it depends altogether upon the kind of meat we are eating, whether we should stop when we are told to do so by men. The flesh of Christ, the very thing every man ought to eat is itself a heinous offence to some who call themselves our "brethren" and the followers of the Lord Jesus." Now, to eat the flesh of Jesus and thus walk charitably toward such people is to employ any means that we know will accomplish a certain end, namely: their repentance and conversion and final salvation.

Charity is the greatest spiritual pearl that is known by the Christian in this life, but there is something beyond which is far greater. Something of which we cannot in this life become conscious. It is as much superior to charity as the kernel is superior to the shell. It is that of which charity is only the "bond," namely: perfectness, that which we will not know until we shall say, "when saw we thee an hungered, &c," and the King shall answer, "Inasmuch as ye have done it unto one of the least of these" it is only then that we become conscious of what is within, but charity we should know and become conscious of here.

J. B. GARVER.

WINTER.

Winter has come with its chilling winds and frosty mornings; the trees are stripped of their beautiful robes of green, and all nature wears a wintry aspect. The flowers that lately decked the earth with beauty, now lies withered and dead, reminding us that another year is rapidly passing away, and with it, how many frail beings have passed to the other shore. Many seats have been made vacant, and many a heart and home has been made sad and gloomy by the entrance of the stern messenger, —death. Many a little cherub has been added to the happy throng in glory. But oh! how fearful to think of the many who have been ushered into the presence of their God unprepared, and are now reaping what they have sown. Sinner, can you not be awakened out of your deep sleep to the reality of things around you? Can you not be induced to make peace with your God? Remember the autumn of your life is drawing on, and soon will come the dark and gloomy winter of everlasting despair, unless you turn your feet Zionward. Then delay not making preparation to meet God. Be obedient unto His commands, that you may have a right to the tree of Life, and enter in through the gates into the city.

JOHN LEISTER.

BE NOT FEARFUL.

Go stand and speak in the temple to the people all the words of this life.—Acts 5:20.

I sometimes fear that we fall short of doing our duty in this respect. We, perhaps, feel too timid about speaking all the words of this life. This should not be. We should not shun to declare the whole counsel of God, and in this we should surely exhibit boldness. This is what the angel commanded the apostles to do, even after they had been imprisoned on account of their speaking forth the words of life with boldness. Then brethren, let us stand up firmly to our post and labor manfully for Jesus. For this purpose we are placed on the walls of Zion; we are to labor for the benefit of souls and the general interests of the Church of Christ, which is the pillar and ground of the truth. We sometimes hear ministers preach whom we have every reason to believe try to preach to suit the people. This is wrong. Jesus never intended that we should be men-pleasers. We are to speak ALL the words of this life.

Let us then wake up to a sense of our duty, and preach only Christ and Him crucified to a dying world. Let us declare all the doctrine of God freely and boldly.

BENJ. FRYFOGLE.

Brimfield, Ind.

GO TO THE PURE FOUNTAIN.

If the fountain is impure, the whole stream becomes impure. Not long ago I received a religious paper with a circular desiring that I should introduce and get subscribers for it. But in looking over the same, I found them not in tenor with the Gospel, did not agree with the Scripture as we understand it. Some pieces were very good, but others would teach us that faith without our works will save us. But the word says, "Faith without works is dead, being alone." I also noticed several articles in regard to playing cards as though some ministers of the Gospel engaged in such games. We would not recognize such as ministers of the Gospel. If they are in their proper place, they will not be found in company with those who engage in such games, and much less engage in it themselves.

This brings to my mind a circumstance related to me by a friend who met a minister at a masked ball. Being somewhat astonished to meet him at such a place, remarked to him, "Well Mr.—we meet at quite a lively place." Well said he "this is the place for a minister of the Gospel to go to get acquainted with human nature." Now if ministers should go to such places, why not private members? and if all would go, it would certainly show a poor light, and how would we be distinguished from the world?

Now in regard to the papers, if we recommend any, we prefer to recommend those that we know originate from the pure fountain head.

ISAAC L. RUDY.

SELECTIONS.

SAINT MARTIN'S TEMPTATION.

For forty-and-five long years
I have followed my Master, Christ,
Through frailty and toils and tears,
Through passions that still enticed;
Through station that came unsought,
To dazzle me, snare, betray;
Through the baits the tempter brought
To lure me out of the way:
Through the peril and greed of power
(The bribe that he thought most sure);
Through the name that hath made me cower,
"*The holy bishop of Tours!*"
Now, tired of life's poor show,
A weary of soul, and sore,
I am stretching my hands to go
Where nothing can tempt me more.

Ah, none but my Lord hath seen
How often I've swerved aside—
How the word or the look serene
Hath hidden the heart of pride.
When a beggar once crouched in need,
I flung him my priestly stole,
And the people did laud the deed,
Withholding the while their dole:
Then I closed my lips on a curse,
Like a scorpion curled within,
On such cheap charity. Worse
Was even than theirs, my sin!
And once when a royal hand
Brake bread for the Christ's sweet grace
I was proud that a queen should stand
And serve in the henchman's place.

But sorest of all bestead
Was a night in my narrow cell,
As I pondered with low-bowed head
A purpose that pleased me well.
'Twas fond to the sense and fair,
Attuned to the heart and will,
And yet on its face it bare
The look of a duty still:
And I said, as my doubts took wing,
"Where duty and choice accord,
It is even a pleasant thing,
To the flesh, to serve the Lord."

I turned and saw a sight
Wondrous and strange to see—
A being as marvelous bright
As the visions of angels be:
His vesture was wrought of flame,
And a crown on his forehead shone,
With jewels of nameless name,
Like the glory about the throne.
"Worship thou me," he said;
And I sought, as I sank, to trace,
Through his hands above me spread,
The lineaments of his face.
I pored on each palm to see
The scar of the *stigma*, where
They had fastened him to the Tree.
But no print of the nails was there.
Then I shuddered, aghast of brow,
As I cried, "Accurst! abhorred!
Get thee behind me! for thou
Art Satan, and not my Lord!"
He vanished before the spell
Of the Sacred Name I named,
And I lay in my darkened cell
Smitten, astounded, shamed.
Thenceforth, whatever the dress
That a seeming duty wear,
I know 'twas a wile, *unless*
The print of the nail was there!

MARGARET J. PRESTON.

—*In Lippincott's Magazine for December*

NEW IN CHRIST JESUS.—The paper manufacturer is not nice in the choice of his materials. All come alike to him. The clean and glancing cloth from the table of the rich, and filthy rags from a beggar's back, are equally welcome. The clean cannot be serviceable without passing thro' the manufacturer's process, and the unclean can be made serviceable with it. He throws both into the same machine, puts both through the same process, and brings out both new creatures. The Pharisees were scandalized on observing that publicans and sinners came in streams to Christ, and were accepted. "This man receiveth sinners," they complained. Yea, receiveth them; sinners are taken between the wheels, at the commencement of this process; but at the end of it saints in white clothing are thrown out, fit for the kingdom of heaven. Christ does not find any pure on earth; he makes them. Those that stand round the throne in white clothing were gathered from the mire.—*Arnot.*

PRAY AND WAIT.—Pray frequently, and wait quietly, and the Lord will make your way plain. Jesus trains up all his servants to waiting; and if you are called to the ministry, He will exercise your soul beforehand with sharp conflicts. Joseph must be first cast into a pit by his own brethren, then into prison by his master, before he rules the kingdom; and David must be hunted as a flea upon the mountains before he gets the scepter. How can you tell what others feel unless you have felt the same yourself? Undertake nothing without first seeking direction from the Lord; and when anything offers that is plausible and inviting, beg of God to disappoint you, if it be not according to His mind. You cannot safely rely on your own judgment, after God has told you, "He that trusteth in his own heart is a fool." This advice relates to all important changes in life.

MANY a discouraged mother folds her tired hands at night, and feels as if she had, after all, done nothing, although she has not spent an idle moment since she rose. Is it nothing that your little children have had some one to come to with all their childish griefs and joys? Is it nothing that your husband feels "safe" when he is away to his business, because your careful hand directs everything at home? Is it nothing, when his business is over, that he has the blessed refuge of a home, which you have done so much to brighten and refine? Oh, weary and faithful mother, you little know your power when you say, "I have done nothing." There is a book in which a fairer record than this is written over against your name.

A soul clothed with Christ, stooping to any sinful delight, or any ardent pursuit of anything earthly, though lawful, doth wonderfully degrade itself.

The Weekly Pilgrim.

JAMES CREEK, PA., Dec. 9, 1873.

☞ How to send money.—All sums over $1.50, should be sent either in a check, draft or postal order. If neither of these can be obtained, have the letter registered.

☞ When Money is sent, *always* send with it the name and address of those who paid it. Write the names and post office as plainly as possible.

☞ Every subscriber for 1874, gets a *Pilgrim Almanac* Free.

Notice.—Please do not mix things. If you send us subscribers, obituaries, essays, correspondence and private notes, put each on a separate sheet or slip of paper. By observing this notice you will much oblige us and prevent mistakes that can scarcely be avoided when everything is mixed on the same sheet of paper.

Preserve a List.—We expect all of our agents to keep for your own use and reference, a complete list of all the names you send us. By so doing you can keep everything in a proper shape with the subscribers, and credit each one as he pays.

Our elder brother, George Brumbaugh, is now on a preaching tour among the brethren of Eld. Moses Miller's charge, Lower Cumberland district, Pa. Bro. G. W. Brumbaugh, of Clover Creek, Pa., is his colleague. Eld Grabill Myers also thought of accompanying them. Hope they may have a pleasant time and be successful in winning souls to Christ.

On Saturday morning, brother Henry Hershberger has made arrangements to meet us at Mt. Dallas Station and convey us out to the Clearridge settlement, where several appointments are made for preaching. This is a little more than was bargained for at this time, but as we have given some of our brethren of that place, several promises at different times, we shall try and meet the engagement if well and the weather does not prove too unfavorable.

On last Sabbath we attended our first regular appointment in the new church at Coffee Run. The congregation was pleasantly, and we hope, profitably entertained by a discourse from the "Ten virgins" by G. B. Brumbaugh. We *felt* that we had a good meeting, and hope we may be permitted to enjoy many more such seasons at that, as well as our other places of holding meetings.

What should be the first prayer of the awakened sinner, seems to be a question among many. This is probably on account of the great abuse to which prayer is now subjected. The abuse is not in praying, but in the subject matter of the prayer. The unregenerated or unborn, are dead and blind, and therefore cannot see. The first desire of the awakened sinner is beautifully set forth in the petition of Bartimeus, "Lord, that I may receive my sight." The first presentiment to the awakened sinner is that of blindness, and the very first desire of a blind man is, to receive sight. Then it follows that the first prayer should be for light, or in other words, "What must I do to be saved?" The terms of salvation should be the first desire, and when they are received, the next should be to comply with them. To pray for the pardon of sins before complying with the terms, is like a laborer asking for the pay before doing the work, and this we all have learned, is extremely bad policy.

Shall we have war? was the great topic of conversation in the large cities for the last few days. Our readers, no doubt have learned, from the secular press long ere this, the cause of this great commotion. The capture of the Virginius and the barbarous butchering of part of its crew, by Spanish desperadoes, has scarcely a parallel in the history of civilized nations, and from all appearance, has set on fire an element which may prove serious, if not fatal to the object which the offending party had in view. At this writing there is a fair prospect of an amicable adjustment of the difficulty between the United States and the Spanish government. But should this be accomplished, it still remains a question whether it will end the Cuban troubles.—The curse of slavery stills reigns there and its advocates seem to be a band of outlaws that live and act independent of reason, government or religion.

ONCE MORE.

Once more! just one number more, we hear our printers say, and we will be through for 1873. Forty-nine times dear brethren, sisters, and kind friends, we have made our pilgrimage to your homes, and once more, and our obligations are fulfilled, and we will cease our visits unless invited to continue them for 1874. If ever we felt concerned and anxious it is just now. Our great wonder is, how many of those whom we have been visiting during the last year, and many, ever since we commenced our pilgrimage, will invite us back again. It is true, and we are conscious of it, in many instances we have failed and come short of our privilege, but who has not? We shall not attempt to justify ourselves by portraying to you, the good we have accomplished as we know it not. We think we did good, we *believe* we did, but God knoweth best, and we feel assured that He will not be unmindful of it. All we know positively is, that we have been indeavoring to labor for the upbuilding of the Church, and final good of our readers. The question, just now with us, is, have our labors been successful, and have our readers thus accepted it? If we have been able to make all our readers feel, that we have thus been laboring, we have no doubt but that we will be invited to continue our visits. How is it dear readers? How we wish we could make this a personal question with you all. How it would do our souls good to hear our thousands of readers say, God bless you and your labors, or if objections are found against us how glad we would be to have the opportunity of answering those objections. It occurs to us that we could plead our cause with acceptance, and persuade you that "To err is human, but to forgive, divine.

Our relation to each other has been such that it makes us feel sad to think that one of you should be missing on our list for 1874. We cannot well afford to do without you. We need your sympathies, your prayers, and your support, and besides all this, we crave your influence. This often amounts to very much, and, when exerted in our favor may greatly encourage us in our arduous labors.

We have scarcely a brother or sister who is now reading the Pilgrim but what could persuade at least one more to take it. This would double our list, and thus enable us to greatly improve our work, both in appearance and value. Will you not give us your influence? We desire it and we hope for it. Disappoint us not, but go to work with a determination and a will. You have neighbors who would be benefited by reading the Pilgrim. Tell them its character and mission, and then ask them to try it a year. It will not only oblige us, but may be the means of converting them to God. Many of you have children who are heads of families, and who are still out of Christ. You cannot make them a better present than to send them the Pilgrim. Many have made good investments by having it sent to their friends. Such favors have been accepted with grateful hearts, and we have the assurance that the givers shall in no wise lose their reward. Think of these things dear reader, and determine not only to send your own name, but send along with it, as many more as you possibly can.

In order that the present closeness of money matters may not be a hindrance or excuse, we have concluded, as usual, to give all honest and good thinking persons their own time to pay, only so it is done as soon as practicable, or within the year. Of course this offer is intended only for such as have not the means at the time of subscribing. Those who can, should pay as near the beginning of the year as possible, as our business requires a considerable amount of money to carry it on, and retain a good character and credit. This we have been enabled to do so far, and hope to continue to do so.

Once more dear reader, and we leave it with you to decide. Make the decision *now*, and let us have your names as soon as possible, thus enabling us to get our books in condition, and send out the Almanacs before the New Year comes in.

HARD TIMES.

The hardness of the times is now the general topic of conversation, and almost everything is being affected by the great crash in pecuniary affairs. The publishing interests will most likely be crippled by it. Some of our agents fear that it will be in the way of procuring subscribers for 1874. It is very natural to complain of hard times when asked to subscribe for a paper, and now as there are some indications of it, this will no doubt be the general exclamation. The missionary cause will also suffer, and the procuring of funds to build churches in which to worship God will be attended with difficulties. All these things the cry of hard times will affect seriously. It is however altogether likely that with many persons the effects are more imaginary than real. Some persons are inclined to become frightened, and even imagine they are hurt, when there is no real danger, and so it is in reference to the late panic, there are those who make a great ado about it, and at the same time may not be affected by it at all. There are certain classes whom it will affect, and are now already realizing what hard times are. In the city of New York there has recently been formed what is called a relief society, and the design is to provide food for young men who are thrown out of employment until they can find work. In order to do this, they have rented a large house in one of the most prominent streets, and it is said that thousands come daily to be fed. Some young men came who were so near exhausted, for want of food, that they fainted at the smell of victuals. Some had nothing to eat for three days, and were without any prospects of obtaining employment. Such persons know what hard times are, and are truthfully realizing the horrors of the financial crisis. But what does farmers and the people generally in the country know about hard times? Have we not all plenty to eat and wear? And does not the Scriptures teach us that when we have this we should be contented? Yes, and when we think of the thousands of men, women and children that would be glad to have the crumbs that fall from our heavy laden tables, should it not close our mouths to any complaint, and call forth our warmest sympathies for those who are in such a fearful dilemma? These are things that we should think of, and just before sitting down to our meals, if our minds could be directed to the many poor, starving men, women and children, would it not cause deeper emotions of gratitude to flow from our hearts for the privilege we enjoy. Ah, yes, there would be no cold formal prayers; deep in our hearts the prayer of devotion would arise, pure and warm.

Let us then, dear readers, who are surrounded with plenty, cease to complain; let us endeavor to feel the relation which we sustain to each other, and the obligations we are under to them in consequence of that relation. It is our duty to help and assist each other, and we should embrace every opportunity to relieve those who are in distress. It is true, money is a little scarce just now and this may put us to a little inconvenience, and may frustrate some of our plans for the future, but as long as we have plenty and to spare there is no reason to complain. Then too do not let the cause of Christ suffer for the want of means. Let us rather deny ourselves of some of the luxuries of life. There is money wanted to build churches, and if we have any money to invest at all, we can not make a better investment than in building churches. It is loaning to the Lord, and in the future we will receive our own with a usury unparalled by anything we have ever realized. Then too, our periodicals must be supported for the disseminating of the Gospel. Do not let the hard times so much impede the promotion of the Gospel through this medium. We are willing, dear brethren and sisters, to economize in every possible way and make all the sacrifice we can, but we cannot do all. There are many of our readers who can do more in way of economizing than we can. Our printing material and paper costs us as much now as any other time, and these things we must have, we cannot do without them, and cannot therefore avoid expenses as persons in other callings can. We hope our readers will think of this, and will help us bear our burdens a little by making a strenuous effort to have all our old subscribers renew their subscription and many more new ones. For this we will hope. J. B. B.

ALMANACS A DEMAND.

Of late we are having quite a number of calls for Almanacs and prospectus for the PILGRIM. These calls are gladly responded to and we hope that those who make them, may be successful in getting up large clubs. Our prospects are quite cheering and the indications are that we will have large accessions of new subscribers. If all our present readers will continue to give us their support we shall have reason to thank God and take courage. Send along your names brethren and sisters. Do not let the cry of hard times cause you to hold back. The harder the times the greater need have you of the consolation and encouragement derived from reading the PILGRIM. If there is need of economy, commence somewhere else. There are many things that you can afford to do without much better than the PILGRIM. Commence with your horses, carriages, houses, tables and clothes, and by the time you lop off all the unnecessaries from them you will have plenty to invest for the PILGRIM. But is it not remarkable that complaints about hard-times seldom come from the poor? If there is no other way, they will scrimp their tables, or put in extra labor to obtain the money. They say that they must have the PILGRIM, and that they cannot do without it. This proves the old adage, "Where there is a will there is a way." Then wake up to the work, and where there is a church without an agent, let some one volunteer his service, send for an *Almanac* and prospectus and got to work. There are hundreds and thousands who would read the PILGRIM had they an opportunity of subscribing for it. Brethren and sisters, give them this opportunity and see what can be done by way of a well directed effort.

ANCIENT BAPTISM.

The following we clip from the *Advent Times*. These Apocryphal books of the Apostles are quite interesting as scraps of ancient history, and their age gives them additional respect. Some of them correspond so nearly with the accepted Scriptures that many of them are thought to be genuine epistles of the Apostles.

That sprinkling is not the accepted mode of baptism, is evident from th apocryphal book of Paul and Thecla, written in the second century, in which it is asserted that in the absence of an opportunity to be baptized by a minister, Thecla "threw herself into the water," while her enemies supposed that the fish would devour her. The point is this: If this had not been the mode practiced, it would have been used as an argument against the genuineness of the book; but this objection was never brought against it and many accepted it as genuine. If the book had realy introduced a new mode of baptism, it would have led to a discussion of that topic, before the book could have been received by any

THE New Constitution of Pennsylvania will be submitted to a vote to its citizens for adoption or rejection on Tuesday, December 16th, 1873. It has been extensively circulated throughout the State, so that all the citizens could have an opportunity of reading it and thus be enabled to vote intelligently on the proposed amendments. As it is a matter of importance to every resident of the Commonwealth, it behooves all those who think it a duty to exercise their privileges to read the new Constitution carefully and not allow themselves to be influenced by designing men, whose object is not to elevate and benefit the government and its people, but to get a grab in the public treasury. For the satisfaction of our readers residing in other States we insert the "preamble" and the four first sections which are as follows:

PREAMBLE.

WE, the people of the Commonwealth of Pennsylvania, grateful to Almighty God for the blessings of civil and religious liberty, and humbly invoking His guidance, do ordain and establish this Constitution.

ARTICLE I.

Declaration of Rights.

That the general, great and essential principles of liberty and free government may be recognized and unalterably established, we declare that

SECTION 1. All men are born equally free and independent, and have certain inherent and indefeasible rights, among which are those of enjoying and defending life and liberty, of acquiring, possessing and protecting property and reputation, and of pursuing their own happiness.

SEC. 2. All power is inherent in the people, and all free governments are founded on their authority and instituted for their peace, safety and happiness. For the advancement of these ends they have at all times an inalienable and indefeasible right to alter, reform or abolish their government in such a manner as they may think proper.

SEC. 3. All men have a natural and indefeasable right to worship Almighty God according to the dictates of their own consciences; no man can of right be compelled to attend, erect or support any place of worship, or to maintain any ministry against his consent; no human authority can, in any case whatever, control or interfere with the rights of conscience, and no preference shall ever be given by law to any religious establishments or modes of worship.

SEC. 4. No person who acknowledges the being of a God and a future state of rewards and punishments shall, on account of his religious sentiments, be disqualified to hold any office or place of trust or profit under this Commonwealth.

Miscellaneous.

THERE are now forty-nine Baptist Churches in Philadelphia.

It is estimated that there are 40,000 people in New York city who are idle, willing to work but can't get it.

AN aged Presbyterian minister died recently in S. C., while in the pulpit. He was commenting on the third chapter of Malachi, when he beckoned to some one in the congregation to come to him, and died immediately.

Something of a sensation in ecclesiastical circles at Rome was created recently by the abandonment of Romanism by a Catholic priest. Having accepted the Baptist faith, his baptism in public, created considerable excitement.

The Evangelical Lutherans of New York have added a new chapter to their Synodical Constitution, making it obligatory upon ministers and congregations to make a regular annual contribution to create a fund from which ministers' worthy widows and orphans are to receive aid.

A BAND of Methodists, in Boston, has been organized under the name of Christian workers. The band now consists of over one hundred persons. Each member is monthly assigned to a particular place where religious meetings are to be held, and there they receive packages of tracts for daily distribution.

The value of three hundred and forty-nine churches in New York is forty-six million dollars, and this does not include the Roman Catholic Cathedral and several other churches in course of erection. It is thought that there are fifty million dollars worth of church property in New York exempt from all taxation.

Quite an excitement has been raised in San Francisco, among the adherents of the Catholic Church in consequence of the Rev. Father Dugan, a Roman Catholic priest, abjuring his old faith and joining the Presbyterians. The recantation and his admission into the Church were made publicly.

The Baltimore *Episcopal Methodist* does not believe the union of the Methodist Church, North and South, practicable or even desirable, believing that the two denominations in their separate capacitity, can accomplish more in advancing the true mission of the Church, than if they were to act conjointly as one organization.

AN English poet and lecturer gave a lecture recently in New York on "Why God Don't Kill the Devil." He thinks that human ignorance, selfishness and superstition has made all the devil there is, and that God does not destroy this man-made power because he wants us to slay him for ourselves.

THE last news from Memphis, Tenn., is that the fever is subsiding. Some thousand persons have died from its effects in a very small district. It is looked upon as being more destructive than a battle, and yet is looked upon as a visitation for which nobody in particular is responsible.

THE ladies of Huntingdon have organized a relief society, and appointed committees to collect funds, and relieve the wants of the distressed poor, and needy. This is a worthy example, and, in view of the approaching Winter, the scarcity of money and the difficulty of obtaining employment, one which it were well to follow in every community. "He that giveth to the poor, lendeth to the Lord." "It is more blessed to give than to receive," then give of your abundance, at least, to God's poor, and He will richly reward you, with abundant blessings.

Correspondence.

A Reporter is wanted from every Church in the brotherhood to send us Church news, Obituaries, Announcements, or anything that will be of general interest. To insure insertion, the writers name must accompany each communication. Our Invitation is not personal but general—please respond to our call.

GREELY, Weld Co., Col. Nov. 28, '73.

Editor Pilgrim:—By your permission, I will concede to the wishes of a number of brethren, that I give through your columns, some general information relative to this Territory, and such advice as would be thought necessary for those contemplating a move in this direction

First I will say, it is difficult for persons in the east to form a correct idea of this country, owing to the many conflicting reports, because persons do not all see alike. Some have their anticipations too high, expecting when they came here to find a land of fenced farms, ploughed lands with fruit trees growing thereon, and irrigating canals everywhere so that they will have nothing to do, but to take a "pre emption" or "homestead" claim and settle down and enjoy all the comforts of life.

Fine pleasant homes may be found here, but they must be paid for just as the farms of Pa., Ohio or any other Eastern state, must have pay for improvements, so those that have made nice homes here, if they sell, expect to be paid for their labor. Others again, look upon Colorado as a wild un-civilized region, simply because it has only been settled a few years, forgetting that this is a fast age, and where the iron horse pushes his way, civilization comes up close to the rear. Many express their surprise on arriving here to find large towns, where a few years ago the red man reveled in the wardance. Large wholesale and retail stores and manufactories, and a society as far along in pride, fashion, and all the doings of civilization much like that of eastern cities. Take for instance this town: three years ago, or a little over, the site upon which it is built, was a desert plain, now it is a town of busy streets, extensive houses, hotels, churches, mills and a school house for free schools, that would be an honor to any community, costing over $30.000. Four departments in the public school have been sustained during the year at a cost for teachers of over $3000, the pupils number hundreds, the population of the town and the surrounding country is about 3000. Farming and gardening here is a success, flour of a superior quality is being shipped from here by the car load to the eastern markets, where it commands the top price over all other.—What has been done here and in other communities in the territory, can be done where yet the land is free, and the buffalo by thousands roam over hill and plane. The South Platte valley offer probably the best inducements for new comers of any other in the territory. A new rail road, branch of the great Union Pacific, running from Julesburg up the South Platte valley to Evans, from this place to the mountains and to the capital of the territory, has been graded and doubtless will be in running order next Summer if not sooner. This valley embraces, it is said the best region in the territory for farming and stock raising. None of these lands have been given to any R. R. company; they are being taken up rapidly, yet there are many good claims to be had, only by preemption or homesteads, or bought of those who have preempted and proven up and paid for them.

Now I will answer a question so often asked me: "How shall I proceed to get a claim?" The law requires the person wanting a claim to select *in person*, make a sign of improvement, such as laying a sod foundation for a house or ploughing a little, put up a stake with name and date of selecting, then it can not be lawfully "jumped" by another party under three months, but before the three months expire it is necessary to put up a small house, and file a declaratory statement, showing which ¼ section has been selected. Then the party should make that his home for six months from the time he commences to improve it, and at the expiration of six months, he can go and "prove up" and get a deed for it by paying $1.25 per acre, or he can remain on it, and pay up at his option any time within thirty months. As soon as it is paid for he can sell it, or do with it what he chooses. If a claim is taken as a homestead, you need not go on it for six months, then it is required that improvements commence on it, and the party must reside on it. After having lived on it for six months if the parties wish, they can get a deed for it by paying $1.25 per acre, or if they live on it five years, get it free. Soldiers can have homesteads selected, and filed through agents. They also only have to reside on the claim long enough to make up five years, including the time they served in the army, when they can get a deed for it. Every person over 21 years of age, or head of a family, can get a claim of 160 acres. After having "proved up" and paid for a preemption claim (160 acres) they can then go and take a homestead of 160 acres,—can take but one of each. Those claims on the Platte, as soon as paid for and a deed procured, are worth $600 without improvements. I know of none that can be bought for less at this time. These farm lands are all river bottom, and susceptible of irrigation from the river. The bottoms are from one to eight miles wide, the soil, of a sandy, gravelly loam, and very productive. Nearest the river the bottoms have a luxuriant crop yearly, of hay grass, further back a short buffalo grass grows. In places there is an abundance of alkali in the soil: in such grounds the grass is short and vegetation does not do well for several years after cultivation, there being an excess of certain constituents necessary for vegetation. After having been "leached" by irrigation a few years, it is said to be the best land.

Another question is, how do you irrigate? As a general thing, the settlers form themselves into an incorporate company, get a canal surveyed, and then a charter is procured, and all hands go to work, take out a quantity of water from the river by a leading canal that is taken back next to the bluffs, so that all the bottom land will be between the canal and the river; then lateral canals or ditches convey the water from the main canal to the farms or gardens; head ditches convey the water along the head or higest part of plats of ground in crop. The water is then let into small furrows, between which the crops are growing, soon the whole surface is saturated, when the water is turned off. In sowing wheat, some take out the middle spout (conductor) of the drill and put in a shovel which makes a furrow along these furrows, when the water is turned on; about two wettings are sufficient for wheat or oats, and three or four for hoed crops. Potatoes and some other vegetables often do well without irrigation, and sometimes there is sufficient rain during the season for all crops. By irrigation the crops are insured from drouth. In the dry warm season, the Platte has the most water, as it is supplied by the melting snow in the mountains, where the snow lies all summer.

As to water other than the rain, we have but few springs any distance from the mountains, but good cool healthful water can be had any where on the bottom lands at a depth of 8 to 30 feet, ordinarily metal pipes are simply driven into the ground until the lower section enters the stratum of quick sand and water. A cast pump is screwed on the top and water, plentiful and good is at hand. Thus well digging is dispensed with, and pumps can be had in the cellar or kitchen.

There is but little timber in the Platt valley. By rail, fuel, lumber and posts can be had from the mountains at fair prices, and excellent coal in abundance at prices ranging from $3 to $6 per ton. There is some stone in the valley in some localities. For buildings, as a substitute for something better, many of the first settlers use *sod* in building houses, stables, and stock inclosures. The walls are about 2½ feet thick, plastered inside and covered with boards. Such houses are warm in winter and cool in summer, are durable and cheap. I see old government forts, the walls of which are sod, and yet standing. others use sun dried brick for building houses. They make a good house. Lumber however is the principle building material.

J. S. FLORY.

ALLENTOWN, PA., Dec. 3. 1873.

Beloved Brethren Editors:—I feel like throwing in my mite of church news. On Sunday last, the 30th ult., brethren Elias Landis, from Juniata county, and Isaac Kulp, and Abram Cassell from Montgomery county, were with us on a mission of love. Brethren Jacob Booze and Moses Scholer were also present. During the day, services were held at Bethlehem, and in the evening at Allentown.

At the latter named place, the brethren did not have any preaching for the last two years. The meeting was held in a large school room. On arriving, contrary to all expectations, the large room was full to overflowing of attentive listeners. The word was held forth by Landis and Cassell in German, and Kulp in the English, from 1 Pet. 3: 12. The brethren tried to show who the righteous are, and that in our natural or unborn state, we were aliens and strangers in the sight of God, unreconciled, out of the ark of safety, on the barren hills of folly and misery, consequently the face of the Lord against us.

They also showed how a person in his unconverted state can become so. When a person, unconscious of his sins, unconcerned about his soul's salvation, wakes up from his slumber, feels the weight and dreadfulness of sin, comes weary and heavy laden to the feet of Jesus, asking what he must do to be saved, and becomes willing to take the easy yoke and light burden of Jesus upon him, embraces the overtures of mercy, fulfills the requirements of the Gospel, makes peace with God on the conditions implied in his holy word, he becomes a child of God; a righteous person on whom is the eye of the Lord, and unto whose prayer the Lord's ear is open. From a babe in Christ he is now to grow to the full measure of the stature, as it is in Christ Jesus by denying himself daily of unrighteousness, ungodliness, and live righteously and soberly, unto the perfect day.

Good impressions were made. It was a season of refreshing showers from on high to the brethren and sisters,—a time long to be remembered. We only hope that God may work wonders in these last, dark and perilous days, and cause many to forsake their evil and sinful ways, and thus be saved. Brethren and sisters we can accomplish something too, if we are right earnest and devoted. Let us take new courage, seeing our labor is not in vain, that is in the Lord. We shall be richly rewarded.

Your weak brother in Christ.

H. F. ROSENBERGER.

Dear Editor:—As it is your desire to have correspondence from each church, I will give you a few items from the Cana Church. Last April it numbered 9 lay members, and now it numbers 28, three speakers and three deacons. We had a Communion meeting here in October. It was the first meeting of this kind ever held in Howard Co., and the people manifested a great interest, and good order prevailed. We have a flattering prospect for a large church here, soon.

For the satisfaction of the readers of the PILGRIM who may wish an item of news from Southern Kansas, I will say that we have a good country, a rich and fertile soil, good water and a mild climate. Timber is rather scarce, but good prospects for coal. This country is quite rolling, consequently it is dry and healthy. Land is very cheap, ranging from $1.25 to $10 per acre, owing to improvements. Any one desiring a home in the West would do well to come and see for themselves. The corn crop was an average one, and wheat very good. Vegetables of all kinds do well. There is plenty of rock for building purposes of both lime and sand-stone. For further information, address,

BURGESS A. HADSELL.

Union Center, Howard Co., Kan.

Dear Pilgrim: The Coventry Congregation, has recently been favored with a visit from Bro. Lemuel Hillery of Iowa. He preached three successive evenings and presented to our minds, from the rich treasury of God's word, things new and old; things if rightly applied will tell to our advantage in eternity. Surely Bro. H. must be one of those who were told to tarry at Jerusalem until they were endued with power from on high, for he is not ashamed to own his Lord, nor defend his cause. May success crown all his efforts to the remotest extent. May he still be enabled by grace divine, to stand firm in defence of the truth as it is in Jesus, before a guilty and gainsaying people, withersoever he may sojourn, that saints may be edified, and sinners may begin to love who never loved before, is the prayer of a weak pilgrim. H. H.

Pottstown, Pa.

NOTICE

I hereby give notice to all the brethren and sisters that intend to go to the next Annual Meeting, which will be held in McCoupin Co. Ill., close to the St. Louis, Alton and Chicago R. R., that the Baltimore & Ohio R. R. Co. grants as favorable rates as we can ask. They grant half fare and give the privilege of getting on at any station, and any number from one up. The treatment is very kind.

At our last A. M., the train was behind time and the conductor telegraphed and had other trains wait, so that brethren could get home the same day. Now as our publication came out too late this year so that many had to pay higher fare than if they had taken the Baltimore & Ohio R. R., I hope that those who were appointed to make arrangements will do so at an early day, and have them published in time. Mr. Smith, the assistant auditor at Columbus Ohio, is a very prompt man, and I have learned from hands along the R. R., that he is a very accommodating man. What little business I have done with the company through Mr. Smith, has proven satisfactory in every respect. All that want to be accommodated, should be prompt. W. SADLER.

NOTICE.—Gideon Bollinger will fill the appointment in Trumble Co., the first of March 1874, instead of David Byers.

CLUBBING LIST.

We will furnish any of the following periodicals with the PILGRIM at the prices indicated:

	Single	*with Pilgrim*
Atlantic Monthly,	$4.00	$4.60
Scribner's "	4.00	4.60
Lippincott's Magazine,	4.00	4.60
Old & New (monthly,)	4.00	4.00
Appleton's Jour. (weekly)	4.00	4.60
Littell's Living Age "	8.00	8.50
Popular Science Monthly	5.00	5.35
Harper's Magazine or Weekly,	4.00	4.85
Nursery Monthly,	1.50	2.60
Wood's Household Magazine $1, with chromo.	1.50	2.50
St. Nicholas,	3.00	3.85
Hearth & Home	3.00	3.85
American Agriculturist	1.50	2.60
Phrenological Journal	3.00	3.00
N. Y. Tribune, weekly,	2.00	3.00
North American Review,	6.00	6.60

MONEY LIST

Alice Hawkins	$1.50	Lewis Workman	1.50
James Guthrie	1.50	Isaac N. Haster	10.50
Marg't Deardorff	1.50	Daniel Brower	3.50
J Barnhart	5.—	J. B. Miller	1.50
John Watts	1.75	Simon Snyder	1.50
Benj. F Stouffer	1.50	John Zigler	.50

MARRIED.

CLAPPER—WIGFIELD.—By the undersigned, at his residence, Nov. 30, 1873, Bro. Jacob S. Clapper to sister Mary Wigfield, all of Yellow Creek, Bedford Co., Pa. S. A. MOORE.

BLOCHER—GARNES.—At my residence, November 6, 1873, Jacob Blocher to Margaret Garnes all of Franklin Co., Penn., both near Upton DANIEL MILLER.

Youth's Department.

WORDS.

Words are only little things,
 Which give life to every day;
Each its pain or pleasure brings
 Passing from our lips away.

These are given for our use,
 They our peace can mar or make;
Little words we oft abuse
 When by them we fond hearts break

Works, like water on the ground,
 Never can be gathered up,
But like the raindrops, fall around,
 Filling evermore life's cup.

Words can wound us, and can pour
 Deadly poison in the sting;
Words are potent to restore,
 And the sweetest pleasures bring.

WHAT WE HAVE.

Last week our department for the boys and girls was unavoidably crowded out, but this week, we hope we have again something that will interest and instruct you. First we have "Knowledge, its use and abuse." All our young readers no doubt have an idea of the value of an education, but you may not know just how to use it rightly. This is very important. There are a great many things that we can obtain that are in themselves very valuable, yet if we do not know how to use them they may be an injury to us, and so it is with education, we may do a great deal of good with it, if we make the right use of it, and a great deal of harm by an improper use of it. Will not then our boys and girls, be interested in learning to know how to make a proper use of their knowledge? You are now no doubt, busily engaged in trying to procure knowledge, & I imagine some of these cold mornings, I can see thousands of boys and girls with books in their arms, wending their way to some school-house. And what for? You all answer to gain knowledge, and many of you are so eager in the pursuit of it, that you will go there through rain and storm. But have you ever thought of how to make use of it? This is just as important a consideration as how to obtain it. We hope then that while you are so busily engaged in the acquisition of knowledge, you will be just as eager to learn how to make a practical use of it in a way that will accomplish the most good. You will then all read our first paper with interest.

Next we have "Usefulness," and this is just what all good boys and girls want to be,—useful. You can not for a moment tolerate the idea of being worthless. But do you all make yourselves as useful as you can? Do you assist father, mother, brothers, sisters and schoolmates whenever you can? We have seen some boys, and girls too, make very ugly faces when their papa or mamma would ask them to help do some work. Now these boys and girls did not want to be worthless, but they were not quite willing to make themselves as useful as they should. You should be willing to assist everybody whenever you can, and by this means you will become the most useful, and this is what you should all desire to be.

Next we have "Unseen yet Loved," and in this is illustrated how we love some one whom we have never seen. We have never seen God, yet he gives us so many things, and is so kind to us every day, that we should surely love him. Our food, raiment, comfortable homes, and every thing that we enjoy is a gift from God. Oh how can we help but love him! We might point out many reasons why we should love God, but we must close our talk with you this time as our printers say they want what we have to say to put it in type.

YOUNG PILGRIM

KNOWLEDGE. ITS USE AND ABUSE.

"What an excellent thing is knowledge!" said a sharp-looking, bustling little man to one who was much older than himself. "Knowledge is an excellent thing," repeated he; "my boys know more at six and seven years of age than I did at twelve. They can read all sorts of books, and talk on all sorts of subjects. This world is a great deal wiser than it used to be. Everybody knows something of everything now. Do you not think, Sir, that knowledge is an excellent thing?"

"Why, sir," replied the old man looking gravely, "that depends entirely upon the use to which it is applied. It may be a blessing or a curse. Knowledge is only an increase of power, and power may be a bad as well as a good thing."

"That is what I cannot understand," said the bustling little man; "how can power be a bad thing?"

"I will tell you," meekly replied the old man, and thus went on: "When the power of a horse is under restraint, the animal is useful, bearing burdens, drawing loads, and carrying his master; but when that power is unrestrained, the horse breaks his bridle, dashes the carriage that he is drawing to pieces, or throws his rider."

"I see! I see!" said the little man.

"When the water of a large pond is properly conducted by trenches, it renders the fields around fertile; but when it bursts through its banks it sweeps everything before it, and destroys the produce of the field."

"I see! I see!" said the little man!"

"When a ship is steered aright, the sail that she hoists up enables her the sooner to get into port; but if steered wrong, the more sail she carries the further she will go out of her course."

"I see! I see!" said the little man, "I see clearly!"

"Well, then," continued the old man, "if you see these things so clearly, I hope you can see too that knowledge, to be a good thing, must be rightly applied. God's grace in the heart will render the knowledge of the head a blessing; but without this it may prove to us no better than a curse."

USEFULNESS.

What is usefulness? I imagine I hear some little one inquiring, as the bright little face suddenly grows thoughtful. I will endeavor to tell you. When we see any of our playmates in need of assistance, can we not lend a helping hand? Our schoolmates may be in trouble in their studies, can we not then offer all the assistance which lies in our power? And would not mamma's heart be lightened to know that the little busy feet that are so willing to run and play, are even more willing to run at mother's bidding? "But I am so little!" still pleads the dear one. I know you are, but although small, you can be useful in many ways.

Rest assured mamma knows better than you how much you can do, and she will not ask you to do anything which it is impossible for you to perform. Then never hesitate when she calls, but leave everything to take care of itself, until the little duties she imposes on you are performed. How much we might lighten her burdens by our little helps, when she is weary with her day's toil; but no one hears her complain. Oh, no! I am afraid we are too apt to think she never tires.

UNSEEN YET LOVED.

A kind mother had once been talking to her little girl about the duty of loving God. The child replied "Mother I have never seen God how can I love Him?" The mother made no reply then. A few days after, she received a package from a friend a great way off; and in the package was a beautiful picture-book for the little girl. The child took the book, and was entirely occupied in looking at the pictures; but soon she exclaimed, "O, Mother! how I do love the good lady that sent me this book!" "But you never saw her, my dear," said the mother. "No" answered the child; "but I love her because she sent me this beautiful present." "My child" said the mother, "you told me the other day that you could not love God, because you had never seen Him. And yet you love this kind lady whom you have never seen, because she has given you a present. Now you have all around you the presents which God has given you. Why cannot you love Him for His presents?"

LITERATURE.

A. B. Brumbaugh, Huntingdon, Pa. Literary Editor.

THE NEWS *versus* PICTURES.—The New York Observer claims to publish the best family newspaper, and repudiates the practice of courting the patronage of readers by the offer of cheap chromos, costing 20 to 30 cents. It says, "We do not propose to go into any competition of this kind, and will ask subscriptions solely on the merits of the paper." While we commend the position the Observer has taken in the matter, we can also heartily endorse it as a most desirable periodical for any household. $3 a year can hardly be made to return as much good, spent in any other way. S. I. PRIME & Co., 37 Park Row, New York.

LARS, *A Pastoral of Norway.* By Bayard Taylor. (James R. Osgood & Co., Boston.) This is a lovely rustic poem, relating the story of Norwegian peasant, who yielding to the custom of his country, fought a duel, then came to Pennsylvania, embraced the faith of the Quakers, and afterward returned to his own country to destroy the custom of duelling. It is a charming poem full of simplicity, dignity, trust, and religious faith. *The Church and State* says, "As a story it is intense and dramatic, abounding in strength of interest; as a lesson, it brings home to the heart truths of profoundest import, with a power that is irresistible. It is a distinctively Christian poem, illustrating in no unworthy manner the influence of simple love and faith."

WE have also from the same house, that wonderful book by H. W. Longfellow entitled CHRISTUS: A *Mystery;* comprising the three volumes, "The Divine Tragedy," "The Golden Legend," and "New England Tragedies" in one. We have a great desire to read these poems, and can assure our readers that they are intensely interesting, but unfortunately the publishers sent us the Diamond edition of the book, and the reading of small type would be suicidal to our eyes. To be had in editions varying in price from $1.00 to $3.50.

NOTHING could be more fitting as a holiday gift than a good and useful book. It is a feast that can be enjoyed every day of the year, and even for many years to come. Old and young share alike in its enjoyment and the benefits resulting therefrom. Many of the leading publishers, in order to meet the great demand for such books, have issued, or are issuing, handsomely executed editions of the most popular works, Poets, &c., finely illustrated. James R. Osgood & Co., of Boston, whose list of holiday books, though not as large as usual, yet abounds in beautiful and valuable works. We called attention to their Red Line Editions of the Poets, &c., a few weeks ago, as being specially suitable for gift-books. Their late work, "CHILD-LIFE IN PROSE," forms a companion to "CHILD-LIFE IN POETRY," published last year, both edited by the poet Whittier. Their books of travel by Warner; "Old Port Days," by Higginson, "Chance Acquaintance," by W. D. Howells; "Whittier's Poems," "Longfellow's Poems," "Snow Bound," "Winter Poems," &c., all beautifully illustrated, form excellent and worthy gift books.

HURD & HOUGHTON, of the Riverside Press, have also just issued several attractive works, which we noticed before, and have nearly ready the "Grammar of Painting and Engraving," and Mrs. Clement's Hand-book of Painter's, Sculptor's, &c. We have from this house a book which was laid on the table among the Christmas presents, last year, entitled BOARDING SCHOOL DAYS, illustrated by Nast & Darly which was pronounced excellent by Gains, for whom it was intended, as well as by all who read it. The book is tastefully bound, characteristically illustrated, and printed in clear, large type so that the reading of it is not an injury to the eyes. And this is a great desideratum in buying a book—that the type be readable. Price $1.50.

THE SCIENCE OF HEALTH for December closes the Third Volume of this practical and independent Magazine. Its leading object is to teach the Science of Life, including all that relates to recovering and Preserving Health, and promoting a higher physical and mental condition. Every family should read this Magazine. Among the contents are "The Potential Sex" in a Review of the Race; "The Model School-Girl, who lost more than she gained, and how," with illustration; "What we want for health, comfort and improvement at this season of the year;" "Woman's Dress," is considered by L. E. L.; "Disease and its Treatment," by different schools; "Conceits of Convalescence;" "Walking as a Medicine," and how to take it; "Occupation as affecting Longevity;" "Seasonable Dishes," on Hygienic principles; "How to go to Bed;" "California Fruits;" "Yellow Fever;" "Cold Feet," and how to keep them warm, and many questions from correspondents are answered, and much general information given. It is published at $2.00 a year. A new volume begins with the next number. Now is the time to subscribe. Address, S. R. WELLS, Publisher, 389 Broadway, New York.

The Weekly Pilgrim.

Published by J. B. Brumbaugh, & Co.

Edited by H. B. & Geo. Brumbaugh.

CORRESPONDING EDITORS.

D. P. Sayler, Double Pipe Creek, Md.

Leonard Furry, New Enterprise, Pa.

The *Pilgrim* is a Christian Periodical, devoted to religion and moral reform. It will advocate in the spirit of *love* and *liberty*, the principles of true Christianity, labor for the promotion of peace among the people of God, for the encouragement of the saints and for the conversion of sinners, avoiding those things which lead toward disunion or sectional feelings.

TERMS.

Single copy, Book paper,	$1.50
Eleven copies, [eleventh for Agt.]	$15.00

Any number above that at the same rate, Address,

H. B. BRUMBAUGH.

James Creek,

Huntingdon county Pa.

The Weekly Pilgrim.

"REMOVE NOT THE ANCIENT LANDMARKS WHICH OUR FATHERS HAVE SET."

VOL. 4. JAMES CREEK, PENNSYLVANIA, DECEMBER 18, 1873. NO. 50

POETRY.

A CHRISTMAS CAROL.

BY ROBERT HERRICK.

Chorus.

What sweeter music can we bring
Than a carol, for to sing
The birth of this our Heavenly King?
Awake the voice! awake the string!
Heart, ear, and eye, and everything
Awake! the while the active finger
Runs division with the finger.

I.

Dark and dull night, fly hence away,
And give the honor to this day,
That sees December turned to May.

II

If we may ask the reason, say
The why, and wherefore all things here
Seem like the spring-time of the year?

III.

Why does the chilling winter's morn
Smile, like a field beset with corn?
Or smell, like a mead new shorn,
Thus, on the sudden?

IV.

Come and see
The cause, why things thus fragrant be:
'T is He is born, whose quickening birth
Gives life and lustre, public mirth,
To Heaven and the under Earth.

Chorus.

We see Him come, and know him ours,
Who with his sunshine and his showers
Turns all the patient ground to flowers.

I.

The darling of the world is come,
And fit it is we find a room
To welcome him.

II.

The nobler part
Of all the house here, is the heart.

Chorus.

Which we will give him, and bequeath
This holly and this ivy wreath,
To do him honor who's our King,
And Lord of all this revelling.

ORIGINAL ESSAYS.

THE THREE FEASTS AND THE BIRTH OF CHRIST.

Three times thou shalt keep a feast unto me in the year.—Ex. 23: 14.

The Jews had to observe a number of feasts besides these, some of which it would appear, were of their own instituting, such as the feast to commemorate the preservation of them from the general massacre projected by Haman. The feast of dedication, which was to commemorate the restoration of the temple, which had been polluted by Antiochus Epiphanes. The feast of branches by which they commemorated the taking of Jericho. The feast of collection on which they made contributions for the services of the temple and synagogue. The feast for the death of Nicanor. The feast for the discovery of the sacred fire, and the feast for carrying wood to the temple. These all appear to be of their own instituting as we find them in the book of Esther, first and second Maccabees, and in the war books of Josephus.

But the feast of the Sabbath which was a weekly feast; the feast of the Sabbathical year, which was a septennial or seventh year feast; the feast of trumpets which was an annual feast; the feast of the new moon which was a monthly feast, and the feast of expiation which was celebrated annually. All these were of divine institution, as we find them in the law given to Moses, and must be observed by divine command. At each of these an offering must be made, and no servile work dare be done on the days of the feast.

In addition to these, the Lord institutes and appoints the keeping of three feasts, to be kept in each year; in which all the males in Israel must take part, and none dare appear before God at their feasts empty. "Three times thou shalt keep a feast unto me in the year. Thou shalt keep the feast of unleavened bread, and the feast of harvest, the first fruits of thy labors which thou hast sown in thy field; and the feast of ingathering which is in the end of the year, when thou hast gathered in thy labors out of the field. Three times in the year all thy males shall appear before the Lord God." "*Old* men, *sick* men, male *idiots* and male *children* under thirteen years of age excepted; for so the Jewish doctors understand this command."—Clark.

The feasts here referred to, are as we have them elsewhere called, first the feast of the passover, instituted (Ex. 12,) and is here called the feast of unleavened bread, because, at this feast, they must eat unleavened bread seven days. The feast of the passover was to be celebrated in commemoration of the wonderful deliverance of the Israelites from the destroying angel which passed over their dwellings when he slew all the first born of the Egyptians, as well as for their deliverance from the house of bondage from under the tyranny of Pharaoh.

2 The feast of weeks called here the feast of harvest, the first fruits of thy labors, called by the Greeks Pentecost.

This feast was celebrated seven weeks after that of the passover, and commenced on the fiftieth day after, and was in commemoration of the giving of the law on Mount Sinai, which took place fifty days after.

The feast of *Tabernacles*, called here *the feast of ingathering.*

This feast was celebrated about the middle of our month September, and was to commemorate the Israelites dwelling in tents for forty years during their stay in the wilderness, See Lev. 23.

"God, out of his great wisdom, says Calmet, appointed several festivals among the Jews, for many reasons: 1 To perpetuate the memory of those great events, and the wonders he has wrought for the people; for example, the *Sabbath* brought to remembrance the *creation* of the world, the *Passover*, the departure out of Egypt, the *Pentecost*, the giving of the law, the Feast of *Tabernacles*, the sojourning of their fathers in the wilderness, &c. 2. To keep them faithful to their religion by appropriate ceremonies, and the splendor of the divine service. 3. To procure their lawful pleasures and necessary rest. 4. To give them instructions, for in their religious assemblies the law of God was always read and explained. 5. To consolidate their social union by renewing the acquaintance of their tribes and families; for, on those occasions, they came together from different parts of the land, to the Holy City."—Clark.

This sounds well, and no doubt has truth in it, but whether we can ever fully understand how so expensive a service, which enjoined so much exemption from labor could be maintained, is doubtful, and well might Peter say, "Now therefore why tempt ye God, to put a yoke upon the neck of the disciples which neither our fathers nor we were able to bear." Acts 5:10. The consumption of hundreds of thousands of the different grades of stock cattle, flocks and herds, with the immense amount of other productions in the use of offerings made by fire, or burnt up, is in itself a problem the Christian world can never solve. And associate with this, the exemption from labor, apparently one half of the time during six years in which they may sow their fields, prune their vineyards, and gather in the fruits thereof; however in part only, for "When ye reap the harvest of your land, there thou shalt not make clean riddance of the corners of thy field where thou reapest, neither shalt thou do any gleaning of thy harvest; thou shalt leave them unto the poor, and to the stranger." The same was required of them in their fruit culture. "But in the seventh year shall be a Sabbath of rest unto the land, a Sabbath for the Lord: thou shalt neither sow thy field nor prune thy vineyard. That which groweth of its own accord of thy harvest thou shalt not reap, neither gather the grapes of thy vine undressed, for it is a year of rest unto the land."—Lev. 25.

The whole of this great mystery may however be understood in this one short sentence, "I am the Lord your God."

God evidently designs the Christian world, with his Church in it, to know, that whatever the faithful observing of his law may cost, he will, in his own way and manner, provide all the necessary means to defray the cost. I have wondered if we were as liberal with his gifts in his services as we ought to be, whether parching droughts, disastrous floods, devouring fires, the ravages of fly and joint worm, rust, blast and mildew in wheat, with enormous doctor bills consequent on sickness &c., would not, to a great extent, be averted, and in the end have even more of the world's goods, though we used much for the Lord, than we so have with all our grasping and hoarding.

It is no uncommon thing for brethren, when called upon to aid in charitable and church wants, to excuse themselves on the ground of short crops, and heavy doctor bills. Let these inquire for a reason why these things are so with them. The reader will please pardon this necessary digression, and I will return to consider the three feasts the Lord enjoined upon his people to keep yearly.

As already observed, the feast of

the passover, which according to our months fall in March and April, and is by us called Easter, was celebrated to keep in remembrance the wonderful deliverance from Egypt, and it was at this feast the Pascal lamb must be killed and eaten as directed in Ex. 12. At the preparation of this feast our Lord was crucified. Seven weeks after this, comes the feast *of harvest or weeks*; called by us *Whitsuntide Pentecost*, and falls in our months May or June. At this feast they must offer their first fruits of the harvest. This feast was celebrated fifty days after the passover, in commemoration of the giving the law on mount Sinai, which took place fifty days after the passover. It was at this feast that the Holy Ghost was shed forth on the assembled disciples in Jerusalem. And the feast of Tabernacles, called also the feast of Ingathering, was celebrated on the 15th day of their month *Tisri*, our September and was to commemorate the Israelites dwelling in tents in the wilderness forty years. On the first day of this feast they must build themselves booths. "And ye shall take you, on the first day, the boughs of goodly trees, branches of palm trees, and the boughs of thick trees, and willows of the brook; and ye shall rejoice before the Lord your God, seven days." Lev. 23: 40, 43.

Now the question is, what occurred at this feast to connect, or associate it with the new, or Christian dispensation? We have already seen that it was at the time of the passover, our Easter, that our Lord was crucified; and at the feast of *Weeks* or *Harvest*, our *Whitsuntide*, the Holy Ghost was shed forth on the assembled disciples. But what occurred at this feast of *Tabernacles*? It was instituted by the same God and was to be kept and observed by the same people, and that too, by all Israel, with the same solemnity as any of the others were kept. It cannot be presumed that it was not intended to stand in connection with an event in the christian dispensation of as much importance as either of the others. I have a theory which fully satisfies my mind, though my proof is presumptive and not direct. I hold that at this feast our Lord was born. At this feast Israel must dwell in booths, and rejoice before the Lord God seven days; and the Savior was born, and laid in a manger, and at his birth, both men and angels rejoiced, before God, singing glory to God in the Highest, on earth, peace, good will toward man. And it was the 15th day of September the early Christians observed as Christ's birth day, till the Latin or Romish church who held herself *supreme* in power, and infallible in judgement, fixed it on the 25th day of December. Good reasons can be given why Christ was not born in December. Because there were in the same country, shepherds abiding in the field, keeping watch by night. "It was a custom among the Jews" (says Clark) "to send out their sheep to the deserts, about the passover, and bring them home at the commencement of the first rain. During the time they were out the shepherds watched them night and day. As the passover occurred in the Spring and the first rain began early in the month, which answers to part of our October and November, we find that the sheep were kept out in the open country during the whole of the summer. And as these shepherds had not yet brought in their flocks, it is a presumptive argument that October had not yet commenced, and that consequently, our Lord was not born on the 25th of December, when no flocks were out in the fields, nor could he have been born later than September, as the flocks were still in the fields by night. On this very ground the nativity in December should be given up. The feeding of the flocks by night in the fields is a chronological fact which casts considerable light upon this disputed point."

My theory is, that at the feast of Tabernacles which commenced on the 15th of our September, at which all Israel must rejoice before God seven days, our Lord was born, at whose birth, men and angels rejoiced before God. And at the feast of the passover, which falls in our months March and April, at which the Paschal lamb must be killed, our Lord was crucified. And at the feast of Harvest or Weeks, which falls in our May and June, at which the first fruits must be offered; at this feast our Lord shed or poured his spirit upon the disciples, which was the first fruits of the Gospel.

D. P. SAYLER.

TIME FLIES. O HOW SWIFTLY!

When we reflect on the time when we entered the year 1873, it seems unto us only a short space, yet many important events mark that period. Changes and vicissitudes almost unnumbered characterizes the year we are now at the eve of closing. O, that these changes only had been for the better, no unpleasant feeling could mar our existence, no gloomy reflecting to cause compunctions of conscience. But weak as our efforts were in doing good, in comparison to what they should have been, causes us to regret that we gave way so much to the weakness and imperfections of the flesh. Naught but the grace and spirit of God can remedy this defect, and just here we find where we are in the fault. Our prayers were either neglected or cold and formal. Let us then have faith in a sin-pardoning God. O, let us come before him in the name of the Great High-Priest and advocate, Jesus Christ in humble submission and with a penitent heart, and acknowledge our sins, our short-comings and negligences, and with uprightness and fervency of mind, soul and spirit, ask him for pardon, strength and power from on high, and that "a double portion of His spirit may fall upon us in order that we may redeem our mis-spent time the coming year, and that grace sufficient may be imparted unto us to regain in that which we have lost in the working out of our soul's salvation.

Brethren and sisters, let us heed this resolve and solemnly reflect that time flies swiftly, and no one knows who will be the next one that will have to exchange time for eternity. Many who bid fair for a long life in the commencement of 1873 are gone the way of all flesh. Where are they now? Echo saith, Where? They have gone to their long homes to reap the reward of their labors according to that which they have done, whether good or evil. Grand-fathers, grand mothers, called from their children and grand-children, though full of years and perfectly satisfied with the ills of life, have caused an aching void in the family household, and forever silenced the sweet conversation passing between them. Fathers and mothers, through the icy hand of the grim monster, death, have been snatched from their dear offspring, leaving a vacancy which this world never can fill, spreading gloom and sorrow, loneliness and mourning around their fireside. Husbands, severed from their wives, wives from their husbands, thus snapping asunder the nearest tie of relationship that can exist on earth, being of one flesh and one bone. Oh! how many deep wounds it has caused to penetrate the dwelling deserted of the one so indispensible for the sweet association, the counsel, the sustenance, the consolation, the aid and support of the family household. Sons and daughters had to leave their parents, the brother his sister, the sister her brother, and so beyond visible association; the closest ties of consanguinity torn asunder, never more on earth to meet. God in his all wise providence thus deals with us as his rational creatures in order to profit thereby, and to bring us nearer to him as our benefactor, protector, and eternal preserver. Have we ever thought of these things? Did the special call of God, by the removal of our most loved associates, pierce our hearts to the forsaking of sin and following after holiness without which no man can see the Lord.

Sinner where are you at the close of this year? Are you still serving sin and satan, the lust of the flesh, the lust of the eye, and the pride of life? Had you not promised God to serve him at the close of last year or at the beginning of this year when you saw that young lady, who a few days before stood in blooming health and gay attire, sinking down to the gloomy grave? Did not your heart faint when that young man, without a moments warning, was ushered into eternity with his brains reeling from intoxicating drink and curses on his lips? Had you not then promised to devote yourself to God, and enter into His service, else you might meet with the same dreadful fate? Where are you now? Are you in the service of the Lord, or still trifling with your God and rejecting the many solemn and special calls? When your sister, or brother or father, or mother laid in the throes of death, raising their hands to heaven and wrestled in fervent prayer to God in behalf of your conversion, did you see them? And do you know that your ministers, the holy watchmen of Zion, incessantly pray to God in behalf of you? Can not, I ask in the name of God, the intercessions of your father, mother, brother, sister, on their dying bed with the united prayers of the Church with their ministers move you and make a lasting impression upon your undying soul, to forsake sin, turn to God with a heart felt repentance, and accept Christ's means of salvation? Young man, young woman, I appeal to you again. Where is now your delight by this time at the close of the year, your engagements? Is it in the service of God, or in the giddy ball room, the gambling hell, or the hell of hells where the inebriate linger and handle the intoxicating bowl around to the full measure of their iniquity? If so, I must say good-by to you. Go on in your mirth, indulge in your folly, "let your heart cheer thee in the days of thy youth, and walk in the ways of thine heart, and in the sight of thine eyes; but know thou for all these things God will bring thee into judgment." Though you may be an abandoned wretch, yet will I not cease to intercede for you, for perhaps God may bring you to repentance the coming year. Brethren and sisters, let us serve God more faithful the coming year than ever. Amen.

LEONARD FURRY.

THERE ARE TWO SIDES TO THIS QUESTION.

The 49th number of the *Christian Standard* is now before me, and contains the following query and answer.

"It is well known that the trine immersionists (Tunkards) believe that faith, repentance, confession, and baptism, are essential to salvation from sin. They baptize for the remission of sins, believing baptism is essential to pardon. Now, then, in case a person has been thus baptized, and afterwards desires to unite with the Christian Church, can he be received upon his baptism, pleading that it was for the remission of sins? Is it therefore valid?"

Answer. "Our opinion is that it ought to be recognized as valid, not because it was administered for the remission of sins—for sprinkling might be administered for the same purpose—but because it is immersion into the name of the Father, and of the Son, and of the Holy Spirit."

Mr. Errett, the editor of the above named paper is a member of what is generally known as the Campbellite Church, though called by themselves the Christian Church. He is a man of more than ordinary ability, and his answer to this query is likely the general sentiment of that body of people. Though the answer is correct, yet at the same time it is very inconsistent with his practice. Mr. Errett uses *backward single immersion*. This he believes to be scriptural baptism, and if correct, then of course *forward trine immersion* is not. The New Testament authorizes but one method, and that alone. Then Mr. Errett's answer certainly would be that *forward trine immersion* is not a scriptural baptism, but he has said that it is valid, now then I want to know where Mr. Errett gets his authority for calling a thing valid which he claims is not taught in the law of Christ. No baptism can be valid unless it is taught in the Testament, Mr. Errett has conceded that trine immersion is valid, hence it is taught in the New Testament. Either it is taught in the law or else Mr. Everett's answer is wrong, there is no middle ground about the matter. But this is the way the thing generally runs. All the leading denominations in christendom are willing to acknowledge that this "general practice of all antiquity" is valid, about this there don't seem to be any doubt. All the doubt in the whole matter is about backward single immersion. It is a well known fact that Mr. Errett's Church has acknowledged that trine immersion is valid, and then turn right round and say it is not taught in the Word. I have puzzled many by asking them for their authority for calling a thing valid that is not taught by Christ, now then let Mr. Errett answer this question.

The Baptists dare not say that forward trine immersion is not valid, for I can prove that used to be their general practice, according to their own books, and if the matter is denied I have the documents in my library to sustain the position beyond question. They aim to trace their Church to the apostles, and yet it is done upon the royal highway of trine immersion. The Methodists dare not repudiate the method, as that, at one time, was John Wesley's preference, and more than that, like the Campbellites, they receive trine immersion into their fellowship and have been known to thus baptize.

The Church of England dare not reject this method, as she at one time would consent to practice no other. Some of her first kings and queens were thus immersed, but she finally laid aside this for sprinkling and pouring. The Roman Catholic Church, with her ancient power and bloody renown, cannot question the validity of this primitive method, as it was her general practice till after the year A. D. 633. At this time the fourth council of Toledo authorized a change from trine to single immersion. It may be worthy of note that this was the first authority ever issued in favor of single immersion.

The Greek and Oriental Churches from the days of the apostles to the present time have continued the general use of trine immersion. With some of the unlearned, the question is, what was the apostolic method? But not so with these Oriental Churches. They were well versed in the Greek language, and all acknowledge that the commission teaches a three-fold immersion, not one of them whose productions have come under my notice say that it teaches single immersion. I presume that Mr. Errett is aware that his backward action in baptism is a human invention, and cannot be traced beyond its origin in the year A. D. 1522. If he can trace it beyond this period, he will now have a chance to do so. I would be pleased to have him try his skill on this point. The idea that the Lord would command a man to come into the church backwards is out of the question. Furthermore, his single immersion was invented by Eunomius in the latter part of the fourth century, and never came into general use till after the 15th.

If Mr. Errett can find single immersion, as a practice, beyond the fourth century, he will do what others have failed to do so far. Of course it must be understood that his authors should have lived at the time that they testify of. When I prove that trine immersion was used in the 2d, 3d, and 4th centuries, I do so by referring to authors who lived and wrote in these centuries. The commission given by Christ, and recorded by (Matt. 28: 19), teaches a three fold immersion; this is affirmed by all ancient Greek scholars who have written on the subject. To this method Paul alludes when he says, "One baptism." All persons admit that trine immersion fills all the grammatical import of the commission, about this there is no doubt, all the trouble is getting single immersion to do the work, we know this three-fold method is right, and is good, hence we will hold fast to it.

J. H. MOORE.

FINISH THY WORK.

The one great difference between God and man, is that *He* has left nothing incomplete, while man labors well for a time, but neglects to gather up and utilize the odds and ends, and thus much of his work goes to waste, or in other words, is **unfinished.**

When God at creations dawning, brought together and combined the elements of a new world, there was nothing imperfect; the stars that shine above us, the trees that wave answer back to Heaven, the flowers, the sweetest thought of the Creator, the grass that clothes the earth in beauty, the cattle on a thousand hills, the merry laughing sparkling water, the rainbow's perfect arch, born of the falling spray, the cloud that catches its golden tint from the sun's last setting ray, each and every one proclaim the work of the Creator finished and sublime. Since the dawn of Creation, nothing has been added, nothing detracted from the completeness of that stupendous perfect work from a perfect hand.

The Christian system! How grand in its sweet simplicity! None but an Infinite God, could have perfected and wrought out such a plan for the redemption of man. The years of sorrow, the night of agony, the death on the Cross ended in the words, "*It is finished.*" The great work is done, the mighty Exampler has triumphed over Death and the Grave, and opened up a way of truth, of holiness. Henceforth, man must take up the burden and go forth, scattering precious seed, working while it is called to-day, lest the night cometh upon his half sown field, and the Lord blame that unworthy servant, who waited for another to do his work. Could we but gain the attention of the whole mass of mankind, and make them sensible of the time they are losing in the worlds great harvest, by loitering at an unfinished task, or by idly doing the Lords behest! Consider the fate of him who hid his Master's talent and take heed that a like fate does not befall you. Each and every one of you have your appointed work in the world, and woe be unto you if you neglect it. It is not for me to tell my neighbor, thus and so, thou shalt do, for in appointing the work of others we but condemn ourselves, judging as we will be judged. Do then the work nearest to you whatever that may be, leave no stone unturned, watch always, work unceasingly, pray ever, and the Master will surely approve thy earnest endeavors. Leave not till the morrow the work your hand should do to-day, the morrow may never be yours, you may say Oh! that I had my life to live over again, how differently would the record be kept! Remember the soul readily takes impressions from outside circumstances, and unless each hour, you each moment is full, Satan will find some mischief for the idle moment, and the beautiful pattern of a perfect work will be marred by a stray or sinful thought. "Ah this life to toil is given" and the tempter ever stands ready to ask a willing service for himself, and oft times, ere we are aware, the work we had determined for Jesus is perverted, and our feet have gone in the way of the ungodly. Whatever thy hand finds to do, do with thy might, putting thy hand resolutely to the plow, and working faithfully till the evening shades fall; then, and not until then, must the work be laid aside, and the weary footsteps turned homeward, seeking the promised rest. Then

"*Finish thy work*; the time is short,
The sun is in the West;
The night is coming down, 'till then
Think not of rest.

Finish thy work; then wipe thy brow,
Ungird thee from thy toil;
Take breath, and from each weary limb
Shake off the soil.

Finish thy work; then go in peace,
Life's battle fought and won;
Hear from the throne the Master's voice,
"Well done, well done!"

LAURA H. MILLER.

West Va.

THE DEFENSE OF DON GRASSI.

The following is the closing part of Don Grassi's, a late convert from Catholic priestism, defense before the Inquisition of Rome. A few years ago, to stand where he stood, and say what he said, would have been to forever bid fare well to the land of the living and take an abode in some dungeon or prison cell, but things in ancient Rome, have changed and the dreaded Inquisition has lost its power as the following plainly shows:

"O you Inquisitors, Pontiffs, Cardinals and prelates; God speaks to you! To what have you brought the true church? She was so pure so beautiful, so glorious, you have betrayed, violated, despoiled, wounded and crucified by your doctrines, superstitions and immorality, and sealed her tomb by your blasphemous 'Dogma of infallibility.' Hear what God says to his suffering children. The God of peace shall bruise Satan under your feet shortly. Do you tremble at these words? Who but Satan instigated and inflicted the tortures of this place? O could these walls within which so many have been burned, speak—could this roof but echo back the cries of agony from your innocent victims, and the vaults beneath us reveal the corpses of those who have been buried alive, no other sentence of condemnation would be required.

But the breath of the Lord has forever extinguished the fires of the Inquisition, and swept away your power; therefore I stand before you to-day and declare these truths, while you dare not touch a hair in my head! Yes God has begun the work and soon this tribunal, these walls and instruments will be bruised under our feet, and scattered as ashes to the four winds, proclaiming to the world that the 'Most Holy Universal Roman Inquisition is dead. Dead because God has crushed it under the feet of His children.

O ye obstinate ones hear me! Hear one of your own brothers who has said mass, and confessed, and preached with you. I am not dead but living and announce the resurrection of that Church which you have tried to drown in blood. Yes she is rising glorious as the morning light and ignorance, superstition, heresy and tyranny flee before her!

"Farewell, church of my youth! Farewell companions of my ministry! alas! alas it has been a ministry of destruction! O if my word has yet any weight with you, I beseech you to open your eyes to the light—to abandon that system of darkness in which you are groping, and accept the true light which Jesus offers you.

SUNDAY SCHOOL REPORT.

The Spring Run Sunday School of the German Baptist Church near McVeytown, Mifflin Co., Pa., opened its 5th session the first Lord's day in May, and closed Sabbath Nov., 23 with a nearly full attendance. Upwards of 125 pupils have attended during the present session.

The books used in our S. S, were the *New Testament*, by all who could read it, and the Union Spelling Book by the ones unable to do so. No Library books were used, although we have a S. S. Library, published by the American Baptist Society, Philada. Hymns, some such as are found in the Brethrens New Hymn Book, were printed on canvass and hung where the audience can see them and join in singing.

The Male pupils committed 2181 verses.

" Female, " " 6411.
" Total, " " 8592,

These were all Scripture except by those who could not read in the scriptures.

The School has done well under the principalship of of our deacon brother Reuben T. Myers, assisted by brethren Jas. S. Hanawalt and Solomon W. Bollinger. all of which were elected by ballot by the Church at a Council meeting in March previous.

On the first day of S. S, the principal appointed sister Eva E. Kinsel Female Supt, and Bro. M. F. H. Kinsel Secty, and Tr. The above corps of officers' assisted by pupils who wished to help make a choice, then procured suitable teachers for the different classes, nearly all of which are members.

Two sisters were appointed to take a subscription to buy rewards and prizes for the last day of school, and $16,00 were paid, and about $10,00 expended for Bibles, Testaments and Scripture cards as prizes for verses committed, and to redeem the tickets.

Now we give the work into God's hands, and hope by his blessing that at least a *little* good may have been done, through the Holy Jesus.

S. W. Bollinger.

Despise not prophesyings.

The Weekly Pilgrim.

JAMES CREEK, PA., Dec. 18, 1873.

☞ How to send money.—All sums over $1.50, should be sent either in a check, draft or postal order. If neither of these can be obtained, have the letter registered.

☞ When Money is sent, *always* send with it the name and address of those who paid it. Write the names and post office as plainly as possible.

☞ Every subscriber for 1874, gets a *Pilgrim Almanac* FREE.

Our agents will please take notice that wherever it is at all convenient, we would prefer to send the Almanacs directly to them, and they distribute them among their subscribers. By so doing all subscribers will be sure to get them. We will gladly furnish our agents with as many as they can use, or need for their subscribers, but want it understood that they are intended for subscribers only and that we have none for sale. They cost us money, therefore we cannot afford to give them to any but actual subscribers. In cases where it is not convenient for our agents to supply their subscribers with Almanacs, we will send directly to them when so ordered. In sending lists where part have Almanacs and part have not, it should be so marked on the list. Please remember this.

Eld. D. P. Saylor.—You appear to be grieved at the blunders in your article in the *Pilgrim Almanac*, but we suppose not more so than ourselves as we are exceedingly sorry that there are so many typographical and other errors in it, but we wish all to know that we are not accountable for them as we had it published away from home, and had not the opportunity of reading the proof, therefore had no control of the work, nor were we aware of the errors until the Almanac was published. We gave the publisher a scolding about it but that does not change the errors—it may help the publisher. To screen Bro. Saylor from such uncalled for blunders, and make his record intelligible, we will give his corrections in next number.

OUR CHANGE OF ADDRESS.

After this date our address will be changed from James Creek to Huntingdon, Pa. This is the last number we expect to publish at James Creek. By the time No. 1, for 1874 appears, we expect to be at our new office at Huntingdon, which is now about ready for us. Of our change in location we will say something in a future number. While we expect it to be of some advantage to us, we feel assured that it will be more to our patrons, as the place affords as good mail facilities as could be found in the United States outside of our large cities. Direct all letters, books, &c., to Box 172, Huntingdon, Pa.

MORE AGENTS WANTED.

We want a live, active agent in every Church district of the brotherhood. Who will volunteer? We will gladly furnish all those who may have a desire to labor for us, with an outfit. It is with our agents that our success mainly depends, therefore we hope that all will leave no effort unmade. If by oversight we have missed sending prospectus and Almanac to any who have been laboring for us, we hope they will inform us of it, and we will supply at once. Go to work at once, and send us all the names you possibly can, so that we can get our books in shape to commence the New Year. The money can be gathered and sent afterwards. Accept all such that you think will pay during the year. We try to be as liberal and as accommodating as possible, so that there can be no reasonable excuse for not subscribing. This kind of liberality would not do well among worldly people, but with our brethren and sisters, we should feel safe in trusting to their honesty.

THE PILGRIM ENLARGED.

We have already received our material for enlarging the Pilgrim for 1874, and our readers can look for a little the largest paper ever published by the brotherhood and that without enlarging the price. We hope to have No. 1 for 1874 ready so that it may reach our readers by the first of the year or soon after. All those who desire No. 1 as soon as issued, should send in their names at once. It promises to be a number of more than usual interest. "An address to our Patrons," a poem of thirty stanzas will lead, on the first page. This alone will be a rich treat, especially to such as admire poetry. Then will follow, "Thoughts on the close of the Old, and beginning of the New Year," by Eld. D. P. Sayler. "Pride and Prudence a Soliloquy," by Eld. J. S. Flory, "These Three," by Eld. C. C. Root, and many other articles that we have not now, before us, with the usual amount of Editorial, Correspondence, Church News, &c. Our enlarged form will give an additional space for reading so that our patrons can feel assured that they will get the worth of their money for 1874 if we are spared to carry out our present plans. The arrangements we have made, and are now making, will enable us to publish a paper of unusual interest and usefulness.

Our brethren have given us a number of valuable suggestions which will be incorporated with improvements that have been suggested to our own minds. If in the multiplicity of counsellors there is wisdom, the Pilgrim ought to be made better by such additional aid and talent. Our object shall be the same as heretofore. The salvation of souls should be the great theme of thought and action. For this, have we launched our bark, and shall endeavor, weekly, to set forth such inducements as may tempt the careless and wayward sinner to take passage with us, so that by the time we reach the desired haven, many may have embarked with us. Not only shall we labor for the conversion of sinners, but also for the peace and good of our beloved Zion, and for the vindication of the "ancient landmarks" so plainly described in the New Testament Scriptures.

Our enlargement will be attended with considerable additional cost of paper, also of composition. This we cannot well afford unless our list is also enlarged. We therefore hope all our readers will be concerned in our behalf and make an effort to largely increase our list of subscribers. There was a call for a larger paper and we have responded, and it now remains for you dear reader, to show your appreciation by giving us such aid as may enable us to carry out our improvements without doing injustice to ourselves.

THE TIME OF THE END.

At the time of the end—the wise shall understand.—Daniel.

Among the wise things that the wise man said is, "There is a time for all things under the sun," a time to begin and a time to end. The time to begin the fourth volume of the Pilgrim is long since past and now "the time of the end has come" and it is said at that time, "the wise shall understand." Giving this a general application, and we have no truer saying. It is true, many wise men have a tolerable understanding of things at the beginning, but at the time of the end all mists of doubts and darkness are blown away and the past with all its hopes, and fears, are laid open before us in its stern realities and we can, thus understand things which, in the beginning were enshrouded in mysteries dark and deep.

Whether we are among the wise or not, is not in our province to say, but this we know, that during the year that is nearly past, we have learned to understand many things that we never understood before. From these things we ought, and hope to profit and we have no doubt but what many of you have been equally fortunate. If so, "the time of the end will be an epoch of general profit."

"The time of the end" is not important only, as closing the fourth volume of the Pilgrim, but it is big with importance to us all as individuals, and calls loudly upon us not only to act wisely but righteously, as there is a "time of the end," in which all shall understand, the ungodly and the sinner, as well as the righteous. The former then, shall only fully comprehend the loss they have sustained in squandering it in gratifying their sinful lust, while the righteous shall fully realize the truth of the saying, "it is no vain thing to serve the Lord."

Time is reckoned by divisions and epochs. A year is one of the most important divisions, as during this space of time, all nature seems to form a complete revolution. Three score and ten of these divisions are allowed as an average of human strength, but we have learned by experience, that thousands never reach this allotted time, and that during any year "the time of the end" may come with us, it therefore behooves us as wise men and women, to consider the number of our days so that the end comes not upon us unawares.

In looking over our obituary notices that were recorded in the present volume, we find that "the time of the end has come" to many, and it now remains for them to understand. If they have entered the kingdom by being born again, and have walked in all the ordinances of the Lord's house blameless, they shall now understand and realize those things which eye hath not seen, ear hath not heard, neither hath entered into the heart of man. But those who have been unwilling to take God at his word shall realize the full force of what Christ meant when He said, "If ye know these things, happy are ye if ye do them." It becomes us, as true and humble servants, to obey God in all things though we cannot, now, fully comprehend the design, in every case, in the time of the end, the wise shall understand, and those only are wise who obey God, as the conclusion of the whole matter is summed up thus, "Fear God and keep His commands for this is the whole duty of man."

The "time of the end" is especially interesting with us, because with it ends, for the present, our obligations to our thousands of readers whom we have been visiting, weekly, during the year that is now closing. Our sojourning together was so pleasant and agreeable that we feel loathe to leave you or discontinue our visits to your homes, but the time of the end has come, and unless invited back again for 1874, this will be our last visit. We have endeavored with all our ability, to make our visits entertaining and instructive, and we feel persuaded from the many expressions of approval and encouragement, that we have not been altogether unsuccessful, that our labors for the Lord have not been in vain. Many have already renewed their invitations by sending in their names for 1874. Some of our lists received have been considerably enlarged by new names. This is quite encouraging, and we hope our agents may be equally successful, so that when the time of the end fully comes, we may have the pleasure of receiving, not only all our old patrons, but many new ones also.

OUR TRIP TO THE SNAKE SPRING CHURCH.

On Saturday morning we left our Office for the purpose of meeting an engagement we had made with Bro. Henry Harshberger to accompany him to the Clear Ridge Settlement, for the purpose of filling some appointments at that place. By making a little extra effort, we were enabled to reach the train just in time to hear our gentlemanly Conductor say, "all aboard," and off we went. Having the late number of the PILGRIM along, we were busily engaged in perusing its pages, forgetting all about high bridges and the danger of toppling over, until disturbed by several talkative gentlemen who were holding a private and confidential conversation in such loud tones, that all within a reasonable distance, could not fail to hear it. We could not see the point, unless they feared that they could not otherwise command observation.

After a pleasant ride, we landed at Mt Dallas Station where, in a short time, we were met by brother Harshberger, who gave us a seat in his buggy, and we started for Clear Ridge. The weather was unusually pleasant and the roads quite good, so that we enjoyed the ride very much, and as we had never traveled in that direction, the sights were all new and interesting. This is especially so when we get into a mountainous country. Our road passed along on top of Clear Ridge, which is sufficiently elevated to afford a view of all the intervening hills between Tussy's and Terrace mountains, which are not a few. In looking over them it reminded us of the remarks of a sister from the West. She said if every other hill of Pennsylvania was turned up side down, she thought it would make a level country. There would be considerable truth in her remarks, providing the hills after being turned could undergo a little shaking together. By one o'clock we reached brother Isaac Ritchey's where we were expected, and a good dinner awaiting our arrival. Brother and sister Ritchey received us kindly and spared no efforts to make us comfortable. Though they reside among the hills, they have plenty to eat and know how to prepare it. After remaining here a short time, Bro. Harshberger informed us that he had made arrangements to take supper with a friend Weimer, some three or four miles farther, so we took leave of our brother and sister, and by sundown we reached our place of destination which was one mile beyond where we were to preach. On our arrival, we were kindly received, and the best they had was not spared to make us feel homelike. After partaking of their hospitality, we were taken to the place for preaching. The house was well filled with attentive listeners, to whom we tried to preach. We do not know how much good was accomplished, but we were somewhat consoled, on hearing several say the sermon was too short. When ministers do not have much to say, the better policy is to stop when they get done. Unfortunately, some do not do this, and the result is, that sermon was too long.

After preaching we again returned to friend Weimer's for the night. If any of our readers have ever learned to enjoy sitting around a blazing fire in the old fashioned chimney, they can have an idea how we spent part of the evening. Friend Weimer worships after the Lutheran mode, but says he is not partial to any form of worship that is anything like right. This we thought rather liberal, but as we were not the spokesman at the time, we allowed it to pass. The man is a good liberal hearted soul, but has not read the Scriptures sufficiently to know that he is responsible to God, and not Lutheranism, Weslyanism or any other ism. Their hospitality was praiseworthy, and we hope they may not lose their reward.

Sunday 10 a. m., there was an appointment in the Clearville Union Church, which we attended and filled. The congregation was not large but quiet and attentive. It may seem strange to some that we talk about congregations being quiet, as it is supposed that all congregations ought to be quiet but this is not always the case, especially when we get out among the hills, away from rail roads telegraphs and schools. While gone we were informed that during a Methodist revival, several young men were thought to take undue liberties during the services. The minister in charge, undertook to teach them better morals by grasping one by the throat and thrusting him out of the house, but such proceedings met with opposition and would have resulted in a regular combat had they not been separated. The minister prosecuted the young man for resisting, and the father of the young man prosecuted the minister for striking his son. There will be a lawsuit in Bedford during next court. So much for modern religion.

After services, we went home with brother John Smith. Brother Smith formerly resided in the Clover Creek congregation, Blair Co., Pa., but has now set his stakes among the hills, where he owns a fine farm and has pleasant surroundings. Sister Smith cared for our bodily wants and sent us away with the consciousness that the laborer is worthy of his meat. From here, brother Harshberger took us to his home, where as usual, we met a welcome reception, and felt rejoiced to enter again the family circle in which we spent a number of pleasant seasons. Everything seemed natural except that sister Fannie was not there. She has cast her lot in another home which to her may be a happier one, if possible, than the one she has left. In the evening there was an appointment in the Meeting-house where we had a good attendance and attention. The congregation was largely of young persons, many of whom are risking their all by remaining outside of the kingdom. We hope the time may soon come when they too will cast their lot with the people of God and labor for His cause.

On our way to church, we called to see Eld. Andrew Snowberger. He has been ailing for some time and the greater part of his time, confined to his house. On Monday morning we were conveyed to the train and in two hours, arrived safely home. Though our trip was short yet it was pleasant, and we hope, profitable. Paul may plant, Apollos may water but God must give the increase.

CHRIST'S YOKE.

"Take my yoke upon you and learn of me; for I am meek and lowly in heart, and you shall find rest to your souls."

In this language of the Savior, we have a very striking illustration of the truth he wished to teach by a metaphor. This was the way in which Christ presented the truth He taught so forcibly and intelligibly, and when we take into consideration this one, we may learn some very beautiful and useful lessons. Let us then turn our attention for awhile to the truths contained in it:

In the days of our Savior's sojourn on earth, the ox was employed to perform the labor that the horse now does, and instead of the harness that is now used to attach the horse to a plow or vehicle of any kind, the yoke was used. The yoke was put on the ox's neck, and this of course could be done only by his resignation or submission to his master. No man could put a yoke on the neck of an ox if he should have any disposition to avoid it. His strength is sufficient to successfully resist any demand that men may make of him, hence it requires a perfect resignation in order that he may be equipped for the performance of labor.

In this we have presented the idea of our resignation to the will of God. We are called to labor in His Vineyard, but in order that we be properly equipped for the labor, we must suffer His yoke to be put upon us. This requires an entire resignation to the will of God. We have the power to resist the yoke of Christ; He does not compel us to take it upon us, but this is the design of God in reference to us, and if we refuse to be subject to His will, we are under His displeasure. Christ while here on earth, taught this entire resignation by the things which He did. For example on one occasion when He drew nigh to Jerusalem, He sent two of His disciples, "saying unto them, Go into the village over against you, and straightway ye shall find an ass tied, and a colt with her: loose them and bring them unto me. And if any man say ought unto you, say the Lord hath need of them." The disciples who were sent for the ass were no doubt entire strangers, and for them to unloose the ass and take him, would seem like unwarrented authority, but Jesus expected all who might interfere, to be satisfied, and submit to their demand by merely saying the "Lord hath need of them." In this act then, we have an example of what He expected when He made a demand, and in the metaphor under consideration designs to teach an entire resignation or submission to His will.

When the ox has submitted to the yoke being placed upon his neck, then it is that he is prepared to labor, and then too, does he expect to be directed and guided by his master. When he is told to go forward, or to the right or left, he is obedient. So it should be with us when we take the yoke of Christ upon us. We must expect to be guided by our Master: we must be willing to go anywhere He may tell us, even though we may not fully understand "whys" and "wherefores." Just as man's knowledge is superior to that of the ox, so is God's knowledge superior to ours. His ways are above our ways, and His thoughts above our thoughts, and therefore it becomes us to render implicit obedience, without inquiring what may be His design. We know by being obedient we will meet His approbation, and when we have the favor and friendship of our Master, then it is that we are happy; we know that we have a right, a title to the mansions above. "Blessed are they that do the commandments that they may have a right to the tree of life and enter in through the gates into the city." Let us then learn from the metaphor a lesson of obedience.

We have also in it the idea of self-denial. While the ox is doing the bidding of his master, there are many things surrounding him that have a tendency to lure him away from his work. For example it would be more agreeable to feast on the beautiful grass by which he is surrounded, or if laboring in the heat of the day it would be more pleasant under the shade of some tree. But the obedient ox must deny himself of what he might enjoy. So must the Christian. When he takes the yoke upon him and becomes obedient unto his Master, he must deny himself of the many things by which he is surrounded. Jesus said unto His disciples, "If any man will come after me, let him deny himself, and take up his cross and follow me." There are many things that attract our attention when we try to perform our Christian duties. The world has many inducements, and if we do not deny ourselves, we are soon found reveling in the fields of sin and folly. How many there are who have taken the yoke upon them, that instead of following Jesus in the path of duty, and complying with His commands, follow their own carnal inclinations. In this it is to be feared thousands make the fatal error. They want to serve God and the world also, but saith Jesus, "No man can serve two masters; for either he will hate the one and love the other, or else he will hold to the one and despise the other." The demands of this world and those of Jesus are directly contrary to each other, and it is impossible for us to meet the demands of both. Therefore if we would be the disciples of Jesus, we must be indifferent to the demands of this world, however congenial they may be to our natures. We must deny ourselves of the transient enjoyments of this life, and not run into the excesses that must finally prove our ruin. The yoke of Christ will restrain us from these things and keep us in obedience to our Divine Master.

We have also in the yoke of Christ the idea of Christian effort. When the ox is yoked he expects to labor, it presents to him the idea of work. When he sees the yoke he no doubt thinks of pulling a wagon or ploughing, and so should the yoke of Christ associate to our minds the idea of labor. We cannot expect to be idle, as the Christian life is one of activity and untiring perseverence. It is one that requires the exertion of all our powers. "Thou shalt love the Lord with all thy heart, and with all thy soul, and with all thy mind." This is the first and great command and implies that our love for God must be so great that we will employ all our strength in His service.

In connection with this idea we have that of Christian experience and our relation to Christ. It is only when we serve Jesus that we learn of the great truths that are essential to our salvation. Christ said on one occasion, "If any man will do his will, he shall know of the doctrine." Some persons have an idea that they can not realize any benefit from the observing of the commandments, but this is a mistake as it is only by doing the will of God that we obtain a knowledge of the experimental part of Christianity. All who have taken the yoke of Christ upon them and are laboring for Jesus, know of the truthfulness of this idea; it affords pleasures, it makes us happy, hence we hear Jesus saying, "If ye know these things, happy are ye if ye do them." But in order that we may perform the will of God acceptably we must have this assistance, saith Jesus, "Without me ye can do nothing." We must be in close relation to Him, and this idea we have in the yoke of Christ. It joins us to Him, and from him we must expect to receive our strength. Paul said on one occasion "I can do all things through Christ who strengtheneth me." Let us then dear reader, endeavor to be yoked with Christ, for He has promised to be our strength in time of need. He says He is meek and lowly of heart, and oh how important that we should learn from him a lesson of meekness. Some of us are perhaps too haughty to take the yoke upon us. Remember God has promised to be with those only who are of a meek and humble spirit. God hateth a proud and haughty spirit. Let us come down meekly to the foot of the cross and take this yoke upon us, ever seeking knowledge from Him to guide our feet in the path of duty, and then finally we shall receive rest unto our souls. This is the final and glorious result. Oh! how weary we sometimes become. Our bodies, mind, and soul becomes weary, and like David, we wish for the wings of a dove to fly away and be at rest. But if we will take the yoke of Jesus upon us He will stand by us in all our trials, and even help us bear our burdens, and at last deliver us on the sunny banks of everlasting deliverance. May God help us all to bear the yoke and obtain this rest.

J. H. B.

VISIT TO CUMBERLAND.

As it may be interesting to some of the readers of the PILGRIM, I will give a brief sketch of a recent visit to the Lower Cumberland Church, by brother G. W. Brumbaugh of Clover Creek, and myself. Leaving my home on the 28th of Nov., and meeting Bro. G. W. B. on the train at our station, Pleasant Grove, we started for Mechanicsburg, where we arrived at about three o'clock, and was here met by our esteemed Bro. Eld. Moses Miller. We were soon conveyed to, and kindly entertained in his house until evening, when we were taken to the Mohler M. H., where we tried to preach to a small congregation of members principally. As the weather was unfavorable, we tried to excuse the people, as we hope the Lord will, and then took hold of our work as best we could with hopes for the better. After services we were taken to the house of brother Springer, which is ever open to the brethren, and whose hospitalities we shared with good grace. Next morning, (Sabbath), we were again taken to the same place, which by the way, is an old community of brethren. After service were taken to Bro. George Brindle's in company with other brethren and sisters, whose friendship and kind associations we will not soon forget. Part of the time was spent in the family of sister Eliza Hurst, whose husband is dead, and who was the former Elder of this congregation. In the evening were taken to Mechanicsburg, where services were held in the Union M. H.,—congregation respectably large and attentive. After service we were kindly escorted to the home of Bro. D. Neiswanger, and comfortably entertained for the night. Brother N. is doing a large mercantile business here, and brethren will find his house a pleasant stopping place. Services next day at the same place, at 10 o'clock, after which we were again taken to brother Moses Millers's, where we always feel at home. In the evening went again to the Mohler M. H. for divine service, after which we lodged for the night with Solomon Mohler, who seems in every respect like a Christian brother, except the name, which we hope he will soon get written upon the great white throne.

Next morning, in company with friend Mohler and wife, we went to Shepherdstown for service in the Union M. H.,—congregation small. After services dined with sister Bealman, mother of our co-laborer Adam Bealman. From here we were taken by brother David Neisly to his house, where we had previously received much kindness, and many tokens of true Christian love, now renewed by the kind reception and entertainment. While here, brother David kindly gave his time and service in conveying us from place to place, and to the meetings which were commenced in the Baker M. H. on Tuesday eve., and continued until Saturday evening. During this time we visited among the different families of the brethren. The Brindles, Bakers, Weberts, and brother John Plank, who is an active agent for the PILGRIM. Among the places of note was that of Boiling Springs, about three miles south of Churchtown, the place of our meetings. These Springs are quite a curiosity, and may yet become a place of notable resort. The waters boil up in great quantities along a ledge of limestone rocks, for a distance of several hundred yards. At several points it gushes out with such force that even at a distance, it resembles a large caldron of boiling water, covering a space of several acres and forming a stream large enough to drive a grist mill and furnace a few rods off, and then makes its way into the Yellow Breeches. Above and close by these springs, is situated a thriving little town called by the same name. In this place lives our kind and enterprising brother George Brindle, who is doing quite a lively mercantile business, and with whom we dined, in company with Eld. M. Miller, D. Neisly, Cyrus Brindle, and their wives. Sister Brindle, daughter of Eld. Jacob Reinhold of Lancaster city, did all in her power to make her guests happy and contented. We also visited an old blind brother, who seemed to be much pleased and cheered up. On Saturday our aged brother, George Brindle, took us to the house of his son, Cyrus Brindle, one of their ministers, who by the way is full of energy, and we hope spiritual life. Here we enjoyed our visit very much. Bro. A. Bealman was in our company. This point however, was made a scene of horror, on the following morning, that is appalling in the extreme. The wife of one of brother B.'s neighbors drowned herself in the creek near by, casting a gloom over the whole community, as such things always do.

On Sabbath Morning we changed our points of labor, Bro. G. W. B. having left me on Saturday morning in company with Eld. Miller for different appointments in the congregation, while I remained here until this morning, when I was taken to Ceckley's M. H., where we tried to preach to an attentive congregation. From this place we had the pleasure to visit the home of brother Adam Bealman, where we also had an appointment at 2 o'clock in a school-house near by, after which we were taken to Mechanicsburg where we had an evening meeting. This closed the term of our labor in this congregation. We were then taken to the house of a friend in town, whose name we have forgotten, but whose kindness we will not forget. We were well cared for and entertained for the night. Next morning started home where we arrived in the evening, meeting our family well and anxiously awaiting our return.

G. B.

PUBLISHERS ITEMS.

POSTAL orders, after January 1st 1874, will cost only 9 cents instead of 15. Our agents will please note this, and send us money in orders when they can be had.

OUR "New Year's Address" for No. 1, 1874, will be a poetical treat. Do not fail to read it.

LOOKOUT for the enlarged PILGRIM for 1874. It will be the largest weekly paper ever published by the Brethren. Only $1.50 per year. If you desire to encourage a cheap and large paper send for the PILGRIM.

ELD. D. P. SAYLER's paper on the closing of the Old, and beginning of the New Year, is complete in practical thoughts, and should be read by all. It will appear in No. 1 for 1874.

WE are informed that Eld. J. R. Hanawalt met with a sad accident lately. His horse became frightened, ran off and he was thrown out of the buggy and badly hurt.

THE *Pilgrim Almanac* for 1874 is of more than ordinary interest, gotten up in the best of style and should be in every home in the Brotherhood. It will be sent FREE to every subscriber for the PILGRIM for 1874.

AGENTS wanted. We would be pleased to employ several hundred more agents to solicit subscribers for the PILGRIM. We intend to make it just the paper the Church and the world needs, *free from wrangling* discussions and full of living Christianity. Every brother, sister or friend that thinks they could gather us a few names, should send for our Almanac and prospectus.

"PRIDE and Prudence," by Eld. J. S. Flory, will be read with interest and profit by all sober minded people. Such papers are especially needful in these days of rank worldlyism—read it—will be published in No. 1 for 1874.

SOME of our agents and patrons in sending money at this late date for 1873, seem to fear that we might feel grieved in waiting so long. Not at all. We are always glad to receive money, and will not complain as long as we get it inside of a year, *i. e.* from such as cannot well pay sooner.

THE *Pilgrim Almanacs* are being sent out by the hundreds. Some of our agents are ordering 30, 40, and 50 copies at a time. Send along your orders, we have a sufficient number to supply all, without money and without price, who read the PILGRIM for 1874.

Correspondence.

A Reporter is wanted from every Church in the brotherhood to send us Church news, Obituaries, Announcements, or anything that will be of general interest. To insure insertion, the writers name must accompany each communication. Our Invitation is not personal but general—please respond to our call.

GREELY, Colorado, Nov. 26, '73.

I will continue such information as I think will best answer the many inquiries about this territory. It is often asked me, "What are the advantages of Colorado over other Western States or Territories, and what are its faults?" I answer, one advantage over many others is its healthfulness, on that head there is no question or discount. The climate is undoubtedly one of the most healthy in the Union. No fever and ague here, the winters are dry and pleasant with the exception of a "squally" day now and then, for a variety. The summers are delightful. Many persons come here from the East with shattered constitutions that receive surprising benefit. The snowy range of mountains, and the high altitude of the territory, causes the air to be pure and invigorating, and the nights cool and pleasant. But little snow or rain falls here in the valley in the winter. Another advantage is, for farm products there is, and will continue to be, a good home market, and good prices, owing to the fact but a small proportion of the land can be farmed, and the mines of the mountains will have thousands of consumers. Another is, stock need but little feed in winter, therefore the farmer can sell his grain, hay and stock, while in the East, the grain and hay, to a great extent, must be fed to the stock during the winter. Another advantage, stock for many years to come can have millions of acres to range over, as it is not likely it will be settled or fenced only along the valleys.

Now for the disadvantages or faults. One is the scarcity of rain, and necessity of irrigation, however some think that a blessing instead of a fault. Another, scarcity of fruit, but that, it is thought, will be overcome in time. Another, the scarcity of timber, and want of sparkling springs and limpid brooks. Timber, it is found, grows rapidly when set out on these bottom lands. Now who should venture to come here? Not he who has a good comfortable home in the East, and can do a good part by his family, such I would advise to stay and let well enough alone The timid "weak-kneed" or doless man or woman, had better stay among their friends. He who has failed for want of energy or tact in the East, will fail here. Men may get renewed strength of body here,—a new lease of life, but they can't get a new set of brains, and he that has inherited laziness there, will doubtless hold his own here. But persons of small means,—enough to come here and have two or three hundred dollars left, with ordinary energy, may do well. Young men with brave hearts, and a will to do and be somebody, may do well, for the chances are in their favor. Men of means coming here, have good opportunities of doing well, and of being useful in helping to develop the country And brave soldiers of the Cross, who will make good *missionaries* by their practical preaching, we need, to help build up a church, that here where the warwhoop of the savage has been heard for centuries, the praise of God may sound from hill to hill. Come brethren, come sisters, you who can, come and help make the "desert bloom as the rose."

"And the homes that arise around us,
Oh! these will grow more and more dear."

As christian associations endear us to each other, and we all work with an eye single to the building up of our Master's cause. Some few brethren are already in the Platte valley, others are making arrangements to come in the spring, others are halting between two opinions, not knowing whether to venture or not. He that delayeth will let good opportunities pass, but let "every one be persuaded in their own mind."

As the "Beaver Colony" we will say, last fall when that organization was effected, we were one among the first to select a claim in that particular locality of the Platte valley. No sooner was it known there was a town site located, and prospect of a settlement, than numbers in this county immediately went there and took claims so the land was soon nearly all entered in that immediate section. But just as good lands and prospects are to be had farther down, and also on the opposite side of the river from Beaver. There are many who do not know the nature of these colonies, so called. As the lands can not be purchased in a body of the government, it is not possible for a company of men to get control of them, consequently they are open to settlement to whoever comes first. There was an organization effected for the purpose of getting reduced rates of transportation on the R. Roads, and to build up a town. This has been accomplished so far as getting cheap transportation, and the prospects are fair for a town being built in that locality. Any one wishing to come to Colorado can get a certificate that will bring them at about half rates from certain points in the east here, and give them privilege to bring 150lbs. of baggage free to each passenger.

Touching this subject we quote from a late No. of the *Greeley Tribune* published here, as follows: "The Green City and Beaver colonies on the Platte, are the only parties we know of through which reduced transportation can be obtained. For new comers, the Platte valley, between Greeley and Julesburg, offers the best inducements to men of moderate means, as they will have a fine stock range." We have a limited supply of Beaver colony certificates. In a former letter I stated that a person selecting a claim must do so in person, such is the letter of the law, yet a claim may be selected by a party here for another and if some little improvement is done on it, nine times out of ten, it will be safe for three months. Many such claims are taken. One more question so often asked I will answer; that is, "Can I get work at good *wages*?" Where there are buildings going up, canals being dug, a railroad being built, farms improving &c., willing hands can generally get work at fair wages. Wages have been high here but since the "panic" times are dull here as elsewhere. I will conclude by making a few pointed quotations from a small circular printed here for the benefit of inquirers.

Don't come with a lot of household goods on which the freight will cost nearly as much as you can buy new furniture with here. Books, choice light furniture, carpets, clothing and bedding should be brought along.

Don't come expecting to see every house as if set in the Garden of Eden. Here as elsewhere homes are first established, then adorned.

Don't come expecting that laws governing supply and demand are different here from what they are in the East; "easy situations," "soft clerkships," "cushioned seats," "school platforms," "plush-covered pulpits," do not abound. But cheap land in abundance, and a home market is waiting for the harvestage. Colorado is a blessing or a curse, as those who come within her borders shape their conduct. The thrifty man prospers, the thriftless man becomes worse than a beggar.

Don't come expecting that it never rains, that the wind never blows, that the sun is never behind a cloud, that zero is never reached by the mercury.

Don't come expecting a man to meet you half way between here and the Missouri River, begging you to come here and work at a big salary. Women might possibly expect this and not be far out of the way, for they are wanted here as house helps, sewers, and as wives. Blessed is the father who, coming to Colorado, has a "quiver full" of grown-up daughters, especially if they are unmarried. "Thou hast all seasons for thine own," Oh, wedding belles, in Colorado.

Don't come expecting Paradise ready made; but come resolved to make your own Paradise, and all the material for it are ready for your hand.

We further quote: "A thumb-nail sketch in Colorado."

Our climate is healthful in an eminent degree.

Our soil is exceedingly rich and wonderfully productive.

The culture of grapes and most kinds of fruits is easy and profitable.

Our rivers and streams afford unlimited water power.

Our mines of gold and silver are known the world over.

Our deposits of iron, coal, lead, and copper, contain a supply of these useful minerals for many generations of men.

Our railways are extending in all directions.

Our churches and schools give excellent facilities for social, religious and intellectual culture.

Our mountains present the grandest scenery in the world.

Our mountains are covered with forests of pine, cedar, and other trees.

Our villages and cities are growing steadily and rapidly.

Stock growing is followed with a success equal to that of any country in the world.

Sheep raising is an easy and sure means of accumulating wealth.

Wheat, Oats, and vegetables are grown to profit.

A good market is ever at hand for the products of the farmer.

Thousands can testify to the relief afforded by our climate to those in search of health.

Pulmonary diseases, if taken in the earlier stages scarcely fail of permanent cure.

Asthma and bronchial affections are cured by residence in Colorado."

I will quote no more now, and will say if there is yet information wanting by those who mean "business" I am ready to respond, but don't forget when sending letters of inquiries that it costs time and money to write and pay postage. A word to the wise is sufficient.

J. S. FLORY.

CLUBBING LIST.

MARRIED.

REPLOGLE—BROWN.—By the undersigned at the bride's residence, Dec. 4, '73, Mr. Jacob Replogle, to Mary Lizzie Brown.

KAGARICE—GUYER.—On the same day by the same, at the bride's parents, S. R. Kagarice, to Nancy Guyer, all of Bedford Co. Pa. S. A. MOORE.

Correspondence Obituaries and Money List crowded out.

LITERATURE.

A. B. Brumbaugh, Huntingdon, Pa. Literary Editor.

The well known publishing house of Scribner, Armstrong & Co., 654 Broadway, New York, have just issued a volume entitled:—"*The Illustrated Library of Favorite Song*," for which we predict a sale never before attained by any similar production. The fact of it being edited by Dr. J. G. Holland, author of "Kathrina," "Bitter-Sweet," &c., is of itself a sufficient guarantee of its sterling merit. As a volume of Poems, it is a store-house of sweets having no rival—and we believe no equal.

Its contents are of a higher order of Poetic Merit—richer, rarer, purer—more touching and tender than any collection ever before attempted. *Every page* bears the evidence of the most discriminating and patient labor, as well as loving care. They are songs for the home and heart, and can but minister to the purest and highest culture of both. In size it is a royal octavo of over 700 pages, printed on the finest tinted paper, and illustrated with 125 thoroughly dainty and delicate engravings from original designs made expressly for this volume by the most eminent artists, and it is said, could not be duplicated for less than twenty thousand dollars. They are indeed Poems in art, and embody the very spirit and sentiment of the text.

Beside the engravings there are 20 full-page fac-similes of the original autograph copies of the most renowned Poems.

Among the number is Longfellow, Tennyson, Bryant, Whittier, Holland, Hood, Willis, and John Howard Payne, the author of "HOME, SWEET HOME," a song known in all languages, and sung in all lands, and is, for its associations alone,—aside from its merit—worth the price of the work, and it seems by us to be by far the cheapest book for its immense cost ever before published in this country.

It is sold only by canvassers and we advise that some one who can appreciate the spirit and beauty of poetry, in every community to write to the publishers, as above for an agency.

ARTHUR BONNICASTLE.—This new book by Dr. J. G. Holland belongs to a class of literature which is gaining in popularity each year. Like all of this favorite author's prose works, it has the merit of clearness, elegance and strength. The story was first given to the public through *Scribner's Monthly*, that justly popular rival of all American Magazines, and is now issued in a handsome volume by Scribner, Armstrong & Co., New York.

Dr. Holland is an author who ventures to think for himself and interprets morality and religion by a different rule from that of most other teachers. It is plainly to be seen that he has no faith in that system of piety which depends upon sudden and violent demonstrations of emotional excitement; but regards the proper religious state of mind in conversion, to be a condition sanctioned by reason and calm judgment. Though we do not fully commend the kind of christianity which he advocates, yet we commend him for the firm stand he has taken against what we consider popular errors in religion. His system seems beautiful. It is a comfortable system and embraces fine sentiments. It is partially free from dogmatic statements, but can be expressed in sweet hymns and eloquent prayers—what might be termed and eclectic christianity. The story though not highly artistic is one which will be read with interest, and the book command a large sale. Price $1.75.

We hereby tender our compliments to our friends "across the water" of "*The Paper and Printing Trades Journal*" published quarterly by Mess. Field and Tuer, London, England, at 1s 6d. a year, and contains much valuable matter. The samples of Tinted, Ribbed Paper accompanying this No. are a real novelty.

THE HARPER'S will receive subscriptions for the forthcoming Evangelical Alliance volume at $5 each up to the first of January 1874.

GAIL HAMILTON'S new volume of social and domestic sketches is now being published by the Harper's: they have also in press "JOSEPH THE JEW," and "Diamond cut Diamond," the last by T. A. Trollope.

SUNDAY MAGAZINE, published in England by W. ISBISTER & Co., London, and in America by J. B. LIPPINCOTT & Co., is an illustrated monthly of recreation and instruction, and aiming especially at bringing out the benignant aspect of the Gospel, and applying it in every available form, to making the world better, brighter and happier. Among the contributors for the new volume of 1873-4, we notice such men as the Archbishop of Canterbury, Dr. Lindsay Alexander, Dr. W. G. Blaikie, &c., The articles in the two numbers (Oct. and Nov.) received are of a high order. Yearly $2.75, with PILGRIM, $3.85.

GOOD BOOKS.

How to read Characteristics. Price,	$1.25
Combe's Moral Philosophy,	1.75
Constitution of Man. Combe,	1.75
Education By Spurzheim.	1.50
Memory—How to Improve it,	1.50
Mental Science, Lectures on,	1.50
Self Culture and Perfection,	1.50
Combe's Physiology, Illus.	1.75
Food and Diet By Pereira,	1.75
Marriage. Muslin, $1.50.	
The Science of Human Life,	3.50
Fruit Culture for the Million,	1.00
Saving and Wasting,	1.50
Ways of Life—Right Way,	1.00
Footprints of Life,	1.25
Conversion of St. Paul,	1.00
Natural Laws of Man,	75
Hereditary Descent,	1.50
Combe on Infancy,	1.50
Sober and Temperate Life,	.50
Children in Health—Disease,	1.75

The Emphatic, Diaglott; or The New Testament in Greek and English. Containing the Original Greek Text of the New Testament, with an Interlineary Word for-word English Translation. Price, $4.00; extra fine binding, $5.00.

Man and Woman: Considered in their Relations to each Other and to the World. 12mo, Fancy cloth, Price $1.00.

Life at Home; or, The Family and its Members. A work which should be found in every family. $1.50. Extra gilt, $2.00.

Hand-book for Home Improvement: comprising "How to Write," "How to Talk," How to Behave," and "How to do Business," in one vol. 2.25.

Man, in Genesis and in Geology; or, the Biblical Account of Man's Creation, tested by Scientific Theories of his Origin and Antiquity. One vol. 12mo, $1.00.

Hopes and Helps for the Young of both sexes, relating to the Formation of Character. Choice of vocation, Health, Conversation, A Social Affection, Courtship and Marriage. Muslin, $1.50.

DYMOND ON WAR.

An Inquiry into the Accordancy of War, with the Principles of Christianity, and an examination of the Philosophical reasoning by which it is defended. With observations on some of the causes of war and on some of its effects. By Jonathan Dymond Sent from this office, post-paid, for 50 cts.

GOOD NEWS!!

FOR THE CHILDREN.

St. Nicholas Has Come!!

He is coming every month.

This beautiful New Magazine published by Scribner & Co., with its Pictures, Stories and Talks, is now ready. $3.00 a year. We will send it with the PILGRIM for one year for $4.00 The PILGRIM and Scribner's Monthly, $4.75. The three for $7.00.

TUNE BOOK.

The Brethren's Tune and Hymn Book, is a compilation of Sacred Music adapted to all the hymns in the Brethren's New Hymn Book. It contains over 250 pages, printed on good paper and neatly bound. We will send it to any address, post paid at $1.25 per copy.

Trine Immersion.

A discussion on Trine Immersion, by letter between Elder B. F. Moomaw and Dr. J. J. Jackson, to which is annexed a Treatise on the Lord's Supper, and on the necessity, character and evidences of the new birth, also a dialogue on the doctrine of non-resistance, by Elder B. F. Moomaw. Single copy 50 cents.

AGENTS WANTED FOR

BEHIND THE SCENES AT WASHINGTON.

The spiciest and best selling book ever published. It tells all about the great Credit Mobilier Scandal, Senatorial Briberies, Congressional Rings, Lobbies, and the wonderful Sights of the National Capitol. It sells quick. Send for specimen pages and see our very liberal terms to agents. Address NATIONAL PUBLISHING Co., Philadelphia, Pa. Oct. 28-8t.

TRACTS.

"ANXIOUS BENCH RELIGION EXAMINED;" BY ELDER J. S. FLORY. A SYNOPSIS OF CONTENTS. An address to the reader: The peculiarities that attend this type of religion. The feelings there experienced not imaginary but real. The key that unlocks the wonderful mystery. The causes by which feelings are excited. How the momentary feelings called "Experimental religion" are brought about, and then concludes by giving that form of doctrine as taught by Jesus Christ and recorded by his faithful witnesses.

COUNTERFEIT DETECTER
OR
BAPTISM—MUCH IN LITTLE

This work is now ready for distribution, and the importance of the subject will speak for it a large demand. It is a short treatise on baptism in tract form intended for general distribution, and is set forth in such a plain and logical manner that a wayfaring man though a fool, cannot err therein. Either of the above tracts sent postpaid on the following terms: Two copies, 10 cts, 10 copies 40 cents, 25 copies 70 cents, 50 copies $1.00, 100 copies $1.50.

THE HELPING HAND.

Containing several hundred Valuable Receipts for cooking well at a moderate expense, making Dyes, Coloring, Cleaning and Cementing. This book also points out in plain language, free from Doctors' terms the diseases of men, women and children, and the latest and most approved means used for their cure, to which is added a description of the Medicinal Roots and Herbs, and how they are to be used in the cure of diseases.

This is a work of considerable importance and we offer it to our readers as being a valuable accession to every household. Send from this office to any address, post. paid, for 25 cents.

FREE TO BOOK AGENTS.

An Elegantly Bound Canvassing Book for the best and cheapest Family Bible ever published, will be sent free of charge to any book agent. It contains Over 600 fine Scripture Illustrations, and agents ar meeting with unprecedented success. Address, stating experience, etc., and we will show you what our agents are doing, NATIONAL PUBLISHING Co., Phila'a Oct. 28-8t.

Trine Immersion

TRACED

TO THE APOSTLES.

The SECOND EDITION is now ready for delivery. The work has been carefully revised, corrected and enlarged.

Put up in a neat pamphlet form, with good paper cover, and will be sent, post-paid, from this office on the following terms: One copy, 25 cts; Five copies, $1.10; Ten copies, $2.00, 25 copies, $4.50; 50 copies, $8.50; 100 copies, $16.00.

Historical Charts of Baptism.

A complete key to the history of Trine, and the ORIGIN of Single Immersion. The most interesting, reliable and comprehensive document ever published on the subject. This Chart exhibits the years of the birth and death of the Ancient Fathers, the length of their lives, who of them lived at the same period, and shows how easy it was for them to transmit to each succeeding generation, a correct understanding of the Apostolic method of baptizing. It is 22x28 inches in size, and extends over the first 400 years of the Christian era, exhibiting at a single glance the impossibility of single immersion ever having been the Apostolic method. Single copy, $1.00; Four copies, $3.25. Sent post paid. Address, J. H. MOORE.

Urbana, Champaign Co., Ill.

1870 1873

DR. FAHRNEY'S
Blood Cleanser or Panacea.

A tonic and purge, for Blood Diseases. Great reputation. Many testimonials. Many ministering brethren use and recommend it. *Ask* or send for the "Health Messenger." Use only the "*Panacea*" prepared at Chicago, Ills., and by

Dr. P. Fahrney's Brothers & Co.,

Feb. 3-pd. *Waynesboro, Franklin Co., Pa*

New Hymn Books, English.

TURKEY MOROCCO.

One copy, postpaid,	$1.00
Per Dozen,	11.25

PLAIN ARABESQUE.

One Copy. post-paid,	75
Per Dozen, "	8.50

Ger'n & English, Plain Sheep.

One Copy, post-paid,	$1.00
Per Dozen	11.25
Arabesque Plain,	1.00
Turkey Morocco,	1.25
Single German, post paid	55
Per Dozen,	5.60

HUNTINGDON & BROAD TOP RAIL ROAD

On and after Nov. 2nd, 1873, Trains will run on this road daily (Sun excepted) as follows:

Trains from Huntingdon South. *Trains from Mt. Dallas moving North.*

EXP'S. P.M.	MAIL. A.M.	STATIONS.	MAIL. P.M.	EXP'S A.M.
5 30	8 05	Huntingdon,	AR 4 00	AR 9 20
5 35	8 10	Long Siding	3 55	9 15
6 05	8 20	McConnelstown	3 45	9 05
6 10	8 26	Pleasant Grove	3 40	8 58
6 25	8 45	MARKLESBURG	3 25	8 45
6 35	8 55	Coffee Run	3 15	8 35
6 40	9 03	Rough & Ready	3 09	8 29
6 48	9 10	Cove	3 01	8 20
6 51	9 13	Fishers Summit	2 58	8 17
7 10	9 30	Saxton	2 45	8 05
7 25	9 45	Riddlesburg	2 25	7 45
7 33	9 52	Hopewell	2 20	7 35
7 45	10 05	Piper's Run	2 09	7 26
8 00	10 17	Tatesville	1 55	7 12
8 10	10 27	Everett	1 43	7 08
8 15	10 30	Mount Dallas	1 40	7 00
8 35	10 50	Bedford	1 20	6 40

SHOUP'S RUN BRANCH.

A. M.	P. M.		P. M.	A. M.
LE 9 40	LE 7 20	Saxton.	AR 2 30	AR 7 50
9 55	7 35	Coalmont.	2 15	7 35
10 00	7 40	Crawford.	2 10	7 30
AR 10 10	AR 7 50	Dudley	LE 2 00	LE 7 20

Bro'd Top City from Dudley 2 miles by stage.

Time of Penna. R. R. Trains at Huntingdon.

***Mail No. 2 makes connection at Huntingdon with Mail going East on Pennsylvania Railroad at 4.15 p. m., and West at 5.45 p. m. Mail No. 1 leaves Huntingdon at 7.40 a. m. on arrival of Pacific Express West.

Trains on this road connect with trains on Bedford & Bridgeport, and Cumberland & Pennsylvania Railroads.

G. F. GAGE, Supt.

The Weekly Pilgrim.

Published by J. B. Brumbaugh, & Co.

Edited by H. B. & Geo. Brumbaugh.

CORRESPONDING EDITORS.

D. P. Sayler, Double Pipe Creek, Md.

Leonard Furry, New Enterprise, Pa.

The *Pilgrim* is a Christian Periodical, devoted to religion and moral reform. It will advocate in the spirit of *love* and *liberty*, the principles of true Christianity, labor for the promotion of peace among the people of God, for the encouragement of the saints and for the conversion of sinners, avoiding those things which tend toward disunion or sectional feelings.

TERMS.

Single copy, Book paper,	$1.50
Eleven copies, [eleventh for Agt.]	$15.00

Any number above that at the same rate, Address,

H. B. BRUMBAUGH,
James Creek,
Huntingdon county Pa.

www.ingramcontent.com/pod-product-compliance
Lightning Source LLC
Chambersburg PA
CBHW032019220426
43664CB00006B/298